PSYCHOLOGY
THEMES AND VARIATIONS

PSYCHOLOGY
THEMES AND VARIATIONS

Wayne Weiten

College of DuPage

Brooks/Cole Publishing Company
Pacific Grove, California

Consulting Editor: Lawrence S. Wrightsman

Brooks/Cole Publishing Company
A Division of Wadsworth, Inc.

Printed in the United States of America

10 9 8 7 6 5 4 3 2

Library of Congress Cataloging-in-Publication Data

Weiten, Wayne, [date]
  Psychology : themes and variations.

  Bibliography: p.
  Includes index.
  1. Psychology. I. Title.
BF121.W38   1989   150   88-26207
ISBN 0-534-08760-4

Sponsoring Editor: Philip L. Curson
Project Development Editors: John Bergez and Janet Hunter
Editorial Assistant: Amy Mayfield
Production Coordinator: Fiorella Ljunggren
Production: Nancy Sjoberg, Del Mar Associates
Production Assistant: Dave Estrada
Manuscript Editor: Linnea Dayton
Interior Design: John Odam and Tom Gould
Cover Art and Design: Flora Pomeroy
Interior Illustration: John Odam, Richard Carter,
  and Kim Fraley
Graphics Consultant: Alastair Norman McLeod, Ph.D.
Photo Researcher and Permissions Editor: Linda L. Rill
Typesetting: Thompson Type
Color Separation: Rainbow Graphic Arts Co., Ltd.
Cover Printing: The Lehigh Press Company
Printing and Binding: Rand McNally & Company

Credits continue on p. 693.

Beth, this one's for you

f I had to sum up in a single sentence what I hope will distinguish this text, the sentence would be this: I have set out to create a *paradox* instead of a *compromise*.

Let me elaborate. An introductory psychology text must satisfy two disparate audiences: professors and students. Because of the tension between the divergent needs and preferences of these audiences, textbook authors usually indicate that they have attempted to strike a compromise between being theoretical versus practical, comprehensive versus comprehensible, research oriented versus applied, rigorous versus accessible, and so forth. However, I believe that many of these dichotomies are false. As Kurt Lewin once remarked, "What could be more practical than a good theory?" Similarly, is rigorous really the opposite of accessible? Not in my dictionary. I maintain that many of the antagonistic goals that we strive for in our textbooks only *seem* incompatible, and that we may not need to make compromises as often as we assume.

In my estimation, a good introductory textbook is a paradox in that it integrates characteristics and goals that appear contradictory. With this in mind, I have endeavored to write a text that is paradoxical in three ways. First, in surveying psychology's broad range of content, I have tried to show that our interests are characterized by diversity *and* unity. Second, I have emphasized both research *and* application and how they work in harmony. Finally, I have aspired to write a book that is challenging to think about *and* easy to learn from. Let's take a closer look at these goals.

Goals

1. *To show both the unity and the diversity of psychology's subject matter.* Students entering an introductory psychology course often are unaware of the immense diversity of subjects studied by psychologists. I find this diversity to be part of psychology's charm, and throughout the book I highlight the enormous range of questions and issues addressed by psychology. Of course, our diversity proves disconcerting for some students who see little continuity between such disparate areas of research as physiology, motivation, cognition, and abnormal behavior. Indeed, in this era of specialization, even some psychologists express concern about the fragmentation of the field.

However, I believe that there is considerable overlap among the subfields of psychology and that we should emphasize their common core by accenting the connections and similarities among them. Consequently, I portray psychology as an integrated whole rather than as a mosaic of loosely related parts. A principal goal of this text, then, is to highlight the unity in psychology's intellectual heritage (the themes), as well as the diversity of psychology's interests and uses (the variations).

2. *To illuminate the process of research and its intimate link to application.* For me, a research-oriented book is not one that bulges with summaries of many studies but one that enhances students' appreciation of the logic and excitement of empirical inquiry. I want students to appreciate the strengths of the empirical approach and to see scientific psychology as a creative effort to solve intriguing behavioral puzzles. For this reason, the text emphasizes not only *what* we know (and don't know) but *how* we attempt to find out. Methods are examined in some detail, and students are encouraged to adopt the skeptical attitude of a scientist and to think critically about claims regarding behavior.

Learning the virtues of research should not mean that students cannot also satisfy their desire for concrete, personally useful information about the challenges of everyday life. Most researchers believe that psychology has a great deal to offer those outside the field and that we should share the practical implications of our work. In this text, practical insights are carefully qualified and closely tied to data, so that students can see the interdependence of research and application. I find that students come to appreciate the science of psychology more when they see that worthwhile practical applications are derived from careful research and sound theory.

3. *To make the text challenging to think about and easy to learn from.* Perhaps most of all, I have sought to create a *book of ideas* rather than a compendium of studies. I consistently emphasize concepts and theories over facts, and I focus on major issues and tough questions that cut across the subfields of psychology (for example, the extent to which behavior is governed by nature, nurture, and their interaction), as opposed to parochial debates (such as the merits of averaging versus adding in impression formation). Chal-

lenging students to think also means urging them to confront the complexity and ambiguity of our knowledge. Hence, the text doesn't skirt around gray areas, unresolved questions, and theoretical controversies. Instead, readers are encouraged to contemplate open-ended questions, to examine their assumptions about behavior, and to apply psychological concepts to their own lives. My goal is not simply to describe psychology but to stimulate students' intellectual growth.

However, students can grapple with "the big issues and tough questions" only if they first master the basic concepts and principles of psychology—ideally, with as little struggle as possible. In my writing, I never let myself forget that a textbook is a tool for teaching. Accordingly, great care has been taken to ensure that the book's content, organization, writing, illustrations, and pedagogical aids work in harmony to facilitate instruction and learning.

Admittedly, these goals are ambitious. If you're skeptical, you have every right to be. Let me explain how I have tried to realize the objectives I have outlined.

Special Features

This text has a variety of unusual features, each contributing in its own way to the book's paradoxical nature. These special features include unifying themes, featured studies, application sections, a didactic illustration program, an integrated running glossary, and concept checks.

Unifying Themes

Chapter 1 introduces six key ideas that serve as unifying themes throughout the text. The themes serve several purposes. First, they provide threads of continuity across chapters that help students to see the connections among different areas of research in psychology. Second, as the themes evolve over the course of the book, they provide a forum for a relatively sophisticated discussion of enduring issues in psychology, thus helping to make this a "book of ideas." Third, the themes focus a spotlight on a number of basic insights about psychology and its subject matter that should leave lasting impressions on your students.

In selecting the themes, the question I asked myself (and other professors) was "What do I really want students to remember 5 years from now?" The resulting themes are grouped into two sets.

THEMES RELATED TO PSYCHOLOGY AS A FIELD OF STUDY

Theme 1: Psychology is empirical. This theme is used to enhance the student's appreciation of psychology's scientific nature and to demonstrate the advantages of empiricism over uncritical common sense and speculation. I also use this theme to encourage the reader to adopt a scientist's skeptical attitude, to engage in more critical thinking about information of all kinds.

Theme 2: Psychology is theoretically diverse. Students are often confused by psychology's theoretical pluralism and view it as a weakness. I don't downplay or apologize for our theoretical diversity, because I honestly believe that it is one of our greatest strengths. Throughout the book, I provide concrete examples of how clashing theories have stimulated productive research, how converging on a question from several perspectives can yield increased understanding, and how competing theories are sometimes reconciled in the end.

Theme 3: Psychology evolves in a sociohistorical context. This theme emphasizes that psychology is embedded in the ebb and flow of everyday life. The text shows how the spirit of the times has often shaped psychology's evolution and how progress in psychology leaves its mark on our society.

THEMES RELATED TO PSYCHOLOGY'S SUBJECT MATTER

Theme 4: Behavior is determined by multiple causes. Throughout the book, I emphasize, and repeatedly illustrate, that behavioral processes are complex and that multifactorial causation is the rule. This theme is used to discourage simplistic, single-cause thinking and to encourage more critical reasoning.

Theme 5: Heredity and environment jointly influence behavior. Repeatedly discussing this theme permits me to air out the nature versus nurture issue in all its complexity. Over a series of chapters, students gradually learn how biology shapes behavior, how experience shapes behavior, and how scientists estimate the relative importance of each. Along the way, students will gain an in-depth appreciation of what we mean when we say that heredity and environment interact.

Theme 6: Our experience of the world is highly subjective. All of us tend to forget the extent to which we view the world through our own personal lens. This theme is used to explain the principles that underlie the subjectivity of human experience, to clarify its implications, and to repeatedly remind the readers that their view of the world is not the only legitimate view.

After all six themes have been introduced in Chapter 1, different sets of themes are discussed in each chapter, as they are relevant to the subject matter. The connections between a chapter's content and the unifying themes are highlighted in a standard section near the end of the chapter, in which I reflect on the "lessons to be learned" from the chapter. The discussions of the unifying themes are largely confined to these sections, entitled "Putting It in Perspective." No effort was made to force every chapter to illustrate a certain number of themes. The themes were allowed to emerge naturally, and I found that one, two, or three surfaced prominently in any given chapter. The accompanying chart shows which themes are highlighted in each chapter.

Featured Studies

Each chapter except the first includes a Featured Study that provides a relatively detailed but clear summary of a particular piece of research. Each Featured Study is presented in the conventional purpose-method-results-discussion format seen in journal articles, followed by a comment in which I discuss why the study is featured (to illustrate a specific method, raise ethical issues, and so forth). By showing research methods in action, I hope to improve students' understanding of how research is done, while also giving them a painless introduction to the basic format of journal articles. Additionally, the Featured Studies show how complicated research can be, so students can better appreciate why scientists may disagree about the meaning of a study. The Featured Studies, incidentally, are fully incorporated into the flow of discourse in the text and are *not* presented as optional boxes.

In selecting the Featured Studies, I assembled a mixture of classics and recent studies that illustrate a wide variety of methods. To make them enticing, I tilted my selections in favor of studies that students find interesting. Thus, readers are given relatively detailed accounts of classics like Sperry's split-brain research, Milgram's work on obedience, Rosenhan's study of pseudopatients, and Schachter's test of his two-factor theory of emotion. They will also encounter recent explorations of personality resemblance between twins, the media-violence question, the ape-language controversy, and the problem of homelessness among the mentally ill.

Application Sections

To reinforce the pragmatic implications of theory and research that are stressed throughout the text, each chapter closes with an Application section that highlights the personal, practical side of psychology. Each Application devotes three to six *pages* of text (rather than the usual box) to a single

issue that should be of special interest to many of your students. Although most of the Application sections have a "how to" character, they continue to review studies and summarize data in much the same way as the main body of each chapter. Thus, they portray research and application not as incompatible polarities, but as two sides of the same coin. Many of the Applications—such as those on finding and reading journal articles, understanding art and illusion, using tests in career planning, and enhancing self-esteem—provide topical coverage unusual for an introductory text.

Unifying Themes Highlighted in Each Chapter

CHAPTER	THEME 1 EMPIRICISM	2 THEORETICAL DIVERSITY	3 SOCIO-HISTORICAL CONTEXT	4 MULTIFACTORIAL CAUSATION	5 HEREDITY AND ENVIRONMENT	6 SUBJECTIVITY OF EXPERIENCE
1. The Evolution of Psychology	■	■	■	■	■	■
2. The Research Enterprise in Psychology	■					■
3. The Biological Bases of Behavior	■				■	
4. Sensation and Perception		■				■
5. Variations in Consciousness		■	■			■
6. Learning Through Conditioning			■		■	
7. Human Memory				■		■
8. Language and Thought	■				■	
9. Intelligence and Psychological Testing			■		■	
10. Motivation and Emotion		■		■	■	
11. Development Across the Life Span					■	
12. Personality: Theory and Research		■	■			
13. Stress, Coping, and Health				■		■
14. Psychological Disorders			■	■	■	
15. Psychotherapy		■				
16. Social Behavior	■					■

A Didactic Illustration Program

When I first outlined my plans for this text, I indicated that I wanted every aspect of the illustration program to have a genuine didactic purpose and that I wanted to be deeply involved in its development. In retrospect, I had no idea what I was getting myself into, but it has been a rewarding learning experience. I was intimately involved in planning every detail of the illustration program, along with another psychologist with experience in these matters (Alastair McLeod) and an editor who was familiar with every nuance of the book (John Bergez). Together, we have worked to create a program of figures, diagrams, photos, and tables that work hand in hand with the prose to strengthen and clarify the main points in the text. As part of this effort, we have designed many original illustrations and revised many old standbys that you have seen before.

The most obvious results of our didactic approach to illustration are the four summary spreads that combine tabular information, photos, diagrams, and sketches to provide exciting overviews of key ideas in the history of psychology, learning, development, and personality theory. But I hope you will also notice the subtleties of the illustration program. For instance, diagrams of important concepts (conditioning, synaptic transmission, EEGs, experimental design, and so forth) are often repeated in several chapters (with variations) to highlight connections among research areas and to enhance students' mastery of key ideas. Numerous easy-to-understand graphs of research results underscore psychology's foundation in research, and we often use photos and diagrams to bolster each other (for example, see the treatment of classical conditioning in Chapter 6). Color is used carefully as an organizational device (see the figures showing psychology's areas of specialization in Chapter 1), and visual schematics are used to simplify hard-to-visualize concepts (see the figure explaining reaction range for intelligence in Chapter 9). All of these efforts were made in the service of one master: the desire to make this an inviting book that is easy to learn from.

Integrated Running Glossary

An introductory text should place great emphasis on acquainting students with psychology's technical language—not for the sake of jargon, but because a great many of our key terms are also our cornerstone concepts (for example, independent variable, reliability, and cognitive dissonance). This text handles terminology with a running glossary embedded in the prose itself. The terms are set off in boldface italics, and the definitions follow in boldface roman type. This approach retains the two advantages of a conventional running glossary: vocabulary items are made salient, and their definitions are readily accessible. However, it does so without interrupting the flow of discourse, while eliminating redundancy between text matter and marginal entries.

Concept Checks

To help students assess their mastery of important ideas, Concept Checks are sprinkled throughout the book (two to four per chapter). In keeping with my goal of making this a book of ideas, the Concept Checks challenge students to apply ideas instead of testing rote memory. For example, in Chapter 6 the reader is asked to analyze realistic examples of conditioning and identify conditioned stimuli and responses, reinforcers, and schedules of reinforcement. Many of the Concept Checks require the reader to put together ideas introduced in different sections of the chapter. For instance, in Chapter 4 students are asked to identify parallels between vision and hearing and in Chapter 11 to analyze interactions between cognitive, moral, emotional, and social development. Some of the Concept Checks are quite challenging, but students find them engaging, and they report that the answers (available in the back of the book) are illuminating.

In addition to the special features just described, the text includes a variety of more conventional, "tried and true" features as well. The back of the book contains a standard *alphabetical glossary*. Opening *outlines* preview each chapter, and a thorough *summary* of key ideas appears at the end of each chapter, along with lists of *key terms* and *key people* (important theorists and researchers). I make frequent use of *italics for emphasis*, and I depend on *frequent headings* to maximize organizational clarity. The preface for students describes these pedagogical devices in more detail.

Content

The text is divided into 16 chapters, which follow a traditional ordering. The chapters are not grouped into sections or parts, primarily because such groupings can limit your options if you want to reorganize the order of topics. The chapters are written in a way that facilitates organizational flexibility, as I always assumed that some chapters might be omitted or presented in a different order.

The topical coverage in the text is relatively conventional, but there are some subtle departures from the norm. For instance, Chapter 1 presents a relatively "meaty" discussion of the evolution of ideas in psychology. This coverage of history lays the foundation for many of the crucial ideas emphasized in subsequent chapters. The historical perspective is also my way of reaching out to the students who find that psychology just isn't what they expected it to be. If we want students to contemplate the mysteries of behavior, we must begin by clearing up the biggest mysteries of them all: "Where did these rats, statistics, synapses, and JNDs come from; what could they possibly have in common; and why doesn't this course bear any resemblance to what I anticipated?" I use history as a vehicle to explain how psychology evolved into its modern form and why misconceptions about its nature are so common.

I also devote an entire chapter (Chapter 2) to the scientific enterprise—not just the mechanics of research methods but the logic behind them. I believe that an appreciation of the nature of empirical evidence can contribute greatly to improving students' critical thinking skills. Ten years from now, many of the "facts" reported in this book will have changed, but an understanding of the methods of science will remain invaluable. An introductory psychology course, by itself, isn't going to make a student think like a scientist, but I can't think of a better place to start the process. Essential statistical concepts are introduced in Chapter 2, but no effort is made to teach actual calculations. For those who emphasize statistics, Appendix B in the back of the book expands on statistical concepts.

Overall, I trust you'll find the coverage up to date, although I do not believe in the common practice of piling up gratuitous references to recent studies to create an impression of currency. I think that an obsession with this year's references derogates our intellectual heritage and suggests to students that the studies we cite today will be written off tomorrow. I often chose to cite an older source over a newer one to give students an accurate feel for when an idea first surfaced or when an issue generated heated debate.

Writing Style

I strive for a down-to-earth, conversational writing style; effective communication is always the paramount goal. My intent is to talk *with* the reader rather than throw information *at* the reader. To clarify concepts and maintain students' interest, I frequently provide concrete examples that students can relate to. As much as possible, I avoid the use of technical jargon when ordinary language serves just as well.

Making learning easier depends, above all else, on clear, well-organized writing. For this reason, I've worked hard to ensure that chapters, sections, and paragraphs are organized in a logical manner, so that key ideas stand out in sharp relief against supportive information.

To keep myself on the path of clarity, I submit my chapters to the ultimate authority: my students, who take great delight in grading *me* for a change. They're given first drafts of chapters and are urged to slash away at pompous language and to flag sources of confusion. They are merciless—and enormously helpful.

The initial drafts of four chapters were written by other psychologists with expertise in those areas of research. Michael Levine (University of Illinois at Chicago) and Stephen Reed (San Diego State University), who both are experienced authors of undergraduate texts in their areas of expertise, each contributed two well-written chapters marked by outstanding scholarship. However, to ensure stylistic consistency and to achieve the substantive goals that I have outlined, I wrote the final versions of all four chapters.

Supplementary Materials

The introductory course in psychology presents inherent difficulties for student and teacher alike. The teaching/learning package that has been developed to supplement *Psychology: Themes and Variations* was designed with these difficulties in mind. The development of all its parts was carefully coordinated so that they are mutually supported.

Study Guide (by Ronald Wasden and Richard Stalling)

For your students, there is an exceptionally thorough Study Guide available to help them master the information in the text. It was written by two of my former professors, Ronald Wasden and Richard Stalling of Bradley University. They have 20 years of experience, as a team, writing study guides for introductory psychology texts, and their experience is readily apparent in the high-quality materials that they have developed.

The review of key ideas for each chapter is made up of an engaging mixture of matching exercises, fill-in-the-blank items, free-response questions, and programmed learning. Each review is organized around learning objectives written by myself and one of the authors of the Test Bank. The Study Guide is closely coordinated with the Test Bank, as the same learning objectives guided the construction of the questions in the Test Bank. The Study Guide also includes a review of key terms, a review of key people, and a self-test for each chapter in the text.

Instructor's Manual (by Stephen Davis, Randolph Smith, and Roger Thomas)

The Instructor's Manual was written by three professors whose extensive activities in the American Psychological Association's Division on the Teaching of Psychology demonstrate their commitment to educational excellence: Stephen Davis (Emporia State University), Randolph Smith (Ouachita Baptist University), and Roger L. Thomas (Texas Christian University).

The first part of the Instructor's Manual contains an eloquent discussion of prospects, problems, and issues in teaching the introductory course. In the second part, you'll find a wealth of resources organized around the content of each chapter in the text, including lecture suggestions, ideas for class demonstrations, discussion questions, suggested readings, and relevant audiovisual materials.

Test Bank (by Susan Shodahl, Robin Lashley, and Wayne Weiten)

Two outstanding young professors have worked with me in developing the Test Bank. Susan Shodahl (San Bernardino Valley College) and Robin Lashley (Kent State University) developed approximately 100 multiple-choice questions for each of the 16 chapters in the text. I gave all of the questions a preliminary critique and a final edit. I also added and deleted questions to achieve the desired balance among types of questions and levels of difficulty.

The questions are closely tied to the chapter learning objectives, written by Robin and myself, and the lists of key terms and key people found in both the text and the Study Guide. The questions are categorized as factual or conceptual. Consistent with my aim of creating a book of ideas, the Test Bank includes a healthy balance of conceptual questions.

Other Teaching Aids

Professors who adopt *Psychology: Themes and Variations* can obtain a number of additional teaching aids. Computerized versions of the Test Bank are available for a variety of computer configurations. The *computerized test bank* is user-friendly and allows you to insert your own questions and to customize those provided. A collection of *transparencies and slides* has been developed to enhance visual presentations in the classroom. A package of *computer simulations*, which can serve a variety of purposes, is also available.

ACKNOWLEDGMENTS

Creating an introductory psychology text is a complicated challenge, and a small army of people have contributed to the evolution of this book. Foremost among them are the psychology editors I have worked with at Brooks/Cole—Claire Verduin, C. Deborah Laughton, and Phil Curson—and the developmental editor for this book, John Bergez. They have helped me immeasurably, and each has become a treasured friend along the way. Claire educated me in the intricacies of textbook publishing in working with me on my adjustment text. Deb provided astute feedback and creative ideas as I laid my plans for this text. Phil's hard work and enthusiastic support were invaluable in converting these plans into reality. I am especially indebted to John, who has devoted countless hours to this project. His exacting tutelage has left an enduring imprint on my writing.

I also want to thank Brooks/Cole's executive editor, Craig Barth, the president of Brooks/Cole, Mike Needham, and the president of Wadsworth Publishing, Dick Greenberg, for giving me the freedom to pursue my personal vision of what an introductory text should be like. They have let me take some chances and have allowed me extensive input regarding every aspect of the book's production. I have never felt constrained by a conservative corporate mentality.

The challenge of meeting a next-to-impossible schedule in producing this book was undertaken by a talented team of people assembled by Nancy Sjoberg at Del Mar Associates. Alastair McLeod, a psychologist with experience in designing textbook graphics, helped John Bergez and me to plan the illustration program. Alastair has many innovative ideas, and I learned a great deal from him. The color scheme for the book and most of the page layouts were designed by John Odam, who showed remarkable ingenuity and creativity (not to mention patience) in juggling the conflicting demands of the illustration program. A similar creative flair was shown by Tom Gould, who designed the chapter openers, the applications, and the four major summary spreads. Linda Rill handled photo research and permissions with efficiency and enthusiasm, and Linnea Dayton did an excellent job in copy editing the manuscript. Finally, Nancy Sjoberg and Dave Estrada provided the organizational glue that held these efforts together.

A host of psychologists deserve thanks for the contributions they made to this book. I am grateful to Mike Levine and Steve Reed for their erudite drafts of Chapters 3 and 4, and 7 and 8, respectively; to Rick Stalling and Ron Wasden for their work on the Study Guide; to Robin Lashley and Susan Shodahl for their work on the Test Bank; to Steve Davis, Randolph Smith, and Roger Thomas for their work on the Instructor's Manual; to Charles Brewer for allowing us to reprint his "Ten Commandments" in the Instructor's Manual; to Larry Wrightsman for his help as consulting editor; and to the 46 reviewers listed on page xiv, who provided insightful and constructive critiques of various portions of the manuscript. I also want to thank the dedicated teachers who gather yearly in Evansville at the Mid-America Conference for Teachers of Psychology, organized by Joe Palladino. I always leave this meeting charged up about teaching and brimming with new ideas (for instance, a comment in a panel discussion by Ruth Ault inspired the thematic organization of this text).

Many other people have also contributed to this project, and I am grateful to all of them for their efforts. At Brooks/Cole, Fiorella Ljunggren monitored the production process, and Vernon Boes, Bill Bokermann, Janet Hunter, Amy Mayfield, Margaret Parks, Adrian Perenon, Mike Sugarman, Jean Vevers, and Linda Wright helped with varied aspects of the book's development and production. At the College of DuPage, the library staff provided me with invaluable assistance in tracking down needed materials. All of my colleagues in psychology provided support and information at one time or another, but I am especially indebted to Barb Lemme and Don Green. Various administrators at the college, including Dick Wood, Walt Packard, Dean Peterson, and Charlyn Fox, went out of their way to facilitate my writing efforts and earned my gratitude. I also want to thank the great many students from my classes who critiqued chapters and Kristi Haxton, a former student, who helped complete the reference entries.

Last, but not least, I am grateful to many friends for their support, especially Jerry Mueller, Bruce Krattenmakker, Carol Ricks, and Cheryl Kasel. My greatest debt is to my wife, Beth Traylor, who has been a steady source of emotional sustenance while enduring my complete preoccupation with this book. Beth, thanks for the patience. This one's for you.

Wayne Weiten

REVIEWERS

Lyn Y. Abramson
University of Wisconsin

Ruth L. Ault
Davidson College

Dan Bellack
Lexington Community College

Robert Bornstein
Miami University

Allen Branum
South Dakota State University

Dan W. Brunworth
Kishwaukee College

William Calhoun
University of Tennessee

Francis B. Colavita
University of Pittsburgh

Stan Coren
University of British Columbia

Stephen F. Davis
Emporia State University

Kenneth Deffenbacher
University of Nebraska

Roger Dominowski
University of Illinois, Chicago

Robert J. Douglas
University of Washington

James Eison
Southeast Missouri State University

Thomas P. Fitzpatrick
Rockland Community College

Donelson R. Forsyth
Virginia Commonwealth University

William J. Froming
University of Florida

Richard Griggs
University of Florida

Arthur Gutman
Florida Institute of Technology

Jane Halonen
Alverno College

Philip L. Hartley
Chaffey College

Glenn R. Hawkes
Virginia Commonwealth University

Lyllian B. Hix
Houston Community College

Robert A. Johnston
College of William and Mary

Alan R. King
University of North Dakota

Mike Knight
Central State University

Ronald Kopcho
Mercer Community College

Robin L. Lashley
Kent State University, Tuscarawas

Peter Leppman
University of Guelph

Wolfgang Linden
University of British Columbia

Donald McBurney
University of Pittsburgh

Ronald K. McLaughlin
Juanita College, Pennsylvania

Sheryll Mennicke
University of Minnesota

Richard Page
Wright State University

Joseph J. Palladino
University of Southern Indiana

Celia Reaves
Monroe Community College

Daniel W. Richards
Houston Community College

Fred Shima
California State University,
Dominguez Hills

Susan A. Shodahl
San Bernardino Valley College

Steven M. Smith
Texas A&M University

Marjorie Taylor
University of Oregon

Donald Tyrrell
Franklin and Marshall College

Wayne Viney
Colorado State University

Keith D. White
University of Florida

Cecilia Yoder
Oklahoma City Community College

BRIEF CONTENTS

CONTENTS

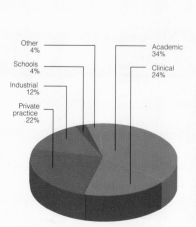

Other
4%
Schools
4%
Industrial
12%
Private
practice
22%
Academic
34%
Clinical
24%

THE RESEARCH ENTERPRISE IN PSYCHOLOGY

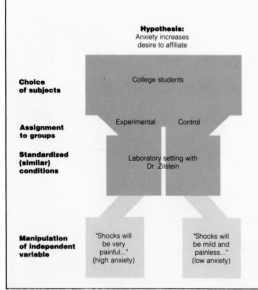

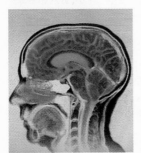

THE BIOLOGICAL BASES OF BEHAVIOR

with Michael W. Levine

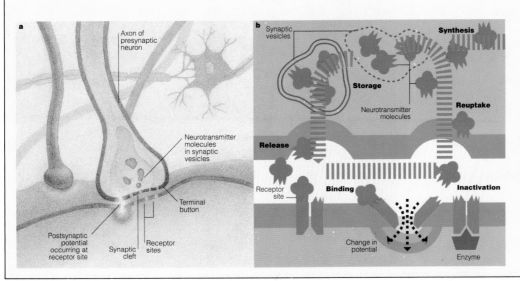

with Michael W. Levine

SENSATION AND PERCEPTION

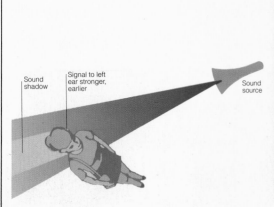

Sound shadow

Signal to left ear stronger, earlier

Sound source

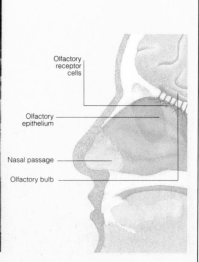

Olfactory receptor cells

Olfactory epithelium

Nasal passage

Olfactory bulb

Variations in Con-sciousness

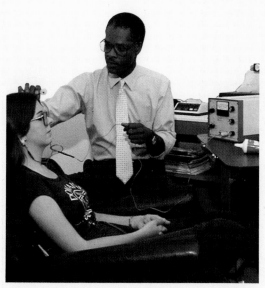

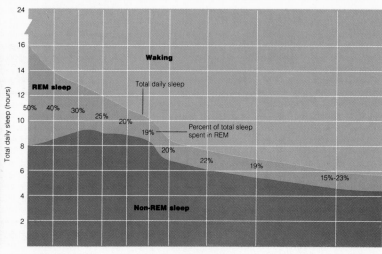

LEARNING THROUGH CONDITIONING

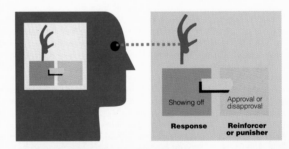

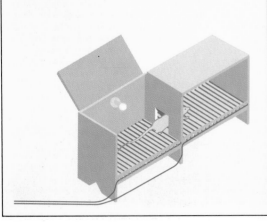

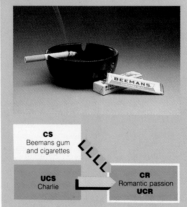

with Stephen K. Reed

HUMAN MEMORY

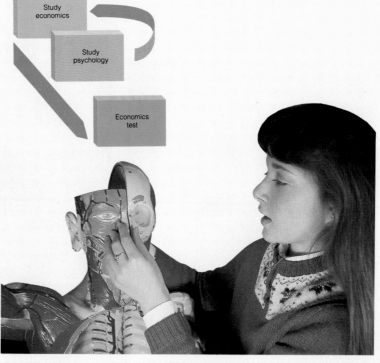

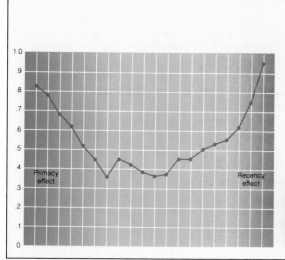

with Stephen K. Reed

LANGUAGE AND THOUGHT

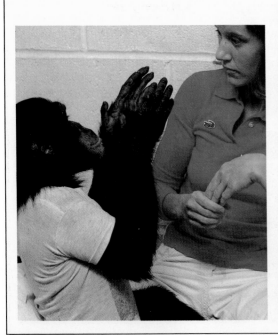

INTELLIGENCE AND PSYCHOLOGICAL TESTING

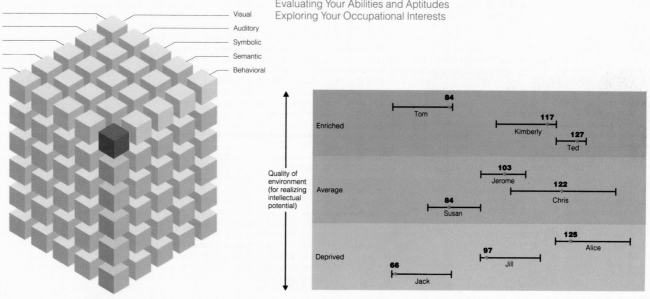

MOTIVATION AND EMOTION

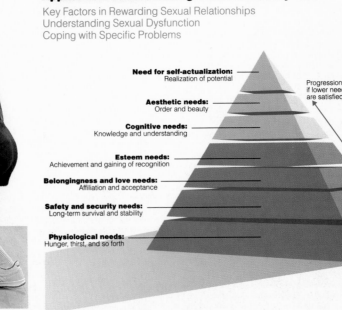

Need for self-actualization: Realization of potential

Aesthetic needs: Order and beauty

Cognitive needs: Knowledge and understanding

Esteem needs: Achievement and gaining of recognition

Belongingness and love needs: Affiliation and acceptance

Safety and security needs: Long-term survival and stability

Physiological needs: Hunger, thirst, and so forth

Progression if lower needs are satisfied

Regression if lower needs are not being satisfied

Human Development Across the Life Span

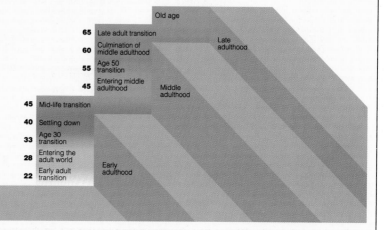

PERSONALITY: THEORY AND RESEARCH

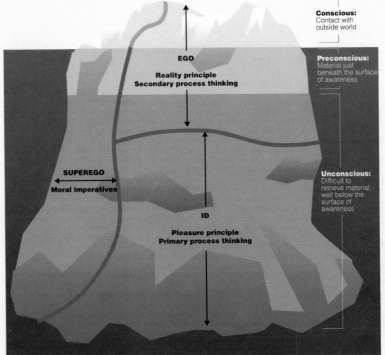

Conscious:
Contact with
outside world

Preconscious:
Material just
beneath the surface
of awareness

Unconscious:
Difficult to
retrieve material;
well below the
surface of
awareness

EGO
Reality principle
Secondary process thinking

SUPEREGO
Moral imperatives

ID
Pleasure principle
Primary process thinking

STRESS, COPING, AND HEALTH

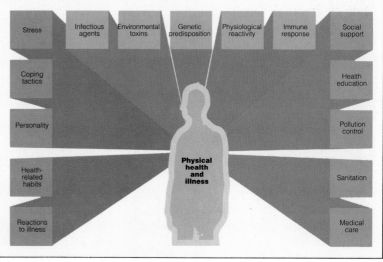

PSYCHO-LOGICAL DISORDERS

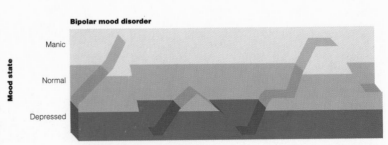

PSYCHO-THERAPY

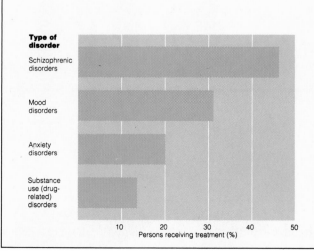

Type of disorder

Schizophrenic disorders

Mood disorders

Anxiety disorders

Substance use (drug-related) disorders

10   20   30   40   50
Persons receiving treatment (%)

SOCIAL BEHAVIOR

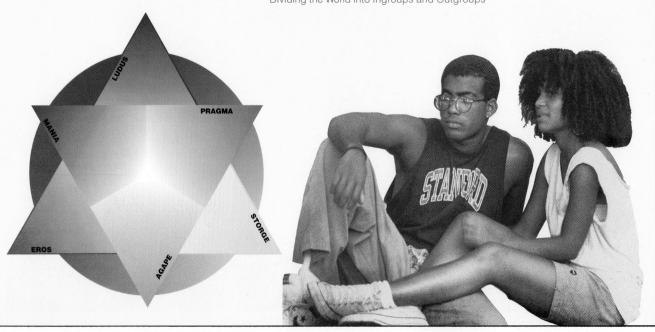

Welcome to your introductory psychology textbook. In most college courses, students spend more time with their textbook than with their professors, so it helps if students *like* their textbooks. Making textbooks likable, however, is a tricky proposition. By its very nature, a textbook must introduce students to many complicated concepts, ideas, and theories. If it doesn't, it isn't much of a textbook, and instructors won't choose to use it. Nevertheless, in writing this book I've tried to make it as likable as possible without compromising the academic content that your instructor demands. I've especially tried to keep in mind your need for a clear, well-organized presentation that makes the important material stand out and yet is interesting to read. Above all else, I hope you find this book challenging to think about and easy to learn from.

Before you plunge into your first chapter, let me introduce you to the book's key features. Becoming familiar with how the book works will help you to get more out of it.

Key Features

You're about to embark on a journey into a new domain of ideas. Your text includes some important features that are intended to highlight certain aspects of psychology's landscape.

UNIFYING THEMES To help you make sense of a complex and diverse field of study, I introduce six themes in Chapter 1 that will reappear in a number of variations as we move from chapter to chapter. These unifying themes are meant to provoke thought about important issues and to highlight the connections between chapters. They are discussed at the end of each chapter in a section called "Putting It in Perspective."

FEATURED STUDIES After Chapter 1, each chapter includes a clearly marked Featured Study, which is an in-depth look at an important, interesting, or provocative piece of research. The Featured Studies are presented as if they were journal articles. I hope they will help you understand how psychologists conduct and report their research.

APPLICATION SECTIONS At the end of each chapter you'll find an Application section that shows how psychology is relevant to everyday life. Some of these sections provide concrete advice that could be helpful to you in school, such as those on improving academic performance, improving everyday memory, achieving self-control, and solving problems systematically. So, you may want to jump ahead and read some of these Applications early.

Learning Aids

This text contains a great deal of information. A number of learning aids have been incorporated into the book to help you digest it all.

An *outline* at the beginning of each chapter provides you with an overview of the topics covered in that chapter. Think of the outlines as road maps, and bear in mind that it's easier to reach a destination if you know where you're going.

Headings serve as road signs in your journey through each chapter. Four levels of headings are used to make it easy to see the organization of each chapter.

Italics (without boldface) are used liberally throughout the text to emphasize crucial points.

Key terms are identified with ***italicized boldface*** type to alert you that these are important vocabulary items that are part of psychology's technical language. The key terms are also listed at the end of the chapter.

An *integrated running glossary* provides an on-the-spot definition of each key term as it's introduced in the text. These formal definitions are printed in **boldface** type. Becoming familiar with psychology's terminology is an essential part of learning about the field. The integrated running glossary should make this learning process easier.

Concept Checks are sprinkled throughout the chapters to let you test your mastery of important ideas. Generally, they ask you to integrate or organize a number of key ideas, or to apply ideas to real-world situations. Although they're meant to be engaging and fun, they do check *conceptual understanding*, and some are challenging. But if you get stuck, don't worry; the answers (and explanations, where they're needed) are in the back of the book in Appendix A.

Illustrations in the text are important elements in your complete learning package. Some illustrations provide enlightening diagrams of complicated concepts; others furnish examples that help to flesh out ideas or provide concise overviews of research results. Careful attention to the tables and figures in the book will help you understand the material discussed in the text.

A *Chapter Review* at the end of each chapter provides a thorough summary of the chapter's *key ideas*, a list of *key terms*, and a list of *key people* (important theorists and researchers). It's wise to read over these review materials to make sure you've digested the information in the chapter.

An *alphabetical glossary* is provided in the back of the book. Most key terms are formally defined in the integrated running glossary only when they are first introduced. So, if you run into a technical term a second time and can't remember its meaning, it may be easier to look it up in the alphabetical glossary than to backtrack to find the definition where the term was originally introduced.

A Few Footnotes

Psychology textbooks customarily identify the studies, theoretical treatises, books, and articles that information comes from. These *citations* occur (1) when names are followed by a date in parentheses, as in "Smith (1972) found that . . ." or (2) when names and dates are provided together within parentheses, as in "In one study (Smith, Miller, & Jones, 1987), the researchers attempted to. . . ." All of the cited publications are listed by author in the alphabetized *References* section in the back of the book. The citations and references are a necessary part of a book's scholarly and scientific foundation. Practically speaking, however, you'll probably want to glide right

over them as you read. You definitely don't need to memorize the names and dates. The only names you may need to know are the handful listed under Key People in each Chapter Review (unless your instructor mentions a personal favorite that you should know).

In addition to the references, you'll find a *Name Index* and a *Subject Index* in the back of the book. The name index tells you the pages on which various names were cited. It's very helpful if you're looking for the discussion of a particular study and you know the name(s) of the author(s). And, if the need arises, the subject index allows you to look up the pages on which a specific topic is covered.

A Word About the Study Guide

A *Study Guide* is available to accompany this text. It was written by two of my former professors, who introduced me to psychology years ago. They have done a great job of organizing review materials to help you master the information in the book. I suggest that you seriously consider using it to help you study.

A Final Word

I'm very pleased to be a part of your first journey into the world of psychology, and I sincerely hope that you'll find the book as thought provoking and as easy to learn from as I've tried to make it. If you have any comments or advice on the book, please write to me in care of the publisher (Brooks/Cole Publishing Company, Pacific Grove, California, 93950). You can be sure I'll pay careful attention to your feedback. Finally, let me wish you good luck. I hope you enjoy your course and learn a great deal.

Wayne Weiten

PSYCHOLOGY
THEMES AND VARIATIONS

THE EVOLUTION OF PSYCHOLOGY

THE EVOLUTION OF PSYCHOLOGY

What is psychology?

If you're like me, your answer to this question probably bears little resemblance to the picture of psychology that would emerge if you glanced through the pages of this book. When I ambled into my introductory psychology course about 20 years ago, I had no idea what psychology involved. I was a pre-law/political science major fulfilling a general education requirement with what I thought would be my one and only psychology course. There were two things I didn't expect. The first was to learn that psychology was about a great many things besides abnormal behavior and ways of winning friends and influencing people. I was surprised to discover that psychology was also about how the eye perceives color, how the brain regulates hunger, whether chimpanzees use insight in solving problems, and a multitude of other topics I'd never thought to wonder about. The second thing I didn't expect was that I would be so completely seduced by the subject. Before long I changed majors and embarked on a career in psychology—a decision I have never regretted.

Why has psychology continued to fascinate me? One reason is that psychology is _practical_. It offers a vast store of information about issues that concern all of us, from broad social questions like the relationship between intelligence and social class, to highly personal questions, such as how to improve your self-control. In a sense, psychology is about you and me. It's about life in our modern world. The practical side of psychology will be apparent throughout this text, and it will be highlighted in the chapter Applications. The Applications focus on everyday problems, such as coping more effectively with stress, improving memory, enhancing self-esteem, and dealing with sleep difficulties.

For me, another element of psychology's appeal is that it represents _a way of thinking_. All of us puzzle about psychological questions, and all of us are exposed to claims about everything, from the differences between men and women to the effects of televised violence on children's behavior. As a science, psychology demands that we ask precise questions and that we test our ideas through systematic observation. Psychology's commitment to testing ideas encourages a healthy brand of critical thinking. In the long run, this means that psychology provides a way of building knowledge that is relatively accurate and dependable.

Of course, psychological research cannot find an easy answer for every interesting question that we ask about the mind and behavior. You won't

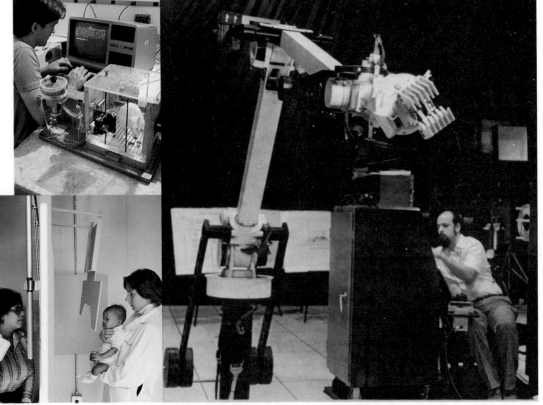

The rich diversity of contemporary psychology embraces a wide range of topics, including the behavior of laboratory animals, perceptual processes in human infants, and such space-age applications as extending the range of our bodies by designing machines for "teleoperating" (manipulating objects in hazardous environments from a safe distance).

find the meaning of life or the secret of happiness in this text. But you will find an approach to investigating questions that has proven very fruitful. The more you learn about psychology as a way of thinking, the better able you will be to evaluate the psychological assertions you encounter in daily life.

There is still another reason for my fascination with psychology. As you proceed through this text, you'll find that psychologists study an enormous diversity of subject matter, from acrophobia (fear of heights) to zoophobia (fear of animals), from language acquisition in apes to the symbolic language of dreams. Psychologists look at all the seasons of human life, from our development in the womb to the emotional stages that we go through in the process of dying. They study observable behaviors such as eating, fighting, and mating, but they also dig beneath the surface to investigate how hormones affect emotions and how the brain registers pain. They probe the behavior of any number of species, from humans to house cats, from monkeys to moths. This rich diversity is, for me, perhaps psychology's most appealing aspect.

Brain chemistry, rats running in mazes, the physiology of vision, the mysteries of love, crea- tivity, and prejudice—what ties all these subjects together in a single discipline? How did psychology come to be such a diverse field of study? Why is it so different from what most people expect? Isn't psychology involved in providing mental health services? Why do psychologists conduct experiments on rats and other animals? If psychology is a social science, why do psychologists study things like brain chemistry and the physiological basis of vision? To answer these questions, we begin our introduction to psychology by retracing its development from philosophical speculations about the mind to a modern behavioral science. By seeing how psychology grew and changed, you will discover why it has the shape it does today.

After our journey into psychology's past, we'll examine a formal definition of psychology and look at psychology as it is today—a sprawling, multifaceted science and profession. To help keep psychology's diversity in perspective, our introduction concludes with a look at six unifying themes that we'll use as connecting threads in the chapters to come. Finally, in the chapter's Application, we'll return to psychology's practical side, as we review some well-researched advice on how to become a more effective student.

FROM SPECULATION TO SCIENCE: HOW PSYCHOLOGY DEVELOPED

Psychology, it has been said, has a long past but a short history. People have always wondered about the mysteries of the mind and behavior, and in that sense, psychology is as old as the human race. But as a scientific discipline, psychology has been in existence for only a little over a hundred years. Psychology's story is a story of people groping toward a better understanding of themselves. As psychology has evolved, its interests, methods, and explanatory models have changed. Let's look at how the transformation from speculation to science took place and at the dramatic transitions the science of psychology has undergone (the highlights are summarized on pages 14–15).

Probing the Mysteries of the Mind: Toward the Birth of Psychology

The term *psychology* comes from two Ancient Greek words, *psyche*, which meant the soul, and *logos*, which referred to the study of a subject. These two Greek roots were first put together to define a topic of study in the 16th century (Boring, 1966). As used then, *psyche* referred to the soul, spirit, or mind, as distinguished from the body. Not until the early 18th century did the term gain more than rare usage among scholars. By that time it had acquired its present literal meaning, *the study of the mind*.

Of course, people speculated about the nature of the soul, spirit, and mind long before the term *psychology* was coined. To take just one example, in ancient Greece the philosopher Aristotle (384–322 B.C.) made intriguing conjectures about thinking, intelligence, motives, and emotions in his work *Peri Psyches (About the Soul)*. These subjects remain at the core of modern psychology. Some of Aristotle's analyses may strike us as primitive today, such as his theory that the heart is the seat of thought. Others, however, were remarkably insightful. For example, at a time when many people thought that mental disorders were due to possession by demons, Aristotle speculated that they might be caused, in part, by biological disturbances. As you will learn later in this book, modern research has shown that Aristotle's guess was a shrewd one.

In speculating about the workings of the mind, Greek scholars such as Aristotle were showing the kind of inquisitive attitude that could eventually

The speculations of the Greek philosopher Aristotle (384–322 B.C.) are just one example of humanity's age-old probings into the mysteries of mind and behavior.

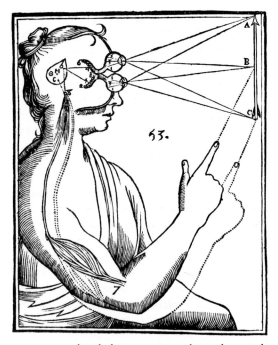

Figure 1.1 Descartes's view of mind and body. Descartes believed in dualism, the idea that the mind and body are separate entities. But how, then, could a thought move an arm? Descartes's answer was that mind and body are linked at the pineal gland, shown in this 1686 woodcut as the tear-shaped object in the middle of the head.

produce a science of psychology. Unfortunately, with the fall of the Greek and Roman civilizations, independent speculations about the mind or soul went into decline for many centuries. Spiritual questions and concerns came to dominate the intellectual scene in medieval Europe, and the Church's authority was supreme. Scholars were expected to verify, not investigate, the revealed truths of the Faith.

A pathway for the eventual emergence of psychology as a subject area was opened by the Renaissance (about 1400–1600). Inspired in part by a renewed interest in Ancient Greek thought, Renaissance artists and thinkers turned to the natural world with a new spirit of active curiosity. This spirit of open-minded investigation, coupled with new methods of observation and measurement, eventually led to revolutionary advances in human knowledge, such as Galileo's mapping of the heavens and Isaac Newton's discovery of the laws of gravity. If the secrets of the physical world could be pried loose by such methods, would the same be true of the secrets of the mind? Only time would tell.

The Parents Meet: Psychology's Origins in Philosophy and Physiology

Two things were needed before psychology could be born as a science: an attitude and a method. First, people had to adopt the attitude that the mind's mysteries could be studied objectively, like any other part of the natural world. Second, they needed to devise ways of investigating psychological questions that allowed them to move beyond speculation or opinion, just as physicists and chemists were finding ways of observing, probing, and measuring physical events. These two requirements were filled by psychology's intellectual parents, philosophy and physiology. Philosophy provided the attitude, and physiology contributed the method.

Philosophy means "the love of wisdom," and historically philosophers have devoted much of their attention to the sources of human knowledge and the nature of reality. Largely a servant of theology during medieval times, by the 17th century philosophy had become an important field of study in its own right. In its new, secular form, philosophy

was soon embroiled in questions about the mind. What are ideas? How are bodily sensations turned into a mental awareness of the outside world? Are our perceptions of the world accurate reflections of reality? Questions about human nature were also open for vigorous debate. For example, do people freely choose their actions? Or are human actions, like the orbits of the planets, inevitably determined by discoverable causes?

One of the most influential philosophers to address such issues was René Descartes (1596–1650), who is often cited as the father of modern philosophy. Descartes was especially interested in the relationship of the mind to the body. This relationship puzzled Descartes, because he believed that mind and body were fundamentally distinct entities—a position called *dualism*. The body, he reasoned, is part of the physical world. It takes up space and obeys physical laws. The mind and its world of ideas seemed to be something entirely different. How, then, do the two interact? For example, how can a *thought* ("move arm") cause a physical effect? Descartes speculated that the mind and the body communicated through the *pineal gland*, a tiny structure located near the base of the brain (see Figure 1.1). Why did Descartes think that mind and body interacted at the pineal gland? Because it appeared to be the only part of the brain that was singular—that is, not duplicated in both the right and left halves.

Descartes and other philosophers who came later were thus deeply involved in psychological issues. What they needed, however, was a better means of resolving them. Intuition and logic could take them only so far. For the most part, philosophers begin with what they believe to be defensible assumptions and *reason* their way to conclusions. The difficulty with this approach is that it amounts to asking how the world *must be* instead of looking to see how it *is*. So, for example, Descartes's conclusion that the mind and body interacted at the pineal gland, arrived at by this reasoning process, was no more accurate than Aristotle's idea that thinking takes place in the heart.

The missing ingredient in the philosophical approach to psychological issues was supplied by psychology's other parent, physiology. *Physiology is a branch of biology concerned with the scientific study of how living organisms function.* By the early 19th century, this interest in function was leading many physiologists to explore some of the same territory as their contemporaries in philosophy. In particular, they were interested in discovering exactly how the mind received and organized information from the senses. Thus, psychological questions became an area of inquiry in physiology as well as in philosophy.

The physiologists, however, employed an entirely different approach. They were trained in the scientific method. As we will see in more detail in the next chapter, the scientific method depends on systematically observing events and testing predictions and explanations to see whether they are supported by the observations. In short, the scientific approach is based on *observation* rather than exclusively on *reasoning*.

The scientific approach paid handsome dividends as physiologists turned to psychological questions. Observation and measurement might not disclose the nature of the soul, but they did produce a series of real discoveries in the first half of the 19th century. For example, Johannes Müller described how signals were conducted along nerves in the body. Herman von Helmholtz shed light on how receptors in the eyes and ears registered and interpreted incoming sensations. Gustav Fechner demonstrated that mental events such as perceptions could be measured with precision.

Such tangible progress showed that the scientific method could be applied successfully to psychological questions. All that remained was for someone to apply the promising methods of the physiologists to the age-old questions of the philosophers.

A New Science Is Born: Wundt's Contributions

By the 1870s a number of philosophers and physiologists were actively exploring psychological issues. However, these scholars viewed such questions as fascinating topics *within* their respective fields. It was a German professor by the name of Wilhelm Wundt (1832–1920) who mounted a relentless campaign to have psychology recognized as an independent discipline with its own subject matter.

The time and place were right for Wundt's appeal. German universities were in a healthy period of expansion, and their intellectual climate favored the scientific approach that Wundt advocated. Hence, his proposals were well received by the academic community, and he succeeded in establishing the first formal laboratory for research in psychology at the University of Leipzig in 1879. In deference to this landmark event, historians have pinpointed 1879 as psychology's "date of birth." Soon afterward, in 1881, Wundt established the first journal devoted to publishing research on psychology. All in all, Wundt's campaign was so successful that today he is widely characterized as the founder of psychology.

Wundt's conception of psychology dominated the field for two decades

"*Physiology* informs us about those life phenomena that we perceive by our external senses.

In *psychology*, the person looks upon himself as from *within* and tries to explain the interrelations of those processes that this internal observation discloses."
WILHELM WUNDT 1832–1920

and was influential for several more. Borrowing from his training in physiology, Wundt (1874) declared that the new psychology should be a science modeled after fields such as physics and chemistry. What was the subject matter of the new science? According to Wundt, it was *consciousness*—one's awareness of immediate experience. *Thus, psychology became the scientific study of consciousness.* This orientation kept psychology focused squarely on the mind, but it demanded that the methods used to explore mental processes should be as scientific as those of chemists or physicists.

Among Wundt's many contributions to psychology, two stand head and shoulders above the others. First, he launched the movement that would eventually make psychology an independent academic discipline, rather than a stepchild

5

The establishment of the first research laboratory in psychology by Wilhelm Wundt (third from left) marked the birth of psychology as a modern science.

Figure 1.2 The first 24 psychological research laboratories established in North American colleges and universities (1883–1893). Many were founded by students of Wilhelm Wundt, G. Stanley Hall (himself a student of Wundt), and William James.

of philosophy or physiology. Second, he successfully shaped that new discipline along the lines of physics, ensuring that psychology would embrace the scientific method.

Wundt was a tireless, dedicated scholar who generated an estimated 53,000 pages of books and articles in his career (Watson, 1971)! His hard work and provocative ideas soon attracted the attention of many outstanding young scholars, who came to Leipzig to study under him and do research on vision, hearing, touch, taste, attention, and emotion. Many of these students then fanned out across Germany and America, establishing laboratories that formed the basis for the new, independent science of psychology.

Indeed, it was in America that Wundt's new science grew by leaps and bounds. In the decade

between 1883 and 1893, some 24 new psychological research laboratories sprang up in the United States and Canada at the schools shown in Figure 1.2 (Garvey, 1929). Many of them were started by Wundt's students, or his students' students.

One of these students, G. Stanley Hall (1844–1924), was a particularly important contributor to the rapid growth of psychology in America. Toward the end of the 19th century, Hall reeled off a series of "firsts" for American psychology. After establishing America's first research laboratory in psychology at Johns Hopkins University in 1883, he launched America's first psychology journal in 1887. More importantly, in 1892 he was the driving force behind the establishment of the American Psychological Association (APA), which remains today as American psychologists' principal organization for the advancement of the discipline. It goes without saying that he was elected the first president of the APA. Today, over 60,000 psychologists belong to the American Psychological Association. It is unlikely that Hall envisioned such a vast membership when he and the other 26 charter members set up their new organization.

Exactly why America took to the new psychology so quickly is hard to say. Perhaps it was because America's relatively young universities were more open to new disciplines than older, more tradition-bound universities elsewhere in the world. In any case, although psychology was born in Germany, it blossomed into adolescence in America. Like many adolescents, however, the

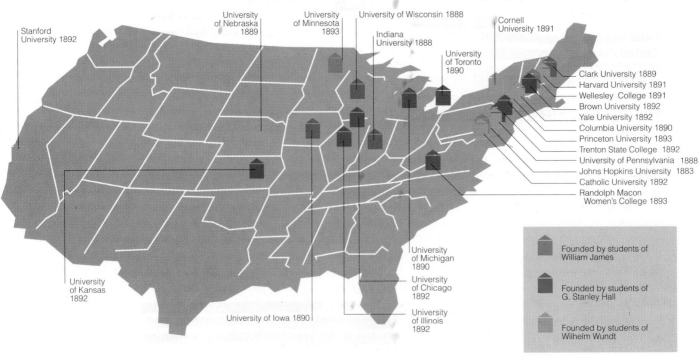

young science was about to enter a period of turbulence and turmoil.

The Battle of the "Schools" Begins: Structuralism Versus Functionalism

When you read that psychology had become a science, you might have imagined that psychologists were now a unified group of scholars busily adding new discoveries to an uncontested store of "facts." In reality, no science works that way. Competing schools of thought exist in most scientific disciplines, and disagreements are sometimes very fundamental. Such diversity in thought is quite natural and often stimulates enlightening debate and dialogue. In psychology, the first two major schools of thought were *structuralism* and *functionalism*. They were entangled in the first great intellectual battle in the field.

Shaped by Wundt's ideas, structuralism was based on the notion that the task of psychology was to analyze consciousness into its basic elements and to investigate how these elements were related. Just as physicists were searching for more and more basic particles of matter, the structuralists wanted to understand conscious experience by breaking it down into its fundamental components, such as sensations, feelings, and images.

While the structuralists explored many questions, most of their work concerned sensation and perception in vision, hearing, and touch. To examine the contents of consciousness, the structuralists depended on introspection. Introspection involves careful, systematic observation of one's own conscious experience. As practiced by the structuralists, introspection required training to make the subject—the person being studied—more objective and more aware. Once trained, subjects were typically exposed to auditory tones, optical illusions, and visual stimuli such as a piece of fruit, and asked to report and analyze what they experienced.

The functionalists took a very different view of psychology's task. Functionalism was based on the belief that psychology should investigate the function or purpose of consciousness, rather than its structure. The chief architect of functionalism was William James (1842–1910), a brilliant, interdisciplinary American scholar. James's training was in medicine, but he was too weak and sickly to pursue a medical practice (he couldn't imagine standing all day long), so he joined the faculty of Harvard University. Medicine's loss proved to be a boon for both psychology and philosophy, as James became an intellectual giant in both fields.

James's thinking illustrates how psychology, like any field, is deeply embedded in a network of cultural and intellectual influences. James had been impressed with Charles Darwin's theory of *natural selection*. According to Darwin, the characteristics of a species come to be "selected" over time because they provide a survival advantage for the species. This cornerstone notion of evolutionary theory suggested that the characteristics of a species must all serve some purpose. James applied this idea to consciousness. Since consciousness was an important characteristic of the human species, James (1890) contended that psychology should investigate the *functions* rather than the *structure* of consciousness.

James also argued that the structuralists' approach missed the real nature of conscious experience. Consciousness, he argued, consists of a continuous *flow* of thoughts. In analyzing consciousness into its "elements," the structuralists were looking at static points in that flow. James wanted to understand the flow itself, which he called the "stream of consciousness." To put James's point in modern terms, it was as if the structuralists set out to view a movie by examining it frame by frame and consequently missed the motion in the motion picture.

Whereas structuralists naturally gravitated to the laboratory, functionalists were more interested in how people adapted their behavior to the demands of the world around them. This practical slant led them to introduce new areas of study into psychology. Instead of focusing on sensation and perception, functionalists such as G. Stanley Hall and John Dewey began to investigate patterns of development in children and the effectiveness of educational practices.

The impassioned advocates of structuralism and functionalism saw themselves as fighting for very high stakes—the definition and future direction of the new science of psychology. Their war of ideas continued energetically for many years. Who won? Neither camp scored a decisive victory, and in time both began to fade in influence as new schools of thought entered the fray.

"It is just this free water of consciousness that psychologists resolutely overlook."
WILLIAM JAMES 1842–1910

For their part, the structuralists eventually ran into difficulties with their method of introspection. They had hoped to discover the universal elements of conscious experience. However, consciousness is highly personal and subjective, and even well-trained introspectionists yielded inconsistent results when presented with the same experience. This inconsistency thwarted the structuralists' efforts to find the basic particles of consciousness (Hearst, 1979). On balance, functionalism left a more enduring imprint on psychology. Although functionalism declined in influence at about the same time as structuralism, its ideas fostered the development of two descendants that remain powerful today—behaviorism and applied psychology.

Watson Alters Psychology's Course as Behaviorism Makes Its Debut

The debate between structuralism and functionalism was only the prelude to other fundamental controversies in psychology. In the early 1900s, a third major school of thought appeared that dramatically altered the course of psychology.

Founded by John B. Watson (1878–1958), *behaviorism is a theoretical orientation based on the premise that scientific psychology should study only observable behavior.* It is important to understand what a radical change is concealed in this definition. Watson (1913) was proposing that psychologists should *abandon the study of consciousness altogether* and focus exclusively on behaviors that they could directly observe. In essence, he was redefining what scientific psychology should be about.

Why did Watson argue for such a fundamental shift in direction? Because to Watson, the power of the scientific method rested on the idea of *verifiability*. In principle, scientific claims can always be verified (or disproved) by anyone who is willing and able to make the required observations. However, this power depends upon studying things that can be observed objectively. Otherwise, the

advantage of using the scientific approach—to replace vague speculation and personal opinion with reliable, exact knowledge—is lost.

For Watson, consciousness and mental processes were not proper subjects for scientific study because they were ultimately private events. After all, no one can see or touch another's thoughts. Since there was no way to directly observe inner mental events, Watson argued that there was no way to verify what anyone concluded about them. Consequently, if psychology was to be a science, it would have to give up consciousness as its subject matter and become instead the *science of behavior.*

By *behavior,* Watson meant any overt responses that can be observed by others. He asserted that psychologists could study anything that people do or say—shopping, playing chess, eating, or complimenting a friend, for example. What they could *not* study scientifically were the thoughts, wishes, and feelings that might accompany these observable behaviors.

Watson's radical reorientation of psychology did not end with his redefinition of its subject matter. He also took an extreme position on one of psychology's oldest and most fundamental questions—the issue of "nature" versus "nurture." This age-old debate is concerned with whether our behavior is determined mainly by our genetic inheritance (nature) or by our environment and experience (nurture). To oversimplify, the question is this: is a great concert pianist or a master criminal born or made?

Watson argued that each is made, not born. In other words, he discounted the importance of genetic inheritance, maintaining that behavior is governed entirely by the environment. Indeed, Watson (1930) boldly claimed,

Give me a dozen healthy infants, well-formed, and my own special world to bring them up in and I'll guarantee to take any one at random and train him to become any type of specialist I might select—doctor, lawyer, artist, merchant-chief, and yes, beggarman and thief (p. 104).

For obvious reasons, Watson's challenge was never put to a test. Nonetheless, his emphasis on the importance of the environment became a basic principle of behaviorism.

Emphasizing the importance of the environment, the behaviorists came to view psychology's mission as an attempt to relate overt behaviors (responses) to observable events in the environment (called stimuli). **A *stimulus* is any detectable input from the environment.** Stimuli can range from light and sound waves to such complex inputs as the words on this page, advertisements on TV, or sarcastic remarks from a friend. Thus, the behaviorists began investigating stimulus-response relationships. For this reason, the behavioral approach is often characterized as *stimulus-response (S-R) psychology.*

Watson's behavioral point of view took hold rapidly. In part, the growth of behaviorism was due to an important discovery by Ivan Pavlov (1849–1936), a Russian physiologist. As you'll learn in Chapter 6, Pavlov showed how dogs could be trained to salivate in response to the auditory stimulus of a bell ringing. This deceptively simple demonstration provided insight into how stimulus-response bonds are created. Such bonds were exactly what behaviorists wanted to investigate, so Pavlov's discovery paved the way for their work.

Behaviorism's stimulus-response approach contributed to the rise of animal research in psychology. Having deleted consciousness from their scope of concern, behaviorists no longer needed to study human subjects who could report on their mental processes. Many psychologists thought that animals would make much better research subjects anyway. Why did they prefer to study animals? A primary reason is that experimental research is often more productive if experimenters can exert considerable *control* over their subjects. Otherwise, too many complicating factors enter into the picture and contaminate the experiment. Obviously, a researcher can exert much more control over a laboratory rat or pigeon than over a human subject, who arrives at a lab with years of uncontrolled experience and who will probably insist on going home at night.

Thus, the lure of increased experimental control led psychologists to turn much of their attention to animal behavior. In this way, the discipline that began its life as the study of mind found itself heavily involved in the study of simple responses made by laboratory animals. Although animal research has its own limitations, this shift in orientation proved productive.

Let's take stock of Watson's impact on psychology. First, he had the audacity to redefine the very subject matter of psychology as behavior rather than consciousness. This view came to dominate psychology and remains highly influential today. Second, by advancing stimulus-response psychology, he helped usher animals into the world's psychology laboratories, thus altering psychology's research focus.

Watson's radical redefinition of psychology did not go unchallenged. In Germany opposition came from an emerging school of thought called *Gestalt psychology.* The Gestalt theorists, who were primarily concerned with perception (we'll discuss their ideas in Chapter 4), argued that psychology should continue to study conscious

experience rather than overt behavior. Another alternative conception of psychology emerged from Austria, where an obscure physician named Sigmund Freud had been contemplating the mysteries of unconscious mental processes. We'll look at Freud's ideas next.

Freud Brings the Unconscious into the Picture

Long before he turned his attention to psychology, Sigmund Freud (1856–1939) dreamed of achieving fame by making an important discovery. His determination was such that in medical school he dissected 400 male eels to prove for the first time that they had testes. His work with eels did not make him famous, but his subsequent work with people did. Indeed, his theories would make him one of the most influential—and controversial—figures of modern times.

In contrast to the laboratory-minded behaviorists, Freud's (1900, 1933) approach to psychology was based on his deep involvement with human beings' problems in living. In his medical practice, Freud treated people troubled by psychological problems such as irrational fears, obsessions, and anxieties. Eventually he devoted himself to treating mental disorders through an innovative procedure that he called *psychoanalysis.*

Psychoanalysis required lengthy verbal interactions with patients in which Freud probed deeply into their lives. Decades of experience with his patients provided much of the inspiration for Freud's theory. He also gathered material by looking inward and examining his own anxieties, conflicts, and desires. For over 40 years, Freud devoted the last half-hour of each workday to self-analysis!

Both his work with patients and his own self-exploration persuaded Freud of the existence and importance of what he called the unconscious.

"The unconscious is the true psychical reality; in its innermost nature it is as much unknown to us as the reality of the external world."

SIGMUND FREUD
1856–1939

According to Freud, **the unconscious contains thoughts, memories, and desires that are well below the surface of conscious awareness, but that nonetheless exert great influence on our behavior.**

Freud's concept of the unconscious was based on a variety of observations. For instance, he noticed that seemingly meaningless "slips of the tongue" (such as "I decided to take a summer school curse") often appeared to reveal a person's true feelings. He also noted that his patients' dreams often seemed to express important feelings that they were unaware of. Knitting these and other observations together, Freud eventually concluded that psychological disturbances were largely caused by personal conflicts that existed at an unconscious level. More generally, his **psychoanalytic theory attempts to explain personality, motivation, and psychological disorders by focusing on unconscious determinants of behavior.**

Freud's concept of the unconscious was not entirely new (it was anticipated by a few earlier theorists), but it was a major departure from conventional thought at the time. Before Freud provided dramatic evidence of unconscious forces at work, most people had assumed that they were fully aware of the forces governing their behavior. To suggest otherwise was to suggest that people were not in control of their lives as much as they imagined. Psychoanalytic theory seemed to pose a threat to the very basis of human dignity. Not surprisingly, Freud was soon engulfed in heated controversy.

As radical as Freud's concept of the unconscious was, it was initially overshadowed by even more startling aspects of psychoanalytic theory. Most important, Freud proposed that our personalities are greatly influenced by how we cope with our sexual urges and the internal conflicts that they often generate. At a time when people were far less comfortable discussing sexual issues than they are today, even scientists were offended and scandalized by Freud's emphasis on sex. But this was not all. Freud further maintained that even infants have sexual urges, and that supposedly rational adults are driven by crude, biological drives, much as lower animals are. Small wonder, then, that many people ridiculed and condemned Freud's theory.

Although Freud began developing his ideas in the 1890s, psychoanalytic theory gained influence within psychology only very gradually. Important public recognition from psychology came in 1909 when G. Stanley Hall invited Freud to America to give a series of lectures at Clark University (see Figure 1.3). By 1920, psychoanalytic theory was widely known around the world, but it continued to meet with considerable resistance in psychology. Why? Two reasons stand out. First, Freudian theory focused on topics that were foreign to mainstream psychology at the time. Freud was interested in personality, motivation, and abnormal behavior; mainstream psychology was primarily interested in sensation, perception, and learning. This mismatch made them awkward bedfellows. Second, psychoanalytic theory conflicted with the spirit of the times in psychology. Many psychologists were becoming uncomfortable with their earlier focus on conscious experience and were turning to the less murky subject of observable behavior. If they felt that *conscious* experience was inaccessible to scientific observation, you can imagine how they felt about trying to study *unconscious* experience. In short, Freudian theory seemed speculative and unscientific. Most psychologists expected it would eventually fade away.

They turned out to be wrong. Psychoanalytic ideas steadily gained acceptance in the culture at large, influencing thought in medicine, the arts, and literature. Then, in the 1930s and 1940s, more and more psychologists found themselves becoming interested in areas Freud had studied— personality, motivation, and abnormal behavior. As they turned to these topics, many of them saw merit in some of Freud's notions (Rosenzweig, 1985). Although psychoanalytic theory continued to generate heated debate, it survived to become an influential theoretical perspective, and many psychoanalytic concepts have filtered into the mainstream of psychology.

Figure 1.3 A portrait taken at the famous Clark University psychology conference, September 1909. Pictured are Freud, G. Stanley Hall, and four of Freud's students and associates. Seated, left to right: Freud, Hall, and Carl Jung; standing: Abraham Brill, Ernest Jones, and Sandor Ferenczi.

Skinner Questions Free Will as Behaviorism Flourishes

While psychoanalytic thought was slowly gaining a foothold within psychology, the behaviorists were temporarily softening their stance on the acceptability of studying internal mental events. Behaviorists were not about to go back to making conscious experience the focus of psychology. However, many behaviorists did admit that stimulus-response connections were made by a living creature—an *organism*—that ought not to be ignored entirely.

Under the leadership of Clark Hull (1884–1952), stimulus-response (S-R) theory evolved into *stimulus-organism-response (S-O-R) theory*. This modified behavioral approach still emphasized the study of observable behavior and stimulus-response relationships. But S-O-R theory permitted careful inferences to be drawn about an organism's internal states, such as drives, needs, and habits. For example, Hull (1943) argued that if an animal ate eagerly when offered food, it was not farfetched to infer the existence of an internal hunger drive.

This movement toward the consideration of internal states was dramatically reversed in the 1950s by the work of B. F. Skinner (1904–   ). Skinner set out to be a writer, but he gave up his dream after a few unproductive years. "I had," he wrote later, "nothing important to say" (1967, p. 395). However, he had many important things to say about psychology, and he went on to become one of the most influential of all American psychologists.

In response to the softening in the behaviorist position, Skinner (1953) championed a return to Watson's strict stimulus-response approach. Of course, Skinner did not deny the existence of internal mental events, but he did insist that they could not be studied scientifically. Moreover, he maintained, psychologists did not *need* to study them. If the stimulus of food is followed by the response of eating, a psychologist can fully describe what is happening without making any guesses about whether the animal is experiencing hunger. According to Skinner, the behavior speaks for itself, and finding out how stimuli and responses are associated is all we need to do to describe, understand, and predict behavior.

The fundamental principle of behavior documented by Skinner is deceptively simple: *organisms tend to repeat responses that lead to positive outcomes, and they tend not to repeat responses that lead to neutral or negative outcomes*. In spite of its simplicity, this principle turns out to be very powerful. Thus, Skinner's voice became influential because he and his followers embarked on a research program that was exceptionally fruitful. In short, they got results. Working primarily with rats and pigeons in highly structured laboratory environments, Skinner showed that he could exert remarkable control over the behavior of his experimental animals by systematically manipulating the outcomes of their responses. He was even able to get animals to perform very foreign behaviors; for example, he trained pigeons to play ping-pong.

Although Skinner himself studied mostly animal behavior, his followers showed that the principles uncovered in their animal research could be applied to complex human behaviors as well. Procedures derived from behavioral principles are now widely used in industry, education, prisons, mental hospitals, and a variety of other settings.

> "I submit that what we call the behavior of the human organism is no more free than its digestion."
>
> B. F. SKINNER 1904–

Skinner's ideas had implications that went far beyond the debate among psychologists about what they should study and how they should study it. Skinner spelled out the full implications of his findings in a controversial book entitled *Beyond Freedom and Dignity* (1971). In it, he asserted that all behavior is fully governed by external stimuli. In other words, your behavior is determined in predictable ways by lawful principles, just as the flight of an arrow is governed by the laws of physics, and if you believe that you *decide* how you will behave, you're wrong. According to Skinner, we are all controlled by our environment, not by ourselves. In short, Skinner arrived at the conclusion that *free will is an illusion*.

As you can readily imagine, such a disconcerting view of human nature was not universally acclaimed. Like Freud, Skinner has been the target of harsh criticism. In spite of the controversy, however, behaviorism flourished as the dominant school of thought in psychology in the 1950s and 1960s (Gilgen, 1982).

The Humanists Revolt

By the 1950s, behaviorism and psychoanalytic theory were firmly established as the leading schools of thought in psychology. However, many psychologists found these theoretical orientations unappealing. The principal charge hurled at both schools was that they were dehumanizing. Psychoanalytic theory was attacked for its belief that behavior is dominated by primitive, animalistic drives. Behaviorism was maligned for its preoccupation with the study of simple animal behavior. Both theories were charged with being too pessimistic about human nature. Above all, many people argued, both schools of thought failed to recognize the *unique* qualities of *human* behavior.

During the 1950s, the diverse opposition to behaviorism and psychoanalytic theory blended into a loose alliance that eventually became a new school of thought called "humanism" (Buhler & Allen, 1972). In psychology, *humanism is a theoretical orientation that emphasizes the unique qualities of humans, especially their freedom and their potential for personal growth*. The most prominent architects of the humanistic movement have been Carl Rogers (1905–1987) and Abraham Maslow (1908–1970).

Humanists such as Rogers (1951) and Maslow (1954) take an *optimistic* view of human nature.

CONCEPT CHECK 1.2
Understanding the Implications of Major Theories: Freud, Skinner, and Rogers

Check your understanding of the implications of some of the major theories reviewed in this chapter by indicating who is likely to have made the statements quoted below. For each quotation, indicate the appropriate theorist, choosing from the following: (a) Sigmund Freud, (b) B. F. Skinner, and (c) Carl Rogers. You'll find the answers in Appendix A at the back of the book.

___ 1. "In the traditional view, a person is free. . . . He can therefore be held responsible for what he does and justly punished if he offends. That view, together with its associated practices, must be re-examined when a scientific analysis reveals unsuspected controlling relations between behavior and environment."

___ 2. "He that has eyes to see and ears to hear may convince himself that no mortal can keep a secret. If the lips are silent, he chatters with his fingertips; betrayal oozes out of him at every pore. And thus the task of making conscious the most hidden recesses of the mind is one which it is quite possible to accomplish."

___ 3. "I do not have a Pollyanna view of human nature. . . . Yet one of the most refreshing and invigorating parts of my experience is to work with such individuals and to discover the strongly positive directional tendencies which exist in them, as in all of us, at the deepest levels."

They maintain that we are not the pawns of either our animal heritage or our environmental circumstances. Furthermore, they say, since humans are fundamentally different from other animals, research on animals has little relevance to the understanding of human behavior. Rogers, for example, argued that human behavior is governed primarily by one's sense of self, or "self-concept"—which animals presumably lack. Both he and Maslow maintained that to fully understand people's behavior psychologists must take into account the fundamental human drive toward personal growth. They claimed that people have a basic need to continue to evolve as human beings and to fulfill their potentials, and that many psychological disturbances are the result of the thwarting of these uniquely human needs.

The humanists' greatest contributions to psychology have been their innovative treatments for psychological problems and disorders. The humanistic movement has provided a fertile breeding ground for the development of creative and successful approaches to psychotherapy. More generally, the humanists have argued eloquently for a different picture of human psychology than those implied by psychoanalysis and behaviorism. We will encounter their influence again, particularly in our discussions of personality (Chapter 12) and psychotherapy (Chapter 15).

Psychology Comes of Age as a Profession

Besides giving rise to humanism, the 1950s also saw psychology come of age as a profession. As you know, psychology is not all pure science. It has a highly practical side, represented by the many psychologists who provide a variety of professional services to the public. Their work falls within the domain of **applied psychology,** **that branch of psychology concerned with everyday, practical problems**.

This branch of psychology, which is so prominent today, was actually slow to develop. Although the first psychological clinic (for evaluating and treating learning problems in children) was established as early as 1896, very few psychologists concerned themselves with applications of their science until World War I (1914–1918) created a huge demand for mental testing of military recruits. The first useful intelligence test had been devised only a few years before by French psychologist Alfred Binet and his colleagues (Binet & Simon, 1905). During the war, the military services seized on intelligence testing as an aid in assigning recruits to jobs in accordance with their abilities. The war thus brought many

psychologists into the applied arena for the first time and established mental testing as a routine professional activity conducted by psychologists.

After World War I, psychology continued to grow as a profession, but only very slowly. The principal professional arm of psychology was *clinical psychology*. As practiced today, **clinical psychology is the branch of psychology concerned with the diagnosis and treatment of psychological problems and disorders**. In the early days, however, the emphasis was almost exclusively on psychological testing for diagnostic purposes, and the number of psychologists involved in clinical work was small. As late as 1937 only about one in five members of the American Psychological Association reported an interest in clinical psychology (Goldenberg, 1983). While that figure was substantially higher than the 4% reported in 1918, clinicians were still a relatively small minority in a field devoted primarily to research.

That picture was about to change with dramatic swiftness. Once again the impetus was a world war. During World War II (1942–1945), a multitude of academic psychologists were pressed into service as clinicians to screen military recruits and to treat soldiers suffering from trauma. Many of these psychologists (often to their surprise) found the clinical work to be challenging and rewarding, and continued to do clinical work after the war. More significantly, some 40,000 American veterans, many with severe psychological scars, returned to seek postwar treatment in Veterans Administration (VA) hospitals. With the demand for clinicians far greater than the supply, the VA stepped in to finance many new training programs in clinical psychology. These new programs, emphasizing training in the treatment of psychological disorders as well as psychological testing, proved attractive. Within a few years, about half of the new Ph.D.'s in psychology were specializing in clinical psychology (Goldenberg, 1983). Thus, by the 1950s the prewar orphan of applied/profes-

"It seems to me that at bottom each person is asking, 'Who am I, *really*? How can I get in touch with this real self, underlying all my surface behavior? How can I become myself?'"
CARL ROGERS 1905–1987

1909 Sigmund Freud's increasing influence receives formal recognition as Hall invites Freud to give addresses at Clark University

1879 Wundt establishes first research laboratory in psychology

1905 Alfred Binet assembles first successful intelligence test

1881 Wundt establishes first journal devoted to research in psychology

1913 John B. Watson writes classic behaviorism manifesto

1875 First demonstration laboratories are set up independently by William James (at Harvard) and Wilhelm Wundt (at the University of Leipzig)

1890 James publishes his seminal work, *The Principles of Psychology*

THE
PRINCIPLES
OF
PSYCHOLOGY

James

1892 G. Stanley Hall founds the American Psychological Association

1920s Gestalt psychology nears its peak influence

1914-1918 Widespread intelligence testing is begun by military during World War I

1904 Ivan Pavlov shows how conditioned responses are created, paving the way for stimulus-response psychology

1880   1890   1900   1910   1920

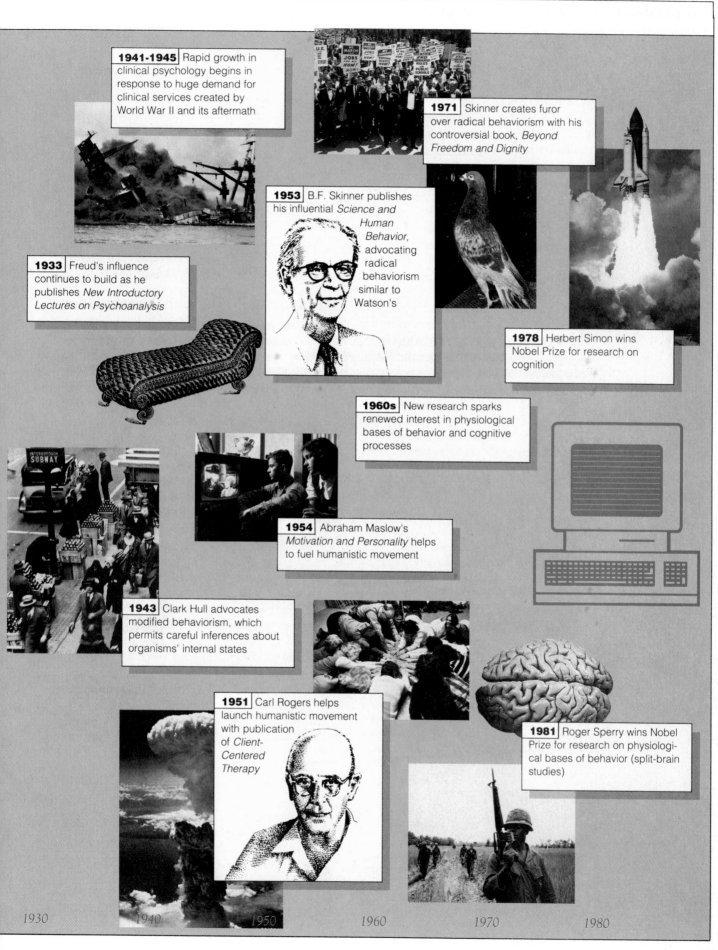

1941-1945 Rapid growth in clinical psychology begins in response to huge demand for clinical services created by World War II and its aftermath

1971 Skinner creates furor over radical behaviorism with his controversial book, *Beyond Freedom and Dignity*

1953 B.F. Skinner publishes his influential *Science and Human Behavior*, advocating radical behaviorism similar to Watson's

1933 Freud's influence continues to build as he publishes *New Introductory Lectures on Psychoanalysis*

1978 Herbert Simon wins Nobel Prize for research on cognition

1960s New research sparks renewed interest in physiological bases of behavior and cognitive processes

1954 Abraham Maslow's *Motivation and Personality* helps to fuel humanistic movement

1943 Clark Hull advocates modified behaviorism, which permits careful inferences about organisms' internal states

1951 Carl Rogers helps launch humanistic movement with publication of *Client-Centered Therapy*

1981 Roger Sperry wins Nobel Prize for research on physiological bases of behavior (split-brain studies)

1930   1940   1950   1960   1970   1980

sional psychology was maturing rapidly into a robust, powerful adult.

There were misgivings about this transformation in some quarters. In the halls of academia, many traditional research psychologists were alarmed by the professionalization of the field. They feared that the energy and resources previously devoted to research would be diluted. Within the medical field, psychiatrists were concerned because the new clinical psychologists were invading their traditional domain. In spite of such reservations, however, the professionalization of psychology has continued at a steady pace. In fact, the trend toward professionalization has spread into additional areas of psychology. Today the broad umbrella of applied psychology covers a variety of new professional specialties, including school psychology, industrial and organizational psychology, and counseling psychology. Whereas psychologists were once almost exclusively research scientists, today roughly two-thirds devote at least some of their time to providing professional services (VandenBos & Stapp, 1983).

Psychology Returns to Its Roots: Renewed Interest in Cognition and Physiology

While applied psychology has blossomed in recent years, research has also continued to evolve. Ironically, two of the latest trends in research hark all the way back to psychology's beginning, when psychologists were principally interested in consciousness and physiology. Today psychologists are showing renewed interest in consciousness (now called cognition) and the physiological bases of behavior (Bruce, 1980; Legge, 1980).

Cognition refers to the mental processes involved in acquiring knowledge. In other words, cognition involves thinking or conscious experience. For many decades, the dominance of behaviorism discouraged investigation of "unobservable" mental processes, and relatively few psychologists showed much interest in cognition. During the 1950s and 1960s, however, this slowly began to change. Major progress in the study of children's cognitive development (Piaget, 1954), memory (Miller, 1956), language (Chomsky, 1957), and problem solving (Newell, Shaw, & Simon, 1958) sparked a surge of interest in cognitive psychology.

Since then, cognitive theorists have argued that psychology must study internal mental events to fully understand behavior (Miller, Galanter, & Pribram, 1960; Neisser, 1967). Advocates of the cognitive orientation point out that our manipulations of mental images surely influence how we behave. Consequently, focusing exclusively on overt, observable behavior yields an incomplete picture of why we behave as we do. Equally important, psychologists investigating decision making, reasoning, and problem solving have shown that methods *can* be devised to study cognitive processes objectively and scientifically. Although the methods are different from those used in psychology's early days, this renewed interest in the inner workings of the mind has put the *psyche* back in contemporary psychology.

The 1950s and 1960s also saw many discoveries that highlighted the interrelationships between mind, body, and behavior. For example, psychologists demonstrated that electrical stimulation of the brain could produce emotional responses like pleasure and rage in animals (Olds, 1956). Other work showed that the right and left halves of the brain are specialized to handle different types of mental tasks (Gazzaniga, Bogen, & Sperry, 1965). Excitement was also generated by the finding that people can exert some self-control over internal physiological processes, including electrical activity in the brain, through a strategy called biofeedback (Kamiya, 1969).

These and many other findings stimulated an increase in research on the physiological bases of behavior. As you know, in the 19th century the young science of psychology was heavily physiological in emphasis. Thus, the recent interest in the biological bases of behavior represents another return to psychology's heritage.

Our review of psychology's past shows how the field has evolved. We have seen psychology develop from philosophical speculation into a rigorous science committed to research. We have seen how a highly visible professional arm involved in

---

CONCEPT CHECK 1.3
Understanding Differing Conceptions of Psychology

Check your understanding of the various schools of thought in psychology's history by matching each conception of psychology's mission with its corresponding school of thought. The answers can be found in Appendix A.

Conception of psychology

___ 1. Psychology should discover relations between environmental stimuli and overt responses.

___ 2. Psychology should analyze the basic elements of conscious experience.

___ 3. Psychology should explain the unique qualities of human behavior.

___ 4. Psychology should discover the purposes of consciousness.

School of thought

A. Structuralism
B. Functionalism
C. Behaviorism
D. Psychoanalysis
E. Humanism

mental health services emerged from this science. We have seen how psychology's focus on physiology is rooted in its 19th-century origins. We have seen how and why psychologists developed their penchant for animal research. We have seen how psychology has evolved from the study of mind and body to the study of behavior—and how the investigation of mind and body has been welcomed back into the mainstream of contemporary psychology. We have seen how different theoretical schools have defined the scope and mission of psychology in different ways. We have seen how psychology's interests have expanded and become increasingly diverse. Above all else, we have seen that psychology is a growing, evolving intellectual enterprise.

Psychology's history is already rich, but its story has barely begun. The century or so that has elapsed since Wilhelm Wundt put psychology on a scientific footing is only an eyeblink of time in the long history of our species. What has been discovered during those hundred years, and what remains unknown, is the subject of the rest of this book.

PSYCHOLOGY TODAY: VIGOROUS AND DIVERSIFIED

We began this chapter with an informal description of what psychology is and the many activities in which psychologists are engaged. Now that you have a feel for how psychology has developed, you can better appreciate a definition of the field that does justice to its modern diversity. We will define psychology as follows: **psychology is the science that studies behavior and the physiological and cognitive processes that underlie it, and the profession that applies the accumulated knowledge of this science to practical problems.**

Contemporary psychology is a vigorous, thriving science and profession. Its growth has been remarkable. One simple index of this growth is the dramatic increase in the membership in the American Psychological Association. Figure 1.4 shows that membership in the APA has increased more than sixfold since 1950! In the United States, psychology now accounts for about 10% of all the doctoral degrees awarded in the sciences and humanities. The comparable figure in 1945 was only 4% (Howard et al., 1986). Of course, psychology is an international enterprise. Today, over 1000 technical journals from all over the world publish research articles on psychology. Thus, by any standard of measurement—the number of people involved, the number of degrees granted, the number of studies conducted, the number of journals published—psychology is a healthy, growing field.

Psychology's vigorous presence in modern society is also demonstrated by the great variety of settings in which psychologists work. The distribution of psychologists employed in various categories of settings can be seen in Figure 1.5. Although psychologists were once found almost exclusively in the halls of academia, Figure 1.5 shows that today only about one-third of American psychologists work in colleges and universities. The remaining two-thirds are found in hospitals, clinics, police departments, research

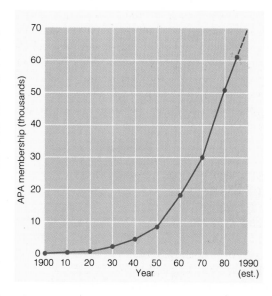

Figure 1.4 Membership in the American Psychological Association, 1900–1990. The steep rise in the number of psychologists in the APA since 1950 testifies to psychology's remarkable growth as a science and a profession.

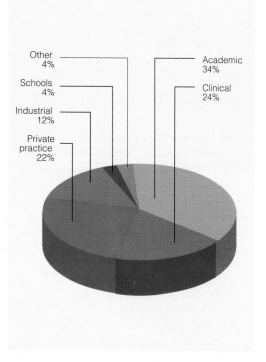

Figure 1.5 Employment of psychologists, by setting. Today only about one-third of American psychologists work primarily in college and university settings.

Figure 1.6 Major research areas in contemporary psychology.

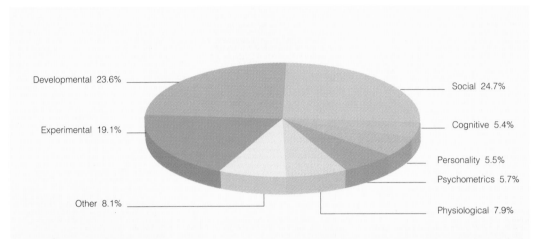

Area	Focus of research
Experimental psychology	Encompasses the traditional core of topics that psychology focused on heavily in its first half-century as a science: sensation, perception, learning, conditioning, motivation, and emotion. Although there is strong emphasis on laboratory experimentation, the name experimental psychology is misleading, as this is not the only area in which experiments are done. Psychologists working in all the areas listed below conduct experiments.
Physiological psychology	Examines the influence of genetic factors on behavior and the role of the brain, nervous system, endocrine system, and bodily chemicals in the regulation of behavior.
Cognitive psychology	Focuses on "higher" mental processes, such as memory, reasoning, information processing, language, problem solving, decision making, and creativity.
Developmental psychology	Looks at human development across the life span. Developmental psychology once focused primarily on child development, but today devotes a great deal of research to adolescence, adulthood, and old age.
Psychometrics	Is concerned with the measurement of behavior and capacities, usually through the development of psychological tests. Involved with the design of tests to assess personality, intelligence, and a wide range of abilities. Psychometrics is also concerned with the development of new techniques for statistical analysis.
Personality	Is interested in describing and understanding individuals' consistency in behavior, which represents their personality. This area of interest is also concerned with the factors that shape personality and with personality assessment.
Social psychology	Focuses on interpersonal behavior and the role of social forces in governing behavior. Typical topics include attitude formation, attitude change, prejudice, conformity, attraction, aggression, intimate relationships, and behavior in groups.

institutes, government agencies, business and industry, schools, nursing homes, counseling centers, and private practice.

Clearly, contemporary psychology is a multifaceted field. This is especially apparent when we consider the many areas of specialization within psychology today. Let's look at the current areas of specialization in both the science and the profession of psychology.

Research Areas in Psychology

Although psychologists generally receive broad training that provides them with knowledge about many areas of psychology, they usually specialize in their research endeavors. This specialization is necessary because the subject matter of psychology has grown so vast over the years. Today it is virtually impossible for anyone to stay abreast of the new research in all specialties. Specialization is also necessary because specific skills and training are required to do research in some areas.

Seven major research areas in modern psychology are (1) experimental psychology, (2) physiological psychology, (3) cognitive psychology, (4) developmental psychology, (5) psychometrics, (6) personality, and (7) social psychology. Figure 1.6 describes these areas briefly and shows the

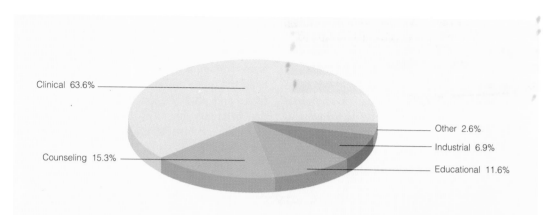

Clinical 63.6%

Counseling 15.3%

Other 2.6%

Industrial 6.9%

Educational 11.6%

Specialty	Focus of professional practice
Clinical psychology	Is concerned with the evaluation, diagnosis, and treatment of individuals with psychological disorders, as well as treatment of less severe behavioral and emotional problems. Principal activities include interviewing clients, psychological testing, and providing group or individual psychotherapy.
Counseling psychology	Overlaps with clinical psychology in that specialists in both areas engage in similar activities — interviewing, testing, and providing therapy. However, counseling psychologists usually work with a somewhat different clientele, providing assistance to people struggling with everyday problems of relatively moderate severity. Thus, they often specialize in family, marital, and career counseling.
Educational and school psychology	Educational psychologists work to improve curriculum design, achievement testing, teacher training, and other aspects of the educational process. School psychologists usually work in elementary or secondary schools, where they test and counsel children having difficulties in school, and aid parents and teachers in solving school-related problems.
Industrial and organizational psychology	Psychologists in this area perform a wide variety of tasks in the world of business and industry. These include: running personnel departments, working to improve staff morale and attitudes, striving to increase job satisfaction and productivity, examining organizational structures and procedures, and making recommendations for improvements.

percentage of research psychologists who identify each area as their primary interest (Stapp & Fulcher, 1983). As you can see, social psychology and developmental psychology have become especially active areas of research.

Professional Specialties in Psychology

At present, there are four clearly identified areas of specialization within the domain of applied psychology. These established professional specialties are (1) clinical psychology, (2) counseling psychology, (3) educational and school psychology, and (4) industrial and organizational psychology. Descriptions of each of these specialties can be found in Figure 1.7 along with the percentage of professional psychologists specializing in each area (Stapp & Fulcher, 1983). As the figure indicates, clinical psychology is currently the most prominent and widely practiced professional specialty in the field.

The distinction between psychology as a research science and psychology as a profession is not absolute. The data in Figures 1.6 and 1.7 are based on psychologists' reports of their single, principal area of specialization, but many psychologists work on both research and application. Some academic psychologists work as consultants, therapists, or counselors on a part-time basis. Similarly, some applied psychologists conduct basic research on issues related to their specialty. For example, many clinical psychologists are involved in research on the nature and causes of abnormal behavior.

The emergence of clinical psychology has left many people confused about the difference between psychology and psychiatry. The confusion is understandable, since both clinical psychologists and psychiatrists are involved in diagnosing and treating mental disorders. Although there is some overlap between clinical psychology and psychiatry, the training and educational requirements for the two fields are quite different. Psychologists go to graduate schools, where they earn one of several doctoral degrees (Ph.D., Ed.D., or Psy.D.) in order to enjoy full status in their profession. Psychiatrists go to medical schools for their postgraduate education, where they receive general training in medicine and earn an M.D. degree. After earning their M.D., they specialize in psychiatry by completing residency training in psychiatry at a hospital. Clinical psychologists and psychiatrists also differ in the way they tend to approach the treatment of mental disorders. We will discuss these differences in Chapter 15.

In short, **psychiatry is a branch of medicine concerned with the diagnosis and treatment of psychological problems and disorders.** In contrast, psychology is concerned with the entire realm of human and animal behavior and the cognitive and physiological processes that underlie that behavior. Thus, psychology's scope of concern is much broader and more diversified than that of psychiatry.

PUTTING IT IN PERSPECTIVE: SIX KEY THEMES

The enormous breadth and diversity of psychology make it a challenging subject for the beginning student. In the pages ahead you will be introduced to many different areas of research and a multitude of new ideas, concepts, and principles. Fortunately, all ideas are *not* created equal. Some are far more important than others. In this section, I will highlight six fundamental themes that will reappear in a number of variations as we move from one area of psychology to another. You have already met some of these key ideas in our review of psychology's past and present. Now we will isolate them and highlight their significance. The remainder of the book will use these organizing themes to help clarify the nature of psychology and the connections between the many different areas of the discipline.

In studying psychology, you are learning about the mind, the body, and behavior, but you are also learning about the scientific discipline that studies it. Accordingly, our six themes come in two sets. The first set consists of three statements highlighting crucial aspects of psychology as a way of thinking and as a field of study. The second set consists of three broad generalizations about psychology's subject matter—behavior and the cognitive and physiological processes that underlie it. As we review what psychologists have learned about behavior, you will encounter these fundamental principles again and again.

Themes Related to Psychology as a Field of Study

Looking at psychology as a field of study, we see three crucial ideas that represent themes 1 through 3: (1) Psychology is empirical. (2) Psychology is theoretically diverse. (3) Psychology evolves in a sociohistorical context. Let's look at each of these ideas in more detail.

THEME 1: PSYCHOLOGY IS EMPIRICAL
We all try to understand behavior. Most of us have our own personal answers for questions such as why some people are lazy, why some are forgetful, and why others stay in demeaning relationships. If all of us are amateur psychologists, what makes scientific psychology different? The critical difference between the two is that scientific psychology is empirical. This aspect of psychology is so fundamental that virtually every page of this book reflects it.

What do we mean by empirical? **Empiricism involves the premise that knowledge should be acquired through observation.** This premise is crucial to the scientific method that psychology embraced in the latter part of the 19th century. When we say that psychology is empirical, we mean that its conclusions are based on systematic observation rather than on reasoning, speculation, traditional beliefs, or common sense. Psychologists are not content with having ideas that sound plausible; they conduct research to *test* their ideas. Is intelligence higher on the average in some social classes than others? Are men more aggressive than women? Rather than speculate or rely on casual observations, the psychologist finds a way to make systematic, objective, and precise observations to answer such questions.

This empirical approach requires a certain attitude—a healthy brand of skepticism. Empiricism is a demanding taskmaster. It demands data and documentation. Psychologists' commitment to empiricism means that they must learn to think critically about generalizations regarding behavior. If someone asserts that people tend to get depressed around Christmas, a psychologist is likely to ask: "How many people get depressed? In what population? In comparison to what baseline rate of depression? How was depression assessed?" Their skeptical attitude reflects the fact that psychologists are trained to ask "Where's the evidence? How do you know?" Hopefully, psychology's empirical orientation will rub off on you, and you will be asking similar questions by the time you finish this book.

THEME 2: PSYCHOLOGY IS THEORETICALLY DIVERSE

Even though psychology is based on observation, a string of unrelated observations would not be terribly enlightening. Psychologists do not set out just to collect facts. They seek to explain and understand what they observe. To achieve these goals, they must construct theories. **A theory is a system of interrelated ideas that is used to explain a set of observations.** In other words, a theory links apparently unrelated observations and provides an explanation of them. As an example, consider Sigmund Freud's observations about slips of the tongue, dreams, and psychological disturbances. On the surface, these observations seemed unrelated. But by devising the concept of the *unconscious*, Freud created a theory that linked and explained these seemingly unrelated aspects of behavior.

Our review of psychology's past should have made one thing abundantly clear: psychology is marked by theoretical diversity. Why do we have so many competing points of view? One reason is that no single theory can adequately explain everything that we know about behavior. Sometimes different theories focus on different aspects of behavior—that is, different collections of observations. Sometimes there is simply more than one way to look at something. Is the glass half empty or half full? Obviously, it is both. To take an example from another science, physicists wrestled for years with the nature of light. Is it a wave, or is it a particle? In the end, it proved useful to think of light sometimes as a wave and sometimes as a particle. Similarly, if a business executive lashes out at her employees with stinging criticism, is she releasing pent-up aggressive urges (a psychoanalytic view)? Is she making a habitual response to the stimulus of incompetent work (a behavioral view)? Or is she scheming to motivate her employees with "mind games" (a cognitive view)? In some cases, all three of these explanations might have some validity.

In short, it is an oversimplification to expect that one view has to be right while all others are wrong. Life is rarely that simple. In view of the immense range of subject areas studied by psychology and their enormous complexity, it would be surprising if there were *not* a number of different theories and points of view.

At present, five broad theoretical perspectives are influential in psychology. Three of these are carryovers from traditional schools of thought wherein far-reaching theories were proposed to explain a huge variety of observations. These are the *behavioral*, *psychoanalytic*, and *humanistic* perspectives. The remaining two viewpoints, the *cognitive* and *physiological* perspectives, are increasingly influential "angles" from which to investigate behavior. You have already seen how each of these five perspectives emerged in psychology. In upcoming chapters you will learn how they can be applied to specific questions about behavior.

It's probably most effective to think of the various theoretical orientations in psychology as complementary viewpoints, each with its own advantages and limitations. Indeed, modern psychologists increasingly recognize that theoretical diversity is a strength rather than a weakness (Wertheimer, 1970). As we proceed through this text, you will see how differing theoretical perspectives often converge on a more thorough understanding of behavior than could be achieved by any one perspective alone.

THEME 3: PSYCHOLOGY EVOLVES IN A SOCIOHISTORICAL CONTEXT

We often think of science as an ivory-tower undertaking that is isolated from the ebb and flow of everyday life. In reality, however, psychology and other sciences do *not* exist in a cultural vacuum. There are dense interconnections between what happens in psychology and what happens in society at large (Braginsky, 1985; Chorover, 1985). Influence travels over these interconnections in both directions. Trends, issues, and values in society influence psychology's evolution, while progress in psychology affects trends, issues, and values in society. To put it briefly, psychology develops in a sociohistorical (social and historical) context.

Let's focus on the impact of society on psychology first. Our review of psychology's past is replete with examples of how social trends leave their imprint on psychology. In the late 19th century, psychology's rapid growth as a laboratory science was due, in part, to a fascination with physics as the model science. Thus, the spirit of the times fostered a scientific approach rather than a philosophical approach to the investigation of the mind. In a similar fashion, Freud's groundbreaking ideas emerged out of a specific sociohistorical context. Cultural values in Freud's era encouraged the suppression of sexuality and tended to make people feel guilty about their sexual urges to a much greater extent than is common today. This climate clearly contributed to Freud's emphasis on the pivotal importance of unconscious sexual conflicts. As a final example, consider the impact of World War II on the development of psychology as a profession. The rapid growth of professional psychology was largely due to the war-related surge in the demand for clinical

Mr. Blank is a graduate student in the Department of Economics and Social Science here at M.I.T. He has had three semesters of teaching experience in psychology at another college. This is his first semester teaching Ec. 70. He is 26 years old, a veteran, and married. People who know him consider him to be a very warm person, industrious, critical, practical, and determined.

Figure 1.8a What is your response to Mr. Blank as a potential new instructor for your class? For example, how considerate, sociable, and good-natured would you expect him to be? (For an explanation, see text, p. 23, and Figure 1.8b).

services. Hence, World War II reshaped the landscape of psychology in a remarkably short time.

If we reverse our viewpoint, we can see that psychology leaves its mark on society. Consider, for instance, the pervasive role of mental testing in modern society. Your own success at school or in your career may well depend in part on how well you weave your way through a complex maze of mental tests. Scholarships and jobs may be on the line as you grapple with intelligence and achievement tests made possible (to the regret of some) by advances in psychology. As another example, let's consider the impact of some of B. F. Skinner's ideas. As you know, Skinner insists that behavior is fully determined by one's environment. Insofar as we believe this, it is difficult for us to hold people responsible for their actions—even actions that we find offensive, such as crimes. Skinner also asserts that punishment is a relatively ineffective method for controlling behavior. These notions helped to promote the idea that prisons should be used to rehabilitate criminals rather than to punish them. While people disagree about the wisdom of this idea, the point is that Skinner's theories have influenced public opinion and official policy on an important issue. This is not unusual. Research and theory in psychology often have an impact on public policy issues, ranging from how much violence should be shown on television to how drug use should be regulated.

In short, society and psychology influence each other in complex ways. In the chapters to come, we will frequently have occasion to notice this dynamic relationship.

Themes Related to Psychology's Subject Matter

Looking at psychology's subject matter, we see three crucial ideas that represent themes 4 through 6: (4) Behavior is determined by multiple causes. (5) Heredity and environment jointly influence behavior. (6) Our experience of the world is highly subjective. Let's look at each of these ideas more closely.

THEME 4: BEHAVIOR IS DETERMINED BY MULTIPLE CAUSES

As psychology has matured, we have accumulated more and more information about behavior and the forces that govern it. Our growing knowledge has led to a deeper appreciation of a simple but important fact: behavior is exceedingly complex, and most aspects of behavior are determined by multiple causes.

The complexity of behavior may seem self-evident, but people often think in terms of single causes. We like simplicity, so we explain behavior by zeroing in on a single cause that stands out. Thus, we offer explanations such as, "Andrea flunked out of school because she is lazy," or "Fred attempted suicide because his girlfriend broke up with him." Single-cause explanations such as these may be accurate as far as they go, but they are usually incomplete. In general, we find that behavior is governed by a complex network of interacting factors. We can refer to this idea as the *multifactorial causation of behavior*.

As a simple illustration of this idea, consider the multiple factors that might influence your performance in your introductory psychology course: your overall intelligence, your reading ability, your memory skills, your motivation to do well in college, your interest in psychology, and the quality of your study skills. These are just some of the *personal* factors that might affect your success. In addition, your grade could be affected by numerous *situational* factors, including whether you like your psychology professor, whether you like your assigned text, whether the class meets at a time when you tend to be alert, whether your work schedule is light or heavy, and whether you're having any personal problems with roommates, friends, or family that interfere with your concentration.

As you proceed through this book, you'll learn that this complexity of causation is the rule rather than the exception. The fact that behavior is complex is one of the reasons for the theoretical diversity we encountered in our survey of psychology's development. Such diversity helps us guard against oversimplified explanations. If we expect to truly understand behavior, we usually have to take into account multiple determinants.

THEME 5: HEREDITY AND ENVIRONMENT JOINTLY INFLUENCE BEHAVIOR

Are we who we are—smart or dumb, athletic or artistic, shy or outgoing, deceitful or honest, hardworking or lazy—because of our genetic inheritance or because of our upbringing? This question about the importance of nature versus nurture, or heredity versus the environment, has been asked in one form or another since ancient times. Historically, the nature versus nurture question was framed as an all-or-none proposition. In other words, some theorists argued that personality characteristics and mental abilities are governed entirely by heredity, while other theorists argued that these traits are determined entirely by one's environment. John B. Watson, for instance, asserted that personality and ability depend on one's environment. In contrast, Sir

Francis Galton, a pioneer in the study of individual differences in mental ability, maintained that intelligence and other traits depend entirely on one's genetic inheritance.

Today, most psychologists agree that heredity and the environment are both very important. A century of research has shown that genetics and experience together influence our intelligence, our temperament, our personality, and our susceptibility to many psychological disorders (Scarr & Kidd, 1983; Schlesinger, 1985). If we ask whether we are born or made, psychology's answer is "Both."

This does *not* mean that nature versus nurture is a dead issue. Lively debate about the *relative influence* of genetics and experience continues unabated. Furthermore, psychologists are actively seeking to understand the complex ways in which genetic inheritance and experience interact to mold behavior.

THEME 6: OUR EXPERIENCE OF THE WORLD IS HIGHLY SUBJECTIVE

It's ironic that one of our enduring insights about behavior contributed greatly to the downfall of structuralism, which was psychology's first major school of thought. Under Wundt's leadership, the structuralists sought to analyze consciousness into its basic elements. However, when they presented exactly the same stimulus to different subjects, they often got different results. Thus, they learned the hard way that our experience of the world is highly subjective.

Even elementary perception—for example of sights and sounds—is not a passive process. We actively process incoming stimulation. We selectively focus on some aspects of that stimulation while ignoring other aspects. Moreover, we impose organization on the stimuli that we pay attention to. These tendencies combine to make our perception of the world personalized and subjective.

The subjectivity of perception was demonstrated nicely in a study by Hastorf and Cantril (1954). They showed students at Princeton and Dartmouth universities a film of a recent Princeton-Dartmouth football game and told them to watch for rules infractions. Both groups saw exactly the same film—but the Princeton students "saw" the Dartmouth players engage in twice as many infractions as the Dartmouth students "saw." The investigators concluded that the game "actually was many different games and that each version of the events that transpired was just as 'real' to a particular person as other versions were to other people" (Hastorf & Cantril, 1954). In

this study, the subjects' perceptions were swayed by their motives. It shows how we sometimes see what we *want* to see.

Other studies reveal that we also tend to see what we *expect* to see. For example, Harold Kelley (1950) showed how perceptions of people are influenced by their reputation. Kelley told students that their class would be taken over by a new lecturer whom they would be asked to evaluate later. Before the class, each student was given a short description of the incoming instructor, but there was one important variation in the descriptions. Half of the students were led to expect a "warm" person, while the other half were led to expect a "cold" one (see Figure 1.8). All the subjects were exposed to exactly the same 20 minutes of lecture and interaction with the new instructor. However, the subjects who *expected* a warm person rated the instructor as more considerate, sociable, humorous, good-natured, informal, and humane than those who expected a cold person.

Thus, it's clear that our motives and expectations color our experiences. To some extent, we see what we want to see or what we expect to see. This subjectivity in perception will surface repeatedly as an explanation for a variety of behavioral tendencies that would otherwise leave us perplexed.

This subjectivity is also precisely what the scientific method is designed to counteract. In using the scientific approach, psychologists strive to make their observations as objective as humanly possible. In some respects, overcoming subjectivity is what science is all about. Otherwise, left to our own subjective experience, we might still believe, for example, that the earth is flat and that the sun revolves around it. Of course, being human, psychologists and other scientists are not immune to the effects of subjective experience. This will become apparent in the next chapter when we discuss how experimenter biases can sometimes influence the conduct of research. Nonetheless, psychologists are committed to the scientific approach because they believe it is the most reliable route to accurate knowledge.

Although accurate knowledge is the foremost goal of the scientific enterprise, psychologists also try to apply the knowledge that they accumulate through their research. Now that you have been introduced to the organizing themes that will guide us as we proceed through the remainder of the book, let's turn to an example of how psychological research can be applied to the challenges of everyday life. In our first Application, we'll focus on a subject that should be highly relevant to you—how to be a successful student.

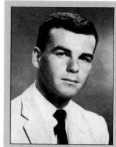

Mr. Blank is a graduate student in the Department of Economics and Social Science here at M.I.T. He has had three semesters of teaching experience in psychology at another college. This is his first semester teaching Ec. 70. He is 26 years old, a veteran, and married. People who know him consider him to be a rather cold person, industrious, critical, practical, and determined.

Figure 1.8b One of two descriptions of a new "instructor" (the other is in Figure 1.8a). Read the accompanying description of Mr. Blank carefully. Is your perception of him the same as it was when you read the description in Figure 1.8a? Only a single word is different in the two versions, but subjects in the Kelley (1950) study perceived the same person very differently depending on which of these descriptions they had been exposed to beforehand.

IMPROVING ACADEMIC PERFORMANCE

Answer the following "true" or "false."

☐ 1. It's a good idea to study in as many different locations (your bedroom or kitchen, the library, lounges around school, and so forth) as possible.

☐ 2. If you have a professor who delivers chaotic, hard-to-follow lectures, there is little point in attending class.

☐ 3. Cramming the night before an exam is an efficient method of study.

☐ 4. In taking lecture notes, you should try to be a "human tape recorder" (that is, take down everything exactly as said by your professor).

☐ 5. You should never change your answers to multiple-choice questions, because your first hunch is your best hunch.

As you will soon learn, all of the above statements are false. If you answered them all correctly, you may already have acquired the kinds of skills and habits that facilitate academic success. If so, however, you are *not* typical. Today, a huge number of students enter college with remarkably poor study skills and habits—and it's not entirely their fault. Our educational system generally does not provide much in the way of formal instruction on good study techniques. In this first Application I will try to remedy this oversight to some extent by sharing with you some insights that psychology can provide on how to improve your academic performance.

Psychologists have been investigating educational processes since the days of G. Stanley Hall in the early part of this century. Today, educational psychology is a major area of specialization in the field. Drawing

mainly from work in this area, we will discuss how to promote better study habits, how to enhance reading efforts, how to get more out of lectures, and how to improve test-taking strategies. You may also want to jump ahead and read the Application for Chapter 7, which focuses on how to improve everyday memory. Many of the ideas in that Application can be helpful when you have to memorize information.

Developing Sound Study Habits

Effective study is crucial to success in college. Although you may run into a few classmates who boast about getting good grades without studying, you can be sure that if they perform well on exams, they study. Students who claim otherwise simply want to be viewed as extremely bright rather than studious.

Learning can be immensely gratifying, but studying usually involves hard work. The first step toward effective study habits is to face up to this reality. You don't have to feel guilty if, like most students, you don't look forward to studying. Once you accept the premise that studying doesn't come naturally, it should be apparent that you need to set up an organized program to promote adequate study. Such a program should include the following elements:

1. *Set up a schedule for studying.* If you wait until the urge to study hits you, you may still be waiting when the exam rolls around. Thus, it's important to allocate definite times to studying. Review your various time obligations (work, housekeeping, and so on) and figure out in advance when you can study. In allotting certain times to studying, keep in mind that you need to be wide awake and alert. It won't do you much good to plan to

study at times when you're likely to be very tired. Be realistic, too, about how long you can study at one time before fatigue wears you down. Allow time for study breaks—they can revive sagging concentration.

It's important to write down your study schedule. Writing it down serves as a reminder and increases your commitment to the schedule. You should begin by setting up a general schedule for the quarter or semester, like the one in Figure 1.9. Then, at the beginning of each week, plan the specific assignments that you intend to work on during each study session. This approach to scheduling should help you to avoid cramming for exams at the last minute. Cramming is an ineffective study strategy for most students (Underwood, 1961; Zechmeister & Nyberg, 1982). Cramming will strain your memorization capabilities and tax your energy level, and it may stoke the fires of test anxiety.

In planning your weekly schedule, try to avoid the tendency to put off working on major tasks such as term papers and reports. Time management experts, such as Alan Lakein (1973), point out that many of us tend to work on simple, routine tasks first, while putting off larger tasks until later, when we supposedly will have more time. This common tendency leads many of us, repeatedly, to delay working on major assignments until it's too late to do a good job. You can avoid this trap by breaking major assignments down into smaller component tasks, which you can schedule individually. Some additional guidelines that promote efficient time management are listed in Figure 1.10.

2. *Find a place to study where you can concentrate.* Where you study can be as important as *when* you study. The key is to find a place where distractions are likely to be minimal. Most people cannot study effectively while watching TV, listening to the stereo, or overhearing conversations. Don't depend

Figure 1.9 One student's general activity schedule for a semester. Each week the student fills in the specific assignments to work on during each study period.

Weekly activity schedule

	Monday	Tuesday	Wednesday	Thursday	Friday	Saturday	Sunday
6 A.M.							
7 A.M.							
8 A.M.						Work	
9 A.M.	History	Study	History	Study	History	Work	
10 A.M.	Psychology	French	Psychology	French	Psychology	Work	
11 A.M.	Study	French	Study	French	Study	Work	
Noon	Math	Study	Math	Study	Math	Work	Study
1 P.M.							Study
2 P.M.	Study	English	Study	English	Study		Study
3 P.M.	Study	English	Study	English	Study		Study
4 P.M.							
5 P.M.							
6 P.M.	Work	Study	Study	Work			Study
7 P.M.	Work	Study	Study	Work			Study
8 P.M.	Work	Study	Study	Work			Study
9 P.M.	Work	Study	Study	Work			Study
10 P.M.	Work			Work			
11 P.M.							

THE EVOLUTION
OF PSYCHOLOGY

Figure 1.10 Hints for managing your time. (Adapted from Johnson, Springer, & Sternglanz, 1982)

- Set aside times and places for work.
- Set priorities and then *do* things in priority order.
- Break large tasks into much smaller ones.
- Keep the tasks planned for a day down to a reasonable number.
- Work on one thing (an important task) at a time.
- Define all tasks specifically (in terms of what you want to have written or want to be able to recall, and so forth).
- Check your progress often.

on willpower to carry you through these distractions. It's much more effective to plan ahead and avoid the distractions altogether. Libraries are usually conducive to study, but they too can become social centers. Hence, it's often a good idea to conceal yourself in an out-of-the-way study carrel where you won't be interrupted by a steady stream of friends.

There is evidence that it helps to set up one or two specific places for study. If possible, your study areas should be used for nothing else. These places may become strongly associated with studying, so that they serve as cues that evoke good study behavior (Beneke & Harris, 1972). In contrast, places that you associate with other activities may serve as cues for these other activities. For example, studying in your kitchen may evoke more eating than reading.

3. *Reward your studying.* One of the reasons it's so difficult to motivate oneself to study regularly is that the payoffs for studying often lie in the distant future. The ultimate reward, a degree, may be years away. Even more short-term rewards, such as an "A" in the course, may be weeks or months away. To combat this problem, it helps to give yourself immediate rewards for studying. It's easier to motivate yourself to study if you reward yourself with a tangible payoff, such as a snack, TV show, or phone call to a friend, when

you finish. Thus, you should set realistic study goals for yourself and then reward yourself when you meet them. This systematic manipulation of rewards involves harnessing the principles of operant conditioning described by B. F. Skinner and other behavioral psychologists. Skinner's followers have refined these principles into powerful methods for the control of behavior. These *behavior modification* procedures, which can be very valuable in increasing study behavior, are described in some detail in the Chapter 6 Application.

Improving Your Reading

Much of your study time is spent reading and absorbing information. *These efforts must be active.* If you engage in passive reading, the information will pass right through you. Many students deceive themselves into thinking that they are studying by running a pastel felt-tip pen through a few sentences here and there in their book. If this isn't done with thoughtful selectivity, the student is simply turning a textbook into a coloring book. Underlining in your text can be useful, but you have to distinguish between important ideas and mere supportive material.

There are a number of ways of actively attacking your reading assignments. One of the more worthwhile strategies is Robinson's (1970) SQ3R method. **SQ3R is a study system designed to promote effective reading by means of five steps: survey, question, read, recite, and review.** Its name is an acronym for the five steps in the procedure:

Step 1: Survey. Before you plunge into the reading itself, glance over the topic headings in the chapter and try to get a general overview of the material. Try to understand how the various chapter segments are related. If there is a chapter outline or summary, consult it to get a general feel for the chapter. The point is, if you know where the chapter is going, you can

better appreciate and organize the information you are about to read.

Step 2: Question. Once you have an overview of your reading assignment, you should proceed through it one section at a time. Take a look at the heading of the first section and convert it into a question. This is usually quite simple. If the heading is "Prenatal Risk Factors," your question should be "What are sources of risk during prenatal development?" If the heading is "Stereotyping," your question should be "What is stereotyping?" Asking these questions gets you actively involved in your reading and helps you to identify the main ideas.

Step 3: Read. Only now, in the third step, are you ready to sink your teeth into the reading. Read only the specific section that you have decided to tackle. Read it with an eye toward answering the question that you just formulated. If necessary, reread the section until you can answer that question. Decide whether the segment addresses any other important questions, and answer these as well.

Step 4: Recite. Now that you can answer the key question for the section, recite the answer out loud to yourself in your own words. It is important to use your own words, because that requires understanding instead of simple memorization. Don't move on to the next section until you understand the main idea(s) of the present section. You may want to write down these ideas for review later. When you have fully digested the first section, then you may go on to the next. Repeat steps 2 through 4 with the next section. Once you have mastered the crucial points there, you can go on again. Keep repeating steps 2 through 4, section by section, until you finish the chapter.

Step 5: Review. When you have read the chapter, test and refresh your memory by going back over the key points. Repeat your questions and try to answer them without consulting your book or notes. This review should fortify your retention of the main ideas and should alert you to any key ideas that you haven't mastered. Going over the main points should also help you to see the relationships between the main ideas.

The SQ3R method does not have to be applied rigidly. For example, it is often wise to break your reading assignment down into smaller segments than those separated by section headings. In fact, SQ3R should probably be applied to many texts on a paragraph-by-paragraph basis. Obviously, applying SQ3R this way will require you to formulate some questions without the benefit of topic headings. However, the headings are not absolutely necessary to use this technique. If you don't have enough headings, you can simply reverse the order of steps 2 and 3. Read the paragraph first, and then formulate a question that addresses the basic idea of the paragraph. Then work at answering the question in your own words. The point is that you can be flexible in your use of the SQ3R technique. *What makes SQ3R effective is that it breaks a reading assignment down into manageable segments*

and requires that you understand them before you move on. Any method that accomplishes these goals should enhance your reading.

Besides topic headings that will help you use the SQ3R method, your textbooks may incorporate various other learning aids you can use to improve your reading. If a book provides a chapter outline and chapter summary, don't ignore them. These aids can help you to recognize the important points in the chapter and to understand how the various parts of the chapter are interrelated. If your book furnishes learning objectives, use them. They tell you what you should get out of your reading. Good learning objectives practically formulate the questions for you in the SQ3R process (learning objectives for this text can be found in the separate *Study Guide*). A lot of thought goes into these and other learning aids. It's wise to take advantage of them.

Getting More out of Lectures

Although lectures are sometimes boring and tedious, it is a simple fact that poor class attendance is associated with poor grades. For example, in one study, Lindgren (1969) found that absences from class were much more common among "unsuccessful" students (grade average "C-minus" or below) than among "successful" students (grade average "B" or above), as shown in Figure 1.11. Even when you

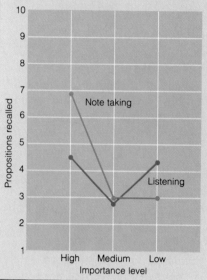

Figure 1.12 Effectiveness of listening only versus note taking during lectures, as measured by recall of high-, medium-, and low-importance propositions. (Data from Einstein, Morris, & Smith, 1985)

have an instructor who delivers hard-to-follow lectures from which you learn virtually nothing, it is still important to go to class. If nothing else, it helps to give you a feel for how the instructor thinks, and this feel can help you to anticipate the content of exams and to respond on exams in the manner expected by your professor.

Fortunately, most lectures are reasonably coherent. Research indicates that accurate note taking is related to better test performance (Palkovitz & Lore, 1980). Good note taking requires you to actively process lecture information in ways that should enhance both memory and understanding.

Studies show that attentive note taking helps students to identify and remember the most important points from a lecture and to weed out ideas of lesser importance. Einstein, Morris, and Smith (1985) conducted a study in which they had undergraduate subjects either just listen to or take notes on a videotaped lecture. Figure 1.12 shows what these researchers found when they measured the students' recall of the lecture material later. Note taking did not produce better recall of information that was of low or medium importance. Instead, it selectively enhanced only the recall of important information. Books on study skills (Pauk, 1984; Sotiriou,

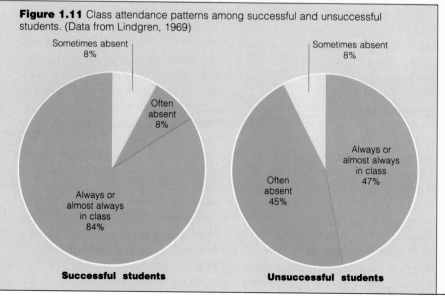

Figure 1.11 Class attendance patterns among successful and unsuccessful students. (Data from Lindgren, 1969)

Sometimes absent 8%
Often absent 8%
Always or almost always in class 84%

Successful students

Sometimes absent 8%
Always or almost always in class 47%
Often absent 45%

Unsuccessful students

1989) offer a number of suggestions on how to take good lecture notes. Some of these are summarized here:

• Extracting information from lectures requires active listening. Focus full attention on the speaker. Try to anticipate what's coming and search for deeper meanings. Pay attention to nonverbal signals that may serve to further clarify the lecturer's intent or meaning.
• When course material is especially complex and difficult, it's a good idea to prepare for the lecture by reading ahead on the scheduled subject in your text. Then you have less brand-new information to digest during the lecture.
• You are not supposed to be a human tape recorder. Insofar as possible, write down the lecturer's thoughts in your own words. This forces you to organize the ideas in a way that makes sense to you. In taking notes, pay attention to clues about what is most important. Many instructors give subtle and not-so-subtle clues about what is important. These clues may range from simply repeating main points to saying things like "You'll run into this again."
• Asking questions during lectures can be very helpful. This practice keeps you actively involved in the lecture. It also allows you to clarify points that you may have misunderstood. Many students are more bashful about asking questions than they should be. They don't realize that most professors welcome questions. Of course, a large class size places some limits on the extent to which each student can question the instructor.
• It's easy to miss points in a fast-paced lecture. Therefore, it's useful to review your notes sometime soon after the class. If something appears to be missing, consult some of your classmates.

Improving Test-Taking Strategies

Let's face it—some students are better than others at taking tests. **Testwiseness is the ability to use the characteristics and formats of a cognitive test so as to maximize one's score.**

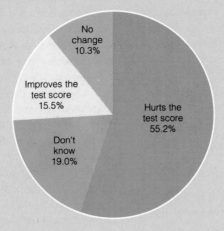

Figure 1.13 Beliefs of 58 college faculty members about the effects of changing initial answers during objective tests. It is interesting to compare the actual results of answer changing reported in Figure 1.14. (Data from Benjamin, Cavell, & Shallenberger, 1984)

No change 10.3%
Improves the test score 15.5%
Don't know 19.0%
Hurts the test score 55.2%

Figure 1.14 Actual effects of changing answers to multiple-choice tests, as found in 20 studies. (Data from Benjamin, Cavell, & Shallenberger, 1984)

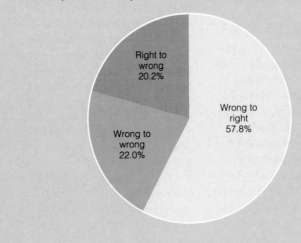

Right to wrong 20.2%
Wrong to wrong 22.0%
Wrong to right 57.8%

Students clearly vary in testwiseness, and these variations are related to performance on exams (Fagley, 1987; Sarnacki, 1979). Testwiseness is not a substitute for knowledge of the subject matter. However, skill in taking tests can help you to show what you know when it's critical to do so.

There are a variety of myths about how to take tests. For instance, many students believe that they shouldn't go back and change their answers to multiple-choice questions. Benjamin, Cavell, and Shallenberger (1984) found that this is the dominant belief among college *faculty* as well as students. Over half of the professors they surveyed thought that answer changing would tend to hurt students' test scores (see Figure 1.13). However,

this old adage that "on tests, your first hunch is your best hunch," has been shown to be wrong.

Formal studies clearly and consistently indicate that, over the long run, changing answers pays off. Benjamin and his colleagues reviewed 20 studies on this question. Figure 1.14 shows the typical (median) results. As you can see, answer changes that go from a wrong answer to a right answer outnumber changes that go from a right answer to a wrong one by a sizable margin. The popular belief that answer changing is harmful is probably attributable to the painful recollections that we have of our right-to-wrong changes. In any case, you can see how it pays to be familiar with sound test-taking strategies.

General Tips

The principles of testwiseness were first described by Millman, Bishop, and Ebel (1965). Let's look at some of their general ideas:

• If effcent use of time appears crucial, set up a mental schedule for progress through the test. Make a mental note to check whether you're one-third finished when one-third of your time is gone. You may want to check again at the two-thirds time mark.

• Do not waste time by pondering troublesome, difficult-to-answer items excessively. If you have no idea of the answer at all, just guess and go on. If you think you need to devote a good deal of time to the item, skip it and mark it so you can return to it later if time permits.

• Adopt the appropriate level of sophistication for the test. Don't "read things into" questions. Sometimes students make things more complex than they were intended to be. Often, simple-looking questions are just what they appear to be—simple.

• Unless it is explicitly forbidden, don't hesitate to ask the examiner to clarify a question when necessary. Many examiners will graciously provide a great deal of useful information.

• If you complete all of the questions and still have some time remaining, review the test. Make sure that you have recorded your answers correctly. If you were unsure of some answers, go back and reconsider them.

Tips for Multiple-Choice Exams

Sound test-taking strategies are especially important on multiple-choice (and true-false) exams. Multiple-choice questions often include clues that may help you to converge on the correct answer (Mentzer, 1982; Weiten, 1984). You may be able to improve your performance on such tests by considering the following points:

• As you read the stem of each multiple-choice question, *anticipate* the answer if you can, before looking at the options. If the answer you anticipated is found among the options, there is a high probability that it's correct.

• Even if you find your anticipated answer among the choices, you should always continue through and read all the options. There may be another option farther down the list that encompasses the one you anticipated. You should always read each question completely.

• It's important to learn how to eliminate highly implausible options quickly. Many questions have only two plausible options, accompanied by "throwaway" options for filler. You should work at spotting these implausible options so that you can quickly discard them and narrow your task.

• Be alert to the fact that examiners sometimes give away information relevant to one question in another test item.

• On items that have "all of the above" as an option, if you know that just two of the options are correct, you should choose "all of the above." If you are confident that one of the choices is incorrect, you should eliminate this option and "all of the above," and choose from the remaining options.

• Although there will always be exceptions, options that are more detailed than the others tend to be correct. Hence, it's a good idea to pay special attention to options that are extra long.

• Options that create broad, sweeping generalizations tend to be incorrect. You should watch out for words such as *always, never, necessarily, only, must, completely, totally,* and so forth, that create these improbable assertions.

• In contrast, options that create carefully qualified statements tend to be correct. Words such as *often, sometimes, perhaps, may,* and *generally* tend to show up in these well-qualified statements.

Tips for Essay Exams

There is little research on testwiseness as it applies to essay exams. This is because there are relatively few clues to take advantage of in the essay format. Nonetheless, various books (Pauk, 1984; Pivar, 1978) offer tips based on expert advice, including the following:

• Time is usually a crucial factor on essay tests. Therefore, you should begin by looking over the questions and making time allocations on the basis of (1) your knowledge, (2) the time required to answer each question, and (3) the points available for answering each question. Usually it's a good idea to answer the questions that you know best first.

• Many students fail to appreciate the importance of good organization in their essay responses. If your instructor can't follow where you are going with your answers, you won't get many points. Test essays are often poorly organized because students feel pressured for time and plunge into answering questions without any planning. It's a good idea to spend a minute getting organized first. Also, many examiners appreciate it if you make your organization quite explicit by numbering the points you're making.

• In writing essays, the trick is to be concise while being complete. You should always try to get right to the point, and you should never pad your answer. Many examiners get cross when they have to wade through excess padding to track down the crucial ideas they're looking for. However, you should avoid writing in such a "shorthand" manner that you leave things ambiguous.

• In many courses you'll learn a great deal of jargon or technical terminology. Demonstrate your learning by using this technical vocabulary in your essay answers.

In summary, sound study skills and habits are crucial to academic success. Intelligence alone won't do the job (although it certainly helps). Good academic skills do not develop overnight. They are acquired gradually, so be patient with yourself. Fortunately, tasks such as reading textbooks, writing papers, and taking tests get easier with practice. Ultimately, I think you'll find that the rewards—knowledge, a sense of accomplishment, and progress toward a degree—are worth the effort.

THE EVOLUTION OF PSYCHOLOGY

From Speculation to Science: How Psychology Developed

• The term *psychology* originally referred to the study of the mind. Although the ancient Greeks speculated about the mind, there was relatively little scholarly contemplation of psychological issues until the Renaissance, when the mind began to attract scholars' interest once again.

• Psychology's intellectual parents were 19th-century philosophy and physiology, which shared an interest in the mysteries of the mind. Philosophy provided the attitude, and physiology provided the method that permitted psychology to evolve from a speculative inquiry into a scientific discipline.

• Psychology was born as an independent discipline in the German university system when Wilhelm Wundt established the first psychological research laboratory in 1879 at Leipzig. Wundt argued, with great influence, that psychology should be the scientific study of consciousness. The new discipline of psychology grew rapidly in America in the latter part of the 19th century, as illustrated by G. Stanley Hall's career.

• With this growth came the first major theoretical war in the field, between structuralism and functionalism. The structuralists believed that psychology should use introspection to analyze consciousness into its basic elements. Functionalists, such as William James, believed that psychology should focus on the purpose and adaptive functions of consciousness. Eventually, both schools faded from the scene, but functionalism left a more enduring imprint on psychology.

• Behaviorists, led by John B. Watson, argued that psychology could scientifically study only observable behavior. Thus, they campaigned to redefine psychology as the science of behavior. Emphasizing the importance of the environment over heredity, the behaviorists began to explore stimulus-response relationships, often using laboratory animals as subjects.

• Sigmund Freud's psychoanalytic theory emphasized the unconscious determinants of behavior and attributed great importance to how people dealt with their sexuality. Freud's ideas were controversial, and they met with resistance in academic psychology. However, as more psychologists developed an interest in personality, motivation, and abnormal behavior, psychoanalytic concepts were incorporated into mainstream psychology.

• Behaviorism continued as a powerful force in psychology, boosted greatly by impressive research by B. F. Skinner and his followers. Like Watson before him, Skinner asserted that psychology should study only observable behavior by analyzing stimulus-response relationships. He also generated controversy by arguing that the notion of free will is an illusion.

• Finding both behaviorism and psychoanalysis unsatisfactory, advocates of a new theoretical orientation called humanism became influential in the 1950s. Humanism emphasizes the unique qualities of human behavior and humans' freedom and potential for personal growth. Led by Carl Rogers and Abraham Maslow, the humanists made a major contribution to psychology—the development of new approaches to psychotherapy.

• Stimulated by the demands of World War II, clinical psychology grew rapidly in the 1950s. Thus, psychology became a profession as well as a science. This movement toward professionalization eventually spread to other areas in psychology, in spite of misgivings felt by many traditional academic psychologists.

• During the 1950s and 1960s there were many advances in the study of cognitive processes and the physiological bases of behavior. These advances led to a renewal of interest in cognition and physiology.

Psychology Today: Vigorous and Diversified

• Contemporary psychology is a diversified science and profession, which has grown rapidly in recent decades. Its vigorous presence in modern society is apparent from the wide variety of settings and roles in which psychologists are found.

• Today, research in psychology requires specialization. Major areas of research in modern psychology include experimental psychology, physiological psychology, cognitive psychology, developmental psychology, psychometrics, personality, and social psychology.

• The division between the science of psychology and the profession of psychology is not absolute, and there is some overlap. Within the domain of applied psychology, there are four established professional specialties: clinical psychology, counseling psychology, educational and school psychology, and industrial and organizational psychology. Although clinical psychology and psychiatry share some of the same interests, they are different professions with different types of training.

Putting It in Perspective: Six Key Themes

• Throughout this book, as we examine psychology in its many variations, we will emphasize six key ideas as unifying themes. Our six key themes come in two sets, as three relate to psychology as a field of study, and three relate to psychology's subject matter.

• Our three key themes having to do with psychology as a field of study are as follows: (1) psychology is empirical, (2) psychology is theoretically diverse, and (3) psychology evolves in a sociohistorical context.

• Themes 4 through 6, related to psychology's subject matter, are these: (4) behavior is determined by multiple causes, (5) heredity and environment jointly influence behavior, and (6) our experience of the world is highly subjective.

Application: Improving Academic Performance

• Educational psychology and other branches of applied psychology have yielded many insights that are relevant to the challenge of doing well in college. To foster sound study habits, you should devise a written study schedule and reward yourself for following it. You should also try to find one or two specific places for studying that are relatively free of distractions.

• You should use active reading techniques to select out the most important ideas from the material you read. SQ3R is one approach to active reading. It breaks a reading assignment down into manageable segments and requires that you understand each segment before you move on.

• Good note taking can help you to get more out of lectures. It's important to employ active listening techniques and to record lecturers' ideas in your own words. It also helps if you read ahead to prepare for lectures, ask questions as needed, and review your notes regularly.

• Being an effective student also requires sound test-taking skills. In general, it's a good idea to set up a schedule for progress through an exam, to adopt the appropriate level of sophistication, to avoid wasting time on troublesome questions, and to review your answers whenever time permits. Many tips specific to multiple-choice exams and to essay exams were also discussed.

KEY TERMS

- Applied psychology
- Behaviorism
- Clinical psychology
- Cognition
- Empiricism
- Functionalism
- Humanism
- Introspection
- Psychiatry
- Psychoanalytic theory
- Psychology
- SQ3R
- Stimulus
- Structuralism
- Testwiseness
- Theory
- Unconscious

KEY PEOPLE

- Sigmund Freud
- G. Stanley Hall
- William James
- Carl Rogers
- B. F. Skinner
- John B. Watson
- Wilhelm Wundt

THE RESEARCH ENTERPRISE IN PSYCHOLOGY

THE RESEARCH ENTERPRISE IN PSYCHOLOGY

Are these popular reports about human sexual behavior accurate? Assertions about behavior are all around us, often expressed in sensational terms. Familiarity with the research enterprise can help you to evaluate many kinds of information.

Can emotional stress lead to physical disease? If so, what kinds of experiences make us more vulnerable to physical illness?

• How does anxiety affect our desire to be with others? Does misery love company?
• Can hypnosis be used to improve the accuracy of eyewitness testimony in court?
• Do young girls and young boys differ in their willingness to take risks?
• What are the psychological characteristics of people who receive the death penalty?
• How common is it for college men to force women into sexual acts against their will?

Questions, questions, questions—we all have questions about behavior. Perhaps the most basic question is "How should we go about investigating these questions?" As noted in Chapter 1, *psychology is empirical*. Psychologists rely on formal, systematic observations to address their questions about behavior. This methodology is what makes psychology a scientific endeavor.

The scientific enterprise is an exercise in creative problem solving. Scientists have to figure out how to make observations that will shed light on the puzzles they want to solve. To make these observations, psychologists employ a variety of research methods because differ-ent questions call for different strategies of study. A research method that is excellent for one question may be entirely inappropriate for another. In this chapter you will see how researchers have employed a variety of methods—including experiments, case studies, surveys, and naturalistic observation—to investigate the questions listed earlier on this page.

Psychology's methods are worth a close look for at least two reasons. First, a better appreciation of the empirical approach will enhance your understanding of the research-based information that you will be reading in the remainder of this book. Second, familiarity with the logic of the empirical approach should improve your ability to think critically about research and make you a more skeptical consumer of information. This is important because we hear about research findings nearly everyday in modern society. The news media constantly report on studies that make assertions about how we should raise our children, improve our health, reform our schools, and enhance our interpersonal relationships. Learning to evaluate these reports with more sophistication can help you to use such information wisely.

In this chapter we'll examine the scientific approach to the study of behavior and then look at the specific research methods that psychologists use most frequently. We'll also discuss why psychologists use statistics in their research. After you learn how research is done, you will also learn how *not* to do it, by being introduced to some common flaws in research. Finally, we'll take a look at ethical issues in behavioral research. In the Application, we'll discuss how to find and read journal articles that report on research.

LOOKING FOR LAWS: THE SCIENTIFIC APPROACH TO BEHAVIOR

Whether the object of study is gravitational forces or people's behavior under stress, *the scientific approach assumes that events are governed by some lawful order.* As scientists, psychologists assume that our behavior is governed by discernible laws or principles, just as the movement of the earth around the sun is governed by the laws of gravity. Although the behavior of living creatures may not seem as lawful and predictable as the "behavior" of planets, the scientific enterprise is based on the belief that there *are* consistencies or laws that can be uncovered through empirical investigation. Fortunately, the plausibility of this fundamental assumption has been supported by the discovery of a great many such consistencies in behavior, some of which provide the subject matter for this text.

Goals of the Scientific Enterprise

What are the key goals of the scientific enterprise? When I ask my students this question, the most common response is that science represents a search for truth. Although this answer is not entirely off the mark, the concept of *truth* has a ring of finality to it that makes scientists uneasy. Scientific discovery is an ongoing process. All of the scientific disciplines have suffered through some embarrassment when one of their basic "truths" has been disproven. In physics, for instance, Newton's laws of gravity were once thought to be the last word on certain characteristics of the universe. However, Einstein later showed that these laws did not apply in certain circumstances.

Scientists are also uneasy with the concept of truth because it sounds absolute. In fact, a great many scientific principles are stated in terms of probability. Whether it is a social scientist discussing behavior ("This approach to child rearing has a high probability of yielding an adolescent troubled by anxiety") or a natural scientist discussing atmospheric conditions ("Current air quality has a high probability of increasing respiratory problems among the elderly"), the statements made on the basis of research are often set forth as matters of probability.

Rather than speak in terms of absolute truth, scientists prefer to state their goals more modestly. Specifically, psychology and other sciences share three sets of interrelated goals: measurement and description, understanding and prediction, and application and control.

MEASUREMENT AND DESCRIPTION

Before we can explain *why* the world works in a certain way, we need to be able to describe *how* it works. Science's commitment to observation usually requires that an investigator figure out a way to measure the phenomenon under study. For example, a psychologist could not investigate whether men are more or less sociable than women without first developing some means of measuring sociability. Thus, the first goal of psychology is to develop measurement techniques that make it possible to describe behavior clearly and precisely.

UNDERSTANDING AND PREDICTION

A higher-level goal of science is understanding. Scientists believe that they understand events when they can explain the reasons for their occurrence. To evaluate their understanding, scientists make and test predictions about relationships between variables. *Variables in a study are any measurable conditions, events, characteristics, or behaviors that are controlled or observed.* Thus, in the investigation mentioned a moment ago, sex and sociability were the variables of interest. If we predicted that putting people under time pressure would lower the accuracy of their time perception, the variables in the study would be time pressure and accuracy of time perception. If we conducted a study of the matter and our prediction was verified, this validation would in-

crease our confidence that we understand the relationship between time pressure and time perception.

APPLICATION AND CONTROL

Ultimately, most scientists hope that the information they gather will be of some practical value in helping to solve everyday problems. Once you understand a phenomenon, you often can use the information you have acquired to exert some control over it. For instance, if a botanist understands the relations between soil type and crop yields, the botanist can influence crop yields by telling people which crops are likely to grow best in which kinds of soil.

Today legions of professional psychologists attempt to apply research findings to practical problems they encounter in schools, businesses, factories, clinics, and mental hospitals. For example, a school psychologist might use new findings about what causes math anxiety to devise a program to help students control their math phobias. Similarly, an organizational psychologist might apply new insights about leadership effectiveness to help a company improve its productivity.

Steps in a Scientific Investigation

Curiosity about a question provides the point of departure for any kind of investigation, scientific or otherwise. Scientific investigations, however, are *systematic*. They follow an orderly pattern. Thomas Holmes and several colleagues studied the effects of stress on physical health. Let's look at how Wyler, Masuda, and Holmes (1971) followed the standard series of steps in their scientific study, as summarized in Figure 2.1.

The following questions concerned Thomas Holmes and his colleagues: Can emotional stress lead to physical disease? If so, what kinds of experiences increase one's vulnerability to physical illness? To investigate these matters, Holmes and his coworkers interviewed thousands of medical patients to find out what kinds of events had preceded the onset of their diseases. Surprisingly, the events that were cited were *not* uniformly negative. The patients reported plenty of the expected negative events, such as divorce, death of a friend, or getting fired at work. However, they also reported many neutral or seemingly positive events, such as getting promoted, getting married, or gaining a new family member. Why would these positive events make people more vulnerable to becoming ill? According to Holmes, it was because they produced *change*. He theorized that change represented the core of stress, and he em-

35

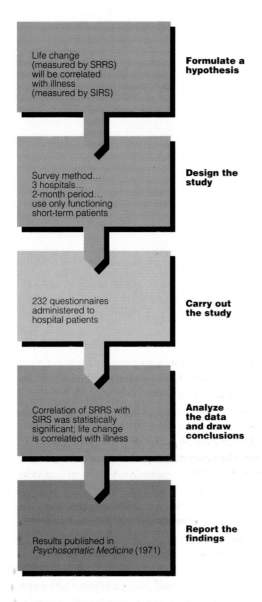

Figure 2.1 Flowchart of steps in a scientific investigation. As illustrated by a study by Wyler, Masuda, and Holmes, a scientific investigation consists of a sequence of carefully planned steps, beginning with the formulation of a testable hypothesis and ending with the publication of the study, if its results are worthy of examination by other researchers.

Life change (measured by SRRS) will be correlated with illness (measured by SIRS)

Formulate a hypothesis

Survey method... 3 hospitals... 2-month period... use only functioning short-term patients

Design the study

232 questionnaires administered to hospital patients

Carry out the study

Correlation of SRRS with SIRS was statistically significant; life change is correlated with illness

Analyze the data and draw conclusions

Results published in *Psychosomatic Medicine* (1971)

Report the findings

barked on a series of studies to explore the relations between life changes and physical health.

STEP 1: FORMULATE A TESTABLE HYPOTHESIS

The cornerstone of the scientific method is its commitment to putting ideas to an empirical test. Thus, the first step in a scientific investigation is to translate a general idea into a testable hypothesis. **A *hypothesis* is a tentative statement about the relationship between two or more variables.** Normally, a hypothesis is expressed as a prediction that explicitly spells out how changes in one variable will be related to changes in another variable. Thus, Holmes hypothesized that increases in life change would be associated with increases in physical illness (see Figure 2.2).

To be testable, scientific hypotheses must be formulated precisely, with clear definitions of the exact nature of the variables under study. Re-

searchers accomplish this precise formulation by providing operational definitions of the relevant variables. **An *operational definition* is one that describes the actions or operations that will be made to measure or control a variable.** Operational definitions establish precisely what each variable in the context of a study means.

To illustrate, let's examine the operational definitions used by Wyler, Masuda, and Holmes (1971). They measured life change as a form of stress with the Social Readjustment Rating Scale (SRRS), devised earlier by Holmes and Richard Rahe (1967). The SRRS is a checklist of 43 common life changes. To each event on the list it assigns a numeric value that is supposed to reflect the magnitude of the readjustment required by the change. The extent of participants' physical illness was assessed with the Seriousness of Illness Rating Scale (SIRS), which had been developed in a previous study by Wyler, Masuda, and Holmes (1968). The SIRS is a checklist of 126 common illnesses that includes numerical values reflecting the severity of each illness. Thus, in the context of this study, the variable of life change was defined as one's score on the SRRS and the variable of physical illness was defined as one's score on the SIRS.

STEP 2: SELECT THE RESEARCH METHOD AND DESIGN THE STUDY

The second step in a scientific investigation involves figuring out just how to put one's hypothesis to an empirical test. The research method chosen depends to a large degree on the nature of the question under study. Different questions require different methods. The various methods—experiments, case studies, surveys, naturalistic observation—all have their advantages and disadvantages. The researcher has to ponder these and then select the strategy that appears most appropriate and most practical. In this case, Wyler, Masuda, and Holmes decided that their question called for a survey—a method that involves administering questionnaires to a large number of people.

Once researchers have chosen a general method, they must plot out the exact plans for executing the study. In this study of stress, Wyler, Masuda, and Holmes had to decide how many people they needed to survey, where they would get their survey respondents, and when they would conduct their survey. They elected to survey patients seen at three local hospitals during a specified two-month period. They excluded patients with long-standing illnesses and those who were too incapacitated to fill out the questionnaires.

STEP 3: CONDUCT THE STUDY

The third step in the research enterprise is to conduct the study itself. Basing their work on previous plans, researchers obtain their sample of subjects and make their formal observations. **Subjects are the persons or animals whose behavior is systematically observed in a study.** This phase of research often involves an enormous amount of time and work. In laboratory experiments investigators may spend many hours exposing subjects to special treatments and observing their responses. In this case Wyler, Masuda, and Holmes spent two months administering their questionnaires to 232 patients who served as the subjects in their study.

STEP 4: ANALYZE THE DATA AND DRAW CONCLUSIONS

The observations made in a study are normally converted into numbers that constitute the raw data of the study. In this instance the subjects' responses to the two questionnaires were scored. This procedure yielded two scores for each subject that indicated the amount of life change and the severity of physical illness each person had experienced.

To be able to draw conclusions, researchers need a means of organizing and analyzing the empirical data collected in a study. This data analysis is done through statistical computations. Statistical analyses play an essential role in the scientific enterprise. *Investigators use statistics to summarize their findings and to decide whether or not their hypotheses have been supported.* Using their statistical analyses, Wyler, Masuda, and Holmes concluded that their data supported their hypothesis. As predicted, they found that high scores on the measure of life change were associated with high scores on the index of physical illness.

STEP 5: REPORT THE FINDINGS

Progress in understanding the world around us can be achieved only if scientists share their findings with one another and the general public. Therefore, the final step in a scientific investigation involves writing up a concise summary of the study and its findings. Typically, scientists prepare a report that can be submitted to a technical journal for publication or delivered at a scientific meeting, such as the annual convention of the American Psychological Association (APA). **A journal is a periodical that publishes technical and scholarly material, usually in a narrowly defined area of inquiry.** The study by Wyler, Masuda, and Holmes (1971) was accepted for publication in a journal called *Psychosomatic Medicine*. It was one of several ground-breaking studies by Holmes and

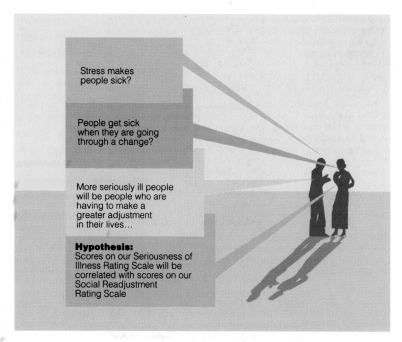

his colleagues linking life stress to physical illness. It set a precedent for hundreds of follow-up studies by other researchers all over the world that have further enhanced our understanding of how stress is related to physical health.

The process of publishing scientific studies allows other experts to evaluate and critique new research findings. Sometimes this process of critical evaluation discloses flaws in a study. If the flaws are serious enough, the results may be discounted or discarded. This evaluation process constitutes a major strength of the scientific approach because it gradually weeds out erroneous findings so that research-based information tends to be relatively dependable and accurate. For this reason, the scientific enterprise is sometimes characterized as "self-correcting."

This self-correcting aspect of science emerged to some extent in the research that followed up on the original findings of Holmes and his colleagues. Their most basic conclusion—that there is a relationship between stress and vulnerability to physical illness—has been supported in hundreds of studies. However, subsequent research has revealed that (1) the association between stress and physical illness is not as strong as Holmes believed and (2) stress is not exclusively a function of change in one's life (Perkins, 1982). These findings are discussed in more detail in Chapter 13.

Advantages of the Scientific Approach

Science is certainly not the only method we use to draw conclusions about behavioral processes. We all use logic, casual observation, and good old-

Figure 2.2 Formulating a hypothesis. Scientific hypotheses usually begin as intuitive ideas or educated guesses about how the world works. To be scientifically testable, however, these preliminary notions must be refined into specific predictions in which each variable is carefully defined in measurable terms.

As discussed in Chapter 1, the scientific approach depends on observation rather than on deductive reasoning or an appeal to authority. In the 13th century, the monk-scholar Roger Bacon anticipated the scientific attitude when he said that the way to find out how many legs a spider has is to count them.

fashioned common sense. Since the scientific method often requires painstaking effort in the collection and analysis of data, it seems reasonable to ask what the advantages of the scientific approach are.

Basically, the scientific approach offers two major advantages. The first is its clarity and precision. Commonsense notions about behavior tend to be vague and ambiguous. Consider the old adage "Spare the rod and spoil the child." What exactly does this generalization about child rearing amount to? How severely should children be punished if we are not to "spare the rod"? How do we assess whether a child qualifies as "spoiled"? A fundamental problem is that sayings like this mean different things to different people. When people disagree about this assertion, it may be because they are assigning entirely different meanings to the adage. In contrast, the scientific approach requires that we specify *exactly* what we are talking about when we formulate hypotheses. This clarity and precision enhance communication about important ideas.

The second and perhaps greatest advantage offered by the scientific approach is its relative intolerance of error. Scientists are trained to be skeptical. They subject their ideas to empirical tests. They also scrutinize one another's findings with a critical eye. They demand objective data and thorough documentation before they accept ideas. When the findings of two studies conflict, the scientist tries to figure out why the studies reached different conclusions, usually by conducting additional research. In contrast, common

sense and casual observation often tolerate contradictory generalizations, such as "Opposites attract" and "Birds of a feather flock together." Furthermore, commonsense analyses involve little effort to verify ideas or detect errors, so that many "truisms" about behavior that come to be widely believed are simply myths.

All this is not to say that science has exclusive ownership of truth. However, the scientific approach does tend to yield more accurate and dependable information than casual analyses and armchair speculation. Knowledge of scientific data can thus provide a useful benchmark against which to judge claims and information from other kinds of sources.

Now that we have an overview of how the scientific enterprise works, we can focus on how specific research methods can provide insights into complex questions about behavior. **A *research* method is a strategy or procedure for collecting empirical data.** No single method is ideal for all purposes and situations. Much of the ingenuity and creativity in research involves selecting and tailoring the method to the question at hand. The next two sections of this chapter discuss the methods that psychologists depend on most. Additional methods that are uniquely suited to certain areas of research will be introduced in later chapters.

The two main types of research methods in psychology are *experimental research methods* and *correlational research methods*. We will discuss them separately because there is an important distinction between them. Experimental research allows us to draw conclusions about whether one variable *causes* changes in another variable. Correlational research only permits us to conclude whether two variables are *related* in some way. Both of these fundamentally distinct approaches have their strengths and weaknesses.

LOOKING FOR CAUSES: EXPERIMENTAL RESEARCH

Does misery love company? This question intrigued social psychologist Stanley Schachter. How does anxiety affect our desire to be with others? When people feel anxious, do they want to be left alone, or do they prefer to have others around? Schachter's review of relevant theories suggested that in times of anxiety people would want others around to help them sort out their feelings. Thus, his hypothesis was that increases in anxiety would cause increases in the desire to be with others, which psychologists call the *need for affiliation*. To test this hypothesis, Schachter

(1959) designed a clever experiment.

The *experiment* is a research method in which the investigator manipulates a variable under carefully controlled conditions and observes whether there are changes in a second variable as a result. The experiment is a relatively powerful procedure that allows a researcher to detect cause-and-effect relationships, and psychologists depend on this method more than any other.

Although its basic strategy is straightforward, in practice the experiment is a fairly complicated technique. A well-designed experiment must take into account a number of factors that could affect the clarity and meaning of the results. To see how an experiment is designed, let's examine the various elements of the experiment, using Schachter's study as an example.

Independent and Dependent Variables

An experiment is designed to find out whether changes in one variable (let's call it X) cause changes in another variable (let's call it Y). To put it more concisely, we want to find out *how X affects Y.* In this formulation, we refer to X as the *independent variable,* and we call Y the *dependent variable.*

An *independent variable* is a condition or event that an experimenter varies in order to see its impact on another variable. The independent variable is the variable that the experimenter controls or manipulates. It is hypothesized to have some effect on the dependent variable, and the experiment is conducted to verify this effect. The *dependent variable* is the variable that is thought to be affected by the manipulation of the independent variable. In psychology studies, the dependent variable usually is a measurement of some aspect of the subjects' behavior that is observed carefully by the experimenter. The independent variable is called *independent* because it is *free* to be varied by the experimenter. The dependent variable is called *dependent* because it is thought to *depend* (at least in part) on manipulations of the independent variable.

In Schachter's experiment, *the independent variable was the subjects' anxiety level.* He manipulated anxiety level in the following way. Subjects assembled in his laboratory were told by a Dr. Zilstein that they would be participating in a study on the physiological effects of electric shock. They were further informed that the upcoming experiment would require that they receive a series of electric shocks while their pulse and blood pressure were monitored. Half of the subjects were warned that the shocks would be very painful. They made up the *high-anxiety* group. The other half of the subjects, assigned to the *low-anxiety* group, were told that the shocks would be mild and painless. In reality, there was no plan to shock anyone at any time. These orientation procedures were simply intended to evoke different levels of anxiety. After the orientation the experimenter indicated that there would be a delay while he prepared the shock apparatus for use, and he asked the subjects whether they would prefer to wait alone or in the company of others. *The subjects' desire to affiliate with others was the dependent variable.*

Experimental and Control Groups

To determine the effect of an independent variable in an experiment, the investigator typically assembles two groups of subjects who are treated differently in regard to the independent variable. These two groups are referred to as the *experimental* and *control* groups. **The *experimental group* consists of the subjects who receive some special treatment in regard to the independent variable. The *control group* consists of similar subjects who do *not* receive the special treatment given to the experimental group.**

Let's return to the Schachter study to illustrate. In this study the subjects in the high-anxiety condition constituted the experimental group. They received a special treatment designed to create an unusually high level of anxiety. The subjects in the low-anxiety condition constituted the control group. They were not exposed to the special anxiety-arousing procedure, so that they would experience a lower level of anxiety.

It is crucial that the experimental and control groups be very similar, except for the different treatment that they receive in regard to the independent variable. This stipulation brings us to the logic that underlies the experimental method. If the two groups are alike in all respects *except for the variation created by the manipulation of the independent variable,* then any differences between the two groups in the dependent variable *must be due to this manipulation of the independent variable.* In this way researchers isolate the effect of the independent variable on the dependent variable. Thus, Schachter isolated the impact of anxiety on need for affiliation. What did he find? As predicted, he found that increased anxiety led to increased affiliation. As Figure 2.3 shows, the

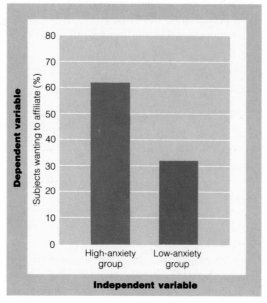

Figure 2.3 Results of Schachter's study of affiliation. The percentage of people wanting to wait with others was higher in the high-anxiety (experimental) group than in the low-anxiety (control) group, consistent with Schachter's hypothesis that anxiety would increase the desire for affiliation. The graphic portrayal of these results allows us to see at a glance the effects of the experimental manipulation on the dependent variable.

percentage of subjects who wanted to wait with others was nearly twice as high in the high-anxiety group as in the low-anxiety group.

That an independent variable has a clear impact on a dependent variable does *not* mean every subject behaves exactly as predicted. In Schachter's study, for instance, the different responses of the two groups showed that the manipulation of anxiety level had a pronounced effect on affiliation behavior. Even so, only 63% of the high-anxiety subjects wanted to wait with others. This lack of uniformity is quite normal, because people are not robots that respond identically to a given situation. Such individual differences are one of the reasons why most psychological principles are expressed in terms of probabilities or tendencies.

Extraneous Variables

As we have seen, the logic of the experimental method rests heavily on the assumption that the experimental and control groups are alike except for their different treatment in regard to the independent variable. Any other differences between the two groups can cloud the situation and can make it impossible to draw solid conclusions about the relationship between the independent variable and the dependent variable.

In practical terms, of course, it is impossible to ensure that two groups of subjects are exactly alike in *every* respect. Therefore, experimenters usually concentrate on making sure that the two groups are alike with regard to a limited number of relevant variables that could have some bearing on the results of the study. These variables are called extraneous, secondary, or nuisance variables. *Extraneous variables* are any variables other than the independent variable that seem likely to influence the dependent variable in a specific study.

In Schachter's study of anxiety and affiliation, one extraneous variable would have been the subjects' tendency to be sociable. Why? Because subjects' sociability could affect their desire to be with others (the dependent variable). If the subjects in one group had happened to be more sociable (on the average) than those in the other group, this difference would have "contaminated" the interpretation of the results.

Of course, the experimenter only has to make sure that the experimental and control groups are alike with regard to variables that are relevant to the dependent variable. Thus, Schachter did not need to worry about whether his two groups were alike in hair color, height, or interest in ballet, because these variables weren't likely to influence the dependent variable, affiliation behavior.

There are several ways to control for extraneous variables, but the most straightforward way is to assign subjects randomly to the experimental and control groups. *Random assignment of subjects occurs when all subjects have an equal chance of being assigned to any group or condition in the study.* When experimenters distribute subjects into groups through some random procedure, they can be reasonably confident that the groups will be similar in most ways. This is a simple and effective way of controlling for a wide range of possible extraneous variables. Thus, random assignment is routinely used in most experiments.

To summarize this discussion of experimental design, Figure 2.4 provides an overview of the various elements in an experiment, using Schachter's study as an example.

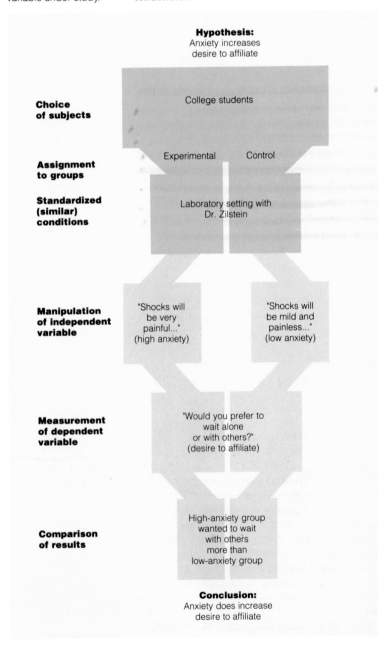

Figure 2.4 The basic elements of an experiment. As illustrated by the Schachter study, the logic of experimental design rests on treating the experimental and control groups exactly alike except for the manipulation of the independent variable. In this way the experimenter attempts to isolate the effects of the variable under study.

Hypothesis:
Anxiety increases desire to affiliate

Choice of subjects — College students

Assignment to groups — Experimental / Control

Standardized (similar) conditions — Laboratory setting with Dr. Zilstein

Manipulation of independent variable — "Shocks will be very painful..." (high anxiety) / "Shocks will be mild and painless..." (low anxiety)

Measurement of dependent variable — "Would you prefer to wait alone or with others?" (desire to affiliate)

Comparison of results — High-anxiety group wanted to wait with others more than low-anxiety group

Conclusion:
Anxiety does increase desire to affiliate

Variations in Designing Experiments

We have discussed the experiment in only its simplest format, in which there is just one independent variable and one dependent variable. Actually, many variations are possible in conducting an experiment. Since you'll be reading about experiments with more complicated designs, these variations merit a brief mention. To illustrate design complexities, let's imagine that you are designing complexities, let's imagine that you are designing some experiments to see how environmental factors influence test performance in the classroom.

First, sometimes it is advantageous to use only one group of subjects who serve as their own control group. The effects of the independent variable are evaluated by exposing this single group to two different conditions—an experimental condition and a control condition. For example, if you wanted to study the effects of extreme heat on test performance, you could have a class take their first exam in an overheated room (experimental condition) and have them take their second exam in the same room at a normal temperature (control condition). The obvious advantage of this approach is that it ensures that the experimental and control groups are alike with regard to any extraneous variables related to subjects' personal characteristics, such as motivation and intelligence. After all, the same people are in both groups.

Second, it is possible to manipulate more than one independent variable in a single experiment. Researchers often manipulate two or three independent variables in an experiment to examine their joint effects on the dependent variable. For example, with a suitable experimental design you could vary both classroom temperature and the amount of distracting noise in the room in a single experiment.

Third, it is also possible to employ more than one dependent variable in a single study. Researchers frequently use a number of dependent variables to get a more complete picture of how the experimental manipulations affect subjects' behavior. Thus, in your studies of test performance, you might use three different kinds of tests, such as a multiple-choice test, an essay test, and a fill-in-the-blank test.

Now that you're familiar with the logic of the experiment, let's turn to our Featured Study for Chapter 2. You will find a Featured Study in each chapter from this point onward. These Featured Studies are intended to give you in-depth examples of how psychologists conduct empirical research. Each one is presented in a way that resembles a journal article, to acquaint you with the format of scientific reports (see the Application at the end of the chapter for more information on this format). The Featured Study for this chapter will give you another example of an experiment in action.

CHAPTER TWO FEATURED STUDY	# Can Hypnosis Improve Eyewitness Memory?

In criminal investigations, hypnosis has occasionally been used successfully to trigger witnesses' recall of information that they were not originally able to remember. In light of this, Sanders and Simmons set out to discover whether hypnosis might also be employed to improve the *accuracy* of eyewitness memory. They were intrigued by this possibility because they knew that eyewitness testimony is frequently riddled with inaccuracies. The hypothesis selected for the study was that hypnotized subjects would show better recall of a simulated crime than nonhypnotized subjects.

Method

Subjects. A total of 100 college students who had volunteered to participate in a study that might involve hypnosis served as subjects. They were assigned to small groups ranging in size from 1 to 8.

Procedure. In the initial session, subjects were told to imagine that they were walking around campus one evening and happened to observe a scene that was about to be shown to them on videotape. The 20-second videotape portrayed a pickpocket stealing someone's wallet (Figure 2.5). The thief, wearing a distinctive black jacket, was on the screen for 8 seconds, and his face was shown clearly for 3 seconds. The subjects were asked to return one week later to provide "testimony" about the crime that they had witnessed on the videotape. In the second session a week later, the subjects were asked to identify the thief in a videotaped police lineup that included six possible suspects. Subjects in the experimen-

Investigators: Glenn S. Sanders and William L. Simmons (State University of New York at Albany)

Source: Use of hypnosis to enhance eyewitness accuracy: Does it work? *Journal of Applied Psychology, 68* (1983), 70–77.

Figure 2.5 One frame from the 20-second videotape used in a study of hypnosis and eyewitness accuracy by Sanders and Simmons. Note the jacket worn by the "thief."

Discussion

The findings indicate that hypnotizing eyewitnesses did *not* improve the accuracy of their testimony. In fact, the results show that hypnosis may actually make eyewitnesses more likely to make mistakes. Sanders and Simmons speculate that hypnosis may make witnesses more error prone by increasing their tendency to focus on highly prominent cues, such as the jacket worn by the thief in their study. Thus, they conclude that use of hypnosis in criminal investigations should probably be limited to helping witnesses to overcome memory blocks.

Comment

This study was featured because it addressed an interesting question with a reasonably straightforward experimental design. It also illustrates the importance of collecting empirical data to answer psychological questions. If asked whether hypnosis would improve the accuracy of eyewitness testimony, many people (including some psychologists) would probably have answered "yes," because of the highly publicized instances in which hypnosis has overcome memory blocks. However, the findings in this experiment suggest that hypnosis is unlikely to enhance the accuracy of eyewitness testimony. Without research data we might be quite likely to speculate otherwise.

Of course, a single study on an issue does not settle the matter once and for all. Follow-up studies are needed to see whether the same results are found with different types of subjects and different types of simulated crimes. In particular, it would be a good idea to present subjects in another study with a more realistic simulation of a crime (acted out by real people, for instance), since watching a videotape is quite different from accidentally witnessing a crime. Thus, more empirical investigation is needed before we close the door on the use of hypnosis to enhance eyewitness memory.

Notice, too, that this study provided examples of some of the variations in experimental design that we have just discussed. Specifically, Sanders and Simmons manipulated two independent variables and measured subjects' responses with three dependent variables.

tal group were hypnotized; subjects in the control group were not.

Design. The experimental design varied two independent variables: (1) whether the subject (witness) was hypnotized and (2) whether the thief was actually in the lineup. Two conditions were set up to manipulate the second independent variable. In one condition the thief, without his jacket, occupied the fourth spot in the lineup. In the other condition the thief was absent from the lineup, but another person wearing the same jacket was in the fourth spot. The dependent variables were the subjects' accuracy in identifying the thief, their confidence in their response, and their performance on a ten-item test that checked their recall of details in the incident.

Results

Figure 2.6 shows the percentage of correct responses (either identifying the thief or indicating that he was not in the lineup, depending on the condition) made by the hypnotized subjects and the control subjects. The control subjects were correct more often than the hypnotized subjects, both when the thief was present and when he was absent. The control subjects expressed confidence in their response more frequently than did the hypnotized subjects, although the difference was small. Data regarding subjects' performance on the ten-item recall test favored the conclusion that control subjects remembered the incident more accurately.

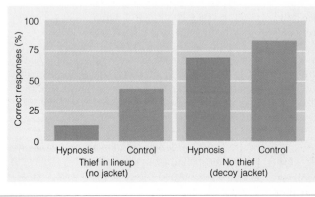

Figure 2.6 Results of the Sanders and Simmons study. In both conditions (thief in the lineup and thief not in the lineup), the control subjects showed more accurate recall than the hypnotized subjects. Instead of improving recall, in this study hypnosis led to more mistakes by "eyewitnesses."

Advantages and Disadvantages of Experimental Research

The experiment is a powerful research method. Its principal advantage is that it allows the researcher to draw conclusions about cause and effect relationships between variables with relatively great confidence. We are able to draw these conclusions about causation because the precise control available in the experiment permits us to isolate the relationship between the independent variable and the dependent variable while neutralizing the effects of extraneous variables. Because no other research method can duplicate this advantage of the experiment, psychologists usually prefer to use the experimental method whenever possible.

For all its power, however, the experiment has limitations. One problem with experiments is that they are frequently artificial. Because experiments require great control over proceedings, researchers often must construct simple, contrived situations in order to isolate the effect of one variable on another. For example, to investigate decision-making processes in juries, psychologists have conducted many experiments in which the subjects have read a brief summary of a trial and then recorded their individual "verdicts" of innocent or guilty. This approach allows the experimenter to manipulate a single variable, such as the race of the defendant, to see if it affects the subjects' verdicts. However, critics have pointed out that having a subject read a short case summary and make an individual decision is terribly artificial in comparison to the complexities of real trials (Weiten & Diamond, 1979). In actual trials, jurors may spend weeks listening to confusing testimony while making subtle judgments about the credibility of witnesses, and then retire for hours of debate to arrive at a verdict. Many researchers have failed to do justice to this complex process in their laboratory experiments. When experiments are highly artificial, doubts arise about whether the findings will apply to everyday behavior outside of the experimental laboratory.

Another disadvantage of the experimental method is the frustrating fact that often it can't be used for a particular research problem. Psychologists are frequently interested in the effect of some variable that cannot be manipulated as an independent variable because of ethical concerns or practical realities. For instance, you might be interested in the effect of a nutritionally poor diet during pregnancy on the likelihood of birth defects. This clearly is a significant issue, but you obviously cannot take 100 pregnant women and assign 50 of them to a condition in which they consume an inadequate diet. The potential risk of birth defects in their children would make this research strategy totally unethical.

In other cases, manipulations of an independent variable would presumably be harmless, but are difficult or impossible to make. For example, you might want to know whether being brought up in an urban area as opposed to a rural area affects people's values. A true experiment would require you to assign similar families to live in urban and rural areas, which obviously is impossible to do. To explore this question, you would have to use correlational research methods, which we turn to next.

CONCEPT CHECK 2.1
Recognizing Independent and Dependent Variables

Check your understanding of the experimental method by identifying the independent variable (IV) and dependent variable (DV) in the following investigations. Note that one study has two IVs and another has two DVs. You'll find the answers in Appendix A in the back of the book.

1. A researcher is interested in how heart rate and blood pressure are affected by viewing a violent film sequence as opposed to a nonviolent film sequence.

IV _Violent_____

DV _Heart rate_____

2. An organizational psychologist develops a new training program to improve clerks' courtesy to customers in a large chain of retail stores. She conducts an experiment to see if the training program leads to a reduction in the number of customer complaints.

IV _____

DV _____

3. A researcher wants to find out how stimulus complexity and stimulus contrast (light/dark variation) affect infants' attention to stimuli. He manipulates stimulus complexity and stimulus contrast and measures how long infants stare at various stimuli.

IV _____

DV _____

4. A social psychologist investigates the impact of group size on subjects' conformity in response to group pressure.

IV _____

DV _____

LOOKING FOR LINKS: CORRELATIONAL RESEARCH

As we just saw, in some situations psychologists cannot exert experimental control over the variables they want to study. Thomas Holmes's research on the relationship between life change and illness provides another example of this problem. Obviously, Holmes could not manipulate the amount of life change experienced by his subjects. Their divorces, retirements, pregnancies, promotions, mortgages, and so forth were far beyond Holmes's control.

In such situations, all a researcher can do is make systematic obervations to see whether there is a link or association between the variables of interest. Such an association is called a *correlation*. **A *correlation* exists when two variables are related to each other.** The results of correlational research are often summarized with a statistic called the *coefficient of correlation*, which we'll discuss later in this chapter.

There are a variety of correlational research methods, including naturalistic observation, case studies, and surveys and psychological tests. The definitive aspect of these methods is that the researcher cannot control the variables under study. This lack of control means that correlational research cannot be used to demonstrate a cause and effect relationship between two variables. *While experimental research can look for causes, correlational research can look only for links or associations between variables.* That is not to suggest that associations are unimportant. You'll see in this section that information about associations between variables can be extremely valuable in our efforts to understand behavior.

Figure 2.7 Naturalistic observation. As the name implies, naturalistic observation allows behavior to unfold naturally, without interference by the researcher. These photographs were taken in 1988 by Harvey Ginsburg during naturalistic observation of boys and girls in a "risky behavior" situation.

Naturalistic Observation

Are males more likely to take risks than females are? Harvey Ginsburg and Shirley Miller wanted to know whether young boys and young girls differ in their willingness to take risks. Popular belief suggests that males are more likely to take risks than females, but there was a notable lack of empirical evidence before Ginsburg and Miller (1982) conducted their study. Ginsburg and Miller probably could have devised an experiment to examine this question, but they wanted to focus on risk taking in the real world, rather than in the laboratory.

They chose as the setting for their study the San Antonio Zoo, where they used naturalistic observation to study children's risk taking. They identified four specific risky behaviors that children might engage in at this zoo: going for a ride on an elephant, petting a burro, feeding animals, and climbing a steep embankment. Without making their presence apparent, they carefully recorded the number of boys and girls who engaged in each of the behaviors. Their observations revealed that there *was* an association between sex and risk taking, at least for these behaviors, as young boys were found to take more risks than young girls (see Figure 2.7 for another example).

In *naturalistic observation* a researcher engages in careful, usually prolonged, observation of behavior without intervening directly with the subjects. This type of research is called *naturalistic* because behavior is allowed to unfold naturally (without interference) in its natural environment—that is, the setting in which it would normally occur.

Case Studies

Are death-row inmates the shrewd, coldly calculating individuals that many people believe them to be? A research team at New York University wanted to investigate the psychological characteristics of people given the death penalty (Lewis, et al., 1986). Until this study, there was no research either confirming or refuting the stereotypic image of criminals sentenced to die.

The research team decided that their question called for a case study approach. **A *case study* is an in-depth investigation of an individual subject.** The researchers compiled case studies on 15 condemned individuals who were chosen as subjects because their execution date was close at hand. The findings were surprising. All 15 in-

mates had histories of severe head injuries, 12 showed signs of brain damage, and most were well below average in intelligence. In other words, the investigators found an unexpected link between suffering from neurological impairment and ending up on death row. Their findings suggest that our legal system doles out its harshest penalty to individuals who are anything but shrewd.

Psychologists typically assemble case studies in clinical settings where an effort is being made to diagnose and treat some psychological problem (see Figure 2.8). The clinician tries to achieve an understanding of an individual's behavior through a variety of procedures, including interviewing the subject, interviewing others who know the subject, making direct observations, examining records, and administering psychological tests. Usually, the clinician is trying to "reason backwards" to determine the causes of the person's difficulties.

Occasionally, a single case study will yield a penetrating insight about human behavior, but usually one case does not provide much basis for deriving general laws of behavior. However, if you have a number of case studies, you can look for threads of consistency among them, and you may be able to draw some general conclusions. This was the strategy employed by the research team that studied death-row inmates.

Surveys and Psychological Tests

How common is it for college men to force women into sexual acts against their will? Are certain attitudes or personality traits in males associated with coercive sexual behavior? These were the questions that Karen Rapaport and Barry Burkhart (1984) set out to answer by administering a survey and several psychological tests to a sample of male undergraduates.

A *survey* is a structured questionnaire designed to solicit information about specific aspects of a subject's behavior. A *psychological test* is a standardized measure of a sample of a person's behavior. Both are typically (although not necessarily) administered to subjects as paper-and-pencil questionnaires that make it relatively easy to collect large amounts of data. Surveys are frequently used to gather data on subjects' attitudes and on aspects of behavior that are difficult to observe directly (such as sexual behavior). Psychological tests are used primarily to gather information on subjects' abilities and personality traits. Tests and surveys are versatile devices heavily used in correlational research. They may also be used to measure dependent variables in experimental research.

Clinical Psychiatric Report — Page 2

Jennie is a 21-year-old single college student with no prior psychiatric history. She was admitted to a short-term psychiatric ward from a hospital emergency room with a chief complaint of "I think I was psychotic." For several months prior to her admission she reported a series of "strange experiences." These included religious experiences, increased anxiety, a conviction that other students were conspiring against her, visual distortions, auditory hallucinations, and grandiose delusions. During the week prior to admission, the symptoms gradually worsened, and eventually she became agitated and disorganized.

A number of stressful events preceded this decompensation. A maternal aunt, a strong and central figure in her family, had died four months previously. As a college senior, she was struggling with decisions about her career choices following graduation. She was considering applying to graduate programs but was unable to decide which course of study she preferred. She was very much involved with her boyfriend, also a college senior. He, too, was struggling with anxiety about graduation, and it was not clear that their relationship would continue. The patient also reported feeling pressured and overextended at school.

The patient's older sister had suffered two psychotic episodes. This sister had slowly deteriorated, particularly after the second episode, and her compliance with treatment had been poor. An older brother and the patient's father also have a history of "emotional problems," although they never had formal psychiatric treatment. Jen____ ____ up ___ ambi_ ____ ____ ____ dd____

Figure 2.8 An example of the case-study technique. As this excerpt illustrates, case studies are particularly appropriate to clinical situations, in which the goal is to achieve an in-depth understanding of a specific individual. In a case study, the data are typically more verbal than mathematical.

In their study, Rapaport and Burkhart (1984) defined coercive sexual behavior as any sexual act engaged in with a woman "against her will." They administered a survey to 201 college men, asking them whether they had ever engaged in any of 11 coercive sexual acts such as placing a hand on a woman's breast or removing her underclothing against her will. What do you suppose they found? As Table 2.1 shows, the survey revealed that a substantial proportion of college men engage in a wide range of sexually coercive acts. The personality testing indicated that the more coercive males tended to be more irresponsible and more aggressive than the less coercive males.

Table 2.1 College Men's Responses to Items on Coercive Sexuality Scale (%)

ITEM	NEVER	ONCE OR TWICE	SEVERAL TIMES	OFTEN
1. Held a woman's hand	57	34	7	1
2. Kissed a woman	47	41	10	2
3. Placed hand on a woman's knee	39	43	15	3
4. Placed hand on a woman's breast	39	37	18	5
5. Placed hand on a woman's thigh or crotch	42	40	16	2
6. Unfastened a woman's outer clothing	51	34	13	2
7. Removed or disarranged a woman's outer clothing	58	31	9	2
8. Removed or disarranged a woman's underclothing	68	27	3	2
9. Removed own underclothing	78	18	3	2
10. Touched a woman's genital area	63	30	6	1
11. Had intercourse with a woman	85	13	2	0

Note: Some rows do not total 100% because of rounding.
Source: Rapaport & Burkhart, 1984

45

Advantages and Disadvantages of Correlational Research

Correlational research procedures offer some unique advantages. The most important one is that correlational methods give us a way to explore questions that we could not examine with experimental procedures. For example, after-the-fact correlational analyses would be the only ethical way to investigate the possible link between poor maternal nutrition and birth defects in humans. In a similar vein, if we hope to learn how urban and rural upbringing relate to people's values, we have to depend on correlational research, since we can't control where subjects grow up. Thus, *correlational research broadens the scope of phenomena that psychologists are able to study.*

A second advantage of correlational research stems from the artificiality frequently seen in experiments. *Correlational procedures often permit us to examine subjects' behavior in natural, real-world circumstances.* For example, if you were interested in the relationship between trial defendants' race and jury verdicts, you could systematically observe the results of real trials over a period of time. This elaborate application of naturalistic observation would take time and effort, but you would be tracking real-world behavior in all of its complexity.

Unfortunately, correlational methods have one very significant disadvantage. As we have seen, in correlational research the investigator does not have the opportunity to control events so as to isolate cause and effect. Consequently, correla-

tional research cannot demonstrate conclusively that two variables are causally related. You may have noticed this problem in our examples of correlational studies. For instance, although Ginsburg and Miller (1982) found an association between sex and risk taking, their data do not permit us to conclude that a child's sex *causes* these differences. Too many factors were left uncontrolled in the study. For example, we have no evidence about how similar the groups of boys and girls were. There could have been differences between the groups in age distribution, for instance, or other factors independent of sex, that might have led to the observed differences in risk taking.

The crux of the problem is that correlation is no assurance of causation. Variables may be closely correlated even though they are not causally related. For example, among young children there is a correlation between the size of their feet and the size of their vocabulary. Larger feet are associated with larger vocabulary. Obviously, increases in foot size do not *cause* increases in vocabulary size. Nor do increases in vocabulary size cause increases in foot size. Instead, both are caused, at least in part, by a third variable—increases in the childrens' age.

When we find that variables X and Y are correlated, we can safely conclude only that X and Y are related. We don't know how X and Y are related. We don't know whether X causes Y, or Y causes X, or whether both are caused by a third variable. To illustrate this interpretive problem, let's examine the correlation found between couples' ratings of their overall marital satisfaction and their satisfaction with their sexual relationship. Survey studies show that high marital satisfaction is associated with high sexual satisfaction and that low marital satisfaction is associated with low sexual satisfaction (Hunt, 1974; Tavris & Sadd, 1977). Although it's clear that good sex and a healthy marriage go hand in hand, it's hard to tell what's causing what. We don't know whether healthy marriages promote good sex, or whether good sex promotes healthy marriages. Moreover, we can't rule out the possibility that both are caused by a third variable (Z). Perhaps sexual satisfaction and marital satisfaction are both caused by compatibility in values. Some plausible causal relationships in this case are diagrammed for you in Figure 2.9, which illustrates the "third variable problem" in interpreting correlations. This is a frequent problem in correlational research, and you'll see this type of diagram again when we discuss other correlations.

Although correlation is *not* equivalent to causation, correlational research *can* contribute to our understanding of causal relations among vari-

---

CONCEPT CHECK 2.2
Matching Research Methods to Questions

Check your understanding of the uses and strengths of various research methods by figuring out which method would be optimal for investigating the questions below about behavioral processes. Choose from the following methods: (a) experiment, (b) naturalistic observation, (c) case study, and (d) surveys and psychological tests. Indicate your choice (by letter) next to each question. You'll find the answers in Appendix A.

_____ 1. Is personality related to how long people usually sleep each night?

_____ 2. Are there certain similarities in regard to early childhood experiences among people who suffer from anxiety disorders?

_____ 3. Do troops of baboons display territoriality? That is, do they mark off an area as their own and defend it from intrusion by other baboons?

_____ 4. Can the presence of food-related cues (delicious-looking food in advertisements, for example) cause an increase in the amount people eat?

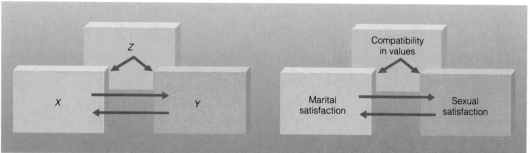

Figure 2.9 Three possible causal relations between correlated variables. If variables X and Y are correlated, does X cause Y, or does Y cause X— or does some hidden third variable, Z, account for the changes in both X and Y? As the relationship between marital and sexual satisfaction illustrates, a correlation alone does not provide the answer. We will encounter this problem of interpreting the meaning of correlations frequently in this text.

ables. Correlational studies that reveal no association between two variables strongly suggest that the variables are not causally related. For example, researchers generally find no association between college students' marijuana use and their grades (Pope, Ionescu-Pioggia, & Cole, 1981). This finding clearly undermines the notion that marijuana use causes poor academic performance. In contrast, correlational studies that uncover an association between variables *raise the possibility* that the variables are causally related. For exam-

ple, when Thomas Holmes and his colleagues repeatedly found correlations between stress and physical health, their findings stimulated research on whether stress causes illness. Eventually, converging lines of experimental and correlational research led investigators to conclude that stress can contribute causally to physical illness. Thus, correlational studies play a role in our efforts to piece together cause and effect relations in the world around us, even though they can't be used to demonstrate causation by themselves.

LOOKING FOR CONCLUSIONS: STATISTICS AND RESEARCH

Whether researchers use correlational methods or experimental methods, they need some way to make sense out of their data. Consider, for instance, the situation encountered by Wyler, Masuda, and Holmes (1971) in their study of the relationship between life change and illness. After collecting their data, they had a life-change score and an illness-severity score for each of their 238 subjects. But how did they determine the meaning of these 476 numbers? How did they figure out whether or not these numbers showed an association between life change and illness? Did they casually scan the data and make a subjective judgment? Of course not. Science is more precise than that. They used statistical analyses to quantify the exact strength of the association between life change and illness.

Statistics involves the use of mathematics to organize, summarize, and interpret numerical data. Researchers use statistics as a tool to analyze their data, because it permits them to draw conclusions based on their observations.

Many students find statistics intimidating, but statistics are an integral part of modern life. Although you may not realize it, you are bombarded with statistics nearly every day. When you read about economists' projections for inflation, when you check a baseball player's batting average, or when you see the popularity ratings of television shows, you are dealing with statistics. In this section we will examine a few basic statistical con-

cepts that will help you to understand the research discussed throughout this book. For the most part, we won't concern ourselves with the details of statistical *computations*. These details and some additional statistical concepts are discussed in Appendix B at the back of the book. At this juncture, we will discuss only the purpose, logic, and value of the two basic types of statistics—descriptive statistics and inferential statistics.

Descriptive Statistics

Descriptive statistics are used to organize and summarize data. They provide an overview of numerical data. Key descriptive statistics include measures of central tendency, measures of variability, and the coefficient of correlation.

MEASURING CENTRAL TENDENCY
In summarizing numerical data, we frequently want to know: What is a typical score? To answer this question, we use three measures of central tendency, or average: the median, the mean, and the mode. The *median* is the score that falls exactly in the center of a distribution of scores. Half of the scores fall above the median, and half fall below it. The *mean* is the arithmetic average of the scores in a distribution. It is obtained by adding up all of the scores and dividing by the number of scores. Finally, the *mode* is the score that occurs most frequently in a distribution.

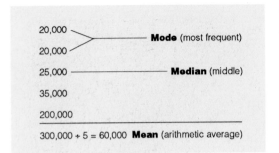

20,000		**Mode** (most frequent)
20,000		
25,000		**Median** (middle)
35,000		
200,000		

300,000 ÷ 5 = 60,000 **Mean** (arithmetic average)

Figure 2.10 Measures of central tendency. The three measures usually converge, but some data produce quite different values for mean, median, and mode. Which measure is most useful depends on what purpose is being served.

	Speed (miles per hour)	
A Perfection Boulevard		B Wild Street
35		21
34		37
33		50
37		28
38		42
40		37
36		39
33		25
34		23
30		48
35	**Mean**	35
2.87	**Standard deviation**	10.39

Figure 2.11 Variability and the standard deviation. These two sets of data produce the same mean, or average, but an observer on Wild Street would see much more variability in the speeds of individual cars than an observer on Perfection Boulevard. The standard deviation is an index of the amount of variability in a set of data.

In general, the mean is the most useful measure of central tendency because we can make additional statistical manipulations with the mean that are not possible with the median or mode. However, the mean is very sensitive to extreme scores in a distribution, which can sometimes make the mean misleading. For instance, let's say that you're interviewing for a sales position at a company where, unbeknownst to you, the five salespeople earned the following incomes in the previous year: $20,000, $20,000, $25,000, $35,000, and $200,000. You ask how much the typical salesperson earns in a year. The sales director proudly announces that her five salespeople earned a *mean* income of $60,000 last year (the calculations are shown in Figure 2.10). However, before you order that expensive new sports car, you had better inquire about the *median* and *modal* income for the sales staff. In this case, one extreme score ($200,000) has inflated the mean, making it unrepresentative of the sales staff's earnings. Therefore, the median ($25,000) and the mode ($20,000) both provide better estimates of what you are likely to earn than the mean.

MEASURING VARIABILITY

When we try to describe a set of data, it is often useful to have some estimate of the *variability* among the scores. **Variability refers to how much the scores tend to vary or depart from the mean score. The *standard deviation* is an index of the amount of variability in a set of data.** This index has a simple relationship to the variability in a data set. When the variability is great, the standard deviation will be relatively large, and when the variability is small, the standard deviation will be relatively small.

This relationship is apparent if you examine the two sets of data in Figure 2.11. The mean is the same for both sets of scores, but variability clearly is greater in Set B than in Set A. This greater variability yields a higher standard deviation for Set B than for Set A. Estimates of variability play a crucial role when researchers use statistics to decide whether the results of their studies support their hypotheses.

CORRELATION

In correlational research, investigators set out to determine whether there is an association between two variables. In this effort, they depend extensively on a very useful descriptive statistic—the correlation coefficient. **A *correlation coefficient* is a numerical index of the degree of relationship that exists between two variables.** A correlation coefficient tells us (1) how strongly related two variables are and (2) the direction (positive or negative) of the relationship.

POSITIVE AND NEGATIVE CORRELATION A *positive* correlation indicates that there is a *direct* relationship between two variables. This means that high scores on variable X are associated with high scores on variable Y, and that low scores on variable X are associated with low scores on variable Y. For example, there is a positive correlation between high school grade-point average (GPA) and subsequent college GPA. That is, people who do well in high school tend to do well in college, and those who perform poorly in high school tend to perform poorly in college (see Figure 2.12).

In contrast, a *negative* correlation indicates

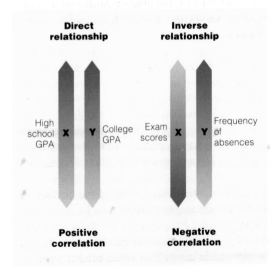

Figure 2.12 Positive and negative correlation. Notice that the terms *positive* and *negative* refer to the *direction* of the relationship between two variables, not to its strength. Variables are positively correlated if they tend to increase and decrease together, and negatively correlated if one tends to increase when the other decreases.

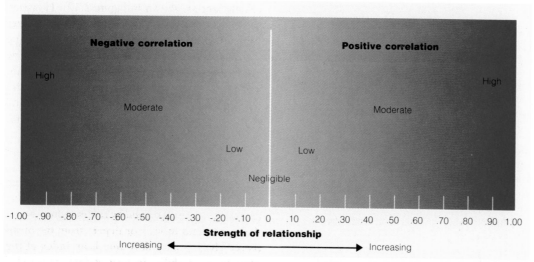

Figure 2.13 Interpreting correlation coefficients. The magnitude of a correlation coefficient indicates the strength of the relationship between two variables. The sign (plus or minus) indicates whether the relationship is direct or inverse. The closer the coefficient to +1 or −1, the stronger the relationship between the variables.

that there is an *inverse* relationship between two variables. This means that people who score high on variable X tend to score low on variable Y, whereas those who score low on X tend to score high on Y. For example, in most college courses, there is a negative correlation between how frequently a student is absent and how well he or she performs on exams. Students who have a high number of absences tend to earn low exam scores, while students who have a low number of absences tend to get higher exam scores (see Figure 2.12).

If a correlation is negative, a negative sign (−) is *always* placed in front of the coefficient. If a correlation is positive, a positive sign (+) may be placed in front of the coefficient, or the coefficient may be shown with no sign. (That is, if there's no sign, the correlation is positive.)

STRENGTH OF THE CORRELATION While the positive or negative sign indicates whether an association is direct or inverse, the size of the coefficient indicates the *strength* of the association between two variables. This coefficient can vary between 0 and +1.00 (if positive) or between 0 and −1.00 (if negative). A coefficient near 0 tells us that there is no relationship between the variables—that is, high or low scores on variable X show no consistent relationship to high or low scores on variable Y. A coefficient of +1.00 or −1.00 indicates that there is a perfect, one-to-one correspondence between the two variables. Most correlations fall between these extremes.

The closer the correlation is to either −1.00 or +1.00, the stronger the relationship is (see Figure 2.13). Thus, a correlation of .90 represents a stronger tendency for variables to be associated than does a correlation of .40. Likewise, a correlation of −.75 represents a stronger relationship than does a correlation of −.45. Keep in mind that the *strength* of a correlation depends only on

the size of the coefficient. The positive or negative sign simply shows whether the correlation is direct or inverse. Therefore, a correlation of −.60 reflects a stronger relationship than a correlation of +.30.

The computation of correlation coefficients allowed Wyler, Masuda, and Holmes (1971) to determine whether their data showed an association between life change and illness. They found a correlation of +.32 between subjects' amount of life change in the year prior to their hospitalization and the severity of their illness. Thus, correlational analyses permitted Holmes and his colleagues to determine that there was a moderate association between life change and illness in their sample of subjects.

CORRELATION AND PREDICTION You may recall that one of the principal goals of scientific research is accurate *prediction*. There is a close link between the magnitude of a correlation and the power it gives us to make predictions. *As a correlation increases in strength (gets closer to either −1.00 or +1.00), our ability to predict one variable based on knowledge of the other variable steadily increases.*

To illustrate, consider how college admissions tests (such as the SAT or ACT) are used to predict college performance. When admissions test scores and college GPA are correlated, researchers generally find correlations in the .40s (College Entrance Examination Board, 1979). This moderate correlation permits college admissions committees to predict with modest accuracy whether prospective students will succeed in college. The predictive power, although far from perfect, is substantial enough to justify the use of the tests as one factor in making admissions decisions. However, *if* this correlation were much higher, say .90, an admissions committee could predict with su-

Check your understanding of correlation by interpreting the meaning of the correlation in item 1 and by guessing the direction (positive or negative) of the correlations in item 2. You'll find the answers in Appendix A.

1. Researchers have found a substantial positive correlation between youngsters' self-esteem and their academic achievement (measured by grades in school). Check any acceptable conclusions based on this correlation.

_____ a. Low grades cause low self-esteem.

_____ b. There is an association between self-esteem and academic achievement.

_____ c. High self-esteem causes high academic achievement.

_____ d. High ability causes both high self-esteem and high academic achievement.

_____ e. Youngsters who score low in self-esteem tend to get low grades, and those who score high in self-esteem tend to get high grades.

2. Indicate whether you would expect the following correlations to be positive or negative.

_____ a. The correlation between age and visual acuity (among adults)

_____ b. The correlation between years of education and income

_____ c. The correlation between shyness and the number of friends one has

---

perb accuracy how students would perform. In contrast, *if* this correlation were much lower, say .20, an admissions committee's ability to predict college performance would be so poor that it would be unreasonable even to consider the test scores as a factor in making decisions.

Inferential Statistics

After researchers have summarized their data with descriptive statistics, they still need to decide whether or not their data support their hypotheses. *Inferential statistics* **are used to interpret data and draw conclusions.** Working with the laws of probability, researchers use inferential statistics to bridge the gap between observations and conclusions.

Let's examine the logic underlying the process of hypothesis testing. To illustrate how this process unfolds, envision a hypothetical experiment on the effects of a computerized tutoring program (the independent variable) on reading achievement (the dependent variable) among sixth-graders. The program is designed to improve students' reading skills. Hence, our hypothesis is that program participants (the experimental group) will score higher than nonparticipants (the control group) on a standardized reading test given near the end of the school year. Let's assume that we compare 60 subjects in each group and

obtain the following results, reported in terms of the subjects' grade level for reading:

Control group		Experimental group
6.3	Mean	6.8
1.4	Standard deviation	2.4

Our hypothesis was that the computerized training program would produce higher reading scores in the experimental group than in the control group. That is indeed the case. However, we have to ask ourselves a critical question: Is this observed difference between the two groups large enough to support the hypothesis? That is, do the higher scores in the experimental group reflect the effect of the reading program, or might a difference of this size have occurred by chance? Obviously, if the results could easily have occurred by chance, then they don't provide meaningful support for the hypothesis. Researchers use inferential statistics to evaluate the possibility that their results may be due to the fluctuations of chance.

When statistical calculations indicate that research results are *not* likely to be due to chance, the results are said to be *statistically significant*. You will probably hear your psychology professor use this term quite frequently. In discussing research, it is routine to note that "statistically significant differences were found." In statistics, the word *significant* has a very precise and special meaning. *Statistical significance* **is said to exist when the probability that the observed findings are due to chance is very low.** "Very low" usually is defined as fewer than 5 chances in 100, which is referred to as the .05 level of significance.

Notice that in this special usage *significant* does not mean "important," or even "interesting." Statistically significant findings may or may not be theoretically significant or practically significant. They are simply results that are unlikely to be due to chance.

We don't need to be concerned here with the details of how statistical significance is calculated, but you should know that a key consideration is the amount of variability in the data. That is why the standard deviation, which measures variability, is such an important statistic. Incidentally, when the necessary computations are made, the difference between the two groups in our hypothetical experiment on the tutoring program does *not* turn out to be statistically significant. Thus, our hypothetical results would not be adequate to demonstrate that our tutoring program leads to improved reading achievement. Psychologists have to do this kind of statistical analysis as part of virtually every study, so inferential statistics are an integral element in the research enterprise.

LOOKING FOR FLAWS: EVALUATING RESEARCH

Although I have emphasized that scientific research is a more reliable source of information than casual observation or popular belief, it would be wrong to conclude that all published research is free of errors. Empirical studies are conducted by fallible human beings, and flawed studies do make their way into the body of scientific literature.

This is one of the reasons scientists often try to replicate studies. **Replication involves the repetition of a study to see whether the earlier results are duplicated.** The replication process helps scientists to identify and purge erroneous findings so that scientific knowledge is relatively reliable. Of course, the replication process sometimes leads to contradictory findings. You'll see plenty of examples in the chapters that follow. Inconsistent results can be frustrating and confusing for students, but they are an unavoidable outgrowth of science's commitment to replication. Fortunately, one of the strengths of the empirical approach is that scientists work to reconcile or explain conflicting results. In fact, new advances in our understanding of behavioral processes sometimes emerge out of these efforts to explain contradictory findings.

Like all sources of information, scientific studies need to be examined with a critical eye. This section describes a number of common methodological problems that spoil studies with some regularity. An awareness of these pitfalls can make you a more skilled evaluator of research and enhance your appreciation of the ingenuity often required in conducting scientific studies. To illustrate the challenges faced by researchers, Figure 2.14 indicates some of the points at which various flaws can enter into the design or execution of an experiment.

Sampling Bias

A *sample* is the collection of subjects selected for observation in an empirical study. In contrast, the *population* is the much larger collection of animals or people (from which the sample is drawn) that we want to generalize about. For example, when political pollsters attempt to predict elections, all of the voters in a jurisdiction represent the population, and those voters surveyed constitute the sample. If a researcher was interested in the ability of 6-year-old children to form concepts, those 6-year-olds actually studied would be the sample, and all similar 6-year-old children (perhaps those in modern Western cultures) would be the population.

The strategy of observing a limited sample in order to generalize about a much broader population rests on the assumption that the sample is reasonably *representative* of the population. A sample is representative if its composition is similar to the composition of the population. If the sample is *not* representative, then the entire reasoning process collapses and the generalizations may be inaccurate. For instance, if political pollsters surveyed people only in posh shopping areas frequented by the wealthy, their generalizations about the voting public as a whole would probably be off the mark most of the time. This kind of methodological flaw is called *sampling bias*.

As an example of the problems that surface when there is a sampling bias, consider the highly publicized surveys concerned with women's sex-

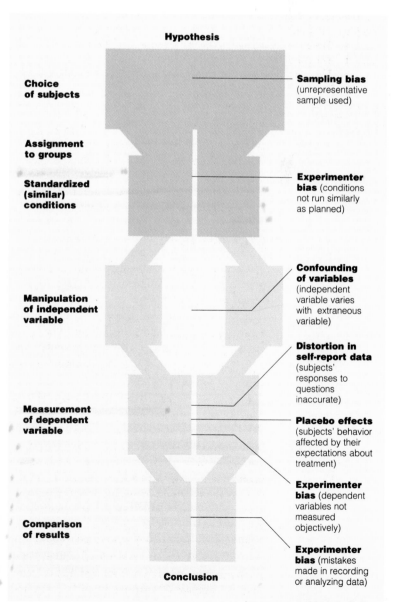

Figure 2.14 Where common flaws in experiments usually occur. The diagram shows the stages at which the research flaws discussed in the text tend to be introduced into experimental studies. As the figure suggests, experimenter bias is a danger that must be guarded against at virtually every stage in the design and execution of an experiment.

51

Social scientists rely on sampling techniques to make generalizations about the behavior of large populations. Companies such as Nielsen and Arbitron use these techniques to produce ratings of the popularity of television shows. Advertisers, producers, networks, and other interested parties depend on these techniques to be free of sampling bias.

uality published by Shere Hite (1976, 1987). The results of these surveys suggest that a large majority of women in the United States are highly dissatisfied with their sex lives, their intimate relationships, and their male partners. Unfortunately, Hite used sampling procedures that make the generality of her findings highly questionable. Her principal means for distributing her first survey was through activist feminist organizations, whose membership rolls are not necessarily representative of the general population of American women. Although Hite's more recent survey received wider distribution, the return rate was only 4.5% (up from 3% in her first study). We can only speculate about any relevant differences between the 4.5% who returned the survey and the 95.5% who did not.

The sampling bias in Hite's study seriously undermines our ability to generalize about American women from her findings. In general, whenever you have doubts about the results of a study, the first thing to examine is the composition of the sample. In case you're wondering, Hite is not a psychologist. She publishes her work in books promoted for sale to the general public rather than in scientific journals. Her sampling procedures appear to have been designed to generate controversial results rather than representative results (controversial results sell books). Her surveys are a rich source of thought-provoking data, but the results have to be viewed with great caution.

Placebo Effects

In pharmacology, a *placebo* is a substance that resembles a drug but that has no pharmacological effect. In studies that assess the therapeutic effects of drugs, placebos are given to some subjects in order to control for the effects of a treacherous extraneous variable—namely, subjects' expectations. Placebos are used because we know that subjects' expectations can influence their feelings, reactions, and behavior. Thus, *placebo effects occur when subjects experience some change from an empty, fake, or ineffectual treatment because of their expectations.* In medicine placebo effects

are legendary. Many physicians tell of patients being "cured" by prescriptions of sugar pills. Similarly, psychologists have found that subjects' expectations can be powerful determinants of their perceptions and behavior when they are "under the microscope" in an empirical study.

In describing placebo effects, I cannot help but recall a friend from my college days who would gulp one drink in a bar and start behaving in a drunken fashion before the alcohol could possibly have taken effect. In fact, this sort of placebo effect has been observed in a number of laboratory experiments on the effects of alcohol (Wilson, 1982). In these studies, the control group subjects are led to believe that they are drinking alcoholic beverages, when in reality the drinks have been cleverly doctored so that they only appear to contain alcohol. Many of the subjects act intoxicated, even though they haven't really consumed any alcohol. Thus, placebo effects can occur even when subjects are quite familiar with the genuine effects of the real drug.

You should be wary of the danger of placebo effects whenever you think that subjects may expect that a treatment will affect them in a certain way. For example, placebo effects must be considered in research on the effects of meditation. A number of published studies suggest that learning to meditate can improve subjects' creativity, energy level, health, and happiness (Bloomfield & Kory, 1976; Henderson, 1975). However, critics have noted that researchers in many of these studies have failed to control adequately for placebo effects (Shapiro, 1981). The problem is that some researchers have assembled their experimental groups with volunteer subjects who were eager to learn meditation, and who often *wanted* and *expected* it to have beneficial effects. The subjects' positive expectations may have colored their subsequent ratings of their creativity, happiness, and so on. Better-designed studies *have* shown that meditation can have positive effects (see Chapter 5), but placebo effects probably contributed to overly favorable results in much of the early research on meditation.

Researchers can assess the possible role of placebo effects by including a placebo group in a study to compare with the experimental group. In evaluating research, then, you should look to see whether the experimenter has taken appropriate precautions to guard against possible placebo effects.

Confounding of Variables

A *confounding of variables* occurs whenever two or more variables vary together in a way that

makes it difficult to sort out their independent effects. The logic of the experiment requires that a researcher isolate the effects of the independent variable. If some extraneous variable covaries with the independent variable, the variables are said to be confounded, and the researcher will not be able to tell which variable is having what effect on the dependent variable.

To illustrate, let's say that you thought that the injection of a certain drug might temporarily enhance memory. You conduct an experiment in which the subjects in the experimental group receive this drug injection just before working on a memory task. To control for possible placebo effects, the subjects in the control group receive a similar injection, but it contains no drug. Let's further suppose that you have to hire a physician to supervise the real drug injections given to the experimental group. The physician is available for this purpose only in the morning, so you decide to run experimental subjects in the morning and control subjects in the afternoon. What is wrong with this experiment?

The problem with this experimental design is that it confounds the independent variable (the drug injection) with an extraneous variable, the time of day when subjects work on the memory task. Those subjects who receive the real drug injection always work on the task in the morning, whereas those who do not get the drug always tackle the task in the afternoon. What if your subjects tend to be more alert in the morning than in the afternoon? Then any superiority in memory performance by the experimental group could be due to the time of day rather than to the effects of the drug. To conduct this experiment properly, you would have to revise your plans so that both groups of subjects were tested in the morning.

As you can see, seemingly harmless differences between experimental and control groups can produce significant confoundings that blur the impact of the independent variable. That is why so much care, planning, and forethought are necessary in designing an experiment, and why published studies contain so much detail about the methodology used. One of the key qualities that separate a talented experimenter from a mediocre one is the ability to foresee troublesome extraneous variables and control for them so as to avoid confounding variables.

Distortions in Self-Report Data

Research psychologists frequently work with self-report data made up of subjects' verbal accounts of their behavior, as opposed to direct behavioral observations. This is the case whenever surveys, questionnaires, attitude scales, or personality inventories are used to measure variables. Self-report data can be very useful; they take advantage of the fact that people have a unique opportunity to observe themselves full time. However, self-reports can be plagued by several kinds of distortion.

One of the most problematic of these distortions is the social desirability bias. **The *social desirability bias* is a tendency to provide socially approved answers to questions about oneself.** Subjects who are influenced by this bias tend to respond to many questions with contrived, edited answers intended to create a favorable impression. For example, many survey respondents report that they voted in an election or gave to a charity, when in fact, it is possible to determine that they did not (Katz, 1951).

Other problems can also produce distortions in self-report data. Subjects sometimes misunderstand questionnaire items, and memory errors can undermine the accuracy of their reports. In re-

---

CONCEPT CHECK 2.4
Detecting Flaws in Research

Check your understanding of how to conduct sound research by looking for methodological flaws in the following studies. You'll find the answers in Appendix A.

Study 1. A researcher announces that he will be conducting an experiment to investigate the detrimental effects of sensory deprivation on perceptual-motor coordination. The first 40 students who sign up for the study are assigned to the experimental group, and the next 40 who sign up serve in the control group. The researcher supervises all aspects of the study's execution. Experimental subjects spend two hours in a sensory deprivation chamber, where sensory stimulation is minimal. Control subjects spend two hours in a waiting room that contains magazines and a TV. All subjects then perform ten 1-minute trials on a pursuit-rotor task that requires them to try to keep a stylus on a tiny rotating target. The dependent variable is their average score on the pursuit-rotor task.

Study 2. A researcher wants to know whether there is a relationship between age and racial prejudice. She designs a survey in which respondents are asked to rate their prejudice against six different ethnic groups. She distributes the survey to over 500 people of various ages who are approached at a shopping mall in a low-income, inner-city neighborhood.

Check the flaws that are apparent in each study.

Methodological flaw	Study 1	Study 2
Sampling bias	_____	_____
Placebo effects	_____	_____
Confounding of variables	_____	_____
Distortions in self-report data	_____	_____
Experimenter bias	_____	_____

sponding to certain kinds of scales, some subjects tend to agree with nearly all of the statements, while other subjects tend to disagree with nearly all of them. Obviously, distortions like these can produce inaccurate results. Although researchers have devised ways to neutralize these problems, one should be especially cautious in drawing conclusions from self-report data.

Experimenter Bias

As scientists, psychologists try to conduct their studies in an objective, unbiased way so that their own views or expectations will not influence the results. However, objectivity is a *goal* that scientists strive for, not an accomplished fact that we can take for granted. In reality, most researchers have an emotional investment in the outcome of their research. Often they are testing hypotheses that they have developed themselves and that they would like to see supported by the data. It is understandable, then, that *experimenter bias* is a possible source of error in research.

Experimenter bias can slip through to influence studies in many subtle ways. One problem is that researchers, like others, sometimes see *what they want to see*. For instance, there is evidence that when experimenters make apparently honest mistakes in recording subjects' responses, the mistakes tend to be heavily slanted in favor of supporting the hypothesis (O'Leary, Kent, & Kanowitz, 1975). As we discussed in Chapter 1, seeing what you want to see is a common human tendency. An accountant in a bank told me that when customers come in to straighten out muddled checkbook records, nearly all of the mathematical errors uncovered are the kinds that lead the customers to believe they have more money than they actually do. Obviously, bank customers have nothing to gain by deliberately pretending that they have extra money. The more likely explanation is that wishful thinking can affect us all, whether in money matters or in research.

Robert Rosenthal has conducted a number of studies that suggest that experimenter bias may

"Quite unconsciously, a psychologist interacts in subtle ways with the people he is studying so that he may get the response he expects to get."
ROBERT ROSENTHAL

lead researchers to unintentionally influence the behavior of their subjects. In one study, Rosenthal and Fode (1963) recruited undergraduate psychology students to serve as the "experimenters" in what was supposed to be a study of how subjects rated the success of people portrayed in photographs. In a pilot study, photos were selected that generated (on the average) neutral ratings on a 20-point scale extending from − 10 (extreme failure) to + 10 (extreme success). Rosenthal and Fode then manipulated the expectancies of their experimenters by telling half of them that they would probably obtain average ratings of − 5, while telling the other half that they would probably obtain average ratings of + 5. The experimenters were forbidden from conversing with their subjects except for reading some standardized instructions. Even though the photographs and instructions were exactly the same for both groups, the experimenters who *expected* positive ratings *obtained* significantly higher ratings than those who expected negative ratings.

How could the experimenters have swayed the subjects' ratings? Rosenthal has suggested that, among other things, the experimenters may have unintentionally influenced their subjects by sending subtle nonverbal signals as the experiment progressed. Without realizing it, they may have smiled, nodded, or sent other positive cues when subjects made ratings that were in line with the experimenters' expectations.

The problems associated with experimenter bias can be neutralized by using a double-blind procedure. **The *double-blind procedure* is a research strategy in which neither subjects nor experimenters know which subjects are in the experimental or control groups.** It's not particularly unusual for subjects to be "blind" about their treatment condition, but the double-blind procedure keeps the experimenter in the dark as well. Of course, a member of the research team who isn't directly involved with subjects keeps track of who is in which group. This procedure controls for sources of error that may be introduced by either subjects or experimenters.

LOOKING AT ETHICS: DO THE ENDS JUSTIFY THE MEANS?

Think back to Stanley Schachter's (1959) study on anxiety and affiliation and imagine how you would have felt if you had been one of the subjects in Schachter's high-anxiety group. You show up at a research laboratory, expecting to participate in a harmless experiment. The room you are sent to is full of unusual electronic equipment. An official-looking man in a lab coat announces that

this equipment will be used to subject you to a series of painful electrical shocks. His statement that the shocks will leave no permanent tissue damage is hardly reassuring. Surely, you think, there must be a mistake. All of a sudden, your venture into research has turned into a nightmare! Your stomach knots up in anxiety. The researcher explains that there will be a delay while he prepares his apparatus, and he asks you to fill out a short questionnaire inquiring about whether you prefer to wait alone or with others. Still reeling in dismay at the prospect of being shocked, you fill out his questionnaire. The researcher collects the questionnaire and then announces that you won't be shocked after all—it was all a hoax! Feelings of relief wash over you, but they're mixed with anger. You feel like the experimenter just made a fool of you, and you're embarrassed and resentful.

Should researchers be allowed to play with your feelings in this way? Should they be permitted to deceive subjects like this? Is this the cost we have to pay to advance scientific knowledge? Do the ends justify the means? As these questions indicate, the research enterprise sometimes presents scientists with difficult ethical issues. In psychological research, the two major ethical dilemmas center on the use of deception and the use of animals. Let's examine these controversial issues.

The Question of Deception

At one time elaborate deception such as that seen in Schachter's study was not particularly unusual in psychological research. Many other studies employed similar deceptive practices. Over the years, psychologists have faked fights, thefts, muggings, faintings, epileptic seizures, rapes, and automobile breakdowns in order to explore a host of issues. They have led subjects to believe that they were hurting others with electrical shocks, that they had homosexual tendencies, and that they were overhearing negative comments about themselves. Why have psychologists used so much deception in their research? Precisely because of the types of methodological problems that we discussed in the last section. Deception is employed to avoid problems such as placebo effects and distortions that can occur in self-report data.

Critics argue against the use of deception on several grounds (Baumrind, 1985; Kelman, 1982). First, they assert that deception is only a nice word for lying, which they see as inherently immoral. Second, they argue that by deceiving unsuspecting subjects, psychologists may undermine many individuals' trust in others. Third, they point out that many deceptive studies produce distress for subjects who were not forewarned about that possibility. Specifically, subjects may experience great stress during a study, or be made to feel foolish when the true nature of a study is explained.

Those who defend the use of deception in research maintain that many important issues could not be investigated if experimenters were not permitted to mislead subjects (Aronson, Brewer, & Carlsmith, 1985). Furthermore, they argue that most research deceptions involve "white lies" that are harmless to participants. Finally, they argue that the benefits—advances in knowledge that often improve human welfare—are worth the cost of occasionally deceiving and distressing subjects.

The issue of deception creates a difficult dilemma for scientists, pitting honesty against the desire to advance knowledge. In recent years, however, there has been a reduction in the use of deception. Today, most institutions that conduct research have formal committees to evaluate the ethics of research proposals before studies are allowed to proceed. These committees have often blocked studies requiring substantial deception. Many psychologists believe that this conservatism has obstructed important lines of research and slowed progress in the field. Although this may be true, it is not easy to write off the points made by the critics of deception. Warwick (1975) states the issue eloquently: "If it is all right to use deceit to advance knowledge, then why not for reasons of national security, for maintaining the Presidency, or to save one's own hide?" (p. 105). That's a tough question regarding a tough dilemma that will probably generate heated debate for a long time to come.

The Question of Animal Research

Psychology's other major ethics controversy concerns the use of animals in research. There are several reasons psychologists use animals as research subjects. Sometimes they simply want to know more about the behavior of a specific type of animal. In other instances they want to identify general laws of behavior that apply to both humans and animals. Finally, in some cases psychologists use animals because they can expose them to treatments that clearly would be unacceptable with human subjects. For example, most of the

The use of animals in scientific research raises difficult ethical issues. The American Psychological Association's ethical guidelines call for humane treatment of experimental animals and clear justification for any procedure that may inflict harm or pain.

55

1. A subject's participation in research should be voluntary and based on informed consent. Subjects should never be coerced into participating in research. They should be informed in advance about any aspects of the study that might be expected to influence their willingness to cooperate. Furthermore, they should be permitted to withdraw from a study at any time if they so desire.

2. Subjects should not be exposed to harmful or dangerous research procedures. This guideline is intended to protect subjects from psychological as well as physical harm. Thus, even stressful procedures that might cause emotional discomfort are largely prohibited. However, procedures that carry a modest risk of moderate mental discomfort may be acceptable.

3. If an investigation requires some deception of subjects (about matters that do not involve risks), the researcher is required to explain and correct any misunderstandings as soon as possible. The deception must be disclosed to subjects in "debriefing" sessions as soon as it is practical to do so without compromising the goals of the study.

4. Subjects' right to privacy should never be violated. Information about a subject that might be acquired during a study must be treated as highly confidential and should never be made available to others without the consent of the participant.

5. Harmful or painful procedures imposed upon animals must be thoroughly justified in terms of the knowledge to be gained from the study. Furthermore, laboratory animals are entitled to decent living conditions that are spelled out in detailed rules that relate to their housing, cleaning, feeding, and so forth.

research on the relationship between deficient nutrition during pregnancy and the incidence of birth defects has been done with animals.

It's this third reason for using animals that generates most of the controversy. Some people maintain that it is wrong to subject animals to harm or pain for research purposes. Citing estimates that roughly 20 million mice, rats, rabbits, cats, dogs, and monkeys die each year for the sake of science, they accuse researchers of unnecessary cruelty to animals. Some of the more militant animals' rights activists have broken into laboratories, destroyed scientists' equipment and research records, and stolen experimental animals (Cunningham, 1985).

In spite of the great furor, only 7% to 8% of all psychological studies involve animals (mostly rodents and birds). Relatively few of these studies require subjecting the animals to painful or harmful manipulations (American Psychological Association, 1984). Psychologists who conduct research with animals point to the many advances of knowledge achieved through such work, including many major breakthroughs that have improved human welfare (Miller, 1985). For example, animal research has led to significant advances in the treatment of psychological disorders, visual defects, and problems with pain. Nonetheless, the manner in which animals can ethically be used for research is a highly charged controversy, and psychologists are becoming increasingly sensitive to this issue. Although animals continue to be used in research, psychologists are taking greater pains to ensure that they receive humane care and to justify their use in relation to the potential benefits of the research.

The ethics issues we have discussed in this section have led the APA to develop a set of ethical standards for researchers (American Psychological Association, 1981). Although most psychological studies are fairly benign, these ethical principles are intended to ensure that both human and animal subjects are treated with dignity. Some of the key guidelines in these ethical principles are summarized in Figure 2.15.

PUTTING IT IN PERSPECTIVE

Two of our six unifying themes have emerged strongly in this chapter. First, the entire chapter is a testimonial to the idea that psychology is empirical (theme 1). Second, our discussion of methodological flaws in research has provided numerous examples of how one's experience of the world can be highly subjective (theme 6). Let's examine each of these points in more detail.

As explained in Chapter 1, the empirical approach entails testing ideas, basing conclusions on systematic observations, collecting data, and relying on a healthy brand of skepticism. All of these features of the empirical approach were apparent in our review of the research enterprise in psychology.

As you have seen, psychologists test their ideas

by formulating clear hypotheses that involve predictions about relations between variables. They then use a variety of research methods—different strategies for observation—to collect data so they can see if their predictions are supported. The various methods are designed to make the researcher's observations highly systematic and precise. The entire endeavor is saturated with skepticism. Psychologists are impressed only by research results that are very unlikely to have occurred by chance. In planning and executing their research, they are constantly on the lookout for methodological flaws, and they publish their findings so that other experts can subject their methods and conclusions to critical scrutiny. Collectively, these procedures represent the essence of the empirical approach.

The subjectivity of personal experience was abundantly apparent in our discussion of methodological problems, especially placebo effects and experimenter bias. When subjects report beneficial effects from a fake treatment (the placebo), it's usually because they want and expect to see these effects. The studies showing that many subjects start feeling intoxicated just because they *think* that they have drunk alcohol are striking demonstrations of the enormous power of our expectations. As I pointed out in Chapter 1, psychologists and other scientists are not immune to the effects of subjective experience. Scientists are human, and some fall prey to experimenter bias. Although they are trained to be objective, it's clear that even scientists may see what they expect to see or what they want to see. This is one reason the empirical approach emphasizes precise measurement of variables and encourages a skeptical attitude. The highly subjective nature of experience is exactly what the empirical approach attempts to neutralize.

The publication of empirical studies allows us to apply our skepticism to the research enterprise. However, you cannot critically analyze studies unless you know where and how to find them. The following Application discusses where studies are published, how to find studies on specific topics, and how to read research reports.

FINDING AND READING JOURNAL ARTICLES

Answer the following "yes" or "no."

1. I have read about scientific studies in newspapers and magazines and sometimes wondered, "How did they come to those conclusions?"

2. When I go to the library, I often have difficulty figuring out how to find information based on research.

3. I have tried to read scientific reports and found them very technical and difficult to understand.

If you responded "yes" to any of these statements, you have struggled with the information explosion in the sciences. We live in a very research-oriented society. The amount of research conducted in most sciences is increasing at a dizzying pace. This increase has been particularly spectacular in psychology (see Figure 2.16). Moreover, psychological research increasingly commands attention from the popular press because it is often immediately relevant to individuals' personal concerns and to the social problems that confront our society.

This Application is intended to

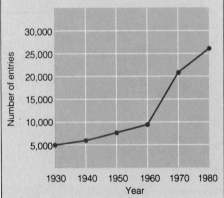

Figure 2.16 The dramatic increase in the number of entries included in *Psychological Abstracts*, a journal that indexes and summarizes the research literature in psychology. *Note:* Figure for 1970 includes dissertations and books; figure for 1980 includes only journal articles.

help you cope with the information explosion in psychology. It assumes that there may come a time when you need to examine original psychological research—whether it is in your role as a student (working on a term paper, for instance), another role (parent, teacher, nurse, administrator), or merely out of curiosity. To facilitate any such effort to look at the research literature in psychology, this Application explains the nature of technical journals and discusses how to find and read journal articles. You can find additional instruction on how to make use of library resources in psychology in an excellent little (137 pages) handbook put out by the APA entitled *Library Use: A Handbook for Psychology* (Reed & Baxter, 1983).

The Nature of Technical Journals

As you will recall from earlier in the chapter, a *journal* is a periodical that publishes technical and scholarly material, usually in a narrowly defined area of inquiry. Scholars in most fields—whether economics, chemistry, physics, education, or psychology—publish the bulk of their work in these journals. Therefore, journal articles represent the core of intellectual activity in any academic discipline.

In general, journal articles are written for other professionals in the field. Hence, authors assume that their readers are other interested economists, psychologists, or chemists. Because journal articles are written in the special professional language unique to a particular discipline, they are often difficult for nonprofessionals to understand. You will be learning a great deal of psychology's special language in this course, which will improve your understanding of journal articles.

There are hundreds of journals devoted exclusively to the publication of psychological research, and over a thousand publish *some* research that is

psychological in nature. Many of these are interdisciplinary journals that bridge the gap between two or more fields. For instance, *Law and Human Behavior* is a psychology-law journal, while *Brain Research* is a psychology-biology journal.

Most journals are highly selective about what they publish. Experts evaluate submissions very carefully, weighing their methodological soundness and their contribution to advancing our knowledge of behavioral processes. Some of the more prestigious psychology journals reject more than 90% of the articles submitted. Some of these are rejected because they aren't considered theoretically important enough to merit publication in a major journal, where space is very limited (they may subsequently be submitted to and accepted by a less prestigious journal). Others are rejected because the research they are reporting contains methodological errors (these may never be published anywhere). Sometimes, a scientifically sound study is rejected because the write-up is confusing and unclear (these may be rewritten and resubmitted).

In psychology most journal articles are reports that describe original empirical studies. These research reports represent the essence of what the science of psychology is all about. They permit researchers to disseminate their findings to the scientific community. Another common type of article is the review article. *Review articles* summarize and reconcile the findings of a large number of studies on a specific issue. Some psychology journals also publish comments or critiques of previously published research, book reviews, theoretical treatises, and descriptions of methodological innovations.

Finding Journal Articles

Reports of psychological research are frequently mentioned in newspapers and many popular magazines. These

summaries can be helpful to readers, but they often present the most sensational conclusions that one might draw from the research, and they sometimes include major factual errors. Hence, if a study mentioned in the press is of considerable interest or relevance to you, you may want to track down the original journal article to ensure that you get accurate information.

Most discussions of research in the popular press do *not* mention where you can find the original technical article. However, there is a way to find out. A very special journal is devoted exclusively to summarizing and indexing the research literature in psychology. This journal, called *Psychological Abstracts*, makes it possible to locate specific articles. It also is invaluable when you want to examine the research literature on a general topic, such as intelligence testing, the effects of day care, or treatments for insomnia.

Psychological Abstracts contains brief summaries, or abstracts, of journal articles, and various kinds of indexes intended to help you find the articles relevant to your interests. Over 1000 journals are scanned regularly to select items to be included in *Psychological Abstracts*. The journal is published monthly, and the summaries are grouped under general headings such as educational psychology, physiological psychology, and developmental psychology. The summaries are concise—about 75 to 175 words. They briefly describe the hypotheses, methods, results, and conclusions of the studies. Each abstract should allow you to determine whether an article is relevant to your research. If it is, you should be able to find the article in your library (or order it), because a complete bibliographic reference is provided (see Figure 2.17).

Your search for a specific article or for information on a broad topic can be greatly aided by judicious use of the *subject* and *author indexes*. These indexes list all articles on a particular topic or by a particular author. The relevant articles are listed according to their index numbers (every article is given its own index number). The subject and author indexes can be found in the back of each monthly issue, and cumulative indexes are published every six months.

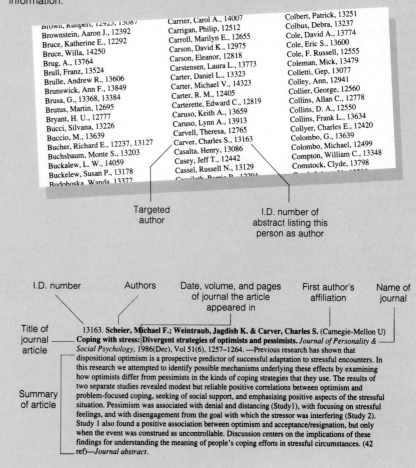

Figure 2.17 Using the author index of *Psychological Abstracts* to locate journal articles. The name of a researcher can be used via the author index (upper portion of figure) to locate abstracts of the researcher's journal articles (example in lower portion). Each abstract provides a summary of the article and complete bibliographical information.

Brown, Rupert, 12923, 13087
Brownstein, Aaron J., 12392
Bruce, Katherine E., 12292
Bruce, Willa, 14250
Brug, A., 13764
Brull, Franz, 13524
Brulle, Andrew R., 13606
Brunswick, Ann F., 13849
Brusa, G., 13368, 13384
Brutus, Martin, 12695
Bryant, H. U., 12777
Bucci, Silvana, 13226
Buccio, M., 13639
Bucher, Richard E., 12237, 13127
Buchsbaum, Monte S., 13203
Buckalew, L. W., 14059
Buckelew, Susan P., 13178
Budohoska, Wanda, 13372

Carrier, Carol A., 14007
Carrigan, Philip, 12512
Carroll, Marilyn E., 12655
Carson, David K., 12975
Carson, Eleanor, 12818
Carstensen, Laura L., 13773
Carter, Daniel L., 13323
Carter, Michael V., 14323
Carter, R. M., 12405
Carterette, Edward C., 12819
Caruso, Keith A., 13659
Caruso, Lynn A., 13913
Carvell, Theresa, 12765
Carver, Charles S., 13163
Casalta, Henry, 13086
Casey, Jeff T., 12442
Cassel, Russell N., 13129
Cassileth, Barrie R., 12204

Colbert, Patrick, 13251
Colbus, Debra, 13237
Cole, David A., 13774
Cole, Eric S., 13600
Cole, F. Russell, 12555
Coleman, Mick, 13479
Colletti, Gep, 13077
Colley, Ann, 12941
Collier, George, 12560
Collins, Allan C., 12778
Collins, D. A., 12550
Collins, Frank L., 13634
Collyer, Charles E., 12420
Colombo, G., 13639
Colombo, Michael, 12499
Compton, William C., 13348
Comstock, Clyde, 13798

Targeted author

I.D. number of abstract listing this person as author

I.D. number — Authors — Date, volume, and pages of journal the article appeared in — First author's affiliation — Name of journal

Title of journal article

13163. Scheier, Michael F.; Weintraub, Jagdish K. & Carver, Charles S. (Carnegie-Mellon U) Coping with stress: Divergent strategies of optimists and pessimists. *Journal of Personality & Social Psychology*, 1986(Dec), Vol 51(6), 1257–1264. —Previous research has shown that dispositional optimism is a prospective predictor of successful adaptation to stressful encounters. In this research we attempted to identify possible mechanisms underlying these effects by examining how optimists differ from pessimists in the kinds of coping strategies that they use. The results of two separate studies revealed modest but reliable positive correlations between optimism and problem-focused coping, seeking of social support, and emphasizing positive aspects of the stressful situation. Pessimism was associated with denial and distancing (Study1), with focusing on stressful feelings, and with disengagement from the goal with which the stressor was interfering (Study 2). Study 1 also found a positive association between optimism and acceptance/resignation, but only when the event was construed as uncontrollable. Discussion centers on the implications of these findings for understanding the meaning of people's coping efforts in stressful circumstances. (42 ref)—*Journal abstract.*

Summary of article

Although news accounts of research rarely mention where a study was published, they often mention the name of the researcher. If you have this information, the easiest way to find a specific article is to look up the author in the *Psychological Abstracts* author index. For example, in June of 1987 a newspaper article summarized an interesting study of optimism as a personality trait. Let's say you were interested in finding the original journal article. The summary in the paper provided no information about which journal the study had been published in. However, the news article did quote Charles Carver, who was one of the researchers. To track down the original article, you would look up Carver's name in the author index. The upper portion of Figure 2.17 shows what you would have found if you had done this soon after publication of the news article. The author index would have revealed that Carver had published one article recently. The abstract for this article, found by its index number (13163), is shown at the bottom of Figure 2.17. As you can see, it shows that the original report was published in the December 1986 issue of the *Journal of Personality and Social Psychology*. Armed with this information, you could obtain the article easily.

A search for articles on a particular subject can be conducted by working through the subject index, which allows you to look up various topics such as achievement motivation, aggressive behavior, alcoholism, animal communication, appetite disorders, and artistic ability. After each subject heading, a list of index numbers refers you to relevant abstracts. For instance, let's say that your psychology professor lectures on endorphins (morphinelike substances produced in the brain) and sparks your interest in this exciting new research. If you wanted to do a term paper on endorphins, the place to start would be in the subject index of *Psychological Abstracts*, where you would find the term and a list of abstract numbers, as seen in Figure 2.18. You could then examine the identified abstracts in order to decide which articles to obtain.

The widespread availability of computers is beginning to revolutionize the task of searching through mountains of technical literature in many disciplines, including psychology. The information contained in *Psychological Abstracts* from 1967 through the present is now stored in a computerized data base, called *PSYCINFO*. Until recently, you had to work with a librarian to arrange a computerized literature search, and it often took several days before you saw the results. Today, however, owners of personal computers can access this data base through phone lines (for a modest fee, of course) and can conduct their own searches almost instantaneously. *PSYCINFO* is also available for immediate searching at some libraries that have purchased the data base stored on a laser disk.

Computerized literature searches can be much more powerful, precise, and thorough than traditional, manual searches. A computer can sift through a half-million articles in a matter of seconds and then print out abstracts of *all* the articles published on a subject—say birth order—since 1967. Obviously, there is no way you can match this efficiency stumbling around in the stacks at your library. Moreover, the computer allows you to pair up topics in order to swiftly narrow your search to exactly those issues that interest you. For example, Figure 2.19 shows a *PSYCINFO* search that identified all the articles on birth order *and* intelligence. If you were preparing a term paper on whether birth order is related to intelligence, this precision would be very valuable.

Reading Journal Articles

Once you find the journal articles that you want, you need to know how to decipher them. You can process the information in journal articles most efficiently if you understand how they are organized. Depending on your needs and purpose, you may be able to simply skim through some of the sections. Journal articles follow a fairly standard organization, which includes the following sections and features.

Abstract

Most journals print a concise summary at the beginning of each article. The

Figure 2.18 Using the subject index of *Psychological Abstracts* to locate journal articles. In a search by subject rather than by author, the subject index is used to locate relevant abstracts by topic.

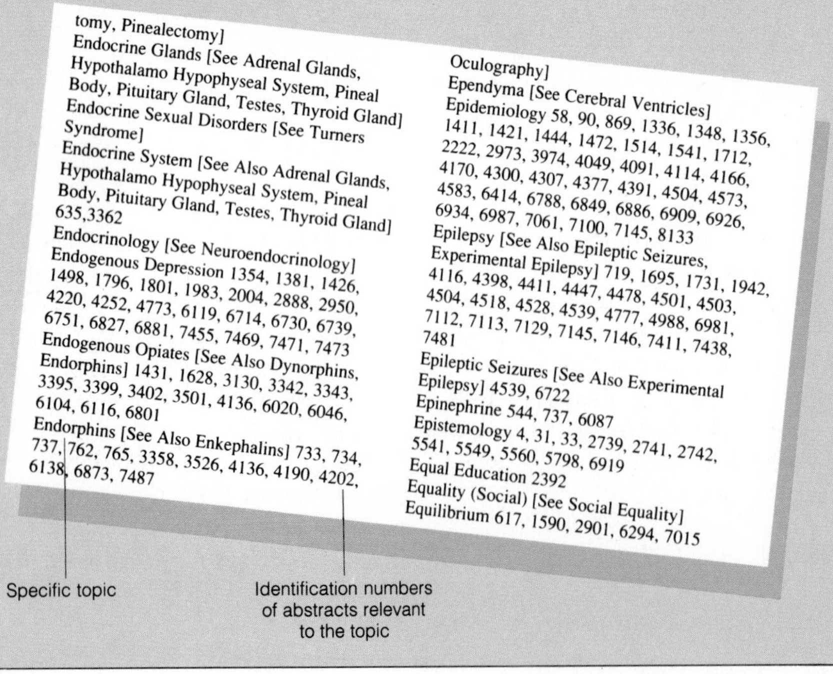

tomy, Pinealectomy]
Endocrine Glands [See Adrenal Glands, Hypothalamo Hypophyseal System, Pineal Body, Pituitary Gland, Testes, Thyroid Gland]
Endocrine Sexual Disorders [See Turners Syndrome]
Endocrine System [See Also Adrenal Glands, Hypothalamo Hypophyseal System, Pineal Body, Pituitary Gland, Testes, Thyroid Gland] 635,3362
Endocrinology [See Neuroendocrinology]
Endogenous Depression 1354, 1381, 1426, 1498, 1796, 1801, 1983, 2004, 2888, 2950, 4220, 4252, 4773, 6119, 6714, 6730, 6739, 6751, 6827, 6881, 7455, 7469, 7471, 7473
Endogenous Opiates [See Also Dynorphins, Endorphins] 1431, 1628, 3130, 3342, 3343, 3395, 3399, 3402, 3501, 4136, 6020, 6046, 6104, 6116, 6801
Endorphins [See Also Enkephalins] 733, 734, 737, 762, 765, 3358, 3526, 4136, 4190, 4202, 6138, 6873, 7487

Oculography]
Ependyma [See Cerebral Ventricles]
Epidemiology 58, 90, 869, 1336, 1348, 1356, 1411, 1421, 1444, 1472, 1514, 1541, 1712, 2222, 2973, 3974, 4049, 4091, 4114, 4166, 4170, 4300, 4307, 4377, 4391, 4504, 4573, 4583, 6414, 6788, 6849, 6886, 6909, 6926, 6934, 6987, 7061, 7100, 7145, 8133
Epilepsy [See Also Epileptic Seizures, Experimental Epilepsy] 719, 1695, 1731, 1942, 4116, 4398, 4411, 4447, 4478, 4501, 4503, 4504, 4518, 4528, 4539, 4777, 4988, 6981, 7112, 7113, 7129, 7145, 7146, 7411, 7438, 7481
Epileptic Seizures [See Also Experimental Epilepsy] 4539, 6722
Epinephrine 544, 737, 6087
Epistemology 4, 31, 33, 2739, 2741, 2742, 5541, 5549, 5560, 5798, 6919
Equal Education 2392
Equality (Social) [See Social Equality]
Equilibrium 617, 1590, 2901, 6294, 7015

Specific topic

Identification numbers of abstracts relevant to the topic

Figure 2.19 Using *PSYCINFO* to locate journal articles. A computerized literature search can be a highly efficient way to locate relevant research. In this example, the first command ("? FIND BIRTH ORDER") asks the computer to find all the entries on birth order in the data base. The computer labels the 1399 articles it finds Set 1 (S1). The second command searches for all the articles on intelligence; the 15,958 such articles make up Set 2 (S2). To identify those articles that deal with *both* birth order and intelligence, the third command searches S1 and S2 to find any articles that are listed in both sets (as depicted in the Venn diagram). The resulting Set 3 (S3) includes 134 such articles. The fourth command directs the computer to print out the titles of all the articles in Set 3, from the most recent to the oldest. The computer can also print out the entire abstract of any article selected from this set.

```
?FIND BIRTH ORDER
     S1    1399      BIRTH ORDER

?FIND INTELLIGENCE
     S2    15958     INTELLIGENCE

?FIND S1 AND S2
           1399      S1
           15958     S2
     S3    134       S1 AND S2

TYPE S3/M

73-22923
    Preventive education and birth order as co-
    determinants of IQ in disadvantaged 5-year-olds.
    Boat, B W; Campbell, F A; Ramey, C T
    U North Carolina School of Medicine, Child Div,
Chapel Hill
    Child Care, Health & Development, 1986 Jan-
Feb Vol 12(1) 25-36
```

abstract allows readers scanning a journal to decide quickly whether articles are relevant to their interests. The abstract also provides an overview of the article that can guide subsequent reading.

Introduction

The introduction presents an overview of the problem studied in the research. It mentions relevant theories and quickly reviews previous research that bears upon the problem, usually citing shortcomings in previous research that necessitate the present study. This review of the current state of knowledge on the topic usually progresses to a very specific and precise statement of the hypotheses under investigation.

Method

The next section provides a thorough description of the research methods used in the study. It provides information on the subjects used, the procedures followed, and any apparatus, surveys, or tests employed. This description is detailed enough to permit another researcher to attempt to replicate the study.

Results

The data obtained in the study are reported in the results section. This sec-tion often creates problems for novice readers because it includes complex statistical analyses and complicated figures, tables, and graphs. It does *not* include any inferences based on the data, because these are supposed to follow in the next section. Instead, it simply contains a concise summary of the raw data and the statistical analyses.

Discussion

In the discussion section you will find the conclusions drawn by the author(s). In contrast with the results section, which is a straightforward summary of empirical observations, the discussion section allows for interpretation and evaluation of the data. Implications for theory and factual knowledge in the discipline are discussed. Conclusions are usually qualified carefully, and any limitations in the study may be acknowledged. This section may also include suggestions for future research on the issue.

References

At the end of an article, you will find full bibliographic references for any studies cited in the text of the article. This list permits the reader to examine first-hand other relevant studies mentioned when the authors compared their results to those found in previous investigations. The references list is often a rich source of "leads" about other articles that are germane to the topic you are looking into.

As noted earlier, the Featured Studies included in this text are summarized in a way that corresponds to the standard organization described here for journal articles, except that the abstract and references are omitted and explanatory comments are added. As in real articles, the introduction section does not have a section heading. Of course, real journal articles are much longer and more detailed than these summaries. Nonetheless, these mini-simulations of journal articles are intended to help you to feel comfortable with the format employed in research reports.

THE RESEARCH ENTERPRISE IN PSYCHOLOGY

KEY IDEAS

Looking for Laws: The Scientific Approach to Behavior

• The scientific approach to acquiring knowledge assumes that there are laws of behavior that can be discovered through empirical research. The goals of the science of psychology include (1) the measurement and description of behavior, (2) the understanding and prediction of behavior, and (3) the application of this knowledge to the task of controlling behavior.

• A scientific investigation follows a systematic pattern that includes five steps: (1) formulate a testable hypothesis, (2) select the research method and design the study, (3) conduct the study, (4) analyze the data and draw conclusions, and (5) report the findings. The two major advantages of the scientific approach are its clarity in communication and its relative intolerance of error.

Looking for Causes: Experimental Research

• Experimental research involves the manipulation of an independent variable to ascertain its effect upon a dependent variable. This research is usually done by comparing experimental and control groups, which must be alike in regard to important extraneous variables. This ensures that any differences between the groups in the dependent variable ought to be due to the manipulation of the independent variable.

• Experimental designs may vary. For example, sometimes an experimental group serves as its own control group. And in many experiments, there is more than one independent variable or more than one dependent variable. Some of these variations in experimental design were seen in our Featured Study. The findings of this experiment suggested that hypnosis is unlikely to improve the accuracy of eyewitness testimony.

• The experiment is a powerful research method that permits one to draw conclusions about cause and effect relationships between variables. However, the experimental method is not usable for some specific problems, and many experiments tend to be too artificial.

Looking for Links: Correlational Research

• Psychologists conduct correlational research when they are unable to exert control over the variables they want to study. The principal correlational methods include naturalistic observation, case studies, and surveys and psychological tests.

• Correlational research allows psychologists to explore issues that may not be open to experimental investigation. Correlational studies also tend to be less artificial than experiments.

• However, correlational research cannot be used to demonstrate that two variables are causally related. Correlation is not equivalent to causation. A correlation only indicates that two variables are related.

Looking for Conclusions: Statistics and Research

• Psychologists use statistics to organize, summarize, and interpret their numerical data. The mean, median, and mode are widely used measures of central tendency. Variability is usually measured with the standard deviation.

• Correlations may be either positive (reflecting a direct association) or negative (reflecting an inverse relationship). The closer a correlation is to either $+1.00$ or -1.00, the stronger the association is. Higher correlations yield greater predictability.

• Hypothesis testing involves deciding whether or not observed findings support one's hypothesis. Statistically significant findings are usually required to provide such support. Findings are significant only when it is very unlikely that they are due to chance.

Looking for Flaws: Evaluating Research

• Scientists often try to replicate research findings to double-check their validity. Although this process of replication inevitably leads to some contradictory findings, science works gradually toward reconciling and explaining inconsistent results.

• Sampling bias occurs when a sample is not representative of the population that the investigator is interested in. Placebo effects occur when subjects experience changes in response to a fake treatment because of their expectations. Variables are said to be confounded when they vary together so that one cannot isolate the effect of the independent variable on the dependent variable.

• Distortions in self-report are a source of concern whenever surveys and personality inventories are used to collect data, especially if the social desirability bias seems likely to influence respondents. Experimenter bias occurs when researchers' expectations and desires sway their observations.

Looking at Ethics: Do the Ends Justify the Means?

• Research sometimes raises complex ethical issues. In psychology the key questions concern the use of deception with human subjects and the use of harmful or painful manipulations with animal subjects. The APA has formulated ethical principles to serve as guidelines for researchers.

Putting It in Perspective

• Two of our unifying themes were especially apparent in our discussion of the research enterprise in psychology. One is that psychology is empirical. The other is that our experience of the world can be highly subjective.

Application: Finding and Reading Journal Articles

• Journals publish technical and scholarly material. Usually they are written for other professionals in a narrow area of inquiry, and they may be highly selective about what they publish. Over a thousand journals publish psychological research.

• *Psychological Abstracts* contains brief summaries of journal articles. Articles on specific topics can be found by using the author and subject indexes or by conducting a computerized literature search.

• Journal articles are easier to understand if one is familiar with the standard format. Most articles include the following elements: abstract, introduction, method, results, discussion, and references.

KEY TERMS

Case study	Mode
Confounding of variables	Naturalistic observation
Control group	Operational definition
Correlation	Placebo effects
Correlation coefficient	Population
Dependent variable	Psychological test
Descriptive statistics	Random assignment
Double-blind procedure	Replication
Experiment	Research method
Experimental group	Sample
Extraneous variables	Social desirability bias
Hypothesis	Standard deviation
Independent variable	Statistical significance
Inferential statistics	Statistics
Journal	Subjects
Mean	Survey
Median	Variability
	Variables

KEY PEOPLE

Thomas Holmes
Robert Rosenthal
Stanley Schachter

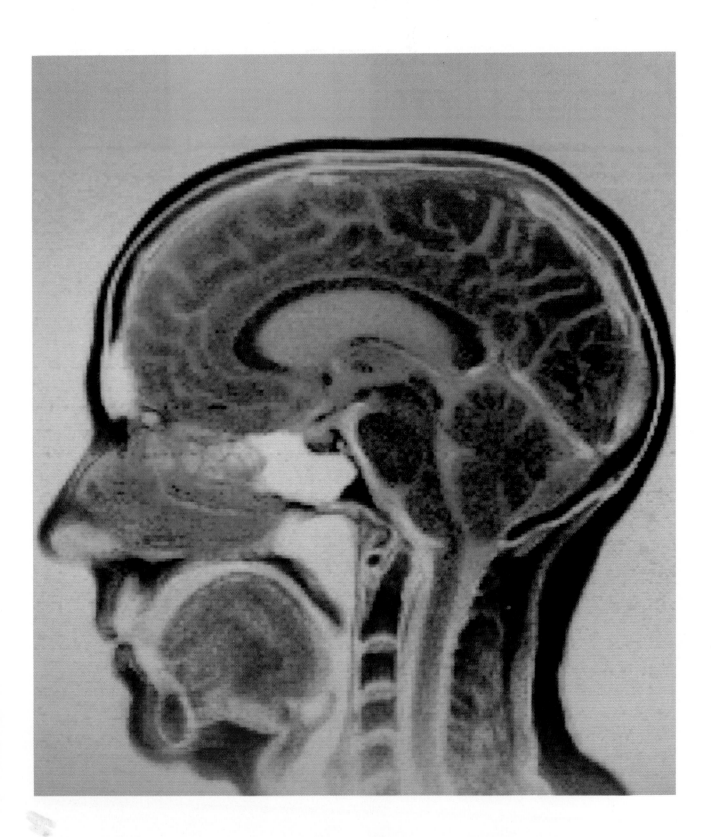

CHAPTER THREE

THE BIOLOGICAL BASES OF BEHAVIOR

With Michael W. Levine
University of Illinois at Chicago

THE BIOLOGICAL BASES OF BEHAVIOR

I f you've ever visited an aquarium, you may have encountered the octopus, one of nature's more captivating animals. Although this jellylike mass of arms and head appears to be a relatively simple creature, it's capable of a number of interesting behaviors. The octopus has highly developed eyes that enable it to respond to stimuli in the darkness of the ocean. When threatened, it can release an inky cloud to befuddle enemies while it makes good its escape by a kind of jet propulsion. If that doesn't work, it can camouflage itself by changing color and texture to blend into its surroundings. Furthermore, the animal is surprisingly intelligent. In captivity, an octopus can learn, for example, to twist the lid off a jar with one of its tentacles to get at a treat inside.

Although it's a talented creature, there are many things an octopus can't do. An octopus can't study psychology, plan a weekend, dream about its future, or discover the Pythagorean theorem. Nonetheless, the biological processes that underlie these uniquely human behaviors are much the same as the biological processes that enable an octopus to escape from a predator or forage for food. Indeed, some of our most important insights about how the nervous system works came from studies of a relative of the octopus, a squid called *Loligo*.

Although organisms as diverse as humans and squid share many biological processes, their unique behavioral capacities depend upon the differences in their physiological makeup. You and I have a larger repertoire of behaviors than the octopus, in large part because we come equipped with a more complex brain and nervous system. Indeed, so complex is the activity of the human brain that no computer has ever come close to duplicating it. In your nervous system there are as many cells busily integrating and relaying information as there are stars in our galaxy. Whether you're scratching your nose or composing a symphony, it's the activity of those cells and their interaction with the rest of the body that enable you to do what you do. It's little wonder, then, that many psychologists have dedicated themselves to exploring the biological bases of behavior.

How is the sensation of a pinprick in your finger registered in your brain? How do mood-altering drugs work? Do different parts of the brain specialize to perform different functions? What happens inside the body when you feel a strong emotion? Are some mental illnesses the result of chemical imbalances in the brain? To what extent is intelligence determined by our biological inheritance? These questions only begin to suggest the countless ways in which biology is fundamental to the study of behavior.

In this chapter we'll examine the principal biological structures and processes that make behavior possible. In the first two sections of the chapter, we'll discuss the workings and organization of the nervous system, the complex communication network that underlies all our activity. We'll then take an extended look at the most important behavioral organ of all, the brain. After completing our review of behavioral physiology with a brief discussion of the endocrine system, we'll consider a key issue raised by the importance of biology—the impact of heredity on behavior. Finally, in the chapter's Application we'll examine the furor about the special abilities of the right and left halves of the brain.

COMMUNICATION IN THE NERVOUS SYSTEM

Imagine that you're watching a scary movie. As the tension mounts, your palms sweat, your heart beats faster, and you begin shoveling popcorn into your mouth, carelessly spilling some in your lap. If someone were to ask you what you were doing at that moment, you would probably say "Nothing—I was just watching the movie." Yet some very complicated things were going on without your thinking about them. A stimulus (the light from the screen) was striking your eye. Almost instantaneously your brain interpreted the stimulus, and signals started to flash to other parts of your body, leading to a flurry of activity—sweat glands released perspiration, your heartbeat quickened, and muscular movements enabled your hand to find the popcorn and, more or less successfully, your mouth.

You can see, even from this simple example, that behavior depends on rapid, complex information processing. Information is traveling from your eye to your brain, from your brain to the muscles of your arm and hand, and from your palms back to your brain. In essence, your nervous system is a complex communication network. It handles *information*, just as your circulatory system handles blood. In this section, we'll take a close look at communication in the nervous system.

Nervous Tissue: The Basic Hardware

Your nervous system is living tissue composed entirely of cells, just like the rest of your body. Like other cells, each cell in your nervous system is a separate entity, set off from the rest of your body by an enclosing *cell membrane*. However, the cells in the nervous system have special properties that distinguish them from those that make up skin, liver, or bone. These properties enable them to carry out the special functions of nervous tissue.

What are those special functions? Cells in the nervous system must do three things:

1. *Receive information.* A cell can't handle information that it doesn't receive. Most cells in the nervous system receive their information from other cells in the nervous system. A privileged few, called *sensory neurons*, receive information from outside the nervous system. The entire nervous system depends on these specialized cells for its information.

2. *Integrate information.* Most cells in the nervous system receive information from many other cells—sometimes thousands of others. These multiple signals must be integrated (put together). In a sense, cells in the nervous system make "computations" based on these multiple inputs before sending a message to another cell.

3. *Transmit information.* Cells in the nervous system also have to transmit signals. The information gathered by your sense organs must be carried to the brain. The cells in your brain have to talk to each other to coordinate your actions. The plans of action formulated by your brain must get from your brain to the muscles of your body. Most cells in the nervous system transmit information

to other nervous system cells. A special few, called *motor neurons*, transmit messages to the muscles that actually move the body.

Now that we know what nervous tissue must do, we can consider the specialized cells of the nervous system. There are two major categories of cells in the nervous system: *glia* and *neurons*.

GLIA: THE SUPPORT SYSTEM

Glia are cells found throughout the nervous system that provide structural support and insulation for neurons. Glia (literally "glue") hold the nervous system together and help maintain the chemical environment of the neurons. Some glia also repair damage to the nervous system (Shepherd, 1983). Some neuroscientists suspect that glia may participate in the nervous system's information processing, although their role is unclear (Funch & Faber, 1984; Karwoski & Proenza, 1980).

NEURONS: THE COMMUNICATION LINKS

Neurons are individual cells in the nervous system that receive, integrate, and transmit information. They are the basic links that permit communication within the nervous system. Figure 3.1 is a highly simplified drawing of a collection of neurons. Actually, neurons come in a tremendous variety of types and shapes that no drawing can adequately represent—trying to draw a "typical" neuron would be like trying to draw the "typical" tree. But Figure 3.1 highlights some common features of neurons. Let's look at these features.

The *soma*, or cell body, contains the cell nucleus and much of the chemical machinery common to most cells (*soma* is from a Greek word for "body"). The rest of the neuron is devoted to handling information.

We usually like to think of information flowing left to right, and so the diagram in Figure 3.1 is

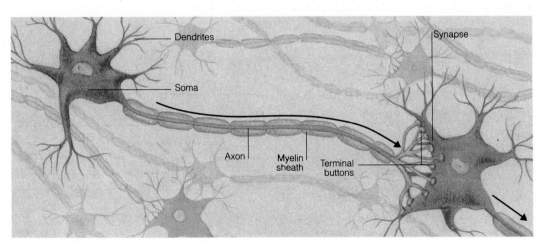

Figure 3.1 Structure of the neuron. Neurons are the communication links in the nervous system. This diagram highlights the key parts of a neuron, including specialized receptor areas (dendrites), the cell body (soma), the fiber along which impulses are transmitted (axon), and the junction across which chemical messengers carry signals to another neuron (synapse). Neurons vary considerably in size and shape and are usually densely interconnected.

set up for just such a flow. At the left is a branched, feelerlike structure called the *dendritic tree* (*dendrite* is a Greek word for "tree"). **Dendrites are branchlike parts of a neuron that are specialized to receive information.**

From the dendrites, information flows into the cell body and then travels along the *axon* (from the Greek for "axle"). **The *axon* is a long, thin fiber that transmits signals away from the soma to other neurons, or to muscles or glands.** Axons may be very long (sometimes several feet), and they may branch off to communicate with a number of other cells.

In humans, many axons are wrapped in a white, fatty substance called *myelin*. **The *myelin sheath* is insulating material, derived from glial cells, that encases some axons.** This insulation speeds up the transmission of signals that move along axons. Furthermore, if certain axons aren't properly insulated from each other, signals in the nervous system can get scrambled. The loss of muscle control frequently seen in the disease *multiple sclerosis* appears to be due to a degeneration of myelin sheaths.

At the end of the axon are terminal buttons. ***Terminal buttons* are small knobs at the end of an axon that secrete chemicals called neurotransmitters.** These chemicals serve as messengers that may activate neighboring neurons. The points at which neurons interconnect are called *synapses*. **A *synapse* is a junction where information is transmitted from one neuron to the next** (*synapse* is from the Greek for "junction").

To summarize, information is received at the dendrites, passed through the soma and along the axon, and transmitted to the dendrites of other cells at meeting points called synapses. Unfortunately, this nice, simple picture has more exceptions than the U.S. Tax Code. For example, some neurons do not have an axon while others may have multiple axons. Also, while neurons typically synapse upon the dendrites of other cells, they may also synapse upon the soma or axon of another cell. Despite these and other complexities, however, the fundamental function of neurons is to do the work of the nervous system by receiving, integrating, and transmitting informational signals.

The Neural Impulse: Using Energy to Send Information

What happens when a neuron is stimulated? What is the nature of the signal—the neural impulse—that moves through the neuron? These were the questions Alan Hodgkin and Andrew Huxley set out to answer in their experiments

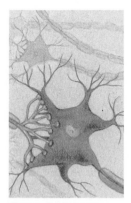

Figure 3.1 (*detail*) Dendritic trees are branching structures specialized to receive signals from many neurons.

junction

cell is polarized

with axons removed from squid. Why did they choose to work with squid axons? Because the squid has a pair of "giant" axons that are about a hundred times larger than those in humans (this still makes them only about as thick as a human hair). These thick axons serve the squid well, because their size speeds up the transmission of messages to the squid's muscles, enabling it to make its remarkable jet-propelled escape from its enemies. They also serve physiologists well. Their large size permitted Hodgkin and Huxley to insert fine wires called *microelectrodes* into the axons without causing any damage. By using the microelectrodes to record the electrical activity in individual neurons, Hodgkin and Huxley (1952a, 1952b, 1952c) unraveled the mystery of the neural impulse.

THE NEURON AT REST: A TINY BATTERY
Hodgkin and Huxley learned that the neural impulse is a complex electrochemical reaction. Both inside and outside the neuron are fluids containing electrically charged atoms and molecules called *ions*. Some of these ions are positively charged, and others are negatively charged. Sodium, potassium, and chloride ions flow back and forth across the cell membrane, but they do not cross at the same rate. The difference in flow rates leads to a slighly higher concentration of negatively charged ions inside the cell. The net result is that the membrane becomes polarized—negatively charged on the inside and positively charged on the outside.

The voltage difference that results from this polarization means that the neuron at rest is a tiny battery, a store of potential energy. **The *resting potential* of a cell is its stable, negative charge when the cell is inactive.** As shown in Figure 3.2a, this charge is about −70 millivolts, roughly ¹⁄₂₀ of the voltage of a flashlight battery.

THE ACTION POTENTIAL
As long as the voltage of a neuron remains constant, the cell is quiet, and no messages are being sent. However, stimuli of sufficient intensity will disrupt this stability by momentarily altering the permeability of the cell membrane. When the cell is stimulated, channels in the membrane open, briefly allowing positively charged sodium ions to rush in. For an instant, the cell's charge is less negative, or even positive. **An *action potential* is a brief change in a neuron's electrical charge.** The firing of an action potential is reflected in the voltage spike you can see in Figure 3.2b.

Like a spark traveling along a trail of gunpowder, the voltage change races down the axon (see Figure 3.2c). The firing of the action potential in

Figure 3.2 The action potential. The electrochemical properties of the neuron allow it to transmit information. The electric charge (voltage) of a neuron can be measured with a pair of electrodes connected to an oscilloscope, as Hodgkin and Huxley showed with a squid axon. At rest, the neuron is like a tiny wet battery with a resting potential of about −70 millivolts (**a**). When a neuron is stimulated, a brief jump in its electric potential occurs, resulting in a spike on the oscilloscope recording of the neuron's electrical activity (**b**). This change in voltage, called an action potential, travels along the axon (**c**). The creature to the right is a squid—an organism often used by scientists to study this process because of its exceptionally large axons.

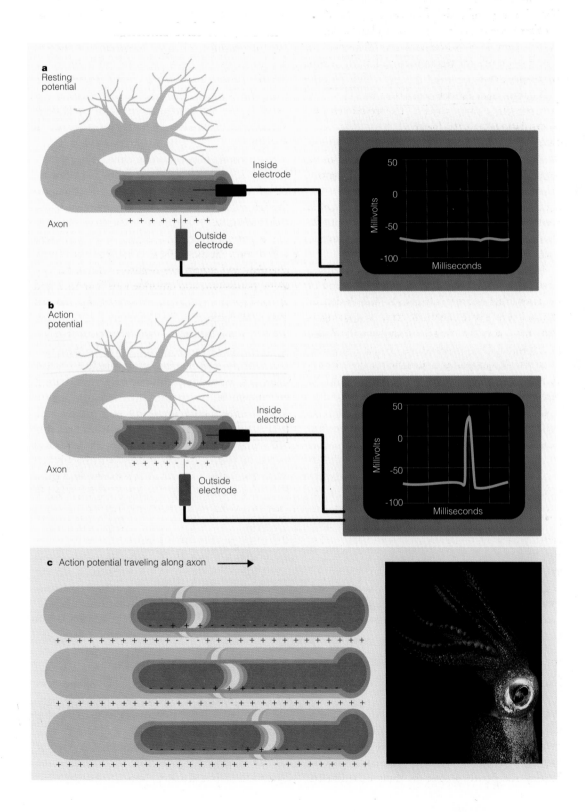

one segment of the axon triggers the firing of the action potential in the next segment and so on down the line, just as a burning grain of gunpowder ignites neighboring grains.

Thus, a neural impulse is an electric current that flows along the axon as a result of an action potential. After the firing of an action potential, the channels in the cell membrane that opened to let in sodium close up, and some time is needed before they are ready to open again. Until they're ready, the cell cannot fire again. **The *absolute refractory period* is the minimum length of time after an action potential during which another action potential cannot begin.**

THE ALL-OR-NONE LAW

The neural impulse is an all-or-none proposition, like firing a gun. You can fire a gun by applying a little pressure to the trigger or by giving it a firm squeeze. Either way, the bullet leaves at full velocity. You can't half-fire a gun. The same is true of the neuron's firing of action potentials. Either the neuron fires or it doesn't. A weaker stimulus does not produce a weaker neural impulse.

Even though the action potential is an all-or-nothing event, neurons *can* convey information about the strength of a stimulus. They do this by varying the *rate* at which they fire action potentials. In general, a stronger stimulus will cause a cell to fire a more rapid volley of neural impulses than a weaker stimulus.

Different neurons transmit neural impulses at different speeds. Thicker axons have less resistance to current and therefore conduct action potentials more rapidly than thinner axons, which is why the squid's thick axons serve their purpose so well. A neural impulse also travels faster on an axon insulated with myelin. Although neural impulses do not travel as fast as electricity along a wire, they *are* very fast. The entire, complicated process takes only a few thousandths of a second. In the time it has taken you to read this description of the neural impulse, billions of them have been transmitted in your nervous system!

The Synapse: Where Neurons Meet

In the nervous system, the neural impulse functions as a signal. For the signal to have any meaning for the system as a whole, it must be transmitted from the neuron to other cells. As noted earlier, this transmission takes place at special junctions between cells called *synapses*. At some junctions, electrical currents pass from cell to cell (Shepherd, 1983). However, most neurons use *chemical* messengers to communicate with each other.

SENDING SIGNALS: CHEMICALS AS COURIERS

A "typical" chemical synapse is shown in Figure 3.3a. The first thing you should note is that the two neurons don't actually touch. They are separated by the **synaptic cleft, a microscopic gap between the terminal button of the sending neuron and the cell membrane of another neuron.** Signals have to jump this gap to permit neurons to communicate. In this situation, the neuron that sends a signal across the gap is called the *presynaptic neuron,* and the neuron that receives the signal is called the *postsynaptic neuron.*

Figure 3.3 Synaptic transmission. (**a**) Neurons transmit information to each other by sending neurotransmitters across a synaptic cleft to receptor sites on another neuron. (**b**) This close-up view summarizes the process of transmission across the synapse. Neurotransmitters must be synthesized, stored, and released. Following release, a neurotransmitter crosses the synapse, binding with a receptor and altering the electrical potential of the postsynaptic neuron. The neurotransmitter may then drift away from the receptor site or be inactivated by enzymes. Most are reabsorbed by the original neuron (reuptake).

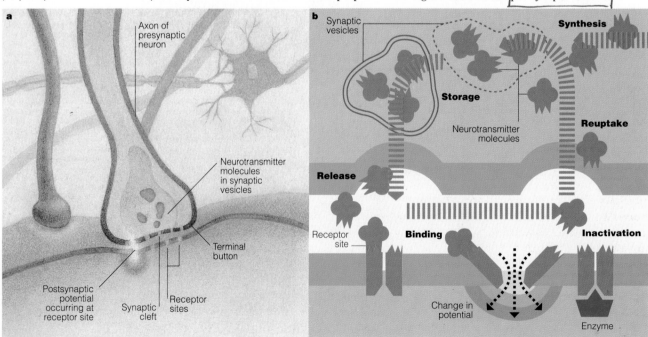

a
Axon of presynaptic neuron

Neurotransmitter molecules in synaptic vesicles

Terminal button

Postsynaptic potential occurring at receptor site

Synaptic cleft

Receptor sites

b
Synaptic vesicles

Synthesis

Storage

Neurotransmitter molecules

Reuptake

Release

Receptor site

Binding

Inactivation

Change in potential

Enzyme

Strychnine!!!

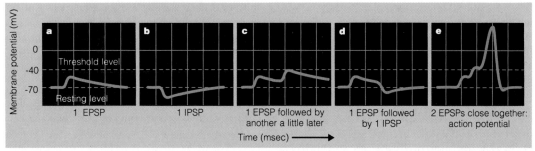

Figure 3.4 Postsynaptic potentials (PSPs). A postsynaptic potential is a change in the voltage of a neuron that occurs when a neurotransmitter binds with a receptor on the neuron. PSPs are either *inhibitory* (IPSP) or *excitatory* (EPSP). (**a**) At some receptor sites, a PSP increases the postsynaptic neuron's voltage (an excitatory effect). (**b**) At other receptor sites, a PSP lowers the neuron's voltage (an inhibitory effect). (**c**) Two excitatory PSPs may add together but still remain below the threshold for causing an action potential in the postsynaptic neuron. (**d**) An excitatory PSP and an inhibitory PSP may balance each other out. (**e**) A series of excitatory PSPs may lead to an action potential.

How are messages transmitted across the gaps between neurons? When an action potential reaches an axon's terminal buttons, it triggers the release of neurotransmitters. **Neurotransmitters are chemicals that transmit information from one neuron to another.** They are stored in small sacs, called *synaptic vesicles.* When a neurotransmitter is released into the synaptic cleft, it diffuses across to the membrane of the receiving cell. There it may bind with special molecules in the postsynaptic cell membrane at various *receptor sites* (see Figure 3.3b). These sites are specifically "tuned" to recognize some neurotransmitters but not others.

RECEIVING SIGNALS: POSTSYNAPTIC POTENTIALS

When a neurotransmitter and a receptor molecule combine, reactions in the postsynaptic cell membrane cause a **postsynaptic potential (PSP), a voltage change at the receptor site.** When a PSP occurs, channels are opened in the cell membrane at this site, allowing specific ions to flood into or rush out of the cell. Postsynaptic potentials do *not* follow the all-or-none law as action potentials do. Instead, postsynaptic potentials are *graded.* That is, they increase or decrease the *probability* of a neural impulse in the receiving cell in proportion to their size (the amount of voltage change).

If the voltage in the postsynaptic neuron shifts in a positive direction, the cell comes closer to its threshold for firing a neural impulse. **An excitatory PSP is an electric potential that increases the likelihood that the postsynaptic neuron will fire action potentials.** If the voltage shifts in a negative direction, the postsynaptic neuron moves farther away from its threshold for firing a neural impulse. This kind of negative shift is an *inhibitory PSP,* **an electric potential that decreases the likelihood that the postsynaptic neuron will fire action potentials**. Both excitatory and inhibitory PSPs are depicted in Figure 3.4. The direction of the voltage shift, and thus the nature of the PSP (excitatory or inhibitory), depends on which receptor sites are activated (Eccles, 1965).

Thus, there are two types of messages that can be sent from cell to cell: excitatory and inhibitory. Both types are essential to the functioning of the nervous system. If cells could only excite other cells, any excitation would grow and reverberate through the nervous system like a nuclear chain reaction. In fact, many kinds of seizures are due to insufficient inhibitory effects at synapses. Strychnine, perhaps the nastiest of poisons, works its deadly effects by disabling many inhibitory synapses; the resulting excitation causes uncontrollable convulsions in which the victim's body literally tears itself apart.

The excitatory or inhibitory effects produced at a synapse last only a fraction of a second. If neurotransmitters remained bound to receptor sites forever, all receptor sites would soon be occupied and cells would remain permanently at a stable electric potential. Information processing in the nervous system would come to a halt! This doesn't happen, however, because neurotransmitters drift away from receptor sites or are inactivated by enzymes that metabolize (convert) them to inactive forms. Most are reabsorbed into the presynaptic neuron through **reuptake, a process in which neurotransmitters are sponged up from the synaptic cleft by the presynaptic membrane**, which allows the synapse to recycle its materials.

The various steps in synaptic transmission are outlined in Figure 3.3b. As you can see, communication at chemical synapses involves: (1) the synthesis of transmitters, (2) the storage of transmitters (3) the release of transmitters into the synaptic cleft, (4) the reception and binding of transmitters at sites on the postsynaptic membrane, (5) the removal or inactivation of transmitters, and (6) the reuptake of transmitters by the presynaptic neuron.

INTEGRATING SIGNALS: A BALANCING ACT

We have seen how neurons receive information and transmit it along axons and ultimately across the synaptic cleft to one another. Keep in mind, however, that a neuron is not linked to only one neuron on either side of it. Most neurons are interlinked in complex, dense networks. In fact, a neuron may have as many as 15,000 synapses re-

71

THE BIOLOGICAL
BASES OF BEHAVIOR

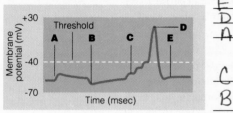
ceiving a symphony of signals from thousands of other neurons, and it may pass its signal to thousands of other neurons as well.

Thus, a neuron must do a great deal more than simply relay messages it receives. It must integrate signals arriving at many synapses before it "decides" whether or not to fire a neural impulse. If many excitatory PSPs occur in a neuron, the electrical currents can add up so that the cell's voltage reaches a certain threshold, as shown in Figure 3.4, and the cell fires an action potential. However, if many inhibitory PSPs also occur, they will tend to cancel the excitatory effect. The state of the neuron is a weighted balance between excitatory and inhibitory influences. The "decision" of the neuron to fire or not to fire is based on a balance sheet of pluses and minuses.

Neurotransmitters and Behavior

We have seen that the nervous system relies on chemical couriers to communicate information between neurons. These neurotransmitters are fundamental to our behavior. They play a key role in everything from our muscle movements to our moods and our mental health.

You might guess that the nervous system would require only two neurotransmitters—one to produce excitatory potentials and one to produce inhibitory potentials. However, there are at least eight chemical substances that clearly qualify as neurotransmitters (Kolb & Whishaw, 1985). These are listed in Table 3.1. Scientists suspect that a number of other substances also function as transmitters, and new candidates are still being discovered. In general, a specific neuron has the chemical factory for making only one of the trans-

mitters, and it releases that transmitter from all of its terminal buttons.

Specific transmitters work at specific kinds of synapses. You may recall that transmitter substances deliver their messages by binding to receptor sites on the postsynaptic membrane. However, a transmitter cannot bind to just any site. The binding process operates much like a lock and key, as shown in Figure 3.5. Just as a key has to fit a lock to work, a transmitter has to fit a receptor, or binding won't occur. Hence, specific transmitters can deliver signals only at certain locations.

Why are there many different transmitters, each of which works only at certain synapses? This specificity is useful because of the density of neurons in the brain. A small area of the brain can be packed with millions of synapses, each releasing chemical transmitters. Some of these transmitters are bound to leak to neighboring synapses. If the neighboring synapses respond to different transmitters, binding won't occur, and the leakage will have no effect. Hence, variety and specificity in neurotransmitters minimizes cross talk between synapses, making the nervous system's communication more precise.

TRACKING TRANSMITTERS: RESEARCH METHODS

Looking for connections between neurotransmitter activity and behavior is very challenging, partly because it's very difficult to measure neurotransmitter activity in an intact human brain. Most of the information on synaptic transmission that we've summarized thus far has been gleaned from laboratory studies of brain tissue extracted from animals. For example, Tom O'Donohue, a researcher exploring neurotransmitter activity, has to visit a Baltimore slaughterhouse about

Table 3.1 Major Neurotransmitters

CHEMICAL FAMILY	NEUROTRANSMITTER	ABBREVIATION
Cholinergic agents	Acetylcholine	ACh
Bioamines	Dopamine	DA
	Norepinephrine	NE
	Serotonin (5-hydroxytryptamine)	5-HT
Amino acids	Gamma-aminobutyric acid	GABA
	Glycine	Gly
	Glutamic acid (glutamate)	Glu
	Aspartic acid (aspartate)	Asp

Figure 3.5 The lock and key model of synaptic receptors. A specific neurotransmitter can bind only to receptor sites into which its molecular structure will fit. Here, binding cannot occur for the neurotransmitter and receptor site on the right.

Neurotransmitters

Receptor sites

lock & key makes communication precise

every 2 weeks to replenish his supply of brain tissue:

We go there to collect hog brains. We use hog brains for a number of reasons. We are trying to isolate a neurotransmitter that exists in very small amounts in brains. In order to isolate enough of the transmitter to learn its chemical structure we have to start with a lot of brains. We take 200 pounds of pig brain, and we homogenize it in about 50 gallons of liquid. Eventually we end up with micrograms of peptide (the possible transmitter substance). (Quoted in Restak, 1984, p. 308)

Although research on animal brain tissue is of the utmost importance, there are limits to how much it can reveal about neurotransmitter activity in the human brain.

In human subjects, researchers usually monitor neurotransmitter activity very indirectly. They typically estimate transmitter levels in a person's brain by measuring metabolic byproducts of their action in specimens of urine, blood serum, and *cerebrospinal fluid* (CSF), a special solution that bathes the brain and spinal cord. At best, this is an imperfect approach, not unlike determining what people eat by going through their garbage cans. CSF samples provide the best information, but the required spinal taps are unpleasant, and even CSF samples provide only rough estimates of transmitter levels in the brain (Nordin, Siwers, & Bertilsson, 1982).

Despite these difficulties, our understanding of how the transmitters work and of what consequences they have for behavior continues to grow. Let's briefly review some of the most significant discoveries researchers have made to date.

ACETYLCHOLINE: A MODEL TRANSMITTER

The discovery that cells communicate by releasing chemicals was first made in connection with the transmitter known by the formidable name *acetylcholine* (abbreviated ACh). ACh has been found throughout the brain and spinal cord. It is the only transmitter between motor neurons and voluntary muscles. Every move you make—typing, walking, talking, breathing—depends upon ACh released to your muscles by motor neurons (Katz, 1966).

An inadequate supply of ACh in the brain has been implicated in the memory losses seen in *Alzheimer's disease*, an affliction endured by about one out of a hundred people over the age of 60 (and some younger people). People with this disease gradually lose their ability to remember anything. Eventually they don't even recognize family members and can't find their way home. This condition is a disease, *not* a normal outcome of the

aging process. Examinations of the brains of people who have died with Alzheimer's disease reveal abnormally low levels of ACh (Coyle, Price, & DeLong, 1983). Researchers believe that some cells responsible for the synthesis of ACh degenerate in victims of Alzheimer's, leaving the brain with a depleted supply of this crucial neurotransmitter.

The activity of ACh (and other neurotransmitters) may be influenced by other chemicals in the brain. Although synaptic receptor sites are sensitive to specific neurotransmitters, sometimes they can be "fooled" by other chemical substances. For example, if you smoke tobacco, some of your ACh synapses will be stimulated by the nicotine that arrives in your brain. At these synapses the nicotine acts like ACh itself; it binds to the receptor, causing a postsynaptic potential (PSP). In technical language, nicotine is an ACh agonist. **An agonist is a chemical that mimics the action of a neurotransmitter.** In other words, an agonist functions as a substitute, producing some of the effects of the regular transmitter.

Not all chemicals that fool synaptic receptors function as agonists. Some chemicals bind to receptors but fail to produce a PSP (the key slides into the lock but doesn't work). In effect, they temporarily *block* the action of the natural transmitter by occupying its receptor sites, rendering them unusable. **An *antagonist* is a chemical that opposes the action of a neurotransmitter.** For example, *curare* is an ACh antagonist that blocks action at the same synapses that are fooled by nicotine. Some South American natives use a form of curare on arrows. If they wound an animal, the curare blocks the synapses from nerve to muscle and paralyzes the animal.

BIOAMINES AND MENTAL ILLNESS

The *bioamines* include three neurotransmitters: dopamine, norepinephrine, and serotonin. Neurons using these transmitters regulate many aspects of everyday behavior. Dopamine, for example, plays a role in the control of voluntary movements. The degeneration of certain neurons that use dopamine apparently causes *Parkinsonism*, a disease marked by tremors, muscular rigidity, and reduced control over voluntary movements. Neural circuits using serotonin appear to play a prominent role in the regulation of sleep (Van Oot, Lane, & Borkovec, 1984). Animals given drugs that deplete serotonin display chronic insomnia within a few days.

Bioamine levels in the brain have been related to the development of certain psychological disorders. One of these is the *bipolar mood disorder*. As we'll discuss in Chapter 14, people who suffer

dopamine
norepinephrin
serotonin

Figure 3.6 Endorphins and "runner's high." When they push their bodies to the limit, some long-distance runners report experiencing feelings of euphoria, called a "runner's high." The euphoria may be a side effect of the release of endorphins in the brain. Endorphins are the body's own internally produced, morphine-like pain relievers. Some investigators speculate that, much like morphine and other opiate drugs, endorphins can produce euphoria.

amino acids

from this disorder experience periods of severe depression and debilitating manic episodes that come and go with little predictability. At one time the evidence suggested that a shortage of norepinephrine (NE) caused depression, while an excess of NE caused manic episodes (Schildkraut, 1965). Subsequent findings revealed that this model was a bit too tidy. Changes in NE *receptors* may be more important than the *levels* of NE found at synapses, and disturbances in dopamine and serotonin activity may also contribute to this disorder (Gerner & Bunney, 1986). Nonetheless, researchers remain convinced that alterations at NE synapses play a key role in the emergence of bipolar mood disorders.

In a similar fashion, alterations at dopamine (DA) synapses have been implicated in the development of *schizophrenic disorders*. These are very severe disorders marked by irrational thought, hallucinations, poor contact with reality, and deterioration of routine adaptive behavior. Many investigators believe that these disorders are caused by overactivity at DA synapses. Why? Primarily because the therapeutic drugs that tame schizophrenic symptoms are known to reduce DA activity (Davidson, Losonczy, & Davis, 1986). Unfortunately, the antagonistic effects of these drugs at dopamine synapses often lead to Parkinsonism-like side effects (tremors and muscular rigidity) that make the drugs unpleasant for some patients.

These are complexities in the dopamine hypothesis of schizophrenia that continue to be debated. Some researchers suspect that NE, serotonin, and other transmitters may also play a role in schizophrenic disorders (Karson, Kleinman, & Wyatt, 1986). In short, it's clear that some forms of mental illness are related to disturbances in the activity of bioamine neurotransmitters, but the details of the picture are still being worked out.

GABA AND ANXIETY

Another group of transmitters consists of small molecules called *amino acids*. Two of these, *gamma-aminobutyric acid* (GABA) and *glycine*, are notable in that they seem to produce only *inhibitory* postsynaptic potentials (PSPs). Some transmitters, such as ACh and NE, can produce either excitatory or inhibitory PSPs, depending on the synaptic receptors they bind to. However, GABA and glycine appear to have inhibitory effects at virtually all synapses where either is present. GABA receptors are widely distributed in the brain. They may be present at 30% of all synapses (Enna & Gallagher, 1983). GABA appears to be responsible for much of the inhibition in the central nervous system.

Recent studies suggest that GABA may regulate the experience of anxiety in humans (Paul, Crawley, & Skolnick, 1986). Generally, the inhibitory effects of GABA keep a lid on neural excitement. However, lowered levels of GABA may permit heightened neural excitement that translates into feelings of anxiety. Consistent with this theory, researchers have found that anti-anxiety drugs, better known as tranquilizers, exert their effects by increasing inhibitory activity at GABA synapses (Olsen, 1982). Ironically, millions of prescriptions were written for tranquilizers such as Valium before scientists discovered their mechanism of action in the late 1970s.

ENDORPHINS AND PAIN

In 1970 after a horse-riding accident, Candace Pert lay in a hospital bed receiving frequent shots of morphine, a pain-killing drug derived from the opium plant. This experience left her with a driving curiosity about how morphine worked. A few years later, she and Solomon Snyder rocked the scientific world by showing that *morphine exerts its effects by binding to specialized receptors in the brain* (Pert & Snyder, 1973).

Pert's discovery raised a perplexing question. Why would the brain be equipped with receptors for morphine, a rare substance that is not normally found in the body? It occurred to Pert and others that the nervous system must have its own endogenous (internally produced) morphinelike substances. Investigators dubbed these as-yet-undiscovered substances *endorphins* (endogenous morphines). A search for the body's natural opium ensued. In short order a number of endogenous opiatelike substances were identified (Hughes et al., 1975).

Research in this area is progressing rapidly, and terminology is evolving as more endogenous opiates are found. We will use the term **endorphins to refer to the entire family of internally produced chemicals that resemble opiates in structure and effects**. All of the endorphins are *neuropeptides*, which are strings of amino acids bound together (Snyder, 1980). Some neuropeptides, such as *substance P*, appear to function as neurotransmitters. Many of the neural circuits that deliver pain signals to the spinal cord and brain seem to use substance P as a transmitter. Although they may serve as transmitters at some synapses, *endorphins seem to function primarily as neuromodulators* (Elliott & Barchas, 1986). **Neuromodulators are chemicals that increase or decrease (modulate) the activity of specific neurotransmitters.** Neuromodulators may work by altering the synthesis, storage, release, reception, removal, or reuptake of a transmitter. Some endorphins, for instance, appear to reduce pain by preventing the release of substance P, so that fewer pain signals are sent to the brain.

The discovery of endorphins has led to revolutionary new theories and findings on the neurochemical bases of pain and pleasure. In addition to their pain-killing effects, opiate drugs produce pleasurable feelings or euphoria. These effects explain why heroin, an opiate, is so widely abused. Researchers suspect that the body's natural endorphins may also be capable of producing feelings of pleasure. This might explain why joggers sometimes experience a "runner's high" (see Figure 3.6). The pain caused by a long run may trigger the release of endorphins, which neutralize some of the pain and create a feeling of exhilaration (Colt, Wardlaw, & Frantz, 1981). Experts can't help wondering whether endorphins might be the chemical basis for other pleasant emotions as well (Blum, 1984).

The existence of endorphins may also shed light on why placebos (substances that resemble a drug but have no real effect) alleviate pain in many medical patients. Perhaps the *belief* that one has taken a pain-killing drug leads to the release of the brain's own pain killers, endorphins. Consistent with this idea, evidence shows that patients who are first given a drug (naloxone) that blocks the action of endorphins do *not* experience pain-killing placebo effects (Fields & Levine, 1984). Acupuncture, an ancient Chinese art involving the insertion of needles into key spots in the body, may also affect pain by stimulating the release of endorphins (Watkins & Mayer, 1982).

"When human beings engage in various activities, it seems that neurojuices are released that are associated with either pain or pleasure. And the endorphins are very pleasurable."
CANDACE PERT

ORGANIZATION OF THE NERVOUS SYSTEM

Clearly, communication within the nervous system is fundamental to behavior. So far, we have looked at how individual cells communicate with one another. In this section we examine the organization of the nervous system as a whole.

Experts believe that there are over 180 *billion* neurons in the human nervous system. Obviously this is an estimate; if you counted them nonstop at the rate of one per second, you'd be counting for about 6000 years! These multitudinous neurons have to work together to keep information flowing effectively. To accomplish this, they are organized into teams, and the various teams have specialized functions and duties that depend primarily on their location in the nervous system.

To see how the nervous system is organized, we'll perform a series of "cuts" that will divide the nervous system into parts. In many instances, the parts will be cut at least once again. An organizational chart that shows the relationships of all the parts can be seen in Figure 3.7.

The Peripheral Nervous System

The first and most important cut separates the *central nervous system* (the brain and spinal cord) from the *peripheral nervous system* (see Figure 3.7). **The *peripheral nervous system* includes all those nerves that lie outside the brain and spinal cord. *Nerves* are bundles of neuron fibers (axons) that travel together in the peripheral nervous system.** This portion of the nervous system is just what it sounds like, the part that extends to the periphery (the outside) of the body.

Figure 3.7 Organization of the human nervous system. The human nervous system is divided into the central nervous system (the brain and spinal cord) and the peripheral nervous system (the remainder). The central and peripheral nervous systems can each be subdivided repeatedly. The *central nervous system* is composed mostly of the brain, which is traditionally divided into three regions: the hindbrain, the midbrain, and the forebrain. All three areas control vital functions, but it's the highly developed forebrain that differentiates humans from lower animals. The reticular formation, listed here as part of the midbrain, actually runs through both the midbrain and hindbrain on its way up and down the brain stem. These and other parts of the brain are discussed in detail later in the chapter. The *peripheral nervous system* is made up of the somatic nervous system, which controls voluntary muscles and sensory receptors, and the autonomic nervous system, which controls smooth muscles, blood vessels, and glands.

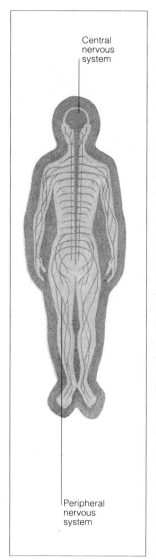

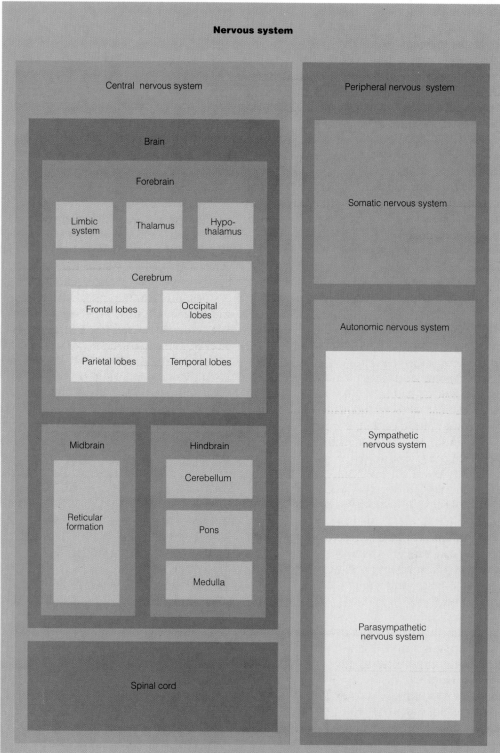

THE SOMATIC NERVOUS SYSTEM

The peripheral nervous system can be subdivided into the *somatic nervous system* and the *autonomic nervous system*. **The somatic nervous system is made up of nerves that connect to voluntary skeletal muscles and sensory receptors.** These nerves are the cables that carry information from receptors in the skin, muscles, and joints to the central nervous system, and that carry commands from motor neurons to the muscles. These functions require two kinds of axons, one for each function. *Afferent fibers* **are axons that carry information inward to the central nervous system from the periphery of the body.** *Efferent fibers* **are axons that carry information outward from the central nervous system to the periphery of the body.** Each body nerve contains many axons of each type. Thus, somatic nerves are "two-way streets" with incoming (afferent) and outgoing (efferent) lanes. Figure 3.8 is a highly simplified diagram of a neural circuit showing this flow of information in and out of the central nervous system. Somatic nerves let you feel the world and move around in it.

THE AUTONOMIC NERVOUS SYSTEM

The autonomic nervous system is made up of nerves that connect to the heart, blood vessels, smooth muscles, and glands. As its name hints, the autonomic system is like a separate (autonomous) system, although it's ultimately controlled by the central nervous system. The autonomic nervous system is somewhat automatic in its operation; that is, it controls involuntary, visceral functions that we don't normally think about, such as heart rate, digestion, and perspiration.

The autonomic nervous system mediates much of the physiological arousal that occurs when we experience emotions. For example, imagine that you are walking home alone one night when a seedy-looking character falls in behind you and begins to follow you. If you feel threatened, your heart rate and breathing will speed up. Your blood pressure may surge, you may get goose bumps, and your palms may begin to get sweaty. These difficult-to-control reactions are aspects of autonomic arousal.

Walter Cannon (1932), one of the first psychologists to study this reaction, called it the *fight-or-flight response*. Cannon carefully monitored this response in cats—after confronting them with dogs. He concluded that many organisms respond to threat by preparing physically for attacking (fight) or fleeing (flight) the enemy. Unfortunately, as you'll see in Chapter 13, this fight-or-flight response can backfire if stress leaves a person in a chronic state of autonomic arousal. Pro-

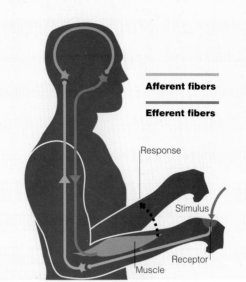

Afferent fibers

Efferent fibers

Response

Stimulus

Receptor

Muscle

Figure 3.8 The nervous system as an information-processing system. The nervous system handles information from the outside world and makes a response. In the simplest case, information in the form of physical energy (the stimulus) is sensed by receptors and converted into a stream of action potentials transmitted along afferent nerve fibers to the brain. After information is processed in the brain, a response is transmitted along the efferent nerve fibers to the muscles.

longed autonomic arousal can eventually contribute to the development of physical diseases (Selye, 1974).

The autonomic nervous system can be subdivided into two branches: the sympathetic division and the parasympathetic division (see Figure 3.9). **The sympathetic division is the branch of the autonomic nervous system that mobilizes the body's resources for emergencies.** It creates the fight-or-flight response. Activation of the sympathetic division slows digestive processes and drains blood from the periphery, lessening bleeding in the case of an injury. Key sympathetic nerves send signals to the adrenal glands, triggering the release of adrenaline, a hormone that readies the muscles for extreme exertion. In contrast, **the parasympathetic division is the branch of the autonomic nervous system that generally conserves bodily resources.** It activates processes that allow the body to save and store energy. For example, actions by parasympathetic nerves slow heart rate, reduce blood pressure, and promote digestion.

The Central Nervous System

The central nervous system is the portion of the nervous system that lies within the skull and spinal column. Thus, **the central nervous system (CNS) consists of the brain and the spinal cord.** It is protected by enclosing sheaths called the *meninges* (hence *meningitis*, the name of the disease in which the meninges become inflamed).

In addition, the central nervous system is bathed in its own special nurtitive "soup," called cerebrospinal fluid. *Cerebrospinal fluid (CSF)* **is a solution that fills the hollow cavities (ventricles) of the brain and circulates around the brain and spinal cord.** This fluid nourishes the brain and

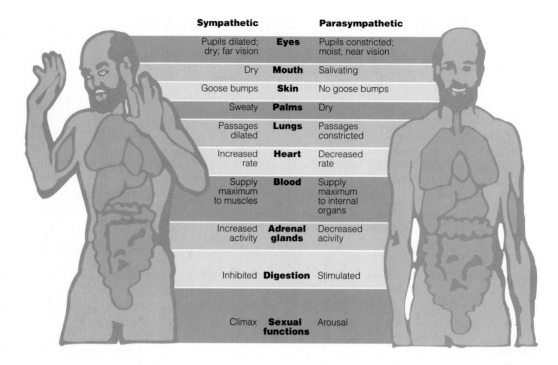

Figure 3.9 The autonomic nervous system (ANS). The ANS is composed of the nerves that connect to the heart, blood vessels, smooth muscles, and glands. The ANS is divided into the sympathetic division, which mobilizes bodily resources in times of need, and the parasympathetic division, which conserves bodily resources. Some of the key functions controlled by each division of the ANS are summarized in the center of the diagram.

	Sympathetic		Parasympathetic
	Pupils dilated; dry; far vision	**Eyes**	Pupils constricted; moist; near vision
	Dry	**Mouth**	Salivating
	Goose bumps	**Skin**	No goose bumps
	Sweaty	**Palms**	Dry
	Passages dilated	**Lungs**	Passages constricted
	Increased rate	**Heart**	Decreased rate
	Supply maximum to muscles	**Blood**	Supply maximum to internal organs
	Increased activity	**Adrenal glands**	Decreased acivity
	Inhibited	**Digestion**	Stimulated
	Climax	**Sexual functions**	Arousal

provides a protective cushion for it. Although derived from the blood, the CSF is filtered very selectively. To enter the CSF, substances in the blood have to cross the **blood-brain barrier, a semipermeable, membranelike mechanism that stops some chemicals from passing between the bloodstream and the brain**. The blood-brain barrier prevents some drugs from entering the CSF and affecting the brain.

THE SPINAL CORD

The *spinal cord* connects the brain to the rest of the body through the peripheral nervous system. Although the spinal cord looks like a simple cable from which the somatic nerves branch, it's a part of the central nervous system. Like the brain, it's enclosed by the meninges and bathed in CSF. In short, the spinal cord is actually a complicated extension of the brain.

The spinal cord runs from the base of the brain to just below the level of the waist. Looked at in cross-section, the spinal cord has two portions. The inner part, shaped roughly like a butterfly, is mainly a collection of cell somas, together with the dendrites and axons that serve them. The outer part consists of bundles of axons running the length of the cord to and from the brain. These axons carry the brain's commands through the spi-

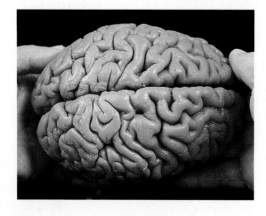

Figure 3.10 The human brain. It's smaller than most people imagine, weighing only three pounds, but the human brain contains billions of neurons that allow us to process an enormous amount of information.

nal cord and relay body sensations to the brain. Indeed, many forms of paralysis are due to spinal cord damage. This fact underscores the critical role that the spinal cord plays in distributing signals from the brain to the motor neurons that move our muscles.

Each level of the spinal cord is concerned with an area of the body. It receives commands from the brain (such as "move hand there" or "step forward with left leg") and feedback from the body nerves (for example, "fingers are pressing on something" or "knee is straight"). By integrating this information to command individual muscle fibers to contract or relax, the spinal cord can mediate some simple responses—spinal reflexes—independently of the brain. One such response is the knee-jerk reflex, tested during physical exams.

THE BRAIN

The crowning glory of the central nervous system is, of course, the brain. Anatomically, the *brain* is the part of the central nervous system that fills the upper portion of the skull. Although it weighs only about 3 pounds and could be held in one hand (see Figure 3.10), the brain contains billions of interacting cells that integrate information from inside and outside the body, coordinate the body's actions, and make it possible for us to talk, to think, to remember, to plan, to create, and to dream.

Because of its central importance for behavior, the brain is the subject of the next three sections of the chapter. We'll begin by looking at the remarkable methods that have enabled researchers to unlock some of the brain's secrets.

LOOKING INSIDE THE BRAIN: RESEARCH METHODS

Suppose you wanted to find out how some part of the brain was related to behavior. How would you attack this formidable task? The geography, or *structure*, of the brain can be mapped out relatively easily by examining and dissecting brains removed from animals or from deceased humans who have donated their bodies to science. Mapping out brain *function*, however, requires a working brain. Hence, special research methods are needed to discover relations between brain activity and behavior.

Investigators who conduct research on the brain or other parts of the nervous system are called *neuroscientists*. Often, such research involves collaboration by neuroscientists from several disciplines, including anatomy, physiology, biology, chemistry, pharmacology, medicine, and, of course, psychology. Much of the excitement in this research comes from the interactions among researchers with different backgrounds and approaches, who learn from one another as they attack a problem from different angles. Neuroscientists use many special techniques to investigate connections between the brain and behavior. Three methods they have depended on heavily are electrical recordings, ablation, and electrical stimulation. In addition, new brain-imaging techniques have recently been developed that may eventually revolutionize brain research.

Electrical Recordings

The electrical activity of the brain can be recorded, much as Hodgkin and Huxley recorded the electrical activity of individual neurons. Recordings of single cells in the brain have proven valuable, but scientists also need ways to record the simultaneous activity of many of the billions of neurons in the brain. Fortunately, in 1929 a German psychiatrist named Hans Berger invented a machine that could record broad patterns of electrical activity in the brain. **The *electroencephalograph (EEG)* is a device that monitors the electrical activity of the brain over time by means of recording electrodes attached to the surface of the scalp** (see Figure 3.11). An EEG electrode sums and amplifies action potentials and graded potentials occuring in many thousands of brain cells.

Usually, six to ten recording electrodes are attached at different places on the skull. The resulting EEG recordings are translated into line tracings, commonly called *brain waves*. These brain waves provide a useful overview of the electrical activity in the brain. Different brain-wave patterns are associated with different states of mental activity, as shown in Figure 3.11. The EEG is frequently used in the clinical diagnosis of brain damage and neurological disorders. In research applications the EEG can be used to identify broad areas of the brain that are especially active when subjects engage in specific behaviors, ranging from daydreaming to working on math problems. As you'll see in Chapter 5, the EEG has been invaluable to researchers exploring the physiology of sleep.

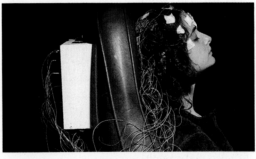

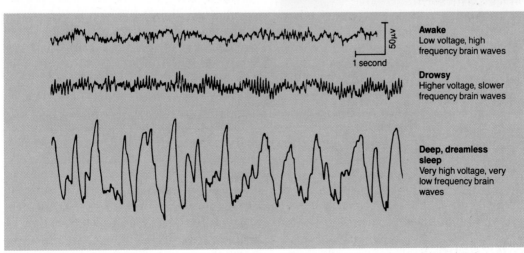

Awake
Low voltage, high frequency brain waves

$50 \mu V$

1 second

Drowsy
Higher voltage, slower frequency brain waves

Deep, dreamless sleep
Very high voltage, very low frequency brain waves

Figure 3.11 The electroencephalograph (EEG). Recording electrodes attached to the surface of the scalp permit the EEG to record the brain's electrical activity over time. The EEG provides output in the form of line tracings called brain waves. Brain waves vary in frequency (cycles per second) and amplitude (measured in voltage). Different states of consciousness are associated with different brain waves. Characteristic EEG patterns for alert wakefulness, drowsiness, and deep, dreamless sleep are shown here. The use of the EEG in research is discussed in more detail in our chapter on states of consciousness (Chapter 5).

THE BIOLOGICAL
BASES OF BEHAVIOR

Ablations and Lesions

To study the relations between brain structures and behavior, scientists often remove structures from animals and then observe whether the animals stop eating, or mating, or hearing, for example. *Ablation* **involves surgically removing a piece of the brain.** If a structure lies deep within the brain, it is often much easier to disable the structure than to remove it. *Lesioning* **involves destroying a piece of the brain.** This is typically done by inserting an electrode into a brain structure and passing a strong electric current through it to burn the tissue and disable the structure.

Lesioning requires researchers to get an electrode to a particular place buried deep inside the brain. They accomplish this with a *stereotaxic* **instrument, a device used to implant electrodes at precise locations in the brain.** The use of this surgical device is described in Figure 3.12.

Obviously, in *research* efforts, ablation and lesioning can be used only with animals. However, lesions sometimes occur naturally in humans—from brain tumors, strokes, head injuries, and other misfortunes. Many major insights about how the brain is related to behavior have resulted from observations of behavioral changes in people who have suffered damage in specific areas of the brain (Gardner, 1975).

Electrical Stimulation of the Brain

Electrical stimulation of the brain (ESB) **involves sending a weak electric current into a** brain structure to stimulate (activate) it. The current is delivered through an electrode implanted with the same stereotaxic techniques used in lesioning procedures, but the current is much weaker. Although this sort of electrical stimulation does not exactly duplicate normal electrical signals in the brain, it's usually a close enough approximation to activate brain structures. Scientists have been using this technique since 1870, when Fritsch and Hitzig triggered muscle movements in a dog by stimulating areas in its brain. Neuroscientists have made extensive use of ESB in their studies of brain function.

Most ESB research is conducted with animals, for obvious reasons (would you volunteer to have your skull opened for electrode implantation?). However, ESB is used on humans in certain kinds of brain surgery required for medical purposes. After a patient's skull is opened, the surgeons may stimulate areas to map the individual patient's brain (to some extent each of us is unique), so that they don't slice through critical areas. The patient describes to the surgical team the feelings produced by each stimulation. As various areas are stimulated, the patient reports visual sensations, muscular twitches, memories, and so forth.

What is the patient doing awake in the midst of major surgery? This condition is not unusual in brain surgery. Neurosurgeons often prefer their patients to be awake to provide feedback, which can have enormous diagnostic value. Hence, they use only a local anesthetic to prevent pain as they open the patient's skull. The electrical stimulations of the brain are not painful because the brain has no pain receptors.

Brain-Imaging Procedures

In recent years, the invention of new brain-imaging devices, or brain scanners, has led to spectacular advances in our ability to look into the brain. Unfortunately, at present these brain scanners remain prohibitively expensive, so their availability for research purposes is limited. Even medical use of these devices is judicious, and some types of scanners are available at only a few hospitals in a region. However, this new technology is gradually opening new horizons in brain research.

The *CAT (computerized axial tomography) scanner* is a computer-enhanced X-ray machine. Multiple X rays are shot from many angles, and the computer assembles these into a vivid picture of brain structure (see Figure 3.13). CAT scans are very useful in pinpointing the location of brain damage in humans. Of the new brain-imaging techniques, the CAT scan is the most widely used in research. For example, recent CAT scan studies

Figure 3.12 An anesthetized rat in a stereotaxic instrument. This rat is undergoing brain surgery. After consulting a detailed map of the rat brain, researchers use the control knobs on the apparatus to implant an electrode in an exact location in the brain.

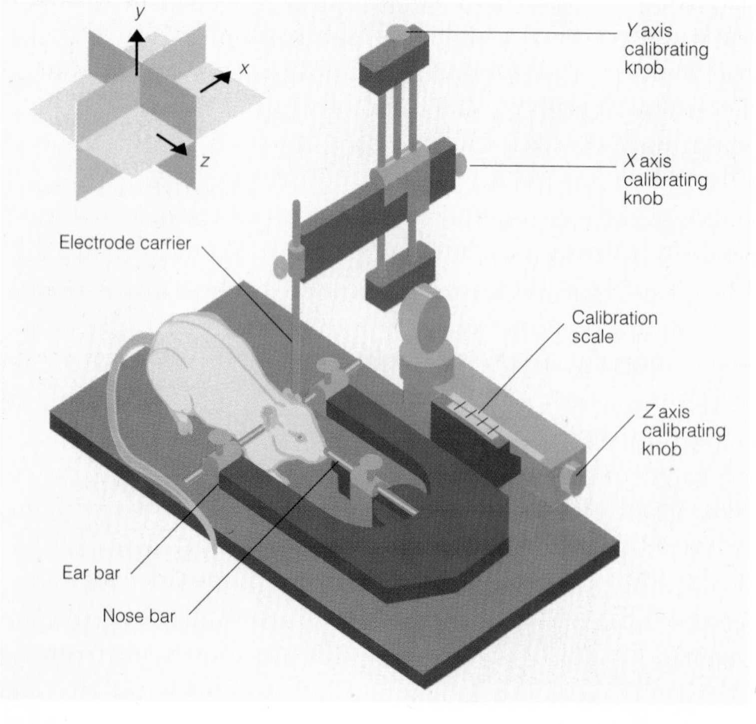

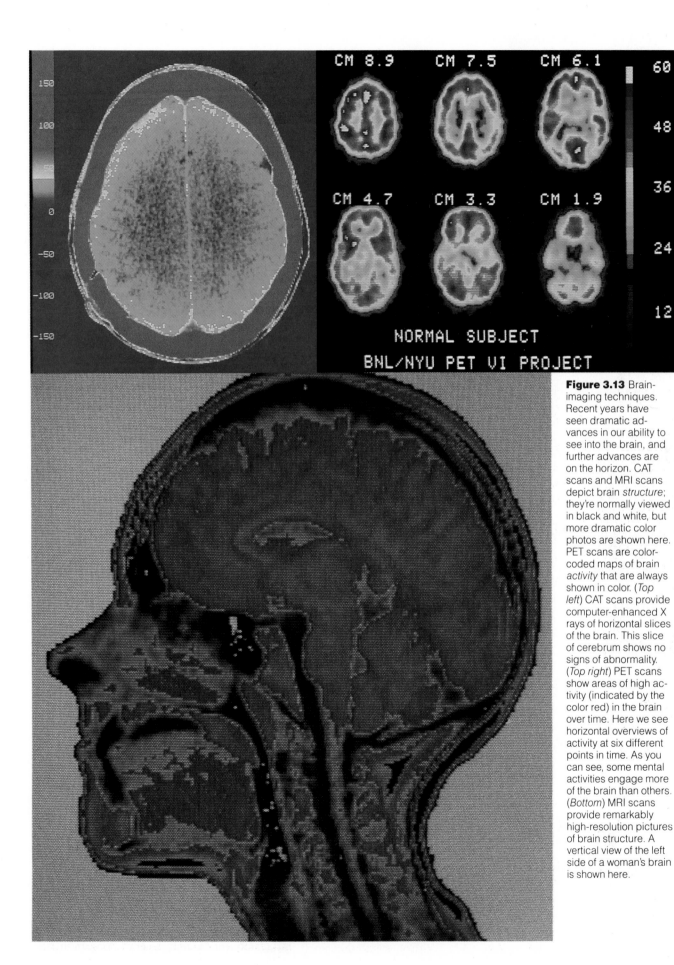

Figure 3.13 Brain-imaging techniques. Recent years have seen dramatic advances in our ability to see into the brain, and further advances are on the horizon. CAT scans and MRI scans depict brain *structure*; they're normally viewed in black and white, but more dramatic color photos are shown here. PET scans are color-coded maps of brain *activity* that are always shown in color. (*Top left*) CAT scans provide computer-enhanced X rays of horizontal slices of the brain. This slice of cerebrum shows no signs of abnormality. (*Top right*) PET scans show areas of high activity (indicated by the color red) in the brain over time. Here we see horizontal overviews of activity at six different points in time. As you can see, some mental activities engage more of the brain than others. (*Bottom*) MRI scans provide remarkably high-resolution pictures of brain structure. A vertical view of the left side of a woman's brain is shown here.

81

have linked schizophrenia to structural abnormalities (enlarged ventricles) in the brain (Jernigan, 1986). Although these findings should be regarded as preliminary, they illustrate the potential of this new technology.

The more recently developed *MRI (magnetic resonance imaging) scanner* uses magnetic fields and computerized enhancement to shoot pictures of brain structure that have remarkably high resolution (see Figure 3.13). MRI scans provide much better images of brain structure than CAT scans. However, this technology is very new and very expensive (the initial cost of an MRI scanner in 1988 was $3 million). Thus far, little behavioral research has been done with the relatively small number of MRI scanners available (Elliott, 1986).

In research on how brain and behavior are related, *PET (positron emission tomography) scanners* may prove to be the most valuable of the new brain-imaging techniques. CAT scans and MRI scans can portray only the *structure* of the brain. PET scans can map *activity* in the brain over time. PET scans take advantage of the fact that the brain "runs on sugar." That is, it replenishes its energy supply by burning sugar with oxygen. In PET scans, radioactively tagged sugars are introduced into the brain. Because the radioactive tags can be detected with X rays, these sugars serve as markers of metabolic activity in the brain. This monitoring technique provides a color-coded map indicating which areas of the brain become active when subjects clench their fists, sing, or contemplate the mysteries of the universe (see Figure 3.13). Since PET scans monitor chemical activity, they can be used to trace the movement of specific neurotransmitters in the brain (Buchsbaum, 1986). For example, researchers have begun to map out the locations of dopamine receptors in the human brain.

THE BRAIN AND BEHAVIOR

Now that we've examined the techniques of brain research, let's look at what research has discovered about the functions of different parts of the brain.

In talking about the brain and its structure, we use a special language, the language of neuroanatomy. Although there is some logic to the names used in neuroanatomy, the logic can be elusive. The early anatomists who charted the brain had no clue as to which structures did what. Consequently, the names they used had little functional meaning. Some anatomical names were derived from the name of the person who first described the structure, and many names were based on what a structure looked like. For example, the names of three parts of the brain are based on their resemblance to an *almond*, a *bridge*, and a *seahorse*. We might expect that such descriptive names would at least be easy to remember, but, unfortunately for most of us, the names were given when science was done in Latin. Thus, the three structures just mentioned are known to us as the *amygdala*, the *pons*, and the *hippocampus*.

The brain can be divided into three major regions: the hindbrain, the midbrain, and the forebrain. The principal structures found in each of these regions are listed in our organizational chart of the nervous system (see Figure 3.7). You can see where these regions are located in the brain by looking at Figure 3.14. They can be found easily in relation to the *brain stem*. The brain stem looks like its name—it appears to be a stem from which the rest of the brain "flowers," like a head of cauliflower. Its lower end is contiguous with the spinal cord; its higher end lies deep within the brain.

We'll begin our tour at the brain's lower end, where the spinal cord joins the brain stem. As we proceed upward, notice how the functions of brain structures go from the regulation of basic bodily processes to the control of "higher" mental processes.

The Hindbrain: Essential Functions

The *hindbrain* includes the cerebellum and two structures found in the lower part of the brain stem: the medulla and the pons. The *medulla*, which attaches to the spinal cord, has charge of largely unconscious but essential functions, such as breathing, maintaining muscle tone, and regulating circulation. The *pons* (literally "bridge") includes a bridge of fibers that connects the brain stem with the cerebellum. The pons contains several clusters of cell bodies that are concerned with sleep and arousal.

The *cerebellum* (literally "little brain") is located adjacent to the back surface of the brain stem. It is a relatively large and deeply folded structure. The cerebellum is involved in the coordination of movement and is also critical to our sense of equilibrium, or physical balance. Although the commands for muscular movements may come from higher brain centers, the cerebellum plays a key role in the execution of these commands. It is your cerebellum that allows you to hold your hand out to the side and smoothly bring your finger to a stop on your nose. This is a

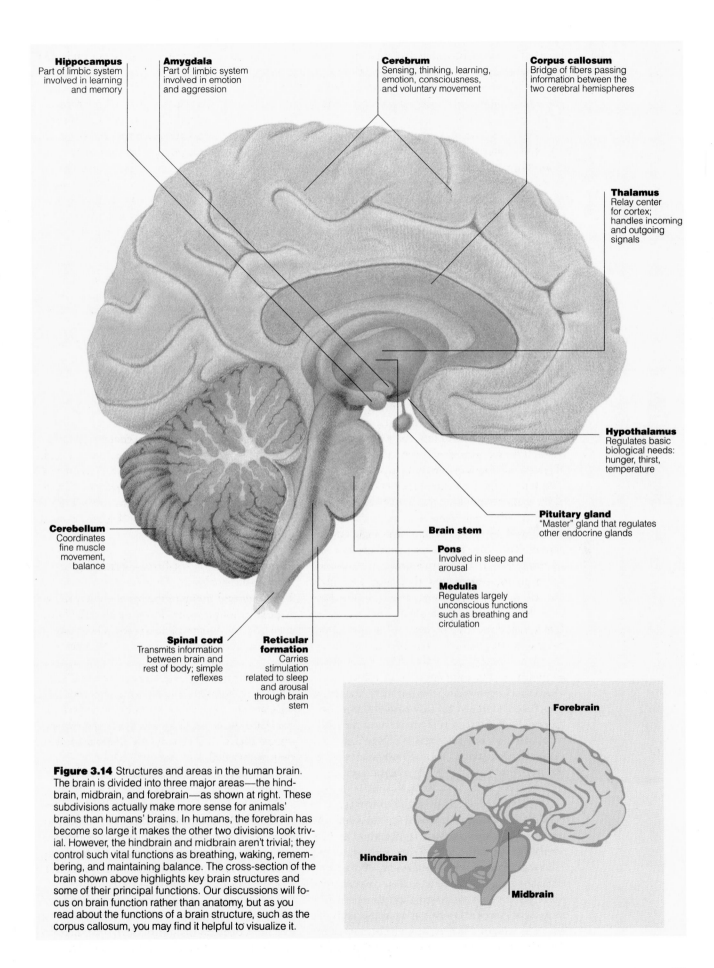

Hippocampus
Part of limbic system involved in learning and memory

Amygdala
Part of limbic system involved in emotion and aggression

Cerebrum
Sensing, thinking, learning, emotion, consciousness, and voluntary movement

Corpus callosum
Bridge of fibers passing information between the two cerebral hemispheres

Thalamus
Relay center for cortex; handles incoming and outgoing signals

Hypothalamus
Regulates basic biological needs: hunger, thirst, temperature

Pituitary gland
"Master" gland that regulates other endocrine glands

Brain stem

Pons
Involved in sleep and arousal

Medulla
Regulates largely unconscious functions such as breathing and circulation

Cerebellum
Coordinates fine muscle movement, balance

Spinal cord
Transmits information between brain and rest of body; simple reflexes

Reticular formation
Carries stimulation related to sleep and arousal through brain stem

Forebrain

Hindbrain

Midbrain

Figure 3.14 Structures and areas in the human brain. The brain is divided into three major areas—the hindbrain, midbrain, and forebrain—as shown at right. These subdivisions actually make more sense for animals' brains than humans' brains. In humans, the forebrain has become so large it makes the other two divisions look trivial. However, the hindbrain and midbrain aren't trivial; they control such vital functions as breathing, waking, remembering, and maintaining balance. The cross-section of the brain shown above highlights key brain structures and some of their principal functions. Our discussions will focus on brain function rather than anatomy, but as you read about the functions of a brain structure, such as the corpus callosum, you may find it helpful to visualize it.

useful roadside test for drunken driving because the cerebellum is one of the structures first depressed by alcohol. Damage to the cerebellum disrupts fine motor skills, such as those involved in writing, typing, or playing tennis.

The Midbrain: Additional Essential Functions

The *midbrain* is the segment of the brain stem that lies between the hindbrain and the forebrain (which is the "flower" above the stem). The midbrain is concerned with sensory processes (possibly with locating where things are) and with the control of voluntary movements. The decline in dopamine synthesis that causes Parkinsonism is due to the degeneration of an area located in the midbrain.

Running through both the hindbrain and the midbrain is the *reticular formation*. The reticular formation lies at the central core of the brain stem. Activity in the ascending fibers of the reticular formation is essential to maintaining an alert brain. Indeed, damage to this area can cause a coma. Signals sent through the reticular formation play a major role in the regulation of sleep and wakefulness.

The Forebrain: Diverse Functions

The *forebrain* is the largest and most complicated region of the brain, encompassing a variety of structures, including the thalamus, hypothalamus, limbic system, and cerebrum. This list is not exhaustive, and some of these structures have their own subdivisions, as you can see in our organizational chart of the nervous system (Figure 3.7). The thalamus, hypothalamus, and limbic system form the core of the forebrain; they are located near the top of the brain stem. Above these structures, we find the *cerebrum*, the seat of awareness and thought. This relatively large structure may contain 70% of the neurons in the CNS! The wrinkled outside surface of the cerebrum is the *cerebral cortex*. It's the outer layer of the brain, the part that looks like a cauliflower.

THE THALAMUS: A WAY STATION

The *thalamus* is a structure in the forebrain through which all sensory information (except smell) must pass to get to the cerebral cortex. This way station is made up of a number of clusters of cell bodies, or somas. Each cluster is concerned with relaying sensory information to a particular part of the cortex. However, it would be a mistake to characterize the thalamus as nothing more than a passive relay station. The thalamus also appears to play an active role in integrating information from different senses.

THE HYPOTHALAMUS: A REGULATOR OF BIOLOGICAL NEEDS

The *hypothalamus* is a structure found near the base of the forebrain that is involved in the regulation of basic biological needs. The hypothalamus lies beneath the thalamus. (*Hypo* means "under," making the hypothalamus the area "under the thalamus.") Although no larger than a kidney bean, the hypothalamus regulates a diverse array of important behavioral functions. One key function of the hypothalamus is to control the autonomic nervous system. In addition, the hypothalamus serves as a vital link between the brain and the endocrine system (our network of glands, discussed later in this chapter). It is located directly above a connecting stalk to the pituitary gland, the "master gland" of the endocrine system.

The hypothalamus plays a major role in the regulation of basic biological drives related to survival, including the so-called four F's—fighting, fleeing, feeding, and mating. For example, when researchers lesion the lateral areas (the sides) of the hypothalamus, animals lose interest in food and frequently starve. In contrast, when electrical stimulation (ESB) is used to activate the lateral hypothalamus, animals eat constantly, ballooning up to grotesque size (Keesey & Powley, 1975; Grossman et al., 1978). Does this mean that the lateral hypothalamus is the "hunger center" in the brain? Not necessarily. The regulation of hunger turns out to be complex and multifaceted, as you'll see in Chapter 10. Nonetheless, it's clear that the hypothalamus is involved in the control of hunger and other basic biological needs.

THE LIMBIC SYSTEM: THE SEAT OF EMOTION

The *limbic system* is a loosely connected network of structures located beneath the cerebral cortex that is involved in the control of emotion, motivation, and memory (see Figure 3.15). These structures include the *hippocampus* and the *amygdala* (remember the "seahorse" and the "almond"?), small parts of the thalamus and hypothalamus, and other structures. The hippocampus appears to play a role in the formation of memories (Berger, 1984). It shows significant damage in patients suffering from Alzheimer's disease (Hyman et al., 1984).

There is ample evidence linking the limbic system to the experience of emotion, although the exact mechanisms of control are not well understood (Pribram, 1981). The limbic system is one

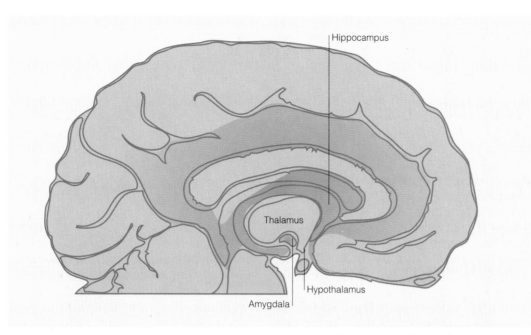

Figure 3.15 The limbic system. The limbic system is a network of structures that plays a role in emotion, motivation, and memory. The shaded area on the brain shows the approximate location of the neural circuits that link most of the structures in the limbic system. These structures fall mostly along the border between the cortex and deeper, subcortical structures (hence the term "limbic," which means edge).

Hippocampus

Thalamus

Hypothalamus

Amygdala

of the areas in the brain where there appear to be emotion-tinged "pleasure centers." This intriguing possibility first surfaced quite by chance, in brain-stimulation research with rats.

James Olds and Peter Milner (1954) accidentally discovered that a rat would press a lever repeatedly to send brief bursts of electrical stimulation to a specific spot in its brain where an electrode was implanted. They thought that they had inserted the electrode in the rat's reticular formation. However, they learned later that the electrode was bent during implantation, so that it ended up elsewhere (probably in the hypothalamus). Much to their surprise, the rat kept "coming back for more" stimulation in this area. Subsequent studies showed that rats and monkeys would press a lever *thousands of times per hour* to stimulate certain brain sites. Although the experimenters obviously couldn't ask the animals about it, they *inferred* that the animals were experiencing some sort of pleasure. Many self-stimulation sites have been found in the limbic system (Olds & Fobes, 1981). The heaviest concentration is located where the *medial forebrain bundle* (a bundle of axons from the brain stem) passes through the hypothalamus.

Brain surgery cases have afforded scientists a few opportunities to probe for similar pleasure centers in human subjects. Since they're often conscious during brain surgery, human subjects *can* be asked about their feelings. Electrically activated pleasure centers *have* been found in these human subjects (Delgado, 1969; Heath, 1964). However, the emotional reactions in humans have not been as consistent nor as strong as anticipated. Given the way laboratory animals work ferociously to earn stimulation of pleasure cen-

ters, researchers expected human subjects to report feelings of spectacular euphoria. Thus far, however, experimenters have struggled to elicit relatively mild feelings of pleasure in humans (Valenstein, 1973). There is a great deal of debate about how pleasure centers in the brain may relate to emotion and motivation (Bindra, 1985).

THE CEREBRUM: THE SEAT OF COMPLEX THOUGHT

The *cerebrum* is the largest and most complicated part of the human brain. It includes the brain areas that are responsible for our most complex mental activities, including learning, remembering, thinking, and consciousness itself. **The *cerebral cortex* is the convoluted outer layer of the cerebrum.** The cortex is folded and bent, so that we pack a large area of cortex—about 1.5 square feet—into the limited volume of the skull (Hubel and Wiesel, 1979).

The cerebrum is divided into two halves called hemispheres. Hence, **the *cerebral hemispheres* are the right and left halves of the cerebrum.** The hemispheres are separated in the center of the brain by a deep fissure. In fact, if one were to slice a human brain down the middle, it would be possible to put the knife all the way down to a thick band of fibers called the *corpus callosum* before cutting any brain tissue. **The *corpus callosum* is the structure that connects the two cerebral hemispheres.** We'll discuss the functional specialization of the two hemispheres in the next section of this chapter.

The cerebral cortex is divided into four parts called *lobes*, more for our convenience than because there really are four distinct pieces. To some extent, each of these lobes is dedicated to specific

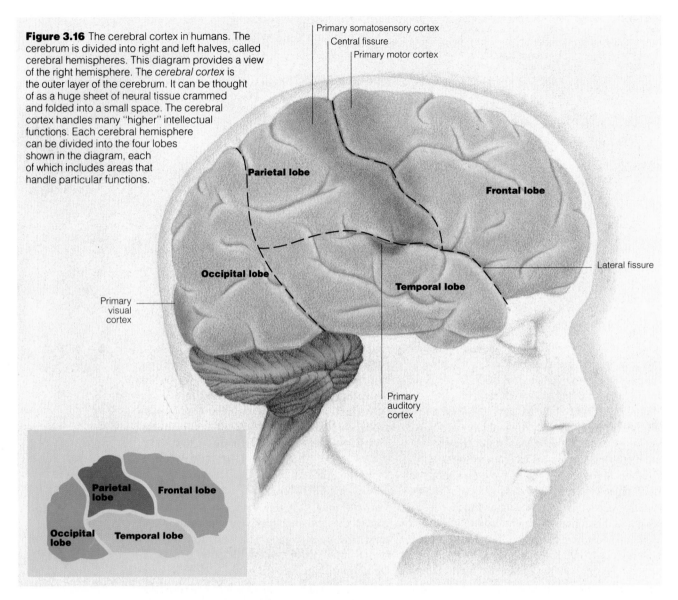

Figure 3.16 The cerebral cortex in humans. The cerebrum is divided into right and left halves, called cerebral hemispheres. This diagram provides a view of the right hemisphere. The *cerebral cortex* is the outer layer of the cerebrum. It can be thought of as a huge sheet of neural tissue crammed and folded into a small space. The cerebral cortex handles many "higher" intellectual functions. Each cerebral hemisphere can be divided into the four lobes shown in the diagram, each of which includes areas that handle particular functions.

Primary somatosensory cortex
Central fissure
Primary motor cortex

Parietal lobe

Frontal lobe

Lateral fissure

Occipital lobe

Temporal lobe

Primary visual cortex

Primary auditory cortex

Parietal lobe

Frontal lobe

Occipital lobe

Temporal lobe

purposes. The location of these lobes can be seen in Figure 3.16.

The *occipital lobe*, at the back of the head, includes the cortical area where most visual signals are sent and processing is begun. This area is called the *primary visual cortex*. In Chapter 4, we'll discuss how it's organized.

The *parietal lobe* is forward of the occipital lobe. It includes the area where we register the sense of touch, called the *primary somatosensory cortex*. Different sections of this area receive signals from different regions of the body. When ESB is delivered in these areas, people report physical sensations—as if someone were actually touching them on the arm or cheek, for example. The parietal lobe is also involved in integrating visual input and in monitoring the body's position in space.

The *temporal lobe* (meaning "near the temples") lies below the parietal lobe. Near its top, the temporal lobe contains an area devoted to

auditory processing, called the *primary auditory cortex*. As we'll see momentarily, damage to an area in the temporal lobe on the left side of the brain can impair the comprehension of speech and language.

Continuing forward, we find the *frontal lobe*, which is the largest lobe in the human brain. The frontal lobe contains the principal areas that control the movement of muscle groups. Together these areas are called the primary motor cortex. ESB applied in these areas can cause muscle contractions. The amount of motor cortex allocated to the control of a body part depends not on the part's size, but on the diversity and precision of its movements. Thus, more cortex is given to parts we have fine control over, like fingers, lips, and the tongue, and less to larger parts that make crude movements, like thighs and shoulders (see Figure 3.17).

The large portion of the frontal lobe to the front

Figure 3.17 The primary motor cortex. If we removed the frontal lobe from the left hemisphere of the human brain (see below) and sliced off the back portion of this section, we would cut out the left half of the primary motor cortex, the area in the brain that controls the movement of muscles. The diagram on the right shows the amount of motor cortex devoted to the control of various muscles and limbs. More cortex is required for muscle groups that must make relatively precise movements.

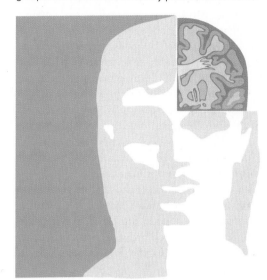

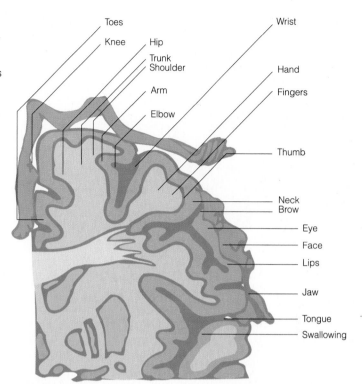

of the motor cortex is something of a mystery. It's the most prominent part of the human brain, and it's the main feature that makes the human brain different from the brain of an ape. But it is apparently not the seat of intelligence, as most mental functions are left intact after damage to this area.

One interesting suggestion is that this area is involved in long-term planning, and predicting the consequences of acts (Furst, 1979). Thus, it may be your frontal cortex that lets you wonder about the future.

RIGHT BRAIN/LEFT BRAIN: CEREBRAL SPECIALIZATION

As we noted a moment ago, the cerebrum—the seat of awareness and thought—is divided into two separate hemispheres (see Figure 3.18). In recent decades, an exciting flurry of research has elucidated the special abilities of the right and left cerebral hemispheres. Some theorists have gone so far as to suggest that we really have two brains in one!

Investigators got their first hint of this specialization many years ago from cases in which one side of a person's brain was damaged, usually by a stroke. In such cases some mental functions were impaired while others were not. For example, *aphasia* **is a disorder marked by language and speech deficits attributable to brain damage.** The lesions that cause aphasia are usually found on the left side of the brain.

The left hemisphere was implicated in the control of language as early as 1861, by Paul Broca, a French surgeon and anthropologist. Broca was treating a patient who had been unable to speak

for 30 years. After the patient died, Broca showed that the probable cause of his speech deficit was a localized lesion on the left side of the frontal lobe. Since then, many similar cases have shown that this area of the brain, known as *Broca's area*, plays an important role in the *production* of speech (see Figure 3.19).

Another major language center, *Wernicke's area*, was found in the temporal lobe of the left hemisphere in 1874. Damage in Wernicke's area (see Figure 3.19) usually leads to aphasia marked by problems with the *comprehension* of speech and language. Patients with lesions in this area may speak with appropriate grammar and pronunciation, but what they say may be nonsense. For example, Geschwind (1979; p. 111) quotes a patient who said, "Mother is away here working her work to get her better, but when she's looking the two boys looking in the other part . . ."

Gradually, accumulating evidence that the left hemisphere usually processes language led scien-

Figure 3.18 The cerebral hemispheres (seen from above). The longitudinal fissure running down the middle of the brain separates the left and right halves of the cerebral cortex.

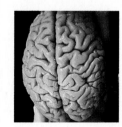

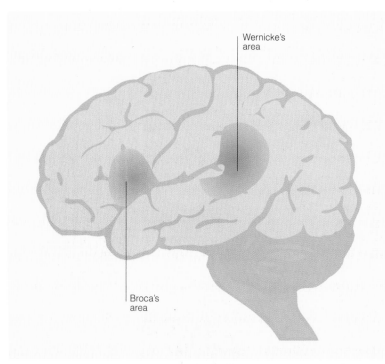

Figure 3.19 Language processing in the brain. This view of the left hemisphere highlights the location of two centers for language processing in the brain: Broca's area, which is involved in speech production, and Wernicke's area, which is involved in language comprehension.

Figure 3.20 Visual input in the split brain. If a subject stares at a fixation point, the point divides the subject's visual field into right and left halves. Input from the right visual field strikes the left side of each eye and is transmitted to the left hemisphere. Input from the left visual field strikes the right side of each eye and is transmitted to the right hemisphere. Normally, the hemispheres share the information from the two halves of the visual field, but in split-brain patients, the corpus callosum is severed, and the two hemispheres cannot communicate. Hence, the experimenter can present a visual stimulus to just one hemisphere at a time.

tists to characterize it as the "dominant" hemisphere. Since our thoughts and ideas are usually coded in terms of language, the left hemisphere was given the lion's share of credit for handling the "higher" mental processes, such as reasoning, remembering, reading, writing, analyzing, planning, and problem solving. Meanwhile, the right hemisphere came to be viewed as the "dumb" hemisphere, lacking any special functions or abilities. Indeed, in 1926 S. E. Henschen was moved to remark "In nature there seems to be a law that in order to attain full development of higher faculties originally distributed over two organs, a concentration of the capacity in only one of them is necessary" (Marshall, 1981, p. 72). Thus, the right hemisphere was seen as the "nondominant" or "minor" hemisphere, which lived off the left hemisphere's far superior talents.

This characterization of the left and right hemispheres as major and minor partners in the brain's work began to change in the 1960s. It all started with landmark research by Roger Sperry, Michael Gazzaniga, and colleagues who studied "split-

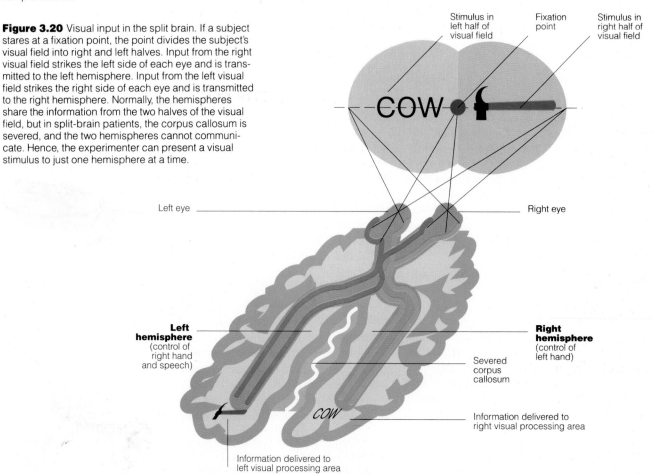

brain" patients, individuals whose cerebral hemispheres were surgically disconnected (Gazzaniga, Bogen, & Sperry, 1965; Gazzaniga, 1970; Levy, Trevarthen, & Sperry, 1972; Sperry, 1982). In 1981 Sperry received a Nobel prize in physiology and medicine for this work and for his many other studies of the brain.

Bisecting the Brain: Split-Brain Research

In *split-brain surgery* **the bundle of fibers that connects the cerebral hemispheres (the corpus callosum) is cut to reduce the severity of epileptic seizures.** It is a radical procedure that is chosen only in exceptional cases that have not responded to other forms of treatment. But the surgery provides scientists with an unusual opportunity to study people who have had their brain literally split in two.

To appreciate the logic of split-brain research, we need to understand how sensory and motor information is routed to and from the two hemispheres. Each *hemisphere's primary connections are to the opposite side of the body.* Thus, the left hemisphere communicates with the right hand, right arm, right leg, right eyebrow, and so on, while the

right hemisphere communicates with the left side of the body.

Vision and hearing are more complex. Both eyes deliver information to both hemispheres, but there still is a separation of input. Stimuli in the right half of your *visual field* are registered by receptors on the left side of each eye, which send signals to the left hemisphere. Stimuli in the left half of your visual field are transmitted by both eyes to the right hemisphere (see Figure 3.20). Auditory inputs to each ear also go to both hemispheres. However, connections to the opposite hemisphere are stronger or more immediate, so that sounds presented to the right ear are registered in the left hemisphere first, while those presented to the left ear are registered more quickly in the right hemisphere.

For the most part, we don't notice this asymmetric, "criss-crossed" organization because the two hemispheres are in close communication with each other. Information received by one hemisphere is readily shared with the other. However, when the two hemispheres are surgically disconnected, the functional specialization of the brain becomes apparent. To illustrate, let's turn to our Featured Study for the chapter. It presents one of the first split-brain studies that led to an avalanche of research on cerebral specialization.

"Both the left and right hemispheres of the brain have been found to have their own specialized forms of intellect."
ROGER SPERRY

WHEN THE RIGHT HAND *REALLY* DOESN'T KNOW WHAT THE LEFT HAND IS DOING

Does splitting the brain mean splitting the mind? Gazzaniga, Bogen, and Sperry set out to determine the extent to which the two hemispheres functioned independently after they were separated. Another goal of their study was to determine whether specialized functions might reside in the right hemisphere.

Previous studies showed that animals experienced no readily apparent ill effects from split-brain surgery. This encouraged neurosurgeons Joseph Bogen and Philip Vogel to try splitting the brain of human patients suffering from severe epilepsy, in the hope that this procedure might suppress their seizures. Medically speaking, the experimental operations were a success; they clearly led to a reduction in seizures. Subsequently, Bogen teamed up with Sperry and Gazzaniga to conduct elaborate tests of mental processing with the first two patients to receive the surgery.

Method

Subjects. The principal subject, operated on in 1962, was a 48-year-old male war veteran

plagued by uncontrollable epileptic seizures. The second subject was a 30-year-old woman with a similar problem who had the surgery in 1963. After the operations, neither showed any obvious changes in personality or general intelligence.

Apparatus and Procedure. The investigators wanted to present visual stimuli such as pictures, symbols, and words to a single visual field, so that the stimuli would be sent to only one hemisphere. The catch is that when people move their eyes, the boundaries of the visual fields shift, so that information about a stimulus ends up being sent to both hemispheres. To get around this problem, the visual stimuli were flashed very briefly onto a screen immediately in front of the subject, who stared at a fixation point (a spot) in the center of the screen (see Figure 3.21). The stimulus could be shown to the right of the fixation point (in which case it projected only to the left hemisphere), or to the left of the fixation point (projecting only to the right hemisphere). Because the stimuli were present for only a split sec-

Investigators: Michael S. Gazzaniga, Joseph E. Bogen (California Institute of Technology), and Roger W. Sperry (California College of Medicine)

Source: Observations on visual perception after disconnexion of the cerebral hemispheres in man. *Brain,* 88 (2) (1965), 221–236.

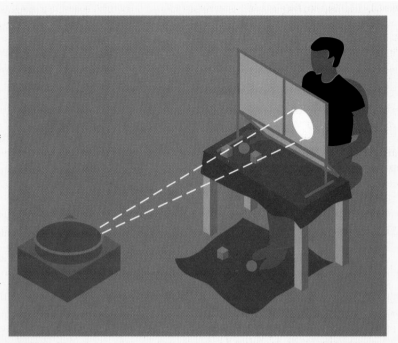

Figure 3.21 Experimental apparatus in split-brain research. On the left is a special slide projector that can present images very briefly, before the subject's eyes can move and thus change the visual field. Images are projected on one half of the screen to present stimuli to just one hemisphere. The portion of the apparatus beneath the screen is constructed to prevent the subject from seeing objects that he may be asked to handle with his right or left hand, another procedure that can be used to send information to just one hemisphere in split-brain patients.

ond, the subjects did not have a chance to move their eyes and allow the "wrong" hemisphere a glimpse of the stimulus.

Other stimuli were presented to a single hemisphere tactually (that is, through the sense of touch). Objects were placed in a subject's right or left hand behind the screen so that the subject couldn't see the objects (see Figure 3.21 again). Immediately after visual or tactual stimuli were presented, the subjects were asked to identify the stimuli. On some trials they were asked to name the stimulus; on other trials they were asked to use their right or left hand to select objects that matched the stimulus. In other tests, the subjects were asked to work on puzzles or copy drawings with a designated hand.

Results

When pictures were flashed in the right visual field and thus sent to the left hemisphere, the subjects were able to name and describe the objects (such as a cup or spoon). However, subjects were not able to name and describe the same objects when they were flashed in the left visual field and sent to the right hemisphere. In fact, since the left hemisphere controls speech, subjects often *said* that they hadn't seen anything! In a similar fashion, an object placed out of view in the right hand (communicating with the left hemisphere) could be named, but the same object placed in the left hand (right hemisphere) could not be. These findings supported the notion that language is housed in the left hemisphere.

Although the right hemisphere was not able to speak up for itself, further tests revealed that it was processing the information presented. If sub-

jects were given an opportunity to *point out a picture* of an object that they had held in their left hand, they were able to do so. They also were able to point out pictures that were flashed to the left visual field (right hemisphere). These findings suggested that the right hemisphere engages in nonverbal information processing.

In the puzzle tests, the right hemisphere turned out to be *superior* to the left hemisphere. These were puzzles in which differently shaped blocks or tiles had to be assembled into a specified pattern (see Figure 3.22). Even though the subjects

Figure 3.22 Visual-spatial tests. To assess visual-spatial processing, split-brain subjects were asked to work puzzles in which they arranged blocks to match a pattern presented on a card.

were right-handed, they could successfully do the puzzles only with the left hand. When forced to use their right hand, they became hesitant and their performance deteriorated. On these trials, the male subject's left hand, which was held behind his back, would make sudden movements, as if it were trying to jump in and help. When he was allowed to use both hands at once, his performance was poor; trying to help, the right hand would mess up what the left was doing correctly! Superior performance by the left hand (and therefore the right hemisphere) was also seen in the tests that required subjects to copy drawings, even though the subjects were right-handed. These findings in the puzzle and drawing tests suggested that the right hemisphere might have a special talent for visual-spatial tasks.

Discussion

Collectively, the results demonstrated that both hemispheres were able to perceive objects and process information. However, with the corpus callosum cut, one hemisphere could not communicate its information to the other. The separated hemispheres operated independently. Hence, under the right conditions, the right hand literally didn't know what the left hand was doing!

Both hemispheres were found to be capable of considerable intellectual activity—although they showed different capabilities. As expected, the left hemisphere proved superior in verbal and linguistic processing. In contrast, the right hemisphere outperformed the left when subjects were asked to think in terms of spatial relationships.

Comment

This classic study produced new insights about how the brain divides its mental chores. It provided the first compelling demonstration that the right hemisphere has its own special talents. Subsequent studies of additional split-brain patients showed that the right hemisphere was better than the left at a variety of visual-spatial tasks, including discriminating colors, arranging blocks, and recognizing faces. Thus, the right hemisphere began to come into its own, and research on the specialization of the cerebral hemispheres has flourished ever since.

In the split-brain studies, the other major finding was that subjects whose hemispheres were disconnected showed signs of having two minds in one brain! Many split-brain patients reported that it sometimes seemed like each hemisphere had a mind of its own. One patient reported that if he shifted a book from his right to his left hand, it would put the book down even though he was wrapped up in it. Apparently his right hemisphere just wasn't interested in reading. Another patient reported that when he angrily reached for his wife with his left hand, his right hand darted out to stop the left! A third patient found her right and left brains competing to dress her, as they chose different clothes to wear. Sometimes her left hand would unbutton a blouse nearly as fast as her right hand buttoned it. Thus, to some extent, split-brain patients experience two independent streams of consciousness.

Hemispheric Specialization in the Intact Brain

The problem with the split-brain operation, of course, is that it creates a very abnormal situation, as evidenced by the independent streams of consciousness just mentioned. The corpus callosum has been cut in only a handful of people. The vast majority of us remain "neurologically intact." Moreover, the surgery is done only with people who suffer from prolonged, severe cases of epilepsy. These people may have somewhat atypical brain organization even before the operation. Thus, theorists couldn't help wondering whether it was safe to generalize broadly from the split-brain studies. For this reason, researchers developed a number of approaches that allowed them to study cerebral specialization in the intact brain.

One approach involves looking at left-right imbalances in visual or auditory processing, called *perceptual asymmetries*. As we just discussed, it's possible to present visual stimuli to just one visual field at a time. In normal individuals, the input sent to one hemisphere is quickly shared with the other. However, subtle differences in the "abilities" of the two hemispheres can be detected by precisely measuring *how long* it takes subjects to recognize different types of stimuli.

For instance, when *verbal* stimuli are presented to the right visual field (and thus sent to the *left hemisphere* first), they are identified more quickly and more accurately than when they are presented to the left visual field (right hemisphere). The faster reactions in the left hemisphere presumably occur because the left hemisphere can recognize verbal stimuli on its own, while the right hemisphere has to take extra time to "consult" the left hemisphere. In contrast, an advantage is typically found for the *right hemisphere* (left visual field) when the stimulus demands are *spatial* in nature, such as locating a dot or recognizing a face (White, 1969; Bradshaw & Nettleton, 1981).

Another approach involves looking at EEG patterns in the two hemispheres as subjects work

Imagine that you are working as a neuropsychologist at a clinic. You are involved in the diagnosis of the cases described below. You are asked to identify the probable cause(s) of the disorders in terms of nervous system malfunctions. Based on the information in this chapter, indicate the probable location of any brain damage or the probable disturbance of neurotransmitter activity, or both. The answers can be found in the back of the book in Appendix A.

Case 1. Miriam is exhibiting language deficits. In particular, she does not seem to comprehend the meanings of words.

_____

Case 2. Camille displays spastic motor coordination and is diagnosed as having Parkinsonism.

_____

Case 3. Neal suffers from Balint's syndrome, which involves defective localization of things in space. He does things like burning his chin when he tries to light a cigarette and missing the glass when he pours his milk.

_____

Case 4. Wendy is highly irrational, has poor contact with reality, and reports hallucinations. She is given a diagnosis of schizophrenic disorder.

_____

on different types of tasks. When subjects work on verbal tasks, brain waves associated with day-dreaming or a lack of mental concentration are pronounced in the right hemisphere. This is thought to reflect "idling" in the right hemisphere while the left hemisphere is actively engaged by the verbal task. The opposite pattern is seen on spatial tasks that presumably engage the right hemisphere. (Galin & Ornstein, 1972). Along with the evidence on perceptual asymmetries, these EEG differences suggest that cerebral specialization in neurologically normal people resembles that found in split-brain patients.

Using these two approaches and a variety of other methods, researchers eventually demonstrated that the right and left halves of the brain are functionally specialized in neurologically intact people. In a nutshell, they concluded that the left hemisphere usually handles verbal processing, such as language, speech, reading, and writing, while the right hemisphere usually handles nonverbal processing, such as that required by spatial, musical, and visual recognition tasks. These findings, which have attracted a great deal of public attention, have interesting implications for our understanding of mental processes. We'll examine these provocative implications in our upcoming Application section at the end of the chapter. For now, however, let's leave the brain and turn our attention to the endocrine system.

THE ENDOCRINE SYSTEM: ANOTHER WAY TO COMMUNICATE

While the major way the brain communicates with the rest of the body is through the nervous system, there is a second communication system that is important to behavior. **The *endocrine system* consists of glands that secrete chemicals into the bloodstream that help control bodily functioning.** The messengers in this communication network are called hormones. **Hormones are the chemical substances released by the endocrine glands.** The endocrine system tends to be involved in the long-term regulation of basic bodily processes, as it can't match the high speed of neural transmission. The major endocrine glands and their chief functions are shown in Figure 3.23.

In a way, endocrine glands are like chemical synapses with distant receptors. Once released, the hormonal transmitters diffuse through the bloodstream and bind to special receptors on distant target cells. In fact, some of the chemical substances that serve as neurotransmitters in the nervous system do double duty—functioning as

hormones when they're released by the endocrine system (norepinephrine, for example). There are many different hormones. Some have very specific target cells; others affect a great many cells throughout the body.

Some hormones are released in response to changing conditions in the body and act to regulate those conditions. For example, hormones released by the stomach and intestines help control digestion, kidney hormones play a part in regulating blood pressure, and pancreatic hormone (insulin) is essential for cells to use sugar from the blood.

Much of the endocrine system is controlled by the nervous system through the *hypothalamus*. This structure at the base of the forebrain has intimate connections with the pea-sized *pituitary gland*, which is located nearby. **The *pituitary gland* releases a great variety of hormones that fan out around the body, stimulating actions in the other endocrine glands.** In this sense, the pituitary is the "master gland" of the endocrine sys-

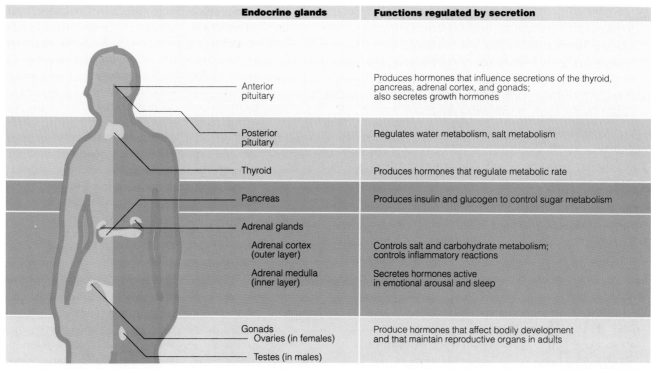

Endocrine glands	Functions regulated by secretion
Anterior pituitary	Produces hormones that influence secretions of the thyroid, pancreas, adrenal cortex, and gonads; also secretes growth hormones
Posterior pituitary	Regulates water metabolism, salt metabolism
Thyroid	Produces hormones that regulate metabolic rate
Pancreas	Produces insulin and glucogen to control sugar metabolism
Adrenal glands	
Adrenal cortex (outer layer)	Controls salt and carbohydrate metabolism; controls inflammatory reactions
Adrenal medulla (inner layer)	Secretes hormones active in emotional arousal and sleep
Gonads Ovaries (in females) Testes (in males)	Produce hormones that affect bodily development and that maintain reproductive organs in adults

tem, although the hypothalamus is the real power behind the throne.

The intermeshing of the nervous system and the endocrine system can be seen in the fight-or-flight response that we described earlier. In times of stress, the hypothalamus sends signals along two pathways—through the autonomic nervous system and through the pituitary gland—to the adrenal glands (Asterita, 1985). In response, the adrenal glands secrete two sets of hormones, catecholamines and corticosteroids. These hormones radiate throughout the body, preparing it to cope with an emergency.

Hormones play important roles in modulating our physiological development. For example, among the more interesting hormones released by the pituitary are the *gonadotropins*. These affect the *gonads*, or sexual glands. Prior to birth, these hormones direct the formation of the external sexual organs in the developing fetus (Money &

Erhardt, 1972). Thus, your sexual identity as a male or female was shaped during prenatal development by the actions of hormones. At puberty, increased levels of sexual hormones are responsible for the emergence of our secondary sexual characteristics, such as males' facial hair and females' breasts. The actions of other hormones are responsible for the spurt in physical growth that occurs around puberty.

These developmental effects of hormones illustrate how our genetic programming has a hand in behavior. Obviously, the hormonal actions that shaped your sex were determined by your genetic makeup. Similarly, the hormonal changes in early adolescence that launched your growth spurt and aroused your interest in sexuality, were preprogrammed over a decade earlier by your genetic inheritance. Thus, we need to discuss the role of heredity in shaping behavior.

Figure 3.23 The endocrine system. The endocrine glands secrete hormones into the bloodstream. These hormones regulate physical functions and may have an impact on behavior.

HEREDITY AND BEHAVIOR: IS IT ALL IN THE GENES?

As you've learned throughout this chapter, your biological makeup is intimately related to your behavior. This is why your genetic inheritance, which shapes your biological makeup, may have much to do with your behavior. Most people realize that physical characteristics such as height, hair color, blood type, and eye color are largely shaped by heredity. But what about psychological characteristics, such as intelligence, moodiness,

impulsiveness, and shyness? To what extent are our behavioral qualities molded by our genes?

As you saw in Chapter 1, questions about the relative importance of heredity versus the environment—nature versus nurture—are very old ones in psychology. One of the first scientists to explore the notion that heredity might influence behavior was Sir Francis Galton, a prominent 19th-century British scholar. Galton (1869) stud-

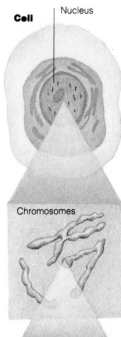

Cell | Nucleus

Chromosomes

DNA

Figure 3.24 Genetic material. This series of enlargements shows the main components of genetic material. *Top:* In the nucleus of every cell are chromosomes, which carry the information needed to construct new human beings. *Center:* Chromosomes are threadlike strands of DNA that carry thousands of genes, the functional units of hereditary transmission. *Bottom:* DNA is a spiralled double chain of molecules that can copy itself for reproduction.

ied family trees and noted that success and eminence appeared consistently in certain families over generations. Galton drew what seemed to be the obvious conclusion: that intelligence was governed entirely by heredity.

Although Galton's methods were innovative for the time, by modern standards they were flawed. He judged intelligence by reputation instead of measuring it objectively. He also failed to control for extraneous variables such as the advantages of higher social class. Nonetheless, Galton launched an intellectual debate that has continued for over 100 years. Scientists are still arguing about how much influence heredity and the environment have on mental ability and many other behavioral traits. To help you appreciate the complexities of this debate, we'll outline some basic principles of genetics and describe the methods that investigators use to assess the effects of heredity.

Basic Principles of Genetics

Every cell in your body contains enduring messages from your mother and father. These messages are found on the *chromosomes* that lie within the nucleus of each cell.

CHROMOSOMES AND GENES

Chromosomes **are threadlike strands of DNA (deoxyribonucleic acid) molecules that carry genetic information** (see Figure 3.24). Every cell in humans, except the sex cells (sperm and eggs), contains 46 chromosomes. These chromosomes operate in 23 pairs, with one chromosome of each pair being contributed by each parent. Parents make this contribution when fertilization creates a *zygote,* **a one-celled organism formed by the union of a sperm and an egg.** The sex cells that

form a zygote each have 23 chromosomes; together they contribute the 46 chromosomes in the zygote and in all the body cells that develop from it. Each chromosome, in turn, contains thousands of biochemical messengers called genes. *Genes* **are DNA segments that serve as the key functional units in hereditary transmission.**

If all offspring are formed by a union of the parents' sex cells, why aren't family members identical clones? They're not clones because a single pair of parents can produce an extraordinary variety of combinations of chromosomes. In each parent, when sex cells form, it is a matter of chance as to which member of each chromosome pair ends up in the sperm or egg. Each parent's 23 chromosome pairs can be scrambled in over 8 million (2^{23}) different ways, yielding roughly 70 trillion possible configurations (2^{46}) when sperm and egg unite. Actually, this is a conservative estimate. It doesn't take into account complexities such as mutations (changes in the genetic code) or crossing over during sex cell formation (an interchange of material between chromosomes). Thus, genetic transmission is a complicated process, and the results are a matter of probability. Except for identical twins, each of us ends up with a unique genetic blueprint.

While different combinations of genes explain why family members aren't exactly alike, the overlap among these combinations explains why family members tend to resemble each other. Members of a family share more of the same genes than nonmembers. Ultimately, each of us shares half of his or her genes with each parent. On the average, full siblings (except identical twins) also share half our genes, and more distant relatives share smaller proportions. Figure 3.25 shows the amount of genetic overlap for various kinship relations. The proportion of shared genes ranges

Relationship	Degree of relatedness	Genetic relatedness	
Identical twins		100%	
• Fraternal twins • Brother or sister • Parent or child	First degree	50%	
• Grandparent or grandchild • Uncle, aunt, nephew, or niece • Half-brother or half-sister	Second degree	25%	
First cousin	Third degree	12.5%	
Second cousin	Fourth degree	6.25%	
Unrelated		0%	

Figure 3.25 Genetic overlap in relatives. Research on the genetic bases of behavior takes advantage of the different degrees of genetic overlap between various types of relatives. If heredity influences a trait, then relatives who share more genes should be more similar with regard to the trait than more distant relatives, who share fewer genes. Comparisons involving various degrees of biological relationships will come up frequently in later chapters.

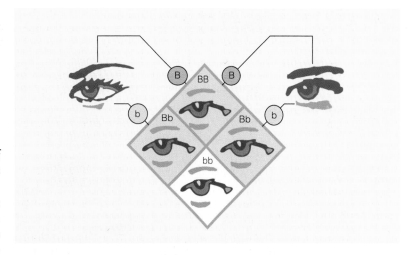

Figure 3.26 Dominant and recessive genes. This diagram shows how two brown-eyed parents (B) with a heterozygous genotype (Bb, denoting brown–blue) have a 25% chance of producing brown-eyed offspring who are homozygous (BB), a 50% chance of producing brown-eyed offspring who are heterozygous (Bb), and a 25% chance of producing blue-eyed offspring, who must be homozygous (bb), since blue eye color is recessive. The genetic bases for behavioral traits appear to be much more complex than the simple rules that govern eye color.

from 100% for identical twins down to a mean of 6.25% for second cousins (children of parents who are cousins).

Like chromosomes, genes operate in pairs, with one gene of each pair coming from each parent. In the simplest scenario, a single pair of genes determines a trait. Eye color provides a nice example. When both parents contribute a gene for the same color (called the *homozygous* condition), the child will have eyes of that color. When the parents contribute genes for different eye colors (the *heterozygous* condition) one gene in the pair, called the *dominant gene*, will override, or mask, the other, called the *recessive gene*. Thus, **a dominant gene is one that is expressed when paired genes are heterozygous (different). A recessive gene is one that is masked when paired genes are heterozygous.**

GENOTYPE VERSUS PHENOTYPE

It might seem that two parents with the same manifest trait, such as brown eyes, should always produce offspring with that trait. However, you can't count on this. For instance, two brown-eyed parents can produce a blue-eyed child (see Figure 3.26). This happens because there are unexpressed recessive genes in the family's gene pool—in this case, genes for blue eyes.

This brings us to the distinction between genotype and phenotype. **Genotype refers to a person's genetic makeup; phenotype refers to the ways in which a person's genotype is manifested in observable characteristics.** Different genotypes (such as two genes for brown eyes as opposed to one gene for brown and one for blue) can yield the same phenotype (brown eyes). Your genotype is determined at conception and fixed forever. In contrast, your phenotypic characteristics (hair color, for instance) may change over time. They may also be modified by your environment.

Genotypes translate into phenotypic characteristics in a variety of ways. Not all gene pairs operate according to the principles of dominance. In some instances, heterozygous gene pairs can produce a blend, an "averaged-out" phenotype. In other cases of heterozygous gene pairs, both characteristics show up phenotypically, as in the case of type AB blood.

POLYGENIC INHERITANCE

Most human characteristics appear to be **polygenic traits, characteristics that are influenced by more than one pair of genes.** For example, it appears that three to five gene pairs interactively determine skin color. Complex physical abilities, such as motor coordination, may be influenced by tangled interactions involving a great many pairs of genes. Most psychological characteristics that appear to be affected by heredity seem to involve complex polygenic inheritance.

Detecting Hereditary Influence: Research Methods

How do we disentangle the effects of genetics and experience in order to determine how heredity affects behavioral traits? Researchers have designed special types of studies to assess the impact of heredity. Of course, with humans we are limited to correlational rather than experimental approaches, as we can't manipulate genetic variables by assigning subjects to mate (this approach, called *selective breeding*, is used in animal studies). The three most important methods in human research are family studies, twin studies, and adoption studies.

FAMILY STUDIES

In *family studies,* researchers assess hereditary influence by examining blood relatives to see how much they resemble each other with regard to a specific trait. If heredity affects the trait under scrutiny, one should find phenotypic similarity among relatives. Furthermore, one should find more similarity among relatives who share more genes. For instance, siblings should exhibit more similarity than cousins (see Figure 3.25).

Illustrative of this method would be the numerous family studies conducted to assess the contribution of heredity to the development

Figure 3.27 Family studies of risk for schizophrenic disorders. First-degree relatives of schizophrenic patients have an elevated risk of developing a schizophrenic disorder (over 8% instead of the baseline 1% for unrelated people). Second- and third-degree relatives have progressively smaller elevations in risk for this disorder. Although these patterns of risk do not prove that schizophrenia is partly inherited, they are consistent with this hypothesis. (Adapted from data in Gottesman & Shields, 1982)

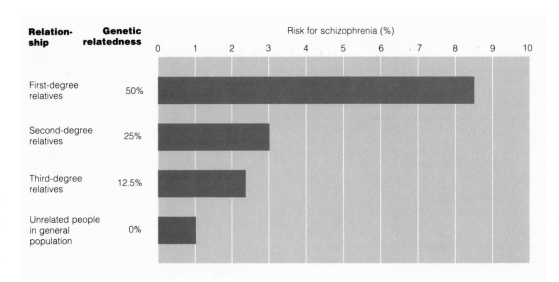

of psychological disorders. The results of many family studies of one such disorder, *schizophrenia*, are summarized in Figure 3.27. This severe mental illness strikes approximately 1% of the population. However, Figure 3.27 reveals that 8.5% of the first-degree relatives of schizophrenic patients exhibit schizophrenia themselves. Thus, first-degree relatives of a patient show an elevated risk for the disorder eight times higher than normal. This risk is greater than that observed for more distantly related, second-degree relatives, which is greater than that found for third-degree relatives. This pattern of results is consistent with the hypothesis that genetic inheritance influences the development of schizophrenic disorders (McGuffin & Reich, 1984).

Family studies can determine whether a trait runs in families. However, when family studies *do* show that a trait runs in families, this correlation does not provide conclusive evidence that the trait is due to the influence of heredity. Why not? Because family members generally share not only genes, but similar environments as well. Furthermore, closer relatives are more likely to live together than more distant relatives. Thus, genetic similarity and environmental similarity *both* tend to be greater for closer relatives. Either of these confounded variables could be responsible when greater phenotypic similarity is found in closer relatives. Family studies can provide useful insights about the possible impact of heredity, but they cannot provide definitive evidence.

TWIN STUDIES

Twin studies can provide better evidence about the possible role of genetic factors. In **twin studies, researchers assess hereditary influence by comparing the resemblance of identical twins and fraternal twins with respect to a trait.** The logic underlying this comparison is as follows. *Identical (monozygotic) twins* emerge from one zygote that splits for unknown reasons. Thus, they have exactly the same genotype; their genetic overlap is 100%. *Fraternal (dizygotic) twins* result when two eggs are fertilized simultaneously, forming two separate zygotes. Thus, fraternal twins are no more alike in genetic makeup than any two siblings born to a pair of parents at different times. Their genetic overlap averages 50%.

Fraternal twins provide a useful comparison to identical twins because in both cases, the twins *usually* grow up in the same home, at the same time, exposed to the same configuration of relatives, neighbors, peers, teachers, events, and so forth. Thus, both kinds of twins normally develop under equally similar environmental conditions, but identical twins share more genetic kinship than fraternal twins. Consequently, if sets of identical twins tend to exhibit more similarity in some trait than sets of fraternal twins, it's reasonable to infer that this greater similarity is probably due to heredity rather than environment. In a sense, fraternal twins serve as a control group in a "natural experiment," where the independent variable is the degree of genetic similarity (of course, this is not a true experiment, and the data are correlational).

Twin studies have been conducted to assess the impact of heredity on many different traits. Some representative results are summarized in Figure 3.28. The higher correlations found for identical twins indicate that they tend to be more similar to each other than fraternal twins on measures of general mental ability, special aptitudes, and personality (Loehlin & Nichols, 1976). These results support the notion that these traits are influenced to some degree by genetic makeup.

ADOPTION STUDIES

Adoption studies **assess hereditary influence by examining the resemblance between adopted children and both their biological and their adoptive parents.** Generally, adoptees are used as subjects in this type of study only if they were given up for adoption at a very early age and raised without having contact with their biological parents. The logic underlying the adoption study approach is quite simple. If adopted children resemble their biological parents with regard to a trait, even though they were not raised by them, this suggests that genetic factors influence that trait. In contrast, if adopted children resemble their adoptive parents, even though they inherited no genes from them, this reflects the influence of their shared environment.

In recent years, adoption studies have contributed to our understanding of how genetics and the environment influence intelligence. The research shows significant similarity between adopted children and their biological parents, as indicated by an average correlation of .36 in recent studies (Vandenberg & Vogler, 1985). Interestingly, however, adopted children resemble their adoptive parents nearly as much (average correlation of .31). These findings clearly indicate that both heredity and the environment influence intelligence. Hence, we can say with confidence that Sir Francis Galton was wrong when he concluded that intelligence was entirely inherited.

The Interplay of Heredity and Environment

We began this section by asking "Is it all in the genes?" When it comes to behavioral traits, the answer clearly is "No." What scientists find is that heredity and experience jointly influence many aspects of behavior. Moreover, their effects are interactive; they play off each other.

For example, consider what researchers have learned about the development of schizophrenic disorders. Although the evidence indicates that genetic factors influence the development of schizophrenia, it does *not* appear that anyone directly inherits the disorder itself. Rather, what people appear to inherit is a certain degree of *vulnerability* to the disorder (Zubin & Spring, 1977). Whether or not this vulnerability is ever converted into the disorder itself depends on each person's experiences in life. As we'll discuss in Chapter 14, certain types of experience seem to trigger the disorder in people who are more vulnerable to it.

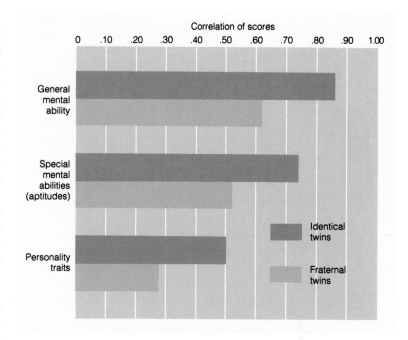

Figure 3.28 Twin studies of mental abilities and personality. Identical twins tend to be more similar than fraternal twins (as reflected in higher correlations) with regard to general mental ability, special aptitudes, and personality traits, suggesting that all these characteristics are influenced by heredity. (Data based on Loehlin & Nichols, 1976)

The interplay of heredity and environment is dramatically highlighted by complex behavioral traits that run in families—such as the acting prowess of the famous Barrymore clan. The Barrymores (shown here in a 1932 photograph) have produced several generations of film and stage stars, from the family patriarch, Maurice Barrymore, who took up acting in the 1870s, to young Drew Barrymore, one of the child stars of Steven Spielberg's *E.T.* a century later.

PUTTING IT IN PERSPECTIVE

Two of our six themes stand out in this chapter. First, as we just discussed, the entire chapter relates to how and why heredity influences behavior—in conjunction with the environment, of course (theme 5). Second, our frequent digressions on the special *methods* employed in research on the biological bases of behavior serve to emphasize that psychology is empirical (theme 1). Let's look at each of these points.

In Chapter 1, when it was first emphasized that heredity and environment jointly shape behavior, you may have been a little perplexed about how your genes could be responsible for your sarcastic wit or your interest in art. In fact, there are no genes for behavior per se. Experts do not expect to find genes for sarcasm or artistic interest, for example. Insofar as your hereditary endowment plays a role in your behavior, it does so *indirectly*, by molding the physiological machine that you work with. Thus, your genes influence your physiological makeup, which influences your personality, temperament, and intelligence, which influence your sense of humor, your interests, and a host of other behavioral traits.

Bear in mind, however, that genetic factors do not operate in a vacuum. Genes exert their effects in an environmental context. As research on schizophrenia demonstrates, the impact of our genetic makeup depends on our environment, and the impact of our environment depends on our genetic makeup. The interactive effects of heredity and environment become intertwined even before a child is born, during prenatal development. Once they are tangled together, there is no way to pry genetics and experience apart. All we can do is use our ingenuity to devise research strategies, such as twin or adoption studies, that allow us to estimate the relative contribution of heredity and environment to specific traits.

The empirical nature of psychology was apparent in our numerous discussions of the special research methods used to study the physiological bases of behavior. As you know, the empirical approach depends on precise observation. If you can't observe and measure something, you can't study it empirically. Thus, when Hans Berger devised a way to monitor brain activity with the EEG, he made it possible for scientists to explore all sorts of new questions about the brain and mental activity. Similarly, when Hodgkin and Huxley figured out a way to measure electric currents in squid axons, it was a major breakthrough that led to rapid progress in our understanding of the neural impulse.

Throughout this chapter, you've seen how investigators have come up with innovative methods to observe and measure elusive phenomena like electrical activity in the brain, neural impulses, neurotransmitter activity, brain function, cerebral specialization and the impact of heredity on behavior. The point is that empirical methods are the lifeblood of the scientific enterprise. When researchers figure out how to better observe something, their discovery usually facilitates major advances in our scientific knowledge. It's because of the crucial importance of observation that neuroscientists are currently excited about new brain-imaging techniques such as CAT scans, PET scans, and MRI scans.

The importance of empiricism will also be apparent in our upcoming Application, which looks at popular ideas about the special abilities of the right and left halves of the brain as they relate to cognitive processes. You'll see that it's important to learn to distinguish between scientific findings and conjecture based on those findings.

RIGHT BRAIN/LEFT BRAIN—TWO MODES OF THINKING?

Answer the following "true" or "false."

☐ **1.** Our right and left brains give us two minds in one.

☐ **2.** Each half of the brain has its own special mode of thinking.

☐ **3.** Some people are left-brained, while others are right-brained.

☐ **4.** The right hemisphere is the creative half of the brain.

☐ **5.** Our schools should devote more effort to teaching the overlooked right side of the brain.

Do we have two minds in one that think differently? Do some of us depend on one side of the brain more than the other? Is the right side of the brain neglected? Should we make more of an effort to exercise it? In recent decades, the apparent specialization in the right and left halves of the brain has been applied to a host of issues. The questions raised here are too complex to answer with a simple "true" or "false," but in this Application we'll take a close look at these provocative attempts to apply the findings on cerebral specialization. You'll learn that some of these ideas are plausible, but in many cases the hype has outstripped the real evidence.

Earlier, we described Roger Sperry's Nobel Prize winning research with "split-brain" patients, whose right and left hemispheres were disconnected (to reduce epileptic seizures), affording scientists a unique opportunity to study the special abilities of each hemisphere. The split-brain studies showed that the previously underrated right hemisphere had some special talents of its own. This discovery detonated an explosion of research on the functional specialization of the cerebral hemispheres.

Cerebral Specialization and Cognitive Processes

Using a variety of methods, scientists have conducted thousands of studies on neurologically intact individuals and compiled mountains of data on the special abilities of the right and left hemispheres. These findings have led to extensive speculation about how the right and left brains might be related to cognitive processes. Some of the more intriguing ideas include the following:

1. *Many theorists have concluded that the two hemispheres are specialized to process different types of cognitive tasks* (Edwards, 1979; Ornstein, 1977). The findings have been widely interpreted as showing that the left hemisphere handles verbal tasks, including language, speech, writing, math, and logic, while the right hemisphere handles nonverbal tasks, including spatial problems, music, art, fantasy, and creativity. These conclusions have attracted a great deal of public interest. For example, Figure 3.29 is an artist's depiction that was printed in *News-week* magazine showing how the brain supposedly divides its work.

2. *Some theorists believe that each hemisphere has its own independent stream of consciousness* (Bogen, 1969; Pucetti, 1981). For instance, Joseph Bogen has asserted, "Pending further evidence, I believe that each of us has two minds in one person" (Hooper & Teresi, 1986, p. 221). Supposedly, this duality of consciousness goes largely unnoticed because of the considerable overlap between the experiences of each independent mind. Ultimately, though, the apparent unity of consciousness is but an illusion. According to some versions of this theory, the two streams of consciousness alternate in the control of overt behavior, sometimes waging a battle for control.

3. *Some theorists also assert that the two hemispheres have different modes of thinking* (Galin, 1974; Bradshaw & Nettleton, 1981). According to this notion, the documented differences between the hemispheres in dealing with verbal and nonverbal materials are due to more basic differences in

Figure 3.29 A popular magazine's oversimplified depiction of hemispheric specialization in the brain.

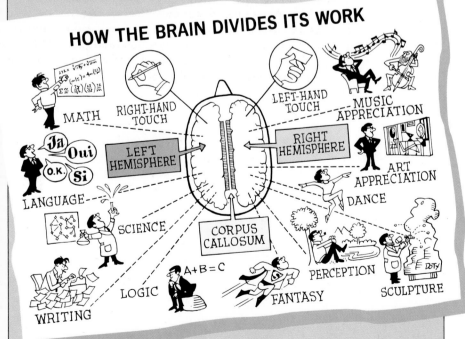

HOW THE BRAIN DIVIDES ITS WORK

Figure 3.30 The yin and yang of experience: proposed differences in thinking modes of left and right hemispheres.

 MODE

 MODE

Verbal: Using words to name, describe, define

Analytic: Figuring things out step by step and part by part

Symbolic: Using a symbol to stand for something; for example, the drawn form ◖●◗ stands for eye, and the sign ＋ stands for the process of addition

Abstract: Taking out a small bit of information and using it to represent a whole thing

Temporal: Keeping track of time; sequencing one thing after another, doing first things first, second things second, and so forth

Rational: Drawing conclusions based on reason and facts

Digital: Using numbers as in counting

Logical: Drawing conclusions based on logic: one thing following another in logical order—for example, developing a mathematical theorem or a well-stated argument

Linear: Thinking in terms of linked ideas, one thought directly following another, often leading to a convergent conclusion

Nonverbal: Showing an awareness of things, but minimal connection with words

Synthetic: Putting things together to form wholes

Concrete: Relating to things as they are at the present moment

Analogic: Seeing likenesses between things; understanding metaphoric relationships

Nontemporal: Being without a sense of time

Nonrational: Not requiring a basis of reason or facts; willing to suspend judgment

Spatial: Seeing where things are in relation to other things and how parts go together to form a whole

Intuitive: Making leaps of insight, often based on incomplete patterns, hunches

Holistic: Seeing whole things all at once; perceiving the overall patterns and structures, which often leads to divergent conclusions

how the hemispheres process information. This theory holds that the left hemisphere handles verbal material well is because it is analytic, abstract, rational, logical, and linear. In contrast, the right hemisphere is thought to be better equipped to handle spatial and musical material because it is synthetic, concrete, nonrational, intuitive, and holistic. These proposed differences between the hemispheres in modes of thinking are summarized in Figure 3.30.

4. *Some theorists further propose that people vary in their reliance on one hemisphere as opposed to the other* (Bakan, 1971; Zenhausen, 1978). Allegedly, some people are "left-brained." Their greater dependence on their left hemisphere supposedly makes them analytic, rational, and logical. Other people are "right-brained." Their greater use of their right hemisphere supposedly makes them intuitive, holistic, and nonrational. Being right-brained or left-brained is thought to explain many personal characteris-

tics—such as whether you like to read, whether you're good with maps, or whether you enjoy music. This notion of "brainedness" has even been used to explain occupational choice. Supposedly, right-brained people are more likely to become artists or musicians, while left-brained people are more likely to become writers or scientists.

5. *Some educators have argued that schools should place more emphasis on teaching the right side of the brain* (Prince, 1978; Samples, 1975). "A real reform of the educational system will not occur until the individual teachers learn to understand the true duality of their students' minds," says Thomas Blakeslee (1980, p. 59). Those sympathetic to his view assert that our schools overemphasize logical, analytic left-hemisphere thinking (required by English, math, and science courses) while shortchanging intuitive, holistic right-hemisphere thinking (required by art and music). After considering the implications of the notion of brainedness, these educators have con-

cluded that modern schools turn out an excess of left-brained graduates. They advocate curriculum reform to strengthen the right side of the brain.

Complexities and Qualifications

The ideas just outlined are the source of considerable debate among psychologists and neuroscientists. They're intriguing ideas, and they clearly have captured the imagination of the general public. However, the research on cerebral specialization is complex, and *these ideas have to be qualified very carefully* (Corballis, 1980; Kinsbourne, 1982; Levy, 1985). Let's examine each point.

1. There *is* ample evidence that the right and left hemispheres are specialized to handle different types of cognitive tasks, *to a degree*. Doreen Kimura (1973) compared the abilities of the right and left hemispheres to quickly recognize letters, words, faces, and melodies in a series of perceptual asymmetry studies like those we described earlier. She found that the superiority of one hemisphere over the other was usually quite modest, as you can see in Figure 3.31, which shows superiority ratios for four cognitive tasks. In a neurologically intact person, the hemispheres don't work alone. For instance, the right hemisphere doesn't shut down entirely so the left hemisphere can read a book by itself. Most tasks probably engage *both* hemispheres, albeit to different degrees. For instance, imagine that you are asked the following question: "In what direction are you headed if you start North and make two right turns and a left turn?" In answering this question, you're confronted with a *spatial* task that should engage the right hemisphere, but first you have to process the wording of the question, a *language* task that should engage the left hemisphere.

Furthermore, there are differences among people in patterns of cerebral specialization (Springer & Deutsch, 1984). For some unknown reason, some people display little hemispheric specialization. That is, their hemi-

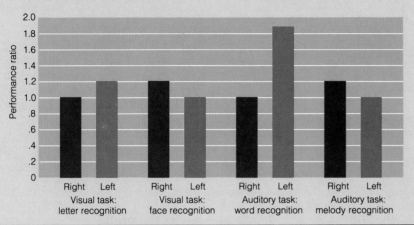

Figure 3.31 Relative superiority of one brain hemisphere over the other in studies of perceptual asymmetry in normal subjects. The performance ratios show the degree to which one hemisphere was "superior" to the other on each type of task. For example, the right hemisphere was 20% better than the left hemisphere in quickly recognizing melodic patterns (ratio 1.2 to 1). Most differences in the performance of the two hemispheres are quite small. (Data from Kimura, 1973)

spheres seem to have equal abilities on some types of tasks. Others even reverse the usual specialization, so that verbal processing might be housed in the right hemisphere. These unusual patterns are especially common among left-handed people. Figure 3.32 shows the results of a study that tested for the localization of speech in 140 right-handed and 122 left-handed subjects (Rasmussen & Milner, 1977). Little specialization (bilateral representation) was found in 15% of the left-handers, and a reversal of the usual specialization (speech handled by the right hemisphere) was found in another 15%. These variations in cerebral specialization are not well understood yet, but they indicate that there is no universal brain organization that is set in concrete.

Figure 3.32 Patterns of speech localization. Speech processing is usually localized in the left hemisphere, but left-handed people show more variety than right-handed people in cerebral specialization for this and other tasks. (Data from Rasmussen & Milner, 1977)

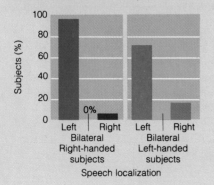

2. The evidence for the idea that we have separate streams of consciousness in each hemisphere is really very weak. There are clear signs of such duality *among split-brain patients*. But this duality probably is a unique by-product of the surgical disconnection of their cerebral hemispheres (Bradshaw, 1981). In fact, many theorists have been impressed by the degree to which even split-brain patients mostly experience *unity* of consciousness. There is little empirical basis for the idea that we all have two independent streams of awareness that are neatly housed in the right and left halves of the brain.

3. In contrast, there *is* extensive evidence supporting the notion that each hemisphere has its own mode of thinking—*if* one simply means that each hemisphere has its own *cognitive style* when its special abilities are engaged by certain kinds of tasks. However, there are important qualifications regarding this point. First, the differences between the hemispheres in cognitive style appear to be a matter of degree rather than either-or differences. Second, there is still a great deal of debate about the essence of these differing cognitive styles. Part of the problem is that aspects of cognitive style, such as analytic versus synthetic, or linear versus holistic, are difficult to define and measure (Brownell & Gardner, 1981).

4. The evidence on the assertion

that some people are left-brained while others are right-brained is inconclusive at present. This notion is plausible—*if* one means only that some people consistently display more activation of one hemisphere than the other. However, we need more research on these possible "preferences" in cerebral activation. The practical significance of any such preferences remains to be determined. At present, we do not have convincing data linking brainedness to musical ability, occupational choice, or the like.

5. The idea that we should reform our schools to better exercise the right side of the brain borders on nonsense. In neurologically intact people it is impossible to teach just one hemisphere at a time, and there is no empirical evidence that it is beneficial to "exercise" a part of the brain (Levy, 1985). There are many sound arguments for reforming our schools to encourage more holistic, intuitive thinking, but these arguments have nothing to do with cerebral specialization.

In summary, the theories linking cerebral specialization to cognitive processes are highly speculative. There's nothing wrong with theoretical speculation. Unfortunately, the tentative, conjectural nature of these ideas about hemispheric specialization has gotten lost in the popular magazine descriptions of research on our right and left brains. Commenting on this popularization, Hooper and Teresi (1986, p. 223) note, "A widespread cult of the right brain ensued, and the duplex house that Sperry built grew into the K-Mart of brain science. Today our hairdresser lectures us about the Two Hemispheres of the Brain." Cerebral specialization is an important and intriguing area of research. However, it is unrealistic to expect that the hemispheric divisions in the brain will provide a biological explanation for every dichotomy or polarity in modes of thinking. Thus, the popular fuss over right and left brains may be a bit premature. There still is much to be learned about the functional organization of the human brain.

THE BIOLOGICAL BASES OF BEHAVIOR

KEY IDEAS

Communication in the Nervous System

• Behavior depends on complex information processing in the nervous system. Cells in the nervous system receive, integrate, and transmit information. Neurons are the basic communication links. They normally transmit neural impulses along an axon to a junction with another neuron. These junctions are called synapses.

• The neural impulse is a brief change in a neuron's electrical charge that moves along an axon. The neural impulse is an all-or-none event, but neurons convey information about the strength of a stimulus by variations in the rate of neural firing.

• Action potentials trigger the release of chemicals called neurotransmitters that diffuse across a synapse to communicate with other neurons. Transmitters bind with receptors in the postsynaptic cell membrane, causing graded excitatory or inhibitory PSPs. Whether the postsynaptic neuron fires a neural impulse depends on the balance of excitatory and inhibitory PSPs occuring at the time. There are a variety of neurotransmitters that bind at specific sites according to a lock-and-key model.

• Transmitter activity in humans is usually measured indirectly. The first transmitter identified was acetylcholine, which has recently been implicated as a factor in Alzheimer's disease. Disturbances in the activity of bioamine transmitters has been related to the development of bipolar mood disorder and schizophrenia. GABA appears to be involved in the regulation of anxiety. Endorphins may work primarily as neuromodulators; in any case, these morphinelike substances play a role in the body's response to pain.

Organization of the Nervous System

• The nervous system can be divided into the central nervous system and the peripheral nervous system. The central nervous system consists of the brain and spinal cord. The spinal cord plays a critical role in distributing signals between the brain and the peripheral nervous system. The brain plays a critical role in virtually all aspects of behavior.

• The peripheral nervous system consists of the nerves that lie outside the brain and spinal cord. It can be subdivided into the somatic nervous system, which connects to muscles and sensory receptors, and the autonomic nervous system, which connects to blood vessels, smooth muscles, and glands. The autonomic nervous system mediates the largely automatic arousal that accompanies emotion and the fight-or-flight response to stress.

Looking Inside the Brain: Research Methods

• Neuroscientists use a variety of methods to investigate brain-behavior relations. The EEG can record broad patterns of electrical activity in the brain. Ablation and lesioning involve removing or destroying a piece of the brain, respectively. Another technique involves electrical stimulation of an area in the brain to activate that area. In recent years, new brain-imaging procedures have been developed, including MRI scans, CAT scans, and PET scans.

The Brain and Behavior

• There are three major regions in the brain: the hindbrain, midbrain, and forebrain. The hindbrain handles essential functions such as breathing, circulation, coordination of movement, and the rhythm of sleep and arousal. The midbrain is involved in the control of voluntary movements and the sleep-arousal cycle.

• The forebrain, the largest region of the brain, includes many structures that handle higher functions. The thalamus is primarily a relay station. The hypothalamus is involved in the regulation of basic biological drives such as hunger and sex, and links the brain to the autonomic nervous system and the endocrine system. The limbic system is a network of structures involved in emotion, motivation, and memory.

• The cerebrum, which is divided into right and left hemispheres joined by the corpus callosum, is the brain area implicated in most complex mental activities. The cortex is the convoluted outer layer, which is subdivided into four areas. These areas (and their primary known functions) are the occipital lobe (vision), the parietal lobe (touch), the temporal lobe (hearing), and the frontal lobe (movement of the body).

Right Brain/Left Brain: Cerebral Specialization

• After the identification of Broca's area and Wernicke's area as speech-language centers, accumulating evidence that the left hemisphere usually processes language led scientists to view it as the dominant hemisphere. This view began to change in the 1960s with the advent of split-brain research.

• Split-brain studies such as our Featured Study, revealed that the right and left halves of the brain have their unique talents, with the right hemisphere specialized to handle visual-spatial functions. Studies of perceptual asymmetries, EEG patterns, and other indicators of brain function have provided extensive evidence of cerebral specialization in neurologically normal people.

The Endocrine System: Another Way to Communicate

• The endocrine system consists of the glands that secrete hormones, which are involved in the regulation of basic bodily processes. The control centers for the endocrine system are the hypothalamus and the pituitary gland.

Heredity and Behavior: Is It All in the Genes?

• The basic units of genetic transmission are genes housed on chromosomes. Genes operate in pairs, and sometimes one is dominant over the other. Although some characteristics are determined by a single pair of genes, most complex behavioral qualities appear to involve polygenic inheritance.

• Researchers assess hereditary influence on a trait through a variety of methods, including family studies, twin studies, and adoption studies. All of these methods attempt to sort out the influence of genetics as opposed to the environment. The preponderance of evidence indicates that most behavioral qualities are influenced by a complex interaction between heredity and environment.

Putting It in Perspective

• Two of our unifying themes stand out in this chapter. First, we saw how heredity interacts with experience to govern behavior by molding the physiological apparatus that executes our behavior. Second, we saw how methodological innovations often lead to progress in understanding behavior, underscoring the empirical nature of psychology.

Application: Right Brain/Left Brain— Two Modes of Thinking?

• Split-brain research stimulated speculation about relations between cerebral specialization and cognitive processes. Some theorists believe that each hemisphere has its own stream of consciousness and mode of thinking, which are applied to specific types of cognitive tasks. Some also believe that people vary in their reliance on the right and left halves of the brain and that schools should work more to exercise the right half of the brain.

• The cerebral hemispheres are specialized for handling different cognitive tasks, but there's also variability among people in patterns of specialization. Evidence for duality in consciousness divided along hemispheric lines is weak, and evidence on brainedness is inconclusive. The two hemispheres may indeed vary in cognitive style, but this conclusion has to be qualified carefully. There is no empirical evidence that it helps to exercise a hemisphere of the brain. Thus, popular ideas about the right and left brain have leapt far beyond actual research findings.

KEY PEOPLE

Alan Hodgkin & Andrew Huxley
James Olds & Peter Milner
Candace Pert & Solomon Snyder
Roger Sperry & Michael Gazzaniga

KEY TERMS

Ablation
Absolute refractory period
Action potential
Adoption studies
Afferent fibers
Agonist
Antagonist
Aphasia
Autonomic nervous system
Axon
Blood-brain barrier
Central nervous system (CNS)
Cerebral cortex
Cerebral hemispheres
Cerebrospinal fluid (CSF)
Chromosomes
Corpus callosum
Dendrites
Dominant gene
Efferent fibers
Electrical stimulation of the brain (ESB)
Electroencephalograph (EEG)
Endocrine system
Endorphins
Excitatory PSP
Family studies
Forebrain
Genes
Genotype
Glia
Hindbrain
Hormones
Hypothalamus
Inhibitory PSP
Lesioning
Limbic system
Midbrain
Motor neurons
Myelin sheath
Nerves
Neuromodulators
Neurons
Neurotransmitters
Parasympathetic division
Peripheral nervous system
Phenotype
Pituitary gland
Polygenic traits
Postsynaptic potential (PSP)
Recessive gene
Resting potential
Reuptake
Sensory neurons
Soma
Somatic nervous system
Split-brain surgery
Stereotaxic instrument
Sympathetic division
Synapse
Synaptic cleft
Terminal buttons
Thalamus
Twin studies
Zygote

CHAPTER FOUR

SENSATION AND PERCEPTION

With Michael W. Levine
University of Illinois at Chicago

Sensation and Perception

Take a look at Figure 4.1. What do you see?

You probably answered "a rose" or "a flower." But is that what you really *see*? No, this isn't a trick question. Let's examine the odd case of "Dr. P." It shows that there's more to seeing than meets the eye.

Dr. P was an intelligent and distinguished music professor who began to exhibit some worrisome behaviors that seemed to be related to his vision. Sometimes he failed to recognize familiar students by sight, though he knew them instantly by the sound of their voices. Sometimes he acted as if he saw faces in inanimate objects, cordially greeting fire hydrants and parking meters as if they were children. On one occasion, reaching for what he thought was his hat, he took hold of his wife's head and tried to put it on! Except for these kinds of visual mistakes, Dr. P was a normal, talented man.

Ultimately Dr. P was referred to Oliver Sacks, a neurologist, for an examination. During one visit, Sacks handed Dr. P a fresh red rose to see if he would recognize it. Dr. P took the rose as if he were being given a model of a geometric solid rather than a flower. "About six inches in length," Dr. P observed, "a convoluted red form with a linear green attachment."

"Yes," Sacks persisted, "and what do you think it *is*, Dr. P?"

"Not easy to say," the patient replied. "It lacks the simple symmetry of the Platonic solids . . ."

"Smell it," the neurologist suggested. Dr. P looked perplexed, as if asked to smell symmetry, but he complied and brought the flower to his nose. Suddenly, his confusion cleared up. "Beautiful. An early rose. What a heavenly smell." (Sacks, 1987, pp. 13–14)

What accounts for Dr. P's strange inability to recognize faces and familiar objects by sight? There was nothing wrong with his eyes. He could readily spot a pin on the floor. If you're thinking that there *must* have been something wrong with his eyes, look once again at Figure 4.1. What you see *is* "a convoluted red form with a linear green attachment." It doesn't occur to you to describe it that way only because, without thinking about it, you instantly perceive that combination of form and color as a flower. This is precisely what Dr. P was unable to do. He could see perfectly well, but he was losing the ability to assemble what he saw into a meaningful picture of the world. Technically, he suffered from a condition called *visual agnosia*, an inability to recognize objects through sight. As Sacks put it, "Visually, he was lost in a world of lifeless abstractions. Indeed, he did not have a real visual world." (Sacks, 1987, p. 15)

As Dr. P's case illustrates, there is much more to your experience of the world than passively receiving information from your senses of sight, hearing, touch, taste, and smell. Everything you know about the world around you, everything you do, every move of your body, is based on information from your senses. But, without active processing of sensory input, you would experience not your familiar world, but a chaos of bewildering sensations.

To acknowledge this need to both take in and process information, psychologists distinguish between sensation and perception. **Sensation is the stimulation of sense organs.** *Perception* **is the selection, organization, and interpretation of sensory input.** Sensation involves the absorption of energy—such as light or sound waves—by sensory organs—such as the eyes and ears. Perception involves organizing and translating sensory input into something meaningful. For example, when you look at Figure 4.1, your eyes are *sensing* the light reflected from the page, including areas of low reflectance where ink has been deposited in an irregular shape. What you *perceive*, however, is a picture of a rose.

The distinction between sensation and perception stands out in Dr. P's case of visual agnosia. His eyes were doing their job of registering sensory input and sending neural impulses to the brain. However, damage in his brain interfered with his ability to organize or integrate this incoming information. Thus, Dr. P's process of visual *sensa-*

Figure 4.1 What do you *see*?

tion was intact, but his process of visual *perception* was severely impaired.

Dr. P's case is unusual, of course. Normally, the processes of sensation and perception are very difficult to separate because the brain automatically starts organizing incoming sensory stimulation the moment it arrives. The distinction between sensation and perception has been useful in helping to organize theory and research in this area, but in operation the two processes merge.

The active role played by our perceptual systems in our experience of the world makes the subject of sensation and perception particularly interesting to psychologists. As you'll discover in this chapter, the relationships between our perceived experience of the world and the objective, physical stimuli that affect our senses are highly complex. We'll begin our discussion by explaining some general concepts and methods that are important in the study of sensation and perception. Next, we'll examine individual senses, in each case beginning with the sensory aspects and working our way through to the perceptual aspects. The chapter's Application explores how principles of visual perception come into play in art and illusion.

PSYCHOPHYSICS: BASIC CONCEPTS AND ISSUES

As you may recall from Chapter 1, the first experimental psychologists were interested mainly in sensation and perception. They called their area of interest *psychophysics—the study of how physical stimuli are translated into psychological (sensory) experience.* A particularly important contributor to psychophysics was Gustav Fechner, who published a seminal work on the subject in 1860. Fechner was a German scientist working at the University of Leipzig, where Wilhelm Wundt later founded the first formal laboratory and journal devoted to psychological research. Unlike Wundt, Fechner was not a "campaigner" interested in establishing psychology as an independent discipline. However, his groundbreaking research laid the foundation that Wundt built upon.

Thresholds: Looking for Limits

Sensation begins with a *stimulus*, any detectable input from the environment. What counts as detectable, though, depends on who or what is doing the detecting. For instance, you might not be able to detect a weak odor that is readily apparent to your dog. Thus, Fechner wanted to know the answer to the following questions: For any given sense, what is the weakest detectable stimulus? For example, what is the minimum amount of light needed for a person to see that there is light?

Implicit in Fechner's question is a concept central to psychophysics: the threshold. **A threshold is a dividing point between energy levels that do and do not have a detectable effect.** For example, hardware stores sell a gadget with a photocell that automatically turns a lamp on when a room gets dark. The level of light intensity at which the gadget clicks on is its threshold.

An *absolute threshold* for a specific type of sensory input is the minimum amount of stimulation that an organism can detect. Absolute thresholds define the boundaries of an organism's sensory capabilities. Fechner used a variety of methods to determine human subjects' absolute threshold for detecting light. The *method of limits* involved flashing lights of dimmer and dimmer intensity, until subjects reported that they were unable to see the lights. Unfortunately, with this method, the subjects quickly learned what to expect on the next trial, and these expectations contaminated their reactions. Fechner's remedy for this problem was to present the test flashes in a random, unpredictable order. He called this the *method of constant stimuli.* Actually, the stimuli were not constant (each flash was of a different strength)—the subjects' *expectations* were held constant.

Using these and other methods, psychologists discovered that absolute thresholds were anything but absolute. There is no single stimulus intensity at which subjects jump from no detection to completely accurate detection. Instead, researchers found that as stimulus intensity increased, subjects' probability of responding to the stimulus *gradually* increased, as shown in Figure 4.2. Thus,

Figure 4.2 The absolute threshold. If absolute thresholds were truly absolute, then at threshold intensity the probability of detecting a stimulus would jump from zero to 100 percent, as in the graph on the left. In reality, the chances of detecting a stimulus increase gradually with stimulus intensity, as in the graph on the right. Accordingly, an "absolute" threshold is defined as the intensity level at which the probability of detection is 50%.

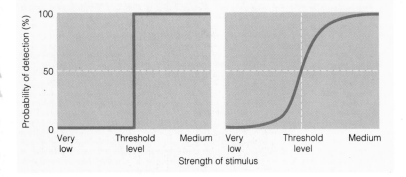

107

Table 4.1 Approximate Absolute Thresholds for Several Senses

SENSORY MODALITY	THRESHOLD
Vision	A candle flame at 30 miles on a dark, clear night
Hearing	The tick of a watch at 20 feet in a quiet room
Taste	One ounce of quinine sulfate in 250 gallons of water
Smell	One drop of perfume diffused throughout a six-room house
Touch	A bee's wing falling on the cheek from a distance of 1 centimeter

they had to arbitrarily define the absolute threshold as the *stimulus intensity detected 50 percent of the time.*

Using this definition, investigators found that under ideal conditions, our abilities to detect weak stimuli are greater than they expected. Some concrete examples of the absolute thresholds for various senses can be seen in Table 4.1. For example, on a clear, dark night, in the absence of other distracting lights, you could see the light of a candle burning 30 miles in the distance! Of course, we're talking about *ideal* conditions—you would have to go out to the "middle of nowhere" to find the darkness required to put this to a suitable test.

Weighing the Differences: The JND

Fechner and his contemporaries were also interested in how sensitive people were to differences between stimuli. **A *just noticeable difference* (JND for short) is the smallest difference in the amount of stimulation that a specific sense can detect.** The methods for measuring JNDs are the

"The method of just noticeable differences consists in determining how much the weights have to differ so that they can just be discriminated."

GUSTAV FECHNER

Table 4.2 Representative (Middle-Range) Values for the Weber Fraction for Various Senses

SENSORY MODALITY	WEBER FRACTION
Vision (brightness, white light)	1/60
Kinesthesis (lifted weights)	1/30
Pain (thermally aroused on skin)	1/30
Hearing (tone of middle pitch and moderate loudness)	1/10
Pressure (cutaneous pressure "spot")	1/7
Smell (odor of India rubber)	1/4

Source: Geldard, 1962

same as those used in measuring absolute thresholds. In fact, an absolute threshold is simply the just noticeable difference from nothing.

You might think that the JND would always have the same value for any given sense. For instance, what do you suppose is the smallest difference in weight that you can detect by lifting different objects? An ounce? Two ounces? Six ounces? As it turns out, the answer varies: it increases with the weight of the objects being compared. However, the smallest detectable difference is a fairly stable *proportion* of the weight of the original stimulus.

This proportion effect was first demonstrated in the early 1800s by Ernst Weber, Fechner's brother-in-law. Weber investigated how much heavier one weight must be than another for the difference to be detectable. He discovered that the JND varies with the magnitude of the stimuli being compared. Fechner later expressed Weber's findings as a general principle, which he called Weber's law. **Weber's law states that the size of a just noticeable difference is a constant proportion of the size of the initial stimulus.**

This constant proportion is called the *Weber fraction.* Weber's law applies not only to the perception of weight but to all the senses. However, different fractions apply to different types of sensory input, as you can see from Table 4.2. For example, the Weber fraction for lifting weights is approximately 1/30. That means that you should be just able to detect the difference between a 30 ounce (oz) weight and a 31 oz weight (the JND for 30 oz is 1 oz). If you started with a 90 oz weight, however, you would *not* be able to tell the difference between it and a 91 oz weight. The JND for 90 oz is 3 oz (1/30 of 90), so the second weight would have to be at least 93 oz for you to distinguish it as heavier. As stimuli increase in magnitude, it takes a larger difference in physical intensity to produce a JND. Although Weber's law does not apply with perfect precision, it provides a good approximation of our ability to detect the differences between sensory stimuli (Engen, 1971).

Psychophysical Scaling

If one light has twice the energy of another, do you necessarily perceive it as twice as bright? When asked to make this kind of judgment, you are being asked to *scale* the magnitude of sensory experiences. Although it might seem that our sensory experiences would correspond exactly to the differences in the stimuli that cause them, the truth turns out to be otherwise. To investigate the magnitude of his subjects' sensory experiences, Fechner used the JND as his unit of measurement.

Reasoning that the JND is the smallest unit of sensation, he represented the perceived magnitude of a sensation by how many JNDs it was above absolute threshold.

Figure 4.3 shows what Fechner found when he related the strength of the physical stimulus (plotted on the horizontal axis) to the expected magnitude of sensation (plotted in JNDs on the vertical axis). As stimulus intensity increases, it takes a greater difference in intensity to produce a JND, as predicted by Weber's law. Hence, the horizontal "steps" in the figure become wider, while the size of the upward jumps stays the same, since each JND presumably has the same sensory effect. The smooth curve drawn through the steps is Fechner's generalized description of the relationship between the intensity of a stimulus and our perception of its magnitude.

The merit of Fechner's approach to this problem has been questioned by S. S. Stevens (1956, 1957), but broadly speaking, other methods of scaling yield reasonably similar results. The important point is that both Fechner and Stevens found that our inner "measurements" of sensory experiences are not a simple linear function of the physical intensity of the stimuli. Instead, as stimuli become more intense, their *perceived* magnitude grows more slowly.

This principle is easy to illustrate. Imagine that you're in a dark room with a single lamp holding three bulbs of the same wattage. You turn the switch, and one bulb lights. After a dark room, that looks pretty impressive. Turn again, and a second bulb comes on. The amount of light is doubled, and the room is certainly brighter, but it does not seems twice as bright. Turn again, and all three bulbs are on. Although you just added as much light on the last turn as on the second, you may barely notice the difference. Thus, three equal increases in the amount of light produce progressively smaller differences in perceived brightness.

What all this means is that in the domain of sensory experience everything is relative. Our perceptions of the differences between stimuli depend on the relative intensities of the stimuli. For instance, your visual system looks mainly at light *contrast*, rather than absolute levels of light. This contrast perception is the reason a photograph looks the same in a dim room and in bright sunlight—we focus on contrasts of light reflectance, rather than absolutes.

Signal-Detection Theory

The notion that everything is relative applies not only to sensory scaling but to sensory thresholds as well. Building on concepts borrowed from radio engineering, **signal-detection theory proposes that sensory sensitivity depends on a variety of factors besides the physical intensity of a stimulus** (Swets, Tanner, & Birdsall, 1961).

What factors besides stimulus intensity does signal-detection theory take into account? One key factor is the "noise" in the system. As a concept, noise is much like the background static you may hear on your radio. Noise makes it harder to detect a signal. The noise in your sensory system is due to the ongoing, spontaneous firing of neurons, which never stops. Sensory inputs are superimposed on this ever-varying background of neural activity. Your detection of sensory input will depend, in part, on the level of noise (neural activity) in the system when the input occurs.

Signal-detection theory also attempts to account for the influence of "higher" mental processes on sensory sensitivity. When subjects are asked to detect weak visual stimuli, they have to decide whether they saw a dim flash or whether they just imagined it. Their responses will depend to some extent on the *criterion* they set for how

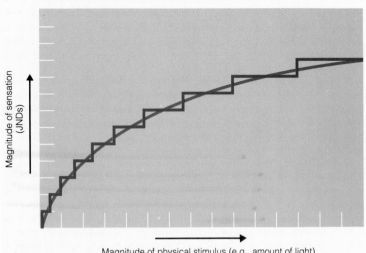

Magnitude of sensation (JNDs)

Magnitude of physical stimulus (e.g., amount of light)

Figure 4.3 Psychophysical scaling. Fechner reasoned that a "just noticeable difference" could be considered a unit of sensation and used Weber's law to find out the relationship between measured physical changes and measured sensation changes. Each upward jump in the figure is the same because it represents 1 sensation unit, but wider and wider "steps" are associated with each jump because larger and larger increases in physical intensity are needed to produce them.

Signal detection is the stock-in-trade of air-traffic controllers, who must continually identify new blips (signals) amidst the "noise" of constantly changing patterns on their radar screens. In part, their detections depend on higher-order mental processes—the criteria they use in deciding quickly whether a detection is "real."

sure they must feel before they respond "yes." The setting of this criterion involves higher mental processes rather than raw sensation. This criterion will depend on subjects' expectations and on the consequences of missing a signal or falsely reporting a signal that wasn't really there. Consider an example from the real world. If your neighborhood has experienced a rash of recent burglaries, your criterion for "hearing" mysterious noises outside your home will change.

The key point is that signal-detection theory replaces Fechner's sharp threshold with the concept of *detectability*, which is measured in terms of the probability of detection under specific circumstances. In comparison to classical models of psychophysics, signal-detection theory is better equipped to explain some of the complexities of perceived experience in the real world.

Sensory Adaptation

Sensory sensitivity is a complex matter that depends on a variety of factors. The process of sensory adaptation is yet another factor that influences our registration of sensory input. **Sensory adaptation involves a gradual decline in sensitivity to prolonged stimulation.** For example, let's say you find that the garbage in your kitchen has started to smell. If you stay in the kitchen without removing the garbage, the stench will soon start to fade. In reality, the stimulus of the odor is stable, but your *sensitivity* to it is decreasing.

Sensory adaptation is a pervasive aspect of everyday life. When you put your stockings on in the morning, you feel them initially, but the sensation quickly fades. If you jump reluctantly into a very cold swimming pool, you'll probably find that the water temperature feels fine in a few moments—after you *adapt* to it.

Sensory adaptation is an automatic, built-in process that keeps us tuned in to the *changes* rather than the *constants* in our sensory input. It allows us to ignore the obvious. After all, we don't need constant confirmation that our stockings are still on, but, like most organisms, we *are* interested in changes in our environment that may signal threats to our safety. Sensory adaptation shows once again that there is no one-to-one correspondence between sensory input and sensory experience.

The general points we've reviewed so far begin to suggest how complex the relationships are between the world outside and our perceived experience of it. As we review each of the principal sensory systems in detail, we'll see repeatedly that our experience of the world depends on both the physical stimuli that we encounter and our active processing of stimulus inputs. We begin our exploration of the senses with vision—the sense that most people think of as nearly synonymous with a direct perception of reality. The case is actually quite different, as you'll see!

OUR SENSE OF SIGHT: THE VISUAL SYSTEM

"Seeing is believing." Good ideas are "bright," and a good explanation is "illuminating." This section is an "overview."

Do you *see* the point? As these common expressions show, we are visual animals. We rely heavily on our sense of sight, and we virtually equate it with what is trustworthy (seeing is believing). Although we take it for granted, you'll see (there it is again) that our **visual system, or sense of sight,** is amazingly complex. Furthermore, as with all the senses, what we "sense" and what we "perceive" may be very different.

The Stimulus: Light

In order for us to see, there must be light. What is light? Light is a form of electromagnetic radiation that travels as a wave moving, naturally enough, at the speed of light. As Figure 4.4a shows, light varies in *amplitude* (the height of the waves) and

in *wavelength* (the distance between peaks of successive waves). Amplitude affects mainly our perception of brightness, and wavelength affects mainly our perception of color. The lights we normally see are mixtures of different wavelengths. Hence, light can also vary in its *purity* (how varied the mix is), which influences our perception of the saturation or richness of colors (saturation is difficult to describe, but if you glance ahead to Figure 4.12, you'll find it clearly illustrated). Of course, most objects we see do not emit light; they *reflect* light (the sun, lamps, and fireflies being some exceptions).

What most of us call light includes only the wavelengths that we humans can see. As shown in Figure 4.4b, that is only a slim portion of the total range of wavelengths. Like the other senses, vision is a filter that permits us to sense only a fraction of the real world. Other animals have capabilities that differ from ours, and so live in a

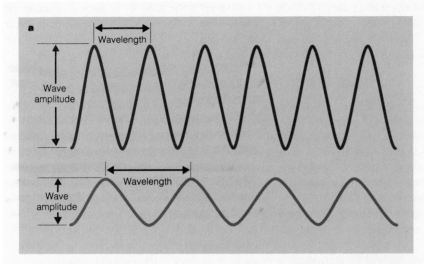

Figure 4.4 Light, the physical stimulus for vision. Light waves vary in amplitude and wavelength (**a**). Within the spectrum of visible light, amplitude (corresponding to physical intensity) affects mainly our experience of brightness. Wavelength affects mainly our experience of color, as we can see by letting white light (such as sunlight) pass through a prism: the prism separates the light into its component wavelengths, and we perceive a rainbow of colors (**b**). However, visible light is only the very narrow band of wavelengths to which our eyes happen to be sensitive. It thus represents a highly selective "window" onto the universe; if we had different sensory capabilities, we would experience a very different world.

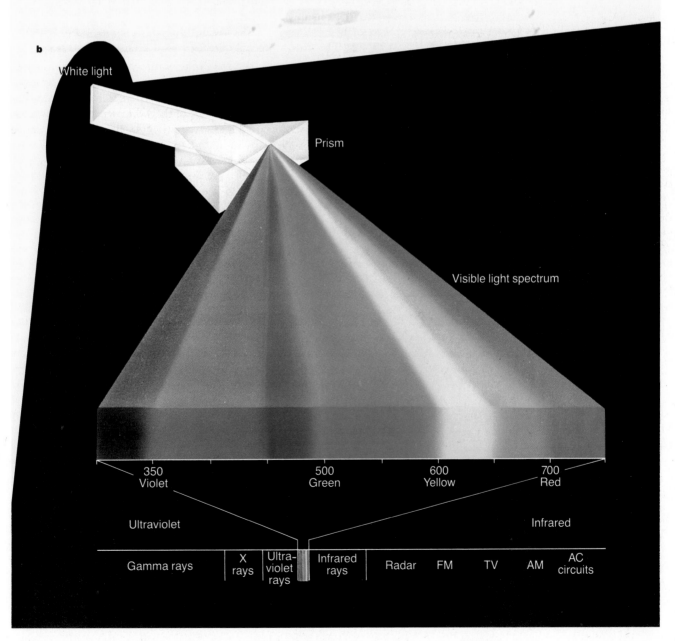

111

quite different visual world. Many insects can see shorter wavelengths than we can see, which we classify as *ultraviolet*. Many fish and reptiles can see longer wavelengths, which we classify as *infrared*.

Although our sense of sight depends upon light waves, for us to *see*, the incoming visual input must be transformed into neural impulses that are sent to the brain. Moreover, for us to see in any useful way, the brain must transform this information into meaningful patterns. The importance of this transformation was made painfully obvious to Dr. P when he began to lose his ability to recognize objects. Let's investigate how these transformations are accomplished.

The Eye: A Living Optical Instrument

Our eyes serve two main purposes: they channel light to the neural tissue that receives it, called the retina, and they house that tissue. The struc-

ture of the eye is shown in Figure 4.5. Each eye is a living optical instrument that creates an image of the visual world on the light-sensitive retina lining its inside back surface.

Light enters the eye through a transparent "window" at the front, called the *cornea*. The cornea and the crystalline *lens*, located behind it, form an upside-down image of objects upon the retina. It might seem disturbing that the image is upside-down, but the arrangement works. It doesn't matter how the image sits on the retina, as long as the brain knows the rule for relating positions on the retina to the corresponding positions in the world. The brain is constantly compensating for changes in the projection of the world upon the retina. For instance, this compensation accounts for the fact that when you cock your head to one side, the world doesn't seem to tilt.

The *lens* is the transparent eye structure that focuses the light rays falling on the retina. The

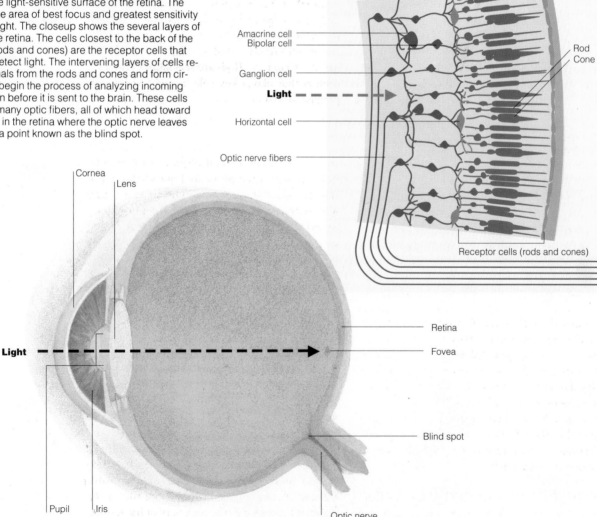

Figure 4.5 The human eye. The eye is a complex optical instrument and information-processing center. Light passes through the cornea, pupil, and lens and falls on the light-sensitive surface of the retina. The fovea is the area of best focus and greatest sensitivity to bright light. The closeup shows the several layers of cells in the retina. The cells closest to the back of the eye (the rods and cones) are the receptor cells that actually detect light. The intervening layers of cells receive signals from the rods and cones and form circuits that begin the process of analyzing incoming information before it is sent to the brain. These cells feed into many optic fibers, all of which head toward the "hole" in the retina where the optic nerve leaves the eye—a point known as the blind spot.

Detail of retina

Amacrine cell
Bipolar cell

Ganglion cell

Light

Horizontal cell

Optic nerve fibers

Rod
Cone

Receptor cells (rods and cones)

Cornea
Lens

Light

Retina
Fovea

Blind spot

Pupil
Iris

Optic nerve

lens is made up of relatively soft tissue, capable of adjustments that facilitate a process called accommodation. *Accommodation* occurs when the curvature of the lens adjusts to alter our visual focus. When we focus on closer objects, the lens gets fatter (rounder) in order to give us a clear image. The lens flattens out to give us a better image of distant objects.

The eye also makes adjustments to alter the amount of light reaching the retina. The *iris* is the colored ring of muscle surrounding the *pupil*, or black center of the eye. **The *pupil* is the opening in the center of the iris that helps regulate the amount of light passing into the rear chamber of the eye.** When the pupil constricts, it lets less light into the eye, but it sharpens the image falling on the retina. When the pupil dilates (opens), it lets more light in, but the image is less sharp. In bright light, our pupils constrict to take advantage of the sharpened image. Since there's plenty of light, we can afford to waste some. But in dim light, our pupils dilate. We sacrifice image sharpness to allow more light to fall on the retina so that we can see more.

The Retina: The Brain's Envoy in the Eye

The *retina* is the neural tissue lining the inside back surface of the eye; it absorbs light, processes images, and sends visual information to the brain. You may be surprised to learn that the retina *processes* images, but it's a piece of the central nervous system that happens to be located in the eyeball. Much as the spinal cord is a complicated extension of the brain (see Chapter 3), the retina is the brain's envoy in the eye. Although the retina is only a paper-thin sheet of neural tissue, it contains a complex network of specialized cells arranged in layers, as shown in Figure 4.5.

The axons that run from the retina to the brain course over the surface of the retina (yes, between the light and the retina) and converge on the spot where they exit the eye. At that point, all the fibers dive through a hole in the retina called the *optic disk* and emerge together from the back of the eye. Since the optic disk is a *hole* in the retina, you cannot see the part of an image that falls on it. It's therefore known as the *blind spot*. You may not be aware that you have a blind spot in each eye. Normally, each eye compensates for the blind spot of the other. You can find your blind spot (it's off center toward your nose) if you follow the instructions in Figure 4.6.

VISUAL RECEPTORS: RODS AND CONES
The retina contains millions of receptor cells that

are sensitive to light. There are two types of retinal receptor cells, called *rods* and *cones*. Their names are based on their shapes, as rods are elongated while cones are stubbier. **Cones are specialized visual receptors that play a key role in daylight vision and color vision.** Although rods outnumber cones by a huge margin—about 120 million to 7 million—the cones handle most of our daytime vision, because bright lights dazzle the rods. The special sensitivities of cones also allow them to play a major role in our perception of color. However, cones do not respond well to dim light. This is why we don't see color very well in low illumination. Nonetheless, cones provide better *visual acuity*—that is, sharpness and precise detail—than rods. **Rods are specialized visual receptors that play a key role in night vision and peripheral vision.** Rods handle night vision because they are more sensitive than cones to dim light.

Rods and cones are *not* uniformly distributed in the retina. Cones are concentrated most heavily in the center of the retina and quickly fall off in density toward its periphery. **The *fovea* is a tiny spot in the center of the retina that contains only cones; visual acuity is greatest at this spot.** When we want to see something sharply, we often move our eyes to center the object in the fovea.

The density of the rods is greatest just outside the fovea, and then the density gradually decreases toward the periphery of the retina. Because of the distribution of rods, when you want to see a faintly illuminated object in the dark, it's best to look slightly above or below the place it should be. Averting your gaze this way moves the image from the cone-filled fovea, which requires more light, to the rod-dominated area just outside the fovea, which requires less light. This trick of averted vision is well known to astronomers, who use it to study dim objects viewed through the eyepiece of a telescope. In addition to handling most of our night vision, the rods are responsible for most of our peripheral vision, since they're the dominant receptor in the periphery of the retina.

Figure 4.6 Demonstration of the blind spot. Close your right eye and stare steadily with your left eye at one detail of the approaching car. Vary the distance from the picture to your eye by moving the book slowly toward or away from you. If you're careful not to let your eye wander, at some point the stop sign will disappear. Its image will have fallen on your blind spot.

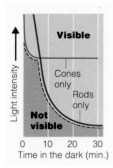

Figure 4.7 The process of dark adaptation. Visual sensitivity improves markedly during the first 5 to 10 minutes, as the eye's bright-light receptors (the cones) rapidly adapt to low levels of light. Further improvement comes from the rods, which are slower to adapt but capable of far greater visual sensitivity in low levels of light.

DARK AND LIGHT ADAPTATION

You've probably noticed that when you enter a dark theater on a bright day, you stumble about almost blindly. But within minutes you can make your way about quite well in the dim light. This adjustment is called *dark adaptation—the process in which the eyes become more sensitive to light in low illumination*. Figure 4.7 maps out the course of this process; the declining absolute thresholds over time indicate increasing visual sensitivity. As you can see, dark adaptation is virtually complete in about 30 minutes, with considerable progress occurring in the first 10 minutes. The curve consists of two segments because cones adapt more rapidly than rods.

When you emerge from a dark theater on a sunny day, you squint to ward off the overwhelming brightness, and the reverse of dark adaptation ensues. *Light adaptation is the process whereby the eyes become less sensitive to light in high illumination.* Like dark adaptation, light adaptation improves your visual acuity under the prevailing circumstances.

INFORMATION PROCESSING IN THE RETINA

In processing visual input, the retina transforms a pattern of light falling onto it into a very different representation of the visual scene. When light strikes the retina's receptors (rods and cones), it triggers neural signals that pass into the intricate network of cells in the retina. Signals move from receptors to bipolar cells to ganglion cells (consult Figure 4.5), which in turn send impulses along the optic nerve to the brain. **The *optic nerve* is a collection of axons from the retina that connect the eye with the brain.** These axons carry visual information, encoded as a stream of neural impulses, to the brain.

A lot of complex information processing goes on in the retina before visual signals are sent to the brain. Ultimately, the information from 127 million rods and cones converges to travel along "only" 1 million axons in the optic nerve. This means that the bipolar and ganglion cells in the intermediate layers of the retina receive, integrate, and compress signals from many receptors.

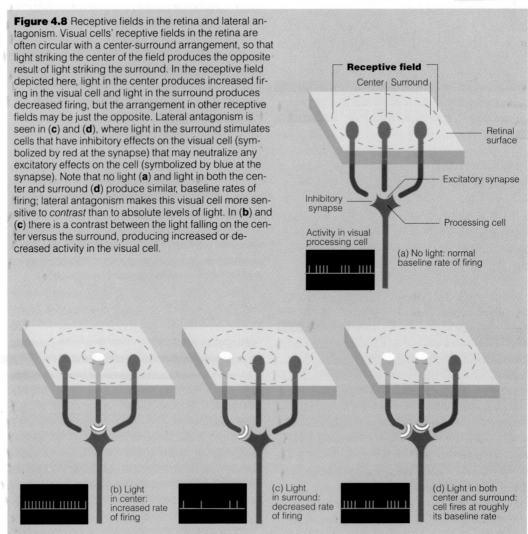

Figure 4.8 Receptive fields in the retina and lateral antagonism. Visual cells' receptive fields in the retina are often circular with a center-surround arrangement, so that light striking the center of the field produces the opposite result of light striking the surround. In the receptive field depicted here, light in the center produces increased firing in the visual cell and light in the surround produces decreased firing, but the arrangement in other receptive fields may be just the opposite. Lateral antagonism is seen in (**c**) and (**d**), where light in the surround stimulates cells that have inhibitory effects on the visual cell (symbolized by red at the synapse) that may neutralize any excitatory effects on the cell (symbolized by blue at the synapse). Note that no light (**a**) and light in both the center and surround (**d**) produce similar, baseline rates of firing; lateral antagonism makes this visual cell more sensitive to *contrast* than to absolute levels of light. In (**b**) and (**c**) there is a contrast between the light falling on the center versus the surround, producing increased or decreased activity in the visual cell.

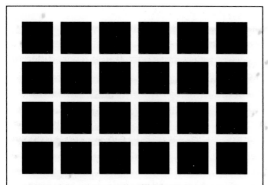

Figure 4.9 The Hermann grid. If you look at this grid, you will see dark spots at the intersections of the white bars, except in the intersection you're staring at directly. This illusion is due to lateral antagonism.

The collection of rod and cone receptors that funnel signals to a particular visual cell in the retina (or ultimately in the brain) make up that cell's *receptive field*. Thus, the **receptive field of a visual cell is the retinal area that, when stimulated, affects the firing of that cell**.

The receptive fields of visual cells come in a variety of shapes and sizes (Kuffler, 1953). Particularly common are circular fields with a center-surround arrangement (Enroth-Cugell & Robson, 1966), where light falling in the center has the opposite effect of light falling in the surrounding area (see Figure 4.8). For example, the rate of firing of a visual cell might be *increased* by light in the *center* of its field and *decreased* by light in the *surrounding area*, as Figure 4.8 shows. Other visual cells may work in just the opposite way. Either way, when receptive fields are stimulated, retinal cells send signals inward toward the brain and *laterally* (sideways) to nearby visual cells. These lateral signals, carried by the horizontal and amacrine cells (see Figure 4.5), allow visual cells in the retina to have interactive effects on each other.

Lateral antagonism is the most basic of these interactive effects. **Lateral antagonism occurs when neural activity in a cell opposes activity in surrounding cells.** Lateral antagonism is responsible for the opposite effects that occur when light falls on the inner versus outer portions of center-surround receptive fields (see Figure 4.8). Lateral antagonism was first described for a simple eye, in a horseshoe crab, by H. K. Hartline and Floyd Ratliff (1957). Lateral antagonism allows the retina to compare the light falling in a specific area (local lighting) against general lighting. This means that the visual system can compute the *relative* amount of light at a point, instead of reacting to *absolute* levels of light. This attention to *contrast* is exactly what we need if a photograph, for instance, is to look the same regardless of the

lighting conditions. If you look at Figure 4.9, you can demonstrate to yourself one perceptual effect of lateral antagonism.

Lateral antagonism is a critical process in vision that underlies a variety of visual phenomena (Levine & Shefner, 1981). Lateral antagonism can occur in various stages of visual processing—in two different layers of the retina, and again later, when signals reach the brain.

Vision and the Brain

Light falls on the eye, but you *see* with your brain. Although the retina does an unusual amount of information processing for a sensory organ, visual input is meaningless until it's processed in the brain.

VISUAL PATHWAYS TO THE BRAIN

How does visual information travel to the brain? Axons leaving the back of each eye form the optic nerves, which project to the visual areas of the brain along the pathways shown in Figure 4.10. As we discussed in Chapter 3, stimuli in the right visual field are registered in the left half of the retina in both eyes, while stimuli in the left visual field go to the right half of the retina in both eyes. Optic nerves from the left half of each retina come together at the *optic chiasm* and then project to the left side of the brain. Optic nerves from the right half of each retina meet at the optic chiasm and then carry their signals to the right side of the brain.

Figure 4.10 Visual pathways to the brain. Light from each side of the visual field strikes the opposite side of the retina in each eye, sending neural impulses along the optic nerve fibers. The nerve fibers from each eye meet at the optic chiasm, but the signals from each eye are not combined until a later stage of processing. Signals from the left side of each retina are combined in the lateral geniculate (not shown) and sent to the primary visual cortex in the left hemisphere. Signals from the right side of each retina are combined and sent to the visual cortex in the right hemisphere.

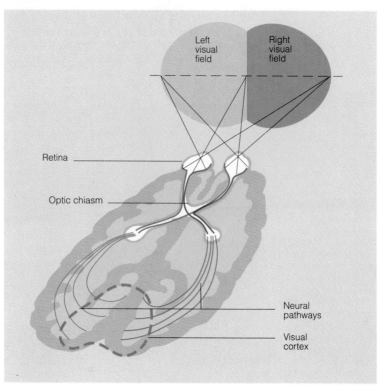

In each half, or hemisphere, of the brain, the optic nerves project into an area of the thalamus. The thalamus is a major relay station where visual signals are processed once again. From here, most visual information is shuttled to the occipital lobe of each hemisphere in the brain. The areas in the occipital lobes that handle the initial cortical processing of visual input make up the *primary visual cortex*.

PROCESSING IN THE VISUAL CORTEX

The cells in the visual cortex communicate with each other extensively in a rich processing network (Gilbert and Wiesel, 1985). The way these cortical cells respond to light once posed a perplexing problem. Researchers investigated the question by placing microelectrodes in the visual cortex of animals to record action potentials from individual cells. They would flash spots of light in the retinal receptive fields that the cells were thought to monitor, but there was rarely any response.

According to David Hubel and Torsten Wiesel (1962, 1963), they discovered the solution to this mystery quite by accident. One of the projector slides they used to present a spot to a cat had a crack in it. The spot elicited no response, but when they removed the slide, the crack moved through the cell's receptive field, and the cell fired like crazy for the moving dark line! It turns out that cortical cells don't really respond much to little spots—they are much more sensitive to lines, edges, and other more complicated stimuli. Armed with slides that had light and dark lines, rather than spots, Hubel and Wiesel embarked on years of painstaking study of the visual cortex (see Figure 4.11). Their work eventually earned them a Nobel Prize in 1981.

Hubel and Wiesel (1962, 1979) identified three major types of visual cells in the cortex, which they called simple cells, complex cells, and hypercomplex cells. *Simple cells* are quite specific about what stimuli will make them fire. A simple cell responds best to a line of the correct width, oriented at the correct angle, and located in the correct position in its receptive field. *Complex cells* also care about width and orientation, but they respond to any position in their receptive fields. Some complex cells are most responsive if a line sweeps across their receptive field—but only if it's moving in the "right" direction. *Hypercomplex cells* are particularly fussy about the length of a stimulus line.

An interesting aspect of this is that the cells in the visual cortex seem to be highly specialized. These cortical cells have been characterized as *feature detectors,* **neurons that respond selectively to very specific features of more complex stimuli.** Ultimately, most visual stimuli could be represented by combinations of lines such as those registered by these feature detectors. Some theorists believe that these feature detectors are registering the basic building blocks of visual perception and that we somehow assemble these into a coherent picture of complex stimuli. Other theorists think that this model is too simple to explain the immense range of our visual capabilities (Levine & Shefner, 1981).

Viewing the World in Color

So far, we've considered only how the visual system deals with light and dark. Let's journey now into the world of color. On the one hand, you can see perfectly well without seeing in color—many animals get by with little or no color vision. There

"One can now begin to grasp the significance of the great number of cells in the visual cortex. Each cell seems to have its own specific duties."

DAVID HUBEL

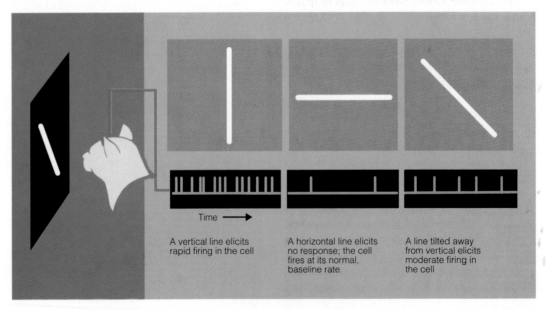

Figure 4.11 Hubel and Wiesel's procedure for studying the activity of neurons in the visual cortex of a cat. As the cat is shown various stimuli, a microelectrode records the firing of a neuron in the cat's visual cortex. The figure shows the electrical responses of a *simple cell* apparently "programmed" to respond to lines oriented vertically.

Time

A vertical line elicits rapid firing in the cell

A horizontal line elicits no response; the cell fires at its normal, baseline rate

A line tilted away from vertical elicits moderate firing in the cell

116

was a time when all photographs, movies, and TV shows were in black-and-white. On the other hand, color adds not only spectacle but information to our perceptions of the world. Emotionally, color clearly is important to many of us. We often spend a great deal of time deciding on the color of the sweater we're going to wear or the color of the car we're going to buy.

THE STIMULUS FOR COLOR

Perceived color is primarily a function of the wavelength of light. In the visible spectrum, lights with the longest wavelengths appear red, while those with the shortest appear violet. Notice the word *appear*. Color is our *psychological* interpretation; it's not a physical property of light itself.

Although wavelength wields the dominant influence, our perception of color depends on complex blends of all three properties of light. Wavelength is most closely related to hue, amplitude to brightness, and purity to saturation. These three dimensions of color are illustrated in the *color solid* shown in Figure 4.12.

As Figure 4.12 demonstrates systematically, we can perceive many different colors. Most of this diversity comes from *mixing* colors. There are two kinds of color mixture: subtractive and additive. You probably became familiar with subtractive mixing as a child by mixing yellow and blue paints to make green. **Subtractive color mixing works by removing some wavelengths of light, leaving less light than was originally there.** Instead of thinking of mixing paints, think of stacking filters. If you look through a sandwich of yellow and blue cellophane filters, they block out, or subtract, certain wavelengths. The middle wavelengths that are left look green.

Additive color mixing works by superimposing lights, putting more light in the mixture than in any one light by itself. If you shine a beam from a blue spotlight and one from a yellow spotlight on the same white surface, you'll have an additive mixture. What color is it? Not green, but very nearly *white*. Additive and subtractive mixtures of the same colors, then, produce different results.

White light actually includes the entire visible spectrum, as Isaac Newton demonstrated (and you can verify) by allowing white light to pass through a prism. Accordingly, when all wavelengths are mixed additively, they yield natural white light. The case is quite different when all colors are combined subtractively. This mixture yields black, as all light is eventually eliminated by the stacked filters (see Figure 4.13).

Our own processes of color perception parallel additive color mixing much more closely than

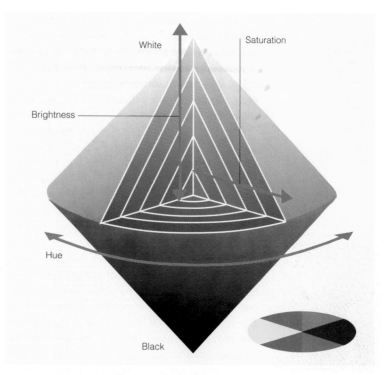

Figure 4.12 The color solid. This figure graphically represents the three dimensions of our experience of color: brightness (increasing from bottom to top of the solid), hue (changing around the solid's perimeter), and saturation (increasing toward the center of the solid). The inset shows the total hue range in relation to the part we can see in the cut-away portion of the solid.

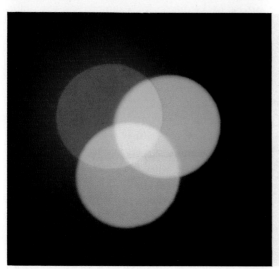

Figure 4.13 Color mixing. Additive color mixing is shown on the left, where red, green, and blue lights are combined, producing white at the intersection of all three colors. Subtractive color mixing is shown on the right, where red, yellow, and blue filters screen out varied portions of the spectrum, producing black at the intersection of all three colors.

117

subtractive mixing, which depends more on the physics of pigments than the psychology of perception. Insights into the principles of additive color mixing inspired the first major theory of color vision, the *trichromatic theory*, back in 1802. An alternative theory that became influential, *opponent process theory*, was proposed in 1878. These competing theories have been pitted against each other in extensive research for over a century. As you'll see, there is much to be learned from this theoretical debate, not only about perceptions of color but about the process by which psychology advances.

TRICHROMATIC THEORY OF COLOR VISION

By the beginning of the 19th century, investigators realized that any colored light could be matched by the additive mixture of three *primary colors:* red, green, and blue. Does it sound implausible that three colors should be adequate for creating all other colors? If so, consider that this is exactly what your color TV does. It fools you into seeing all the colors of a natural scene by mixing the three colors of red, green, and blue.

If all colors can be matched with additive mixtures of no more than three primaries, could it be that we have only three channels for color perception? This notion was first stated by Thomas Young in 1802, and modified slightly by Hermann von Helmholtz (1852) 50 years later. Their theory came to be known as the *Young-Helmholtz theory*, or the *trichromatic theory* of color vision (*tri* for "three," *chroma* for "color"). **The trichromatic theory of color vision proposes that the human eye has three types of receptors with differing sensitivities to different wavelengths.** According to this model, our perceptions of all colors are produced through combinations of activity by these three types of receptors.

Trichromatic theory meshes reasonably well with many of the known principles of color perception. For example, some aspects of *color blindness* suggest that we have a three-channel system for color vision. People who see a full range of colors are called *trichromats*, because they register all three color channels. Most people who are color blind are *dichromats*; that is, they make do with only two color channels.

There are three types of dichromats, who display three different defects in color perception (Le Grand, 1957). The three types of deficiencies seen among dichromats suggest that there are three channels for color vision, providing support for trichromatic theory. The most common type of dichromat has difficulty distinguishing red from green, seeing both as yellowish. Many other dichromats struggle to differentiate yellow and blue.

Color blindness is much more frequent in males than in females. We now know that most types of color blindness are due to errors or omissions at specific locations on the X chromosome (Nathans et al., 1986). Hence, color blindness usually is a sex-linked hereditary trait. Women who are not color blind themselves carry the gene for color blindness and may pass this visual defect on to their sons. Incidentally, complete blindness to differences in colors is quite rare. People with this condition are called *monochromats* because their vision operates in just one color channel, so they can't tell any colors apart.

OPPONENT PROCESS THEORY OF COLOR VISION

Although researchers found that the trichromatic theory explained some facets of color vision well, it ran aground in other areas. Nothing in the trichromatic theory explains why red looks redder against a green background than against a gray or yellow background, for example, or why blue looks bluer against yellow than against any other color. Notice that red-green and blue-yellow are **complementary colors—pairs of colors that, when mixed together, produce gray tones.** The various pairs of complementary colors are arranged in a color circle in Figure 4.14.

If you stare at a strong color and then look at a gray background, you'll see a colored **after-image—a visual image that persists after a stimulus is removed.** The color of the afterimage will be the complement of the color you originally stared at. You can demonstrate this for yourself by following the instructions in Figure 4.15. Trichromatic theory cannot account for the striking contrasts of complementary colors or for the appearance of complementary afterimages.

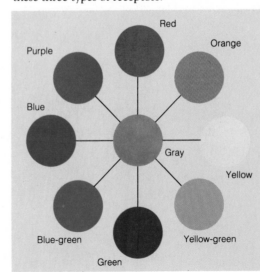

Figure 4.14 Complementary colors. We experience colors opposite each other on this color circle as complements, or "opposites." Additively mixing complementary colors produces gray. Opponent-process principles help to explain this effect as well as the other peculiarities of complementary colors noted in the text.

Figure 4.15 Demonstration of a complementary afterimage. Stare at the dot in the center of the flower for at least 60 seconds, and then quickly shift your gaze to the dot in the white rectangle. You should see an afterimage of the flower—but in complementary colors.

Here's another peculiarity to consider. If you ask people to describe colors, but restrict them to using three names, they run into difficulty. For example, using only red, green, and blue, they simply don't feel comfortable describing yellow as "reddish green." However, if you let them have just one more name, they usually choose to use yellow, and then they can describe any color quite well (Boynton & Gordon, 1965). This is not just a peculiarity of the English language; all cultures that describe colors require at least *four* basic names (Ratliff, 1976). If we reduce colors to three channels, why do we require four different color names?

In an effort to answer questions such as these, Ewald Hering proposed the *opponent process theory* of color vision in 1878. The **opponent process theory of color vision holds that color is perceived in three channels, where an either-or response is made to pairs of antagonistic colors.** Like trichromatic theory, opponent process theory allows for three channels, but it suggests that each channel has two modes of operation. One channel is red versus green, the second is yellow versus blue, and the third is black versus white. The antagonistic processes in this theory provide plausible explanations of things such as complementary colors in afterimages and the need for four names (red-green and blue-yellow) to describe colors. Opponent process theory also explains some aspects of color blindness. For instance, it can explain why it's red-green or blue-yellow that dichromats typically find indistinguishable.

RECONCILING THEORIES OF COLOR VISION

Advocates of trichromatic theory and opponent process theory argued about the relative merits of their models for about a century. Most researchers assumed that one theory must be wrong and one must be right. In recent decades, however, it's become clear that *it takes both theories to explain color vision.*

Eventually a physiological basis for both theories was found. Researchers showed that, consistent with the trichromatic theory, *the eye has three types of cones*, each type being most sensitive to a different band of wavelengths, as shown in Figure 4.16 (Marks, Dobelle, & MacNichol, 1964; Wald & Brown, 1965). In light bright enough to suppress the activity of the rods, the three cone types

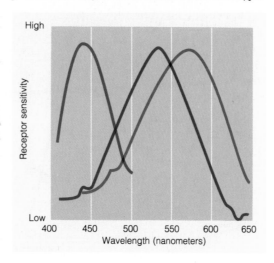

Figure 4.16 The relative sensitivities of three kinds of cones to different wavelengths of light. Notice (1) the amount of overlap in the areas covered by the curves (for example, a light of wavelength 475, which we experience as a bluish-green, excites all three types of cones about equally) and (2) the differences in the wavelengths to which each type of cone is *most* sensitive.

represent the three color channels predicted by the trichromatic theory.

Researchers also discovered a biological basis for opponent processes. They found visual cells in the retina and thalamus *that respond in opposite ways to complementary colors* (DeValois, Abramov, & Jacobs, 1966). For example, some of these cells are excited by green and inhibited by red. Others work in just the opposite way, as predicted in opponent process theory.

Our perception of color appears to involve sequential stages of information processing. The receptors that do the first stage of processing seem to follow the principles outlined in trichromatic theory. In later stages of processing, cells in the retina and visual cortex seem to follow the principles outlined in opponent process theory. As you can see, vigorous theoretical debate about color vision produced a solution that went beyond the contributions of either theory alone. We will return to this demonstration of the value of theoretical diversity at the end of the chapter.

Perceiving Forms and Patterns

The drawing in Figure 4.17 is a poster for a circus act involving a trained seal. Take a good look at it. What do you see?

If you tried the experiment, you probably saw a seal balancing a ball on its nose and a trainer holding a fish and a whip. But suppose you're told that the drawing is actually a poster for a costume ball. What do you see this time?

If you focused on the idea of a costume ball (stay with it a minute if you still see the seal and trainer), you probably saw a costumed man and woman. She's handing him a hat, and he has a

sword in his right hand (look again if you didn't see them on your own). This tricky little sketch was made ambiguous quite intentionally. It's a *reversible figure, a drawing that is compatible with two different interpretations that can shift back and forth*.

The point of this demonstration is simply this: *exactly the same sensory input can result in radically different perceptions*. There is no one-to-one correspondence between sensory input and what we perceive. *This is a principal reason why our experience of the world is subjective*. Perception involves much more than passively receiving signals from the outside world. Perception involves imposing organization on these signals. We *interpret* sensory input.

As reversible figures show, our interpretations of the same input can be quite different. These variations are influenced by many factors. In this case, you saw two different "realities" because your *expectations* were manipulated. Information given to you about the drawing created a *perceptual set—a readiness to perceive a stimulus in a particular way*. A perceptual set creates a certain slant in how we interpret sensory input.

Thus, to understand how we perceive forms, patterns, figures, and objects, we need to find out how we *organize* and *interpret* visual input. Several influential approaches to this question emphasize *feature analysis*.

FEATURE ANALYSIS: ASSEMBLING FORMS

The information received by our eyes would do us little good if we couldn't recognize objects and forms—ranging from words on a page to mice in our cellar and friends in the distance. This was exactly the fate that befell Dr. P. As you recall, Dr. P could "see" perfectly well and yet could not make sense out of the world because he was unable to translate what he saw into the recognition of objects and faces. Even without visual defects, form perception can be challenging. For example, professors reading essay exams routinely complain about having difficulty recognizing the letter forms that make up their students' handwriting.

According to some theories (Lindsay & Norman, 1977; Selfridge, 1959), our perceptions of form and pattern entail *feature analysis—a process in which we detect specific elements in visual input and assemble these elements into a more complex form*. In other words, we start with the components of a form, such as lines, edges, and corners, and build from them perceptions of squares, triangles, stop signs, bicycles, ice cream cones, and telephones. An application of this model of form perception is diagrammed in Figure

Figure 4.17 A poster for a trained seal act. Or is it? The picture is an ambiguous figure, which can be interpreted as either of two scenes.

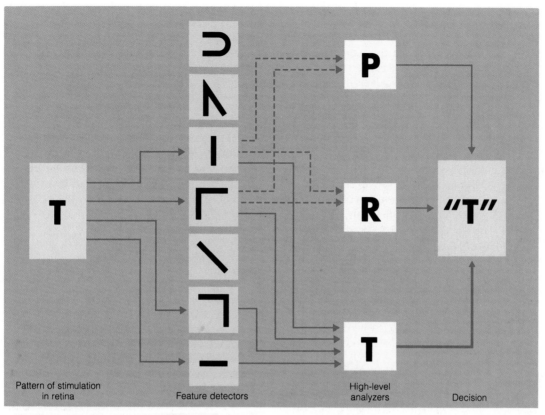

Figure 4.18 Feature analysis in form perception. How do we recognize forms from patterns of light falling on our retinas? One vigorously debated theory, suggested by the work of Hubel and Wiesel (see Figure 4.11), is that the brain has cells that respond to specific aspects or features of stimuli, such as lines and angles. Groups of neurons functioning as higher-level analyzers then respond to input from these "feature detectors." The more input each analyzer receives, the more active it becomes. Finally, another group of neurons weighs signals from these analyzers and makes a "decision" about the stimulus. In this way we arrive at the perception of a form by assembling its elements from the bottom up.

Pattern of stimulation in retina

Feature detectors

High-level analyzers

Decision

4.18. It shows how, in theory, we might recognize the letter T by registering and assembling the configuration of features that make up this letter.

Feature analysis assumes that form perception involves **bottom-up processing, a progression from elements to the whole.** The plausibility of this model was bolstered greatly when Hubel and Wiesel showed that cells in the visual cortex operate as highly specialized feature detectors. Indeed, their findings strongly suggest that at least some aspects of form perception involve feature analysis.

Can feature analysis provide a complete account of how we perceive forms? Probably not. A crucial problem for the theory is that form perception often does *not* involve bottom-up processing. There is ample evidence that our perceptions of form sometimes involve **top-down processing, a progression from the whole to the elements,** as our Featured Study illustrates.

Do we build some perceptions from the top down?

Studies of visual information processing typically present subjects with isolated stimuli (such as single letters) or unrelated stimuli (such as random strings of letters), but outside of the perception laboratory, stimuli are usually part of larger wholes. Using a letter-recognition task, this study examined the effects of telling subjects to pay attention to a stimulus as a whole.

Method

The subjects were 32 undergraduate students at the University of Pennsylvania. The stimuli were sets of four letters that were presented to subjects with a *tachistoscope*, a device that exposes

visual material on a screen for very brief intervals. On each presentation the subjects were told in advance that they would be asked to identify the letter that appeared in a particular position (in other words, they were asked to name the first, second, third, or fourth letter). The dependent variable was the subjects' accuracy in identifying the specified letter, after a very short exposure (about 35/1000 of a second).

Half of the subjects were shown displays consisting of four random letters (like S P B K). The other half of the subjects worked on the same task with sets of letters that formed words. Thus, a display might be either W O R K or W O R D, for

Investigators: James C. Johnston and James L. McClelland (University of Pennsylvania)

Source: Perception of letters in words: Seek not and ye shall find. *Science, 184* (1974), 1192–1194.

example. On half of the trials, the subjects in both groups were instructed to focus their attention on the position where the critical letter would appear. On the other half of the trials, the subjects were told to fixate on the middle of the stimulus array and pay attention to the stimulus as a whole. After an extensive series of practice trials, the subjects' responses on 128 test trials were analyzed.

Results

The results are summarized in Figure 4.19, which shows subjects' average accuracy in each of the four conditions in the study. The results for subjects who saw unrelated letters can be seen on the right. These subjects were more accurate when they were instructed to focus on the position where the critical letter would appear than they were when they were instructed to view the stimulus as a whole. The results for the subjects who saw letters that made up words (shown on the left) were just the opposite. These subjects did better when they were instructed to focus on the stimulus array as a whole.

Discussion

The results for the subjects who worked with words were interesting. Normally, it's advantageous for subjects to focus their attention on the exact spot where a critical stimulus will be presented. The usual advantage for this strategy was observed for the subjects who saw random sets of letters. But the opposite pattern of results was observed when the stimuli consisted of words. The investigators noted, "As far as we know, this is the only case ever reported in which knowing what part of an array contains the relevant stimulus makes that stimulus harder to see" (p. 1193). The superiority of the instructions to focus on the whole suggests that we can perceive a word before its individual letters, and that we can identify the letters from a word faster and more accurately than we can read the letters separately.

Comment

The subjects who saw words clearly were depending on top-down processing, working from the whole (the word) to the elements (the letters). The results in the words (whole stimulus) condition show that top-down processing can be superior to bottom-up processing. It seems unlikely that bottom-up processing can account for our ability to rapidly process words in reading. If we depended exclusively on bottom-up processing in reading, we would have to analyze the features of each letter to recognize that letter and then assemble the letters into words. This would be a terribly time-consuming task for each word, and it would slow our reading speed to a snail's pace.

Many researchers have concluded that both top-down and bottom-up processing have their niches in perception. Moreover, the two different types of processing are not necessarily incompatible. Since this study, McClelland has proposed a model of reading that incorporates both bottom-up processing and top-down processing (McClelland & Rumelhart, 1981).

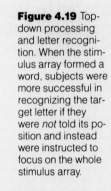
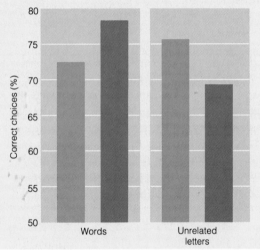

Figure 4.19 Top-down processing and letter recognition. When the stimulus array formed a word, subjects were more successful in recognizing the target letter if they were *not* told its position and instead were instructed to focus on the whole stimulus array.

Position condition

Whole-stimulus condition

Correct choices (%)

80 75 70 65 60 55 50

Words   Unrelated letters

LOOKING AT THE WHOLE PICTURE: GESTALT PSYCHOLOGY

Sometimes a whole, as we perceive it, may have qualities that don't exist in any of the parts. This insight became a basic tenet of *Gestalt psychology*, an influential school of thought that originally emerged out of Germany during the first half of this century. **Gestalt psychology was a theoretical orientation with a strong interest in perception that emphasized that the whole may be greater than the sum of its parts** (*Gestalt* is a German word for "form" or "shape").

A simple example of this principle, which you've experienced innumerable times, is the *phi phenomenon*, first described by Max Wertheimer

in 1912. **The phi phenomenon is the illusion of movement created by presenting visual stimuli in rapid succession.** We see examples of the phi phenomenon nearly every day. For example, movies and TV consist of separate still pictures projected rapidly one after the other. We *see* smooth motion, but in reality the "moving" objects merely take a slightly different position in successive frames. The same principle is illustrated by electric signs in which bulbs in a succession of positions flash in turn, like the arrows directing you to another lane at road-construction sites (see Figure 4.20). The bulbs going on and off with the appropriate timing give the impression of motion. Of course, nothing in the sign really moves; the

Figure 4.20 The phi phenomenon. The illusion of movement in a highway construction sign is an instance of the phi phenomenon, which is also at work in "motion pictures" and television. The phenomenon illustrates the Gestalt principle that the whole can have properties that are not found in any of its parts.

elements (the bulbs) are stationary. Working as a whole, however, they have a property (motion) that isn't evident in any of the parts.

ORGANIZING VISUAL INPUT: GESTALT PRINCIPLES

We have been assuming that it's simple to select out the forms in a visual display. But as the computer programmers who have tried to design robots with artificial vision have discovered, just deciding which features of a scene belong together and which are parts of other objects is a highly sophisticated task. The Gestaltists formulated a series of principles by which they believed the visual system sorts a scene into discrete forms. Let's examine some of these principles.

FIGURE AND GROUND Take a look at Figure 4.21. Do you see the figure as two silhouetted faces against a white background, or as a white vase against a black background? When you see the two faces, they appear to be solid, and to stand in front of the white; the border between black and white "belongs" to the faces. But if you switch to seeing the vase, the white stands solidly in front, "owning" the border.

This reversible figure illustrates the Gestalt principle of *figure and ground*. Dividing visual displays into figure and ground is a fundamental way in which we organize visual perceptions. The *figure* is the thing being looked at and the *ground* is the background against which it stands. The figure seems to have substance and appears to stand

out in front of the ground. Furthermore, the border separating figure and ground seems to belong to the figure, not the ground.

More often than not, your visual field may contain many figures sharing a background. The following Gestalt principles relate to how we group these elements into higher-order figures.

PROXIMITY Things that are near each other seem to belong together. The way in which you group the closer dots in Figure 4.22 illustrates the principle of proximity.

SIMILARITY We also tend to group stimuli that are similar. This principle is apparent in Figure 4.22, where we group elements of similar lightness into the number two.

CONTINUITY The principle of continuity reflects our tendency to follow in whatever direction we've been led. Thus we tend to psychologically connect points that result in a straight or gently curved line, as shown in Figure 4.22.

COMMON FATE Elements that move together tend to be grouped together, a principle called common fate by the Gestaltists. If you've ever seen clouds rushing by at two levels—low fast

"The fundamental 'formula' of Gestalt theory might be expressed in this way: There are wholes, the behaviour of which is not determined by that of their individual elements."

MAX WERTHEIMER

Figure 4.21 The Gestalt principle of figure and ground. Whether you see two faces or a vase depends on which part of this drawing you see as figure and which as background. Although this reversible drawing allows us to switch back and forth between two ways of organizing our perception, we can't perceive the drawing both ways at once.

Figure 4.22 Gestalt principles of perceptual organization. Gestalt principles help explain how we subjectively organize perceptions. *Proximity:* These dots might well be organized in columns (that is, top to bottom) rather than horizontal rows, but because of proximity (the dots are closer together horizontally), we tend to perceive rows. *Closure:* Even though the figure is incomplete, we organize it into a triangle. *Similarity:* Because of similarity of color, we see dots organized into the number 2 instead of a random array. *Simplicity:* We tend to see figure (**a**) as made up of the elements shown in the simplest alternative (**b**), instead of the more complex alternatives shown in (**c**) and (**d**), even though these could represent its structure equally well. *Continuity:* We tend to group these dots in a way that produces a smooth path rather than an abrupt shift in direction.

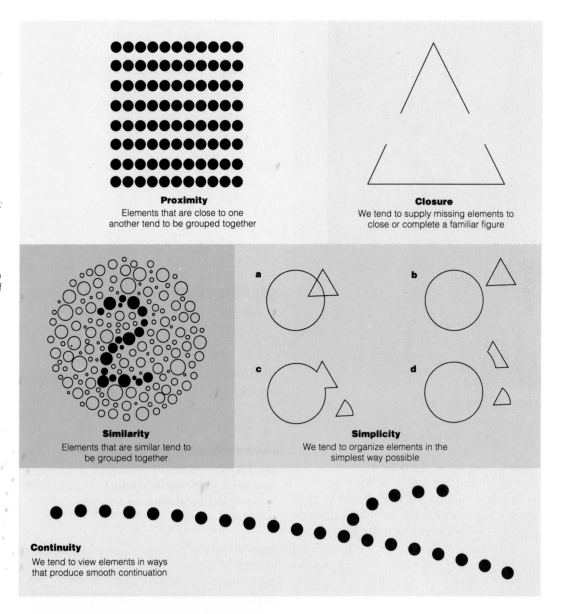

Proximity
Elements that are close to one another tend to be grouped together

Closure
We tend to supply missing elements to close or complete a familiar figure

Similarity
Elements that are similar tend to be grouped together

Simplicity
We tend to organize elements in the simplest way possible

Continuity
We tend to view elements in ways that produce smooth continuation

clouds and high slower-moving clouds—you know how distinctly the clouds at each level stand apart from each other.

CLOSURE We often group elements so that they create a sense of closure, or completeness. Thus, we may "complete" figures that actually have gaps in them (consult Figure 4.22 once again).

SIMPLICITY The Gestaltists' most general, but obscure, principle was the law of *pragnanz*, which translates from German as "good form." The idea is that we tend to group elements that combine to form a good figure. The principle is obscure in that it's difficult to spell out what makes a figure good. Some theorists maintain that goodness is largely a matter of simplicity, asserting that we tend to organize forms in the simplest way possible (see Figure 4.22 for an example).

FORMULATING
PERCEPTUAL HYPOTHESES

The Gestalt principles provide some indications of how we organize visual input. However, we're still one step away from understanding how these organized perceptions result in a representation of the real world. To understand the problem, we need to distinguish between two kinds of stimuli. **Distal stimuli are stimuli that lie in the distance (that is, in the world outside us).** In vision, these are the objects that you're looking at. They are "distant" in that your eyes don't touch them. What your eyes *do* "touch" are the images formed by patterns of light falling on your retinas. These images are the **proximal stimuli, the stimulus energies that impinge directly on your sensory receptors.** The distinction is important, because there are great differences between the object you perceive and the image by which you perceive it.

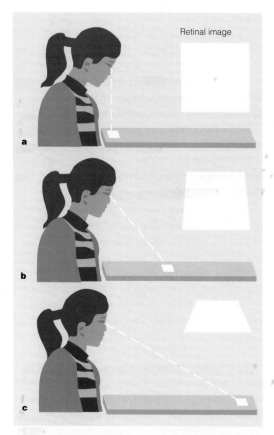

Retinal image

Figure 4.23 Distal and proximal stimuli. Proximal stimuli are often distorted, shifting representations of distal stimuli in the real world. If you look directly down at a small, square piece of paper on a desk (**a**), the distal stimulus (the paper) and the proximal stimulus (the image projected on your retina) will both be square. But as you move the paper away on the desktop (**b** and **c**), the square distal stimulus projects an increasingly trapezoidal image on your retina, making the proximal stimulus more and more distorted. Nevertheless, you continue to perceive a square.

In visual perception, the proximal stimuli are distorted, two-dimensional versions of their actual, three-dimensional counterparts. For example, consider the distal stimulus of a square. As shown in Figure 4.23, if a square object is lying on a desk at some distance from you, it is actually projecting a trapezoid (the proximal stimulus) on your retinas, because the top of the square is farther from your eyes than the bottom. Obviously, the trapezoid is a distorted representation of the square. If what we have to work with is so distorted a picture, how do we get an accurate view of the world out there?

One explanation is that we bridge the gap between distal and proximal stimuli by constantly making and testing *hypotheses* about what's out there in the real world. In effect, our perceptions of forms require us to make educated guesses about what forms could be responsible for a pattern of stimulation registered by our senses (Gregory, 1973). Thus, a **perceptual hypothesis is an inference about what distal stimuli could be responsible for the proximal stimuli sensed.** If the hypothesis is consistent with the proximal stimuli, it's accepted, and that is what we perceive. The square in Figure 4.23 may project a trapezoidal image on your retinas, but your perceptual system "guesses" correctly that it's a square—and that's what you see.

Let's look at another ambiguous drawing to fur-

ther demonstrate the process of making a perceptual hypothesis. Figure 4.24 is a famous reversible figure, first published as a cartoon in a humor magazine. Perhaps you see it as a drawing of a young woman looking back over her right shoulder. Alternatively, you might see it as an old woman with her chin down on her chest. The ambiguity exists because there isn't enough information to force your perceptual system to accept only one of these hypotheses.

If you can see only one of the women, you may be wondering where the other is. To guide you, Figure 4.25 shows unambiguous drawings of the young woman on the top and of the old woman on the bottom. Now you should be able to find either woman in Figure 4.24, and switch back and forth between them at will. You just needed some guidance as to how to make the other perceptual hypothesis. Incidentally, studies show that people who are led to *expect* the young woman or the old woman generally see the one they expect to see (Leeper, 1935). This is another example of how perceptual sets influence what we see.

Psychologists have used a variety of reversible figures to study how people formulate their perceptual hypotheses. Another example can be seen in Figure 4.26, which shows the *Necker cube*. The shaded surface can appear as either the front or the rear of the transparent cube. If you look at the

Figure 4.24 A famous reversible figure. What do you see?

Figure 4.25 Unambiguous drawings of the young and old woman in Figure 4.24.

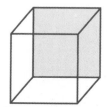

Figure 4.26 The Necker cube. The tinted surface can become either the front or the back of the cube.

top down

THE CHT

Figure 4.27 The effect of context on perceptual hypotheses.

cube for awhile, your perception will alternate between these possibilities. Later, in our Application on art and illusion, you'll see how M. C. Escher used the Necker cube to create a fascinating piece of art.

The *context* in which something appears often guides our perceptual hypotheses. To illustrate, take a look at Figure 4.27. What do you see?

You probably saw the words "THE CAT." But look again; the middle characters in both words are identical. You identified an "H" in the first word and an "A" in the second because of the surrounding letters, which created an expectation. This is another example of top-down processing in visual perception.

In summary, we go through life making "guesses" on the basis of proximal stimuli about what lies out there in the real world. The guessing process is largely automatic and we take it for granted. We have ample experience with most of the visual stimuli that we encounter, so our hypotheses are easily formulated and generally accurate. Nonetheless, it's sobering to realize that they are merely *hypotheses* and they can be wrong.

Perceiving Depth or Distance

More often than not, forms and figures are objects in space. Spatial considerations add a third dimension to visual perception. **Depth perception involves our interpretation of visual cues that tell us how near or far away objects are.** In essence, depth perception involves making inferences about distance. To make judgments of distance, we rely on two types of cues: binocular cues and monocular cues.

BINOCULAR CUES

We have a range finder built into our heads: two eyes set 6 to 7 centimeters apart. Because they're set apart, each eye has a slightly different view of the world. **Binocular cues are clues about distance that are obtained by comparing the differing views of the two eyes.** "Stereo" viewers like the Viewmaster toy you may have had as a child make use of this principle by projecting slightly different flat images of the same scene to each eye. The brain then supplies the "depth," and the viewer sees a three-dimensional scene.

To demonstrate the different views your eyes have, point at something across the room. Without moving your pointing arm, cover first one eye and then the other with your free hand. Your right eye should see you pointing to the left of the target, and your left eye should see you pointing to the right of it. If you are right on target with one eye and widely off with the other, you suffer from *stereoblindness*. This means that you make little or no use of binocular depth cues.

The principal binocular depth cue is *retinal disparity*. Objects within 25 feet project images to slightly different locations on your right and left retinas. Closer objects project to locations a little farther apart. These variations in retinal disparity give us information about distance (see Figure 4.28). Another binocular cue is *convergence*, which involves sensing your eyes converging toward each other as they focus on closer objects.

Binocular cues are really just frosting on the cake—you don't need them to see depth. If you cover one eye, the world does *not* collapse into a flat sheet. In fact, many people are *stereoblind* (perhaps you just discovered in the pointing test that you are one of them). Such people have to

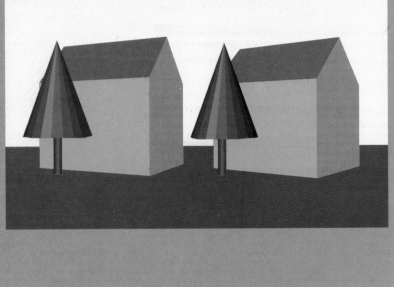

Figure 4.28 Retinal disparity and depth perception. Hold the edge of a piece of cardboard against your nose so that your left eye sees only the left drawing, and your right eye only the right. You should see two similar images floating about. Let them blend into one (it may help to concentrate on a particular point, such as the tip of the tree). When you succeed in superimposing the image, you should see a single image with a three-dimensional quality. This effect mimics the retinal disparity your brain uses to generate depth.

make do with monocular cues, which can provide adequate depth perception.

MONOCULAR CUES

Monocular cues are clues about distance that are obtained from the image in either eye alone. There are two kinds of monocular cues to depth. One kind involves active use of the eye in viewing the world. For example, when an object is close, you may sense the accommodation that must occur for the eye to adjust its focus. Similarly, if you cover one eye and move your head from side to side, closer objects appear to move more than distant objects.

The other kind of monocular cue is *pictorial*— a cue that can be given in a flat picture. There are many pictorial cues to depth, which is why paintings and photographs can seem so realistic that you feel you can climb right into them. Table 4.3 lists eight pictorial depth cues. Prominent pictorial cues include *texture gradient* (small details are too small to see when they are far away), *linear perspective* (lines converge in the distance), *interposition* (if an object comes between you and another object, it must be closer to you), *relative size* (closer objects appear larger), and *height in plane* (distant objects appear higher in the picture). Some of the monocular cues are illustrated in Figure 4.29. You can check your understanding of pictorial depth cues by following the instructions in Concept Check 4.1.

Table 4.3 Monocular Cues to Depth

1. Interposition	The shapes of near objects overlap or mask those of more distant ones.
2. Height in plane	Near objects are low in the visual field, more distant ones are higher up.
3. Texture gradient	A texture, such as the pattern of stones, is coarser for near areas and finer for more distant ones.
4. Relative size	If separate objects are expected to be of the same size, the larger ones are seen as closer.
5. Light and shadow	Patterns of light and dark suggest which objects are in front of which others.
6. Linear perspective	Parallel lines that run away from the viewer seem to get closer together.
7. Aerial haze	With distance, objects seem increasingly hazy and bluish in color.
8. Object familiarity	Objects that seem to be familiar are assumed to be their usual size.

Source: Ruch (1984)

Figure 4.29 Four monocular cues to depth. From top to bottom: interposition, light and shadow, linear perspective, and texture gradient. In most of our visual experience, several monocular cues are present at once. The world rarely looks "flat," even through only one eye.

Perceptual Constancies in Vision

When a person approaches you from the distance, the image of the person on your retinas gradually changes in size. Do you perceive that the person is growing right before your eyes? Of course not. Our perceptual system constantly makes allowances for this kind of variation in visual input. The task of the perceptual system is to provide an accurate rendition of distal stimuli based on distorted, ever-changing proximal stimuli. In doing

so, it relies in part on perceptual constancies. A *perceptual constancy* is a tendency to experience a stable perception in the face of continually changing sensory input.

We have already run into a perceptual constancy in vision, although we didn't label it as such. As you learned, the retina compares the light reflected from an object with the general illumination, registering contrast rather than the absolute level of light. This is why white paper looks white in sunlight, artificial light, or moonlight, even though the absolute amount of light falling on the retina is different in each situation. This stable perception of lightness in varied levels of illumination is called *lightness constancy*.

Size constancy refers to our tendency to view objects as stable in size even though the size of their images on the retina changes when they are viewed from different distances. This perceptual constancy explains why people approaching you aren't perceived as changing in size. Likewise, you perceive a car moving away from you as receding rather than shrinking.

The other major perceptual constancy in vision compensates for distortions due to the three-dimensional nature of the world. For example, it's responsible for your seeing a square as a square instead of as the trapezoid projected on your retinas. Stability in the perception of shapes, in spite of distortions in the proximal stimuli, is called, logically enough, *shape constancy*. It explains why we perceive a door, for instance, as the same shape, even though its retinal image changes drastically when it's opened and closed (see Figure 4.30).

Figure 4.30
Shape constancy. Trace the outline of the door with your finger, and notice how much the shape of this object changes as the door opens—yet we perceive the door as having a constant shape. This built-in talent for overriding sensory input creates stability in our perceptual world.

Imagine how bewildering our visual world would be if our perceptions were always exact reflections of frequently distorted and constantly changing proximal stimuli. Perceptual constancies help to impose some order on what would otherwise be chaos.

The Power of Misleading Cues: Optical Illusions

In general, perceptual constancies, depth cues, and principles of visual organization (such as the Gestalt laws) help us to view the world around us accurately. Sometimes, however, our perceptual systems make inappropriate assumptions. The result is a kind of erroneous perception called an *optical illusion*.

One of the most famous illusions, one that has appeared on cereal boxes and placemats the world over, is the *Müller-Lyer illusion*, which can be seen in Figure 4.31. The two vertical lines in this figure are equally long, but they certainly don't look that way. Why not?

Actually, it's likely that several mechanisms play a role in the illusion (Day, 1965; Gregory, 1978). The figure on the left looks like the outside of a three-dimensional, rectangular object, such as a booklet, thrust toward the viewer, while the one on the right looks like the inside of such an object thrust away (see Figure 4.32). The vertical line in the left figure therefore seems closer. If two lines cast equally long retinal images, but one seems closer, the closer one is assumed to be shorter. Thus, the Müller-Lyer illusion may be due largely to a combination of size constancy and misperception of depth.

These factors also seem critical to the *Ponzo illusion* (shown in Figure 4.33, along with a number of other heavily studied geometric illusions). The upper and lower horizontal lines are the same length, but the upper one appears longer. This probably occurs because the converging lines convey linear perspective, a key depth cue suggesting that the upper line lies farther in the distance. The Ponzo illusion and the other geometric illusions shown in Figure 4.33 demonstrate that visual stimuli can be highly deceptive.

Adelbert Ames designed a striking illusion that makes use of misperception of distance. It's called, appropriately enough, the *Ames Room*. It's a specially contrived room built with a trapezoidal rear wall and a sloping floor and ceiling (see Figure 4.34). When viewed from the correct point, as in the picture, it looks like an ordinary rectangular room. In reality, the left corner is much taller and much farther from the viewer than the right corner. Hence, bizarre illusions unfold in the Ames

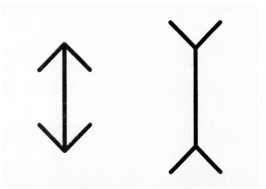

Figure 4.31 The Müller-Lyer illusion. Go ahead, measure them: The two vertical lines are equal in length.

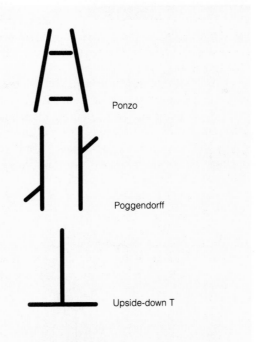

Figure 4.32 An example of the kind of visual experience that may give rise to the Müller-Lyer illusion. This illusion may occur because we impose a sense of depth on the lines and assume that one vertical line is closer than the other.

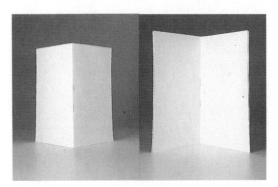

Zollner

Figure 4.33 Four geometric illusions. *Ponzo:* The horizontal lines are the same length. *Poggendorff:* The two diagonal segments lie on the same straight line. *Upside-down T:* The vertical and horizontal lines are the same length. *Zollner:* The long diagonals are all parallel (try covering up some of the short diagonal lines if you don't believe it).

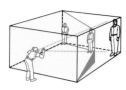

Figure 4.34 The Ames room. The diagram shows the room as it is actually constructed and as our brains construe it—as having a rectangular shape. Because of this reasonable perceptual hypothesis, the normal adjustments we make to preserve size constancy lead us into the bizarre perceptions described in the text. For example, naive viewers "conclude" that one man is much larger than the other, when in fact he is merely closer.

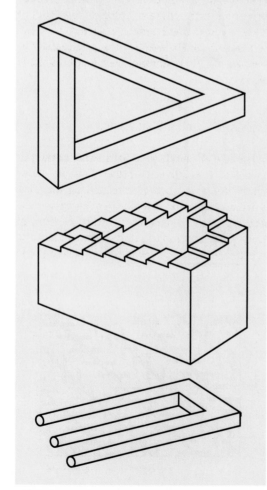

Figure 4.35 Three impossible figures. The figures are impossible, yet they clearly exist—on the page. What makes them impossible is that they appear to be three-dimensional representations, yet they are drawn in a way that frustrates our attempts to "assemble" their features into possible objects. It's difficult to see the drawings simply as lines lying in a plane—even though this perceptual hypothesis is the only one that resolves the contradiction.

room. People standing in the right corner appear to be giants, while people standing in the left corner appear to be midgets. Even more disconcerting, a person who walks across the room from right to left appears to shrink before your very eyes! The Ames room creates these misperceptions by toying with our perfectly reasonable perceptual hypothesis that the room is vertically and horizontally rectangular.

Impossible figures create another form of illusion. While these figures may look fine at first glance, a closer look reveals that they are geometrically inconsistent or impossible. Three of these impossible constructions are shown in Figure 4.35. Notice that specific portions of these figures are reasonable, but they don't add up to a sensible whole. The parts don't interface properly. The initial illusion that the figures make sense is probably due to bottom-up processing. We perceive specific features of the figure as acceptable, but are baffled as they are built into a whole. Our perceptual hypothesis about one portion of the figure turns out to be inconsistent with our hypothesis about another portion.

Obviously, illusions like the impossible figures and their real-life relative, the Ames room, involve a conspiracy of cues intended to deceive the viewer. Many visual illusions, however, occur quite naturally. A well-known example is the *moon illusion*. When overhead, the full moon appears to be much smaller than that huge harvest moon looming at the horizon. The illusion is so strong that many people find it hard to accept that neither the moon nor its image actually changes in size or distance from us. Like many of the other illusions we have discussed, the moon illusion is due mainly to misperception of distance (Kaufman & Rock, 1962). The moon illusion shows that optical illusions are part of everyday life. Indeed, many people are virtually addicted to an optical illusion—called television.

What do optical illusions tell us about visual perception? They drive home the point made earlier—that we go through life formulating perceptual hypotheses about what lies out there in the real world. The fact that we're only working with hypotheses becomes especially striking when our hypotheses are wrong, as they are when we see illusions. Optical illusions also show how context factors such as depth cues shape perceptual hypotheses. Finally, like ambiguous figures, illusions clearly demonstrate that our perceptions are *not* simple reflections of objective reality. Once again, we see that our perception of the world is subjective.

These insights do not apply to visual perception only. We will encounter these lessons again as we examine other sensory systems, such as hearing, which we turn to next.

OUR SENSE OF HEARING: THE AUDITORY SYSTEM

Stop reading for a moment, close your eyes, and listen carefully. What do you hear?

Chances are that if you concentrate on listening to your environment, you'll discover that you're immersed in sounds: street noises, a high-pitched laugh from the next apartment, perhaps some background music you put on a while ago but have long since ceased to be aware of. You might even hear a sound that you momentarily cannot place—and then you do (oh, that's the refrigerator motor). As this little demonstration shows, physical stimuli producing sound are present almost constantly, but we're not necessarily aware of these sounds.

Like vision, our **auditory system, or sense of hearing,** tells us about the world "out there," but not until we have actively processed incoming information. A distal stimulus—a screech of tires, someone laughing out loud, the hum of the refrigerator—produces a proximal stimulus in the form of sound waves reaching our ears. As in vision, our perceptual system must somehow transform this stimulation into the psychological experience of sound. To do so, our perceptual system must form a perceptual hypothesis about what is out in the world that could be producing the proximal stimulus. (What *is* that sound? Oh, the refrigerator.)

The Stimulus: Sound

Sound waves are vibrations of molecules, which means that they must travel through some physical medium, such as air. They move at a fraction of the speed of light. Sound waves usually are generated by vibrating objects, such as a guitar string, a loudspeaker cone, or your vocal cords, although they can also be generated by forcing air past a chamber (as in a pipe organ), or by suddenly releasing a burst of air (as when you clap).

Like light waves, sound waves are characterized by their *amplitude* (height), their *wavelength* (usually expressed by their *frequency*), and their *purity* (the extent to which they are a mixture of waves of different frequencies). The physical properties of amplitude, wavelength, and purity affect mainly the perceived (psychological) qualities of loudness, pitch, and timbre, respectively. However, the physical properties of sound interact in complex ways to produce our perceptions of these sound qualities.

Human Hearing Capacities

In the case of sound, we usually speak of the *frequency* of a sound wave rather than its wavelength. Since frequency is related to the time between peaks of successive waves, it measures the same property as wavelength does (see Figure 4.36). The frequency of a sound wave is measured in cycles per second, commonly called *hertz* (Hz).

Figure 4.36 Sound, the physical stimulus for hearing. Like light, sound travels in waves—in this case, waves of air pressure. A smooth curve similar to those shown earlier for light would represent a pure tone, like that produced by a tuning fork. Most sounds, however, are complex. For example, the wave shown here is for C played on a piano. The sound wave for the same note played on a violin would have the same wavelength (or frequency) as this one. But the "wrinkles" in the wave would be different, corresponding to the differences in timbre between the two sounds.

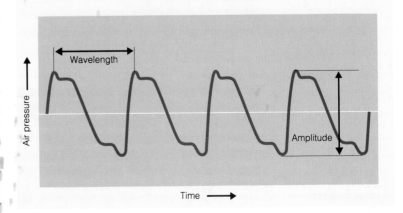

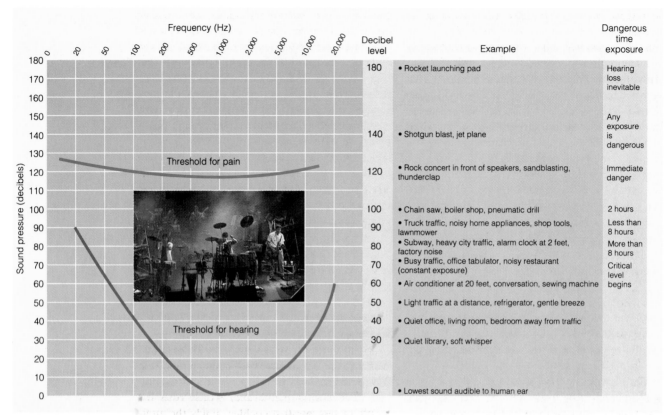

Figure 4.37 Sound pressure and auditory experience. Sound pressure, measured in decibels, interacts with frequency to produce different auditory effects. For example, the threshold for human hearing is a function of both decibel level and frequency. Our hearing is keenest for sounds at a frequency of about 1000 Hz; at other frequencies, it takes higher decibel levels to produce sounds we can detect (lower curve in graph). On the other hand, our threshold for pain is almost purely a function of decibel level (upper curve). Some common sounds corresponding to various decibel levels are listed to the right, together with the amount of time at which exposure to higher levels becomes dangerous.

For the most part, we perceive higher frequencies as having higher pitch. That is, if you strike the key for high C on a piano, it will produce higher-frequency sound waves than the key for low C. Although our perception of pitch depends mainly on frequency, the amplitude of the sound waves also influences pitch.

Just as the visible spectrum is only a portion of the total spectrum of light, so too we can hear only a portion of the available range of sounds. Humans can hear sounds ranging in frequency from a low of 20 Hz up to a high of about 20,000 Hz. Sounds at either end of this range are harder to hear, and sensitivity to high-frequency tones declines as adults grow older. Other organisms have different capabilities. Low-frequency sounds under 10 Hz are audible to homing pigeons, for example, while bats and porpoises can hear frequencies well above 20,000 Hz.

In general, the greater the amplitude of sound waves, the louder the sound we perceive. The range between the weakest sounds we can hear and the strongest we can tolerate is enormous. Whereas frequency is measured in Hertz, amplitude is measured in *decibels (dB)*. The decibel scale is logarithmic, so each increment of 10 dB represents a tenfold increase in amplitude. The relationship between decibels (which measure a physical property of sound) and loudness (a psychological quality) is complex, but a very approximate rule of thumb is that perceived loudness

doubles about every 10 decibels (Stevens, 1955). To make this less abstract, Figure 4.37 shows the approximate amplitude of the sound waves corresponding to various common sounds.

Very loud sounds can jeopardize the quality of your hearing. Even brief exposure to sounds over 120 decibels in amplitude can be painful and may cause damage to your auditory system (Henry, 1984). Because of this potential for pain and damage, the ground crews at airports must wear protective gear over their ears. Chronic exposure to sounds in the 90–120 dB range, often found in factories, mills, and other industrial settings, may also contribute to a gradual loss in hearing sensitivity. Exposure to excessive noise is the most common cause of constant "ringing in the ears," although there are other causes also.

As shown in Figure 4.37, the absolute thresholds for the weakest sounds we can hear are different for sounds of different frequencies. The human ear is most sensitive to sounds at frequencies between 1000 and 5000 Hz; that is, these frequencies yield the lowest absolute thresholds. Hence, amplitude is the principal determinant of loudness, but our perceptions of loudness ultimately depend on an interaction between amplitude and frequency.

We are also sensitive to variations in the complexity of sounds. The purest sound is one that has only a single frequency of vibration, such as that produced by a tuning fork. Most of the sounds we hear are complex mixtures of many frequencies. The purity or complexity of a sound influences how we perceive timbre, or the quality of a sound. To understand timbre, think of a note with precisely the same loudness and pitch played on a French horn and then on a violin. The difference you perceive in the sounds is a difference in timbre.

Sensory Processing in the Ear

Like your eyes, your ears channel energy to the neural tissue that receives it. Figure 4.38 shows that the human ear can be divided broadly into three sections: the external ear, the middle ear, and the inner ear. The way sound is conducted is different in each section. The external ear depends on the *vibration of air molecules*. The middle ear depends on the *vibration of movable bones*. The inner ear depends on *waves in a fluid*, which are finally converted into a stream of neural signals sent to the brain.

The *external ear* is largely made up of the *pinna*, a sound-collecting cone. When you cup your hand behind your ear to try to hear better, you are augmenting that cone. Many animals have large external ears that they can aim directly toward

a sound source, but we can adjust our aim only very crudely, by turning our heads. Sound waves collected by the pinna are funneled along the auditory canal as variations in air pressure. Ultimately, they strike the *eardrum*, a taut membrane that vibrates in response.

In the *middle ear*, the vibrations of the eardrum are transmitted inward by a mechanical chain made up of the three tiniest bones in your body (the hammer, anvil, and stirrup), known collectively as the *ossicles*. The ossicles form a three-stage lever system that converts relatively large movements with little force into smaller motions with greater force.

The *inner ear* consists largely of the **cochlea, a fluid-filled, coiled tunnel within the bone of your skull** (*cochlea* comes from the Greek word for a spiral-shelled snail, which this chamber resembles). Sound enters the cochlea through the *oval window*, which is vibrated by the bones in the middle ear. The ear's neural tissue, analogous to the retina in the eye, lies within the cochlea. This neural tissue sits on the basilar membrane that divides the cochlea into upper and lower chambers. **The basilar membrane, which runs the length of the spiralled cochlea, holds the auditory receptors, called hair cells.** Waves in the fluid of the inner ear stimulate the hair cells,

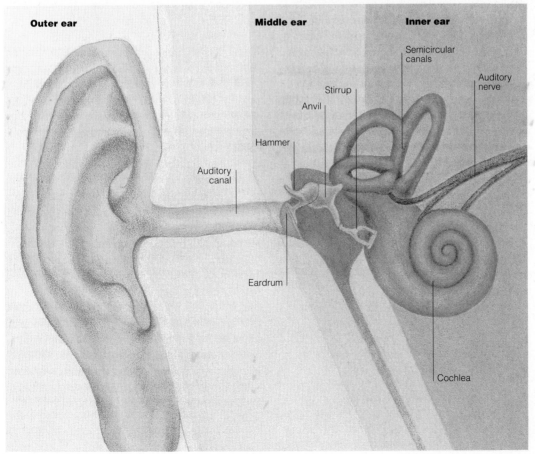

Outer ear **Middle ear** **Inner ear**

Semicircular canals

Auditory nerve

Stirrup

Anvil

Hammer

Auditory canal

Eardrum

Cochlea

Figure 4.38 The human ear. Converting sound pressure to information processed by the nervous system involves a complex relay of stimuli: Waves of air pressure create vibrations in the eardrum, which in turn cause oscillations in the tiny bones in the inner ear (the hammer, anvil, and stirrup). As they are relayed from one bone to the next, the oscillations are magnified and then transformed into pressure waves moving through a liquid medium in the cochlea. These waves cause the basilar membrane to oscillate, stimulating the hair cells that are the actual auditory receptors (see Figure 4.39). As we'll see later in the chapter, the semicircular canals, while anatomically part of the auditory system, are actually involved in our sense of balance rather than hearing (see Figure 4.45).

which, like the rods and cones in the eye, convert this physical stimulation into neural signals that are sent to the brain.

Explaining Auditory Perception: Theories of Hearing

Theories of hearing need to account for how we physiologically translate sound waves into our auditory perceptions of pitch, loudness, and timbre. To date, most of the theorizing about hearing has focused on the perception of pitch, which is reasonably well understood. Researchers' understanding of how we perceive loudness and timbre is primitive by comparison. Hence, we'll discuss loudness and timbre only very briefly, after reviewing how theories of pitch perception have evolved.

PLACE THEORY

There have been two influential theories of pitch perception: *place theory* and *frequency theory*. You'll be able to follow the development of these theories more easily if you can imagine the spiralled cochlea unraveled, so that the basilar membrane becomes a long, thin sheet, lined with about 25,000 individual hair cells (see Figure 4.39). Long ago, Hermann von Helmholtz (1863) proposed that different sound frequencies vibrate different portions of the basilar membrane, producing different pitches, just as plucking different strings on a harp produces sounds of varied pitch. This model, called **place theory, holds that our perception of pitch corresponds to the vibration of different portions, or places, along the basilar membrane.** Place theory assumes that hair cells at different places respond independently and that different sets of hair cells are vibrated by different sound frequencies. The brain then detects the frequency of a tone according to which area along the basilar membrane is most active.

FREQUENCY THEORY

Other theorists in the 19th century proposed an alternative theory of pitch perception, called *frequency theory* (Rutherford, 1886). **Frequency theory holds that our perception of pitch corresponds to the rate, or frequency, at which the entire basilar membrane vibrates.** This theory views the basilar membrane as being more like a drumhead than a harp. According to frequency theory, *all* of the membrane vibrates in unison in response to sounds. However, a particular sound frequency, say 3000 Hz, causes the basilar membrane to vibrate *at a corresponding rate* of 3000 times per second. The brain detects the frequency of a tone by the rate at which the auditory nerve fibers fire.

RECONCILING PLACE AND FREQUENCY THEORIES

The competition between these two theories of hearing is reminiscent of the dispute between the trichromatic and opponent-process theories of color vision. Like that argument, the debate between place and frequency theories generated roughly a century of research. Although both theories proved to have some flaws, *both turned out to be valid in part.*

Helmholtz's place theory was basically on the mark except for one detail. The hair cells along the basilar membrane are *not* independent; they vibrate together, as suggested by frequency theory. The actual pattern of vibration, predicted and observed by Georg von Bekesy (1947), is a traveling wave that moves along the basilar membrane. Place theory is correct, however, in that the wave *peaks* at a particular place, depending on the frequency of the sound wave. Interestingly, a process analogous to lateral antagonism in vision helps the auditory system to determine the place of maximum vibration along the basilar membrane (Weiss, 1964).

Frequency theory was also found to be flawed when investigators learned that neurons were hard-pressed to fire at a maximum rate of about 1000 impulses per second. How, then, could frequency theory account for the translation of 3000 Hz or 10,000 Hz sound waves, which would require 3000 or 10,000 impulses per second? The answer, suggested by Wever and Bray (1937), is that *groups* of hair cells operate according to the volley principle. **The volley principle holds that groups of auditory nerve fibers fire neural impulses in rapid succession, creating volleys of impulses.** These volleys exceed the 1000 per second limit. Studies suggest that auditory nerves can team up like this to generate volleys of up to 5000 impulses per second (Zwislocki, 1981).

Although the original theories have had to be revised, the current thinking is that pitch perception depends on both place and frequency coding

Figure 4.39 The basilar membrane. The figure shows the cochlea unwound and cut open to reveal the basilar membrane, which is covered with thousands of hair cells (the auditory receptors). Pressure waves in the fluid filling the cochlea cause oscillations to travel in waves down the basilar membrane, stimulating the hair cells. Although the entire membrane vibrates, as predicted by frequency theory, the point in the membrane where the wave peaks depends on the frequency of the sound stimulus, as suggested by place theory.

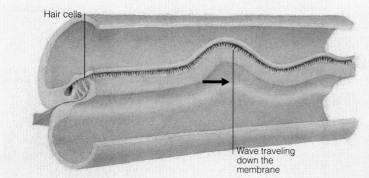

Hair cells

Wave traveling down the membrane

of vibrations along the basilar membrane. Sounds under 1000 Hz appear to be translated into pitch through frequency coding. For sounds between 1000 and 5000 Hz, our perception of pitch seems to depend on a combination of frequency and place coding. Sounds over 5000 Hz seem to be handled through place coding only. Once again, we find that theories that were pitted against each other for decades are complementary rather than contradictory.

EXPLAINING PERCEPTIONS OF LOUDNESS

The mechanisms responsible for the perception of loudness are not well understood, although there are some plausible theories. Loudness appears to depend largely on two factors: the *breadth* of the area of rapid firing along the basilar membrane and the activation of certain "high-threshold" neurons that respond to very high amplitudes only (Von Bekesy, 1960). However, this theory doesn't account for how sound frequency and complexity interact with amplitude to influence our perception of loudness. The mechanisms responsible for the perception of timbre remain even more obscure.

Auditory Pathways to the Brain

Unlike the visual system, the auditory system does most of its information processing in the central headquarters of the brain, instead of at the satellite facilities, the ears. After leaving the ears, the auditory nerves travel to the lower *brain stem*, where synapses interconnect in a complex pattern. Many pathways cross to the other side of the brain, so that input from each ear projects more directly and immediately to the *opposite* side of the brain than to the side the ear is on.

The auditory pathways ascend through the brain stem to the auditory portion of the *thalamus*. From here, auditory signals are shuttled to the *primary auditory cortex*, in the temporal lobe of each hemisphere of the brain. Studies suggest that the auditory cortex has specialized cells—similar to the feature detectors found in the visual cortex—that show special sensitivity to certain features of sound (Abeles & Goldstein, 1970).

Investigators are a bit perplexed about the role of the auditory cortex in hearing (Durrant & Lovrinic, 1977). When the auditory cortex is removed from both sides of a cat's brain, the cat shows surprising hearing ability. Typically, the cat can still respond to variations in sound amplitude and frequency. This suggests that much of the processing of loudness and pitch may occur in lower brain centers (the brain stem and the thal-

amus). So, what's left for the auditory cortex to handle? Theorists speculate that cortical processing may be critical to our ability to locate the source of sounds in space, the topic we turn to next. (Cortical processing also appears to play a major role in speech perception.)

Perceiving Sources of Sound: Auditory Localization

You're driving along the highway when suddenly you hear a siren wailing in the distance. As the sound grows louder, you glance around you, cocking your ear to the sound. Where is it coming from? Behind you? In front of you? From one side? As this example shows, recognizing where a sound is coming from is another common perceptual task. Called *auditory localization*, this process is analogous to depth perception in vision; both involve spatial aspects of sensory input. The fact that our ears are set *apart* contributes to our ability to locate sounds in space, just as the separation of our eyes contributes to our perception of depth.

Unlike our eyes, our ears can't compare images, but they can compare sounds in terms of their *intensity* or loudness. For example, a sound source to one side of the head produces a greater intensity at the ear nearer to the sound than at the farther ear. This is due partly to the loss of sound intensity with distance and partly to the "shadow," or partial sound barrier, cast by the head itself (see Figure 4.40). The intensity difference between the two ears is greater when the sound source is well to one side. Our perceptual system uses this difference as one clue in localizing sounds.

Amazingly enough, we also localize sounds by comparing the *timing* of their arrival at each ear. Since the path to the farther ear is longer, the sound takes longer to reach that ear. Our comparisons of the timing of sounds are remarkably sensitive: we can detect timing differences as small as

Figure 4.40 Cues in auditory localization. A sound coming from the left reaches the left ear sooner than the right. When the sound reaches the right ear it also is less intense because it has traveled a greater distance and because it is in the sound shadow produced by the listener's head. We use these cues to localize the sources of sound in space.

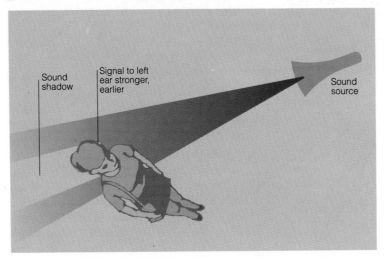

Sound shadow

Signal to left ear stronger, earlier

Sound source

Check your understanding of both vision and audition by comparing key aspects of sensation and perception in these senses. The dimensions of comparison are listed in the first column below. The second column lists the answers for the sense of vision. You can fill in the answers for the sense of hearing in the third column. These answers can be found in Appendix A in the back of the book.

Dimension	Vision	Hearing
1. Stimulus	Light waves	_____
2. Elements of stimulus and related perceptions	Wavelength/hue Amplitude/brightness Purity/saturation	_____
3. Receptors	Rods and cones	_____
4. Location of receptors	Retina	_____
5. Main location of processing in brain	Occipital lobe Visual cortex	_____
6. Spatial aspect of perception	Depth perception	_____
7. Typical Weber fraction	$\frac{1}{60}$ (brightness)	_____

1/100,000 of a second (Durlach & Colburn, 1978).

We also attempt to get a fix on the source of a sound by turning our head or by moving about. The resulting changes in our perception of the sound provide clues about where the sound is coming from. These processes are much like the active process of moving our eyes that provide monocular cues about depth in visual perception.

Speaking of visual perception, we often localize sounds with our eyes! How can we hear with our eyes? The key is that we usually don't listen with our eyes closed. We often make use of joint information from two or more senses to make our perceptual model of the world. Most sound sources have visible components (someone's lips moving, for instance). For a demonstration of the influence of visual input on auditory localization, pay attention to where the sound seems to come from the next time you're shown a movie in a classroom. The sound seems to come from the objects and people on the screen, not the rear or middle of the room where the speaker usually is. Thus, auditory localization cues can sometimes be misleading, just like clues to depth perception. In fact, the erroneous perception that the movie's sound comes from the front of the room is essentially an auditory equivalent of an optical illusion.

OUR OTHER SENSES

In humans the visual and auditory senses are especially important, and psychologists have devoted most of their attention to these sensory systems. However, our other senses also play a critical role in our experience of the world. Imagine how dull life would be without your sense of taste. Or imagine how difficult life would be if you lacked a sense of balance. In the remainder of the chapter, we'll take a brief look at what psychologists have learned about our other senses: taste, smell, touch, and balance.

Our Sense of Taste: The Gustatory System

True wine lovers go through an elaborate series of steps when they are served a good bottle of wine. Typically, they begin by drinking a little water to clean their palate. Then they sniff the cork from the wine bottle, swirl a small amount of the wine around in a glass, sniff the odor emerging from the glass, take a sip of the wine, and roll the wine around in their mouth for a short time before finally swallowing it. At last they are ready to confer their approval or disapproval. Is all this activity really a meaningful way to put the wine to a sensitive test? Or is it just a harmless ritual passed on through tradition? You'll find out in this section.

Your **gustatory system, or sense of taste,** relies on sensory structures called *taste buds* that line the trenches around tiny bumps on your tongue. They contain the gustatory receptors, called *taste cells*, which fire neural impulses when they absorb chemicals dissolved in your saliva (Kimura and Beidler, 1961). Interestingly, taste cells have a short life, spanning only a matter of days, and they are constantly being replaced (Beidler, 1963). New cells are born at the edge of the taste bud and migrate inward to die at the center.

It's generally (but not universally) agreed that there are four fundamental tastes: sweet, sour, bitter, and salty (Bartoshuk, 1971). Sensitivity to these tastes is distributed somewhat unevenly across the tongue, with sweet and salty near the front, sour near the sides, and bitter at the back (Figure 4.41). When we eat, we are constantly

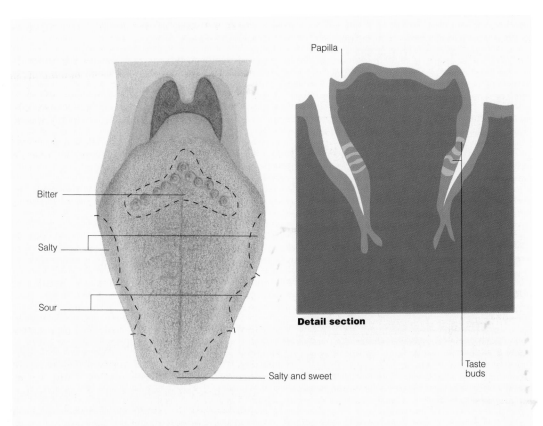

Bitter

Salty

Sour

Salty and sweet

Papilla

Detail section

Taste buds

Figure 4.41 The tongue and taste. The taste buds sensitive to certain basic tastes are distributed unevenly across the tongue, as shown here. The detail on the right shows a blowup of a vertical cross section of one of the tiny bumps (papillae) on the tongue. Most of our taste buds are found in the little trenches around papillae.

mixing food and saliva and moving it about the mouth, so the stimulus is constantly changing. However, if a flavored substance is placed in a single spot on the tongue, *sensory adaptation* occurs and the taste fades until it vanishes (Krakauer and Dallenbach, 1937). Sensory adaptation in our taste system can leave *aftereffects*. Adapting to a sour solution makes water taste sweet, and adaptation to a sweet solution makes water taste bitter (Bartoshuk, 1968). We encounter these aftereffects frequently. For instance, if you take a sip of orange juice right after a taste of a sweet roll, the orange juice will seem extra sour.

So far, we've been discussing taste, but we are really interested in the *perception of flavor*. Flavor depends not only on the constellation of tastes in a food, but on the texture, appearance, and odor of the food. A food's texture depends on its feel as the tongue, teeth, and palate caress each morsel. People who must have all their food homogenized in a blender miss texture more than you might guess.

The way food looks is also important. We don't usually think about appearance as part of flavor, but it is. Try to imagine yourself eating green eggs or a blue steak. The importance of appearance was underscored in a study in which blindfolded people found brown chocolate and white chocolate equally tasty—until they removed their blindfolds. Without blindfolds, they rated the same white samples as less "chocolatey" than before (Duncker, 1939).

You probably won't be surprised to learn that odor contributes greatly to flavor (Sekuler & Blake, 1985). Although taste and smell are distinct sensory systems, they interact extensively. You might have noticed this interaction when you ate a favorite meal while enduring a severe head cold. That food you were looking forward to savoring probably tasted bland, because your stuffy nose impaired your sense of smell. Our ability to identify flavors is severely handicapped by eliminating odor perception (Mozell et al., 1969). With your nose pinched and your eyes shut, you can be given a piece of onion and think it's an apple!

Now that we've explored the dynamics of taste, we can return to our opening question about the value of the elaborate ritual involved in wine tasting. This ritual *is* an authentic way to put the wine to a sensitive test. The aftereffects associated with sensory adaptation make it wise to clean your palate before tasting the wine; otherwise, contrast effects from food just eaten may throw off your sense of taste. Sniffing the cork, and the wine in the glass, is important because odor is a major determinant of flavor. Swirling the wine in the glass helps to release the wine's odor inside the glass. Rolling the wine around in your mouth is especially critical because it distributes the wine over the full diversity of taste cells and forces the wine's odor up into your nasal passages. Thus, each action in this age-old ritual makes a meaningful contribution to the tasting.

Our Sense of Smell: The Olfactory System

Humans are usually characterized as being relatively insensitive to smell. In this regard we often are compared unfavorably to dogs, who are renowned for their ability to track a faint odor over long distances. Are humans really inferior in the sensory domain of smell? Let's examine the facts.

In many ways, your **olfactory system, or sense of smell**, is much like your sense of taste. Chemical stimuli dissolved in fluid (the mucus of your nose) are absorbed by receptors. In this case, the stimuli are molecules plucked from the air, and the receptors line your nasal passages (see Figure 4.42). Unlike the taste cells, the *olfactory receptors* have axons that synapse directly with cells in the *olfactory bulb* at the base of the brain. This arrangement is unique. Smell is the only sensory system that does not project upward to the cortex through the thalamus.

Odors cannot be classified as neatly as tastes. If there are primary odors, there must be a fairly large number of them, and olfactory receptors must be able to recognize a variety of different molecules in the mucus. Amoore (1970) suggested a "lock-and-key" mechanism, in which the shape of a molecule would determine which receptor would respond to it. However, the responses of the olfactory receptors do not show the kind of specificity that a lock-and-key theory would require (Schiffman, 1974). Individual cells respond better to certain odors, but most cells respond to more than one odor (Gesteland, 1978).

Figure 4.42 The olfactory system. Odor molecules travel through the nasal passages and stimulate receptors in the olfactory epithelium (the surface layer of cells). The olfactory nerve transmits neural impulses through the olfactory bulb to the brain.

Like the other senses, the sense of smell shows sensory adaptation (Mozell, 1971). After a period of exposure, strong odors usually fade from notice. Adaptation apparently occurs at different rates for different odors (Pfaffmann, 1951).

Overall, humans have greater olfactory capacities than widely believed (Cain, 1979). For example, people are able to determine from odors left in clothing whether the wearer was male or female. In one interesting study (Russell, 1976), subjects were asked to wear an undershirt for 24 hours, forgoing deodorant, soap, and perfume for both the day of the experiment and the day before. The undershirts were then placed in bags and the subjects were each presented with three bags to smell. First, each was asked which of the three shirts was his or her own; 75% chose correctly. Then each was asked to pick which of two shirts was worn by a male and which by a female. Once again, 75% were correct. Thus, we may have a better sense of smell than we're given credit for. Admittedly, we can't track the faint smell of a timber wolf through a mountain range, but we can track the weak odor of a pizza stand through a crowded street fair. Although there are some species whose sense of smell is superior, ours compares favorably with that of many animals.

Our Sense of Touch: The Tactile System

If there is any sense that we trust almost as much as sight, it is the sense of touch. Yet, like all the senses, touch involves converting the sensation of physical stimuli into a psychological experience—and it can be fooled.

Your skin houses your **tactile system, or sense of touch**. It's saturated with sensory receptors that are responsive to the pressure of touch, to warmth and cold, and to pain. There are many different kinds of skin receptors. It seems that these ought to be specialized for different functions, such as pressure, vibration, hot, cold, and so forth, but the distinctions are not as clear as researchers originally expected (Sinclair, 1955).

TOUCH: FEELING THE PRESSURE

Cells in the nervous system that respond to touch are sensitive to a specific patch of skin. These patches of skin are the functional equivalents of receptive fields in vision. They vary in size and in what they are sensitive to (see Figure 4.43).

Signals about touch are mostly sent to the *primary somatosensory cortex* in the brain's parietal lobe. Although the entire body is sensitive to touch, in humans the bulk of the somatosensory cortex is devoted to processing touch sensations

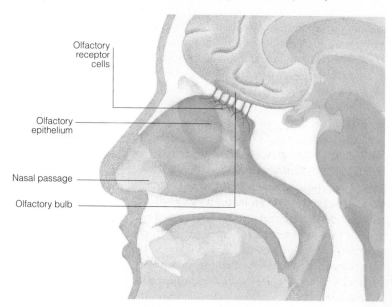

Olfactory
receptor
cells

Olfactory
epithelium

Nasal passage

Olfactory bulb

coming from the fingers, lips, and tongue. That's why you can make much finer discriminations with your fingers than you can with your toes or the small of your back. Some cells in the somatosensory cortex function like the feature detectors discovered in vision (Hyvarinen and Poranen, 1978). They respond to specific features of touch, such as a movement across the skin in a particular direction.

We have been talking about touch as if it were simply a matter of allowing objects to press against the skin. Of course, touch often is an *active* process, as when you move your fingers across an object, much as you use your eyes to scan a scene (Gibson, 1962). Perhaps the best demonstration of our own participation in feeling touch is tickling. No one knows exactly what a tickle is, or why it makes most of us giggle, but we do know that you can't tickle yourself. This is true even if you use a tickling machine that does tickle you when someone else operates it (Weiskrantz, Elliott, & Darlington, 1971).

TEMPERATURE: FEELING THE HEAT

Although skin receptors are not as specialized as researchers once believed, there apparently *are* nerve fibers specific for warmth and cold (Duclaux & Kenshalo, 1980). Spots that respond to cold don't respond to warmth, and vice versa. Ironically, touching something really hot, like a stove, activates *both* the warm and cold receptors.

Sensory systems are best at *comparisons*, so when we say "warm" we really mean "warmer than the skin," and "cold" means "cooler than the skin." In fact, your perception of temperature is definitely relative. If you place your left hand in a pan of cool water and your right hand in a pan of warm water for a minute, and then place both hands in a pan of lukewarm (body temperature) water, the lukewarm water will seem warm to your left hand and cool to your right. Notice once again that *context* and *contrast* are critical to our perceptions.

If you do the experiment with the two pans of water, you may notice something else: just before you take your hands out of the first pans to place them in the lukewarm water, the two pans may feel like they are the same temperature. You may think that they both have come to room temperature, but that is not so. The temperatures feel similar because of sensory adaptation (Kenshalo, 1970). The thermal stimulus is unchanging, so the sensory system stops signalling the temperature.

PAIN: FEELING THE HURT

As unpleasant as pain is, the sensation of pain is crucial to survival. Pain is a marvelous warning system. It tells us when we should stop shoveling snow, or it lets us know that we have a pinched nerve that requires treatment. Without it we would frequently be unaware of danger to our bodies. Just how the perception of pain works, however, presents a number of puzzles.

Pain messages are transmitted to the brain via two pathways that pass through slightly different areas in the thalamus. One is a *fast pathway* that registers localized pain and relays it directly to the cortex in a fraction of a second. This is the system that hits you with sharp pain when you first cut your finger. The second system uses a *slow pathway*, routed through the limbic system, that lags a second or two behind the fast system. This system conveys the less localized, longer lasting, aching pain that comes after the initial injury.

Like other perceptions, pain is not an automatic result of certain types of stimulation. The perception of pain can be influenced greatly by psychological factors such as expectations, personality, and mood. For instance, in one study, researchers manipulated subjects' mood and then asked them to fill out a scale on which they rated their personal pain in 25 body areas (Stalling et al., 1985). As predicted, subjects in the negative mood condition reported more pain than those in the positive mood condition.

The psychological element in pain is clear when something distracts you from the perception of pain and the pain temporarily disappears. For example, imagine that you've just hit your thumb with a hammer and it's throbbing with pain. Suddenly, your child cries out that there's a fire in the laundry room. As you race to deal with this emergency, you'll probably forget about the pain in your thumb. Placebo effects in pain relief also illustrate the subjective nature of pain. As we mentioned in Chapters 2 and 3, many people suffering from pain report relief from a placebo—an inert "sugar pill" that is presented to them as if it were a painkiller. As you can see, then, the relationships between sensory input and our perceptual response are particularly complicated in the case of pain.

Some of these perplexing relationships are explained well by the gate-control theory of pain (Melzak, 1973). **Gate-control theory holds that incoming pain sensations pass through a "gate" in the spinal cord that can be open or closed.** It appears that this imaginary gate may be closed by signals either from peripheral receptors or from the brain (see Figure 4.44). Signals being sent from the brain would explain how factors such as emotional state, attention, and expectations might contribute to shutting off pain signals.

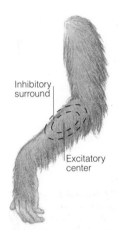

Inhibitory surround

Excitatory center

Figure 4.43 Receptive fields for touch. A receptive field for touch is an area on the skin surface that, when stimulated, affects the firing of a cell that responds to pressure on the skin. Shown here is a center-surround receptive field for a cell in the thalamus of a monkey.

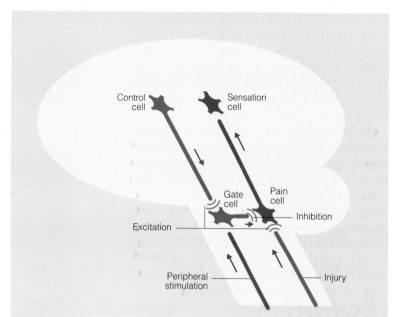

Control
cell

Sensation
cell

Gate
cell

Pain
cell

Excitation

Inhibition

Peripheral
stimulation

Injury

Figure 4.44 The gate-control theory of pain. According to this model of pain perception, incoming pain signals can be blocked or "gated" on their way up the spinal cord. The gate is *not* an actual anatomical structure that opens and shuts. The gating effect probably depends on neural impulses that inhibit the activity of cells in the ascending pathway for pain signals.

The pain-blocking signals from the brain may originate in the midbrain and the limbic system (Mantyh, 1983). Interestingly, these areas show relatively dense concentrations of *endorphins*, the brain's own natural, morphinelike painkillers discussed in Chapter 3. Thus, endorphin activity in the midbrain or limbic system may activate a mechanism that gates pain signals in the spinal cord, reducing our discomfort (Basbaum & Fields, 1984).

Like other sensory systems, the pain system shows sensory adaptation to unchanging stimuli, as long as they are not too severe (Kenshalo, 1971). However, many painful stimuli may not show adaptation, because the stimulus is not actually unchanging. Every time we move, we tend to irritate a wound. Even if we lie still, every heartbeat changes the pressure and the chemical concentrations at the injury, which may account for the throbbing often associated with pain.

Figure 4.45 The vestibular system. The semicircular canals in the inner ear are the sensory organ for balance and head movement. Fluid movements in these canals stimulate neural impulses that travel along the vestibular nerve to the brain.

KINESTHESIS: FEELING MOVEMENT

Your tactile system also includes a **kinesthetic sense that monitors the positions of the various parts of your body.** To some extent, you know where your limbs are because you commanded the muscles that put them there. Nonetheless, your sense of touch allows you to double-check these locations. Your kinesthetic sense monitors two kinds of receptors: receptors residing in the joints that indicate the bend of the joints and receptors residing within the muscles that register their tautness, or extension. Together, these two types of kinesthetic receptors allow you to keep track of the position of your limbs.

Our Sense of Balance: The Vestibular System

When you're jolting along in a bus, the world outside the bus window doesn't seem to jump about as your head bounces up and down. Yet a movie taken with a camera fastened to the bus *would* show a bouncing world. How are you and the camera different? Unlike the camera, you are equipped with a **vestibular system, which responds to gravity and keeps you informed of your body's location in space.** Your vestibular system provides your sense of balance, or equilibrium, compensating for changes in your body's position (Parker, 1980). Thus, your perception of the world includes your knowledge of where you are within it.

The vestibular system shares space in your inner ear with the auditory system. The *semicircular canals* make up the largest part of the vestibular system, which is shown in Figure 4.45. They look like three inner tubes joined at the base. Any rotational motion of your head is uniquely represented by the combination of fluid flows in the semicircular canals. These shifts in fluid are detected by hair cells similar to those found along the basilar membrane in the cochlea.

Your perceptual system integrates the vestibular organs' input about your body's position with information from other senses—you can see where you are, and you know where you've instructed your muscles to take you. Nevertheless, without the interaction of all these senses, you could become very disoriented, as anyone who has been on an amusement park thrill ride can testify.

The interaction among the senses is illustrated by the phenomenon of motion sickness. Although stimulation of the vestibular system is thought to be the main cause of motion sickness, other senses also come into play. When you're seasick, for example, the problem may be the disagreement between your vestibular system, which correctly senses motion, and your visual system, which sees the entire ship as a stationary world. To alleviate this problem, sailors often advise sea-faring novices to focus their gaze on the horizon, so that vestibular and visual input mesh better.

The interaction of the vestibular and visual senses in motion sickness raises a point that merits emphasis as we close our tour of the human sensory systems. Although we have discussed the various sensory modalities separately, it's important to remember that all the senses send signals to the same brain, where the information is pooled. We have already encountered examples of sensory integration. It's at work when the sight and smell of food influences its taste. It's also at work in pinpointing the source of sounds, when we "hear with our eyes."

This kind of sensory integration is the norm in our perceptual experience. For example, when you sit around a campfire, you *see* it blazing, you *hear* it crackling, you *smell* it burning, you feel its *touch* in its warmth, and if you cook something over it, you may even *taste* it. Thus, perception involves building a unified model of the world out of integrated input from all the senses.

PUTTING IT IN PERSPECTIVE

In this chapter, two of our six unifying themes stand out in sharp relief. First, the way in which competing theories of color vision and hearing have been reconciled in recent years shows how psychology's theoretical diversity can pay dividends (theme 2). Second, the entire chapter relates to our experience of the world as highly subjective (theme 6). Let's discuss the value of theoretical diversity first.

Contradictory theories about behavior can be disconcerting and frustrating for theorists, researchers, teachers, and students alike. Theoretical diversity may not seem like much of an advantage when we struggle to make sense out of diametrically opposed explanations of the same phenomenon. Most of us show a natural human tendency to want to tie things up in a neat, sensible package. As the Gestaltists would have put it, we prefer closure and simplicity.

Yet this chapter provides two dramatic demonstrations of how theoretical diversity can lead to progress in the long run. The trichromatic and opponent process theories of color vision and the place and frequency theories of pitch perception were viewed as fundamentally incompatible for many decades. These competing theories generated and guided the research that now provides us with a fairly solid understanding of how we perceive color and pitch. As you know, in each case, the evidence eventually revealed that the opposing theories were not really incompatible and that both were needed to fully explain the sensory processes that each sought to explain individually. If it hadn't been for these theoretical debates, our understanding of color vision and pitch perception might be far more primitive, as our understanding of timbre still is.

Thus, theoretical diversity can be a very positive force that promotes progress in a scientific discipline. Diverse theoretical perspectives are necessary to fully understand some phenomena. Sometimes these multiple perspectives converge and are integrated in ways that clear up enduring questions about behavior.

This chapter should also have enhanced your appreciation of why our experience of the world is highly subjective. We've seen again and again that there is no one-to-one correspondence between sensory input and our perceived experience of the world. As ambiguous figures and optical illusions clearly show, the same sensory input can result in differing "realities." Perception is an active process in which we organize and interpret the information received by our senses. Our interpretations are shaped by a host of factors, including the environmental context and our perceptual sets. Furthermore, in experiencing the world, we construct perceptual hypotheses from shifting, often distorted proximal stimuli. Small wonder, then, that different people often perceive the same event in very different ways. The gap between sensory input and perceptual experience allows for a lot of interpretation. Our experience of the world is subjective because the process of perception is inherently subjective.

The following Application demonstrates this subjectivity once again. It focuses on how painters have learned to make use of the principles of visual perception to achieve a variety of artistic goals.

THINKING ABOUT
ART AND ILLUSION

Answer the following multiple-choice question: Artistic works such as paintings

☐ **a.** render an accurate picture of reality.

☐ **b.** create an illusion of reality.

☐ **c.** provide an interpretation of reality.

☐ **d.** make us think about the nature of reality.

☐ **e.** All of the above.

The answer to our question is (e), all of the above. Historically, artists have had many and varied purposes, including each of those listed in the possible answers to the question. To realize their goals, artists have had to use a number of principles of perception—sometimes quite deliberately, and sometimes not. To explore the role of perceptual principles in art and illusion, let's use the example of painting.

The goal of most early painters was to produce a believable picture of reality. This goal immediately suggests a problem familiar to most of us who have attempted to draw realistic pictures; the real world is three-dimensional, but a canvas or a sheet of paper is flat. Paradoxically, then, painters who set out to recreate reality must do so by creating an *illusion* of three-dimensional reality. In other words, options (a) and (b) in our opening question are one and the same.

Prior to the Renaissance, these efforts to create a convincing illusion of reality were awkward by modern standards because the artists did not understand how to make use of depth cues. This is apparent in Figure 4.46, a depiction of a religious scene painted

Figure 4.46 *The Kiss of Judas* by Jacopo Torriti (circa 1300). Notice how the absence of depth cues makes the painting seem flat and unrealistic.

around 1300. The painting clearly lacks a sense of depth. The people seem paper-thin. They have no real position in space.

Many of the principles of geometric perspective that relate to depth perception were discovered during the Renaissance. Figure 4.47 dramatizes the resulting transition in art. It shows a scene depicted by Gentile and Giovanni Bellini, Italian Renaissance painters. It seems more realistic and lifelike than the painting in Figure 4.46 because it employs monocular cues to depth. Notice how the buildings on the sides converge to make use of linear perspective. And distant objects are smaller than nearby ones, an

application of relative size. This painting also makes use of height in a plane, as well as interposition. By taking advantage of pictorial depth cues, the artists enhance the illusion of reality.

In the centuries since the Renaissance, painters have adopted a number of viewpoints about the portrayal of reality. For instance, the French Impressionists of the 19th century did not want to recreate the photographic "reality" of a scene. They set out to interpret a viewer's fleeting perception or *impression* of that reality. To accomplish this, they worked with color in unprecedented ways.

Claude Monet, a French impressionist, began to work with separate daubs of pure, bright colors that blurred together to create an alternating perceptual experience. If you view his paintings up close, you perceive only a shimmering mass of color. When you step back, however, the adjacent colors begin to blend, and forms begin to take shape, as you can see in Figure 4.48. Monet achieved this duality through careful use of color mixing and by working systematically with complementary colors.

Similar methods were used even more precisely and systematically by Georges Seurat, a French artist who employed a technique called *pointillism*. Seurat carefully studied what scientists knew about the composition of color in the 1880s. He ap-

Figure 4.47 A painting by the Italian Renaissance artists Gentile and Giovanni Bellini (circa 1480). In this painting, a number of depth cues—including linear perspective, relative size, height on a plane, and interposition—enhance the illusion of three-dimensional reality.

Figure 4.48 Claude Monet's *Palazzo da Mula, Venice* (1908), an example of Impressionist use of daubs of color. Monet often used complementary colors to achieve his visual effects.

Figure 4.49 Georges Seurat's *Sunday Afternoon on the Island of La Grande Jatte* (without artist's border) (1884–1886). Seurat's "pointillist" technique used thousands of tiny dots of color and principles of color mixing (see detail at the right); the eye and brain combine the points into the colors the viewer actually sees.

plied this knowledge in a manner so calculated and laboratorylike that critics in his era dubbed him the "little chemist." Seurat constructed his paintings out of tiny dots of pure, intense colors. Even more so than Monet, he made use of additive color mixing, a departure from the norm in painting, which usually depends on subtractive mixing of pigments. A famous result of Seurat's "scientific" approach to painting, his renowned *Sunday Afternoon on the Island of La Grande Jatte*, is shown in Figure 4.49.

As the work of Monet and Seurat illustrates, modern painters were moving away from attempts to recreate the world we literally see. If 19th-century painters liberated color, their successors at the turn of the 20th century

the grapes together in the bottom right corner. Closure accounts for your being able to see the essence of the violin.

Other Gestalt principles are the key to the effect achieved in the painting in Figure 4.51. This painting, by Marcel Duchamp, a French artist who blended cubism and a style called futurism, is titled *Nude Descending a Staircase*. The effect clearly depends on the Gestalt principles of continuity and common fate.

The surrealists toyed with reality in a different way. Influenced by Sigmund Freud's writings on the unconscious, the surrealists explored the world of dreams and fantasy. Specific elements in their paintings often are depicted realistically, but the strange juxtaposition of elements yields a disconcerting irrationality reminiscent of dreams. A prominent example of this style is

liberated form. This was particularly true of cubism. This style was begun in 1909 by Pablo Picasso, a native of Spain, who went on to experiment with other styles in his prolific career. The cubists didn't try to *portray* reality so much as to *reassemble* it. They attempted to reduce everything to combinations of geometric forms (lines, circles, triangles, rectangles, and such) laid out in a flat space, lacking depth. In a sense, *they applied the theory of feature analysis to canvas,* as they built their figures out of simple features.

The resulting paintings were decidedly unrealistic, but Picasso would leave realistic fragments that provided clues about the subject. He liked to challenge his viewers to decipher the subject of his paintings. Take a look at the painting in Figure 4.50 and see if you can figure out what Picasso was portraying.

The work in Figure 4.50 is titled *Violin and Grapes.* Note how Gestalt principles of perceptual organization are at work to create these forms. Proximity and similarity serve to bring

Figure 4.50 A 1912 painting (*Violin and Grapes*) by Pablo Picasso that makes use of Gestalt principles of perceptual organization. What is depicted in the painting? (Collection, The Museum of Modern Art, New York, Mrs. David M. Levy Bequest)

Figure 4.51 Marcel Duchamp's *Nude Descending a Staircase, No. 2* (1912), a painting that makes use of the Gestalt principles of continuity and common fate. (Philadelphia Museum of Art: The Louise and Walter Arensberg Collection)

Figure 4.52 Salvador Dali's *Slave Market with the Disappearing Bust of Voltaire* (1940), which playfully includes a reversible figure (two nuns form the bust of Voltaire, a philosopher known for his stringent criticisms of the Church).

Spanish artist Salvador Dali's *Slave Market with the Disappearing Bust of Voltaire*, shown in Figure 4.52. Notice the reversible figure near the center of the painting. The "bust of Voltaire" is made up of two human figures in the distance, standing in front of an arch. Dali often used reversible figures to enhance the ambiguity of his bizarre visions.

Perhaps no one has been more creative in manipulating perceptual ambiguity than M. C. Escher, a modern Dutch artist. Escher was not interested in representing a slice of the world so much as he was interested in stimulat-

ing the viewer to think about the nature of reality and the process of visual perception itself. Interestingly, Escher readily acknowledged his debt to psychology as a source of inspiration (Teuber, 1974). He followed the work of the gestaltists carefully after reading Kurt Koffka's (1935) *Principles of Gestalt Psychology*. Escher would even cite specific journal articles that served as the point of departure for his works. For example, the woodcut *Day and Night* (see Figure 4.53) is largely a manipulation of the figure and ground phenomenon. Escher based it on an article by Molly Harrower (1936) in

the *British Journal of Psychology*.

Waterfall, a 1961 engraving by Escher, is an impossible figure that appears to defy the law of gravity (see Figure 4.54). The puzzling problem here is that a level channel of water terminates in a waterfall that "falls" into the same channel two levels "below." This drawing is made up of two of the impossible triangles shown in Figure 4.35. In case you need help seeing them, the waterfall itself forms one side of each triangle.

The Necker cube, a reversible figure mentioned earlier, was the inspiration for Escher's 1958 lithograph *Belvedere*, shown in Figure 4.55. You have to look carefully to realize that this is an *impossible figure* like those you saw when we discussed optical illusions (see Figure 4.35). Note that the top story runs at a right angle from the first story. Note also how the pillars are twisted around. The pillars that start on one side of the building end up supporting the second story on the other side! Escher's debt to the Necker cube is manifested in several places. For in-

Figure 4.53 M. C. Escher's woodcut *Day and Night* (1938), in which figure is gradually transformed into ground and ground into figure.

Figure 4.54 Escher's engraving *Waterfall* (1961). Escher's use of depth cues and impossible triangles deceives the brain into seeing water flow uphill.

stance, there's a drawing of a Necker cube on the floor next to the seated boy (on the lower left).

While Escher challenges us to think about perception, Belgian artist René Magritte challenges us to think about the conventions of painting. Many of his paintings depict paintings on an easel, with the "real" scene continuing unbroken at the edges. The painting in Figure 4.56 is such a picture within a picture. In addition, there are two identical triangles in the painting. One represents a road, and the other is a nearby tower. Notice how the identical triangles are perceived differently, primarily because of the variations in *context* and secondarily because of variations in light and shadow and texture gradient.

Ultimately, Magritte's painting blurs the line between the real world and the illusory world created by the artist, suggesting that there is no line—that everything is an illusion. In this way, Magritte "frames" the ageless, unanswerable question: what is reality?

Figure 4.55 (Below) Escher's lithograph *Belvedere* (1958), which depicts an impossible figure inspired by the Necker cube. The cube appears in the architecture of the building, in the model held by the boy on the bench, and in the drawing lying at his feet.

Figure 4.56 René Magritte's *Les Promenades d'Euclide* (1955). Notice how the pair of nearly identical triangles look quite different in different contexts. (The Minneapolis Institute of Arts, The William Hood Dunwoody Fund)

SENSATION AND PERCEPTION

Psychophysics: Basic Concepts and Issues

• Psychophysicists use a variety of methods to relate sensory inputs to subjective perceptions. They have found that thresholds are not really absolute. Differences between the perceived magnitudes of stimuli are measured in terms of just noticeable differences (JNDs). As physical stimuli increase in intensity, their perceived magnitude grows more slowly.

• According to signal-detection theory, the detection of sensory inputs depends on a variety of factors besides the physical intensity of the stimuli. Foremost among these factors are the noise in your sensory system and considerations that influence how you set your response criterion. Prolonged stimulation may lead to sensory adaptation, which involves a reduction in sensitivity.

Our Sense of Sight: The Visual System

• Light, the stimulus for vision, varies in terms of wavelength, amplitude, and purity. Light enters the eye through the cornea and is focused on the retina by the lens. The pupil controls the amount of light falling on the neural tissue of the retina.

• Rods and cones are the visual receptors found in the retina. Cones play a key role in daylight vision and color perception; rods are critical to night vision and peripheral vision. Dark adaptation and light adaptation both involve changes in the sensitivity of the retinal receptors.

• The retina transforms light into neural impulses that are sent to the brain along the optic nerve. Receptive fields are areas in the retina that affect the firing of visual cells. They vary in shape and size, but center-surround arrangements are common. Lateral antagonism occurs when activity in one cell diminishes signals from a nearby cell.

• Visual signals are transmitted from the retina along optic nerves through the optic chiasm. From there they are shuttled through the thalamus to the primary visual cortex in the occipital lobe of each hemisphere in the brain. The visual cortex contains cells that appear to function as feature detectors, responding to specific elements in complex stimuli.

• Perceptions of color are primarily a function of light wavelength, while amplitude affects brightness and purity affects saturation. Our perceptions of many varied colors depend on processes that resemble additive color mixing. The trichromatic theory of color vision holds that we have three types of receptors that are differentially sensitive to different wavelengths. The opponent process theory holds that we have three channels for color perception that respond to red versus green, blue versus yellow, and black versus white. The evidence now suggests that both theories are necessary to account for our color vision.

• According to feature analysis theories, we detect specific elements in stimuli and build them into recognizable forms through bottom-up processing. However, studies such as our Featured Study show that form perception also involves top-down processing.

• In contrast to feature analysis, Gestalt psychology emphasized that the whole may be greater than the sum of its parts (features). The Gestaltists described various principles that guide our perception of forms, including figure and ground, proximity, similarity, continuity, common fate, closure, and simplicity.

• The process of pattern perception illustrates that we work with perceptual hypotheses about the distal stimuli that could be responsible for the proximal stimuli we sense. Ambiguous figures show that a stimulus can generate alternative perceptual hypotheses.

• Depth perception depends primarily on monocular cues such as texture gradient, linear perspective, interposition, relative size, and height in plane. Binocular cues such as retinal disparity and convergence can also contribute to depth perception.

• Perceptual constancies in vision, such as lightness constancy, size constancy, and shape constancy, help us to deal with the ever-shifting nature of proximal stimuli. Optical illusions demonstrate that our perceptual hypotheses can be inaccurate and that our perceptions are not simple reflections of objective reality.

Our Sense of Hearing: The Auditory System

• Sound, the stimulus for hearing, varies in terms of wavelength (frequency), amplitude, and purity. These properties affect mainly perceptions of pitch, loudness, and timbre, respectively.

• Sound is transmitted through the external ear via air conduction to the middle ear. In the inner ear, fluid conduction vibrates hair cells along the basilar membrane in the cochlea. These hair cells are the receptors for hearing that are analogous to the rods and cones in the eye.

• Place theory proposed that pitch perception depends on where vibrations occur along the basilar membrane. Frequency theory countered with the idea that pitch perception depends on the rate at which the basilar membrane vibrates. Modern evidence suggests that these theories are complementary rather than incompatible.

• Auditory signals are transmitted through the brain stem and thalamus to the primary auditory cortex in the temporal lobe of each hemisphere. Cortical processing appears to be important to auditory localization. We pinpoint the source of sounds by comparing interear differences in the intensity and timing of sounds and by active efforts such as turning our head.

Our Other Senses

• The taste buds found on the tongue are sensitive to four basic tastes: sweet, sour, bitter, and salty. Sensitivity to these tastes is distributed unevenly across the tongue. The perception of flavor is influenced by the texture, appearance, and odor of food. Odor is particularly influential.

• Like taste, smell is a chemical sense. Chemical stimuli activate olfactory receptors that line the nasal passages. Olfactory receptors show some specificity, but most cells respond to more than one odor. Our sense of smell is inferior to that of many animals, but our olfactory capabilities are often underestimated.

• Our tactile system is multifaceted, responding to pressure, temperature, pain, and muscular movement. Although the entire body is sensitive to pressure, the bulk of the somatosensory cortex is devoted to signals from the fingers, lips, and tongue. Separate nerve fibers respond specifically to warmth and cold.

• Pain signals are sent to the brain along two pathways that are characterized as fast and slow. The perception of pain is highly subjective and may be influenced by mood, attention, personality, and placebo effects. Gate-control theory holds that incoming pain signals can be blocked in the spinal cord by a gating mechanism that may be activated in a variety of ways.

• Our sense of balance depends primarily on activity in the vestibular system. The semicircular canals make up the largest part of the vestibular system.

Putting It in Perspective

• This chapter underscored two of our unifying themes. The resolution of the theoretical debates about color vision and pitch perception illustrated the potential strength of theoretical diversity. The repeated demonstration that there is no one-to-one correspondence between sensory input and perception shed light on why our experience of the world is highly subjective.

Application: Thinking About Art and Illusion

• The principles of visual perception are often applied to artistic endeavors. Painters routinely use pictorial depth cues to make their scenes more lifelike. Color mixing, feature analysis in form perception, Gestalt principles, reversible figures, and impossible figures also surfaced in our discussion of art and illusion.

KEY TERMS

Absolute threshold
Additive color mixing
Afterimage
Auditory system
Basilar membrane
Binocular cues
Bottom-up processing
Cochlea
Complementary colors
Cones
Dark adaptation
Depth perception
Distal stimuli
Feature analysis
Feature detectors
Fovea

Frequency theory
Gate-control theory
Gestalt psychology
Gustatory system
Just noticeable
    difference (JND)
Kinesthetic sense
Lateral antagonism
Lens
Light adaptation
Monocular cues
Olfactory system
Opponent process
    theory of color vision
Optic nerve
Perception
Perceptual constancy

Perceptual hypothesis
Perceptual set
Phi phenomenon
Place theory
Proximal stimuli
Psychophysics
Pupil
Receptive field of a
    visual cell
Retina
Reversible figure
Rods
Sensation
Sensory adaptation
Signal-detection theory
Subtractive color mixing

Tactile system
Threshold
Top-down processing
Trichromatic theory of
    color vision
Vestibular system
Visual system
Volley principle
Weber's law

KEY PEOPLE

Gustav Fechner
Hermann von Helmholtz
David Hubel &
    Torsten Wiesel
Ernst Weber
Max Wertheimer

Variations in Consciousness

A young woman sits alone in a room. Attached to her scalp are recording electrodes from an *electroencephalograph* (EEG), a device that monitors the electrical activity in her brain. Connected to the EEG is another device that sounds a tone every time the EEG registers a particular pattern of brain waves. As long as the pattern persists, the tone fills the room, and when the pattern changes, the room falls silent. As the woman sits quietly, the tone gradually begins to sound more and more frequently. What's going on here?

The young woman was a subject in one of a series of experiments conducted by Joe Kamiya. Kamiya set out to see whether people could learn to control the electrical activity in their brains by altering their mental states (Kamiya, 1969; Nowlis & Kamiya, 1970). The tone provided the subjects with *biofeedback*—information about internal bodily changes. In the experiment described here, the tone sounded whenever the young woman produced a specific pattern of brain waves called *alpha waves*. What did Kamiya find? He found that when people are provided with EEG biofeedback, the vast majority *can* learn to alter their brain-wave activity to some extent (see Figure 5.1).

In the course of this research, Kamiya also made some other interesting observations. Although subjects could increase alpha activity, they had difficulty explaining *how* they did it. When pressed, subjects would offer explanations, but the explanations tended to be tentative and vague. Their responses were equally hazy when Kamiya asked them to describe *what it felt like* when they were producing alpha-wave activity. Most of them agreed that the alpha state was quite pleasant, but, beyond that, they had great difficulty describing it. When questioned, one subject replied, "You keep asking me to describe this darned alpha state. I can't do it. It has a certain feel about it, sure, but really, it's best left undescribed" (Kamiya, 1969, p. 515).

The difficulty that Kamiya's subjects experienced when asked to describe their mental state during alpha activity is hardly unique. Researchers find that people also have difficulty describing the states of consciousness associated with hypnosis, meditation, and the use of mind-altering drugs. Even everyday mental states can defy description. Can you provide a lucid description of exactly how you feel when you daydream? Ironically, the very thing we are most intimately acquainted with—our ever-changing conscious experience—eludes our best efforts to describe it. The problem may be that states of consciousness are the ultimate in subjective experience. Your consciousness can be directly experienced by only one person—you. You cannot merge or share consciousness with someone else in order to compare notes.

In a sense, conscious experience would seem to be what psychology is all about. Indeed, psychology began in the 19th century as the science of

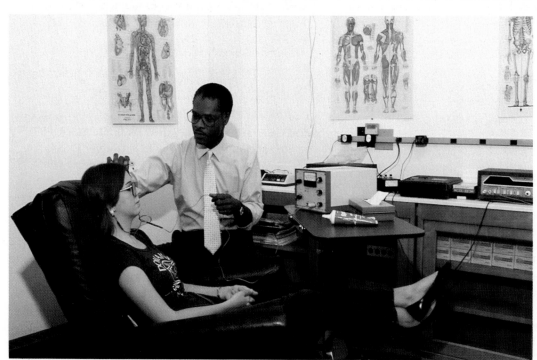

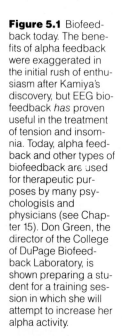

Figure 5.1 Biofeedback today. The benefits of alpha feedback were exaggerated in the initial rush of enthusiasm after Kamiya's discovery, but EEG biofeedback *has* proven useful in the treatment of tension and insomnia. Today, alpha feedback and other types of biofeedback are used for therapeutic purposes by many psychologists and physicians (see Chapter 15). Don Green, the director of the College of DuPage Biofeedback Laboratory, is shown preparing a student for a training session in which she will attempt to increase her alpha activity.

consciousness. However, as we discussed in Chapter 1, pioneering researchers found that the private, highly subjective nature of consciousness made it difficult to study empirically. Science requires observation and measurement, but we cannot observe consciousness from the outside. For this reason many psychologists concluded that consciousness simply could not be studied scientifically. For many decades it appeared that consciousness was, for scientific purposes, a lost world whose mysteries could never be probed.

The prevailing attitudes shifted, however, in the 1950s and 1960s. Gradually, the subject of consciousness, in all its variations, began to attract new interest and respect. As expected, it proved to be a challenging subject for scientific study, and, as you'll see, many fundamental questions remain unanswered. Nonetheless, with a good deal of ingenuity, researchers have found ways to explore the hidden worlds of consciousness. What they have discovered in the last few decades is the subject of this chapter.

Our review will begin with a few general points about the nature of consciousness. After that, the largest section of the chapter will be a "bedtime story," as we take a long look at the much-researched subject of sleep and dreams. We'll continue our tour of variations in consciousness by examining hypnosis, meditation, and the effects of mind-altering drugs. Finally, our Application will address a number of practical questions about sleep and dreams.

ON THE NATURE OF CONSCIOUSNESS

What is consciousness? **Consciousness is our awareness of internal and external stimuli.** Your consciousness includes (1) your awareness of external events ("the professor just asked me a difficult question about medieval history"), (2) your awareness of your internal sensations ("my heart is racing, and I'm beginning to sweat"), (3) your awareness of your *self* as the unique being having these experiences ("why me?"), and (4) your awareness of your thoughts about these experiences ("I'm going to make a fool of myself!"). To put it concisely, consciousness is personal awareness. But as you can see, awareness is a complex phenomenon. In this section, we'll build on ideas from previous chapters to make some general points about the nature of consciousness.

The Stream of Consciousness

The contents of your consciousness are continually changing. Rarely does consciousness come to a standstill; it moves, it flows, it fluctuates, it wanders. Recognizing this, William James (1902) christened this continuous flow the *stream of consciousness.* If you could tape-record your thoughts, you would find an endless flow of ideas that might zigzag all over the place. Try to monitor this flow sometime when you're listening to a lecture in class. You'll probably find yourself shifting back and forth between the lecture and daydreaming. As you'll soon learn, your consciousness continuously moves through a series of transitions, even when you sleep. To be constantly shifting and changing seems to be part of the essential nature of consciousness.

Variations in Levels of Awareness

While William James emphasized the continuous flow of consciousness, Sigmund Freud (1900) wanted to examine what went on beneath the surface of this stream. As explained in Chapter 1, Freud believed that *unconscious* needs, wishes, and conflicts can influence our feelings and behavior. However, Freud did not imply that the distinction between conscious and unconscious processes is absolute or that we are completely sealed off from the unconscious. For instance, he saw dreams as clear examples of unconscious processes, but he recognized that people often have conscious recollections of their dreams. To Freud, the stream of consciousness had depth: conscious and unconscious processes were different *levels of awareness.*

Freud was one of the first theorists to recognize that consciousness is not an all-or-none phenomenon. Instead, levels of awareness vary along a continuum between alert, focused awareness and the minimal awareness characteristic of sleep. Like other aspects of consciousness, this continuum is difficult to describe, but a few examples will illustrate some of the levels it includes.

Near the top of the continuum of awareness we find the states of consciousness that we experience during activities that demand high concentration, such as taking an exam, planning a move in chess, or playing a video game. Posner and Snyder (1975) call these kinds of activities *controlled processes.* **Controlled processes require alert awareness, absorb our limited attention, and interfere with other ongoing activities.** For example, suppose you're accustomed to driving a car with an automatic transmission and you want to learn to drive a car with a stick shift. If you're smart, you'll probably take your first lessons in a deserted parking lot, because initially working the stick shift will require so much attention that it will interfere with other activities associated with driving, such as paying attention to the flow of traffic. The state of focused awareness described in this example is the mark of controlled processes.

Once you learn to drive with a stick shift, however, working the shift will no longer require your concentrated attention. As you drive, you won't usually be thinking to yourself, "I need to lift my foot off the floor and depress the clutch pedal now." You'll just do it automatically. Presumably you'll make the appropriate moves at the right times, which will mean you have some awareness of what is going on, but it will be a lower level of awareness than that seen in controlled processes.

Posner and Snyder use the term *automatic processes* to refer to the states of consciousness that we experience when we're awake but on "automatic pilot." **Automatic processes occur with little awareness, require minimal attention, and do not interfere much with other activities.** For instance, most people can walk, talk, and chew gum at the same time, because these are automatic processes that demand little attention.

Daydreams are another familiar example of lowered awareness. *Daydreaming* involves drifting off into a world of fantasy. Although we remain awake, our awareness of the world around us tends to be reduced. Much of our daydreaming occurs while we're engaged in automatic processes.

Daydreams are often characterized as an "escape from reality" and have traditionally been regarded as an immature waste of time. However, Jerome Singer (1975) has concluded that virtually all of us daydream frequently. Moreover, studies looking for a possible link between frequent, vivid daydreaming and poor mental health have *not* found one (Klinger, 1987). On the contrary, psychologists who have studied them maintain that daydreams can serve a variety of important functions. They can help us to relax, to endure frustration, to alleviate boredom, and to rehearse how we're going to handle real-life challenges.

Further down the continuum of levels of awareness are the states of consciousness you experience when you sleep or when you are put under anesthesia for surgery. It might seem strange to describe these states as variations of consciousness. Clearly, when you are asleep, you are more inert than alert, and any information processing you do is decidedly passive. Yet you continue to maintain a low level of awareness. How do we know? Because some stimuli *do* penetrate your awareness. For example, people under surgical anesthesia occasionally hear comments made during their surgery, which they later repeat to their surprised surgeons (Rymer, 1987). Similarly, in laboratory studies of sleep, people sometimes remember hearing words that were spoken while they were unquestionably asleep (Bonnet, 1982).

Not only are we aware of some stimuli when we are largely unconscious, we can also discriminate among different stimuli. A good example is the new parent who can sleep through a loud thunderstorm, or even the raucous buzz of an alarm clock, but who immediately hears the muffled sound of the baby crying down the hall. The parent's selective sensitivity to different sounds means that some mental processing must be going on even during sleep. This minimal awareness marks the lower end of the continuum of our levels of awareness.

Consciousness and Brain Activity

Variations in consciousness are intimately related to changes in electrical activity in the brain. Investigators have been exploring this relationship ever since Hans Berger (1929) invented the EEG. As explained in Chapter 3, an **electroencephalograph (EEG) is a device that monitors the electrical activity of the brain over time by means of recording electrodes attached to the surface of the scalp.** The EEG records and amplifies electrical activity in the outer layer of the brain, called the *cortex*.

Ultimately, the EEG summarizes the rhythm of cortical activity in the brain in terms of line tracings called *brain waves*. The brain-wave tracings vary in *amplitude* (height) and *frequency* (cycles per second, abbreviated *cps*). Human brain-wave activity is usually divided into four principal bands based on the frequency of the brain waves.

Table 5.1 EEG Patterns Associated with States of Consciousness

WAVE PATTERNS	FREQUENCY (CYCLES/SEC)	TYPICAL STATES OF CONSCIOUSNESS
β Beta	13–24	Normal waking thought, alert problem solving
α Alpha	8–12	Deep relaxation, blank mind, meditation
θ Theta	4–7	Light sleep
Δ Delta	0–3	Deep sleep

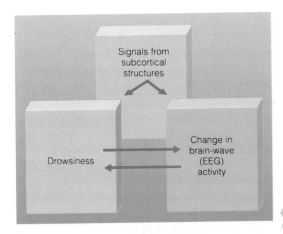

Figure 5.2 The "third variable" problem applied to mental states and electrical activity in the brain. As discussed in Chapter 2, correlations alone do not establish causation. For example, there are strong correlations between drowsiness and a particular pattern of brain-wave activity. But does drowsiness cause a change in brain waves, or do changes in brain waves cause drowsiness? Or does some third variable account for the changes in both?

These EEG bands, named after letters in the Greek alphabet, are *beta* (13–24 cps), *alpha* (8–12 cps), *theta* (4–7 cps), and *delta* (under 4 cps).

Different patterns of cortical EEG activity are associated with different states of consciousness, as is summarized in Table 5.1. For instance, when you are alertly engaged in problem solving, beta waves tend to dominate. When you are relaxed and resting, alpha waves increase. When you slip into deep, dreamless sleep, delta waves become more prevalent. Although these correlations are far from perfect, changes in brain activity are closely related to variations in consciousness (Guyton, 1981).

As is often the case with correlations, researchers are faced with a chicken-or-egg puzzle when it comes to the relationship between mental states and the brain's electrical activity. If you become drowsy while you are reading this page, your brain-wave activity will probably change. But are the changes in your brain-wave activity causing your drowsiness, or is your drowsiness causing the changes in your brain-wave activity? Or are the drowsiness and the shifts in brain-wave activity both caused by a third factor (see Figure 5.2)—perhaps signals coming from a subcortical area in the brain, such as the brain stem? Frankly, no one knows. All we know for sure is that variations in consciousness are correlated with variations in brain activity.

The link between consciousness and brain activity is particularly evident in studies of our sleep and waking cycle. Measures of EEG activity have provided investigators with a method for mapping out that most private of mental domains, the world of sleep. As we will see in the next section, that world is far more complex and varied than you might expect.

THE SLEEP AND WAKING CYCLE

Sleep is a variation in consciousness that is familiar to everyone. If you live to be 75, you probably will have spent somewhere between 18 and 25 years lost in sleep. Although it is a familiar state of consciousness, sleep is widely misunderstood. Generally, people view sleep as a single, uniform state of physical and mental inactivity. In reality, we evolve through a variety of different states of consciousness as we sleep, and quite a bit of both physical and mental activity occurs. Scientists have learned a great deal about sleep since the 1950s. In this section we'll discuss some of their insights.

Conducting Sleep Research

The advances in our understanding of sleep are the result of hard work by researchers who have spent countless nighttime hours watching other people sleep. This work is done in sleep laboratories, where volunteer subjects come to spend the night. Sleep labs have one or more "bedrooms" in which the subjects retire, usually after being hooked up to a variety of physiological recording devices. In addition to an EEG, these devices typically include an *electromyograph (EMG)*, **which records muscular activity and tension; an *electro-oculograph (EOG)*, which records eye movements; and and an *electrocardiograph (EKG)*, which records the contractions of the heart.** Other instruments monitor breathing, pulse rate, and body temperature. The researchers observe the sleeping subject through a window (or with a video camera) from an adjacent room, where they also monitor their elaborate physiological recording equipment (see Figure 5.3).

With this basic setup, researchers are able to study many aspects of the sleep process. Usually the researchers wait until a subject's second or third night in the lab before formally collecting data, because it takes most people a night or two to adapt to the strange bedroom and the recording devices (Antrobus et al., 1978). After a subject adapts to the lab, data collection begins and con-

Figure 5.3 The observation room of a sleep laboratory. Researchers in a sleep laboratory can observe subjects via video monitors while using elaborate equipment to record physiological changes during sleep. This kind of research has disclosed that sleep is a complex series of physical and mental states.

tinues over a period of days and sometimes weeks. Many kinds of observations can be made to see how certain variables such as age, sleep deprivation, and drug administration are related to patterns of sleeping.

Sleep as a Biological Rhythm

A rhythmic quality pervades the world around us. The daily alternation of light and darkness, the annual pattern of the seasons, and the phases of the moon all reflect this rhythmic quality of repeating cycles. Humans and many other animals display biological rhythms that are tied to these planetary rhythms (Luce, 1971). **Biological rhythms are periodic fluctuations in physiological functioning.** Birds beginning a winter migration or raccoons going into hibernation are showing the influence of a yearly cycle, just as a student trying to fight off sleep while studying late at night is showing the influence of a daily cycle of activity and rest. The existence of these rhythms means that organisms have biological clocks that somehow monitor the passage of time.

Table 5.2 Some Circadian Rhythms in Humans

PHYSIOLOGICAL MEASURES	TYPICAL TRENDS
Mental performance, time estimation	Highest in morning, declines slowly throughout day
Body temperature, skin temperature	Highest in late afternoon, lowest before waking
Respiration rate, rate of oxygen consumption	Lowest at night
Output of adrenal hormones	High during day, low at night
Output of urine; levels of sodium, potassium, and other elements in urine	High during day, low at night
Muscular coordination and strength, reaction times	Highest in early afternoon
Heart rate, blood pressure, number of red and white blood cells, level of blood sugar and other blood constituents	Lowest at night
Pain sensitivity	Highest at night, lowest in afternoon

Source: Adapted from Ruch, 1984

BIOLOGICAL RHYTHMS IN HUMANS

Four time cycles appear to be related to behavior in humans. Our biological rhythms include cycles corresponding roughly to periods of 1 year, 28 days, 24 hours, and 90 minutes (Aschoff, 1981). The yearly, or seasonal, cycle has been related to patterns of sexual activity and the onset of mood disorders such as depression (Smolensky et al., 1981; Wehr et al., 1986). Women's menstrual cycles are tied to the 28-day lunar month. This cycle has been related to fluctuations in mood, although the data are complex and controversial. Men may experience similar but less obvious 28-day cycles that affect their hormonal secretions (Parlee, 1973, 1982). The 90-minute cycle appears related to fluctuations in alertness and daydreaming (Lavie, 1982). Our yearly, monthly, and 90-minute time cycles appear to exert only a modest influence over our mental states and behavior. In contrast, our daily rhythms appear to exert considerably more influence.

CIRCADIAN RHYTHMS

Our most obvious biological rhythms are our daily cycles, or circadian rhythms. The term *circadian* is derived from two Latin roots: *circa* (about) and *dies* (a day). Thus, **circadian rhythms are the 24-hour biological cycles found in humans and many other species.** In humans, circadian rhythms are particularly influential in regulating sleep (Webb, 1982), but they also produce variations in body temperature, blood pressure, urine production, and hormone secretion, as well as other physical functions highlighted in Table 5.2 (Aschoff & Wever, 1981). For instance, your body temperature varies by about 3 degrees Fahrenheit over the period of a day, usually peaking in the afternoon and descending to a low in the depths of the night.

A study by Charles Czeisler and his colleagues indicates that we generally fall asleep as our body temperature begins to drop and awaken as it begins to ascend once again (Czeisler et al., 1980). Researchers have concluded that our circadian rhythm can leave us physiologically primed to fall asleep most easily at a particular time of day. This optimal time varies from one person to another, depending on unique personal schedules, but it's interesting to learn that each of us may have an "ideal" time for going to bed.

Our circadian clocks are apparently regulated internally, because they continue to run even when we're cut off from exposure to the cycle of day and night. For instance, when people stay in a cave or a closed-off room without windows or clocks, their circadian rhythms generally persist even though information about the light-dark cycle is eliminated. Interestingly, however, when people are isolated in this way, *they tend to drift toward a 25-hour cycle* (Aschoff & Wever, 1981). This peculiar trend is charted for one experimental subject in Figure 5.4. Investigators aren't sure why this drift occurs. It may have something to do with the 24.8-hour period of the moon's orbit around the earth, but this hypothesis is based on conjecture.

Although our biological clocks continue to function when we're cut off from the daily cycle of light and darkness, our biological rhythms tend to become more erratic or less rhythmic. This observation led many theorists to conclude that exposure to daylight *readjusts* our biological clocks. The readjustments may be necessary to correct for our tendency to drift toward a 25-hour cycle.

Scientists aren't sure how our basic timekeeping mechanism works. One theory is that the body's ability to track time is tied to the synthesis of proteins (Jacklet, 1978). However, researchers do have a pretty good idea of how the day-night cycle resets our biological clocks. There is evidence that exposure to sunlight affects the activity of the *pineal gland* (Binkley, 1979). The pineal gland's secretion of a neurotransmitter (serotonin) and a hormone (melatonin) is closely related to the cycle of light and darkness. The connection between the day-night cycle and activity in the pineal gland probably accounts for how our biological clocks are readjusted.

IGNORING OUR CIRCADIAN RHYTHMS

What happens when you ignore your biological clock and go to sleep at a time that is unusual for you? Typically, the quality of your sleep suffers. This is the reason for what we call *jet lag*. When you fly across several time zones, your biological clock keeps time as usual, even though official clock time changes. You then go to sleep at the "wrong" time and are likely to experience agitated, poor-quality sleep (Tepas, 1982). This inferior sleep, which can continue to occur for several days, can make people sluggish and irritable.

People differ in how quickly they can readjust their biological clocks to compensate for jet lag (Colquhoun, 1984). In addition, the speed of readjustment depends on several factors, including the distance and direction traveled. Generally, it's easier to fly westward and lengthen your day than it is to fly eastward and shorten it (Klein et al., 1977). It takes longer to resynchronize after flying east. Why? Perhaps because of our curious tendency to drift toward a 25-hour cycle. Apparently,

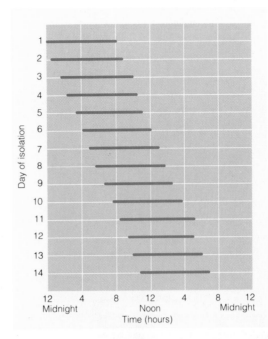

Figure 5.4 Changes in sleep periods of a subject isolated from the day-night cycle. The drift of the sleep periods to the right is characteristic of studies in which subjects are deprived of information about day and night. Subjects typically drift toward a 25-hour "day," retiring later and later with each day spent in isolation. When subjects are reexposed to light-cycle cues, they quickly return to a 24-hour rhythm.

there is a natural drift toward lengthening the daily cycle, which is exactly what you do when you fly westward. Flying eastward goes against this drift, much like swimming against a river current. Researchers are currently investigating whether certain drugs can be used to help people reset their biological clocks and so reduce the effects of jet lag. Thus far, the results are promising but inconclusive (Rosenfeld, 1986).

The findings on jet lag have led researchers to distinguish between two types of alterations in

Jet travel enables us to change time zones quickly, but our biological clocks are not so easily reset. The result is jet lag.

157

Figure 5.5 Circadian rhythms and jet lag. Air travelers generally adjust to local time more slowly after flying east (which shortens their day) than after flying west (which lengthens it). The explanation for this phenomenon may be our natural drift toward a longer daily cycle; it is easier to extend our biological cycle than to shorten it. (Data reported in Moore-Ede, Sulzman, & Fuller, 1982)

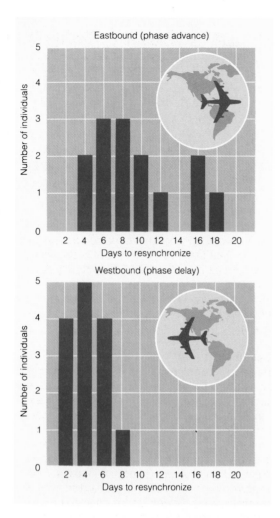

Eastbound (phase advance)

Westbound (phase delay)

circadian rhythm. When your schedule is altered so that you lengthen your day, you are said to experience a *phase-delay* shift. If you shorten your day, you go through a *phase-advance* shift. The evidence on jet lag suggests that we can accommodate phase-delay changes more easily than phase-advance changes (see Figure 5.5).

Of course, you don't have to hop a jet to get out of sync with your biological clock. Just going to bed a couple of hours later than usual can affect how you sleep. For instance, Charles Czeisler and his colleagues found that people who were at home but out of phase with their usual sleep schedule tended to sleep much longer than those who were in phase (Czeisler et al., 1980).

Rotating time shifts that force people to keep changing their sleep schedule also play havoc with biological rhythms. Rotating shifts are common among nurses, pilots, police officers, and many kinds of industrial workers. People who rotate shifts often complain bitterly about their sleep problems, and scientific research indicates that their complaints are well founded. Studies show that shift rotation can have a negative impact on the quality of employees' sleep, not to mention their productivity at work and their physical and mental health (Bell & Telman, 1980; Webb, 1975). This point brings us to our Featured Study, in which Charles Czeisler and his coworkers attempted to reduce the problems caused by rotating shifts.

Manipulating our Biological Clocks

Investigators: Charles A. Czeisler, Martin C. Moore-Ede (Harvard University), and Richard M. Coleman (Stanford University)

Source: Rotating shift work schedules that disrupt sleep are improved by applying circadian principles. *Science, 217* (1982), 460–463.

Over one-quarter of the U.S. work force has to endure shift changes with some regularity. Ample evidence shows that these rotating shifts disrupt sleep patterns, are unpleasant for the workers, and have a modest negative impact on the workers' mental and physical health. The purpose of this study was to see whether the negative effects of shift rotation could be reduced by using knowledge acquired in the study of biological rhythms. In effect, the investigators wanted to find out whether workers' biological clocks could be manipulated more effectively.

Research on biological rhythms suggested that it would be easier for shift workers to rotate through phase-delay changes (progressively later starting times) rather than phase-advance changes (progressively earlier starting times). Evidence also suggested that the periods between changes to a new starting time should be as long as feasible. The investigators hypothe-

sized that these kinds of alterations in rotation schedules would increase workers' satisfaction, health, and productivity.

Method

Subjects. The subjects were males, aged 19 to 68, who worked at an industrial plant in Utah. Comparisons were made between 85 rotating shift workers and a control group of 68 nonrotating workers who held comparable jobs.

Procedure. The rotating workers had been on a phase-advance schedule, moving successively through starting times of midnight, 4 P.M., and 8 A.M., with shift changes occurring weekly. The direction of shift rotation was changed to phase-delay for all of the rotating workers in the study. Some of these subjects remained on a weekly rotation, while others were moved to a 3-week period between shift changes. The dependent

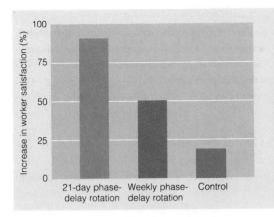

Figure 5.6 Effects on worker satisfaction of changes to a phase-delay shift rotation. Changing shifts by starting work at progressively later instead of earlier times markedly improved workers' satisfaction with their schedules. Improvement was greater for workers who had more time to adjust to each change in schedule.

variables of workers' satisfaction and health were measured 3 months after the change of schedules, while worker productivity was assessed 9 months after the change.

Results

The changeover to a phase-delay schedule led to improved worker satisfaction in both the 1-week and 3-week rotation groups. The 3-week rotation group, which had been exposed to *two* potentially beneficial alterations in schedule (the change to phase-delay and the change to a longer rotation), reported a larger increase in satisfaction than the 1-week group (see Figure 5.6). The 3-week group also showed greater improvements in health and work productivity than the 1-week group.

Discussion

The results support the hypothesis that the negative effects of shift rotation can be reduced by making workers' schedules more compatible with human circadian rhythms. The relationship found between work schedules and sleep quality provides additional evidence that human biological rhythms are important determinants of patterns of sleep quality, as well as daytime alertness and efficiency.

Comment

This study is an example of research that is important from both a practical and a theoretical standpoint. It tested basic theories about the advantages of phase-delay as opposed to phase-advance changes in circadian rhythm. At the same time it gathered information on practical questions about how to design optimal schedules in the real world of commerce and industry. Thus, it shows how the theoretically oriented science of psychology and the application-oriented profession of psychology can be united in a single creative endeavor.

As you can see from our brief review of research on biological rhythms, these cycles are more significant than most people realize. However, it's important to understand that the influence of our biological rhythms is subtle rather than overpowering. Our circadian rhythms may make a particular time of day ideal for falling asleep, but they don't knock us out. Obviously, to some degree we can ignore or override our biological clocks.

It's also important to realize that scientists are just beginning to understand the subtle relations between biological rhythms and behavior, and that some popular claims about biological rhythms are not supported by scientific data. In particular, there are *no* data that allow us to make predictions about fluctuations in individuals' moods or abilities based on birth date. In other words, the biorhythm advice found in newspaper columns and elsewhere has no empirical basis (Palmer, 1982). Nothing we have discussed lends any credibility to biorhythm predictions.

Cycling Through the Stages of Sleep

Not only does sleep occur in a context of daily rhythms, but subtler rhythms are evident within the experience of sleep itself. Since the 1950s, when pioneers such as Nathaniel Kleitman and William Dement made some major breakthroughs studying the physiology of sleep, researchers have learned a great deal about what goes on when we sleep. Kleitman and Dement found that when we sleep, we cycle through a series of five distinct stages. Let's take a look at what researchers have learned about the changes that occur during these stages of sleep (Borbely, 1986; Dement, 1978).

STAGES 1–4

The transitions between the first four stages of sleep are gradual rather than abrupt, and the divisions between these stages are somewhat arbitrary. When you first fall asleep, your sleep is relatively light, and you can be awakened easily. Stage 1 is a brief transitional stage that usually lasts only 5–10 minutes. Your breathing and heart rate slow down as your muscle tension and body temperature decline. The alpha waves that probably dominated your EEG activity just before you fell asleep give way to lower-frequency EEG activity in which theta waves are prominent. Figure 5.7 illustrates the differences between wide-awake beta waves, the alpha waves associated with relaxation and drowsiness, and the theta waves seen in stage 1 sleep (along with EEGs from other stages).

As you descend through stages 2, 3, and 4 of the sleep cycle, your respiration rate, heart rate, muscle tension, and body temperature continue to decline. Your sleep deepens, and it takes progressively stronger stimuli to awaken you. During stage 2, brief bursts of higher-frequency brain waves, called *sleep spindles*, appear against a background of mixed, mostly lower-frequency EEG activity (consult Figure 5.7 once again). Gradually, high-amplitude, low-frequency delta waves become more common. When such delta waves account for at least 20% of your EEG activity, you are said to be in stage 3. When more than 50% of your EEG activity consists of these delta waves, you have reached stage 4, which is dominated by slow-wave activity. Typically you reach stage 4 in less than an hour and stay there for roughly a half hour. Then the cycle reverses itself, and you gradually move upward through progressively lighter stages of sleep. That's when things start to get very interesting.

REM SLEEP

When you reach what should be stage 1 once again, you usually go into the fifth stage of sleep, which is most widely known as *REM sleep*. REM is an abbreviation for *rapid eye movements*. This name is derived from the most obvious outer sign associated with this stage of sleep—rapid lateral eye movements that take place beneath your closed eyelids. Researchers monitor these eye movements precisely in the sleep lab with an electro-oculograph, but you can also observe them yourself if you have an opportunity to watch closely when someone is sleeping. In the REM stage, you'll see little ripples moving back and forth across the sleeper's closed eyelids.

REM sleep was discovered accidentally by Nathaniel Kleitman and his colleagues at the University of Chicago in the 1950s (Aserinsky & Kleitman, 1953; Dement & Kleitman, 1957). One of Kleitman's graduate students, Eugene Aserinsky, was assigned to record sleeping subjects' slow, rolling eye movements because they were thought to accompany the onset of sleep. He was astonished when he found vigorous, rapid, coordinated eye movements at periodic intervals during subjects' sleep. The term *REM sleep* was coined by William Dement, another student in Kleitman's lab, who went on to become one of the world's most prominent sleep researchers. As Dement (1978) noted later in his book *Some Must Watch While Some Must Sleep*, "This was *the* breakthrough—the discovery that changed the course of sleep research." As investigators explored the characteristics of the REM stage, they found that it was a very special and very different kind of sleep.

Their research showed that the REM stage is a deep stage of sleep in the conventional sense that it is relatively hard to awaken a person from this stage. The REM stage is also marked by irregular breathing and pulse rate. Muscle tone is extremely relaxed, so much so that bodily movements are minimal and the sleeper is virtually paralyzed.

Although REM sleep is a deep stage of sleep, EEG activity is dominated by high-frequency, low-amplitude beta waves that resemble those observed when people are alert and awake (see Figure 5.7 again). This pairing of deep sleep with "wide-awake" brain waves is a perplexing paradox. In fact, the contradiction is so fundamental that the REM stage is often referred to as *paradoxical sleep*.

Scientists aren't sure how to explain this paradox, but they assume that it must be related to the most fascinating feature of REM sleep—namely, that *this is the stage of sleep during which most dreaming occurs*. How do we know that? In sleep studies, researchers have systematically awakened subjects

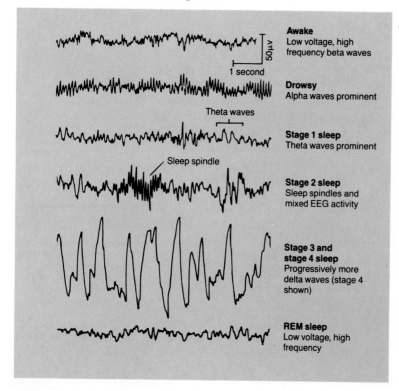

Figure 5.7 EEG patterns in sleep and wakefulness. Our characteristic brain waves vary depending on our state of consciousness. Generally, as we move from an awake state through deeper stages of sleep, our brain waves decrease in frequency (cycles per second) and increase in amplitude (height). However, brain waves during REM sleep resemble "wide-awake" brain waves.

Awake
Low voltage, high frequency beta waves

50μV

1 second

Drowsy
Alpha waves prominent

Theta waves

Stage 1 sleep
Theta waves prominent

Sleep spindle

Stage 2 sleep
Sleep spindles and mixed EEG activity

Stage 3 and stage 4 sleep
Progressively more delta waves (stage 4 shown)

REM sleep
Low voltage, high frequency

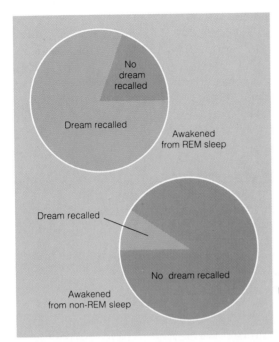

Figure 5.8 REM sleep and dream activity. The graph portrays the results of a number of dream-recall studies. Subjects recalled dreams far more often when awakened from REM sleep than from non-REM sleep, indicating that most of our dreaming occurs during the REM stage. (Based on data from Dement, 1978)

To summarize, **REM sleep is a deep stage of sleep marked by rapid eye movements, high-frequency brain waves, and dreaming.** It is such a special stage of sleep that the other four stages are generally lumped together simply as "non-REM sleep." **Non-REM (NREM) sleep consists of sleep stages 1 through 4, which are marked by an absence of rapid eye movements, relatively little dreaming, and systematic variations in EEG activity.**

REPEATING THE CYCLE

During the course of a night, we usually repeat the entire sleep cycle about four times. Since each cycle runs roughly 90 minutes, this regular pattern in sleep is an example of the 90-minute biological rhythms we discussed earlier.

As the night wears on, the sleep cycle changes gradually. While the first REM period is relatively short, lasting perhaps 5 or 10 minutes, subsequent REM periods get progressively longer, peaking at around 40 minutes in length. In addition, the NREM intervals tend to get shorter, and each descent into the deeper NREM stages tends to become more shallow. These trends can be seen in Figure 5.9, which charts the sleep cycle of a subject observed in one study.

"[The discovery of REM sleep] was the breakthrough—the discovery that changed the course of sleep research."
WILLIAM DEMENT

from the various stages of sleep to ask whether a dream was interrupted. (Life in a sleep lab can be a rude awakening.) In doing so, they found that most dream reports came from awakenings during the REM stage. Figure 5.8 shows William Dement's (1978) compilation of the results of eight early studies of this sort, involving nearly 1500 awakenings of subjects. REM awakenings produced dream recall 78% of the time, while awakenings from other stages were accompanied by dream recall only 14% of the time. Although some dreaming occurs in other stages, dreaming is most frequent, vivid, and memorable during REM sleep.

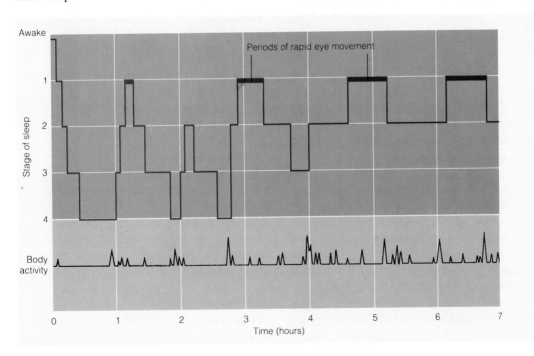

Figure 5.9 The cycle of sleep. The graph shows one subject's sleep cycle and associated amount of body activity during the course of a night. Notice how the sleeper cycles through several descents into progressively shallower stages of sleep and how periods of REM sleep become longer as the night goes on.

Figure 5.10 Changes in sleep patterns over the life span. Both the total amount of sleep per night and the proportion of REM sleep change with age. Sleep patterns change most dramatically during infancy, with total sleep time and amount of REM sleep declining sharply in the first 2 years of life. After a noticeable drop in the average amount of sleep in adolescence, sleep patterns remain relatively stable, although total sleep and REM sleep continue to decline gradually with age. (Adapted from Roffwarg, Muzio, & Dement, 1966, revised by authors since publication)

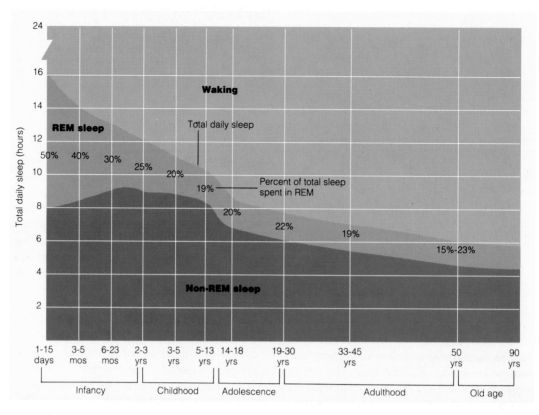

These trends mean that NREM sleep tends to predominate early in your sleep cycle, gradually giving way to periods of REM sleep and dreaming that dominate the latter part of a night's sleep. Of course, individuals show unique variations on this typical pattern. However, a particular person tends to cycle through a night of sleep in much the same way night after night, providing that nothing happens to throw off the person's circadian rhythm (Webb, 1975). Thus, each of us has a unique "trademark" pattern of sleeping.

AGE AND THE SLEEP CYCLE

Age alters the sleep cycle. What we have described so far is the typical pattern of sleeping for adults. Children, however, display different patterns (Parmelee & Stern, 1972; Williams, Karacan, & Hursch, 1974).

Newborns sleep six to eight times in a 24-hour period, so that total sleeping time often exceeds 16 hours. Furthermore, they spend much more of their sleep time than adults do in the REM stage. In the first few months of life, REM accounts for about half of babies' sleep, as compared to one-fifth of adults' sleep. During the remainder of the first year, children move toward fewer but longer sleep periods, and the REM portion of their sleep gradually declines to roughly 30%. The REM portion of sleep continues to decrease very gradually until it levels off at about 20% during adolescence (see Figure 5.10). After that, age-related changes in sleep patterns are modest, although disturbances in the sleep cycle tend to occur more frequently among the elderly than among the middle-aged.

The Neural Bases of Sleep

EEG recordings only provide us with global overviews of cortical activity that we can relate to patterns of sleep and waking. Although the EEG has been invaluable in the investigation of sleep, these global overviews permit little insight into the neural mechanisms that may actually cause us to fall asleep. Investigators have used a variety of research methods to explore the neural bases of sleep—methods such as ablation, lesioning, electrical stimulation, and tracking neurotransmitters (see Chapter 3). The results of this research indicate that the neural bases of sleep are complex and multifaceted.

If one brain structure stands out as especially important to sleep and wakefulness, it's the *reticular formation* in the core of the brain stem. The ***ascending reticular activating system (ARAS)* consists of the afferent fibers running through the reticular formation that influence physiological arousal.** As you can see from Figure 5.11, the ARAS projects diffusely into many areas of the cortex. Wakefulness depends on neural stimulation traveling upward through this system (Moruzzi & Magoun, 1949). When these ascend-

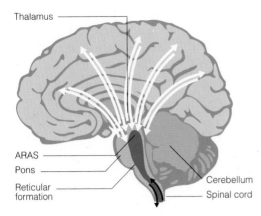

Thalamus

ARAS
Pons
Reticular
formation

Cerebellum
Spinal cord

Figure 5.11 The ascending reticular activating system (ARAS). A number of brain areas and structures interact to regulate sleep and waking. Particularly important is the ARAS, which conveys neural stimulation to many areas of the cortex.

ing fibers are cut in the brain stem of a cat, the result is continuous sleep. Electrical stimulation along the same pathways produces arousal and alertness.

Although the ARAS plays a central role in the neural regulation of sleep and waking, many other brain structures are also involved. Lesions in specific areas of the pons, medulla, thalamus, hypothalamus, limbic system, and other structures can have dramatic effects on sleep and waking in animals (Vertes, 1984; see Chapter 3 for the locations of these brain structures). Thus, the ebb and flow of sleep and waking are regulated through activity in a constellation of interacting brain centers.

Efforts to identify the neurotransmitters involved in the regulation of sleep and waking have uncovered similar complexity and diffusion of responsibility. At least four neurotransmitters—serotonin, norepinephrine, dopamine, and acetylcholine—influence the course of our sleep and arousal, and several other chemicals may play a contributing role (Van Oot, Lane, & Borkovec, 1984). In summary, there isn't any single structure in the brain that serves as a "sleep center" nor any one neurotransmitter that serves as a "sleep chemical." Instead, it appears that sleep depends on the interplay of a great many neural centers and neurotransmitters.

Doing Without: Sleep Deprivation

At one time or another, you probably have had to get through a day with too little sleep. If you suffered from fatigue, drowsiness, headaches, and poor concentration, you know from personal experience just how unpleasant the lack of sleep can be. Interestingly, however, scientific research on sleep deprivation suggests that it is not as detrimental as most people subjectively feel that it is.

COMPLETE DEPRIVATION

What happens when people go completely without sleep for a period of days? The answer varies a great deal depending on the person and the task at hand. As you might expect, complete deprivation of sleep has been related to various negative effects, including weariness, poor concentration, reduced motivation, irritability, and lapses in attention (Johnson, 1982). Some people show severe mental disorientation and even suffer from hallucinations, usually after about 60 hours of staying awake.

Severe effects from sleep deprivation would probably be more common, except that most of us have a hard time going very long without sleep. Most people experience great difficulty getting beyond a third or fourth day without any sleep. In the laboratory, after subjects have gone about 72 hours without sleep, it becomes impossible to prevent them from drifting off into "microsleep" periods—moments of drowsiness during which their EEG activity resembles stage 1 sleep (although they appear to be awake).

Despite the negative effects of sleep deprivation, researchers have been impressed by how *well* sleep-deprived subjects can perform if they are motivated to do so (Webb & Cartwright, 1978). In 1965 a 17-year-old student named Randy Gardner, who wanted to set a world record, managed to stay awake for 264 consecutive hours. Gardner's accomplishment was astonishing enough by itself, but he did it *without experiencing any major ill effects* (Dement, 1978).

Although Randy Gardner's story is atypical, it appears that the only consistent effect of complete sleep deprivation is an increase in subjective feelings of tiredness or weariness. In other words, the main effect of sleep loss is sleepiness! Even this tiredness fluctuates throughout the day with one's biological rhythms, rather than increasing steadily.

PARTIAL DEPRIVATION

Partial sleep deprivation occurs when we consistently make do with substantially less sleep than normal over a period of time. For example, Haslam (1981) studied soldiers who agreed to

Figure 5.12 Awakenings of one subject from REM sleep over a period of three nights. The pattern of awakenings illustrates how a REM-deprived subject tends to compensate by repeatedly slipping back into REM sleep. Notice how the awakenings of this subject became more frequent during the course of each night and from night to night. (Based on data from Borbely, 1986)

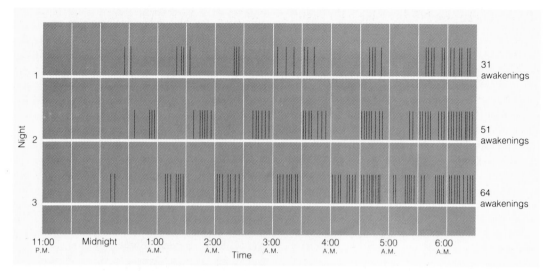

31 awakenings

51 awakenings

64 awakenings

work on only 1.5 or 3 hours of sleep per day. This kind of partial sleep deprivation probably occurs much more often in everyday life than complete deprivation.

Clearly, partial sleep deprivation can have negative effects, but most studies find that the declines in performance are inconsistent and modest in size. According to Johnson (1982), the impact of partial sleep deprivation on performance depends to a large degree on the task at hand. The negative effects due to sleep loss are greater when subjects are asked to work on long-lasting tasks, difficult tasks, or uninteresting tasks.

When subjects reduce their nightly sleep time gradually (for instance, by a half hour each week), the negative effects of sleep loss tend to be modest. However, many of the sleep-deprived subjects still complain of feeling fatigued, even when their performance on tasks remains unaffected (Friedmann et al., 1977).

Insofar as sleep deprivation makes us feel weary, research indicates that we can quickly make up for the feelings of weariness that come from sleep loss. Randy Gardner, for example, appeared to recover from his 264 hours without sleep in just one 15-hour night of sleep! After either partial or complete sleep deprivation, most people compensate by getting a few hours of extra sleep for one to three nights. This extra sleep is usually enough to fuel their recovery, and they then return to their normal sleep patterns. We definitely do *not* need to make up for lost sleep on a one-to-one basis.

REM DEPRIVATION

The unique quality of REM sleep has led researchers to investigate the effects of a special type of partial sleep deprivation—*REM deprivation*. In a number of laboratory studies, subjects were awak-

ened over a period of nights whenever they began to go into the REM stage. These subjects often got a decent amount of sleep in NREM stages, but they were systematically deprived of REM sleep.

What are the effects of REM deprivation? Early studies reported that REM deprivation led to major negative effects such as heightened anxiety, irritability, and fatigue. However, these early reports have not stood the test of time and replication (Pearlman, 1982). The accumulated evidence suggests that the effects of REM deprivation on daytime functioning are mild.

However, REM deprivation *does* have some interesting effects on subjects' patterns of sleeping. As the nights go by in REM-deprivation studies, it becomes necessary to awaken the subjects more and more often to deprive them of their REM sleep, because they spontaneously shift into REM more and more frequently. While subjects normally go into REM about four times a night, REM-deprived subjects start slipping into REM every time the researchers turn around. In one study, researchers had to awaken a subject 64 times by the third night of REM deprivation (Borbely, 1986; see Figure 5.12). Furthermore, when a REM-deprivation experiment comes to an end and subjects are allowed to sleep without interruption, they experience **REM rebound, which involves spending extra time in REM periods for one or more nights after REM deprivation.**

What do theorists make of these spontaneous pursuits of REM sleep? They conclude that REM sleep is a very important form of sleep and that we must have a specific *need* for it—and a rather strong need, at that. Unfortunately, theorists remain perplexed about *how* it's important and *why* we need it. The function of REM sleep is one of many unsolved mysteries that continue to fascinate sleep researchers.

Problems in the Night: Sleep Disorders

Not everyone consistently enjoys the luxury of a good night's sleep. Many people are troubled by sleep disorders, ranging from occasional or chronic insomnia to its rare opposite, narcolepsy, in which people fall irresistibly into deep sleep even during normal waking hours. In this section we will briefly discuss what is currently known about a variety of sleep disorders.

INSOMNIA

Insomnia is the most common sleep disorder. **Insomnia involves chronic problems in getting adequate sleep.** There are three basic patterns of insomnia: (1) difficulty in falling asleep initially, (2) difficulty in remaining asleep, and (3) persistent early morning awakening. Insomnia often sounds like a minor problem to people who haven't struggled with it, but it can be a very unpleasant malady. Insomniacs toss and turn in restless frustration as they watch their precious sleep time tick away (see Figure 5.13).

PREVALENCE How common is insomnia? Nearly everyone suffers occasional sleep difficulties due to stress, disruptions of biological rhythms, or other temporary circumstances. Fortunately, these problems clear up spontaneously for most of us. However, as many as 30% of adults may have chronic problems with insomnia (Hartmann, 1985).

Some of these people may be suffering from *pseudoinsomnia*, which means that they just *think* that they are getting an inadequate amount of sleep. When monitored in a sleep clinic, some people who complain vigorously about insomnia show perfectly sound sleep patterns (Mitler et al., 1975). In one well-known case of exaggerated complaining, a British insomniac claimed that he hadn't slept in 10 years! When invited to stay at a sleep clinic for observation, he seemed determined to prove his chronic sleeplessness. However, by the second night he nodded out for 20 minutes. By the fourth night, he could barely keep his eyes open and soon he was snoring blissfully for hours (Oswald & Adam, 1980).

The discrepancy between individuals' feelings about how much they sleep and objective reality shows once again that states of consciousness are highly subjective. Actually, this discrepancy is not unique to insomniacs. Normal sleepers also tend to underestimate how much sleep they get (Lewis, 1969). Apparently, many of us desire sleep so strongly that we routinely feel we're not getting enough.

Figure 5.13 Insomnia. Nothing is more natural than sleep, yet chronic difficulty in falling and staying asleep is the most common sleep problem. Unfortunately, insomnia can be self-perpetuating if improperly treated (see Figure 5.14).

CAUSES Insomnia has a number of causes (Kales & Kales, 1984). Perhaps the most common cause is excessive anxiety and tension that make it difficult to relax and go to sleep. Insomnia is frequently a side effect of emotional problems, such as depression, or of significant stress, such as heavy pressure at work or marital conflict. Understandably, health problems like back pain, ulcers, and asthma can lead to insomnia as a side effect. The use of certain drugs, especially stimulants such as cocaine and amphetamines, may also lead to problems in sleeping.

TREATMENT The most frequently used approach to the treatment of insomnia is the prescription of sedative drugs, commonly known as sleeping pills. Unfortunately, this treatment is probably used *too* frequently. Sleep experts are virtually unanimous in maintaining that in the past physicians have prescribed sleeping pills far too readily. As a result of this criticism from sleep researchers, prescriptions for sleeping pills declined about 50% between 1971 and 1982 (Lamberg, 1986).

According to sleep expert Ernest Hartmann (1978), sleeping pills are a poor long-range solution for insomnia for a number of reasons. For example, there is some danger of overdose, and many people become dependent on sedatives in order to fall asleep. Moreover, with continued use, sedatives gradually lose their effectiveness, so people need to increase their dose to more dangerous levels, creating a vicious circle of escalating dependency (see Figure 5.14). Ironically, sedatives also interfere with the normal cycle of sleep.

Figure 5.14 The vicious circle of dependence on sleeping pills. Because of the body's ability to develop tolerance to drugs, using sedatives routinely to "cure" insomnia can lead to a vicious circle of escalating dependency as larger and larger doses of the sedative are needed to produce the same effect.

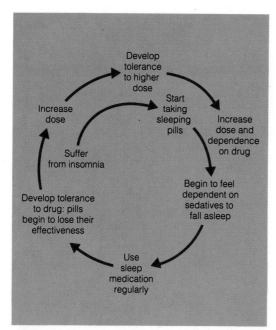

Although sedatives promote sleep, they *reduce* the proportion of sleep time spent in the important REM stage.

In short, while there is a role for sedatives in the treatment of insomnia, they need to be used very cautiously and conservatively. They should be used primarily for short-term treatment of sleep problems.

A much safer alternative for treating insomnia is *L-tryptophan*, an amino acid found in many foods. This natural substance, which can be obtained as a dietary supplement in health food stores, helps to promote the synthesis of serotonin, one of the neurotransmitters involved in the regulation of sleep. As is often the case with health fads, the effectiveness of L-tryptophan has probably been exaggerated. Research to date suggests that the sedative effects of L-tryptophan are mild and inconsistent (Borbely, 1986). However, it seems to help some people, and it's largely risk free.

Beyond discouraging the use of drugs, it is hard to generalize about how chronic insomnia should be treated, because its many different causes call for different solutions. A number of sleep clinics have been established in recent years to help people who suffer from insomnia and other sleep disorders (Hales, 1987). Work in these clinics has generated some insights about strategies that people can apply on their own when grappling with insomnia. Some of these insights are reviewed in the Application at the end of this chapter.

OTHER SLEEP PROBLEMS

While insomnia is the most common difficulty associated with sleep, people are plagued by many other types of sleep problems as well. This section briefly summarizes the symptoms, causes, and prevalence of six additional sleep disorders and problems, as described by Hartmann (1985) and Van Oot, Lane, and Borkovec (1984).

Narcolepsy is a disease marked by sudden and irresistible onsets of sleep during normal waking hours. A person suffering from narcolepsy goes directly from wakefulness into the REM stage of sleep. This is a potentially dangerous condition, since some victims fall asleep instantly, even while driving a car or operating a machine. Narcolepsy is quite rare. Its causes are unknown, but there is evidence that people may be genetically predisposed to the disease. Stimulant drugs have been used to treat narcolepsy with modest success, but as you will see in the upcoming discussion of drugs, stimulants carry many problems and dangers of their own.

Sleep apnea involves frequent, reflexive gasping for air that awakens a person and then disrupts sleep. Some victims are awakened from their sleep hundreds of times a night. Apnea occurs when a person literally stops breathing for 15–60 seconds. The causes of this rare condition are unknown. As you might expect, sleep apnea

---

CONCEPT CHECK 5.1
Comparing REM and NREM Sleep

A table here could have provided you with a systematic comparison of REM sleep and NREM sleep, but that would have deprived you of the opportunity to check your understanding of these sleep phases by creating your own table. Try to fill in each of the blanks below with a word or phrase highlighting the differences between REM and NREM sleep with regard to the various characteristics specified. As usual, you can find the answers in the back of the book in Appendix A.

Characteristic	REM *sleep*	NREM *sleep*
Type of EEG activity	_____	_____
Eye movements	_____	_____
Dreaming	_____	_____
Depth (difficulty in awakening)	_____	_____
Percentage of total sleep (in adults)	_____	_____
Increases or decreases with age (as percentage of sleep)	_____	_____
Timing in sleep cycle (dominates early or late)	_____	_____

often leads to insomnia as a side effect. Severe cases may also cause heart and lung damage. Apnea can be treated with surgery or drug therapy.

***Night terrors* are abrupt awakenings from NREM sleep accompanied by intense autonomic arousal and feelings of panic.** Night terrors usually occur during stage 3 or stage 4 sleep (see Figure 5.15). Victims typically let out a piercing cry and sit bolt upright. Usually they then stare into space, with no recall of any dream. The panic normally fades quickly, and a return to sleep is fairly easy. Night terrors can occur at any age, but they are especially common in children aged 3 to 8. Night terrors are *not* indicative of an emotional disturbance, and treatment is generally unnecessary as they are usually a temporary problem.

***Nightmares* are anxiety-arousing dreams that lead to awakening, usually from REM sleep.** Typically, the person who awakens from a nightmare recalls the dream vividly and may find it difficult to get back to sleep. Although adults have nightmares, these frightening episodes are mainly a problem among children. Most youngsters have occasional nightmares, but *persistent* nightmares may reflect an emotional disturbance. If nightmares are very persistent and unpleasant, counseling may be helpful. Otherwise, treatment is unnecessary as most children outgrow the problem.

***Somnambulism,* or sleepwalking, occurs when a sleeping person arises and wanders about in deep NREM sleep (stage 3 or 4).** Despite what you may have heard, sleepwalkers are not acting out a dream. They may awaken during their journey, or they may return to bed without any recollection of their excursion. The causes of this unusual disorder are unknown, although there does appear to be a genetic predisposition to it.

Sleepwalking occurs mostly in children, but it

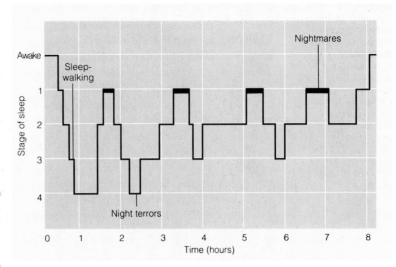

Figure 5.15 Sleep problems and the cycle of sleep. Different sleep problems tend to occur at different points in the sleep cycle. Whereas sleepwalking and night terrors are associated with deep, non-REM stages of sleep, nightmares are associated with the heightened dream activity of REM sleep.

is occasionally seen in adults. Children usually outgrow the problem, so professional intervention isn't required. However, sleepwalkers *are* prone to having accidents. For example, one sleepwalking auto mechanic fell off his second-story porch and broke his back. Children have been known to fall down stairs and into swimming pools, so parents may need to take some precautionary measures if the problem persists, such as locking the child in an accident-proofed bedroom. Contrary to popular myth, it is safe to awaken people (gently) from a sleepwalking episode—much safer than letting them wander about.

***Hypersomnia* is a condition marked by a consistent need for an excessive amount of sleep.** Hypersomniacs are chronically lethargic and may routinely sleep 12–16 hours, or even more, a day. Hypersomnia may result from severe depression, drug dependence, and some physical diseases, among other causes. It is a good idea for people suffering from hypersomnia to seek professional consultation.

THE WORLD OF DREAMS

"I had a discussion with a man about investing in the stock market. I gave him all my money for this. Then I searched for a woman to clean my apartment. A next-door neighbor, a man, took over to find one. I came home and found my neighbor in my apartment, asleep.

"The cleaning woman came in and started to act in a very disturbed manner. She wanted me to give her my sweater. I was afraid of her. She threw me on the floor. Then I pulled off my green sweater.

"Then I remembered that stocks were bad and they were about to go into a depression and I wanted to make some arrangements. Oh yes, the woman had already taken another sweater while I was not there.

"Ann, a policeman, and I were seated. The policeman said I should get the key back and not to worry

about anything the woman stole because the government would reimburse me. Just then the madwoman walked in at that point and just sat down in a very relaxed manner. She had a small round case with a key. In her presence, the policeman insisted that I give him the details about the sweaters. I told the policeman, but I stuttered because I feared the madwoman. As I gave the description of the green sweater, the policeman asked the woman if she stole it. She casually said yes, that she intended to return the sweater. As she took out the sweater, she took out a gun, too, and aimed it at the policeman. She pulled the trigger but there was no ammunition. As the madwoman and the policeman wrestled, I woke up." (Caligor & May, 1968, pp. 32–33)

One of the most fascinating aspects of sleep is the state of dreaming. **A *dream* is a mental experience during sleep that includes vivid visual images.** As the preceding dream account illustrates, dreams are not strongly restrained by logic or rationality. They often are disorganized and highly unrealistic, as their plots take unpredictable and even impossible turns.

People have always been intrigued by dreams, seeking to find hidden meanings in this seemingly magical world of consciousness. Only in recent years have dreams been subjected to empirical study. In the laboratory, psychologists investigate dreaming by awakening subjects from sleep to ask them whether they were dreaming and what they were dreaming about. As you have already learned, this kind of study has shown that most dreaming occurs during REM sleep.

Psychologists also learn about dreams by instructing research subjects or therapy patients to try to awaken during the night at home to record their dreams. This was the method employed by therapist Leopold Caligor, who obtained the "madwoman" dream from one of his patients. These kinds of studies have cast some light on when we dream and what we dream about. What remains obscure is *why* we dream.

Table 5.3 Common Dreams of College Students and the Percentage Having Each Type of Dream

TYPE OF DREAM	PERCENTAGE OF STUDENTS
Falling	83
Being attacked or pursued	77
Trying repeatedly to do something	71
School, teachers, studying	71
Sexual experiences	66
Arriving too late	64
Eating	62
Being frozen with fright	58
The death of a loved one	57
Being locked up	56
Finding money	56
Swimming	52
Snakes	49
Being inappropriately dressed	46
Being smothered	44
Being nude in public	43
Fire	41
Failing an examination	39
Seeing self as dead	33
Killing someone	26

Source: Griffith, Miyago, & Tago, 1958

The Contents of Our Dreams

What do we dream about? Overall, our dreams are not as exciting as advertised. Perhaps we view dreams as exotic because we are more likely to remember our more bizarre nighttime dramas. After analyzing the contents of more than 10,000 dreams, Calvin Hall (1966) concluded that most dreams are in fact relatively mundane. They tend to unfold in familiar settings with a cast of characters dominated by family, friends, and colleagues, with a sprinkling of strangers.

Hall found that certain themes are more common than others in our dreams. Examples of dreams commonly reported by college students can be found in Table 5.3. If you glance through this table, you'll see that we dream quite a bit about sex, aggression, and misfortune. According to Hall, our dreams tend to center on classic sources of internal conflict, such as the conflict between taking chances and playing it safe. Hall was struck by how little we dream about public affairs and current events. Typically, our dreams are very self-centered; we dream mostly about ourselves.

Links Between Our Dream World and the Real World

Though dreams can seem to belong in a world of their own, what we dream about is affected by what is going on in our lives (Hall & Van de Castle, 1966). If you're struggling with financial problems, worried about an upcoming exam, or fantasizing about an attractive classmate, for example, these themes may very well show up in your dreams. Freud noticed long ago that the contents of our waking life tend to spill into our dreams, and he labeled this spillover the *day residue*.

The contents of our dreams can also be affected by stimuli that are experienced during the dream. For example, William Dement sprayed water on one hand of sleeping subjects while they were in the REM stage (Dement & Wolpert, 1958). Subjects who weren't awakened by the water were awakened by the experimenter a short time later and asked what they were dreaming about. Dement found that 42% of the subjects incorporated the water into their dreams. When awakened, they said that they had dreamt that they were in rainfalls, floods, baths, swimming pools, and the like. Some people report that they occasionally experience the same thing at home when the sound of their alarm clock fails to awaken them. The alarm is incorporated into their dream as a loud engine, a siren, or some other sound. Like the day residue, the incorporation of external stimuli into dreams shows that our dream world is not entirely separate from our waking world.

Theories of Dreaming

Why do we dream? Many theories have been proposed regarding the purposes of dreaming. Sigmund Freud (1900), who analyzed clients' dreams in therapy, believed that the principal purpose of dreams was *wish fulfillment*. He thought that people fulfilled needs that went ungratified during waking hours through wishful thinking in dreams. For example, someone who was sexually frustrated would tend to have highly erotic dreams, and an unsuccessful person would dream about great accomplishments.

Other theorists, such as Rosalind Cartwright (1977), have proposed that dreams provide us with an opportunity to work through the major problems in our lives. According to this cognitive, *problem-solving* view of dreams, there is considerable continuity between waking and sleeping thought. Proponents of this view believe that dreams allow us to engage in creative thinking about our problems, because dreams are not restrained by logic or realism.

An influential *physiological view* of dreaming argues that dreams are simply the byproduct of bursts of activity in the brain (Hobson & McCarley, 1977). The architects of this model argue that dreams are side effects of neural activation (the "wide-awake" brain waves) during REM sleep. In contrast to the theories of Freud and Cartwright, this theory obviously downplays the role of emotional factors as determinants of dreams.

These are only three of at least seven major theories about the functions of dreams. All seven theories are based more on conjecture than on research. Webb and Cartwright (1978) point out that none of the theories has been tested adequately. In part, this is because the private, subjective nature of dreams makes it difficult to put the theories to an empirical test. Like the question of why we need REM sleep, the question of why we dream remains one of the many mysteries in the investigation of consciousness.

HYPNOSIS AND MEDITATION

Ever restless, consciousness moves through many variations: from alert concentration to daydreams, from waking to sleep, from nightmares to pleasant dreams. Because the shifts from one of these kinds of awareness to another are largely spontaneous and familiar to us all, they do not seem mysterious to most people. However, the subjects we turn to next are neither spontaneous nor generally familiar. Hypnosis and meditation involve deliberate efforts to alter states of awareness. They seem to involve exotic worlds of consciousness—true "altered states"—that many people never experience. Let's examine hypnosis and meditation and see what scientists have discovered about them.

Hypnosis: Altered Consciousness or Role Playing?

Have you ever seen a show put on by a stage hypnotist? If so, you probably saw some unusual demonstrations that you may have found perplexing. For instance, I once saw a stage hypnotist tell a hypnotized subject that he had just returned from Mars and that he should tell the audience what it was like—in his native Martian tongue. The young man started speaking energetically, but in absolute gibberish (at least to earthling ears). Another subject frantically dropped a pencil when informed that it was a red-hot piece of iron, and a third began to crawl about the stage as if she were a mountain lion.

What's going on here? The power of theatrical hypnotists to produce foolish behavior in members of the audience symbolizes for many what hypnosis is all about. In the classic explanation of hypnosis, its effects are achieved by putting subjects into a special state of consciousness, commonly called a *hypnotic trance*. As you will soon see, this explanation has been hotly debated.

Hypnosis has a long and checkered history. It all began with a flamboyant 18th-century Austrian physician named Franz Anton Mesmer. Working in Paris, Mesmer claimed to cure people of paralysis and other illnesses through an elaborate routine involving a "laying on of hands." Although Mesmer had some complicated theories about how he had harnessed "animal magnetism," he had simply stumbled onto the power of suggestion. It was rumored that the French government offered him a princely sum to disclose how he effected his cures. He refused, probably because he didn't really know. Eventually he was dismissed as a charlatan and run out of town by the local authorities.

Although officially discredited, Mesmer in-

"[Dreams are] the royal road to the unconscious"
SIGMUND FREUD

Figure 5.16 Distribution of scores of more than 500 subjects on the Stanford Hypnotic Susceptibility Scale. As the graph indicates, responsiveness to hypnotism varies widely, and many people are not very susceptible to hypnotic induction. (Based on data from Hilgard, 1965)

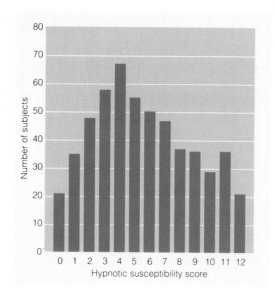

"Many psychologists argue that the hypnotic trance is a mirage. It would be unfortunate if this skeptical view were to gain such popularity that the benefits of hypnosis are denied to the numbers of those who could be helped."

ERNEST HILGARD

spired followers—practitioners of "mesmerism"—who continued to ply their trade, putting interested people into apparent trance states. To this day, our language preserves the memory of Franz Mesmer: when we are "under the spell" of an event or a story, we are *mesmerized*.

Eventually, a Scottish physician, James Braid, became interested in the trancelike state that could be induced by the mesmerists. He thought that perhaps the trance could be used to produce anesthesia for surgeries. It was Braid who popularized the term *hypnotism* in 1843, borrowing it from the Greek word for sleep. With a new name and a modest bit of scientific credibility, hypnotism gained some acceptance within the medical profession. However, just as it was catching on as a technique for producing general anesthesia, more powerful and reliable drug anesthetics were discovered, and interest in hypnotism dwindled.

Since then, hypnotism has led a curious dual existence. On the one hand, it has been the subject of numerous scientific studies. Furthermore, it has enjoyed considerable use as a clinical tool by physicians, dentists, and psychologists for over a century. Meanwhile, an assortment of entertainers and quacks have continued in the less respectable tradition of mesmerism, using hypnotism for parlor tricks and chicanery. It is not surprising, then, that most people don't know what to make of the whole subject. In this section, we'll work on clearing up some of the confusion surrounding hypnosis.

HYPNOTIC INDUCTION AND SUSCEPTIBILITY

Hypnosis is a systematic procedure that typically produces a heightened state of suggestibility. Hypnosis may also lead to passive relaxation, narrowed attention, and enhanced fantasy.

If only in popular films, virtually everyone has seen a *hypnotic induction* enacted with a swinging pendulum. But this is only one of a variety of hypnotic induction techniques—Kroger (1977) lists over 20. Generally, it is the hypnotist's verbal behavior that plays the crucial role in the induction. Usually, the hypnotist suggests to the subject that he or she is relaxing. Repetitively, softly, subjects are told that they are getting tired, drowsy, or sleepy. Often, the hypnotist vividly describes bodily sensations that should be occurring. Subjects are told that their arms are going limp, their feet are getting warm, their eyelids are getting heavy. Gradually, most subjects succumb and become hypnotized.

People differ in how well they respond to hypnotic induction. Ernest and Josephine Hilgard have done extensive research on this variability in *hypnotic susceptibility*. Not everyone can be hypnotized. About 10% of the population doesn't respond well at all. At the other end of the continuum, about 10% of people are exceptionally good hypnotic subjects (Hilgard, 1965). Responsiveness to hypnotism can be estimated with the Stanford Hypnotic Susceptibility Scale (SHSS). The distribution of scores on the SHSS is portrayed graphically in Figure 5.16. As you can see, we differ markedly in our hypnotic susceptibility.

What makes some people highly susceptible to hypnosis? Josephine Hilgard (1970) has sketched a general picture of the type of people who respond well to hypnosis. People who can become deeply engrossed in an intense experience tend to be more susceptible. People with vivid imagination and strong fantasy involvement also tend to score high on the SHSS. Interestingly, people who experienced much severe punishment in childhood also tend to show good hypnotic susceptibility (Nash, Lynn, & Givens, 1984). Theorists speculate that childhood punishment may have led such people to rely heavily on fantasy and to be relatively submissive.

THE EFFECTS OF HYPNOSIS

Many interesting effects can be produced through hypnosis. The following list describes some of the more prominent ones:

1. *Anesthesia.* Under the influence of hypnosis, some subjects can withstand treatment that would normally cause remarkable amounts of pain (Finer, 1980). As a result, some physicians and dentists have used hypnosis as a substitute for anesthetic drugs. Although drugs are quicker, stronger, and more reliable, hypnosis is a surpris-

ingly effective anesthetic for some people (see Figure 5.17).

2. *Sensory distortions and hallucinations.* Hypnotized subjects may be led to experience auditory or visual hallucinations. They may hear sounds or see things that are not there, or fail to hear or see stimuli that are present (Brady & Levitt, 1966). Subjects' sensations may also be distorted so that something sweet tastes sour or an unpleasant odor smells fragrant.

3. *Disinhibition.* Generally, it's difficult to get hypnotized subjects to do things that they normally would consider immoral or unacceptable. Nonetheless, hypnosis *can* sometimes reduce inhibitions that would normally prevent subjects from acting in ways they would see as socially undesirable. In experiments, hypnotized subjects have been induced to throw what they believed to be nitric acid into the face of a research assistant. Similarly, stage hypnotists are sometimes successful in getting people to disrobe in public. One lay hypnotist even coaxed a man into robbing a bank (Deyoub, 1984). This disinhibition effect makes hypnosis look very powerful, but it may not be quite so mysterious as it seems. The disinhibition effect may occur simply because hypnotized people feel that they cannot be held responsible for their actions while they are hypnotized.

4. *Posthypnotic suggestions and amnesia.* Suggestions made during hypnosis may influence a subject's behavior later (Evans, 1980). The most common posthypnotic suggestion involves creating *posthypnotic amnesia*. Subjects are told that they will remember nothing that happened while they were hypnotized. Such subjects usually claim to remember nothing, as ordered.

THEORIES OF HYPNOSIS

Although a number of theories have been developed to explain hypnosis, it is still not well understood. The most crucial theoretical issue is whether hypnosis involves a unique altered state of consciousness or a normal state of consciousness characterized by dramatic role playing.

HYPNOSIS AS ROLE PLAYING Theodore Barber (1969, 1979) has been a leading advocate of the view that hypnosis produces a normal mental state in which suggestible people act out the role of a hypnotic subject. According to this notion, good hypnotic subjects get caught up in their role and try to behave as they think hypnotized people are supposed to. Barber argues that it is subjects' role expectations that produce hypnotic effects rather than a special trancelike state of consciousness.

Two lines of evidence support the role-playing

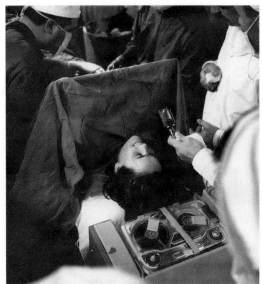

Figure 5.17 Hypnosis and anesthesia. The only anesthetic being used with this appendectomy patient is hypnotic suggestion, delivered by means of tape-recorded messages telling the patient that she can feel no pain.

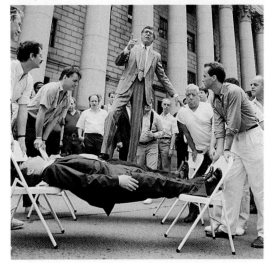

Figure 5.18 Debunking the "human plank" feat. Some feats supposedly performed under hypnosis can be performed equally well by nonhypnotized subjects. Here, the "Amazing Kreskin"—who is arguing against the use of hypnosis in court cases—demonstrates that proper positioning is the only requirement for the famous human plank feat.

view. First, many of the seemingly amazing effects of hypnosis can be duplicated by nonhypnotized subjects. This finding leads Barber to argue that we do not need to hypothesize a special state of consciousness to explain hypnotic feats. For example, much has been made of the fact that hypnotized subjects can be suspended rigidly between two chairs with only their heads and feet supporting them and that subjects suspended just a little differently can serve as "human planks" (see Figure 5.18). These feats seem impressive only because people haven't tried them. It turns out that nonhypnotized subjects can easily match most of the feats associated with hypnosis (Meeker & Barber, 1971).

The second line of evidence involves demonstrations that hypnotized subjects often are acting out a role. For example, Martin Orne (1951) regressed hypnotized subjects back to their sixth birthday and asked them to describe it. As usual, they responded with detailed descriptions that appeared to represent great feats of hypnosis-enhanced memory. However, instead of accepting this information at face value, Orne compared it with information that he obtained from the subjects' parents. It turned out that many of the subjects' memories were inaccurate and invented!

In a similar study, Orne (1959) intentionally gave a group of students some inaccurate information about hypnosis, telling them that a person's preferred hand often became rigid during hypnosis. Later, during a demonstration of hypnosis, many of these students displayed the mythical rigid hand while hypnotized. Thus, misleading information affected the subjects' enactments of their hypnotic role.

In summary, the role-playing explanation of hypnosis suggests that situational factors lead some subjects to act out a certain role in a highly cooperative manner. The exceptional cooperation induced through hypnosis is no small accomplishment, so this explanation does not indicate that hypnosis is meaningless or useless. However, it does take away some of the romance and mystery.

"Thousands of books, movies and professional articles have woven the concept of 'hypnotic trance' into the common knowledge. And yet there is almost no scientific support for it."

THEODORE BARBER

HYPNOSIS AS AN ALTERED STATE OF CONSCIOUSNESS In spite of the doubts raised by Barber and Orne, many prominent theorists maintain that hypnotic effects *are* attributable to a special, altered state of consciousness (Beahrs, 1983; Fromm, 1979; Hilgard, 1986). These theorists argue that role playing probably cannot explain all hypnotic phenomena. For instance, they assert that even the most cooperative subjects are unlikely to endure surgery without an anesthetic drug just to please their physician and live up to their expected role.

Of late, the most influential explanation of hypnosis as an altered state is Ernest Hilgard's (1986) theory, which holds that hypnosis creates a dissociation in consciousness. **Dissociation involves a splitting off of mental processes into two separate, simultaneous streams of awareness.** In other words, Hilgard theorizes that hypnosis splits consciousness into two streams. One of these is in communication with the hypnotist and the external world, while the other is a difficult-to-detect "hidden observer." Hilgard believes that many hypnotic effects are a product of this divided consciousness. For instance, he suggests that a hypnotized subject might appear unresponsive to pain because the pain isn't registered in the portion of consciousness that communicates with other people.

One appealing aspect of Hilgard's theory is that the divided consciousness that he proposes to explain hypnosis is a common, normal experience. For example, people often drive a car a great dis-

tance, responding to traffic signals and other cars, with no recollection of any conscious effort to do so. In such cases, consciousness is clearly divided between the actions required by driving and the driver's conscious train of thought. Interestingly, this common driving experience has long been known as *highway hypnosis*. In this condition, there is even a sort of amnesia for the component of consciousness that drove the car, similar to posthypnotic amnesia. In summary, Hilgard's theory of hypnosis involves an altered state of consciousness, but a plausible one that has continuity with everyday modes of consciousness, rather than a mysterious, less plausible trance state.

The debate about whether hypnosis involves an altered or normal state of consciousness appears likely to continue for the foreseeable future. As you will see momentarily, a similar debate has dominated the scientific discussion of meditation.

Meditation: Pure Consciousness or Relaxation?

Recent years have seen an explosion of interest in meditation in North America. Although a relative newcomer to our shores, meditation has a centuries-old heritage in ancient Eastern cultures. Once associated with the occult, meditation has been demystified through extensive research in the last two decades.

Meditation refers to a family of mental exercises in which a conscious attempt is made to focus attention in a nonanalytical way. There are many different approaches to meditation. In the United States the most widely practiced approaches are those associated with yoga, Zen, and transcendental meditation (TM). Although all three of these approaches are rooted in Eastern religions (Hinduism, Buddhism, and Taoism), meditation can be divorced entirely from religious beliefs. In fact, most Americans who practice meditation have only vague ideas regarding its religious significance. Of interest to us is the fact that meditation involves a deliberate effort to alter consciousness.

Most meditative techniques are deceptively simple. For example, a person practicing TM is supposed to sit in a comfortable position with eyes closed and silently focus attention exclusively on a *mantra*, a specially assigned Sanskrit word that creates a resonant sound. This exercise in mental self-discipline is to be practiced twice daily for 20 minutes. The technique has been described as "diving from the active surface of the mind to its quiet depths" (Bloomfield & Kory, 1976, p.49). Most proponents of TM believe that it involves an altered state of "pure consciousness." Many

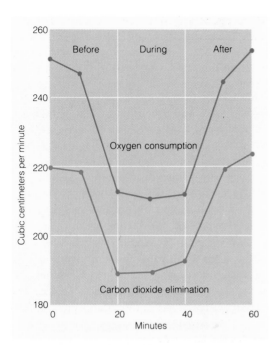

Figure 5.19 The suppression of physiological arousal during transcendental meditation. The physiological changes shown in the graph are evidence of physical relaxation during the meditative state. However, such changes can also be produced by systematic relaxation procedures. (Based on data from Wallace & Benson, 1972)

skeptics counter that meditation is simply an effective relaxation technique.

Advocates of TM claim that it can improve learning, creativity, perceptiveness, energy level, health, interpersonal relationships, and general happiness, while reducing tension and anxiety caused by stress (Bloomfield & Kory, 1976; Schwartz, 1974). These are not exactly humble claims. Moreover, TM advocates assert that they can back up their claims with scientific evidence. Let's look at the evidence.

PHYSIOLOGICAL EFFECTS

What happens physically when an experienced meditator goes into the meditative state? An intriguing finding in some studies is that alpha waves become more prominent in EEG recordings. Most studies also find that a subject's heart rate, respiration rate, oxygen consumption, and carbon dioxide elimination tend to decline (see Figure 5.19). Many researchers have also observed increases in skin resistance and decreases in blood lactate, two physiological indicators associated with relaxation (Davidson, 1976; Woolfolk, 1975). Taken together, all these bodily changes suggest that meditation leads to a potentially beneficial physiological state characterized by relaxation and suppression of arousal. These findings generated quite a bit of excitement in the 1970s. Enthusiastic advocates concluded that meditation produced a unique state of pure consciousness and physical serenity. This conclusion lent credence to the numerous claims about the psychological benefits of meditation.

However, additional research using better experimental controls soon dampened some of the enthusiasm. It turns out that these physical changes are not unique to meditation. A variety of systematic relaxation training procedures can produce similar results (Shapiro, 1984). After reviewing numerous studies, David Holmes (1984) concluded that meditation can reduce physiological arousal, but no more so than relaxation. A subsequent review (Dillbeck & Orme-Johnson, 1987) found that TM was slightly better than relaxation in reducing somatic arousal. Taken together, these reviews suggest that meditation is simply an exotic way to achieve effective relaxation.

PSYCHOLOGICAL EFFECTS

The evidence regarding the psychological effects of meditation is rather similar to the findings about its physical effects. Meditation appears to produce some favorable effects, but these are neither unique to meditation nor nearly so spectacular as some proponents have claimed. There is some evidence that meditation can improve mood, lessen fatigue, and reduce troublesome anxiety (Smith, 1975). However, meditation does not appear to be any more effective in achieving these goals than other systematic relaxation procedures (Shapiro, 1984). It seems fair to conclude that meditation can be a worthwhile relaxation strategy, but there is no evidence that it produces a unique state of pure consciousness.

CONCEPT CHECK 5.2
Relating EEG Activity to Variations in Consciousness

Early in the chapter we emphasized that there is an intimate relationship between brain activity and variations in consciousness. Check your understanding of this relationship by indicating the kind of EEG activity (beta, alpha, theta, or delta) that *probably* would be dominant in each of the following situations. The answers are in Appendix A.

_____ 1. You are playing a video game.
_____ 2. You are deep in meditation.
_____ 3. You have just fallen asleep.
_____ 4. You are sleepwalking across the lawn.
_____ 5. You are in the midst of a terrible nightmare.
_____ 6. You are a novice typist, practicing your typing.

Like hypnosis and meditation, drugs are frequently used in deliberate efforts to alter consciousness. In this section, we focus on the use of drugs for their pleasurable effects, commonly referred to as *drug abuse* or *recreational drug use*, in contrast to medical or therapeutic drug use.

Drug abuse has leveled off since the mid-1970s, after increasing dramatically in the 1960s and early 1970s. Figure 5.20 tracks the yearly results of a large national survey on drug use among high school seniors in the United States (Johnston, O'Malley, & Bachman, 1987, 1988). The survey suggests that recreational drug use has largely remained stable in the 1980s, and that the use of two drugs—marijuana and sedatives—even declined a little. These declines are encouraging, but viewed as a whole, the survey results suggest that widespread recreational drug use is here to stay for the foreseeable future.

Like other controversial social problems, recreational drug use often inspires more rhetoric than reason. For instance, a former president of the American Medical Association made headlines when he declared that marijuana "makes a man of 35 sexually like a man of 70." In reality, the research findings do not support this assertion. This influential physician later retracted his statement, admitting that he had made it simply to campaign against marijuana use (Leavitt, 1982). Unfortunately, such scare tactics can backfire

by undermining the credibility of drug education efforts.

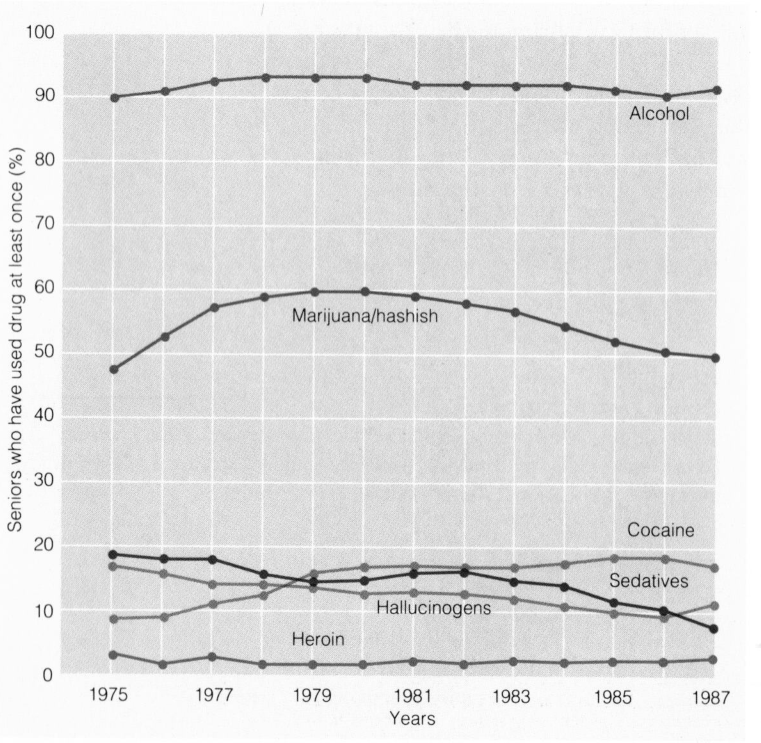

Recreational drug use involves personal, moral, political, and legal issues that are not matters for science to resolve. However, the more knowledgeable you are about drugs, the more informed your decisions and opinions about them will be. Accordingly, this section describes the types of drugs that are most commonly used for recreational purposes, and summarizes their effects on consciousness, behavior, and health.

Principal Abused Drugs and Their Effects

The drugs that people use recreationally are psychoactive. **Psychoactive drugs are chemical substances that modify mental, emotional, or behavioral functioning.** Not all psychoactive drugs produce effects that lead to recreational use or drug abuse. Generally, people prefer drugs that elevate their mood or produce other pleasurable alterations in consciousness.

The principal types of recreational drugs are described in Table 5.4. The table lists representative drugs in each of six categories, and indicates how the drugs are taken, their medical uses, their effects on consciousness, and their most common side effects (based on Blum, 1984; Julien, 1985). The six categories of recreational drugs that we will discuss here are narcotics (or opiates), sedatives, stimulants, hallucinogens, cannabis, and alcohol.

Narcotics, or *opiates,* **are drugs derived from opium that are capable of relieving pain.** In its legal application, the term *narcotic* is misused in a haphazard way to refer to a variety of drugs besides opiates. We'll focus on heroin and morphine, although less potent opiates such as codeine, Demerol, and methadone are also abused. In addition to their painkilling capabilities, in sufficient dosages these drugs can produce an overwhelming sense of euphoria, or well-being. This euphoric effect has a relaxing, apathetic, "Who cares?" quality to it that makes the heroin high an attractive escape from reality.

Sedatives **are sleep-inducing drugs that tend to decrease central nervous system activation and behavioral activity.** Over the years, the most widely abused sedatives have been the *barbiturates,* which are compounds derived from barbituric acid. People abusing sedatives, or downers, generally consume larger doses than are prescribed for medical purposes. The desired effect is a eu-

Figure 5.20 Self-reported drug use among high school seniors in the United States, 1975–1987. Although the rapid escalation of drug use among young people has tapered off since the early 1970s, recreational use of drugs remains widespread (Based on data from Johnston, O'Malley, & Bachman, 1987, 1988)

phoria similar to that produced by drinking large amounts of alcohol. Feelings of tension, anxiety, and depression are temporarily replaced by a relaxed, pleasant state of intoxication, in which inhibitions are loosened.

Stimulants are drugs that tend to increase central nervous system activation and behavioral activity. These range from mild, widely available stimulants, such as caffeine and nicotine, to stronger, carefully regulated stimulants, such as cocaine. We will focus on cocaine, which comes from the coca shrub, and amphetamines (speed), which are synthesized in a pharmaceutical laboratory. These drugs have fairly similar effects, ex-

cept that cocaine produces a very brief high unless more is taken. Stimulants produce a euphoria very different from that created by narcotics or sedatives. They produce a buoyant, elated, enthusiastic, energetic, "I can conquer the world!" feeling accompanied by increased alertness.

Hallucinogens are a diverse group of drugs that have powerful effects on mental and emotional functioning, marked most prominently by distortions in sensory and perceptual experience. The principal hallucinogens are LSD, mescaline, and psilocybin, which have similar effects, although they vary in potency. These drugs increase sensory awareness and produce profound, dream-

Table 5.4 Psychoactive Drugs: Methods of Ingestion, Medical Uses, and Effects

DRUGS	METHODS OF ADMINISTRATION	PRINCIPAL MEDICAL USES	DESIRED EFFECTS	SHORT-TERM SIDE EFFECTS
Narcotics (opiates) Morphine Heroin	Injected, smoked, oral	Pain relief	Euphoria, relaxation, anxiety reduction, pain relief	Lethargy, drowsiness, nausea, impaired coordination, impaired mental functioning, constipation
Sedatives Barbiturates (e.g., Seconal) Nonbarbiturates (e.g., Quaalude)	Oral, injected	Sleeping pill, anticonvulsant	Euphoria, relaxation, anxiety reduction, reduced inhibitions	Lethargy, drowsiness, severely impaired coordination, impaired mental functioning, emotional swings, dejection
Stimulants Amphetamines Cocaine	Oral, sniffed, injected, freebased	Treatment of hyperactivity and narcolepsy, local anesthetic (cocaine only)	Elation, excitement, increased alertness, increased energy, reduced fatigue	Increased blood pressure and heart rate, increased talkativeness, restlessness, irritability, insomnia, reduced appetite, increased sweating and urination, anxiety, paranoia, increased aggressiveness
Hallucinogens LSD Mescaline Psilocybin	Oral	None	Increased sensory awareness, euphoria, altered perceptions, hallucinations, insightful experiences	Dilated pupils, nausea, emotional swings, paranoia, jumbled thought processes, impaired judgment, anxiety, panic reaction
Cannabis Marijuana Hashish THC	Smoked, oral	Treatment of glaucoma; other uses under study	Mild euphoria, relaxation, altered perceptions, enhanced awareness	Bloodshot eyes, dry mouth, reduced short-term memory, sluggish motor coordination, sluggish mental functioning, anxiety
Alcohol	Drinking	Antiseptic	Mild euphoria, relaxation, anxiety reduction, reduced inhibitions	Severely impaired coordination, impaired mental functioning, increased urination, emotional swings, depression, quarrelsomeness, hangover

Note: The principal omission from this table is PCP (phencyclidine hydochloride), which does not fit neatly into any of the listed categories. PCP has stimulant, hallucinogenic, and anesthetic effects. Its short-term side effects can be very dangerous. Common side effects include agitation, paranoia, confusion, and severe mental disorientation that has been linked to accidents and suicides.

like, "mystical" feelings of euphoria that are very difficult to describe. Because of the latter effect, they have been used in religious ceremonies for centuries in some cultures. Unfortunately, at the other end of the emotional spectrum, hallucinogens can also produce nightmarish feelings of anxiety, fear, and paranoia, commonly called a "bad trip."

Cannabis **is the hemp plant from which marijuana, hashish, and THC are derived.** Marijuana is a mixture of dried leaves, flowers, stems, and seeds taken from the plant, while hashish comes from the plant's resin. THC is the active chemical ingredient in cannabis. It can be synthesized for research purposes (for example, to give to animals who can't very well smoke marijuana or hashish). When smoked, cannabis has an almost immediate impact that may last several hours. The desired effects of the drug are a mild, relaxed euphoria, accompanied by enhanced sensory awareness and a distorted sense of time.

Alcohol **encompasses a variety of beverages containing ethyl alcohol,** such as beers, wines, and distilled spirits. The concentration of ethyl alcohol varies from about 4% in most beers up to 40% in 80-proof liquor, and occasionally more in higher-proof liquors. When people drink heavily, the central effect is a "Who cares?" kind of euphoria that temporarily boosts self-esteem as problems seem to melt away and inhibitions diminish. Alcohol is the most widely used recreational drug in our society. It is estimated that there are about 10 million alcoholics—people with severe drinking problems—in the United States. Contrary to what many people believe, alcoholics are not mostly skid-row bums. Alcoholics are found in all walks of life (Schuckit, 1986). They live down the block from you, they work with you, they even represent you in Congress.

Factors Influencing Drug Effects

The effects of various drugs summarized in Table 5.4 are the *typical* effects. Drug effects are different for different people and even for the same person in different situations. The impact of any drug depends in part on the user's mood, motivation, personality, previous experience with the drug, body weight, and physiology, as well as the dose and potency of the drug, the method of administration, and the setting in which the drug is taken (Leavitt, 1982). Our theme of *multifactorial causation* clearly applies to the effects of drugs.

So too, does our theme emphasizing the *subjectivity of experience*. Expectations are potentially powerful factors that can influence the user's perceptions of a drug's effects. You may recall from our discussion of placebo effects in Chapter 2, that some people who are misled to *think* that they are drinking alcohol show signs of intoxication (Wilson, 1982). Similarly, if you *expect* a drug to make you feel giddy, serene, happy, or profound, your expectation may contribute to the feelings that you experience.

A drug's effects can also change as one's body develops a tolerance for the chemical as a result of continual use. *Tolerance* **refers to a progressive decrease in a person's responsiveness to a drug.** Tolerance effects usually lead people to consume larger and larger doses of a drug to attain the effects they are accustomed to. Most drugs produce tolerance effects, but some do so more rapidly than others. For example, tolerance to the effects of alcohol usually builds slowly, whereas tolerance to the effects of heroin increases much more quickly. The second column in Table 5.5 indicates whether various categories of drugs tend to produce tolerance rapidly or gradually.

Mechanisms of Drug Action

Psychoactive drugs are transported through the bloodstream to the brain, where they exert their main effects. Once in the brain, a drug diffuses and acts on target cells in a variety of ways. After a while, the drug may drift away and affect other cells. Or it may cross back into the bloodstream, perhaps returning to the brain later.

Once they are in the body, drugs may be metabolized (used and converted), inactivated, or eliminated. For example, ethyl alcohol is metabolized into the chemical acetaldehyde, which is converted into acetate. Some of these chemicals may contribute to the hangover that can follow drinking. Alcohol is metabolized mostly by the liver, which can suffer damage from high concentrations of the metabolic byproducts associated with alcohol. Along with the liver, the kidneys play a key role in removing most drugs from the body. This is why urine tests are used to check for drug use.

How rapidly a drug is metabolized and removed influences how long lasting its effects will be. For example, the effects of cocaine are not as long-lived as the effects of amphetamines because cocaine is metabolized much more rapidly (in just 5–15 minutes). In contrast, some barbiturate sedatives leave hangover effects of drowsiness that may last for several days because the drug is eliminated slowly.

Although most of them have effects that reverberate throughout the body, psychoactive drugs

Table 5.5 Psychoactive Drugs: Tolerance, Dependence, Potential for Fatal Overdose, and Health Risks

DRUGS	TOLERANCE	RISK OF PHYSICAL DEPENDENCE	RISK OF PSYCHOLOGICAL DEPENDENCE	FATAL OVERDOSE POTENTIAL	HEALTH RISKS
Narcotics (opiates)	Rapid	High	High	High	Infectious diseases, accidents
Sedatives	Rapid	High	High	High	Accidents
Stimulants	Rapid	Moderate	High	Moderate	Sleep problems, malnutrition, nasal damage, hypertension, stroke, liver disease
Hallucinogens	Gradual	None	Very low	Very low	Accidents
Cannabis	Gradual	None	Low to moderate	Very low	Accidents, lung cancer, respiratory disease, pulmonary disease
Alcohol	Gradual	Moderate	Moderate	Low to high	Accidents, liver disease, malnutrition, brain damage, neurological disorders, heart disease, stroke, hypertension, ulcers, cancer, birth defects

work primarily by altering neurotransmitter activity in the brain. As we discussed in Chapter 3, *neurotransmitters* are chemicals that transmit signals between neurons at junctions called *synapses*. Different drugs have different effects largely because they act selectively on specific types of synapses that are sensitive to particular neurotransmitters. Most psychoactive drugs appear to have complex, multiple effects on neural transmission at chemical synapses.

Let's look at the actions of amphetamines to see how drugs exert selective, multiple effects on neurotransmitter activity. Amphetamines act mostly on synapses sensitive to two bioamine transmitters, norepinephrine (NE) and dopamine (DA). Indeed, the name amphet*amines* reflects the kinship between these drugs and the bio*amines*. Amphetamines appear to mimic the action of NE, directly stimulating some NE receptors (Berger & Dunn, 1986). They also have additional effects on NE activity, some of which are summarized in Figure 5.21. For example, they increase the release of NE and inhibit the activity of an enzyme called *monoamine oxidase* (MAO) that metabolizes NE and DA. This inhibition of MAO activity slows the removal of NE and DA from synaptic clefts, thus making more of these transmitters available (Cooper, Bloom, & Roth, 1986). The key point is that amphetamines selectively influence NE and DA activity in a *variety* of ways. Cocaine shares some of these actions, which is why cocaine and amphetamines produce similar stimulant effects.

Alcohol and sedatives tend to depress activity in the central nervous system (CNS). This effect may be largely due to their impact on GABA activity. GABA is a neurotransmitter found at inhibitory synapses. Barbiturates seem to mimic GABA by directly stimulating GABA receptors (Nicoll & Madison, 1982). Alcohol appears to amplify the effects of naturally released GABA (Nestoros, 1980). Both actions inhibit neural activity in the brain. With barbiturates stimulating GABA receptors and alcohol amplifying this

Figure 5.21 Amphetamines and neurotransmitters. Like other psychoactive drugs, amphetamines alter neurotransmitter activity at specific synapses in a variety of ways. Depicted here are three ways (there may be more) in which amphetamines appear to increase norepinephrine (NE) activity at NE synapses.

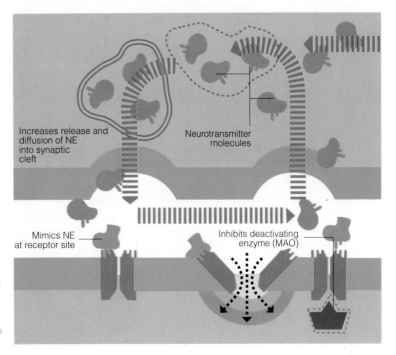

Increases release and diffusion of NE into synaptic cleft

Neurotransmitter molecules

Mimics NE at receptor site

Inhibits deactivating enzyme (MAO)

stimulation, the combination of the two drugs can be especially potent. The drugs' actions are *synergistic*, which means that their combined effect can be much greater than the sum of the effects of each one alone. Synergistic effects explain why alcohol and barbiturates are a very dangerous mixture. The combination of these drugs has caused many fatal overdoses by depressing CNS activity excessively. Many other combinations of drugs may also be dangerous because of their synergistic impact on neural activity.

The discovery of endorphins—opiatelike chemicals that are produced naturally in the brain—has led to new insights about the actions of opiate, or narcotic, drugs. A variety of endorphins act on specific receptors. Opiate drugs apparently bind to these receptors and mimic the actions of endorphins. The various opiate drugs have somewhat different effects because they tend to bind to different receptors (Snyder, 1984).

The impact of hallucinogens on neurotransmitter activity is not well understood. They appear to exert their key effects on serotonin activity (Jacobs, 1987). The neural effects of cannabis remain very obscure (Cooper, Bloom, & Roth, 1986).

Drug Dependence

People can become either physically or psychologically dependent on a drug. Physical dependence, sometimes called *addiction*, is a common problem with narcotics, sedatives, and alcohol, and an occasional problem with stimulants. **Physical dependence exists when a person must continue to take a drug to avoid withdrawal illness.**

The symptoms of withdrawal illness depend on the specific drug. Withdrawal from heroin, barbiturates, and alcohol can produce fever, chills, tremors, convulsions, seizures, vomiting, cramps, diarrhea, and severe aches and pains. Withdrawal from stimulants leads to a more subtle syndrome, dominated by fatigue, apathy, irritability, depression, and disorientation. The severe distress associated with withdrawal understandably motivates a person who is physically dependent on a drug to continue using it.

Psychological dependence exists when a per-

Our society encourages some types of drug use more than others, but all drugs have side effects and carry risks.

son must continue to take a drug in order to satisfy intense mental and emotional craving for the drug. Whereas physical dependence leads to continued drug use to avoid negative effects, psychological dependence leads to continued drug use to experience positive effects. Psychological dependence is more subtle than physical dependence, but the need it creates can be powerful. Cocaine, for instance, can produce an overwhelming psychological need for continued use. Psychological dependence is possible with all recreational drugs, although it seems to be rare for hallucinogens.

Both types of dependence are established gradually with repeated use of a drug. Different drugs have different potential for creating either physical or psychological dependence. The third and fourth columns in Table 5.5 provide estimates of the risk of each kind of dependence for the six categories of recreational drugs covered in our discussion.

Drugs and Physical Health

The use of some recreational drugs can be very damaging to physical health. In a dramatic illustration of this risk, Michael Bozarth and Roy Wise (1985) conducted a study of rats that were given unlimited access to heroin or cocaine. The rats "earned" drug injections delivered through tubes implanted in their bodies by pressing a lever in an experimental chamber.

Even though unlimited food and water were available, rats on cocaine lost an average of 29% of their body weight. Their health deteriorated rapidly, and by the end of the 30-day study, 90% of them had died. The health of the rats on heroin deteriorated less rapidly, but 36% of them also died during the study. As is true for many human drug users, serious physical effects did not deter the rats from continuing their "drug abuse." Many of the rats on cocaine experienced severe seizures, but they would resume their lever pressing as soon as their convulsions subsided!

In humans, recreational drug use can affect physical health in a variety of ways. The three principal risks are (1) overdose, (2) tissue damage (direct effects), and (3) health-impairing behavior that results from drug use (indirect effects).

OVERDOSE

Any drug can be fatal if a person takes enough of it, but some drugs are much more dangerous than others. The fifth column in Table 5.5 shows estimates of the risk of accidentally consuming a *lethal* overdose of each listed drug. Drugs that are CNS depressants—sedatives, narcotics, and al-

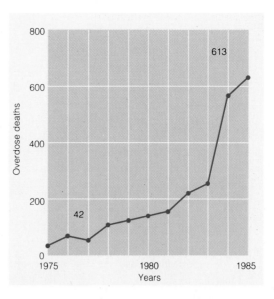

Figure 5.22 Deaths attributed to cocaine overdose in 25 major metropolitan areas of the United States, 1975–1985. The growing popularity of cocaine and new methods of ingesting the drug have led to a more than tenfold increase in reported deaths from cocaine overdose in recent years. (Based on data from the National Institute on Drug Abuse)

cohol—carry the greatest risk of overdose. It's important to understand that the effects of depressant drugs are synergistic with each other. Many overdoses involve lethal *combinations* of CNS depressants. What happens when a person overdoses on these drugs? The respiratory system usually grinds to a halt, producing coma, brain damage, and death within a brief period.

Fatal overdoses with CNS stimulants usually involve a heart attack, stroke, or cortical seizure. Death due to an overdose of stimulants used to be relatively infrequent (Kalant & Kalant, 1979), but cocaine overdoses are increasing as more people experiment with more dangerous methods of cocaine consumption, such as freebasing and smoking crack (see Figure 5.22). *Freebasing* is chemical treatment that is used to extract nearly pure cocaine concentrate from ordinary street cocaine. *Crack* is the most widely distributed byproduct of this process, consisting of little chips of pure cocaine, which are usually smoked. Smoking crack is far more dangerous than snorting cocaine powder because of crack's greater purity and because smoking leads to a more rapid absorption of the drug into the bloodstream (Cregler & Mark, 1986).

DIRECT EFFECTS

In some cases, drugs cause tissue damage directly. For example, snorting cocaine can damage nasal membranes or alter cardiovascular functioning in ways that increase the risk of stroke. Long-term, excessive alcohol consumption can cause a number of physical problems, including liver damage, neurological disorders, and heart disease.

INDIRECT EFFECTS

Surprisingly often, the negative effects of drugs on physical health are indirect results of the drugs'

179

impact on behavior. For instance, people using stimulants often do not eat or sleep properly. Sedatives increase the risk of accidental injuries because they severely impair motor coordination, leading some users to trip down stairs, fall off stools, and suffer other mishaps. Many drugs impair driving ability, increasing the risk of automobile accidents. Alcohol is notorious for this effect, and in fact, may contribute to roughly *half* of all automobile fatalities. Intravenous drug users risk contracting infectious diseases, including AIDS (acquired immune deficiency syndrome), that can be spread by unsterilized needles.

The sixth column in Table 5.5 lists the major health risks (other than overdose) associated with the use of recreational drugs. As you can see, alcohol appears to have the most diverse negative effects on physical health. The irony, of course, is that alcohol is the only recreational drug listed that is legal.

CONTROVERSIES CONCERNING MARIJUANA

The possible health risks associated with the use of marijuana have been the subject of considerable controversy in recent years. The preponderance of evidence suggests that heavy use of marijuana increases the chances for respiratory and pulmonary disease, including lung cancer. There is also reasonably convincing evidence that marijuana increases the risk of accidents in some users. These dangers are listed in Table 5.5, but many other widely publicized dangers are omitted because the findings on these other risks remain controversial. Here is a brief overview of the evidence on the controversies surrounding some of the other risks:

• *Does marijuana cause brain damage?* The handful of studies linking marijuana to brain damage have been shown to be methodologically unsound (Kuehnle et al., 1977). Marijuana affects EEG activity (Heath, 1976), but there is no clear evidence that these changes in brain activity are permanent or pathological (Fried, 1977).
• *Does marijuana cause chromosome breakage?* Findings on this issue are inconsistent, but Cohen (1980) concludes that marijuana does not appear to increase chromosomal breakage. High doses of THC have been shown to cause birth defects in animals, but there is no evidence that marijuana causes birth defects in humans (Blum, 1984). Of course, caution dictates that pregnant women avoid using any drug.
• *Does marijuana reduce one's immune response?* Cannabis may suppress the body's natural immune response slightly (Nahas, 1976). However, infectious diseases are no more common among marijuana smokers than among nonsmokers, so this effect apparently is too small to have any practical importance (Relman, 1982).
• *Does marijuana lead to impotence and sterility in men?* Cannabis appears to produce a small, reversible decline in sperm count among male smokers and may have temporary effects on hormone levels (Kolodny et al., 1974). Although the popular media have frequently implied that marijuana therefore makes men sterile and impotent, there is no evidence that temporary changes in sperm and hormone levels produce any discernible impact on male smokers' fertility or sexual functioning (Relman, 1982).

Drugs and Psychological Health

Does drug abuse lead to mental illness? There is a clear association between excessive drug use and the occurrence of mental disorders. However, it's difficult to sort out cause and effect. For example, narcotics (opiate) users have high rates of mental illness, but researchers are unsure whether narcotics use *causes* this higher rate of mental disorders (Sutker & Archer, 1984). It may be that people with psychological problems are drawn to narcotics, so that the drug abuse is a symptom of mental disorder rather than a cause of it. In short, it may be that psychological disorders cause drug abuse, rather than vice versa.

In spite of these interpretive problems, there is reasonably clear evidence that at least two kinds of drugs, stimulants and alcohol, *can* cause psychological disorders. The use of stimulants occasionally leads to the onset of a severe disorder called *amphetamine, or cocaine, psychosis*, which is marked by paranoia, hallucinations, and hyperactivity (Sadava, 1984). Alcoholism can lead to a variety of psychological disorders, such as *Korsakoff's syndrome*, a condition marked by mental confusion, hallucinations, and memory losses (Nathan & Hay, 1984). Other drugs probably contribute to the development of some psychological disorders through a complex interactive process in which drug abuse and poor mental health feed off each other.

To summarize, although the dangers of drug abuse have sometimes been exaggerated, recreational drugs carry many genuine psychological and physical health risks. As a means of altering conciousness, psychoactive drugs should be treated with a heavy dose of respect.

PUTTING IT IN PERSPECTIVE

Three of our unifying themes have emerged in this chapter. First, we can see how psychology evolves in a sociohistorical context (theme 3). Twenty-five years ago you wouldn't have found a chapter on consciousness in an introductory psychology text. However, in the 1960s people began to turn inward, showing a new interest in altering their consciousness through drug use, meditation, hypnosis, biofeedback, and other methods. Psychologists responded to these social trends by beginning to study variations in consciousness in earnest. This renewed interest in conciousness shows once again how social forces can have an impact on psychology's evolution.

A second prominent theme that surfaced in the chapter is the idea that our experience of the world is highly subjective (theme 6). We encountered this theme at the start of the chapter when we discussed the difficulty that people have in describing their states of consciousness. The subjective nature of consciousness was apparent elsewhere in the chapter as well. For instance, we found that the states of consciousness produced by drugs depend significantly on each individual's personal expectations.

Finally the chapter illustrated psychology's theoretical diversity (theme 2). We discussed conflicting theories about dreams, hypnosis, and meditation, and we skirted a quagmire of current theories about the purpose of sleep. For the most part, we did not see opposing theories converging toward reconciliation, as we did in the previous chapter. However, it's important to emphasize that rival theories do not always, or even usually, merge neatly into tidy models of behavior. Competing theories sometimes converge, but many theoretical controversies go on indefinitely. This reality does not negate the value of theoretical diversity. While it's always nice to resolve a theoretical debate, the debate itself advances our knowledge by stimulating and guiding research.

In many respects, our upcoming Application demonstrates that we do not have to resolve theoretical debates in order to advance our knowledge. The Application summarizes practical information that researchers have accumulated about sleep and dreams. What is interesting is how much our knowledge about these phenomena has advanced in the last few decades without our resolving any of the major theoretical issues in the area. Although there is no shortage of theories, we still do not understand the purpose of sleep, why we need REM sleep, or why we dream. In spite of these enduring mysteries, researchers have acquired a great deal of fascinating and valuable information about sleeping and dreaming.

ADDRESSING PRACTICAL QUESTIONS ABOUT SLEEP AND DREAMS

Answer the following "true" or "false."

☐ **1.** Everyone needs 8 hours of sleep a night to maintain sound mental health.

☐ **2.** Naps rarely have a refreshing effect.

☐ **3.** Some people never dream.

☐ **4.** When people cannot recall their dreams, it's because they are trying to repress them.

☐ **5.** Only an expert in symbolism, such as a psychoanalytic therapist, can interpret the latent meaning of dreams.

The preceding assertions were all drawn from the Sleep and Dreams Information Questionnaire (Palladino & Carducci, 1984), which measures practical knowledge about sleep and dreams. Are they true or false? You'll learn the answers in this Application.

Common Questions About Sleep

How much sleep do people need? Young adults average about 7.5 hours of sleep per night. However, sleep needs vary greatly from person to person. Figure 5.23 shows that there is considerable variability in how long people sleep. Asking how much sleep the average person needs is like asking what shoe size the average person needs. (If we gave the average shoe size to everyone, most of us would be very uncomfortable.)

How much sleep do you need? Wilse Webb, a prominent sleep researcher, suggests that you can estimate your personal need for sleep in the following way: Select a night and go to sleep only a few hours before your normal time to get up. Get accustomed to how you feel after this (presumably)

inadequate amount of sleep. On succeeding nights, increase your sleep time by going to bed an hour earlier each night until you reach a length of time that allows you to awaken spontaneously and feel well rested during the day. That length of time should reflect your personal need for sleep (Goleman, 1982).

Can people learn to get by with less sleep? Some of us can. There are well-documented cases of people who have learned to live with less than 3 hours of sleep per night for years without any ill effects (Jones & Oswald, 1968). Thus, the first statement in our series of true-false items is false. The evidence on partial sleep deprivation that we reviewed in this chapter suggests that many of us could sleep less without noticeably harming our daytime efficiency. If you want to spend less time sleeping, try reducing your sleep time gradually and see how you feel. In one study of subjects who gradually reduced their sleep time, some continued to sleep an hour or two less after the study was finished (Friedmann et al., 1977).

Can short naps be refreshing? Some naps are beneficial, and some are not.

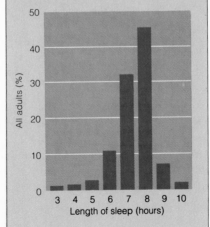

Figure 5.23 Hours of sleep per night reported in a survey of nearly 1 million adults. Although most adults sleep for an average of 7 to 9 hours per night, some people need less and some people need more sleep. (Based on data from Kripke et al., 1979)

The effectiveness of a nap varies from person to person and also depends upon the time of day and the amount of recent sleep (Gillberg, 1984). A crucial consideration is probably where the nap occurs in one's biological rhythm. Midday naps were the most refreshing in one study (Naitoh, 1981).

You may want to try napping at different times of the day to see which times are most beneficial to you. In general, though, you should realize that naps are *not* very efficient ways to sleep because you're often just getting into the deeper stages of sleep when your napping time is up. Nonetheless, there have been many highly productive people, including Thomas Edison, Winston Churchill, and John F. Kennedy, who made effective use of naps.

The award for the most bizarre napping, however, must go to Salvador Dali, the surrealist painter. Dali would relax in an armchair, holding a spoon between his thumb and index finger. The instant he nodded off, the spoon would fall from his hand, hitting a plate placed on the floor, and the clatter would awaken him. Dali claimed that these instant naps were invigorating, but one can never be sure whether a surrealist is being realistic. In any case, naps often can have a refreshing effect, so statement 2 is also false.

How do alcohol and drugs affect sleep? Obviously, stimulants such as cocaine and amphetamines make it difficult to sleep. More surprising is the finding that CNS-depressant drugs that facilitate sleep (such as alcohol, analgesics, sedatives, and tranquilizers) also disrupt the normal sleep cycle. The principal problem is that they all suppress REM sleep. Thus, many drugs have negative effects on sleep.

Is there such a thing as sleep learning? Yes, but it won't get you through college. As you know, we do have a primitive, low level of awareness while we

Figure 5.24 Ten suggestions for better sleep. (From Hales, 1987)

1. Keep regular hours.
2. Remember that quality of sleep matters more than quantity.
3. Exercise every day—but not in the evening.
4. Don't smoke.
5. Don't have coffee late in the day.
6. Don't drink alcohol after dinner.
7. Don't nap during the day.
8. Unwind in the evening.
9. Don't go to bed starved or stuffed.
10. Develop a bedtime sleep ritual.

sleep. This raises the legitimate possibility that we could learn while we sleep. Indeed, *very simple* learning, such as the development of a conditioned reflex, can occur during the lighter stages of sleep. However, your ability to assimilate information of any complexity while asleep is minimal at best (Bonnet, 1982). It would be nice if we could learn Spanish or chemistry by listening to an audiotape while we slept, but the evidence unequivocally indicates that trying to do so is pointless.

What can be done to avoid sleep problems? There are many ways to improve your chances of getting satisfactory sleep (see Figure 5.24). Most of them involve developing sensible daytime habits that won't interfere with your sleep at night (Hales, 1987; Kales & Kales, 1984). For example, if you've been having trouble sleeping at night,

it's a good idea to avoid the temptation of daytime naps, so that you're tired when your bedtime arrives. Some people find that daytime exercise helps them to fall asleep more readily at bedtime.

It's also wise to minimize your consumption of stimulants such as coffee or cigarettes. Because they aren't prescription drugs, we often fail to appreciate how much impact caffeine and nicotine can have on our physical arousal. Many foods and beverages contain more caffeine than people realize (see Table 5.6). Also, bear in mind that unwise eating habits can interfere with sleep. Try to avoid going to bed hungry, or uncomfortably stuffed, or soon after eating foods that disagree with you.

In addition to these prudent habits, two other preventive measures are worthy of mention. First, try to establish a reasonably regular bedtime. This allows you to take advantage of your circadian rhythm, so that you're trying to fall asleep at a time when your body is primed to cooperate by drifting into sleep more easily.

Second, create a favorable environment for sleep. This advice belabors what should be obvious, but many people fail to heed it. Make sure that you have a good bed that is comfortable for you. Take steps to ensure that your bedroom is quiet enough and that the humidity and temperature are to your liking.

What can be done about insomnia? First, don't panic if you run into a little trouble sleeping. An overreaction to sleep problems can begin a vicious circle of escalating problems, like that depicted in Figure 5.25. If you jump to the conclusion that you are becoming an insomniac, you may approach sleep with anxiety that will aggravate the problem. The harder you work at falling asleep, the less success you're likely to have.

As we noted earlier, temporary sleep problems are common, and they generally clear up on their own. If you have trouble falling asleep, try to suppress negative, anxiety-arousing thoughts like those shown in the left column of Table 5.7 with calmer thoughts like those in the right column.

One sleep expert, Dianne Hales (1987), lists 101 suggestions for combatting insomnia in her book *How to Sleep Like a Baby.* Many involve "boring yourself to sleep" by playing alphabet games, taking an imaginary stroll through your neighborhood, reciting poems, or listening to your clock.

Another recommended strategy is to engage in some not-so-engaging activity. For instance, you might try

Table 5.6 Average Caffeine Content of Various Foods and Beverages

Instant coffee (5 oz), 64 mg
Percolated coffee (5 oz), 108 mg
Drip coffee (5 oz), 145 mg
Decaffeinated coffee (5 oz), 3 mg
Black tea (5 oz), 42 mg
Canned iced tea (17 oz), 30 mg
Cocoa drink (6 oz), 8 mg
Chocolate drink (8 oz), 14 mg
Sweet chocolate (1 oz), 20 mg
Colas (12 oz), 50 mg
Other soft drinks (12 oz), 0–52 mg

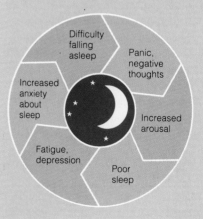

Figure 5.25 The vicious circle of anxiety and sleep difficulty. Anxiety about sleep difficulties leads to poorer sleep, which increases anxiety further, which in turn leads to even greater difficulties in sleeping.

183

Table 5.7 Cognitive Reactions to Sleep Problems

ANXIETY-AROUSING THOUGHTS	CALMING THOUGHTS
"I've been lying here for an hour already. I'll bet this is going to be a miserable night."	"That's okay. The house is peaceful and I am resting. I'll be asleep soon."
"Oh, brother. Here it is 3:30 A.M. and I'm awake. I bet I'll never get back to sleep."	"I'll get back to sleep if I just stay calm and don't worry about it."
"I need to get to sleep. I'll be no good tomorrow if I don't."	"I'll get to sleep. Losing a half hour's sleep is not going to make *that* much difference."

Note: Difficulties in sleeping can be reduced if anxiety-arousing thoughts are replaced with calming thoughts.
Source: Coates & Thoresen, 1977

reading your dullest textbook; it could turn to be a superb sedative. It's often a good idea to simply launch yourself into a pleasant daydream. This is a normal presleep process that can take your mind off your difficulties.

Whatever you think about, try to avoid ruminating about the current stresses and problems in your life. Research has shown that the tendency to ruminate in bed is one of the key differences between insomniacs and people with normal sleep patterns (see Figure 5.26).

Anything that relaxes you—whether it's music, meditation, prayer, or a warm bath—can aid you in falling asleep. Experts have also devised systematic relaxation procedures that can make relaxation efforts more effective. You may want to go to the trouble of learning about techniques such as *progressive relaxation training* (Jacobson, 1938), *autogenic training* (Schultz & Luthe, 1959), or the *relaxation response* (Benson, 1975). We'll return to the last of these techniques when we discuss stress and coping in Chapter 13.

Common Questions About Dreams

Does everyone dream? Yes. Some people report that they never remember any

dreams. However, when these people are brought into a sleep lab and awakened from REM sleep, they report interrupted dreams—much to their surprise (Hall & Nordby, 1972). Apparently, some people just don't *remember* their dreams. Thus, statement 3 at the start of this Application is false.

Why is it that some people do not remember their dreams? The evaporation of dreams appears to be quite normal. Given our lowered level of awareness during sleep, it's understandable that our memory of dreams is mediocre. Our dream recall seems to be best when we are awakened during or soon

after a dream. Most of the time, people who *do* recall dreams upon waking the next morning are probably remembering either the *last* dream from their final REM period or a dream that awakened them earlier in the night. In other words, most of us probably forget most of our dreams, and not because we are repressing them (statement 4 is false). People who never remember their dreams may simply cycle through the stages of sleep in a way that puts too much time between their last REM/dream period and awakening, so that their last dream is forgotten (Webb & Kersey, 1967).

Can people improve their recall of dreams? Yes. Most of us don't have any significant reason to work at recalling our dreams, so we just let them float away. However, some therapists who believe that dreams are important instruct their clients to work at improving their dream recall. Many of their clients have found that they can remember more dreams merely by placing that goal upppermost in their minds as they go to sleep. So if you decide to work at it, you may be able to remember more of your dreams.

Are dreams instantaneous? No. There has long been speculation that dreams flash through our consciousness almost

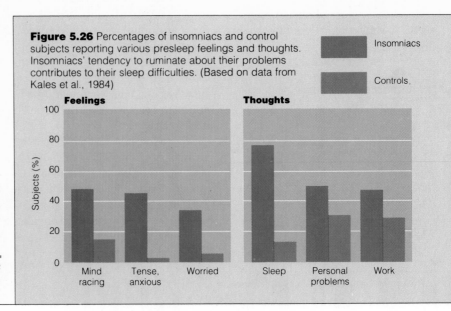

Figure 5.26 Percentages of insomniacs and control subjects reporting various presleep feelings and thoughts. Insomniacs' tendency to ruminate about their problems contributes to their sleep difficulties. (Based on data from Kales et al., 1984)

instantaneously. According to this notion, complicated plots that would require 20 minutes to think through in waking life can bolt through our dreaming mind in a second or two. However, modern research has shown that this "speed dreaming" doesn't occur. When researchers awaken a subject who has been dreaming (in REM) for 15 minutes and ask him or her to recount the dream, the subject tends to produce approximately 15 minutes' worth of plot (Webb & Bonnet, 1979).

Do people dream in color? Although some people report that they dream exclusively in black-and-white, evidence suggests that most dreams do include color (Schwartz, Weinstein, & Arkin, 1978).

Do dreams require interpretation? Yes, but interpretation may not be as difficult as generally assumed. People have long believed that dreams are symbolic and that it is necessary to interpret the symbols to understand what the dreams mean. Freud, for instance, made a distinction between the manifest content and the latent content of a dream. **The *manifest content* consists of the plot of a dream at a surface level. The *latent content* is the hidden or disguised meaning of the events in the plot.** Thus, Freudian therapists interpreting a dream might equate a dream event like walking into a tunnel or riding a horse with sexual intercourse. Table 5.8 lists some additional examples of supposed symbols of sexual organs and urges. Theorists who see dreams as symbolic are likely to assert that dream interpretation is an extremely complicated task requiring considerable knowledge of symbolism.

More recently, however, many dream theorists have argued that symbolism in dreams is less deceptive and mysterious than Freud thought (Faraday, 1974; Foulkes, 1985; Hall, 1979). Calvin Hall makes the point that dreams require some interpretation simply because they are more visual than verbal; that is, we need to translate the pictures into ideas. Hall argues that because dream symbolism is highly personal, the dreamer may be the person best equipped to decipher a dream. Thus, like the first four statements at the start of the Application, number 5 is false. It is not unreasonable for you to try to interpret your own dreams. Unfortunately, though, you'll never know

for sure whether you were correct, because there is no definitive way to judge the validity of different dream interpretations.

Can people learn to influence their dreams? Quite possibly, but it is not easy. When researchers in a number of studies have instructed subjects to try to dream about a particular topic, the dreamers have been successful often enough to suggest that some dream control is possible. However, there have been many failures as well, suggesting that dream control may be quite difficult (Tart, 1979).

Thus far, the most impressive work on influencing dreams has been reported by Rosalind Cartwright (1974). She instructed subjects to dream about a particular personality trait—assertiveness, say—and found that their dreams *were* influenced by the instructions. Even more intriguing is Cartwright's (1978) work with depressed women who were instructed to alter the plots in their dreams. Some of these women were successful in tilting the plots in their dreams toward happier endings. Cartwright speculates that these happier endings might carry over to affect waking mood and thus have therapeutic value.

Could a shocking dream be fatal? According to folklore, if you fall from a height in a dream, you'd better wake up on the plunge downward. Supposedly, if you hit the bottom and die in your dream, the shock to your system will be so great that you will actually die in your sleep.

Think about this one for a moment. *If* it were a genuine problem, who would have reported it? You can be sure that no one has ever testified to experiencing a fatal dream. This myth presumably exists because many people do awaken during the downward plunge, thinking that they have narrowly avoided death. In reality, the evidence indicates that quite a few people dream of their own death—and live to tell about it.

Table 5.8 Examples of Possible Sexual Meanings of Dream Symbols as Suggested by Freudian Analysis

FEMALE ORGANS	MALE ORGANS	INTERCOURSE
Enclosed spaces	Elongated objects	Climbing steps
Boxes	Tree trunks	Climbing a ladder
Ovens	Umbrellas	Going up a staircase
Hollow objects	Knives	Driving a car
Ships	Neckties	Riding an elevator
Closets	Airplanes	Riding a horse
Wagons	Trains	Crossing a bridge
Caves	Snakes	Riding a roller coaster
Hats	Hoses	Flying in an airplane
Pockets	Flames	Movement (or combination) of male and female symbols
Drawers	Bullets	

Note: The interpretations shown are hypothetical; Freudian interpretation emphasizes that the analysis of actual dreams is quite complex.
Source: Houston, Bee, & Rimm, 1983

VARIATIONS IN CONSCIOUSNESS

KEY IDEAS

On the Nature of Consciousness

• The private nature of consciousness makes it difficult to investigate, but we have begun to advance our knowledge of this subject in recent years. Consciousness is our continually changing stream of mental activity. Consciousness varies along a continuum of levels of awareness. Controlled processes require heightened awareness; automatic processes occur with little awareness. Minimal awareness continues even when we sleep. Variations in consciousness are intimately related to brain activity, as measured by the EEG.

The Sleep and Waking Cycle

• Sleep is influenced by biological rhythms, especially our 24-hour circadian rhythms. Our biological clock is an internally regulated mechanism that runs even when we are cut off from the light-darkness cycle. Exposure to light may reset our biological clock by affecting the activity of the pineal gland.

• Ignoring your biological clock by going to sleep at an unusual time may have a negative effect on your sleep. This is one reason for jet lag and for the unpleasant nature of rotating shift work. Studies indicate that we can accomodate phase-delay changes in our sleep cycle more easily than phase-advance changes. In our Featured Study investigators successfully applied this information to reduce problems associated with shift rotation.

• When you fall asleep, you evolve through a series of stages in cycles of approximately 90 minutes. During the REM stage you experience rapid eye movements, a brain wave that is characteristic of waking thought, and most of your dreaming. The sleep cycle tends to be repeated about four times in a night, as REM sleep gradually becomes more predominant and NREM sleep dwindles. These patterns of sleeping are influenced to some extent by an individual's age.

• The neural bases of sleep are very complex. Arousal depends on activity in the ascending reticular activating system, but other brain structures also contribute to the regulation of our sleep and waking cycle. A variety of neurotransmitters appear to be involved in the modulation of sleep.

• Many studies have examined the effects of complete, partial, and REM sleep deprivation. This research indicates that we need REM sleep, although scientists are not sure why. The impact of sleep loss on performance is highly variable, with the typical effects being less damaging than expected. The only consistent effect of sleep deprivation is sleepiness.

• People are troubled by a great variety of sleep disorders. Foremost among these is insomnia, which has a variety of causes. Sleeping pills are generally a poor solution for insomnia. The optimal treatment for insomnia depends on its apparent cause. Other less common sleep problems include narcolepsy, sleep apnea, night terrors, nightmares, somnambulism, and hypersomnia.

The World of Dreams

• Dreams are a routine accompaniment to sleep, but our theories of dreaming remain largely untested, and we do not really know why we dream. Research on dream content indicates that most of our dreams are not as exotic as widely believed. The content of one's dreams may be affected both by events in one's life and by external stimuli that are experienced during the dream.

Hypnosis and Meditation

• Hypnosis has a long and curious history. People vary greatly in their susceptibility to hypnosis. People who are easily hypnotized tend to have a vivid imagination and strong fantasy involvement. Among other effects, hypnosis can produce anesthesia, sensory distortions, disinhibition, and posthypnotic amnesia. Two major theoretical approaches view hypnosis either as an altered state of consciousness or as a normal state of consciousness in which subjects assume a hypnotic role.

• Claims for the benefits of meditation have created some excitement in recent decades, and evidence does suggest that meditation can be beneficial. However, the more recent studies suggest that these benefits are not unique to meditation as much as they are a product of any effective relaxation procedure.

186

CHAPTER FIVE

Altering Consciousness with Drugs

• Most recreational drug use involves an effort to alter consciousness with psychoactive drugs. The principal categories of abused drugs are narcotics, sedatives, stimulants, hallucinogens, cannabis, and alcohol. Although it's possible to describe the typical effects of various drugs, the effect on any individual depends on a host of factors including subjective expectations and tolerance to the drug.

• Drugs are transported to the brain by the bloodstream. Psychoactive drugs exert their main effects in the brain, where they alter neurotransmitter activity at synaptic sites in a variety of ways. Eventually, drugs are metabolized, inactivated, or eliminated. These processes influence the duration of a drug's effects.

• Drugs vary in their potential for creating psychological and physiological dependence and for damaging one's physical health. Recreational drug use can prove harmful to health by producing an overdose, by causing tissue damage, or by increasing health-impairing behavior. There is an association between drug use and poor mental health, but it's hard to tell how the two are related.

Putting It in Perspective

• Three of our unifying themes were highlighted in this chapter. First, we saw how psychology's study of consciousness reflected concurrent social trends, showing that psychology evolves in a sociohistorical context. Second, we saw that states of consciousness are highly subjective. Third, we saw that extensive theoretical diversity continues to generate vigorous debate about many issues related to consciousness.

Application: Addressing Practical Questions About Sleep and Dreams

• Sleep needs vary greatly and some people can learn to get by with less sleep than they are accustomed to. The value of short naps depends on many factors, including one's biological rhythm. Alcohol and many other widely used drugs have a negative effect on sleep. Sleep learning is possible, but only very primitive kinds of learning.

• People can do many things to avoid or reduce sleep problems. Mostly, it's a matter of developing good daytime habits that do not interfere with nighttime sleep. A regular bedtime and a good sleep environment are also helpful. People troubled by transient insomnia should avoid panic, pursue effective relaxation, and try to distract themselves so they don't work too hard at falling asleep, since working at it can be counterproductive.

• Everyone dreams, but some people cannot remember their dreams, probably because of the nature of their sleep cycle. Dream recall can be improved, and some people have even been taught to influence the course of their dreams. Dreams are not instantaneous, and there's no evidence that dreams of death can be fatal. Most theorists believe that dreams require some interpretation, but this interpretation may not be as complicated as once assumed.

KEY TERMS

- Alcohol
- Ascending reticular activating system (ARAS)
- Automatic processes
- Biological rhythms
- Cannabis
- Circadian rhythms
- Consciousness
- Controlled processes
- Dissociation
- Dream
- Electrocardiograph (EKG)
- Electroencephalograph (EEG)
- Electromyograph (EMG)
- Electro-oculograph (EOG)
- Hallucinogens
- Hypersomnia
- Hypnosis
- Insomnia
- Latent content
- Manifest content
- Meditation
- Narcolepsy
- Narcotics
- Nightmares
- Night terrors
- NREM sleep
- Opiates
- Physical dependence
- Psychoactive drugs
- Psychological dependence
- REM rebound
- REM sleep
- Sedatives
- Sleep apnea
- Somnambulism
- Stimulants
- Tolerance

KEY PEOPLE

Theodore Barber
William Dement
Sigmund Freud
Calvin Hall
Ernest Hilgard
William James
Nathaniel Kleitman
Anton Mesmer

LEARNING THROUGH CONDITIONING

You're sitting in the waiting room of your dentist's office. You cringe when you hear the sound of a dental drill coming from the next room.

• A young girl goes to the front closet, takes out a chain leash for her dog, and jingles the chain loudly. The dog leaps off the couch and comes running, wagging its tail with excitement.

• A 4-year-old boy pinches his hand in one of his toys and curses loudly. His mother looks up in dismay and says to his father, "Where did he pick up that kind of language?"

• A seal waddles across the stage, bows ceremoniously, and "doffs his cap" by flipping it into the air and catching it in his mouth. The spectators at the aquatic show clap appreciatively as the trainer tosses the seal a fish as a reward.

• A helicopter pilot carefully maneuvers his craft over a capsized boat in the bay. He courageously battles the gusting wind, trying to position the craft for a challenging rescue.

• The crowd hushes as an Olympic diver prepares to dive. In a burst of bodily motion, she propels herself into the air and glides smoothly through a dazzling corkscrew somersault.

What do all of these scenarios have in common? At first glance, very little; they form a diverse collection of events, some trivial, some impressive. However, they do share one common thread—*they all involve learning*. This statement may surprise you. When most people think of learning, they envision students reading textbooks or novices working to acquire a specific skill, such as riding a bicycle or skiing. Although these activities do involve learning, to psychologists they represent only the tip of the learning iceberg.

Learning is a relatively durable change in behavior or knowledge that is due to experience. This broad definition means that learning is one of the most fundamental concepts in all of psychology. Learning includes our acquisition of knowledge and skills, but learning also shapes personal habits like nail biting, personality traits like shyness, emotional responses like a fear of storms, and personal preferences like a taste for tacos or a distaste for formal clothes. Most of your behavior is the result of learning. If it were possible to strip away your learned responses, there would be very little behavior left. You wouldn't be able to read this book, find your way home, or cook yourself a hamburger. You would be about as complex and exciting as a turnip.

Although you and I depend on learning, it is *not* an exclusively human process. Most organisms are capable of learning. Even the lowly flatworm can acquire a learned response. As this chapter unfolds, you may be surprised to see that much of the research on learning has been conducted using lower animals as subjects. Why? Because researchers can exert much better experimental control over animals than over humans. As we saw in Chapter 1, improved experimental control was one of the main reasons why the noted behaviorist John B. Watson advocated the study of animal behavior. For the most part, Watson's plan has worked out well. Decades of research have shown that many principles of learning discovered in animal research apply quite well to humans.

In this chapter, we'll focus our attention on a specific kind of learning: conditioning. **Conditioning is the simplest form of learning; it involves learning associations between stimuli and responses.** In investigating conditioning, psychologists study learning at a very fundamental level. This strategy has paid off with insights that have laid the foundation for the study of much more complex forms of learning, which we'll examine in later chapters.

Most of this chapter will be devoted to explaining the two major types of conditioning: *classical conditioning* and *operant conditioning*. After discussing the essentials of classical and operant conditioning, which have been known for some time, we'll look at new directions in the study of conditioning. In our chapter Application you'll see how you can harness the principles of conditioning in powerful ways to improve your self-control.

CLASSICAL CONDITIONING

Do you get weak in the knees at the thought of standing on the roof of a tall building? Does your heart race when you imagine encountering a harmless garter snake? If so, you can understand, at least to some degree, what it's like to have a phobia. **Phobias are irrational fears of specific objects or situations.** Mild phobias are commonplace (Costello, 1982). Over the years, students in my classes have described having at least mildly phobic responses to a diverse array of stimuli, including bridges, elevators, tunnels, heights, dogs, cats, bugs, birds, snakes, professors, doctors,

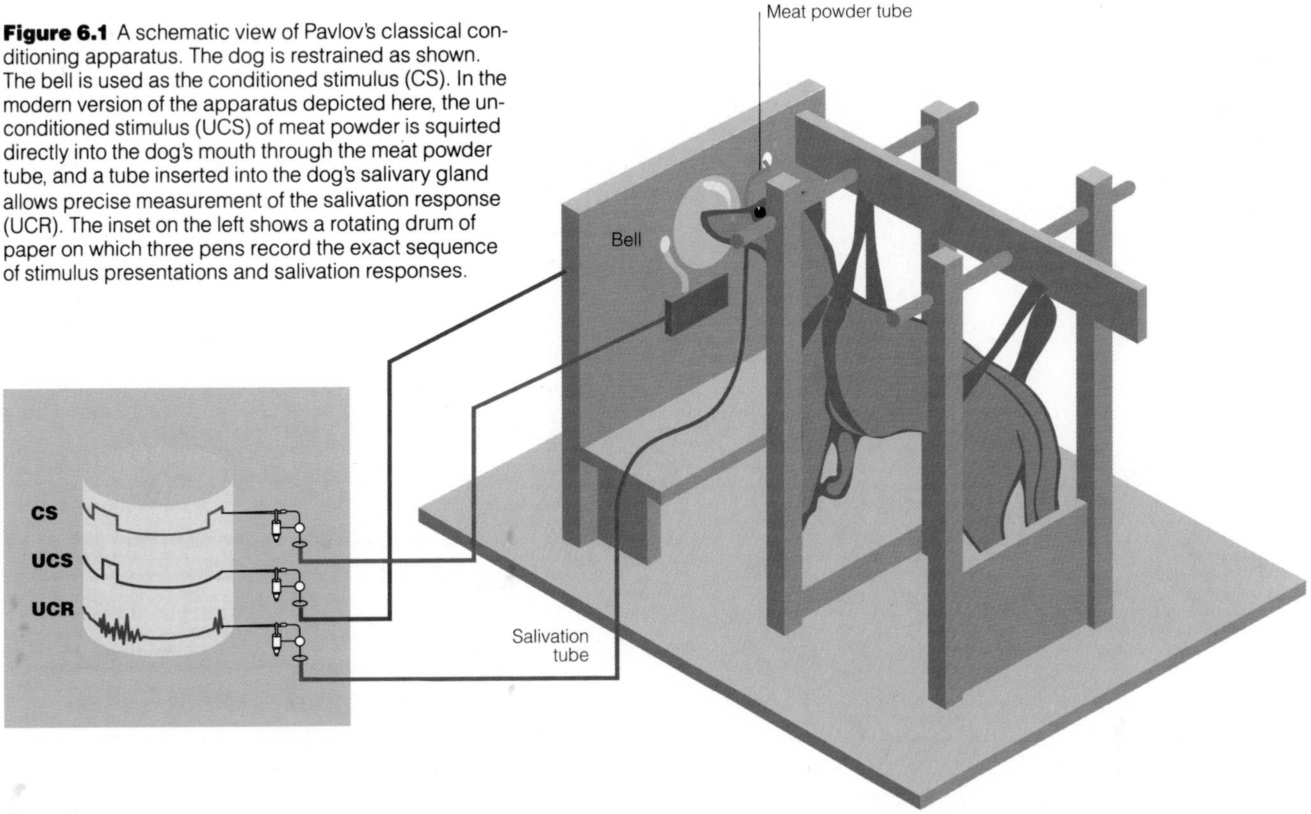

Figure 6.1 A schematic view of Pavlov's classical conditioning apparatus. The dog is restrained as shown. The bell is used as the conditioned stimulus (CS). In the modern version of the apparatus depicted here, the unconditioned stimulus (UCS) of meat powder is squirted directly into the dog's mouth through the meat powder tube, and a tube inserted into the dog's salivary gland allows precise measurement of the salivation response (UCR). The inset on the left shows a rotating drum of paper on which three pens record the exact sequence of stimulus presentations and salivation responses.

strangers, darkness, thunderstorms, and germs. If you have a phobia, you may have wondered just how you managed to acquire such a foolish, irrational fear. Chances are, it was through classical conditioning.

Classical conditioning is a type of learning in which a neutral stimulus acquires the ability to evoke a response that was originally evoked by another stimulus. The process was first described in 1903 by Ivan Pavlov, and it is sometimes called *Pavlovian conditioning* in tribute to him. The term *conditioning* comes from Pavlov's determination to discover the "conditions" that produced this kind of learning. The process came to be known as *classical conditioning* in order to differentiate it from other forms of conditioning that were subsequently described by other theorists. Over the years this form of learning also acquired another name, *respondent conditioning*, so make a mental note that classical conditioning, Pavlovian conditioning, and respondent conditioning are the same process.

Pavlov's Demonstration: "Psychic Reflexes"

Ivan Pavlov was a prominent Russian physiologist who did Nobel Prize winning research on digestion. Something of a "classic" himself, he was an absent-minded but brilliant professor obsessed with his research. Pavlov apparently was so naive

about everyday financial matters that his wife allowed him to carry only a little pocket change. Yet he ran an exceptionally efficient research laboratory in which he was a demanding taskmaster. Legend has it that Pavlov once severely reprimanded an assistant who was late for an experiment because he was trying to steer clear of street fighting in the midst of the Russian Revolution. The assistant defended his tardiness, saying, "But, Professor, there's a revolution going on with shooting in the streets!" Pavlov supposedly replied, "What the hell difference does a revolution make when you've work to do in the laboratory? Next time there's a revolution, get up earlier!" Pavlov also found it annoying that assistants had to waste valuable time picking up their monthly wages (Fancher, 1979; Gantt, 1975).

Pavlov was studying digestive processes in dogs when he stumbled onto what he called "psychic reflexes" (Pavlov, 1906). Like many great discoveries, Pavlov's was partly accidental, although he had the insight to recognize its significance. He was examining the role of saliva in digestion. His subjects were dogs that were restrained in a harness in an experimental chamber (see Figure 6.1). A thin tube was surgically inserted into the salivary gland so that their saliva ran out into a small cylinder in which it was collected. Pavlov would present meat powder to a dog and then collect the resulting saliva. As his research progressed, he noticed that the dogs that were accustomed to the

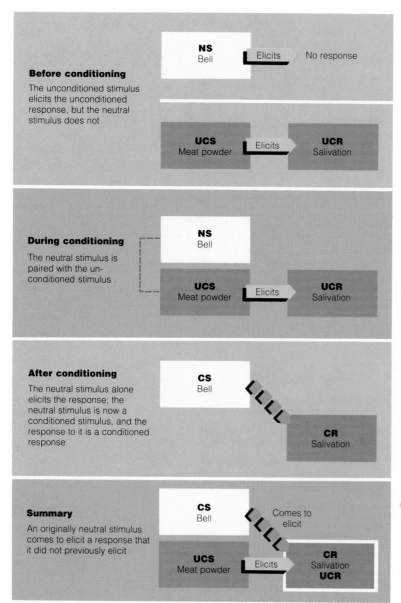

Before conditioning

The unconditioned stimulus elicits the unconditioned response, but the neutral stimulus does not

NS Bell — Elicits — No response

UCS Meat powder — Elicits → **UCR** Salivation

During conditioning

The neutral stimulus is paired with the unconditioned stimulus

NS Bell

UCS Meat powder — Elicits → **UCR** Salivation

After conditioning

The neutral stimulus alone elicits the response; the neutral stimulus is now a conditioned stimulus, and the response to it is a conditioned response

CS Bell

CR Salivation

Summary

An originally neutral stimulus comes to elicit a response that it did not previously elicit

CS Bell — Comes to elicit

UCS Meat powder — Elicits → **CR** Salivation **UCR**

Figure 6.2 The sequence of events in classical conditioning. As we encounter new examples of classical conditioning throughout the book, we will see many diagrams like the one in the fourth panel, which summarizes the process.

procedure started salivating *before* the meat powder was presented. For instance, they would salivate in response to a clicking sound made by the device that was used to present the powder.

Intrigued by this unexpected finding, Pavlov decided to investigate further. To clarify what was happening, he decided to pair the presentation of the meat powder with a single stimulus that would stand out in the laboratory situation. For this purpose he chose a simple, auditory stimulus—the ringing of a bell. After the bell and the meat powder were presented together a number of times, Pavlov presented the bell alone. What happened? The dogs responded to the sound of the bell by itself (refer to Figure 6.1).

What was so significant about a dog salivating when a bell was rung? The key is that the bell started out as a *neutral* stimulus; that is, it did not originally produce the response of salivation.

However, Pavlov managed to change that by pairing the bell with a stimulus (meat powder) that did produce the salivation response. Through this process the bell acquired the capacity to trigger the response of salivation. What Pavlov had demonstrated was *how learned reflexes are acquired.*

Terminology

There is a special vocabulary associated with classical conditioning. It often looks intimidating to the uninitiated, but it's really not terribly mysterious. The bond between the meat powder and salivation is a natural, unlearned association that does not have to be created through conditioning. It is therefore called an *unconditioned* association. In unconditioned bonds, **the unconditioned stimulus (UCS) is a stimulus that evokes an unconditioned response without previous conditioning. The *unconditioned response* (UCR) is an unlearned reaction to an unconditioned stimulus that occurs without previous conditioning.**

In contrast, the link between the bell and salivation was established through conditioning and is therefore called a *conditioned association.* In conditioned bonds, **the *conditioned stimulus* (CS) is a previously neutral stimulus that has, through conditioning, acquired the capacity to evoke a conditioned response. The *conditioned response* (CR) is a learned reaction to a conditioned stimulus that occurs because of previous conditioning.** Ironically, the names for the four key elements in classical conditioning (the UCS, UCR, CS, and CR) are the byproduct of a poor translation of Pavlov's writing into English. Pavlov actually used the words condition*al* and uncondition*al* to refer to these concepts (Gantt, 1975).

To help you understand how these four elements of classical conditioning are related, it is worth noting that the unconditioned response and conditioned response often involve virtually the same behavior, although there may be subtle differences between them. In Pavlov's initial demonstration, the UCR and CR both involved salivation. When evoked by the UCS (meat powder), salivation is an unconditioned response; when evoked by the CS (the bell), salivation is a conditioned response. The procedures involved in classical conditioning are outlined in Figure 6.2.

Pavlov's *psychic reflex* came to be called the *conditioned reflex.* Classically conditioned responses are viewed as reflexes because most of them are relatively automatic or involuntary. Because they are reflexive, classically conditioned responses are said to be *elicited.* **To *elicit* means to draw out or bring forth.** Finally, **a *trial* in classical condition-**

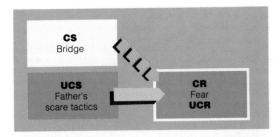

Figure 6.3 Classical conditioning of a fear response. Many emotional responses that would otherwise be puzzling can be explained as a result of classical conditioning. In the case of one woman's bridge phobia, the fear originally elicited by her father's scare tactics has become a conditioned response to the stimulus of bridges.

ing consists of any presentation of a stimulus or pair of stimuli. Psychologists are often interested in how many trials are required to establish a particular conditioned bond. The number of trials needed to form an association varies considerably. Classical conditioning generally proceeds gradually, but it *can* occur very quickly, sometimes in just one pairing of the CS and UCS.

Classical Conditioning in Everyday Life

In laboratory experiments on classical conditioning, researchers have generally worked with extremely simple responses made by animals, mainly dogs, pigeons, and rats. Besides salivation, frequently studied favorites include eyelid closure, knee jerks, the flexing of various limbs, and fear responses. Although the study of such simple responses has proven both practical and productive, these responses don't even begin to convey the rich diversity of everyday behavior that is regulated by classical conditioning. Let's look at some examples of classical conditioning drawn from everyday life.

CONDITIONED FEAR AND ANXIETY

Classical conditioning plays a key role in shaping emotional responses such as fear and anxiety. Phobias are a good example of such responses. Clinical studies of patients suffering from phobias suggest that many phobias can be traced back to experiences that involve classical conditioning (Goldstein & Chambless, 1978). It's easy to imagine how such conditioning can take place outside the laboratory. For example, a student of mine was troubled by a bridge phobia so severe that she couldn't drive on interstate highways because of all the viaducts that had to be crossed. She was able to pinpoint as the source of her phobia something that had happened many years before. When her family would drive to visit her grandmother, they had to cross a little-used, rickety, dilapidated bridge out in the countryside. Her father, in a misguided attempt at humor, made a major production of these crossings. He would stop short of the bridge and carry on about the enormous danger. Obviously, he thought the bridge was safe because otherwise he wouldn't

have driven across it. However, the naive young girl was terrified by her father's scare tactics, and the bridge became a conditioned stimulus eliciting great fear (see Figure 6.3). Unfortunately, the fear extended to *all* bridges, and 40 years later she was still carrying the burden of this phobia. Although a number of processes seem to be able to cause phobias (Marks, 1977), it's clear that classical conditioning is responsible for a great many of our irrational fears.

Everyday anxiety responses that are less severe than phobias may also be a product of classical conditioning. For instance, your cringing in response to the sound of a dentist's drill involves classical conditioning. In this case the pain caused by drilling was the UCS that was paired with the sound of the drill, which became a CS eliciting your cringe.

Not every frightening experience leaves a conditioned fear in its wake. As we will discuss, a variety of factors influence whether a particular situation results in a conditioned response. We should probably be thankful that conditioning is not an inevitable process, because if every scare produced a conditioned anxiety or a phobia, we would all be emotional wrecks.

OTHER CONDITIONED EMOTIONAL RESPONSES

Classical conditioning is not limited to the production of unpleasant emotions such as fear and anxiety. Many pleasant emotional responses are also acquired through classical conditioning. Consider the following example, described by a 53-year-old woman who wrote a letter to newspaper columnist Bob Greene about the news that a company was bringing back a discontinued product—Beemans gum. She wrote:

That was the year [1949] I met Charlie. I guess first love is always the same. . . . Charlie and I went out a lot. He chewed Beemans gum and he smoked. . . . We would go to all the passion pits—the drive-in movies and the places to park. We did a lot of necking, but we always stopped at a certain point. Charlie wanted to get married when we got out of high school . . . [but] Charlie and I drifted apart. We both ended up getting married to different people.

And the funny thing is . . . for years the combined smell of cigarette smoke and Beemans gum made my

"Next time there's a revolution, get up earlier!"

IVAN PAVLOV

Figure 6.4 (Below) Classical conditioning and romance. Pleasant emotional responses can be acquired through classical conditioning, as illustrated by one woman's unusual conditioned response to the aroma of Beemans gum and cigarettes.

Figure 6.5 (Right) Classical conditioning in advertising. Many advertisers attempt to make their products conditioned stimuli that elicit pleasant emotional responses.

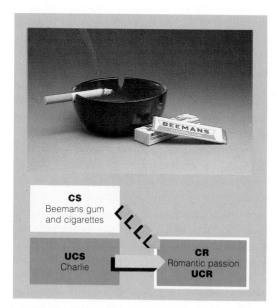

knees weak. Those two smells were Charlie to me. When I would smell the Beemans and the cigarette smoke, I could feel the butterflies dancing all over my stomach.

The writer clearly had a unique and long-lasting emotional response to the smell of Beemans gum and cigarettes. The credit for this *pleasant* response goes to classical conditioning (see Figure 6.4).

Preferences for specific kinds of sexual activities may also be shaped by classical conditioning. An extreme example is **fetishism, a form of sexual deviance in which a person is aroused by certain inanimate objects** (such as shoes, boots, leather, or undergarments). One enterprising young man with a shoe fetish managed to collect over 15,000 pictures of shoes for his sexual pleasure! There is evidence that fetishes may be acquired through classical conditioning (Rachman, 1966). Some researchers think that the fetish object happens to get paired with an instance of intense sexual arousal, usually when the person is relatively young. The fetish object then becomes a conditioned stimulus that can elicit arousal on its own.

Advertising campaigns sometimes try to take advantage of classical conditioning. Advertisers fairly routinely pair their products with UCSs that elicit pleasant emotions. The most common strat-

egy is to present a product in association with an attractive person (see Figure 6.5). The advertisers hope that these pairings will make their products conditioned stimuli that evoke good feelings.

CONDITIONING AND PHYSIOLOGICAL RESPONSES

Classical conditioning may have an impact not only on overt behaviors but also on physiological processes. Consider, for example, the functioning of your body's immune system. When an infectious agent invades your body, your immune system attempts to repel the invasion by producing specialized proteins called *antibodies*. The immune response is critically important. It is the disabling of the immune system that produces the disease AIDS (Acquired Immune Deficiency Syndrome).

Recent research has shown that the functioning of our immune system can be influenced by psychological factors, including conditioning. Robert Ader and Nicholas Cohen (1981, 1984) have repeatedly shown that classical conditioning procedures can lead to *immunosuppression*—a decrease in the production of antibodies. In a typical study, animals are injected with a drug (the UCS) that *chemically* causes immunosuppression and are simultaneously given an unusual-tasting liquid to drink (the CS). Days later, after the chemical immunosuppression has ended, the animals are injected with an infectious agent that triggers an immune response. Some of the animals are then re-exposed to the CS, by being given the unusual solution to drink. Measurements of antibody production indicate that the animals exposed to the CS show a reduced immune response (see Figure 6.6).

Immune resistance is only one example of the physiological processes that can be influenced by classical conditioning. Other recent studies suggest that classical conditioning may also elicit the release of *endorphins*, the brain's opiatelike painkillers that we discussed in Chapters 3 and 4 (Fanselow & Baackes, 1982). Release of endorphins may be one reason why chemically empty placebo drugs can relieve pain. Fake "painkilling pills" may somehow become a CS eliciting endorphin release in some individuals. Because of findings about the conditioning of immune processes and endorphin release, experts are reappraising our traditional theories of health, pain, and disease to include a larger role for psychological factors. This trend is discussed further in Chapter 13.

Basic Processes in Classical Conditioning

Probably because most conditioned responses *are* reflexive and difficult to control, classical conditioning is often portrayed as a mechanical process that inevitably leads to a certain result. Pavlov's dogs would have been hard-pressed to withhold their salivation. Similarly, most people with phobias have great difficulty suppressing their fear. However, an understanding of classical conditioning as an "irresistible force" is misleading because it fails to consider the many factors involved in classical conditioning. In this section we'll look at basic processes in classical conditioning to expand on the rich complexity of this form of learning.

ACQUISITION: FORMING NEW RESPONSES

We have already discussed *acquisition* without attaching a formal name to the process. **Acquisition is the formation of a new conditioned response tendency.** Pavlov theorized that the acquisition of a conditioned response depended on stimulus *contiguity*, which literally means "touching." **Stimulus contiguity occurs when there is a temporal (time) association between two events.** Thus, Pavlov thought that the key to classical conditioning was the pairing of stimuli in time.

Stimulus contiguity *is* important, but learning

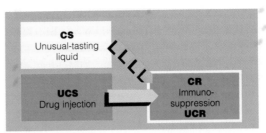

Figure 6.6 Classical conditioning of immunosuppression. The diagram shows how even our immune response can be influenced by classical conditioning.

theorists now realize that contiguity doesn't tell the entire story. We are bombarded daily by countless stimuli that could be perceived as being paired, yet only some of these pairings produce classical conditioning. Consider the woman who developed a conditioned emotional reaction to the smell of Beemans gum and cigarettes. Certainly there were other stimuli that shared contiguity with Charlie. He smoked, so there were probably ashtrays present, but she doesn't get weak in the knees at the sight of an ashtray.

If conditioning does not occur in response to all the stimuli that are present in a situation, what determines when it does occur? Evidence suggests that stimuli that are novel, unusual, or especially intense have more potential to become CSs than routine stimuli, probably because they are more likely to stand out among other stimuli. Thus, stimulus contiguity alone does not automatically produce conditioning.

A number of other factors also influence whether acquisition occurs. Timing is an important consideration. Many different CS–UCS timing arrangements have been investigated. Three such temporal arrangements are diagrammed in Figure 6.7. In *simultaneous conditioning*, the CS

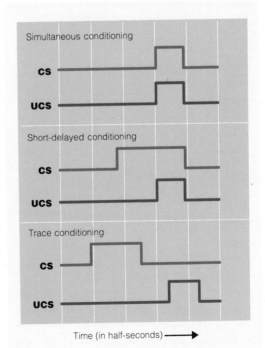

Figure 6.7 Temporal relations of stimuli in classical conditioning. The effects of classical conditioning depend in part on the timing of the stimuli. Three different ways of pairing the CS and UCS are diagrammed here. The most effective arrangement is short-delayed conditioning, in which the CS begins a half-second before the UCS.

and UCS begin and end together. In *short-delayed conditioning*, the CS begins just before the UCS and stops at the same time as the UCS, so the CS and UCS overlap. In *trace conditioning*, the CS begins and ends before the UCS is presented.

Which temporal arrangement works best? The most obvious approach, simultaneous presentation, is *not* particularly effective in establishing a new conditioned response. Nor is trace conditioning. Short-delayed conditioning is the temporal arrangement that best facilitates the acquisition of most conditioned responses, as long as the delay between the onset of the CS and that of the UCS is very brief, ideally about one-half second (Heth & Rescorla, 1973; Kamin, 1965). Later in our discussion of new directions in the study of conditioning, we'll see some striking exceptions to this rule of thumb, and some additional factors that influence acquisition.

EXTINCTION: WEAKENING CONDITIONED RESPONSES

Fortunately, a newly formed stimulus-response bond does not necessarily last indefinitely. If it did, learning would be inflexible, and organisms would have difficulty adapting to new situations. Instead, the right circumstances produce **extinction, the gradual weakening and disappearance of a conditioned response tendency.**

What leads to extinction in classical conditioning? The consistent presentation of the conditioned stimulus *alone*, without the unconditioned stimulus; in other words, it comes from the situation in which the CS and UCS are no longer paired. For example, when Pavlov consistently presented *only* the bell to a previously conditioned

dog, the bell gradually lost the capacity to elicit the response of salivation. Such a sequence of events is depicted in the left portion of Figure 6.8, which graphs the amount of salivation by a dog over a series of trials. Note how the salivation response declines during extinction.

For an example of extinction from outside the laboratory, let's assume that you cringe at the sound of a dentist's drill, which has been paired with pain in the past. You take a job as a dental assistant, and you start hearing the drill (the CS) day in and day out without experiencing any pain (the UCS). Your cringing response will gradually diminish until it is extinguished altogether.

How long it takes to extinguish a conditioned response depends on many factors. Foremost among them is the strength of the conditioned bond when extinction begins. Some conditioned responses are extinguished very quickly, while others are very difficult to weaken.

SPONTANEOUS RECOVERY: RESURRECTING RESPONSES

Some conditioned responses display the ultimate in tenacity by "reappearing from the dead" after being extinguished. Learning theorists use the term *spontaneous recovery* to describe such a resurrection from the graveyard of conditioned associations. **Spontaneous recovery is the reappearance of an extinguished response after a period of nonexposure to the conditioned stimulus.**

Pavlov observed spontaneous recovery in some of his early studies. He fully extinguished a dog's CR of salivation to a bell and then returned the dog to its home cage. On a subsequent day, when the dog was brought back to the experimental

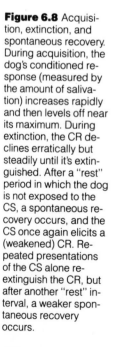

Figure 6.8 Acquisition, extinction, and spontaneous recovery. During acquisition, the dog's conditioned response (measured by the amount of salivation) increases rapidly and then levels off near its maximum. During extinction, the CR declines erratically but steadily until it's extinguished. After a "rest" period in which the dog is not exposed to the CS, a spontaneous recovery occurs, and the CS once again elicits a (weakened) CR. Repeated presentations of the CS alone reextinguish the CR, but after another "rest" interval, a weaker spontaneous recovery occurs.

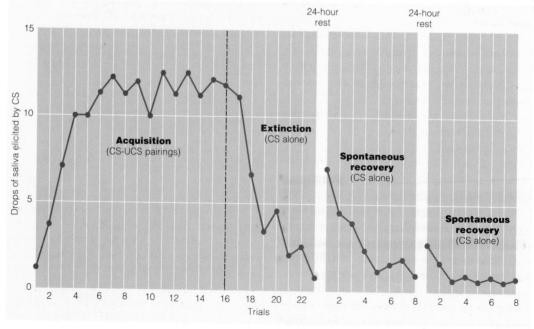

chamber for retesting, the bell was rung and the salivation response reappeared. Although it had returned, the rejuvenated response was weak. There was less salivation than when the response had been at its peak strength. If Pavlov consistently presented the CS by itself again, the response was re-extinguished quickly. However, in some dogs the response made still another spontaneous recovery (typically even weaker than the first) after the dogs had spent another period in their cages (consult Figure 6.8 once again).

The theoretical meaning of spontaneous recovery is complex and hotly debated, but its practical meaning is quite simple. Even if you manage to rid yourself of a conditioned response (like cringing when you hear a dental drill), it may make a surprise reappearance later. This is particularly likely if you are not exposed for a while to the CS that elicited the response. For example, suppose you quit your job as a dental assistant and are not exposed to the sound of a dentist's drill for a year or so. There's an excellent chance that if you stop by a dentist's office to pick up a friend, you'll cringe once again at the sound of the drill.

STIMULUS GENERALIZATION AND THE CASE OF LITTLE ALBERT

After conditioning has taken place, organisms often show a tendency to respond not only to the exact CS used, but also to other, similar stimuli. For example, Pavlov's dogs might have salivated in response to a different bell, or you might cringe at the sound of a jeweler's drill as well as a dentist's drill. These responses are examples of stimulus generalization. **Stimulus generalization occurs when an organism responds to new stimuli that are similar to the original stimulus used in conditioning.**

Stimulus generalization is commonplace. We have already discussed a real-life example: the woman who acquired a bridge phobia during her childhood because her father scared her whenever they went over a particular old bridge. The original CS for her fear was that specific bridge, but her fear was ultimately *generalized* to all bridges.

John B. Watson, the founder of behaviorism, conducted an influential early study of generalization. Watson and a colleague, Rosalie Rayner, examined the generalization of conditioned fear in an 11-month-old boy known in the annals of psychology as "Little Albert." Like many babies, Albert was initially unafraid of a live white rat. Then Watson and Rayner (1920) paired the presentation of the rat with a loud, startling sound (the gong of a steel bar struck with a hammer behind Albert's back). Albert *did* show fear in response to this auditory stimulus, and after seven

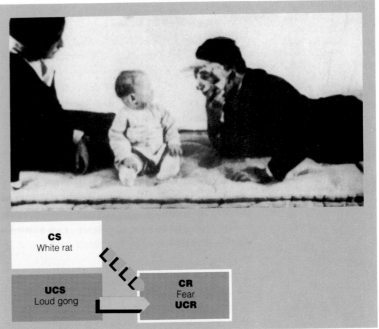

pairings the rat was established as a CS eliciting a fear response even when the gong was not sounded (see Figure 6.9).

Five days later, Watson and Rayner exposed the youngster to other stimuli that resembled the rat in that they were white and furry. They found that Albert's fear response was generalized to a variety of stimuli, including a rabbit, a dog, a fur coat, a Santa Claus mask, and Watson's hair. Most of these conditioned fears were still apparent a month after the original conditioning.

What happened to Little Albert? Did he grow up with a phobia of Santa Claus? Unfortunately, we have no idea. He was taken from the hospital where Watson and Rayner (1920) conducted their study before they got around to extinguishing the conditioned fears they had created, and he was never heard of again. Thus, although Watson and Rayner provided a nice demonstration of stimulus generalization in a human subject, they were roundly criticized in later years for failing to ensure that Albert experienced no lasting ill effects. Their failure to do so clearly was deficient by today's much stricter code of research ethics.

Like conditioning itself, stimulus generalization does not occur in just any set of circumstances. Stimulus generalization depends on the similarity between the new stimulus and the original. The basic law governing generalization is this: *The more similar new stimuli are to the original CS, the greater the likelihood of generalization.* Conversely, generalization becomes less likely as the similarity between the new stimulus and the original decreases. For example, Little Albert's conditioned fear did *not* generalize to wooden blocks that bore no resemblance to the original CS, the rat.

Figure 6.9 The conditioning of Little Albert. The diagram shows how Little Albert's fear response to a white rat was established. Albert's fear response to other white, furry objects illustrates generalization. In the photo, made from a 1919 film, Rosalie Rayner and John Watson (behind the mask) test Albert for stimulus generalization. (Photo courtesy of Prof. Benjamin Harris)

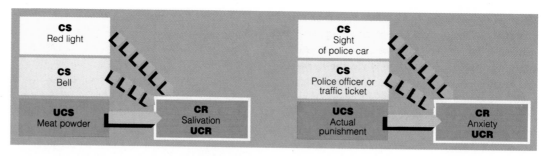

Figure 6.10 Higher-order conditioning. In higher-order conditioning, a neutral stimulus comes to elicit a conditioned response by being paired with an already established CS.

STIMULUS DISCRIMINATION

Stimulus discrimination is just the opposite of stimulus generalization. **Stimulus discrimination occurs when an organism does *not* respond to stimuli that are similar to the original stimulus used in conditioning.** Organisms can gradually learn to discriminate between the original CS and very similar stimuli if they have adequate experience with both. For instance, let's say your new pet dog runs around excitedly wagging its tail whenever it hears your car pull up in the driveway.

Initially it will probably respond to *all* cars that pull into the driveway (stimulus generalization). However, if there is anything distinctive about the sound of your car, your dog may gradually respond with excitement only to your car and not other cars (stimulus discrimination).

The development of stimulus discrimination usually requires that the original CS (your car) continues to be paired with the UCS (your arrival), while other similar stimuli (the other cars) are not paired with the UCS. As with generalization, a basic law governs discrimination. *The less similar new stimuli are to the original CS, the greater the likelihood (and ease) of discrimination.* Conversely, if a new stimulus is quite similar to the original CS, learning to discriminate will be relatively difficult.

HIGHER-ORDER CONDITIONING

Imagine that you were to conduct the following experiment. First, you condition a dog to salivate in response to the sound of a bell. Once the bell is firmly established as a CS, you pair the bell with a new stimulus, let's say a red light, for 15 trials. You then present the red light alone, without the bell. Will the dog salivate in response to the red light?

The answer is "yes." Even though the red light has never been paired with the meat powder, it will acquire the capacity to elicit salivation by virtue of being paired with the bell (see Figure 6.10). This is a demonstration of **higher-order conditioning, in which a conditioned stimulus functions as if it were an unconditioned stimulus.** Higher-order conditioning shows that classical conditioning does not depend on the presence of a genuine, natural UCS; an already established CS will do just fine. In higher-order conditioning, new conditioned responses are built on the foundation of already established conditioned responses.

For instance, when you're driving, you may react to the sighting of a police car with a conditioned response of anxiety, even if you're under the speed limit. If so, your response is probably due to higher-order conditioning. The mere sight of a police car shouldn't by itself produce anxiety,

---

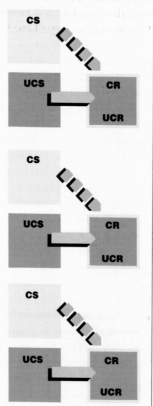

unless it has in the past been paired with some anxiety-producing stimulus—perhaps a police officer or a traffic ticket. Neither a policeman nor a traffic ticket is an unconditioned stimulus for anxiety, however. If either of them elicits anxiety, it's again because of previous conditioning. At some point in your past, the officer or ticket may have been paired with punitive measures, which are the real UCS (see Figure 6.10). As a result, the policeman or the traffic ticket is an established CS that in turn is paired with the sight of a police car. Thus, conditioning can occur when a neutral stimulus is paired with a previously established CS. This phenomenon of higher-order conditioning greatly extends the reach of classical conditioning.

OPERANT CONDITIONING

Even Pavlov recognized that classical conditioning was not the only form of conditioning. Classical conditioning best explains reflexive responding that is largely controlled by stimuli that *precede* the response. However, both animals and humans make a great many responses that don't fit this description. Consider the response you are engaging in right now—studying. It is definitely not a reflex (life might be easier if it were), and the stimuli that govern it (exams and grades) do not precede it. Instead, your studying response is mainly influenced by stimulus events that follow it—specifically, its *consequences*.

This kind of learning was christened *operant conditioning* by B. F. Skinner in the 1930s. The term was derived from his belief that in this type of responding, an organism "operates" on the environment instead of simply reacting to a stimulus. Learning occurs because responses come to be influenced by the consequences that follow them. Thus, **operant conditioning is a form of learning in which voluntary responses come to be controlled by their consequences.** Operant conditioning probably governs a larger share of human behavior than classical conditioning, since most of our responses are voluntary rather than reflexive.

Thorndike's Law of Effect

Another name for operant conditioning is **instrumental learning**, a term introduced earlier by Edward L. Thorndike (1913), who wanted to emphasize that this kind of responding is often *instrumental* in obtaining some desired outcome. Thorndike's pioneering work provided the foundation for many of Skinner's ideas. Thorndike began studying animal learning around the turn of the century. Setting out to determine whether animals could think, he conducted some classic studies of problem solving in cats. In these studies a hungry cat was placed in a small cage, or "puzzle box," with food available just outside. The cat could escape to obtain the food by performing a simple response such as pulling a wire or depressing a lever (see Figure 6.11). After each escape, the cat was rewarded with a small amount of food and then returned to the cage for another trial. Thorndike monitored how long it took the cat to get out of the box on each trial—over a long series of trials. If the cat could think, Thorndike reasoned, there would be a sudden drop in the time required to escape when the cat recognized the solution to the problem.

Instead of a sudden drop, Thorndike observed a very gradual, uneven decline in the time it took the cats to escape from his puzzle boxes (see Figure 6.11). The decline in solution time showed that the cats *were learning*, but Thorndike concluded that their learning did *not* depend on thinking and understanding. Instead, he attributed this learning to a principle he called *the law of effect*. According to the **law of effect, if a response in the presence of a stimulus leads to satisfying effects, the association between the stimulus and the response is strengthened.** Thorndike viewed instrumental learning as a mechanical process in which successful responses are gradually "stamped in" by their favorable effects. His law of effect became the cornerstone of Skinner's theory, although Skinner employed different terminology.

Figure 6.11 The learning curve of one of Thorndike's cats. The inset shows one of Thorndike's puzzle boxes. The cat had to perform three separate acts to escape the box, including depressing the pedal on the right. The learning curve shows how the cat's escape time declined (erratically) over a number of trials.

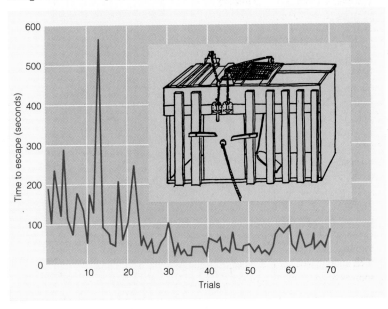

Figure 6.12 Skinner box and cumulative recorder. In this Skinner box designed for rats, the response under study is lever pressing. Food pellets, which may serve as reinforcers, are delivered into the food cup on the right. The speaker and light permit manipulations of visual and auditory stimuli, and the electric grid gives the experimenter control over negative consequences (shock) in the box. A cumulative recorder connected to the box keeps a continuous record of responses and reinforcements. Each lever press moves the pen up a step, and each reinforcement is marked with a slash.

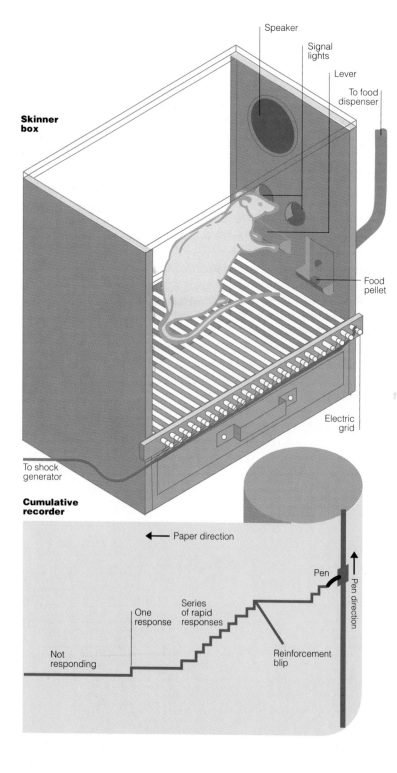

Skinner's Demonstration: It's All a Matter of Consequences

Like Pavlov, Skinner conducted some deceptively simple research that became enormously influential, although he got off to an inauspicious start. His first book, *The Behavior of Organisms* (Skinner, 1938), sold only 80 copies in its first four years in print. Nonetheless, he went on to become, in the words of historian Albert Gilgen (1982), "without question the most famous American psychologist in the world" (p. 97).

The fundamental principle of operant conditioning is uncommonly simple and was anticipated by Thorndike's law of effect. *Skinner demonstrated that organisms tend to repeat those responses that are followed by favorable consequences.* He moved beyond Thorndike by arguing and showing that this principle governs complex human learning as well as simple animal learning. The fundamental principle of operant conditioning is embodied in Skinner's concept of reinforcement. **Reinforcement occurs when an event following a response strengthens the tendency to make that response.** In other words, we are more likely to repeat behaviors that lead to a desirable outcome—some kind of payoff. Favorable outcomes come in many forms, and later we will distinguish between *positive reinforcers* and *negative reinforcers*. For now, though, you can think of reinforcement as a matter of being rewarded.

The principle of reinforcement may be simple, but it is immensely powerful. Skinner and his followers have shown that much of our everyday behavior is regulated by reinforcement. For example, you study hard because good grades are likely to follow as a result. You go to work because this behavior leads to your receiving paychecks. Perhaps you work extra hard because respect, promotions, and raises tend to follow that behavior. You tell jokes, and your friends laugh with you—so you tell some more. You can readily recognize the pervasive role of reinforcement in our lives if you imagine what would happen if these reinforcements did *not* occur.

Skinner's demonstration of the power of reinforcement has affected the motivational strategies used in child care, education, business, and industry. In all these areas, there has been a trend toward increased emphasis on rewarding desirable behavior rather than punishing undesirable behavior. Insofar as people have a choice between using "the carrot or the stick" to motivate people, Skinner's work has led to more dependence on the carrot. In the world of business, for instance, consultants are placing a new emphasis on the use of carefully planned incentives to improve productivity. The intriguing paradox is that these new approaches to problems involving complex human behavior emerged out of Skinner's research on the behavior of rats and pigeons in exceptionally simple situations. Let's look at that research.

Terminology and Procedures

Like Pavlov, Skinner created a prototype experimental procedure that has been repeated (with variations) thousands of times. In this procedure, an animal, typically a rat or a pigeon, is placed in an *operant chamber* that has come to be better known as a *Skinner box*. **A Skinner box is a small enclosure in which an animal can make a specific response that is systematically recorded and in which the consequences of the response are controlled.** In the boxes designed for rats, the key response typically made available is pressing a small lever mounted on one side wall (see Figure 6.12). The boxes made for pigeons have a small disk mounted on a side wall, and the designated response is pecking this disk.

Operant responses such as lever pressing and disk pecking are said to be *emitted* rather than *elicited*. **To emit means "to send forth."** This word was chosen to describe operant responses because operant conditioning governs mainly *voluntary* responses. In contrast, classical conditioning governs mainly *involuntary*, reflexive responses.

The Skinner box permits the experimenter to control the reinforcement contingencies that are in effect for the animal. **Reinforcement contingencies are the circumstances or rules that determine whether responses lead to presentation of a reinforcer.** Typically, the experimenter manipulates whether positive consequences occur when the animal makes the designated response. The positive consequences usually involve delivering a small bit of food into a food cup mounted in the chamber. The animals are deprived of food in advance, so their hunger virtually ensures that the food serves as a reinforcer that will increase responding.

The key dependent variable in most research on operant conditioning is the subjects' *response rate* over time. An animal's rate of lever pressing or disk pecking in the Skinner box is monitored continuously by a device known as a *cumulative recorder* (see Figure 6.12). **The cumulative recorder creates a graphic record of operant responding as a function of time.** The recorder works by means of a roll of paper that moves at a steady rate underneath a movable pen. When there is no responding, the pen stays still and draws a straight horizontal line, reflecting the passage of time. Each time the designated response

occurs, however, the pen moves upward a notch. The pen's motion relative to the movement of the paper produces a graphic summary of the animal's responding over time. Thus, the cumulative recorder device automatically maintains an accurate chronicle of responding and reinforcement in a Skinner box.

The results of operant conditioning studies are usually portrayed graphically. As shown in Figure 6.13, the horizontal axis is used to mark the passage of time, and the vertical axis is used to plot the accumulation of responses. In interpreting these graphs, the key consideration is the *slope* of the line that represents the record of responding. *A rapid response rate produces a steep slope, whereas a slow response rate produces a shallow slope.* Because the response record is cumulative, the line never goes down. It can only go up as more responses are made or flatten out and continue horizontally if the response rate slows to zero. The magnifications in Figure 6.13 show how slope and response rate are related.

Basic Processes in Operant Conditioning

Although the principle of reinforcement is strikingly simple, many other processes involved in operant conditioning make this form of learning just as complex as classical conditioning. In fact,

Figure 6.13 A graphic portrayal of operant responding. The results of operant conditioning are often summarized in a graph of cumulative responses over time. The insets magnify small segments of the curve to show how an increasing response rate yields a progressively steeper slope (bottom), a high, steady response rate yields a steep, stable slope (middle), and a decreasing response rate yields a progressively flatter slope (top).

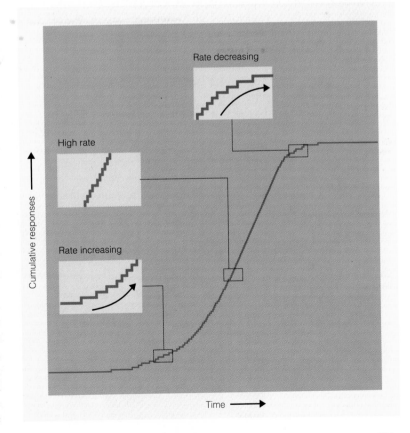

Figure 6.14 Shaping. A circus bear performing unbearlike tricks is showing the results of shaping, an operant technique in which an organism is rewarded for closer and closer approximations of the desired response.

some of the same processes are involved in both types of conditioning. In this section we'll discuss how the processes of acquisition, extinction, generalization, and discrimination occur in operant conditioning.

ACQUISITION AND SHAPING

As in classical conditioning, *acquisition* in operant conditioning is the formation of a response tendency. However, the procedures used to establish a tendency to emit a voluntary operant response are different from those used to create a reflexive CR. Operant responses are established through a gradual process called **shaping—the reinforcement of closer and closer approximations of the desired response.**

Shaping is necessary when an organism does not, on its own, emit the desired response. For example, when a rat is first placed in a Skinner box, it may not press the lever at all. In this case an experimenter begins shaping by releasing food pellets whenever the rat moves toward the lever. As this response becomes more frequent, the experimenter starts requiring a closer approximation of the desired response, possibly releasing food

Figure 6.15 Shaping and complex human behavior. Shaping is at work in the Suzuki method of teaching children to play the violin. The children gradually produce closer and closer approximations of the desired results.

only when the rat actually touches the lever. As reinforcement increases the rat's tendency to touch the lever, the rat will spontaneously press the lever on occasion, finally providing the experimenter with an opportunity to reinforce the designated response. These reinforcements will gradually increase the rate of lever pressing.

Shaping is the key to training animals to perform impressive tricks. When you go to a zoo, circus, or marine park and see bears riding bicycles, monkeys playing the piano, or whales leaping through hoops, you're witnessing the results of shaping (see Figure 6.14). To demonstrate the power of shaping techniques, Skinner once trained some pigeons so that they appeared to play ping pong! They would run about on opposite ends of a ping pong table and peck the ball back and forth. Armed with their knowledge of shaping and other operant techniques, Keller and Marian Breland, two psychologists influenced by Skinner, went into the business of training animals for advertising and entertainment purposes. One of their better-known feats involved training "Priscilla, the Fastidious Pig" to turn on a radio, eat at a kitchen table, put dirty clothes in a hamper, run a vacuum, and then "go shopping" with a shopping cart. Of course, Priscilla picked the sponsor's product off the shelf in her shopping expedition (Breland & Breland, 1961).

Shaping can also be used to mold complex human behavior. For example, the Suzuki method of teaching young children to play the violin uses shaping techniques (see Figure 6.15). Programmed learning is an application of the shaping principle to educational efforts (Keller, 1968). **Programmed learning is an approach to self-instruction in which information and questions are arranged in a sequence of small steps to permit active responding by the learner.** Questions are set up so that material presented in previous steps makes them easy to answer. The technique may sound foreign to you, but you probably have used it. Many study guides that accompany textbooks use this approach, and most computer-aided instruction also depends on it. Programmed learning provides for rapid and frequent reinforcement of learning efforts by giving the student immediate feedback (the assumption is that correctly answering questions is reinforcing). It involves shaping in that it helps the learner acquire more complex responses through gradual, orderly reinforcement of smaller component responses.

EXTINCTION

In operant conditioning, *extinction* refers to the gradual weakening and disappearance of a response tendency because the response is no longer followed by a reinforcer. Extinction begins in operant conditioning whenever previously available reinforcement is terminated. In laboratory studies with rats, this usually means that the experimenter stops delivering food when the rat presses the lever. When extinction is begun, there often is a brief surge in the rat's responding, followed by a gradual decline in response rate until it approaches zero (see Figure 6.16).

The same effects are generally seen in the extinction of human behavior. Let's say that a child routinely cries at bedtime and that this response is reinforced by attention from mom and dad. If the parents decided to cut off further reinforcement by ignoring all such crying episodes, they would be attempting to extinguish this undesirable response. Typically, the child increases such crying behavior for a few days, and then the crying tapers off fairly quickly (Williams, 1959).

A key question in operant conditioning concerns how much *resistance to extinction* an organism will display when reinforcement stops. **Resistance to extinction occurs when an organism continues to make a response after delivery of the reinforcer for it has been terminated.** The greater the resistance to extinction, the longer the responding continues. Thus, if a researcher stops reinforcing lever pressing and the response tapers off very slowly, the response has shown high resistance to extinction. However, if the response tapers off quickly, the response has shown relatively little resistance to extinction.

Resistance to extinction may sound like a matter of purely theoretical interest, but actually it's very practical. We often want to strengthen a response in such a way that it is relatively resistant to extinction. For instance, most parents want to see their child's studying response survive even if the child hits a rocky stretch when studying consistently fails to lead to good grades. Similarly, a casino wants to see patrons continue to gamble, even if they encounter a lengthy losing streak. Thus, a high degree of resistance to extinction can be desirable in many situations. Resistance to extinction is mainly a function of the *schedule of reinforcement* used during the acquisition phase of conditioning, a matter that we will discuss a little later in this chapter.

STIMULUS CONTROL: GENERALIZATION AND DISCRIMINATION

Although operant responding is ultimately controlled by its consequences, stimuli that *precede* a response can also influence operant behavior. When a response is consistently followed by a reinforcer in the presence of a particular stimulus, that stimulus comes to serve as a signal indicating

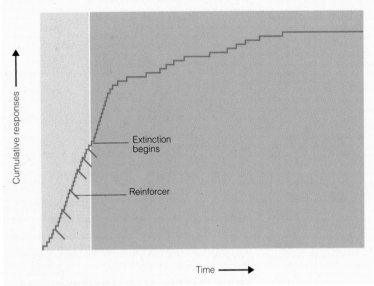

that the response is likely to lead to a reinforcer. Once an organism learns these signals, it tends to respond accordingly. For example, a routine manipulation in operant studies is to reinforce the designated response only when it occurs in the presence of a stimulus. For example, a pigeon's disk pecking may be reinforced only when a small light behind the disk is lit (see Figure 6.17). When the light is out, pecking does not lead to the reward. Pigeons quickly learn to peck the disk only when it is lit. The light that signals the availability of a reinforcer is called a discriminative stimulus. **Discriminative stimuli are cues that influence operant behavior by indicating the probable consequences (reinforcement or nonreinforcement) of a response.**

Figure 6.16 Extinction in operant conditioning. Extinction begins when a response is no longer followed by a reinforcer. Responding persists for a time, but extinction eventually produces a gradual decline in response rate. Responses that are highly resistant to extinction taper off very slowly.

Figure 6.17 An example of a discriminative stimulus. The pigeon is learning that pecking the disk pays off only if the disk is lit. The light that signals the availability of the food reinforcer is a discriminative stimulus.

Figure 6.18 Reinforcement in operant conditioning. In operant conditioning, a *response* is followed by a *reinforcer* in a particular *stimulus context*. As a result of the reinforcement, the organism's tendency to emit the response in that context is strengthened. The example in this figure involves positive reinforcement; negative reinforcement is diagrammed in Figure 6.21.

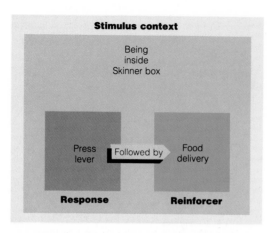

Ultimately, then, operant conditioning depends on the juxtaposition of three key elements: (1) a response, (2) a reinforcer, and (3) a stimulus context in which they occur (see Figure 6.18). This juxtaposition means that stimulus situations play a key role in the regulation of operant behavior. Birds learn that hunting for worms is likely to be reinforced after a rain. Children learn to ask for sweets when their parents are in a good mood. Drivers learn to slow down when the highway is wet.

Human social behavior is regulated extensively by discriminative stimuli. Consider the behavior of asking someone out for a date. Many people emit this response only very cautiously, after receiving many signals (such as eye contact, smiles, and encouraging conversational exchanges) that reinforcement (a favorable answer) is fairly likely. In fact, learning to read subtle discriminative stimuli in social interaction is a major part of

developing good social skills. Socially unskilled people have difficulty decoding social cues from others (Goldenthal, 1985).

Reactions to a discriminative stimulus are governed by the processes of stimulus *generalization* and *discrimination*, just like reactions to a CS in classical conditioning. For instance, envision a cat that comes running into the kitchen whenever it hears the sound of a can opener because that sound has become a discriminative stimulus signaling a good chance of its getting fed. If the cat also responded to the sound of a new kitchen appliance (a blender, for example), this would represent *generalization*—responding to a new stimulus as if it were the original. *Discrimination* would occur if the cat learned to respond only to the can opener and not to the blender.

As you have learned in this section, the processes of acquisition, extinction, generalization, and discrimination in operant conditioning parallel these same processes in classical conditioning. Table 6.1 compares these processes in the two kinds of conditioning.

Consequences That Strengthen Responses: Reinforcement

Although it's convenient to think of reinforcement in terms of rewards, desirable outcomes, and the experience of pleasure, strict behaviorists object when reinforcement is equated with pleasure. Why? They're uncomfortable because the experience of pleasure is an event that may be unobservable within the organism. Generally, behaviorists believe that scientific assertions must be limited to what can be observed.

In keeping with this orientation, Skinner says that reinforcement occurs whenever an outcome strengthens a response, as measured by an increase in the rate of the responding. This definition avoids the issue of what the organism is feeling. Notice also that reinforcement is defined *after the fact*, in terms of its *effect* on behavior. Thus, to know whether something is reinforcing, we must observe whether an organism's rate of responding goes up after the supposed reinforcer has been presented. The central process in reinforcement, then, is the *strengthening of a response tendency*.

Something that is clearly reinforcing for an organism at one time may not function as a reinforcer later. Food will reinforce lever pressing by a rat only if the rat is hungry. Similarly, something that serves as a reinforcer for one person may not function as a reinforcer for another person. For example, parental approval is a potent reinforcer for most children, but not all. Consequently, the

Table 6.1 Comparison of Basic Processes in Classical and Operant Conditioning

PROCESS AND DEFINITION	DESCRIPTION IN CLASSICAL CONDITIONING	DESCRIPTION IN OPERANT CONDITIONING
Acquisition: The formation of a conditioned response tendency	CS and UCS are paired, gradually resulting in CR.	Responding gradually increases because of reinforcement, possibly through shaping.
Extinction: The gradual weakening and disappearance of a conditioned response tendency	CS is presented alone until it no longer elicits CR.	Responding gradually slows and stops after reinforcement is terminated.
Stimulus generalization: An organism's response to stimuli other than the original stimulus used in conditioning	CR is elicited by new stimulus that resembles original CS.	Responding increases in the presence of new stimulus that resembles original discriminative stimulus.
Stimulus discrimination: An organism's failure to respond to stimuli that are similar to the original stimulus used in conditioning	CR is not elicited by new stimulus that resembles original CS.	Responding does not increase in the presence of new stimulus that resembles original discriminative stimulus.

question is not "Is X a reinforcer?" but, rather, "Will X serve as a reinforcer for a particular response made by a particular organism at a particular time?" The only way to know is to observe the effect of the potential reinforcer on behavior in a specific context.

DELAYED REINFORCEMENT

In operant conditioning, a favorable outcome is much more likely to strengthen a response if the outcome follows *immediately*. If there is a delay between a response and the positive outcome, the response may not be strengthened. Furthermore, studies show that the longer the delay between the designated response and the delivery of the reinforcer, the more slowly conditioning proceeds, if it proceeds at all (Lett, 1975). In operant conditioning, then, it is the *contiguity* between a response and the presentation of a reinforcer that is critical (just as in classical conditioning, the contiguity between the CS and UCS is important).

The relative weakness of a delayed reinforcer is easy to understand in animals, because the delay may obscure the connection between the response and the reinforcer. However, a delayed reinforcer is also less effective with *humans*, who are well aware of the link between their response and the eventual presentation of the reinforcer. Although we sometimes manage to bridge long delays, we prefer immediate gratification. This is one reason many people find it difficult to lose weight. The reward for eating is immediate, while the reward for not eating (a trimmer, healthier you) is months away.

CONDITIONED REINFORCEMENT

Operant theorists make a distinction between unlearned, or primary, reinforcers and conditioned, or secondary, reinforcers. **Primary reinforcers are stimulus events that are inherently reinforcing because they satisfy biological needs.** The number of primary reinforcers for a species is limited because primary reinforcers are closely tied to physiological needs. Primary reinforcers for humans include food, water, warmth, sex, and perhaps affection expressed through hugging and close bodily contact.

Secondary, or conditioned, reinforcers **are stimulus events that acquire reinforcing qualities by being associated with primary reinforcers.** The events that function as secondary reinforcers vary among members of a species because they depend on learning. Examples of common secondary reinforcers in humans are money, good grades, attention, flattery, praise, and applause. Most of the material things that people work hard to earn are secondary reinforcers. For example, we learn to find stylish clothes, flashy cars, large diamonds, elegant china, acclaimed paintings, and state-of-the-art stereos reinforcing.

Schedules of Reinforcement

We make innumerable responses that do *not* lead to favorable consequences. It might be nice if we were reinforced every time we took an exam, watched a movie, hit a golf shot, went on a date, or made a sales call. However, in the real world most responses are reinforced only some of the time. How does this reality affect the potency of reinforcers? To find out, operant psychologists have devoted an enormous amount of attention to how schedules of reinforcement influence operant behavior (Ferster & Skinner, 1957; Skinner, 1938, 1953).

A *schedule of reinforcement* **is a specific pattern of presentation of reinforcers over time.** The simplest pattern is continuous reinforcement. *Continuous reinforcement* **occurs when every instance of a designated response is reinforced.** In the laboratory, experimenters often use continuous reinforcement to shape and establish a new response before moving on to more realistic schedules involving intermittent reinforcement. **Intermittent,** or *partial,* **reinforcement occurs when a designated response is reinforced only some of the time.**

Which do you suppose leads to longer-lasting effects—being reinforced every time you emit a response or being reinforced only some of the time? Studies show that, given an equal number of presentations of a reinforcer, *intermittent* reinforcement makes a response more resistant to extinction than continuous reinforcement (Robbins, 1971). In other words, organisms continue responding longer after reinforcements are no longer presented when they have originally been conditioned by being reinforced only *some* of the time.

In fact, intermittent schedules of reinforcement that provide only sporadic delivery of reinforcers can yield great resistance to extinction. This explains why behaviors that are reinforced only occasionally can be very durable. Consider parents whose child persists in throwing temper tantrums on a regular basis. The parents may be proud of the fact that they give in to these temper tantrums (reinforcing them) only about one in seven times. They believe they are working toward eliminating the tantrums, and they may be mystified when the the tantrums persist. Parents in this situation usually fail to realize that they are

"Operant conditioning shapes behavior as a sculptor shapes a lump of clay."
B. F. SKINNER

Figure 6.19 Reinforcement schedules in everyday life. Complex human behaviors are regulated by schedules of reinforcement. Participation in frequent-flyer programs is reinforced on a fixed-ratio schedule. Playing slot machines involves variable-ratio reinforcement. Watching the clock at work is rewarded on a fixed-interval basis (the arrival of quitting time is the reinforcer). Waiting for a bus is likely to involve variable-interval reinforcement because most buses adhere to their schedules erratically.

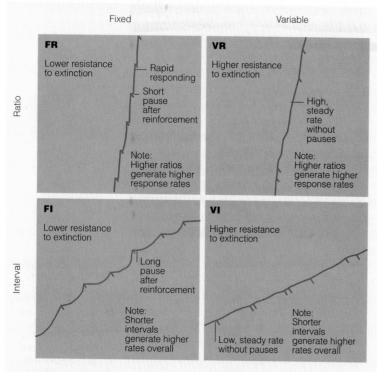

Figure 6.20 Schedules of reinforcement and patterns of response. Each type of reinforcement schedule tends to generate a characteristic pattern of responding. In general, ratio schedules tend to produce more rapid responding than interval schedules (note the steep slopes of the FR and VR curves). In comparison to fixed schedules, variable schedules tend to yield steadier responding (note the smoother curves for the VR and VI curves on the right) and greater resistance to extinction.

providing steady intermittent reinforcement for the tantrums, a pattern that will make the behavior relatively difficult to eliminate.

Reinforcement schedules come in many varieties, but four particular types of intermittent schedules have attracted the most interest. These four types of schedules are described here along with examples drawn from the laboratory and from everyday life (see Figure 6.19 for additional examples):

• In a *fixed-ratio (FR) schedule,* the reinforcer is given after a fixed number of nonreinforced responses. *Examples:* (1) A rat is reinforced for every tenth lever press. (2) A salesman receives a bonus for every fourth set of encyclopedias he sells.

• In a *variable-ratio (VR) schedule,* the reinforcer is given after a variable number of nonreinforced responses. The number of nonreinforced responses varies around a predetermined average. *Examples:* (1) A rat is reinforced for every tenth lever press on the average, but the exact number of responses required for reinforcement varies from one time to the next. (2) A slot machine in a casino pays off once every six tries on the average, with the number of nonwinning responses in between payoffs varying greatly from one time to the next.

• In a *fixed-interval (FI) schedule,* the reinforcer is given for the first response that occurs after a fixed time interval has elapsed. *Examples:* (1) A rat is reinforced for the first lever press after a 2-minute time interval has elapsed and then repeatedly has to wait 2-minute intervals to earn additional reinforcements. (2) Students can earn grades (let's assume the grade is reinforcing) by turning in a paper every 2 weeks.

• In a *variable-interval (VI) schedule,* the reinforcer is given for the first response after a variable time interval has elapsed. The interval length varies around a predetermined average. *Examples:* (1) A rat is reinforced for the first lever press after a 1-minute interval has elapsed, but the following intervals are 3 minutes, 2 minutes, 4 minutes, and so on—with the preset intervals having an average length of 2 minutes. (2) A person repeatedly dials a busy phone number (getting through is the reinforcer).

Over 40 years of research has yielded an enormous volume of data on how schedules of reinforcement are related to patterns of responding (Reynolds, 1975; Zeiler, 1977). Some of the more important findings are summarized in Figure 6.20, which depicts typical response patterns generated by each schedule. In general, ratio schedules tend to produce more rapid responding than interval schedules because when a ratio schedule is in effect, faster responding leads to quicker reinforcement. Also, variable-interval and variable-ratio schedules tend to generate steadier response rates and greater resistance to extinction than their fixed-interval and fixed-ratio counterparts because they are less predictable.

Although most of the research on reinforcement schedules was conducted on rats and pigeons in Skinner boxes, operant psychologists have found that humans react to schedules of reinforcement in much the same way as lower animals (de Villiers, 1977). For example, when animals are placed on ratio schedules, shifting to a higher ratio (that is, requiring more responses per reinforcement) tends to generate faster responding. People who run factories that pay on a piecework basis (a fixed-ratio schedule) have seen the same reaction in humans. For this reason, piecework factories often try to increase the amount of work required to earn reinforcement (raising the ratio from three buttons sewn per dollar to four per dollar, for instance). Shifting to a higher ratio usually stimulates harder work and greater productivity.

There are many other parallels between animals' and humans' reactions to different schedules of reinforcement. For instance, rats and pigeons on variable-ratio schedules tend to show rapid, steady responding, and the responses show relatively great resistance to extinction. People who gamble routinely show similar effects. Most gambling is reinforced according to variable-ratio schedules, which tend to produce rapid, steady responding and great resistance to extinction—exactly what casino operators want.

In summary, schedules of reinforcement are powerful determinants of patterns of responding. Although most of us are unaware of their operation, our behavior is routinely regulated by these schedules.

Positive Reinforcement Versus Negative Reinforcement

According to Skinner, reinforcement can occur in two very different ways, which he called *positive reinforcement* and *negative reinforcement*. **Positive reinforcement occurs when a response is strengthened because it is followed by the arrival of a (presumably) pleasant stimulus.** Thus far, for purposes of simplicity, our examples of reinforcement have involved positive reinforcement. Good grades, good meals, paychecks, scholarships, promotions, nice clothes, nifty cars, attention, flattery, and respect are all positive reinforcers. Their presentation or arrival can strengthen a response.

CONCEPT CHECK 6.2
Recognizing Schedules of Reinforcement

Check your understanding of schedules of reinforcement in operant conditioning by indicating the type of schedule in effect in each of the examples below. In the spaces on the left, fill in FR for fixed ratio, VR for variable ratio, FI for fixed interval, and VI for variable interval. The answers can be found in Appendix A.

_____ 1. Sarah is paid a commission for selling computer systems. She gets a bonus for every third sale.

_____ 2. Artie's parents let him earn some pocket money by doing yard work *approximately* once a week.

_____ 3. Martha has gone fly-fishing. Think of each time that she casts her line as the response that may be rewarded.

In contrast, **negative reinforcement occurs when a response is strengthened because it is followed by the removal of a (presumably) unpleasant stimulus.** Don't let the word *negative* confuse you. Negative reinforcement *is* reinforcement; like all reinforcement it *strengthens* a response tendency. However, this strengthening takes place because a response leads to the removal of an aversive stimulus rather than the arrival of a pleasant stimulus. The negative reinforcement procedure is diagrammed in Figure 6.21.

In laboratory studies, negative reinforcement is usually accomplished as follows. While a rat is in a Skinner box, a moderate electric shock is delivered to the animal through the floor of the box. When the rat presses the lever, the shock is turned off for a period of time. Thus, lever pressing leads to the removal of an unpleasant stimulus (shock). Although this sequence of events is quite different from positive reinforcement, be assured that it strengthens the rat's lever-pressing response.

Everyday human behavior is regulated extensively by negative reinforcement. Consider a handful of examples. You rush home in the winter to get out of the cold. You clean house to get rid of a disgusting mess. You give in to a child's beg-

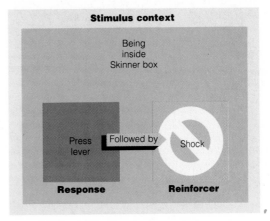

Figure 6.21 Negative reinforcement in operant conditioning. In negative reinforcement, the removal of an aversive stimulus (symbolized here by the "No" sign) serves as a reinforcer. Negative reinforcement produces the same result as positive reinforcement: the organism's tendency to emit the reinforced response in a specific stimulus context is strengthened.

ging to halt the whining. You give in to a roommate or spouse to bring an unpleasant argument to an end.

Negative Reinforcement and Avoidance Behavior

As you have probably noticed, many people tend to avoid facing awkward situations, difficult challenges, and sticky personal problems. Consistent reliance on avoidance is unfortunate; it's not a very healthy or effective coping strategy. How do we learn such a strategy? Often we learn it through negative reinforcement.

ESCAPE LEARNING

The roots of avoidance lie in escape learning. **In *escape learning* an organism engages in a response that brings aversive stimulation to an end.** Psychologists study escape learning in the laboratory with dogs or rats that are conditioned in a *shuttle box*. The shuttle box has two compartments connected by a doorway with a door that can be opened and closed by the experimenter (see Figure 6.22a). In a typical study, the experimenter opens the door, places an animal in one

compartment, and turns on the shock in the floor of that chamber. The animal quickly learns to escape the shock by running to the other compartment. This escape response leads to the removal of an unpleasant stimulus, so it is strengthened through negative reinforcement. Similarly, if you left a party where you were getting "needled" heavily by peers, you would be engaging in an escape response.

AVOIDANCE LEARNING

Escape learning often leads to avoidance learning. **In *avoidance learning* an organism engages in a response that prevents aversive stimulation from occurring.** In other words, the organism doesn't let the aversive stimulation happen in the first place. In laboratory studies of avoidance learning, the experimenter simply gives the animal a signal that shock is forthcoming. The typical signal is a light that goes on a few seconds before the shock. At first the dog or rat will run only when shocked (escape learning), but gradually the animal learns to run to the safe compartment as soon as the light comes on, demonstrating avoidance learning. Similarly, if you quit going to parties because of your concern about being needled by peers, you would be demonstrating avoidance learning.

Avoidance learning is actually a bit puzzling. Avoidance responses tend to be long lasting even though the mechanism of reinforcement is obscure. For example, when an animal in a shuttle box learns to avoid shock entirely, there would seem to be no opportunity for continued negative reinforcement. Specifically, once it acquires the avoidance response, the animal does not experience any more shock. In theory, the avoidance response should gradually be extinguished because it is no longer reinforced (by the removal of shock). However, avoidance responses usually remain strong. The best explanation of this paradox is O. Hobart Mowrer's (1947) two-process theory of avoidance.

TWO-PROCESS THEORY OF AVOIDANCE

Mowrer's explanation is known as the *two-process theory* of avoidance behavior because it integrates the processes of both classical and operant conditioning. According to this theory, the light going on in the shuttle box becomes a CS (through classical conditioning) eliciting conditioned fear in the animal. The response of fleeing to the other side is operant behavior. In Mowrer's scheme, this response produces negative reinforcement, even after shock is no longer experienced, *because it reduces conditioned fear.* Fear is decidedly unpleasant, and a response that reduces fear will usually be strengthened through negative reinforcement.

Figure 6.22 A shuttle box (**a**). Escape and avoidance learning are often studied in an apparatus of this type. Warning signals, shock, and the animal's ability to flee from one compartment to another can be controlled by the experimenter. According to two-process theory (**b**), avoidance *begins* because classical conditioning leads to the acquisition of a new fear (panel 1). Avoidance *continues* because it's maintained by operant conditioning (panel 2). Specifically, the avoidance response leads to the removal of conditioned fear, resulting in negative reinforcement.

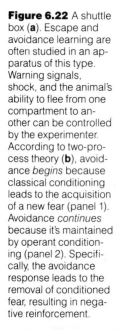
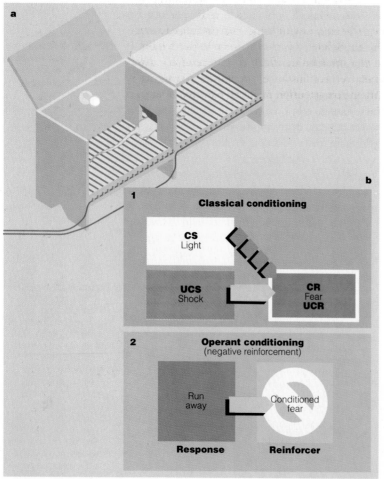

1 Classical conditioning

CS
Light

UCS
Shock

CR
Fear
UCR

2 Operant conditioning
(negative reinforcement)

Run away

Conditioned fear

Response   **Reinforcer**

In short, two-process theory appears to solve our riddle by asserting that the avoidance response removes an *internal* aversive stimulus—conditioned fear—rather than an external aversive stimulus such as shock (see Figure 6.22b).

There are some "holes" in the two-process theory of avoidance. For instance, there is little correlation between the apparent intensity of an animal's fear and its avoidance performance (Mineka, 1979). Although the two-process theory of avoidance learning is still being refined (Bolles & Fanselow, 1980; Hineline, 1981), it is widely used to explain why phobic responses are so persistent (Seligman & Johnston, 1973).

For example, suppose you have a phobia of elevators. According to two-process theory, you acquired your phobia through classical conditioning. Somewhere along the way, elevators were paired with a scary stimulus event. Now, whenever you need to use an elevator, you experience conditioned fear. If your phobia is severe, you probably take the stairs instead. Taking the stairs is an avoidance response that should lead to consistent negative reinforcement by relieving your conditioned fear.

Thus, phobias are thought to be highly resistant to extinction because (1) they lead to avoidance responses that earn negative reinforcement for each instance of the response, and (2) the avoidance responses prevent any opportunity to unlearn the conditioned fear because you never expose yourself to the conditioned stimulus (in this case, riding in the elevator). Thus, the two-process theory of avoidance behavior accounts nicely for the surprising durability of irrational phobic responses.

Consequences That Weaken Responses: Punishment

We have defined reinforcement in terms of its effect on behavior. The presentation of a pleasant stimulus or the removal of an unpleasant one *strengthens* a tendency to make a certain response. Are there also consequences that *discourage* an organism's tendency to make a response? Yes, there are, and in Skinner's model of operant behavior, such consequences are called *punishment*.

Punishment occurs when an event that follows a response weakens or suppresses the tendency to make that response. In laboratory studies, the administration of punishment is very simple. When the rat presses the lever or the pigeon pecks the disk, it gets zapped with a brief shock. This procedure usually leads to a rapid decline in the animal's response rate.

Punishments can occur in two different ways that parallel the distinction between positive and negative reinforcement that we noted earlier. In *positive punishment*, a response is followed by the presentation of an aversive stimulus (for instance, a child is spanked). In *negative punishment*, a response is followed by the removal of a pleasant stimulus (for instance, a child's TV-watching privileges are reduced). One widely used approach to negative punishment is the *time-out* procedure. In this procedure, a person is temporarily removed from a situation in which certain reinforcers are available. For instance, an unruly sixth-grader thriving on attention might be removed from the class. Figure 6.23 compares the procedures and results of both types of punishment and both types of reinforcement.

Figure 6.23 Positive and negative reinforcement and punishment. Both reinforcement and punishment can be accomplished in two ways, depending on whether a response is followed by the presentation or removal of a pleasant or aversive stimulus. Notice that *reinforcement* strengthens a response; *punishment* weakens it. Remember, the "no" signs on the right side of the diagram mean that a response has led to the *removal* of a stimulus, so you get rid of glare when you don your sunglasses and lose your audience when you tell boring stories.

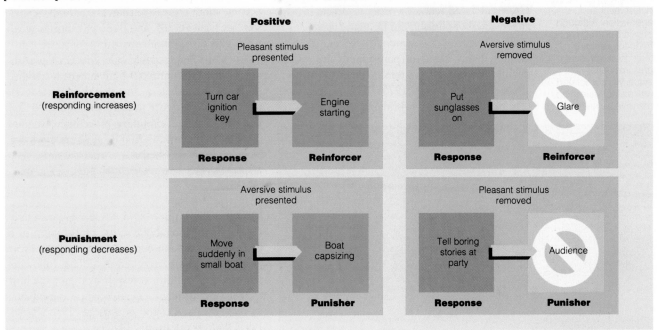

The concept of punishment in operant conditioning confuses many students on two counts. First, it is often confused with negative reinforcement, which is entirely different. As Figure 6.23 shows, punishment and negative reinforcement are different procedures, and, by definition, they produce opposite results. Negative reinforcement strengthens responses, while punishment weakens responses.

The second source of confusion involves viewing punishment as only a disciplinary procedure used by parents, teachers, and other authority figures. In the operant model, however, punishment occurs any time consequences weaken a response tendency. Defined in this way, the concept of punishment goes far beyond actions like parents spanking children and teachers handing out detentions. For example, if you wear a new outfit and your friends promptly make fun of it, your behavior is punished and your tendency to emit this response (to wear the same clothing) will probably decline. Similarly, if you go to a restaurant and have a horrible meal, your response is punished and your tendency to go to that restaurant will probably decline.

Although he touted the power of reinforcement, Skinner argued that punishment is *not* a particularly influential determinant of behavior (Skinner, 1938, 1953). He based his assertion mainly on studies that manipulated the punishment of lever pressing by rats. Skinner found that the strength of the lever-pressing response recovered quickly once the punishment was halted. He concluded that punishment only *temporarily suppressed* responding rather than producing a genuine, durable weakening of response strength. His research led many theorists to downplay the effectiveness of punishment for many years.

After decades of research, however, it's now clear that the effects of punishment are just as durable as the effects of reinforcement (Fantino, 1973; Hilgard & Bower, 1975). The reappearance of a response when punishment stops seems no

different than the disappearance of a response when positive reinforcement stops. Operant theory predicts that behavior will change when its consequences change. Thus, most current views assume that punishment *can* be just as influential as reinforcement.

Although, as we have seen, punishment in operant conditioning involves far more than disciplinary acts, research on punishment takes on special significance because punishment is so frequently used for disciplinary purposes. Let's look at the implications of operant research for the use of punishment as a disciplinary measure.

SIDE EFFECTS OF PUNISHMENT

A key problem with punishment is that even when it is effective in weakening a response, it can have unintended side effects (Newsom, Favell, & Rincover, 1983; Van Houten, 1983). One of these effects is the *general suppression of behavioral activity.* That is, sometimes punishment suppresses many responses besides the punished response. In the laboratory, punished rats may simply freeze up. Similarly, some children who are punished frequently and severely become withdrawn, inhibited, and less active than other children. It is also common for punishment to trigger *strong emotional responses*, including fear, anxiety, anger, and resentment. Strong emotions can temporarily disrupt normal functioning and generate hostility toward the source of the punishment, such as a parent.

Finally, studies show that *physical* punishment often leads to an increase in *aggressive behavior.* There is ample evidence that children who are subjected to a lot of physical punishment tend to become more aggressive than the average youngster (see Figure 6.24). You'll see why shortly, when we discuss observational learning.

All of the undesirable side effects of punishment can be minimized if punishment is handled skillfully. Nonetheless, the truckload of side effects associated with punishment makes it less than ideal as a disciplinary procedure. Operant psychologists maintain that disciplinary goals can often be accomplished more effectively by *reinforcing desirable behavior* than by *punishing undesirable behavior.*

MAKING PUNISHMENT MORE EFFECTIVE

Although we probably overuse punishment as a means of behavioral control, it does have a role to play in disciplinary efforts. The following guidelines summarize research evidence on how to make punishment effective while minimizing its side effects (Axelrod & Apsche, 1983; Parke, 1977; Walters & Grusec, 1977).

Figure 6.24 Physical punishment and aggression. Although physical punishment is frequently administered to suppress aggressive behavior, it actually is associated with an increase in aggressive behavior.

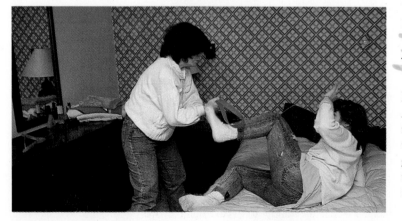

1. *Apply punishment swiftly.* A delay in delivering punishment—like a delay in delivering a reinforcer—undermines its impact. When a mother says, "Wait until your father gets home . . . ," she is making at least one fundamental mistake in the use of punishment. This problem with delayed punishment also explains the ineffectiveness of punishing a pet hours after it has misbehaved, when the owner finally returns home. For instance, it won't do any good to beat your dog with a newspaper while shoving its face in the feces it left on your carpet. This punishment doesn't teach the pet not to defecate on your carpet; it teaches your dog to keep its face out of its feces.

2. *Use punishment just severe enough to be effective.* Intense punishment can be a two-edged sword. Although more severe punishments tend to be more effective in suppressing unwanted responses, they also increase the chance of undesirable side effects. Thus, it's best to use the least severe punishment that seems likely to have some impact.

3. *Make punishment consistent.* With respect to the effect of consistency, punishment differs markedly from reinforcement. If you want to eliminate a response, you should punish it every time it is emitted. Intermittent schedules of punishment are not very effective in suppressing a response. When parents are inconsistent about punishing a particular behavior, they create more confusion than learning.

4. *Explain the punishment.* When children are punished, the reason for their punishment should be explained as fully as possible given the constraints of their age. The more children understand why they were punished, the more effective the punishment tends to be.

5. *Make an alternative response available and reinforce it.* One shortcoming of punishment is that it tells a child only what *not* to do. Operant responses usually help to attain some kind of goal. Thus, the response you want to eliminate through

---

CONCEPT CHECK 6.3
Recognizing Outcomes in Operant Conditioning

Check your understanding of the various types of consequences that can occur in operant conditioning by indicating whether the examples below involve positive reinforcement (PR), negative reinforcement (NR), or punishment (P). The answers can be found in Appendix A.

_____ 1. Lyle gets a speeding ticket.
_____ 2. Diane's supervisor compliments her on her hard work.
_____ 3. Leon goes to the health club for a rare workout and pushes himself so hard that his entire body aches and he throws up.
_____ 4. Audrey lets her dog out so she won't have to listen to its whimpering.
_____ 5. Richard shoots up heroin to ward off tremors and chills associated with heroin withdrawal.

---

punishment probably has a purpose. If you can make another response available that serves the same purpose, doing so should hasten the weakening of the punished response. For example, many of the troublesome behaviors of children are primarily attention-seeking devices. Punishment of such attention-seeking responses will be more effective if you can also provide children with more acceptable ways to gain attention.

6. *Minimize dependence on physical punishment.* Modest physical punishment may be necessary when children are too young to understand a verbal reprimand or the withdrawal of privileges. A light slap on the hand or bottom should suffice. Otherwise, physical punishment should be avoided because, as we discussed, it tends to increase aggressive behavior in children. Also, physical punishment often isn't as effective as most parents assume. Even a vigorous spanking isn't felt by a child an hour later. In contrast, withdrawing valued privileges can give children hours to contemplate the wisdom of changing their ways.

NEW DIRECTIONS IN THE STUDY OF CONDITIONING

As you learned in Chapter 1, science is constantly evolving and changing in response to new research and new thinking. Such change has certainly occurred during the study of conditioning. As Domjan and Burkhard (1986) note, "Our basic ideas of classical and instrumental conditioning have undergone profound changes in the past 15 years, and this vigorous progress continues" (p. vii). In this section we will examine two major changes in thinking about conditioning and the research that set each shift in motion. These changes involve (1) the recognition that an organism's biological heritage can limit or channel conditioning and (2) an increased appreciation of the role of cognitive processes in conditioning.

Recognizing Biological Constraints on Conditioning

Learning theorists have traditionally assumed that the fundamental laws of conditioning are very general—that they apply to a wide range of species. Although no one ever suggested that hamsters could learn physics, until the 1960s most psychologists assumed that associations could be conditioned between any stimulus an organism could register and any response it could make. However, findings in recent decades have demonstrated that there are limits to the generality of conditioning principles—limits imposed by an organism's biological heritage.

INSTINCTIVE DRIFT:
THE CASE OF THE MISERLY RACCOONS

One biological constraint on learning is instinctive drift. **Instinctive drift occurs when an animal's innate response tendencies interfere with conditioning processes.** Instinctive drift was first described by the Brelands, the operant psychologists who went into the business of training animals for commercial and entertainment purposes (Breland & Breland, 1966). They have described many amusing examples of their failures to control behavior through conditioning. For instance, they were once training some raccoons to deposit coins in a piggy bank. They were successful in shaping the raccoons to pick up a coin and put it into a small box, using food as the reinforcer. However, when they gave the raccoons two coins, they ran into an unexpected problem. The raccoons wouldn't give the coins up! Regardless of

the reinforcer available for depositing the coins, they would sit and rub the coins together like so many little misers.

What had happened to disrupt the conditioning program? Apparently, associating the coins with food had brought out the raccoons' innate food-washing behavior. Raccoons often rub things together to clean them. Try as they might, the Brelands could not succeed in shaping the raccoons' behavior so that they consistently deposited their coins. Although it seems that the response should have been easy to learn, the raccoons kept drifting back to their more natural, instinctive response tendencies. The Brelands have reported that they have run into this sort of instinct-related interference on many occasions with a wide variety of species.

CONDITIONED TASTE AVERSION: THE "SAUCE BEARNAISE SYNDROME"

A number of years ago, a prominent psychologist, Martin Seligman, dined out with his wife and enjoyed a steak with sauce bearnaise. About 6 hours afterwards, he developed a wicked case of stomach flu and endured severe nausea. Subsequently, when he ordered his old favorite, sauce bearnaise, he was chagrined to discover that its aroma alone nearly made him throw up.

Seligman's experience was not unique. Many people develop similar aversions when food is followed by nausea from illness, alcohol intoxication, or food poisoning. However, Seligman was puzzled by what he called his "sauce bearnaise syndrome" (Seligman & Hager, 1972). On the one hand, it appeared to be the straightforward result of classical conditioning. A neutral stimulus (the sauce) had been paired with an unconditioned stimulus (the flu) which caused an unconditioned response (the nausea), so that the sauce bearnaise became a conditioned stimulus eliciting nausea (see Figure 6.25).

On the other hand, Seligman recognized that his aversion to the taste of bearnaise sauce violated certain basic principles of conditioning. First, the lengthy delay of 6 hours between the CS (the sauce) and the UCS (the illness) should have prevented conditioning from occurring. In laboratory studies, a delay of more than *30 seconds* between the CS and the UCS makes it very difficult to establish a conditioned response, yet this conditioning occurred in just one pairing. Second, why was it that *only* the bearnaise sauce became a CS eliciting nausea? Why not other stimuli that were present in the restaurant? Shouldn't plates, knives, tablecloths, or his wife, for example, also trigger Seligman's nausea?

The riddle of Seligman's sauce bearnaise syn-

Figure 6.25 Conditioned taste aversion. Taste aversions can be established through classical conditioning, as in the "sauce bearnaise syndrome." Even the aroma of someone else's food is enough to spoil this diner's meal. However, as the text explains, taste aversions can be acquired in ways that violate basic principles of classical conditioning.

CS
Sauce bearnaise

UCS
Flu

CR
Nausea
UCR

drome was solved by John Garcia and his colleagues, who conducted a series of laboratory studies on *conditioned taste aversion* (Garcia & Koelling, 1966; Garcia, Clarke, & Hankins, 1973; Garcia & Rusiniak, 1980). They systematically manipulated the kinds of stimuli preceding the onset of nausea and other noxious experiences in rats, using radiation to artificially induce the nausea. They found that when taste cues were followed by nausea, rats quickly acquired conditioned taste aversions. However, when taste cues were followed by other types of noxious stimuli (such as shock), rats did *not* develop conditioned taste aversions. Furthermore, visual and auditory stimuli followed by nausea also failed to produce conditioned aversions.

In short, Garcia and his coworkers found that taste aversions were conditioned *only* through the pairing of taste stimuli and nausea. When taste stimuli were paired with other responses or nausea was paired with other stimuli, minimal conditioning occurred. In contrast, the taste-nausea connection was made so readily that conditioned taste aversions could develop in spite of remarkably long CS–UCS delays. These findings contradicted the long-held belief that associations could be created between virtually any stimulus and any response. Garcia found that it was almost impossible to create certain associations, while taste-nausea associations were almost impossible to prevent.

What is the theoretical significance of this unique readiness to make connections between taste and nausea? Garcia argues that it is a byproduct of the evolutionary history of mammals. Animals that consume poisonous foods and survive must learn not to repeat their mistakes. Natural selection will favor organisms that quickly learn what *not* to eat. Thus, evolution may have equipped some organisms, including humans, with a biologically built-in tendency to learn taste-nausea associations very easily.

Not all species are equipped in this way, however. For instance, quail, which depend heavily on their vision, learn associations between visual cues and nausea more readily than taste-nausea associations (Wilcoxon, Dragoin, & Kral, 1971). Thus, it appears that different species are biologically programmed to learn some kinds of stimulus-response associations more readily than others.

Conditioned taste aversion has practical as well as theoretical significance. After learning how easy it was to condition food aversions, Garcia decided to apply this discovery to a challenging practical problem: the control of predators' attacks on livestock. We will examine his work in our Featured Study to give you a concrete example of field research in psychology.

CHAPTER
SIX
FEATURED
STUDY

Pulling a Gag on Hungry Coyotes

In some areas of the western United States, coyotes have plagued sheep ranchers by killing off many of their valuable sheep. For ecological reasons, killing the coyotes in retaliation is both difficult and controversial. The purpose of this study was to see whether conditioned taste aversion could be employed to make sheep unappetizing to coyotes and thereby reduce sheep ranchers' herd losses without harming the coyote population.

As a pilot study the researchers conducted an experiment with captive animals. Six coyotes and two wolves were given the opportunity to consume specially treated pieces of sheep and rabbit carcass. The researchers had treated the carcasses with a chemical (lithium chloride) that causes nausea and illness when eaten. The researchers intended to create a conditioned taste aversion to sheep and rabbits (see Figure 6.26). They made a comparison of the predators' attack behavior before and after the predators ate the treated carcasses.

After the treated carcasses had been eaten, attacks on live rabbits and sheep placed in a pen with the coyotes and wolves were greatly reduced. In fact, some of the coyotes vomited at the sight of a rabbit. One wolf tested with a live

Investigators: Carl R. Gustavson, Daniel J. Kelly, Michael Sweeney (Eastern Washington State College), & John Garcia (University of California, Los Angeles)

Source: Prey-lithium aversions I: Coyotes and wolves. *Behavioral Biology, 17* (1976), 61–72.

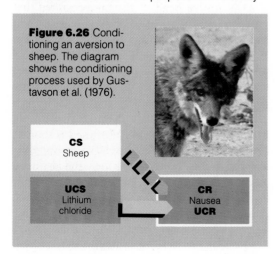

Figure 6.26 Conditioning an aversion to sheep. The diagram shows the conditioning process used by Gustavson et al. (1976).

CS
Sheep

UCS
Lithium
chloride

CR
Nausea
UCR

sheep seemed to be intimidated by the sheep (much to the surprise of the sheep)! Meanwhile, attacks on other prey (chickens) placed in the pen remained unchanged. Encouraged by the success of their pilot study, the researchers went ahead with their field study of coyotes in the wild.

Method
The field study was conducted on a 3000-acre sheep ranch in Washington to see whether these techniques could affect the attack behavior of freely roaming coyotes. The subjects were an unknown number of wild coyotes inhabiting the area.

The research team set up twelve bait stations around the ranch in areas where tracks suggested heavy coyote activity. Lithium-treated dog food wrapped in sheep's hide and lithium-treated sheep carcasses (from natural losses) served as the bait in these traps. Missing bait was replaced regularly. Researchers carefully inspected animal tracks near the bait stations to make sure the bait was consumed by coyotes and not other predators, such as weasels or badgers.

The dependent variable was the number of sheep on the ranch killed by coyotes during the test period. Garcia and his coworkers compared this number to the herd losses during the previous year.

Results
The researchers were able to make only rough estimates of the program's effectiveness. Difficulties in verifying whether killed sheep had in fact been attacked by coyotes were greater than anticipated. In addition, the rancher's records of herd losses in previous years were less than perfect. However, the best estimates available suggested that the number of sheep killed by coyotes declined somewhere between 30% and 60% during the test period. Figure 6.27 shows a conservative estimate of the program's effectiveness.

Discussion
The results suggest that conditioned taste aversion can be used to reduce predators' attacks on livestock. The failure to stop the attacks com-

pletely in this instance was attributed to turnover in the coyote population on the ranch. The researchers speculated that many of the coyotes that consumed tainted food may have moved on to other areas, while new, naive coyotes with normal attack habits moved into the treated area. This turnover would limit the success of a program that was confined to a single ranch. A geographically broader program would seem to be necessary for more thorough suppression of the attacks.

Comment
This study illustrates the kinds of problems that researchers run into when they leave their well-controlled laboratories and move out into the "real world." In this field study the researchers were never sure exactly how many subjects (coyotes) they had. Nor were they sure how much migration changed the subject pool with time. It was also hard to tell whether the treatment (the tainted bait) had actually been received by the subjects, and the dependent variable of sheep killed by coyotes turned out to be tricky to measure. These problems created major headaches and interpretive difficulties for the researchers. You can see why psychologists are so fond of their laboratories, where they can exert precise experimental control over the proceedings! Nonetheless, this study is a nice example of applied research in which a behavioral intervention was tested in a challenging real-world situation.

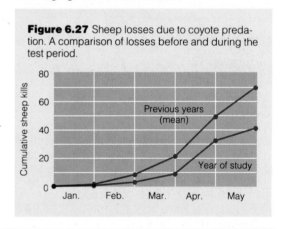

Figure 6.27 Sheep losses due to coyote predation. A comparison of losses before and during the test period.

PREPAREDNESS AND PHOBIAS
Scientists always seek to identify similarities and explain relationships among observations. In this spirit Martin Seligman has proposed a concept called *preparedness* to explain his sauce bearnaise syndrome, Garcia's findings, and a variety of other phenomena. **Preparedness involves a species-specific predisposition to be conditioned in certain ways and not in others.** Seligman believes that preparedness is a biologically programmed result of evolution. Instinctive drift and conditioned taste aversion both appear to involve prepared-

ness. In addition, Seligman believes that phobic responses in humans are influenced by preparedness (De Silva, Rachman, & Seligman, 1977).

Although people can acquire phobias for almost anything, certain phobias are vastly more common than others. People tend to develop phobias for snakes, spiders, heights, and darkness much more readily than for flies, desks, erasers, or electrical outlets, for example. What characteristic do common phobic objects share? Most were once genuine threats to our ancestors. Consequently, a fear response to such objects had survival value for our species. According to Seligman's theory of preparedness, evolutionary forces gradually programmed humans to acquire fears of these objects very easily and rapidly.

The concept of preparedness does *not* conflict with previously discussed ideas about the origins of phobias. Seligman still believes that phobic responses may be created through classical conditioning and maintained through operant conditioning (negative reinforcement). The concept of preparedness builds on these ideas to explain why phobic conditioning seems to be selective.

Laboratory simulations of phobic conditioning have largely supported the theory of preparedness (Hygge & Ohman, 1978; Ohman, Erixon, & Lofberg, 1975). In these studies, slides of common phobic stimuli (snakes and spiders) and stimuli with little phobic potential (flowers and houses) were paired with shock. Physiological monitoring of the people who served as subjects indicated that the common phobic stimuli produced more rapid conditioning, stronger fear responses, and conditioned fears that were more resistant to extinction. These results are consistent with what the theory of preparedness would predict.

In summary, several lines of research suggest that there are species-specific biological constraints on conditioning. We humans are not immune to the influence of these biological forces. Although it is still reasonable to search for general laws of conditioning, it is now clear that an organism's biological heritage can channel conditioning in certain directions.

Recognizing Cognitive Processes in Conditioning

Pavlov, Skinner, and their followers traditionally viewed conditioning as a mechanical process in which stimulus-response associations are stamped in by experience. According to this view, conditioning is orchestrated by the environment and the organism plays a passive role. Learning theorists asserted that if a flatworm can be conditioned, then conditioning can't depend on higher mental processes. Although this viewpoint did not go entirely unchallenged (e.g., Tolman, 1922, 1932), mainstream theories of conditioning did not assign a major role to cognitive processes.

In recent decades, however, there has been a shift toward more cognitive explanations of conditioning that emphasize mental processes. This shift is largely due to new empirical findings that undermine the old, mechanical view of conditioning. Let's review some of these findings and the more cognitive models of conditioning that have resulted.

BLOCKING

Imagine conducting a seemingly simple study of classical conditioning in rats. In phase one we pair a tone with shock so that the tone becomes a CS eliciting fear. In phase two, we pair the same tone *and* a light with shock. Two stimulus signals are now associated with shock, and when we present them together (without the shock) this combination elicits fear. In phase three, we present only the light to see if it elicits conditioned fear by itself. What would you predict? The light *has* been paired with shock. According to conventional theories of conditioning, the light should trigger fear. However, this is *not* what Leon Kamin (1968, 1969) found. The light, by itself, is not an effective CS. It evokes either no response at all or else a very weak one.

This phenomenon is called *blocking*, because something is blocking the usual conditioning that should take place when the light and shock are paired. For some reason, a basic conditioning procedure has failed to bring about conditioning. Why? Research suggests that it is because the light is a *redundant* stimulus that adds no new information. Shock has always been preceded by the tone. The tone is all the rat needs to pay attention to in order to know when to expect shock. Thus, **blocking occurs when a stimulus paired with a UCS fails to become a CS because it is redundant with an established CS.**

The significance of blocking is subtle, but immense. The existence of blocking suggests that the rat is not a passive recipient of mechanical conditioning. The rat actively filters out a redundant stimulus, apparently because the light doesn't improve the predictability of the shock. Consider the concepts employed to explain blocking—redundancy, information, attention, expectation, and predictability. We're talking about cognitive processes, such as they are, in a rat!

SIGNAL RELATIONS

The cognitive element in conditioning has also been the focus of research conducted by Robert Rescorla (1980, 1987; Rescorla & Wagner, 1972). Rescorla asserts that environmental stimuli serve as signals and that some stimuli are better, or more dependable, signals than others. Hence, he has manipulated *signal relations* in classical conditioning—that is, CS–UCS relations that influence whether a CS is a "good" signal. A good signal is one that allows accurate prediction of the UCS.

In essence, Rescorla manipulates the *predictive value* of a conditioned stimulus. How does he do

"In the last 20 years attention has shifted to the study of Pavlovian conditioning. That shift has been richly rewarded."
ROBERT RESCORLA

this? He varies the proportion of trials in which the CS and UCS are paired. Consider the following example. A tone and a shock are paired 20 times for one group of rats. Otherwise, these rats are never shocked. This is the usual Pavlovian conditioning procedure. For these rats the CS (tone) and UCS (shock) are paired in 100% of the experimental trials. Another group of rats also receives 20 pairings of the tone and shock. However, this group is also exposed to the shock on 20 other trials when the tone does not precede it. For this group, the CS and UCS are paired in only 50% of the trials. Thus, the two groups of rats have had an equal number of CS–UCS pairings, but the CS is a better signal or predictor of shock for the 100% CS–UCS group than for the 50% CS–UCS group.

What did Rescorla find when he tested the rats for conditioned fear? He found that the CS elicits a much stronger response in the 100% CS–UCS group than in the 50% CS–UCS group. Given that the two groups received an equal number of CS–UCS pairings, this difference in conditioning must be due to the greater predictive power of the CS for the 100% group.

Numerous studies of signal relations have shown that the predictive value of a CS is very influential in classical conditioning (Rescorla, 1978). These studies of signal relations suggest that classical conditioning may involve information processing rather than reflexive responding.

RESPONSE-OUTCOME RELATIONS AND REINFORCEMENT

Let's turn to operant behavior for one more example of cognitive processes in conditioning. Imagine that it's the night before an important exam, and you study very hard while repeatedly playing a Bruce Springsteen album. The next morning you earn a high A on your exam. Does this result strengthen your tendency to play Springsteen albums before exams? Probably not. Chances are, you will recognize the logical relation between the response of studying hard and the reinforcement of a good grade, and only the response of studying will be strengthened.

However, it's not out of the realm of possibility that you will develop a habit of playing Springsteen before big exams. Skinner (1948) has argued that superstitious behavior can be established through noncontingent reinforcement. **Noncontingent reinforcement occurs when a response is strengthened even though delivery of the reinforcer was not a result of the response.** There are many anecdotal reports of athletes acquiring superstitious responses (wearing a special pair of socks, eating the same lunch, and so on) through noncontingent reinforcement (Gmelch, 1978). Although we do seem to acquire some superstitions in this way, recent studies suggest that noncontingent reinforcement is not as powerful or influential as Skinner originally believed (Killeen, 1981).

In any case, it is clear that reinforcement is *not* automatic when favorable consequences follow a response. Instead, the evidence indicates that we actively reason out the causal relations between our responses and the outcomes that follow. Some relations are more plausible than others. When a response is followed by a positive outcome, the response is more likely to be strengthened if we think that the response was *caused* by the outcome.

Once more, cognitive processes are affecting the process of conditioning. You might guess that only humans would engage in causal reasoning about response-reinforcer relations. However, evidence suggests that under the right circumstances even pigeons can learn to recognize causal relations between responses and their outcomes (Killeen, 1981).

CONDITIONING AS CONTINGENCY DETECTION

The evidence on blocking, signal relations, and response-outcome relations has provoked psychologists to develop new models of conditioning that have a stronger cognitive flavor than before (Catania, 1979; Rescorla, 1978, 1988). These reformulated models view conditioning as a matter of detecting the *contingencies* among environmental events. According to these theories, organisms actively try to figure out what leads to what (the contingencies) in the world around them. Stimuli are viewed as signals that help organisms to minimize their noxious experiences and maximize their pleasant ones.

Newer theories of conditioning emphasize that organisms engage in active information processing. These cognitively oriented theories are quite a departure from older theories that viewed conditioning as a mindless, mechanical process. We can also see this new emphasis on cognitive processes in our next subject, observational learning.

OBSERVATIONAL LEARNING

Can classical and operant conditioning account for all of our learning? Absolutely not. Consider how we learn a fairly basic skill such as driving a car. People do not hop naively into an automobile and start emitting random responses until one leads to favorable consequences. On the contrary, most people learning to drive know exactly where to place the key and how to get rolling. How are these responses acquired? Through *observation*. Most new drivers have years of experience observing others driving, and they put these observations to work. Learning through observation accounts for a great deal of learning in both animals and humans.

Observational learning occurs when an organism's responding is influenced by the observation of others, who are called *models*. This process has been described and investigated extensively by Albert Bandura (1977, 1986). Bandura does not view observational learning as entirely separate from classical and operant conditioning. Instead, he asserts that it greatly extends the reach and relevance of these conditioning processes. Whereas older conditioning theories emphasized the organism's direct experience, Bandura has demonstrated that both classical and operant conditioning can take place vicariously through observational learning.

Essentially, observational learning involves being conditioned indirectly by observing another's conditioning (see Figure 6.28). To illustrate, suppose you observed a friend behaving assertively with a car salesman and being reinforced by the exceptionally good buy she obtained on a car. Your own tendency to behave assertively with salespeople might well be strengthened as a result. Notice that the favorable consequence is experienced by your friend, not by you. The good buy should reinforce your friend's tendency to bargain assertively. But your tendency to bargain assertively may also be reinforced indirectly.

Basic Processes

Bandura has identified four key processes that are crucial in observational learning. The first two—attention and retention—highlight the importance of cognition in this type of learning.

- *Attention.* To learn through observation, you must pay attention to another person's behavior and its consequences.
- *Retention.* Because you may not have occasion to use the modeled response for weeks, months, or even years, you also have to store in your memory a mental representation of what you have witnessed.
- *Reproduction.* The enactment of a modeled response depends on your ability to reproduce the response by converting your stored mental images into overt behavior. For some responses this may not be easy. For example, this requirement explains why most of us cannot execute a breathtaking windmill dunk even though we've watched Michael Jordan do it in a basketball game.
- *Motivation.* Finally, you are unlikely to reproduce an observed response unless you are motivated to do so. Your motivation depends on whether you encounter a situation in which you

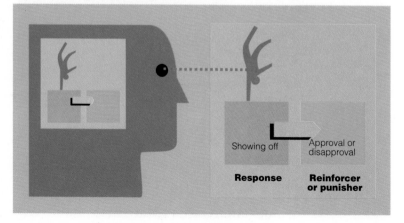

Figure 6.28 Observational learning. In observational learning, an observer attends to and stores a mental representation of a model's behavior (for example, showing off by doing handstands) and its consequences (such as approval or disapproval from others).

Through observation, the English titmouse has learned how to break into containers to swipe milk from its human neighbors. The boy in the photograph below is already beginning to *perform* the behavior that he is acquiring through observation.

believe the response is likely to pay off for you.

Observational learning has proven especially valuable in explaining complex human behaviors, but animals can also learn through observation. A simple example is the thieving behavior of the English titmouse, a small bird renowned for its early-morning raids on its human neighbors. The titmouse has learned how to open cardboard caps on the bottles of milk delivered to the porches of many homes in England. Having opened the cap, the titmouse skims the cream from the top of the milk. This clever learned behavior has been passed down from one generation of titmouse to the next through observational learning.

Acquisition Versus Performance

Bandura points out that there is often a gap between what people have learned and what they do. For instance, anyone knows how to show up at a party. Introverts who avoid parties do so because they don't expect to find the parties very reinforcing. People have many acquired responses that they may or may not perform, depending on the situation. Thus, Bandura distinguishes between the *acquisition* of a learned response and the *performance* of that response. Because of their cognitive abilities, humans can store away many learned responses and select from them as needed.

Bandura maintains that reinforcement affects which responses we perform more than which responses we acquire. We emit those responses that we think are likely to be reinforced. For instance, you may study hard in a class for which the professor gives sound, sensible exams, because you expect that studying will be reinforced with a good grade. In contrast, you may hardly open the text in a class in which the professor gives arbitrary, unpredictable exams, because you don't expect studying to be reinforced. In both cases you know how to execute the response (studying). However, you perform differently in the two situations because you think the reinforcement contingencies are different. Thus, Bandura concurs with Skinner about the great importance of reinforcement, but Bandura does not view reinforcement as a mechanical process. He assumes that people are active agents who pursue reinforcements because of their expectations.

Applications

Bandura's theory of observational learning has shed light on many important aspects of human behavior. For example, it explains why physical punishment tends to increase aggressive behavior in children, even when it is intended to do just the opposite. Parents who depend on physical punishment frequently punish their children for hitting other children—by hitting the child. The parents may sincerely intend the punishment to reduce such aggressive behavior by the children, but they are unwittingly serving as *models* of aggressive behavior. Although a parent may tell a child that "hitting people won't accomplish anything," the parent is at that very moment in the midst of hitting the child in order to accomplish something. Since parents usually accomplish their immediate goal of stopping the child's hitting, the child sees that aggression is reinforced. Empirical studies clearly show that in this situation actions speak louder than words—because of observational learning.

It is the power of observational learning that makes television a very influential determinant of behavior. Young children are especially impressionable, and there is extensive evidence that they pick up many responses from viewing models on TV (Huston & Wright, 1982). Because of this evidence, the amount of aggressive behavior that should be allowed on TV shows is a very controversial subject. We'll discuss evidence linking television violence to aggressive behavior—through observational learning—in our upcoming chapters on human development (Chapter 11) and personality (Chapter 12). In the chapter on development, you will also see that observational learning contributes to the acquisition of gender roles. Clearly, observational learning is important in human behavior.

"Most human behavior is learned by observation through modeling."

ALBERT BANDURA

PUTTING IT IN PERSPECTIVE

Two of our six unifying themes stand out in this chapter. First, you can see how nature and nurture interactively govern behavior (theme 5). Second, looking at psychology in its sociohistorical context, you can see how progress in psychology spills over to affect trends and values in society at large (theme 3). Let's examine each of these points in more detail.

In regard to nature versus nurture, research on learning clearly demonstrates the enormous power of the environment in shaping behavior. Pavlov's model of classical conditioning shows how our experiences can account for our everyday fears and anxieties as well as many other emotional responses. Skinner's model of operant conditioning shows how environmental contingencies of reinforcement and punishment can mold everything from a child's bedtime whimpering to an adult's restaurant preferences. Indeed, the research linking environment to behavior has been so impressive that many behaviorists once believed that *all* aspects of behavior could be explained in terms of environmental determinants.

In recent decades, however, new evidence has shown that there are biological constraints on conditioning processes. The phenomena of instinctive drift, conditioned taste aversion, and preparedness in the learning of phobias all illustrate how an organism's biological heritage can channel conditioning in certain directions. Thus, even in explanations of learning, an area once dominated by "nurture" theories, we see once again that heredity and the environment jointly influence behavior.

The history of psychologists' investigations of conditioning also shows how progress in the field can seep into other aspects of society. For example, Skinner's ideas about the power of reinforcement and the ineffectiveness of punishment have influenced our society's norms regarding discipline. Today's parents and educators appear to depend less on punitive measures than did previous generations. Research on operant conditioning has also affected management styles in the business world, leading to an increased emphasis on systematic manipulations of positive reinforcement. In the educational arena, the concept of individualized, programmed learning is a spinoff from behavioral research. The fact that the principles of conditioning are routinely applied in our homes, our businesses, our schools, and our factories clearly shows that psychology is far from an ivory-tower endeavor.

In the Application that follows, you will see how you can apply the principles of conditioning to improve your self-control, as we discuss the technology of behavior modification.

Type of learning	Procedure	Diagram	Result
Classical conditioning Ivan Pavlov	A neutral stimulus (for example, a bell) is paired with an unconditioned stimulus (such as food) that elicits an unconditioned response (salivation)	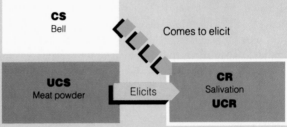	The neutral stimulus becomes a conditioned stimulus that elicits the conditioned response (for example, a bell triggers salivation)
Operant conditioning B. F. Skinner	In a stimulus situation, a response is followed by favorable consequences (reinforcement) or unfavorable consequences (punishment)	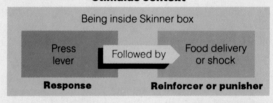	If reinforced, the response is strengthened (emitted more frequently); if punished, the response is weakened (emitted less frequently)
Observational learning Albert Bandura	An observer attends to a model's behavior (for example, showing off) and its consequences (for example, approval or disapproval by others)	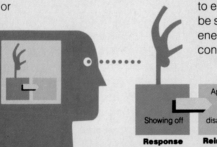	The observer stores a mental representation of the modeled response; the observer's tendency to emit the response may be strengthened or weakened, depending on the consequences observed

Typical kinds of responses	Examples in animals	Examples in humans

Involuntary, reflex responses usually governed by the autonomic nervous system

Coyotes given tainted sheep develop a conditioned response of nausea elicited by the sight of sheep

Little Albert learns to fear a white rat and other white furry objects through classical conditioning

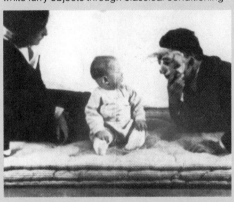

Voluntary, sponta-neous responses usually governed by the somatic nervous system

Circus bears perform remarkable feats because they have been reinforced for gradually learning closer and closer approximations of responses they do not normally emit

A casino patron emits rapid responses on a slot machine that has been programmed to dole out reinforcers according to a complex variable-ratio schedule of reinforcement

A young boy tries to perform a response that he is acquiring through observational learning

Usually voluntary responses, often consisting of novel and complex sequences

An English titmouse learns to break into humans' milk bottles by observing the thievery of other titmice

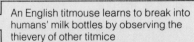

ACHIEVING SELF-CONTROL THROUGH BEHAVIOR MODIFICATION

Answer the following "yes" or "no."

☐ **1.** Do you have a hard time passing up food, even when you're not hungry?

☐ **2.** Do you wish you studied more often?

☐ **3.** Would you like to reduce your smoking or drinking?

☐ **4.** Do you experience difficulty in getting yourself to exercise regularly?

☐ **5.** Do you wish you had more will power?

If you answered "yes" to any of these questions, you have struggled with the challenge of self-control. This Application discusses how you can use the techniques of behavior modification to improve your self-control. If you stop to think about it, self-control—or rather a lack of it—underlies many of the personal problems we struggle with in everyday life.

Behavior modification is a systematic approach to changing behavior through the application of the principles of conditioning. Advocates of behavior modification assume that our behavior is a product of learning, conditioning, and environmental control. They further assume that *what is learned can be unlearned.* Thus, they set out to "recondition" people to produce more desirable patterns of behavior.

Behavior modification can be a powerful tool. Advocates of behavior modification began in the 1960s to apply their technology with great success in schools, businesses, hospitals, factories, child-care facilities, prisons, mental health centers, and drug abuse programs (Goodall, 1972; Kazdin, 1982).

One nice thing about behavior modification is that anyone can learn to use it with only a moderate amount of instruction. It involves a fairly straightforward application of the principles of conditioning introduced in this chapter. Moreover, you can use behavior modification to alter your own behavior—to engage in self-modification. The technology of behavior modification can be particularly helpful in your efforts to improve self-control.

Our discussion will borrow liberally from an excellent book on self-modification by David Watson and Roland Tharp (1989). There are five steps in the process of self-modification. These steps are outlined in a flowchart in Figure 6.29.

Specifying Your Target Behavior

The first step in any systematic effort at self-modification is to specify the *target behaviors*, or *target responses.* These are the behaviors you will try to change in some way. This crucial step can be more complicated than it sounds.

A behavior modification program can be applied only to a clearly defined, overt behavioral response. However, many of us tend to be vague in describing our problems and can be hard-pressed to identify the exact nature of the behavior we want to change.

We tend to think in terms of negative personality *traits* rather than undesirable *behaviors.* For example, asked what behaviors he would like to change, a man might say, "I'm too irritable." That may well be accurate, but it doesn't help much in designing a self-modification program. To use a behavioral approach, we need to translate vague statements about traits into clear descriptions of the specific be-

haviors that lead us to think we have those traits.

The best way to identify behaviors is to ponder past behavior or closely observe current behavior and to list specific *examples* of responses that lead to the trait description. For instance, the man who characterizes himself as "too irritable" might identify two overly frequent responses, such as arguing with his wife and snapping at his children. These are specific responses for which he could design a self-modification program.

Figure 6.29 Flowchart of steps in executing a self-modification program.

Step 1 — Specify your target behavior

Step 2 — Gather baseline data
- Identify possible controlling antecedents
- Determine initial level of response
- Identify possible controlling consequences

Step 3 — Design your program
- Select strategies to increase response strength *or* Select strategies to decrease response strength

Step 4 — Execute and evaluate your program

Step 5 — Bring your program to an end

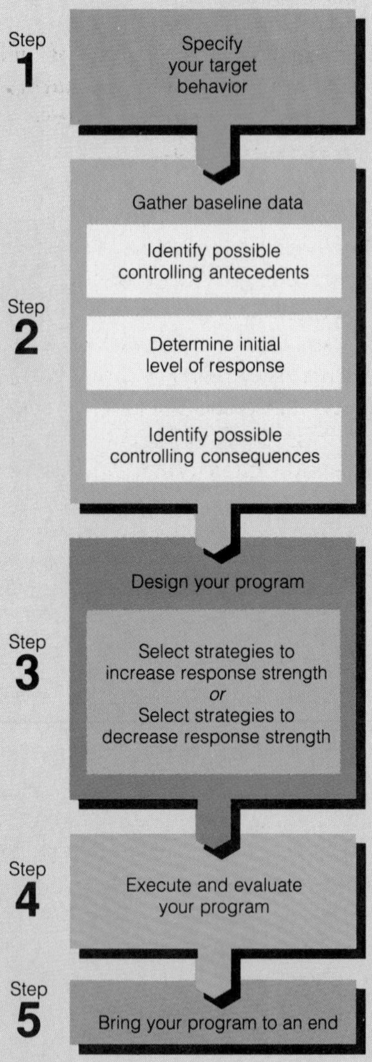

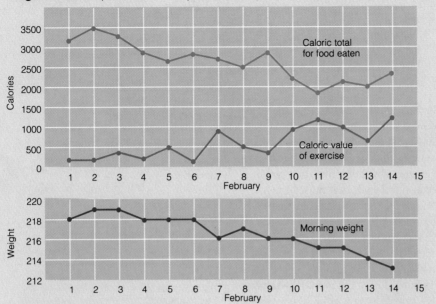

Figure 6.30 Graphic record of daily food consumption, exercise, and weight.

Gathering Baseline Data

The second step in a behavior modification effort is to gather baseline data. **The *baseline period* is a span of time before your program begins, during which you systematically observe your target behavior.** People are often tempted to skip this step and move ahead. But it is imperative to resist this temptation, because you need to know the original response level of your target behavior to evaluate your progress. You can't tell whether your program is working effectively unless you have a baseline for comparison. In gathering your baseline data, you need to monitor three things: (1) the initial response level of the target behavior, (2) the typical antecedents of the target behavior, and (3) the typical consequences of the target behavior.

Initial Response Level

In most cases, you simply need to keep track of how often the target response occurs. For example, you might count the daily frequency of smoking cigarettes, biting your fingernails, snapping at your children, or whatever the target behavior happens to be.

The appropriate unit of measurement depends on the nature of the target response. If studying is your target behavior, you will probably monitor hours of study. If you want to modify your eating habits, you will probably want to keep track of how many calories you consume. Whatever the unit of measurement, *it is crucial to gather accurate data*. You may need to carry some sort of portable device for recording your behavior, such as a hand-held counter or an index card on which you make notes. You should keep permanent written records, and it is usually best to portray these records graphically (see Figure 6.30). There are no simple guidelines for how long you should gather baseline data. Generally, you need to gather data until you can identify a *pattern* of responding.

Antecedents

Antecedents are events that typically precede your target behavior. Often these events play a major role in governing your target response. If classical conditioning controls the behavior, antecedents may literally trigger your target response. If operant conditioning controls the behavior, antecedents may serve as discriminative stimuli that affect the probability of your emitting the target response. In either case, recognizing links between antecedents and target behaviors can be very helpful in designing your program. For example, if your target is overeating, you might discover that most of your overeating occurs late in the evening after you've had a couple of beers. Once you pinpoint this kind of antecedent-response connection, you can design your program to circumvent it or to break it down.

Consequences

Finally, you need to identify the reinforcer that is maintaining a target behavior or the punishment that is suppressing it. In trying to identify reinforcers, first, remember that sometimes the response itself is the reinforcer. For example, consummatory responses such as smoking or eating are intrinsically reinforcing. Second, remember that avoidance behavior is usually maintained by negative reinforcement. That is, the payoff for avoidance is usually the removal of something aversive, such as anxiety or a threat to self-esteem. Third, recall that some responses are reinforced only intermittently. You can avoid unnecessary confusion in your search for reinforcers by being aware that a response may not be reinforced every time.

Designing Your Program

Once you have selected a target behavior and gathered adequate baseline data, it's time to assemble your program. Generally speaking, your program will be designed either to increase or to decrease the frequency of a target response. These are somewhat different tasks, and we'll discuss each type of program separately.

Increasing Response Strength

Efforts to increase the frequency of a target response depend largely on the use of positive reinforcement. In other words, you reward yourself for behaving properly. Although the basic strategy is quite simple, there are a number of considerations in rewarding yourself skillfully.

Selecting a reinforcer. If you intend to reward yourself for increasing a response, you need to find an effective reinforcer. Your choice will depend on your unique personality and situation. Reinforcement is subjective; some-

223

thing that is reinforcing for one person may not be reinforcing for another. Figure 6.31 lists questions you can ask yourself to discover what your personal reinforcers are. Be sure to be realistic and choose a reinforcer that is really available to you.

You don't have to come up with spectacular new reinforcers that you've never experienced before. *You can use reinforcers you are already getting.* However, you have to restructure the contingencies so that you get them only if you behave appropriately. For example, I own a sports car that I am fond of driving. It serves as a key reinforcer in a self-modification program that I have designed to increase my writing behavior so that I can get this book finished on time. I keep track of exactly how many hours I spend working on this book each day. Each week, I have to *earn* the privilege of driving my sports car by working a certain

minimum number of hours on this book (otherwise my wife gets it, and I drive our other car). Thus, reinforcers that are already available to you can be made contingent upon your target behavior in order to strengthen that behavior.

Arranging the contingencies. Once you've chosen your reinforcer, you have to set up reinforcement contingencies. Your reinforcement contingencies will describe the exact behavioral goals that must be met and the reinforcer that may then be awarded. For example, in a program to increase exercise, you might make spending $25 on clothes (the reinforcer) contingent upon jogging 15 miles during the week (the target behavior). In a program to increase study behavior, you might make listening to your stereo each night contingent upon studying 3 hours each day.

Try to set behavioral goals that are both challenging and realistic. You want your goals to be challenging so that they lead to improvement in your behavior. However, setting unrealistically high goals—a common mistake in self-modification—often leads to unnecessary discouragement.

One way to avoid the satiation problem is to put yourself on a token economy. **A *token economy* is a system for doling out symbolic reinforcers that are exchanged later for a variety of genuine reinforcers.** Thus, you might develop a point system for exercise behavior, accumulating points that can be spent on albums, movies, restaurant meals, and so forth (see Table 6.2). You can also use a token economy to reinforce a variety of related target behaviors, rather than a single specific response. For example, the token economy in Table 6.2 is set up to strengthen three different, although related, responses (jogging, tennis, and sit-ups).

Shaping. In some cases you may want to reinforce yourself for a response you are not presently capable of making, such as speaking in front of a large group, smoking no cigarettes whatsoever, or jogging 10 miles a day. As

Table 6.2 Example of a Token Economy Designed to Reinforce Exercise

RESPONSES EARNING TOKENS

RESPONSE	AMOUNT	NUMBER OF TOKENS
Jogging	½ mile	4
Jogging	1 mile	8
Jogging	2 miles	16
Tennis	1 hour	4
Tennis	2 hours	8
Sit-ups	25	1
Sit-ups	50	2

REDEMPTION VALUE OF TOKENS

REINFORCER	TOKENS REQUIRED
Purchase one record album of your choice	30
Go to movie	50
Go to nice restaurant	100
Take a special weekend trip	500

you'll have to build gradually toward your ultimate behavioral goal, this kind of situation calls for shaping, reinforcing closer and closer approximations of the desired response. Thus, you might start jogging 2 miles a day, and add ½ mile each week until you reach your goal of 10 miles a day. In shaping your behavior, you should set up a schedule spelling out how and when your target behaviors and reinforcement contingencies should change. Generally, it's a good idea to move forward very gradually.

Decreasing Response Strength

Let's turn now to the challenge of reducing the frequency of an undesirable response. You can do this in a number of ways. Sometimes it's best to combine several strategies. You might guess that *extinction* would be the obvious strategy for decreasing the strength of a response. This is often true when you're designing a program to modify someone else's behavior. However, self-modification programs often center on unwanted responses that are inherently reinforcing, making it impossible to cut off the reinforcer for the response. In such cases,

Figure 6.31 Questions to help you find out what your personal reinforcers are.

1. What will be the rewards of achieving your goal?
2. What kind of praise do you like to receive, from yourself and others?
3. What kinds of things do you like to have?
4. What are your major interests?
5. What are your hobbies?
6. What people do you like to be with?
7. What do you like to do with those people?
8. What do you do for fun?
9. What do you do to relax?
10. What do you do to get away from it all?
11. What makes you feel good?
12. What would be a nice present to receive?
13. What kinds of things are important to you?
14. What would you buy if you had an extra $20? $50? $100?
15. On what do you spend your money each week?
16. What behaviors do you perform every day? (Don't overlook the obvious or the commonplace.)
17. Are there any behaviors you usually perform instead of the target behavior?
18. What would you hate to lose?
19. Of the things you do every day, which would you hate to give up?
20. What are your favorite daydreams and fantasies?
21. What are the most relaxing scenes you can imagine?

your principal options include the use of reinforcers, the control of antecedents, and punishment.

Reinforcers. Reinforcers can be used in an indirect way to decrease the frequency of a response. This may sound paradoxical since you've learned that, by definition, reinforcement strengthens a response. The trick lies in how you define the target behavior. For example, in the case of overeating you could define your target behavior as eating more than 1600 calories a day (an excess response to be decreased) or eating less than 1600 calories a day (a deficit response to be increased). You can choose the latter definition and reinforce yourself whenever you eat less than 1600 calories in a day. Thus, you can reinforce yourself for not emitting a response, or for emitting it less, and thereby decrease a response through reinforcement.

Control of antecedents. Antecedents increase the likelihood of many unwanted responses. Therefore, a worthwhile strategy for decreasing the occurrence of an undesirable response is to identify its antecedents and avoid exposure to them. This strategy is especially useful when you are trying to decrease the frequency of a consummatory response, such as smoking or eating.

In the case of overeating, for instance, the easiest way to resist temptation is to avoid having to face it, so a good behavioral program to reduce overeating often depends on controlling exposure to antecedents that promote extravagant eating.

Control of antecedents can also be helpful in a program to increase studying. Although the core of such a program should involve reinforcing good study behavior, you may need to control antecedents to reduce loafing, daydreaming, and socializing when you should be studying. The key often lies in *where* you study. You can reduce excessive socializing by studying somewhere away from people. Similarly, you can reduce loafing by studying someplace where there is no TV, stereo, or phone to distract you.

Punishment. The strategy of decreasing unwanted behavior by punishing yourself for that behavior is an obvious option, and one that people tend to overuse. The biggest problem with punishment in a self-modification effort is that it is difficult to follow through and punish oneself. Nonetheless, there may be situations in which your manipulations of reinforcers need to be bolstered by the threat of punishment.

If you're going to use punishment, keep two guidelines in mind. First, don't use punishment alone; use it in conjunction with positive reinforcement. If you set up a program in which you can earn only negative consequences, you probably won't stick to the program. Thus, make sure you have the opportunity to earn some positive outcomes, too. Second, use a relatively mild punishment, so that you will actually be able to administer it to yourself. Nurnberger and Zimmerman (1970) developed a creative method of self-punishment. They had subjects write out a check to an organization the subjects hated (for instance, the campaign of a political candidate they despised). The check was held by a third party. If the subjects failed to meet their behavioral goals, the third party mailed the check. Such a punishment is relatively harmless, but can serve as a strong source of motivation.

Executing and Evaluating Your Program

Once you have designed your program, the next step is to put it to work by enforcing your carefully planned contingencies. During your intervention period, continue to record the frequency of your target behavior accurately so you can evaluate your progress. The success of your program depends on your not cheating—for example, rewarding yourself when you haven't earned the reward.

You can do two things to increase the likelihood that you will comply with your program. One is to write up a **behavioral contract**—**a written agreement outlining a promise to**

adhere to the contingencies of a behavior modification program. The formality of signing such a contract in front of friends or family seems to make many people take their program more seriously. You can further reduce the likelihood of cheating by having someone other than yourself dole out the reinforcers and punishments. When a spouse, friend, or family member is monitoring your behavior, it's much harder to cheat.

Behavior modification programs often turn out to need some fine tuning once you set them into action. So don't be surprised if you need to make a few adjustments. Several flaws are especially common in designing self-modification programs. Among those you should look out for are (1) depending on a weak reinforcer, (2) permitting lengthy delays between appropriate behavior and delivery of the reinforcer, and (3) trying to do too much too quickly by setting unrealistic goals. Often, a small revision or two can turn a failing program around and make it a success.

Ending Your Program

Generally, when you design your program, you should spell out the conditions under which you will end it. In other words, you should set terminal goals such as reaching a certain weight, studying with a certain regularity, or going without cigarettes for a certain length of time. Often it's a good idea to phase out your program by planning a gradual reduction in the frequency or potency of your reinforcement for appropriate behavior.

If your program is successful, it may fade away without a conscious decision on your part. New, improved patterns of behavior often become self-maintaining—responses such as eating right, exercising regularly, or studying diligently may become habitual, so that you no longer need to support them with an elaborate program. Whether you end your program intentionally or it fades out spontaneously, you should always be prepared to reinstitute it if you find yourself slipping back to your old patterns of behavior.

LEARNING THROUGH CONDITIONING

KEY IDEAS

Classical Conditioning

• Classical conditioning explains how a neutral stimulus can acquire the capacity to elicit a response originally evoked by another stimulus. This kind of conditioning was originally described by Ivan Pavlov, who conditioned dogs so that they salivated when a bell was rung.

• Many kinds of everyday responses are regulated through classical conditioning, including phobias, anxiety responses, and pleasant emotional responses. Even subtle physiological processes such as immune system functioning and endorphin release respond to classical conditioning.

• Stimulus contiguity plays a key role in the acquisition of new conditioned responses. Short-delayed conditioning is the temporal arrangement that works best for acquisition. A conditioned response may be weakened and extinguished entirely when the CS is no longer paired with the UCS. In some cases spontaneous recovery occurs, and an extinguished response reappears after a period of nonexposure to the CS.

• Conditioning may generalize to additional stimuli that are similar to the original CS. The opposite of generalization is discrimination, which involves not responding to stimuli that resemble the original CS. Higher-order conditioning occurs when a CS functions as if it were a UCS, to establish new conditioning.

Operant Conditioning

• Operant conditioning involves largely voluntary responses that are governed by their consequences. Following the lead of E. L. Thorndike, B. F. Skinner investigated this form of conditioning, working mainly with rats and pigeons conditioned in Skinner boxes. His work showed that organisms tend to repeat those responses that are followed by reinforcers.

• The key dependent variable in operant conditioning is the rate of response over time. When this is shown graphically, steep slopes indicate rapid responding. New operant responses can be shaped by gradually reinforcing closer and closer approximations of the desired response.

• In operant conditioning, when reinforcement is terminated, response rate usually declines and extinction may occur. There are variations in how long an organism continues to make a response that is no longer reinforced.

• Operant responses are regulated by discriminative stimuli that are cues for the likelihood of obtaining reinforcers. These stimuli are subject to the same processes of generalization and discrimination that occur in classical conditioning.

• The central process in reinforcement is the strengthening of a response. Something that is reinforcing for an organism at one time may not be reinforcing later. Delayed reinforcement slows the process of conditioning. Primary reinforcers are not learned; they are closely tied to the satisfaction of physiological needs. In contrast, secondary reinforcers acquire their reinforcing quality through conditioning.

• Schedules of reinforcement influence patterns of operant responding. Intermittent schedules produce greater resistance to extinction than similar continuous schedules. Ratio schedules tend to yield higher rates of response than interval schedules. Shorter intervals and higher ratios are associated with faster responding.

• Responses can be strengthened either through the presentation of positive reinforcers or through the removal of negative reinforcers. Negative reinforcement regulates escape and avoidance learning. Once learned, avoidance responses tend to be efficient and long-lasting. The two-process theory provides the best explanation of avoidance behavior and may shed light on why phobias are so difficult to unlearn.

• Punishment involves unfavorable consequences that lead to a decline in response strength. Some of the problems associated with the application of punishment are an increase in aggressive behavior and decreases in social behaviors. Punishment is more effective when it is swift, severe, consistent, explained, and accompanied by an opportunity to earn reinforcement with an alternate response. The removal of positive reinforcers can be used as punishment.

New Directions in the Study of Conditioning

• Recent decades have brought profound changes in our understanding of conditioning. Research on instinctive drift, conditioned taste aversion, and preparedness in the conditioning of phobias has led to the recognition of biological constraints on conditioning. Our Featured Study showed how conditioned taste aversion can be used to reduce predatory attacks on livestock.

• Studies of blocking, signal relations in classical conditioning, and response-outcome relations in operant conditioning suggest that cognitive processes play a larger role in conditioning than researchers originally believed. Modern theories hold that conditioning involves detecting the contingencies that govern events.

Observational Learning

• In observational learning an organism is conditioned vicariously by watching a model's conditioning. Both classical and operant conditioning can occur through observational learning, which depends on the processes of attention, retention, reproduction, and motivation.

• According to Bandura, reinforcement influences which of several already acquired responses we perform more than it influences the acquisition of new responses. The principles of observational learning have been used to explain why physical punishment increases aggressive behavior. Observational learning also can account for the influence of mass media (such as television) on behavior.

Putting It in Perspective

• Two of our key themes were especially apparent in our coverage of learning and conditioning. One theme involves the interaction of heredity and the environment in governing behavior. The other involves the way progress in psychology affects society at large.

Application: Achieving Self-Control Through Behavior Modification

• In behavior modification, the principles of learning are used to change behavior directly. Behavior modification techniques can be employed to increase one's self-control.

• The first step in self-modification involves specifying the overt target behavior to be increased or decreased. The second step involves gathering baseline data about the initial rate of the target response and identifying any typical antecedents and consequences associated with the behavior.

• The third step is to design a program. If you are trying to increase the strength of a response, you'll depend on positive reinforcement. The reinforcement contingencies should spell out exactly what you have to do to earn your reinforcer. A number of strategies can be used to decrease the strength of a response, including reinforcement, control of antecedents, and punishment.

• The fourth step involves executing and evaluating your program. Self-modification programs often require some fine tuning. The final step is to determine how and when you will phase out your program.

KEY TERMS

Acquisition
Antecedents
Avoidance learning
Baseline period
Behavioral contract
Behavior modification
Blocking
Classical conditioning
Conditioned reinforcers
Conditioned response (CR)
Conditioned stimulus (CS)
Conditioning
Continuous reinforcement
Cumulative recorder
Discriminative stimuli
Elicit
Emit
Escape learning
Extinction
Fetishism
Fixed-interval (FI) schedule

Fixed-ratio (FR) schedule
Higher-order conditioning
Instinctive drift
Instrumental learning
Intermittent reinforcement
Law of effect
Learning
Negative reinforcement
Noncontingent reinforcement
Observational learning
Operant conditioning
Partial reinforcement
Pavlovian conditioning
Phobias
Positive reinforcement
Preparedness
Primary reinforcers
Programmed learning
Punishment
Reinforcement
Reinforcement contingencies

Resistance to extinction
Respondent conditioning
Schedule of reinforcement
Secondary reinforcers
Shaping
Skinner box
Spontaneous recovery
Stimulus contiguity
Stimulus discrimination
Stimulus generalization
Token economy
Trial
Unconditioned response (UCR)
Unconditioned stimulus (UCS)
Variable-interval (VI) schedule
Variable-ratio (VR) schedule

KEY PEOPLE

Albert Bandura
Ivan Pavlov
Robert Rescorla
Martin Seligman
B. F. Skinner
E. L. Thorndike
John B. Watson

227

Human Memory

With Stephen K. Reed
San Diego State University

Human Memory

I f you live in the United States, you've undoubtedly handled thousands upon thousands of American pennies. Surely, then, you remember what a penny looks like—or do you? Take a look at Figure 7.1. Which drawing corresponds to a real penny?

Did you have a hard time selecting the real penny? If so, you're not alone. Nickerson and Adams (1979) found that most people can't recognize the real penny in this collection of drawings. How can that be? Why do most of us have so poor a memory for an object we see every day?

Let's try another exercise. A definition of a word follows. It's not a particularly common word, but there's a good chance that you're familiar with it. Try to think of the word.

Definition: Favoritism shown or patronage granted by persons in high office to relatives or close friends.

If you can't think of the word, perhaps you can remember what letter of the alphabet it begins with, or what it sounds like, or how many syllables it has. If so, you're experiencing the *tip-of-the-tongue phenomenon,* in which forgotten information feels like it's just out of reach. In this case, the word you may be reaching for is *nepotism.*

You've probably endured the tip-of-the-tongue phenomenon while taking exams. You blank out on a term that you're sure you know. You may feel like you're on the verge of remembering the term,

but you can't quite come up with it. Later, perhaps while you're driving home, the term suddenly comes to you. "Of course," you may say to yourself, "how could I forget that?" That's an interesting question. Clearly, the term was stored in your memory. How can you "remember" something yet be unable to recall it when you need it?

As these examples suggest, memory involves more than storing information in some mental compartment. In fact, psychologists probing the workings of memory have had to grapple with three enduring questions: (1) How do we get information *into* memory? (2) How do we *maintain* information in memory? (3) How do we get information *back out* of memory?

These three questions are the key to understanding what psychologists have learned about memory—and about forgetting. They correspond to the three processes illustrated in Figure 7.2: *encoding* (getting information in), *storage* (maintaining it), and *retrieval* (getting it out).

Encoding involves forming a memory code. For example, when you form a memory code for a word, you might emphasize how it looks, how it sounds, or what it means. Encoding usually requires attention, which is why you may not be able to recall exactly what a penny looks like. Most of us don't pay much attention to the appearance of a penny. However, as you'll see throughout this chapter, memory is an active process, and we're unlikely to remember something unless we make a conscious effort to do so. **Storage involves maintaining encoded information in**

Figure 7.1 A simple memory test. Nickerson and Adams (1979) presented these 15 versions of an object most people have seen hundreds or thousands of times and asked "Which one is correct?"

memory over time. Psychologists have focused much of their memory research on trying to identify just what factors help or hinder our memory storage. But, as the tip-of-the-tongue phenomenon shows, information storage isn't enough to guarantee that we'll remember something; we need to be able to get information out of storage. *Retrieval* **involves recovering information from memory stores.** Research issues concerned with retrieval include the study of how people search memory and why some retrieval strategies are more effective than others.

Most of this chapter is devoted to an examination of memory encoding, storage, and retrieval. As you'll see, these basic processes help to explain the ultimate puzzle in the study of memory: why we forget. Just as memory involves more than storage, forgetting involves more than "losing" something from the memory store. Forgetting may be due to deficiencies in any of the three key processes in memory—encoding, storage, or retrieval. After our review of theories of forgetting,

Figure 7.2 The computer as an information-processing system. Information is *encoded* by keystrokes and mouse movements, *stored* as tiny "on" and "off" voltages on microchips, and *retrieved* as images on the monitor.

we take a brief look at "brain chemistry" and what psychologists are learning about the physiological basis for memory. The chapter's Application extracts some practical advice from memory research on how to improve your memory.

ENCODING: GETTING INFORMATION INTO MEMORY

Have you ever been embarrassed because you couldn't remember someone's name? Perhaps there have been times when you realized only 30 seconds after you had met someone that you had already "forgotten" his name. More often than not, this familiar kind of forgetting is due to a failure to form a memory code for the name. When we're introduced to people, we're often very busy sizing them up and thinking about what we're going to say. With our attention diverted in this way, the person's name goes "in one ear and out the other." We don't remember it because it was never encoded for storage into memory.

Like the illustration of the penny that started this chapter, the problem of forgetting names illustrates that active encoding is the first important process in memory. In this section, we discuss the role of attention in encoding, different types of encoding, which reflect different levels of processing information, and ways to enrich the encoding process.

The Role of Attention

To form a memory code, you must pay attention to the information you want to remember. If you attend a class lecture, but pay attention to what your friend is whispering, you're not likely to remember much of the lecture. Focused attention is critical to encoding.

THE SELECTIVITY OF ATTENTION
As we meander through life, we're bombarded by an endless array of stimuli. For instance, at this moment you might be sitting in a library somewhere reading this book. Now, when it comes to stimulus input, a library is not exactly Times

Can you imagine how hard it is for these brokers in a European stock exchange to figure out which phone is ringing and to focus on their own conversation? We would endure similar chaos all the time if our attention weren't selective.

231

Square. Yet there surely are many stimuli competing for your attention. Visually, there are the lights above, the print symbols on this page, books on display nearby, pictures on the wall, and people walking around. In the auditory domain, you might hear the buzz of the lights, the whirring of the air circulation system, the wind whistling through the trees outside, cars driving by, a conversation a few feet away, or the sound of your heart beating. Through some of your other senses, you might notice the feel of the clothes on your body, the taste of your chewing gum in your mouth, and the rumblings of hunger in your stomach. And those are just a few of the physical stimuli! We haven't even mentioned competition from other lines of thought, such as your annoyance with your roommate, your anxiety about an upcoming exam, and your eager anticipation of Friday's date.

Thus, even in the relative quiet of a library, you may be deluged by so many stimuli that it seems almost miraculous that you ever manage to study. Fortunately, most of us *are* able to study under such conditions because we deploy our *attention* in a very selective, almost miserly fashion.

Attention involves focusing awareness on a narrowed range of stimuli or events. We routinely talk about "selective attention," but the words are really redundant. Attention *is* selection of input. If you pause to devote a little attention to the matter, you'll realize that selective attention is critical to everyday functioning. If our attention were distributed equally among all stimulus inputs, life would be utter chaos. If you weren't able to filter out most of the potential stimulation around you, you wouldn't be able to read a book, converse with a friend, or even carry a coherent train of thought.

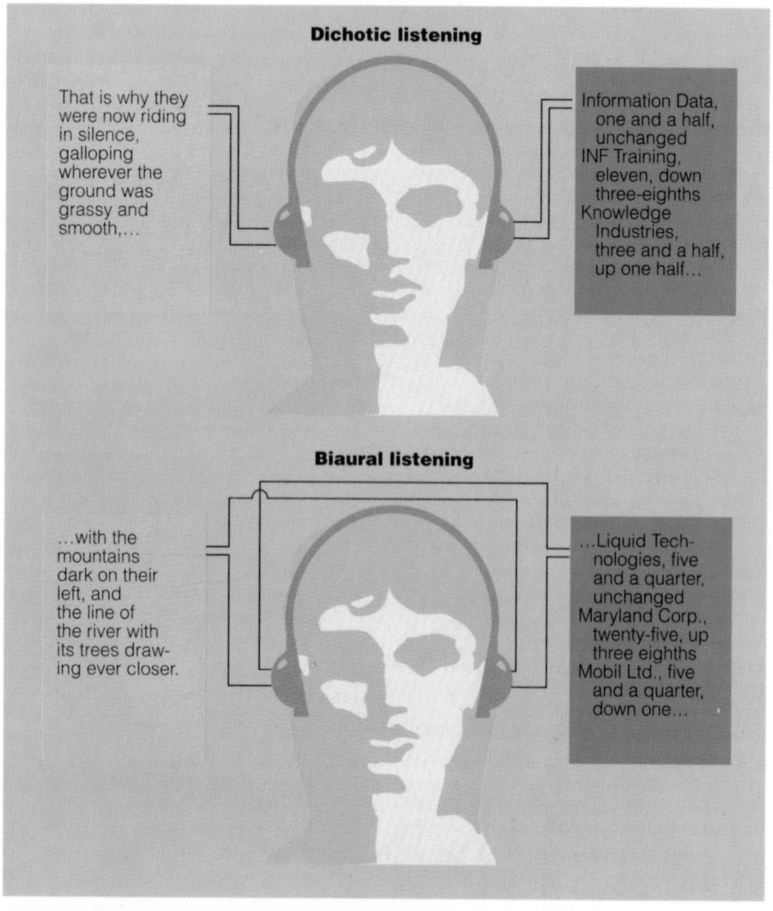

EARLY VERSUS LATE SELECTION

Most theories of attention liken it to a *filter* that screens out most potential stimuli while allowing a select few to pass through into conscious awareness. However, there's been a great deal of debate about *where* the filter is located in our information-processing system. The key issue in this debate is whether stimuli are screened out early, during sensory input, or late, after the brain processes the meaning or significance of the input. Hence, models of attention are often characterized as *early selection* or *late selection* theories.

Donald Broadbent (1958) proposed an influential theory of attention that emphasized early selection during sensory processing. He had participants listen to two taped messages presented *simultaneously* in carefully controlled ways, through headphones, to one or both ears (Broadbent, 1954; Cherry, 1953). As you can imagine, presenting the messages simultaneously made paying attention much more difficult than it is ordinarily. In **biaural listening a subject hears two separate auditory inputs that are both sent simultaneously to both ears. In *dichotic listening* a subject hears two separate auditory inputs that are sent simultaneously, but each is sent to only one ear** (see Figure 7.3).

But how does either method of listening relate to early or late selection? Broadbent and others found that subjects generally were able to focus their attention more effectively in dichotic listening than in biaural listening. In *biaural presentations*, if the two oral messages were equally meaningful and spoken by the same voice, subjects experienced great difficulty focusing their attention on one of the messages while ignoring the other. Subjects exposed to *dichotic presentations* had more success attending to one of the messages. The separation at the point of sensory reception (in the ears) apparently made it much easier for subjects to allocate their attention in the dichotic listening task. Researchers have also found that subjects are less confused in biaural listening if the two messages vary in sensory quality—if, for instance, they are spoken by different voices.

Figure 7.3 Dichotic and biaural listening. In both types of listening, subjects hear two messages simultaneously and attempt to focus their attention on only one. The task proves to be easier in dichotic listening, in which each message goes to just one ear.

Dichotic listening

That is why they were now riding in silence, galloping wherever the ground was grassy and smooth,...

Information Data, one and a half, unchanged INF Training, eleven, down three-eighths Knowledge Industries, three and a half, up one half...

Biaural listening

...with the mountains dark on their left, and the line of the river with its trees drawing ever closer.

...Liquid Technologies, five and a quarter, unchanged Maryland Corp., twenty-five, up three eighths Mobil Ltd., five and a quarter, down one...

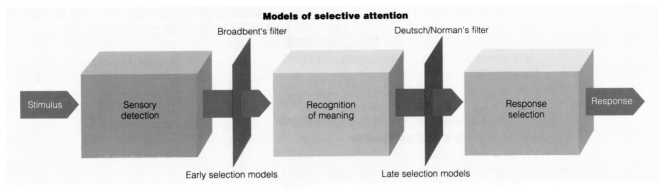

Models of selective attention

Broadbent's filter

Deutsch/Norman's filter

Stimulus → Sensory detection → Recognition of meaning → Response selection → Response

Early selection models

Late selection models

Thus, if simultaneous messages differ at the stage of sensory reception (for example, coming to different ears or spoken by different voices), we can better focus our attention on one message and filter out the other. Considering this kind of evidence, Broadbent concluded that we make an early selection of stimulus input based on its sensory qualities.

Broadbent's model seemed plausible, but it did not explain the "cocktail party problem." What's that? Well, there probably are many "cocktail party problems," such as getting drunk or behaving obnoxiously, but psychologists interested in attention mean something else. Imagine yourself at a crowded party where many conversations are taking place. You're paying attention to one companion's conversation and filtering out the others. However, if someone across the room *mentions your name*, you'll probably notice it even though you were ignoring that conversation. If selection is early, how can you register input you've been blocking out when it suddenly becomes personally meaningful? This filtering requires *late* selection, *after* sensory input, based on the *meaning* of the input.

Various theorists have devised late selection models of attention (Deutsch & Deutsch, 1963; Norman, 1976). These models assume that all incoming information makes its way to the brain and is processed in terms of meaning before a late selection of input is made. According to this view, all inputs are registered but quickly forgotten unless they're selected into memory. In this model, attention influences only what we try to remember—not what we perceive. The difference between early and late selection models of attention is diagrammed in Figure 7.4.

Late selection models can account for the allocation of attention based on the *meaning* or significance of the incoming information. They explain how you can react to parts of another conversation—your name, a favorite topic, or juicy gossip, to name but a few—that you are, at least on one level, ignoring. The late selection models recognize that we deploy attention according to the personal significance of various inputs.

Which view is supported by the weight of evidence—early selection or late selection? There is ample evidence for *both* early selection and late selection; which of the two occurs seems to depend on the circumstances (Johnston & Dark, 1986). Efforts are currently under way to reconcile early and late selection theories of attention. For example, Johnston and Heinz (1978) have theorized that our attention filter may not be in a fixed position. They suggest that we can decide "where" to place our attention filter in the various stages of processing incoming information, and that this ability to move the filter affords some flexibility in the point at which we screen out irrelevant input.

Levels of Processing

Attention is critical to encoding, but not all attention is created equal. We can attend to things in different ways, focusing on different aspects of the stimulus input. According to some theorists, these qualitative differences in *how* we attend to information are the main factors influencing how much we remember. For example, Fergus Craik and Robert Lockhart (1972) argue that different rates of forgetting occur because some methods of encoding create more durable memory codes than others.

According to Craik and Lockhart, there are different "levels" at which we process incoming information. For instance, they maintain that in dealing with verbal information, we engage in three progressively deeper levels of processing: structural encoding, phonemic encoding, and semantic encoding. They assert that our initial, relatively shallow processing results in a **structural code, a memory code that emphasizes the physical structure of the stimulus** (in this case, a word). Structural codes depend on the sensory features of the stimulus. For example, if words are flashed on a screen, the structural encoding level of processing registers things like how they were

Figure 7.4 Two models of selective attention. According to early selection models of attention, the brain filters out irrelevant stimulus information on the basis of its sensory qualities. According to late selection models, filtering is done only after the meaning or significance of the stimulus has been registered.

printed (capital, lowercase, script, and so on) or the length of the words (how many letters). Further analysis may result in a **phonemic code, a memory code that emphasizes what a word sounds like**. This involves naming or saying (perhaps silently) the words. After naming the words, we may engage in deeper processing that results in a **semantic code, a memory code that emphasizes the meaning of verbal input**. In semantic processing, we think about the objects and actions the words represent.

Levels of processing theory proposes that **deeper levels of processing result in longer-lasting memory codes.** Structural coding is a shallow level of processing, so when only the physical features of a stimulus have been analyzed, memory of the stimulus should quickly evaporate. When the stimulus is named, the phonemic memory code should last longer. A still better memory code should result when the person considers the meaning of the stimulus. The levels of processing theory has been evaluated in many studies; our Featured Study presents one of the groundbreaking investigations.

CHAPTER SEVEN FEATURED STUDY

LOOKING FOR A DEEPER MEANING

Investigators: Fergus I. M. Craik and Endel Tulving (University of Toronto)

Source: Depth of processing and the retention of words in episodic memory. *Journal of Experimental Psychology: General, 104* (1975), 268–294.

Craik and Tulving conducted a series of experiments to evaluate Craik and Lockhart's levels of processing theory. In one experiment they compared the durability of structural, phonemic, and semantic memory codes. They directed subjects' attention to particular aspects of stimulus words by asking them to make judgments about different characteristics of words. The questions were designed to engage the subjects in different levels of processing. The key hypothesis was that retention of the stimulus words would increase as subjects moved from structural to phonemic to semantic encoding.

Method

Subjects. The subjects were 24 students of both sexes who were tested individually and paid for participating. They were told that the experiment would measure their perception and speed of reaction.

Procedure. Stimulus words were presented briefly, and the subjects were asked to make the following three types of judgments about the words: (1) Is the word in capital letters? (2) Does the word rhyme with *weight*? (3) Would the word fit in the sentence "He met a _____ in the street"?

The first question asks about physical structure and should result in a structural code. The second question asks about pronunciation and should result in a phonemic code. The third question requires the consideration of meaning and should result in a semantic code.

Subjects made 60 judgments: 20 regarding whether a word was in uppercase, 20 regarding whether a word rhymed with another word, and 20 regarding whether a word would fit into a sentence. The different types of questions occurred in a random order. For each type of question, the correct response was "yes" on half of the trials

Figure 7.5 Speed and accuracy at three levels of processing. Craik and Tulving theorized that structural (appearance), phonemic (sound), and semantic (meaning) encoding represent progressively deeper levels of processing in memory. Consistent with this idea, as a level of processing gets *deeper*, quickness of response goes *down*, but retention goes *up*.

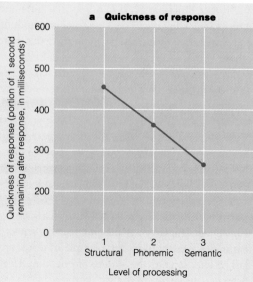

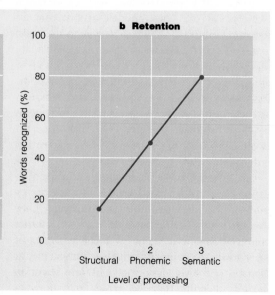

and "no" on half of the trials. The subjects listened to the question first and 2 seconds later saw the word appear on a small screen. They then responded as rapidly as possible by pressing either the "yes" or the "no" response key.

After making the 60 judgments, the students received an unexpected test on their memory for the words. The test consisted of a typed list of 180 words including the 60 words presented in the experiment. Subjects were instructed to check all the words that they had seen during the experiment.

Results

Figure 7.5a shows how quickly subjects responded to the different types of questions. Specifically, Figure 7.5a graphs how much of a second remained (on the average) after a subject responded "yes" to each kind of question. (If a subject took a *whole* second to respond, the score would be 0.) The results show that subjects were quick in responding about the print style of the word and progressively slower in responding about its sound and meaning. A similar pattern was observed for "no" responses.

Figure 7.5b shows the average proportion of words remembered by the subjects in each of the three conditions. Again, these data are for "yes" responses, but the trends were similar for "no" responses. As predicted, the subjects recognized the most words in the sentence condition, followed by the rhyme condition, and then the print style condition.

Discussion

The results provided striking support for the levels of processing theory of memory. The differences in reaction time indicated that semantic coding took longer than phonemic coding, which took longer than structural coding. The additional time required by phonemic and semantic coding was consistent with the idea that these are deeper levels of processing. Furthermore, the three different methods of encoding had a clear impact on subjects' retention of the stimulus words. The findings support the notion that semantic codes are more effective than phonemic codes, which are in turn more effective than structural codes. Thus, Craik and Tulving concluded that deeper levels of processing produce more durable memory codes, which result in better retention.

Comment

The levels of processing theory has proven to be a very useful and influential model of memory. Craik and Lockhart (1972) initially proposed the levels of processing theory as an alternative to storage-oriented theories of memory (which we'll discuss later in this chapter). However, many psychologists believe that the two kinds of theories are not necessarily incompatible. Given the multifaceted nature of memory, it's reasonable to expect that several different theoretical perspectives will be needed to arrive at a thorough understanding of memory. The levels of processing model provides a promising way of thinking about the encoding process.

Although it has proven fruitful, the levels of processing model is not without its weaknesses. What exactly is a "level" of processing and how do we determine whether one level is deeper than another? Craik and Tulving had hoped that the *time required for processing* would prove to be a good indicator of depth. Equating longer processing with deeper processing worked out acceptably in our Featured Study, but in other studies Craik and Tulving (1975) found that it's possible to design a task in which decisions about the physical structure of a word (structural coding) take longer than decisions about its meaning (semantic coding). Instead of asking whether a word was in uppercase letters, Craik and Tulving asked their subjects whether words consisted of two consonants followed by two vowels followed by a consonant. For example, the word *stoop* should receive a positive response; the word *black*, a negative response. This type of structural coding produced less retention of the words than semantic processing, but it took twice as long. Thus, the time required for processing is not a reliable index

of depth of processing, and the concept of levels of processing remains vaguely defined.

Enriching Encoding

Structural, phonemic, and semantic encoding do not exhaust our options when it comes to forming memory codes. There are other dimensions to encoding, dimensions that can enrich the encoding process and thereby improve memory.

ELABORATION

Semantic coding can often be enhanced through a process called elaboration. **Elaboration involves linking a stimulus to other information at the time of encoding.** The additional associations usually help people remember the items. Differences in elaboration can help explain why different approaches to semantic processing result in varied amounts of retention.

The effect of elaboration was seen in one of the experiments conducted by Craik and Tulving

Figure 7.6 The effect of visual imagery on retention. Subjects given pairs of words to remember showed better recall for high-imagery pairings, demonstrating that visual imagery enriches encoding. (Data from Paivio, Smythe, & Yuille, 1968)

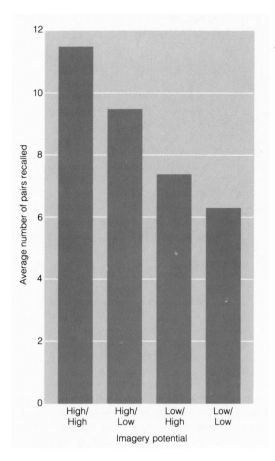

(1975). In this experiment, subjects were once again asked to decide whether words would fit in a sentence, but the complexity of the sentence was manipulated. For example, before subjects were shown the word *tomato*, they were shown one of the following sentences.

Simple: She cooked the _____.
Medium: The ripe _____ tasted delicious.
Complex: The small lady angrily picked up the red _____.

Craik and Tulving hypothesized that if elaboration improves memory, then the more complex sentences should result in better recall. Their findings supported this hypothesis. When the words fit the sentence, recall improved as the sentences became more complex and elaborate. But is it only the length and complexity of the third sentence that makes the information more memorable? Or might it be that you are more likely to retain a mental picture of a tomato that may be hurled than one that is being eaten or cooked? The visual images elicited by ideas are important factors in memory. We consider their importance next.

VISUAL IMAGERY
Visual imagery—the creation of visual images to represent the words to be remembered—can also be used to enrich the encoding process. Using visual imagery is similar to elaboration, in that it involves linking a stimulus to additional material.

Of course, some words are easier to create images for than others. If you were asked to remember the word *juggler*, you could readily form an image of someone juggling balls. However, if you were asked to remember the word *truth*, you would probably have more difficulty forming a suitable image. The difference is that *juggler* refers to something concrete and *truth* refers to an abstract concept. Allan Paivio (1969) points out that we can form images of concrete objects more easily than abstract concepts and that this ease of image formation affects memory.

The beneficial effect of imagery on memory was demonstrated in a study by Paivio, Smythe, and Yuille (1968). They asked subjects to learn a list of 16 pairs of words. They manipulated whether the words were concrete, high-imagery words or abstract, low-imagery words. In terms of imagery potential, the list contained four types of pairings: high-high (juggler-dress), high-low (letter-effort), low-high (duty-hotel), and low-low (quality-necessity). Figure 7.6 shows the recall for each type of pairing. The impact of imagery is quite evident. The best recall was of high-high pairings; the worst recall was of low-low pairings. Pairings of a low-imagery word and a high one resulted in intermediate retention, which was better if the high-imagery word came first.

According to Paivio (1986), visual imagery facilitates memory because it provides a second kind of memory code and two codes are better than one. His **dual-coding theory holds that memory is enhanced by forming semantic and visual codes since either can lead to recall.** For example, if you encode both the image and the meaning of the word *dress*, you have two routes to recall.

SELF-REFERENCE
Making material *personally* meaningful can also enrich encoding. For example, if you ride a bus regularly, you've probably heard the bus driver call out the names of the stops day in and day out for months. Do you remember all of the stops? If you haven't made an effort to memorize them, probably not. But you could probably list those that you've used, or even the ones where your friends

Students learning anatomy must tax their memories to store an enormous amount of information. The use of brightly colored plastic models enriches visual encoding and thus facilitates retention.

get on. So, somewhere along the way, you made an effort to remember the information relevant to you.

Self-referent encoding involves deciding how or whether information is relevant to you. This approach to encoding was compared to structural, phonemic, and semantic encoding in a study by Rogers, Kuiper, and Kirker (1977). Their verbal stimuli were forty adjectives that could be applied to people, like *sly, timid,* and *shrewd.* Like Craik and Tulving (see the Featured Study), these researchers manipulated encoding by giving their subjects special instructions. To induce encoding that emphasized self-reference, they asked subjects to decide whether the adjectives flashed on a screen "describe you." Their results showed that encoding involving self-reference led to a dramatic increase in retention in comparison to structural encoding, phonemic encoding, and even semantic encoding.

This power of self-reference demonstrates once again the critical role encoding plays in memory. But encoding is only one of the three key processes in memory. We turn next to the process of storage, which is for many people virtually synonymous with memory.

STORAGE: MAINTAINING INFORMATION IN MEMORY

In their efforts to understand memory storage, people have historically related it to the technologies of their age (Roediger, 1980). One of the earliest models used to explain memory storage was the wax tablet. Both Aristotle and Plato compared memory to a block of wax that differed in size and hardness for different individuals. Remembering, according to this analogy, was like stamping an impression into the wax. As long as the image remained in the wax, the memory would remain intact.

Current theories of memory reflect the technological advances of the 20th century. Wax tablets have been replaced by computers, as many modern theories draw an analogy between information storage by computers and information storage in memory. These *information-processing theories* of memory emphasize how information flows through a series of separate memory stores. According to this analogy, our memory systems, much like computers, have temporary storage buffers and permanent storage areas. The challenge for psychologists has been to describe the different kinds of memory stores and the operations that are used to transfer information from one store to another.

The most prominent information-processing model of memory holds that we have three different kinds of memory store: a *sensory store,* a *short-term store,* and a *long-term store.* Many psychologists have contributed to this theory, but Richard Atkinson and Richard Shiffrin (1968; 1971) were especially influential. They integrated many findings on memory into a coherent, broad model of information processing. We will use their model, which is diagrammed in Figure 7.7, as a general guide in our discussion of memory storage.

Sensory Memory

The *sensory memory* preserves information in its original sensory form for a very brief time, usually only a fraction of a second. Sensory stores

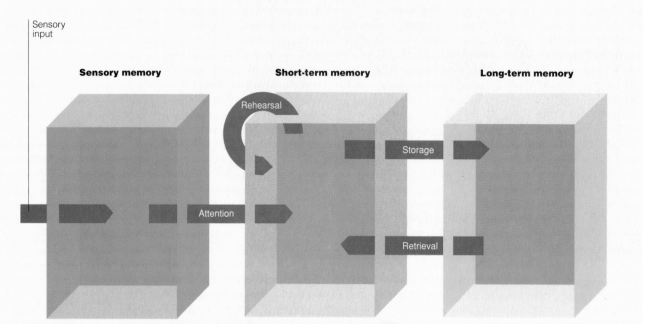

Figure 7.7 The Atkinson and Shiffrin model of memory storage. Atkinson and Shiffrin propose that our memory is made up of three information stores. *Sensory memory* can hold a huge amount of information just long enough for a small portion of it to be selected for longer storage. *Short-term memory* is our low-capacity "working memory." It receives input from both sensory memory (through attention) and long-term memory (through retrieval). Except when aided by rehearsal, its storage duration is very brief. *Long-term memory* can store an apparently unlimited amount of information for indeterminate periods, but to be used the information must be retrieved and transferred back into our working memory.

exist for each of the different senses, such as vision, hearing, and touch. Sensory memory allows the sensation of a visual pattern, sound, or touch to linger on for a brief moment after the termination of the stimulus. In fact, the key difference between the sensory store and the short- and long-term stores is that the stimulus seems to still be present.

Figure 7.8 A demonstration of sensory memory. Because the image of the sparkler persists briefly in sensory memory, when the sparkler is moved fast enough, the blending of afterimages causes us to see a continuous circle instead of a succession of individual points.

In the case of vision, we're really perceiving an *afterimage* rather than the actual stimulus. You can demonstrate the existence of afterimages for yourself by rapidly moving a lighted sparkler in circles in the dark. If you move the sparkler fast enough, you should see a complete circle even though the light source is only a single point (see Figure 7.8). Your sensory memory preserves the sensory image long enough for you to perceive a continuous circle rather than separate points of light.

The sensory image that follows the termination of a stimulus gives you additional time to try to recognize the stimulus. Imagine that you are in a psychology experiment and you're told that you'll briefly see a string of five letters on a screen in front of you. Your task is to recall the five letters a short time later. You then see the letters

O V L B H

and are asked to recall them 30 seconds later. In order to be able to recall the letters, you must first recognize them. If the letters were on the screen for only a brief time—such as 1/100 of a second—you would not have time to recognize them unless you could use your sensory store to preserve an image of the letters.

However, you'd better take advantage of that sensory afterimage immediately, because it doesn't

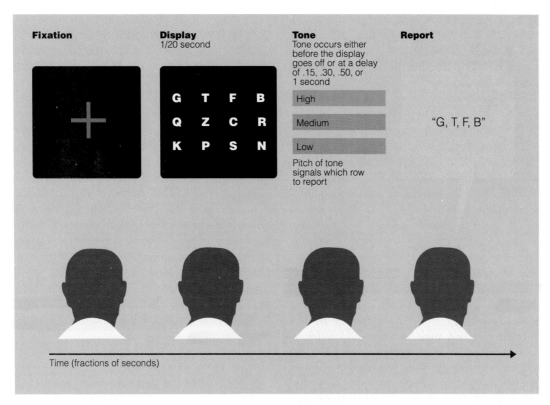

Fixation

Display
1/20 second

Tone
Tone occurs either before the display goes off or at a delay of .15, .30, .50, or 1 second

High

Medium

Low

Pitch of tone signals which row to report

Report

"G, T, F, B"

G T F B
Q Z C R
K P S N

Time (fractions of seconds)

Figure 7.9 Sperling's (1960) study of sensory memory. After the subjects had fixated on the cross, the letters were flashed on the screen just long enough to create a visual afterimage. High, medium, and low tones signalled which row of letters to report. Because subjects had to rely on the afterimage to report the letters, Sperling was able to measure how rapidly the afterimage decayed by varying the delay between the display and the signal to report.

last very long. This was demonstrated in a classic experiment by George Sperling (1960). Sperling briefly flashed three rows of letters on a screen. A tone following the exposure signalled which row of letters the subject should report to the experimenter (see Figure 7.9). Subjects were fairly accurate when the signal occurred immediately after the brief exposure, but their accuracy steadily declined as the delay of the tone increased from 0 seconds to 1 second.

Why should a delay of only 1 second influence the subjects' accuracy? According to Sperling, the 1-second delay is significant because the memory trace in the visual sensory store decays in less than a second. Research has shown that the maximum duration of sensory storage varies from about ¼ second in vision up to about 2 seconds in other senses.

The sensory store has a very large capacity. When subjects are shown a large array of 25 letters, all of the letters enter the sensory store, but subjects don't have enough time to recognize them all before the sensory image decays (Rumelhart, 1970). The duration, rather than the capacity, therefore limits the usefulness of the sensory store.

To summarize, stimuli in the sensory memory consist of sensations that need to be analyzed and combined into patterns that make up recognizable letters, words, sounds, and so forth. The sensory store has a very large capacity and provides an approximate copy of the stimulus input, but the

duration of storage is measured in scant fractions of a second. Information processing at this stage therefore depends on how quickly you can recognize patterns before the sensory trace fades away.

Assuming that you do recognize some of the stimuli, how do you go about remembering them? According to Atkinson and Shiffrin, the next step in the storage process involves keeping the information alive in the short-term memory store.

Short-Term Memory

***Short-term memory (STM)* is a limited-capacity store that can maintain unrehearsed information for about 20 to 30 seconds.** The 30-second maximum duration of STM may not seem short when contrasted with the even shorter duration of sensory storage, but the *short* in short-term memory is meant to be contrasted with the *long* in long-term memory. Information stored in long-term memory may last weeks, months, perhaps an entire lifetime. In comparison to this longevity, short-term memory looks very short indeed.

Actually, you can maintain information in your short-term store for longer than 30 seconds. Theoretically, you can retain material in your STM indefinitely. How? Primarily, by engaging in ***rehearsal**—the process of repetitively verbalizing or thinking about the information*. You surely have used the rehearsal process on many occasions. For instance, when you obtain a phone number from the information operator, you probably recite it over and over until you can dial the number. Rehearsal keeps recycling the information through your short-term memory (Craik & Watkins, 1973). In theory this recycling could go on indefinitely, but in reality something eventually will distract you and break the recycling process.

Our dependence on verbal rehearsal to maintain information in short-term memory is apparent from the kinds of mistakes we tend to make when our efforts break down. For example, suppose that you were asked to remember a list of random letters such as

Q P L H S X

presented very briefly on a screen. Mistakes on this task usually involve *acoustic confusions*, in which the incorrect answers *sound* like the correct answers (Conrad, 1964; Sperling, 1967). For instance, you might mistakenly convert P to E because they sound alike. Notice, you are far less likely to convert P to R because they *look* alike. Even when information is presented visually, we tend to make acoustic mistakes, because we usually keep information alive in STM through recitation. Rehearsal is not the only way to maintain information in STM, but it's the strategy that we rely on most when working with verbal material.

DURABILITY OF STORAGE
Without rehearsal or some other maintenance effort, information in short-term memory decays very rapidly. This rapid decay was demonstrated in a study by Peterson and Peterson (1959), who measured how long undergraduates could remember three consonants if they couldn't rehearse them. To prevent rehearsal, the Petersons required the students to count backward by threes from the time the consonants were presented until the recall test (see Figure 7.10). For example, subjects might hear the letters C J L followed by the number 547. They would then count backward from 547 by threes until they saw a light, which was a signal for recalling the three consonants. The light occurred either 3, 6, 9, 12, 15, or 18 seconds after the subject began counting. Figure 7.11 plots subjects' average accuracy in recalling the three consonants as a function of the time elapsed. The results indicate that when people cannot rehearse unfamiliar material, the material is quickly lost from STM. Without rehearsal, the maximum duration of STM storage is only about 20–30 seconds.

CAPACITY OF STORAGE
In addition to being limited in how long it can hold information, short-term memory is limited in the number of items it can hold. The limited capacity of STM was pointed out by George Miller (1956) in a famous paper called "The magical number seven, plus or minus two: Some limits on our capacity for processing information." Miller noticed that people could recall only about seven items in tasks that required them to remem-

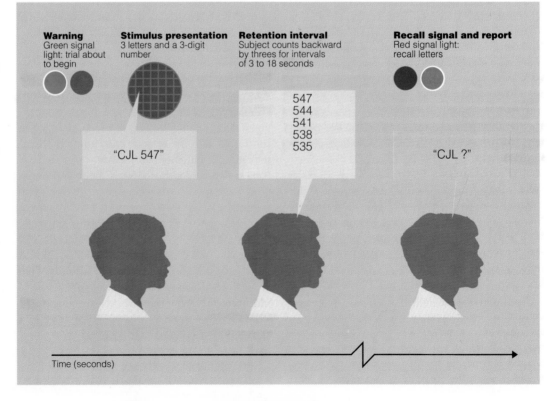

Figure 7.10 Peterson and Peterson's (1959) study of short-term memory. After a warning light was flashed, the experimenters gave the subjects three consonants to remember. They prevented rehearsal by giving the subjects a three-digit number at the same time and telling them to count backward by threes from that number until given the signal to recall the letters. By varying the amount of time between stimulus presentation and recall, the experimenters were able to measure the rate of decay in short-term memory.

Warning
Green signal light: trial about to begin

Stimulus presentation
3 letters and a 3-digit number

"CJL 547"

Retention interval
Subject counts backward by threes for intervals of 3 to 18 seconds

547
544
541
538
535

Recall signal and report
Red signal light: recall letters

"CJL ?"

Time (seconds)

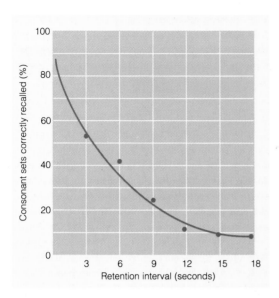

Figure 7.11 The rapid decay of short-term memory. Unaided by rehearsal, subjects' short-term memory for the target consonants declined rapidly. The actual data points (the dots) closely fit the theoretical curve shown here. (Data from Peterson & Peterson, 1959)

ber unfamiliar material. The common thread in these tasks, Miller argued, was that they required the use of STM. If STM can hold only five to nine items, then performance on all tasks that require the use of STM will be constrained by this limit.

You can demonstrate this limitation for yourself by measuring your ability to recall strings of letters in a *memory span* task. After reading each of the following rows of letters, close your eyes, and try to recall the letters in the correct order.

B R Q L Z N
K Y C T M F J
W P K T L D R V
B X M H G S N C Q

You were probably able to recall the letters from the first two lines but may have found it difficult to recall all the letters from the last two lines. Why? The last two lines contain more than seven letters and exceed the capacity of the average person's short-term memory.

When our short-term memory is filled to capacity, the insertion of new information into STM apparently leads to a *displacement* of some of the information currently in STM. In other words, if you're memorizing a ten-item list of basic chemical elements, the eighth, ninth, and tenth items in the list will begin to "bump out" earlier items. Similarly, if you're reciting the phone number of a pizza parlor you're about to call and someone asks you "How much is this pizza going to cost?" your retrieval of the cost information into STM may knock part of the phone number out of STM.

The limited capacity of STM is an important constraint, because we use STM in many tasks, such as reading, problem solving, and decision making. If you were shopping for cat food and wanted to mentally calculate how much you would have to pay to buy eight cans at 43 cents

per can, you could perform the multiplication in your head. But calculating the cost of 28 cans would probably exceed the capacity of your STM. This limited capacity represents how much information we can keep active in our conscious awareness. The limit constrains our ability to use STM to accomplish tasks in which we need to juggle various pieces of information mentally (Baddeley & Hitch, 1974).

CHUNKING

We can increase the capacity of short-term memory somewhat by combining stimuli into larger, possibly higher-order units (Simon, 1974). George Miller (1956) recognized this possibility and therefore proposed that STM capacity should be measured in chunks. **A chunk is a group of familiar stimuli stored as a single unit.** Each chunk is considered to be one item even though it consists of more than one potential stimulus.

You can demonstrate the effect of chunking by asking someone to recall a sequence of 12 letters grouped in the following way:

FB - ITW - AC - IAIB - M

As you read the letters aloud, pause at the hyphens. Your subject will probably attempt to remember each letter separately because there are no obvious groups or chunks. But a string of 12 letters is too long for STM, so errors are likely. Now present the same string of letters to another person, but place the pauses in different locations:

FBI - TWA - CIA - IBM

The letters now form four familiar chunks that should occupy only four slots in STM, resulting in successful recall (Bower & Springston, 1970).

To successfully chunk the letters I B M, your subject must first recognize these letters as a familiar unit, and this familiarity has to come from somewhere in long-term memory. Hence, in this case, information was transferred from long-term into short-term memory. This is not unusual. We routinely draw information out of our long-term memory banks to evaluate and understand information that we're working with in short-term memory.

The concept of chunking—combining stimuli into larger units—is not limited to verbal ma-

"The Magical Number Seven, Plus or Minus Two."
GEORGE MILLER

terial. Chunking is also effective for spatial information. For example, one reason skilled electronics technicians can understand and remember circuit diagrams is that they have learned to view meaningful groups of symbols in the circuit drawings as chunks. As a result, after a brief viewing of a circuit diagram, experienced technicians are more accurate than novices in reconstructing the diagram (Egan & Schwartz, 1979).

Our short-term memory is our *working memory*. It holds the information we're currently manipulating. Much of that information may come from sensory input, but it would be mostly nonsense if we couldn't analyze it using concepts, ideas, and recollections drawn from our long-term memory. In fact, our mental capabilities would border on pathetic if our memory consisted only of our sensory and short-term stores. Small wonder, then, that a great deal of attention has been devoted to the nature and operation of our long-term memory.

Figure 7.12 The *Challenger* explosion. Schoolchildren throughout the United States were watching on television when the *Challenger* space shuttle exploded in the skies over Florida in 1986. For these children, and for many other observers, their experience of the *Challenger* tragedy is likely to be a *flashbulb memory*—one that will persist in vivid detail.

Long-Term Memory

Long-term memory (LTM) is an unlimited capacity store that can hold information over lengthy periods of time. Long-term memory therefore has two important advantages over STM. First, it's not limited in its storage capacity. There will always be room in long-term memory for more information. Second, unlike sensory and short-term memory, which decay rapidly with time, LTM is not limited in terms of how long information can be stored. Long-term memories are durable; some may remain in LTM across an entire lifetime!

DURABILITY: IS STORAGE PERMANENT?
In fact, one point of view is that *all* information stored in long-term memory lasts an entire lifetime, and forgetting occurs only because people sometimes cannot *retrieve* needed information from LTM. To draw an analogy, imagine that memories are stored in LTM like marbles in a barrel. According to this view, none of the marbles ever leak out. When you forget, you just aren't able to dig out the right marble, but it's there—somewhere. An alternative point of view assumes that some memories stored in LTM do vanish forever. According to this view, the barrel is leaky and some of the marbles roll out, never to return.

The notion that LTM storage may be permanent is certainly intriguing. It's based on several lines of evidence. One is that we all have some memories that have lasted over a great many years. Think about it. You probably have some vivid recollections that date back to kindergarten or before. You may also have a grandparent who describes events from 50 years ago in exquisite detail.

Flashbulb memories are unusually vivid and detailed recollections of momentous events. They provide striking examples of seemingly permanent storage (Brown & Kulik, 1977). Many American adults, for instance, can remember exactly where they were, what they were doing, and how they felt when they were told that President Kennedy had been assassinated. You may have a similar recollection related to the explosion of the *Challenger* spacecraft (see Figure 7.12).

Evidence that appears to support the notion of permanent memory storage also comes from the frequent reports of exceptional recall through hypnosis. Many hypnotized subjects have been regressed back to early childhood and have described in remarkable detail childhood events that they thought they had forgotten (Spiegel & Spiegel, 1985). These hypnosis-aided recoveries of lost memories suggest that our normal forgetfulness is just a matter of poor retrieval.

Finally, there are the widely cited studies by Canadian neuroscientist Wilder Penfield, who reported triggering long-lost memories through electrical stimulation of the brain (ESB) during surgical operations (Penfield & Perot, 1963). As we discussed in Chapter 3, patients often remain conscious during brain surgery. Penfield used ESB to map brain function in surgical patients. He found that stimulation of the temporal lobe sometimes elicited vivid descriptions of events long past. Patients would describe events that apparently came from their childhood—like "being in a lumberyard" or "watching Mom make a phone call"—as if they were there once again. Penfield and others inferred that these descriptions were exact playbacks of long-lost memories unearthed by electrical stimulation of the brain.

Do these lines of evidence demonstrate that LTM storage is permanent? No, there are problems with each line of evidence (Loftus & Loftus, 1980). Although we all have some highly durable, seemingly permanent memories, like flashbulb memories, this does *not* mean that *all* our memories are chiseled into granite. The hypnosis-aided recoveries of lost memories have usually been taken at face value and accepted uncritically. But researchers who have followed up on recovered memories have often discredited the accuracy of these hypnosis-aided recollections simply by double-checking them. The Penfield findings can be interpreted in a variety of ways. The "memories" activated by ESB often included factual impossibilities and dreamlike elements of fantasy. For instance, the person who recalled being in a lumberyard had never actually been to one. The apparent recollections of Penfield's subjects may have been hallucinations, dreams, or loose reconstructions of events rather than exact replays of the past.

After a thorough review, Elizabeth and Geoffrey Loftus (1980) concluded that there is no convincing evidence that all our memories are stored away permanently. The fact that *some* forgetting is due to retrieval failure does not demonstrate that *all* forgetting involves a breakdown in retrieval.

TRANSFERRING INFORMATION INTO LONG-TERM MEMORY

How is information transferred from STM into LTM? Atkinson and Shiffrin (1971) distinguished among several different mechanisms for transferring material into LTM, but their emphasis was on *verbal rehearsal*. They proposed that the probability of recalling an item from LTM increases each time the item is rehearsed. According to their model, information that is being maintained in short-term memory through verbal rehearsal is gradually absorbed into long-term memory.

Dewey Rundus, then a graduate student working in Atkinson's laboratory at Stanford, tested this hypothesis by asking undergraduates to recall a list of words after they had rehearsed the words aloud. Rundus (1971) presented a list of 20 nouns to the subjects, one word at a time. The words were presented slowly, so that the subjects had time to rehearse some of the words before hearing a new one. Following the presentation of the entire list, students were told to try to recall the words in any order.

Figure 7.13 shows the probability of recall for each word as a function of its position in the list. The resultant U-shaped curve, called the serial position effect, is often seen when subjects are tested on their memory of a list. **The *serial position effect* occurs when subjects show better recall for items at the beginning and end of a list than for items in the middle.** This effect includes two component effects—primacy and recency—that are often seen in memory research. **A *primacy effect* occurs when items at the beginning of a list are recalled better than other items. A *recency effect* occurs when items at the end of a list are recalled better than other items.**

What accounts for the serial position effect? Why does it include the seemingly incompatible primacy and recency effects? According to Rundus, the primacy and recency effects appear together because the short-term and long-term memory stores operate separately. The primacy effect reflects LTM storage. The words at the be-

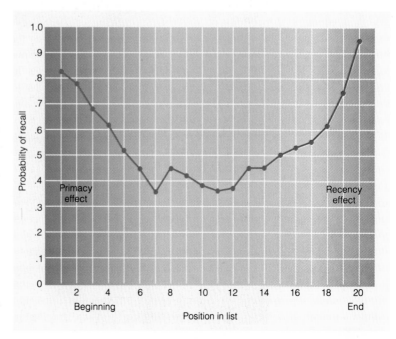

Figure 7.13 The serial position effect. After hearing a list of items to remember, people reliably recall more of the items from the beginning (primacy effect) and the end (recency effect) of the list than from the middle, producing the characteristic U-shaped curve shown here. Blue shading represents decreasing probability that the item is in LTM; gray, increasing probability that it is in STM. (Data from Rundus, 1971)

ginning of the list get rehearsed more often than the others and so they're more likely to be transferred into LTM than later words. In contrast, the recency effect reflects STM storage. Since the words at the end of the list are the ones most recently presented, they're still available in STM when subjects are asked to recall the list.

Subsequent research has provided some support for this explanation. If the primacy effect is caused by the extra rehearsals, it should be eliminated if the initial words on the list do not receive extra rehearsals. In fact, the primacy effect disappears when subjects are instructed to rehearse all words equally often (Fischler, Rundus, & Atkinson, 1970). This supports the assumption by Atkinson and Shiffrin that verbal rehearsal plays a key role in the transfer of information from short-term memory into long-term memory.

Divisions of Long-Term Memory

Information that is transferred into long-term memory is bound to have a lot of company. Although it appears that *not all* LTM storage is permanent, your long-term memory undeniably houses a vast amount of information. Some theorists believe that this information is distributed among a number of separate divisions in long-term memory. In other words, they think that long-term memory consists of several storehouses rather than just one storehouse.

DECLARATIVE VERSUS PROCEDURAL MEMORY

The most basic division breaks memory into declarative and procedural memory (Winograd,

Our recall of perceptual-motor skills such as typing depends on procedural memory— our memory for actions and operations.

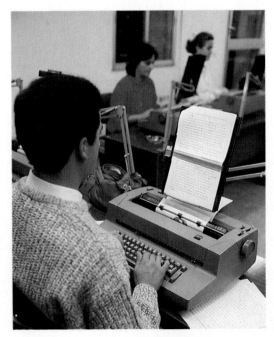

1975). *Declarative memory* is memory for factual information. It contains your recollections of words, definitions, names, dates, faces, events, concepts, and ideas. *Procedural memory* is memory for actions, skills, and operations. It contains your memory of how to execute such actions as riding a bike, typing, and tying your shoes. To illustrate the distinction, if you know the rules of tennis (the number of games in a set, scoring, and such), this factual information is stored in declarative memory. If you remember how to hit a serve and swing through a backhand, these perceptual-motor skills are stored in procedural memory.

Procedural memory is viewed as a relatively primitive type of memory; it can be observed even in lower animals. Among the "operations" thought to be stored in procedural memory are automatic glandular and muscular reflexes governed by classical conditioning. Declarative memory involves more complex mental processes that are seen only in higher organisms.

The evidence that declarative and procedural memories are separate comes primarily from studies of people suffering from amnesia due to brain damage. *Amnesia* involves a significant memory loss that is too extensive to be due to normal forgetting. Different patterns of forgetting are seen in cases of amnesia. In many cases, declarative memory is severely impaired while procedural memory is left largely intact (Squire, 1987). For example, a victim of amnesia may remember how to brush his teeth and drive a car, but can't recall the name of the President or what month it is. Cases such as these suggest that procedural and declarative memories may be stored separately. However, at present the evidence for separate storage is inconsistent, and a great deal of additional research is needed.

SEMANTIC VERSUS EPISODIC MEMORY

Endel Tulving (1986) has further subdivided declarative memory into semantic and episodic memory (see Figure 7.14). Both contain factual information, but episodic memory contains *personal facts* and semantic memory contains *general facts*. *Episodic memory* is made up of chronological, or temporally dated, recollections of personal experiences. Episodic memory is a record of things you've done, seen, and heard; it includes information about *when* you did these things, saw them, or heard them. It contains recollections like your memory of being in a ninth-grade play, visiting the Grand Canyon, hearing a Fleetwood Mac concert, or going to a movie last weekend.

Semantic memory contains general knowledge that is not tied to the time when the information was learned. Semantic memory contains infor-

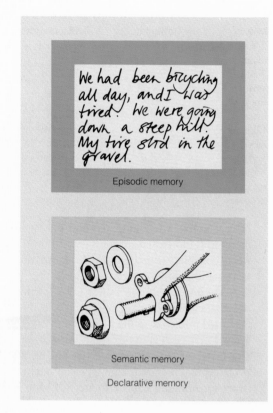

Episodic memory

Semantic memory

Declarative memory

Procedural memory

Long-term memory

Figure 7.14 Divisions of long-term memory. There is some evidence that different types of information are stored separately in the brain. This is surprising because our knowledge of many subjects—bicycling, for example—draws on all three types of memory at once.

mation such as the following: Christmas is December 25th, dogs have four legs, Phoenix is located in Arizona, and an axon is part of a neuron. You probably don't remember when you learned that dogs have four legs or that Phoenix is in Arizona. Information like this is usually stored undated. Unless your learning it was especially important to you, you probably did not date-stamp your memory. The distinction between episodic and semantic memory can be better appreciated by drawing an analogy to books: episodic memory is like an autobiography, and semantic memory is like an encyclopedia.

The patterns of memory loss seen in some cases of amnesia suggest that episodic and semantic memories may be stored separately (Wood, Ebert, & Kinsbourne, 1982). For instance, an amnesiac might forget many personal facts, like where she went to school and when she graduated, but her recall of general facts, such as the fact that milk comes from cows, may be largely unaffected. However, the evidence for separate storage of episodic and semantic memory is hotly debated.

Current evidence is inconclusive, but the idea that long-term memory may be divided into a collection of separate storehouses is an intriguing one to scientists. This promises to be a fertile area for future research.

Organization in Long-Term Memory

Consider what your plight would be if your college or local library did not organize its holdings, which might well be a quarter of a million volumes. Imagine searching for a specific book on 17th-century Canadian history in a collection of 250,000 randomly shelved books. Your term paper would probably be long overdue before you found the needed book.

Large information stores are usable only to the extent that they are organized. This is equally true of libraries, computer disks, and brains. Damage to the organizational operations can easily cause massive losses of information.

Figure 7.15 Clustering. The words in this list fall into four conceptual classes: animals, men's names, vegetables, and professions. Even when the words are presented in mixed order, people tend to recall them in groupings that fall in the same class. This phenomenon is called *clustering*.

Giraffe	Plumber	Owen	Lettuce
Parsnip	Otto	Parsley	Donkey
Zebra	Noah	Otter	Blacksmith
Radish	Chipmunk	Grocer	Eggplant
Diver	Adam	Badger	Garlic
Broker	Chemist	Camel	Wildcat
Spinach	Turnip	Baboon	Jason
Baker	Simon	Florist	Leopard
Woodchuck	Howard	Rhubarb	Printer
Dancer	Milkman	Melon	Bernard
Weasel	Gerard	Mustard	Carrot
Pumpkin	Panther	Wallace	Sherman
Amos	Oswald	Dentist	Waiter
Typist	Druggist	Muskrat	Moses
Byron	Reindeer	Mushroom	Cabbage

Organization is just as important for long-term memory. Although there's been some debate about whether long-term memory is really divided into separate stores, it *is* clear that we impose some organization on the information housed in long-term memory. Without at least some organization, the huge amount of information stored in LTM would be virtually useless to us. Unfortunately, our long-term memory stores do not appear to be organized as systematically as a well-run library. Research suggests that we use a hodgepodge of overlapping organizational frameworks in long-term memory.

CONCEPTUAL HIERARCHIES

If you were to memorize the list of 60 words in Figure 7.15, your recall of the list at a later time would demonstrate the presence of organization in long-term memory. Each of the words in this list fits into one of four categories: animals, men's names, vegetables, or professions. Bousfield (1953) showed that subjects recalling this list engage in clustering. **Clustering refers to our tendency to remember similar or related items in groups.** Even though the words on the list are not organized, you would tend to remember them in bunches that belong together conceptually—perhaps a string of professions, followed by a handful

of vegetables, a few animals, and maybe a few more professions. Clustering demonstrates that, when possible, we impose some organization on material stored in long-term memory.

According to Gordon Bower (1970), information that can be placed in categories is likely to be organized into conceptual hierarchies. **A conceptual hierarchy is a multilevel classification system based on common properties among items.** A conceptual hierarchy that a person might construct for minerals can be found in Figure 7.16. Clustering is thought to occur because we sort information into conceptual bins as part of the memory storage process. Conceptual hierarchies appear to be particularly useful for the kind of information found in semantic memory.

SEMANTIC NETWORKS

Of course, not all the information found in semantic memory can be fitted neatly into conceptual hierarchies. Much of our knowledge seems to be organized into less systematic frameworks, called semantic networks (Collins & Loftus, 1975). **A semantic network consists of concepts joined together by links that show how the concepts are related.** Figure 7.17 shows a small semantic network. The words in the ovals are the concepts, and the lines connecting the concepts

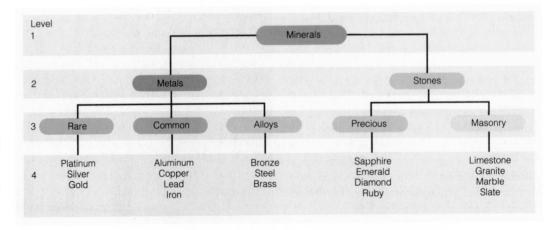

Figure 7.16 A conceptual hierarchy for words related to *minerals*. One way in which we facilitate the storage and retrieval of information in long-term memory is by organizing it in logical categories of this type.

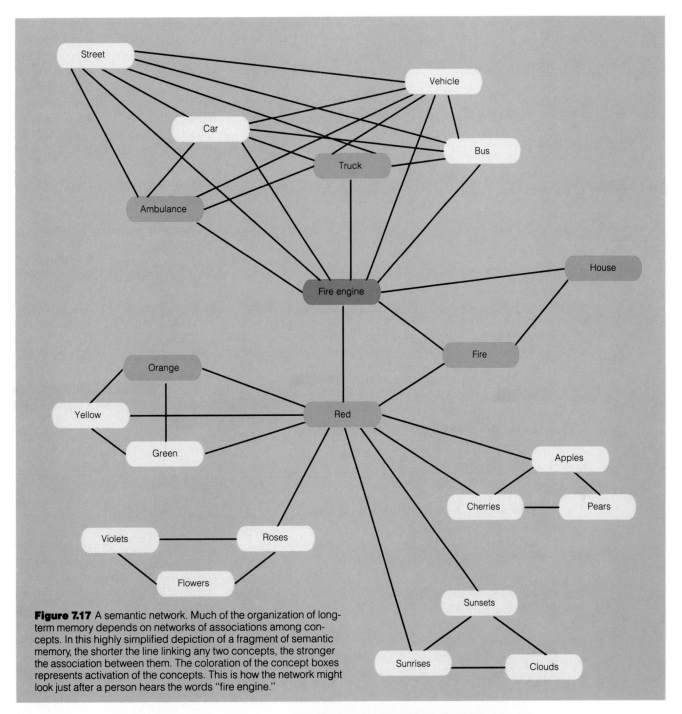

Figure 7.17 A semantic network. Much of the organization of long-term memory depends on networks of associations among concepts. In this highly simplified depiction of a fragment of semantic memory, the shorter the line linking any two concepts, the stronger the association between them. The coloration of the concept boxes represents activation of the concepts. This is how the network might look just after a person hears the words "fire engine."

are the links. A more detailed figure would contain labels for the links to show how concepts are related to each other; however, in this instance, the relations should be fairly clear. For example, *fire engine* is linked to *red* because of its color, to *vehicle* because it's a vehicle, and to *house* because fires often occur in houses. The length of each link represents the degree of association between two concepts. Shorter links imply stronger associations.

Semantic networks have proven useful in explaining why thinking about one word can make it easier to remember a closely related word. In a *lexical decision task,* **people see a string of letters and must decide as quickly as they can whether the string of letters forms a word.** Some of the strings do (such as *butter*) and some of the strings don't (such as *nart*). People are faster in deciding that a letter string is a word if the preceding string formed a closely related word (Meyer & Schvaneveldt, 1976). For example, people verify more quickly that the string *butter* is a word when it is preceded by the related word *bread* than when it is preceded by the unrelated word *nurse*.

According to Collins and Loftus (1975), when we think about a word, our thoughts naturally go

Check your understanding of the three memory stores by filling in the blanks in the table below. The answers can be found in the back of the book in Appendix A.

FEATURE	SENSORY MEMORY	SHORT-TERM MEMORY	LONG-TERM MEMORY
Maintenance of information	Not possible	Continued attention; rehearsal	Repetition; organization
Encoding format	Copy of input	_____	Largely semantic
Storage capacity	Large	Small (7 ± 2 chunks)	_____
Storage duration	_____	Up to 30 seconds	Minutes to years

after you toss a rock into a pond or a lake.

Consider again the semantic network shown in Figure 7.17. If subjects performing a lexical decision task see the word *red*, words that are linked to *red* should become activated, making them easier to remember than other words. Since the activation decreases as it travels outward, words that are closely linked to *red* (such as *orange*) will be easier to recall than words that have longer links (such as *sunrises*).

SCHEMAS AND SCRIPTS

The spreading activation model has been used to describe fairly complex behavior, such as how people produce sentences (Dell, 1986) or how people combine ideas when they read a short story (J. L. Myers et al., 1984). Although semantic networks are very useful for analyzing the associations among words, they are less useful for showing how knowledge is clustered together into a coherent whole. Thus, it appears that we rely on other organizational devices in long-term memory, such as schemas (Bartlett, 1932; Thorndyke & Hayes-Roth, 1979). **A *schema* is an organized cluster of knowledge about a particular object or sequence of events.**

For example, imagine that you've visited Professor Smith's office several times and you're now trying to describe it to a friend. You have a schema, based on experience, for what professors' offices are like. Thus, your recall of Professor Smith's office will be influenced by both the actual details of her office and your general knowledge of offices. You might therefore falsely recall that she had filing cabinets because filing cabinets are part of your general schema for professors' offices.

A particular kind of schema called a script may be especially relevant to episodic memory. **A *script* organizes what people know about common activities**—such as going to a restaurant or visiting a doctor (Schank & Abelson, 1977). A script is like an outline of a play in that it specifies the standard roles, objects, events, and results of some activity. For example, going to a restaurant involves fairly standard roles (customer, chef, waiter), objects (tables, plates, menus), sequences of events (looking at the menu, ordering the food, eating, paying the bill), and results (hunger is satisfied). People show considerable agreement on the scripts for many common activities such as attending a lecture, getting up in the morning, going grocery shopping, or visiting a doctor (Bower, Black, & Turner, 1979).

The value of scripts in information storage was demonstrated in a study by Bransford and Johnson (1973), who had subjects read the story reprinted in Figure 7.18. The story describes a very familiar

to related words. They call this process *spreading activation* within a semantic network. They assume that activation spreads out along the paths of the semantic network surrounding the word. They also theorize that the strength of this activation decreases as it travels outward, much as ripples decrease in size as they radiate outward

The procedure is actually quite simple. First you arrange things into different groups. Of course, one pile may be sufficient depending on how much there is to do. If you have to go somewhere else due to lack of facilities, that is the next step; otherwise you are pretty well set. It is important not to overdo things. That is, it is better to do too few things at once than too many. In the short run this may not seem important, but complications can easily arise. A mistake can be expensive as well. At first the whole procedure will seem complicated. Soon, however, it will become just another facet of life. It is difficult to foresee any end to the necessity for this task in the immediate future, but then one never can tell. After the procedure is completed, one arranges the materials into different groups again. Then they can be put into their appropriate places. Eventually they will be used once more, and the whole cycle will then have to be repeated. However, that is part of life.

Figure 7.18 An abstract passage used to study the role of scripts in long-term memory. Knowing what activity the passage is describing greatly improves recall of the ideas in the passage.

activity, but the ideas are presented so abstractly that the activity is difficult to recognize. People who read the passage without being told what the activity is show poor recall of the ideas in the story. People who are told in advance that the passage is about washing clothes recall over twice as much. Now that you know what the paragraph is about, you can use your script for washing clothes to organize the passage's abstract ideas.

Schemas and scripts provide us with skeletons that we "flesh out" with our actual experiences. While they serve as organizational devices in memory storage, they also play a key role in retrieval efforts, the subject we turn to next.

RETRIEVAL: GETTING INFORMATION BACK OUT OF MEMORY

Entering information into long-term memory is a worthy goal, but an insufficient one if we can't get the information back out again when we need it. Fortunately, recall often occurs without much effort, but occasionally we need to make a planned search of LTM. For instance, if you were asked to recall the names of all 50 states in the United States, you might organize your memory search by alphabetical order or by geographical location. Similarly, if you were asked to name your favorite TV shows, you might search systematically by the day of the week or by the type of show (dramas, comedies, and so on). As these examples illustrate, retrieval depends to a great extent on the organizational frameworks used in LTM storage.

Using a Schema to Guide a Search

The importance of organizational frameworks to storage and retrieval was demonstrated in an experiment by Anderson and Pichert (1978). They asked subjects to read a story that contained many ideas that would be relevant for someone interested in buying a house and many other ideas that would be relevant for someone interested in robbing the house. For example, a potential home buyer would be interested in knowing that the house had a leaky roof; a potential burglar would be interested in knowing that the family owned a valuable coin collection.

Some of the subjects were told to read the story from the perspective of a potential home buyer. Others were told to read it from the perspective of a potential burglar. As you might expect, the subjects' perspective was related to the kind of information they recalled later. The group that had the burglar perspective recalled more burglar information, and the group that had the home-buyer perspective recalled more home-buyer information. This difference suggested that subjects' perspective or schema influenced the kind of information *stored* in LTM.

However, Anderson and Pichert took their study one step further. They checked whether, given a new perspective, subjects could recall additional information—without seeing the story again. They hypothesized that a change in perspective might suggest a new plan for searching LTM. Switching perspectives *did* result in the recall of additional ideas on the second recall attempt. In contrast, a control group that was not encouraged to take a new perspective recalled slightly less information on their second attempt than they had on their first. Thus, a new schema helped people recall more ideas from the story, even without rereading it. This finding shows that a schema can influence *retrieval* as well as storage.

Using Cues to Aid Retrieval

At the beginning of the chapter we discussed the **tip-of-the-tongue phenomenon, which is a temporary inability to remember something you know accompanied by a feeling that it's just out of reach.** The tip-of-the-tongue phenomenon clearly is due to a failure in retrieval. Fortunately, we can often jog our memories with *retrieval cues*—stimuli that help us to gain access to memories. This was apparent when Roger Brown and David McNeill (1966) studied the tip-of-the-tongue phenomenon by giving subjects definitions of obscure words and asking them to think of the words. The example word *nepotism* at the beginning of the chapter was taken from their study. Brown and McNeill found that subjects groping for obscure words were correct in guessing the first letter of the missing word 57% of the time! This far exceeds chance and shows that our partial recollections are often headed in the right direction.

Read and Bruce (1982) studied the tip-of-the-tongue phenomenon and retrieval cues by giving people pictures or verbal descriptions of entertainers. For example, the verbal description of Ray Bolger was "On Broadway he created the role of Charley in *Charley's Aunt*, but is perhaps best remembered as the scarecrow in the Judy Garland movie *The Wizard of Oz*." The experimenters obtained nearly 500 cases in which subjects thought they knew the answer, but could not immediately retrieve the name. These names were tested again in 11 sessions over a 3-week period until they were remembered, sometimes with the help of additional information. After recalling the names, subjects answered questions about how they finally retrieved the names.

The most frequently reported strategy for recalling the names was to make use of partial information, such as the length of a name or letters or sounds within the name. (Ray . . . Ray Olger . . . Ray Folger . . . Ray *Bolger*!) People also used information associated with the entertainer, such as additional movie and television roles. Or a person might concentrate on one part of the clue. A person might, for instance, recall the last—or most memorable—time of watching *The Wizard of Oz* in the hope that this would spark a memory. This recollection could even go as far as imagining watching the credits roll by. Although the person might not literally catch a glimpse of the name as it rolled by, the attempt might be all that was needed for retrieval. Only infrequently did subjects report that they spontaneously recalled a name without a planned search of their memory.

Retrieval cues appear to aid our memory efforts in a variety of ways. In some cases they may allow us to narrow our search of long-term memory. In other instances they may trigger a series of associations that leads to the missing word. In other words, a cue may lead us into the maze of associations surrounding the forgotten information.

Reinstating the Context of an Event

Let's test your memory: what did you have for breakfast two days ago? If you can't immediately

In court, lawyers routinely try to stimulate a witness's memory by asking the witness to reinstate the context of an event. Although hypnosis also depends on reinstatement of context to enhance memory, hypnosis-aided recollections are generally inadmissible in court because hypnosis makes a witness highly suggestible.

answer, you might begin by imagining yourself sitting at the breakfast table. Trying to recall an event by putting yourself back in the context in which it occurred involves working with *context cues* to aid retrieval.

The technique of reinstating the context of an event is frequently used in legal investigations to enhance eyewitness recall. The eyewitness may be encouraged to retrieve information about a crime by replaying the sequence of events.

The value of reinstating the context of an event may help to account for how hypnosis occasionally stimulates eyewitness recall. Hypnosis has been used in a number of cases to help witnesses remember additional details about a crime (Block, 1976). When hypnosis is used for this purpose, the hypnotist usually attempts to reinstate the context of the event by telling the witness to imagine being at the scene of the crime once again.

There are, however, major problems associated with the use of hypnosis in legal investigations (Smith, 1983). As we saw in the Featured Study for Chapter 2 and in our discussion of hypnosis in Chapter 5, hypnosis seems to increase subjects' tendencies to report incorrect information. Thus, serious doubts about the accuracy of hypnosis-aided recall have led courts to be very cautious about allowing hypnosis-aided recollections as admissible testimony.

Because of these problems, some researchers have asked whether reinstating context *without* hypnosis might be as valuable as reinstating context under hypnosis. To answer this question, a group of psychologists asked hypnotized and non-hypnotized subjects to recall information about a simulated crime (Geiselman et al., 1985). Subjects saw a 4-minute film of a violent crime and were interviewed 2 days later by law-enforcement personnel. Subjects were randomly assigned to one of three interview conditions. The *standard* interview followed questioning procedures that law enforcement personnel would normally use. The *hypnosis* interview involved asking hypnotized subjects to state what they remembered from the film. In the *cognitive* interview, subjects were encouraged to use specific memory retrieval techniques to reinstate the context of the incident. For instance, the investigator might foster context cues by saying, "Picture yourself back in the room where you saw the film. The film is just beginning. What do you see?"

Both the cognitive and hypnosis procedures resulted in significantly greater recall than the standard interview. The investigators attributed this finding to the memory-guidance techniques that are common to both of these procedures. Al-

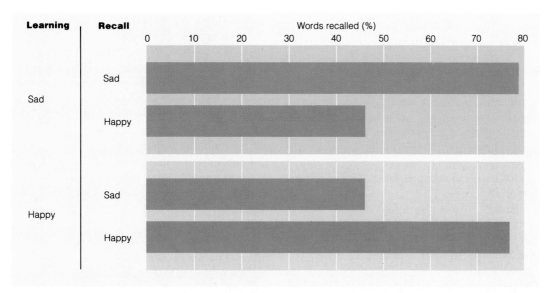

Learning	Recall	Words recalled (%)

Figure 7.19 State-dependent memory. Subjects in Bower's (1981) study remembered information better when they were in the same mood during recall as they were during the original learning, or encoding, of the information. Later experiments have not consistently found this result.

though the cognitive interview did not result in better recall than the use of hypnosis, it yielded comparable results and was easier for the law-enforcement personnel to learn and administer. This study suggests that reinstatement of context can aid recall with or without hypnosis. It also implies that reinstatement of context is one of the key factors at work when hypnosis facilitates eyewitness recall.

State-Dependent Memory

So, we know that reinstating the context of an event can often aid recall. Would it also be helpful to recreate the *mood* we were in when the original event took place? Some theorists believe so, and because retrieval seems to depend, in part, on being in the same emotional state as when the original learning occurred, they call this phenomenon *state-dependent memory*.

State-dependent memory is improved recall that is attributed to being in the same emotional state during encoding and subsequent retrieval. A state-dependent memory effect was observed by Gordon Bower (1981), who manipulated subjects' mood state to be happy or sad while they learned a list of words and while they attempted to recall the words later. If the initial learning occurred during a happy state, recall was better in a happy state. Similarly, subjects who memorized the list in a sad mood recalled more when they were in a sad mood at the time of retrieval (see Figure 7.19). Theorists speculate that state-dependent memory may occur because our mood at the time of learning is associated with the information learned, so that the mood state becomes part of our memory code.

State-dependent memory has also been seen in studies in which emotional states were induced by drugs. In one study, subjects smoked marijuana or a placebo cigarette that tasted like marijuana, just before they began to learn a list of 48 words, and just before they attempted to recall the words at a later time (Eich et al., 1975). As predicted, the group that learned under the influence of marijuana showed better recall when retrieval also occurred under the influence of marijuana (as opposed to the placebo condition). Before you get the wrong idea, however, it's worth noting that the best recall in the study was seen when subjects were *not* high (the placebo condition) during both learning and retrieval.

These intriguing studies suggest that our emotional states may be important context factors that can influence the ease with which we retrieve information. However, there are doubts about the strength and consistency of state-dependent memory effects. Blaney (1986) recently reviewed the research on state-dependent memory and concluded that the results are mixed. Although some studies (like those we just described) have found that retention is better when people have the same mood during learning and recall, a great many studies have *not* found evidence of state-dependent memory. At present, then, the balance of evidence suggests that state-dependent memory effects are inconsistent.

The Reconstructive Nature of Memory

When we retrieve information from long-term memory, we're not able to pull up a "mental videotape" that provides an exact replay of the past. To some extent, our memories are sketchy *reconstructions* of the past. The reconstructive nature of memory was first highlighted many years ago by Sir Frederic Bartlett, a prominent English psychologist. Bartlett (1932) had his subjects read

"It is in the nature of the mind to forget and in the nature of man to worry over his forgetfulness."
GORDON BOWER

THE WAR OF THE GHOSTS

One night two young men from Egulac went down to the river to hunt seals, and while they were there it became foggy and calm. Then they heard war cries, and they thought: "Maybe this is a war party." They escaped to the shore, and hid behind a log. Now canoes came up, and they heard the noise of paddles, and saw one canoe coming up to them. There were five men in the canoe, and they said:

"What do you think? We wish to take you along. We are going up the river to make war on the people."

One of the young men said: "I have no arrows."

"Arrows are in the canoe," they said.

"I will not go along. I might be killed. My relatives do not know where I have gone. But you," he said, turning to the other, "may go with them."

So one of the young men went, but the other returned home.

And the warriors went up the river to a town on the other side of Kalama. The people came down to the water, and they began to fight, and many were killed. But presently the young man heard one of the warriors say: "Quick, let us go home: that Indian has been hit." Now he thought: "Oh, they are ghosts." He did not feel sick, but they said he had been shot.

So the canoes went back to Egulac, and the young man went ashore to his house, and made a fire. And he told everybody and said: "Behold I accompanied the ghosts, and we went to fight. Many of our fellows were killed, and many of those who attacked us were killed. They said I was hit, and I did not feel sick."

He told it all, and then he became quiet. When the sun rose he fell down. Something black came out of his mouth. His face became contorted. The people jumped up and cried.

He was dead.

The End

Figure 7.20 A story used in a study of reconstructive memory (Bartlett, 1932). Subjects recalling the story tended to change details and to "remember" elements that are not in the original at all.

the tale called *The War of the Ghosts,* which is reproduced in Figure 7.20. After subjects had read it twice and had waited 15 minutes, they were asked to recall and write down the tale as best they could.

What did Bartlett find? The recalled tales tended to be shorter than the original. As you might expect, subjects condensed the story, leaving out elements they considered boring, as well as various details. Of greater interest to Bartlett was the fact that subjects inevitably *changed* the tale to some extent. The canoe might become a boat or the two young men might be hunting beavers instead of seals. Subjects often introduced entirely *new elements* and twists. For instance, in one case, the death at the end was attributed to fever and the character was described as "foaming at the mouth" (instead of "something black came out of his mouth").

Bartlett concluded that his subjects reconstructed the tale in ways that helped them to make sense out of it. He believed that the distortions in recall occurred because subjects tried to fit the tale into their established schemas.

Current schema theories also emphasize the partially reconstructive nature of memory (Brewer & Nakamura, 1984). The partial reconstruction view holds that part of what we recall about an event is the details of that particular event, and part of what we recall is a reconstruction based on our general knowledge about that type of event. (Remember your visit to Professor Smith's office?) According to this view, our more general, schematic knowledge becomes more influential in determining our recall as the details of an event blur with the passage of time.

Sulin and Dooling (1974) illustrated the reconstructive nature of memory by asking subjects to read the following biographical passage:

Adolf Hitler strove to undermine the existing government to satisfy his political ambitions. Many of the people of his country supported his efforts. Current political problems made it relatively easy for Hitler to take over. Certain groups remained loyal to the old government and caused Hitler trouble. He confronted these groups directly and so silenced them. He became a ruthless, uncontrollable dictator. The ultimate effect of his rule was the downfall of his country (Sulin & Dooling, 1974, p. 256).

Either 5 minutes or 1 week after reading the passage, the subjects were given a true-false memory test on information in the story. The test included seven sentences taken from the passage randomly mixed with seven sentences that were not in the passage. If people reconstruct the passage based on their knowledge of Hitler, they should falsely "recall" sentences that fit with their knowledge of Hitler. People who were tested 5 minutes after reading the passage made relatively few false recollections because they were able to remember the details of the passage. However, people who were tested 1 week later used their general knowledge more in reconstructing the passage. They were much more likely to falsely recall reading sentences such as "He was obsessed with the desire to conquer the world," which reflected their general knowledge of Hitler rather than the content of the passage.

Elizabeth Loftus and her colleagues have shown that reconstructive distortions show up frequently in eyewitness testimony (Loftus & Palmer, 1974). In one study, subjects saw a videotape of an auto accident and then were "grilled" as if they were providing eyewitness testimony. Some subjects were asked, "How fast were the cars going when they *hit* each other?" Other subjects were asked, "How fast were the cars going when they *smashed* into each other?" A week later, these subjects were asked if they remembered seeing any broken glass in the accident (there was none). Subjects who had earlier been asked about the cars *smashing* into each other were more likely than the other subjects to "recall" broken glass. Why would they add this detail to their reconstructions of the accident? Probably because broken glass is consistent with their schemas for cars *smashing* together.

The evidence clearly shows that our memories are not exact replicas of our experiences. However, a basic problem with reconstructive models of memory is that distinguishing between reconstructive and constructive errors is very difficult. *Reconstructive* errors are distortions that are introduced during *retrieval*, as we fill in gaps based on our schemas and scripts. *Constructive* errors are distortions introduced during *encoding and storage*, as we rearrange events to mesh with our schemas and scripts. For example, in the Hitler passage, when you read the phrase "to satisfy his political ambitions," you might immediately have recoded and stored it as "to satisfy his obsession to rule the world."

Thus, some distortions may occur because we read things into information as we encode and store it; distortions are not due solely to loose reconstruction during retrieval. The difficulty in sorting out the source of distortions in memory shows that encoding, storage, and retrieval are closely intertwined processes, more easily separated in principle than in practice. This interdependence of encoding, storage, and retrieval will be particularly apparent in our discussion of forgetting.

"One reason most of us, as jurors, place so much faith in eyewitness testimony is that we are unaware of how many factors influence its accuracy."

ELIZABETH LOFTUS

FORGETTING: WHEN MEMORY LAPSES

Why do we forget information—even information that we would like to remember? What causes forgetting? Many theorists believe that there isn't one simple answer to this question. They point to the complex, multifaceted nature of memory, and assert that forgetting can be caused by deficiencies in encoding, storage, retrieval, or some combination of these processes.

How Quickly We Forget: Ebbinghaus's Forgetting Curve

The first person to conduct scientific studies of forgetting was Hermann Ebbinghaus, who published a series of insightful memory studies way back in 1885. As a young man, Ebbinghaus stumbled onto a copy of Gustav Fechner's epic work, *Elements of Psychophysics* (see Chapter 4), in a secondhand bookstore. He was excited and impressed by Fechner's application of precise measurement methods to the study of perception. He decided to apply the same kind of empirical precision to higher mental processes and embarked on the study of memory.

Ebbinghaus studied only one subject—himself. To give himself lots of new material to memorize, he invented *nonsense syllables—consonant-vowel-consonant letter arrangements that do not correspond to words*, such as BAF, XOF, VIR, and MEQ. He used nonsense syllables because he wanted to work with largely meaningless materials that would be uncontaminated by his previous learning.

Ebbinghaus tirelessly memorized over 150 lists of nonsense syllables and then tested his memory of these lists after various time intervals had elapsed. Figure 7.21 shows what he found. This diagram, called a *forgetting curve*, graphs retention and forgetting over time. His widely cited forgetting curve shows a precipitous drop in retention during the first few hours after the nonsense syllables were memorized. He forgot more than 60% of the syllables in less than 9 hours! Thus, Ebbinghaus concluded that most forgetting occurs very rapidly after we learn something.

That's a depressing conclusion. What, then, is the point of memorizing information if you're going to forget it all right away? Fortunately, subsequent research showed that Ebbinghaus's forgetting curve was unusually steep (Postman, 1985). Although the basic shape of the curve has been replicated in hundreds of studies, forgetting usually isn't as swift or as extensive as Ebbinghaus thought. One problem was that he was working with such meaningless material. When subjects memorize more meaningful material, forgetting is

Figure 7.21 Ebbinghaus's forgetting curve for nonsense syllables. From his experiments on himself, Ebbinghaus concluded that forgetting is extremely rapid immediately after the original learning and then levels off. However, subsequent research has suggested that this forgetting curve is unusually steep. (Data from Ebbinghaus, 1885)

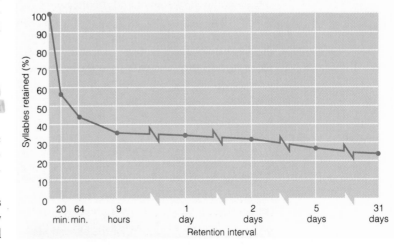

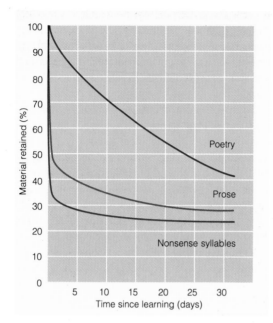

Figure 7.22 Forgetting curves for three kinds of material. The shallower forgetting curves for prose and poetry represent the fact that meaningful material is forgotten more slowly than Ebbinghaus's nonsense syllables. Poetry, containing internal cues like rhyme and rhythm, is forgotten less quickly than prose. (Based on Guilford, 1939)

less rapid. Figure 7.22 shows typical forgetting curves for written prose, poetry, and nonsense syllables. The curves for prose and poetry are much less steep than Ebbinghaus's original forgetting curve (for nonsense syllables). Also, different methods of measuring forgetting yield varied estimates of how quickly we forget. This underscores the importance of the methods used to measure forgetting, the matter we turn to next.

Measures of Forgetting

To study forgetting empirically, psychologists need to be able to measure it with some precision. Their efforts to measure forgetting inevitably measure retention as well. **Retention refers to the proportion of material retained (remembered).** In studies of forgetting, the results may be reported in terms of the amount forgotten by subjects or its opposite, the amount retained. In these studies, the *retention interval* is the length of time between the presentation of stimuli and the measurement of forgetting.

There are three different methods of measuring forgetting. Each of these methods—recall, recognition, and relearning—usually provide somewhat different estimates of forgetting and retention.

RECALL

Who is the current Secretary of State in the United States? What movie won the Academy Award for best picture last year? What is the capacity of STM? These questions require recall, perhaps the most common measure of forgetting used by psychologists. **A *recall* measure requires subjects to reproduce information on their own without any cues.** If you were to take a recall test on a list of 25 words you had memorized, you would simply be told to write down on a blank sheet of paper as many of the words as you could remember.

RECOGNITION

In contrast, in a recognition test you might be asked to *choose* the 25 words that you memorized from a list of 100 words. **A *recognition* measure requires subjects to select previously learned information from an array of options.** Subjects not only have cues to work with, they have the answers right in front of them. You might remember the distinction between recall and recognition this way: an eyewitness to a crime is initially asked to describe the suspect (recall) and later attempts to identify the suspect in a police lineup (recognition). In educational testing, essay questions and fill-in-the-blanks questions are recall measures of retention; multiple-choice, true-false, and matching questions are recognition measures.

If you're like most students, you probably prefer multiple-choice tests over essay tests. This is understandable, because evidence shows that recognition measures tend to yield higher estimates of retention than recall measures (Nelson, 1978). There are two ways of looking at this difference. One view is that recognition tests are especially *sensitive* measures of retention. The other view is that recognition tests are excessively *easy* measures of retention.

Actually, there is no guarantee that a recognition test will be easier than a recall test. This tends to be the case, but the difficulty level of a recognition test can vary greatly, depending on how the test is constructed. For instance, the difficulty level of a multiple-choice question depends on the number, similarity, and plausibility of the options provided as possible answers. Two questions that test for retention of exactly the same information can be dramatically different in difficulty. To illustrate, see if you know the answer to the following multiple-choice question:

> The capital of Washington is
> a. Seattle   c. Tacoma
> b. Spokane   d. Olympia

Most students who aren't from Washington find this a fairly difficult question. The answer is Olympia. Now take a look at the next question:

> The capital of Washington is
> a. London   c. Tokyo
> b. New York   d. Olympia

Virtually anyone can answer this question because the incorrect options are readily dismissed. Although this illustration is a bit extreme, it shows that recognition measures of retention can vary immensely in difficulty.

RELEARNING

The third method of measuring forgetting is relearning. **A *relearning* measure requires a subject to memorize information a second time to determine how much time or effort is saved by having learned it before.** To use this method, a researcher measures how much time (or how many practice trials) a subject needs to memorize information the first time. At a later time the subject is asked to relearn the information, and the researcher measures how much more quickly the material is memorized. Subjects' *savings scores* provide an estimate of their retention. For example, if it takes you 20 minutes to memorize a list of words the first time and only 5 minutes to memorize the same list a week later, you've saved 15 minutes, which is 75% ($^{15}/_{20} = \frac{3}{4} = 75\%$) of the original 20 minutes. Your savings score of 75% suggests that you retained 75% of the information and forgot the remaining 25%. Studies show that relearning measures can detect retention that is overlooked by recognition tests (Nelson, 1978). Thus, the relearning method is a sensitive measure of retention.

Why We Forget

Measuring forgetting is only the first step in the long journey toward explaining why forgetting occurs. In this section, we explore the possible causes of forgetting, looking at factors that may affect encoding, storage, and retrieval processes.

INEFFECTIVE ENCODING

A great deal of our forgetting may only *appear* to be forgetting. The information in question may never have been inserted into memory in the first place. Since you can't really forget something you never learned, this phenomenon is sometimes called *pseudoforgetting*. We opened the chapter with an example of pseudoforgetting. People usually *assume* that they know what a penny looks like, but most of us have actually failed to encode this information. As with the penny, a *lack of attention* usually underlies our failures to encode information.

Even when we do form memory codes for new information, subsequent forgetting may be due to *ineffective* encoding. The research on levels of processing shows that some approaches to encoding lead to more forgetting than others (Craik & Tulving, 1975). For example, if you're distracted while you read your textbooks, you may be do-

ing little more than saying the words to yourself. This is *phonemic coding*, which is inferior to *semantic coding* of verbal material. When you then can't remember the information that you've read, your forgetting may be due to ineffective encoding.

DECAY

Instead of focusing on encoding, decay theory attributes forgetting to the impermanence of memory *storage*. After Ebbinghaus showed that memory declines rapidly with time, most people concluded that memories simply waste away. **Decay theory proposes that forgetting occurs because memory traces fade with time.** The implicit assumption is that there is a decay in the physiological mechanisms responsible for memories. According to decay theory, the mere passage of time produces forgetting. This notion meshes nicely with commonsense views of forgetting.

As we saw earlier, decay clearly accounts for the loss of information from sensory stores. The rapid evaporation of unrehearsed information in short-term memory suggests that decay *may* contribute to forgetting from our STM store as well (there's some debate about this). However, the critical task for theories of forgetting is to explain the loss of information stored in long-term memory, and it has proven terribly difficult to demonstrate that decay causes LTM forgetting.

If decay theory is correct, the principal cause of forgetting should be the passage of time. In studies of long-term memory, however, researchers have found that the passage of time is not as influential as what happens during the time interval. This was first shown in a clever experiment by Jenkins and Dallenbach (1924). Their subjects memorized a list of nonsense syllables and were tested for recall after either 1, 2, 4, or 8 hours. The catch was that half the subjects slept during the retention interval and the other half went about their normal waking activities. According to decay theory, if the same amount of time—say, 8 hours—has elapsed for both groups, they should display an equal amount of forgetting. However, as you can see in Figure 7.23, the subjects who remained awake forgot more than those who slept.

Why did the subjects who remained awake forget more? Their greater forgetting was blamed on interference from the competing information that they had to process while awake. Many subsequent studies have shown that forgetting depends not on the amount of time that has passed since learning, but on the amount, complexity, and type of information that subjects have had to assimilate during the retention interval. This negative impact of competing information on retention is called *interference*.

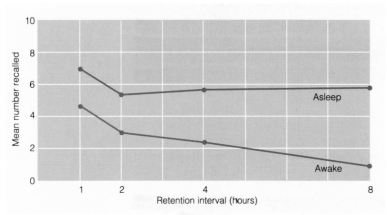

Figure 7.23 Interference and retention. By sending some of their subjects off to bed after learning a list of nonsense syllables while allowing others to engage in their normal waking activities, Jenkins and Dallenbach (1924) demonstrated that much of forgetting is attributable to interference. The subjects who slept forgot the least.

Interference effects in long-term memory create a fundamental problem in testing decay theory. A straightforward test would be to give subjects some information, tell them not to think about it, and test them later, hoping that nothing occurred during the retention interval to interfere with the information. Simple, right? Wrong. The experimenter cannot control what people think about during the retention interval. Let's say you're one of the subjects. If you think about the test material, this rehearsal will ward off forgetting and there will be no opportunity for decay. If you think about something else, your thoughts could interfere with the retention of the test material. The experiment can succeed only if you think about nothing at all during the retention interval. Try it. Take some time out right now to see how long you can go without thinking about anything. Don't worry—it won't take you long to find out.

In summary, we aren't sure whether decay causes LTM forgetting. Admittedly, plenty of studies show a gradual decrease in the retention of

material with the passage of time, as decay theory would predict. However, as time passes, there is more opportunity for interference to build up. Because of this, we can't be sure whether the gradual decline in retention is due to the decay of memory traces or to the cumulative effects of interference.

INTERFERENCE

Interference theory proposes that people forget information because of competition from other material. Although demonstrations of decay in long-term memory have remained elusive, hundreds of studies have shown that interference influences forgetting (Postman, 1971). If interference and decay are twisted together and confounded over time, why then is interference theory testable and decay theory not? The difference is this: researchers haven't figured out how to manipulate decay in an experiment, but it's easy to manipulate interference. Although it's probably impossible to completely eliminate interference, psychologists can control the *amount* of interfering material to determine whether increasing the amount of interference increases forgetting. In the experiment on interference that we mentioned earlier, Jenkins and Dallenbach (1924) manipulated the amount of interference by having their subjects sleep or remain awake during the retention interval.

In many other studies, researchers have controlled interference by varying the *similarity* between the original material given to subjects (the test material) and the intervening material that will cause interference. According to interference theory, interference is greatest when new material is very similar to the test material. Decreasing the similarity should reduce interference and cause

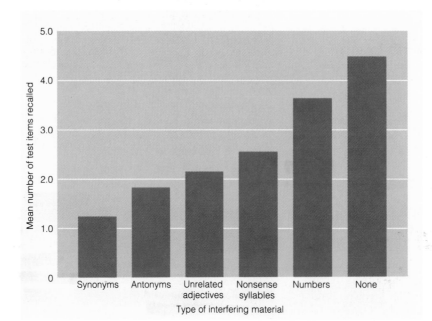

Figure 7.24 Effects of interference. According to interference theory, more interference from competing information should produce more forgetting. Mc-Geoch and McDonald (1931) controlled the amount of interference by varying the similarity of an intervening learning task to the original learning task. The results were consistent with interference theory. The amount of interference is greatest at the left of the graph and so is the amount of forgetting. As interference decreases (moving to the right on the graph), retention improves.

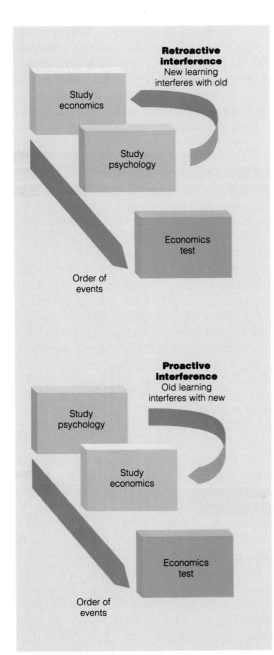

Retroactive interference
New learning interferes with old

Study economics

Study psychology

Economics test

Order of events

Proactive interference
Old learning interferes with new

Study psychology

Study economics

Economics test

Order of events

Figure 7.25 Retroactive and proactive interference. Retroactive interference occurs when learning produces a "backward" effect, reducing recall of previously learned material. Proactive interference occurs when learning produces a "forward" effect, reducing recall of subsequently learned material.

active interference occurs when new information impairs the retention of previously learned information. Retroactive interference occurs in between the original learning and the retest on that learning, during the retention interval. For example, the interference manipulated by McGeoch and McDonald (1931) was retroactive interference. In contrast, proactive interference occurs when previously learned information interferes with the retention of new information. Proactive interference is rooted in learning that comes *before* the information that must be remembered. In retrospect, it's clear that both kinds of interference contributed to Ebbinghaus's unusually steep forgetting curve. Memorizing over 150 lists of similar nonsense syllables had to create *massive* interference for Ebbinghaus.

To illustrate the distinction between retroactive and proactive interference, imagine that you have to memorize a great deal of information for an economics test tomorrow. If you memorize the information on economics and then study psychology, the interference from the psychology study will be retroactive interference. However, if you study psychology first and then memorize the information on economics, the interference from the psychology study will be proactive interference. The distinction between the two kinds of interference is diagrammed in Figure 7.25.

The evidence indicates that both types of interference can have powerful effects on how much we forget. At present, theorists aren't sure whether competing memories interfere with the *storage* or with the *retrieval* of forgotten information. Some studies suggest that retrieval is disrupted (Tulving & Psotka, 1971). If retrieval is the victim, interference is only one of several factors that can lead to retrieval failures, which we turn to next.

RETRIEVAL FAILURE
We often remember things that we were unable to recall at an earlier time. This may be obvious only when we struggle with the tip-of-the-tongue phenomenon, but it happens frequently. In fact, a great deal of our forgetting may be due to breakdowns in the process of retrieval.

Why does an effort to retrieve something fail

"Left to itself every mental content gradually loses its capacity for being revived. . . . Facts crammed at examination time soon vanish."
HERMANN EBBINGHAUS

less forgetting. This is exactly what McGeoch and McDonald (1931) found in an influential study. They had subjects memorize test material that consisted of a list of two-syllable adjectives. They varied the similarity of intervening learning by having subjects then memorize one of five lists. In order of decreasing similarity to the test material, they were the following: synonyms of the test words, antonyms of the test words, unrelated adjectives, nonsense syllables, and numbers. Later, subjects' recall of the test material was measured. Figure 7.24 shows that as the similarity of the intervening material decreased, the amount of forgetting also decreased—because of reduced interference.

There are two kinds of interference: *retroactive* interference and *proactive* interference. **Retro-**

Check your understanding of why we forget by identifying the probable causes of forgetting in each of the following scenarios. You will find the answers in Appendix A.

1. Ellen can't recall the reasons for the Webster-Ashburton Treaty because she was daydreaming when it was discussed in history class.

_____

2. Arnold hates his job at Taco Heaven and is always forgetting when he is scheduled to work.

_____

3. Ray's new assistant in the Shipping Department is named John Cocker. Ray keeps calling him Joe, mixing him up with the rock singer, Joe Cocker.

_____

4. Tania studied history on Sunday morning and sociology on Sunday evening. It's Monday, and she's struggling with her history test because she keeps mixing up prominent historians with influential sociologists.

_____

snow." Because subjects emphasized the phonemic aspects of the word, the phonemic retrieval cue (hint 1) should be more effective than the semantic retrieval cue (hint 2). However, when semantic encoding is used, semantic cues should be more effective (Fisher & Craik, 1977).

A general statement of the principle at work here was formulated by Tulving and Thomson (1973). Their **encoding specificity principle** states that the value of a retrieval cue depends on how well it corresponds to the memory code. This principle provides one explanation for the inconsistent success of our retrieval efforts.

Many years ago, Sigmund Freud (1901) came up with an entirely different explanation. As we noted in Chapter 1, Freud asserted that people often keep embarrassing, unpleasant, or painful memories buried in their unconscious. For example, a person who was deeply wounded by perceived slights at a childhood birthday party might *repress* all recollection of that party. In his therapeutic work with patients, Freud recovered many of these buried memories. This suggests that the memories were there all along, but something was preventing retrieval. Freud theorized that retrieval was blocked by unconscious avoidance tendencies.

Our tendency to forget things we don't want to think about is called motivated forgetting. **Motivated forgetting** involves purposeful suppression of memories. When we forget things like a dental appointment, a promise to help a friend move, or a term paper deadline, motivated forgetting is often at work.

Assuming that motivated forgetting accounts for only a portion of what you forget, what happens to the rest of the things you learn—and then forget? Lest the content of this section join their ranks, refresh your memory of the factors that influence forgetting: ineffective encoding, decay, interference, and retrieval failure. Indeed, forgetting is so complex, we have three different ways of measuring it. Can you *recall* them? Perhaps you could *recognize* them and then *relearn* them more quickly than the first time around.

on one occasion and succeed on another? That's a tough question. One theory is that retrieval failures may be more likely when there is a mismatch between the retrieval cues that you're working with and the coding of the information you're searching for. According to Tulving and Thomson (1973), a good retrieval cue is consistent with the original encoding of the information to be recalled. If the sound of a word—its phonemic quality—was emphasized during encoding, an effective retrieval cue should emphasize the sound of the word. If the meaning of the word was emphasized during encoding, semantic cues should be best.

Imagine an experiment in which subjects' attention during encoding is focused on the phonemic aspects of the words to be remembered. For instance, a word such as *hail* is preceded by the question "Rhymes with *pail*?" Later, subjects take a recall test and are given one of two hints: (1) "Rhymes with *bail*" or (2) "Associated with

IN SEARCH OF THE MEMORY TRACE: THE PHYSIOLOGY OF MEMORY

For decades, psychologists and neuroscientists have ventured forth in search of the physiological basis for the memory trace. This great abstraction in the study of memory has proven elusive. On several occasions scientists have been excited by new leads, only to find that they led down blind alleys. For example, Wilder Penfield's ESB studies

suggested that the cortex houses exact tape recordings of past experiences (Penfield & Perot, 1963). At the time, scientists believed that this was a major breakthrough; ultimately, it was not.

Similarly, James McConnell rocked the world of science when he reported that he had chemically transferred a specific memory from one flatworm to another. McConnell (1962) created a conditioned reflex (contraction in response to light) in flatworms and then transferred RNA from the trained worms to untrained worms, who then showed evidence of "remembering" the conditioned reflex. The implication was that it would be only a matter of time before neuroscientists could identify the chemical basis for complex memories. (Imagine: a pill containing the information for Physics 201 or History 101 might be developed.) Unfortunately, the chemical transfer studies proved difficult to replicate, and it now seems unlikely that RNA provides the chemical code for memories (Squire, 1987).

Investigators continue to explore a variety of leads about the physiological basis for memory. In light of past failures, these lines of research should probably be viewed with guarded optimism, but let's look at some of the more promising leads (consult Chapter 3 if you need to refresh your memory about the physiological processes and structures discussed in this section).

Work by Eric Kandel and his colleagues suggests that memory formation results in *alterations in neurotransmitter secretions* at specific synaptic sites (Kandel & Schwartz, 1982). Like McConnell, Kandel studied conditioned reflexes in a simple organism—a sea slug. He has shown that specific forms of learning in the sea slug result in an increase or decrease in the release of neurotransmitters by presynaptic neurons. Kandel believes that durable changes in synaptic transmission may be the neural building blocks of complex memories as well. Of course, there are critics who think it's risky to generalize from a sea slug to a human.

Richard F. Thompson and his colleagues have shown that specific memories may depend on *localized neural circuits* in the brain (McCormick & Thompson, 1984). In other words, memories may create unique, reusable pathways in the brain along which signals flow. Thompson has traced the pathway that accounts for a rabbit's memory of a conditioned eyeblink response. The key link in this circuit is a microscopic spot in the *cerebellum*, a structure in the hindbrain. When this spot is destroyed, the conditioned eyeblink response vanishes, but all other aspects of behavior remain unchanged. This does *not* mean that the cerebellum is the key to memory. Thompson theorizes that other memories probably create entirely different pathways in other areas of the brain. The key implication of Thompson's work is that it may be possible to map out specific neural circuits that correspond to specific memories.

Cases of *amnesia* due to head injury are another source of clues about the physiological bases of memory. Although many patterns of forgetting are seen in cases of amnesia, there are two basic types of amnesia. **In *retrograde amnesia* a person loses memories of events that occurred prior to the injury.** For example, a 25-year-old gymnast who sustained a head trauma might find 3 years, or 7 years, or perhaps her entire lifetime erased. **In *anterograde amnesia* a person loses memories of events that occur after the injury.** For instance, after her accident, the injured gymnast might suffer impaired ability to remember people she meets, what she has for breakfast, and where she parks her car.

Because victims' current memory functioning is impaired, cases of *anterograde* amnesia have proven to be especially rich sources of information on how brain damage is related to memory deficits. One well-known case, that of H. M., has been followed since 1953 (Corkin, 1984; Scoville & Milner, 1957). H. M. had surgery to relieve debilitating epileptic seizures. Unfortunately, the surgery inadvertently wiped out most of his long-term memory capability. H. M.'s short-term memory is fine, but he has no recollection of anything that has happened since 1953 (other than about the most recent 30 seconds of his life). He doesn't recognize the doctors treating him, he can't remember routes to and from places, and he doesn't know his age. He can't remember what he did yesterday, let alone what he has done for the last 35 years.

H. M.'s memory losses have been attributed to the removal of his *hippocampus*, a forebrain structure that's part of the limbic system (the location of the hippocampus is shown in Figure 7.26). Damage to the hippocampus has also been implicated in other cases of anterograde amnesia (Milner, 1974). Neuroscientists believe that the hippocampus plays a key role in memory, but the

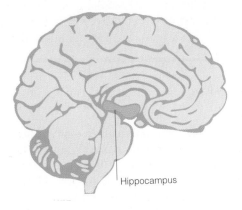

Hippocampus

Figure 7.26 The location of the hippocampus. The hippocampus is part of the limbic system and is believed to play a key role in memory.

nature of that role remains obscure. Theorists are perplexed, because some subtle long-term memory capabilities have recently been found in humans with hippocampal lesions, and because hippocampal lesions in animals do not reliably produce the global memory deficits expected (Corkin, 1984; Squire, 1987).

Various other lines of research have related memory functioning to (1) activity in the thalamus (Mishkin, 1982), (2) synthesis of acetylcholine, the neurotransmitter that's depleted by Alzheimer's disease (Bartus et al., 1982), (3) hormonal fluctuations (McGaugh, 1983), and (4) protein synthesis in the brain (Davis & Squire, 1984).

Does all this sound confusing? It should, because it is. The bottom line is that neuroscientists are still assembling the pieces of the puzzle that will explain the physiological basis of memory. At present, they're not sure how the pieces fit together, and they suspect that there are still many pieces missing. This difficulty is probably due to the complex, multifaceted nature of memory. Looking for the physiological basis for memory is only slightly less daunting than looking for the physiological basis for thought.

PUTTING IT IN PERSPECTIVE

Figure 7.27 An overview of memory processes. Memory processes in encoding, storage, retrieval, and forgetting are illustrated using Atkinson and Shiffrin's model of three memory stores as an organizational device.

One of our integrative themes—the idea that our experience of the world is subjective (theme 6)—stood head and shoulders above the rest in this chapter. Let's briefly review how the study of memory has illustrated and illuminated this idea.

First, our discussion of attention as inherently selective should have shed light on why our experience of the world is highly subjective. To a great degree, what you see in the world around you depends on where you focus your attention. This is one of the main reasons that two people can be exposed to the "same" events and walk away with entirely different perceptions. For instance, if you and a friend met a prominent politician at a fundraiser, you might come away with one impression because you attended to the meaning of what was

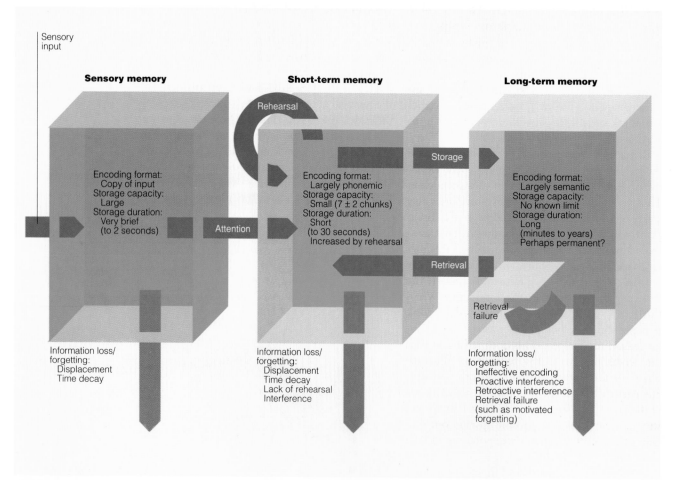

said and your friend, who paid attention to the politician's body language, might have an entirely different impression.

Second, our dependence on schemas and scripts to organize information in memory helps to explain the subjective nature of our personal experiences. For instance, the study in which subjects assumed the perspective of either a home buyer or a burglar showed that different schemas can lead to very different recollections based on the same information.

Third, the reconstructive nature of memory should further explain our tendency to view the world with a subjective slant. When you observe an event, you don't store an exact copy of the event in your memory. Instead, you store a rough, "bare bones" approximation of the event that may be reshaped some more during retrieval, especially if a long time has gone by. Thus, with the passage of time, you—and all of us—tend to put more and more of a personal, subjective imprint on memories.

Finally, we often forget those things that we don't want to remember. This propensity for motivated forgetting introduces yet another source of personal bias into our views of the past. In short, a host of natural human tendencies in the processes of attention and memory conspire to make our experience of the world highly subjective.

Another of our unifying themes also surfaced in this chapter. The multifaceted nature of memory demonstrated once again that behavior is governed by multiple causes (theme 4). Your memory of a specific event may be influenced by many factors, including:

- The amount of attention you devote to it.
- The level at which you process the incoming information.
- Whether you enrich your encoding with some form of elaboration.
- Whether you have an opportunity to transfer the information into long-term memory.
- How you organize the information.
- How you search through your memory store.
- The extent to which you use schemas to reconstruct the event.
- The amount of interference you experience.

The multifaceted nature of memory is diagrammed in Figure 7.27, which provides an overview of memory processes organized around the three types of memory stores.

Given the multifaceted nature of memory, it should come as no surprise that there are many different ways to improve memory. We discuss a variety of strategies in our Application section.

IMPROVING EVERYDAY MEMORY

Answer the following "true" or "false."

☐ **1.** Memory strategies were recently invented by psychologists.

☐ **2.** Imagery can be used to remember concrete words only.

☐ **3.** Overlearning information leads to poor retention.

☐ **4.** Outlining reading is not likely to affect retention.

☐ **5.** Massing practice in one long study session is more efficient than distributing practice across several shorter sessions.

Mnemonic devices are strategies for enhancing memory. They have a long and honorable history, so the first statement is false. In fact, one of the mnemonic devices that we cover in this application—the method of loci—was described in Greece as early as 86–82 B.C. (Yates, 1966). Actually, mnemonic devices were even more crucial in ancient times than today. In ancient Greece and Rome, for instance, paper and pencils were not readily available so people could write down things that they needed to remember. People had to depend heavily on mnemonic devices.

In this Application, we consider how the principles of memory can be employed to enhance your ability to remember things. We discuss everyday memory in general, but emphasize how principles relate to effective studying in school. In the process, you'll learn that *all* of the true-false statements above are false. So, without further ado, let's begin our coverage by discussing the value of rehearsal.

Engage in Adequate Rehearsal

Practice makes perfect, or so you've heard. In reality, practice is not likely to guarantee perfection, but it usually leads to improved retention. Studies show that retention improves with increased rehearsal. Presumably this improvement occurs because rehearsal helps transfer the information to be remembered into long-term memory.

Continued rehearsal may also pay off by improving your *understanding* of assigned material. As you go over information again and again, your increased familiarity with the material may permit you to focus selectively on the most important points. Bromage and Mayer (1986) examined the effects of repetition in a study in which undergraduate subjects listened to an audiotaped lecture on photography, from one to three times. Information in the lecture was classified into three levels of importance. As Figure 7.28 shows, increased repetition led to increased recall for information at all three levels of importance. However, repetition had its greatest impact on the retention of the *most important* information, yielding enhanced understanding of the lecture.

There is evidence that it even pays to overlearn material. **Overlearning refers to continued rehearsal of material after you first appear to master it.** In one study, after subjects mastered a list of nouns (they recited the list without error), Krueger (1929) required them to continue rehearsing for 50% or 100% more trials. Measuring retention at intervals up to 28 days, Krueger found that greater overlearning was related to better recall of the list (see Figure 7.29). The practical implication of this finding is simple: you should not quit rehearsing material as soon as you appear to have mastered it.

Schedule Your Rehearsal as Distributed Practice

Let's assume that you are going to study 9 hours for an exam. Is it better to "cram" all of your study into one 9-hour period (massed practice) or to distribute it among, say, three 3-hour periods on successive days (distributed practice)? The evidence indicates that retention tends to be greater after distributed practice than after massed practice, especially if the intervals be-

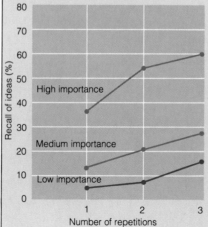

Figure 7.28 Effects of repetition on recall of high-, medium-, and low-importance ideas. In this study, repetition most aided the recall of high-importance ideas. (Data from Bromage & Mayer, 1986)

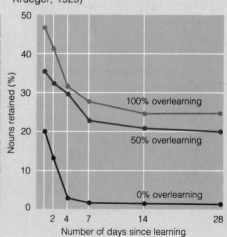

Figure 7.29 Effects of overlearning on retention. A comparison of the three forgetting curves suggests that overlearning enhances retention even over lengthy periods of time. (Data from Krueger, 1929)

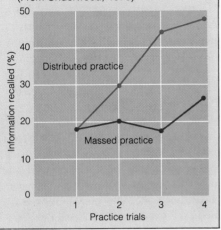

Figure 7.30 Effects of massed versus distributed practice on retention. Children in this study showed better recall of information when practice sessions were distributed over time. (From Underwood, 1970)

tween practice periods are fairly long, such as 24 hours (Zechmeister & Nyberg, 1982). Figure 7.30 shows the results of one study on massed versus distributed practice. Studying children (aged 9–14) who practiced a list of words four times, Underwood (1970) found that distributed practice led to larger increases in recall than a similar amount of massed practice.

Why is distributed practice better? This may seem strange, but Keppel (1967) suggests that it's because distributed practice allows *forgetting* to occur. If you wait a day before going over material again, you'll probably forget some of it. This allows you to identify the material that you haven't learned very well, so you can devote extra practice to it or form new memory codes that are more effective.

Minimize Interference

Research suggests that interference is a major cause of forgetting, so you'll probably want to think about how you can minimize interference. This is especially important for students, because memorizing information for one course can interfere with the retention of information in another course. It may help to allocate study for specific courses to specific days. Thorndyke and Hayes-Roth (1979) found that similar material produced less interference when it was learned on different days. Thus, the day before an exam in a course, it's probably best to study for

that course only—if possible. If demands in other courses make that impossible, study the test material last.

Of course, studying for other classes is not the only source of interference in a student's life. Other normal waking activities also produce interference. Therefore, it's a good idea to conduct one last, thorough review of material as close to exam time as possible (Anderson, 1980). This helps you to avoid memory loss due to interference from intervening activities.

Engage in Deep Processing

Although it's important to engage in adequate rehearsal, the research by Craik and Tulving (1975) on levels of processing suggests that how *often* you go over material is less critical than the *depth* of processing that you engage in when you go over it. Thus, if you expect to remember what you read, you have to wrestle fully with its meaning. Many students could probably benefit if they spent less time on rote repetition and devoted more effort to analyzing the meaning of their reading assignments.

Enrich Encoding with Verbal Mnemonics

When working with verbal material, deeper processing usually entails working harder to make information meaningful. But evidence shows that the effort is worthwhile: retention improves as material becomes more meaningful. A very useful strategy is to make material *personally* meaningful. When you read your textbooks, try to relate information to your own life and experience. For example, when you read about classical conditioning, try to think of responses that you make that are due to classical conditioning.

Of course, it's not always easy to make something personally meaningful. For instance, when you study chemistry you may have a hard time relating to polymers at a personal level. Thus, many mnemonic devices—such as acrostics, acronyms, and narrative methods—are designed

to make abstract material more meaningful.

Acrostics and Acronyms

Acrostics are phrases (or poems) in which the first letter of each word (or line) functions as a cue to help you recall more abstract words that begin with the same letter. For instance, you may remember the order of musical notes with the saying "Every good boy does fine" (or "deserves favor"). A slight variation on acrostics is the *acronym*—a word formed out of the first letters of a series of words. Students memorizing the order of colors in the light spectrum often store the name "Roy G. Biv" to remember red, orange, yellow, green, blue, indigo, and violet. Notice that this acronym takes advantage of chunking.

Narrative Methods

Another useful way to remember a list of words is to create a story that includes the words in the correct order. The narrative increases the meaningfulness of the words and links them in a specific order. Examples of this technique can be seen in Table 7.1.

Table 7.1 Word Lists to Be Memorized and Stories Constructed from Them

WORD LISTS	STORIES
Bird Costume Mailbox Head River Nurse Theater Wax Eyelid Furnace	A man dressed in a *Bird Costume* and wearing a *Mailbox* on his *Head* was seen leaping into the *River*. A *Nurse* ran out of a nearby *Theater* and applied *Wax* to his *Eyelids*, but her efforts were in vain. He died and was tossed into the *Furnace*.
Rustler Penthouse Mountain Sloth Tavern Fuzz Gland Antler Pencil Vitamin	A *Rustler* lived in a *Penthouse* on top of a *Mountain*. His specialty was the three-toed *Sloth*. He would take his captive animals to a *Tavern* where he would remove *Fuzz* from their *Glands*. Unfortunately, all this exposure to sloth fuzz caused him to grow *Antlers*. So he gave up his profession and went to work in a *Pencil* factory. As a precaution he also took a lot of *Vitamin* E.

Source: Bower & Clark, 1969

Figure 7.31 Effects on recall of using narrative methods of remembering. In this study of recall, 12 lists of words were presented. Subjects in the "narrative group" were asked to recall the words by constructing a story out of them; subjects in the control group were not given any special instructions. Recoding the material in story form dramatically improved recall, with the control group recalling an average of 14% of the words and the narrative group recalling an average of 94%. (Data from Bower & Clark, 1969)

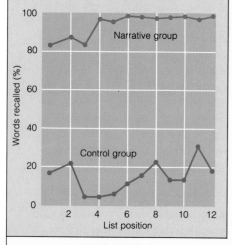

Bower and Clark (1969) found that this procedure greatly enhanced subjects' recall of lists of unrelated words. Figure 7.31 summarizes some of their results.

Why—and how—would you use the narrative method? Let's assume that you always manage to forget to put one item in your gym bag on your way to the pool. Short of pasting a list on the inside of the bag, how can you remember everything you need? You could make up a story that includes the items you need:

The wind and rain in COMBINATION LOCKed out the rescue efforts—nearly. CAP, the flying ace, TOWELed the SOAP from his eyes, pulled his GOGGLES from his SUIT pocket and COMBed the BRUSH for survivors.

Rhymes

Another verbal mnemonic that we often rely on is rhyming. You've probably repeated, "I before E except after

C . . ." thousands of times. Perhaps you also remember the number of days in each month with the old standby, "Thirty days hath September. . . ." Rhyming something to remember it is an old and very useful trick.

Enrich Encoding with Visual Imagery

Memory can be greatly enhanced by the use of visual imagery. As you may recall, Allan Paivio (1986) believes that visual images create a second memory code and that two codes are better than one. Many popular mnemonic devices depend on visual imagery, including the following examples.

Link Method

The *link method* involves forming a mental image of items to be remembered in a way that links them together. For instance, suppose that you're going to stop at the drugstore on the way home and you need to remember to pick up a news magazine, shaving cream, film, and pens. To remember these items, you might visualize a public figure likely to be in the magazine shaving with a pen while being photographed. There is evidence that the more bizarre you make your image, the more helpful it will be (McDaniel & Einstein, 1986).

Method of Loci

The *method of loci* involves taking an imaginary walk along a familiar path where you have associated images of items you want to remember with certain locations. The first step is to commit to memory a series of loci, or places along a path. Usually these loci are specific locations in your home or neighborhood. Then envision each thing you want to remember in one of these locations. Try to form distinctive, vivid images. When you need to remember the items, imagine yourself walking along the path. The various loci on your path should serve as cues for the retrieval of the images that you formed (see Figure 7.32).

The method of loci assures that

Figure 7.32 The method of loci. In this example from Bower (1970), a person about to go shopping pairs items to remember with familiar places (*loci*) arranged in a natural sequence: (1) hot dogs/driveway; (2) cat food/garage interior; (3) tomatoes/front door; (4) bananas/coat closet shelf; (5) whiskey/kitchen sink. The shopper then used imagery to associate the items on the shopping list with the loci, as shown in the drawing: (1) giant *hot dog* rolls down a *driveway*; (2) a cat noisily devours *cat food* in the *garage*; (3) ripe *tomatoes* are splattered on the *front door*; (4) bunches of *bananas* are hung from the *closet shelf*; (5) the contents of a bottle of *whiskey* gurgle down the *kitchen sink*. As the last panel shows, the shopper recalls the items by mentally touring the loci associated with them. (From Bower, 1970)

items are remembered in their correct order because the order is determined by the sequence of locations along the pathway. The potential effectiveness of this method was demonstrated by Crovitz (1971) who asked subjects to remember a list of 32 words. The subjects instructed in the method of loci recalled an average of about 26 words, compared to only about 7 words for subjects in the control group, who received no special instructions.

Keyword Method

Visual images are also useful when we need to form an association between a pair of items such as a person's name and face, or a foreign word and its English translation. However, there is a potential problem that you may recall from our earlier discussion of visual imagery: it's difficult to generate images to represent abstract words (Paivio, 1969). A way to avoid this problem is to employ the **keyword method, in which you associate a concrete word with an abstract word and generate an image to represent the concrete word.**

A very practical use of this method is to help you remember the names of people you meet. Just convert the name into a visual image and then link the image to a prominent feature of the person's face (Morris, Jones, & Hampson, 1978). The utility of this technique obviously depends on how easy it is to form an image from a name. Some names should be fairly easy, such as Smith (form an image of a blacksmith, perhaps hammering out a crooked nose). Other names, such as Gordon or Detterman, may require associating a concrete word to the name and then forming an image of the associated word. The associated word, which is the keyword, should sound like the name that's being learned. *Garden* is an example of a keyword for *Gordon*. And *debtor man* might be a good keyword for Detterman, if you formed an image of Mr. Detterman dressed in ragged clothes.

The keyword method has been used to enhance students' memory of foreign words (Atkinson & Raugh,

1975). For example, imagine that you're having difficulty remembering that *boulangerie* is French for *bakery*. To remember this French word you might use the keyword, *boo-lingerie*, and picture a ghost hanging lingerie in your favorite bakery.

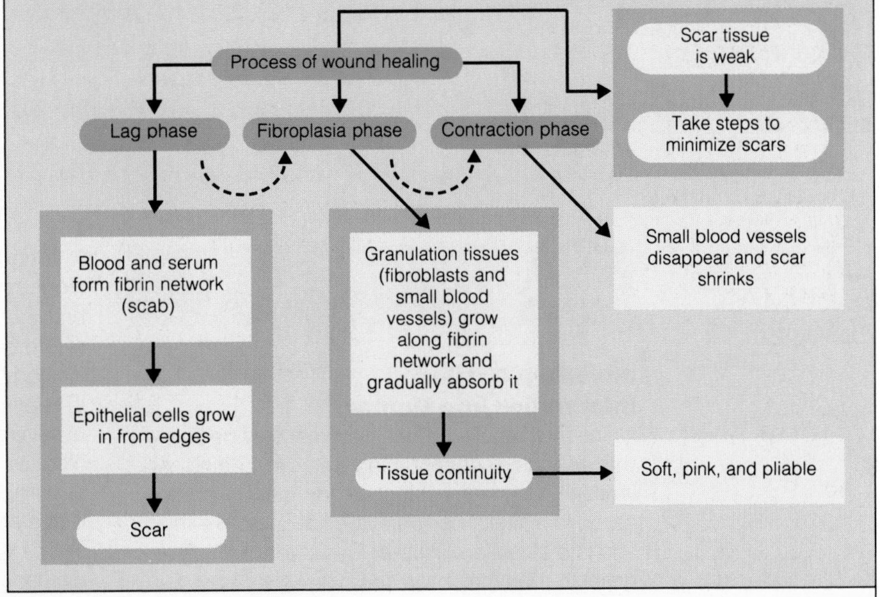

Organize Information

As you've learned, organizational frameworks play a critical role in long-term memory. Retention tends to be greater when information is well organized. Gordon Bower (1970) has shown that hierarchical organization is particularly helpful. It may therefore be a good idea to *outline* reading assignments, since outlining forces you to organize material hierarchically.

Along similar lines, Dansereau (1985) has experimented with a technique called networking in helping students to master information gleaned from textbooks. *Networking* involves organizing information into networks consisting of nodes and links. These networks resemble the *semantic networks* described by Collins and Loftus (1975). As students read a text, they try to identify important concepts or ideas (nodes) and represent their interrelationships (links) to form the network. Students are instructed to diagram their networks to create visual and spatial representations of how the material is organized.

Figure 7.33 A networking of ideas applied to material from a nursing textbook.

Figure 7.33 shows an example of a network from a chapter in a nursing textbook.

The advantage of networking was demonstrated in a study in which students read a 3000-word excerpt from a geology textbook (Holley et al., 1979). Students who were taught how to construct networks did significantly better on an essay test than students who used their normal study methods. However, the two groups did not differ in performance on short-answer or multiple-choice tests. This suggests that networking may help you to organize main ideas more than to improve your memory for details.

Take Advantage of Retrieval Cues

When your memory lapses, try to take advantage of any retrieval cues that happen to surface. For instance, if you think you know the first letter of a word that you're groping for, use that letter to guide your memory search. "Hunches" like this often *are* related to the forgotten information (Read & Bruce, 1982). Many people fail to appreciate the potential value of these retrieval cues and don't devote much thought to them. Also, remember the value of context cues. You may be able to jog your memory by reinstating the context in which you learned the forgotten information.

265

Human Memory

KEY IDEAS

Encoding: Getting Information into Memory

• The multifaceted process of memory begins with encoding. Attention facilitates encoding. Attention is inherently selective and has been compared to a filter. There is evidence of both early and late selection of input. This evidence suggests that we may have some flexibility in where we place our attention filter.

• According to the levels of processing theory, the kind of memory codes people create depends on which aspects of a stimulus are emphasized. A structural code, emphasizing physical structure, results in a rapid forgetting rate; a phonemic code, emphasizing pronunciation, results in an intermediate rate; and a semantic code, emphasizing meaning, results in a slow forgetting rate. These differences were apparent in our Featured Study.

• Elaboration enriches encoding by linking a stimulus to other information. Visual imagery works in much the same way, and creates two memory codes rather than just one. Encoding that emphasizes personal self-reference may be especially useful in facilitating retention.

Storage: Maintaining Information in Memory

• Information-processing theories of memory assert that people have three different kinds of memory stores: a sensory memory, a short-term memory, and a long-term memory. The sensory store preserves information in its original sensory form. Its maximum duration varies from about ¼ second to 2 seconds. Short-term memory is a limited-capacity memory that can maintain unrehearsed information for about 20 to 30 seconds. Short-term memory has a capacity of about seven (plus or minus two) chunks of information.

• Long-term memory is an unlimited capacity store that may hold information indefinitely. Several lines of evidence suggest that LTM storage may be permanent, but the evidence is not convincing. Information is transferred from STM to LTM primarily through rehearsal. LTM may consist of several divisions or separate stores. Declarative memory is memory for facts, while procedural memory is memory for actions and skills. Declarative memory can be subdivided into episodic memory, for personal facts, and semantic memory, for general facts.

• Psychologists have proposed several structures to represent the way people organize information in LTM. Conceptual hierarchies may be useful in handling categorical information. Semantic networks consist of concepts joined together by links that show how the concepts are related. A spreading activation model proposes that when a word is recognized, activation spreads along the paths of a network to activate closely associated words. A schema is an organized cluster of knowledge about a particular object or sequence of events. A particular kind of schema, called a script, specifies what people know about common activities such as visiting a doctor.

Retrieval: Getting Information Back Out of Memory

• A schema can provide a plan for searching memory when a person recalls associated ideas. Recall is often guided by partial information about the word or contextual information associated with the word. Reinstating the context of an event can facilitate recall. This factor may account for cases in which hypnosis appears to aid recall of previously forgotten information.

• Context cues may also play a role in state-dependent memory. State-dependent memory occurs when recall is facilitated because mood during encoding matches mood during retrieval. Our memories are not exact replicas of our past experiences. Memory is partially reconstructive.

Forgetting: When Memory Lapses

- Ebbinghaus's early studies of nonsense syllables suggested that we forget very rapidly. Subsequent research showed that Ebbinghaus's forgetting curve was exceptionally steep. Forgetting can be measured by asking people to either recall, recognize, or relearn information. Different methods often produce different estimates of forgetting and retention.
- Some forgetting, including pseudoforgetting, is due to ineffective encoding of information. Decay theory proposes that forgetting occurs spontaneously with the passage of time. It has proven difficult to show that decay occurs in long-term memory.
- Interference theory proposes that memory for other material causes forgetting. Evidence that either prior (proactive interference) or subsequent (retroactive interference) material can cause forgetting supports interference theory.
- Forgetting may also be a matter of retrieval failure. Retrieval may be prevented by motivated forgetting. According to the encoding specificity principle, the effectiveness of a retrieval cue depends on how well it corresponds to the memory code that represents the stored item.

In Search of the Memory Trace: The Physiology of Memory

- Memory traces may involve alterations in neurotransmitter release at specific locations or in localized neural circuits. Research on amnesia has implicated the hippocampus as a brain structure involved in memory. Research on the physiological basis of memory has provided many interesting leads, but the picture remains confusing.

Putting It in Perspective

- Our discussion of attention and memory enhances our understanding of why our experience of the world is highly subjective. Work in this area also shows that behavior is governed by multiple causes.

Application: Improving Everyday Memory

- Rehearsal, even when it involves overlearning, facilitates retention. Distributed practice tends to be more efficient than massed practice. It is wise to plan study sessions so as to minimize interference. Deep processing during rehearsal is critical. This deep processing may involve making the material personally meaningful. Meaningfulness can also be enhanced through the use of verbal mnemonics like acrostics, acronyms, and narrative methods.
- Visual imagery is a powerful device for improving memory. The link method, the method of loci, and the keyword method are mnemonic devices that depend on the value of visual imagery. Evidence also suggests that organization enhances retention, so strategies like outlining and networking may be valuable. When memory fails, partial information should be used as a cue to aid retrieval.

KEY TERMS

Amnesia
Anterograde amnesia
Attention
Biaural listening
Chunk
Clustering
Conceptual hierarchy
Decay theory
Declarative memory
Dichotic listening
Dual-coding theory
Elaboration
Encoding
Encoding specificity
  principle
Episodic memory
Flashbulb memories
Forgetting curve
Information-processing
  theories
Interference theory

Keyword method
Levels of processing
  theory
Lexical decision task
Link method
Long-term memory (LTM)
Method of loci
Mnemonic devices
Motivated forgetting
Nonsense syllables
Overlearning
Phonemic code
Primacy effect
Proactive interference
Procedural memory
Recall
Recency effect
Recognition
Rehearsal
Relearning

Retention
Retrieval
Retroactive interference
Retrograde amnesia
Schema
Script
Semantic code
Semantic memory
Semantic network
Sensory memory
Serial position effect
Short-term memory
  (STM)
State-dependent
  memory
Storage
Structural code
Tip-of-the-tongue
  phenomenon

KEY PEOPLE

Richard Atkinson &
  Richard Shiffrin
Gordon Bower
Fergus Craik & Robert
  Lockhart
Hermann Ebbinghaus
Elizabeth Loftus
George Miller
Wilder Penfield
Endel Tulving

CHAPTER EIGHT

LANGUAGE AND THOUGHT

With Stephen K. Reed
San Diego State University

LANGUAGE AND THOUGHT

D r. Watson—Mr. Sherlock Holmes," said Stamford, introducing us.

"How are you?" he said, cordially, gripping my hand with a strength for which I should hardly have given him credit. "You have been in Afghanistan, I perceive."

"How on earth did you know that?" I asked, in astonishment. (From *A Study in Scarlet* by Arthur Conan Doyle)

If you've ever read any Sherlock Holmes stories, you know that the great detective continually astonishes his stalwart companion, Dr. Watson, with his extraordinary deductions. Obviously, Holmes could not arrive at his conclusions without a chain of reasoning. Yet, to the detective, even an elaborate reasoning process is a simple, everyday act. Consider his feat of knowing at once, when he first meets Watson, that the doctor has been in Afghanistan. As Holmes explains later,

"I knew you came from Afghanistan. From long habit the train of thought ran so swiftly through my mind that I arrived at the conclusion without being conscious of the intermediate steps. There were such steps, however. The train of reasoning ran: 'Here is a gentleman of a medical type, but with the air of a military man. Clearly an army doctor, then. He has just come from the tropics, for his face is dark, and that is not the natural tint of his skin, for his wrists are fair. He has undergone hardship and sickness, as his haggard face says clearly. His left arm has been injured. He holds it in a stiff and unnatural manner. Where in the tropics could an English army doctor have seen much hardship and got his arm wounded? Clearly in Afghanistan.' The whole train of thought did not occupy a second."

Admittedly, Sherlock Holmes's deductive feats are fictional. But even to read about them appreciatively—let alone imagine them, as Sir Arthur Conan Doyle did—is a remarkably complex and sophisticated mental act. Our everyday thought processes seem ordinary to us only because we take them for granted, just as Holmes saw nothing extraordinary in what to him was a simple deduction.

Suppose we change our point of view and imagine what it would take to program a computer to mimic a relatively simple cognitive activity—say, finding a clock and reading the time. How hard would it be to design a computer that could perform this task? According to Naomi Weisstein, it would border on impossible:

If we gave the computer a list of states which would correspond to a clock, there would be an indefinite list through which the computer would have to search. As

the computer got closer to a clock, the size of the clock would change; hence each step towards the clock would . . . [produce] a new array [of stimuli] . . . But even if these problems could be solved, clocks can be any size or shape: modern "sunbursts," digital clocks, red streaks running around a hexagonal block, and so forth. An enumeration of all possible shapes and sizes, or even of all possible standard shapes and sizes just is not possible. (Quoted in Solso, 1988, pp. 467–468)

Some theorists would disagree with Weisstein's pessimistic conclusion about the possibility of programming a computer to recognize and read clocks. However, even those who believe that computers have unlimited potential to simulate human thought acknowledge that highly complex programs are required for computers to duplicate our performance of routine mental tasks. (Developing such programs is a field of research in its own right, called *artificial intelligence*.) In short, in comparison to computers, we're all Sherlock Holmeses, continually performing magical feats of thought. As we discussed in Chapter 4, even elementary perception involves elaborate cognitive processes: we must sort through distorted, constantly shifting perceptual inputs and deduce what's out there in the real world. Imagine then, the complexity of thought required to balance a checkbook, read a book, fix an automobile, or write a poem.

Of course, all this is not to say that our cognitive processes are flawless or unequaled. Computers are far superior to us at performing some types of tasks, and even your $10 calculator can surely run circles around you when it comes to computing square roots. As we'll see, some of the most interesting cognitive research focuses on ways in which our thinking can be limited, simplistic, or outright illogical.

As we noted in Chapter 1, the study of cognitive processes began to re-emerge in psychology during the 1950s. For many decades before the 1950s, the theoretical dominance of behaviorism discouraged the study of "unobservable" mental processes. Herbert Simon, one of the leading architects of the cognitive revolution in psychology, recalls that even as late as the early 1960s "you couldn't use a word like *mind* in a psychology journal—you'd get your mouth washed out with soap" (Holden, 1986). However, the 1950s saw major advances in the study of cognitive development (Piaget, 1954), memory (Miller, 1956), language (Chomsky, 1957), and other mental processes. Simon, for instance, helped develop the first computer programs designed to simulate human problem-solving strategies (Newell, Shaw, & Simon, 1958) and conducted research on decision

"You couldn't use a word like 'mind' in a psychology journal—you'd get your mouth washed out with soap."
HERBERT SIMON

Electronic circuits can be designed to produce *artificial intelligence*—a machine simulation of human or animal behavior. The circuitry in this "micromouse" enables it to find its way through a maze by detecting relevant aspects of its surroundings and controlling its movements to reach the goal. As impressive as this "behavior" is, the micromouse has a long way to go before it's smart enough to run away from a cat.

making that eventually earned him a Nobel Prize (in 1978).

In the previous chapter, we examined the process in human cognition that psychologists have studied the most—memory. In this chapter, we'll look at the other cognitive processes that have been the principal interests of psychologists—language use and development, problem solving and decision making (cognitive development is covered in an upcoming chapter [11] on human development). In exploring these topics, we'll address a variety of interesting questions, including the following:

• What, exactly, is language? Is it unique to humans?
• How do children develop the ability to use lan-

guage? Are we biologically programmed to acquire language?
• What makes written material easy or difficult to understand?
• How do we reason our way through problems? Do experts and novices approach problems differently?
• How are creative people different from others?
• How rational are we in making decisions?

We'll begin with an exploration of language, because language is clearly critical to such human activities as problem solving and decision making. Indeed, if you were to ask people, "What characteristic most distinguishes humans from other living creatures?" a great many would reply, "language." Would they be right? Let's find out.

LANGUAGE: TURNING THOUGHTS INTO WORDS

Consider the following conversation.

Teacher: What want you?
Student: Eat more apple.
Teacher: Who want eat more apple?
Student: Me Nim eat more apple.
Teacher: What color apple?
Student: Apple red.
Teacher: Want you more eat?
Student: Banana, raisin.

The sophistication of this exchange might not impress you—until you learn that the "student" is a 2½-year-old chimpanzee named Nim. The

conversation sounds odd in part because it was conducted in sign language. Herbert Terrace (1986) taught Nim to use sign language while raising the chimp like a human child in a human family.

If you look again at the conversation, you can see that Nim's responses are appropriate and apparently intelligent. Does this mean that language is *not* uniquely human? This question provides our point of departure for discussing *psycholinguistics—the study of the psychological mechanisms underlying the acquisition and use*

of language. Among the concerns of psycholinguists are how language is structured, how our understanding and use of language develops, and what factors account for our ability to acquire language in the first place. We'll complete our examination of language by looking at the highly complex activity you're engaged in right now—attempting to understand written text.

Communicating with Chimpanzees

Suppose you wanted to discover whether you could teach language to an animal. It's a good bet you'd pick an animal like the chimpanzee, an intelligent primate widely regarded as humans' closest cousin. But how would you go about teaching language to a chimp?

In early studies, researchers tried to teach chimps to *speak*. These efforts were not very fruitful. For instance, after 6 years of patient hard work, Hayes and Hayes (1951) managed to train a chimp named Viki to say a grand total of three words (*mama, papa,* and *cup*). Investigators concluded that chimps simply didn't have the appropriate vocal apparatus to acquire human speech.

But is speech the only way to use language? Of course not. At this moment you're reading a written expression of language. Writing may not be a realistic form of expression for chimps, either, but what about other nonoral expressions of language? Once researchers working with apes shifted away from using speech as the vehicle for teaching language, some interesting things began to happen.

David Premack (1971), for example, used small, plastic symbols of various colors and shapes

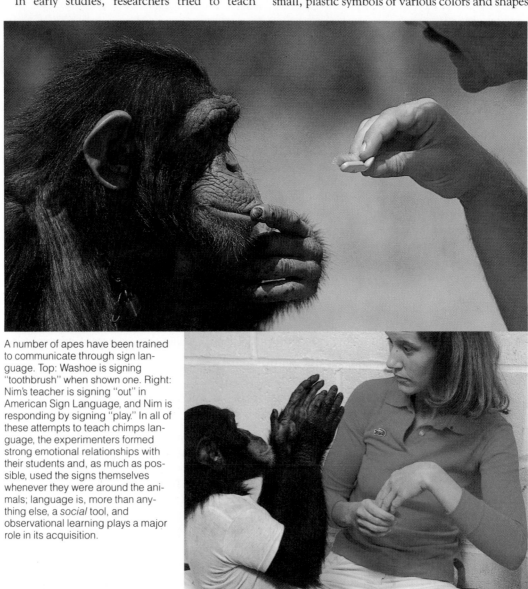

A number of apes have been trained to communicate through sign language. Top: Washoe is signing "toothbrush" when shown one. Right: Nim's teacher is signing "out" in American Sign Language, and Nim is responding by signing "play." In all of these attempts to teach chimps language, the experimenters formed strong emotional relationships with their students and, as much as possible, used the signs themselves whenever they were around the animals; language is, more than anything else, a *social* tool, and observational learning plays a major role in its acquisition.

as substitutes for written words. Premack taught a chimp named Sarah to arrange these arbitrary symbols on a magnetic board to construct simple "sentences" (see Figure 8.1).

Other researchers tried training chimps to use a nonoral human language: American Sign Language (ASL). ASL is a complex language of hand gestures and facial expressions used by thousands of deaf people in the United States. The first effort of this sort was begun by Allen and Beatrice Gardner (1969), who worked with a female chimp named Washoe. The Gardners approached the task as if Washoe were a deaf child. They signed to her regularly, rewarded her imitations, and taught her more complex signs by physically moving her hands through the required motions.

In 4 years, Washoe acquired a sign vocabulary of roughly 160 words. She learned to combine these words into simple sentences, such as "Washoe sorry," "Gimme flower," and "More fruit." Occasionally, these sentences included as many as five words, such as "You me go there in." The Gardners concluded that Washoe's language development was roughly equivalent to that of a 3-year-old human.

Although we can evidently communicate with chimpanzees through sign language, scientists heatedly debate whether the chimps are genuinely acquiring language. For example, despite his apparent success with Nim, Herbert Terrace (1986) doubts whether chimps can really form sentences. Initially Terrace believed that his research showed that a chimp could create a sentence. However, he began to reconsider after carefully examining videotapes of Nim's conversations. Nim's constructions were far less original than those of a

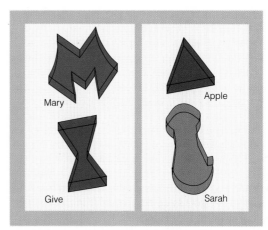

Figure 8.1 Four symbols used by Sarah, the chimpanzee in the Premack (1971) study. Since animals lack the vocal apparatus needed to produce human speech, psychologists have tried a number of devices to give animals the means of producing or manipulating words. After experimenting with a joystick like those used in computer games, Premack settled on distinctive plastic shapes as Sarah's word equivalents.

young child, and the chimp showed little progress toward mastering the *rules* of language. Many of Nim's signs repeated, at least in part, the signs made by a caretaker. Terrace concluded that Nim's sentences were the products of imitation and operant conditioning, rather than spontaneous generations based on the rules of language. After watching films of the Gardners' training efforts, he drew the same conclusion about Washoe. Terrace believes that Washoe, Nim, and other chimps have simply learned to make certain responses to earn reinforcement, much as a pigeon can learn to peck a disk for a food reward (Terrace et al., 1979).

In spite of these reservations, Terrace has argued that research on communicating with chimps should continue in order to determine how much progress chimps can make. The Featured Study for this chapter describes how one bright young chimp learned to communicate at a more advanced level than other chimpanzees, including Nim and Washoe.

CHAPTER
EIGHT
FEATURED
STUDY

Can Chimps Learn Language?

The purpose of this study was to provide a developmental account of how a chimpanzee acquired the ability to communicate with his caretakers by touching geometric symbols on a keyboard. Each symbol represented a word.

The chimp, named Kanzi, was born at the Yerkes Primate Research Center in Atlanta and remained with his mother until he was 2½ years old. His mother was trained to communicate with her caretakers by using the keyboard. Kanzi was permitted to attend his mother's training sessions, but his interest in the keyboard was sporadic. Following separation from his mother, Kanzi's attitude

toward the keyboard showed an unexpected change. He appeared to search for particular symbols and his behavior suggested that he had learned that particular symbols referred to particular items. This report summarizes Kanzi's language development from 2½ years to 4 years of age.

Method

Subject. The subject was a male pygmy chimpanzee. The *Pan paniscus* species has not been studied much for its ability to acquire language, although evidence suggests that pygmy chim-

Investigators: Sue Savage-Rumbaugh, Kelly McDonald, Rose A. Sevcik, William D. Hopkins, and Elizabeth Rupert (Yerkes Regional Primate Research Center, Emory University and the Language Research Center, Georgia State University)

Source: Spontaneous symbol acquisition and communicative use by pygmy chimpanzees (*Pan paniscus*). *Journal of Experimental Psychology: General, 115* (1986), 211–235.

panzees may be more intelligent than other apes.

Procedure. Researchers kept a complete record of all of Kanzi's utterances over a 17-month period beginning when he was 2½ years old. The symbols were automatically recorded by a computer-monitored keyboard when the chimp was indoors. When outdoors, Kanzi pointed to the symbols on a thin laminated "pointing board"; these utterances were recorded by hand and entered into the computer later. During all daily activities with Kanzi (playing, eating, resting, traveling in the woods, and so forth), the caretakers used the graphic symbols to communicate with each other and with Kanzi (see Figure 8.2).

Results

Kanzi made rapid progress in his ability to communicate appropriately with symbols. At the end of the 17-month study he had acquired 50 words and had used them in 800 different combinations. The symbols primarily described foods, actions (such as chase, groom, grab), and locations (trailer, treehouse, refrigerator). Kanzi's ability to combine symbols occurred very early, but he did not often use this skill. Symbol combinations accounted for only 6% of his utterances.

A large proportion of Kanzi's combinations were spontaneous (see Figure 8.3); that is, they were not elicited by the teacher. A second important aspect of Kanzi's efforts is related to the issue of whether chimpanzees can construct a sentence. In contrast to Nim, whose three-word constructions almost always involved Nim receiving something ("Banana eat Nim"), Kanzi produced three-word combinations in which he distinguished between the doer and the recipient of the action. To do this, Kanzi had to make use of word

Figure 8.2 Communicative use of symbols by a pygmy chimpanzee. Kanzi learned to use computer-controlled symbol boards by watching his mother and his caretaker use them—an example of observational learning. Top: Chasing was one of Kanzi's favorite activities, and the symbol for chase was the first one he learned to use. Bottom left: Kanzi selecting the symbol for another game, "grab." Bottom right: One of Kanzi's portable boards.

order to distinguish between statements such as "Person chase Kanzi" and "Kanzi chase Person." To specify whether he wanted to chase or be chased, Kanzi had to differentiate between these combinations in a way that seems to involve the use of grammatical rules.

Discussion

This study extends previous studies of chimpanzees' ability to acquire a language. It provides stronger support for the hypothesis that chimps may be able to follow rules of language in generating spontaneous sentences. The report also describes the first instance in which a chimp used symbols without specific training. Kanzi first acquired the use of symbols through observing his mother's responses at the keyboard.

Comment

Kanzi's accomplishments are impressive. Nonetheless, theorists still wonder whether chimps like Kanzi are really using gestural signs and computer keys as symbols in the same way that humans use words. In essence, the critics chorus, "But is it *really* language?" To shed more light on this controversy, let's examine the properties and structure of language and then reconsider the question.

Figure 8.3 Examples of Kanzi's utterances. This excerpt includes examples of Kanzi's appropriate and apparently spontaneous utterances ("chase" and "yes chase"), together with the investigators' coding of them.

Utterance: Kanzi seems disappointed when Liz and Patty stop chasing him, and he runs back toward them and asks them to continue, by touching "chase" at the keyboard, and then runs again down the road with the keys. They refuse, indicating "no chase" at the keyboard and commenting in English that they are tired and do not feel like chasing anymore. Kanzi, not wanting to take no for an answer, repeats his request in the same manner three more times. Finally, Liz states very emphatically "no chase," speaking firmly and tapping the symbols loudly. Kanzi just as firmly then replies "yes chase." Because Kanzi is not often so adamant, Liz and Patty give in and chase him a little farther down the road even though they are quite winded at this point.

Coding: These utterances are all coded as spontaneous correct requests.

What Is Language?

A *language* is a collection of symbols, and rules for combining those symbols, that can be used to create an infinite variety of messages. This definition includes three critical properties.

First, language is *symbolic*. We use spoken sounds and written words to represent objects, actions, events, and ideas. The word *lamp*, for instance, refers to a class of objects that have certain properties. Our use of language symbols is flexible and complex. This flexibility is apparent when you consider the diversity of objects that may be called by the same name (consider the diversity of lamps, for example).

Notice also that the symbols used in a language are arbitrary. That is, there is typically no built-in relationship between the look or sound of words and the objects or actions they stand for. Take, for instance, the writing object that you may well now have in your hand. It's represented by the word *pen* in English, *stylo* in French, and *pluma* in Spanish. While the symbols employed in a language are arbitrary, each has a shared meaning for the people who use that language, even though a word may not mean precisely the same thing to everyone.

Second, language is *generative*. That is, a limited number of symbols can be combined in an infinite variety of ways to *generate* an endless array of messages. We all have some "stock sayings," but every day we create sentences that we have never spoken before and understand sentences we

have never before encountered (like this one).

Third, language is *structured*. In other words, we follow rules in combining symbols to make meaningful utterances. For example, you might say, "The swimmer jumped into the pool," but you would never recombine the same words to say, "Pool the into the jumped swimmer."

For the most part, we learn to follow the rules of language automatically, with little conscious effort. These rules allow us to be spontaneous and inventive with language and still understand each other. Structure, then, is one of the key properties of a genuine language. Let's examine it in more detail.

The Structure of Language

Human languages have a hierarchical structure. As Figure 8.4 shows, sounds are combined into meaningful units, which are combined into words, which are combined into phrases, which are combined into sentences.

PHONEMES

At the base of the language hierarchy are ***phonemes*, the smallest units of sound in a spoken language.** Considering that a standard unabridged dictionary of the English language (*Webster's Third New International*) contains more than 450,000 word entries, you might imagine that there must be a huge number of phonemes. In fact, linguists estimate that humans are capable of producing only about 100 such basic sounds.

Figure 8.4 An analysis of a simple English sentence. As this example shows, verbal language has a hierarchical structure. At the base of the hierarchy are the *phonemes*, which are units of vocal *sound* that do not, in themselves, have meaning. The smallest units of *meaning* in a language are *morphemes*, which include not only root words but such meaning-carrying units as the past-tense suffix *-ed* and the plural *-s*. Complex rules of syntax govern how the words constructed from morphemes may be combined into phrases, and phrases into meaningful statements, or sentences.

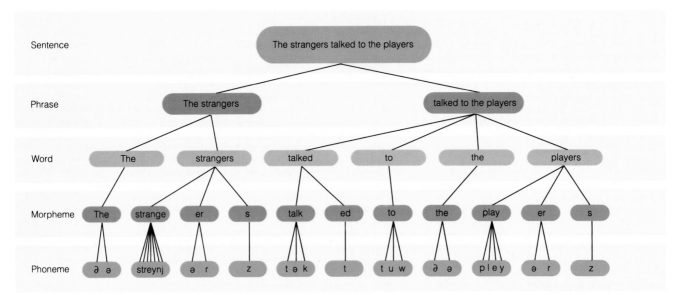

Moreover, no one language uses all of these sounds; different languages use different subsets of the total collection of phonemes.

For all its rich vocabulary, the English language is composed of about 40 phonemes, corresponding roughly to the 26 letters of the alphabet plus several variations. Some representative English phonemes are listed in Table 8.1. A letter in the alphabet is represented by more than one phoneme if it has more than one pronunciation. For example, the letter *e* has two pronunciations: the long-*e* sound in *decoy* and the short-*e* sound in *depth*. The letter *a* is pronounced differently in the words *father, had, call,* and *take*. Each of these pronunciations is represented by a different phoneme. In addition, some phonemes are represented by combinations of letters, such as *ch* and *th*. From this handful of basic sounds, English speakers are able to generate all the words in the English language—and to invent new ones besides.

MORPHEMES

To generate meaning, we combine phonemes into **morphemes, the smallest units of meaning in a language.** Morphemes include root words as well as prefixes and suffixes. Many words, like *fire, guard,* and *friend,* consist of a single morpheme. Many others represent combinations of morphemes. For example, the word *unfriendly* consists of three morphemes—the root word *friend,* the prefix *un,* and the suffix *ly.* Each of the morphemes contributes to the meaning of the entire word.

The suffix changes the noun *friend* into the adjective *friendly* and the prefix produces an adjective (*unfriendly*) with the opposite meaning.

SYNTAX

Of course, most of our utterances consist of more than a single word. As we've already noted, we don't combine words randomly. **Syntax is a sys-**

Table 8.1 Examples of Some English-Language Phonemes

SYMBOL	EXAMPLES
p	*p*at, a*pp*le
b	*b*at, am*b*le
d	*d*ip, love*d*
g	*g*uard, o*g*re
f	*f*at, *ph*ilosophy
s	*s*ap, pa*ss*, pea*c*e
z	*z*ip, pad*s*, *x*ylophone
y	*y*ou, ba*y*, fe*u*d
w	*w*itch, q*u*een
l	*l*eaf, pa*l*ace
i	b*ee*t, b*ea*t, bel*ie*ve
i	b*i*t, *i*njury
e	*a*te, b*ai*t, *eigh*t
u	b*oo*t, tw*o*, thr*ough*
U	p*u*t, f*oo*t, c*ou*ld
oy	b*oy*, d*oi*ly
ay	b*i*te, s*igh*t, *i*sland
š	*sh*oe, mu*sh*, deduc*t*ion

Source: Adapted from Moates & Schumacher, 1980

tem of rules that specify how words can be combined into phrases and sentences. A simple rule of syntax is that declarative sentences (sentences that make a statement) must have both a *subject* (what the speaker is talking about) and a *predicate* (a statement about the subject). "The sound of cars is annoying" is a sentence, but one phrase, "The sound of cars" is not, because it lacks a predicate.

Rules of syntax underlie all our language use, even though we may not be aware of them. For example, even if they can't verbalize the rule, virtually all English speakers know that an *article* (such as *the*) comes before the word it modifies (you would never say *swimmer the* instead of *the swimmer*). How we learn the sometimes complicated rules that govern our use of language is one of the major puzzles investigated by psycholinguists.

Having reviewed the properties and structure of language, what can we conclude about the ape-language controversy? Have chimpanzees such as Sarah, Washoe, Nim, and Kanzi genuinely begun to acquire language? Let's take another look.

Another Look at the Ape-Language Controversy

We noted that language is characterized by three key properties: it's symbolic, generative, and structured. The communication abilities of the trained chimps appear to meet the first two criteria. The chimps have acquired the use of symbols, and they have generated many different combinations of these symbols. (Admittedly, their combinations have generally been limited to two or three words, but no one expected them to win literary prizes.) Until recently, however, there was little reason to believe that the chimps *followed rules* in generating their word combinations. Researchers who called these word combinations "sentences" were using the concept loosely. This is what makes Kanzi's apparent mastery of some syntax so dramatic (see Figure 8.5). If replicated with other chimps, this finding would suggest that true language use is not a uniquely human characteristic.

Even if language is not unique to humans, however, we do appear to be *uniquely well suited* for learning and using language. There's no comparison between our linguistic abilities and those of apes or other animals. As remarkable as the language studies with apes are, they should make us even more impressed with the fluency, flexibility, and complexity of human language. A normal human toddler quickly surpasses even the most verbal and carefully trained ape. In mastering language, children outstrip chimps the way jet air-

Figure 8.5 Three levels of language structure. These sentences display increasingly complex syntax and thus greater structure. Nim's utterance is a string of words without any apparent rules for combining them. To Nim, "banana eat Nim" and "Nim eat banana" are the same sentence. Kanzi's utterance displays more structure, because the *order* of the words is significant. For example, the recipient of the action occupies the last position in the sentence. Even relatively simple human sentences introduce more complex rules of syntax, as in the ordered combination of a verb and an adverb to make a single predicate.

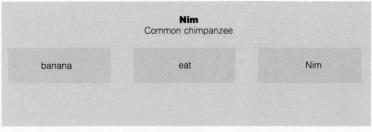

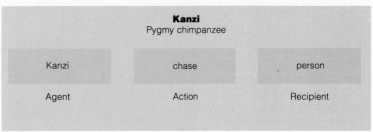

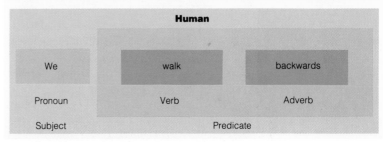

planes outrace horse-drawn buggies. By the time most children enter school, they already have a vocabulary of thousands of words that they can combine in statements much longer and more complex than the simple combinations produced by chimpanzees.

How does this remarkable development of language happen? What stages do children go through in progressing from babbling to sophisticated speech? The next section takes up these questions.

Milestones in Language Development

Learning to use language requires learning a number of skills that become important at different points in a child's development (Siegler, 1986). Before babies can be understood (at least by people other than their immediate family), they need to produce phonemes clearly enough to make recognizable words. After children learn to pronounce words, they have to decide which ones to use, as the meaning of words becomes important. About 6 months after children start to say single words, they begin to combine words, and rules of

Table 8.2 Overview of Typical Language Development

AGE	GENERAL CHARACTERISTICS
Months	
1–3	*Undifferentiated crying.* Vocalizes randomly and coos.
4–6	*Babbling.* Verbalizes in response to speech of others; responses approximate human intonational patterns.
7–11	Moves tongue with vocalizations (lalling); vocalizes recognition; babbling "drifts" toward using phonemes of native language.
12	*First word.*
18	*One-word sentence stage.* Has developed well-established jargon; uses nouns primarily.
Years	
2	*Two-word sentence stage.* Speaks functionally complete sentences; uses more pronouns and verbs.
2.5	*Three-word sentence stage.* Uses telegraphic speech.
3	Uses complete simple active sentence structure; uses sentences to tell stories that are understood by others; uses plurals.
3.5	*Expanded grammatical forms.* Expresses concepts with words; uses four-word sentences.
4	Uses imaginary speech; uses five-word sentences.
5	*Well-developed and complex syntax.* Uses more complex syntax. Uses more complex forms to tell stories.

Source: Adapted from Hull & Hull, 1973

syntax become important. We'll examine this sequence of development by looking first at how children learn to pronounce words, then at their use of single words, and finally at their ability to combine words to form sentences. Consult Table 8.2 for an overview of the developmental sequence we are about to examine.

MOVING TOWARD PRODUCING WORDS

Babies can't talk right away, in part because of their limited ability to produce sounds. Before they can start to use language, they must learn to produce specific sounds at will and then to combine them with other sounds to produce words. How does this ability to make sounds develop? Kaplan and Kaplan (1971) suggest that this progression involves four stages:

1. *Crying.* As new parents know all too well, a baby's first sounds are produced by crying. What the cries mean is often difficult to determine on the basis of the sounds alone. Often we must consider the context to identify whether the baby is bored, hungry, or wet.

2. *Cooing.* By the end of their first month, babies

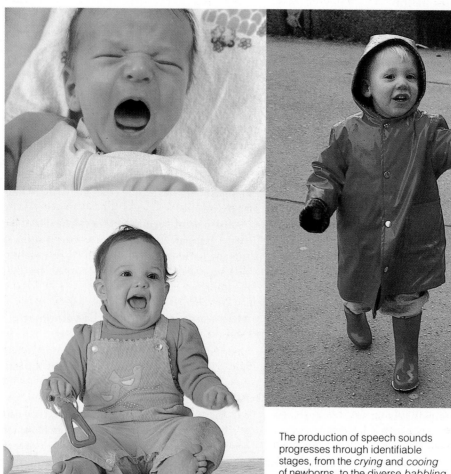

The production of speech sounds progresses through identifiable stages, from the *crying* and *cooing* of newborns, to the diverse *babbling* sounds of a 6-month-old, to the more communicative *speech* of a toddler.

Table 8.3 Examples of Children's First Words and Overextensions Based on Shape

WORD	FIRST REFERENT	DOMAIN OF APPLICATION
buti	ball	toy, radish, stone spheres on park gates
nénin	breast	button on garment, point of bare elbow, eye in portrait, face in portrait, face in photo
gumene	coat button	collar stud, door handle, light switch, anything small and round
ticktock	watch	clocks, all clocks and watches, gas meter, firehose wound on spool, bath scale with round dial
baw	ball	apple, grapes, eggs, squash, bell clapper, anything round
kotibaiz	bars of cot (crib side)	large toy abacus, toast rack, picture of building with columned facade
tee	stick	cane, umbrella, ruler, (old-fashioned) razor, board of wood, all sticklike objects
mum	horse	cow, calf, pig, moose, all four-legged animals

Source: Clark, 1983

make sounds other than crying. They produce cooing sounds by placing the tongue near the back of the mouth and rounding the lips.

3. *Babbling.* By 6 months, infants can produce a wide variety of sounds that correspond to phonemes used in many different languages. They can also form their first syllables by combining vowel and consonant sounds.

4. *Speech.* The variety of phonemes babies produce decreases toward the end of the first year. Infants gradually produce sounds that occur in the language they hear around them more frequently and use sounds that do not occur in that language less frequently. This movement toward the phonemes used in the child's native tongue is called *babbling drift.* At around 10 to 12 months, most children begin to utter sounds that correspond to words.

This developmental sequence helps to explain why most infant's first words are similar—even in different languages (Siegler, 1986). The initial words resemble the syllables that infants most often babble spontaneously. For example, words such as *dada, mama,* and *papa* are names for parents in many languages because they consist of sounds that are easy to produce. The babbles of French, American, and Chinese babies are, in fact, indistinguishable at 5 months (Nakazima, 1962). Beginning at about 6 months, however, the sounds become differentiated, and by the end of the first year they resemble many of the characteristics of the native language. By this time, children produce sounds that have meaning for them even though they may differ from adult words (see Table 8.3 for examples). These sounds serve as children's first words and, if used consistently, are understood by parents.

USING WORDS

Children usually utter their first words around their first birthday. After this milestone, their vocabulary grows slowly at first. Most youngsters can say between 3 and 50 words by 18 months. Soon, however, their vocabularies begin to grow at a dizzying pace. By the age of 6, an average child has a vocabulary of 8000 to 14,000 words (Carey, 1977). To build such a large vocabulary, a child must learn about 5 to 8 new words every day!

Until they accumulate large vocabularies, toddlers must try to express themselves with only a few words. This results in **overextensions, in which a word is incorrectly used to describe a wider set of objects or actions than it is meant to.** For example, a child might use the word *ball* for anything round—oranges, apples, even the moon. Overextensions usually appear in children's speech between age 1 and 2½ and last up to several months (Clark, 1983). These mistakes show that toddlers are actively trying to learn the rules of language—albeit with mixed success.

As Table 8.3 indicates, overextensions are usually based on the appearance of objects, particularly an object's shape. For example, a child who learned to call a watch a *ticktock* used the same word to refer to a gas meter and a bath scale with a round dial.

A major cause of overextensions is that children simply lack the appropriate words for many objects. For example, a child who uses the word *apple* to refer to a variety of round objects—balls, tomatoes, cherries, and so on—may be able to consistently identify an apple among these objects (Thomson & Chapman, 1977), which suggests that the child knows what the word *apple* should refer to, but hasn't yet learned what to call the other objects and so calls them apples also. As children acquire larger vocabularies, they use overextensions less often (Clark, 1983).

While very young children increase their ability to communicate as they learn new words, they remain unable to express themselves in sentences. They compensate for this limitation by using single words to express complex thoughts. **Holophrases are single-word utterances that represent the meaning of several words.** Young children use single words as adults use sentences because they lack the knowledge of syntax necessary to form a sentence (Greenfield & Smith, 1976).

Children's one-word phrases often communicate meaning effectively, particularly when they accompany gestures or changes in intonation (Barrett, 1982). Children's use of these words suggests that they are careful to select the word that will convey their intentions. For example, a child who wants a banana will say *banana* rather than *want* because *banana* is the more informative term (Greenfield & Smith, 1976)—there are many things a child could want, but relatively few reasons why a child would be interested in a banana. Thus, even before children know syntax, they can express complete thoughts by naming those aspects of a situation that are the most critical (Greenfield, 1982).

COMBINING WORDS

Emphasis on the most critical elements of meaning continues when children begin to combine words. Usually near the end of their second year (Carroll, 1986), they begin to make simple constructions such as *allgone baby*. These early combinations have been characterized as "telegraphic" because they resemble telegrams, in which nonessential words are left out. **Telegraphic speech consists mainly of content words; articles, prepositions, and other less critical words are omitted.** Thus, a child might say, "Give doll" rather than "Please give me the doll."

CONCEPT CHECK 8.1
Tracking Language Development

Check your understanding of how language skills progress in youngsters. Number the utterances below to indicate the developmental sequence in which they would probably occur. The answers can be found in Appendix A in the back of the book.

_____ 1. "Doggie," while pointing to a cow.
_____ 2. "The dogs runned away."
_____ 3. "Doggie run."
_____ 4. "The dogs ran away."
_____ 5. "Doggie," while pointing to a dog.

After children begin to combine words, their vocal expressions steadily become longer (Brown, 1973). By the end of their third year, most children can express complex ideas such as the plural (*the girls walk*) or the past tense (*the girl walked*). However, their efforts to learn the rules of language continue to generate revealing mistakes. They routinely overgeneralize rules and use them in irregular cases where they do not apply. For example, children will say things like "The girl goed home" or "I hitted the ball."

Children don't learn the fine points of grammar and usage in a single leap, but gradually acquire them in several small steps. For example, in learning to ask questions, children begin by changing only the intonation (*Daddy go?* rather than the factual statement *Daddy go*). Later, they add words such as *what* or *where* at the beginning of a sentence to produce questions (*Where daddy go?*). It's not until after 3 years of age that children use auxiliary ("helping") verbs (*be, can, do, have*) to produce proper questions (*Where did daddy go?*) (Klima & Bellugi, 1966).

REFINING LANGUAGE SKILLS

Youngsters make their largest strides in language development in their first 4 to 5 years, but they continue to refine their language skills during their school-age years also. They generate longer and more complicated sentences as they receive formal training in written language.

As their language skills develop, school-age children begin to appreciate ambiguities in language and can, for instance, recognize two possible meanings in sentences such as "Visiting relatives can be bothersome." This interest in ambiguities indicates that they're developing **metalinguistic awareness—the ability to reflect on the use of language.** They begin to think about language as a system of rules. As metalinguistic awareness grows, children begin to "play" with language, coming up with puns and jokes.

In the final analysis, what's most striking about children's language development is how swiftly it occurs. Bright, mature college students often struggle mightily to learn a foreign language, yet toddlers acquire a decent mastery of their native tongue in a mere 30 months or so. How do they do it? Theorists have proposed several explanations of language acquisition. We examine these theories in the next section.

Theories of Language Acquisition

One of the perplexing aspects of the first 60 or 70 years of psychology's history is how little interest psychologists showed in language (Lachman, Lachman, & Butterfield, 1979). Psychologists interested in "verbal learning" mostly studied how subjects learned and remembered meaningless associations, such as an arbitrary pairing of the number 63 and the letter L. Natural language acquisition was virtually ignored. By the mid-1950s, however, the behaviorists began to extend the principles of conditioning and reinforcement to new problems, one of them being how we acquire language. Their provocative ideas stimulated rejoinders from two other theoretical perspectives, which can be characterized as nativist and cognitive perspectives. You'll see that the attempts to explain our grasp of language remain theoretical: so far there is no one theory that has all the answers.

LEARNING THEORIES

The behaviorist approach to language was first outlined by the influential American psychologist B. F. Skinner. In his book *Verbal Behavior*, Skinner (1957) argued that children learn a language the same way that they learn everything else: through imitation, reinforcement and the other established principles of learning.

According to Skinner, vocalizations that are not reinforced drop out, and the remainder are shaped by conditioning until they are correct. Behaviorists assert that by withholding reinforcement parents can encourage their children to correctly pronounce words and learn other aspects of language (Staats & Staats, 1963). For example, a parent may initially give a child a drink of water when the child is only approximately correct in pronunciation (*wahwah*). But as the child grows older, the parent may wait for a closer approximation (*watah*) and finally the correct pronunciation before supplying the drink.

Learning theories also use the principles of imitation and reinforcement to explain how children learn syntax. According to the behaviorists' view, children learn how to construct sentences by imitating the sentences of adults and older children. If children's imitative statements are understood, parents are able to answer their questions or respond to their requests, thus reinforcing their verbal behavior. Learning theory asserts that parents also directly shape their children's language by providing feedback, translating understandable but ungrammatical statements into correct grammatical form.

According to behavioral theory, children learn to produce sentences by learning associations between adjacent words in the sentence. Skinner (1957) maintains that each word in a sentence serves as a stimulus for the word that follows it. In the sentence *The boy hit the ball*, the word *the* is a stimulus for the response *boy*, and the word *boy* is a stimulus for the word *hit*. According to Skinner, then, the speaker of a language would have to learn which words (possible responses) could follow any other word (stimulus) in a sentence.

NATIVIST THEORIES

Early in his career, Noam Chomsky subscribed to the behavioral view of language. However, he soon uncovered basic shortcomings in Skinner's explanation of language acquisition. Chomsky (1959, 1965) pointed out that there are an infinite number of sentences in a language. It's therefore unreasonable to expect that people could learn a language by learning associations between all possible adjacent words. Consider a word like *the*. There are countless words that could follow *the*; we never learn all of them. When you consider all the words that can possibly occur in a sentence and all the words that could possibly follow each word, you can see that learning associations would be a very inefficient way to learn a language.

Research findings have also challenged the behaviorist position that children learn to construct correct sentences through reinforcement. Most of the evidence indicates that parents respond to meaning and factual accuracy in their youngsters' speech rather than to grammar. Unless they are making a conscious attempt to teach proper grammar, parents reinforce factually accurate statements and correct factually inaccurate statements regardless of the grammar used. If a mother is curling her daughter's hair, she might approve the ungrammatical statement *Her curl my hair*. In other words, parents appear to engage in little of the language shaping that is critical to the explanation of language development proposed by learning theory (Brown & Hanlon, 1970; Maratsos, 1983).

An alternative theory favored by Chomsky (1968, 1975) is that humans are born with an innate or "native" capacity to learn language (in this sense, *native* is a variation on the word *nature* as it's used in the "nature versus nurture" debate). According to *nativist theory*, we have special abilities that equip us with a biologically "built-in" *language acquisition device*. Why does Chomsky believe that children possess an innate capacity for learning language? One reason is that children acquire language so quickly. How could they acquire so complex a skill in such a short time unless they have a built-in capacity for it? Another reason is that the general course of language development is rather similar for all languages, suggesting that children all over the world are guided by the same innate capabilities.

"Even at low levels of intelligence, at pathological levels, we find a command of language that is totally unattainable by an ape."
NOAM CHOMSKY

Figure 8.6 Phrase-structure and transformational rules. According to Chomsky, our mastery of rules of syntax explains how we quickly learn to produce an enormous variety of meaningful statements. Phrase-structure rules allow us to combine words and phrases into sentences, while transformational rules allow us to convert sentences to new statements with a shared core of meaning.

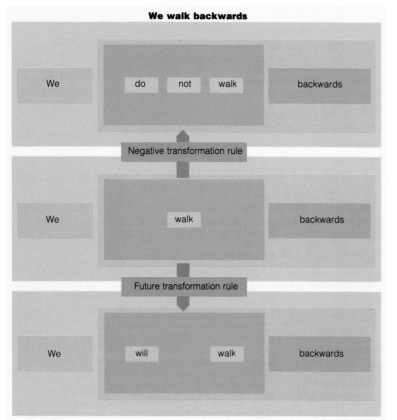

According to Chomsky, the language acquisition device helps children learn the *rules of language*, not specific verbal responses and associations, as Skinner had proposed. Chomsky asserts that youngsters' application of rules explains many of their early errors in language. For example, a standard rule for constructing the past tense is to add *-ed* to the end of a verb. The overuse of this rule produces incorrect verbs such as *goed*, *eated*, and *thinked*. These kinds of errors are commonplace, and they indicate that rules affect children's acquisition of language (Brown, 1973). Furthermore, mistakes such as these are inconsistent with Skinner's emphasis on imitation because most adult speakers don't use ungrammatical words like *goed*. Children can't imitate things they don't hear.

In his effort to account for our acquisition of syntax, Chomsky proposed that children gradually master two sets of rules: *phrase-structure* rules and *transformational* rules (see Figure 8.6). **Phrase-structure rules specify how we can combine words into phrases and phrases into sentences.** Does this bring back vague memories of

diagramming sentences in school? If so, you're remembering how you used these rules. You may have been taught how to break down a sentence into parts by first dividing it into a noun phrase and a verb phrase and then dividing the noun phrase into an adjective and a noun, and the verb phrase into an adverb and a verb. In performing these divisions, we identify which words in a sentence are grouped together.

Phrase-structure rules do not explain how to modify a sentence to form a similar sentence. For example, how can we change (1) an active statement into a passive statement, (2) a positive statement into a negative statement, or (3) an assertion into a question? Given the sentence *The boy hit the ball*, a change to the passive produces *The ball was hit by the boy*. A change to a negative statement produces *The boy did not hit the ball*. A change to a question produces *Did the boy hit the ball?* In each case the modification transforms an entire sentence into another, closely related sentence. To account for such changes, **transformational rules specify how simple declarative sentences can be rearranged into questions, negatives, and other types of sentences.**

COGNITIVE THEORIES

Many psychologists who study cognitive development view language development differently than Chomsky. The nativist theory advocated by Chomsky has been criticized on two counts. First, it isn't much of an explanation. Chomsky proposes that humans have an innate "language acquisition device," but what *is* a language acquisition device, how does it work, and what are the neural mechanisms involved? The concept is terribly vague. Second, efforts to verify that children learn transformational rules have not been very successful. Children undeniably learn rules of language, but the rules they acquire appear to be different from the transformational rules Chomsky proposed (Carroll, 1986).

To Chomsky, language acquisition has its own unique and separate pattern and laws of development. In contrast, *cognitive theories* of language acquisition argue (1) that language and thought are intertwined throughout development, (2) that language reflects the quality of thought as the child becomes more mature, and (3) that, consequently, to understand how language develops, we need to study the overall course of children's cognitive development.

Jean Piaget (1983) is a prominent advocate of the cognitive view. Piaget asserts that language development depends on cognitive development. According to this notion, as children begin to think in terms of symbols representing absent objects, they begin to use language. Further developments in language use reflect further progress in thinking. For instance, if children begin to add *-ed* to verbs to express past tense, it's because they understand the *idea* of the past, not a linguistic rule.

A central assumption of cognitive theories of language acquisition is that children are born with limited information-processing capacities. Like other complex tasks, language places great demands on those limited capacities (Siegler, 1986). Speaking effectively requires clear pronunciation, the correct ordering of words, and the communication of coherent thoughts. Children develop this skill by listening carefully to pronunciation, paying attention to and remembering the order of words, and emphasizing meaning in their conversations.

At present, the cognitive perspective guides the lion's share of research on language acquisition. Whether it will succeed in providing a more complete account of language acquisition than the behavioral and nativist perspectives remains to be seen. The cognitive perspective holds promise, but thus far our understanding of language acquisition remains unsatisfactory.

Cognitive psychologists' interest in how people produce and understand meaningful statements applies to adults as well as to children. To understand a text or a speech, we have to understand the ideas in a sentence, and we have to be able to relate the ideas in one sentence to the ideas in another sentence. The next section describes how psychologists measure understanding as a step in constructing theories of how we comprehend ideas contained in text.

Understanding Text

It may be difficult to single out any one cognitive skill as more important than the others, but if we had to make a choice, *comprehension* would be a prime contender for the honor. Much of what we learn depends on our ability to understand written or spoken material.

Pretend for a minute that you've been selected to be a member of a jury in a murder trial. Before the trial begins, the judge instructs you and the other jury members about how to evaluate the proceedings. Since you're a conscientious juror, you listen carefully as the judge begins:

You must not consider as evidence any statement of counsel made during the trial; however, if counsel for the parties have stipulated to any fact, or any fact has been admitted by counsel, you will regard that fact as being conclusively proved as to the party or parties making the stipulation or admission.

Are you starting to feel lost? If so, you're not alone. Charrow and Charrow (1979) studied the effects of improving jury instructions. One group of prospective jury members listened to the instructions you've just read. Another group listened to a modified set of instructions:

Ordinarily, any statement made by the lawyers in this case is not evidence. However, if all the lawyers agree that some particular thing is true, you must accept it as the truth.

Both groups were then asked to recall in their own words the instructions given by the judge. The jury members who listened to the modified instructions recalled about 50% more information than the group that listened to the original instructions. These results demonstrate that restating ideas in a clearer form can make them easier to understand and recall.

Fortunately, this kind of interest in comprehension has resulted in attempts to rewrite legal regulations and instructions to make them easier to understand. When Jimmy Carter was President, he issued an order requiring each federal regulation to be written in plain English so it would be understandable to those who had to comply with it (the federal government still has a long way to go to meet this goal, as you may have noticed if you've filed a tax return lately).

MEASURING UNDERSTANDING

Some cognitive psychologists want to learn precisely how people attempt to understand written or spoken material. To study the understanding of text, they have devised two primary measures of text comprehension. One measure, used in the jury study, is the number of ideas that people can recall from a text. This measure assumes that subjects who have really understood the ideas should be able to recall more ideas than subjects who haven't understood the ideas. A second measure of comprehension is more subjective but also more direct. People simply rate how easy various texts are to understand, or they read a passage and push a button as soon as they understand it. The response-time measure is based on the assumption that people will take less time if the text is easy to comprehend.

INTEGRATION OF IDEAS

Ease of comprehension is influenced not only by the particular sentence we're reading, but by the sentences that precede it. We rarely have to comprehend a sentence in isolation, because sentences usually occur within a context. In fact, a sentence that's very difficult to understand alone may be perfectly clear in its context (Haviland & Clark, 1974). *George thinks vanilla* is a rather

Example 1

The ants ate the jelly. The ants were hungry. The ants were in the kitchen. The kitchen was spotless. The jelly was grape. The jelly was on the table. The table was wooden.

Example 2

The kitchen was spotless. The table was wooden. The ants were hungry. The ants were in the kitchen. The jelly was grape. The jelly was on the table. The ants ate the jelly.

bizarre statement in isolation, but is understandable when preceded by the question *What kind of ice cream does Vivian like?* Understanding should therefore depend on how easy it is to relate the ideas in a sentence to the ideas that came before it.

Recent research has focused on how people relate or *integrate* ideas in a sentence to ideas that occurred in previous sentences. These studies attempt to discover what makes the integration easy or difficult. Research on the integration of ideas has dealt with three questions: (1) Are the ideas familiar ones or new ones? (2) Does integration require searching long-term memory? (3) Is it necessary to infer how ideas are related? Let's examine each of these questions.

1. *Familiar ideas versus new ideas.* Familiar ideas are ideas that have occurred previously in the text. New ideas are ones that have not been previously mentioned. A text that consisted entirely of new ideas would be very difficult to comprehend because it would not be obvious how the ideas were related.

The disadvantage of introducing many unfamiliar terms in a short text was demonstrated in a study by Kieras (1978). Figure 8.7 shows two examples of short texts, each consisting of seven sentences. Read both of these examples. Which is easier to comprehend?

In the figure "new" sentences are shown highlighted. A sentence is classified as new if both of its two concepts are being mentioned for the first time (such concepts are underlined in the figure). Example 1 contains only one new sentence by this definition; all the sentences but the first refer to at least one concept used in preceding sentences. Example 2 contains four sentences representing entirely new information. As Kieras (1978) predicted, the ideas in the first example were easier to integrate and recall than the ideas in the second example.

2. *Short-term memory versus long-term memory.* In the previous chapter, you learned the distinction between short-term memory (STM) and long-term memory (LTM). Short-term memory was characterized as our "working memory," which can hold about seven chunks of information for

up to 20–30 seconds. Research suggests that text comprehension is easier when relevant information is still active in STM, and does not have to be retrieved from LTM. Consider the following two sentences:

A thick cloud of smoke hung over the forest. The forest was on fire.

These sentences are easy to integrate because information from the first sentence should still be available in STM when you encounter the second sentence. Now compare this passage:

A thick cloud of smoke hung over the forest. Glancing to one side, Carol could see a bee flying around the back seat. Both of the kids were jumping around but made no attempt to free the insect. The forest was on fire.

This passage should be more difficult to comprehend because we have inserted two sentences that change the topic and make it less likely that information about the smoke is still in STM when you learn about the fire. The difficulty is not just that the passage is longer; it's that it contains irrelevant information, making it more difficult to preserve the important information in STM. In comparison, consider this third example:

A thick cloud of smoke hung over the forest. The smoke was thick and black and began to fill the clear sky. Up ahead Carol could see a ranger directing traffic to slow down. The forest was on fire.

This passage is nearly as long as the preceding one, yet it should be easier to comprehend. Why?

The two inserted sentences continue the initial idea, making it easier to keep information about the cloud of smoke active in STM. In a study using these passages, readers did in fact comprehend the final sentence more quickly in the third case than they did in the second one (Lesgold, Roth, & Curtis, 1979).

3. *Direct relation versus inference.* A third variable that influences the integration of ideas is whether there is a direct relation between two ideas, or whether a relation must be inferred. This distinction is illustrated by the following pairs of sentences:

Ed was given an alligator for his birthday. The alligator was his favorite present.

Ed was given lots of things for his birthday. The alligator was his favorite present.

At first glance it appears that both cases provide the same information, but there's an important difference. In the first case, we are directly told that Ed received an alligator for his birthday; in the second case we must infer it. People took significantly longer to comprehend the second sentence when they had to infer its relation to the first sentence (Haviland & Clark, 1974). Thus, it appears that if we have to make inferences, comprehension is slower and more difficult.

These studies of the integration of ideas demonstrate that a number of variables influence comprehension. Walter Kintsch (1979) has developed a model of text comprehension that includes the three variables just discussed. Its central assumption is that incoming information can be understood more easily when it can be integrated with information that the reader has already encountered. Comprehension is easiest when the new information can be related to information that's still active in STM. If this fails, the reader attempts to relate the new information to information stored in LTM. Failing that, an inference is required to integrate the ideas in the text. According to Kintsch, having to use each of these additional steps makes comprehension more difficult.

PREDICTING READABILITY

Kintsch's model has been applied to the prediction of **readability—the ease of reading different kinds of text.** Predicting readability is an important practical problem, because the developers of educational materials want to be assured that their materials can be understood by the students who read them.

According to Kintsch and Vipond (1979), the earliest formulas for predicting the readability of text material appeared in the 1920s. There are now about 50 readability formulas. Most base their predictions on the average number of words in the sentences (the sentence length) and the percentage of uncommon or unfamiliar words. As you might expect, the formulas predict that passages with longer sentences and more uncommon words will be relatively difficult to read.

However, recent studies raise serious doubts about how well these formulas can predict reading ease. Many studies have failed to find a relationship between readability estimates based on these formulas and subjects' comprehension of the text (Bruce, Rubin, & Starr, 1981). Also, readability predictions based on these formulas correlate only modestly with students' subjective ratings of the readability of text material (Griesinger & Klene, 1984). The problem appears to be that these formulas ignore flow, cohesiveness, and repetition of ideas—factors related to the ease of integrating ideas.

In contrast, Kintsch's comprehension model is sensitive to how these organizational factors influence the integration of ideas in text material. For example, how often you need to search your LTM or make an inference depends in part on the material's organization. Kintsch's model allows estimation of how often you as a reader must search your LTM to relate new information to previous information. It also permits estimation of how many inferences are required to understand information.

In one study, Kintsch and Vipond (1979) used these measures, along with more traditional readability measures, to predict the relative difficulty of reading 20 paragraphs. They found that the two best predictors of readability were the percentage of uncommon words and the number of LTM searches required. The number of inferences required also influenced readability, although not as much as uncommon words or the number of LTM searches did. The inferences required by Kintsch's sample of 20 paragraphs were fairly easy; the effect of inferences might increase if they were more difficult. In any case, this study suggests that we can better predict readability if we consider organizational factors in text material.

The prediction of readability provides a nice example of a highly complex problem requiring a solution, and Kintsch's work illustrates the value of creative, new approaches to a problem. Most of the problems that we tackle are far less complex than the task of predicting readability, but we all grapple with a diverse array of problems every day. Psychologists have a long-standing interest in problem solving, which is the topic we turn to next.

Since we've just discussed the importance of understanding text, let's look at two problems that depend on understanding text. Can you can solve them?

In the Thompson family there are five brothers, and each brother has one sister. If you count Mrs. Thompson, how many females are there in the Thompson family?

Fifteen percent of the people in Topeka have unlisted telephone numbers. You select 200 names at random from the Topeka phone book. How many of these people can be expected to have unlisted phone numbers?

These problems, borrowed from Sternberg (1986), are exceptionally simple, but many people fail to solve them. The answer to the first problem is two. The only females in the family are Mrs. Thompson and her one daughter, who is a sister to each of her brothers. The answer to the second problem is none. You won't find people with un-

listed phone numbers in the phone book.

Why do many people fail to solve these problems? The catch is that they contain *irrelevant information* that leads them astray. In the first problem, the number of brothers is irrelevant. In the second problem, since all the names came out of the phone book, the figures of 15% and 200 names are irrelevant.

Effective problem solving requires that you consider a problem carefully and decide what information is relevant and what is irrelevant. This insight will surface again as we discuss the cognitive processes involved in problem solving.

Classifying Problems

According to some psychologists, such as Jim Greeno (1978), problems can be categorized into three basic classes:

Figure 8.8 Six standard problems used in studies of problem solving. As the text explains, the problems fall into three classes, each of which calls for its own type of solution. Try solving the problems and identifying which class each belongs to before reading further.

A. Analogy
What word completes the analogy?
Merchant : Sell : : Customer : _____
Lawyer : Client : : Doctor : _____

B. String problem
Two strings hang from the ceiling but are too far apart to allow a person to hold one and walk to the other. On the floor are a book of matches, a screwdriver, and a few pieces of cotton. How could the strings be tied together?

C. Missionaries and cannibals
Three missionaries and three cannibals who have to cross a river find a boat, but the boat is so small that it can hold no more than two people. If the missionaries on either bank of the river are outnumbered at any time by cannibals, they will be eaten. Find the simplest schedule of crossings that will allow everyone to cross safely. At least one person must be in the boat at each crossing.

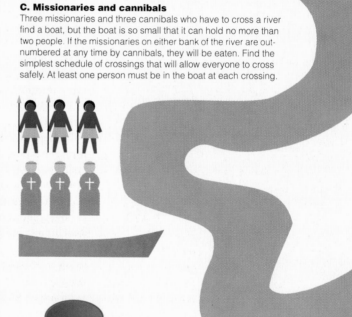

D. Water jar
You have an 8-gallon pail and a 5-gallon pail. How could you obtain 2 gallons of water?

E. Anagram
Rearrange the letters in each row to make an English word.
RWAET
KEROJ

F. Series completion
What number or letter completes each series?
1 2 8 3 4 6 5 6 ____
A B M C D M ____

1. *Inducing structure.* The problem solver must discover the relations among the parts of the problem.

2. *Arrangement.* The problem solver must arrange the parts in a way that satisfies some criterion.

3. *Transformation.* The problem solver must carry out a sequence of transformations in order to reach a specific goal.

Greeno's list is not exhaustive, but it does provide a useful scheme for understanding the nature of problems. Figure 8.8 shows six examples of problems that psychologists have studied. Look over Figure 8.8 and see if you can solve the problems, but don't spend too much time on any one. When you're finished, try to classify them using Greeno's system. Here's a hint: there are two examples of each type of problem. We'll analyze these examples to see how the three basic types of problems differ.

INDUCING STRUCTURE

The *series-completion problems* in Figure 8.8 are examples of *inducing structure.* In problems that involve inducing structure, the solution requires discovering how numbers or words are related. For example, in the first series-completion problem given, the task is to find the next number in the series: 1 2 8 3 4 6 5 6 ___. To do so, you must first find a pattern in the sequence of numbers. Once you notice that there are two series in this example, the answer is close at hand. One series is the increasing series 1 2, 3 4, 5 6; the other is the decreasing series 8, 6, ___. So the correct answer is 4. Did you solve the other series-completion problem in Figure 8.8? The answer is the letter E.

The *analogy problems* in Figure 8.8 also involve inducing structure (the answers are *Buy* and *Patient*). Analogy problems are often used in intelligence tests, which we'll discuss in the next chapter. A widely used admissions test for graduate school, the Miller Analogies Test, is composed *exclusively* of verbal analogies. Many other tests of cognitive abilities include analogies among the test items.

The psychological processes used in solving an analogy or series-completion problem involve identifying relations among the parts and fitting the relations together to form a pattern. Robert Sternberg (1977) has highlighted the importance of discovering the relations among the parts of an analogy. Consider this problem:

Washington is to 1 as Lincoln is to ___ (10 or 5).

The task requires choosing either 10 or 5 to complete the analogy. What processes are in-volved in completing the task? First, we must determine how Washington and 1 are related. Washington was the first president of the United States, and his portrait appears on the $1 bill. Next, how are Washington and Lincoln related? Both were presidents and both appear on currency, so either of these relations could form the basis of the analogy. Finally, how is Lincoln related to 10 or 5? Since Lincoln was the 16th president of the United States, neither answer fits the presidential relation. However, Lincoln's portrait appears on a $5 bill, so the choice of 5 is consistent with the currency relation.

ARRANGEMENT PROBLEMS

The relations among the numbers or words in a series-completion or analogy problem are fixed. You have only to figure out what these relations are, rather than create new relations. In contrast, the parts of an *arrangement problem* have to be rearranged in order to satisfy some criterion. The parts can usually be arranged in many different ways, but only one or a few of the arrangements forms a solution.

The *string problem* in Figure 8.8 is an example of an arrangement problem. One factor that makes it difficult to find a solution to this problem is **functional fixedness—the tendency to perceive an item only in terms of its most common use.** The string problem requires finding a *novel* use for one of the objects—the screwdriver. Instead of focusing on its usual functions, you need to view the screwdriver as a weight. If you attach the screwdriver to one string and set it swinging as a pendulum, you can hold the other string and catch the screwdriver. Then you have only to untie the screwdriver and tie the strings together.

Studies have shown that this particular problem is usually solved with a burst of insight. **Insight is the sudden discovery of the correct solution following incorrect attempts based primarily on trial and error.** The key factor distinguishing insight from other forms of discovery is its suddenness. In contrast to solutions that are achieved through careful planning or a series of small steps, solutions based on insight seem to occur "in a flash."

A recent study by Metcalfe (1986) supports the idea that solutions to problems often occur quite suddenly. Metcalfe gave her subjects *anagram problems* to solve. Anagrams are a type of arrangement problem (the answers to those in Figure 8.8 are *water* and *joker*). The subjects were asked to assess how close they were to solving the problem, on a scale from 1 to 10, during the course of working on the anagrams. Subjects recorded their ratings every 10 seconds. The ratings remained very low until the discovery of the solution, suggesting that the correct answer appeared suddenly.

A sudden solution does *not* usually occur in transformation problems, which are solved by carrying out a planned sequence of steps. The contrast between arrangement problems and transformation problems is discussed in the next section.

TRANSFORMATION PROBLEMS

In some respects, *transformation problems* are similar to arrangement problems. Both consist of an initial state and a goal. The difference is that the problem solver knows exactly what the goal is for transformation problems. The *missionaries and cannibals problem* and the *water jar problem* in Figure 8.8 are examples of transformation problems. When the missionaries and cannibals problem is finished, three missionaries and three cannibals should be across the river. When the water jar problem is finished, one of the pails should contain 2 gallons of water.

In contrast, the problem solver doesn't know how the outcome of an arrangement problem will look after the problem has been solved. For example, if you were given an anagram presented as a transformation problem (for instance: rearrange the letters KEROJ to spell JOKER), you wouldn't have a problem to solve! Transformation problems are challenging because even though we know exactly what the goal is, it's not obvious how the goal can be achieved.

To solve transformation problems you must find a sequence of transformations that will produce the goal state. According to Allen Newell and Herbert Simon (1972), this requires skill in a method called means/end analysis. **Means/end analysis involves identifying differences that exist between the current state and the goal state, and making changes that will reduce these differences.** However, means/end analysis may not always lead to optimal progress in problem solving.

Consider the missionaries and cannibals problem, which requires transporting everyone across the river. A good strategy would be to take as many people as possible across the river on each trip and bring as few as possible back. It's usually possible to bring only one person back in the boat, but to maintain the requirements of the problem, at one point it's necessary to bring two people back. This is a difficult move for most of us because it seems to take us away from the goal (Thomas, 1974). In general, problems become difficult whenever we have to make moves that violate the means/end strategy (Atwood & Polson, 1976). The missionaries and cannibals problem and the water jar problem, which are solved in Figure 8.9, both require deviation from the means/end strategy; this is one reason they're difficult for most of us.

The means/end strategy is an example of a heuristic. **A *heuristic* is a strategy or guiding principle used in solving problems.** Heuristics are often useful, but they don't guarantee success. Although reducing differences between the current state and the goal state often brings us closer to a solution, as we've seen, occasionally we must make a move that seems to take us away from our goal. We discuss some other examples of heuristics in the next section.

Problem-Solving Stategies

We use a great variety of heuristics in attempting to solve problems. Three very general problem-solving strategies that are often useful are these:

1. *Form subgoals.* Try breaking a problem into several parts, represented by subgoals.

Figure 8.9 Solutions to the *missionaries and cannibals* and *water jar* problems. The difficulty presented by both of these transformation problems is the necessity of temporarily working "away" from the goal, which frustrates a straightforward means-end strategy.

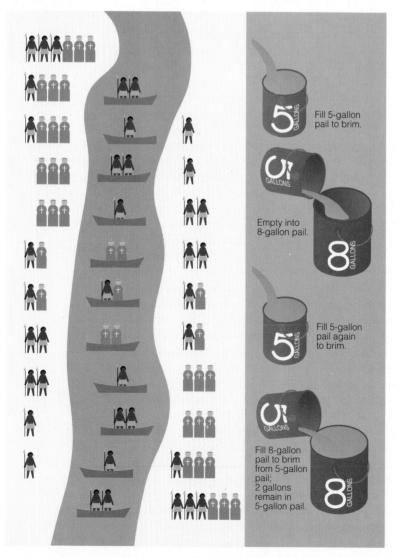

Fill 5-gallon pail to brim.

Empty into 8-gallon pail.

Fill 5-gallon pail again to brim.

Fill 8-gallon pail to brim from 5-gallon pail; 2 gallons remain in 5-gallon pail.

2. *Work backwards.* It may be advantageous to start at the goal state and work backwards toward the initial state.

3. *Search for analogies.* It may be helpful to recognize that one problem is similar to others that you've solved.

FORMING SUBGOALS

A commonly suggested heuristic for solving problems is to formulate *subgoals*, intermediate steps in solving a problem. When you reach a subgoal, you've solved part of the problem. Some problems have fairly obvious subgoals, and research has shown that people take advantage of them. For instance, in analogy problems, the first subgoal usually is to figure out the possible relations between the first two parts of the analogy.

A limitation of the subgoal strategy is that it may not be obvious how to divide a solution into its parts. In such cases, someone else may have to suggest a subgoal. For example, Simon and Reed (1976) asked students to solve a complex version of the missionaries and cannibals problem in which there are five missionaries, five cannibals (instead of three each), and a boat that can hold three people. Some students were given a subgoal: they were told that at some point there would be three cannibals across the river, by themselves, without the boat. These students solved the problem in an average of 20 moves, compared to an average of 30 moves for students who weren't given the subgoal.

WORKING BACKWARDS

If you're working on a problem that has a well-specified goal, you may find the solution more readily if you begin at the goal and work backwards. Try this strategy with the following problem:

Try to arrange four 7s to make the number 56. You can add, subtract, multiply, and divide, and you can use parentheses to group 7s, but you must use all four 7s.

This problem is difficult because there are so many ways of combining the 7s. It's easier to solve if you work backward from the number 56. There are relatively few ways of breaking up 56, such as 28×2, 14×4, and 7×8. The advantage of 7×8 is that it uses one of the 7s, giving us a subgoal: Combine three 7s to make the number 8. Do you see the solution now?

You can express 8 as $7 + 1$, using up another 7, so all that's left is to use two 7s to express the number 1. Since $7/7 = 1$, the answer to the subgoal is $7/7 + 7$, and the answer to the problem is $(7/7 + 7) \times 7$.

Working backwards is a good strategy when you

can see that although you have many options available at the beginning of a problem, you'll have relatively few options available near the end (J. R. Anderson, 1980). It's also worth considering when you stop making progress by working forward.

SEARCHING FOR ANALOGIES

Searching for analogies is another of the major heuristics for solving problems. If you can spot an analogy between problems, you may be able to use the solution to a previous problem to solve a current one. Of course, this depends on recognizing the similarity between two problems, which may itself be a challenging problem. We often are unable to recognize that two problems are similar, but once informed of the similarity, we do reasonably well in making use of the analogous solution

---

CONCEPT CHECK 8.2
Thinking About Problem Solving

Check your understanding of problem solving by answering some questions about the following problem. Begin by trying to solve the problem.

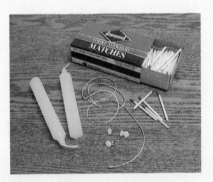

The candle problem. Using the objects shown—candles, a box of matches, string, and some tacks—figure out how you could mount a candle on a wall so that it could be used as a light.

Work on the problem for a while before you turn the page to see the solution. After you've seen the solution, respond to the following questions. The answers are in Appendix A.

1. If it didn't occur to you that the matchbox could be converted from a container to a platform, this illustrates _____
_____.

2. While working on the problem, if you thought to yourself, "How can I create a platform attached to the wall," you used the heuristic of _____ _____.

3. If it occurred to you suddenly that the matchbox could be used as a platform, this realization would be an example of _____.

4. If you had a hunch that there might be some similarity between this problem and the string problem in Figure 8.8 (the similarity is the novel use of an object), your hunch would illustrate the heuristic of _____ _____.

5. In terms of Greeno's three types of problems, the candle problem is a(n) _____ problem.

(Gick & Holyoak, 1980; Reed, Ernst, & Banerji, 1974). Try to apply this strategy to these two problems:

A teacher had 23 pupils in his class. All but 7 of them went on a museum trip and thus were away for the day. How many students remained in class that day?

Susan gets in her car in Boston and drives toward New York City, averaging 50 miles per hour. Twenty minutes later, Ellen gets in her car in New York City and starts driving toward Boston, averaging 60 miles per hour. Both women take the same route, which extends a total of 220 miles between the two cities. Which car is nearer to Boston when they meet?

These problems resemble the problems that opened our discussion of problem solving. Each has an obvious solution that's hidden in irrelevant quantitative information (Sternberg, 1986). If you recognized this similarity, you probably solved the problems easily. If not, take another look now that you know what the analogy is.

Neither problem requires any calculation whatsoever. The answer to the first problem is 7. As for the second problem, when the two cars *meet* they're in the same place; they have to be the same distance from Boston.

The problems described thus far have consisted primarily of puzzles in which you could search for a solution without having special knowledge. In contrast, games such as chess and problems encountered in the classroom require knowledge about a particular subject matter. When this is the case, you need both subject-matter knowledge and strategies to become proficient (Glaser, 1984). To learn how people acquire expertise, psychologists have studied how experts and novices differ in their efforts to solve problems.

The solution to the *candle problem* in Concept Check 8.2

Acquiring Expertise

To understand the development of expertise, psychologists have tried to identify what experts have learned that makes them experts. How, for instance, could the chess master Koltanowsky keep track of enough information to be able to play 34 chess games simultaneously—while blindfolded? One way to investigate expertise is to look closely at how experts and novices (people with little experience) solve problems and to determine how the two groups differ. Let's look at some of these differences.

CHUNKING

One of the classic studies on expertise was conducted by a Dutch psychologist, Adriaan de Groot, during the 1940s and was later published in his book, *Thought and Choice in Chess* (de Groot, 1965). The main conclusion of the study was that master chess players have an advantage over weaker players because their view of a chess game is organized into thousands of chunks. As we discussed in Chapter 7, a *chunk* is a familiar stimulus grouping that is stored in memory as a single unit. According to de Groot, the analysis of the game into configurations of several chess pieces forms the basis for selecting the appropriate moves.

Support for de Groot's conclusion came from a clever series of memory studies that compared experts' and novices' ability to recall pieces on a chessboard as it might appear 20 moves into a game (see Figure 8.10). The subjects had 5 seconds to view the board, the pieces were removed, and the subjects were asked to place the pieces back on the board to reproduce what they had just

Figure 8.10 An illustration of chunking. Asked to reproduce these chessboard configurations after seeing them for only a few seconds, chess masters would outperform ordinary players by a wide margin—but only for the configuration shown on the left. For the one on the right, masters do no better than weaker players, even though the number of pieces is the same. The reason? The configuration on the right is impossible under the rules of chess and thus lacks the familiar patterns that the master has stored in memory as "chunks."

seen. The master players correctly placed about 90% of the pieces, compared to only 40% for the weaker players.

Another experiment by de Groot (1966) suggested that master players' better memory was the result of their ability to remember locations by dividing the pieces into familiar groups or chunks. When pieces were placed randomly on the board (thereby eliminating familiar groups), the master players were no longer better than weaker players at reproducing the board (consult Figure 8.10 once again). Based on more detailed studies of chess players, Simon and Gilmartin (1973) estimate that chess masters may store between 10,000 and 100,000 chunks of information on chess in long-term memory! This estimate indicates that there is no shortcut to becoming a chess master.

PLANNING

Another difference between experts and novices is the effective use of planning (Miller, Galanter, & Pribram, 1960). A *plan* consists of a sequence of actions for carrying out some task. When we plan, we construct the sequence before beginning the task.

In chess, a plan requires thinking several moves ahead. Perhaps surprisingly, de Groot (1966) did not find that expert chess players planned further ahead than novice chess players. The experts selected better moves by taking advantage of the many chunks of chess knowledge stored in memory, rather than by formulating more extensive plans.

However, experts *do* seem to plan more than novices in solving complex problems such as physics problems (Larkin & Reif, 1979). Planning uses the subgoal heuristic described in the previous section. We formulate a plan by constructing subgoals that divide the solution into its various parts. Successful planning requires that we place the subgoals in the correct order. For example, if you want to paint your ceiling and your ladder, you should paint the ceiling first so you can use your ladder. In more complex problems, the order of subgoals can be less obvious and can require careful planning (Sacerdoti, 1974).

RECOGNIZING ANALOGIES

One of the heuristics we've discussed involved thinking of an analogous problem. Ideally, the analogous problem should have a solution (method of solving) that's identical to that of the problem you want to solve. As you may recall, we're not very good at recognizing analogous problems because they describe different situa-

Table 8.4 A Word Problem and Related Problems

TYPE OF PROBLEM	PROBLEM STATEMENT
Word problem	A farmer is counting the hens and rabbits in his barnyard. He counts a total of 50 heads and 140 feet. How many hens and how many rabbits does the farmer have?
Related structure	Bill has a collection of 20 coins that consists entirely of dimes and quarters. If the coins total $4.10, how many of each kind of coin are in the collection?
Related context	A farmer is counting the hens and rabbits in his barnyard. He counts six coops with four hens in each, two coops with three hens in each, five cages with six rabbits in each, and three cages with four rabbits in each. How many hens and how many rabbits does the farmer have?

Source: Silver, 1981

tions and may—at least at a superficial level—look very dissimilar.

However, as we acquire expertise, we become better at recognizing that problems may have identical solutions even when they describe different situations. The distinction between an identical solution and an identical situation is illustrated by the three problems in Table 8.4. Take a moment to think about these problems before reading further.

The first two problems in Table 8.4 have identical solutions. The first is about hens and rabbits and the second is about coins, but the structure of the equation is the same. The first and third problems describe the same situation but have different solutions.

To study subjects' recognition of analogous problems, Chi, Glaser, and Rees (1982) asked eight novices and eight experts to sort 24 physics problems into categories. Novices tended to categorize problems on the basis of common objects, such as placing inclined-plane problems in one category and spring problems in another category. Experts tended to categorize problems on the basis of the physics principles relevant to solving the problem. Thus, novices formed groups that described identical *situations*; experts formed groups that had identical *solutions*. This supports the idea that expertise often includes an enhanced ability to recognize analogous solutions.

Creativity in Problem Solving

Like expertise, *creativity* can be important in solving many of the problems we encounter. Consider the dilemma that the well-known attorney, Vincent Bugliosi, found himself in during a murder trial (as related by Bransford and Stein, 1984). As the prosecuting attorney, Bugliosi was handicapped because there were no eyewitnesses. He had built a solid case against the defendant, but it rested entirely on circumstantial evidence. Near the end of the trial, the defense lawyer made a penetrating argument that seemed to undermine the prosecution's case. The defense attorney argued that circumstantial evidence is like a chain, and that a chain is only as strong as its weakest link. He then proceeded to show that there were several weak links in the circumstantial chain constructed by Bugliosi.

If you were the prosecuting attorney, how would you counter this argument? Bugliosi realized that there *were* weak links in his case, but he did not want to lose the case to a clever analogy. He needed his own analogy—one that would make the evidence appear stronger. What was his solution? He argued that circumstantial evidence is like a *rope* rather than a chain. A rope is made up of a number of independent strands. Bugliosi pointed out that a few strands can break without affecting the overall strength of the rope very much. He acknowledged that his case included some weak strands, but he asserted that they were not fatal the way that weak links in a chain would be. His rebuttal must have been convincing, because he won the case.

Faced with a difficult problem, Bugliosi came up with a creative solution. But what is it that makes his strategy creative? To answer this question, we have to examine the nature of creativity.

THE NATURE OF CREATIVITY

What makes creative thought creative? **Creativity involves the generation of ideas that are original, novel, and useful.** First and foremost, creativity involves seeing the world in a new and different light. Creative thinking is fresh, innovative, and inventive. But novelty, by itself, is not enough. If bizarre thinking were the only mark of creativity, severely disturbed psychotics would be the most creative people around. Thus, in addition to being unusual, creative thinking must be adaptive; it must be appropriate to the situation and problem. Bugliosi's rope analogy, for example, was an adaptive response to a tough situation. Bugliosi could have compared circumstantial evidence to a bassett hound or a windshield wiper. These analogies certainly would have been novel, but they wouldn't have solved his problem.

According to many theorists, the key to creativity lies in *divergent thinking*—thinking "that goes off in different directions," as J. P. Guilford (1959, p. 381) puts it. Most of our training in school encourages convergent thinking. **In convergent thinking we try to narrow down a list of alternatives to converge on a single correct answer.** For example, when you take a multiple-choice exam, you try to eliminate incorrect options until you hit upon the correct response. **In *divergent thinking* we try to expand the range of alternatives by generating many possible solutions.** Imagine that you work for an advertising agency. To come up with as many slogans as possible for a client's product, you must use divergent thinking. Some of your slogans may be clear losers, and eventually you would have to engage in convergent thinking to pick the best. But it's the divergent thinking involved in dreaming up the possibilities that's critical to creativity.

MEASURING CREATIVITY

The concept of divergent thinking forms the basis for many psychological tests that measure creativity. The items on these tests give respondents a specific starting point and then require them to generate as many possibilities as they can in a short period of time. Typical items might require you to: (1) list as many uses as you can for a newspaper, (2) think of as many fluids that burn as you can, (3) write as many words as you can that are similar in meaning to the word *tough*, or (4) imagine that people no longer need sleep and think of as many consequences as you can (see Figure 8.11 for additional examples). Subjects' scores on these tests depend on the *number* of alternatives they generate and the *originality* and *usefulness* of the alternatives.

How well do psychological tests predict creative productivity in the real world? This is a tricky research issue because it's hard to come up with good measures of creative productivity. Researchers have used many different kinds of measures, ranging from the number of journal articles produced by scientists to ratings of architects' cre-

Figure 8.11 Examples of problems used to measure creativity. Tests of creativity contain problems like these, which require divergent thinking. Respondents attempt to generate a large number of solutions in a short amount of time.

1. Many words begin with an L and end with an N. List as many words as possible, in a 1-minute period, that have the form L _____ N. (They can have any number of letters in between the L and the N.)
2. Suppose that people reached their final height at the age of 2, and so normal adult height was less than 3 feet. In a 1-minute period, list as many consequences as possible that would result from this change.
3. Here are four shapes. Combine them to make each of the following objects: a face, a lamp, a piece of playground equipment, a tree. Each shape may be used once, many times, or not at all in forming each object, and it may be expanded or shrunk to any size.

ative production by other architects. In general, these studies find that creativity tests are moderately good predictors of creative achievement in the real world (Barron & Harrington, 1981).

Why aren't tests of creativity better predictors of actual creative achievement? A major reason is that creative achievement depends on many factors besides creativity. Creative productivity over the course of an individual's career will depend on the person's motivation, intelligence, training, and good fortune.

Recent research by Benjamin Bloom (1985) and his colleagues on the development of talent highlights the importance of training and hard work. Investigators from the University of Chicago put together richly detailed case histories for 120 exceptionally successful young people from six fields, including concert pianists and sculptors. In all fields, they found that great success depended on high-quality training. The accomplished pianists and sculptors had moved through a succession of outstanding teachers and mentors during their formative years. The study also found that creative success was attributable to dogged determination. Typical remarks from those interviewed include, "What I got at [school] was the absolute determination to be an artist no matter what," and "I had to pursue it—I had to push," and "You have to have discipline and . . . total belief in what you're doing" (Sloane & Sosniak, 1985, pp. 135–136).

CORRELATES OF CREATIVITY

What are creative people like? Are they brighter than average? Is there a particular personality profile associated with creativity? Much of the research on creativity has sought to discover the correlates of creativity.

Creative people exhibit the full range of personality traits, but investigators *have* found that certain personality characteristics are associated with creativity (Barron & Harrington, 1981). At the core of this set of personality characteristics are the related traits of independence, autonomy, self-confidence, and nonconformity. Creative people tend to think for themselves and are less easily influenced by the opinions of others than the average person. Creative people also tend to be more tolerant of complexity, contradiction, and ambiguity than others. They don't feel compelled to simplify everything, and they're not as troubled by uncertainty as are many of us.

But are they smarter? The evidence indicates that creativity and intelligence are only weakly related (Horn, 1976; Wallach & Kogan, 1965). As you'll see in the next chapter, intelligence tests tap convergent rather than divergent thinking.

Creativity can be displayed in many ways and in many fields of endeavor, as these three highly creative people illustrate: Steven Jobs, electronics engineer and innovative founder of Apple Computer; Mikhail Baryshnikov, master ballet dancer; and Gloria Steinem, pioneering feminist and founder of *Ms.* magazine. As diverse as these individuals are, one thing they share is a trait common among people of significant creative achievement—a dedication to sheer hard work.

Thus, creativity and intelligence appear to represent different types of mental ability. They're not entirely unrelated, however. Creative thinking requires a certain minimum level of intelligence. Hence, most highly creative people are average or above average in intelligence.

If divergent thinking is a mark of creativity, why do we emphasize convergent thinking so much in our schools and training? On a daily basis, life more often demands decisions than creativity, and convergent thinking is more important in decision making. As you might expect, cognitive psychologists have shown great interest in the process of decision making, which is our next subject.

293

Decisions, decisions. Life is full of them. You decided to read this book today. Earlier today you decided when to get up, whether to eat breakfast, and if so, what to eat. Usually you make routine decisions like these with little effort, but on occasion you need to make important decisions that require more thought. Big decisions—such as selecting a car, a home, or a job—are often difficult because each alternative has a number of facets or attributes, and only seldom does the best alternative excel on all of them.

Most of us try to be systematic and rational in our decision making. However, the work that earned Herbert Simon the 1978 Nobel Prize in economics showed that we don't always live up to these goals. Before Simon's work, most traditional theories in economics assumed that people made rational choices to maximize their economic gains. Simon (1957) showed that we have a limited ability to evaluate many possible alternatives. He noted that we tend to focus on only a few aspects of our available options and that we often make "irrational" decisions that are far from optimal. In this section, we examine research on decision making to better understand how this happens.

Selecting an Alternative

Boris has lived in a dormitory for three years. Now that he's in his senior year, he feels it's time to enjoy the greater freedom that an apartment can offer. He has found two reasonably attractive apartments and is trying to decide between them. Assuming that Boris intends to make a deliberate choice and not leave the decision to chance (throw darts or wait and see which apartment is still available in a week), how does he go about selecting between his alternatives? Let's look at some strategies Boris might use in trying to make his choice.

If Boris used an *additive strategy* to make his decision, he would first list the attributes that influence his decision, and then rate the desirability of each apartment on each attribute. For example, let's say that Boris wants to consider four attributes: rent, noise level, distance to campus, and cleanliness. He might make the ratings that you see in Table 8.5, on a scale of -3 (a very negative impression) to $+3$ (a very positive impression). The additive strategy consists of adding the ratings for each alternative and selecting the alternative with the largest sum.

Given the ratings in Table 8.5, Boris will select apartment B.

One limitation of a purely additive strategy is that it doesn't allow any attributes to be more important than others. For example, distance to campus might be far more important to Boris than noise level or rent. To make the additive strategy more useful, Boris can *weight* attributes differently (Dawes, 1979). For example, if he considers distance to campus to be twice as important as the other attributes, he can multiply his ratings of this attribute by 2. The distance rating would then be $+6$ for apartment A and -2 for apartment B. If Boris is now satisfied that he has weighted the attributes properly, he'll find that apartment A has a larger sum ($+7$) than apartment B ($+5$) and that it should be the preferred choice. Of course, Boris could further refine his strategy by more elaborate weightings of each attribute.

Additive strategies are examples of compensatory models in decision making. **Compensatory decision models allow attractive attributes to compensate for unattractive attributes.** For example, even though small cars are not as safe in collisions as large cars, you might allow their attractive attributes (lower cost, better gas mileage, easier maneuverability) to compensate for the lower safety ratings. In contrast, **noncompensatory decision models do not allow some attributes to compensate for others.** A single bad rating can result in the elimination of that alternative. We next discuss an example of a noncompensatory model.

We often make choices by gradually eliminating less attractive alternatives (Tversky, 1972). This strategy is called *elimination by aspects* because it assumes that we eliminate alternatives by evaluating them on each attribute or aspect in turn. Whenever any alternative fails to satisfy

Table 8.5 Application of the Additive Model to Choosing an Apartment

ATTRIBUTE	APARTMENT	
	A	B
Rent	$+1$	$+2$
Noise level	-2	$+3$
Distance to campus	$+3$	-1
Cleanliness	$+2$	$+2$
	$+4$	$+6$

some minimum criterion for an attribute, we eliminate it from further consideration.

To illustrate, suppose Juanita is looking for a new car. If she has only $10,000 to spend, she may first eliminate all cars that cost over $10,000. She may also be interested in gas economy and eliminate cars that don't average at least 20 miles per gallon of gas. By continuing to select attributes and reject choices that don't satisfy some minimum criterion, she can gradually eliminate alternatives until there's only a single car remaining that satisfies all her criteria.

The final choice, based on this procedure, depends on the order in which she evaluates the attributes. If one of the last attributes Juanita evaluates is the price of the car, she could have previously eliminated all cars that cost under $10,000; if she has only $10,000 to spend, her evaluative process would not have brought her far. Her plight would not be unusual, though. Without realizing it, people often seek the impossible—such as a sleek, new, fancy, large, safe automobile for under $10,000. Thus, when using elimination by aspects, it's best to evaluate attributes in the order of their importance.

Both the additive and the elimination-by-aspects strategies have strengths and weaknesses. The additive strategy allows good attributes to compensate for bad attributes, but it requires quite a bit of effort to use. The elimination by aspects strategy is easy to use, but a single bad attribute is sufficient to eliminate an alternative.

In a study to determine how people select a strategy, John Payne (1976) gave individual subjects information about apartments and asked them to select one of them. The information about each attribute of each apartment was typed on a card, as shown in Figure 8.12. The cards were placed on the table face down so the subject would have to turn a card over to see its value. This step allowed Payne to see the order in which each subject evaluated the attributes. Payne was able to determine people's decision strategies by watching how they turned over the cards and by listening to what they said (subjects were told to think aloud as they did the task). The task included many variations in which people had to choose from either 2, 6, or 12 apartments, and each apartment had either 4, 8, or 12 attributes.

When the task involved few apartments and attributes, people mainly used a compensatory model, like an additive strategy, to select an apartment. However, as the task became more complex, people shifted to a noncompensatory model like elimination by aspects. People therefore adapted their strategy to the demands of the task. The additive strategy is very thorough but is very demanding when the task contains a lot of information. For complex tasks, a simpler, noncompensatory strategy was preferred.

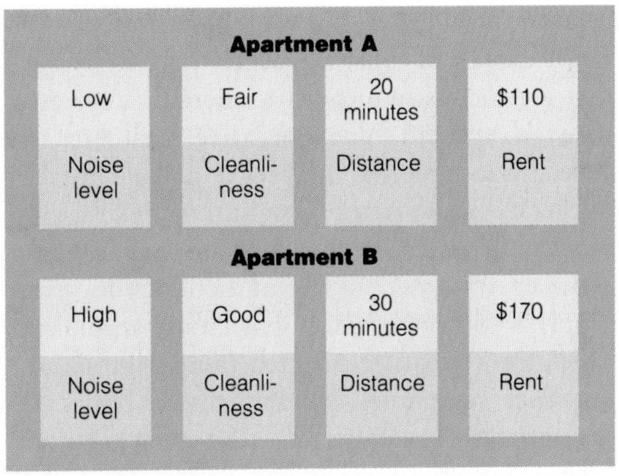

Figure 8.12 Examples of cards used in the Payne (1976) study of decision making. Face down, the cards read "Noise level," "Cleanliness," and so on; to discover their value, the subjects had to turn the cards face up. The procedure used in this study is an excellent example of the ways in which psychologists try to make cognitive processes observable and thus open to scientific investigation.

Risky Decision Making

Suppose you have the chance to play a dice game in which you might win some money. You must decide whether it would be to your advantage to play. You're going to roll a fair die. If the number 6 appears, you win $5. If one of the other five numbers appears, you win nothing. It costs you $1 every time you play. Should you participate?

This problem calls for a different decision strategy from those appropriate for selecting alternatives. **Risky decision making involves making decisions under conditions of uncertainty.** Uncertainty exists when we don't know what will happen. At best, we know the probability that a particular event will occur.

For our game, one way to decide would be to figure out the *expected value* of participation in the game. To do so, you would need to calculate the average amount of money you can expect to win or lose every time you play. The value of a win is $4 ($5 minus the $1 entry fee). The value of a loss is $-\$1$. To calculate expected value, you also need to know the probability of a win. Since a die has six faces, the probability of a win in this case is one out of 6, or $\frac{1}{6}$; the probability of a loss is $\frac{5}{6}$.

Thus, on five out of every six trials, you lose $1; on one out of six, you win $4. The game is beginning to sound unattractive, isn't it? We can figure out the precise expected value as follows:

$$\text{Expected value} = (\tfrac{1}{6} \times 4) + (\tfrac{5}{6} \times -1) = \tfrac{4}{6} + (-\tfrac{5}{6}) = -\tfrac{1}{6}$$

The expected value of this game is $-\frac{1}{6}$ of a dollar, which means that you lose an average of about 17 cents every turn in the game. Now that you know the expected value, surely you won't agree to play. Or will you?

If we want to understand why people make the

295

decisions they do, the concept of expected value is not enough. People frequently behave in ways that are inconsistent with expected value. Any time the expected value is negative, a gambler can expect to lose money. Yet people gamble at racetracks and casinos and buy lottery tickets even though, in all cases, the odds are against them and they can expect to lose in the long run. Even people who don't gamble buy house insurance, which has a negative expected value. (If it didn't, insurance companies couldn't stay in business.) The rational expectation when you buy house insurance is that you will lose money. Moreover, even those people who collect more than they pay in premiums would hardly consider insurance reimbursement as winnings.

One way of explaining decisions that violate expected value is to replace the objective value of an outcome by its *subjective utility*. Subjective utility represents what an outcome is personally worth to an individual. For example, buying a few lottery tickets may allow you to dream about becoming wealthy, and buying house insurance may give you a sense of security. Subjective utilities like these vary from one person to another. If we know an individual's subjective utilities, we'll bet-

ter understand that person's risky decision making. Another way of improving our predictions of individuals' risky decision making is to consider the *subjective probabilities* of events. If you don't know actual probabilities, you must rely on your personal estimates of what the probabilities are. As we see in the next section, subjective probabilities introduce another bit of illogic into our decision making.

Estimating Probabilities

What is the more likely cause of death—asthma or tornadoes?

Are there more words in the English language that start with the letter K or that have K as their third letter?

These questions ask you to make probability estimates. Amos Tversky and Daniel Kahneman (1973, 1980) have shown that people base probability estimates on heuristics that sometimes yield reasonable estimates, but often do not.

Tversky and Kahneman hypothesized that people estimate the probability of an event by judging the ease with which relevant instances come to mind. For example, you may assess the divorce rate in the community in which you grew up by recalling divorces among your friends' parents. Tversky and Kahneman refer to this strategy as the *availability heuristic* because it depends on the availability of examples in our memories.

Recalling specific instances of an event is a reasonable strategy to use in estimating the event's probability. However, if instances occur frequently but you have difficulty retrieving them from memory, your estimate will be biased. For instance, because it's easier to think of words that begin with a certain letter than words that contain that letter at some other position, people should be biased toward responding that there are more words that start with the letter K than have a K in the third position.

To test this hypothesis, Tversky and Kahneman (1973) selected five consonants (K, L, N, R, V) that occur more frequently in the third position of a word than in the first. The subjects were informed that they would be given several letters of the alphabet and that they should judge whether each of the letters appears more often in the first or third position. Most of the subjects erroneously believed that all five letters were more frequent in the first than in the third position. In fact, on the average, subjects estimated that there were twice as many words that started with the letter as had the letter in the third position.

The frequency with which events appear in the media has become a major factor in our estimating probabilities. Many of the events reported on the news are not a part of our daily lives, but reports of them do affect our view of the world. When people were asked to judge the relative frequency of causes of death, they greatly overestimated the frequency of events that receive heavy media coverage (Slovic, Fischhoff, & Lichenstein, 1976). The frequency of accidents, cancer, and tornadoes were overestimated. Fatalities due to asthma and diabetes, which receive less media coverage, were underestimated. For instance, a majority of subjects thought that tornadoes kill more people than asthma. In reality, asthma fatalities outnumber tornado fatalities by a ratio of over 20 to 1.

Another guide in estimating probabilities that Tversky and Kahneman identified is the *representativeness heuristic*. This heuristic captures our tendency to estimate the probability of an event according to how similar it is to the typical prototype of that event (Tversky & Kahneman, 1980). For example, imagine that you're going to meet a man who is an articulate, ambitious, power-hungry wheeler-dealer. Do you think it's more likely that he's a college teacher or a college teacher who's also a politician? You'll probably respond "college teacher who's a politician" be-

cause the description fits the common stereotype of politicians. In reality, however, it would be better to guess that the mystery man is a college teacher, because this group (college teachers) is far larger than and completely includes college teachers who are politicians.

In evaluating probabilities, another consideration is the *framing of questions* (Kahneman & Tversky, 1984). People often allow a decision to be framed by the language or context in which it's presented, rather than exploring it from different perspectives. For example, when told that a business decision has an 80% chance of success, most subjects support the decision. However, if told that the decision has a 20% risk of failure, subjects usually vote against it. Notice that the 80% success rate and 20% failure rate represent exactly the same probability situation. But stating the probability in terms of success leads to acceptance, whereas stating the probability in terms of failure leads to rejection.

In summary, the evidence on decision making suggests that we try to follow systematic and logical strategies, but we often aren't as rational as we could be—even when we think we are.

PUTTING IT IN PERSPECTIVE

Two of our unifying themes seem especially appropriate to this chapter. The first is the continuing question about the relative influence of heredity and the environment (theme 5). The controversy about how we acquire language skills replays the nature versus nurture debate. Skinner's theory, that we learn language through imitation and reinforcement, emphasizes the importance of the environment. Chomsky's theory, that we have an innate language acquisition device, argues for the importance of biology. The debate is far from settled, but the evidence suggests that both theories may contain a kernel of truth. Our unique ability to master language (in comparison to the ability of apes, for example) and our remarkably rapid acquisition of language must have a biological basis, although psychologists have not yet identified it. Nonetheless, environment is also relevant. For instance, the tendency of infants to drift toward using the phonemes employed in their native tongue reflects the influence of environment. Thus, it appears that language development depends on both nature and nurture, which is an

intermediate position consistent with cognitive theories of language acquisition.

The second pertinent theme is the empirical nature of psychology (theme 1). As we discussed in Chapter 1, psychologists paid little attention to cognitive processes for many decades because most of them assumed that the private experience of thought could not be studied scientifically. During the 1950s and 1960s, however, psychologists began to devise creative new ways to study thinking. As you saw in this chapter, cognitive psychologists figured out ways to measure mental processes, such as the understanding of text and language competence. They also devised methods for observing problem solving and decision making in action. These innovations in research methods launched a "cognitive revolution" that put the *psyche* (the mind) back in psychology.

You've seen some of the fruits of this cognitive revolution in this chapter. You'll see more in the upcoming Application, which discusses new insights into how we can improve our problem solving and decision making.

"People treat their own cases as if they were unique, rather than part of a huge lottery. You hear this silly argument that 'The odds don't apply to me.' Why should God, or whoever runs this lottery, give you special treatment?"
AMOS TVERSKY

SOLVING PROBLEMS SYSTEMATICALLY

Answer the following "true" or "false."

☐ 1. Identifying the problem is always easy; solving it is difficult.

☐ 2. The facts needed to solve a problem are always stated with the problem.

☐ 3. All the quantitative information in a problem should be used in its solution.

☐ 4. People should critically evaluate ideas as soon as they are suggested.

☐ 5. Problem solving is finished once a course of action has been selected.

The logistics of problem solving has been one of our key topics in this chapter. In this application, we outline a general set of guidelines for improving problem solving. You'll learn that all of the true-false statements above are false.

Let's begin with a problem.

Two train stations are 50 miles apart. At 1 P.M. on Sunday a train pulls out from each of the stations and the trains start toward one another. Just as the trains pull out from the stations a hawk flies into the air in front of the first train and flies ahead to the front of the second train. When the hawk reaches the second train, it turns around and flies toward the first train. The hawk continues in this way until the trains meet. Assume that both trains travel at the speed of 25 miles per hour and the hawk flies at a constant speed of 100 miles per hour. How many miles will the hawk have flown when the trains meet?

What's your reaction to this problem? Many of us react with immediate dismay and emotional distress (Bransford & Stein, 1984). We think things like, "Oh, no—not another mathematical word problem," or "I can never solve these," or "This kind of problem makes me crazy!" Negative emotional reactions like these interfere with effective problem solving. They disrupt concentration and prevent you from attacking the problem. Thus, the first guideline for effective problem solving is to avoid negative thinking. Think positively about your ability to solve problems. See if you can reason your way through the *bird and train problem* just described. You'll find the answer in Figure 8.13.

Figure 8.13 Solution to the bird-train problem. (Adapted from Bransford & Stein, 1984)

The problem asks how far the bird will fly in the time it takes the trains to meet. Since we know how fast the bird flies, to solve the problem all we need to know is how long it takes the trains to meet.

1. The train stations are 50 miles apart. Since the trains are traveling toward each other at the same speed, they will each travel 25 miles before they meet.
2. The trains are traveling at 25 miles per hour, so the time it takes them to meet is one hour.
3. Since the bird flies at a speed of 100 miles per hour, it will fly 100 miles in the time it takes the trains to meet.

Even with a positive attitude, you still need to approach problems systematically. In an excellent book entitled *The Complete Thinker*, Barry Anderson (1980) described a five-step program of actions for attacking problems. This program, which will serve as our organizational framework, is outlined in Figure 8.14. The remainder of this Application shows how each of these steps is applied in specific examples.

State the Problem

The first step in problem solving is to identify the problem. If your car is running poorly, you need to decide whether it needs a timing adjustment, new distributor points, or better gas.

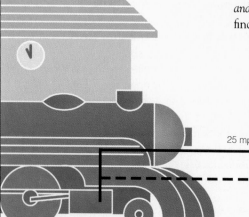

25 mph

50 miles

Figure 8.15 The nine-dot problem. Without lifting your pencil from the paper, draw no more than four lines that will cross through all nine dots.

Successful relations between parents and teenagers require the ability to isolate the real problems among the many apparent ones. Designers occasionally become so involved in trying to create the perfect design that they lose sight of alternative approaches; for example, countless hours were spent on the mechanical design of a tomato picker that wouldn't damage the crop, before it was decided that a tougher-skinned tomato was a more practical solution.

A clear statement of a problem requires specifying all the constraints on the solution *without assuming any con-straints that don't exist.* An example of a problem in which people place an unnecessary constraint on the solution is shown in Figure 8.15 (Adams, 1980). Without lifting your pencil from the paper, try to draw no more than four straight lines that will cross through all nine dots.

Most people will not draw lines outside the imaginary boundary that surrounds the dots. Notice that this constraint is not part of the problem statement; it's imposed only by the problem solver. Correct solutions, two of which are shown in Figure 8.16, extend outside the imaginary boundary.

Get the Facts

Once the problem is clearly stated, we need to get the facts necessary to solve it. We frequently fail to recognize all the information at our disposal.

Consider the following riddle (Gardner, 1969):

There once was a horse
That won great fame.
What-do-you-think
Was the horse's name.

If you have difficulty solving this riddle, you haven't taken all the facts into account. Notice that there's no question mark at the end of the second sentence and that there are hyphens connecting *what, do, you,* and *think*. Do these facts help you find the solution? Perhaps now you see that the second sentence simply states that the name of the horse was What-do-you-think.

In real-life problems, it can take a long time to gather all the facts. This is true for problems in scientific research, personal problems such as

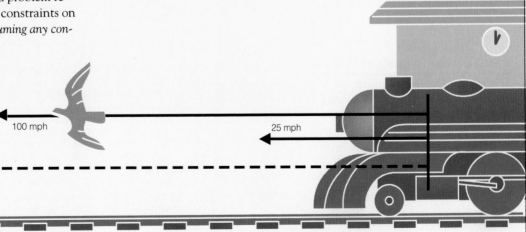

100 mph

25 mph

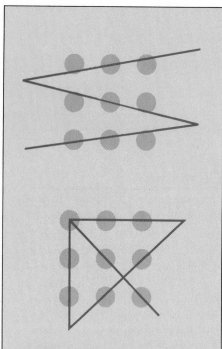

Figure 8.16 Two solutions to the nine-dot problem. The key to solving the problem is to recognize that nothing in the problem statement forbids going outside the imaginary boundary surrounding the dots.

trying to find out why you don't feel well, or global problems such as why the world's economy is sluggish (B. F. Anderson, 1980). When gathering facts, it may be necessary to form hypotheses to guide the collection of information. For example, physicians often form hypotheses very early during a diagnosis in order to guide the acquisition of additional data (Elstein, Shulman, & Sprafka, 1978). There are many different medical tests that can be performed. If physicians didn't impose some limits on what facts to gather, they would be overwhelmed with too much information and their patients would be overwhelmed with medical costs.

Focus on the Important Facts

When you have a lot of information, you can simplify the problem-solving task by focusing on the relevant facts. Complex problems can be simplified by focusing on their important aspects and ignoring some of the details. In fact, not all the information in a problem may be helpful in solving it. Try to solve the following problem as an illustration of this point.

You have black socks and blue socks in a drawer, mixed in a ratio of 4 to 5. Because it's dark you're unable to see the colors of the socks that you take out of the drawer. How many socks do you have to take out of the drawer to be assured of having a pair of socks of the same color?

You've seen this type of problem before. The key is to realize that it contains irrelevant information. People who answer the problem incorrectly tend to focus on irrelevant facts such as the ratio of black socks to blue socks. Sternberg (1986) points out that people often incorrectly assume that all the quantitative information in a problem is necessary to solve it. They therefore try to figure out how to use the quantitative information before they even consider whether it's relevant.

By the way, the answer to the socks problem is three. At worst, one sock

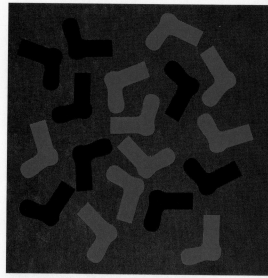

will be black and one sock will be blue after two selections. The third sock will match either the black or the blue sock, assuring a pair of one color or the other.

Table 8.6 Checklist for Generating Variations on an Idea

POSSIBLE SOLUTION	RELEVANT QUESTIONS
Adapt	What else is like this? What other ideas does this suggest? Does the past offer a parallel? What could I copy? Whom could I emulate?
Put it to other uses	What would be some new ways to use it as is? How else could it be used if modified?
Modify	Could I use a new twist? What if I change the meaning, color, motion, sound, odor, form, shape? Are there other changes I could make?
Magnify	What could I add? Could it be used more often, for a longer time? Could it be stronger, higher, longer, thicker? Could I add an extra ingredient, give it a "plus" value? Could I duplicate it, multiply it, exaggerate it?
Minify	What could I subtract? Could I make it smaller, condense it, miniaturize it? Could I make it lower, shorter, lighter? Could I omit something, streamline it, split it up, understate it?
Substitute	Who or what else would work instead? Could I use other ingredients, other materials, another process, a different source of power? Would another approach, another tone of voice, another place work better?
Rearrange	Could I interchange components, use another pattern or another layout? Could I change the sequence, transpose cause and effect, change the pace, modify the schedule?
Reverse	Could I transpose positive and negative, use opposites, turn it backwards, turn it upside down? Should I reverse roles, change shoes, turn the tables, turn the other cheek?
Combine	Could I put together a blend, an alloy, an assortment, an ensemble? Could I combine units, purposes, appeals, ideas?

Source: Adapted from Osborn, 1963

Table 8.7 Criteria for Judging Ideas

CRITERION	RELEVANT ISSUES
Is it effective?	Effectiveness means results. Will the idea fill the bill? Will it do the job? Will it work? Is it good enough to make a meaningful contribution?
Is it efficient?	Given that an idea is effective, another question arises. Is it a significant improvement over the status quo? Have you come up with an idea where a great deal is to be gained from implementing it, or have you reinvented the wheel?
Is it compatible with human nature?	Your idea may be effective, efficient, and a tremendous boon to mankind. It may solve a very pressing problem or fill a universal need. But if people have to modify or radically alter their behavior to adopt your idea, its chances for success are slim or nil.
Is it compatible with your goals?	In effect, this criterion is asking you, "How badly do you want to try this idea?" Does it go against the grain of what you want out of life? If so, forget it. However, if you find yourself consumed by an idea, take charge and give it all you've got. The more you want to do something, the more you'll automatically and willingly give of yourself to the task at hand. This greatly increases your chances of success.
Is the timing right?	In judging the timing of an idea, start first with the present. Would it be practical right now as conditions exist? How long will it take to turn the idea into a reality? What's the future going to be like when it's implemented? Are there any trends developing that will make this idea more or less valuable in the future than today? Be sure to consider every idea from the standpoint of the time frame in which it will be implemented. There's no such thing as the right idea at the wrong time.
Is it feasible?	The feasibility criterion asks two questions: (1) Can it be done? and (2) If it can be done, is it worth it? Some ideas may be very effective solutions to problems, but the means to implement them may not be available to you—they may not even exist.
Is it simple?	Today, simplicity is at a premium due to its scarcity, and it's a valuable criterion for judging ideas. Given two or more relatively equal ideas, choose the simpler one first.

Source: Adapted from LeBoeuf, 1980

Generate Ideas

The next step, once you've identified the important facts, is to engage in divergent thinking to generate ideas for solving the problem. A checklist to help you generate variations on an idea is provided in Table 8.6.

As we saw earlier when we discussed writing slogans for an advertising agency, one trick in generating a large number of ideas is to put your critical thinking on hold—at least temporarily (Osborn, 1963). **Brainstorming involves free expression of ideas while withholding criticism and evaluation.** This approach is particularly effective during group problem-solving sessions. If group members immediately criticize each others' ideas, the generation of ideas—especially risky, offbeat, and potentially innovative ideas—is inhibited. Brainstorming can be helped by trying to think what's good about each idea and building on previous ideas.

Choose the Best Idea

At some point it's necessary to switch from generating ideas (divergent thinking) to evaluating ideas (using convergent thinking) so that you can select a course of action. Now is the time to be critical and evaluate strengths and weaknesses. Decision techniques such as the additive and expected value models discussed in this chapter can be helpful in selecting the best idea from a batch of alternatives. Table 8.7 lists some additional guidelines for evaluating ideas.

Since we may not always select the best idea, it's important to try to monitor the application of our solutions and to revise them if necessary. Sternberg (1986) lists a number of examples in which solution monitoring is required. For instance, teachers or lecturers need to be aware of whether their audience is understanding the material they present. If understanding or interest is waning, good teachers attempt to figure out why and make corrections. Business executives must monitor the success of their products and possibly discontinue or change a product as a result of declining sales.

Sternberg (1986) recommends several steps that you can take to improve your solution monitoring.

1. *Be aware of the need for solution monitoring.* The most important step you can take is simply to recognize the need to monitor your solutions and change strategies when necessary.

2. *Beware of justification of effort.* It's natural that once you've invested a substantial amount of time or effort in a given course of action, you'll seek reasons to justify your effort. Watch out for this tendency—in yourself and others.

3. *Avoid impulsiveness in solution monitoring.* Solution monitoring is also subject to error. Be careful to determine that the initial solution is not working before switching solutions.

4. *Actively seek external feedback.* It may be necessary to actively seek feedback. You may have little idea about what your colleagues, boss, spouse, or friends really think of your solutions.

In summary, it's wise to maintain flexibility while implementing a solution to a problem. Keep in mind that few choices in life are truly irreversible, and don't get "locked into" a particular course of action. Monitor results closely, and be willing to revise your strategy as needed.

LANGUAGE AND THOUGHT

KEY IDEAS

Language: Turning Thoughts into Words

• Psychologists' interest in language acquisition has been extended to include the study of whether chimpanzees can learn a language. Chimpanzees can learn signs or symbols to represent words and can combine them to communicate with their caretakers. However, some theorists doubt whether chimps can generate sentences and really learn the rules of language.

• Our Featured Study, which followed the language development of a chimp named Kanzi, was relevant to this issue. Sue Savage-Rumbaugh and her colleagues concluded that Kanzi was capable of generating spontaneous sentences that followed language rules relating to the ordering of words. Kanzi is also the first chimp to acquire the use of symbols incidentally, through the observation of another chimp's training.

• Languages are symbolic, generative, and structured. Human languages are structured hierarchically. At the bottom of the hierarchy are the basic sound units, called phonemes. At the next level are morphemes, the smallest units of meaning in a language. Words are morphemes or are formed of morphemes. Words are combined into sentences according to the rules of syntax.

• Chimps' use of language appears to be symbolic and generative, but until recently, there was little evidence that chimps could acquire language rules. Kanzi's ability to form sentences that use correct word order strengthens the argument that apes can learn a genuine, albeit simple, language. Although language may not be uniquely human, humans do appear uniquely well suited for learning language.

• Language in humans begins with infants' attempts to produce sounds. The initial sounds are similar across languages, but beginning when the child is about 6 months of age, the sounds begin to resemble the surrounding language. Children utter their first words at around 10 to 12 months and can usually say between 3 and 50 words by 18 months.

• These early words are often overextended to refer to objects that look similar to the correctly named object. Single words, called holophrases, are also used to express the meaning of several words. Children begin to combine words by the end of their second year. Their early sentences are telegraphic, in that they omit many nonessential words. Over the next several years, children gradually learn the complexities of syntax.

• There are three major theories of language acquisition. According to Skinner's learning theory, children acquire a language through imitation and reinforcement. A nativist theory favored by Chomsky is that children have an innate capacity to learn the rules of a grammar, and that learning a language is different from other kinds of learning. Cognitive psychologists, however, claim that the development of language and the development of thought are closely related. They emphasize the information processing aspects of language.

• Understanding the meaning of a speech or a text is an important cognitive skill, requiring the integration of ideas across sentences. Integration is easiest when the ideas (1) have been expressed earlier in the passage, (2) are still in short-term memory, and (3) can be directly related to new ideas without an inference. A model of comprehension proposed by Walter Kintsch has been successful in improving the prediction of readability.

Problem Solving: In Search of Solutions

• In studying problem solving, some psychologists have differentiated between several types of problems. Transformation problems, such as the missionaries/cannibals puzzle, require that the problem solver carry out a sequence of transformations (moves) in order to reach a specific goal. Arrangement problems, such as anagrams, require the problem solver to arrange the parts in a way that satisfies a general goal. In problems that require inducing structure, such as the series completion task, the problem solver must discover the relations among the parts of a problem.

• A variety of strategies, or heuristics, are useful for solving problems. Means/end analysis requires reducing the differences between the current problem state and the goal state. When people form subgoals, they try breaking the problem into several parts. Sometimes it is useful to start at the goal state and work backwards toward the initial state. Another general strategy involves searching for analogies between new problems and old problems.

• The solution of many kinds of problems requires learning both subject-matter knowledge and general strategies. Experts are better than novices in solving these kinds of problems because they have more organized chunks of knowledge in memory and because they construct superior plans for reaching the goal. Experts also tend to be more capable of identifying useful analogies between problems.

• Creativity is often useful in problem solving. The generation of original, novel, and useful ideas seems to be facilitated by divergent thinking. Most creativity tests attempt to measure divergent thinking skills. These tests are moderately good predictors of creative productivity in the real world. Creativity and intelligence are only weakly related. Creative people tend to display certain personality traits, such as independence and tolerance of ambiguity.

Decision Making: Choices and Chances

• Decision making is another example of the cognitive processes studied by psychologists. The additive model is used when people make decisions by rating the attributes of each alternative and selecting the alternative that has the highest sum of ratings. When elimination by aspects is used, people gradually eliminate alternatives if their attributes fail to satisfy some minimum criterion. To some extent, people adapt their decision-making strategy to the situation.

• Risky decision making is making decisions under conditions of uncertainty. Psychological models of how people make risky decisions are based on the expected values of the different outcomes and the probabilities that these outcomes will occur. Some models also consider the subjective utility and subjective probability of various outcomes. People use a number of heuristics in estimating probabilities. These heuristics do not always lead to realistic estimates.

Putting It in Perspective

• Two of our unifying themes surfaced in the chapter. Our discussion of language acquisition revealed once again that all aspects of behavior are shaped by both nature and nurture. The recent progress in the study of cognitive processes showed how progress in psychology depends upon the application of empirical methods.

Application: Solving Problems Systematically

• To solve problems effectively, it helps to suppress negative emotional reactions and to approach problems systematically. Anderson recommends five steps in systematic problem solving: (1) state the problem, (2) get the facts, (3) focus on the important facts, (4) generate ideas, and (5) choose the best idea.

KEY TERMS

Brainstorming
Compensatory decision
 models
Convergent thinking
Creativity
Divergent thinking
Functional fixedness
Heuristic
Holophrases
Insight
Language
Means/end analysis
Metalinguistic awareness
Morphemes
Noncompensatory
 decision models
Overextensions
Phonemes
Phrase-structure rules
Psycholinguistics
Readability
Risky decision making
Syntax
Telegraphic speech
Transformational rules

KEY PEOPLE

Noam Chomsky
Herbert Simon
B. F. Skinner
Amos Tversky &
 Daniel Kahneman

Intelligence and Psychological Testing

INTELLIGENCE AND PSYCHOLOGICAL TESTING

Have you ever thought about the role that psychological testing has played in your life? In all likelihood your years in grade school and high school were punctuated with a variety of intelligence tests, achievement tests, creativity tests, aptitude tests, and occupational interest tests. In the lower grades, you were probably given standardized achievement tests once or twice a year. For instance, you may have taken the Iowa Tests of Basic Skills, which measured your progress in reading, language, vocabulary, mathematics, and study skills. Perhaps you still have vivid memories of the serious atmosphere in the classroom, the very formal instructions ("do not break the seal on this test until your examiner tells you to do so"), and the heavy pressure to work fast (personally, I can still see Sister Dominic marching back and forth with her intense gaze riveted on her stopwatch).

Where you're sitting at this very moment may have been influenced by your performance on standardized tests, in that your choice of a college to attend may have hinged on your SAT or ACT test scores. Moreover, your interactions with standardized tests may be far from finished. Even at this point in your life, you may be selecting your courses to "gear up" for the Graduate Record Exam (GRE), the Law School Admission Test (LSAT), the Medical College Admission Test (MCAT), or required certification tests in fields such as accounting, nursing, radiologic technology, or hotel-motel management. After graduation, when you go job-hunting, you may find that prospective employers expect you to take still more batteries of psychological tests as they attempt to assess your personality, your motivation, and your talents.

The vast enterprise of modern standardized testing evolved from psychologists' pioneering efforts to measure *general intelligence*. The first useful intelligence tests, which were created soon after the turn of the century, have left a great many

"descendants." Today, we have over 2600 published psychological tests that measure a diverse array of mental abilities and other behavioral traits. Indeed, psychological testing has become a big business. The revenues of the largest American testing company (ETS) exceed $100 million a year (Hothersall, 1984).

Clearly, American society has embraced psychological testing. Each year in the United States alone, people take *hundreds of millions* of intelligence and achievement tests (Anderson, 1982). Scholarships, degrees, jobs, and self-concepts are on the line as we attempt to hurdle a seemingly endless succession of tests. It's apparent that our lives are affected by how we perform on psychological tests, so it pays to be aware of their strengths and limitations. In this chapter we'll explore many questions about testing, including the following:

- How did psychological testing become so prevalent in our society?
- How do psychologists judge the validity of their tests?
- What exactly do intelligence tests measure?
- Is intelligence inherited? If so, to what extent?
- How are tests used to measure aspects of personality?
- What role can occupational interest tests play in vocational decisions?

We'll begin by introducing some basic concepts in psychological testing. Then we'll explore the history of intelligence tests because they provided the model for subsequent psychological tests. Next we'll address practical questions about how intelligence tests work. After examining the nature versus nurture debate as it relates to intelligence, we'll discuss some new directions in the study of intelligence. Toward the end of the chapter, we'll take a look at personality tests. In the Application, you'll find out how psychological tests can be helpful in career planning.

KEY CONCEPTS IN PSYCHOLOGICAL TESTING

A *psychological test* is a standardized measure of a sample of a person's behavior. Psychological tests are measurement instruments. They're used to measure the *individual differences* that exist among people in abilities, aptitudes, interests, and aspects of personality.

Your responses to a psychological test represent a *sample* of your behavior. The word *sample* should

alert you to one of the key limitations of psychological tests. It's always possible that a particular behavior sample is not representative of your characteristic behavior. We all have our bad days. A stomachache, a fight with a friend, a problem with your car—all might affect your responses to a particular test on a particular day.

The problem of obtaining a representative sam-

Figure 9.1 The sampling process in testing. A psychological test obtains a sample of behavior, just as the Viking 2 spacecraft was designed to obtain a sample of Martian soil. Sampling is a necessary measurement technique: we can't measure an individual's behavior in its entirety anymore than we can sift through the entire surface of Mars. However, it's always possible that a sample is unrepresentative and misleading. The results of psychological tests should therefore be interpreted with caution.

ple is *not* unique to testing (see Figure 9.1). It's an unavoidable problem for any measurement technique that relies on sampling. For example, a physician taking your blood pressure might get an unrepresentative reading, just as a football scout clocking a prospect's 40-yard sprint time might get a misleading figure. Because of the limitations of the sampling process, test scores should always be interpreted *cautiously*. Many psychological tests are very precise measurement devices, but, because of the ever present sampling problem, test results should *not* be viewed as the "final word" on one's personality and abilities.

Principal Types of Tests

Psychological tests are used extensively in research, but most of them were developed to serve some very practical purpose outside of the laboratory. Most tests can be placed in one of two very broad categories: (1) mental ability tests and (2) personality tests.

MENTAL ABILITY TESTS
Psychological testing originated with efforts to measure general mental ability. Today, tests of mental abilities remain the most common kind of psychological test. This broad class of tests includes three principal subcategories: intelligence tests, aptitude tests, and achievement tests.

Intelligence tests measure general mental ability. They're intended to assess intellectual potential rather than previous learning or accumulated knowledge. Aptitude tests are also designed to measure intellectual potential, but they break

mental ability into separate components. Thus, **aptitude tests assess talent for specific kinds of learning.** In other words, aptitude tests measure particular types of mental ability, such as numerical ability, spatial reasoning, or mechanical reasoning. Like aptitude tests, achievement tests have a specific focus, but they're supposed to measure previous learning instead of potential. Thus, **achievement tests gauge a person's mastery and knowledge of various subjects** (such as reading, English, or mathematics).

PERSONALITY TESTS
If you had to describe yourself in a few words, what words would you use? Are you introverted? Independent? Ambitious? Enterprising? Conventional? Assertive? Domineering? Words such as these refer to personality *traits*. These traits can be assessed systematically with over 500 personality tests. **Personality tests measure various aspects of personality, including motives, interests, values, and attitudes.** Many psychologists prefer to call these tests personality *scales*, since, unlike tests of mental abilities, the questions do not have right and wrong answers. We'll look at the different types of personality scales later in the chapter.

Standardization and Norms

Both personality scales and tests of mental abilities are *standardized* measures of behavior. **Standardization refers to the uniform procedures used in the administration and scoring of a test.** All subjects get the same instructions, the same questions, and the same time limits, so that

Figure 9.2 Test reliability. Subjects' scores on the first administration of an assertiveness test are represented on the left, and their scores on a second administration of the same test a few weeks later on the right. If subjects obtain similar scores on both administrations, the test measures assertiveness consistently and has high reliability. If they get very different scores on the second administration, the test has low reliability.

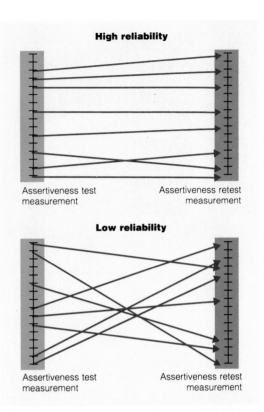

High reliability

Assertiveness test measurement   Assertiveness retest measurement

Low reliability

Assertiveness test measurement   Assertiveness retest measurement

their scores can be compared meaningfully. This means, for instance, that a person taking the Differential Aptitude Test (DAT) in 1968 in San Diego, and another taking the DAT in 1977 in Atlanta, and another taking it in 1985 in Peoria all confront exactly the same test-taking task.

The standardization of a test's scoring system includes the development of test norms. **Test norms provide information about where a score on a psychological test ranks in relation to other scores on that test.** Why do we need test norms? Because in psychological testing, everything is relative. Psychological tests tell you how you score *relative to other people.* They tell you, for instance, that you are average in creativity, or slightly above average in clerical ability, or extremely below average in anxiety. These interpretations are derived from the test norms that help you to understand what your test score means.

Usually, test norms allow you to convert your "raw score" on a test into a *percentile score,* **which indicates the percentage of people who score below the score you obtained.** For example, you might take a 40-item assertiveness scale and obtain a raw score of 26 (in other words, you indicate a preference for the assertive option on 26 of the questions). That score of 26 has little meaning until you consult the test norms and find out that it places you at the 82nd percentile. This normative information would indicate that you appear to be more assertive than 82% of the sample of people that provided the basis for the test norms.

The sample of people that the norms are based on is called a test's *standardization group.* Ideally, test norms are based on a large sample of people who were carefully selected to be representative of the broader population. In reality, the representativeness of standardization groups varies considerably from one test to another.

Reliability

Any kind of measuring device, whether it's a tire gauge, a stopwatch, or a psychological test, should be reasonably consistent. That is, repeated measurements should yield reasonably similar results—a quality that psychologists call *reliability.*

To better appreciate the importance of reliability, think about how you would react if a tire pressure gauge gave you several very different readings for the same tire. You would probably conclude that the gauge was broken and toss it into the garbage, because consistency in measurement obviously is essential to accuracy in measurement.

Reliability **refers to the measurement consistency of a test (or other kinds of measurement techniques).** A reliable test is one that yields similar results upon repetition of the test (see Figure 9.2). Like most other types of measuring devices, psychological tests are not perfectly reliable. That is, they usually don't yield exactly the same scores when repeated. A certain amount of inconsistency is unavoidable because human behavior is variable. For example, if you take the Beck Depression Inventory on two different occasions, you're not likely to respond to all 21 items in exactly the same way both times.

Although a test's reliability can be estimated in several ways, the most widely used approach is to check test-retest reliability. ***Test-retest reliability is estimated by comparing subjects' scores on two administrations of a test.*** If we wanted to check the test-retest reliability of a newly developed test of assertiveness, we would ask a group of subjects to take the test on two occasions, probably a few weeks apart. The underlying assumption is that assertiveness is a fairly stable aspect of personality that won't change in a matter of a few weeks. Thus, changes in subjects' scores across

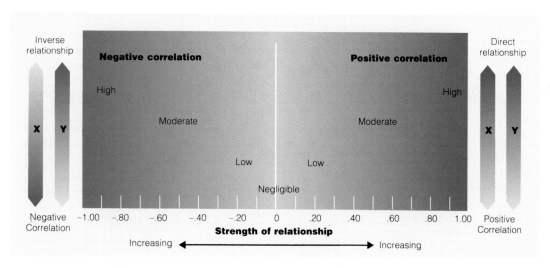

Figure 9.3 Correlation and reliability. As you recall from Chapter 2, a positive correlation means that two variables are directly related; a negative correlation means that the variables are inversely related. The closer the correlation coefficient gets to either −1.00 or +1.00, the stronger the relationship. At a minimum, reliability estimates for psychological tests must be moderately high positive correlations.

the two administrations of the test presumably reflect inconsistency in measurement.

Reliability estimates require the computation of correlation coefficients, which we introduced in Chapter 2. Correlation plays a critical role in research on testing, so let's re-examine the concept briefly (see Figure 9.3). **A correlation coefficient is a numerical index of the degree of relationship that exists between two variables.** A *positive* correlation indicates that there's a direct relationship between two variables: high scores on variable X are associated with high scores on variable Y, and low scores on X tend to go with low scores on Y. A *negative* correlation indicates that there's an inverse relationship between two variables: high scores on X are associated with low scores on Y, and high scores on Y go with low scores on X. The actual coefficient of correlation can vary between 0 and ±1.00. The closer a correlation comes to either +1.00 or −1.00 (that is, the farther it is from 0), the stronger the association between the two variables.

In estimating test-retest reliability, the two variables that must be correlated are the two sets of scores from the two administrations of the test. If people get fairly similar scores on the two administrations of our assertiveness test, this consistency yields a substantial positive correlation. The magnitude of the correlation gives us a precise indication of the test's consistency. The closer the correlation comes to +1.00, the more reliable the test is.

There are no absolute guidelines about acceptable levels of reliability, since what's acceptable depends to some extent on the nature and purpose of the test. The reliability estimates for most psychological tests are above .70. Many exceed .90. The higher the reliability coefficient, the more consistent the test is. As reliability goes down, concern about measurement error increases.

Validity

Even if a test is quite reliable, we still need to be concerned about its validity. **Validity refers to the ability of a test to measure what it was designed to measure.** If we develop a new test of assertiveness, we have to provide some evidence that it really measures assertiveness. Validity can be estimated in a variety of ways, depending on the nature of the test.

CONTENT VALIDITY
Achievement tests and educational tests such as classroom exams should have adequate content validity. **Content validity refers to the degree to which the content of a test is representative of the domain it's supposed to cover.** If you take a physics exam and the professor sloppily throws in questions on material that was not covered in class or in assigned reading, the professor has compromised the content validity of the exam. Content validity is evaluated with logic more than with statistics.

CRITERION-RELATED VALIDITY
Psychological tests are frequently used to make predictions about specific aspects of individuals' behavior. We use them to predict performance in college, job capability, and suitability for training programs, as just a few examples. Criterion-related validity is a central concern in such cases. **Criterion-related validity is estimated by correlating subjects' scores on a test with their scores on an independent criterion (another measure) of the trait assessed by the test** (see Figure 9.4).

For example, if you developed a test to measure aptitude for becoming an airplane pilot, you could check its validity by correlating subjects' scores on your aptitude test with subsequent ratings of their performance in their pilot-training program.

309

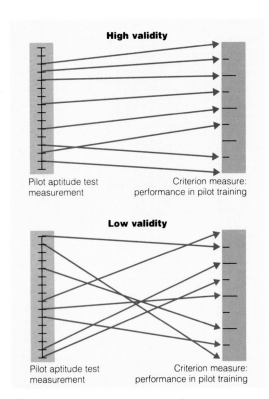

Figure 9.4 Correlation and criterion-related validity. To evaluate the criterion-related validity of a pilot aptitude test, a psychologist would correlate subjects' test scores with a criterion measure of their behavior, such as ratings of their performance in a pilot training program. Test validity is high if scores on the two measures are highly correlated. If there's little or no relationship between the two sets of scores, validity is low, which means that the aptitude test does not measure what it is supposed to measure.

High validity

Pilot aptitude test measurement

Criterion measure: performance in pilot training

Low validity

Pilot aptitude test measurement

Criterion measure: performance in pilot training

The ratings of performance in the training program would be the independent criterion of pilot aptitude. If your test has reasonable validity, people who score high on the test should tend to earn high performance ratings during training, and low scorers should tend get low ratings. In other words, there ought to be a reasonably strong positive correlation between the test and the criterion measure, which would validate the test's predictive ability.

CONSTRUCT VALIDITY

Many psychological tests attempt to measure abstract personal qualities, such as creativity, intelligence, or independence. There are no obvious criterion measures for these abstract qualities, which are called *hypothetical constructs*. In measuring abstract qualities, we're concerned about **construct validity—the extent to which there is evidence that a test measures a particular hypothetical construct.**

The process of demonstrating construct validity can be a complicated matter. It usually requires a series of studies that examine the correlations between scores on the test and various measures thought to be *related* to the trait in question. For example, the construct validity of intelligence tests has been investigated by correlating intelligence test scores with grades in school. No one would argue that grades in school are a pure criterion of intelligence. However, they are undoubtedly related to intelligence. Hence, we can reason that if an intelligence test really measures intelligence, there should be a positive correlation between scores on the test and school grades. If this is found to be the case, the results provide support for the test's construct validity.

A thorough demonstration of construct validity requires that we look at the relations between a test and as many related measures as we can find. Ultimately, it's the overall pattern of correlations that provides convincing (or unconvincing) evidence of a test's construct validity.

The complexities involved in demonstrating construct validity will be apparent in our upcoming discussion of intelligence testing. The ongoing debate about the construct validity of intelligence tests is one of the oldest debates in psychology. Let's look now at the origins of intelligence tests, to provide some background to help you appreciate the current controversies about intelligence testing.

"Imagine a Utopia . . . in which a system of competitive examinations . . . had been so developed as to embrace every important quality of mind and body, and where a considerable sum was allotted to the endowment of such marriages as promised to yield children who would grow into eminent servants of the State."

Sir Francis Galton

THE EVOLUTION OF INTELLIGENCE TESTING

Psychological tests play a prominent role in our society, but this wasn't always so. The first primitive psychological tests were invented only a little over a hundred years ago. Since then, our reliance on psychological tests has grown gradually. In this section, we discuss the pioneers who launched psychological testing with their efforts to measure general intelligence.

Galton's Studies of Hereditary Genius

It all began with the work of a British scholar, Sir Francis Galton, in the latter part of the 19th century. Galton, a precocious child who was reciting Shakespeare at age 6, counted the eminent naturalist Charles Darwin among his cousins. Thus, it was natural that he took an interest in how intellectual genius seemed to run in families. Galton studied family trees and found that success and eminence appeared consistently in some families over generations. For the most part, these families were very much like Galton's family—well-bred, upper-class families with access to superior schooling and social connections that pave the way to success. Yet Galton discounted the advantages of an upper-class upbringing. In his book, entitled *Hereditary Genius*, Galton (1869) concluded that success ran in families because great intelligence was passed from generation to generation through genetic inheritance.

Galton's conviction about the genetic basis of intelligence and his disdain for the lower classes were so strong that he advocated eugenic programs. **Eugenics involves efforts to control reproduction to gradually improve hereditary characteristics in a population** (the term *eugenics* comes from the Greek word *eugenes*, meaning "wellborn"). Galton wanted to encourage intellectually superior people to mate together to improve the quality of the human race. He envisioned a "golden book of natural nobility" that would list Britain's brightest young marital candidates. More disturbingly, Galton wanted to discourage (or prevent) people of lesser intelligence from having children. Fortunately, Galton never saw his dream realized. However, his ideas show that the concept of intelligence has had controversial social and political implications from the very beginning.

To show that intelligence was governed by heredity, Galton needed an objective measure of intelligence. His approach to this problem was guided by the theoretical views of his day, which assumed that the contents of the mind were built out of elementary *sensations*. Thus, Galton hypothesized that exceptionally bright people should exhibit exceptional sensory acuity. Working from this premise, he tried to assess innate mental ability by measuring simple sensory processes, such as sensitivity to high-pitched sounds, color perception, and reaction time (the speed of one's response to a stimulus). As you might guess, his efforts met with little success. It turned out that sensory abilites were largely unrelated to other criteria of mental ability that he was trying to predict (such as success in school or professional life).

In pursuing this line of investigation, Galton invented the concept of *correlation*, the statistical measure that has since played an enormously important role in psychological testing and in many other lines of research. Although Galton's mental tests were a failure, his work created an interest in the measurement of mental ability. It set the stage for a subsequent breakthrough by Alfred Binet, a prominent French psychologist.

Binet's Breakthrough

In 1904, a commission on education in France asked Alfred Binet to devise a test that could be used to identify mentally subnormal children, who were assumed to be unable to profit from a normal education. The commission was motivated by admirable goals. It wanted to identify youngsters in need of special training, and it wanted to avoid complete reliance on teachers' evaluations because these might often be subjective and biased.

In response to this need, Binet and a colleague, Theodore Simon, published the first useful test of general mental ability in 1905. Their test proved useful because they had the insight to load it with items that required verbal reasoning and the manipulation of information, rather than the sensory skills Galton had measured. From the very beginning, then, intelligence tests were designed to predict whether children could perform adequately in school. Binet's test predicted school performance fairly well, and its use spread across Europe and America.

The Binet-Simon scale expressed a child's score in terms of "mental level" or "mental age." **A child's *mental age* indicated that he or she displayed the mental ability typical of a child of that chronological (actual) age.** Thus, a child with a mental age of 6 performed like the average 6-year-old on the test. Of course, if the child's chronological age was 10, this wasn't a good sign. When youngsters were found to have a mental age substantially lower than their actual age, it was inferred that they were low in intelligence. For example, if the test indicated that a 12-year-old child had a mental age of 7, the child was considered to be subnormal.

Realizing that his scale was a somewhat crude initial effort at measuring mental ability, Binet revised it in 1908 and again in 1911. Unfortunately, *his* revising came to an abrupt end with his death in 1911. However, other psychologists continued to build on Binet's work, especially in America, where Lewis Terman and David Wechsler "picked up the torch" for the testing movement.

Terman and the Stanford-Binet

In America, Binet's test was initially put into use by Henry Goddard (1908), who translated it into English with virtually no changes in content. However, Lewis Terman and his colleagues at Stanford University soon went to work on a major expansion and revision of the test. Their work led to the 1916 publication of the Stanford-Binet Intelligence Scale (Terman, 1916). Although this revision was quite loyal to Binet's original conception of mental ability, it incorporated a new scoring scheme based on the "intelligence quotient" originally suggested by William Stern (1914). **An *intelligence quotient (IQ)* is a child's mental age divided by chronological age, multiplied by 100.** This formula depends on an actual quotient.

"The intelligence of anyone is susceptible of development. With practice, enthusiasm, and especially with method one can succeed in increasing one's attention, memory, judgment, and in becoming literally more intelligent than one was before."
ALFRED BINET

$$IQ = \frac{\text{Mental age}}{\text{Chronological age}} \times 100$$

The ratio of mental age to chronological age created a more elegant scoring system than Binet's, a system that made it possible to compare children of different ages. In Binet's system, such comparisons were awkward. It was not clear, for example, whether a 12-year-old with a mental age of 9 was more or less intelligent than a 9-year-old with a mental age of 6, although both showed the same 3-year lag in mental development. The IQ ratio placed all children (regardless of age) on the same scale, which was centered at 100 if their mental age corresponded to their chronological age. Thus, in our examples, the 12-year-old would receive an IQ score of 75; the 9-year-old, an IQ score of 67 (see Table 9.1 for the calculations).

Although other revisions of Binet's scale were developed around the same time as Terman's, the Stanford-Binet quickly became the world's foremost intelligence test and the standard of comparison for virtually all intelligence tests that followed (Zimmerman & Woo-Sam, 1984). When new IQ tests were developed in subsequent years, their validity was often demonstrated simply by showing that they correlated strongly with the Stanford-Binet. Although many new IQ tests geared to specific populations, age groups, and purposes have been developed, the apparent variety is somewhat misleading: most tests remain loyal to the conception of intelligence originally formulated by Binet and Terman.

Like Galton, Terman was keenly interested in people who showed extremely high intelligence. Although his view wasn't as one-sided as Galton's, he too believed that intelligence was largely inherited. In 1921 he began a major study of gifted children that has been continued through today by other researchers (Terman & Oden, 1959; Sears, 1977). This nearly 70-year-old research project represents psychology's longest-running study.

In this study, over 250,000 California school children were given IQ tests, and 1528 highly gifted youngsters, with an average IQ of about 150, were identified. These gifted children were followed through grade school, high school, college, and their entire careers, right on through to their retirements. Terman discovered that the classic stereotype of gifted children—that they are weak, sickly, socially inept bookworms—was decidedly inaccurate. In comparison to normal subjects, Terman's gifted children were found (1) to be above average in height, weight, strength, and physical health, (2) to display superior emotional adjustment and mental health, and (3) to be socially adept and well liked. Although there were exceptions to the general rule, Terman's subjects continued to enjoy better-than-average health and social-emotional adjustment throughout their adult years.

Collectively, the gifted children in Terman's sample grew up to be very successful. By mid-life, they had produced 92 books, 235 patents, and nearly 2200 scientific articles (Goleman, 1980). Interestingly, one of the children, Robert Sears, went on to head the psychology department at Stanford University, the same department that Terman had once headed. Today, Sears and his wife, Pauline, oversee the follow-up studies of Terman's gifted group.

Wechsler's Innovations

While Terman was following gifted children, David Wechsler was busy working with a very different clientele. As chief psychologist at New York's massive Bellevue Hospital, Wechsler was charged with overseeing the psychological assessment of thousands of adult patients. He found the Stanford-Binet somewhat unsatisfactory for this purpose. Although Terman had added items to extend the test's use to adults, the test had originally been designed with children in mind.

Thus, Wechsler set out to improve on the measurement of intelligence *in adults*. In 1939 he published an IQ test designed for adults, which came to be known as the Wechsler Adult Intelligence Scale (WAIS). Judging from the success that his test enjoyed, Wechsler had filled an important need. Ironically, Wechsler (1949, 1967) eventu-

"It is the method of tests that has brought psychology down from the clouds and made it useful to men; that has transformed the 'science of trivialities' into the 'science of human engineering.'"

LEWIS TERMAN

Table 9.1 Calculating the Intelligence Quotient

MEASURE	CHILD 1	CHILD 2	CHILD 3	CHILD 4
Mental age (MA)	6 years	6 years	9 years	12 years
Chronological age (CA)	6 years	9 years	12 years	9 years
$IQ = \frac{MA}{CA} \times 100$	$\frac{6}{6} \times 100 = 100$	$\frac{6}{9} \times 100 = 67$	$\frac{9}{12} \times 100 = 75$	$\frac{12}{9} \times 100 = 133$

Wechsler Adult Intelligence Scale (WAIS)

Test	Description	Example
VERBAL SCALE		
Information	Taps general range of information	On what continent is France?
Comprehension	Tests understanding of social conventions and ability to evaluate past experience	Why are children required to go to school?
Arithmetic	Tests arithmetic reasoning through verbal problems	How many hours will it take to drive 150 miles at 50 miles per hour?
Similarities	Asks in what way certain objects or concepts are similar; measures abstract thinking	How are a calculator and a typewriter alike?
Digit span	Tests attention and rote memory by orally presenting series of digits to be repeated forwards or backwards	Repeat the following numbers backwards: 2 4 3 5 1 8 6
Vocabulary	Tests ability to define increasingly difficult words	What does *audacity* mean?
PERFORMANCE SCALE		
Digit symbol	Tests speed of learning through timed coding tasks in which numbers must be associated with marks of various shapes	Shown: 1 2 3 4 Fill in: 1 4 3 2
Picture completion	Tests visual alertness and visual memory through presentation of an incompletely drawn figure; the missing part must be discovered and named	Tell me what is missing: 
Block design	Tests ability to perceive and analyze patterns by presenting designs that must be copied with blocks	Assemble blocks to match this design: 
Picture arrangement	Tests understanding of social situations through a series of comic-strip-type pictures that must be arranged in the right sequence to tell a story	Put the pictures in the right order: 
Object assembly	Tests ability to deal with part/whole relationships by presenting puzzle pieces that must be assembled to form a complete object	Assemble the pieces into a complete object: 

ally devised *downward extensions* of his scale for children, assembling a version of the test for children aged 6 to 17 and another version for children aged 4 to 6.

The Wechsler scales were characterized by at least two major innovations (Frank, 1983). First, Wechsler made his scales less dependent on subjects' verbal ability than the Stanford-Binet by adding many items that required nonverbal reasoning (see Figure 9.5). To highlight the distinction between verbal and nonverbal ability, he formalized the computation of separate scores for verbal IQ, performance (nonverbal) IQ, and full-scale (total) IQ. The Wechsler tests are also divided into 11 smaller subtests that determine the verbal and performance IQ scores.

Second, Wechsler discarded the intelligence quotient in favor of a new scoring scheme based on the *normal distribution*. This scoring system has since been adopted by most other IQ tests, including the Stanford-Binet. Although the term *intelligence quotient* lingers on in our vocabulary, scores on intelligence tests are no longer based on an actual quotient or ratio. We'll take a close

Figure 9.5 Subtests on the Wechsler Adult Intelligence Scale (WAIS). Unlike the Stanford-Binet, the WAIS is subdivided into a series of tests that yield separate verbal and performance (nonverbal) IQ scores. Sample test items that closely resemble those on the WAIS are shown on the right.

CONCEPT CHECK 9.1
Recognizing Basic Concepts in Testing

Check your understanding of basic concepts in psychological testing by answering the questions below. Select your responses from the following concepts:

Test norms   Criterion-related validity
Test-retest reliability   Construct validity
Content validity

The answers are in Appendix A.

1. At the request of the HiTechnoLand computer store chain, Professor Charlz develops a test to measure aptitude for selling computers. Two hundred applicants for sales jobs at HiTechnoLand stores are asked to take the test on two occasions, a few weeks apart. A correlation of + .82 is found between applicants' scores on the two administrations of the test. Thus, the test appears to possess reasonable _____.

2. All 200 of these applicants are hired and put to work selling computers. After 6 months Professor Charlz correlates the new workers' aptitude test scores with the dollar value of the computers that each sold during the first 6 months on the job. This correlation turns out to be − .21. This finding suggests that the test may lack _____.

3. Back at the university, Professor Charlz is teaching a course in Theories of Personality. He decides to use the same midterm exam that he gave last year, even though the exam includes questions about theorists that he did not cover or assign reading on this year. There are reasons to doubt the _____ of Professor Charlz's midterm exam.

Intelligence Testing Today

Today, psychologists and educators have many IQ tests available for their use. Basically, these fall into two categories: *individual tests* and *group tests*. Individual IQ tests are administered only by psychologists who have special training for this purpose. A psychologist works with a single examinee at a time. The Stanford-Binet and the Wechsler scales are both individual IQ tests, and they continue to be the most widely used tests in this category.

The problem with individual IQ tests is that they're rather expensive and time-consuming to administer. Therefore, researchers have developed a number of IQ tests that can be administered to a large group of people at once by a person with minimal training in testing (the interpretation of test results should still be done by a psychologist). Because they're much more cost-effective, group tests such as the Henmon-Nelson Tests of Mental Ability and the California Test of Mental Maturity are now used more frequently than individual tests. If you've taken an IQ test, chances are that it was a group test. As you'll see in the next section, many school districts routinely administer group tests.

BASIC QUESTIONS ABOUT INTELLIGENCE TESTING

There are many misconceptions about intelligence tests. In this section we'll use a question-and-answer format to explain the essential principles involved in intelligence testing.

Why Are People Given Intelligence Tests?

Most IQ testing is conducted by school districts, which are largely free to formulate their own unique testing programs because there is little federal or state policy regarding ideal patterns of testing. Some districts administer group IQ tests to all students at regular and frequent intervals; others administer only individual IQ tests on an occasional basis, as needed. Boehm (1985) lists three major functions of IQ testing in educational settings:

1. *Screening and diagnosis.* Children who are troubled by learning problems in school are most likely to be helped if their problems can be diagnosed early and accurately. IQ tests usually play a

key role in these diagnostic efforts. They can be very useful in distinguishing mental retardation from specific learning disabilities.

2. *Selection and placement.* Many districts use IQ scores to sort students into appropriate programs and courses. For instance, IQ tests usually play a key role in identifying "gifted" children, who are then funneled into accelerated programs. IQ tests may also be used by districts that group all students according to their academic ability. Evidence regarding the value of this "tracking" is inconclusive, but many school administrators believe that it facilitates more effective teaching.

3. *Evaluation and research.* The highly standardized nature of IQ tests also makes them useful in the evaluation of educational programs. The well-known Headstart program, for instance, was evaluated in part by examining changes in participants' IQ scores.

It should also be noted that clinical psychologists use IQ tests frequently in their diagnostic activities (Matarazzo & Herman, 1985). Clinicians use individual IQ tests not only to measure general intelligence, but to assess strengths, weaknesses, and peculiarities in a client's cognitive functioning. Individual IQ tests can also be used to help differentiate between organic brain damage and other kinds of mental disorders.

What Kinds of Questions Are on Intelligence Tests?

The nature of the questions found on IQ tests will vary somewhat from test to test, depending on whether the test is intended for children or adults (or both), and whether the test is designed to be administered to individuals or groups. Overall, the questions are fairly diverse in format. The Wechsler scales, with their numerous subtests, provide a representative example of the kinds of items that appear on most IQ tests. As you saw in Figure 9.5, the items in the Wechsler subtests require subjects to furnish information, recognize vocabulary, demonstrate basic memory, and manipulate words, numbers, and images through abstract reasoning.

What Do Modern IQ Scores Mean?

As we discussed, scores on intelligence tests once represented a ratio of mental age to chronological age, but this system has given way to one based on the normal distribution and the standard deviation statistic (see Chapter 2). **The *normal distri-**

***bution* is a symmetric, bell-shaped curve that represents the pattern in which many human characteristics are dispersed in the population.** When a trait is normally distributed, most cases fall near the center of the distribution (an average score) and the number of cases gradually declines as one moves away from the center in either direction, as shown in Figure 9.6.

The normal distribution was first discovered by 18th-century astronomers who found that their measurement errors were distributed in a predictable way that resembled a bell-shaped curve. Since then, research has shown that many human traits, ranging from height to running speed to spatial ability, also follow a normal distribution.

Psychologists eventually recognized that intelligence scores fall into a normal distribution, just as many other human characteristics do. This insight permitted David Wechsler to devise a more sophisticated scoring system for his tests that has been adopted by virtually all IQ tests. In this system, raw scores are translated into ***deviation IQ scores* that locate subjects precisely within the normal distribution, using the standard deviation as the unit of measurement.**

For most IQ tests, the mean of the distribution is set at 100 and the standard deviation (SD) is set at 15. These choices were made to provide continuity with the original IQ ratio (mental age to chronological age) that was centered at 100. In this system, which is depicted in Figure 9.7, a score of 115 means that a person scored exactly

"The subtests [of the WAIS] are different measures of intelligence, not measures of different kinds of intelligence."
DAVID WECHSLER

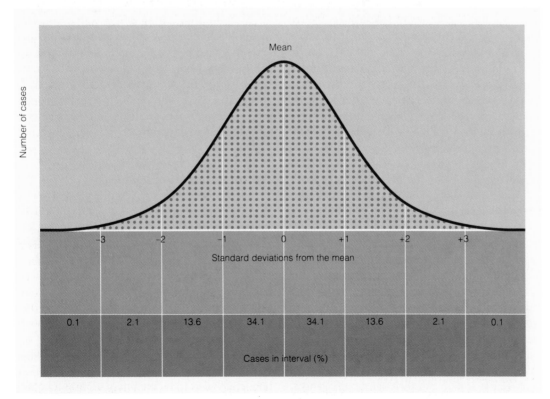

Number of cases

Mean

| 0.1 | 2.1 | 13.6 | 34.1 | 34.1 | 13.6 | 2.1 | 0.1 |

Standard deviations from the mean

Cases in interval (%)

Figure 9.6 The normal distribution. Many characteristics are distributed in a pattern represented by this bell-shaped curve. The horizontal axis shows how far above or below the mean a score is (measured in plus or minus standard deviations). The vertical axis is used to graph the number of cases obtaining each score. In a normal distribution, the cases are distributed in a fixed pattern. For instance, 34.1% of the cases fall between the mean and +1 or −1 standard deviation. Raw scores on psychological tests are often converted into a form that shows where each score falls in the normal distribution for the trait measured. (Consult Appendix B for a more detailed explanation of the normal distribution.)

Figure 9.7 Deviation IQ scores. Modern IQ scores indicate where a person's measured intelligence falls in the normal distribution. On the WAIS and most other IQ tests, the mean is set at an IQ of 100 and the standard deviation at 15. Thus, an IQ of 130 means that a person scored 2 standard deviations above the mean. Because of the fixed distribution of cases in the bell-shaped curve, any deviation IQ score can be converted into a percentile score, which indicates the percentage of cases obtaining a lower score. For instance, 98% of the population scores below 130 (the 98th percentile). The mental classifications at the bottom of the figure are descriptive labels that roughly correspond to ranges of IQ scores.

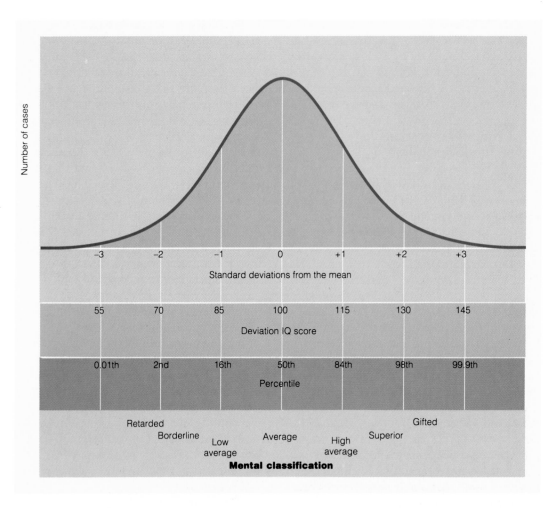

one SD (15 points) above the mean. A score of 85 means that a person scored one SD below the mean. A score of 100 means that a person showed average performance. You don't really need to know how to work with standard deviations to understand this system (but if you're interested, consult Appendix B). *The key point is that modern IQ scores indicate exactly where you fall in the normal distribution of intelligence.* Thus, a score of 120 does not indicate that you have 120 "units" of intelligence or that you answered 120 questions correctly. It places you at a specific point in the normal distribution of intelligence.

IQ scores are always based on how people perform in comparison to the test norms for their own age group, so that 5-year-olds are compared to other 5-year-olds, 12-year-olds to 12-year-olds, and adults to adults (everyone is lumped together in adulthood after age 15 to 18, depending on the test). Thus, an IQ score is always indicative of individuals' *relative standing* in their own age group. This is why IQ scores don't routinely increase as children grow older. Obviously, most children are growing more intelligent as they grow older, but their IQ scores remain constant unless their relative standing in their age group changes.

Deviation IQ scores can be converted into percentile scores (see Figure 9.7). In fact, a major advantage of this scoring system is that a specific score on a specific test always translates into exactly the same percentile score, regardless of the person's age group (the old system of IQ ratio scores lacked this consistency). These precisely comparable scores allow experts to set exact cutoffs for mental subnormality and giftedness that are independent of age.

How Is IQ Related to Retardation and Giftedness?

What are the cutoffs for extremes in intelligence—retardation and giftedness? On the low end, scores more than two standard deviations below the mean are regarded as subnormal. Thus, on most IQ tests, a score below 70 is thought to be indicative of mental retardation. However, diagnoses of mental retardation should *not* be based exclusively on IQ test results. **Mental retardation refers to subnormal general mental ability accompanied by deficiencies in everyday living skills originating prior to age 18.** The age limitation is included to define retardation as a condi-

Table 9.2 Characteristics of the Mentally Retarded

CATEGORY OF RETARDATION	ESTIMATED INCIDENCE IN U.S. AND PERCENTAGE OF RETARDED POPULATION	EDUCATION POSSIBLE	LIFE ADAPTATION POSSIBLE
Mild 50–70 IQ (equivalent to 8–12-year-old)	4,200,000 70%	Sixth grade (maximum) by late teens; special education helpful	Can be self-supporting in nearly normal fashion if environment is stable and supportive; may need help with stress
Moderate 35–50 IQ (equivalent to 6–8-year-old)	1,200,00 20%	Second to fourth grade by late teens; special education necessary	Can be semi-independent in sheltered environment; needs help with even mild stress
Severe 20–35 IQ (equivalent to 3–6-year-old)	400,000 6.7%	Limited speech, toilet habits, and so forth with systematic training	Can help contribute to self-support under total supervision
Profound below 20 IQ (equivalent to 0–3-year-old)	200,000 3.3%	Little or no speech; not toilet trained; relatively unresponsive to training	Requires total care

Source: Ruch, 1984

tion originating during childhood. Everyday living skills include dressing oneself, taking care of personal hygiene, and communicating effectively with others. The criterion of deficiencies in such skills is included so that retardation is not determined solely by a person's test ability and academic performance. This requirement acknowledges that "school learning" is not the only kind of important learning.

The American Association on Mental Deficiency (AAMD) has devised a system that classifies retardation as mild, moderate, severe, and profound. Table 9.2 lists the IQ range for each category, the percentage of retarded people falling into each category, and typical behavioral characteristics of individuals at each level. This table shows that the vast majority of retarded people (about 70%) are only mildly retarded. Individuals in this category are not readily distinguishable from the rest of the supposedly normal population. The common belief that most retarded people are dramatically different from the rest of us is inaccurate.

In principle, designations of giftedness should be based on superior potential in any of six areas: general intelligence, specific academic aptitudes (in math, for example), creativity, leadership, performing arts, or athletics. In practice, efforts to identify gifted children depend heavily on IQ test performance. School districts vary in terms of how selective they want to be about who qualifies as gifted. Generally, children whose IQ scores are more than two or three standard deviations above the mean are regarded as intellectually gifted. Thus, the minimum IQ score for accelerated programs usually falls somewhere between 130 and 145. Obviously, these cutoffs, and any other cutoffs that might be chosen, are arbitrary.

Do Intelligence Tests Measure Potential or Knowledge?

Intelligence tests are intended to be measures of intellectual potential. They attempt to assess potential by presenting novel questions that require you to "think on your feet," rather than questions that simply tap factual knowledge. However, we all have very different backgrounds, and it's not easy to devise items that are completely unaffected by differences in what we, as individuals, already know. Test developers try to circumvent this problem by requiring subjects to *apply* relatively *common* knowledge. Nevertheless, IQ tests unavoidably contain items that are influenced by the test taker's knowledge based on previous learning. *Hence, IQ tests measure a blend of potential and knowledge.* Test developers try to tilt the balance toward the assessment of potential as much as possible, but factual knowledge clearly has an impact on intelligence test scores (Zigler & Seitz, 1982).

Do Intelligence Tests Have Adequate Reliability?

Do IQ tests produce consistent results when people are retested? Yes. Most IQ tests report commendable reliability estimates, correlations that often range into the .90s. In comparison to most other types of psychological tests, IQ tests are exceptionally consistent measurement instruments. However, like other tests, they *sample* behavior, and a specific testing may yield an unrepresentative score.

Variations in examinees' motivation to take an IQ test or in their anxiety about the test can sometimes produce misleading scores (Zimmerman & Woo-Sam, 1984). The most common problem is that low motivation or high anxiety may drag a person's score down on a particular occasion. For instance, a fourth-grader who is made to feel that the test is terribly important may get jittery and be unable to concentrate. The same child might score much higher on a subsequent administration of the test by another examiner who creates a more comfortable, low-key atmosphere. Although the reliability of IQ tests is excellent, caution is always in order in interpreting test scores. IQ scores should be viewed as estimates of "true" intelligence that are generally accurate within plus or minus five points.

Do Intelligence Tests Have Adequate Validity?

Do intelligence tests measure what they're supposed to measure? Yes, but this answer has to be qualified very carefully. IQ tests are valid measures of the kind of intelligence that's necessary to do well in academic work, but if you want to assess intelligence in a broader sense, the validity of IQ tests is questionable.

As you may recall, intelligence tests were originally designed with a relatively limited purpose in mind: to predict school performance. This has continued to be the principal purpose of IQ testing. Efforts to document the validity of IQ tests have usually concentrated on their relationship to grades in school. Typically, positive correlations in the .50s and .60s are found between IQ scores and school grades. Even higher correlations (in the .70s) are found between IQ scores and the number of years of school that people complete (Brody, 1985).

These correlations are about as high as one could expect given that many factors besides a

These accomplished individuals illustrate the three basic types of intelligence recognized by most people (based on the research by Sternberg et al., 1981). Jesse Jackson's 1988 presidential campaign highlighted his interpersonal skills, or *social intelligence*. Chrysler executive Lee Iacocca's success in reviving his troubled company exemplifies *practical intelligence*. Superb *verbal intelligence* was necessary for Sandra Day O'Connor to become a justice on the United States Supreme Court.

person's intelligence are likely to affect grades and school progress. For example, school grades may be influenced by a student's motivation, diligence, or personality, not to mention teachers' subjective biases. Thus, IQ tests are reasonably valid indexes of school-related intellectual ability or academic intelligence.

However, a misconception has developed over the years: people have come to believe that IQ tests measure mental ability in a truly general sense. In reality, IQ tests have always focused on the abstract reasoning and verbal fluency that are essential to academic success. The tests do not tap social competence, practical problem solving, creativity, mechanical ingenuity, or artistic talent.

When Robert Sternberg and his colleagues asked laypeople to list examples of intelligent behavior, they found that the examples fell into three basic categories representing three types of intelligence (Sternberg et al., 1981). These were (1) *verbal intelligence* (common examples: "reads with high comprehension," "displays a good vocabulary"), (2) *practical problem-solving intelligence* ("sizes up situations well," "poses problems in an optimal way"), and (3) *social intelligence* ("accepts others for what they are," "thinks before speaking and doing").

For the most part, IQ tests assess only the first of the three types of intelligence that people think about in everyday life (as identified by Sternberg and his co-workers). Although IQ tests are billed as measures of *general* mental ability, they actually focus somewhat narrowly on a specific type of intelligence—academic/verbal intelligence. Hence, IQ tests do not appear to be valid indicators of intelligence in a truly general sense.

Do Intelligence Tests Predict Vocational Success?

Intelligence tests can predict vocational success, but not to a degree that's practically useful. "Vocational success" is a vague, value-laden concept that's difficult to quantify. Nonetheless, researchers have attacked this question by examining the correlations between IQ scores and specific indicators of vocational success, such as the prestige of a person's occupation, or ratings of subjects' job performance.

On the positive side of the ledger, it's clear that IQ is related to occupational attainment. People who score high on IQ tests are more likely than those who score low to end up in high-prestige jobs (Harrell & Harrell, 1945; Thorndike & Hagen, 1959). Since IQ tests measure school ability

fairly well and school performance is important in reaching certain occupations, this link between IQ scores and job status makes sense.

Of course, the relations between IQ and occupational attainment are moderate, and there are plenty of exceptions to the general trend. Some people plow through the educational system with bulldog determination and hard work, in spite of limited academic ability as measured by IQ tests. Such people may go on to prestigious jobs, while people who are brighter according to the IQ test, but who are less highly motivated, settle for lower-status jobs.

On the negative side of the ledger, IQ scores are rather mediocre predictors of performance *within* a particular occupation or job category (Ghiselli, 1966). For instance, if you have the IQ scores of 100 freshly graduated attorneys, these scores will not be much help in predicting which graduates will go on to become the best lawyers. Why not? In part, the problem is statistical. The range of IQ scores among the attorneys will be restricted, with most scores probably falling between 115 and 135. In other words, most of the attorneys will be "bunched together" with fairly similar scores. Without much variation in the predictor variable (here, IQ scores), you don't have much to work with in making predictions—about vocational success or anything else. Consider an analogy: could you predict basketball ability based on height if all your subjects were between 6 feet and 6 feet 2 inches?

Other considerations may also undermine IQ tests' prediction of occupational success. For instance, after a person graduates from school, practical and social intelligence (which are not assessed by IQ tests) may become more important determinants of success than academic/verbal intelligence.

The poor ability of IQ tests to predict job performance has led to controversy over the use of IQ tests in employee selection. Over the years, many companies have used IQ tests to help them sort through job candidates and decide whom to hire or promote. However, there's little evidence that IQ tests are valid indexes of a person's job potential in most occupational areas (Berg, 1970). Hence, the use of IQ testing in making employment decisions has been challenged on legal grounds and appears to be declining (Wigdor & Garner, 1982). Essentially, the courts have ruled that testing for employment selection is acceptable only if the tests that are used measure specific abilities that are clearly and directly related to performance of the jobs in question. Psychological tests that measure abilities relevant to specific jobs *can* be valuable tools in selecting employees

"To understand intelligent behavior, we need to move beyond the fairly restrictive tasks that have been used both in experimental laboratories and in psychometric tests of intelligence."
ROBERT STERNBERG

(Schmidt & Hunter, 1981), but IQ tests are not well suited for this purpose.

Is Intelligence a Stable Personal Attribute?

You've probably heard of hopeful parents who have their 2-year-old or 3-year-old preschoolers tested to see if they're exceptionally bright. These parents would have been better off saving the money spent on preschool testing. IQ scores are relatively unstable during the preschool years, and infants' IQ tests are not very good predictors of IQ

scores in adolescence and adulthood. As children grow older, their IQ scores eventually stabilize (Sontag, Baker, & Nelson, 1958). By age 7 or 8, IQ tests are reasonably accurate, but far from perfect, predictors of adult IQ.

Although IQ scores tend to stabilize after early childhood, they are *not* set in concrete. The widespread notion that IQ scores are unchangeable is based on the belief that IQ tests measure innate ability. However, we now understand that this isn't true. In the next section we'll discuss evidence that IQ scores are influenced by environment as well as genetic inheritance.

HEREDITY AND ENVIRONMENT AS DETERMINANTS OF INTELLIGENCE

"Despite more than half a century of repeated efforts by psychologists to improve the intelligence of children, particularly those in the lower quarter of the IQ distribution relative to those in the upper half of the distribution, strong evidence is still lacking as to whether or not it can be done."
ARTHUR JENSEN

Many early pioneers of intelligence testing, such as Sir Francis Galton and Lewis Terman, simply *assumed* that intelligence was inherited. Small wonder then that this view lingers on among many people. Gradually, however, it has become clear that both heredity and environment influence intelligence (Scarr & Carter-Saltzman, 1982; Sternberg & Powell, 1983). Does this mean that the nature versus nurture debate has been settled with respect to intelligence? Absolutely not. Theorists and researchers continue to argue vigorously about which is more important.

The nature versus nurture debate becomes especially heated when the topic is intelligence. Presumably, this is because the issue has such far-reaching social and political implications. Theorists such as Arthur Jensen (1969, 1980), who believe that intelligence is largely inherited, maintain that special educational programs for underprivileged groups are pointless. Jensen argues against spending tax dollars to improve educational opportunities for groups that generally do poorly in school. He believes that their poor academic performance is their genetic destiny.

Theorists who believe that intelligence is shaped by experience are highly critical of this view. Lewontin, Rose, and Kamin assert that "the IQ test in practice has been used both in the United States and England to shunt vast numbers of working-class and minority children into inferior and dead-end educational tracks" (1984, p. 87). Such critics maintain that we should allocate even more funds for remedial education programs, improved schooling in lower-class neighborhoods, and college financial aid for the underprivileged.

The debate about whether intelligence is largely inherited has direct relevance to important social issues and political decisions; therefore we'll

take a detailed look at this complex controversy. In succession, we'll review evidence about how intelligence is influenced by heredity, by environment, and by the interaction of heredity and environment. Finally, we'll examine a specific component of the nature versus nurture debate— the controversy over cultural differences in IQ scores.

Evidence for Hereditary Influence

Galton's observation that intelligence runs in families was quite accurate. However, *family studies* can determine only whether genetic influence on a trait is plausible, not whether it is certain. Family members share not just genes, but similar environments. If high intelligence (or low intelligence) appears in a family over several generations, this could reflect the influence of either shared genes or shared environment. Because of this problem, we have to turn to *twin studies* and *adoption studies* to obtain more definitive evidence on whether heredity affects intelligence.

TWIN STUDIES
Our best evidence regarding the role of genetic factors comes from studies that compare identical and fraternal twins as to their similarity in intelligence. The rationale for twin studies is that both identical and fraternal twins normally develop under generally similar environmental conditions, but identical twins share more genetic kinship than fraternal twins. Hence, if pairs of identical twins are more similar in intelligence than pairs of fraternal twins, it's presumably because of their greater genetic similarity (see Chapter 3 for a more detailed explanation of the logic underlying twin studies).

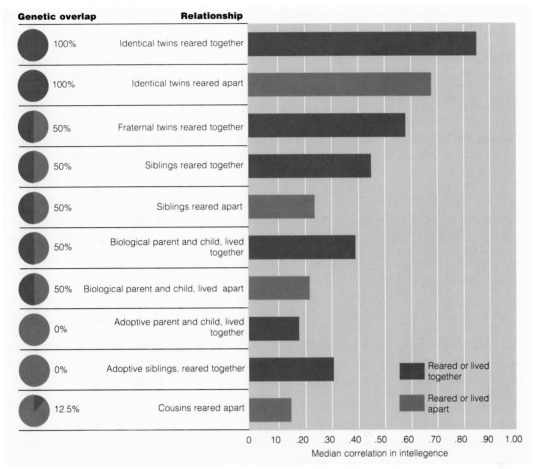

Figure 9.8 Studies of IQ similarity. The graph shows the median correlations in IQ scores for people of various types of relationships, as obtained in studies of IQ similarity. Higher correlations indicate greater similarity. The results show that greater genetic similarity is associated with greater similarity in IQ, suggesting that intelligence is partly inherited (compare, for example, the correlations for identical and fraternal twins). However, the results also show that living together is associated with greater IQ similarity, suggesting that intelligence is partly governed by environment (compare, for example, the scores of siblings reared together and reared apart). (Data from Bouchard & McGue, 1981)

What are the findings of twin studies regarding intelligence? Bouchard and McGue (1981) reviewed the results of 111 studies of intellectual similarity for various kinds of kinship relations and child-rearing arrangements. The key findings from their review are highlighted in Figure 9.8, which plots the median correlation observed for various types of relationships. As you can see, the median correlations reported for identical twins are very high (.85 and .67), indicating that identical twins tend to be very similar in intelligence. The median correlation for fraternal twins is significantly lower (.58). This correlation indicates that fraternal twins also tend to be quite similar in intelligence, but noticeably less so than identical twins. These results support the notion that IQ is inherited to a considerable degree (Nichols, 1978; Vandenberg & Vogler, 1985).

Critics have tried to poke holes in this line of reasoning by arguing that identical twins are more alike in IQ because parents and others treat them more similarly than fraternal twins. This environmental explanation of the findings has some merit, since identical twins are always the same sex, and gender influences how a child is raised. However, a clever study (Scarr & Carter-Saltzman, 1979) of twins who were mislabeled as

identical or fraternal suggests that this environmental hypothesis cannot account for identical twins' greater IQ similarity.

In this study, IQ tests were given to 400 pairs of same-sex twins. The sample included identical twins who had mistakenly been thought to be fraternals, and fraternal twins who had mistakenly been thought to be identicals, as well as twins of both types who had been correctly labeled. If identical twins are more similar in intelligence because they are treated more alike, then fraternal twins reared as identicals should also be highly similar in intelligence. Furthermore, identical twins mistakenly raised as fraternals should be less similar in intelligence than identical twins raised as identicals. Neither of these hypotheses was borne out by the results. Intellectual similarity depended not on whether the twins were raised as identical or fraternal, but on whether they really *were* identical or fraternal.

Evidence favorable to the genetic hypothesis also comes from a handful of studies that have focused on identical twins who were reared apart because of family breakups or adoption. Although reared in different environments, these twins still display greater similarity in IQ (median correlation of .67) than fraternal twins reared together!

THE BURT AFFAIR AND ITS AFTERMATH

In recent years, the best known study of intelligence in identical twins reared apart has been discredited as fraudulent. It turns out that Sir Cyril Burt (1955), one of England's most prominent psychologists, fabricated much of his data (Dorfman, 1978; Hearnshaw, 1979). This episode of scientific fraud is worth examining because it highlights the sociopolitical implications of the IQ debate and the importance of empirical skepticism to the scientific enterprise.

Burt was a great admirer of Sir Francis Galton. When Burt was a child, his father, who knew members of the Galton family, waxed eloquent about Galton's brilliance. Said Burt, "I heard more about Francis Galton than anyone else" (Fancher, 1985; p. 170). Following in Galton's footsteps, Burt was convinced that intelligence was inherited, and he had little sympathy for children from disadvantaged environments who performed poorly on IQ tests. Since intelligence was inherited, Burt reasoned, it was their genetic makeup, not their environment, that was to blame. Burt was so persuaded of the iron rule of genetic inheritance that he saw little hope of solving the problem of chronic poverty "without the forcible detention of the wreckage of society or otherwise preventing them from propagating their species" (Lewontin, Rose, & Kamin, 1984, p. 87).

Burt's views were influential in shaping an educational policy in Britain that tended to exclude the underprivileged from higher education opportunities, basing progression to higher levels of education on a series of standardized tests taken by all school children at age 11. When many critics began questioning the assumptions underlying this educational system, Burt apparently felt the need to fabricate his twin study findings to provide dramatic support for the policy he believed in. In 1955 he wrote that during the previous 20 years he and two colleagues had located and tested 21 rare pairs of identical twins reared apart. He reported that the twins' IQ scores showed a correlation of .88, indicating that they were remarkably similar in intelligence. By the mid-1960s he reported that his sample of identical twins reared apart had grown to 53 pairs and that the data continued to support the idea that intelligence is inherited (Burt's data are *not* included in Figure 9.8).

Shortly after Burt's death in 1971, Leon Kamin of Princeton University noted some peculiarities in Burt's data and began to question their authenticity (Kamin, 1974). When a cloud of suspicion arose around Burt's findings, his family authorized a biography by an admirer of Burt's, Leslie Hearnshaw, who was given full access to all of Burt's private papers and records. Hearnshaw (1979) discovered, much to his dismay, that Burt's colleagues in the twin research, the twins, and the data, had never existed.

How could faked findings go undetected by the scientific community for almost two decades? The main reason was that Burt's fabricated data were fairly similar to what was actually found in genuine studies (Rimland & Munsinger, 1977; Vernon, 1979). Although his figures were somewhat higher than those found in genuine studies, they were close enough that they did not raise many doubts. Fraudulent studies are usually detected when they cannot be replicated, so Burt's fraud went unnoticed for a long time.

More than anything else, the Burt fiasco illustrates how far some people will go to "win" the emotionally charged IQ debate. Although it's heartening that empirical skepticism eventually exposed Burt's deception, his story is a reminder of how difficult it can be to maintain objectivity about issues that have profound social and political ramifications. The Burt affair is a low point in the annals of science, but empirical skepticism *did* win out in the long run. Even the world's most eminent scientists are not exempt from the critical scrutiny of their peers.

ADOPTION STUDIES

Research on adopted children also provides evidence about the effects of heredity (and the environment, as we shall see). If adopted children resemble their biological parents in intelligence even though they were not reared by these parents, this finding supports the genetic hypothesis. The relevant studies indicate that there *is* more than chance similarity between adopted children and their biological parents, as indicated by the median correlation of .22 (refer to Figure 9.8).

HERITABILITY ESTIMATES

Various experts have sifted through mountains of correlational evidence and have used statistical methods to estimate the *heritability* of intelligence. **A *heritability ratio* is an estimate of the proportion of trait variability in a population that is determined by variations in genetic inheritance.** Given the strong views that experts bring to the IQ debate, it should come as no surprise that heritability estimates for intelligence vary considerably.

At the high end, theorists such as Arthur Jensen (1980) and Hans Eysenck (1981) maintain that the heritability of IQ is about 80%, with only 20% of the variation in intelligence being attributable to environmental factors. A great many researchers in this area characterize the 80% figure as a higher estimate than the data really support. However, even the estimates at the low end of the range suggest that the heritability of intelligence appears to be at least 40% (Henderson, 1982; Jencks et al., 1972).

These estimates are interesting, and, either way, they suggest that heredity has a substantial impact on intelligence. However, it's important to understand that heritability estimates have certain limitations.

First, a heritability estimate is a *group statistic* based on studies of trait variability within a specific group, and it cannot be applied meaningfully to *individuals*. In other words, even if the heritability of intelligence truly is 80%, this does not mean that each individual's intelligence is 80% inherited.

Second, the heritability of a specific trait may vary from one group to another depending on a variety of factors. For instance, in a group with a given gene pool, heritability will increase if there's a shift toward raising group members in more similar circumstances, since the extent of environmental differences will be reduced. To date, heritability estimates for intelligence have been based largely on research with white, middle-class subjects and should be applied only to such groups.

Evidence for Environmental Influence

Heredity unquestionably influences intelligence, but a great deal of evidence indicates that our upbringing also affects our mental ability. We'll examine three lines of research—concerning adoption, environmental deprivation or enrichment, and home environment—that show how life experiences shape intelligence.

ADOPTION STUDIES

Research with adopted children provides useful evidence about the impact of experience as well as heredity (Bouchard & McGue, 1981; Plomin & DeFries, 1980). Many of the correlations in Figure 9.8 reflect the influence of the environment. For example, adopted children show some resemblance to their foster parents in IQ. This similarity can be attributed only to the fact that their foster parents shape their environment. Adoption studies also indicate that siblings reared together are more similar in IQ than siblings reared apart. This is true even for identical twins,

Youngsters raised in deprived environments (that is, environments that are unlikely to foster intellectual development) typically show a gradual decline in IQ. Their slippage relative to more fortunate peers supports the idea that the quality of one's environment influences IQ.

who have the same genetic endowment. Moreover, entirely unrelated children who are raised in the same home also show a significant resemblance in IQ. All of these findings indicate that environment influences intelligence.

ENVIRONMENTAL DEPRIVATION AND ENRICHMENT

Remember that your IQ is measured relative to your age group. If your IQ was tested when you were 8, you were compared to other 8-year-olds; at 16, to other 16-year-olds. If environment affects intelligence, then children who are raised in clearly substandard circumstances should experience a gradual decline in IQ as they grow older (since other children will be progressing more rapidly). This cumulative deprivation hypothesis was tested decades ago by studying children consigned to understaffed orphanages and children raised in the poverty and isolation of the back hills of Appalachia (Sherman & Key, 1932; Stoddard, 1943). Generally, investigators *did* find that environmental deprivation led to the predicted erosion in intelligence.

Conversely, children who are removed from a deprived environment and placed in circumstances more conducive to learning should benefit from their environmental enrichment. Their IQ scores, which were depressed by their environmental deprivation, should gradually increase.

This hypothesis has been tested by studying children who have been moved from understaffed orphanages or disadvantaged homes into high-quality, middle-class adoptive homes (Scarr & Weinberg, 1977, 1983; Skodak & Skeels, 1947). The IQs of these children tend to increase noticeably, providing support for the potential impact of environmental enrichment.

HOME-ENVIRONMENT STUDIES

In the studies just discussed, the evaluations of environments as good or bad were based on crude, global judgments. These global evaluations were adequate since the investigators were comparing *extreme* variations. In recent years, however, researchers have examined the influence of environment on intelligence in another way. The new approach involves going into intact homes (mother and father living together with their children) to make an elaborate, systematic assessment of the quality of the intellectual environment in the homes. If environment shapes intelligence, then these assessments of home environments should correlate with youngsters' IQ scores. They do. Bradley and Caldwell (1980) found significant correlations between their assessments of the intellectual environment of homes and children's IQ scores.

What kind of home environment nurtures the development of intelligence? Many factors appear to be involved (Bradley & Caldwell, 1980; Hanson, 1975). It helps if parents run an orderly household *and* encourage exploration, experimentation, and independence. In the ideal home, parents are warm, affectionate, and highly involved with their children. They provide a diverse array of age-appropriate toys, as well as more formal learning materials (such as books). The parents speak articulately and are interested in intellectual pursuits (and therefore serve as role models for these behaviors). When children reach school age, parents encourage them to work hard in school and reward them when they make progress. Throughout childhood, the parents emphasize achievement motivation and provide tangible assistance with school work.

The Interaction of Heredity and Environment

Clearly, heredity and environment both influence intelligence to a significant degree. Indeed, many theorists now assert that the question of which is more important ought to take a back seat to the question of just how they *interact* to govern IQ.

The current thinking is that heredity may set certain limits on intelligence and that environ-

"My research has been aimed at asking in what kind of environments genetic differences shine through and when do they remain hidden?"
SANDRA SCARR

mental factors determine where we fall within these limits (Cronbach, 1975; Scarr & Carter-Saltzman, 1982). According to this proposal, genetic makeup places an upper limit on a person's IQ that can't be exceeded even when environment is ideal. Heredity is also thought to place a lower limit on an individual's IQ, although extreme circumstances (for example, being locked in an attic until age 20) could drag one's IQ beneath this boundary. Theorists use the term *reaction range* **to refer to these genetically determined limits on IQ.** Sandra Scarr, who has conducted a number of important studies on the inheritance of intelligence, is one theorist who emphasizes the reaction-range concept. She explains:

Each person has a range of potential in development. For example, a person with "medium-tall" genes for height who grows up in a poor environment may be shorter than average. In a good nutritional environment, the person would grow up taller than average. But no matter how well-fed, someone with "short" genes will never be taller than average. It works the same way with shyness, intelligence, and almost any other aspect of personality and behavior. (Quoted in Hall, 1987, p. 18)

According to the reaction-range model, children raised in high-quality environments that nurture the development of intelligence should score near the top of their potential IQ range. Children raised under less ideal circumstances should score lower in their reaction range. The reaction range for most people is *estimated* to be around 20–25 points on the IQ scale. Thus, most people are probably born with a reaction range of roughly 90 to 110. Their actual score within this range will then depend on the quality of their intellectual environment. Of course, other people are assumed to be born with ranges such as 70–90, 80–105, 110–130, 120–145, and so forth (see Figure 9.9).

The concept of a reaction range can explain why high-IQ children sometimes come from very poor environments and why low-IQ children sometimes come from very good environments—without discounting the role that environment undeniably plays. But how do we measure the genetic boundaries on a person's intelligence? That's the problem with the reaction range concept: there is no readily apparent way to measure the range. This makes it very difficult to test the reaction range model empirically. The impossibility of measuring individuals' genetically determined intellectual potential also makes it difficult to resolve the debate about the causes of ethnic or cultural differences in IQ scores. We'll try to sort through this complex issue in the following pages.

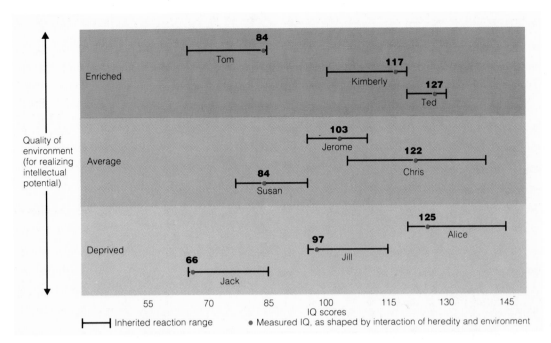

Figure 9.9 Reaction range. The concept of reaction range posits that heredity sets limits on our intellectual potential (represented by the horizontal bars), while the quality of our environment influences where we score within this range (represented by the dots on the bars). People raised in enriched environments should score near the top of their reaction range, while people raised in poor-quality environments should score near the bottom of their range. Genetic limits on IQ can be inferred only indirectly, so theorists aren't sure whether reaction ranges are narrow (like Ted's) or wide (like Chris's). The concept of reaction range can explain how two people with similar genetic potential can be quite different in intelligence (compare Tom and Jack) and how two people reared in environments of similar quality can score quite differently (compare Alice and Jack).

Cultural Differences in IQ Scores

The age-old quarrel about the importance of nature versus nurture lies at the core of the current controversy about the causes of differences between ethnic groups in average IQ. The full range of IQ scores is seen in all ethnic groups, but the *average* IQ for some minority groups in the United States is about 12–15 points lower than the average observed for whites. There is no debate about the existence of these group differences, variously referred to as racial, ethnic, or cultural differences in intelligence. The controversy concerns *why* the differences are found. There is a vigorous argument about whether cultural differences in intelligence are due to the influence of heredity or environment.

JENSEN'S HERITABILITY EXPLANATION
In 1969, Arthur Jensen sparked a heated war of words by arguing that cultural differences in IQ are due to heredity. The cornerstone for Jensen's argument was his analysis suggesting that the heritability of intelligence is about 80%. Essentially, he asserted that (1) intelligence is largely genetic in origin and (2) therefore, genetic factors are "strongly implicated" as the cause of ethnic differences in intelligence. Jensen's article triggered a flurry of rebuttals and research that shed additional light on the determinants of intelligence.

Some of Jensen's critics pointed to crucial weaknesses in his reasoning (Kagan, 1969; Lewontin, 1976; Mackenzie, 1984). For example, a heritability estimate applies only to the specific group on which the estimate was based. Jensen's

data were drawn from studies dominated almost entirely by white subjects. His heritability estimate for IQ (80%) is viewed by many as a "high-end" estimate based on these data, and there is doubt about the validity of applying his estimate to other cultural groups.

Moreover, even if you accept Jensen's assumption that the heritability of IQ is about 80%, it does *not* follow logically that average differences between groups must be due largely to heredity. Leon Kamin, the person who first uncovered Cyril Burt's fraudulent data, has outlined a compelling analogy that highlights the logical fallacy in Jensen's reasoning (see Figure 9.10):

We fill a white sack and a black sack with a mixture of different genetic varieties of corn seed. We make certain that the proportions of each variety of seed are identical in each sack. We then plant the seed from the white sack in fertile Field A, while that from the black sack is planted in barren Field B. We will observe that within Field A, as within Field B, there is considerable variation in the height of individual corn plants. This variation will be due largely to genetic factors (seed differences). We will also observe, however, that the average height of plants in Field A is greater than that in Field B. That difference will be entirely due to environmental factors (the soil). The same is true of IQs: differences in the average IQ of various human populations could be entirely due to environmental differences, even if *within* each population all variation were due to genetic differences! (Kamin, 1981, p. 97)

Kamin's analogy shows that even if the heritability of intelligence is high, average differences between groups in IQ *could* still be due entirely or in part to the influence of the environment. Other critics of Jensen's position have approached the

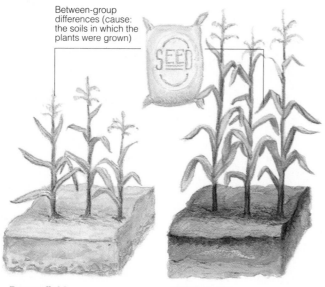

Between-group differences (cause: the soils in which the plants were grown)

SEED

Barren field
Within-group differences (cause: genetic variations in the seeds)

Fertile field
Within-group differences (cause: genetic variations in the seeds)

Figure 9.10 Genetics and between-group differences on a trait. Kamin's analogy (see text) shows how between-group differences on a trait (the height of corn plants) could be due to environment, even if the trait is largely inherited. The same reasoning presumably applies to the trait of human intelligence.

issue by trying to show that ethnic differences in IQ *are* due to the environment.

CULTURAL DISADVANTAGE AS AN EXPLANATION

Many social scientists argue that minority students' IQ scores are depressed because they tend to grow up in deprived environments that create a cultural disadvantage—both in school and on IQ tests. There is no question that, on the average, whites and minorities tend to be raised in very different circumstances. Most minority groups have endured a long history of economic discrimination and are greatly overrepresented in the lower social classes. A lower-class upbringing tends to carry a number of disadvantages that work against the development of a youngster's full intellectual potential (Blau, 1981). In comparison to the middle and upper classes, lower-class children tend to be exposed to fewer books, to have fewer learning supplies, to have less privacy for concentrated study, to get less parental assistance in learning, to have poorer role models for language development, to experience less pressure to work hard on intellectual pursuits, and to attend poorer-quality schools (Wolf, 1965).

In light of these disadvantages, it's not surprising that there's a positive correlation between social class and intelligence: children from higher classes tend to get higher IQ scores (Bouchard & Segal, 1985; White, 1982). The average IQ in the lowest social classes runs about 10–20 points lower than the average IQ in the highest social classes. This is true even if race is factored out of the picture by studying whites exclusively. Given the overrepresentation of minorities in the lower classes, many researchers argue that ethnic differences in intelligence are really social-class differences in disguise.

CULTURAL BIAS ON IQ TESTS AS AN EXPLANATION

Some critics of IQ tests have argued that cultural differences in IQ scores are due, in part, to cultural bias built into IQ tests. They assert that IQ tests are slanted in favor of white middle-class Americans, at the expense of lower-class ethnic minorities. According to Jane Mercer (1975),

Black Intelligence Test of Cultural Homogeneity

Like many other minorities, blacks who speak an urban black dialect may be at a disadvantage on IQ tests, which are written in white, middle-class language. To illustrate the potential significance of this problem, Robert Williams (1974) developed a tongue-in-cheek "IQ test" written in black dialect. Here are some items from this test.

Instructions: Circle the letter that indicates the correct meaning of the word or phrase.

1. *the bump*
   a. a condition caused by a forceful blow
   b. a suit
   c. a car
   d. a dance

2. *running a game*
   a. writing a bad check
   b. looking at something
   c. directing a contest
   d. getting what one wants from another person or thing

3. *to get down*
   a. to dominate
   b. to travel
   c. to lower a position
   d. to have sexual intercourse

4. *cop an attitude*
   a. leave
   b. become angry
   c. sit down
   d. protect a neighborhood

5. *leg*
   a. a sexual meaning
   b. a lower limb
   c. a white
   d. food

Answers: 1-d; 2-d; 3-d; 4-b; 5-a

Figure 9.11 The Black Intelligence Test of Cultural Homogeneity. As you might guess, blacks get higher scores than whites on this culturally slanted test. Although this test reverses the cultural bias of IQ tests to an exaggerated degree, for many nonblacks it provides a forceful illustration of what it would be like to take an IQ test in another ethnic group's language—a challenge that many minority children have to grapple with routinely in educational settings.

when IQ tests are given to minorities, they measure both mental ability *and assimilation into the mainstream culture*. She assessed the degree to which Mexican-American and black children came from homes that were assimilated into the dominant Anglo-American culture. She found that the IQ scores of these ethnic children were correlated with the "Anglicization" of their home backgrounds.

What are the sources of cultural bias on IQ tests? Critics argue that IQ tests are biased against minorities in a number of ways, including the following (Hilliard, 1984; Mercer, 1984; Williams et al., 1980):

1. The vast majority of psychologists are upper- and middle-class whites. When administering one-on-one IQ tests, they may often have difficulty establishing good rapport with minority students. This poor rapport could have a negative effect on both the examinees' motivation and the examiners' scoring of their test responses.
2. Since IQ tests are constructed by white middle-class psychologists, they naturally draw on experience and knowledge typical of white, middle-class lifestyles. For instance, an item that asks very young children "How is a piano like a violin?" may favor middle-class examinees who are more likely to be familiar with these objects at a young age.
3. IQ tests employ language and vocabulary that reflect the white, middle-class origins of their developers. Obviously, bilingual children who have to take an IQ test in their "second language" have a disadvantage. This language gap may also affect many blacks who speak an urban black dialect, which is an unconventional form of English (see Figure 9.11).

The charges of cultural bias on IQ tests have received some empirical support (Bernal, 1984; Cole, 1981), and IQ test results for minority students clearly should be interpreted with extra caution. However, the balance of evidence suggests that the cultural slant on IQ tests is modest, producing only weak and inconsistent effects on the performance of minority examinees (Kaplan, 1985; Oakland & Parmelee, 1985). Thus, cultural bias on IQ tests appears to be less of a problem than the cultural disadvantage associated with a lower-class upbringing.

Taken together, the various rebuttals of Jensen's views provide serious challenges to his theory. Genetic explanations for ethnic differences in IQ appear weak at best—and suspiciously racist at worst. In fairness to Jensen, his writings focus

---

CONCEPT CHECK 9.2
Understanding Correlational Evidence on the Heredity-Environment Question

Check your understanding of how correlational findings relate to the nature versus nurture issue by indicating how you would interpret the meaning of each "piece" of evidence described below. The figures inside the parentheses are the median IQ correlations observed for the relationships described (based on Bouchard & McGue, 1981), which are shown in Figure 9.8.

In the spaces on the left, enter the letter H if the findings suggest that intelligence is shaped by heredity, enter the letter E if the findings suggest that intelligence is shaped by the environment, and enter the letter B if the findings suggest that intelligence is shaped by both (or either) heredity and environment. The answers can be found in Appendix A.

_____ 1. Identical twins reared apart (.67) are more similar than fraternal twins reared together (.58).
_____ 2. Identical twins reared together (.85) are more similar than identical twins reared apart (.67).
_____ 3. Siblings reared together (.45) are more similar than siblings reared apart (.24).
_____ 4. Biological parents and the children they raise are more similar (.39) than unrelated persons who are reared apart (no correlation if sampled randomly).
_____ 5. Adopted children show similarity to their biological parents (.22) and to their adoptive parents (.18).

---

squarely on empirical data and theoretical issues, and he studiously avoids racist rhetoric, but Block and Dworkin (1976) note that others have cited his conclusions while advocating eugenic programs with racist overtones.

Unfortunately, since the earliest days of IQ testing, some people have used IQ tests to further their elitist views and goals. The current controversy about ethnic differences in IQ is just another replay of a record that has been heard many times before. For instance, beginning in 1913, Henry Goddard tested a great many immigrants to the United States at Ellis Island in New York. Goddard reported that 79% of the Italian immigrants, 80% of the Hungarian immigrants, and 83% of the Jewish immigrants tested out as "feeble-minded." As you can see, claims about ethnic deficits in intelligence are nothing new; only the victims have changed.

The debate about cultural differences in intelligence illustrates how IQ tests have often become entangled in thorny social conflicts. This is unfortunate because it brings politics to the testing enterprise. Intelligence testing has many legitimate and valuable uses, but the controversy associated with intelligence tests has undermined their value, leading to some of the new trends that we discuss in the next section.

NEW DIRECTIONS IN THE ASSESSMENT AND STUDY OF INTELLIGENCE

Intelligence testing has been through a period of turmoil, and changes are on the horizon. In fact, many changes have occurred already. We'll discuss some of the major new trends and projections for the future in this section.

Reduced Reliance on IQ Tests

In 1982, a task force assembled by the National Academy of Sciences recommended a reduced emphasis on standardized tests in the United States. A reduction in reliance on IQ tests is clearly under way. Many school districts are shifting from IQ tests to achievement tests. The problem is not so much that IQ tests are flawed; they are reasonably sound measurement instruments. However, they are terribly misunderstood by the general public. Far too many people believe that IQ tests measure an innate, fixed mental capacity that is truly general in scope and of the utmost significance for success in life. Achievement tests, on the other hand, are not burdened with these mythical qualities. Some authorities (Reschly, 1981; Turnbull, 1979) have argued that the concept of IQ is so bound up in myth that it has outlived its usefulness. They suggest that we should do away with the term IQ and relabel intelligence scales as tests of scholastic ability or

academic aptitude. Movement in this direction is apparent.

Increased Emphasis on Specific Abilities

As we decrease our emphasis on the measurement of *general* mental ability, many scholars are advocating more assessment of *specific* mental abilities (Carroll & Horn, 1981; Gardner, 1983). Intelligence testing grew out of a particular theoretical climate in the first few decades of this century. At that time, Charles Spearman's (1904, 1923) ideas about the structure of intellect were dominant. Spearman developed an advanced statistical procedure called factor analysis. In **factor analysis, correlations among many variables are analyzed to identify closely related clusters of variables.** If a number of variables correlate highly with each other, the assumption is that a single factor is influencing all of them. Factor analysis attempts to identify these hidden factors.

Spearman used factor analysis to examine the correlations between tests of many specific mental abilities. He concluded that all cognitive abilities share an important core factor, which he labeled "g" for general mental ability. Although Spearman recognized that there were also "special" abilities (such as numerical reasoning or memory), he thought that one's ability in these specific areas was largely determined by one's general mental ability (see Figure 9.12). Thus, test developers came to see *g* as the "Holy Grail" in their quest to measure mental ability. Since then, intelligence tests have always been designed to tap as much of *g* as possible.

A very different view of the structure of intellect began to emerge in the 1940s. Using a somewhat different approach to factor analysis, L. L. Thurstone (1938, 1955) concluded that intelligence involves multiple abilities. Thurstone argued that Spearman and his followers placed far too much emphasis on *g*. In contrast, Thurstone found that he could carve intelligence into seven distinct factors called *primary mental abilities*: word fluency, verbal comprehension, spatial ability, perceptual speed, numerical ability, inductive reasoning, and memory. Following in this tradition, J. P. Guilford (1959, 1985) "upped the ante" with a prominent theory that divided intelligence into *150 separate abilities*—and did away with *g* entirely (see Figure 9.13).

Thurstone's and Guilford's theories attracted

Figure 9.12 Spearman's *g*. In his analysis of the structure of intellect, Charles Spearman found that *specific* mental talents (S_1, S_2, S_3, and so on) were highly intercorrelated. Thus, he concluded that all cognitive abilities share a common core, which he labeled *g* for general mental ability.

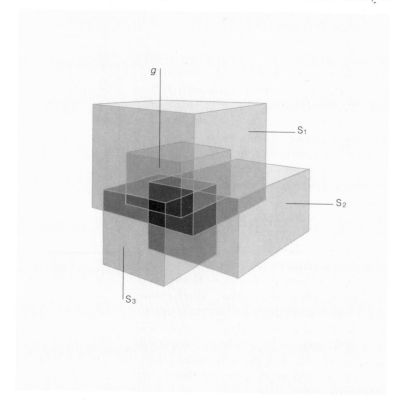

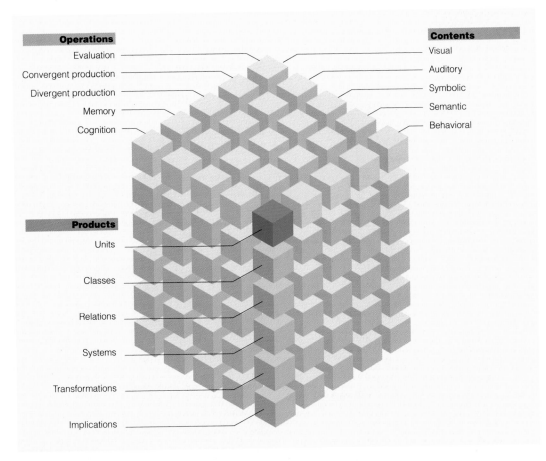

Operations
- Evaluation
- Convergent production
- Divergent production
- Memory
- Cognition

Contents
- Visual
- Auditory
- Symbolic
- Semantic
- Behavioral

Products
- Units
- Classes
- Relations
- Systems
- Transformations
- Implications

Figure 9.13 Guilford's model of mental abilities. In contrast to Spearman (see Figure 9.12), J. P. Guilford concluded that intelligence is made up of many separate abilities. According to his analysis, we may have as many as 150 distinct mental abilities that can be characterized in terms of the operations, contents, and products of intellectual activity.

favorable attention, but their ideas had relatively little impact on the day-to-day enterprise of intelligence testing (Horn, 1979). Test developers continued to stalk g with single-minded determination. However, the recent crisis in intelligence testing may finally provide the impetus for change. There is a new trend toward devising tests of mental ability that assess a variety of specific abilities. In part, this trend is due to the recognition that the g measured by IQ tests is not really all that general in scope. The trend is also motivated by the belief that assessments of specific abilities may be more useful than assessments of general mental ability. In any case, the next generation of mental ability tests may focus more on specific abilities than previous generations did.

A Cognitive View of Intelligence: Sternberg's Theory

Psychologists are increasingly employing a cognitive perspective in their efforts to study various topics—including intelligence. For over a century, the investigation of intelligence has been approached primarily from a *testing perspective*. This perspective emphasizes measuring the *amount of intelligence people have* and figuring out why some have more than others. In contrast, the *cognitive perspective* focuses on *how we use our intelligence*. The interest is in process rather than amount. In particular, cognitive psychologists focus on the information-processing strategies that underlie intelligence. This new perspective is generating intriguing insights that are changing the way we think about intelligence.

How is the cognitive perspective being applied to the understanding of intelligence? Robert J. Sternberg (1984, 1985), who views intelligence as "mental self-government," has devised a model known as the *triarchic* (government by three rulers) theory of intelligence. As its name suggests, the theory proposes that intelligent thought is governed by three sets of mental processes—metacomponents, performance components, and knowledge-acquisition components.

METACOMPONENTS
Sternberg calls metacomponents "executive" processes because they give directions to the other two kinds of components. They are high-level processes used in planning how to attack a problem. Metacomponents include processes such as defining the nature of a problem, selecting the steps needed to solve a problem, allocating resources (attention) to problems, and monitoring solutions to problems.

329

INTELLIGENCE AND
PSYCHOLOGICAL TESTING

PERFORMANCE COMPONENTS

According to Sternberg, "metacomponents decide what to do, performance components actually do it." For purposes of illustration, consider an analogy problem: LAWYER is to CLIENT as DOCTOR is to _____. Some of the processes involved in solving this problem include *encoding* the concepts in the problem, *inferring* the relationship between LAWYER and CLIENT, and *applying* the inferred relation to a new domain, arriving at the answer of PATIENT. Performance components vary depending on the nature of the problem. Sternberg assumes, however, that there are certain performance components upon which we depend heavily. Much of his research is intended to identify these crucial performance components.

KNOWLEDGE-ACQUISITION COMPONENTS

These are the processes involved in learning and storing information. The strategies that you may use to help memorize things exemplify the processes that fall in this category. A mnemonic device such as using a rhyme to remember something (for example: "Thirty days hath September . . .") represents a knowledge-acquisition component.

Sternberg's analysis has interesting implications for intelligence testing. According to Stern-

berg, traditional intelligence tests focus heavily on performance components. He asserts that they tap an examinee's prior knowledge, but that they do little to test knowledge-acquisition skills. Sternberg maintains that it would be more effective to design intelligence tests that sample evenly from the three components of intelligence. According to Sternberg, tests designed in this way would measure intelligence in a much more general sense than current IQ tests because the three basic components are relevant to all kinds of problem-solving situations. Thus, such a test could measure social and practical intelligence, as well as the academic and verbal intelligence assessed by traditional IQ tests.

A great deal of additional research needs to be done before the cognitive approach to intelligence yields a useful test of intelligence. However, the new approach is refreshing, the research program is ambitious, and the "dream" is exciting. Only time will tell whether the dream will be realized.

It appears that tests of mental abilities may be entering a period of transition. Certainly there's a great deal of tension, debate, and pressure for change. In contrast, the theoretical and intellectual climate is much more tranquil in the domain of personality testing, which we'll focus on in the remainder of the chapter.

PERSONALITY TESTING

We all engage in efforts to size up our own personality as well as that of others. When you think to yourself that "this salesman is untrustworthy," or when you say to a co-worker that "Mary Ann is shrewd and poised," or when you remark to a friend that "Howard is too timid and submissive," you're making personality assessments. In a sense then, personality assessment is an ongoing part of daily life. Given our interest in personality assessment, it's not surprising that psychologists have been asked to devise formal measures of personality.

Personality tests can be divided into two broad categories that are based on their measurement approach. *Self-report inventories* take a relatively direct approach and ask people to describe how they behave in specific situations. *Projective tests* take an indirect approach, interpreting subjects' responses to ambiguous stimuli, such as inkblots. In this section, we examine representative tests from both categories and discuss their strengths and weaknesses.

The Uses of Personality Scales

Why do we use psychological tests to measure personality? There are a variety of reasons. Benjamin Kleinmuntz (1975) lists four principal uses of personality tests: clinical diagnosis, counseling, personnel selection, and psychological research.

1. Personality tests are used extensively by mental health professionals in the *clinical diagnosis* of psychological disorders. Although diagnoses are not made on the basis of test results alone, personality scales can be very helpful in arriving at diagnostic decisions.
2. Personality measurement may be done for the purpose of *counseling* individuals about a variety of normal, everyday problems. Counselors often use personality scales to help people chart career plans and make vocational decisions. We discuss the use of occupational interest inventories in vocational counseling in the Application at the end of the chapter.

3. Formal personality assessment often plays a key role in *personnel selection* in business, industry, government, and the military services. This use of personality testing has been questioned in recent years, but many organizations continue to use personality scales to assess applicants' suitability for various jobs.

4. Personality scales are frequently used in *psychological research*. Empirical studies on a great variety of issues require precise measurement of some aspect of personality. For instance, if you want to investigate whether a specific trait (let's say, introversion) is related to a certain style of child rearing, your task is simplified greatly if you have a personality test that measures this trait.

Both self-report inventories and projective tests may be used for all four of the purposes outlined.

Self-Report Inventories

Consider the following statements:

I get a fair deal from most people.
I have the time of my life at parties.
My way of doing things is apt to be misunderstood by others.
I'm glad that I'm alive.
Several people are following me everywhere.

These statements are all found in a widely used self-report personality test, known as the Minnesota Multiphasic Personality Inventory (MMPI). The vast majority of personality scales are self-report inventories like the MMPI. **Self-report inventories are personality tests that ask individuals to answer a series of questions about their characteristic behavior.** When you take a self-report personality scale, you endorse statements as true or false as applied to you, or indicate how often you behave in a particular way, or rate yourself with respect to certain qualities. The logic underlying this approach is very simple. Who knows you better? Who has known you longer? Who has more access to your private feelings? Of course, your self-reports are subject to conscious and unconscious distortion. As you'll see, however, test developers have devised strategies to minimize this problem.

MULTITRAIT INVENTORIES
Some self-report inventories measure many dimensions of personality simultaneously. These multidimensional tests may assess a dozen or more personality traits, providing a comprehensive overview of a respondent's personality. Multitrait inventories are used extensively in clinical, counseling, and personnel work; single-trait scales are used more in research. There are many multitrait personality inventories. We'll look at two representative examples, the MMPI and the 16PF.

MMPI The most widely used multitrait scale is the MMPI, which was developed in the 1940s (Hathaway & McKinley, 1943). The MMPI was designed to aid clinicians in the diagnosis of psychological disorders. Consequently, it measures mostly aspects of personality that, when manifested to an extreme degree, are thought to be symptoms of disorders. Examples include personality traits such as paranoia, depression, and hysteria. The MMPI yields scores on the 14 subscales described in Table 9.3. Four of the subscales are *validity scales* that provide indications about whether a subject has been careless or deceptive in taking the test. The remaining ten are *clinical scales* that measure various aspects of personality.

The MMPI is a rather lengthy test, consisting of 550 statements to which the subject answers "true," "false," or "cannot say." The items for the various subscales on the MMPI were selected by comparing the responses of normal subjects with those of people who had been diagnosed as having specific disorders. For example, the items selected for the depression scale were those that tended to be answered differently by normal subjects and subjects suffering from depression. Likewise, the items chosen for the schizophrenia scale were those that differentiated between the normal subjects and those diagnosed as schizophrenic.

Are the MMPI scales valid? That is, do they measure what they were designed to measure? The validity of the MMPI has been investigated in hundreds of studies (Butcher & Keller, 1984). Originally, it was assumed that the ten clinical subscales would provide direct indexes of specific types of disorders. In other words, a high score on the depression scale would be indicative of depression, a high score on the paranoia scale would be indicative of a paranoid disorder, and so forth. However, research revealed that the relations between MMPI scores and various types of pathology are much more complex than originally anticipated. People with most types of disorders show elevated scores on *several* MMPI subscales. This means that certain score *profiles* are indicative of specific disorders (see Figure 9.14). Thus, the interpretation of the MMPI is quite complicated.

Nonetheless, the MMPI can be a very helpful diagnostic tool for the clinician. The fact that the inventory has been translated into more than 90 foreign languages is a testimonial to its usefulness (Butcher, 1984). Furthermore, it has recently undergone a major revision and modernization, which should increase its value.

Table 9.3 Personality Characteristics Associated with High MMPI Scores

SCALE	CHARACTERISTICS ASSOCIATED WITH HIGH SCORES
Validity scale	
Cannot say (?)	May indicate evasiveness.
Lie scale (L)	Indicates a tendency to present oneself in an overly favorable or highly virtuous light.
Fake bad scale (F)	Suggests carelessness, confusion, or "faking illness." Random responding also will result in an elevated F score.
Subtle defensiveness (K)	Measures defensiveness of a subtle nature.
Clinical scale	
Hypochondriasis (Hs)	Indicates person is cynical, defeatist, preoccupied with self, complaining, hostile, and presenting numerous physical problems.
Depression (D)	Indicates person is moody, shy, despondent, pessimistic, and distressed; one of the most frequently elevated scales in clinical patients.
Hysteria (Hy)	Indicates person is repressed, dependent, naive, and outgoing, has multiple physical complaints, and expresses psychological conflict through vague and unbased physical complaints.
Psychopathic deviation (Pd)	May indicate rebelliousness, impulsiveness, hedonism, antisocial behavior, difficulty in marital or family relationships, and trouble with the law or authority in general.
Masculinity/femininity (MF)	Indicates males are sensitive, esthetic, passive, or feminine, and indicates females are aggressive, rebellious, and unrealistic.
Paranoia (Pa)	Often indicates scorer is suspicious, aloof, shrewd, guarded, worrisome, and overly sensitive and likely to project or externalize blame.
Psychasthenia (Pt)	Indicates scorer is tense, anxious, ruminative, preoccupied, obsessional, phobic, rigid, and frequently self-condemning and feeling inferior and inadequate.
Schizophrenia (Sc)	Often indicates scorer is withdrawn, shy, unusual, or strange and has peculiar thoughts or ideas, poor reality contact and perhaps delusions and hallucinations.
Hypomania (Ma)	Indicates scorer is social, outgoing, impulsive, overly energetic, optimistic, and in some cases amoral, flighty, confused, and disoriented.
Social introversion (Sie)	Indicates modesty, shyness, withdrawal, and inhibition. Persons with low scores are spontaneous, sociable, and confident.

Figure 9.14 MMPI profiles. Scores on the 10 clinical scales of the MMPI are often plotted as shown here to create a profile for a client. The normal range for scores on each subscale is 40 to 60. People with disorders frequently exhibit elevated scores on several clinical scales rather than just one.

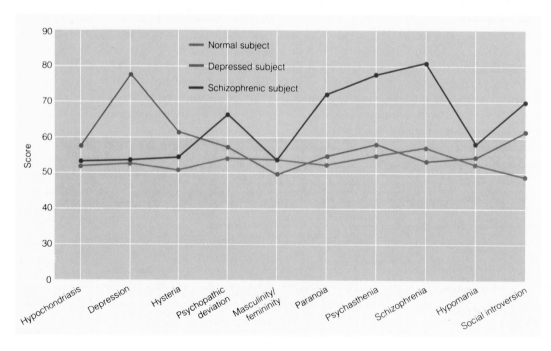

16PF Raymond Cattell and his colleagues employed a different approach to test construction in developing the Sixteen Personality Factor (16PF) Questionnaire. Cattell set out to measure the *basic dimensions* of the *normal* personality. His first challenge was to identify these basic dimensions. Cattell had studied under Charles Spearman, the "father of factor analysis." He reasoned that if factor analysis could be used to explore the structure of intellect, it could also be used to explore the structure of personality.

Cattell started with a previously compiled list of 4504 personality traits! This massive list was reduced to 171 traits by weeding out terms that were virtually synonymous. Cattell then used factor analysis to identify clusters of closely related traits and the factors underlying them. Eventually, he reduced the list of 171 traits to just 16 distinct factors that he called *source traits* (1957, 1965).

The 16PF is a 187-item self-report scale that was devised to assess these 16 source traits (Cattell, Eber, & Tatsuoka, 1970). According to Cattell, one can describe an individual's personality quite thoroughly by measuring these 16 basic dimensions of personality, which are listed in Figure 9.15.

While Cattell aspired to provide a complete description of an individual's personality, many other test developers have been content to focus on one aspect of personality at a time. Their efforts have yielded many self-report measures of individual traits, as you'll see in the next section.

SINGLE-TRAIT INVENTORIES

Multitrait inventories typically are marketed commerically for use in a variety of applied settings. They often are the product of decades of research by entire teams of psychologists. In contrast, single-trait scales are typically developed to facilitate research on specific aspects of personality. Although some of the better-known single-trait scales have evolved through decades of research, most of these scales are assembled through a brief series of studies. There are a huge number of single-trait scales.

Some examples of single-trait scales are the State-Trait Anxiety Inventory (Spielberger, Gorsuch, & Lushene, 1970), the Self-Esteem Scale (Rosenberg, 1965), the Power Motivation Scale (Good & Good, 1972), the Achievement Orientation Questionnaire (Herrenkohl, 1972), and the Mosher Guilt Scale (Persons, 1970). The names of these scales give a good sense of the traits they measure.

New single-trait scales are being developed all the time, as needed for research purposes. A relatively new single-trait measure of personality is the Chronic Self-Destructiveness Scale, which, as you can guess, measures the tendency to behave in a self-destructive manner. Its development reflects psychologists' increasing interest in how behavioral factors are related to physical health. Our Featured Study for this chapter concerns the development and validation of this interesting new personality scale.

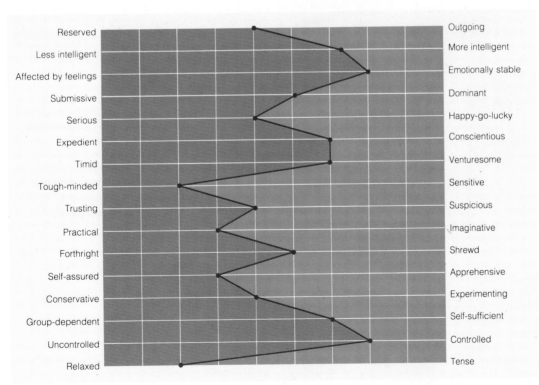

Figure 9.15 The Sixteen Personality Factor Questionnaire (16PF). Unlike the MMPI, Cattell's 16PF is designed to assess normal aspects of personality. The pairs of traits listed across from each other in the figure define the sixteen factors measured by this self-report inventory. The profile shown is the average profile seen among a group of airline pilots who took the test.

DEVELOPING A YARDSTICK FOR SELF-DESTRUCTIVENESS

Investigators: Kathryn Kelley, Donn Byrne, D. P. J. Przybyla (State University of New York at Albany), Bruce Eberly, Carole Eberly (VA Medical Center, Richmond, Virginia), Virginia Greendlinger, Choi K. Wan, and Janet Gorsky (State University of New York at Albany)

Source: Chronic self-destructiveness: Conceptualization, measurement, and initial validation of the construct. *Motivation and Emotion,* 9(2) (1985), 135–151.

The investigators defined chronic self-destructiveness as a general tendency to act in ways that increase the probability of future negative consequences and decrease the likelihood of future positive consequences—in other words, a tendency to put yourself at risk without increasing your chances for pleasant outcomes. Examples of such behavior include reckless driving, gambling, excessive drug use, careless spending, and not complying with medical recommendations. This investigation set out to devise and validate a scale to measure this hypothesized personality trait.

Method

The article reports on six separate studies that were conducted to develop and validate the

Self-destructive behavior comes in many forms, from compulsive gambling to chronic overeating to using dangerous drugs. Our Featured Study investigated whether a distinct personality type underlies the diverse manifestations of self-destructive behavior.

Chronic Self-Destructiveness Scale (CSDS). In Study 1, 189 actions that appeared to reflect self-destructiveness were examined for possible inclusion in the test, and the test-retest reliability of the newly formed scale was estimated.

In Study 2, correlations between the CSDS and other potentially related measures were examined. It was predicted that self-destructiveness would correlate positively with two measures of a trait called *external locus of control.* As we'll discuss in Chapter 12, people with an external locus of control feel that they have little control over their fate and that there's little connection between their own actions and their outcomes. The investigators also predicted that the CSDS would correlate negatively with a personality syndrome known as the *Type A personality* (characterized as achievement-oriented, time conscious, and diligent), which we'll discuss in Chapter 13. A negative correlation was also predicted between the CSDS and the *need for achievement,* because high need for achievement requires self-control and the ability to delay gratification.

Study 3 looked at the predicted link between the CSDS and subjects' anonymous reports of how much they cheated in school. Study 4 focused on the expected association between the CSDS and risky driving habits. In Study 5, the CSDS was used to predict adolescent rebelliousness. In Study 6, it was used to predict delaying a health test. Overall, 990 subjects were involved in one or more of the studies. Most of the subjects were college undergraduates.

Results

Study 1 compared responses on individual items describing specific self-destructive actions with subjects' total scores based on all 189 items. Only those items that correlated significantly with subjects' total scores were retained for use in the new scale. This analysis was done separately for each sex, yielding two slightly different 52-item scales. The two forms of the scale overlap, as many items appear on both versions (see Figure 9.16 for some examples). Test-retest reliability for a 1-month time period was found to be quite high (in the .90s) for both the male and female versions of the scale.

In Study 2, the predicted correlations between the CSDS and the established personality tests were found for all but one of the tests examined. The one exception was the predicted association between CSDS scores and the need for achievement.

In Study 3, high scorers on the CSDS reported

___ **39.** I sometimes forget important appointments I wanted to keep.

___ **40.** It's easy to get a raw deal from life.

___ **41.** I know who to call in an emergency.

___ **42.** I can drink more alcohol than most of my friends.

___ **43.** I seem to keep making the same mistakes.

___ **44.** I lose often when I gamble for money.

___ **45.** Using contraceptives is too much trouble.

cheating more on classroom exams than low scorers. In Study 4, a strong positive correlation was found between self-destructiveness and subjects' tendency to accumulate traffic tickets. Self-reports of adolescent rebelliousness were found to correlate with the CSDS in Study 5. In Study 6, women who had gone 2 or more years without a Pap smear (gynecological checkup) were found to score higher in self-destructiveness than women who had undergone this health test in the past year.

Discussion

The results suggest that chronic self-destructiveness is a generalized personality trait that leads people to engage in a variety of counterproductive behaviors that are otherwise unrelated. The authors speculate that the tendency to seek im-mediate pleasure and avoid immediate discomfort lies at the core of this personality trait. The pattern of correlations between the CSDS and various other personality measures and self-destructive behaviors suggests that the scale has reasonable construct validity.

Comment

This series of studies is a fairly representative example of how psychologists go about the business of generating a new scale to measure a specific aspect of personality. Generally, the key steps are to (1) conceptualize the trait to be measured, (2) generate a large pool of possible test items, (3) whittle the test down to a reasonable size by selecting only those items that provide the best prediction of the trait, (4) check reliability, and (5) attempt to demonstrate the scale's construct validity.

The final step is the most complex. This study illustrates a typical strategy for demonstrating construct validity. The investigators correlated their new scale with various measures that ought to be related to scores on the scale—if the scale really measures what it's intended to measure. Work on the final step often continues through a series of investigations. Although Kathryn Kelley and her colleagues mustered impressive support for the validity of the CSDS in this initial report, additional investigations have been conducted (Kelley et al., 1985), and more are still under way to obtain further evidence on the construct validity of the scale.

STRENGTHS AND WEAKNESSES OF SELF-REPORT INVENTORIES

To appreciate the strengths of self-report inventories, consider how else you might inquire about an individual's personality. For instance, if you want to know how assertive someone is, why not just ask the person? Why administer an elaborate 50-item personality inventory that measures assertiveness? The advantage of the personality inventory is that it can provide a more objective and more precise estimate, one that is better-grounded in extensive comparative data.

Take a moment to consider: how assertive are you? You probably have some vague idea of how assertive you tend to be. But can you accurately estimate how your assertiveness compares to others'? To do that, you need a great deal of comparative information about others' usual behavior—information that most of us lack. In contrast, a self-report inventory inquires about your typical behavior in a wide variety of circumstances requiring assertiveness and generates an exact comparison with the typical behavior reported by many other respondents for the same circumstances.

Although self-report inventories are much more thorough, precise, and systematic than our casual observations, they are only as accurate as the information that we give them. The principal shortcomings of self-report inventories are that they are susceptible to certain sources of error, including deliberate deception, the influence of social desirability, and response sets (Kleinmuntz, 1975).

DELIBERATE DECEPTION Some self-report inventories are dominated by questions that are easy to figure out, making it simple to fake a particular personality trait. Intentional deception is most likely when there is something to be gained from fraudulent responding. Thus, it plagues employment screening more than research.

SOCIAL DESIRABILITY BIAS **The** *social desirability bias* **is a tendency seen in some people to respond to questions in ways that make them "look good."** In other words, some individuals consistently provide socially acceptable or valued responses to the questions. They routinely indicate "yes" for statements like "I always admit my

Figure 9.17 The Rorschach test. Subjects are shown a series of 10 inkblots and are asked to describe the forms that they see in these ambiguous stimuli. Evidence on the reliability and validity of the Rorschach is controversial.

mistakes" or "I am always courteous." People who display this bias often have no intention of being deceptive. They may be unaware of their tendency to slant their answers in a socially desirable direction.

RESPONSE SETS Other people display response sets that distort the results of their tests. **A *response set* is a systematic tendency to respond in a particular way that is unrelated to the content of the questions.** For instance, some people, called "yea-sayers," tend to agree with virtually every statement on a test, regardless of what the statements say. Other people, called "nay-sayers," tend to disagree with nearly every statement.

REDUCING THE IMPACT OF SELF-REPORT PROBLEMS Test developers have devised a number of strategies to reduce the impact of deliberate deception, social desirability bias, and response sets (Jackson, 1973). For instance, it's possible to insert a "lie scale" into a test to assess the likelihood that a respondent is engaging in deception. The MMPI has a lie scale made up of 15 items that ask the subject to acknowledge minor faults that virtually all of us have. For instance, one item reads "Once in a while I put off until tomorrow what I ought to do today." Subjects who report themselves to be nearly faultless on these questions are probably engaging in conscious deception. There are test norms for this lie scale that indicate the extent to which a subject is engaging in deception.

Test developers try to reduce the problem of social desirability bias in several ways. The best way is to identify items that are sensitive to this bias and drop them from the test. Another approach involves the use of "forced-choice" items that require a subject to choose between two statements that are similar in social desirability, but different in their implications regarding the respondent's personality. For example, the 225 items on the Edwards Personal Preference Schedule require respondents to make choices between pairs of statements like the following:

a. I like to sympathize with my friends when they are hurt or sick.
b. I like to say what I think about things.

Problems with response sets can be reduced by systematically varying the way in which test items are worded. The key is to balance the items so that the responses of agreement and disagreement are equally likely to be indicative of the trait being measured.

Although the problems associated with the self-report approach can't be eliminated entirely, self-report inventories can provide excellent measurement of personality when they are constructed appropriately. In light of the potential for distortion, however, the results of self-report personality scales should be interpreted with caution. Of course, prudence is *always* in order when we interpret psychological test results of any kind.

Projective Tests

Projective tests, which share a rather indirect approach to the assessment of personality, are used extensively in clinical work. **Projective tests ask subjects to respond to vague, ambiguous stimuli in ways that may reveal the subjects' needs, feelings, and personality traits.** For example, in the Rorschach test, a series of ten inkblots are presented to subjects who are asked to describe what they see in the inkblots (see Figure 9.17). In the Thematic Apperception Test (TAT), a series of pictures of simple scenes (such as a boy contemplating a violin resting on a table or the scene shown in Figure 9.18) are presented to subjects who are asked to tell stories about what is happening in the scenes and what the characters are feeling.

Figure 9.18 The Thematic Apperception Test (TAT). In taking the TAT, respondents are asked to tell stories about scenes depicted on cards such as this one. The themes apparent in each story can·be scored to provide insight about the respondent's personality.

The number of projective tests available is very small in comparison to the number of self-report inventories in use. Table 9.4 lists representative examples of projective tests. The Rorschach and TAT are the most widely used projective tests.

THE PROJECTIVE HYPOTHESIS

Projective tests are based on the assumption that a subject's personality will inevitably color his or her response to intentionally ambiguous stimuli (Frank, 1939). Thus, a competitive person who is shown the TAT card of the boy at the table with the violin might concoct a story about how the boy is contemplating an upcoming musical com-

petition at which he hopes to excel. The same card shown to a person who is high in impulsiveness might elicit a story about how the boy is planning to sneak out the door to go dirt-bike riding with friends. The "projective hypothesis" is that ambiguous materials can serve as a blank screen onto which people project their characteristic concerns, conflicts, and desires.

The scoring and interpretation of projective tests is very complicated. Rorschach responses may be analyzed in terms of content, originality, the feature of the inkblot that determined the response, and the amount of the inkblot used, among other criteria. In fact, five different systems exist for scoring the Rorschach. TAT stories are examined in terms of heroes, needs, themes, and outcomes. Although elaborate scoring guidelines have been devised for the Rorschach and the TAT, individual clinicians tend to develop their own interpretive styles.

STRENGTHS AND WEAKNESSES OF PROJECTIVE TESTS

Proponents of projective tests assert that they possess two unique strengths. First, they are not transparent to subjects—that is, the subject doesn't know how the test provides information

Table 9.4 Representative Projective Tests

TEST	STIMULI PRESENTED	RESPONSE REQUEST
Rorschach test (Rorschach, 1942)	10 cards, each with a bilaterally symmetric inkblot	"Tell me what this might be."
Thematic Apperception Test (TAT) (Murray, 1943)	10 to 12 (out of 30 available) cards depicting simple scenes	"Tell me a story about each picture. Tell me what is happening, what the characters are thinking and feeling . . ."
Menninger Word Association Test (Rapaport, Gill, & Shafer, 1968)	60 nouns	"Tell me the first word that comes to mind."
Rotter Incomplete Sentence Blank (Rotter & Rafferty, 1950)	40 sentence stems such as, "My greatest fear is . . ."	"Finish the sentence in writing as rapidly as possible."
Draw-a-Person Test (Machover, 1949)	Blank sheet of paper	"Draw a whole person." (When finished: "Draw a person of the other sex.")

to the tester—so it's very difficult for people to engage in intentional deception. Second, the indirect approach used in these tests may allow them to circumvent conscious defenses, thus making them especially sensitive to unconscious, latent features of personality.

Critics of projective tests maintain that they are poorly standardized, so that different clinicians administer and score them differently, making the reliability of the tests distressingly low. Critics also maintain that there is inadequate evidence for the validity of projective measures. In spite of these problems, projective tests continue to be widely used by clinicians, many of whom depend heavily on projective techniques (Piotrowski, Sherry, & Keller, 1985). Over 20 years ago, a reviewer characterized the critics of projective tests as "doubting statisticians" and the users of projective tests as "enthusiastic clinicians" (Adcock, 1965); little has changed since then.

The continued popularity of projective techniques suggests that they are effective in eliciting information that is valuable to many clinicians. The subjectivity of the tests is a legitimate concern, but some projective measures have shown adequate reliability and validity when users agree on a systematic scoring procedure. For instance, adaptations of the Thematic Apperception Test have yielded reliable measurements of human needs and the test has been invaluable in research on motivation.

The task of personality assessment has been approached from a number of different angles. However, all approaches share the same goal: accurate description of individuals' characteristic behavior. Considering the uses to which personality scales are put—ranging from clinical diagnosis to personnel selection—the reliability and validity of the tests is becoming increasingly important.

PUTTING IT IN PERSPECTIVE

As you probably noticed, two of our integrative themes dominated this chapter. Our discussions repeatedly illustrated that psychology evolves in a sociohistorical context (theme 3) and that heredity and environment jointly influence behavior (theme 5). Let's discuss theme 5 first.

Human intelligence is shaped by a complex interaction of hereditary and environmental factors. We've drawn a similar conclusion before in other chapters where we examined other aspects of behavior. However, this chapter should have enhanced your appreciation of this idea in at least two ways.

First, we examined more of the details of how we arrive at the conclusion that heredity and environment jointly shape behavior. These details are available to us because psychologists have researched the interplay of heredity and environment as it relates to intelligence more thoroughly than any other human characteristic. Thus, you saw how psychologists have conducted family studies, twin studies, adoption studies, environmental enrichment studies, environmental deprivation studies, and home environment studies in their efforts to document the influence of genetics and experience on intelligence.

Second, we saw dramatic illustrations of the immense importance attached to the nature versus nurture debate. Cyril Burt, Britain's most distinguished psychologist, was willing to risk scandal and disgrace by faking research results to influence this critical debate. When Leon Kamin first suggested that Burt's findings were fraudulent, he was attacked in the London *Times* by Arthur Jensen, who characterized Kamin's work as "desperate, scorched-earth style of criticism" and "unfounded defamation." As more evidence on Burt's deceit became available, Jensen had to concede that Kamin's charges were valid, but his initial comments show how bitter the nature-nurture debate can get.

Jensen, too, has been the target of savage criticism. After his controversial 1969 article, he was widely and unfairly characterized as a racist, and when he gave speeches, he was often greeted by protestors carrying signs such as "Kill Jensen" and "Jensen Must Perish." As you can see, the debate about the inheritance of intelligence inspires passionate feelings in many people. In part, this is because the debate has far-reaching social and political implications, which brings us to the other prominent theme in the chapter.

There may be no other area in psychology where the connections between psychology and society at large are so obvious. Prevailing social attitudes have always exerted some influence on testing practices and the interpretation of test results. In the first half of the 20th century, a strong current of racial and class prejudice was apparent in the United States and Britain. This prejudice supported the beliefs that IQ tests measured innate ability and that "undesirable" groups scored poorly because of their genetic inferiority. Although these beliefs did not go unchallenged within psychology, their widespread acceptance in the field reflected the social values of the time.

Racial and class prejudice have yet to become relics of the past, but there certainly has been a trend away from old prejudices in the last few decades. This trend has been accompanied by an increased appreciation of how the environment contributes to poor IQ test performance in underprivileged groups. Thus, we see once again that trends in psychology often mirror trends in society.

Of course, this influence runs both ways. Research and theory in psychology leave their mark on our society as well. The ebb and flow of the nature versus nurture debate has often spilled over to affect governmental social policies. For example, Burt's views on the inheritance of intelligence clearly influenced the evolution of the British educational system. Henry Goddard's reports of high rates of feeble-mindedness among certain groups of immigrants may have influenced a shift in U.S. immigration policy in 1924, when immigration from Southern and Eastern Europe was temporarily curtailed (there's quite a debate about the extent of Goddard's influence).

More generally, the development of mental ability tests has had an enormous impact on educational systems in America and Europe. Many school districts use standardized tests as a yardstick to measure the effectiveness of their teaching programs. Standardized tests also serve as gateways to educational and career opportunities. Thus, events in psychology often have an effect on public policy and the nature of life in modern society.

Today, psychological tests serve many diverse purposes. One of their less controversial uses is for the purpose of vocational counseling. This is the use that we focus on next, in this chapter's Application.

USING TESTS TO AID CAREER PLANNING

Answer the following "true" or "false."

☐ **1.** There are limits on your career options.

☐ **2.** You have the potential for success in a variety of occupations.

☐ **3.** Vocational choice is a developmental process that extends throughout life.

☐ **4.** Some vocational decisions are not easily undone.

☐ **5.** Vocational choice is an expression of one's personality.

"What do you do for a living?" This question is a popular conversation opener among adults meeting for the first time. Its popularity illustrates the central role that work plays in our lives. Besides

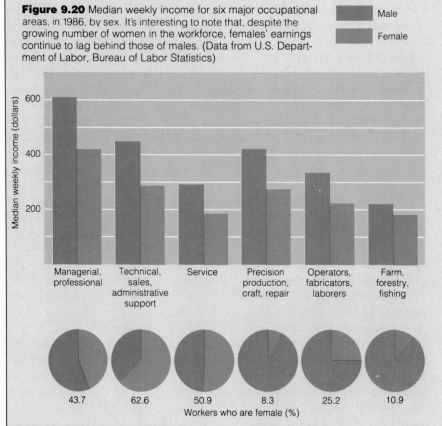

Figure 9.20 Median weekly income for six major occupational areas, in 1986, by sex. It's interesting to note that, despite the growing number of women in the workforce, females' earnings continue to lag behind those of males. (Data from U.S. Department of Labor, Bureau of Labor Statistics)

Male
Female

Median weekly income (dollars)

Managerial, professional | Technical, sales, administrative support | Service | Precision production, craft, repair | Operators, fabricators, laborers | Farm, forestry, fishing

43.7 | 62.6 | 50.9 | 8.3 | 25.2 | 10.9
Workers who are female (%)

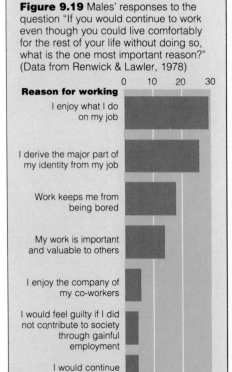

Figure 9.19 Males' responses to the question "If you would continue to work even though you could live comfortably for the rest of your life without doing so, what is the one most important reason?" (Data from Renwick & Lawler, 1978)

Reason for working

0   10   20   30

I enjoy what I do on my job

I derive the major part of my identity from my job

Work keeps me from being bored

My work is important and valuable to others

I enjoy the company of my co-workers

I would feel guilty if I did not contribute to society through gainful employment

I would continue out of habit

the obvious need for money, why *do* we work? Figure 9.19 highlights some of the key reasons. Many people report that they find their work enjoyable and interesting, that it gives them a sense of identity, and that it's valuable to society. Given that you probably will spend a sizable portion of your adult life working (if you haven't already), it pays to devote some thought to vocational planning, in the hopes that you, too, may find a career that's enjoyable, interesting, and valuable.

A *vocation* is an urge or commitment to work in a particular occupational area. Psychologists have studied how we arrive at vocational choices, what determines vocational success and satisfaction, and how patterns of career development evolve. In this Application, we look at issues related to *vocational choice* and discuss how psychological tests can be used as an aid in making decisions about careers.

Vocational Choice: General Principles

All of our opening questions were concerned with general principles related to the process of vocational choice. All five of the statements are true. Let's take a closer look at these principles.

1. *There are limits on your career options.* Entry into a particular occupation is not simply a matter of choosing what you want to do. It's a two-way street. You get to make choices, but you also have to persuade schools and employers to choose you. Your career options will be limited to some extent by your personality, your abilities, your financial resources, and fluctuations in the economy and the job market.
2. *You have the potential for success in a variety of occupations.* Vocational counselors stress that people have multiple potentials (Gilmer, 1975). There

are over 20,000 different occupations to choose from! Employment and income data on six major groups of occupations are summarized in Figure 9.20. In light of the huge variety in occupational opportunities, it's foolish to believe that only one career would be right for you. If you expect to find one job that fits you perfectly and provides you with total satisfaction, you may spend your entire lifetime searching for it.

3. *Vocational choice is a developmental process that extends throughout life.* Vocational choice involves not a single decision, but a series of decisions. Many people assume that this developmental process comes to an end in one's twenties, but studies of career patterns show that vocational development continues over the entire lifespan (Ginzberg, 1972). People in their 30s, 40s, and 50s are frequently faced with important decisions about their career paths.

4. *Some vocational decisions are not easily undone.* Although vocational development is a lifelong process, it's important to realize that many decisions are not readily reversed (Ginzberg, 1972). Once you invest time, money, and effort in moving along a particular career path, it may not be easy to change directions. This reality was illustrated in a survey in which 44% of the respondents indicated that they felt "trapped" in their current job (Renwick & Lawler, 1978). This potential problem highlights why it's so important for you to devote systematic thought and planning to the issue of vocational choice.

5. *Vocational choice is an expression of your personality.* Most theories of vocational choice agree that we express our personality in making our career choices (Roe, 1956; Super, 1972). According to an influential theory devised by John Holland (1985), we have stereotypic views of the work environments associated with various occupations. Holland asserts that we each search for a work environment that will fit our personality. Holland has identified six broad personality types, which he calls *personal orientations*. These personal orientations—realis-

tic, investigative, artistic, social, enterprising, and conventional—are described in Table 9.5, along with work environments that tend to mesh nicely with each orientation.

In the final analysis, vocational choice is a matching process. The goal is to find a good match between your personal characteristics and the characteristics of an occupation. Thus, the first step in systematic career planning is self-examination. You need to get a clear picture of your abilities and your personality (Shertzer, 1977). Because psychological tests can help assess abilities and personality, they can be useful in vocational planning. They usually can provide more objective and precise information about your personal characteristics than your own subjective estimates can.

Evaluating Your Abilities and Aptitudes

In thinking about careers, you need to be realistic about your abilities. If you're in college, it's likely that you've already taken many tests to evaluate your abilities. Thus, you may not need to go out of your way to take special tests. As we discussed earlier, most school districts routinely administer intelligence, aptitude, and achievement tests. Moreover, you can look back at 12 or more years of work in school to gauge your abilities. Thus,

Table 9.5 Personal Orientations and Related Work Environments

THEMES	PERSONAL ORIENTATIONS	WORK ENVIRONMENTS
Realistic	Values concrete and physical tasks. Perceives self as having mechanical skills and lacking social skills.	Setting: concrete, physical tasks requiring mechanical skills, persistence, and physical movement. Careers: machine operator, truck driver, draftsperson, and barber.
Investigative	Wants to solve intellectual, scientific, and mathematical problems. Sees self as analytical, critical, curious, introspective, and methodical.	Settings: research laboratory, diagnostic medical case conference, or work group of scientists. Careers: marine biologist, computer programmer, clinical psychologist, architect, and dentist.
Artistic	Prefers unsystematic tasks or artistic projects: painting, writing, or drama. Perceives self as imaginative, expressive, and independent.	Settings: theater, concert hall, library, and radio or TV studio. Careers: sculptor, actor, designer, musician, author, or editor.
Social	Prefers educational, helping, and religious careers. Enjoys social involvement, church, music, reading, and dramatics. Is cooperative, friendly, helpful, insightful, persuasive, and responsible.	Settings: school and college classrooms, psychiatrist's office, religious meetings, mental institutions, and recreational centers. Careers: counselor, nurse, teacher, social worker, judge, minister, and sociologist.
Enterprising	Values political and economic achievements, supervision, and leadership. Enjoys leadership control, verbal expression, recognition, and power. Perceives self as extroverted, sociable, happy, assertive, popular, and self-confident.	Settings: courtroom, political rally, car sales room, real estate firm, and advertising company. Careers: realtor, politician, attorney, salesperson, and manager.
Conventional	Prefers orderly, systematic, concrete tasks with verbal and mathematical data. Sees self as conformist and having clerical and numerical skills.	Settings: bank, post office, file room, business office, and Internal Revenue office. Careers: banker, accountant, timekeeper, financial counselor, typist, and receptionist.

Source: Adapted from Holland, 1985

you may already know whether you're strong in numerical ability, writing ability, social science, natural science, graphic arts, spatial reasoning, mechanical reasoning, and so forth.

If you do *not* feel that you have adequate information about your abilities, you may want to take a test that measures *multiple aptitudes*. You can often arrange to take such tests through your college counseling office. The most thoroughly validated multiple-aptitude batteries are the Differential Aptitude Test (DAT) and the General Aptitude Test Battery (GATB). The eight aptitudes measured by the DAT are listed in Figure 9.21.

Multiple aptitude batteries provide only very general clues about whether you might be successful in specific occupations. The DAT and GATB measure eight and nine aptitudes respectively, but remember, there are over 20,000 different occupations to choose from. Thus, as Zunker (1982) notes, "Multiaptitude test batteries should not be expected to pinpoint careers. The tests cannot answer specific questions: 'Will I be a good architect?'" (p. 39). Part of the problem is that many occupations use several of the abilities measured by aptitude batteries, so relations between aptitudes and occupational success are terribly complex. Nonetheless, aptitude tests may yield useful information. If you were thinking about becoming an architect and you scored low on the GATB subscales that measure spatial aptitude, form perception, and motor coordination, these scores would certainly make you wonder whether your career plans were realistic.

Although aptitude tests are only moderately useful in vocational counseling, some personality scales can be quite valuable. Perhaps this is because

Figure 9.21 Aptitudes measured by the Differential Aptitude Test (DAT).

1. Verbal reasoning
2. Numerical ability
3. Abstract reasoning
4. Clerical speed and accuracy
5. Mechanical reasoning
6. Space relations
7. Spelling
8. Language usage

most of us haven't taken many personality tests, so they yield more new information for our consideration.

Exploring Your Occupational Interests

The personality tests used in vocational counseling focus primarily on interests. **These *occupational interest inventories* are self-report scales that examine interests as they relate to various vocations.** There are many tests in this category. The most widely used are the Strong-Campbell Interest Inventory (SCII) and the Kuder Occupational Interest Survey (KOIS), both of which can be taken at most college counseling centers.

Occupational interest inventories do not attempt to predict whether you would be successful in various occupations. They relate more to the likelihood of job *satisfaction* than job *success*. The tests are based on the assumption that if your interests are similar to the typical interests of people already in a particular occupation, then you might enjoy working in that occupational area.

Most occupational interest inventories share the following general strategy. The test developer begins by measuring the interests of people who are already established in various occupations and who report that they enjoy their work. Typical interest profiles are compiled for many occupational groups. When you take an occupational interest inventory, your interests are compared with these occupational profiles. You receive many scores indicating how similar your interests are to the typical interests of people in various occupations. For example, a high score on the accountant scale of a test indicates that your interests are similar to those of the average accountant. This correspondence in interests does not *ensure* that you would enjoy a career in accounting, but it's a moderately good predictor of job satisfaction (Campbell & Hansen, 1981).

The most recent revision of the Strong-Campbell Interest Inventory groups occupations into six broad cat-

egories that correspond to the six types of work environments identified by John Holland (1985). Holland's six prototype work environments are called *general occupational themes*. Scores on these general themes indicate whether you have a realistic, investigative, artistic, social, enterprising, or conventional personality, as described by Holland. As you can see in Figure 9.22, the SCII divides each theme into a few basic interest scales and then breaks basic interests down into 162 specific occupational scores.

Interest inventories like the SCII can provide worthwhile food for thought about possible careers. The results may confirm your subjective guesses about your interests and strengthen already existing vocational preferences. Or the test results may inspire you to investigate career possibilities that you had never thought of before. Unexpected results may stimulate you to rethink your vocational plans.

Although interest inventories can be helpful in working through career decisions, several precautions are worth noting. First, you may score high on some occupations that you're sure you would hate. Given the sheer number of occupational scales on the tests, this can easily happen by chance. However, you shouldn't dismiss the remainder of the test results just because you're sure that a few specific scores are "wrong." Second, don't let the test make career decisions for you. Some students naively believe that they should pursue whatever occupation yields their highest score. This is not how the tests are meant to be used. They merely provide information for you to consider. Ultimately, you have to think things out for yourself.

Third, you should be aware that there is a lingering sex bias on most occupational interest inventories. Many of these scales were originally developed 30–40 years ago, when outright discrimination or more subtle discouragement prevented women from entering many traditionally "male" occupations. Critics assert that

Figure 9.22 The Strong-Campbell Interest Inventory. The SCII estimates the similarity between the respondent's interests and the interests of people working in various occupations grouped into six categories, based on the six types of work environments described by Holland. The first page of a two-page score report for W. B. is shown. It is normal to get high scores on many specific occupational scales (shown on the right side), and the test results should not be discounted merely because some of these may seem far-fetched (for example, W. B. may be sure that she doesn't want to be a farmer, chef, or librarian). Broad patterns of interest captured by scores on the general occupational themes and basic interest scales (shown on the left side) often are more informative. For instance, W. B.'s high scores on science, mathematics, and nature may stimulate her to think about occupations that could satisfy all three of these interests.

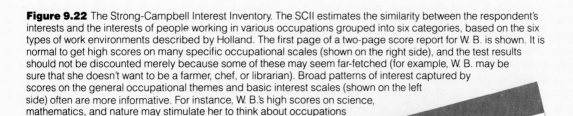

interest inventories have helped to channel women into sex-typed careers, such as nursing and secretarial work, while guiding women away from more prestigious "male" occupations such as medicine and engineering (Diamond, 1979). Undoubtedly, this was true in the past. In recent years, progress has been made toward reducing sex bias in occupational tests, but the bias has not been eliminated yet. Thus, in interpreting interest inventory results, be wary of letting old stereotypes limit your career options. A good career counselor should be able to help women—and men—sort through the effects of sex bias on their test results.

INTELLI-GENCE AND PSYCHOLOGICAL TESTING

Key Concepts in Psychological Testing

• Psychological tests are standardized measures of behavior—usually mental abilities or aspects of personality. Test scores are interpreted by consulting test norms to find out what represents a high or low score. As measuring devices, psychological tests should produce consistent results, a quality called reliability.

• Validity refers to the degree to which there is evidence that a test measures what it was designed to measure. Content validity is crucial on classroom tests. Criterion-related validity is critical when tests are used to predict performance. Construct validity is critical when a test is designed to measure a hypothetical construct.

The Evolution of Intelligence Testing

• The first crude efforts to devise intelligence tests were made by Sir Francis Galton, who wanted to show that intelligence was inherited. He invented the correlation statistic and set the stage for Alfred Binet. Modern intelligence testing began with the work of Binet, who devised a scale to measure a child's mental age.

• Lewis Terman revised the original Binet scale to produce the Stanford-Binet in 1916. It introduced the intelligence quotient and became the standard of comparison for subsequent intelligence tests. David Wechsler devised an improved measure of intelligence for adults and a series of IQ tests that reduced the emphasis on verbal ability and employed a new scoring system based on the normal distribution. Today, there are many individual and group intelligence tests.

Basic Questions About Intelligence Testing

• IQ tests are mostly administered in schools, but patterns of use vary greatly from one school district to another. Intelligence tests are useful in screening for learning problems, in student placement and research, and in clinical assessment. Intelligence tests contain a diverse mixture of questions.

• In the modern scoring system, deviation IQ scores indicate where people fall in the normal distribution of intelligence for their age group. Scores more than two standard deviations below the mean of 100 are usually diagnostic of mental retardation, but these diagnoses should not be based solely on IQ test scores. Children who score two standard deviations above the mean may be viewed as gifted, but cutoff scores for accelerated programs vary.

• Although they are intended to measure potential for learning, IQ tests inevitably assess a blend of potential and knowledge. IQ tests are exceptionally reliable. They are reasonably valid measures of school-related intellectual ability, but they do not tap social or practical intelligence. Thus, IQ tests do not measure intelligence in a truly general sense.

• IQ scores are correlated with occupational attainment. Nonetheless, they do not predict performance within an occupation very well. There is little evidence for their validity in selecting employees. IQ scores become fairly stable during the grade-school years.

Heredity and Environment as Determinants of Intelligence

• In spite of Cyril Burt's fraudulent data, twin studies show that identical twins are more similar in IQ than fraternal twins, suggesting that intelligence is inherited, at least in part. Studies that show that adopted children's IQ scores correlate modestly with their biological parents' scores also suggest that genetic factors affect IQ. Estimates of the heritability of intelligence range from 40% to 80%, but heritability ratios apply to groups rather than individuals, and estimates of heritability are group-specific.

• Many lines of evidence indicate that environment is also an important determinant of intelligence. The IQ resemblance between adopted children and their foster parents can reflect only the influence of environment. Studies of environmental deprivation and environmental enrichment demonstrate that experience affects intelligence. Research relating the quality of home environments to IQ scores also suggests that intelligence is shaped, in part, by environment.

- The key question today is this: how do heredity and environment interact to mold intelligence? Some theorists employ the concept of a reaction range to explain this interaction. According to this notion, heredity places limits on one's intellectual potential, and the environment determines where one falls within these limits.
- Genetic explanations for cultural differences in IQ have been challenged on a variety of grounds. Even if the heritability of IQ is great, group differences in intelligence may be due to something other than heredity. Moreover, ethnicity varies with social class, so cultural disadvantage may account for low IQ scores among minority students. Furthermore, critics have asserted that there are various sources of cultural bias in IQ tests.

New Directions in the Assessment and Study of Intelligence

- In the future, our schools and our society may place less emphasis on intelligence tests because of the widespread misconceptions about the meaning of IQ scores. There probably will be more emphasis on the measurement of specific mental abilities rather than general mental ability. Future research also seems more likely to employ a cognitive perspective similar to Sternberg's, looking at how we use our intelligence to solve problems.

Personality Testing

- Personality assessment is useful in clinical diagnosis, counseling, personnel selection, and research. Self-report inventories, such as the MMPI, ask subjects to describe themselves. The MMPI has proven useful in clinical diagnosis, although its interpretation is more complex than originally expected.
- Multitrait inventories are used extensively in applied work, while single-trait scales are used more in research. Our Featured Study described the development of a new single-trait inventory measuring chronic self-destructiveness. Self-report inventories are vulnerable to certain sources of error, including deception, the social desirability bias, and response sets. Like all psychological tests, they should be interpreted with caution.

- Projective tests, such as the Rorschach or TAT, assume that subjects' responses to ambiguous stimuli reveal something about their personality. Projective tests may discourage deception by subjects and facilitate the exploration of unconscious dimensions of personality. While the projective hypothesis seems plausible, projective tests' reliability and validity are disturbingly low.

Putting It in Perspective

- Two of our integrative themes stood out in the chapter. Our discussions of intelligence showed how heredity and environment interact to shape behavior. Our discussions also showed how trends in psychology often mirror societal trends, and how events in psychology leave their mark on our society.

Application: Using Tests to Aid Career Planning

- There are limits on career options, although people have the potential for success in a variety of occupations. Vocational choice is a lifelong developmental process and some decisions are not easily reversed. Vocational choices are shaped by personality.
- Most people have some insight into their abilities because they have taken many tests of mental abilities during their progression through school. Additional information can be gained through multiple aptitude batteries, although these are not very precise predictors of occupational success.
- Occupational interest inventories are fairly good predictors of job satisfaction. They assess the similarity between your interests and the interests of people already working in various careers. Although interest inventories can be helpful, you have to make your own vocational decisions, and you should be wary of sex bias on occupational interest tests.

KEY TERMS

Achievement tests
Aptitude tests
Construct validity
Content validity
Correlation coefficient
Criterion-related validity
Deviation IQ score
Eugenics
Factor analysis
Heritability ratio
Intelligence quotient (IQ)

Intelligence tests
Mental age
Mental retardation
Normal distribution
Occupational interest inventories
Percentile score
Personality tests
Projective tests
Psychological test
Reaction range

Reliability
Response set
Self-report inventories
Social desirability bias
Standardization
Test norms
Test-retest reliability
Validity
Vocation

KEY PEOPLE

Alfred Binet
Sir Cyril Burt
Raymond Cattell
Sir Francis Galton
Arthur Jensen
Sandra Scarr
Robert Sternberg
Lewis Terman
David Wechsler

MOTIVATION AND EMOTION

MOTIVA-TION AND EMOTION

In September 1983, for the first time in 132 years, the United States lost the America's Cup, the foremost trophy in the sport of sailing. An Australian team with a superior new boat design won the Cup. The Australians were understandably ecstatic. In contrast, the U.S. team was devastated by its abrupt and unexpected defeat. Dennis Conner, the team's skipper, wept openly in despair after the last race.

Within months, however, Conner began a relentless campaign to recapture the America's Cup in the next race in 1987. Working 365 days a year, he secured an unprecedented $15 million in financial backing, investigated hundreds of new boat designs, supervised the building of four boats, assembled and trained a crackerjack crew, and sailed in hundreds of races to prepare. Describing his frantic pace, Conner's wife said, "He never relaxes, and we never go on vacations. Hell to Dennis would be a day on the beach." Conner's crew would certainly agree with his wife. Working 12 to 15 hours a day, 6 or 7 days a week, they were pushed through a grueling training regimen for 17 months. Training in the Pacific, thousands of miles from their homes, most of them saw their wives or girlfriends only once during this time.

In 1987, the long hours of hard work and sacrifice paid off. Conner and his crew trounced their opponents and recaptured the America's Cup. The jubila-tion of victory is readily apparent in Conner's face in the photo in Figure 10.1.

The saga of Dennis Conner and his crew is packed with motivational riddles. What motivated these men to dedicate their lives to the pursuit of a yachting trophy? Money? No, the well-educated crew members were paid a mere $75 per week during their brutal, monastic months of training. Fame? For Conner perhaps, but the other crew members knew that their names wouldn't become household words. A deep-rooted love of sailing? Maybe for some of them, but Conner noted, "I don't like to sail. I like to compete." That was the key theme for most of the crew. More than anything else, they seemed to be propelled by the excitement of competition and the thrill of victory. As Conner put it, "The bottom line is, people like to win."

Dennis Conner's story is also filled with strong emotions. When he lost the America's Cup in 1983, Conner experienced tremendous dejection and disappointment. When he won the Cup back in 1987, he experienced enormous joy and happiness. His tale illustrates the intimate relation between motivation and emotion—the topics we'll examine in this chapter.

We'll begin by discussing theoretical perspectives on motivation. You'll learn that our behavior is energized by a diverse collection of motives that have both biological and social origins. We'll then take a close look at a handful of selected motives that have been studied extensively, including hunger, sex, affiliation, and achievement. To close, we'll analyze the elements of emotion and examine theories that attempt to explain the emotional experience. In the Application we'll expand on the dynamics of sexual behavior, addressing practical issues.

Figure 10.1 Dennis Conner hoisting the America's Cup in celebration.

MOTIVATIONAL THEORIES AND CONCEPTS

Why did many of Dennis Conner's crew members give up good jobs to join his quest for the Americas Cup? Why did Senator Gary Hart risk his presidential ambitions for a weekend of romance? Why did Greta Garbo suddenly retire from making movies at the peak of her highly acclaimed career? Why did you decide to attend college? Why did you start reading this chapter today? In asking these questions, we're looking for the *motives* underlying the actions. Motives are the needs, wants, interests, and desires that propel us in certain directions. In short, **motivation involves goal-directed behavior.**

There are a number of different theoretical ap-proaches to motivation. Above all other differences, motivational theories differ in their emphasis on the innate, biological basis of motivation as opposed to the learned, social basis of motivation. Let's look at some motivational theories and the concepts they employ.

Instinct Theories

What motivates a mother to stay up all night long caring lovingly for a cranky, sick infant? Is it her maternal *instinct*? Since the 19th century, psychologists have used the concept of instincts to explain motivation in terms of innate biological programming. William McDougall's (1908) instinct theory was psychology's most influential theory of motivation in the first third of the 20th century.

Instinct theories are rooted in the study of animal behavior. Instincts appear to explain why squirrels bury nuts, why certain species of birds migrate to the south in the autumn, and why many animals mark off and defend a home territory. What makes a response instinctive? *Instincts* are behavioral patterns that are (1) unlearned, (2) uniform in expression, and (3) universal in a species. For instance, if all members of a particular species of bird build their nests in the same way, even when raised in isolation (indicating the response is unlearned), then this nest-building behavior is instinctive.

Look at the photo in Figure 10.2. Why are the young ducklings following the eminent Dr. Lorenz? And what does this picture have to do with instincts? Many birds and a variety of other animals exhibit an instinctive behavior called imprinting. *Imprinting* occurs when an animal makes a strong social attachment (usually to its mother) during a critical period shortly after birth. This species of duck forms a social attachment to the first moving object it sees between about 10 and 20 hours after birth. Under normal conditions, this moving object is the mother duck. As part of an influential study conducted in 1937, Konrad Lorenz made sure that *he* was the first moving object that the ducklings saw during the critical time period. Thus, the ducklings imprinted on Lorenz rather than their mother.

As the example of imprinting suggests, instinctive behaviors are automatic and relatively rigid in expression. Consider the spider *Cupiennius salei*, which instinctively goes through a rigid program of 6400 spinning movements to create its cocoon. It cannot learn any shortcuts. If its silk glands dry out during the spinning, it continues to weave a nonexistent cocoon (Eibl-Eibesfeldt, 1975).

In contrast, humans generally display far more flexibility and diversity in behavior. Even fundamental maternal urges are far from universal or automatic. Many mothers *learn* to love their newborn infants; some never do. Mothers express their love in different ways. Thus, maternal "instincts" in humans aren't really instincts. Human maternal affection isn't necessarily innate, automatic, or rigid in its expression.

When subjected to close scrutiny, the instinct concept did not explain human behavior very well. Critics showed that human instincts proposed by McDougall, such as jealousy and cleanliness, were heavily dependent on personal

Figure 10.2 Imprinting. These young ducklings are following the eminent scientist Konrad Lorenz because this species of duck forms a strong social attachment to the first moving object seen between 10 and 20 hours after birth—usually the mother duck, but in this case Lorenz. This process of imprinting is an example of instinctive behavior in animals.

experience. In fact, researchers eventually demonstrated that even animals' instinctive behaviors can be influenced by learning (Tinbergen, 1951). For example, many theorists came to view imprinting as a form of perceptual learning because research showed that imprinting isn't as automatic or as closely tied to a critical period as Lorenz originally believed.

Today, some theorists continue to advocate "instinct-oriented" explanations of human motivation (Ardrey, 1966; Eibl-Eibesfeldt, 1979; Lorenz, 1981). But these theorists merely emphasize the biological roots of some motives; they don't suggest that the motives are true instincts. In recent years, the most prominent instinct-oriented model of human motivation has been Edward Wilson's theory of sociobiology, which we turn to next.

Sociobiology's View

According to Wilson, *sociobiology* is the study of the biological basis of social behavior in all organisms, including humans. Sociobiologists believe that human social motives have genetic and evolutionary bases. Although Wilson does not make much use of the concept of instinct per se, his theory is descended from instinct theories in that it proposes that human social motives are genetically programmed.

Sociobiologists argue that natural selection favors social behaviors that maximize survival (Trivers, 1971; Wilson, 1980). Thus, they explain social motives such as competition, dominance, aggression, and sexual activity in terms of their evolutionary purpose and value. If humans are intensely competitive, sociobiologists say it's because competitiveness gives a survival advantage, so that proportionately more competitive genes are passed on to the next generation.

You may wonder: if behavior is as selfish as sociobiologists make it sound, how do they explain self-sacrifice? Why does a soldier throw himself on a hand grenade to protect a comrade? Why does a blackbird risk death to signal the approach of a hawk to others in the flock? Sociobiologists offer an interesting explanation for this apparent paradox. They point out that an organism may contribute to passing on its genes by sacrificing itself to save others that share the same genes. Altruistic (self-sacrificing) behavior that evolves as members of a species protect their own offspring, for example, can be extended to other, more distantly related members of the species. Thus, the principle of genetic selfishness may operate to produce behavior that seems remarkably unselfish.

Sociobiology's basic thesis—that evolution has influenced human motivation—seems reasonable. However, sociobiology has generated a highly charged debate. Critics argue that Wilson's theory overemphasizes the influence of biology on social behavior and that it can be used to ordain the status quo in society as the inevitable outcome of evolutionary forces (Lewontin, Rose, & Kamin, 1984). For example, if males have dominant status over females, an advocate of sociobiology might assert that natural selection must have favored this arrangement. Indeed, in discussing the genetic basis for human sex roles, Wilson has said:

My own guess is that the genetic bias is intense enough to cause a substantial division of labor even in the most free and egalitarian of future societies. . . . Thus, even with identical education and equal access to all professions, men are likely to continue to play a disproportionate role in political life, business, and science. (Wilson, 1975, pp. 48, 50)

You can probably see why some advocates of change and reform in modern society are concerned by the political implications of this line of thought. Wilson has tried to address these concerns by asserting that sociobiology should try to avoid "the naturalistic fallacy of ethics, which uncritically concludes that what is, should be." However, Wilson's disclaimers have not satisfied sociobiology's critics.

The debate on sociobiology is complex, and we won't settle it here. Of interest to us, however, is the way in which the debate about the scientific merit of sociobiology has become intertwined with debate about the political implications of the theory. This shows us once again how psychology evolves in a sociohistorical context and how psychological theories can have far-reaching social and political ramifications.

Drive Theories

Many theories view motivational forces in terms of *drives*. The drive concept appears in a diverse array of theories that otherwise have very little in common, such as psychoanalytic (Freud, 1915) and behaviorist formulations (Hull, 1943). This approach to understanding motivation was explored most fully by Clark Hull in the 1940s and 1950s.

Hull's concept of drive was derived from the observation that organisms seek to maintain **homeostasis, a state of physiological equilibrium or stability.** Our bodies maintain homeostasis in various ways. For example, human body temperature normally fluctuates around 98.6 degrees Fahrenheit. If your body temperature rises or drops noticeably, automatic responses occur. If your temperature goes up, you'll perspire. If your temperature goes down, you'll shiver. These reactions are designed to move your temperature back toward 98.6 degrees. Thus, our bodies react to many disturbances in physiological stability by trying to restore equilibrium.

Drive theories apply the concept of homeostasis to behavior. **A *drive* is an internal state of tension that motivates an organism to engage in activities that should reduce this tension.** These unpleasant states of tension are viewed as disruptions of the preferred equilibrium. According to drive theories, when we experience a drive, we're motivated to pursue actions that will lead to *drive reduction*. The hunger motive provides a simple example of drive theory in action. If you go without food for a while, you begin to experience some discomfort. This internal tension (the drive) motivates you to obtain food. Eating reduces the drive and restores physiological equilibrium.

Most drive theories assume that we begin life with a small set of unlearned, biological drives, and that we gradually develop a larger, more diverse set of acquired drives through learning. Behaviorists' drive theories maintain that we acquire new drives, such as those for approval or achievement, because we learn that there are associations between approval or achievement and the satisfaction of our biological drives. In other words, they use the principles of conditioning that we discussed in Chapter 6 to explain the acquisition of learned drives. Other drive theories assume that

Animal species as diverse as wolves, chimpanzees, and geese form complex social structures, comparable to human families or tribes. Behaviors such as courting, playing, fighting, and the grooming shown here are examples of social behavior in animals. Many biologists and psychologists believe that social and emotional behavior patterns are products of evolution in the same way that anatomical and physiological characteristics are.

we acquire learned drives through socialization as our elders teach us to value approval or achievement. Although drive theories allocate a role to learning, they ultimately use a biological (homeostatic) model to explain motivation.

Drive theories have been very influential, and the drive concept continues to be widely used in modern psychology. *However, drive theories cannot explain all motivation.* Homeostasis appears irrelevant to some human motives, such as a "thirst for knowledge." Also, motivation may exist without drive arousal. This point is easy to illustrate. Think of all the times that you've eaten when you weren't the least bit hungry. You're driving home from school, amply filled by a solid lunch, when an ice cream parlor beckons seductively. You pull in and have a couple of scoops of your favorite flavor. Not only are you motivated to eat in the absence of internal tension, you may very well *cause* yourself some internal tension (from overeating). Because drive theories assume that we always try to reduce internal tension, they can't explain this behavior very well. Incentive theories, which represent a different approach to motivation, can account for this behavior more readily.

Incentive Theories

Incentive theories propose that external stimuli regulate motivational states (Bolles, 1975; McClelland, 1975; Skinner, 1953). **An incentive is an external goal that has the capacity to motivate behavior.** Ice cream, a juicy steak, a monetary prize, approval from friends, an A on an exam, and a promotion at work are all incentives. Some of these incentives may reduce drives, but others may not.

Drive and incentive models of motivation are often contrasted as *push versus pull* theories. Drive theories emphasize how *internal* states of tension *push* us in certain directions. Incentive theories emphasize how *external* stimuli *pull* us in certain directions. According to drive theories, the source of motivation lies *within* the organism. According to incentive theories, the source of motivation lies *outside* the organism, in the environment. This means that incentive models don't operate according to the principle of homeostasis, which hinges on internal changes in the organism. Thus, in comparison to drive theories, incentive theories emphasize environment and learning and downplay the biological bases of human motivation.

As you're painfully aware, we can't always obtain the incentives or goals that we desire, such as good grades or choice promotions. *Expectancy-value models* of motivation are incentive theories that take this reality into account (Atkinson & Birch, 1978). According to expectancy-value models, our motivation to pursue a particular course of action will depend on two factors: (1) our expectancy about our chances of attaining the incentive and (2) the value of the desired incentive.

Thus, your motivation to pursue a promotion at work will depend on your estimate of the likelihood that you can snare the promotion (expectancy), and how appealing the promotion is to you (value). In a similar fashion, your motivation to buy lottery tickets will depend on the size of the prize and your belief about your chances to win. State-run lotteries clearly recognize this reality. To lure people into playing these lotteries, officials make incentive value high by offering games with huge financial prizes (but with very low odds of winning). They also elevate the expectancy of winning by offering games in which there are many daily winners (of small prizes).

The Range and Diversity of Human Motives

Motivational theorists of all persuasions agree on one point: humans display an enormous diversity of motives. As we've seen, most theories distinguish between *biological motives* that originate in bodily needs, such as hunger and thirst, and *social motives* that originate in social experiences, such as needs for achievement, orderliness, and understanding.

We have a limited number of biological needs. According to K. B. Madsen (1968, 1973), most theories list 10 to 15 such needs. After comparing 20 motivational theories, Madsen compiled a list of 12 biological motives that are recognized by most theorists. His list, which appears in Figure 10.3, shows that most of our biological motives

---

Biological Needs in Humans

- Hunger motive
- Thirst motive
- Sex motive
- Nurturance motive (parenting)
- Temperature motive (appropriate body temperature)
- Pain-avoidance motive
- Excretory motive (elimination of bodily wastes)
- Oxygen motive
- Rest and sleep motive
- Activity motive (for optimal levels of stimulation and arousal)
- Security motive (need to avoid fear)
- Aggression motive

Figure 10.3 Human biological motives identified by Madsen (1973).

reflect needs that are essential to our survival, such as the needs for food, water, oxygen, elimination of bodily wastes, and maintenance of body temperature within an acceptable range. Two of our biological motives—sex and nurturance (parenting)—are critical to long-range group survival, rather than individual survival. Some of the biological motives on Madsen's list—for instance, the security and activity motives—reflect innate preferences for certain "states of comfort" rather than survival needs.

We all share the same biological needs, but our social needs vary depending on our personal experience. For example, some of us acquire a need for orderliness, and some of us don't. Although we have a limited number of biological needs, we can acquire an unlimited number of social needs through learning and socialization. Thus, it's impossible to assemble an exhaustive list of human social needs.

Nonetheless, Henry Murray (1938) compiled an influential catalog of common needs acquired

Table 10.1 Human Social Needs: Murray's Psychogenic Needs

NEED	DEFINITION
Abasement	To submit passively to external force. To accept injury, blame, criticism, punishment. To surrender. To become resigned to fate. To admit inferiority, error, wrong-doing, or defeat. To confess and atone. To blame, belittle, or mutilate the self. To seek and enjoy pain, punishment, illness, and misfortune.
Achievement	To accomplish something difficult. To master, manipulate, or organize physical objects, human beings, or ideas. To do this as rapidly and as independently as possible. To overcome obstacles and attain a high standard. To excel one's self. To rival and surpass others. To increase self-regard by the successful exercise of talent.
Affiliation	To form friendships and associations. To greet, join, and live with others. To cooperate and converse sociably with others. To love. To join groups.
Aggression	To overcome opposition forcefully. To fight. To revenge an injury. To attack, injure, or kill another. To oppose forcefully or punish another.
Autonomy	To get free, shake off restraint, break out of confinement. To resist coercion and restriction. To avoid or quit activities prescribed by domineering authorities. To be independent and free to act according to impulse. To be unattached, unconditioned, irresponsible. To defy convention.
Blamavoidance	To avoid blame, ostracism, or punishment by inhibiting asocial or unconventional impulses. To be well-behaved and obey the law.
Counteraction	Proudly to refuse admission of defeat by restriving and retaliating. To select the hardest tasks. To defend one's honor in action.
Defendance	To defend oneself against blame or belittlement. To justify one's actions. To offer extenuations, explanations, and excuses. To resist "probing."
Deference	To admire and support a superior other. To praise, honor, or eulogize. To yield eagerly to the influence of an allied other. To emulate an exemplar. To conform to custom.
Dominance	To influence or control others. To persuade, prohibit, dictate. To lead and direct. To restrain. To organize the behavior of a group.
Exhibition	To make an impression. To be seen and heard. To excite, amaze, fascinate, entertain, shock, intrigue, amuse, or entice others.
Harmavoidance	To avoid pain, physical injury, illness, and death. To escape from a dangerous situation. To take precautionary measures.
Infavoidance	To avoid humiliation. To quit embarrassing situations or to avoid conditions that may lead to belittlement: the scorn, derision, or indifference of others. To refrain from action because of the fear of failure.
Nurturance	To nourish, aid, or protect a helpless other. To express sympathy. To "mother" a child.
Order	To put things in order. To achieve cleanliness, arrangement, organization, balance, neatness, tidiness, and precision.
Play	To relax, amuse oneself, seek diversion and entertainment. To "have fun," to play games. To laugh, joke, and be merry. To avoid serious tension.
Rejection	To snub, ignore, or exclude another. To remain aloof and indifferent. To be discriminating.
Sentience	To seek and enjoy sensuous impressions.
Sex	To form and further an erotic relationship. To have sexual intercourse.
Succorance	To seek aid, protection, or sympathy. To cry for help. To plead for mercy. To adhere to an affectionate, nurturant parent. To be dependent.
Understanding	To analyze experience, to abstract, to discriminate among concepts, to define relations, to synthesize ideas.

Source: From Murray, 1938

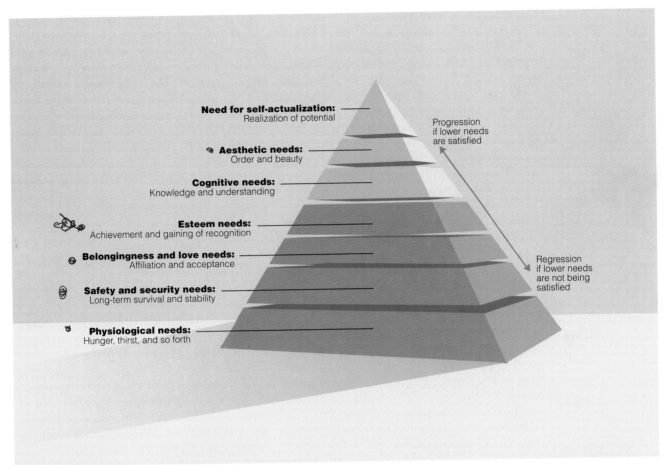

Need for self-actualization:
Realization of potential

Aesthetic needs:
Order and beauty

Cognitive needs:
Knowledge and understanding

Esteem needs:
Achievement and gaining of recognition

Belongingness and love needs:
Affiliation and acceptance

Safety and security needs:
Long-term survival and stability

Physiological needs:
Hunger, thirst, and so forth

Progression
if lower needs
are satisfied

Regression
if lower needs
are not being
satisfied

through social mechanisms, which he called "psy-chogenic needs." Murray's list, which included 28 social motives exhibited by most people, is summarized in Table 10.1. Murray theorized that most of us have needs for achievement, recognition, affiliation, dominance, acquisition (of possessions), exhibition, and play, among other things. Murray's list shows that we're motivated by a great variety of needs that depend on learning rather than biological necessity. Of course, the strength of these needs varies from one person to another, depending on personal history.

The distinction between biological needs and social needs is *not* clear-cut. A specific motive may be viewed as a biological motive by one theorist and as a social motive by another. For instance, you may have noticed that aggression and nurturance appear on both Madsen's list of biological motives and Murray's list of social motives. These differences of opinion exist because human motives vary in the *degree* to which they depend on biology. Even a heavily biological motive like hunger is shaped to some extent by social factors. Sexual motivation clearly has both biological and social origins. Furthermore, sociobiologists and other theorists maintain that many social needs, such as dominance, affiliation, and curiosity, have biological foundations that are not fully appreciated.

Although the distinction between biological and social needs is not absolute, this dichotomy allows us to impose some organization on the diverse motives seen in human behavior. We turn next to a theory that provides a more elaborate scheme for organizing human motives.

Arranging Needs in a Hierarchy: Maslow's Theory

Abraham Maslow (1962, 1970), a prominent humanistic theorist, has proposed a sweeping overview of human motivation that strikes a unique balance between biological and social needs and integrates many of the motivational concepts that we've discussed.

Maslow echoes Murray's point that our needs are many and diverse. He assumes that these needs compete for expression. At this very moment, your need for sleep may be pitted against your need for achievement, as you work to earn a good grade in Psychology. Of course, not all needs are created equal. Maslow proposes that human motives are organized into a **hierarchy of needs, a systematic arrangement of needs according to priority, that assumes that basic needs must be met before less basic needs are aroused.**

This hierarchical arrangement is usually portrayed as a pyramid (see Figure 10.4). The needs

Figure 10.4 Maslow's hierarchy of needs. According to Maslow, our needs are arranged in a hierarchy, and we must satisfy our basic needs before we can satisfy our higher needs. In the diagram, higher levels in the pyramid represent progressively less basic needs. We progress upward in the hierarchy when lower needs are satisfied reasonably well, but we may regress back to lower levels if basic needs are no longer satisfied. The motives in the lower portion of the diagram (colored a darker shade) are deficiency needs that operate like drives. The motives in the upper portion (colored a lighter shade) are growth needs, which do not function like drives.

at the bottom of the pyramid are the most basic. They are fundamental physiological needs that are essential to survival, such as the need for oxygen, food, water, and so on. They must be satisfied fairly well before we become concerned about needs at higher levels in the hierarchy. When we manage to satisfy a level of needs reasonably well (complete satisfaction is not necessary), *this satisfaction activates needs at the next level.*

The second tier in Maslow's pyramid is made up of safety and security needs. These needs reflect concern about *long-term* survival. People seek to live in an orderly, stable, safe world where they're protected from assault, mayhem in the streets, environmental poisons, economic chaos, and so forth. Safety and security needs motivate adults to seek a stable job, to buy insurance, and to put money in their savings accounts. When safety and security needs are met adequately, needs for love and belongingness become more prominent. These needs lead people to seek affection—from family, from friends, and in intimate relationships. When these needs are gratified, esteem needs are activated. People then become more concerned about their achievements and the recognition, respect, and status that they earn.

Maslow's key point is that lower levels of needs must be satisfied reasonably well before higher needs are aroused. An example of this hierarchical principle emerged in a study of hunger (Keys et al., 1950). The subjects were men excused from required military duty because they were conscientious objectors. They agreed to go on virtually a starvation diet to investigate the effects of severe food deprivation (modern ethical standards for research would rule out such a study today). With their basic hunger motive largely thwarted, the men gradually became apathetic about nearly everything but eating. They talked about food constantly, and cookbooks became their favorite reading material. Eventually, they even lost interest in their girlfriends. Many of them removed pictures of their girlfriends from their lockers, replacing them with "pinups" of favorite foods! Thus, when basic needs go unmet, our concern usually shifts from higher needs to the lower needs that are being thwarted.

Maslow characterized our lower, basic needs as *deficiency needs*, and he assumed that they operated like drives. However, he proposed that humans also have *growth needs* that cannot be explained by drive theories (or incentive theories, for that matter). Remember, Maslow was committed to the humanistic theoretical perspective. As we discussed in Chapter 1, the humanists maintain that humans are unique organisms that

---

CONCEPT CHECK 10.1
Applying Motivational Concepts

Check your understanding of the motivational concepts that we've discussed by analyzing the examples of motivated behavior described here. In the first column of blank spaces, indicate which theoretical approach seems to provide the best explanation for the behavior. In the second column, indicate which level of needs in Maslow's hierarchy has been activated. The answers are in Appendix A.

Scenario	Relevant theory	Level of needs
1. You're alone in a strange city, and you feel lonely. You yearn for someone to talk to. You go for a walk along the waterfront, hoping to meet someone.	_____	_____
2. You're working 2 hours overtime every night. You don't like staying late, but your company really needs to get the work done and you can't pass up the substantial bonus (triple pay) they're offering.	_____	_____
3. You become fascinated by modern architecture, so you go get a bunch of books out of the library because you want to understand the thinking behind postmodernism.	_____	_____
4. You're among the nation's poor, and you can't put adequate food on the table for your family. You give your children all of the food available for dinner, telling them you don't feel hungry, when you're really starving.	_____	_____

have the capacity for *personal growth*—that is, evolution toward a higher state of being. According to Maslow, growth needs emerge only when lower needs are gratified adequately. Growth needs include the need for knowledge, understanding, and aesthetic beauty. These growth needs are found in the uppermost reaches of Maslow's hierarchy.

Foremost among growth needs is the **need for self-actualization, which is the need to fulfill one's potential; it is the highest need in Maslow's motivational hierarchy**. Maslow summarized this concept with a very simple statement: "What a man *can* be, he *must* be." According to Maslow, people will be frustrated if they are unable to fully use their talents or pursue their true interests. For example, if you have great musical talent but must work as an accountant, or if you have scholarly interests but must work as a sales clerk, your need for self-actualization will be thwarted. Maslow's own experiences may have influenced his emphasis on the need for self-actualization. He endured some frustration because his family pressured him to study law, although he soon managed to turn to his true interest, psychology.

Maslow theorized that the various levels of needs are ordered in the same way for nearly everyone. He asserted that this ordering was "instinctoid," by which he meant that it was biologically built-in as part of human nature. However, he recognized that some people might get their hierarchies scrambled due to unusual factors in their personal history. He speculated that the most common rearrangement of levels occurs when adults put higher priority on their esteem needs than on their love and belongingness needs. Such people are more concerned about prestige and their career advancement than they are about their intimate relationships or family. They may let their marriage or personal life deteriorate while they pour all of their energy into their career.

In suggesting that the ordering of our needs is innate but subject to rearrangement based on experience, Maslow emphasizes both the biological and the social bases of human motivation. Moreover, his hierarchy systematically organizes needs according to their biological and social foundations. As we move upward in the hierarchy, each level of needs becomes less biological and more social in origin. Thus, according to Maslow, the degree to which our behavior is dominated by biological needs depends on which level of needs is activated, and this, in turn, varies depending on the person and the circumstances.

Maslow's theory has proven very influential. However, aspects of his theory are difficult to test empirically. In particular, growth needs such as self-actualization have proven difficult to measure and study, so portions of Maslow's theory rest on only a thin foundation of research (Geller, 1982). Nonetheless, Maslow contributed to our understanding of motivation by suggesting a hierarchical principle that takes both the biological and social foundations of human motives into consideration.

Maslow's theory has its strengths and its weaknesses—just like all the other motivational theories that we've discussed. Thus far, no one theory has come to dominate the investigation of motivation in contemporary psychology. Perhaps it's unrealistic to expect a single theory to explain the huge variety of motives that inspire our goal-directed behavior. In any case, in the remainder of the chapter, you'll see the influence of all the motivational theories that we've discussed.

Our next task is to take a closer look at selected motives. To a large degree, our choices reflect the motives psychologists have studied most heavily. Given the range and diversity of human motives, we can only examine a handful in depth, so we'll draw two examples each from the two broad classes of human needs (biological motives and social motives). We'll focus on hunger and sexual motivation to show how researchers have dissected biological needs. Then we'll examine affiliation and achievement to illustrate how psychologists have analyzed social motives. As we explore these four motives—hunger, sex, affiliation, and achievement—we'll be moving upward through Maslow's hierarchy. Thus, you'll see the influence of physiological factors gradually declining, giving way to social and evironmental factors.

"What a man *can* be, he *must* be."
ABRAHAM MASLOW

THE MOTIVATION OF HUNGER AND EATING

Why do we eat? Because we're hungry. What makes us hungry? A lack of food. Any grade-school child can explain these basic facts. So hunger is a simple motivational system, right? Wrong! Hunger is deceptive. It only looks simple. Ac- tually, it's a terribly puzzling and complex motivational system, so complex that despite extensive studies on the subject, psychologists and other scientists are still struggling to better understand hunger.

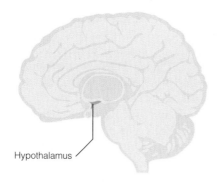

Figure 10.5 The hypothalamus. This small structure at the base of the forebrain plays a role in regulating a variety of human biological needs, including hunger. (Consult Figure 3.14 for a more detailed view.)

Hypothalamus

Biological Factors in the Regulation of Hunger

The first scientific theories of hunger were fairly simple. Cannon and Washburn (1912) found a strong association between stomach contractions and subjective reports of hunger. Based on this correlation, they theorized that stomach contractions cause hunger. However, as we've seen before, correlation is no assurance of causation. Stomach contractions may accompany hunger, but they don't cause it. How do we know? Because research showed that people continue to experience hunger even after their stomach is removed out of medical necessity (Wangensteen & Carlson, 1931). If hunger can occur without a stomach, then stomach contractions can't be the cause of hunger. This realization led to more elaborate theories of hunger that focus on (1) the role of the brain, (2) blood sugar level, and (3) hormones.

BRAIN REGULATION

Research with laboratory animals eventually suggested that the experience of hunger is controlled in the brain—specifically, in the hypothalamus. As we discussed in Chapter 3, the *hypothalamus* is a tiny structure in the forebrain, involved in the regulation of a variety of biological needs related to survival (see Figure 10.5). Researchers typically investigate the role of the hypothalamus in behavior by subjecting animals to *electrical stimulation of the brain* (ESB). They implant an electrode in the hypothalamus and then pass different currents through the electrode to either destroy (lesion) or activate the area of the brain at the base of the electrode (see Chapter 3).

A great many animal studies have shown that the activation and destruction of two areas in the hypothalamus are associated with changes in eating. Investigators have found that when they activate the *lateral hypothalamus* (LH) through ESB, animals promptly begin to eat, even if they're already full. The animals stop eating when the electrical stimulation of the LH is halted. In contrast, when researchers destroy the LH, animals ignore

available food and frequently starve (Anand & Brobeck, 1951; Teitelbaum & Epstein, 1962). The opposite pattern is seen when researchers stimulate or lesion the *ventromedial nucleus of the hypothalamus* (VMH) (Brobeck, Tepperman, & Long, 1943; Wyrwicka & Dobrzecka, 1960). Activation of the VMH curtails eating behavior. Lesioning the VMH leads to extensive overeating and gross obesity. Indeed, it is not unusual for animals with VMH lesions to balloon up to three times their original weight!

The typical results of these studies of hypothalamic manipulations and eating are summarized in Figure 10.6. Given these results, investigators concluded that activation of the lateral hypothalamus *started* the experience of hunger and that activation of the ventromedial hypothalamus *stopped* the experience of hunger. They weren't entirely sure what normally led to the activation of these areas in the absence of artificial electrical stimulation. But they concluded that the LH and VMH were the brain's on-off switches or start-stop centers that controlled hunger.

Doubts about this conclusion soon surfaced, however. Physiologists noticed that hypothalamic stimulation and lesioning led to some peculiarities in the eating behavior of experimental animals. For example, rats with VMH lesions usually engage in massive overeating leading to obesity. However, they're *lazy*, and if they're forced to work for their food (by pressing a lever), they end up eating less than normal. They also are *picky* and reject food that doesn't taste good. Critics argued that if the animals were really hungry, they wouldn't be so lazy or picky.

Researchers shed some light on these riddles when they found that the effects of LH and VMH manipulations *were not unique to hunger.* For instance, LH stimulation, which triggers eating when food is present, will elicit drinking if water alone is present, and running if neither food nor water is available. Thus, Elliot Valenstein (1973) reasoned that LH stimulation did not produce hunger, but rather a *generalized arousal.* He argued that this arousal led to eating in many studies simply because the animals were confined to cages with food present—what else could they do? In a similar fashion, Valenstein argued that VMH activation blocked eating by inhibiting general arousal. Finally, he asserted that hypothalamic manipulations led to peculiarities in eating because the animals weren't experiencing genuine hunger. Although Valenstein's theory is the subject of debate, several other lines of evidence support the idea that the activation or destruction of hypothalamic areas influences eating *indirectly* (Grossman, 1979).

Valenstein's theory has muddied the waters quite a bit. Most theorists still believe that the LH and VMH are involved in the control of hunger. However, the exact nature of their role in the regulation of hunger is unclear. The once popular notion that they are on-off centers for hunger has been discarded as too simple (Logue, 1986). As you'll soon learn, other physiological mechanisms have been implicated in the regulation of hunger.

BLOOD GLUCOSE REGULATION

Much of our food intake is converted into *glucose*, which circulates in the blood. **Glucose is a simple sugar that is an important source of energy.** Manipulations that decrease blood glucose level can increase hunger; manipulations that increase glucose level can make people feel satiated (full). Based on these findings, Jean Mayer (1955, 1968) proposed that our hunger is regulated by the rise and fall of our blood glucose levels.

According to Mayer, fluctuations in blood glucose level are monitored in the brain by **glucostats—neurons sensitive to glucose in the surrounding fluid.** These glucostats are thought to control the experience of hunger. This model is complicated by the fact that diabetics often have very high glucose levels (which should make them feel full) but still feel quite hungry. Mayer accounts for this apparent contradiction by reasoning that the glucostats must monitor glucose *utilization*, rather than glucose *level*.

Reliable associations between blood glucose fluctuations and hunger have been found in numerous studies. Although, there's little doubt that hunger is regulated, at least in part, through glucostatic mechanisms, the *location* of the glucostats remains open to debate. Neurons sensitive to glucose have been found in the hypothalamus (Oomura, 1976), but glucose fluctuations in the brain seem too slow and too small to account for our swings in hunger.

Some studies suggest that the glucostatic regulation of hunger may be accomplished through the liver (Niijima, 1982; Novin et al., 1983). Glucose-sensitive receptors in the liver may send their signals to the hypothalamus by way of the vagus nerve that connects the liver with the brain. The liver may also monitor other physiological changes that affect hunger.

HORMONAL REGULATION

Insulin, a hormone secreted by the pancreas, must be present for cells to extract glucose from the blood. A lack of insulin causes sugar diabetes. Diabetics are unable to use the glucose in their blood unless they are given insulin injections. In nondiabetic individuals, an injection of insulin

Section of hypothalamus	Destroyed (by lesioning)	Activated (by electrical stimulation)
Lateral area	Animal stops eating	Animal overeats
Ventromedial nucleus	Animal overeats	Animal stops eating

leads to a decline in blood glucose level and an increase in hunger. Normal secretion of insulin by the pancreas is also associated with increased hunger (Rezek, 1976).

These findings indicate that insulin fluctuations contribute to the experience of hunger. Indeed, research suggests that insulin may not be the only hormone involved in hunger regulation. For instance, there's evidence that a hormone called cholecystokinin (CCK) is secreted when food enters the digestive system. Some investigators suspect that CCK enters the bloodstream and carries a *stop-eating* message to the brain (Kraly, 1981).

Environmental Factors in the Regulation of Hunger

Hunger clearly is a biological need, but eating is not regulated by biological factors alone. Studies show that social and environmental factors govern eating to a considerable extent. Three key environmental factors are (1) learned preferences and habits, (2) food-related cues, and (3) stress.

LEARNED PREFERENCES AND HABITS

Are you fond of eating calves' brains? How about eels? Could we interest you in some dog meat? Probably not, but these are delicacies in some regions of the world. Arctic Eskimos like maggots! You probably prefer beef, chicken, apples, lettuce, potato chips, pizza, cornflakes, or ice cream. These preferences are acquired through learning. People from different cultures display very different patterns of food consumption. If you doubt this, just visit a neighborhood grocery store in an ethnic urban neighborhood (not your own, of course).

Humans do have some innate taste preferences of a very general sort (for sweet over sour, for instance). But learning wields a great deal of influence over *what* we prefer to eat (Logue, 1986).

Figure 10.6 The hypothalamus and eating behavior. Researchers found that destroying or activating the lateral hypothalamus (LH) or ventromedial hypothalamus (VMH) in rats and other animals caused opposite effects on eating. These results suggested that the LH and VMH were the brain's on-off centers for hunger, but the text discusses doubts raised by subsequent studies.

357

Learned habits also influence *how much* we eat. Consider what happens when artificial sugar is substituted for real sugar in subjects' diets *without their knowledge*. Due to this substitution, subjects get far fewer calories, which should lead to increased eating to compensate for the caloric loss. But most people don't increase their food intake for at least 6 days (Bellisle, 1979). They continue to eat in their usual way—out of habit.

Even the feeling of fullness or satiation that we experience after we eat may be caused by learning rather than physiological changes (Booth, 1977). When we eat, the absorption of nutrients into the body takes a while. Usually, we stop eating *before* physiological mechanisms could signal satiation. Why? Probably because certain eating experiences have consistently been associated with eventual satiation, so that feeling full becomes a conditioned response to these food stimuli. In other words, we *learn* that a steak and eggs or three pieces of pizza will lead to satiation. Thus, these patterns of eating trigger a conditioned response of satiation. People who routinely overeat may have been conditioned so that only very large amounts of food produce this conditioned response.

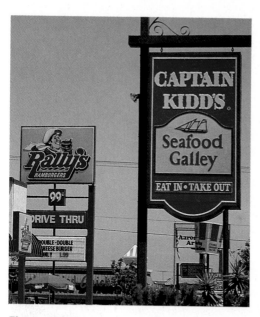

Figure 10.7 Food-related cues, such as these advertisements signaling the ready availability of fast food, are major determinants of our eating behavior.

FOOD-RELATED CUES

Many of us have had our hunger aroused by television commercials for delicious-looking food or by seductive odors coming from the kitchen. These experiences illustrate how food-related cues can trigger hunger. Stanley Schachter (1971) conducted numerous studies on how external cues influence hunger. In one study, Schachter and Gross (1968) manipulated the apparent time by altering the clock in a room so that it ran fast or slow. The subjects had been asked to remove their watches, so they were misled about the time of day. When offered crackers, obese subjects ate nearly twice as many when they thought (erroneously) that it was late rather than early in the afternoon. Non-obese subjects ate fewer crackers when they thought it was late—because they didn't want to spoil their appetite for dinner. Thus, the control of time cues affected eating in both groups, but with opposite results. In other

studies Schachter manipulated external cues such as how tasty and appealing food appeared, how obvious its availability was, and how much effort was required to eat (see Figure 10.7). All of these external cues were found to influence eating behavior to some extent (Schachter & Rodin, 1974). Thus, it's clear that hunger is governed in part by a variety of food-related cues.

STRESS AND EATING

When I have an exceptionally stressful day, I often head for the refrigerator, a grocery store, or a restaurant—usually in pursuit of something chocolate. In other words, I sometimes deal with life's hassles by stuffing myself with my favorite foods. My response is not particularly unusual. Research indicates that stress leads many people to overeat (Slochower, Kaplan, & Mann, 1981). Thus, stress is another environmental factor that can influence hunger (see Chapter 13 for a formal definition of stress).

Eating and Weight: The Roots of Obesity

We just saw that hunger is regulated by a complex interaction of biological and psychological factors. The same kinds of complexities emerge when investigators explore the roots of weight problems or obesity.

Although we live in a culture that seems obsessed with being slender, more and more people are struggling with the problem of obesity. Estimates indicate that 25% to 45% of American adults are overweight (Grinker, 1982). If obesity merely frustrated our vanity, there would be little cause for concern. Unfortunately, obesity is cause for great concern because it's a significant health problem. Overweight people are more vulnerable than others to cardiovascular diseases, diabetes, hypertension, respiratory problems, stroke, arthritis, and back problems (Jeffrey & Lemnitzer, 1981).

SENSITIVITY TO EXTERNAL CUES

Stanley Schachter (1971) advanced the hypothesis that obese people are extra sensitive to external cues that affect hunger and are relatively insensitive to internal physiological signals. According to this notion, fat people pay little attention to messages from their bodies but respond readily to environmental cues such as the availability of food, the attractiveness of food, and the time of day. Schachter argued that obese people eat excessively because they can't ignore food-related cues that trigger eating. Such people may walk into a shopping mall intending to eat nothing, just to shop in a few stores; instead they eat because their hunger is aroused by the sight and aroma of others' ice cream cones, hot dogs, and tacos.

Schachter and others conducted many studies that provided support for his theory that obesity is promoted by sensitivity to external food cues. For example, one study compared the eating of obese and underweight subjects who were offered ice cream (Nisbett, 1968). Some subjects received tasty ice cream; others received ice cream that didn't taste very good. As Figure 10.8 shows, this external factor did not have much impact on the eating of the underweight subjects, but it made an enormous difference to the obese subjects, who ate nearly five times as much when the ice cream tasted good.

Although Schachter's theory has received support, follow-up studies have led to some modifications in the theory. Judith Rodin's (1978, 1981) research has blurred Schachter's key distinction between the internal and external determinants of hunger. Rodin demonstrated that the sight, smell, and sound of a grilling steak (external determinants) could elicit insulin secretions (internal determinants) that led to increased hunger. She also found that food-related stimuli produced the largest insulin responses in people who tended to respond to food-related cues by eating. Rodin's findings raise the possibility that people who are responsive to external food cues may really be responding to internal signals (insulin). Their problem may be that they secrete insulin too readily in response to the food-related cues.

After reviewing the accumulated evidence, Rodin also argues that the link between sensitivity to external cues and obesity is weaker than Schachter believed. Many obese people are not exceptionally responsive to food-related stimuli. Moreover, many people who are very responsive to food cues are slender or normal in weight. Thus, Rodin asserts that obesity must depend on factors besides sensitivity to external food cues. She theorizes that responsiveness to external cues contributes to obesity, but only in conjunction with metabolic and other genetic factors, such as those we are about to discuss.

GENETIC PREDISPOSITION
It may be that sensitivity to food-related cues leads to obesity only in people who are genetically predisposed to weight problems. You may know some people who can eat constantly without gaining weight, and other, less fortunate people who grow chubby eating far less. Differences in physiological makeup must be the cause of this paradox. Recent research suggests that these differences may have a genetic basis.

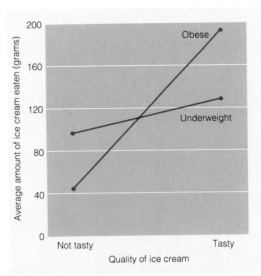

"People's metabolic machinery is constituted in such a way that the fatter they are, the fatter they are primed to become."
JUDITH RODIN

Figure 10.8 Obesity and eating habits. Overweight and underweight subjects were given an opportunity to eat ice cream. The tastiness of the ice cream had far more impact on the eating behavior of the overweight subjects than on that of the underweight subjects, supporting Schachter's theory that obese people are overly sensitive to food cues that have little to do with the satisfaction of nutritional needs. (Based on data from Nisbett, 1968)

In a recent study, adults raised by foster parents were compared to their biological and foster parents in regard to weight (Stunkard et al., 1986). The investigators found that the adoptees resembled their biological parents but not their adoptive parents in this respect. This finding meshes with research indicating that there are genetic strains of rats and mice that are prone to obesity (Bray & York, 1979). Thus, our weight seems to be influenced by our genetic makeup, and some of us may inherit a vulnerability to obesity.

What, exactly, is inherited by people who are prone to obesity? It may be a sluggish metabolism. Your **basal metabolic rate is your body's rate of energy output at rest after a 12-hour fast.** People vary in their basal metabolic rate. This means that some of us burn off calories faster than others. Calories that are burned off won't be stored as fat.

There also is reason to believe that heredity affects the number of fat cells that we develop. Studies show that obese people have more fat cells than other people do (Knittle & Hirsch, 1968). Hence, some people may be predisposed to weight problems because they're genetically programmed to develop an excessive number of fat cells (Grinker, 1982). This intriguing notion brings us to set-point theory, which concerns how our bodies might regulate fat deposits.

THE CONCEPT OF SET POINT
People who lose weight on a diet have a rather strong (and depressing) tendency to gain back the weight they lose. The reverse is also true. People who have to work to put weight on often have trouble keeping it on. According to Richard Nisbett (1972), these observations suggest that your body may have a **set point, a natural point of stability in body weight.**

359

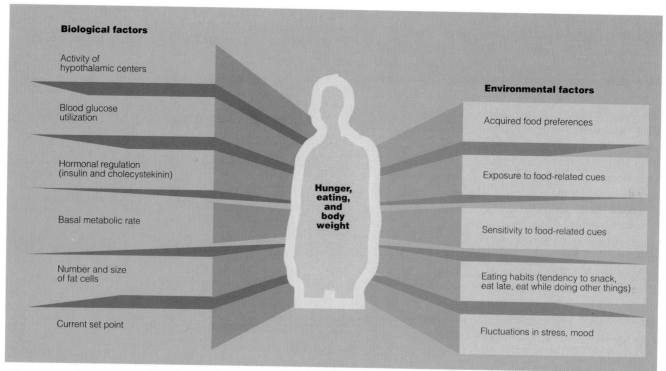

Biological factors

Activity of
hypothalamic centers

Blood glucose
utilization

Hormonal regulation
(insulin and cholecystekinin)

Basal metabolic rate

Number and size
of fat cells

Current set point

**Hunger,
eating,
and
body
weight**

Environmental factors

Acquired food preferences

Exposure to food-related cues

Sensitivity to food-related cues

Eating habits (tendency to snack,
eat late, eat while doing other things)

Fluctuations in stress, mood

Figure 10.9 The factors influencing hunger, eating, and body weight. Multifactorial causation is readily apparent in the regulation of hunger, eating, and weight, which are shaped by a complex array of interacting biological and environmental factors.

According to set-point theory, our bodies monitor levels of fat stores to keep them fairly stable (Keesey & Powley, 1975, 1986). Supposedly, when fat stores slip below a crucial set point, some mechanism increases our tendency to experience hunger. The location and nature of the cells that monitor fat stores are unknown. Some proponents of this theory believe that the hypothalamus is involved (Keesey et al., 1984). In fact, they maintain that the stimulation and destruction of hypothalamic centers in animals affect eating by altering the animals' set point.

What determines your set point? Advocates of set-point theory suspect that it depends on the number of fat cells in your body. They note that when people diet and lose weight, the weight loss does *not* lead to a decrease in the *number* of fat cells. Instead, fat cells shrink in average *size*. This curious stability suggests that the number of fat cells has something to do with one's set point. Although the number of fat cells in the body can be increased at any age (through persistent overeating), the count typically stabilizes in early

childhood (Knittle, 1975). This finding suggests that fat cell number depends on a combination of heredity and early patterns of eating. Thus, your set point may have been set early in life.

The relevance of set-point theory to obesity should be readily apparent. Weight problems may be terribly difficult to avoid if one has a high set point. This does *not* mean that all obese people are doomed to remain obese forever. However, it may explain why most overweight people have to fight a lengthy, uphill battle to keep weight off.

Many of us, even if we aren't obese, also struggle to maintain a weight that we consider ideal. Our hunger and weight are governed by the same considerations that underlie hunger and weight in the obese: blood glucose levels, insulin secretion, activity in hypothalamic centers, liver functioning, acquired food preferences, learned eating habits, sensitivity to food cues, stress, metabolic rate, fat cell distribution, and body weight set point (see Figure 10.9). Hunger is basic, but it's *not* simple. Neither is sex, the biological motive that we'll consider next.

SEXUAL MOTIVATION AND BEHAVIOR

How does sex resemble food? Sometimes it seems that people are obsessed with both. We joke and gossip about sex constantly. Our magazines, novels, movies, and television shows are saturated with sexual activity and innuendo. The advertising industry uses sex to sell us everything from

mouthwash to designer jeans to automobiles. Our intense interest in sex reflects the importance of sexual motivation. In this portion of the chapter, we'll examine the factors that influence sexual desire, and we'll describe the physiology of the human sexual response. In the Application, we'll return to the topic of sexuality and discuss some of the factors that promote rewarding sexual relationships.

Determinants of Sexual Desire

Sex is essential for the survival of a species, but it's *not* essential to an *individual's* survival. Sexual motivation is not driven by deprivation to the extent that hunger is—you can live out your life without sex, but without food your life will be very short. Like hunger, sexual desire is influenced by a complicated network of biological and social factors.

HORMONAL REGULATION

The biological influence on sexual desire is shown quite vividly in the animal kingdom. In many species, females are sexually receptive only just prior to ovulation. Their heightened interest in sex depends on the elevation in circulating levels of certain hormones. Hormones exert similar effects in males. For instance, if the source of a male rat's sex hormones is removed, the rat's interest in sex usually dwindles. Injections of hormones can revive sexual desire in most of these animals. Thus, it's clear that hormones regulate sex drive in animals, although their effects are less pronounced among higher primates (Feder, 1984).

The biological tyranny that rules sexuality in many animals has far less influence on human sexuality, yet there are some interesting relations between hormone levels and sexual activity in humans. The hormones that play a special role in sexual motivation are secreted by the ovaries in females and the testes in males. Estrogens are the principal class of female sex hormones. Androgens are the principal class of male sex hormones. Actually, both classes of hormones are produced in both sexes, but the relative balance is much different. The hypothalamus and the pituitary gland regulate these hormonal secretions (Hoyenga & Hoyenga, 1979).

Androgen fluctuations seem related to sexual motivation in *both* sexes. High levels of testosterone (a key androgen) in female and male subjects correlate with higher rates of sexual activity, although the relations are weaker for women (Daitzman & Zuckerman, 1980; Persky et al., 1978). Curiously, *estrogen* levels among women do *not* correlate well with sexual interest and activity. Hence, in humans there is only a very weak association between sex drive and the ovulation/menstruation cycle (Sanders & Bancroft, 1982).

The correlations between hormone levels and sexual activity in humans are interesting, but they do *not* prove that hormonal surges *cause* sexual

desire under normal circumstances. We must be cautious about this conclusion because the *direction* of the possible causal relationships underlying this correlation is ambiguous. Some evidence suggests that sexual arousal may cause hormonal surges rather than vice versa (Purvis et al., 1976). Thus, there are serious doubts about whether normal hormonal swings have any causal relation to human sexual desire (Persky, 1983).

PHEROMONES

The female gypsy moth can lure males for sexual liaisons from up to 2 miles away (Hopson, 1979). How does she do it? She secretes a powerful pheromone. A *pheromone* is a chemical secreted by one animal that affects the behavior of another. These chemical messengers are usually detected through the sense of smell; they influence various aspects of behavior in lower animals, including sexuality.

Do pheromones influence human behavior? Possibly, but not in the way that many popular articles have suggested. Some popular magazines imply that humans secrete pheromones that incite compelling sexual desire. Some "adult" magazines even advertise pheromone substances that supposedly serve as sexual stimulants. At present, however, there is no convincing evidence that pheromones exert any impact on sex drive in humans or other higher primates such as monkeys (Quadagno, 1987).

Nonetheless, human pheromones *may* cause a very interesting phenomenon. When women live together (in a sorority, for example), their menstrual cycles gradually tend to become more synchronized (McClintock, 1971). This ovulatory synchronization also occurs among some animals (such as mice) when they are housed together, and it has been linked to pheromones (Bronson & Whitten, 1968).

In a clever study, Russell, Switz, and Thompson (1980) showed that pheromones may be responsible for ovulatory synchronization in humans, as well. They collected samples of underarm sweat from women and dissolved these samples in alcohol. A second set of women regularly rubbed these sweat-and-alcohol preparations on their lips; a control group used alcohol-only preparations. The ovulatory cycles of the women who received the sweat preparations began to synchronize with the cycles of the women who donated the sweat. Thus, humans may indeed respond to pheromones, but the response isn't necessarily related to sex drive.

Pheromones are the substances most recently touted for their aphrodisiac value. But fascination with *aphrodisiacs—substances thought to in-*

crease sexual desire—dates back to prehistoric times. Today, most people realize that supposed aphrodisiacs ranging from oysters to vitamin E have no real impact on sex drive.

In recent years, new myths have grown up surrounding the aphrodisiac effects of various drugs. Although certain drugs may facilitate sexual desire in *some* people *some* of the time, this occurs through *indirect psychological mechanisms* (Gawin, 1978). Alcohol, for instance, affects sexual motivation in some people by weakening their sexual inhibitions. However, this psychological effect is accompanied by a physiological effect that decreases actual sexual responsiveness. Indeed, a great many drugs have negative effects on sexual arousal. Long (1987) lists 39 drugs that may have a negative effect on sexual responsiveness in men; many of these can also impair arousal in women. At present, there are no known substances that can reliably increase sexual desire through any direct physical mechanism. In other words, no genuine aphrodisiacs are known.

ATTRACTION TO A PARTNER
Although we habitually use the term *sex drive*, human sexual motivation seems to operate in accordance with an incentive model more than a drive model. Thus, key considerations are the availability of a potential partner and attraction to that partner. Humans are not unique in this regard. Many organisms respond to the external stimulus of an available partner.

In fact, a *new* partner can revive dwindling sexual interest in many animals. This phenomenon has a curious name, *the Coolidge effect*, which derives from the following story. President Coolidge and his wife were touring a farm. Mrs. Coolidge was informed that a rooster on the farm often copulated 20 or more times in a day. "Tell that to Mr. Coolidge," she supposedly said. When informed of the rooster's feat, the President asked if it was always with the same hen. He was told that the rooster enjoyed a different hen each time. "Tell *that* to Mrs. Coolidge," was his reply. Today, no one is sure whether the story is true, but the Coolidge effect is seen in many animals, including rats, bulls, and monkeys (Bermant & Davidson, 1974). Anecdotal evidence suggests that the Coolidge effect may also occur in humans.

Many species of animals are *selective* in their attraction, often choosing to mate with the largest or most colorful of the available candidates. Most humans are selective too. Human selectivity is influenced greatly by learning, which explains why people differ substantially in what they find physically attractive (Wiggins, Wiggins, & Conger, 1968). Of course, humans further complicate

sexual attraction by considering a host of factors besides physical beauty. Our sexual interest may be influenced by a potential partner's personality, competence, social status, and values, not to mention our affection for the person (Symons, 1979).

For many animals, sexual overtures from a potential partner usually increase sexual desire. For example, a male chimpanzee usually will respond with interest when a female chimp bends over to present her genitals. Humans tend to be more subtle. We signal our interest with extended eye contact, hushed vocal tones, romantic music, dimmed lights, affectionate caressing, and so forth (Scheflen & Scheflen, 1972).

EROTIC MATERIALS
A potential partner is not the only external stimulus that can awaken our sexual interest. Erotic reading material, photographs, and films can stimulate sexual desire (Heiman, 1977). The intensity of sexual arousal generally increases as the depictions of sexual activity become more explicit (Miller, Byrne, & Fisher, 1980). Of course, we don't all respond favorably to sexually explicit media.

Women are more likely than men to report that they dislike erotic materials (Kenrick et al., 1980). However, when physiological responses to erotic stimuli are measured in laboratory studies, men and women usually are equally responsive (Fisher & Byrne, 1978; Heiman, 1977). How do we explain this paradox? It may be a comment on the nature of the pornography industry. Erotic materials generally are scripted to appeal to men and often portray women in degrading roles (Dworkin, 1981). In formal studies, however, researchers usually present less sexist material to their subjects (unless they are specifically exploring the effects of sexist erotica).

How much impact does erotic material have on actual sexual behavior? Research suggests that exposure to erotic material elevates the likelihood of overt sexual activity for a few hours immediately after the exposure (Cattell, Kawash, & DeYoung, 1972). This modest effect may explain why investigators have failed to find a statistical link between the availability of erotica and sex crime rates. In fact, researchers found that sex crimes *declined* after pornographic materials were made readily available in Denmark in the 1960s (Kutchinsky, 1985; see Figure 10.10).

Although erotic materials don't appear to incite overpowering sexual urges, they may alter *attitudes* in ways that eventually influence sexual behavior. Zillmann and Bryant (1984) found that subjects exposed to a large dose of pornography developed more liberal attitudes about acceptable sexual practices.

Recent studies of *aggressive pornography* have raised concerns about its effects. Aggressive pornography typically depicts violence against women. Some studies indicate that this type of material increases male subjects' aggressive behavior toward women, at least in the context of the research laboratory (Malamuth & Donnerstein, 1982). Exposure to aggressive pornography may also change males' attitudes about sexual aggression by perpetuating the myth that women enjoy being raped and ravaged (Malamuth, 1984). Thus, there is worrisome evidence that aggressive pornography may contribute to sexual violence against women.

PERSONALITY, AGE, AND ATTITUDES

The ease with which sexual motivation is aroused varies from one person to another and from one situation to another. Factors such as personality, age, and attitudes influence these individual differences in sex drive. In regard to *personality*, evidence suggests that extroverts are more sexually active than introverts (Eysenck, 1976). In regard to *age*, sexual activity tends to decline steadily during middle and late adulthood (Wilson, 1975). However, it doesn't decline nearly as much as most younger people assume (Pocs & Godow, 1977), and many people continue to be quite active in their 70s and 80s.

In regard to *attitudes*, studies show that people who experience a lot of guilt about sexual urges are less active sexually than others (Mosher & Cross, 1971). One research team (Fisher et al., 1988) has distinguished between **erotophobes, people who have very negative attitudes about sex,** and **erotophiles, people who have very favorable attitudes about sex.** Erotophobes tend to feel embarrassed when discussing sex, condemn premarital sex, dislike erotic materials, and view sex as unimportant in their lives. Erotophiles are more comfortable discussing sex, more liberal about premarital sex, more responsive to erotic materials, and more likely to view sex as important in their lives. As you might anticipate, erotophiles are more sexually active than erotophobes (Fisher, 1984). Thus, erotophiles tend to be more responsive to sexual stimuli than erotophobes.

The impact that attitudes can have on our sexual behavior underscores the fact that hormones and pheromones don't exert full control in humans. Our sex drive is not as simple as that of lower animals—we don't go into heat to preserve the species. Our desires are influenced by many social factors that vary from person to person.

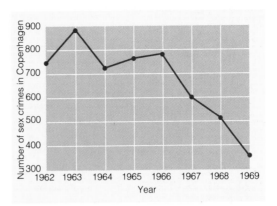

Figure 10.10 Pornography and sexual offenses. Starting in 1965, pornography was made readily available in Denmark, creating a unique opportunity to see whether legalization of pornography would result in more sex crimes. As the graph shows, the number of sex crimes went down instead of up, suggesting that erotic materials do not incite sexual offenses. The Danish findings undermine the proposed link between pornography and sex crimes, although some experimental studies have suggested that there may still be cause for concern. (Data from Kutchinsky, 1985)

The Human Sexual Response

Assuming one is motivated to engage in sexual activity, exactly what happens physically? This may sound like a very simple question, but we really knew very little about the physiology of the human sexual response before William Masters and Virginia Johnson did ground-breaking research in the 1960s. Although our society seems obsessed with sex, until relatively recently we did *not* encourage scientists to study sex. At first Masters and Johnson even had difficulty finding journals that were willing to publish their studies.

Masters and Johnson used physiological recording devices to monitor the bodily changes of volunteers engaging in sex. They even equipped an artificial penile device with a camera to study physiological reactions inside the vagina! Their observations and interviews with their subjects yielded a detailed description of the human sexual response and won them widespread acclaim.

Masters and Johnson (1966, 1970) divide the sexual response cycle into four stages: excitement, plateau, orgasm, and resolution. Figure 10.11 shows how the intensity of sexual arousal changes as women and men progress through these stages. Let's take a closer look at these phases in the human sexual response.

EXCITEMENT PHASE

During the initial phase of excitement, the level of arousal usually escalates rapidly. In both sexes, muscle tension, respiration rate, heart rate, and blood pressure increase quickly. **Vasocongestion—engorgement of blood vessels—**produces penile erection and swollen testes in males. In females, vasocongestion leads to a swelling and hardening of the clitoris, expansion of the vaginal lips, and vaginal lubrication.

PLATEAU PHASE

During the plateau phase, physiological arousal usually continues to build, but at a much slower

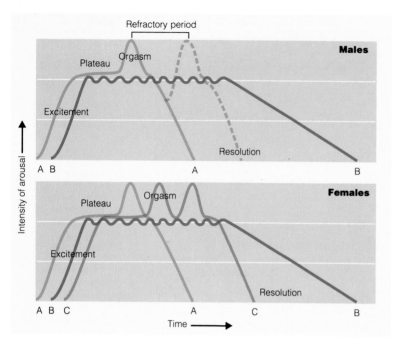

Figure 10.11 The human sexual response cycle. There are similarities and differences between men and women in patterns of sexual arousal. Pattern A, which culminates in orgasm and resolution, is the most typical sequence for both sexes. Pattern B, which involves sexual arousal without orgasm, followed by a slow resolution, is also seen in both sexes, although it is more common among women. Pattern C, which involves multiple orgasms, is seen only in women, as men go through a refractory period before they are capable of another orgasm. (Based on Masters & Johnson, 1966)

pace. In women, further vasocongestion produces a tightening of the vaginal entrance, as the clitoris withdraws under the clitoral hood. Many men secrete a bit of fluid at the tip of the penis. This is not ejaculate, but it may contain sperm. When foreplay is lengthy, it's normal for arousal to fluctuate in both sexes. This fluctuation is more apparent in men; erections may increase and decrease noticeably.

ORGASM PHASE

Orgasm **occurs when sexual arousal reaches its peak intensity and is discharged in a series of muscular contractions that pulsate through the pelvic area.** Heart rate, respiration rate, and blood pressure increase sharply as one experiences this exceedingly pleasant spasmodic response. In males, orgasm is accompanied by ejaculation of the seminal fluid. The subjective experience of orgasm is very similar for men and women. When

subjects provide written descriptions of what their orgasms feel like (without using specific words for genitals), even psychologists and physicians can't tell which came from women and which came from men (Vance & Wagner, 1976; Wiest, 1977).

In contrast, there are some interesting sex differences in the patterns of the orgasm phase. Some women are multiorgasmic. They may experience a series of moderately intense orgasms culminating in a very intense climax. Or they may have two or more orgasms of full intensity. Multiple orgasms are very rare in men. Masters and Johnson also found that women are more likely than men to engage in intercourse without experiencing an orgasm.

RESOLUTION PHASE

During the resolution phase, the physiological changes produced by sexual arousal subside. If one has not had an orgasm, the reduction in sexual tension may be relatively slow and sometimes unpleasant. After orgasm, men experience a *refractory period,* **a time following male orgasm during which males are largely unresponsive to further stimulation.** The refractory period varies from a few minutes to a few hours and increases with age.

Masters and Johnson's exploration of the human sexual response led to major new insights about the nature and causes of sexual problems. Ironically, although Masters and Johnson broke new ground in studying the physiology of sexual arousal, their research demonstrated that sexual problems are due largely to social and psychological factors, rather than to physical malfunctions (this is discussed further in the chapter Application). Their conclusion shows once again that human sexuality involves a fascinating blend of biological and social needs. We turn next to a related motive—affiliation—that is more social in origin.

AFFILIATION: IN SEARCH OF BELONGINGNESS

How would you like to spend the rest of your life alone on a pleasant but deserted island? Most of us would find this to be a terrible fate. Why? Because our fundamental need to be with others would be thwarted. Some animals (bears, tigers, and bald eagles, for example) don't mind going it alone. Humans, however, react very badly to prolonged periods of social isolation. We are social animals and we have to have meaningful contact with others. Think about the amount of time that you spend interacting with other people. Latané

and Bidwell (1977) observed college students around campus and found that they were with someone 60% of the time.

The *affiliation motive* **involves the need to associate with others and maintain social bonds.** Affiliation encompasses our needs for companionship, friendship, love, and a feeling that we belong to a social group. Abraham Maslow (1970) called this motive the need for love and belongingness. He thought that it was a very basic motive, and he placed it at the third level in his hierarchy of needs. When the affiliation motive is frustrated, people often experience considerable distress. The importance of affiliation is demonstrated by the strong correlation observed between feelings of loneliness and depression (Bradburn, 1969).

Some theorists believe that there are biological foundations for our affiliation motive. For example, John Bowlby (1980) claims that infants are biologically programmed to develop emotional bonds with their caretakers. He points out that infants show a need for human contact from the earliest days of life, before such a need could be learned. Bowlby's theory is controversial and difficult to prove. Although affiliation *may* be partly biological in origin, it's primarily a social motive that is shaped through learning and personal experience.

Situational Determinants of Affiliation Behavior

Relatively little research has been done on how situational factors influence affiliation behavior. Nonetheless, investigators have identified two situational determinants—anxiety and embarrassment—that have opposite effects on the motivation to be with others.

In a classic study described in Chapter 2, Stanley Schachter (1959) demonstrated that anxiety can increase affiliation behavior. As you may recall, subjects in the *high-anxiety* group were told that they would receive a series of very painful electrical shocks, while subjects in the *low-anxiety* group were told that the shocks would be painless. When subsequently asked whether they would prefer to wait alone or with others while the experimenter prepared the shock apparatus, subjects in the high-anxiety group showed more interest in having company. Subsequent studies showed that anxiety increases affiliation because having other people around allows subjects to "compare

notes" to evaluate their concerns (Shaver & Klinnert, 1982). Subjects want to share their feelings and see if others are as worried as they are.

In contrast, potentially embarrassing situations decrease our desire to be with others. When researchers tell subjects that they'll have to engage in embarrassing activities (sucking on a large nipple, for instance), most subjects choose to remain alone (Sarnoff & Zimbardo, 1961; Teichman, 1973). Understandably, most of us are not interested in having an audience when we're about to make a fool of ourselves.

Individual Differences in the Need for Affiliation

Some people have stronger affiliation needs than others. Some of us are *joiners*, while others are *loners*. Much of the research on affiliation has looked into these individual differences. In this research, investigators usually measure subjects' need for affiliation with some variant of Henry Murray's Thematic Apperception Test (Morgan & Murray, 1935; Murray, 1943).

The Thematic Apperception Test (TAT) has played a crucial role in the study of affiliation and a variety of other social motives. Social needs vary greatly in strength from one person to another. Hence, psychologists need a way to measure the strength of social motives, and the TAT has proven very useful for this purpose. As we noted in Chapter 9, the TAT is a *projective test*. The stimulus materials are pictures of people in ambiguous scenes open to interpretation. Examples include a man working at a desk and a woman seated in a chair staring off into space. Subjects are asked to write or tell stories about what's happening in the scenes and what the characters are feeling. The themes of these stories are then scored to measure the strength of various needs. Figure 10.12 shows examples of stories dominated by affiliation and achievement themes.

Affiliation arousal
George is an engineer who is working late. He is *worried that his wife will be annoyed* with him for neglecting her. She has been *objecting* that he cares more about his work than his wife and family. He seems *unable to satisfy* both his boss and his wife, but he *loves her* very much and will do his best to *finish up* fast and get home to her.

Achievement arousal
George is an engineer who *wants to win* a competition in which the man with *the most practicable drawing* will be awarded the contract to build a bridge. He is taking a moment to think *how happy he will be* if he wins. He has been *baffled by how to make such a long span strong*, but remembers *to specify a new steel alloy* of great strength, submits his entry, but does not win, and *is very unhappy*.

Figure 10.12 Measuring motives with the Thematic Apperception Test (TAT). Subjects taking the TAT tell or write stories about what is happening in a scene, such as this one showing a man at work. The two stories shown here illustrate strong affiliation motivation and strong achievement motivation. The italicized parts of the stories are thematic ideas that would be identified by a TAT scorer.

How do people who score high in the need for affiliation differ from those who score low? First, *they devote more time to interpersonal activities.* For example, they join more social groups such as clubs and church organizations (Smart, 1965). They make more phone calls and visits to friends (McClelland & Winter, 1969), and they devote more time to conversation and letter writing than others (McAdams & Constantian, 1983). Second, *people with strong affiliation needs worry more about acceptance than those with low affiliation drive.* For example, they experience greater anxiety when they're being evaluated socially by peers (Byrne, 1961). They also go out of their way to avoid being argumentative in groups because they fear rejection (Exline, 1962).

The Need for Intimacy

The affiliation motive encompasses a variety of related needs. In recent years, investigators have begun to examine specific elements of affiliation motivation. For example, Dan McAdams (1980, 1982) has argued that our need for intimacy is an important component of our affiliation motive.

The *intimacy motive* involves the need to have warm, close exchanges with others, marked by open communication. In contrast to the broader affiliation motive, the intimacy motive reflects a desire for a particular *quality* of social interaction. Individual differences in the need for intimacy can be measured with the TAT. The scorer simply looks for different themes in the stories than when scoring for affiliation need.

McAdams (1980) found that people who scored high on the intimacy motive were rated by peers as relatively warm, sincere, and loving, while those who scored low were seen as more self-centered and domineering. The same subjects' need for affiliation failed to predict these differences in interpersonal behavior. Additional studies indicate that students high in intimacy motivation disclose more about themselves to their friends, and laugh, smile, and look at others more than people low in intimacy motivation (McAdams, Healy, & Krause, 1984; McAdams, Jackson, & Kirshnit, 1984). Thus, it appears that our need for intimacy is an important factor in our interpersonal behavior, and it deserves further study.

ACHIEVEMENT: IN SEARCH OF EXCELLENCE

"People with a high need for achievement are not gamblers; they are challenged to win by personal effort, not by luck."
DAVID MCCLELLAND

At the beginning of this chapter, we discussed Dennis Conner's lengthy, laborious, and tenacious pursuit of the America's Cup. He and his crew made great sacrifices and worked uncounted hours to achieve their goal. What motivates people to push themselves so hard? In all likelihood, it's a very strong need for achievement. The *achievement motive* involves the need to master difficult challenges, to outperform others, and to meet high standards of excellence. Above all else, the need for achievement involves the desire to excel—especially in competition with others. In Maslow's hierarchy of needs, achievement is found at the fourth level, among the esteem needs. Although some people have tried to link achievement to biological factors such as hormonal fluctuations (Baker, 1980), the need for achievement is generally viewed as a product of social training.

David McClelland and his colleagues (McClelland et al., 1953; McClelland, 1985) have been studying the achievement motive for about 40 years. McClelland believes that achievement motivation is of the utmost importance. He notes that estimates of the average need for achievement in entire societies at specific times correlate with progress and productivity in those societies

(McClelland, 1961). For example, estimates of changes in achievement motivation in ancient Greece relate closely to the rise and fall of Greek civilization. Also, estimates of achievement need in the United States have fluctuated in tandem with inventive activity as measured by the U.S. Patent Index (deCharms & Moeller, 1962). This remarkable correspondence between achievement motivation and patent activity is graphed in Figure 10.13.

McClelland views the need for achievement as the spark that ignites economic growth, scientific progress, inspirational leadership, and masterpieces in the creative arts. It's difficult to argue with his assertion about the immense importance of achievement motivation. Consider how much poorer our culture would be if people such as Charles Darwin, Thomas Edison, Ernest Hemingway, Pablo Picasso, Abraham Lincoln, Susan B. Anthony, Winston Churchill, and Martin Luther King hadn't had a fire burning in their hearts.

Individual Differences in the Need for Achievement

We've all heard the stories of Lincoln as a young boy, reading through the night by firelight. Find

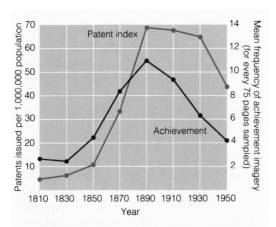

Figure 10.13 Achievement need and inventive activity. Applying TAT-like scoring techniques to popular American literature, deCharms and Moeller (1962) concluded that Americans' need for achievement began to decline around 1890. They also found some correspondence between achievement motivation and inventive activity, as measured by the U.S. Patent Index, suggesting that a culture's need for achievement may affect its productivity.

a biography of any high achiever, and you'll find a similar drive—throughout the person's life. Achievement doesn't suddenly become a driving force for us; the need for achievement is a fairly stable aspect of personality. Hence, research in this area has focused mostly on individual differences in achievement motivation. Investigators usually measure subjects' need for achievement with the Thematic Apperception Test. In the studies that have estimated achievement motivation for *entire societies*, TAT-like scoring procedures were used to assess the themes in representative examples of popular literature from those societies (rather than individuals' stories).

The research on individual differences in achievement motivation has yielded interesting findings on the characteristics of people who score high in the need for achievement. They tend to work harder and more persistently on tasks than people low in the need for achievement (French & Thomas, 1958). They also are more likely than others to delay gratification in order to pursue long-term goals (Mischel, 1961). In terms of careers, they typically go into competitive occupations that provide them with an opportunity to excel (McClelland, 1965). Apparently, their persistence and hard work often pays off: high achievement motivation correlates positively with measures of career success and with upward social mobility among lower-class men (Crockett, 1962; Veroff et al., 1960).

Situational Determinants of Achievement Behavior

But your achievement drive is not the only determinant of how hard you work. Situational factors can also have an effect on achievement strivings. John Atkinson (1974, 1981) has elaborated extensively on McClelland's original theory of achievement motives and has identified some important situational determinants of achievement behavior.

Atkinson uses an expectancy-value model of motivation. He theorizes that the tendency to pursue achievement in a particular situation depends on the following factors:

• The strength of one's *motivation to achieve success*. This is viewed as a stable aspect of personality.
• One's estimate of the *probability of success* for the task at hand. This varies from task to task.
• The *incentive value of success*. This depends on the tangible and intangible rewards for success on the specific task.

The latter two variables are situational determinants of achievement behavior; that is, they vary from one situation to another. According to Atkinson, the pursuit of achievement increases as the probability of success and the incentive value of success go up.

Let's apply Atkinson's model to a simple example. According to this theory, your tendency to pursue a good grade in Calculus should depend on your general motivation to achieve success, your estimate of the probability of getting a good grade in the class, and the value you place on a good grade in Calculus. Thus, given a certain motivation to achieve success, you will pursue a good grade in Calculus more vigorously if you have a high expectancy of success and if you place a high value on that good grade. In contrast, given the *same* motivation to achieve success, your pursuit of a good grade in Chemistry will be less vigorous if you have an outrageously demanding professor (this lowers your expectancy of success) or if a good grade in Chemistry is not required for your major (this lowers the incentive value of success). These examples demonstrate how your achievement behavior may vary as a function of situational factors even though your motivation to achieve success remains stable across the two situations.

Factoring in the Fear of Failure

According to Atkinson, we also must consider a person's fear of failure to understand achievement behavior (Atkinson & Birch, 1978). He maintains that people vary in their *motivation to avoid failure*. This motive is considered a stable aspect of personality. Together with situational factors such as the probability of failure and the negative value placed on failure, it influences our achievement strivings. Figure 10.14 diagrams the factors in Atkinson's model that are thought to govern achievement behavior.

Like the motive to achieve success, the motive to avoid failure can stimulate achievement. For example, you might work very hard and very persistently in Calculus primarily because you couldn't tolerate the shame associated with failure. In other words, you might work more to avoid a bad grade than to earn a good grade.

The relative strengths of the motive to achieve success and the motive to avoid failure influence the risks that people prefer to take (Atkinson & Litwin, 1960; Weiner, 1978). Hence, in some situations, the motivation to avoid failure may *inhibit* achievement. A strong fear of failure could prevent you from pursuing a goal altogether. For example, an intense fear of failure might stop you from ever enrolling in Chemistry if it's not required. Unfortunately, many people shy away from worthwhile challenges in life because their fear of failure is so strong.

Factoring in the Fear of Success

One's *fear of success* may also affect achievement behavior. This variable surfaced in research on sex differences in achievement motivation. The first

2 decades of research on achievement focused heavily on males. The handful of studies using female subjects suggested that the need for achievement was lower in women than in men. In an effort to explain these apparent sex differences, Matina Horner (1968) hypothesized that *achievement strivings in many women are suppressed by an underlying fear of success*.

In a ground-breaking study, Horner (1968) found dramatic support for her hypothesis. She assessed achievement using a projective technique that resembled the TAT. Specifically, she asked subjects to complete a story that placed the character in an achievement-oriented situation. The story began, "After first-term finals, Anne [or John, for the male subject] finds herself [himself] at the top of her [his] medical school class." A great many of the female subjects (65%) wrote stories with negative themes, such as those that follow.

Although Anne is happy with her success, she fears what will happen to her social life. The male med students don't seem to think very highly of a female who has beaten them in their field.

Anne is pretty darn proud of herself, but everyone hates and envies her.

Unfortunately, Anne no longer feels so certain that she really wants to be a doctor. She is worried about herself and wonders if perhaps she isn't normal.

The female subjects in Horner's study tended to write stories in which Anne's success led to unfortunate consequences for her. They expressed

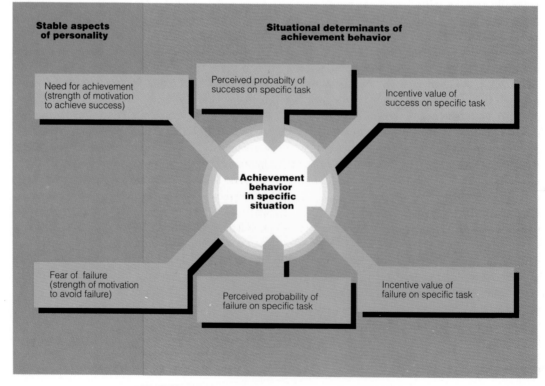

Figure 10.14 Determinants of achievement behavior. According to John Atkinson, our pursuit of achievement in a particular situation depends on several factors. Some of these factors, such as our need for achievement or fear of failure, are relatively stable motives that are part of our personalities. Many other factors, such as the likelihood and value of success or failure, vary from one situation to another, depending on the circumstances.

Stable aspects of personality

Situational determinants of achievement behavior

Need for achievement (strength of motivation to achieve success)

Perceived probabilty of success on specific task

Incentive value of success on specific task

Achievement behavior in specific situation

Fear of failure (strength of motivation to avoid failure)

Perceived probability of failure on specific task

Incentive value of failure on specific task

Although originally viewed as a unique problem for women, research has shown that fear of success may affect achievement behavior in either sex. Women are most likely to have their achievement strivings inhibited when they compete against men in a traditionally masculine domain—such as sports.

fears of social rejection and concerns about being seen as unfeminine. In contrast, most of Horner's male subjects wrote stories with positive themes; only 10% showed any apparent fear of success.

Horner also had her subjects work on an intellectual task alone and in competition with a member of the same sex or the opposite sex. She found that the women who showed fear of success performed worse in competition with a man than when they worked alone. In other words, many of these women seemed to "take a dive" so that they wouldn't show up a male. On the basis of these findings, Horner (1968, 1972) concluded that fear of success is more common in women than men and that this fear of success inhibits the pursuit of achievement in many women.

Horner's thought-provoking research generated many follow-up studies. Collectively, they suggest some revisions of Horner's original conclusions along the following lines (Bremer & Wittig, 1980; Hoffman, 1974; Karabenick, 1977; Tresemer, 1976; Zuckerman & Wheeler, 1975):

1. Fear of success actually appears to be nearly as common in men as it is in women. Subsequent studies have found more fear of success among men and less fear of success among women than originally seen in the Horner study. Thus, sex differences in the prevalence of fear of success seem negligible.

2. However, there are differences in *why* men and women fear success. Subjects of both sexes are concerned that females' success may lead to social rejection and loneliness. Subjects worry that males' success won't be worth all the effort and sacrifice.

3. When aroused, fear of success is somewhat more likely to inhibit achievement behavior in women than in men. In other words, men seem to brush aside their fear of success more often than women do. This inhibition of achievement in women is especially likely when they're competing with men on traditionally masculine tasks.

4. Fear of success among women may not be a *motive* as much as an understandable reaction to *situational factors*. Given the discrimination against women that occurs in our society, some women may be prone to make low estimates of the probability that they'll succeed in certain situations. Negative side effects associated with success for women may also lower the incentive value of

success in some situations. Thus, potentially realistic evaluations of situations may restrain females' quest for achievement.

In conclusion, fear of success is not as big a roadblock to women's achievement as Matina Horner originally thought. Indeed, Horner's own career exemplifies the earnest pursuit of success, as she went on to become president of Radcliffe College. It's now clear that fear of success can suppress the pursuit of achievement in *either* sex. This inhibition of achievement seems to occur more often in females than males, but the sex differences are much smaller than early evidence suggested.

The relationships between achievement behavior and *fear* of success and *fear* of failure illustrate the intimate connection between motivation and emotion, since fear is one of our most fundamental emotions. Emotion and motivation are often intertwined. On the one hand, *emotion can cause motivation*. For example, *anger* about your work schedule may motivate you to look for a new job. *Jealousy* of an ex-girlfriend may motivate you to ask out her roommate. On the other hand, *motivation can cause emotion*. For example, your motivation to win a photography contest may lead to great *anxiety* during the judging, and either great *joy* if you win or great *gloom* if you don't. Thus, motivation and emotion are closely related, although they're *not* the same thing. We'll analyze the nature of emotion in the next section.

"The motive to avoid success has an all-too-important influence on the intellectual and professional lives of women in our society."
MATINA HORNER

THE ELEMENTS OF EMOTIONAL EXPERIENCE

Our most profound and important experiences in life are saturated with emotion. Think of the *joy* that people feel at weddings, the *grief* at funerals, the *ecstasy* when they fall in love. Emotions also color our everyday experiences. For instance, you might experience *anger* when a professor treats you rudely, *dismay* when you learn that your car needs expensive repairs, and *happiness* when you see that you aced your Economics exam. In some respects, emotions lie at the core of our mental health. The two most common complaints that lead people to seek psychotherapy are excessive *depression* and *anxiety*. Clearly, emotions play a pervasive and central role in our lives.

Exactly what is an emotion? We all have plenty of personal experience with emotion, but it's an elusive concept to define. Most formal definitions include cognitive, physiological, and behavioral components, which may be summarized as follows: **emotion involves (1) a subjective conscious experience (the cognitive component) accompanied by (2) bodily arousal (the physiological component) and by (3) characteristic overt expressions (the behavioral component).** That's a pretty complex definition. Let's take a closer look at each of these three components of emotion.

The Cognitive Component: Subjective Feelings

Over 400 words in the English language refer to emotions (Davitz, 1969), but people often have difficulty describing their emotions to others (Zajonc, 1980). Emotion is a very personal, subjective experience. In studying emotions, we often have to rely on subjects' verbal reports of what they're experiencing. Their reports indicate that emotions are potentially intense internal feelings that sometimes seem to have a life of their own. Although some degree of control is possible, we can't click our emotions on and off like our bedroom light.

The conscious experience of emotion includes an *evaluative* aspect. We characterize our emotions as pleasant or unpleasant (Schlosberg, 1954). Of course, we often experience "mixed emotions" that include both pleasant and unpleasant qualities (Polivy, 1981). For example, an executive just given a promotion with challenging new responsibilities may experience both happiness and anxiety. A young man who has just lost his virginity may experience a mixture of apprehension, guilt, and delight.

The Physiological Component: Autonomic Arousal

Imagine your reaction as your car spins out of control on an icy highway. Your fear is accompanied by a variety of physiological changes. Your heart rate and breathing accelerate. Your blood pressure surges, and your pupils dilate. The hairs on your skin stand erect, giving you "goose bumps," and you start to perspire. Although your reactions may not always be as obvious as in this scenario, *emotions are accompanied by physiological arousal.* Surely, you've experienced a "knot in your stomach" or a "lump in your throat"—thanks to anxiety.

The physiological arousal associated with emotion occurs mainly through the actions of the *autonomic nervous system,* which regulates the activity of our glands, smooth muscles, and blood vessels. The autonomic nervous system is responsible for our fight-or-flight response to stress. As you may remember from Chapter 3, these autonomic responses are ultimately controlled in the brain by the hypothalamus and adjacent structures in the limbic system.

One prominent part of emotional arousal is the galvanic skin response. **The *galvanic skin response (GSR)* is an increase in the electrical conductivity of the skin that occurs when sweat glands increase their activity.** GSR is a convenient and sensitive index of autonomic arousal and is used as a measure of emotion in many laboratory studies.

The connection between emotion and autonomic arousal provides the basis for the ***polygraph,* or *lie detector,* a device that records autonomic fluctuations while a subject is questioned.** A polygraph can't actually detect lies; it's really an emotion detector. It detects emotions by monitoring key indicators of autonomic arousal, typically heart rate, blood pressure, respiration rate, and GSR (see Figure 10.15). The assumption is that when subjects lie, they experience emotion (presumably anxiety) that produces noticeable changes in these physiological indicators. The polygraph examiner asks a subject a number of nonthreatening questions to establish the subject's baseline on these autonomic indicators. Then the examiner asks the critical questions (for example, "Where were you on the night of the burglary?") and observes whether the subject's autonomic arousal changes.

The polygraph is a potentially useful tool that can help police to check out leads and alibis, but

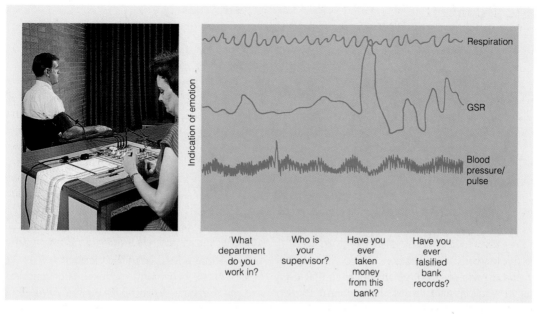

Figure 10.15 Emotion and the polygraph. A lie detector measures the autonomic arousal that most people experience when they tell a lie. After using non-threatening questions to establish a baseline, a polygraph examiner looks for signs of arousal (such as the sharp change in GSR shown here) on incriminating questions.

its capacity to assess truthfulness is *far* from perfect (Lykken, 1981). Part of the problem is that people who are telling the truth may experience emotional arousal when they respond to incriminating questions. Thus, polygraph tests often lead to accusations against people who are really being honest. Another problem is that some people can lie without experiencing anxiety or autonomic arousal.

A study by Benjamin Kleinmuntz and Julian Szucko (1984) suggests that polygraph exams are inaccurate about one-quarter to one-third of the time. They arranged for lie detector tests for theft suspects, including 50 suspects who ultimately confessed their guilt and 50 suspects who were ultimately proven innocent by others' confessions. As you can see in Figure 10.16, the lie detector tests would have led to guilty verdicts for about one-third of the suspects who were proven innocent. Furthermore, about one-quarter of the suspects who later confessed would have been judged innocent based on their lie detector results. Because of this high error rate, most courts do not allow polygraph results to be submitted as evidence. Many companies used to administer lie detector tests to prospective and current employees to weed out thieves. However, the Kleinmuntz and Szucko study helped to stimulate the passage of a new federal law that severely restricts this use of polygraph exams.

The Behavioral Component: Nonverbal Expressiveness

At the behavioral level, we reveal our emotions through characteristic overt expressions such as smiles, frowns, furrowed brows, clenched fists,

and slumped shoulders. In other words, *our emotions are expressed in our "body language," or nonverbal behavior.*

We can distinguish among a variety of basic emotions displayed in facial expressions. Ekman and Friesen (1975) asked subjects to identify what emotion a person was experiencing on the basis of facial cues in photographs. Their subjects were generally successful in identifying fundamental emotions such as happiness, sadness, anger, fear, surprise, and disgust (see Figure 10.17). Some theorists believe that muscular feedback from our own facial expressions makes a major contribution to our conscious experience of our emotions (Tomkins, 1980).

The facial expressions that go with different emotions may be largely innate (Eibl-Ebesfeldt, 1975). People who have been blind since birth smile and frown much like everyone else, even though they've never seen a smile or frown

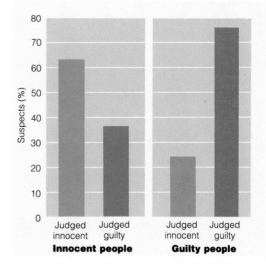

Figure 10.16 The accuracy of lie detectors. In the study by Kleinmuntz and Szucko (1984), one-third of the theft suspects who were proven innocent (left panel) would have been found guilty on the basis of results of their polygraph examinations. About one-quarter of the suspects who eventually confessed their guilt (right panel) appeared innocent in their polygraph tests.

371

Figure 10.17 Emotion and facial expressions. Ekman and Friesen (1975) found that people in highly disparate cultures showed fair agreement on the emotions portrayed in these photos. This consensus across cultures suggests that facial expression of emotions may have a biological basis.

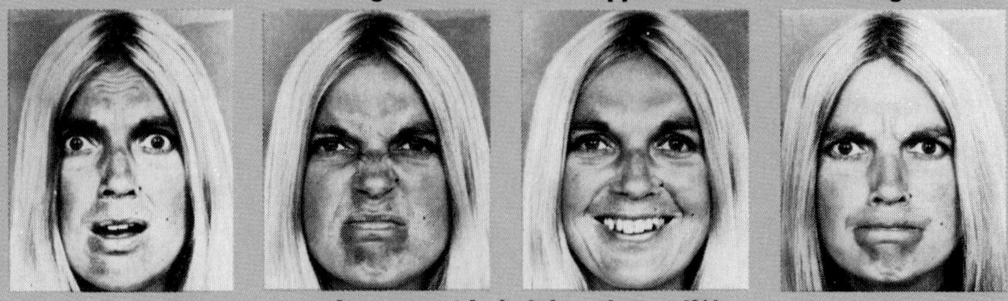

Country	Fear	Disgust	Happiness	Anger
		Agreement in judging photos (%)		
United States	85	92	97	67
Brazil	67	97	95	90
Chile	68	92	95	94
Argentina	54	92	98	90
Japan	66	90	100	90
New Guinea	54	44	82	50

(Charlesworth & Kreutzer, 1973). Emotional facial expressions also are strikingly similar even in very different cultures. Ekman and Friesen (1975) took their facial-cue photographs to New Guinea and showed them to natives in remote rural areas with no contact with Western culture. The natives did a fair job of identifying the differ-ent emotions portrayed in the pictures.

Of course, behavioral expressions of emotion are also shaped by learning, so researchers do find cultural differences in nonverbal expressions of emotions. In Tibet, for instance, people display happiness as they greet their friends by sticking out their tongues at them (Ekman, 1975).

THEORIES OF EMOTION

How do we explain the experience of emotion? A variety of theories and conflicting models exist. Some have been vigorously debated for over a century. As we describe these theories, you'll recognize a familiar bone of contention. Like theories of motivation, theories of emotion differ in their emphasis on the innate biological basis of emotion versus the social, environmental basis.

James-Lange Theory

William James, the prominent functionalist who urged psychologists to explore the purposes of consciousness (see Chapter 1), developed a theory of emotion over 100 years ago that remains influential today. At about the same time, James (1884) and Carl Lange (1885) independently proposed that *the conscious experience of emotion results from one's perception of autonomic arousal* (see Figure 10.18). Their theory stood common sense on its head. Everyday logic suggests that when you stumble onto a rattlesnake in the woods, the conscious experience of fear leads to visceral arousal. The James-Lange theory of emotion asserts that the perception of visceral arousal leads to the conscious experience of fear. In other words, while you might assume that your pulse is racing because you're fearful, James and Lange argue that you're fearful because your pulse is racing.

The James-Lange theory emphasizes the phys-iological determinants of emotion. According to this view, *different patterns of autonomic activation lead to the experience of different emotions.* Hence, people supposedly distinguish emotions such as fear, joy, and anger based on the exact configura-tion of their physical reactions.

Cannon-Bard Theory

Walter Cannon (1927) found the James-Lange theory unconvincing. Cannon, who developed the concepts of homeostasis and the fight-or-flight response, pointed out that physiological arousal may occur without the experience of emotion (if you exercise vigorously, for instance). He also ar-gued that visceral changes are too slow to precede the conscious experience of emotion. Finally, he argued that people experiencing very different emotions, such as fear, joy, and anger, exhibit very similar patterns of autonomic arousal.

Thus, Cannon espoused a different explanation of emotion; later, Philip Bard (1934) elaborated on it. The Cannon-Bard theory argues that emo-tion occurs when the *thalamus* sends signals *simul-taneously* to the cortex (creating the conscious experience of emotion) and to the autonomic ner-vous system (creating visceral arousal). The Can-non-Bard model is compared to the James-Lange model in Figure 10.18. Cannon and Bard were off the mark a bit in pinpointing the thalamus as the

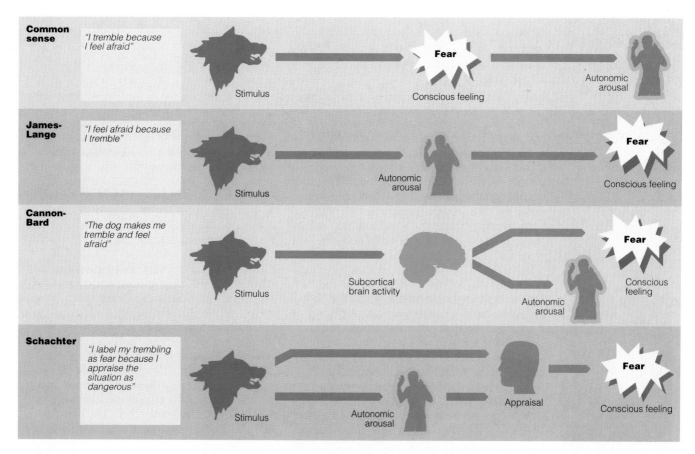

Common sense	"I tremble because I feel afraid"	Stimulus	Fear / Conscious feeling	Autonomic arousal
James-Lange	"I feel afraid because I tremble"	Stimulus	Autonomic arousal	Fear / Conscious feeling
Cannon-Bard	"The dog makes me tremble and feel afraid"	Stimulus	Subcortical brain activity	Autonomic arousal / Fear / Conscious feeling
Schachter	"I label my trembling as fear because I appraise the situation as dangerous"	Stimulus	Autonomic arousal	Appraisal / Fear / Conscious feeling

neural center for emotion. As we discussed in Chapter 3, the limbic system, the hypothalamus, and other neural structures have been implicated as the seats of emotion. However, many modern theorists agree with the Cannon-Bard view that emotions originate in subcortical brain structures (Izard, 1984; Lindsley, 1970; Tomkins, 1980).

Ultimately, the key issue in the James-Lange–Cannon-Bard debate turned out to be whether different emotions are associated with different patterns of autonomic arousal. The research findings mostly supported the Cannon-Bard point of view for several decades. Investigators found that different emotions were *not* reliably associated with different patterns of autonomic activation (Strongman, 1978). However, more recent studies have detected some subtle differences in the patterns of visceral arousal that accompany basic emotions such as happiness, sadness, anger, and fear (Ekman, Levenson, & Friesen, 1983; Schwartz, Weinberger, & Singer, 1981).

The debate continues, however, because there are doubts about whether people can actually *distinguish* between these slightly different patterns of physiological activation (Zillmann, 1983). Humans are not particularly adept at recognizing their autonomic fluctuations. Thus, there must be some other explanation for how we differentiate various emotions.

Schachter's Two-Factor Theory

Stanley Schachter believes that we look at situational cues to differentiate between alternative emotions. According to Schachter (1964; Schachter & Singer, 1979), the experience of emotion depends on two factors: (1) autonomic arousal and (2) your cognitive interpretation of that arousal. Schachter proposes that when you experience visceral arousal, you search your environment for an explanation (see Figure 10.18). If you're stuck in a traffic jam, you'll probably label your arousal as anger. If you're taking an important exam, you'll probably label it anxiety. If you're celebrating your birthday, you'll probably label it happiness.

Schachter agrees with the James-Lange view that emotion is inferred from arousal. However, he also agrees with the Cannon-Bard position that different emotions yield indistinguishable patterns of arousal. He reconciles these views by arguing that people look to external rather than internal cues to differentiate and label their specific emotions. Schachter's theory allocates a larger role to social and environmental factors than other theories of emotion do. The original evidence for Schacter's two-factor theory came from a classic experiment, which is our Featured Study.

Figure 10.18 Theories of emotion. Three influential theories of emotion are contrasted here with each other and with the common-sense view. The James-Lange theory was the first to suggest that our feelings of arousal cause emotion, rather than vice versa. Schachter built on this idea by adding a second factor—our interpretation (appraisal and labeling) of our arousal.

Emotions as Labels for Arousal

Investigators: Stanley Schachter and Jerome E. Singer

Source: Cognitive, social, and physiological determinants of emotional state. *Psychological Review, 69* (1962), 379–399.

"Cognitive factors play a major role in determining how a subject interprets his bodily feelings."
STANLEY SCHACHTER

The two-factor theory proposes that emotions consist of autonomic arousal and labels for that arousal that depend on situational factors. In essence, Schachter suggests that we think along the following lines: "If I'm aroused and you're obnoxious, I must be angry." Schachter and Singer tested this theory by independently manipulating autonomic arousal and situational factors to see whether they jointly determined subjects' emotions.

Method

The subjects were male college students who were led to believe that they were participating in a study of the effects of a vitamin injection on vision. Some subjects were injected with adrenaline, which causes temporary autonomic arousal; other subjects received a placebo injection (saline solution) that had no impact on arousal.

Expectation based on information about the effects of the adrenaline injection was manipulated as follows. *Informed subjects* were led to expect some symptoms of autonomic arousal. They were told that the vitamin produced certain side effects, such as a pounding heart, tremors, and a flushed feeling (the genuine side effects of adrenaline). Two groups of *misinformed subjects* were not led to expect any arousal. One of these groups was told that the vitamin had no side effects, while the other was led to expect irrelevant side effects (numb feet and itching). *Placebo subjects* who got the saline injection were also told (accurately) not to expect any side effects.

After the injection, subjects were asked to wait in another room while the vitamin was absorbed. Each subject waited with one other person who was introduced as another subject in the experiment. This person was actually a member of the experimental team. He was responsible for manipulating situational factors by creating either a euphoric or angry emotional atmosphere. In the

euphoric condition, the confederate was very playful. He made paper airplanes and tossed paper "basketballs" into a wastebasket. In the *angry condition*, the confederate was disagreeable, grumbling and groaning about having to fill out an annoying questionnaire. Thus, the independent variables were whether subjects expected symptoms of physiological arousal and whether they were exposed to situational cues for euphoria or anger.

Subjects' emotional responses were assessed in two ways. First, overt expressions of emotion were observed by the experimenters through a one-way mirror. Second, subjects responded to a questionnaire that inquired about their feelings. The observation of emotion and the questionnaire served as the dependent variables in the study.

The experimenters hypothesized that the two groups of subjects who were misinformed about the side effects of the drug would infer that they were experiencing emotional arousal and that they would label that arousal as either euphoria or anger, depending on the situational factors. The other two groups were not expected to experience much emotion: the placebo subjects did not have any autonomic arousal to explain, and the informed subjects, who expected arousal, could attribute it to the injection.

Results

Figure 10.19 summarizes the results of the study. The informed subjects showed few signs of emotion in their behavior or their self-reports. The two groups of misinformed subjects displayed and reported more emotion. As expected, they typically described and labeled their mood in accordance with the situational manipulations. Thus, they tended to feel euphoric or angry, depending on the confederate's behavior. The placebo subjects reported less emotion than the misinformed subjects, but more than expected. The differ-

Figure 10.19 The Schachter and Singer (1962) results. As predicted, misinformed subjects labeled their arousal in accordance with the situation. (Note that this figure compares only the key conditions in the study; the results for the placebo and control groups are omitted.)

Situational cues	Subjects' expectations	
	Informed subjects (expected symptoms of arousal)	Misinformed subjects (did not expect symptoms of arousal)
Actor is angry	Subjects' emotions are generally unaffected	Subjects tend to exhibit anger
Actor is euphoric (happy)	Subjects' emotions are generally unaffected	Subjects tend to exhibit euphoria

ences between the misinformed and placebo groups in reported emotion were not statistically significant.

Discussion

The investigators concluded that the results supported the two-factor theory of emotion. As predicted, misinformed subjects who experienced unexplained arousal inferred that they were experiencing emotion. Moreover, they tended to label their arousal as euphoria or anger in accordance with the situational cues. Thus, they distinguished specific emotions based on their cognitive explanations for their arousal. For the most part, similar tendencies were not seen in the informed or placebo subjects.

Comment

This study exerted enormous influence over subsequent theory and research in several areas of psychology. In fact, it became one of the most widely cited studies ever conducted, even though the results provided only modest support for the hypothesis. Most of the differences between the groups were in the predicted directions, but many were quite small and some failed to reach statistical significance. In their discussion of the study, Schachter and Singer highlighted the significant results that supported

their theory and softpedaled the failures to find significant differences. They were later heavily criticized for this in some quarters (Marshall & Zimbardo, 1979; Maslach, 1979).

To some extent, the criticism was unfair: it's quite normal for investigators to interpret the results of a study in as favorable a light as possible. This falls within the rules of science as long as investigators report their procedures and results accurately. The "Method" and "Results" sections of research reports should be straightforward summaries of what was done and what was observed, but the "Discussion" sections inevitably involve some subjective interpretation about what the results mean. It's always up to the reader to decide whether investigators' conclusions (in the "Discussion" section) are reasonable in light of the results obtained.

In retrospect, the Schachter-Singer study deserves its place in history. It was influential not because the results were clear and convincing, but because the two-factor theory that it tested seemed insightful, plausible, and powerful. However, there *is* a lesson to be learned in the overly enthusiastic acceptance that the Schachter-Singer study enjoyed for many years. The discerning reader should always examine the results of a study very carefully to see how well they support the researchers' conclusions.

The ultimate verdict on the two-factor theory of emotion was a split decision (Reisenzein, 1983). Many follow-up studies supported parts of the cognitive-arousal model of emotion. A naturalistic study of interpersonal attraction by Dutton and Aron (1974) provides a particularly clever example of research that supported the two-factor theory.

Dutton and Aron (1974) arranged for young men crossing a footbridge in a park to encounter a young woman who asked them to stop briefly to fill out a questionnaire. The woman offered to explain the research at some future time and gave the men her phone number. Autonomic arousal was manipulated by enacting this scenario on two very different bridges. One was a long suspension bridge that swayed precariously 230 feet above a river (see Figure 10.20). The other bridge was a

Figure 10.20 In their naturalistic study of the two-factor theory of emotion, Dutton and Aron (1974) manipulated emotional arousal by arranging for males to encounter a female confederate on this precarious-looking bridge.

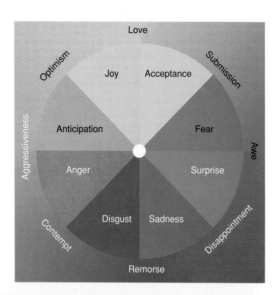

Figure 10.21 Mixing primary emotions. Eight primary emotions (shown inside the circle) are identified in Robert Plutchik's model of emotion. Plutchik's theory assumes that additional emotions (such as those shown here on the outside of the circle) are created by blending primary emotions. For example, awe is viewed as a blend of fear and surprise. Many more combinations are possible than are shown here.

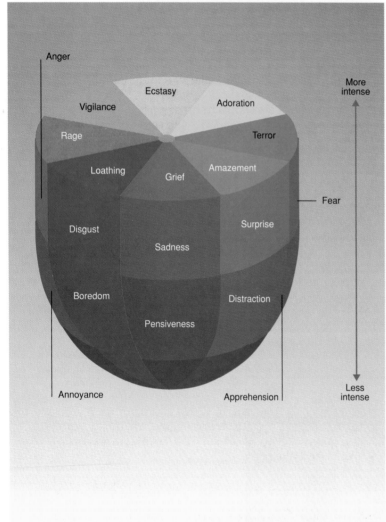

Figure 10.22 Emotional intensity in Plutchik's model. According to Plutchik, diversity in human emotion is a product of variations in emotional intensity, as well as a blending of primary emotions. Each vertical slice in the diagram is a primary emotion that can be subdivided into emotional expressions of varied intensity, ranging from most intense (top) to least intense (bottom).

solid, safe structure a mere 10 feet above a small stream. The experimenters reasoned that the men crossing the shaky, frightening bridge would be experiencing emotional arousal and that some of them might attribute that arousal to the woman rather than to the bridge. If so, they might mislabel their emotion as lust rather than fear and infer that they were attracted to the woman. The dependent variable was how many of the men later called the woman to pursue a date. As predicted, more of the men who met the woman on the precarious bridge called her for a date than of those who met her on the safe bridge.

The Dutton and Aron study supports the hypothesis that we often infer emotion from our physiological arousal and label that emotion in accordance with our cognitive explanation for it. The fact that these explanations may be inaccurate sheds light on why people frequently seem confused about their own emotions.

Although the two-factor theory has received support, follow-up studies have revealed some limitations as well (Leventhal & Tomarken, 1986). Situations can't mold our emotions in just any way at any time. When subjects experience autonomic arousal of unknown origin, their explanations usually have a negative slant. That is, subjects tend to infer that they're experiencing unpleasant emotions (Marshall & Zimbardo, 1979). Also, in searching to explain arousal, subjects don't limit themselves to the immediate situation. They may consider memories of past events (Maslach, 1979). For example, a subject injected with adrenaline might interpret his arousal as disgust because he loathes shots. Finally, the misperceptions of emotions that provide the foundation for two-factor theory seem to occur mostly in novel situations when arousal is moderate (Cotton, 1981). Thus, our emotions are not as pliable as the two-factor theory initially suggests.

Evolutionary Theories of Emotion

As the limitations of the two-factor theory were exposed, theorists turned to ideas espoused by Charles Darwin long ago. Darwin (1872) believed that emotions developed because of their adaptive value. Fear, for instance, would help an organism avoid danger and thus would aid in survival. Hence, Darwin viewed human emotions as a product of evolution. This assumption serves as the foundation for several newly prominent theories of emotion developed independently by S. S. Tomkins (1980), Carroll Izard (1984), and Robert Plutchik (1984).

These evolutionary theories view emotions as

Figure 10.23 Primary emotions. Evolutionary theories of emotion attempt to identify primary emotions. Three leading theorists—Silvan Tompkins, Carroll Izard, and Robert Plutchik—have compiled different lists of primary emotions, but this chart shows that there is great overlap among the basic emotions identified by these theorists. (Based on Mandler, 1984)

Primary Emotions in Three Evolutionary Theories		
Silvan Tomkins	Carroll Izard	Robert Plutchik
Fear	Fear	Fear
Anger	Anger	Anger
Enjoyment	Joy	Joy
Disgust	Disgust	Disgust
Interest	Interest	Anticipation
Surprise	Surprise	Surprise
Contempt	Contempt	
Shame	Shame	
	Sadness	Sadness
Distress		
	Guilt	
		Acceptance

largely innate reactions to certain stimuli. As such, emotions are thought to be immediately recognizable under most conditions without much thought. After all, primitive animals that are incapable of complex thought seem to have little difficulty in recognizing their emotions. Evolutionary theorists believe that emotion evolved before thought. They assert that thought plays a relatively small role in emotion, although they admit that learning and cognition may have some influence on human emotions. Evolutionary theories of emotion generally assume that emotions originate in subcortical brain structures (such as the hypothalamus and most of the limbic system) that evolved before the cortical structures associated with complex thought.

The principal question that evolutionary theories of emotion wrestle with is—*what are the fundamental emotions?* These theories assume that evolution equips us with a small number of primary emotions with proven adaptive value. According to this view, *the many different emotions that we experience are (1) blends of primary emotions and (2) variations in intensity.* For example, Robert Plutchik (1980) has devised an elegant model of how primary emotions such as fear and surprise may blend into secondary emotions such as awe (see Figure 10.21). Plutchik's model also shows how various emotions, such as apprehension, fear, and terror, may involve one primary emotion experienced at different levels of intensity (see Figure 10.22). Thus, evolutionary theories of emotion attempt to identify the primary emotions. As Figure 10.23 shows, Tomkins, Izard, and Plutchik have not come up with identical lists, but there is considerable agreement among them.

Solomon's Opponent Process Theory

Richard Solomon's (1982) opponent process theory applies a homeostatic model to the experience of emotion. Solomon assumes that emotions have what he calls *hedonic value:* that is, they vary in terms of being pleasant or unpleasant. *According to Solomon, an emotional response will be followed shortly by its hedonic opposite.* For example, fear will give way to relief, anger to calm, euphoria to depression, interest to boredom. Solomon believes that the brain automatically activates these

opponent processes to protect itself from emotional extremes and to restore equilibrium.

Normally, the opponent emotional states are of roughly equal intensity, so that they balance each other out. However, Solomon theorizes that when a stimulus repeatedly evokes the same emotion, the initial reaction gradually weakens in intensity and the opponent reaction gets stronger. For example, among sky divers, prejump anxiety gradually declines while postjump exhilaration increases (Solomon & Corbitt, 1974). In this case, the eventual dominance of the opponent reaction (exhilaration) explains why sky divers find their hobby very enjoyable. Solomon suspects that the eventual dominance of opponent emotional pro-

---

CONCEPT CHECK 10.2
Understanding Theories of Emotion

Check your understanding of theories of emotion by matching the theories we discussed with the statements below. Let's borrow William James's classic example: assume that you just stumbled onto a bear in the woods. The first statement expresses the commonsense explanation of your fear. Each of the remaining statements expresses the essence of a different theory; indicate which theory in the spaces provided. The answers are provided in Appendix A.

1. You tremble because you're afraid.   common sense

2. You're afraid because you're trembling.   _____

3. You're afraid because situational cues (the bear) suggest that's why you're trembling.   _____

4. You're afraid because the bear has elicited an innate primary emotion.   _____

cesses may explain why people engage in a variety of risky, thrill-seeking behaviors, ranging from gambling to running river rapids.

Solomon's theory seems to provide a viable explanation of thrill-seeking, as well as some other phenomena. The other theories presented in this section—the James-Lange, Cannon-Bard, two-factor, and evolutionary theories—also contribute to our understanding of emotion. Thus far, however, no one theory has emerged that can account for all the facets of our emotional experiences.

PUTTING IT IN PERSPECTIVE

Three of our organizing themes were particularly prominent in this chapter: psychology's theoretical diversity (theme 2), the joint influence of heredity and environment (theme 5), and the multiple causes of behavior (theme 4).

We began the chapter with a discussion of various theoretical perspectives on motivation and ended with a review of different theories of emotion. Obviously, this area of inquiry is marked by great theoretical diversity, and there has been little movement toward reconciling the contradictory theories. Some issues, such as whether different emotions generate different patterns of physiological arousal, have generated vigorous debate for nearly a century. Why are there so many conflicting theories of motivation and emotion? In this case, theoretical diversity appears to exist because motivation and emotion are such broad areas of study. Motivation, for instance, encompasses a wide range of disparate needs. It's probably unrealistic to expect one theory to apply equally well to such different kinds of needs as those for oxygen, food, sex, affiliation, achievement, understanding, and self-actualization. Many of the competing theories that we discussed in this chapter focused on different facets of motivation and emotion.

The age-old nature versus nurture question was at the center of many of the theoretical debates in the chapter. Although there's plenty of room for continued debate about the relative importance of heredity and environment, we repeatedly saw that biological and social factors jointly govern motivation and emotion. For example, we learned that eating behavior depends on a complicated interaction between biological determinants (such as blood sugar fluctuations, set point, number of fat cells, inherited metabolic rate, and insulin secretion) and environmental determinants (such as food-related cues, learned eating habits, acquired tastes, and exposure to stress). We saw similar interactions between biological and environmental factors in the regulation of sexual desire and the experience of emotion.

Indeed, complicated interactions permeated the entire chapter, demonstrating that if we want to fully understand behavior, we have to take multiple causes into account. For instance, we saw that achievement behavior is a function of the motive to achieve success, the probability of success, the value of success, the motive to avoid failure, the probability of failure, the negative impact of failure, and the fear of success. Similarly, we discussed how human sexual desire may be influenced by hormones, attraction to a partner, erotic materials, personality, age, and attitudes.

In the upcoming Application, the complexity of human sexuality will be apparent once again, as we focus on issues that relate to sexual satisfaction. We'll look at advances in the understanding of sexual problems and their treatment, to extract some practical suggestions about enhancing sexual relationships.

UNDERSTANDING HUMAN SEXUALITY

Answer the following "true" or "false."

☐ **1.** Sexual problems are very resistant to treatment.

☐ **2.** Sexual problems belong to couples more than to individuals.

☐ **3.** Partners often disagree about how often they should have sexual relations.

☐ **4.** It's not a good idea for partners to openly discuss sex because this creates unhealthy pressures.

☐ **5.** Sexual fantasies about people other than one's partner are normal.

The answers for the true-false questions above are (1) false, (2) true, (3) true, (4) false, and (5) true. If you answered several of the questions incorrectly, you have misconceptions about sexuality that may at some point affect your sexual relations. If so, you're not unusual. Although our modern society seems obsessed with sex, misconceptions about sexuality are commonplace. In this Application, we'll take a practical look at sex—a very important motive that generates some of our most powerful emotions.

Sexual intercourse is really a pretty simple activity. Most animals execute the act with a minimum of difficulty. However, humans manage to make sexual relations terribly complicated, and many people suffer from sexual problems. Fortunately, recent advances in our understanding of sexual functioning have yielded many useful ideas on how to improve sexual relationships (Barbach, 1975, 1982; Hyde, 1986; Nass & Fisher, 1988).

In the interests of simplicity, our advice is directed to heterosexual couples. Obviously, many readers may not be involved in a sexual relationship at present, but if not, we'll assume that someday you will be. We'll also assume that your sexual partnership will be (or is) based on a sincere bond of affection. Clinical interviews and surveys suggest that affection is very important to rewarding sexual relations.

Key Factors in Rewarding Sexual Relationships

Let's begin with some general points about some of the factors that promote rewarding sexual relationships.

1. A surprisingly great number of people are ignorant about the realities of sexual functioning. So, the first step in promoting sexual satisfaction is to acquire accurate information about sex. The shelves of most bookstores are bulging with popular books on sex, but many of them are loaded with inaccuracies. The best source of information is probably a college textbook on human sexuality. Enrolling in an entire course on sexuality is also a good idea. More and more colleges are offering such courses today.

2. The sexual value systems that people acquire incidentally during childhood are likely to affect them as adults. Negative values may be derived from the "conspiracy of silence" that surrounds the topic of sex in many homes. Unfortunately, sexual problems can be caused by a negative sexual value system in which people associate sex with immorality and depravity. The guilt feelings caused by this orientation can interfere with sexual functioning. Given this possibility, experts on sexuality often encourage adults to examine the sources and implications of their sexual values.

3. As children, people often learn that they shouldn't talk about sex. Many people carry this attitude into adulthood and have great difficulty discussing sex, even with their partner. Good communication is extremely important in a sexual relationship. Figure 10.24 lists common problems in sexual relations reported by a sample of 100 couples (Frank, Anderson, & Rubinstein, 1978). Many of the problems reported by the couples—such as choosing an inconvenient time, too little foreplay, and too little tenderness after sex—are largely due to poor communication. People can't expect their partners to be mind readers. Sexual partners have to share their thoughts and feelings to promote mutual satisfaction.

4. The mind is the ultimate erogenous zone, and fantasizing during a sexual

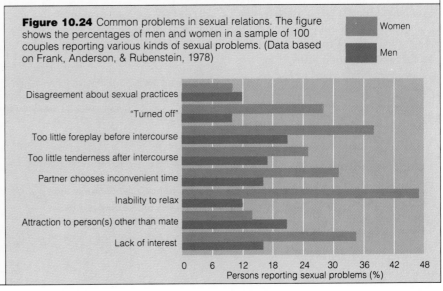

Figure 10.24 Common problems in sexual relations. The figure shows the percentages of men and women in a sample of 100 couples reporting various kinds of sexual problems. (Data based on Frank, Anderson, & Rubenstein, 1978)

Women
Men

Disagreement about sexual practices
"Turned off"
Too little foreplay before intercourse
Too little tenderness after intercourse
Partner chooses inconvenient time
Inability to relax
Attraction to person(s) other than mate
Lack of interest

0 6 12 18 24 30 36 42 48
Persons reporting sexual problems (%)

Table 10.2 Fantasies During Intercourse

THEME	% OF FANTASIES	
	MALES	FEMALES
A former lover	42.9	41.0
An imaginary lover	44.3	24.3
Oral-genital sex	61.2	51.4
Group sex	19.3	14.1
Being forced or overpowered into a sexual relationship	21.0	36.4
Others observing you engage in sexual intercourse	15.4	20.0
Others finding you sexually irresistible	55.2	52.8
Being rejected or sexually abused	10.5	13.2
Forcing others to have sexual relations with you	23.5	15.8
Others giving in to you after resisting at first	36.8	24.3
Observing others engaging in sex	17.9	13.2
A member of the same sex	2.8	9.4
Animals	0.9	3.7

Note: For comparison, the responses of "frequently" and "sometimes" were combined for both males and females to obtain the percentages above. The number of respondents answering for a specific fantasy ranged from 103 to 106 for males and from 105 to 107 for females.

encounter is normal for both sexes (Sue, 1979). Both males and females report that their sexual fantasies increase their arousal. Some common sexual fantasies are listed in Table 10.2. Note that it's not abnormal to fantasize about people other than one's lover or about sexual activities that one wouldn't actually engage in.
5. Sexual encounters generally work out best when people have privacy, a relaxed atmosphere, and genuine interest. Realistically, people can't count on (or insist upon) having ideal situations all the time, but it's wise to be aware of the value of being selective. It also helps to understand that it's quite common for partners to disagree about how often they should have sex. In one study, 54% of couples reported some disagreement on this issue (Levinger, 1966). This sort of disagreement is normal and should not be a source of resentment. Couples simply need to work toward a reasonable compromise.

Understanding Sexual Dysfunction

Many people struggle with *sexual dysfunctions*—impairments in sexual functioning that cause subjective distress. Figure 10.25 shows the percent-

age of subjects in one study reporting the principal kinds of dysfunctions that we'll discuss (Frank et al., 1978). The data suggest that roughly half of both women and men are troubled to some degree by sexual problems.

Traditionally, people have assumed that a sexual problem lies in *one partner*. Although it's convenient to refer to a man's erectile difficulties or a woman's orgasmic difficulties, research indicates that most sexual problems emerge out of partners' unique ways of relating to each other. Masters and Johnson argue convincingly that *sexual problems belong to couples rather than to individuals*.

In this section, we'll examine the symptoms and causes of the three most common sexual dysfunctions: erectile

difficulties, premature ejaculation, and orgasmic difficulties. In the next section, we'll discuss possible ways to overcome these problems.

Erectile difficulties occur when a man is persistently unable to achieve or maintain an erection adequate for intercourse. *Impotence* is the traditional name for this problem. However, sex researchers prefer to avoid this term because of its demeaning connotation.

The most common cause of erectile difficulties is anxiety about sexual performance. What leads to this troublesome anxiety? Its cause can range from a man's doubts about his virility to conflict about the morality of his sexual desires. Anxiety about sexual performance can also be caused by an overreaction to a specific incident in which a man could not achieve sexual arousal. Many temporary conditions, such as fatigue, worry about work, an argument with his partner, a depressed mood, or too much alcohol can also cause such incidents.

Recent research suggests that physiological factors (other than those produced by anxiety) may also contribute to erectile difficulties. A host of common diseases (such as diabetes) can produce erectile problems as a side effect (Melman & Leiter, 1983). Many experts now estimate that organic factors may contribute to erectile dysfunction in as many as one-quarter of the cases.

Premature ejaculation occurs when sexual relations are impaired because a man consistently reaches orgasm too quickly. What is "too quickly"? Any time requirement is

Figure 10.25 Sexual dysfunction in normal couples. The graph shows the prevalence of sexual dysfunction as reported by a sample of 100 couples, 80% of whom reported having happy or satisfying marriages. (Data based on Frank, Anderson, & Rubenstein, 1978)

Erectile difficulties in men
Difficulty getting an erection
Difficulty maintaining an erection
Premature ejaculation in men
Orgasmic difficulties in women
Difficulty in reaching orgasm
Inability to have an orgasm

Frequency of self-reported sexual problems (%)

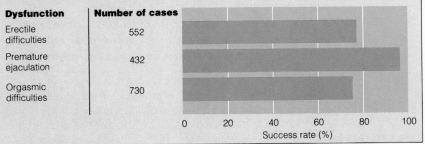

Figure 10.26 Success rates reported by Masters and Johnson in the treatment of sexual dysfunctions. The figure shows results for cases treated between 1959 and 1977. Treatment was categorized as successful only if the change in sexual function was clear and enduring. The minimum follow-up period was two years. (Data based on Masters & Johnson, 1970; Kolodny, Masters, & Johnson, 1979)

Dysfunction	Number of cases
Erectile difficulties	552
Premature ejaculation	432
Orgasmic difficulties	730

hopelessly arbitrary. The subjective feelings of the partners are the critical consideration. If either partner feels the ejaculation is persistently too fast for sexual gratification, there's a problem.

What causes premature ejaculation? Some men simply don't exert much effort to prolong intercourse. Most of these men don't view their ejaculations as premature (but their partners often feel quite differently). Among men who *are* concerned about their partners' satisfaction, problems may occur because their early sexual experiences emphasized the desirability of a rapid climax. Furtive sex in the back seat of a car, quick efforts at masturbation, and experiences with prostitutes are situations in which men typically attempt to achieve orgasm very quickly. A pattern of rapid ejaculation may be entrenched by these formative experiences.

Orgasmic difficulties **occur when people experience sexual arousal but have persistent problems in achieving orgasm.** When this problem occurs in men, it's often called *retarded ejaculation.* The traditional name for this problem in women, *frigidity,* is no longer used because of its derogatory implications. Since the problem is more common among women, we limit this discussion to females.

Negative attitudes about sex are the primary cause of orgasmic difficulties among women. A woman who has been taught that sex is dirty and depraved will be likely to approach sex with shame and guilt. These negative attitudes can inhibit expression of her sexuality and thus impair orgasmic responsiveness. A lack of authentic affection for her partner, fear of pregnancy, or concern about achieving orgasm may also contribute to orgasmic difficulties.

Coping with Specific Problems

With the advent of modern sex therapy, sexual problems no longer have to be chronic sources of shame and frustration. *Sex therapy* **involves the professional treatment of sexual dysfunctions.** With professional assistance, most sexual difficulties can be resolved effectively (Arentewicz & Schmidt, 1983). Masters and Johnson have reported very high success rates for their treatments of specific problems, which are shown in Figure 10.26. Some critics argue that the cure rates reported by Masters and Johnson are overly optimistic in comparison with those of other investigators (Zilbergeld & Evans, 1980). Nonetheless, there is clear consensus that sexual dysfunctions can be conquered with encouraging regularity.

Of course, sex therapy isn't for everyone. It can be expensive and time-consuming. In some locations, it's difficult to find. However, many people can benefit from ideas drawn from the professional practice of sex therapy (Hartman & Fithian, 1974; Kaplan, 1979, 1983; Masters & Johnson, 1980). In this section, we'll briefly discuss a few of the experts' recommendations for dealing with erectile difficulties, premature ejaculation, and orgasmic difficulties.

The key to overcoming psychologically based erectile difficulties is to decrease the man's performance anxiety.

It's a good idea for a couple to openly discuss the problem so that the woman can be reassured that it's not due to a lack of affection for her. Obviously, it's crucial for her to be emotionally supportive.

Masters and Johnson use a procedure called sensate focus in the treatment of erectile difficulties and other dysfunctions. *Sensate focus* **is an exercise in which partners take turns pleasuring each other with guided verbal feedback, while certain kinds of stimulation are temporarily forbidden.** One partner stimulates the other, who simply lies back and enjoys it, while giving instructions and feedback about what feels good. Initially, the partners are not allowed to touch each other's genitals or to attempt intercourse. This prohibition should free the man from feelings of pressure to perform. Over a number of sessions, the couple gradually include genital stimulation in their sensate focus, but intercourse is still banned. With the pressure to perform removed, a man may experience arousals that begin to restore his confidence in his sexual response.

Men troubled by premature ejaculation range from those who climax almost instantly to those who can't last as long as their partner would like. In the latter case, simply slowing down the tempo of intercourse may help. The problem of instant ejaculation is more challenging to remedy. Sex therapists rely primarily on certain sensate focus exercises in which the man is repeatedly brought to the verge of orgasm. These sensate focus exercises can help him to gradually improve control over his ejaculation response.

Orgasmic difficulties among women are often due to negative attitudes about sex. Thus, a restructuring of values frequently is the key to dealing with problems in achieving orgasm. Sensate focus exercises can also help a woman to better get in touch with her sexual response and preferences. In sensate focus, the guided verbal feedback that she gives to her partner can improve his appreciation of her erotic preferences.

Motivation and Emotion

KEY IDEAS

Motivational Theories and Concepts

• Motivation involves goal-oriented behavior. Some motivational theories emphasize the biological roots of motives; others emphasize the social roots. Instincts appear to explain the motivation of some aspects of animal behavior, but their relevance to human motivation is controversial. Like instinct theorists, sociobiologists maintain that there is an evolutionary basis for many human motives.

• Drive theories apply a homeostatic model to motivation. They assume that organisms seek to reduce unpleasant states of tension called drives. In contrast, incentive theories emphasize how external goals energize behavior. Madsen's list of biological needs and Murray's list of social needs illustrate that a diverse array of motives govern human behavior.

• Maslow's hierarchy of needs assumes that basic needs must be satisfied reasonably well before higher needs are activated. His model integrates biological and social needs, as well as deficiency and growth needs. According to Maslow, our growth needs include the need to realize our full potential, a motive called the need for self-actualization.

The Motivation of Hunger and Eating

• Eating is regulated by a complex interaction of biological and environmental factors. In the brain, the lateral and ventromedial areas of the hypothalamus appear to be involved in the control of hunger, but their exact role is unclear. Fluctuations in blood glucose also seem to play a role, but the exact location of the glucostats and their mode of functioning are yet to be determined. Hormonal regulation of hunger depends primarily on insulin secretions.

• Learned habits also exert a great deal of influence over both what we eat and how much we eat. For example, culture influences food preferences. Food-related cues in the environment can trigger eating. Stress may also influence eating in some people.

• Schachter hypothesizes that obesity develops mainly in people who are overly sensitive to external cues that trigger eating. However, Rodin concludes that oversensitivity to external cues is only one factor among many determinants of obesity. Evidence indicates that there is a genetic predisposition to obesity. Weight problems can also be caused by an elevated set point for body weight. According to set-point theory, our bodies monitor fat stores to keep them fairly stable.

Sexual Motivation and Behavior

• Hormones exert considerable influence over sexual motivation in many animals. Although some interesting correlations exist between hormonal fluctuations and sexual activity in humans, we are not sure whether normal hormonal swings have much impact on human sexual desire. In a similar manner, pheromones appear to be important determinants of sexual desire in lower animals but of limited relevance to humans.

• Attraction to a potential partner is a critical determinant of sexual interest in humans. People also respond to a variety of erotic materials. In laboratory studies, women are just as responsive as men. There are great individual differences among people in sex drive that depend on personality, attitudes, and age.

• The human sexual response cycle can be divided into four stages: excitement, plateau, orgasm, and resolution. The subjective experience of orgasm is fairly similar for both sexes. Intercourse leads to orgasm in women less consistently than in men, but women are much more likely to be multiorgasmic. Men experience a refractory period after an orgasm.

Affiliation: In Search of Belongingness

• Affiliation encompasses our various needs for social bonds. Affiliation tends to increase in anxiety-arousing situations and decrease in embarrassing situations. Individual differences in the need for affiliation are usually measured with the TAT.

• People who are relatively high in the need for affiliation tend to devote more time to interpersonal activities and worry more about acceptance than others. Our need for intimacy (close, warm, open relations) appears to be an important component of our affiliation motive.

Achievement: In Search of Excellence

• Achievement involves the need to excel, especially in competition with others. The need for achievement is usually measured with the TAT. People who are relatively high in the need for achievement work harder and more persistently than others. They delay gratification well and pursue competitive careers.

• Our pursuit of achievement tends to increase when the probability of success and the incentive value of success are high. However, the pursuit of achievement can be inhibited by either a fear of success or a fear of failure. Fear of success appears to be equally common in men and women, but it may inhibit achievement a little more in women.

The Elements of Emotional Experience

• Emotion is made up of cognitive, physiological, and behavioral components. The cognitive component involves subjective feelings that have an evaluative aspect. The physiological component is dominated by autonomic arousal. This is the basis for the lie detector, which is really an emotion detector. At the behavioral level, our emotions are expressed through our body language, with facial expressions being particularly prominent.

Theories of Emotion

• The James-Lange theory asserts that emotion results from one's perception of autonomic arousal. The Cannon-Bard theory counters with the proposal that emotions originate in subcortical areas of the brain. According to Schachter's two-factor theory, we infer emotion from arousal and then label it in accordance with our cognitive explanation for the arousal. Early support for this theory was provided by our Featured Study, which manipulated arousal and the apparent reasons for arousal. Evolutionary theories of emotion maintain that emotions are innate reactions that require little cognitive interpretation. Solomon's opponent process theory applies a homeostatic model to emotion.

Putting It in Perspective

• Three of our organizing themes were especially salient in this chapter. Our look at motivation and emotion showed once again that psychology is characterized by theoretical diversity, that biology and environment shape behavior interactively, and that behavior is governed by multiple causes.

Application: Understanding Human Sexuality

• Rewarding sexual relationships are more likely when partners have genuine affection for each other, sound knowledge about sexual functioning, favorable attitudes toward sex, and good communication. It is also helpful to enjoy sexual fantasy and to be selective about when you engage in sexual activities.

• Sexual dysfunctions involve impairments in sexual functioning. Erectile difficulties are primarily due to anxiety about performance. Premature ejaculation is frequently due to formative sexual experiences that emphasized rapid climax. Negative attitudes about sex are the most common cause of orgasmic difficulties. A variety of suggestions were also discussed for coping with specific sexual problems.

KEY TERMS

Achievement motive
Affiliation motive
Androgens
Aphrodisiac
Basal metabolic rate
Drive
Emotion
Erectile difficulties
Erotophiles
Erotophobes
Estrogens
Galvanic skin response (GSR)

Glucose
Glucostats
Hierarchy of needs
Homeostasis
Imprinting
Incentive
Instinct
Insulin
Intimacy motive
Lie detector
Motivation
Need for self-actualization

Orgasm
Orgasmic difficulties
Pheromone
Polygraph
Premature ejaculation
Refractory period
Sensate focus
Set point
Sex therapy
Sexual dysfunction
Sociobiology
Vasocongestion

KEY PEOPLE

John Atkinson
Matina Horner
Abraham Maslow
William Masters & Virginia Johnson
David McClelland
Henry Murray
Judith Rodin
Stanley Schachter
Edward Wilson

Human Development Across the Life Span

Human Development Across the Life Span

HUMAN
DEVELOP-
MENT
ACROSS THE
LIFE SPAN

Archie Leach grew up in a lower-middle-class British home that was saturated with frustration and unhappiness. Archie's mother was obsessed with money and felt that her husband never earned enough. When Archie wanted anything, she constantly harped on the fact that money didn't "grow on trees." As a youngster, Archie was a frail, sad-eyed boy; he was often sullen and wrapped up in himself. His parents were miserable with each other, and his mother suffered from depression. When Archie was 10, his father had his mother committed to a mental hospital. Archie was bewildered by his mother's disappearance; his father gave him only a vague explanation, saying that she had gone away for a "rest." Archie, who didn't learn the truth for more than 20 years, thought that his mother had abandoned him. Understandably, he was deeply hurt and felt betrayed.

As a young man, Archie tried to break into theater in New York. However, at the age of 25, "Archie Leach possessed a low opinion of himself as an actor . . . Archie was still the confused, troubled boy from Bristol, who through his work sought but did not find the affection he had never received from his parents" (Harris, 1987, p. 42). He was a shy, moody young man who was especially awkward with the opposite sex. One acquaintance remarked, "He was literally tongue-tied around women."

In spite of these humble beginnings, Archie Leach eventually enjoyed great success in the

Archie Leach's evolution into Cary Grant is a developmental story marked by both continuity and transition.

world of entertainment. Blessed with classic good looks, he began to cultivate the image of an elegant man-about-town. "He looked graceless at first, but he knew that to succeed he had to become someone else, and he was not to be put off" (Wansell, 1983, p. 50).

Archie moved to Los Angeles and started working in films. He made remarkable progress in his effort to transform himself into a sophisticated ladies' man. He earned leading roles in better and better films and went on to star in 72 movies spanning 4 decades, using the stage name Cary Grant. He became a matinee idol, involved in romances with some of the world's most beautiful and desirable women. As one of his biographers put it, by the end of his career, Cary Grant had come to personify adjectives like "dapper, debonair, charming, jaunty, ageless, dashing, blithe, witty, [and] stylish" (Harris, 1987, p. 4).

Archie Leach's transformation into Cary Grant was a stunning triumph, but many remnants of Archie's past were apparent beneath the surface of Cary Grant's public persona. Having felt betrayed by his mother when she mysteriously disappeared, he had lifelong difficulties trusting women. This lack of trust and the moody self-absorption that he had shown as a child contributed greatly to his four failed marriages. Although he could be glib and charming, he continued to feel strained in social encounters, and he spent much of his time in seclusion. In spite of his acclaimed brilliance as a movie star, he remained terribly insecure. He was never able to shake his mother's obsessive concern about money; his miserliness was legendary. He amassed a fortune estimated to be worth 40 million dollars, but he "saved the string from parcels and the tinsel from the Christmas tree, cut the buttons off the shirts he was about to discard in order to save them for future use, [and] marked the wine bottle to make sure that none was drunk while he was not there" (Wansell, 1983, p. 233).

What does Cary Grant have to do with developmental psychology? His story provides an interesting illustration of the two themes that permeate the study of human development: *continuity* and *transition*. In investigating human development, psychologists try to shed light on how people arrive at their various destinations in life. They focus on how people evolve through transitions over time. In looking at these transitions, developmental psychologists inevitably find continuity with the past. This continuity may be the most fascinating element in the story of Cary Grant's personal development. The metamorphosis of shy, awkward little Archie Leach into urbane, debonair Cary Grant was a more radical transformation than most people go through. Nonetheless, the threads of continuity connecting Archie's childhood to the development of Cary Grant's adult personality were quite obvious.

Development refers to the sequence of age-related changes that occur as a person progresses from conception to death. Development is a reasonably orderly, cumulative process that includes both the biological and behavioral changes that take place as we grow older. An infant's newfound ability to grasp objects, a child's gradual mastery of grammar, an adolescent's spurt in physical growth, a young adult's increasing commitment to a vocation, and a middle-aged person's struggle with a mid-life crisis all represent development. All of these transitions are predictable changes that are related to age.

Development is a multifaceted process; progress unfolds concurrently in many different areas. In this chapter we'll discuss physical development, perceptual development, motor development, emotional development, cognitive development, moral development, personality development, and social development. In the Application we'll examine the development of sex roles. As we proceed, you'll see that the pacing of development varies across different areas of development. During a particular age span, development in one area (say, cognitive abilities) might be very rapid, while development in another area (social relations, for example) might be relatively slow.

Traditionally, psychologists have been most interested in development during childhood. Our coverage reflects this emphasis. However, you should be aware that development is a lifelong process. As Cary Grant's story illustrates, significant changes in personality can occur well into adulthood. We'll divide the life span into four broad periods: (1) the prenatal period, between conception and birth, (2) childhood, (3) adolescence, and (4) adulthood. We'll examine aspects of development that are especially dynamic during each period. Let's begin by looking at events that occurred before your birth, during prenatal development.

PROGRESS BEFORE BIRTH: PRENATAL DEVELOPMENT

Development begins with conception. Conception occurs when fertilization creates a **zygote, a one-celled organism formed by the union of a sperm and an egg**. All of the other cells in your body developed from this single cell. Each of your cells contains enduring messages from your parents carried on the *chromosomes* that lie within the cell's nucleus. Each chromosome houses many genes. *Genes* are the functional units in hereditary transmission. They carry the details of our genetic blueprints, which are revealed gradually throughout life (see Chapter 3 for more information on genetic transmission).

The *prenatal period* extends from conception to birth, usually encompassing 9 months of pregnancy. A great deal of very important development occurred before your birth. In fact, development during the prenatal period is remarkably rapid. If you were an average-sized newborn and your physical growth had continued during the first year of your life at a prenatal pace, by your first birthday you would have weighed 200 pounds! Fortunately, you didn't grow at that rate—and no human does—because in the final weeks before birth the frenzied pace of prenatal development tapers off dramatically.

In this section, we'll examine the usual course of prenatal development and discuss how environmental events can leave their mark on development even before birth exposes the newborn to the outside world.

The Course of Prenatal Development

The prenatal period is divided into three phases: (1) the germinal stage (the first 2 weeks), (2) the embryonic stage (2 weeks to 2 months), and (3) the fetal stage (2 months to birth). Some of the key developments in these phases are outlined here.

GERMINAL STAGE

The *germinal stage* is the first phase of prenatal development, encompassing the first 2 weeks after conception. This brief stage begins when a zygote is created through fertilization. Within 36 hours rapid cell division begins, and the zygote becomes a microscopic mass of multiplying cells. This mass of cells slowly migrates along the mother's fallopian tube to the uterine cavity. On about the seventh day, the cell mass begins to implant itself in the uterine wall. This implantation process takes about a week and is far from automatic. As many as half of all zygotes are rejected at this point (Roberts & Lowe, 1975).

During the implantation process, the placenta begins to form. **The *placenta* is the structure that connects the circulation of the fetus and that of the mother.** The placenta allows oxygen and nutrients to pass into the fetus and bodily wastes to pass out to the mother. This critical exchange takes place across thin membranes that block the passage of blood cells, keeping the fetal and maternal bloodstreams separate.

EMBRYONIC STAGE

The *embryonic stage* is the second stage of prenatal development, lasting from 2 weeks until the end of the second month. During this stage, most of the vital organs and bodily systems begin to form in the developing organism, which is now called an *embryo*. Structures such as the heart, the spine, and the brain emerge gradually as cell division becomes more specialized. Although the

Development is rapid during the prenatal period. *Top left:* This 5½-week-old embryo is only ⅔ of an inch long. The large umbilical vein supplies the embryo with blood, which brings oxygen and nourishment. *Top right:* At 11 weeks, this fetus is 2 inches long. Note the well-developed fingers. The fetus can now move its legs, feet, hands, and head and displays a variety of basic reflexes. *Bottom:* After 5½ months of prenatal development, this male fetus is nearly 12 inches long. Facial features are already well defined, and arms and legs move vigorously when the fetus is not asleep.

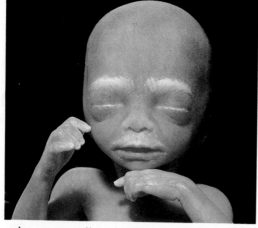

embryo is typically only about an inch long at the end of this stage, it's already beginning to look human: arms, legs, hands, feet, fingers, toes, eyes, and ears are discernible.

The embryonic stage is a period of great vulnerability because virtually all the basic physiological structures are being formed. If anything interferes with normal development during the embryonic phase, the effects can be devastating. Most miscarriages occur during this period (Pernoll, 1982), and most major birth defects are believed to be due to problems that occur during the embryonic stage.

FETAL STAGE

The *fetal stage* is the third stage of prenatal development, lasting from 2 months through birth. Early in this stage muscles and bones begin to form. The developing organism, now called a *fetus*, becomes capable of physical movements as

skeletal structures harden. Organs formed in the embryonic stage continue to grow and gradually begin to function. Sex organs start to develop during the third month.

By approximately the end of the sixth month, the fetus may be able to survive on its own in the event of a premature birth. During the final 3 months of the prenatal period, brain cells multiply at a brisk pace, a layer of fat is deposited under the skin to provide insulation, and the respiratory and digestive systems mature. All of these changes ready the fetus for life outside the cozy, supportive environment of its mother's womb.

Environmental Factors and Prenatal Development

Although an unborn child develops in the protective buffer of its mother's womb, events in the external environment can affect it indirectly through the mother. Because the developing organism and its mother are linked intimately through the placenta, a mother's eating habits, drug use, and physical health, among other things, can affect prenatal development. Figure 11.1 shows the periods of prenatal development during which various structures are most vulnerable to damage.

MATERNAL NUTRITION

The developing fetus needs a variety of essential nutrients. Thus it's not surprising that severe maternal malnutrition increases the risk of birth complications and neurological deficits (Stechler & Halton, 1982). Effects of severe malnutrition are a major problem in underdeveloped nations where food shortages are common. The impact of moderate malnutrition, which is more common in modern societies, is more difficult to gauge. However, some studies have found a correlation between moderate prenatal dietary deficits and poor motor skills, apathy, and irritability during infancy (Bhatia, Katiyar, & Agarwal, 1979; Zeskind & Ramey, 1981). These studies suggest that it's important for pregnant women to have nutritionally balanced diets. In addition to monitoring the nutritional quality of their diets, pregnant women need to be aware of other substances they consume.

MATERNAL DRUG USE

A major source of concern about fetal and infant well-being is the mother's consumption of drugs, including widely used substances like tobacco and alcohol, as well as prescription and recreational drugs. Unfortunately, most drugs consumed by a pregnant woman can slip through the membranes

Figure 11.1 Periods of vulnerability in prenatal development. Generally, structures are most susceptible to damage when they are undergoing rapid development. The darker regions of the bars indicate the most sensitive periods for various organs and structures, and the lighter regions indicate periods of continued, but lessened, vulnerability. As a whole, sensitivity is greatest in the embryonic stage, but some structures remain somewhat vulnerable throughout prenatal development.

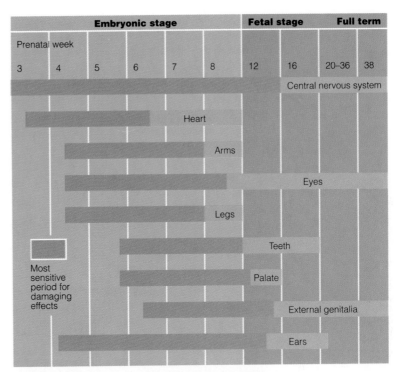

of the placenta. The dangers of drug use during the prenatal period were made tragically apparent in the early 1960s, when a drug called thalidomide was prescribed for many women in Europe to minimize their morning sickness during pregnancy. It turned out that thalidomide interfered with embryonic development, and thousands of babies were born with stunted limbs before investigators were able to pinpoint the cause of the deformities.

Since then, research has revealed that many drugs are potentially harmful to the embryo or fetus, including virtually all widely abused drugs (see Chapter 5), many drugs prescribed for legitimate medical reasons, and even some over-the-counter drugs (Vaughn, McKay, & Behrman, 1979). The impact of drugs on the embryo or fetus varies greatly depending on the drug, the dose, and the phase of prenatal development. Table 11.1 summarizes the risks associated with the use of various drugs.

Women who drink alcohol while pregnant may also expose their unborn children to unnecessary risks. It has long been clear that *heavy* drinking by a mother can be hazardous to a fetus. **Fetal**

alcohol syndrome is a collection of congenital (inborn) problems associated with excessive alcohol use during pregnancy. Typical problems include microcephaly (a small head), heart defects, irritability, hyperactivity, and retarded mental and motor development. Previously, the available evidence suggested that it was safe for women to drink in moderation during pregnancy. However, some studies in the last decade indicate that even normal social drinking *may* be harmful to the fe-

---

Table 11.1 Some Drugs That May Affect the Embryo, Fetus, or Newborn

DRUG	POSSIBLE DANGERS
Antibiotics	Heavy use of streptomycin by pregnant women can produce hearing loss in their infants. Terramycin and tetracycline may be associated with premature delivery, retarded skeletal growth, and cataracts.
Aspirin	If used in large quantities, aspirin can cause neonatal bleeding and gastrointestinal discomfort.
Anticonvulsants	Anticonvulsants can produce heart problems and defects such as cleft lip.
Barbiturates	In normal doses barbiturates cause the fetus or newborn to be lethargic. In large doses they can cause anoxia (oxygen starvation) or can interfere with the baby's breathing.
Hallucinogens	Hallucinogens are suspected to cause spontaneous abortion as well as behavioral abnormalities among newborn infants.
Narcotics	Maternal addiction to narcotics increases the risk of premature delivery. Moreover, the fetus is often born addicted to the narcotic agent, and this addiction results in a number of complications.
Sex hormones	Sex hormones contained in birth control pills and drugs for prevention of miscarriage can have a number of harmful effects, including heart malformations, cervical cancer (in female offspring), and masculinization of the fetus.
Tranquilizers (other than thalidomide)	Tranquilizers may produce respiratory distress in newborns.

Source: Adapted from Shaffer, 1989

tus, especially during the last few months of pregnancy (Haynes, 1982).

Tobacco use during pregnancy may also be harmful to the fetus. Smoking appears to produce a number of subtle physiological changes in the mother that collectively reduce the flow of oxygen to the fetus (Quigley et al., 1979). This is probably the main reason that pregnant women who smoke have an increased risk for miscarriage and other birth complications (Niswander, 1982).

MATERNAL ILLNESS
The fetus is largely defenseless against infections because its immune system matures relatively late in the prenatal period. The placenta screens out quite a number of infectious agents, but not all. Thus, many maternal illnesses can interfere with prenatal development. Diseases such as rubella (German measles), syphilis, cholera, smallpox, mumps, and even severe cases of the flu can be very hazardous to the fetus (Nesbitt & Abdul-Karim, 1982). The nature of any damage depends on when the mother contracts the illness. Different diseases are particularly dangerous during different phases of prenatal development. For instance, rubella is most dangerous early in pregnancy, whereas cholera becomes more dangerous in the later part of the prenatal period.

We have a long way to go before we understand all the factors that shape development before birth. For example, the effects of fluctuations in maternal emotions are not well understood. Nonetheless, it's clear that critical developments unfold quickly during the prenatal period. In the next section, you'll learn that development continues at a fast pace during the early years of childhood.

THE WONDROUS YEARS OF CHILDHOOD

There's a certain magic associated with childhood. Young children have an extraordinary ability to captivate adults' attention, especially their parents'. Legions of new parents apologize repeatedly to friends and strangers alike as they talk on and on about the cute things their kids do. Most wondrous of all are the rapid and momentous developmental changes of the childhood years. Helpless infants become curious toddlers almost overnight. Before parents can catch their breath, these toddlers are schoolchildren engaged in spirited play with young friends. Then, suddenly, they're insecure adolescents, asking about dates, part-time jobs, cars, and colleges. The whirlwind transitions of childhood often seem miraculous.

Of course, the transformations that occur in childhood only *seem* magical. In reality, they reflect an orderly, predictable, gradual progression. In this section you'll see what psychologists have learned about this progression, as we examine various aspects of development that are especially dynamic during childhood. Language development, which is very rapid during early childhood, is omitted here only because we covered it in the chapter on language and thought (refer to Chapter 8). Let's begin by looking at infants' perceptual abilities.

Experiencing the World: Perceptual Development

Studies of infants' perception have focused heavily on vision, just like studies of adults' perception. Ironically, the newborn child's visual capability appears to be mediocre compared to its hearing.

VISUAL ACUITY AND DEPTH PERCEPTION
The newborn child sees blurred images, since visual acuity initially is only about 20/500 (versus the adult norm of 20/20). This means that what a newborn can see at a distance of 20 feet, an adult with normal vision can see at 500 feet. Part of the problem is that the eye muscles that control visual accommodation (adjustment of the curvature of the lens) are still developing, so that 1-month old infants' visual focus is "fixed" at about 8 inches.

Infants are far from blind, however. They can follow a moving object at close range at about 2 months—albeit with rather jerky eye movements. At around 3 months of age, most infants begin to recognize their mother's face (Barerra & Maurer, 1981). Accommodation is adequate at about 4 months, and visual acuity gradually improves to about 20/100 by 6 months and reaches 20/20 at around age 4.

Infants' ability to perceive depth has been ex-

Figure 11.2 The visual cliff. No, this infant is not crawling on air. He's crawling on a glass platform after being coaxed past the drop-off on a visual cliff, a device used to study depth perception in infants. Generally, infants balk at crawling over the edge of the cliff at around 6 months of age.

amined extensively in research with an apparatus called a visual cliff. The **visual cliff is a glass platform that extends over a several-foot drop-off (the cliff)** (see Figure 11.2). If a child crawls across the shallow or "top" side of the apparatus, but refuses to crawl over the drop-off to the deep side, researchers conclude that the child can perceive depth. Eleanor Gibson and Richard Walk found that babies start balking at crawling over the edge at around 6 months of age (Gibson & Walk, 1960). This indicates that most infants are capable of depth perception around the middle of their first year.

Experiments with younger children who can't yet crawl *suggest* that depth perception may be present even earlier. To test for depth perception in younger infants, researchers set them down on each side of the visual cliff and monitor their heart rate to see if it varies from side to side. Surprisingly, heart rate in 2-month-old children *decreases* when they're on the deep side. This suggests, with some ambiguity, that they can perceive the difference between the two sides, but are not yet afraid of the drop-off (Campos, Langer, & Krowitz, 1970). Thus, there is evidence that some primitive depth perception may exist by 2 months of age.

HEARING AND OTHER SENSES

Generally, a newborn's hearing is more fully developed than its vision. Immediately after birth, newborns show some ability to tell where sounds are coming from, a process called *auditory localization*. Newborns' ability to locate sounds was demonstrated by Michael Wertheimer (1961), an enterprising psychologist who started performing experiments as soon as he entered the delivery room after his daughter's birth. Wertheimer used a clicker device to make noises from different locations in the delivery room and noted that his daughter consistently turned her head in the direction of the noise.

Infants only a few days old are easily startled by sudden bursts of noise and are comforted by rhythmic sounds. Babies can distinguish their mothers' voices within the first week of life (DeCasper & Fifer, 1980). This probably explains why infants are comforted by their mother's presence even before they can recognize her face. At 1 month of age babies can already discriminate basic speech sounds. This capability is critical to the rapid language development that occurs during the first year of life.

Early development in the other senses has not yet been studied extensively. However, it's clear that newborns can taste the differences in sweet, sour, salty, and bitter subtances, that they can smell strong odors such as alcohol, and that they're sensitive to even relatively light touches (Acredolo & Hake, 1982). Thus, basic sensory capabilities seem to develop reasonably early in the senses of taste, smell, and touch. Overall, the perceptual abilities of very young infants are advanced in comparison to their motor abilities, which we'll consider next.

Exploring the World: Motor Development

Motor development refers to the progression of muscular coordination required for physical activities. Basic motor skills include grasping and reaching for objects, manipulating objects, sitting up, crawling, walking, running, and so forth. Motor development lags behind perceptual development to some degree, so that infants often have a lot of information from sensory input that they can't act upon very effectively (Bruner, 1968). For instance, a baby may see an intriguing toy but be unable to get to it or hold onto it until motor development proceeds further.

BASIC PRINCIPLES

A number of principles are apparent in motor development. One is the *cephalo-caudal trend—the head-to-foot direction of motor development.* Children tend to gain control over the upper part of their bodies before the lower part. You've seen this trend in action if you've seen an infant learn to crawl: children gradually shift from using their arms for propelling themselves to using their legs. The *proximo-distal trend is the center-outward direction of motor development.* Children gain control over their central torso before their extremities. Thus, infants initially reach for things by twisting their entire torso, but gradually they learn to extend just their arms.

Early progress in motor skills is largely attributable to maturation. *Maturation* refers to development that reflects the gradual unfolding of one's genetic blueprint. Maturation is a product of genetically programmed physical changes—as opposed to experience and learning. Early motor development is primarily due to maturation, but it can also be influenced by environmental factors. For example, if children get little opportunity to practice motor skills because they're confined to their cribs, their motor development may be slowed (Dennis, 1960). As children grow older and acquire specialized motor skills, maturation becomes less influential and experience becomes more critical. Obviously, maturation by

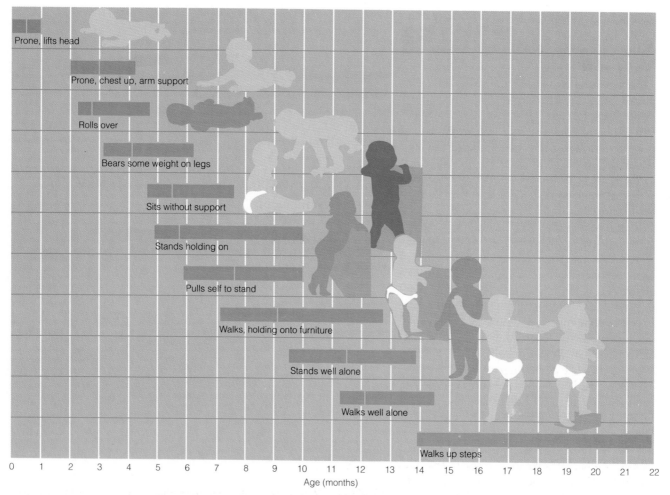

Prone, lifts head

Prone, chest up, arm support

Rolls over

Bears some weight on legs

Sits without support

Stands holding on

Pulls self to stand

Walks, holding onto furniture

Stands well alone

Walks well alone

Walks up steps

0 1 2 3 4 5 6 7 8 9 10 11 12 13 14 15 16 17 18 19 20 21 22

Age (months)

Figure 11.3 Landmarks in motor development. The left edge, interior mark, and right edge of each bar indicate the age at which 25%, 50%, and 90% of infants have mastered each motor skill shown. Developmental norms typically report only the median age of mastery (the interior mark), which can be misleading in light of the variability in age of mastery that is apparent in this chart.

itself will never lead to the development of ballet or football skills, for example, without exposure to appropriate training.

UNDERSTANDING DEVELOPMENTAL NORMS

Parents often pay close attention to early motor development, comparing their child's progress with developmental norms. **Developmental norms indicate the average age at which people display various behaviors and abilities.** For example, the generalizations that "average children" say their first word at about 12 months and start combining words into sentences between 18 and 24 months are developmental norms. Developmental norms are useful benchmarks as long as parents don't expect their children to progress exactly at the pace specified in the norms. Some parents get unnecessarily alarmed when their children fall behind developmental norms.

What these parents overlook is that developmental norms are group *averages*; variations from the average are entirely normal. This normal variation stands out in Figure 11.3, which shows norms for many basic motor skills. The left edge, interior mark, and right edge of the bars in the

diagram indicate the age at which 25%, 50%, and 90% of youngsters can demonstrate various motor skills. Typically, information on developmental norms includes only the median age of attainment indicated by the interior (50%) mark in each bar. This exclusive focus on average progress fails·to convey the immense variability seen in youngsters' development. As Figure 11.3 shows, a substantial portion of children often don't achieve a particular milestone until long after the average time cited in norms. For example, the average child can walk holding onto furniture at 9 months, but 10% of children still haven't mastered this 3 months later. Thus, there is considerable variability among children in motor development, just as there is in all other areas of development.

Easy and Difficult Babies: Differences in Temperament

Infants also show great variability in temperament. **Temperament refers to characteristic mood, energy level, and reactivity.** From the very beginning, some babies seem animated and cheerful and others seem sluggish and ornery. Infants show consistent differences in emotional tone, tempo of activity, and sensitivity to environmental stimuli very early in life (Rothbart & Derryberry, 1981).

Alexander Thomas and Stella Chess have conducted a major *longitudinal* study of the development of temperament (Thomas, Chess, & Birch, 1970; Thomas & Chess, 1977). **In a *longitudinal* study investigators observe one group of subjects repeatedly over a period of time.** This approach to the study of development is often contrasted with the cross-sectional approach (the logic of both approaches is diagrammed in Figure 11.4). **In a *cross-sectional study* investigators compare groups of subjects of differing age who are observed at a single point in time.** For example, in a cross-sectional study an investigator tracing the growth of children's vocabulary might compare 50 6-year-olds, 50 8-year-olds, and 50 10-year-olds. In contrast, an investigator using the longitudinal method would assemble one group of 50 6-year-olds and measure their vocabulary at age 6, again at age 8, and once more at age 10.

Both methods are well suited to the challenge of mapping out relations between age and changes in behavior. Each method has its advantages. Cross-sectional studies can be completed more quickly, easily, and cheaply than longitudinal studies, which often extend over many years. But longitudinal studies tend to be more sensitive to developmental changes (Nunnally, 1982).

Each method also has its disadvantages. In cross-sectional research, age trends are valid only if the subjects in different age groups are similar in all respects except their age. In our hypothetical study of vocabulary growth, for instance, we would get misleading results if our 6-year-olds were more intelligent (on the average) than our 8-year-olds. Entirely different problems surface in longitudinal research. When a longitudinal study goes on for a number of years, subjects tend to drop out as they lose interest or move away. The drop-outs often differ from the subjects who remain in the study, complicating the interpretation of age comparisons. In addition, those who remain in the study may be affected by their participation. A frequent test of your vocabulary, for instance, may foster an interest in language and make your language development atypical.

To some extent, the choice between the longitudinal approach and the cross-sectional approach depends on what the investigators want to learn about development. Thomas and Chess wanted to learn about the long-term stability of children's temperaments. Given this goal, they needed to follow the same children in a longitudinal study to assess their temperamental stability

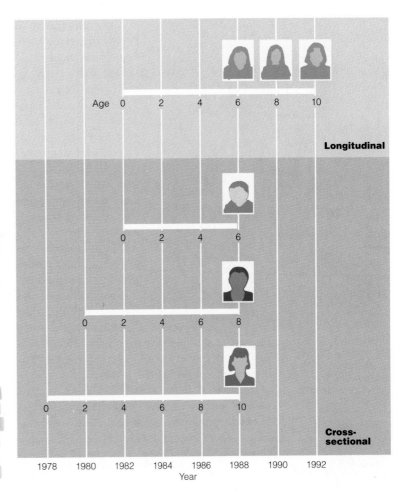

over time. They began their study in 1956 with a group of 141 middle-class children; in 1961 they added a second group of 95 children of working-class parents. They tracked the development of most of these children through adolescence, relying primarily on interviews with their parents and secondarily on interviews with the children and their teachers.

Thomas and Chess found that "temperamental individuality is well established by the time the infant is 2 to 3 months old" (Thomas & Chess, 1977, p. 153). They identified three basic styles of temperament that were apparent in most of the children. About 40% of the youngsters were *easy children* who tended to be happy, regular in sleep and eating, adaptable, and not readily upset. Another 15% were *slow-to-warm-up children* who tended to be less cheery, less regular in their sleep and eating, slower in adapting to change, more wary of new experiences, and moderate in reactivity (their reactions to stimuli were intermediate in intensity). *Difficult children* who tended to be glum, erratic in sleep and eating, resistant to change, easily irritated, and intense in their reactions constituted 10% of the group. The remaining 35% of the children showed mixtures of these temperaments.

Figure 11.4 Longitudinal versus cross-sectional research. In a longitudinal study of development between ages 6 and 10, the same children would be observed at 6, again at 8, and again at 10. In a cross-sectional study of the same age span, a group of 6-year-olds, a group of 8-year-olds, and a group of 10-year-olds would be compared simultaneously. Note that data collection could be completed immediately in the cross-sectional study, whereas the longitudinal study would require 4 years to complete.

393

Temperamental individuality and stability are apparent in the first few months of life. The rapid emergence of individuality suggests that temperament is partly biological in origin.

These differences in temperament were found to be moderately stable over time. A child's temperament at 3 months was a fair predictor of the child's temperament at age 10. Infants who were categorized as "difficult" were found to develop more emotional problems requiring counseling than other children. Although basic changes in temperament were seen in some children, Thomas, Chess, and Birch concluded that "Our long-term study has now established that the original characteristics of temperament tend to persist in most children over the years" (1970, p. 104).

Nonetheless, Thomas and Chess maintain that parents' reactions to their children and their styles of child rearing can influence a child's temperament. These parental reactions may promote either stability or change in a child's temperament, depending on how the child's emotional tone meshes with the parents' preferences. The match between a child's temperament and a parent's expectations can also influence early emotional bonding, which is our next subject.

Early Emotional Bonding: Attachment

Do mothers and infants forge lasting emotional bonds in the first few hours after birth? Does emotional bonding have to occur during an early, critical period of life? Do early emotional bonds affect later development? These are just some of the questions investigated by psychologists interested in attachment.

Attachment refers to a close, emotional bond of affection between an infant and its caregiver. Researchers have shown a keen interest in how infant-mother attachments are formed early in life. Although children eventually form attachments to many people, including their fathers, siblings, grandparents, and others, the mother is often the target of the first important attachment because she is often the principal provider of care in the early months of life.

Contrary to popular belief, infants' attachment to their mothers is *not* instantaneous. Initially, babies show little in the way of a special preference for their mothers. They can be handed over to strangers such as babysitters with relatively little difficulty. This typically changes at around 6 to 8 months of age (Lamb, 1982). Infants begin to show a preference for their mother's company and often protest when separated from her. This is the first manifestation of *separation anxiety*—emotional distress seen in many infants when they are separated from people with whom they have formed an attachment. Separation anxiety, which may occur with other familiar caregivers as well as the mother, typically peaks around 14 to 18 months and then begins to decline.

THEORIES OF ATTACHMENT
Why do children gradually develop special attachments to their mothers? This question sounds simple enough, but it has been the subject of a lively theoretical dialogue.

Behaviorists have argued that the infant-mother attachment develops because mothers are associated with the powerful, reinforcing event of being fed. Thus, the mother becomes a conditioned reinforcer. This reinforcement theory of attachment came into question as a result of Harry and Margaret Harlow's famous studies of attachment in infant rhesus monkeys (Harlow & Harlow, 1962).

The Harlows removed newborn monkeys from their mothers at birth and raised them in the lab-

Figure 11.5 Attachment and contact-comfort in monkeys. Even if fed by a wire surrogate mother, the Harlows' infant monkeys cuddled up with a terry-cloth surrogate that provided contact-comfort. When threatened by a frightening toy (as shown on the right), the monkeys sought security from their terry-cloth mothers.

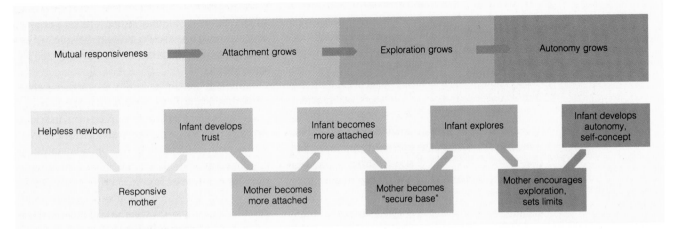

Mutual responsiveness → Attachment grows → Exploration grows → Autonomy grows

| Helpless newborn | Infant develops trust | Infant becomes more attached | Infant explores | Infant develops autonomy, self-concept |

| Responsive mother | Mother becomes more attached | Mother becomes "secure base" | Mother encourages exploration, sets limits |

oratory with two types of artificial "substitute mothers." One artificial mother was made of terry cloth and could provide "contact-comfort," while the other artificial mother was made of wire (see Figure 11.5). A feeding bottle was attached to just one of the substitute mothers, so that half of the monkeys were fed by their wire mother and the other half were fed by a cloth mother. This allowed the Harlows to isolate the importance of feeding as a reinforcer in comparison to the pleasure of cuddling up with the comfortable terry cloth mother.

The young monkeys' attachment to their substitute mothers was tested by introducing a frightening stimulus, such as a strange toy (see Figure 11.5). If reinforcement through feeding was the key to attachment, the frightened monkeys should have scampered off to the mother that had fed them. This was not the case. The young monkeys scrambled for their cloth mothers, even if they were *not* fed by them! Only the cloth mothers, which the monkeys would cling to, were able to provide security. Thus, the Harlows concluded that the contact-comfort provided by a mother plays a critical role in the development of attachment.

The Harlows' work made a simple reinforcement explanation of attachment unrealistic for animals, let alone for more complex human beings. An alternative explanation of attachment was then proposed. John Bowlby (1969, 1973, 1980) was impressed by the importance of contact-comfort to the Harlows' monkeys and by the apparently *unlearned* nature of this preference. He concluded that there must be a biological basis for attachment. According to his view, infants are biologically programmed to emit behavior (smiling, cooing, clinging, and so on) that triggers an affectionate, protective response from adults, and adults are biologically programmed to be captivated by this behavior and to respond with warmth and love.

At present we have only circumstantial evidence to support Bowlby's hypothesis that there is a biological basis for attachment. However, Bowlby's theory has proven influential because it accurately casts the infant in an *active* role pursuing contact with the mother, and because it accurately emphasizes the reciprocal, interactive way in which the attachment relationship grows.

Current evidence indicates that attachment emerges out of a complex, mutual interplay between infant and mother (Lamb et al., 1985; see Figure 11.6). Studies reveal that mothers who are sensitive and responsive to their child's needs tend to evoke stronger attachments than mothers who are relatively insensitive or inconsistent in their responding (Ainsworth, 1979). However, an infant is not a passive bystander as this process unfolds. Infants are active participants who influence the process with their crying, smiling, fussing, and babbling. Difficult infants who spit up most of their food, make bathing a major battle, refuse to go to sleep, and rarely smile may sometimes slow the process of attachment in the mother by undermining her responsiveness (Greene, Fox, & Lewis, 1983). Hence, an infant's temperament and the personality of the mother can both influence the emergence of attachment.

EFFECTS OF ATTACHMENT AND EMOTIONAL DEPRIVATION

As you can see from this discussion, and may have seen in life, the attachment process is less than automatic, and some children have better bonds with their mothers than other children do. Evidence suggests that a strong infant-mother attachment can be beneficial for a child. Infants with a relatively secure attachment tend to be more obedient and to respond better to unfamiliar people (Londerville & Main, 1981). They also display more persistence, curiosity, self-reliance, and leadership in the preschool years (Joffe & Vaughn, 1982). Ironically, secure attachment

Figure 11.6 The evolution of attachment. The unfolding of attachment depends on the mutual interaction between a mother (or other caregiver) and an infant.

"Important theoretical and practical questions in this realm of interest can be resolved by the use of monkeys."
HARRY & MARGARET HARLOW

also makes children more apt to explore the world around them. Apparently, a solid attachment gives a young child a secure base of operations from which to venture forth.

If solid early attachments are so important, you won't be surprised to learn that psychologists have been concerned about the effects of emotional deprivation. **Emotional deprivation occurs when infants get little attention from adult caregivers and when circumstances prevent normal bonding.** John Bowlby has theorized that infants deprived of normal attachment to a caregiver in the first year or so will be deficient in forming affectionate bonds with others *throughout* life.

Underlying Bowlby's theory is the idea that there are "critical periods" in development. **A critical period is a brief time in development during which certain experiences must occur if development is to unfold normally.** Critical periods have been observed in the development of some animals. For example, in the previous chapter we discussed how baby ducklings form a strong social attachment with the first moving object they see between 10 and 20 hours after birth (see Figure 10.2). Konrad Lorenz (1937) called this automatic attachment *imprinting*, and he concluded that it could occur only during a brief time interval shortly after birth, which represented a critical period.

To support the hypothesis that there are critical periods in human social development, some theorists cite evidence on children reared in overcrowded "warehouse" orphanages that were commonplace before effective contraceptives became available. During infancy many of these children received little one-on-one care and thus had little opportunity for meaningful attachment to a caregiver. Consistent with Bowlby's theory, many of these children *did* tend to show enduring difficulties in forming affectionate relationships with others (Goldfarb, 1947; Provence & Lipton, 1962). Their language and cognitive development was also noticeably slower during childhood than that of other children.

Do these findings prove that there are critical periods in human social development? In a word, no. More recent studies show that the effects of early emotional deprivation can be reversed (Clarke & Clarke, 1976). When emotionally deprived youngsters are placed in warm, supportive homes, many recover and go on to enjoy normal social relations. If early deprivation can be reversed, this shows that normal development does not depend on experiences that *must* occur during a *critical* time period. Consequently, most theorists have discarded the idea that we go through critical periods of development. Instead, many

"Human personality in principle develops according to steps predetermined in the growing person's readiness to be driven toward, to be aware of, and to interact with, a widening social radius."
ERIK ERIKSON

theorists prefer the more limited hypothesis that we go through *sensitive periods*—time intervals during which specific forms of development can unfold most readily and quickly, if certain experiences occur.

Although we don't appear to go through periods that are critical in a strict sense, early experiences can certainly leave their mark on development in later stages of life. Our attachments play an important role in our emotional development and may affect our social interactions for many years to come. In the next section, we'll examine a systematic theory of personality development that links early childhood experiences to adult personality.

Becoming Unique: Personality Development

How do we develop our unique constellations of personality traits over time? Many theories have addressed this question. The first major theory of personality development was put together by Sigmund Freud back around the turn of the century. Freud's theory startled the world. As we'll discuss in Chapter 12, he claimed that the basic foundation of an individual's personality is firmly laid down by age 5. Half a century later, Erik Erikson (1963) proposed a sweeping revision of Freud's theory that has proven very influential. Like Freud, Erikson concluded that events in early childhood leave a permanent stamp on adult personality. However, unlike Freud, Erikson theorized that personality continues to evolve over the entire life span.

Building on Freud's earlier work, Erikson devised a stage theory of personality development. As you'll see in reading this chapter, many theories describe development in terms of stages. **A stage is a developmental period during which characteristic patterns of behavior are exhibited and certain capacities become established.** Stage theories assume that (1) we must progress through specified stages in a particular order because each stage builds on the previous stage and (2) our progress through these stages is strongly related to age.

ERIKSON'S STAGE THEORY
Erikson partitioned the life span into eight stages. Each stage is assumed to bring a *psychosocial crisis* involving transitions in important social relationships. According to Erikson, our personality is shaped by how we deal with these psychosocial crises. Each crisis is viewed as a potential turning point that can yield different outcomes. The

stages are described in terms of these alternative outcomes, which represent personality traits that people display over the remainder of their lives. All eight stages in Erikson's theory are charted in Table 11.2. We describe the first four childhood stages here and discuss the remaining stages in the upcoming sections on adolescence and adulthood.

TRUST VERSUS MISTRUST Erikson's first stage encompasses the first year of life, when an infant has to depend completely on adults to take care of its basic needs for such necessities as food, a warm blanket, and changed diapers. If an infant's basic biological needs are adequately met by its caregivers and sound attachments are formed, an optimistic, trusting attitude toward the world should be created. However, if the infant's basic needs are taken care of poorly, a more distrusting, insecure personality may result.

AUTONOMY VERSUS SHAME AND DOUBT Erikson's second stage unfolds during the second and third years of life, when parents begin toilet training and other efforts to regulate a child's behavior. A child must begin to take some personal responsibility for feeding, dressing, and bathing. If all goes well, the child acquires a sense of self-sufficiency. However, if parents are never satisfied with the child's efforts and there are constant parent-child conflicts, the child may develop a sense of personal shame and self-doubt.

INITATIVE VERSUS GUILT In Erikson's third stage, lasting roughly from the fourth through sixth years, the challenge facing children is to function socially within their families. If children think only of their own needs and desires, family members may begin to instill feelings of guilt, and self-esteem may suffer. But if children learn to get along well with siblings and parents, a sense of self-confidence should begin to grow.

INDUSTRY VERSUS INFERIORITY In the fourth stage (age 6 through puberty), the challenge of learning to function socially is extended beyond the family to the broader social realm of the neighborhood and school. Children who are able to function effectively in this less nurturant social sphere where productivity is highly valued should develop a sense of competence.

EVALUATING ERIKSON'S THEORY

The strength of Erikson's theory is that it accounts for both continuity and transition in personality development. It accounts for transition by showing how new challenges in social relations stimulate personality development throughout life. It accounts for continuity by drawing connections between early childhood experiences and aspects of adult personality.

On the negative side, Erikson's theory discusses only selected aspects of personality. Also, it's an "idealized" description of "typical" developmental patterns; it's not well suited for explaining the enormous personality differences that exist among people. Inadequate explanation of individual differences is a common problem with stage theories of development. This shortcoming surfaces again in the next section, where we'll describe Jean Piaget's stage theory of cognitive development.

Table 11.2 Stages of Psychosocial Development

STAGES	PSYCHOSOCIAL CRISES	SIGNIFICANT SOCIAL RELATIONSHIPS	FAVORABLE OUTCOME
1. First year of life	Trust versus mistrust	Mother or mother substitute	Trust and optimism
2. Second and third years	Autonomy versus doubt	Parents	A sense of self-control and adequacy
3. Fourth through sixth years	Initiative versus guilt	Basic family	Purpose and direction; ability to initiate one's own activities
4. Age 6 through puberty	Industry versus inferiority	Neighborhood; school	Competence in intellectual, social, and physical skills
5. Adolescence	Identity versus confusion	Peer groups and outgroups; models of leadership	An integrated image of oneself as a unique person
6. Early adulthood	Intimacy versus isolation	Partners in friendship and sex; competition, cooperation	An ability to form close and lasting relationships, to make career commitments
7. Middle adulthood	Generativity versus self-absorption	Divided labor and shared household	Concern for family, society, and future generations
8. The aging years	Integrity versus despair	"Mankind"; "my kind"	A sense of fulfillment and satisfaction with one's life; willingness to face death

Source: Erikson, 1963

The Growth of Thought: Cognitive Development

Four-year-old Susan was asked where she got her name. She answered, "My mommy named me." "What if your mother had called you Jack?" "Then I'd be a boy." . . . Susan also claimed that if the name of the sun were changed and it was called the moon, "then it would be dark in the daytime."

A three-year-old girl, with a gleam in her eye, approached a plant. Her mother cautioned her not to touch it. "Why not?" "Because you might hurt it." "No, I won't, 'cause it can't cry." (Ault, 1977, p. 3)

These are just a few examples of how young children's thinking differs from that of adults. These examples illustrate why people speak of the freshness of seeing the world through children's eyes. Their view is different. And it's not just because children are less informed (or shorter) than you or I. Children's thought processes are fundamentally different from ours.

Cognitive development refers to transitions in youngsters' patterns of thinking, including reasoning, remembering, and problem solving. The investigation of cognitive development has been dominated in recent decades by the theory of Jean Piaget (1929, 1952, 1983), a Swiss scholar who studied children's thinking from the 1920s until his death in 1980. Most of our discussion of cognitive development is devoted to Piaget's theory and the research it generated, although we'll also delve into information-processing approaches to cognitive development.

OVERVIEW OF PIAGET'S STAGE THEORY

Jean Piaget was an interdisciplinary scholar whose own cognitive development was exceptionally rapid. In his early teens, he worked part-time at a local museum of natural history and became fascinated by mollusks, which are shell-bearing invertebrates such as snails and clams. While still a

"It is virtually impossible to draw a clear line between innate and acquired behavior patterns."

JEAN PIAGET

teenager, he published 21 articles on mollusks in scientific journals. Assuming that he was a mature adult, one museum wrote to offer him a curatorship, which he had to turn down because he was still in high school!

In his early 20s, after he had earned a doctorate in natural science and published a novel, Piaget's interest turned to psychology. He met Theodore Simon, who had collaborated with Alfred Binet in devising the first useful intelligence tests (Binet & Simon, 1905). Working in Simon's Paris laboratory, Piaget administered intelligence tests to many children to develop better test norms. In doing this testing, Piaget discovered that he was intrigued by the reasoning underlying the children's *wrong* answers. He decided that measuring children's intelligence was less interesting than studying how children *use* their intelligence. In 1921 he moved to Geneva, where he spent the remainder of his life studying cognitive development.

Like Erikson's theory, Piaget's model is a *stage theory* of development. Piaget proposed that children's thought processes advance through a series of four major stages: (1) the *sensorimotor period* (birth to age 2), (2) the *preoperational period* (ages 2 to 7), (3) the *concrete operations period* (ages 7 to 11), and (4) the *formal operations period* (age 11 onward). Table 11.3 provides a brief overview of each of these periods. Piaget regarded his age norms as approximations and acknowledged that transitional ages may vary from one child to another.

Noting that children actively explore the world around them, Piaget asserted that interaction with the environment and maturation gradually alter the way children think. According to Piaget, children progress in their thinking through the complementary processes of assimilation and accommodation. *Assimilation* involves interpreting new experiences in terms of mental

Table 11.3 A Summary of Piaget's Stages

APPROXIMATE AGE RANGE	STAGE	MAJOR CHARACTERISTICS
Birth to 2 years	Sensorimotor period	Coordination of sensory input and motor responses Development of object permanence Little or no capacity for symbolic representation
2 to 7 years	Preoperational period	Development of symbolic thought Irreversible, egocentric thinking
7 to 11 years	Concrete operations period	Mental operations applied to concrete objects and events Development of conservation, mastery of concept of reversibility
11 through adulthood	Formal operations period	Mental operations applied to abstractions Development of logical and systematic thinking

structures already available, without changing them. A child may, for instance, know something about how Velcro operates from putting on and taking off a bib. Presented with shoes with Velcro fasteners, the same child is likely to pick up the new task (fastening the shoes) very easily.

Accommodation **involves changing existing mental structures to explain new experiences.** Accommodation and assimilation often occur interactively. For instance, a child accustomed to popping the caps off soda bottles with a bottle opener may try to use the opener in this way the first time she or he encounters a twist-off cap. When this strategy (of assimilation) fails to yield results, the child may try other approaches in a trial-and-error fashion. When the solution (twisting the cap) is discovered, the child's mental structures for handling soda bottles may be altered. If so, these alterations in mental structures involve accommodation. With the companion processes of assimilation and accommodation in mind, let's turn now to the four stages in Piaget's theory.

SENSORIMOTOR PERIOD

One of Piaget's foremost contributions was to greatly enhance our understanding of mental development in the earliest months of life. The first stage in Piaget's theory is the *sensorimotor period*, which lasts roughly from birth to age 2. Piaget calls this stage *sensorimotor* because children are developing the ability to coordinate their sensory input with their motor actions.

The major development during the sensorimotor stage is the gradual appearance of symbolic thought. At the beginning of this stage, a child's behavior is dominated by innate reflexes. But by the end of the stage, a child can use mental symbols to represent objects (for example, a mental image of a favorite toy). The key to this transition is the acquisition of the concept of object permanence.

Object permanence **develops when a child recognizes that objects continue to exist even when they are no longer visible to the child.** Although you surely take the permanence of objects for granted, infants aren't aware of this permanence at first. If you show a 4-month-old child an eye-catching toy and then cover it with a pillow, the child will not attempt to search for the toy. Piaget inferred from this observation that the child does not understand that the toy continues to exist under the pillow. The notion of object permanence does not dawn on children overnight. The first signs of this insight usually appear between 4 and 8 months of age, when children will often pursue an object that is *partially* covered in their

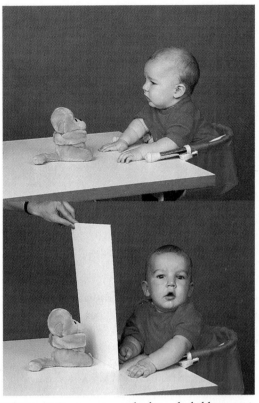

When this young boy's view of a toy is blocked, he doesn't attempt to search for the toy, because he doesn't yet understand that the toy continues to exist behind the barrier. According to Piaget, the eventual acquisition of the concept of object permanence is the foremost development during the sensorimotor period.

presence. Progress is gradual, and children typically don't master the concept of object permanence until they're about 18 months old.

The significance of object permanence is immense. Once children realize that disappearing objects continue to exist, they begin to use mental images to represent the absent objects. This is the primitive beginning of symbolic thought, which will gradually expand the boundaries of youngsters' thinking.

PREOPERATIONAL PERIOD

During the *preoperational period*, which extends roughly from age 2 to age 7, children gradually improve in their use of mental images. Although progress in symbolic thought continues, Piaget emphasized the *shortcomings* in preoperational thought.

Consider a simple problem that Piaget presented to youngsters. He would take two identical beakers and fill each with the same amount of water. After the child agreed that the two beakers contain the same amount of water, he would pour the water from one of the beakers into a much taller and thinner beaker (see Figure 11.7). He then asked the child whether the two differently shaped beakers still contained the same amount of water. Confronted with a problem like this, children in the preoperational period generally say "no." They typically focus on the higher water line in the taller beaker and insist that there is more water in the slender beaker. They have not

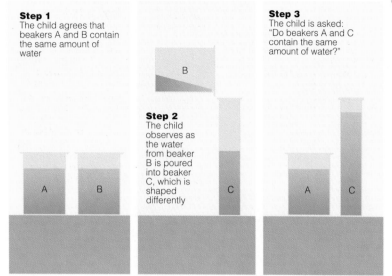

Step 1
The child agrees that beakers A and B contain the same amount of water

Step 2
The child observes as the water from beaker B is poured into beaker C, which is shaped differently

Step 3
The child is asked: "Do beakers A and C contain the same amount of water?"

Figure 11.7 Piaget's conservation task. After watching the transformation shown, a preoperational child will usually answer that the taller beaker contains more water. In contrast, the child in the concrete operations period tends to respond correctly, recognizing that the amount of water in beaker C remains the same as the amount in A.

yet mastered the principle of **conservation, Piaget's term for the awareness that physical quantities remain constant in spite of changes in their shape or appearance.**

Why are preoperational children unable to solve conservation problems? According to Piaget, this inability to understand conservation is due to some basic flaws in preoperational thinking. Preoperational flaws include centration, irreversibility, and egocentrism.

CENTRATION **Centration is the tendency to focus on just one feature of a problem, thus neglecting other important aspects.** When working on the conservation problem with water, preoperational children tend to concentrate on the height of the water while ignoring the width. They have difficulty focusing on several aspects of a problem at once.

IRREVERSIBILITY **Irreversibility is the inability to envision reversing an action.** Preoperational children can't mentally "undo" something. For instance, in grappling with the conservation of water, they don't think about what would happen if the water were poured back from the tall beaker into the original beaker.

EGOCENTRISM **Egocentrism in thinking is characterized by a limited ability to share another person's viewpoint.** Indeed, preoperational children fail to appreciate that there are points of view other than their own. For instance, if you ask a preoperational girl whether her sister has a sister, she'll probably say no if they are the only two girls in the family. She's unable to view sisterhood from her sister's perspective (this also shows irreversibility).

A notable feature of egocentrism is **animism—**

the belief that all things are living, just like oneself. Thus, youngsters attribute lifelike, human qualities to inanimate objects, asking questions such as, "When does the ocean stop to rest?" or "Why does the wind get so mad?"

As you can see, Piaget emphasized the weaknesses that are apparent in *pre*operational thought. Indeed, this is why he called this stage *pre*operational. The ability to perform **operations—internal transformations, manipulations, and reorganizations of mental structures—** emerges in the next stage.

CONCRETE OPERATIONS PERIOD

The development of mental operations marks the beginning of the *concrete operations period*, which usually lasts from about age 7 to 11. Piaget called this stage *concrete* operations because children can only perform operations on images of tangible objects and actual events.

Among the operations that children master in this stage are reversibility and decentration. *Reversibility* permits a child to mentally undo an action. *Decentration* allows the child to focus on more than one feature of a problem simultaneously. The newfound ability to coordinate several aspects of a problem helps the child to appreciate that there are several ways to look at things; this ability in turn leads to a decline in egocentrism.

As children master concrete operations, they develop a variety of new problem-solving capacities. Let's examine another problem studied by Piaget. Give a preoperational child seven carnations and three daisies. Tell the child the names for the two types of flowers and ask the child to sort them into carnations and daisies. There should be no problem. Ask the child whether there are more carnations or more daisies. Most children will correctly respond that there are more carnations. Now ask the child whether there are more carnations or more flowers. At this point, most preoperational children will stumble, and respond incorrectly that there are more carnations than flowers. Generally, preoperational children can't handle *hierarchical classification* problems that require them to focus simultaneously on two levels of classification. However, the child who has advanced to concrete operations is not as limited by centration and can work successfully with hierarchical classification.

Children in the concrete operations period are also able to grasp the principle of *conservation* as it applies to liquid, mass, number, volume, area, and length (see Figure 11.8). Children master some conservation problems (conservation of number, for instance) earlier than others (such as

Typical tasks used to measure conservation	Typical age of mastery
 **Conservation of number** Two equivalent rows of objects are shown to the child, who agrees that they have the same number of objects One row is lengthened, and the child is asked whether one row has more objects	6-7
 **Conservation of mass** The child acknowledges that two clay balls have equal amounts of clay The experimenter changes the shape of one of the balls and asks the child whether they still contain equal amounts of clay	7-8
Conservation of length The child agrees that two sticks aligned with each other are the same length After moving one stick to the left or right, the experimenter asks the child whether the sticks are of equal length	7-8
 **Conservation of area** Two identical sheets of cardboard have wooden blocks placed on them in identical positions; the child confirms that the same amount of space is left on each piece of cardboard The experimenter scatters the blocks on one piece of cardboard and again asks the child whether the two pieces have the same amount of unoccupied space	8-9

Figure 11.8 The gradual mastery of conservation. Children master Piaget's conservation problem during the concrete operations period, but their mastery is gradual. As outlined here, children usually master the conservation of number at age 6 or 7, but they may not understand the conservation of area until age 8 or 9.

volume). Although this difference in mastery may be due in part to differences in the complexity of the concepts involved, this piecemeal progress also illustrates the very *gradual* nature of cognitive development. Children in the concrete operations period also begin to appreciate the logic of relations. Unlike preoperational children, they can understand that if Sue is younger than Sara and Sara is younger than Sandy, then Sue is younger than Sandy.

FORMAL OPERATIONS PERIOD

The final stage in Piaget's theory is the *formal operations period*, which typically begins around 11 years of age. In this stage, children begin to apply their operations to *abstract* concepts in addition to concrete objects. Indeed, during this stage, youngsters come to *enjoy* the heady contemplation of abstract concepts. Many adolescents spend hours mulling over hypothetical possibilities related to abstractions such as justice, love, and free will.

According to Piaget, youngsters graduate to relatively adult modes of thinking in the formal operations stage. He did *not* mean to suggest that there is no further cognitive development once children reach this stage. However, he believed that after children achieve formal operations, further developments in thinking are changes in *degree* rather than fundamental changes in the *nature* of thinking.

Adolescents in the formal operations period become more *systematic* in their problem-solving efforts. Children in earlier developmental stages tend to attack problems quickly with a trial-and-error approach. In contrast, children who have achieved formal operations are more likely to "think things through." They envision possible courses of action and try to use logic to reason out the likely consequences of each possible solution before they act. Thus, thought processes in the formal operations period can be characterized as abstract, systematic, logical, and reflective.

EVALUATING PIAGET'S THEORY

Jean Piaget made a landmark contribution to our understanding of children in general and their cognitive development in particular. Above all else, he sought answers to new questions. As he acknowledged in a 1970 interview, "It's just that no adult ever had the idea of asking children about conservation. It was so obvious that if you change the shape of an object, the quantity will be conserved. Why ask a child? The novelty lay in asking the question" (Hall, 1987, p. 56). Piaget's daring ideas sparked an explosion of research that continues through today. This research has supported a great many of Piaget's central propositions (Siegler, 1986). In such a far-reaching theory, however, there are bound to be some weak spots. Let's briefly examine some of the criticism of Piaget's theory.

1. In some areas, Piaget may have underestimated children's cognitive development. Some researchers have found evidence that children begin to develop object permanence at a younger age than Piaget thought (Bower, 1982; Harris, 1983). Others have marshaled evidence that preoperational children are not as egocentric as Piaget believed (Flavell et al., 1981), and that they can handle some conservation problems before achieving concrete operations (Field, 1981).
2. Critics have also questioned the generality and finality of the formal operations period. Many adults show little evidence of formal operational reasoning as measured by Piaget; those who do reach formal operations generally achieve this at a later age than Piaget thought (Neimark, 1982). Some theorists also believe that there are higher stages of thinking that go beyond formal operational thought (Commons, Richards, & Kuhn, 1982).
3. Piaget's model suffers from problems that plague most stage theories. Like Erikson, Piaget has little to say about individual differences in development. Also, people often simultaneously display patterns of thinking that are characteristic of several different stages. For instance, even well-educated adults who have clearly achieved formal operations often show decidedly egocentric thought. This "mixing" of stages calls into question the value of organizing development in terms of stages (Flavell, 1982).

Like any theory, Piaget's is not flawless. However, without Piaget's theory to guide research, many crucial questions about cognitive development might not have been confronted until decades later (if at all). Thus, in his critique of Piaget's career and contributions, David Cohen asserts that "Piaget is, without doubt, the great child psychologist of the twentieth century, and really has no competition for this title" (1983, p. 66).

PROGRESS IN INFORMATION PROCESSING

Piaget's ideas continue to be very influential, but in recent years, an information-processing perspective has been used more and more frequently in the study of cognitive development (Klahr & Wallace, 1976; Siegler, 1984). We discussed information-processing models of cognition in Chapters 7 and 8. As you may recall, *information-processing theories* draw an analogy between the mind and the computer; they focus on how we receive, encode, store, organize, retrieve, and use information. Hence, investigators have explored age-related changes in attention, memory, concept formation, and problem solving. The information-processing perspective has proven especially fruitful in accounting for developmental changes in attention and memory.

ATTENTION Attention involves focusing awareness on a narrowed range of stimuli. Preschool children have very short attention spans and are easily distracted. At age 2 or 3, most children have a hard time focusing on a task for more than a few minutes (Wellman, Ritter, & Flavell, 1975). As children grow older, their attention spans lengthen and they acquire more conscious control over what they pay attention to (Odom, 1978). Throughout childhood, progress also occurs in youngsters' ability to focus their attention *selectively*. Between the ages of 7 and 13, children are still improving in their ability to filter out irrelevant input (Miller & Weiss, 1981). For example, they gradually become more adept at focusing on a story being read to them while ignoring the noise in the background and other activity in the room.

CONCEPT CHECK 11.1
Recognizing Piaget's Stages

Check your understanding of Piaget's theory by indicating the stage of cognitive development illustrated by each of the examples below. For each scenario, fill in the letter for the appropriate stage in the space on the left. The answers are in Appendix A.

a. Sensorimotor period
b. Preoperational period
c. Concrete operations period
d. Formal operations period

_____ 1. Upon seeing a glass lying on its side, Sammy says, "Look, the glass is tired. It's taking a nap."
_____ 2. Maria is told that a farmer has nine cows and six horses. The teacher asks: "Does the farmer have more cows or more animals?" She answers, "More animals."
_____ 3. Alice is playing in the living room with a small red ball. The ball rolls under the sofa. She stares for a moment at the place where the ball vanished and then turns her attention to a toy truck sitting in front of her.

MEMORY Memory ability also improves gradually throughout childhood. The key question is *why*. The answer seems to center on the fact that older children acquire deliberate strategies that improve their storage and retrieval of information. What are these strategies? The first to appear is *rehearsal*, which involves repetitively verbalizing or thinking about material. Children start using rehearsal around age 5; most children use it routinely by about age 9 (Kail & Hagen, 1982). Around the age of 9 or 10, some children begin to use *organization* to improve their recall (Paris & Lindauer, 1982). At first, this simply involves grouping things into categories based on similarities. *Elaboration*, which involves building additional associations onto information to be recalled, tends to show up only during adolescence (Pressley, 1982). Thus, an accumulation of new strategies seems to account for much (not all) of children's improvement in active memorization.

The information-processing perspective on cognitive development has added to our understanding of how children progress in their thinking. Like Piaget's theory, the computer analogy has stimulated researchers to ask new questions and explore new issues. Moreover, the application of the information-processing approach to cognitive development has barely begun; its greatest contributions probably lie in the future. However, the influence of Piaget's much older theory will be felt in the next section, which examines moral development.

The Development of Moral Reasoning

In Europe, a woman was near death from cancer. One drug might save her, a form of radium that a druggist in the same town had recently discovered. The druggist was charging $2,000, ten times what the drug cost him to make. The sick woman's husband, Heinz, went to everyone he knew to borrow the money, but he could only get together about half of what it cost. He told the druggist that his wife was dying and asked him to sell it cheaper or let him pay later. But the druggist said, "No." The husband got desperate and broke into the man's store to steal the drug for his wife. Should the husband have done that? Why? (Kohlberg, 1969, p. 379)

What's your answer to Heinz's dilemma? Would you have answered the same way 3 years ago? In the fifth grade? Can you guess what you might have said at age 6?

By asking similar questions and studying subjects' responses, Lawrence Kohlberg (1964, 1976, 1981) has developed a model of *moral development*.

What is morality? That's a terribly complicated question that philosophers have debated for centuries. For our purposes, it will suffice to say that morality involves the ability to discern right from wrong and to behave accordingly.

KOHLBERG'S STAGE THEORY

Kohlberg's model is the most influential of a number of competing theories that attempt to explain how youngsters develop a sense of right and wrong. His work is descended from much earlier work by Jean Piaget (1932). Piaget theorized that moral development is determined by cognitive development. By this he meant that the way we think out moral issues depends on our level of cognitive development. This assumption provided the springboard for Kohlberg's research.

Kohlberg's theory focuses on moral *reasoning* rather than overt *behavior*. This point is best illustrated by describing Kohlberg's method of investigation. He presents his subjects with thorny moral questions such as Heinz's dilemma. Kohlberg asks his subjects what the actor in the dilemma should do, and more importantly, why. It's the *why* that interests Kohlberg. He examines the nature and progression of subjects' moral reasoning.

The result of this work is the stage theory of moral reasoning outlined in Table 11.4. Kohlberg found that people progress through a series of three levels of moral development, each of which can be broken into two sublevels, yielding a total of six stages. Each stage represents a different approach to thinking about right and wrong. Examples of how people reason out Heinz's dilemma in each of Kohlberg's six stages are shown in Table 11.4.

Younger children at the *preconventional level* think in terms of external authority. Acts are wrong because they are punished, or right because they lead to positive consequences. Older children who have reached the *conventional level* of moral reasoning see rules as necessary for maintaining social order. They therefore accept these rules as their own. They "internalize" these rules not to avoid punishment but to be virtuous and to win approval from others. Moral thinking at this stage is relatively inflexible; rules are viewed as absolute guidelines that should be enforced rigidly.

During adolescence, some youngsters move

Amy Carter, the daughter of former President Jimmy Carter, was arrested for her participation in protests of apartheid in South Africa. Her violation of official rules in order to be faithful to her personal ethics illustrates the postconventional level of moral reasoning described by Kohlberg.

Table 11.4 Kohlberg's Levels of Moral Development

KOHLBERG'S LEVELS AND STAGES	DESCRIPTION	EXAMPLE OF CHARACTERISTIC REASONING REGARDING HEINZ'S DILEMMA
Level I. Preconventional morality		
Stage 1: Punishment orientation	Compliance with rules to avoid punishment	"If he steals the drug, he might go to jail." (Punishment is the primary consideration.)
Stage 2: Naive reward orientation	Compliance with rules to get rewards, sharing in order to get returns	"He can steal the drug and save his wife, and he'll be with her when he gets out of jail." (Act is motivated by its hedonistic consequences for the actor.)
Level II. Conventional morality		
Stage 3: Good-boy/good-girl orientation	Conformity to rules that are defined by others' approval/disapproval	"People will understand if you steal the drug to save your wife, but they'll think you're cruel and a coward if you don't." (Reactions of others and the effects of the act on social relationships become important.)
Stage 4: Authority orientation	Rigid conformity to society's rules, law-and-order mentality, avoid censure for rule-breaking	"It is the husband's duty to save his wife even if he feels guilty afterwards for stealing the drug." (Institutions, law, duty, honor, and guilt motivate behavior.)
Level III. Postconventional morality		
Stage 5: Social-contract orientation	More flexible understanding that we obey rules because they are necessary for social order, but the rules could be changed if there were better alternatives	"The husband has a right to the drug even if he can't pay now. If the druggist won't charge it, the government should look after it." (Democratic laws guarantee individual rights; contracts are mutually beneficial.)
Stage 6: Morality of individual principles and conscience	Behavior conforms to internal principles (justice, equality) to avoid self-condemnation, and sometimes may violate society's rules	"Although it is legally wrong to steal, the husband would be morally wrong not to steal to save his wife. A life is more precious than financial gain." (Conscience is individual. Laws are socially useful but not sacrosanct.)

Source: Adapted from Kohlberg, 1969

on to the *postconventional level*, which involves working out a personal code of ethics. Acceptance of rules is less rigid, and moral thinking shows some flexibility. Subjects at the postconventional level allow for the possibility that one might not comply with some of society's rules if they conflict with personal ethics. For example, subjects at this level might applaud a newspaper reporter who goes to jail rather than reveal a source of information who was promised anonymity.

EVALUATING KOHLBERG'S THEORY

How has Kohlberg's theory fared in research? The central ideas have received reasonable support. Youngsters generally do progress through Kohlberg's stages of moral reasoning in the order that he proposed (Carroll & Rest, 1982). Studies also show that progress in moral reasoning is closely tied to cognitive development (Rest & Thoma, 1985). Furthermore, there's a link between level of moral *reasoning* and actual moral *behavior* (Blasi, 1980). For example, Kohlberg (1975) found that when subjects had an opportunity to engage in cheating, youngsters in higher stages of moral reasoning cheated less than youngsters in lower stages. The association between moral rea-

soning and overt behavior is far from perfect, but that's exactly what Kohlberg expected.

Like all influential theorists, Kohlberg has his critics. They have raised the following issues:

1. It's not unusual to find that a person shows signs of several adjacent levels of moral reasoning at a particular point in development (Rest, 1983). For instance, a subject might display a mixture of stage 3, stage 4, and stage 5 reasoning. As we noted in our critique of Piaget, this mixing of stages is a problem for virtually all stage theories. The stage concept is a very useful organizational device, but development is not as orderly and uniform as the idealized descriptions in these theories imply.

2. The relations between age and level of moral reasoning are moderately strong. Representative age trends are shown in Figure 11.9. The trends are in the predicted directions. As children get older, stage 1 and stage 2 reasoning decline, while stage 3 and stage 4 reasoning increase. However, there is great variation in the age at which people reach specific stages. Furthermore, only a small percentage of people ever reach stage 6.

3. There is concern that Kohlberg's theory captures the essence of moral development in males

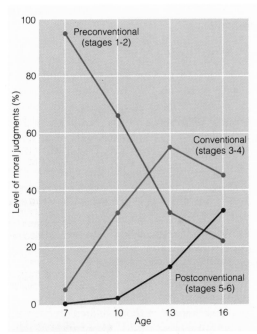

Preconventional
(stages 1-2)

Conventional
(stages 3-4)

Postconventional
(stages 5-6)

Level of moral judgments (%)

Age

Figure 11.9 Age and moral reasoning. The percentages of different types of moral judgments made by subjects at various ages are graphed here (based on Kohlberg, 1963, 1969). As predicted, preconventional reasoning declines as children mature, conventional reasoning increases during middle childhood, and postconventional reasoning begins to emerge during adolescence; but at each age, children display a mixture of different levels of moral reasoning.

better than in females. According to Carol Gilligan (1982), females are socialized to equate "goodness" with self-sacrifice more than are males. Because Kohlberg's model doesn't consider this factor, it may have a built-in bias that leads to underestimates of moral development in female subjects.

Gilligan (1982) believes that females go through a different series of moral stages than males. She describes three stages of moral reasoning in females. The first stage involves a selfish orientation. Decisions about suitable behavior are ruled by one's own needs and desires. Females in the second stage show great concern for the welfare of others. They assume that a good person should make personal sacrifices for the benefit of others. In the third stage, women strive to achieve a balance between concern for their own welfare and concern for the welfare of others.

Moral reasoning is just one of several areas of development in which there appear to be some differences between males and females. You'll see another example in the next section, which is concerned with selected aspects of social development. Our Application will further explore the nature and meaning of gender differences in development and behavior.

Interacting with Others:
Social Development

Chances are that your memories of childhood are dominated by recollections of playing with friends. Your social development began in your home with your family, but it soon extended beyond that sanctuary of support. Your interactions with peers began in your preschool years.

Early social encounters are limited in depth because of younger children's egocentrism. Often, preschoolers who appear to be playing together actually are not. If you watch closely, you'll see that much of their play is *parallel play—side-by-side play that goes on with little shared interaction.* By the time children are brought together in grade school, declining egocentrism and improved communication make for more meaningful social interaction. During the remainder of childhood, most children spend more and more time socializing with peers as their social sphere becomes less centered around their family (Ellis, Rogoff, & Cromer, 1981).

Psychologists have studied many aspects of social development. In sampling from this domain, we'll look at two kinds of social behavior that have been the focus of much research—altruism

---

CONCEPT CHECK 11.2
Analyzing Moral Reasoning

Check your understanding of Kohlberg's theory of moral development by analyzing hypothetical responses to the following moral dilemma.

A midwest biologist has conducted numerous studies demonstrating that simple organisms such as worms and paramecia can learn through conditioning. It occurs to her that perhaps she could condition fertilized human ova to provide a dramatic demonstration that abortions destroy adaptable, living human organisms. This possibility appeals to her, as she is ardently opposed to abortion. However, there is no way to conduct the necessary research on human ova without sacrificing the lives of potential human beings. She desperately wants to conduct the research, but obviously, the sacrifice of human ova is fundamentally incompatible with her belief in the sanctity of human life. What should she do? Why? (Submitted by a student [age 13] to Professor Barbara Banas at Monroe Community College)

In the spaces on the left of each numbered response indicate the level of moral reasoning shown, choosing from the following: (a) preconventional level, (b) conventional level, (c) postconventional level. The answers are in Appendix A.

_____ 1. She should do the research. Although it's wrong to kill, there's a greater good that can be realized through the research.

_____ 2. She shouldn't do the research because people will think that she's a hypocrite and condemn her.

_____ 3. She should do the research because she may become rich and famous as a result.

Preschoolers who seem to be playing together often are not. Much of their play is parallel play; that is, they play side by side but with little genuine interaction.

and aggression. **Altruism is selfless concern for the welfare of others that leads to helping behavior (without any expectation of personal gain). Aggression involves any behavior that is intended to hurt someone, either physically or verbally** (through insults, for instance). These two very different kinds of interpersonal behavior tend to show opposite developmental trends.

PATTERNS OF ALTRUISM AND AGGRESSION

Altruism tends to increase as children grow older, at least through the grade-school years (Rushton, 1980). Interestingly, there's a positive correlation between a child's altruism and level of moral reasoning. Thus, children who are at higher stages of moral development tend to be more helpful and concerned about others than children in lower stages (Underwood & Moore, 1982).

In contrast, aggression generally declines with age, although this generalization has to be qualified carefully because aggression changes in form as children grow older. Younger children display more *instrumental aggression*, which is intended to achieve some goal such as retrieving a toy. Older children display more *hostile aggression*, which is intended solely to hurt another (Hartup, 1974). With increasing age, aggression also tends to become less physical and more verbal.

In spite of these age trends, there are huge differences in altruism and aggression among children of the same age. Some children are much more altruistic or more aggressive than other children. Although Gilligan's theory of moral development suggests that there *may* be gender differences in altruism, the hypothesized differences are not well documented at present. However, there is ample evidence of gender differences in aggression: at all ages, boys tend to be more aggressive than girls.

THE ROOTS OF ALTRUISM AND AGGRESSION

Altruism and aggression both appear to be influenced by (1) genetic predisposition, (2) parental modeling, and (3) portrayals of role models in the mass media.

Your genetic makeup may create a predisposition toward either altruistic or aggressive behavior. Identical twins were found to be much more similar to each other than fraternal twins on measures of both altruism and aggression in a recent *twin study* (Rushton et al., 1986). This finding suggests that heredity influences individual differences in altruism and aggression. How can heredity mold our interpersonal behavior? Investigators aren't sure, but inherited differences in *temperament* could be the bridge between our genes and our social behavior. Aspects of temperament, such as characteristic mood, activity level, and emotional reactivity, may foster a predisposition toward helpful or hurtful behavior.

Through the process of *observational learning*, which we described in Chapter 6, parents can have a great impact on their children's tendencies to be altruistic or aggressive. Parents who are cooperative, helpful, and generous with other adults (including each other) promote altruism in their children (Rushton, 1980). In the same fashion, parents who are belligerent with others and parents who use physical punishment to discipline their children tend to raise more aggressive offspring (Eron, 1982). In regard to both altruism and aggression, the evidence clearly indicates that what parents *do* is more influential than what they *say*. It doesn't do any good for parents to preach the value of altruism if they then refuse to help a neighbor who needs a ride or a relative who needs a babysitter.

Altruism and aggression are also influenced by a child's exposure to role models in the mass media, especially television (Huston & Wright, 1982). Children spend an enormous amount of time watching television. On the positive side, televised portrayals of altruistic behavior have been shown to increase helpfulness and cooperation in children. Unfortunately, the power of television works both ways, and most children are fed far more aggression than altruism in their video diet.

Children's television shows are extremely aggressive, averaging 25 incidents of violence per hour (Gerbner et al., 1980). It has been estimated that the typical child has vicariously witnessed 13,000 television murders by age 16 (Waters & Malamud, 1975)! A number of studies suggest that this extensive exposure to media violence contributes to the development of aggressiveness in some children (Liebert, Sprafkin, & Davidson, 1982). This terribly important issue, which has been the subject of a great deal of research, brings us to our Featured Study for this chapter.

DOES MEDIA VIOLENCE RUB OFF ON CHILDREN?

Earlier research by Leonard Eron and his colleagues showed that there is an association between the amount of violence in a third-grader's television diet and the child's aggressiveness both in the third grade and ten years later at the age of 19 (Eron, 1963; Eron et al., 1972; Lefkowitz et al., 1977). The connection between television violence and aggression was found to be much stronger for males than for females. This study was designed to expand on the earlier research in two ways. First, given that the link between television violence and aggression was already apparent in the third grade, the research team decided to focus on even younger children, beginning in the first grade. Second, given the substantial changes in sex roles in our society since the original research began in 1960, the investigators wanted to take another look at possible gender differences.

Method

Subjects and design. The subjects were 758 grade-school children drawn primarily from the public schools in a socially diversified suburb of Chicago. An "overlapping" longitudinal design was employed over a period of 3 years. Thus, the researchers followed one set of children from the first through the third grade and simultaneously followed another set of children from the third through the fifth grade.

Measures. The two key measures focused on the children's television viewing habits and their level of aggressiveness. The children were asked to in-

dicate (in age-appropriate booklets on colored paper) how often they watched any of 80 television shows that were popular among children. The amount of violence in each of these 80 shows was rated independently by graduate students. The violence ratings for each child's eight favorite shows were added to produce an index of exposure to media violence for each young subject. The children's aggressiveness was measured by obtaining peer ratings from the youngsters' classmates. Every child in each grade-school class that was studied rated the aggressiveness of every other child in the class (on age-appropriate forms that inquired about ten specific types of aggressive acts). The classmates' pooled ratings provided the index of each subject's aggressiveness.

Results

As is usually the case in longitudinal research, the number of subjects declined over time as some children left the school system. Although the sample shrank to 505 children, the loss of subjects created few problems in interpreting the results because the loss was spread evenly across both sexes and all grades. Positive correlations were found between the measures of exposure to media violence and peer-rated aggressiveness in all five grades. The correlations were small (median = .23), but all were statistically significant. In contrast to earlier results, the correlations between television violence and aggressiveness were significant for both boys and girls. Indeed, the correlations were a little stronger for the girls.

Investigators: Leonard D. Eron, L. Rowell Huesmann, Patrick Brice, Paulette Fischer, and Rebecca Mermelstein (University of Illinois at Chicago)

Source: Age trends in the development of aggression, sex typing, and related television habits. *Developmental Psychology, 19*(1) (1983), 71–77.

The effect of television violence on children has been the subject of heated debate since the advent of TV. In the 1960s, research by Leonard Eron and his colleagues suggested that TV violence had more impact on boys than on girls. The Featured Study was designed, in part, to see whether similar gender differences would be found in the 1980s.

Discussion

The results replicate previous findings linking media violence to aggressive behavior in children. The results also suggest that this link may be forged at a very young age, even in the first grade. The roughly similar correlations found for girls and boys suggest that both sexes may be equally subject to the influence of media violence. This is a new finding that may be due to shifting sex roles or to the emergence of aggressive female role models on television, which were rare in the 1960s when the original research was begun.

Comment

This study was featured because it focused on an important social issue in a realistic way. Most studies of media violence have been laboratory experiments that sacrifice realism for the power of experimental control and the ability to draw conclusions about cause and effect. Such experiments are extremely important, but their dependent measures of aggression (such as pressing a button labeled "hurt" or hitting an inflated plastic doll) have often been criticized as unrealistic. In contrast, this study looked at real-world viewing habits and actual everyday aggression—in all their complexity.

Of course, this was a correlational study, and we always have to be cautious in drawing causal conclusions based on correlational data. Theorists have pointed out that a number of possible causal relationships could account for the correlation between high exposure to media violence and high aggressiveness. One possibility is that exposure to media violence causes higher aggressiveness. Another possibility is that high aggressiveness causes an increased interest in violent television shows. Alternatively, a third variable, such as a genetic predisposition to aggressiveness, could cause both elevated aggressiveness and increased interest in media violence.

Standing alone, this study would *not* allow us to conclude that exposure to television violence *causes* an increase in aggressive tendencies. However, the study does not stand alone. It's part of a vast body of research on media violence and aggression that includes a wealth of experimental studies (including one discussed in the next chapter). Viewed as a whole, this research provides convincing evidence that media violence makes a modest but real contribution to causing aggressive behavior in our society.

In summary, a multiplicity of factors shape the development of altruism and aggression. In this section, we highlighted the role of heredity, parental models, and television; but the development of altruism and aggression may also be influenced by cultural ideals and youngsters' physique, moral education, and peer group relations (Parke & Slaby, 1983).

Our social behavior continues to evolve throughout adolescence as peer relations become increasingly important. Next, we'll turn our attention to the transition of adolescence.

CONCEPT CHECK 11.3
Recognizing Links Between Areas of Development

Check your understanding of interrelations among different aspects of development by identifying the connections between areas of development as shown in the figure below.

We discussed various areas of development separately, but development in one area often influences development in another area. In fact, there are intimate relations between all areas of development. The diagram below identifies a few links mentioned in our discussion of the childhood years. The direction of each arrow indicates the *probable* direction of the potential causal relationship.

In the space provided, describe the possible influences indicated by the arrows. To illustrate the nature of the task, the answers for (d) are provided. The remaining answers can be found in Appendix A.

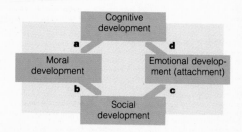

a. _____

b. _____

c. _____

d. Emotional deprivation may cause slower cognitive development. Securely attached infants display more curiosity.

THE TRANSITION OF ADOLESCENCE

Adolescence is a bridge between childhood and adulthood. During this time, we continue to make significant progress in cognitive, moral, and social development. However, the most dynamic areas of development involve physical changes and related transitions in emotional and personality development.

Puberty and the Growth Spurt

Puberty is the period of early adolescence marked by rapid physical growth and the development of sexual (reproductive) maturity. Puberty is brought on by hormonal changes that lead to accelerated physical growth and sexual differentiation (Chumlea, 1982), as outlined in Figure 11.10. Youngsters experience sudden increases in height and weight, as well as shifts in body proportions. For example, males tend to become more broad shouldered and females develop wider hips. The growth spurt around puberty is often unevenly distributed across the various parts of the body and can result in a temporary increase in clumsiness.

As puberty continues, adolescents become capable of reproduction. Puberty is also marked by the emergence of *secondary sex characteristics—physical features that are associated with gender but that are not directly involved in reproduction*. Adolescent females closely monitor the development of their breasts; males search for evidence of facial hair and a voice change. Females experience a landmark transition, *menarche*, which is the first occurrence of menstruation.

Youngsters vary somewhat in the age at which they experience the onset of puberty. The average age of onset is around 11 for girls and 13 for boys. Those who mature particularly early or particularly late often feel uneasy about it. As you may recall, most adolescents aren't fond of looking different from others physically. Girls who mature early and boys who mature late seem to feel especially awkward about their looks (Siegel, 1982).

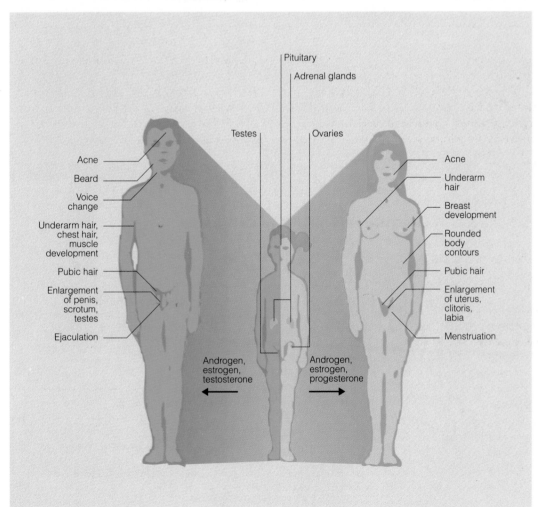

Acne
Beard
Voice change
Underarm hair, chest hair, muscle development
Pubic hair
Enlargement of penis, scrotum, testes
Ejaculation

Pituitary
Adrenal glands
Testes
Ovaries

Acne
Underarm hair
Breast development
Rounded body contours
Pubic hair
Enlargement of uterus, clitoris, labia
Menstruation

Androgen, estrogen, testosterone

Androgen, estrogen, progesterone

Figure 11.10 Physical development at puberty. Hormonal changes during puberty lead not only to a growth spurt but also to the development of secondary sexual characteristics. The pituitary gland sends signals to the adrenal glands and gonads (ovaries and testes), which secrete hormones responsible for various physical changes that differentiate males and females.

409

Figure 11.11 Adolescent suicide. (**a**) The suicide rate for adolescents and young adults (15–24 years old) has increased in recent decades far more than the suicide rate for the population as a whole. (**b**) Nonetheless, suicide rates remain lower for adolescents than for adults. (**c**) One study (Hawton et al., 1982) of the problems that precipitate suicide attempts among adolescents found that social difficulties are often a factor. [Data in (**a**) and (**b**) from the National Center for Health Statistics]

Late-maturing boys tend to feel anxious, inferior, and socially inadequate in comparison to their early-maturing counterparts. Girls who mature early often feel self-conscious.

The consequences of maturing early or late may carry on into adulthood. In one influential study, Mary Cover Jones (1965) found that males who matured late tended to display less leadership and have more feelings of inferiority than males who matured early—even after they reached their 30s. Many of the personality differences between early- and late-maturing boys that were seen during adolescence eventually disappeared during the adult years, but a few of the differences lingered on. Once again, we see that development usually is characterized by both continuity and change.

Time of Turmoil? Adolescent Suicide

Back around the turn of the century, G. Stanley Hall (1904), one of psychology's great pioneers (see Chapter 1), proposed that the adolescent years are characterized by convulsive instability and disturbing inner turmoil. Hall attributed this turmoil to adolescents' erratic physical changes and resultant confusion about self-image. Over the decades, a host of theorists have agreed with Hall's view of adolescence as a stormy period.

The recent surge in *adolescent suicide* would seem to support the idea that adolescence is a time marked by turmoil, but the figures can be interpreted in different ways. On the one hand, suicide rates among adolescents *have* risen alarmingly in recent decades. This is apparent in Figure 11.11a, which shows a 137% increase in suicide among young people aged 15–24 between 1960 and 1982—a period during which suicide rates for the population as a whole increased only slightly. On the other hand, even with this steep increase, the suicide rate for adolescents is low in comparison to the rates for older age groups. Figure 11.11b plots suicide rates as a function of age. The figure reveals that the incidence of suicide in the 15–19 age group is lower than in any older age group and only about half that of the 20–24 age group.

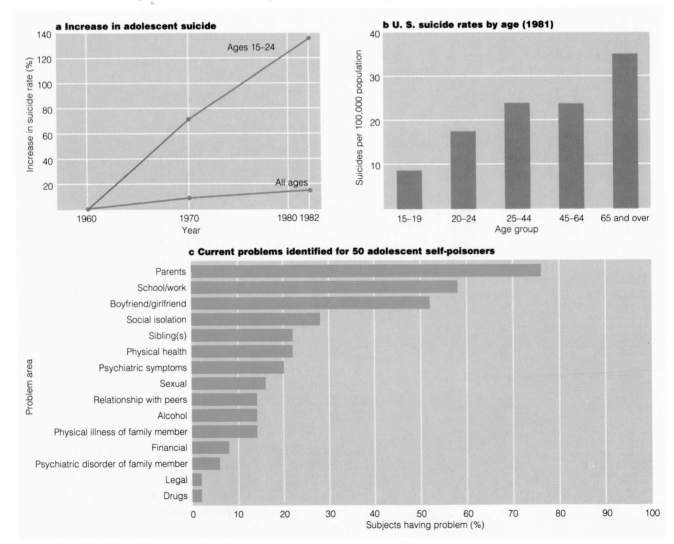

Actually, the suicide crisis among teenagers involves *attempted* suicide more than *completed* suicide. It's estimated that when all age groups are lumped together, suicide attempts outnumber actual suicidal deaths by a ratio of about 8:1 (Cross & Hirschfeld, 1986). However, this ratio of attempted to completed suicides is much higher among adolescents than for any other age group. It's hard to obtain accurate figures on suicide attempts because many attempts are covered up, but studies estimate that the ratio of attempted to completed suicides among adolescents may be 100:1 and possibly even higher (Sheras, 1983).

Thus, David Curran (1987) concludes that among adolescents "attempted suicide has become a phenomenon of truly epidemic proportions" (p. 14). According to Curran, suicide attempts by adolescents tend to be a "communicative gesture designed to elicit caring" (p. 12). Put another way, they are desperate cries for attention, help, and support.

What drives an adolescent to such a dramatic but dangerous gesture? Research by Jacobs (1971) suggests that the "typical" suicidal adolescent has a long history of stress and personal problems extending from childhood. Unfortunately, for some teenagers these problems—conflicts with parents, difficulties in school, loneliness (see Figure 11.11c)—escalate during adolescence. As their efforts to cope with these problems fail, many teenagers rebel against parental and school authority, withdraw from social relations, and make dramatic gestures such as running away from home. These actions often lead to progressive social isolation.

When the individual is thus isolated, a pressing problem with great emotional impact may precipitate an attempted suicide. The precipitating problem—a lousy grade in school, not being allowed to go somewhere or buy something special, a spat with a boyfriend or girlfriend—may appear trivial to an objective observer. But the seemingly trivial problem may serve as the final thread in a tapestry of frustration and distress.

Returning to our original question, does the weight of evidence support the idea that adolescence is usually a period of turmoil and turbulence? Overall, the consensus of the experts appears to be that it is not. The increase in adolescent suicide is a disturbing social tragedy that requires attention from parents, schools, and the helping professions (see the Chapter 14 Application for a discussion of suicide prevention). But even with the recent increases in suicidal behavior, fewer than 1% of adolescents attempt suicide.

What about the remaining 99% of the adolescent population? Research suggests that most teenagers navigate through adolescence without any more turmoil than one is likely to encounter in other periods of life. In one widely cited study of adolescent boys, a distinct minority (22%) went through a turbulent, crisis-dominated adolescence (Offer & Offer, 1975). Basing her conclusion on her extensive studies of adolescents, Anne Petersen (1987) aserts, "the adolescent's journey toward adulthood is inherently marked by change and upheaval but need not be fraught with chaos or deep pain" (p. 34).

Although turbulence and turmoil are not *universal* features of adolescence, this *is* a period during which challenging adaptations have to be made. In particular, most adolescents struggle to some extent in their effort to achieve a sound sense of identity.

The Search for Identity

Erik Erikson was especially interested in personality development during adolescence, which is the fifth of the eight major life stages he describes. The psychosocial crisis during this stage pits *identity* against *confusion* as potential outcomes. According to Erikson (1968), the premiere challenge of adolescence is the struggle to form a clear sense of identity. This involves working out a stable concept of oneself as a unique individual and embracing an ideology or system of values that provides a sense of direction. Erikson asserts that adolescents grapple with questions such as "Who am I, and where am I going in life?"

Erikson recognizes that the process of identity formation begins before adolescence and often extends beyond it, as his own life illustrates (Coles, 1970; Roazen, 1976). Erikson's mother, who was Jewish, was abandoned by his Danish father before his birth in 1902 in Germany. Within a few years, his mother married a Jewish doctor and the two of them raised Erik in the Jewish faith as Erik Homburger. Erik was viewed as a Jew by his gentile schoolmates, but he was viewed as a gentile at his temple because of his decidedly Scandinavian appearance. Thus, Erikson struggled with identity confusion early in life.

During adolescence Erikson began to resist family pressures to study medicine. Instead, he wandered about Europe until he was 25, trying to "find himself" as an artist. His interest in psychoanalysis was sparked by an introduction to Sigmund Freud's youngest daughter, Anna, a pioneer of child psychoanalysis. After his psychoanalytic training, he moved to the United States; when he became a naturalized citizen in 1939, he changed his surname from Homburger to Erikson. Clearly, Erikson was struggling with the question of "Who am I?" well into adulthood. Small wonder, then, that he focused a great deal of attention on identity formation.

Although the struggle for a sense of identity neither begins nor ends in adolescence, it does tend to be especially intense during this period. Why? For many reasons, including the following: (1) rapid physical changes stimulate thought about self-image, (2) changes in cognitive processes (in Piaget's terminology, the arrival of formal operations) promote personal introspection, and (3) decisions about vocational directions require self-contemplation. One influential study (Coleman, Herzberg, & Morris, 1977) suggests that the crucial question is not "Who am I?" as much as "Who will I become?" Thus, adolescents are understandably preoccupied with concerns about their future.

Adolescents grapple with identity formation in a variety of ways. Descriptions of some of the more common patterns follow. An individual may get locked into one of these patterns or go through several of them during different phases (Marcia, 1966, 1980).

• *Foreclosure* involves a premature commitment to visions, values, and roles prescribed by one's parents. This path allows a person to circumvent much of the "struggle" for an identity, but it may backfire and cause problems later.

• A *moratorium* involves delaying commitment for a while to experiment with alternative ideologies and careers. Such experimentation can be valuable. Unfortunately, some people remain indefinitely in what should be a temporary phase.

• *Identity diffusion* is a state of rudderless apathy. Some people simply refuse to confront the challenge of charting a life course and committing to an ideology. Although this stance allows them to evade the struggle, their lack of direction can become problematic.

• *Identity achievement* involves arriving at a sense of self and direction after some consideration of alternative possibilities. Commitments have the strength of some conviction, although they're not absolutely irrevocable.

Erikson and many other theorists believe that adequate identity formation is a cornerstone of sound psychological health. Identity confusion can interfere with important developmental transitions that should happen during the adult years, as you'll see in the next section, which explores developmental trends during adulthood.

THE EXPANSE OF ADULTHOOD

Prior to the 1970s, psychologists showed relatively little interest in adult development. It was widely assumed that developmental processes slowed to a crawl as people moved into adulthood. However, when researchers began to devote more attention to adult development, they discovered that the traditional view was only half right. They found a good deal of stability, as expected, but they also found a good deal of change.

The pace of development *does* taper off in the adult years, but everyone continues to develop, and many people go through major transitions. Examples of profound transitions in adulthood are commonplace. At mid-life, Jerry Rubin went from an outraged, radical, political activist to a subdued, conventional, Wall Street businessman. Over a period of 40 years, Claire Booth Luce went through a remarkable series of different careers as a magazine editor, newspaper columnist, novelist, playwright, congresswoman, and U.S. ambassador. The distinguished graphic artist, Erté, embarked on his very successful career in sculpture at the age of 87!

Personality Development

The stories of Jerry Rubin, Claire Booth Luce, and Erté show that one's personality can continue to evolve throughout life. But are their stories typical? How stable is personality over the life span?

THE STABILITY QUESTION
Is a grouchy 20-year-old going to be a grouchy 40-year old and a grouchy 65-year-old? Psychologists have engaged in spirited debate about the stability of personality during adulthood. After tracking subjects through adulthood, many researchers have been impressed by the amount of change observed. Roger Gould (1975) studied two samples of men and women and concluded that "the evolution of a personality continues through the fifth decade of life." In a study following women from their college years through their 40s, Helson and Moane (1987) found that "personality does change from youth to middle age in consistent and often predictable ways."

Major transitions in adulthood are common, as illustrated by the life of one-time radical Jerry Rubin.

In contrast, many other researchers have been struck by how much persistence and durability they have found in personality. The general conclusion, emerging from several longitudinal studies based on large samples and objective assessments of personality, was that personality tends to be quite stable over periods of 20 to 40 years (Block, 1981; Costa & McCrae, 1980; Stevens & Truss, 1985). These studies found that personality in early adulthood was an excellent predictor of personality right through to late adulthood. Paul Costa, one of the psychologists involved in this research, maintains that, "the assertive 19-year-old is the assertive 40-year-old is the assertive 80-year-old" (Rubin, 1981, p. 20).

How do we reconcile these contradictory conclusions? Perhaps it's best to split the difference. This appears to be a debate in which researchers are essentially looking at the same findings but from different perspectives, so that some conclude that "the glass is half full," and others conclude that "it's half empty." In his discussion of this controversy, Zick Rubin (1981) notes, "when pressed, people on both sides of the debate agree that personality is characterized by *both* stability and change" (p. 24).

ERIKSON'S VIEW OF ADULTHOOD

Insofar as personality changes, Erik Erikson's (1963) theory offers some clues about the nature of changes we can expect. In his eight-stage model of development over the life span, Erikson divided adulthood into three stages, each with a specific psychosocial crisis that must be resolved (see Table 11.2):

- *Intimacy versus isolation.* In early adulthood, the psychosocial crisis centers on whether one can develop the capacity to share intimacy with others. Successful resolution of this crisis should promote empathy and openness, rather than manipulativeness and social isolation.
- *Generativity versus self-absorption.* In middle adulthood, the key challenge is to acquire a genuine concern for the welfare of future generations, which results in providing unselfish guidance to younger people. Self-absorption is characterized by self-indulgent concerns with meeting one's own needs and desires.
- *Integrity versus despair.* During the aging years, the challenge is to avoid the tendency to dwell on the mistakes of the past and on one's imminent death. The crisis involves finding meaning and satisfaction in one's life, rather than wallowing in bitterness and resentment.

Erikson's theory paved the way for a flurry of research on stages of adult development in the 1970s. In the next section, we'll look at two newer theories that have proven influential.

Stages of Adult Development: Gould and Levinson

Two independent studies of adult development attracted an enormous amount of attention beginning in the late 1970s. These two studies were summarized in a pair of widely read books: *Transformations* by Roger Gould (1978) and *The Seasons of a Man's Life* by Daniel Levinson and colleagues (1978). Both Gould and Levinson concluded that adults progress through a series of predictable stages. They analyzed the transitions of early and middle adulthood in great detail. Levinson, for instance, broke the adult years into the stages diagrammed in Figure 11.12. Gould and Levinson's findings were not identical, but they did include many similarities. Their descriptions focus on a mixture of personality, social, and vocational development. In this section, we'll review their findings and highlight some points of agreement.

EARLY ADULTHOOD

Both Gould and Levinson emphasize that the key transition in one's late teens and early 20s is the movement out from the safe shelter of the family. This transition requires confronting insecurity about the future as young people attempt to achieve psychological independence from their parents and to master the practical demands involved in learning to live on their own. According to Levinson, it's during this phase that a young adult begins to shape a "Dream"—a vision of what he or she would like to accomplish as an adult. Initially, this aspect of identity may be

Figure 11.12 Levinson's stages of adult development. According to Levinson, adults progress through predictable stages of development, just as children do. Levinson believes that phases of relative stability (shown in solid colors) alternate with transitional phases (shown in blended colors) marked by turmoil and self-examination.

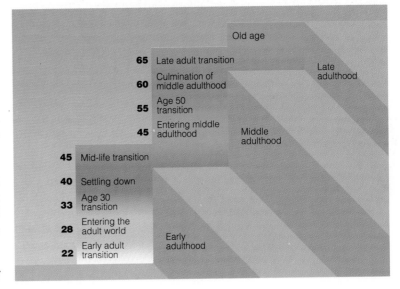

vague and unrealistic. However, as young adults move through their 20s, they typically add definition, detail, and some realism to this vision of the future.

The remainder of the 20s is typically devoted to completing the transition into the adult world. This tends to be a relatively stable phase, as tentative decisions regarding marriage, family, and career are converted into deeper commitments. According to Levinson, the key conflict at this time is between the urge to continue *exploring* various options and the desire to make firm *commitments* to vocations and intimate relationships.

Levinson believes that a very special relationship is often formed during this phase. This is the relationship with a *mentor*—an older, more experienced person who serves as a teacher, advisor, role model, and sponsor. Usually, the mentoring relationship emerges in a work setting with a senior colleague and lasts about 2 to 10 years.

Around the age of 30, give or take a few years, many of both Gould's and Levinson's subjects exhibited signs of increased inner turmoil. Levinson estimated that over 60% of his subjects experienced a "crisis" around this time. These crises centered on doubts about the commitments made in the previous stage. Levinson found that during their 30s, many of his subjects broke away from the people who had been their mentors.

MIDDLE ADULTHOOD

A major landmark of adult development is the mid-life transitional period, which occurs in the vicinity of age 40. This transition is often characterized by reappraisal of one's life and some emotional turbulence. Most of the subjects in Levinson's study had not fulfilled their Dream, and had to rework their expectations at this time. Even many of those who *had* fulfilled their Dream experienced a crisis as they realized that success does not arrest the inevitable process of aging. Gould reports that many people are forced to confront their mortality at this time as their parents, colleagues, or friends die. Gould also emphasizes that during this period many people feel pressed by time. They hear the clock ticking loudly as they work to accomplish their goals in life.

The instability of the mid-life transition tends to be followed by a period of relative calm as people move through their mid and late 40s. Although most people are not entirely satisfied with their lives at this point, Gould notes that they begin to accept their fate with less resistance. Levinson found a tendency to shift some energy away from career concerns in favor of family concerns during this period.

Gould suggests that the 50s are a period of "mellowing," as people continue to become more accepting of their past. Levinson makes similar projections, although he also theorizes that people who don't have a mid-life crisis around age 40 may have a delayed transitional crisis around age 50.

EVALUATING GOULD AND LEVINSON

Although Gould's and Levinson's theories have achieved great popularity, both theories have notable limitations. Their "ages and stages" approach to understanding adult development has been criticized on the following grounds:

1. Gould and Levinson have created an appealing model of *typical* development, but they have little to say about *atypical* development. Like other stage theorists, they ignore the great individual differences that exist among people. Adult development is not as orderly and predictable as they suggest. For instance, both imply that a mid-life crisis is inevitable, but other studies show that *some* people sail through the mid-life period with ease (Livson, 1976; Vaillant, 1977).

2. Both theories describe the development of mainly middle- and upper-class males born in a particular historical period—just before or during the Depression of the 1930s. What these people went through may not be what their children will go through; today's children are evolving in a very different world. In particular, developmental patterns for women seem likely to change in light of alterations in sex roles in the last 2 decades.

As an alternative to the ages-and-stages approach to adult development, many psychologists have simply set out to identify developmental trends across the expanse of adulthood. We'll summarize some of these trends on the following pages.

Aging and Physical Changes

It's readily apparent that we experience many physical changes as we progress through adulthood. In both sexes, hair tends to thin out and become gray, and many males confront receding hairlines and baldness. To the dismay of many, the proportion of body fat tends to increase with age. Overall, weight tends to increase in most adults through the mid 50s, when a very gradual decline may begin. These changes have little functional significance, but in our youth-oriented society, they often lead people to view themselves as less attractive.

The number of active neurons in the brain declines steadily during adulthood. Although the rate of loss is hard to measure, *estimates* of this loss range as high as 100,000 brain cells *per day* after age 30! As startling as these losses may seem, they apparently are "a drop in the bucket." As we noted in Chapter 3, estimates of the number of neurons in our nervous system run as high as *180 billion*. There is no clear evidence that the normal loss of brain cells has any functional significance (Larue & Jarvik, 1982). It doesn't appear to contribute to **senility, which is an abnormal deterioration in mental faculties seen in about 5% of people over 65**.

In the sensory domain, the key developmental changes occur in vision and hearing. The proportion of people with 20/20 visual acuity declines with age. Farsightedness, difficulty adapting to darkness, and poor recovery from glare are common among older people (Kline & Schieber, 1985). Noticeable hearing losses requiring corrective treatment show up in about one-third of older adults, usually after age 50. These sensory losses could have functional significance, but in our modern society we can usually compensate for them with glasses and hearing aids.

There also are age-related changes in hormonal functioning during adulthood. Among women, these changes lead to *menopause*. This ending of menstrual periods, accompanied by a loss of fertility, typically occurs between the ages of 47 and 51. Women's reactions to menopause vary greatly. Some women experience psychological distress, but emotional problems appear to be less common than widely believed (Weg, 1978). Although people sometimes talk about "male menopause," men don't really go through the equivalent of menopause. Middle-aged males experience hormonal changes, but they're very gradual.

The hormonal changes experienced by men and women don't appear to be the chief cause of the decline in sexual activity typically seen during the later years (Solnick & Corby, 1983). Declining sexual activity seems to be due primarily to the influence of age role definitions suggesting that older people shouldn't be very interested in sex. The vast majority of older adults remain capable of rewarding sexual encounters, although arousal tends to become slower and less intense. Married couples who remain sexually active in old age generally are those who had a particularly good sexual relationship when they were younger (Pfeiffer & Davis, 1972). This is yet another example of continuity in human development across the life span.

Aging and Cognitive Changes

Mental abilities and memory are relatively stable throughout most of adulthood. Decreases in the efficiency of long-term memory start to show up in some people after the age of 55, but they tend to be small (Walsh, 1983). The memory lapses commonly associated with old age may often be due to a lack of interest rather than memory failure per se (Schaie & Geiwitz, 1982).

In the cognitive domain, age seems to take its toll on *speed* first. Many studies indicate that one's *speed* in learning, solving problems, retrieving memories, and processing information tends to decline with age (Birren, Woods, & Williams, 1980). This decline in mental speed may begin in middle adulthood, and it appears to be very gradual. Although mental speed may decrease, problem-solving ability remains fairly stable until late in life.

Although there clearly are some decreases in mental efficiency after middle adulthood, many people remain capable of great intellectual accomplishment well into their later years. Agatha Christie was still grinding out mysteries in her 80s, and Andrés Segovia continued to give concerts in his 90s. A study by Dennis (1966) tracked the scholarly, scientific, and artistic productivity of 738 men who lived to the age of at least 79. Figure 11.13 plots the percentage of professional works completed by these men in their 20s, 30s, 40s, 50s, 60s, and 70s. As you see in the graph,

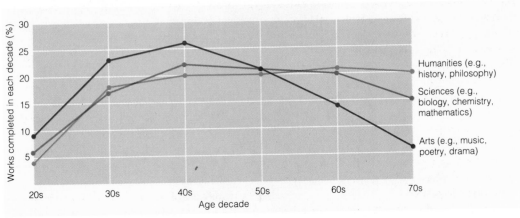

Figure 11.13 Professional productivity over the life span. Dennis (1966) compiled the percentage of professional works completed in each decade of life by 738 men who lived to be at least 79 years old. Productivity peaked in the 40s decade, but professional output remained strong through the 60s decade and, for the humanities and sciences, even into the 70s decade.

AN OVERVIEW OF HUMAN DEVELOPMENT

Stage of development	Infancy (birth–2)	

Physical and sensorimotor development

Rapid brain growth; 75% of adult brain weight attained by age 2

Ability to localize sounds apparent at birth; ability to recognize parent's voice within first week

Visual acuity progresses from 20:500 at birth to 20:40 by age 2; depth perception present by 6 months or earlier

Landmarks in motor development: infants sit without support around 6 months, walk around 12–14 months, run freely around 2 years

Major stage theories	Piaget	Sensorimotor	
	Kohlberg	Premoral	
	Erikson	Trust vs. distrust	Autonomy vs. shame
	Freud	Oral	Anal

Cognitive development

Gradual development of object permanence; by age 2, infants understand that absent objects continue to exist

Shows orienting response (pupils dilate, head turns) and attention to new stimulus; habituation (reduced orienting response) to repeated stimulus

Babbling "drifts" toward use of phonemes in native language at 7–11 months

First word used around age 1; holophrases (one-word "sentences") used around 18 months; frequent overextensions (words applied too broadly)

Social and personality development

Temperamental individuality established by 2–3 months; infants tend to be easy, difficult, or slow to warm up

Attachment to caregiver(s) usually evident around 6–8 months; secure attachment facilitates exploration

"Stranger anxiety" often appears around 6–7 months; separation anxiety common at 7–12 months

Information compiled by Barbara Hansen Lemme, College of DuPage

Early childhood
(2–6)

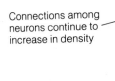
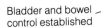

Connections among neurons continue to increase in density

Visual acuity reaches 20:20 around 4 years

Bladder and bowel control established

Hand preference usually solidified by 3–4 years; coordination improves; children learn to dress themselves

Middle childhood
(6–12)

In girls, growth spurt begins around age 10½, bringing dramatic increases in height and weight

Increased level of pituitary activity and sex hormones

In girls, puberty begins around age 12; menstruation starts

Girls' secondary sexual characteristics (such as breast development and widening hips) begin to emerge

Preoperational	Concrete operations
Preconventional	Conventional
Initiative vs. guilt	Industry vs. inferiority
Phallic	Latency

Development of symbolic thought (use of symbols to represent objects and activities); thought marked by egocentrism (limited ability to view world from another's perspective)

Thought marked by centration (inability to focus on more than one aspect of a problem at a time) and irreversibility (inability to mentally undo an action)

Telegraphic speech (omitting nonessential words) at 2–3 years; well-developed syntax by age 5; dramatic increase in vocabulary

Short-term memory capacity increases from two items at age 2 to five items around age 6–7; attention span improves

Gradual mastery of conservation (understanding that physical quantities can remain constant in spite of transformations in shape)

Development of decentration (ability to focus on more than one feature of a problem at a time) and reversibility (ability to mentally undo an action)

Metalinguistic awareness (ability to reflect on use of language) leads to play with language, use of puns, riddles, metaphors

Long-term memory improves with increasing use of encoding strategies of rehearsal and organization

Realization that gender does not change; child begins to learn gender roles and form gender identity; social behavior influenced by observational learning, resulting in imitation

Progression from parallel (side-by-side, noninteractive) play to cooperative play

Social world extended beyond family; first friendships formed

Great increase in social skills, improved understanding of others' feelings; social world dominated by same-sex peer relationships

Role-taking skills emerge; fantasy is basis for thoughts about vocations and jobs

Altruism tends to increase, aggression tends to decrease; aggression tends to become verbal more than physical, hostile more than instrumental

417

Adolescence
(12–20)

Young adulthood
(20–40)

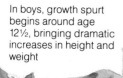

In boys, growth spurt begins around age 12½, bringing dramatic increases in height and weight

Increased level of pituitary activity and sex hormones

In boys, puberty begins around age 14; boys become capable of ejaculation

Boys' secondary sexual characteristics (such as voice change and growth of facial hair) begin to emerge

Reaction time and muscular strength peak in early to mid-20s

External signs of aging begin to show in 30s; skin loses elasticity; hair is thinner, more likely to be gray

Maximum functioning of all body systems, including senses, attained; slow decline begins in 20s

Lowered metabolic rate contributes to increased body fat relative to muscle; gain in weight common

Formal operations

Postconventional (if attained)

Identity vs. confusion

Intimacy vs. isolation

Genital

Deductive reasoning improves; problem solving becomes more systematic, with alternative possibilities considered before solution is selected

Thought becomes more abstract and reflective; development of ability to mentally manipulate abstract concepts as well as concrete objects

Idealistic contemplation of hypotheticals, "what could be"

Long-term memory continues to improve as elaboration is added to encoding strategies

Intellectual abilities and speed of information processing are relatively stable

Greater emphasis on application, rather than acquisition, of knowledge

Some evidence of trend toward dialectical thought (ideas stimulate opposing ideas), leading to more contemplation of contradictions, pros and cons

Increased interactions with opposite-sex peers; dating begins

Attention devoted to identity formation, questions such as "Who am I?" and "What do I want out of life?"

Realistic considerations about abilities and training requirements become more influential in thoughts about vocations and jobs

Energies focused on intimate relationships, learning to live with marriage partner, starting a family, managing a home

Trial period for occupational choices followed by stabilization of vocational commitment; emphasis on self-reliance, becoming one's own person

For many, development of close relationship with mentor (older person who serves as role model, adviser, and teacher)

Middle adulthood
(40–65)

Changes in vision; increased farsightedness and difficulty recovering from glare; slower dark adaptation

The number of active brain cells declines, but the significance of this neural loss is unclear

In women, menopause occurs around age 50; in both sexes, sexual activity declines, although capacity for arousal changes only slightly

Reduced sensitivity to high-frequency sounds, especially in males after age 55

Late adulthood
(65 and older)

Height decreases slightly because of changes in vertebral column; decline in weight also common

Noticeable decrease in sensitivity of vision, hearing, and taste

Increase in chronic diseases, especially heart disease, cancer, and stroke

Rate of aging is highly individualized

Generativity vs. self-absorption

Integrity vs. despair

Some evidence for trend toward improved judgment or "wisdom" based on accumulation of life experience

Effectiveness of retrieval from long-term memory begins slow decline, usually not noticeable until after age 55

Gradual decline in speed of learning, problem solving, and information processing

In spite of decreased speed in cognitive processes, intellectual productivity and problem-solving skills usually remain stable

Continued gradual decline in cognitive speed and effectiveness of long-term memory

Intellectual productivity depends on psychological factors, such as health and lifestyle; many people in 60s and 70s remain quite productive

Terminal drop: marked decrease in intellectual performance in the 2–3 years preceding death

Decision making tends to become more cautious

Mid-life transition around age 40 leads to reflection, increased awareness of mortality and passage of time; may or may not be personal crisis

"Sandwich generation" caught between needs of aging parents and children reaching adulthood

Career development peaks; some tendency to shift energy from career concerns to family concerns

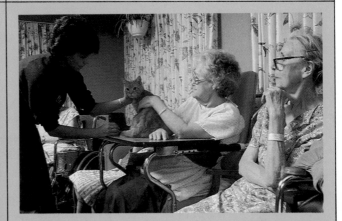

Physical changes associated with aging require adjustments that affect life satisfaction

Marital satisfaction often increases, but eventually death of spouse presents coping challenge

Living arrangements are a significant determinant of satisfaction as 60–90% of time is spent at home

productivity peaked in the 40s decade, but the subsequent decreases generally were small. Many of these men remained very productive in their 70s.

Aging and Social Changes

Prominent theories about late adulthood suggest that a process of *social disengagement* often takes place (Kahana, 1982). According to this notion, older people gradually turn inward and withdraw psychologically and socially from the world around them. Supposedly, they reduce their emotional investment in current events and their actual interactions with other people as well.

There is evidence of a trend toward disengagement during late adulthood, but this generalization has to be qualified carefully. Palmore (1975) notes that (1) disengagement is not inevitable, (2) disengagement that does occur may be imposed on older people by society rather than being a matter of choice, and (3) elderly people who maintain a *high* level of activity tend to be more satisfied than those who do not. It's possible that, in general, development may flow in the direction of disengagement; but a portion of the elderly with certain values and personality characteristics resist this undercurrent successfully.

PUTTING IT IN PERSPECTIVE

Most of our six integrative themes surfaced to some degree in our coverage of human development. We saw theoretical diversity (theme 2) in the debates about the basis for attachment, the progression of moral reasoning, and the stages of adult development. We saw that research in developmental psychology leaves its mark on society (theme 3), affecting things like child-care practices and the controversy about televised violence. We saw multifactorial causation of behavior (theme 4) in our examination of the development of temperament, attachment, altruism, and aggression. But above all else, we saw how heredity and environment jointly mold behavior (theme 5); we'll concentrate on this theme in our discussion.

We've encountered the dual influence of heredity and environment before, but this theme is rich in complexity, and each chapter draws out different aspects and implications. In previous chapters, we saw that heredity and environment are both important determinants of behavior. However, our discussion of development amplified the point that genetics and experience work *interactively* to shape behavior. As Thomas, Chess, and Birch put it, "The paramount conclusion from our studies is that the debate over the relative importance of nature and nurture only confuses the issue. What is important is the interaction between the two" (1970, p. 107).

What does it mean to say that heredity and environment interact? To put it metaphorically, it means that they're entangled in the dance of development from the very beginning. To quote Piaget, "It is virtually impossible to draw a clear line between innate and acquired behavior patterns" (Hall, 1987, p. 62). During prenatal development, environmental factors such as maternal nutrition, illness, and drug use can affect the unfolding of a child's genetic blueprint even before birth exposes the newborn to the outside world.

In the language of science, an interaction means that the effects of one variable depend on the effects of another. In other words, heredity and environment do not operate independently. Children with "difficult" temperaments will elicit different reactions from different parents, depending on the parents' personalities and expectations. Likewise, a particular pair of parents will affect different children in different ways, depending on the inborn characteristics of the children. There's a mutual interplay, or feedback loop, between biological and environmental factors. For instance, a temperamentally difficult child may elicit negative reactions from parents, which serve to make the child more difficult, which evokes more negative reactions. If this child develops into an ornery 11-year-old, which do we blame—genetics or experience? Clearly, this outcome is due to their reciprocal effects.

The interaction of genetics and experience is not limited to the early years. It occurs across the entire life span. For example, maturing late in adolescence or going bald at age 30 are determined by genetic inheritance. But their impact on an individual's social and personality development depend on a host of environmental considerations.

All aspects of development are shaped jointly by heredity and experience. We often estimate their relative weight or influence, as if we could cleanly divide behavior into genetic and environmental components. Although we can't really carve up behavior that neatly, such comparisons can be of great theoretical interest, as you'll see in our upcoming Application, which discusses the nature and origins of gender differences in behavior.

UNDERSTANDING GENDER DIFFERENCES

Answer the following "true" or "false."

☐ **1.** Females are more socially oriented than males.

☐ **2.** Males outperform females on spatial tasks.

☐ **3.** Females are more irrational than males.

☐ **4.** Males are less sensitive to nonverbal cues than females.

☐ **5.** Females are more emotional than males.

Are there genuine behavioral differences between the sexes similar to those mentioned above? If so, why do these differences exist? How do they develop? These are the complex and controversial questions that we'll explore in this Application.

Sex-related stereotypes are very prevalent in our society. **Stereotypes are widely held beliefs that people have certain characteristics because of their membership in a particular group.** We have stereotypes not only of men and women, but of ethnic groups, such as Mexicans and Germans, and occupational groups, such as lawyers and professors. Table 11.5 lists some characteristics that are part of the masculine and feminine stereotypes in our society. The table shows something you may have already noticed on your own: the male stereotype is much more flattering, suggesting that men have virtually cornered the market on competence and rationality. After all, we all know that females are more dependent, emotional, irrational, submissive, and talkative than males. Or do we? Let's look at the research.

How Do the Sexes Differ in Behavior?

Gender differences **(also known as sex differences) refer to behavioral (rather than biological) disparities between females and males.** Mountains of research, literally thousands of studies, exist on gender differences. It's difficult to sort through this huge body of research, but fortunately, many review articles on gender differences have been published in recent years. As noted in Chapter 2, *review articles* summarize and reconcile the findings of a large number of studies on a specific issue.

What does gender research show? Are the stereotypes of males and females accurate? For the most part, no. The research indicates that there *are* genuine behavioral differences between the sexes, but they are far fewer in number than stereotypes suggest. As you'll see, only two of the differences mentioned in our opening true-false questions (the even-numbered items) have been supported by the research.

Cognitive Abilities

In the cognitive domain, several independently conducted reviews of hundreds of studies reveal three well-documented gender differences in mental abilities (Hyde, 1981; Linn & Petersen, 1986; Maccoby & Jacklin, 1974). First, on the average, females perform somewhat better than males on tests of *verbal ability*. Second, on tests of *mathematical ability*, males show an advantage. Third, males tend to score high in *visual-spatial ability* more often than females. For all three of these cognitive abilities, the gap between males and females doesn't open up until early adolescence.

Social Behavior

In regard to social behavior, research findings support the existence of three more gender differences. First, a review of 143 studies indicates that

Table 11.5 Elements of Traditional Sex-Related Stereotypes

FEMININE	MASCULINE
Not at all aggressive	Very aggressive
Not at all independent	Very independent
Very emotional	Not at all emotional
Very easily influenced	Not at all easily influenced
Very submissive	Very dominant
Very excitable in a minor crisis	Not at all excitable in a minor crisis
Very passive	Very active
Very illogical	Very logical
Very home oriented	Very worldly
Easily hurt emotionally	Not easily hurt emotionally
Generally indecisive	Decisive
Very easily moved to tears	Never moved to tears
Very dependent	Not at all dependent
Very conceited about appearance	Never conceited about appearance
Very talkative	Not at all talkative
Very tactful	Very blunt
Very gentle	Very rough
Very aware of feelings of others	Not at all aware of feelings of others
Very interested in own appearance	Not at all interested in own appearance
Very desirous of security	Not very desirous of security

Source: Adapted from Broverman et al., 1972

males tend to be more *aggressive* than females, both verbally and physically (Hyde, 1984). This disparity shows up early in childhood. Its continuation into adulthood is supported by the fact that men account for a grossly disproportionate number of the violent crimes in our society. Second, there are gender differences in *nonverbal communication*. Based on a review of 75 studies, Hall (1978) concluded that females are more sensitive than males to subtle nonverbal cues. Females also smile and gaze at others more than males (Hall & Halberstadt, 1986). Third, two separate reviews conclude that there are gender differences in *influenceability* (Becker, 1986; Eagly & Carli, 1981). Females appear to be slightly more susceptible to persuasion and conforming to group pressure than males.

Qualifications

Although there are some genuine gender differences in behavior, bear in mind that they are *group* differences that tell us nothing about individuals. Essentially, we are comparing the "average man" with the "average woman." However, you are—and every individual is—unique; the average female and male are ultimately figments of our imagination. Furthermore, the genuine group differences noted are relatively small. Figure 11.14 shows how scores on a trait, perhaps verbal ability, might be distributed for

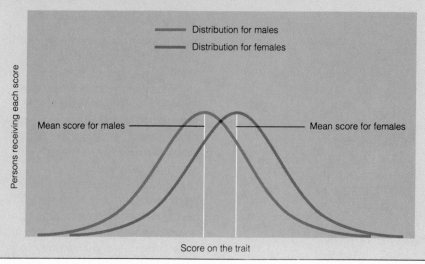

Figure 11.14 Hypothetical example of score distributions that could produce statistically significant sex differences. For a given trait, one sex may score higher *on the average*, but that does not mean the two sexes are completely dissimilar in regard to that trait. Typically there is considerable overlap in the distributions of scores and greater variability within each sex than between the two sexes.

men and women. Although the group averages are detectably different, you can see that there is great variability within each group (sex) and a huge overlap between the two group distributions.

One way to look at the strength of the association between gender and a specific trait is to estimate the proportion of variation (on the trait) that is accounted for by a person's sex. Estimates of these proportions can be made through meta-analyses, which are special types of research reviews. **Meta-analysis combines the statistical results of many studies of the same question, yielding an estimate of the size and consistency of a vari-**

able's effects. Many of the review articles that we've cited thus far were reports of meta-analyses.

Table 11.6 summarizes the findings of meta-analyses on gender effects. These meta-analyses suggest that sex accounts for only about 1% of the variation among people in verbal ability, mathematics ability, and influenceability. Furthermore, for the traits with the largest gender differences, sex accounts for only about 4–6% of the variation among individuals.

To summarize, the behavioral differences between males and females are fewer and smaller than popular stereotypes suggest. Many supposed gender differences, including those in social orientation, emotional reactivity, self-esteem, analytic ability, and dependence, have turned out to be more mythical than real (Maccoby & Jacklin, 1974). Nonetheless, there are some genuine gender differences that require explanation, which is the matter we'll attend to next.

Biological Origins of Gender Differences

What accounts for the development of the gender differences that do exist? Are they the product of learning, or are they biological in origin? This question is yet another manifestation of the nature versus nurture issue. Investigations of the biological origins of

Table 11.6 Meta-Analyses of Gender Differences

CHARACTERISTIC	RESEARCHER	NUMBER OF STUDIES ANALYZED	SEX SHOWING HIGHER LEVELS	VARIANCE ACCOUNTED FOR BY SEX (%)
Verbal abilities	Hyde (1981)	27	F better	1
Mathematical abilities	Hyde (1981)	16	M better	1
Visual/spatial abilities	Hyde (1981)	10	M better	4.5
Aggression	Hyde (1984)	143	M greater	6
Decoding of nonverbal cues	Hall (1978)	75	F better	4
Susceptibility to social influence	Eagly & Carli (1981)	148	F more	1

Source: Adapted from Brigham (1986)

gender differences have centered on hormones and brain organization.

Hormones

Traditionally, biological explanations of gender differences have focused on the probable role of hormones. We know that hormones play a key role in sexual differentiation during prenatal development. Gender is determined by one's sex chromosomes, with an XX pairing producing a female and an XY pairing producing a male. However, both male and female embryos are essentially the same until about 8 to 12 weeks after conception, when male and female gonads (sex glands) begin to produce different hormonal secretions. The high level of androgens (the principal class of male hormones) in males and the low level of androgens in females lead to the differentiation of male and female genital organs. This developmental sequence is outlined in Figure 11.15.

The critical role of prenatal hormones in sexual differentiation becomes apparent when something interferes with normal prenatal hormonal secretions. John Money and his colleagues have tracked the development of a small number of females who were exposed to high levels of androgens during their prenatal development. The girls were born to mothers who either had a hormonal malfunction during pregnancy or were given an androgenlike drug to prevent miscarriage. These *androgenized females* were born with masculinized genitals. The degree of masculinization of their genitals varied, depending on the extent of their prenatal hormonal imbalance. In some cases, the masculinization was so subtle that it went unnoticed for months and even years. Once it was noticed, most cases were treated with a combination of hormone (cortisone) therapy and surgical correction of the genitals.

Money and his colleagues wondered whether the prenatal dose of male hormones had affected the behavioral tendencies of these androgenized females. When they researched this question, they found that the androgenized females showed "tomboyish"

interests in vigorous outdoor activities, and preferences for male playmates and "male" toys (Money & Erhardt, 1972).

The findings on androgenized females suggested to many theorists that prenatal hormones shape behavioral differences between the sexes, but there are—naturally—a few problems. First, it's always dangerous to draw conclusions about the general population based on a handful of people who have an abnormal condition. Second, most of the androgenized girls received drug treatments (cortisone) for their condition; these treatments could have influenced their activity levels. Third, the girls were born with masculine-looking genitals that often were not surgically corrected until age 2 or 3. Hence, their families may not have *raised* them quite the same way they would have raised "normal" girls. In light of this, research on androgenized females cannot conclusively demonstrate that prenatal hormones influence gender differences in behavior.

Brain Organization

Interpretive problems have also cropped up in efforts to link gender differences to the specialization of the cerebral hemispheres in the brain. As you may recall from Chapter 3, in most people the left hemisphere is more actively involved in verbal processing, and the right hemisphere, in visual-spatial processing (Sperry, 1982; Springer & Deutsch, 1984). After these findings surfaced, various theorists began to wonder whether there might be a connection between this division of labor in the brain and the gender differences in verbal and spatial skills. Consequently, they began looking for disparities in brain organization between males and females.

They found that males tend to exhibit more cerebral specialization than females (McGlone, 1980). In other words, there's a trend for males to depend more heavily than females do on the left hemisphere in verbal processing and more heavily on the right in spatial processing. Many theorists believe that this difference in brain organization is responsible for gender differences in verbal and spatial ability (Goleman, 1978).

This idea is intriguing, but we have a long way to go before we can explain

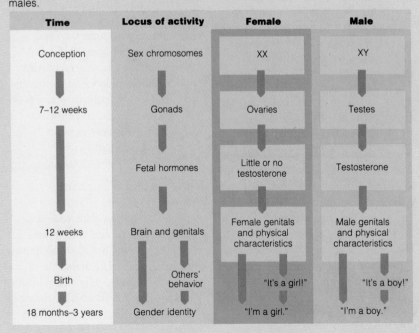

Figure 11.15 The diagram outlines how gender identity depends on a biological foundation laid down during prenatal development, as well as reactions from others during early childhood. Normal sexual differentiation in the fetus depends on a low level of testosterone (a key androgen) in females and a high level of testosterone in males.

Time	Locus of activity	Female	Male
Conception	Sex chromosomes	XX	XY
7–12 weeks	Gonads	Ovaries	Testes
	Fetal hormones	Little or no testosterone	Testosterone
12 weeks	Brain and genitals	Female genitals and physical characteristics	Male genitals and physical characteristics
Birth	Others' behavior	"It's a girl!"	"It's a boy!"
18 months–3 years	Gender identity	"I'm a girl."	"I'm a boy."

gender differences in terms of right brain/left brain specialization. Studies have not been very consistent in finding that males have more specialized brain organization than females (Harris, 1980; Kinsbourne, 1980). Moreover, even if men *do* show stronger cerebral specialization than women, no one is really sure just how that would account for the observed gender differences in cognitive abilities. It seems peculiar that strong specialization would produce an advantage for males on one kind of task (spatial) and a disadvantage on another kind of task (verbal). Thus, the theory linking cerebral specialization to gender differences in mental abilities remains highly speculative.

In summary, researchers have made relatively little progress in their efforts to document the biological roots of gender differences in behavior. The idea that "anatomy is destiny" has proven difficult to demonstrate. After decades of research, we still don't have solid evidence linking obvious hormonal differences between the sexes to behavioral differences.

Theorists remain convinced that biological factors contribute to gender differences. However, the overall evidence, or rather the lack of it, suggests that biology must play a relatively minor role, creating predispositions that are largely shaped by experience. In contrast, efforts to link gender differences to disparities in the way males and females are raised have proven more fruitful.

Environmental Origins of Gender Differences

Socialization refers to the acquisition of the norms, roles, and behaviors expected of people in a particular society (or smaller social group). It includes all the efforts made by a society to ensure that its members learn to behave in a manner that's considered appropriate. The socialization process has traditionally included efforts to train children about gender roles. *Gender roles* (also known as sex roles) are expectations about what is appropriate behavior for each sex. Investigators have identified three key processes involved in the socialization of gender roles: operant conditioning, observational learning, and self-socialization. First we'll examine these processes; then we'll look at the principal sources of gender role socialization.

Operant Conditioning

In part, gender roles are shaped by the power of reward and punishment—the key processes in operant conditioning. Parents, teachers, peers, and others often reinforce (usually with tacit approval) "sex-appropriate" behavior and respond negatively to "sex-inappropriate" behavior (Fagot, 1978). If you're a man, you might recall getting hurt as a young boy and being told that "men don't cry." If you succeeded in inhibiting your crying, you may have earned an approving smile or even something tangible like an ice-cream cone. The reinforcement probably strengthened your tendency to "act like a man" and suppress emotional displays. If you're a woman, chances are your crying wasn't discouraged as sex-inappropriate.

Studies suggest that parents may use *punishment* more than *reward* in socializing gender roles (O'Leary, 1977). Many parents take sex-appropriate behavior for granted and don't go out of their way to reward it. But they may react very negatively to sex-inappropriate behavior. Thus, a 10-year-old boy who enjoys playing with dollhouses may elicit strong disapproval from his parents. Parents devote more attention and effort to discouraging sex-inappropriate behavior in boys than in girls.

Observational Learning

As a young girl, did you imitate the behavior of your mother, your aunts, your older sisters, and your female peers? As a young boy, did you imitate your father and other male role models? Such behaviors reflect observational learning, in which behavior is shaped by the observation of others' behavior and its consequences. In everyday language, observational learning results in *imitation*.

Children imitate both males and females, but most children tend to imitate same-sex role models more than opposite-sex role models (Perry & Bussey, 1979). Thus, imitation often leads young girls to play with dolls, dollhouses, and toy stoves; young boys are more likely to tinker with toy trucks, miniature gas stations, or tool kits.

Self-Socialization

Children are not merely passive recipients of gender role socialization. According to Lawrence Kohlberg (1966), once children recognize the permanent quality of their gender (around ages 5 to 7), they begin to actively pursue information about how males and females are supposed to behave. Thus, they get involved in their own socialization, working diligently to discover the "rules" that are supposed to govern their behavior.

Sources of Gender Role Socialization

There are three *main* sources of influence in gender role socialization: families, schools, and the media. Of course, we are now in an era of *transition* in sex roles, so the generalizations that follow may say more about how you were socialized than about how your children will be. We'll discuss this transition after describing the traditional picture.

Families. A great deal of sex role socialization takes place in the home (Huston, 1983). Fathers engage in rougher play with their infant sons than with their infant daughters. As children grow, boys and girls are encouraged to play with different types of toys. As Figure 11.16 shows, substantial gender differences are found in toy preferences. Generally, boys have less leeway to play with "feminine" toys than girls do with "masculine" toys.

When children are old enough to help with household chores, the assignments tend to depend on sex—for example, girls wash dishes and boys mow the lawn. Likewise, the leisure

424

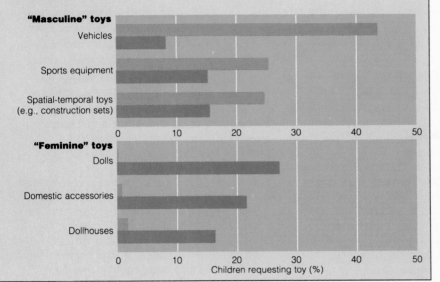

Figure 11.16 Percentages of boys and girls requesting "masculine" and "feminine" toys from Santa Claus. Children's preferences in regard to traditionally masculine and feminine toys show the effects of sex-role socialization. The results were obtained from an analysis of children's letters to Santa Claus. (Adapted from Richardson & Simpson, 1982)

activities that children are encouraged to engage in vary by sex—Johnny plays in Little League and Mary practices the piano. Given these patterns, it's not surprising that parents' traditional or nontraditional attitudes about gender roles have been shown to influence the gender roles acquired by their children (Repetti, 1984).

Schools. Schools also make a major contribution to the socialization of gender roles (Busch-Rossnagel & Vance, 1982; Etaugh & Harlow, 1975). Books that children use in learning to read (grade-school readers) influence youngsters' ideas about what is suitable behavior for males and females. One survey of 134 readers found that boys were typically portrayed as clever, heroic, and adventurous; girls were typically found in the kitchen doing domestic chores (Women on Words and Images, 1972).

As youngsters progress through the school system, they often are channeled in different career directions considered appropriate for their sex. For example, males have been more likely to be encouraged to study mathematics and to work toward becoming engineers or doctors. Females have often been encouraged to take classes in home economics and to work toward becoming nurses or homemakers.

Media. Television is another source of gender role socialization. Television shows have traditionally depicted men and women in highly stereotypic ways (Tedesco, 1974). Women are often portrayed as submissive, passive, and emotional. Men are more likely to be portrayed as independent, assertive, and competent. Even the commercials on television contribute to the socialization of sex roles. Women are routinely shown worrying about trivial matters such as a ring around their husband's shirt collar and the shine of their dishes.

One study demonstrates strikingly just how influential television can be. Many children's shows on public/educational television strive to promote nontraditional gender roles. Repetti

(1984) found that children who watch a great deal of educational television tend to be less traditional in their views of gender roles than other children. Thus, media content influences the gender roles acquired by children.

Gender Roles in Transition

Gender roles are in a period of transition in our society. Many women and men are rebelling against traditional role expectations based on sex. Many parents are trying to raise their children with fewer preconceived notions about how males and females "ought" to behave. Some social critics view this as a healthy trend because they believe that traditional roles have been too narrow and restrictive for both sexes (Bem, 1975; Fasteau, 1974; Goldberg, 1983). Such theorists argue that conventional sex roles lock people into rigid "straitjackets" that prevent them from realizing their full potential. Other social critics, such as George Gilder (1986), believe that changes in gender roles may harm intimate relationships between men and women and hurt the quality of family life. Thus, there's vigorous debate about the effects of changing gender roles.

In this era of transition and debate, we're faced with complex personal questions about the roles we want to assume and about how we want to raise our children. Our review of the nature and origins of gender differences may help you to work through these decisions.

"And now, back to our anchor*man* . . ." Although gender roles are in transition, many of us continue to associate such qualities as calm authoritativeness with males more readily than with females. Our views are shaped by many factors, including the roles in which we see men and women. (From left: ABC's Peter Jennings, NBC's Tom Brokaw, and PBS's Jim Lehrer and Robert MacNeil.)

425

Human Development Across the Life Span

KEY IDEAS

Progress Before Birth: Prenatal Development

• Development is a lifelong process marked by continuity and transition. Prenatal development proceeds through the germinal, embryonic, and fetal stages as the zygote is differentiated into a human organism potentially capable of survival about 6 months after conception. During the prenatal period, development may be affected by maternal drug use, maternal malnutrition, and some maternal illnesses.

The Wondrous Years of Childhood

• Research on the development of vision indicates that acuity improves throughout the first year, and depth perception is clearly established by around 6 months of age. In comparison, hearing is more advanced during the early months of life. Motor development lags behind sensory-perceptual development at first. Motor development follows cephalo-caudal (head-to-foot) and proximo-distal (center-outward) trends. Early motor development appears to depend more on maturation than learning, although both clearly play a role.

• Developmental norms for motor skills and other aspects of development can be useful benchmarks. But they are only group averages, and there is great variability in the pacing of development. Both cross-sectional and longitudinal studies are well suited to developmental research. Longitudinal studies are more sensitive to developmental changes, but interpretive problems can surface with either approach.

• Temperamental differences among children are apparent during the first few months of life. Thomas and Chess found that most infants could be classified as easy, slow-to-warm-up, or difficult children. These differences in temperament are fairly stable and may have far-reaching effects because of the reactions they tend to elicit from parents.

• Infants' attachment to their mothers develops gradually. Separation anxiety usually surfaces around 6 to 8 months of age. Reinforcement explanations of attachment appear inadequate in light of the Harlows' research with infant monkeys. They showed that infant monkeys' attachments to artificial mothers were based on contact-comfort rather than feeding. Bowlby's theory that attachment is biologically programmed has been influential, although the evidence is circumstantial.

• Research shows that attachment emerges out of a mutual interplay between infant and mother. A relatively secure infant-mother attachment appears to be beneficial to a child's development. In contrast, emotional deprivation during infancy may have negative effects on future social bonding, although these effects can be reversed.

• Erik Erikson's theory of personality development proposes that we evolve through eight stages over the life span. In each stage we wrestle with changes (crises) in social relationships. The outcomes of these psychosocial crises leave their mark on adult personality. Successful progress through Erikson's four childhood stages should yield a trustful, autonomous person with a sense of initiative and industry.

• Research on cognitive development has been dominated by Jean Piaget's stage theory. The key development during the sensorimotor period is the child's gradual recognition of the permanence of objects. The preoperational period is marked by certain deficiencies in thinking—notably centration, irreversibility, and egocentrism. During the concrete operations period, children develop the ability to perform operations on mental representations, which makes them capable of conservation and hierarchical classification. The formal operations period ushers in more abstract, systematic, and logical thought.

• Although critics have identified some problems with Piaget's theory, there is no doubt that his work has greatly improved our understanding of cognitive development. The other major approach to the study of cognitive development is rooted in information-processing models of thinking. The information-processing perspective has proven especially useful in explaining progress in attention and memory ability.

• Recent research on moral development has been dominated by Kohlberg's stage theory of moral reasoning. According to Kohlberg, moral reasoning progresses through three levels that are related to age and determined by cognitive development. Research has identified age-related progress in moral reasoning, although there is a great deal of overlap between the developmental stages described by Kohlberg. Gilligan has argued that females progress through a somewhat different series of moral reasoning stages than males.

• Altruism and aggression, two important aspects of social behavior, tend to increase and decrease, respectively, with age. The development of altruism and aggression are affected by genetic inheritance, parental training, and role models in the mass media. Our Featured Study showed how exposure to television violence correlates with peer-rated aggression, even in very young children.

The Transition of Adolescence

• The growth spurt at puberty is a prominent event involving the development of reproductive maturity and secondary sexual characteristics. Early or late maturation during adolescence affects youngsters' self-concepts and may have lasting effects on their personalities.

• Many theorists have asserted that adolescence is a period of turmoil. Although the recent surge in suicide and attempted suicide by adolescents appears to support this notion, the statistics are open to varying interpretations. Other sources of evidence suggest that adolescence is no more tumultuous than other periods of life.

• According to Erikson, the key challenge of adolescence is to make some progress toward a sense of identity. There are four patterns of identity formation: foreclosure, moratorium, identity diffusion, and identity achievement.

The Expanse of Adulthood

• Research on adult development has blossomed in recent decades. During adulthood, personality is marked by both stability and change. Gould and Levinson maintain that there are predictable patterns of change in adults that can be broken into stages. Both suggest that there is a great deal of developmental change during adulthood. Both also believe that a mid-life crisis is a normal developmental transition.

• During adulthood, age-related physical transitions include changes in appearance, neuron losses, sensory losses (especially in vision and hearing), and hormonal changes. Menopause is not as problematic as widely suggested, and sexual activity need not decline during the later years. In the cognitive domain, mental speed declines first, followed in late adulthood by decreases in memory and problem-solving ability. Nonetheless, many people in their 60s and 70s remain quite capable mentally. In the social sphere, there may be a trend toward disengagement, but it is far from universal.

Putting It in Perspective

• One of our integrative themes stood out among the others in this chapter. Our discussion of development showed how heredity and environment interactively shape behavior. They are entangled even before birth, and the effect of one depends upon the other.

Application: Understanding Gender Differences

• Gender differences in behavior are fewer in number and smaller in magnitude than sex-related stereotypes suggest. Research reviews suggest that there are genuine gender differences in verbal ability, mathematical ability, spatial ability, aggression, nonverbal communication, and influenceability. Some of these differences tend to become more or less pronounced with age.

• There is research linking gender differences in humans to hormones and brain organization, but the research is marred by interpretive problems. Efforts to link gender differences to socialization processes have been more successful. Operant conditioning, observational learning, and self-socialization contribute to the development of gender differences. Families, schools, and the media are among the main sources of gender-role socialization.

KEY TERMS

Accommodation	Irreversibility
Aggression	Longitudinal study
Altruism	Maturation
Animism	Meta-analysis
Assimilation	Motor development
Attachment	Object permanence
Centration	Operations
Cephalo-caudal trend	Parallel play
Cognitive development	Placenta
Conservation	Prenatal period
Critical period	Proximo-distal trend
Cross-sectional study	Puberty
Development	Secondary sex
Developmental norms	characteristics
Egocentrism	Senility
Embryonic stage	Separation anxiety
Emotional deprivation	Socialization
Fetal alcohol syndrome	Stage
Fetal stage	Stereotype
Gender differences	Temperament
Gender roles	Visual cliff
Germinal stage	Zygote

KEY PEOPLE

John Bowlby	Daniel Levinson
Erik Erikson	Jean Piaget
Roger Gould	Alexander Thomas &
Harry & Margaret Harlow	Stella Chess
Lawrence Kohlberg	

Personality: Theory and Research

PERSONALITY: THEORY AND RESEARCH

I have a close friend who has to be one of the world's great optimists. A few years ago, he was riding an all-terrain vehicle in a California desert and flipped it into the air. The vehicle landed on him, shattering one of his legs. Two days later, he called me in Chicago (from the hospital) to tell me about the accident. Still in great pain from extensive surgery, and facing more operations, not to mention a year or two on crutches, he was joking about it. He was in his usual—make that unalterable—cheerful, lighthearted mood! Most of us, of course, would have been rather dejected and gloomy under such circumstances. Consider another example. A few years ago, I went with the same friend to see the Chicago Cubs play a doubleheader. For most Cubs fans such as ourselves, the baseball that day was terribly boring and depressing. In the first game, the Cubs were shut out, losing 1 to 0. In game two, after eight innings, they still hadn't scored a single run and were getting trounced, 9 to 0, when I said, "Let's get out of here. This is disgusting." He turned to me in genuine surprise, saying, "What? Leave? We're gonna rally!"

My friend's optimism is a key facet of his *person-*

ality. In fact, it dominates his behavior to such an extent that Gordon Allport, an influential personality theorist, would call it his *cardinal trait*. In this chapter, we'll explore the mystery of personality. What exactly is personality? How does personality develop over time? For instance, how does someone like my friend get to be so upbeat and optimistic? Is personality largely biological in origin, or is experience critical? What makes for a healthy personality?

Traditionally, the study of personality has been dominated by "grand theories" that are very broad in scope, attempting to explain a great many facets of behavior. Our discussion will reflect this emphasis, as we'll devote most of our time to the sweeping theories of Sigmund Freud, Carl Jung, B. F. Skinner, Carl Rogers, and several others. However, in recent years the study of personality has shifted toward narrower research programs that examine specific aspects of personality (Singer & Kolligian, 1987). The latter portion of the chapter will reflect this trend, as we review several contemporary empirical approaches to personality. In the chapter Application, we'll analyze the nature and importance of self-esteem, review how it develops, and discuss advice on how to improve it.

THE NATURE OF PERSONALITY

Personality is a complex hypothetical construct that has been defined in a variety of ways. Let's take a close look at the concepts of personality, personality traits, and personality theories.

Defining Personality: Consistency and Distinctiveness

What does it mean to say that my friend has an optimistic personality? This assertion indicates that he has a fairly *consistent tendency* to behave in a cheerful, hopeful, enthusiastic way, looking at the bright side of things, across a wide variety of situations. In a similar vein, if you note that a friend has an outgoing personality, you mean that she or he consistently behaves in a friendly, open, and extraverted manner in a variety of circumstances. Although none of us is entirely consistent in behavior, this quality of *consistency across situations* lies at the core of the concept of personality.

Distinctiveness is also central to the concept of personality. We use personality to explain why we

don't all act alike in similar situations. If you were stuck in an elevator with three people, each might react differently. One might crack jokes to relieve tension. Another might make ominous predictions that "we'll never get out of here," while the third person might calmly think about how to escape from the elevator. These varied reactions to the same situation occur because each person has a different personality. We all have traits that are also seen in other people, but we each have our own, distinctive *set* of personality traits that makes each of us unique.

These two qualities of *consistency* and *distinctiveness* in individual behavior make up the essence of the personality concept. In other words, we use the concept of personality to explain (1) the stability in a person's behavior over time and across situations (consistency) and (2) the behavioral differences among people reacting to the same situation (distinctiveness). When we attempt to describe an individual's personality, we usually do so in terms of specific aspects of personality, which are called *traits*. Combining these ideas into a definition, *personality* **refers to an individual's unique constellation of consistent behavioral traits.**

Personality Traits: Dispositions and Dimensions

We all make remarks like "Jan is very *conscientious*," or "Bill is too *timid* to succeed in that job," or "I wish I could be as *outgoing* as Marlene." These descriptive statements all refer to personality traits. **A *personality trait* is a durable disposition to behave in a particular way in a variety of situations.** Adjectives such as honest, dependable, moody, impulsive, suspicious, anxious, excitable, domineering, and friendly describe dispositions that represent personality traits.

Personality traits are abstractions that we can't observe directly. Rather, we *infer* traits from behavior—which, of course, we can observe. For example, you might choose to describe a friend as insecure because you've observed his tendency to make negative remarks about himself, his inability to ask out dates because of his often-voiced fear of rejection, and his repeated requests for reassurance that you really like him. Your friend's insecurity is not a tangible characteristic like his hair color. It's an abstraction that you infer from certain patterns in his behavior.

Most approaches to personality assume that some traits are more basic than others. According to this notion, a small number of fundamental traits determine other, more superficial traits. For example, a person's tendency to be impulsive, restless, irritable, boisterous, and impatient might all be derived from a more basic tendency to be excitable.

Gordon Allport (1937, 1961) was one of the first theorists to make systematic distinctions between traits in terms of their importance. After sifting through an unabridged dictionary, Allport identified over 4500 personality traits. To impose some order on this chaos, he distinguished three levels of traits. **A *cardinal trait* is a dominant trait that characterizes nearly all of a person's behavior.** The influence of a cardinal trait is overwhelming. Mother Teresa's altruism, Machiavelli's manipulativeness and William F. Buckley's arrogance would be examples of cardinal traits. According to Allport, cardinal traits are rare; only a small minority of people display them.

In Allport's model, **central traits are prominent, general dispositions found in anyone.** They're the basic building blocks of personality. Central traits are very influential, but they don't rule our behavior in the way that cardinal traits do. How many central traits do we usually have?

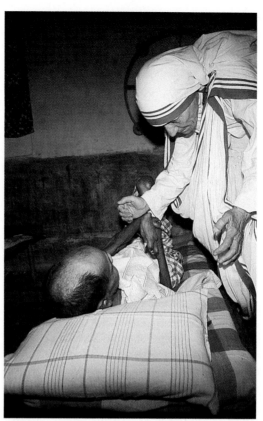

According to Gordon Allport, a minority of people exhibit cardinal traits that thoroughly dominate their behavior. Mother Teresa's altruism is an example of a cardinal trait.

Allport's research led him to conclude that most of us have only five to ten central traits.

At the bottom of Allport's hierarchy are secondary traits. **Secondary traits are less consistent dispositions that surface in some situations, but not others.** For example, a person might be passive in most circumstances, but highly aggressive in dealing with subordinates at work. This occasional aggressiveness would be a secondary trait.

Following Allport's lead, a number of psychologists have taken on the challenge of identifying the basic traits that form the core of personality. As we discussed in Chapter 9, Raymond Cattell (1950, 1966) has used the statistical procedure of factor analysis to reduce Allport's list of traits to just 16 basic dimensions of personality that he calls *source traits*. Cattell believes that all our other traits are derived from our source traits, and that we can thoroughly describe an individual's personality by measuring these 16 traits. Indeed, they're the 16 dimensions of personality measured by Cattell's widely used Sixteen Personality Factor Questionnaire (consult Figure 9.15).

More recently, Robert McCrae and Paul Costa (1985, 1987) have used factor analysis to arrive at an even simpler, *five-factor model of personality*. McCrae and Costa maintain that most personality traits are derived from just five critical traits: (1) neuroticism, (2) extraversion, (3) openness to experience, (4) agreeableness, and (5) conscientiousness. These dimensions of personality are de-

Table 12.1 McCrae and Costa's Five-Factor Model of Personality

FACTOR	DESCRIPTION
Neuroticism	Anxious, insecure, guilt-prone, self-conscious
Extraversion	Talkative, sociable, fun-loving, affectionate
Openness to experience	Daring, nonconforming, showing unusually broad interests, imaginative
Agreeableness	Sympathetic, warm, trusting, cooperative
Conscientiousness	Ethical, dependable, productive, purposeful

Source: McCrae & Costa, 1987

scribed in Table 12.1. Like Cattell, McCrae and Costa maintain that personality can be described adequately by measuring the basic traits that they've identified. Their bold proposal to reduce the complexity of personality to just five fundamental dimensions is currently generating considerable debate.

The debate about how many dimensions are necessary to describe personality is likely to continue for many years to come. It's an example of an important theoretical issue in the study of personality. As you'll see throughout the chapter, the study of personality is an area in psychology that has a long history of "dueling theories."

Perspectives on Personality: Dueling Theories

There's quite a variety of different theoretical approaches to the understanding of personality. **Personality theories** are systems of related ideas used to explain the development, structure, and functioning of personality. We'll describe nine theo-

retical systems in this chapter, and we'll only be scratching the surface. In spite of all the diversity, we can organize theories of personality into groups that share certain assumptions, emphases, and interests. We'll divide personality theories into four groups, each with its own perspective: (1) a psychodynamic perspective, (2) a behavioral perspective, (3) a humanistic perspective, and (4) a biological perspective.

In constructing theories, scientists always make certain assumptions. Later in the chapter, we'll compare the crucial assumptions underlying the major theoretical approaches to personality. In particular, we'll look at the assumptions made regarding the following issues:

1. *Freedom versus determinism.* Is our behavior determined by forces that lie beyond our control (an assumption called *determinism*)? Or are we free to chart our own courses of action?
2. *Nature versus nurture.* Is personality shaped primarily by our genetic inheritance (nature)? Or is personality largely molded by experience (nurture)?
3. *Conscious versus unconscious.* Is our behavior governed by our conscious, rational thought? Or is it a product of unconscious, irrational thought processes?
4. *Person versus situation.* Does behavior depend primarily on the person or the situation? In other words, is our behavior highly consistent over times, places, and situations (indicating that the person is critical)? Or are we heavily influenced by environmental demands (indicating that the situation is critical)?

You'll see these issues surface again and again as we scrutinize prominent theories of personality. We'll begin our discussion of personality theories by examining the life and work of Sigmund Freud.

PSYCHODYNAMIC PERSPECTIVES

Psychodynamic theories include all the diverse theories descended from the work of Sigmund Freud, which focus on unconscious mental forces. Freud inspired many brilliant scholars who followed in his intellectual footsteps. Some of these followers simply refined and updated Freud's theory. Other theorists veered off in new directions and established independent, albeit related, schools of thought. Today, the psychodynamic umbrella covers a large collection of loosely related theories that we can only sample from in this text. We have already discussed the psycho-

dynamic theories of Erik Erikson (1963) and John Bowlby (1969) in our chapter on human development (see Chapter 11). In this section, we'll examine the ideas of Sigmund Freud in some detail and then take a brief look at the theories of Carl Jung and Alfred Adler.

Freud's Psychoanalytic Theory

Born in 1856, Sigmund Freud grew up in a middle-class Jewish home in Vienna, Austria. He showed an early interest in intellectual pursuits

Freud's psychoanalytic theory was based on decades of clinical work. He treated a great many patients in the consulting room pictured here. The room contained numerous artifacts from other cultures—and the original psychoanalytic couch.

and became an intense, hard-working young man, driven to achieve fame. He experienced his share of inner turmoil and engaged in regular self-analysis for over 40 years. He lived in a "Victorian" era, marked by sexual repression. Freud's life was also affected by the first great World War, which devastated Europe, and by the growing anti-Semitism of the times. We'll see that the sexual repression and aggressive hostilities that Freud witnessed left their mark on his view of human nature.

Freud was a physician practicing neurology in Vienna at the end of the 19th century. In his practice, he saw some patients who had apparent physical problems (partial paralysis, tremors, hearing loss, and such) for which he could find no organic basis. It was recognized even then that physical symptoms were sometimes caused by emotional disturbances. At the time, this syndrome was called *hysteria.*

Inspired by a colleague named Josef Breuer, Freud stumbled onto a new treatment for hysteria. Breuer had treated a young woman whose hysterical symptoms (severe headaches and loss of feeling in one arm) cleared up when she talked out certain emotionally charged issues. Breuer didn't feel comfortable with some aspects of this "talking cure" and abandoned the method. However, Freud recognized the method's potential and began to use it regularly. His interest turned to psychiatry, and he spent many years refining his new treatment method, which he christened *psychoanalysis.* It eventually became a leading approach to psychotherapy.

Freud's (1901, 1924, 1940) *psychoanalytic theory* grew out of his decades of interactions with his clients in psychoanalysis and also out of his own self-analysis. Psychoanalytic theory attempts to explain personality, motivation, and psychological disorders by focusing on the influence of early childhood experiences, unconscious motives and

conflicts, and how people cope with their sexual and aggressive urges.

Freud's theory attracted relatively little attention at first. It took 8 years to sell the 600 copies of the first printing of his classic book, *The Interpretation of Dreams,* which was published in 1900—a humble beginning for a theorist who would greatly influence modern intellectual thought! After this slow beginning, Freud's ideas gradually gained prominence, but his success was not without its costs.

Most of Freud's contemporaries were uncomfortable with his theory for at least three reasons. First, in arguing that our behavior is governed by unconscious factors that we're not aware of, Freud made the disconcerting suggestion that we're not masters of our own minds. Second, in claiming that our adult personalities are shaped by childhood experiences and other factors beyond our control, he embraced a strong brand of determinism, suggesting that we're not masters of our own destinies. Third, by emphasizing the great importance of how people cope with their sexual urges, he offended those who held the conservative, Victorian values of his time.

Thus, Freud endured a great deal of criticism, condemnation, and outright ridicule, even after his work began to attract more favorable attention. As he explained, "No one who, like me, conjures up the most evil of those half-tamed demons that inhabit the human breast, and seeks to wrestle with them, can expect to come through the struggle unscathed" (Freud, 1905). Let's examine the ideas that generated so much controversy.

STRUCTURE OF PERSONALITY

Freud divided personality structure into three components: the id, the ego, and the superego. He saw a person's behavior as the outcome of interactions among these three components.

The *id* is the primitive, instinctive component of personality that operates according to the pleasure principle. Freud referred to the id as the reservoir of psychic energy. By this he meant that the id houses the raw biological urges (to eat, sleep, defecate, copulate, and so on) that energize our behavior. The id operates according to the ***pleasure principle,* which demands immediate gratification of its urges.** The id engages in *pri-*

433

mary-process thinking, which is primitive, illogical, irrational, and fantasy oriented.

The *ego* is the decision-making component of personality that operates according to the reality principle. The ego mediates between the id, with its forceful desires for immediate satisfaction, and the external social world, with its expectations and norms regarding suitable behavior. The ego considers social realities—society's norms, etiquette, rules, and customs—in deciding how to behave. The ego is guided by the *reality principle,* **which seeks to delay gratification of the id's urges until appropriate outlets and situations can be found.** In short, to stay out of trouble, the ego often works to tame the unbridled desires of the id. As Freud put it, the ego is "like a man on horseback, who has to hold in check the superior strength of the horse" (Freud, 1923, p. 15).

In the long run, the ego wants to maximize gratification, just as the id does. However, the ego engages in *secondary-process thinking,* which is relatively rational, realistic, and oriented toward problem solving. Thus, the ego strives to avoid negative consequences from society and its representatives (for example, punishment by parents or teachers) by behaving "properly." It also attempts to achieve long-range goals that sometimes require putting off gratification.

While the ego concerns itself with practical realities, the *superego* **is the moral component of personality that incorporates social standards about what represents right and wrong.** Throughout our lives, but especially during childhood, we receive training about what constitutes good and bad behavior. Many social norms regarding morality are eventually internalized. Internalization means that we truly *accept* certain principles, and then *we* put pressure on *ourselves* to live up to these standards. The superego emerges out of the ego at around 3 to 5 years of age. In some people, the superego can become irrationally demanding in its striving for moral perfection. Such people are plagued by excessive feelings of guilt.

According to Freud, the id, ego, and superego are distributed differently across three levels of awareness, which we'll descibe next.

LEVELS OF AWARENESS

Perhaps Freud's most enduring insight was his recognition of how unconscious forces can influence behavior. He inferred the existence of the unconscious from a variety of observations that he made with his patients (see Table 12.2). For example, he noticed that "slips of the tongue" often revealed a person's true feelings. He also realized that his patients' dreams often expressed hidden desires. Most importantly, through psychoanalysis he often helped patients to discover feelings and conflicts that they had previously been unaware of. Thus, Freud concluded that "the news that reaches your consciousness is incomplete and often not to be relied on" (Freud, 1917, p. 143).

Freud contrasted the unconscious with the conscious and preconscious, creating three levels of awareness. **The *conscious* consists of whatever you are aware of at a particular point in time.** For example, at this moment your conscious may include the present train of thought in this text and a dim awareness in the back of your mind that your eyes are getting tired and you're beginning to get hungry. **The *preconscious* contains material just beneath the surface of awareness that can easily be retrieved.** Examples might include your middle name, what you had for supper last night, or an argument you had with a friend yesterday. **The *unconscious* contains thoughts, memories, and desires that are well below the surface of conscious awareness, but which nonetheless ex-**

Table 12.2 Examples of Behaviors Motivated by Unconscious Feelings

BEHAVIOR	UNCONSCIOUS FEELINGS	TRANSFORMATION INVOLVED
Slip of tongue: "May I *insort* (instead of escort) you."	Wish to insult	Condensation (insult + escort = "insort")
Slip of tongue: "Gentlemen, I declare a quorum present and herewith declare the session *closed.*"	Desire to close the meeting	Association of opposites (open = closed)
A woman dreams of being disappointed in the quality of some theater tickets as a result of having gotten them too soon.	Regret at having married too soon (could have gotten a better husband by waiting)	Symbolism (getting tickets = marrying)
A man dreams of breaking an arm.	Desire to break marriage vows	Conversion into visual imagery (breaking vows = breaking an arm)

Source: Freud, 1920

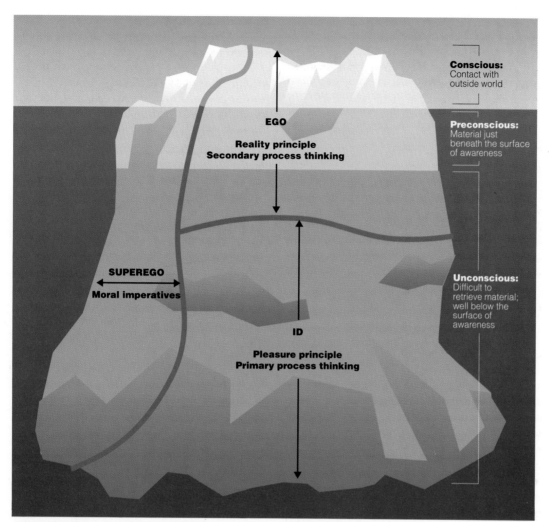

Figure 12.1 Freud's model of personality structure. Freud theorized that we have three levels of awareness—the conscious, the preconscious, and the unconscious. To dramatize the enormous size of the unconscious, he compared it to the portion of an iceberg that lies beneath the water's surface. Freud also divided personality structure into three components—id, ego, and superego—which operate according to different principles and exhibit different modes of thinking. In Freud's model, the id is entirely unconscious, but the ego and superego operate at all three levels of awareness.

ert great influence on our behavior. Examples of material that might be found in your unconscious include a forgotten trauma from childhood, hidden feelings of hostility toward a parent, and repressed sexual desires that you're unaware of.

Freud compared the mind to an iceberg that has most of its mass hidden beneath the water's surface (see Figure 12.1). He believed that our unconscious (the mass below the surface) is much larger than our conscious or preconscious. As you can see in Figure 12.1, he proposed that the ego and superego operate at all three levels of awareness, while the id is entirely unconscious, expressing its urges at a conscious level through the ego. Of course, the id's desires for immediate satisfaction often trigger internal conflicts with the ego and superego. These conflicts play a key role in Freud's theory.

CONFLICT AND THE TYRANNY OF SEX AND AGGRESSION

Freud assumed that our behavior is the outcome of an ongoing series of internal conflicts. Internal battles between the id, ego, and superego are thought to be routine. Why? Because the id wants

to gratify its urges immediately, but the norms of civilized society frequently dictate otherwise. For example, your id might feel an urge to clobber a coworker who constantly irritates you. However, society frowns on such behavior, so your ego would try to hold this urge in check, and you would find yourself in a conflict. You may be experiencing conflict at this very moment. In Freudian terms, your id may be secretly urging you to abandon reading this chapter so that you can fix a snack and watch some television. Your ego may be weighing this appealing option against your society-induced need to excel in school.

Freud believed that our lives are dominated by conflict. He asserted that we career from one conflict to another. The following scenario provides a concrete illustration of how the three components of personality interact to create constant conflicts:

Imagine lurching across your bed to shut off your alarm clock as it rings obnoxiously. It's 7 A.M. and time to get up for your history class. However, your id (operating according to the pleasure principle) urges you to return to the immediate gratification of additional sleep. Your ego (operating according to the reality principle) points

435

out that you really *must* go to class since you haven't been able to decipher the textbook on your own. Your id (in its typical unrealistic fashion) smugly assures you that you *will* get the A grade that you need and suggests lying back to dream about how impressed your roommates will be. Just as you're relaxing, your superego jumps into the fray and tries to make you feel guilty about all the money your parents paid in tuition for the class that you're about to skip. You haven't even gotten out of bed yet, but there's already a pitched battle in your psyche.

Let's say your ego wins the battle. You pull yourself out of bed and head for class. On the way, you pass a donut shop and your id clamors for cinnamon rolls. Your ego reminds you that you're getting overweight and that you're supposed to be on a diet. Your id wins this time. After you've attended your history lecture, your ego reminds you that you need to do some library research for a paper in philosophy. However, your id insists on returning to your apartment to watch some sitcom reruns. As you reenter your apartment, you're overwhelmed by how messy it is. It's your roommates' mess, and your id suggests that you tell them off. As you're about to lash out, however, your ego convinces you that diplomacy will be more effective. Three sitcoms later you find that you're in a debate with yourself about whether to go to the gym to work out, or to the student union to watch MTV. It's only mid-afternoon—and already you've been through a series of internal conflicts.

Although Freud believed that conflicts were commonplace, he thought that some conflicts were far more significant than others. In particular, he believed that conflicts centering on sexual and aggressive impulses were especially likely to have far-reaching consequences. Why did he emphasize sex and aggression? Two reasons were prominent in his thinking.

First, Freud thought that sex and aggression were subject to more complex and ambiguous social controls than other basic motives. The norms governing sexual and aggressive behavior are subtle, and we often get inconsistent messages about what's appropriate. Thus, he believed that these two drives are the source of much confusion.

Second, Freud noted that the sexual and aggressive drives are thwarted more regularly than other basic, biological urges. Think about it: If you get hungry or thirsty, you can simply head for a nearby vending machine or a drinking fountain. But, if a department store clerk infuriates you, you aren't likely to reach across the counter and slug the clerk, because this is socially unacceptable behavior. Likewise, when you see an attractive person who inspires lustful urges, you don't normally walk up and propose a tryst in a nearby broom closet. There's nothing comparable to vending machines or drinking fountains for the satisfaction of our sexual and aggressive urges.

Thus, Freud ascribed great importance to these needs because social norms dictate that they're routinely frustrated.

ANXIETY AND DEFENSE MECHANISMS

Most of our conflicts are trivial and quickly resolved one way or the other. Occasionally, however, a conflict will linger on for days, months, and even years, creating internal tension. More often than not, such prolonged and troublesome conflicts involve sexual and aggressive impulses that society wants to tame. These conflicts are often played out entirely in the unconscious. Although you may not be aware of these unconscious battles, they can produce *anxiety* that slips to the surface of conscious awareness. The anxiety can be attributed to your ego worrying about (1) the id getting out of control and doing something terrible that leads to severe negative consequences or (2) the superego getting out of control and making you feel terribly guilty about a real or imagined transgression.

The arousal of anxiety is a crucial event in Freud's theory of personality functioning. Anxiety is distressing, so people try to rid themselves of this unpleasant emotion any way they can. This effort to ward off anxiety often involves defense mechanisms (see Table 12.3). **Defense mechanisms are largely unconscious reactions that protect a person from unpleasant emotions such as anxiety and guilt.** Typically, they're mental maneuvers that work through self-deception. Consider **rationalization, which involves creating false but plausible excuses to justify unacceptable behavior.** For example, after cheating someone in a business transaction, you might reduce your guilt by rationalizing that "everyone does it."

According to Freud, the most basic and widely used defense mechanism is repression. **Repression involves keeping distressing thoughts and feelings buried in the unconscious.** We tend to repress desires that make us feel guilty, conflicts that make us anxious, and memories that are painful. Repression has been called "motivated forgetting." If you forget a dental appointment or the name of someone you don't like, repression may be at work.

Self-deception can also be seen in projection and displacement. **Projection involves attributing your own thoughts, feelings, or motives to another.** Usually, the thoughts we project onto others are thoughts that would make us feel guilty. For example, if your lust for a coworker makes you feel guilty, you might attribute any latent sexual tension between the two of you to the *other person's* desire to seduce you. **Displacement involves diverting emotional feelings (usually anger) from**

Table 12.3 Defense Mechanisms, with Examples

DEFINITION	EXAMPLE
Repression involves keeping distressing thoughts and feelings buried in the unconscious.	A traumatized soldier has no recollection of the details of a close brush with death.
Projection involves attributing one's own thoughts, feelings, or motives to another.	A woman who dislikes her boss thinks she likes her boss, but feels that the boss doesn't like her.
Displacement involves diverting emotional feelings (usually anger) from their original source to a substitute target.	After parental scolding, a young girl takes her anger out on her little brother.
Reaction formation involves behaving in a way that is exactly the opposite of one's true feelings.	A parent who unconsciously resents a child spoils the child with outlandish gifts.
Regression involves a reversion to immature patterns of behavior.	An adult has a temper tantrum when he doesn't get his way.
Rationalization involves creating false but plausible excuses to justify unacceptable behavior.	A student watches TV instead of studying, saying that "additional study wouldn't do any good anyway."
Identification involves bolstering self-esteem by forming an imaginary or real alliance with some person or group.	An insecure young man joins a fraternity to boost his self-esteem.

their original source to a substitute target. If your boss gives you a hard time at work and you come home and slam the door, kick the dog, and scream at your spouse, you're displacing your anger onto irrelevant targets. Unfortunately, social constraints often force us to hold back our anger, and we end up lashing out at the people we love the most.

Other prominent defense mechanisms include reaction formation, regression, and identification. **Reaction formation involves behaving in a way that's exactly the opposite of one's true feelings.** Guilt about sexual desires often leads to reaction formation. Freud theorized that many males who ridicule homosexuals are defending against their own latent homosexual impulses. The telltale sign of reaction formation is the exaggerated quality of the opposite behavior. **Regression involves a reversion to immature patterns of behavior.** When anxious about their self-worth, some adults respond with childish boasting and bragging (as opposed to subtle efforts to impress others). For example, a fired executive having difficulty finding a new job might start making ridiculous statements about his incomparable talents and achievements. Such bragging is regressive when it's marked by massive exaggerations that virtually anyone can see through. **Identification involves bolstering self-esteem by forming an imaginary or real alliance with some person or group.** For example, youngsters often shore up precarious feelings of self-worth by identifying with rock-star heroes, movie stars, or famous athletes. Adults may join exclusive country clubs or civic organizations.

CONCEPT CHECK 12.1
Identifying Defense Mechanisms

Check your understanding of defense mechanisms by identifying specific defenses in the story below. Each example of a defense mechanism is underlined, with a number beneath it. Write in the defense at work in each case in the numbered spaces after the story. The answers are in Appendix A.

My boyfriend recently broke up with me after we had dated seriously for several years. At first, I cried a great deal and locked myself in my room, where I pouted endlessly. I was sure that my former boyfriend felt as miserable as I did. I told several friends that he was probably lonely and depressed. Later, I decided that I hated him. I was happy about the breakup and talked about how much I was going to enjoy my newfound freedom. I went to parties and socialized a great deal and just forgot about him. It's funny—at one point I couldn't even remember his phone number! Then I started pining for him again. But eventually I began to look at the situation more objectively. I realized that he had many faults and that we were bound to break up sooner or later, so I was better off without him.

1. _____
2. _____
3. _____
4. _____
5. _____

Additional examples of the defense mechanisms we've described here can be found in Table 12.3. If you see defensive maneuvers that you've employed, you shouldn't be surprised. According to Freud, we all use defense mechanisms to some extent. They become problematic only when we depend on them excessively. The seeds for psychological disorders are sown only when our defenses lead to wholesale distortion of reality.

The defense mechanism has become a widely used concept in psychology, and various theorists have added to Freud's original list of defenses. We'll examine some of these additional defense mechanisms in the next chapter when we discuss the role of defenses in coping with stress. For now, however, let's turn our attention to Freud's ideas about the development of personality.

DEVELOPMENT: PSYCHOSEXUAL STAGES

Freud believed that "the child is father to the man." In fact, he made the rather startling assertion that the basic foundation of an individual's personality has been laid down by the tender age of 5! To shed light on these crucial early years, Freud formulated a stage theory of development that emphasized how young children deal with their immature but powerful sexual urges (he used the term "sexual" in a general way to refer to many urges for physical pleasure). According to Freud, these sexual urges shift in focus as children progress from one stage of development to another. Indeed, the names for the stages (oral, anal, genital, and so on) are based on where children are focusing their erotic energy at the time. Thus, *psychosexual stages* are developmental periods with a characteristic sexual focus that leave their mark on adult personality.

Freud theorized that each psychosexual stage has its own, unique developmental challenges or tasks (see Table 12.4). The way these challenges are handled supposedly shapes personality. The notion of *fixation* plays an important role in this process. **Fixation involves a failure to move forward from one stage to another as expected.** Essentially, the child's development stalls for a while. Fixation is caused by *excessive gratification* of needs at a particular stage, or by *excessive frustration* of those needs. Either way, fixations left over from childhood affect adult personality. Generally, fixation leads to an overemphasis on the psychosexual needs that were prominent during the fixated stage. Freud described a series of five psychosexual stages. Let's examine some of the highlights in this developmental sequence.

ORAL STAGE This stage usually encompasses the first year of life, during which the main source of erotic stimulation is the mouth (in biting, sucking, chewing, and so on). The handling of the child's feeding experiences is supposed to be crucial to subsequent development. Considerable importance is attributed to the manner in which the child is weaned from the breast or the bottle. According to Freud, fixation at the oral stage could form the basis for obsessive eating or smoking later in life (among many other things).

ANAL STAGE In their second year, children supposedly get their erotic pleasure from their bowel movements, through either the expulsion or retention of the feces. The crucial event at this time involves toilet training, which represents society's first systematic effort to regulate the child's biological urges. Severely punitive toilet training is thought to lead to a variety of possible outcomes. For example, excessive punishment might produce a latent feeling of hostility toward the "trainer," usually the mother, and this hostility might generalize to women as a class. Another possibility is that heavy reliance on punitive mea-

---

Table 12.4 Summary of Freud's Stages of Psychosexual Development

STAGE	APPROXIMATE AGES	EROTIC FOCUS	KEY TASKS AND EXPERIENCES
Oral	0–1	Mouth (sucking, biting)	Weaning (from breast or bottle)
Anal	1–3	Anus (expelling or retaining feces)	Toilet training
Phallic	3–6	Genitals (masturbating)	Identifying with adult role models; coping with Oedipal crisis
Latency	6–12	None (sexually repressed)	Expanding social contacts
Genital	Puberty onward	Genitals (being sexually intimate)	Establishing intimate relationships; contributing to society through working

sures might lead to an association between genital concerns and the anxiety that the punishment arouses. This genital anxiety derived from severe toilet training could evolve into anxiety about sexual activities later in life.

PHALLIC STAGE Around the ages of 3 through 6, the genitals become the focus for the child's erotic energy, largely through self-stimulation. During this very pivotal stage, the *Oedipal complex* emerges. Little boys develop an erotically tinged preference for their mother. They also feel hostility toward their father, whom they view as a competitor for mom's affection. Little girls develop a special attachment to their father. Around the same time, they learn that little boys have very different genitals, and they supposedly develop *penis envy*. According to Freud, young girls feel hostile toward their mother because they blame her for their anatomical "deficiency."

To summarize, **in the *Oedipal complex* children manifest erotically tinged desires for their opposite-sex parent, accompanied by feelings of hostility toward their same-sex parent**. The name for this syndrome was taken from a tragic myth from ancient Greece: Oedipus is separated from his parents at birth, and, not knowing the identity of his real parents, he inadvertently kills his father and marries his mother.

According to Freud, the way parents and children deal with the sexual and aggressive conflicts inherent in the Oedipal complex is of paramount importance. The child has to resolve the Oedipal dilemma by purging the sexual longings for the opposite-sex parent and by crushing the hostility felt toward the same-sex parent. Healthy psychosexual development is supposed to hinge on the resolution of the Oedipal conflict. Why? Because continued hostility with the same-sex parent may prevent the child from identifying adequately with that parent. Freudian theory predicts that without such identification many aspects of the child's development won't progress as they should.

LATENCY AND GENITAL STAGES From around age 6 through puberty, the child's sexuality is largely suppressed—it becomes *latent*. Important events during this *latency stage* center on expanding social contacts beyond the immediate family. With the advent of puberty, the child progresses into the *genital stage*. Sexual urges reappear and focus on the genitals once again. At this point, the sexual energy is normally channeled toward peers of the other sex, rather than toward oneself, as in the phallic stage.

In arguing that the early years shape personality, Freud did not mean that personality development comes to an abrupt halt in middle childhood. However, he did believe that the foundation for one's adult personality had been solidly entrenched by this time. He maintained that future developments are rooted in early, formative experiences and that significant conflicts in later years are replays of crises from childhood.

In fact, Freud believed that unconscious sexual conflicts rooted in childhood experiences cause most personality disturbances. His steadfast belief in the psychosexual origins of psychological disorders eventually led to bitter theoretical disputes with two of his most brilliant colleagues—Carl Jung and Alfred Adler. Jung and Adler both argued that Freud overemphasized sexuality. Freud summarily rejected their ideas, and the other two theorists felt compelled to go their own way, developing their own psychodynamic theories of personality.

Jung's Analytical Psychology

Carl Jung was born to middle-class Swiss parents in 1875. The son of a Protestant pastor, he was a deeply introverted, lonely child, but an excellent student. Jung had earned his medical degree and was an established young psychiatrist in Zurich when he began to write to Freud in 1906. When the two men had their first meeting, they were so taken by each other's insights, they talked nonstop for 13 hours! They exchanged 359 letters before their friendship and theoretical alliance were torn apart in 1913.

Given that Freud was exploring new and uncharted frontiers in psychodynamics, it was understandable that Jung felt the need to propose revisions and refinements of psychoanalytic theory. Indeed, Freud himself modified his ideas in many ways during his 50 years of theory building. Nonetheless, Freud expressed great displeasure when his disciples proposed their own revisions. The relationship between Jung and Freud was ruptured irreparably when Jung could no longer accept the immense importance that Freud placed on sexuality. As Jung put it, "What I seek is to set bounds to the rampant terminology of sex which vitiates all discussion of the human psyche, and to put sexuality itself in its proper place" (Jung, 1917). He called his new approach *analytical psychology* to differentiate it from Freud's psychoanalytic theory.

Jung's analytical psychology eventually attracted many followers. Unlike Freud, Jung encouraged his followers to develop their own theoretical views. Perhaps because of his conflict with Freud, he deplored the way schools of

"I am not a Jungian . . . I do not want anybody to be a Jungian. I want people above all to be themselves."
CARL JUNG

Figure 12.2 Jung's vision of the collective unconscious. Much like Freud, Jung theorized that each person has conscious and unconscious levels of awareness. However, he also proposed that the entire human race shares a collective unconscious, which exists in the deepest reaches of our awareness. He saw the collective unconscious as a storehouse of hidden ancestral memories, called archetypes. Jung believed that important cultural symbols emerge from these universal archetypes. Thus, he argued that remarkable resemblances among symbols from very disparate cultures (such as the mandalas shown here) are evidence of the existence of the collective unconscious.

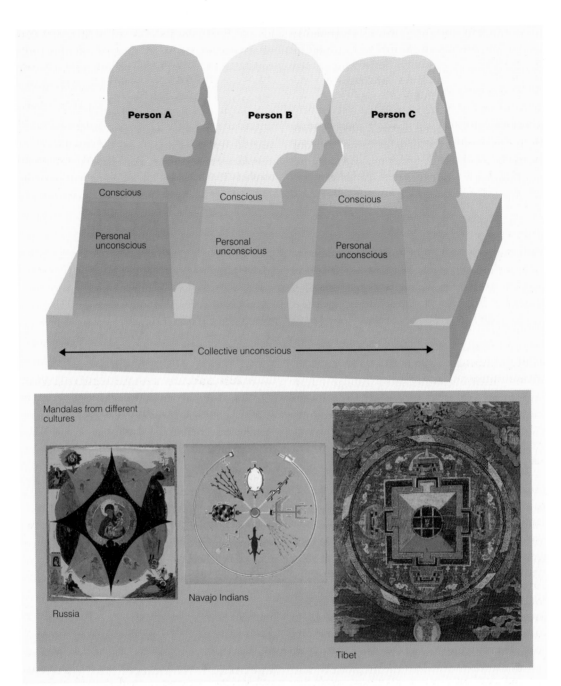

thought often become dogmatic, discouraging creative, new ideas. Although many theorists came to characterize themselves as "Jungians," Jung himself often remarked "I am not a Jungian," and "I do not want anybody to be a Jungian. I want people above all to be themselves" (van der Post, 1975).

Like Freud, Jung (1921, 1933) emphasized the unconscious determinants of personality. However, he proposed that the unconscious consists of *two* layers. The first layer, called the personal unconscious, is essentially the same as Freud's version of the unconscious. **The *personal unconscious* houses material that is not within one's conscious awareness because it has been** repressed or forgotten. In addition, Jung theorized the existence of a deeper layer he called the collective unconscious. **The *collective unconscious* is a storehouse of latent memory traces inherited from our ancestral past.** According to Jung, we share our collective unconscious with the entire human race (see Figure 12.2). It contains the "whole spiritual heritage of mankind's evolution, born anew in the brain structure of every individual" (Jung quoted in Campbell, 1971, p. 45).

Jung called these ancestral memories archetypes. They are not specific memories of actual, personal experiences. Instead, *archetypes* are **emotionally charged images and thought forms** that have **universal meaning**. These archetypal images and ideas show up frequently in dreams and are often manifested in a culture's use of symbols in art, literature, and religion. According to Jung, symbols from very different cultures often show striking similarities because they emerge from archetypes that are shared by the entire human race. For instance, Jung found numerous cultures in which the *mandala* or "magic circle" served as a symbol of the unified wholeness of the self (see Figure 12.2).

To better understand archetypal symbolism, Jung traveled widely, researching artistic, literary, and religious symbolism in a great variety of cultures. He studied Navajo Indians as well as cultures in India and in Sudan, Egypt, and other parts of Africa. Jung felt that an understanding of archetypal symbols helped him to make sense out of his patients' dreams. This was of great concern to him, as he thought that dreams contained important messages from the unconscious. Like Freud, he depended extensively on dream analysis in his treatment of patients.

Jung's unusual ideas about the collective unconscious did not have much impact on the mainstream of thinking in psychology. Their influence was felt more in other fields, such as anthropology, philosophy, art, and religious studies. Ironically, Freud was sympathetic to Jung's concept of the collective unconscious, but he was reluctant to incorporate this highly unconventional idea into his psychoanalytic theory because he thought that his theory was already too controversial.

However, many of Jung's other ideas *have* been incorporated into the mainstream of psychology. For instance, Jung was the first to describe the introverted (inner-directed) and extraverted (outer-directed) personality types. **Introverts** tend to be preoccupied with the internal world of their own thoughts, feelings, and experiences. Like Jung himself, they generally are contemplative and aloof. In contrast, **extraverts** tend to be interested in the external world of people and things. They're more likely to be outgoing, talkative, and friendly, instead of reclusive.

Jung was also the first personality theorist to argue that to be psychologically healthy, people need to fulfill their potential. Thus, 30 years before the advent of humanistic theory in psychology, he anticipated the humanists' emphasis on personal growth and self-actualization, which we'll discuss later in this chapter.

Adler's Individual Psychology

Like Freud, Alfred Adler grew up in Vienna in a middle-class Jewish home. He was a sickly child who struggled to overcome rickets and an almost fatal case of pneumonia. At home, he was overshadowed by an exceptionally bright and successful older brother. Nonetheless, he went on to earn his medical degree, and he practiced ophthalmology and general medicine before his interest turned to psychiatry. He was a charter member of Freud's inner circle—the Vienna Psychoanalytic Society. However, he soon began to develop his own theory of personality, perhaps because he didn't want to be dominated once again by an "older brother" (Freud). His theorizing was denounced by Freud in 1911, and Adler was forced to resign from the Psychoanalytic Society. He took 9 of its 23 members with him to form his own organization. Adler's new approach to personality was christened *individual psychology*.

Like Jung, Adler (1917, 1927) argued that Freud had gone overboard in centering his theory around sexual conflicts. According to Adler, the foremost source of human motivation is a striving for superiority. For Adler, this striving did not necessarily translate into the pursuit of dominance or high status. Adler viewed **striving for superiority as a universal drive to adapt, improve oneself, and master life's challenges**. He noted that young children understandably feel weak and helpless in comparison with more competent older children and adults. These early inferiority feelings supposedly motivate us to acquire new skills and develop new talents. Thus, Adler maintained that striving for superiority was the prime goal of life, rather than physical gratification (as suggested by Freud).

Adler asserted that everyone has to work to overcome some feelings of inferiority. **Compensation involves efforts to overcome imagined or real inferiorities by developing one's abilities.** Adler believed that compensation was entirely normal. However, inferiority feelings can become excessive in some people. The result is an *inferiority complex*—**exaggerated feelings of weakness and inadequacy.** Adler thought that either parental pampering or parental neglect could cause an inferiority complex. Thus, he agreed with Freud on the importance of early childhood, although he focused on different aspects of parent-child relations.

According to Adler, "All neurotic symptoms are safeguards of persons who don't feel adequately equipped or prepared for the problems of life" (Adler, 1964, p. 95). Thus, Adler explained personality disturbances by noting that an inferiority complex can pervert the normal process of striving for superiority. He asserted that some people engage in *overcompensation* in order to conceal, even from themselves, their feelings of inferiority.

"The goal of the human soul is conquest, perfection, security, superiority."
ALFRED ADLER

Instead of working to master life's challenges, people with an inferiority complex work to achieve status, gain power over others, and acquire the trappings of success (fancy clothes, impressive cars, or whatever looks important to them). They tend to flaunt their success in an effort to cover up their underlying inferiority complex. However, the problem is that such people engage in unconscious self-deception, worrying more about *appearances* than *reality*.

Adler's theory stressed the social context of personality development. For instance, it was Adler who first focused attention on the possible importance of birth order as a factor governing personality. He noted that only children, firstborns, second children, and subsequent children enter very different social environments that are likely to affect their personality. Thus, he theorized that children without siblings are often spoiled by excessive attention from parents. He thought that firstborns often are problem children because they become upset when they're "dethroned" by a second child. He hypothesized that second-born children would tend to be competitive because they have to struggle to catch up with an older sibling. Adler's hypotheses stimulated hundreds of studies on the effects of birth order. This research has proven very interesting, although the effects of birth order have turned out to be weaker and less consistent than Adler expected (Schooler, 1972).

Adler's interest in birth order was just one manifestation of his emphasis on the importance of the social environment in shaping personality.

Adler's theory has been used to analyze the tragic life of the legendary sex symbol Marilyn Monroe (Ansbacher, 1970). During her childhood, Monroe suffered from parental neglect that left her with acute feelings of inferiority and a lack of social interest. Her inferiority feelings led her to overcompensate by flaunting her beauty, marrying celebrities (Joe DiMaggio and Arthur Miller), keeping film crews waiting for hours, and seeking the adoration of her fans. Her lack of social interest made her aloof, manipulative, and self-centered—traits that probably contributed to her failed marriages.

The tragedies and heroism that he witnessed as a physician assigned to the Russian front during World War I increased his appreciation of the social context that we evolve in. He concluded that human nature includes a unique **social interest—an innate sense of kinship and belongingness with the human race.** He saw this social interest as the source of humans' willingness to work together, in a spirit of cooperation, for the common good of the society.

Evaluating Psychodynamic Perspectives

The psychodynamic approach has given us a number of far-reaching, truly "grand" theories of personality. These theories yielded some bold new insights. Although one might argue about exact details of interpretation, psychodynamic theory and research have demonstrated (1) that unconscious forces can influence behavior, (2) that internal conflict often plays a key role in generating psychological distress, and (3) that early childhood experiences can influence adult personality. Psychodynamic models have also been praised because they probe beneath the surface of personality and because they focus attention on how personality develops over time. Many widely used concepts in psychology emerged out of psychodynamic theories, including the unconscious, defense mechanisms, introversion-extraversion, and the inferiority complex.

But in addition to being praised, psychodynamic formulations have also been criticized on several grounds, including the following:

1. *Lack of testability.* Scientific investigations require testable hypotheses. Psychodynamic ideas have often been too vague to permit a clear scientific test. For instance, no one has figured out how to either prove or disprove the existence of the collective unconscious described by Jung.

2. *Inadequate evidence.* The empirical evidence on psychodynamic theories has often been characterized as "inadequate." There has been too much dependence on clinical case studies in which it's much too easy for clinicians to see what they expect to see based on their theory. There's also a problem in that the subjects observed in clinical situations are not particularly representative of the population at large. Insofar as we have accumulated evidence on psychodynamic theories, the evidence has provided only modest support for the central hypotheses.

3. *Sexism.* Many critics have argued that psychodynamic theories are characterized by a sexist bias against women. Freud believed that females' penis envy made them feel inferior to men. He also

thought that females tended to develop weaker superegos and to be more prone to neurosis than men. He dismissed female patients' reports of sexual molestation during childhood as mere fantasies. Although the sex bias in modern Freudian theories has been reduced to some degree, the psychodynamic approach has generally provided a rather male-centered view of behavior.

It's easy to ridicule Freud for concepts such as penis envy, and it's easy to point to Freudian ideas that have turned out to be wrong. However, you have to remember that Freud, Jung, and Adler began to fashion their theories about a century ago. It's not entirely fair to compare these theories to other models that are only a decade old. That's like asking the Wright brothers to race the Concorde. Freud and his colleagues deserve great credit for breaking new ground with their speculations about psychodynamics. Standing at a distance a century later, one has to be impressed by the extraordinary impact that psychodynamic theory has had upon modern intellectual thought. In psychology as a whole, no other school of thought has been as influential, with the exception of behaviorism, which we turn to next.

BEHAVIORAL PERSPECTIVES

Behaviorism is a theoretical orientation based on the premise that scientific psychology should study only observable behavior. Behaviorism has been a major school of thought in psychology since 1913, when John B. Watson began campaigning for the behavioral point of view. Research in the behavioral tradition has focused largely on learning, and for many decades behaviorists devoted relatively little attention to the study of personality. However, their interest in personality began to pick up after John Dollard and Neal Miller (1950) attempted to translate selected Freudian ideas into behavioral terminology. Dollard and Miller showed that behavioral concepts could provide enlightening insights about the complicated subject of personality.

In this section, we'll examine three behavioral views of personality, as we discuss the ideas of B. F. Skinner, Albert Bandura, and Walter Mischel. For the most part, you'll see that behaviorists explain personality the same way they explain everything else—through *learning*.

Skinner's Ideas Applied to Personality

As we noted in Chapters 1 and 6, modern behaviorism's most prominent theorist has been B. F. Skinner, an American psychologist born in 1904. After earning his doctorate in 1931, Skinner spent most of his career at Harvard University, where he achieved renown for his research on learning in lower organisms, mostly rats and pigeons. Although Skinner's (1953, 1957) principles of *operant conditioning* were never meant to be a theory of personality, his ideas have affected thinking in all areas of psychology and have been applied to the explanation of personality. We'll examine Skinner's views as they relate to personality structure and development.

PERSONALITY STRUCTURE:
A VIEW FROM THE OUTSIDE
Unlike most personality theorists, Skinner makes no provision for internal personality structures similar to Freud's id, ego, and superego because such structures can't be observed. Following in the tradition of Watson, Skinner is not interested in what's going on "inside" a person. He argues that it's useless to speculate about private, unobservable cognitive processes. Instead, he focuses on how the external environment molds our overt behavior. Indeed, he argues for a strong brand of *determinism*, asserting that our behavior is fully determined by environmental stimuli. He claims that free will is but an illusion, saying, "There is no place in the scientific position for a self as a true originator or initiator of action" (Skinner, 1974, p. 225).

If our behavior is governed by the ever-changing environment around us, where does the consistency in our behavior come from? How does Skinner explain the stability that we see in individuals' behavior? According to Skinner, we show some consistent patterns of behavior because we have some stable *response tendencies* that we have acquired through experience. Our response tendencies may change in the future, as a result of new experience, but they're enduring enough to create a certain degree of consistency in our behavior.

Implicitly, then, Skinner views an individual's personality as a *collection of response tendencies that are tied to various stimulus situations*. A specific situation may be associated with a number of response tendencies that vary in strength, depending on past conditioning (see Figure 12.3). As an example, consider the rather general stimulus situation of a large party where you know relatively few people. Your response tendencies in this situ-

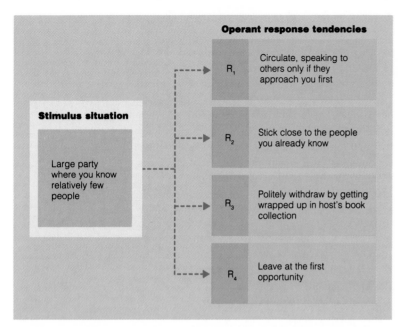

Operant response tendencies

Stimulus situation

Large party where you know relatively few people

R₁ — Circulate, speaking to others only if they approach you first

R₂ — Stick close to the people you already know

R₃ — Politely withdraw by getting wrapped up in host's book collection

R₄ — Leave at the first opportunity

Figure 12.3 A behavioral view of personality. Skinner and other staunch behaviorists devote little attention to the structure of personality because it is unobservable, but they implicitly view personality as an individual's collection of response tendencies. A possible hierarchy of response tendencies for a specific stimulus situation is shown here.

ation, in order of strength, might be (1) to circulate, speaking to others only if they approach you first, (2) to stick close to the few guests you already know, making no effort to meet anyone new, (3) to politely withdraw by getting wrapped up in your host's book or record collection (or whatever else is available), and (4) to leave as soon as you can.

If you showed similar response patterns in other social situations, most personality theorists would probably label you introverted. But Skinner avoids trait labels like introverted, optimistic, or assertive, because he sees personality traits as imaginary, internal determinants of behavior. Skinner is content with his view from the outside; he maintains that we should simply describe the relationships that we observe between stimulus situations and your patterns of responding.

Stimulus context

Party

Telling jokes — Followed by → Attention, compliments

Response — **Reinforcer**

Figure 12.4 Personality development and operant conditioning. According to Skinner, our characteristic response tendencies are shaped by reinforcers and other consequences that follow behavior. Thus, if your joking at a party leads to attention and compliments, your tendency to be witty and humorous will be strengthened.

PERSONALITY DEVELOPMENT AS A PRODUCT OF CONDITIONING

Skinner accounts for personality development by explaining how our various response tendencies are acquired through learning. He acknowledges that some of our characteristic responses are the product of classical conditioning as described by Pavlov, but he believes that most of our responses are shaped by the type of conditioning that he described: operant conditioning.

As we discussed in Chapter 6, Skinner maintains that environmental consequences—reinforcement, punishment, and extinction—determine our patterns of responding. On the one hand, when our responses are followed by favorable consequences (reinforcement), they are strengthened. For example, if your joking at a party pays off with favorable attention, your tendency to joke at parties will increase (see Figure 12.4). On the other hand, when our responses lead to negative consequences (punishment), they are weakened. Thus, for example, if your impulsive decisions always backfire, your tendency to make quick decisions will decline.

Since our response tendencies are constantly being strengthened or weakened by new experiences and the consequences they bring, Skinner views personality development as a continuous, lifelong journey. Unlike Freud and many other theorists, he sees no reason to break the developmental process into stages, and he doesn't attribute special importance to early childhood experiences.

According to Skinner, conditioning in humans operates much the same as it does in the rats and pigeons that he has studied in his laboratory. Hence, he assumes that conditioning strengthens and weakens our response tendencies "mechanically," that is, without our conscious participation. In Skinner's eyes, the mechanical nature of conditioning allows us to explain consistencies in behavior (personality) without being concerned about individuals' cognitive processes.

Skinner's ideas continue to be very influential, but his mechanical, deterministic, noncognitive view of personality has not gone unchallenged by other behaviorists. Theorists such as Albert Bandura and Walter Mischel have developed somewhat different behavioral models with a more cognitive emphasis.

Bandura and Social Learning Theory

Albert Bandura is a contemporary theorist who has helped to reshape the theoretical landscape of behaviorism. Bandura grew up in Canada and earned his doctorate in psychology at the Univer-

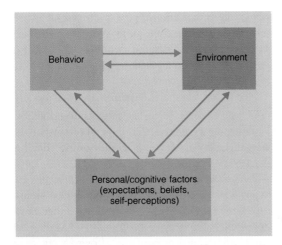

Figure 12.5 Bandura's reciprocal determinism. Bandura rejects Skinner's highly deterministic view that freedom is an illusion and argues that internal mental events, external environmental contingencies, and overt behavior all influence one another.

sity of Iowa, where he studied under Kenneth Spence, a prominent behaviorist. He has spent his entire academic career at Stanford University, where he has conducted influential research on behavior therapy and the determinants of aggression.

COGNITIVE PROCESSES AND RECIPROCAL DETERMINISM

Bandura is one of several behaviorists who have added a cognitive flavor to behaviorism since the 1960s. Bandura (1977), Walter Mischel (1973), and Julian Rotter (1982) take issue with Skinner's "pure" behaviorism. They point out that humans obviously are conscious, thinking, feeling beings. Moreover, they argue that in neglecting cognitive processes, Skinner ignores the most distinctive and important feature of human behavior. Bandura disagrees with Skinner's claim that mental processes can't be studied scientifically, noting that "Cognitive processes are not publicly observable, but they . . . can become known indirectly" (1986, p. 14). Bandura and like-minded theorists call their modified brand of behaviorism *social learning theory.*

Bandura (1982, 1986) agrees with the fundamental thrust of behaviorism in that he believes that personality is largely shaped through learning. However, he contends that conditioning is not a mechanical process in which we are passive participants. Instead, he maintains that we actively seek out and process information about our environment in order to maximize favorable outcomes. In focusing on information processing, he brings unobservable cognitive events into the picture.

Comparing his theory to Skinner's highly deterministic view, Bandura advocates a position that he calls *reciprocal determinism.* According to this notion, the environment does determine behavior (as Skinner would argue). However, behavior also determines the environment (in other words, we can act to alter our environment). Moreover, personal factors (cognitive structures such as beliefs and expectancies) determine and are determined by both behavior and the environment (see Figure 12.5). Thus, *reciprocal determinism* **involves the assumption that internal mental events, external environmental events, and overt behavior all influence one another.** According to Bandura, we are neither masters of our own destiny nor hapless victims buffeted about by the environment. Instead, the truth lies somewhere in between these two extremes.

OBSERVATIONAL LEARNING

Bandura's foremost theoretical contribution has been his description of observational learning, which we introduced in Chapter 6. *Observational learning* **occurs when an organism's responding is influenced by the observation of others, who are called models.** According to Bandura, both classical and operant conditioning can take place vicariously when one person observes another's conditioning. For example, if you watched your sister get "burned" by a rubber check when she sold her old stereo, this could strengthen your tendency to be suspicious of others. Although your sister would be the one actually experiencing the negative consequences, they might also influence you—through observational learning.

Skinner's theory makes no allowance for this type of indirect learning. After all, observational learning requires that you pay *attention* to your sister's behavior, that you *understand* its consequences, and that you store a mental representation of what you've witnessed in *memory.* Obviously, attention, understanding, and memory involve cognition, something that Skinner isn't interested in.

Bandura maintains that our characteristic patterns of behavior are shaped by the *models* that we're exposed to. He isn't referring to the attractive fashion models who dominate our mass media—although they might also qualify. In observational learning, **a *model* is a person whose behavior is observed by another.** At one time or another, we all serve as models for others. Bandura's key point is that many of our response tendencies are the product of imitation. The effort of some individuals to emulate fashion models is just a special instance of a very general phenomenon.

In recent decades, the potential influence of models has been dramatically and tragically demonstated by the occurrence of "copycat crimes." One person hijacks an airliner, sticks a razor blade in Halloween candy, or slips cyanide into drug capsules, and before you know it, a half-dozen copycats are showing the power of observational learning. The power of models is often in evidence at rock concerts. Many rock fans try to emulate their favorite performers, so that concert audiences are choked with Madonna "wanna-be's" and a surplus of Prince, Billy Idol, and David Byrne look-alikes.

As social learning theory has been refined, it has become apparent that some models are more influential than others. Both children and adults tend to imitate people they like or respect more than people they don't. We also are especially prone to imitate the behavior of people whom we consider attractive or powerful (such as rock stars). In addition, imitation is more likely when we see similarity between our models and ourselves. Thus, children tend to imitate same-sex role models somewhat more than opposite-sex models. Finally, as noted before, we are more likely to copy a model if we observe that the model's behavior leads to positive outcomes.

According to social learning theory, models have a great impact on personality development. Children learn to be assertive, conscientious, self-sufficient, dependable, easy-going, and so forth by observing others behaving in these ways. Parents, teachers, relatives, siblings, and peers serve as models for young children. Bandura and his colleagues have done extensive research showing how models influence the development of aggressiveness, sex roles, and moral standards in children (Bandura, 1973; Bussey & Bandura, 1984; Mischel & Mischel, 1976). Their research on modeling and aggression has been particularly influential.

MODELING AND AGGRESSION

In a classic study, Bandura, Ross, and Ross (1963) showed how the observation of filmed models can influence the learning of aggressive behavior in

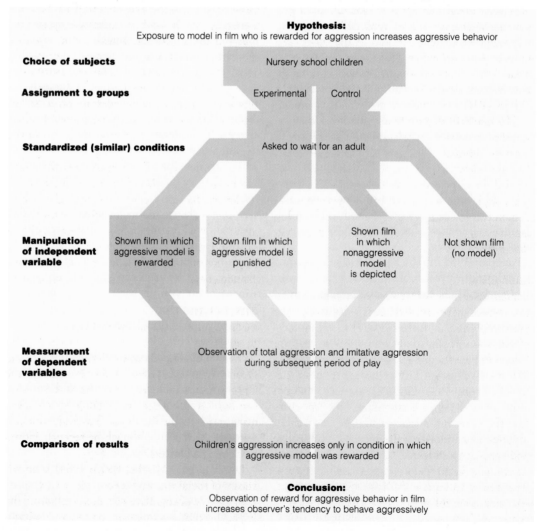

Figure 12.6 Design of the experiment by Bandura, Ross, and Ross (1963). The four conditions run in this classic study of modeling and aggression are outlined here.

children. They manipulated whether or not the subjects saw an aggressive model on film and whether the aggressive model experienced positive or negative consequences (see Figure 12.6). Nursery school children who were asked to watch TV while waiting for an adult saw one of three 5-minute film sequences. In the *Aggressive-Model-Rewarded* condition, Rocky and Johnny are playing with toys and Rocky attacks Johnny, striking him and dragging him off to a far corner of the room. The final scene shows Rocky having a great time with the toys while helping himself to pop and cookies. In the *Aggressive-Model-Punished* condition, Rocky engages in the same aggression, but Johnny thrashes Rocky, who is shown cowering in a corner in the final scene. In the *Nonaggressive-Model-Control* condition, Rocky and Johnny are simply shown engaged in vigorous play without any aggression. There also was a *No-Model-Control* condition in which subjects were not shown a film while they waited for their adult escort.

Soon after the manipulations, the children were taken to a toy room where their play was observed through a one-way mirror. Children who saw the aggressive model rewarded engaged in more aggression than children in the other conditions. Also, as Figure 12.7 shows, there was a clear elevation of imitative aggression (specific aggressive acts similar to Rocky's) only among the children who saw aggression pay off for the model.

The results of this study suggested that the portrayal of aggression on televison shows is likely to increase habitual aggressiveness among children, because television role models are frequently rewarded for their aggressive behavior. This landmark study was one of the earliest experimental demonstrations of a cause-and-effect relationship between aggressive behavior and exposure to media violence.

SELF-EFFICACY

Bandura discusses how a variety of personal factors (aspects of personality) govern behavior. The most important of these personal factors is **self-efficacy—our belief about our ability to perform behaviors that should lead to expected outcomes**. When self-efficacy is high, we feel confident that we can execute the responses necessary to earn reinforcers. When self-efficacy is low, we worry that the necessary responses may be beyond our abilities. Perceptions of self-efficacy are subjective and specific to different kinds of tasks. For instance, you might feel extremely confident about your ability to handle difficult social situations, but very doubtful about your ability to handle academic challenges.

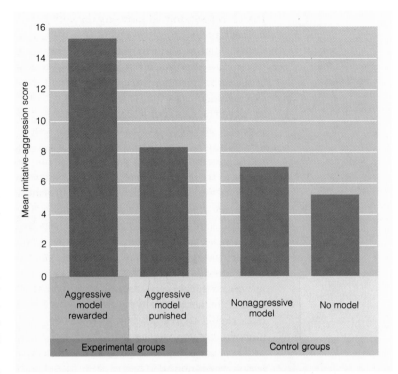

Perceptions of self-efficacy can influence which challenges we tackle and how well we perform. Generally, you'll tend to undertake those tasks that you think you can handle, while avoiding those that you think are beyond your ability. Moreover, your feelings of confidence may influence your persistence on a task and the emotions that you experience while working on it. When your confidence is high, you'll tend to work longer and harder while experiencing fewer disruptive emotions such as anxiety or despair.

With its heavy emphasis on learning, Bandura's theory is firmly grounded in the tradition of behaviorism, but its cognitive element allows it to account for aspects of human behavior that Skinner's theory can't explain. A similar brand of cognitive-oriented behaviorism is apparent in the theorizing of Walter Mischel, whose ideas we'll examine next.

Mischel and the Person-Situation Controversy

Walter Mischel was born in Vienna, not far from Freud's home. His family immigrated to the United States in 1939, when he was 9. After earning his doctorate in psychology, he spent many years on the faculty at Stanford, as a colleague of Bandura's, although he recently moved to Columbia University.

Like Bandura, Mischel (1973; 1984) is an advocate of social learning theory. He, too, emphasizes the role of cognitive factors in mediating the impact of reinforcement on behavior. Mischel's

Figure 12.7 Results of the study by Bandura, Ross, and Ross (1963). Of the four treatments run in this study, only one produced a clear increase in aggression—the condition in which children saw aggressive behavior pay off for a filmed model. The results suggest that observational learning shapes personality, including the trait of aggressiveness.

chief contribution to personality theory has been to focus attention on the extent to which situational factors govern behavior. This contribution has embroiled him in a fundamental controversy about the consistency of human behavior across varying situations.

According to social learning theory, we make responses that we think will lead to reinforcement in the situation at hand. We try to gauge the reinforcement contingencies and adjust our behavior to the circumstances. Thus, if you believe that hard work in your job will pay off by leading to raises and promotions, you'll probably be diligent and industrious. But if you think that hard work in your job is unlikely to be rewarded, you may behave in a lazy and irresponsible manner.

Thus, social learning theory predicts that people will often behave differently in different situations. Mischel (1968, 1973) reviewed decades of research and concluded that, indeed, people exhibit far less consistency across situations than widely assumed. For example, studies show that a person who is honest in one situation may be dishonest in another. Someone who wouldn't dream of being dishonest in a business deal might engage in wholesale cheating in filling out tax returns. Similarly, some people are quite shy in one situation and very outgoing in another. In light of these realities, Mischel maintains that behavior is characterized by more *situational specificity* than consistency.

Mischel's position has generated great controversy because it strikes at the heart of the concept of personality itself. As we discussed at the beginning of the chapter, we use the concept of personality to explain consistency in our behavior over time and situations. If there isn't much consistency—then there isn't much need for the concept of personality.

Mischel's views have attracted many critics who have sought to defend the value of the personality concept. For instance, Epstein (1980) argued that the methods used in much of the research reviewed by Mischel led to an underestimate of cross-situational consistency. Block (1981) marshaled data indicating that personality traits are reasonably stable over periods of many years. Other researchers argued that Mischel failed to consider that some people are more consistent than others in behavior and that a particular person will be more consistent on some traits than on other traits (Bem & Allen, 1974; Kenrick & Stringfield, 1980). Thus, Mischel's provocative theories have sparked a robust debate about the relative importance of the *person* as opposed to the *situation* in determining behavior.

This debate has led to a growing recognition

"It seems remarkable how each of us generally manages to reconcile his seemingly diverse behaviors into one self-consistent whole."
WALTER MISCHEL

that both the person and the situation are very important determinants of behavior. The concept of personality doesn't require anything approaching *complete* consistency in behavior. There clearly is enough cross-situational consistency in humans' behavior to warrant interest in person variables, or personality. In fact, Mischel never advocated that we should discard the personality concept. He merely asserted that we should pay more attention to the situational determinants of behavior and how they interact with personality variables. His arguments and the ensuing debate have led many psychologists to do just that (Kenrick & Funder, 1988).

Evaluating Behavioral Perspectives

Behavioral theories are firmly rooted in extensive empirical research rather than clinical intuition. This commitment to research has kept the behavioral approach open to new findings and new ideas. Thus, it has continued to evolve while some theoretical approaches have been stagnant in comparison.

Skinner's ideas have shed light on how environmental consequences and conditioning mold our characteristic behavior. Bandura's social learning theory has expanded the horizons of behaviorism and increased its relevance to the study of personality. Mischel deserves credit for increasing our awareness of how situational factors interact with personality to govern behavior. Of course, each theoretical approach has its shortcomings, and the behavioral approach is no exception. Major lines of criticism include the following:

1. *Overdependence on animal research.* Many principles in behavioral theories have been discovered through research on animals. Some critics argue that behaviorists have depended too much on animal research and that they have indiscriminately generalized from animal behavior to human behavior.

2. *Neglect of biological factors.* Most behaviorists, including Skinner, don't deny that biological factors influence our behavior. However, the behaviorists have made little effort to integrate biological factors into their theories.

3. *Fragmentation of personality.* Behaviorists have also been criticized for providing a fragmented view of personality. The behavioral approach carves personality up into stimulus-response associations. There are no unifying structural concepts (such as Freud's ego) that tie these pieces together. Humanistic theorists, whom we shall cover next, have been particularly vocal in criticizing this piecemeal analysis of personality.

Humanistic theory emerged in the 1950s as something of a backlash against the behavioral and psychodynamic theories that we have just discussed. The principal charge hurled at these two models was that they were dehumanizing. Freudian theory was criticized for its belief that behavior is dominated by primitive, animalistic drives. Behaviorism was criticized for its preoccupation with animal research and for its mechanistic, fragmented view of personality. Critics argued that both schools of thought were too deterministic and that both failed to recognize the unique qualities of human behavior. Many of these critics blended into a loose alliance that was christened the "third force" in psychology because it surfaced as an alternative to the two dominant "forces" at the time (the psychodynamic and behavioral orientations).

This third force came to be known as humanism because of its exclusive interest in human behavior. **Humanism is a theoretical orientation that emphasizes the unique qualities of humans, especially their free will and their potential for personal growth.** Humanistic psychologists are interested only in issues that are important to human existence—like love, creativity, loneliness, and personal growth. They don't believe that we can learn anything of any significance about the human condition from animal research.

In contrast to most psychodynamic and behavioral theorists, humanistic theorists take an optimistic view of human nature. Besides assuming that we have the freedom to chart our own courses of action and an innate drive toward personal growth, humanistic theories assume (1) that we can rise above our primitive animal heritage and control our biological urges and (2) that we are largely conscious and rational beings who are not dominated by unconscious, irrational needs and conflicts.

Humanistic theorists also maintain that one's subjective view of the world is more important than objective reality. According to this notion, if you *think* that you're homely, or bright, or sociable, then these beliefs will influence your behavior more than the realities of how homely, bright, or sociable you are. Therefore, the humanists embrace the *phenomenological approach*, **which assumes that we have to appreciate individuals' personal, subjective experiences to truly understand their behavior.** As Carl Rogers puts it, "The best vantage point for understanding behavior is from the internal frame of reference of the individual himself" (Rogers, 1951, p. 494).

The humanistic approach clearly provides a different perspective on personality than either the psychodynamic or the behavioral approach. In this section we'll review the ideas of the two most influential humanistic theorists, Carl Rogers and Abraham Maslow.

Rogers's Person-Centered Theory

Carl Rogers (1951, 1961, 1980) is one of the fathers of the human potential movement, which emphasizes self-realization through sensitivity training, encounter groups, and other exercises intended to foster personal growth. Rogers grew up in a religious, upper-middle-class home in the suburbs of Chicago. He was a bright student, but he had to rebel against his parents' wishes in order to pursue his graduate study in psychology, earning a doctorate from Columbia University in 1931. While he was working at the University of Chicago in the 1940s, Rogers devised a major new approach to psychotherapy. Like Freud, Rogers based his personality theory on his extensive therapeutic interactions with many clients. Because of its emphasis on a person's subjective point of view, Rogers calls his approach a *person-centered theory*.

THE SELF

Rogers views personality structure in terms of just one construct. He called this construct the *self*, although it's more widely known today as the *self-concept*. **A self-concept is a collection of beliefs about one's own nature, unique qualities, and typical behavior.** Your self-concept is your own mental picture of yourself. It's a collection of self-perceptions. For example, a self-concept might include beliefs such as, "I'm easy-going" or "I'm sly and crafty" or "I'm pretty" or "I'm hard-working." According to Rogers, we're aware of our self-concept; it's not buried in our unconscious.

Rogers stresses the subjective nature of the self-concept. Your self-concept may not be entirely consistent with your experiences. To put it more bluntly, your self-concept may be inaccurate. Most of us tend to distort our experiences to some extent to promote a relatively favorable self-concept. For example, you may believe that you're quite bright, but your grade transcript might suggest otherwise. Rogers calls this gap between your self-concept and reality incongruence. **Incongruence refers to the degree of disparity that exists between one's self-concept and one's actual experience.** In contrast, if a person's self-concept is

Figure 12.8 Rogers's view of personality structure. In Rogers's model, the self-concept is the only important structural construct. However, Rogers acknowledges that one's self-concept may not be consistent with the realities of one's actual experience—a condition called incongruence.

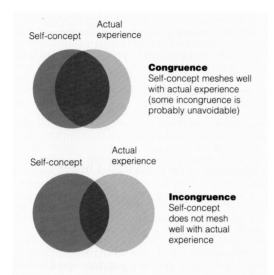

Self-concept / Actual experience

Congruence
Self-concept meshes well with actual experience (some incongruence is probably unavoidable)

Self-concept / Actual experience

Incongruence
Self-concept does not mesh well with actual experience

reasonably accurate, it's said to be *congruent* with reality (see Figure 12.8). Everyone experiences *some* incongruence; the crucial issue is how much. As we'll see, Rogers maintains that too much incongruence undermines our psychological well-being.

DEVELOPMENT OF THE SELF

In terms of personality development, Rogers was concerned with how childhood experiences promote congruence or incongruence between one's self-concept and one's experience. According to Rogers, we have a strong need for affection, love, and acceptance from others. Early in life, parents provide most of this affection. Rogers maintains that some parents make their affection very *conditional*—it depends on the child's behaving well and living up to expectations. When parental love seems conditional, children often block out of their self-concept those experiences that make them feel unworthy of love. They do this because they're worried about parental acceptance, which appears precarious. At the other end of the spectrum, Rogers asserts that some parents make their affection very *unconditional*. Their children have less need to block out unworthy experiences because they've been assured that they're worthy of affection, no matter what they do.

Hence, Rogers believes that unconditional love from parents fosters congruence and that conditional love fosters incongruence. He further theorizes that if we grow up believing that affection from others is very conditional, we go on to distort more and more of our experiences to feel worthy of acceptance from a wider and wider array of people.

A person's self-concept evolves throughout childhood and adolescence. As our self-concept gradually stabilizes, we begin to feel comfortable with it and we usually are loyal to it. This loyalty produces two effects. First, our self-concept be-

comes a "self-fulfilling prophecy" in that we tend to behave in ways that are consistent with it. If you see yourself as an even-tempered, reflective person, you'll consciously work at behaving in these ways. If you happen to behave impulsively, you'll probably feel some discomfort because you're "acting out of character." Second, we become resistant to information that contradicts our self-concept. Contradictory information threatens our comfortable equilibrium. If your experiences begin to suggest that you're not as even-tempered as you thought, you'll probably find ways to dismiss this evidence.

ANXIETY AND DEFENSE

According to Rogers, experiences that threaten our personal views of ourselves are the principal cause of troublesome anxiety. The more inaccurate your self-concept is, the more likely you are to have experiences that clash with your self-perceptions. Thus, people with highly incongruent self-concepts are especially likely to be plagued by recurrent anxiety.

To ward off this anxiety, we often behave defensively in an effort to reinterpret our experience so that it appears consistent with our self-concept. Thus, we ignore, deny, and twist reality in order to protect and perpetuate our self-concept. Consider a young lady who, like most of us, considers herself a "nice person." Let's suppose that in reality she is rather conceited and selfish, and she gets feedback from both boyfriends and girlfriends that she is a "self-centered, snotty brat." How might she react in order to protect her self-concept? She might ignore or block out those occasions when she behaves selfishly and deny the accusations by her friends that she is self-centered. She might attribute her girlfriends' negative comments to their jealousy of her good looks and blame the boyfriends' negative remarks on their disappointment because she won't get more serious with them. Meanwhile, she might start doing some kind of charity work to show everyone (including herself) that she really is a nice person. As you can see, we sometimes go to great lengths to defend our self-concept.

Rogers's theory can explain defensive behavior and personality disturbances, but he believes that it's also important to focus attention on psychological health. Rogers asserts that psychological health is rooted in a congruent self-concept. In turn, congruence is rooted in a sense of personal worth, which stems from a childhood saturated with unconditional affection from parents and others. These themes are very similar to those emphasized by the other major humanistic theorist, Abraham Maslow.

Maslow's Theory of Self-Actualization

Abraham Maslow grew up in Brooklyn and described his childhood as "unhappy, lonely, [and] isolated." To follow through on his interest in psychology, he had to resist parental pressures to go into law. In light of his later criticism of animal research, it's ironic that Maslow began his career studying the social behavior of monkeys under the guidance of Harry Harlow at the University of Wisconsin. He eventually moved on to Brandeis University, where he created an influential theory of motivation and provided crucial leadership for the fledgling humanistic movement.

Like Rogers, Maslow (1968, 1970) argued that psychology should take an optimistic view of human nature instead of dwelling on the causes of disorders. "To oversimplify the matter somewhat," he said, "it's as if Freud supplied to us the sick half of psychology and we must now fill it out with the healthy half" (Maslow, 1968, p. 5). Maslow's key contribution to personality theory was his description of the *self-actualizing person* as an example of psychological health.

THE NEED FOR SELF-ACTUALIZATION

Maslow's theory of motivation, which we discussed in Chapter 10, provided the basis for his views on the nature of the healthy personality. Maslow theorized that human needs are organized in a hierarchy and that lower needs must be satisfied before higher needs are activated. He also proposed that humans are driven by a **need for self-actualization, which is the need to fulfill one's potential; it's the highest need in Maslow's motivational hierarchy.** Thus, Maslow agreed with Rogers that we have an innate drive toward fulfillment and personal growth. Moreover, he believed that this fulfillment was crucial to psychological health, saying, "A musician must make music, an artist must paint, a poet must write, if he is to be ultimately at peace with himself. What a man *can* be, he *must* be" (Maslow, 1970, p. 46).

CHARACTERISTICS OF
SELF-ACTUALIZING PEOPLE

Working from this premise, Maslow set out to discover the nature of the healthy personality. He tried to identify people of exceptional mental health, so that he could investigate their characteristics. In one case, he used psychological tests and interviews to sort out the healthiest 1% of a sizable population of college students. He also studied admired historical figures (such as Thomas Jefferson and William James) and personal acquaintances characterized by superior adjustment. Over a period of years, he accumulated his case histories and gradually sketched, in broad strokes, a picture of ideal psychological health.

According to Maslow, **self-actualizing persons are people with exceptionally healthy personalities, marked by continued personal growth.** Maslow identified various traits that were characteristic of self-actualizing people; many of these traits are listed in Figure 12.9.

In brief, Maslow found that self-actualizers are accurately tuned in to reality and that they're at peace with themselves. He found that they're open and spontaneous and that they retain a fresh appreciation of the world around them. Socially, they're sensitive to others' needs and enjoy rewarding interpersonal relations, but they're not dependent upon others for approval or uncomfortable with solitude. They thrive on their work, and they enjoy their sense of humor. Maslow also noted that they enjoy "peak experiences" (profound emotional highs) more often than others. Finally, he found that they strike a nice balance between many polarities in personality, so that they can be both childlike and mature, rational and intuitive, conforming and rebellious.

Evaluating Humanistic Perspectives

The humanists added a refreshing new perspective to the study of personality. Their argument that a person's subjective views may be more important than objective reality has proven compelling. As we noted earlier, even behavioral theorists have begun to consider subjective personal factors such as beliefs and expectancies. The humanistic approach also deserves credit for making the self-concept an important construct in psychology. Today, theorists of many persuasions use the self-concept in their analyses of personality. Finally, the humanists have often been applauded for focusing attention on the issue of what constitutes a healthy personality.

Of course, there's a negative side to the balance sheet as well. Critics have identified some weak-

Characteristics of Self-Actualizing People

- Clear, efficient perception of reality and comfortable relations with it
- Spontaneity, simplicity, and naturalness
- Problem centering (having something outside themselves they "must" do as a mission)
- Detachment and need for privacy
- Autonomy, independence of culture and environment
- Continued freshness of appreciation
- Mystical and peak experiences
- Feelings of kinship and identification with the human race
- Strong friendships, but limited in number
- Democratic character structure
- Ethical discrimination between means and ends, between good and evil
- Philosophical, unhostile sense of humor
- Balance between polarities in personality

Figure 12.9 Maslow's view of the healthy personality. Humanistic theorists emphasize psychological health instead of maladjustment. Maslow's description of characteristics of self-actualizing people evokes a picture of the healthy personality.

"It is as if Freud supplied to us the sick half of psychology and we must now fill it out with the healthy half."
ABRAHAM MASLOW

nesses in the humanistic approach to personality, including the following.

1. *Lack of testability.* Like psychodynamic theorists, the humanists have been criticized for generating hypotheses that are very difficult to put to a scientific test. Humanistic concepts such as personal growth and self-actualization are difficult to define and measure.

2. *Unrealistic view of human nature.* Critics also charge that the humanists have been unrealistic in their assumptions about human nature and their descriptions of the healthy personality. For instance, Maslow's self-actualizing people sound *perfect.* In reality, Maslow had a very hard time finding such people. When he searched among the living, the results were so disappointing that he turned to the study of historical figures. Thus, humanistic portraits of psychological health are perhaps a bit too optimistic.

3. *Inadequate evidence.* For the most part, humanistic psychologists haven't been particularly research oriented. Some are scornful of efforts to quantify human experience to test hypotheses. Humanistic theories are based primarily on clinical observation. More experimental research is needed to catch up with the theorizing in the humanistic camp. This is precisely the opposite of the situation that we'll encounter in the next section, on biological perspectives, where more theorizing is needed to catch up with the research.

BIOLOGICAL PERSPECTIVES

"Personality is determined to a large extent by a person's genes."

HANS EYSENCK

Like many identical twins reared apart, Jim Lewis and Jim Springer found they had been leading eerily similar lives. Separated four weeks after birth in 1940, the Jim twins grew up 45 miles apart in Ohio and were reunited in 1979. Eventually, they discovered that both drove the same model blue Chevrolet, chain-smoked Salems, chewed their fingernails and owned dogs named Toy. Each had spent a good deal of time vacationing at the same three-block strip of beach in Florida. More important, when tested for such personality traits as flexibility, self-control, and sociability, the twins responded almost exactly alike (Leo, 1987, p. 63).

So began a *Time* magazine summary of a major twin study conducted at the University of Minnesota Center for Twin and Adoption Research, where since 1979 investigators have been studying the personality resemblance of identical twins reared apart. Thanks in part to publicity like the *Time* article, the investigators have managed to locate and complete testing on 44 rare pairs of identical twins separated early in life.

Not all the twin pairs have been as similar as Jim Lewis and Jim Springer, but many of the parallels have been uncanny. Identical twins Oskar Stohr and Jack Yufe were separated soon after birth, and Oskar was sent to a Nazi-run school in Czechoslovakia while Jack was raised in a Jewish home on a Caribbean island. When they were reunited for the first time during middle age, they both showed up wearing similar moustaches, haircuts, shirts, and wire-rimmed glasses! A pair of previously separated female twins both arrived at the Minneapolis airport wearing seven rings on their fingers. One had a son named Richard Andrew and the other had a son named Andrew Richard! Still another pair of separated twin sisters shared the same phobia of bodies of water, and they dealt with it in the same peculiar way—backing into the ocean.

Could personality be largely inherited? These anecdotal reports of striking resemblances between identical twins reared apart certainly raise

this possibility. As you'll see, this idea is not entirely new. In this section we'll discuss early biological theories of personality, review Hans Eysenck's modern theory, which emphasizes the influence of heredity, and look at the Minnesota study of twins reared apart.

Early Theories of Physique and Personality

In the first half of this century, Ernst Kretschmer (1921) and William Sheldon (1940) independently proposed theories that linked personality to physique on the grounds that both are governed by genetic endowment. Sheldon (1942) conducted elaborate research in which he rated male subjects' bodies along three dimensions and found high correlations between body types and clusters of personality traits (see Figure 12.10). In Sheldon's scheme, *endomorphy* referred to the degree to which one's body was fat, round, and soft; it was associated with a sociable, relaxed, affectionate personality. *Ectomorphy* referred to a thin, flat, frail body type, which was associated with an inhibited, apprehensive, intellectual personality. *Mesomorphy* referred to a hard, strong, muscular body type, which was associated with an energetic, competitive, domineering personality.

Sheldon's findings initially appeared to provide impressive support for his theory, but his research was marred by a fatal flaw. Sheldon had made all the ratings of both physique and personality himself. In retrospect, there's little doubt that he fell prey to experimenter bias. In making the personality ratings, he was influenced by subjects' readily apparent physiques, and he saw what he expected to see. His findings were not replicated in subsequent studies by other researchers. Ultimately,

the idea that physique and personality go hand in hand was abandoned in favor of more sophisticated biological theories of personality, such as the one devised by Hans Eysenck.

Eysenck's Theory

Hans Eysenck was born in Germany, but fled to London during the era of Nazi rule. He went on to become one of Britain's most prominent psychologists. Eysenck is drawn to controversy like a moth to a flame. He is best known for his central role in two of psychology's most heated debates—on the heritability of intelligence and on the effectiveness of psychotherapy. He has argued that intelligence is mostly determined by heredity, and that traditional, verbal therapies, especially Freudian therapy, have little or no value in the treatment of mental disorders. Both of these positions have been unpopular in the field, as Eysenck has acknowledged. "I have usually been against the establishment and in favor of the rebels" (Eysenck, 1982, p. 298).

Eysenck's (1967, 1982) biologically oriented theory of personality, which he first proposed while behaviorism was at the zenith of its influence, also went against the spirit of the times. According to Eysenck, "Personality is determined to a large extent by a person's genes" (1967, p. 20). How is heredity linked to personality in Eysenck's model? In part, through conditioning concepts borrowed from behavioral theory. Eysenck theorizes that some people can be conditioned more readily than others because of inherited differences in their physiological functioning. These variations in "conditionability" are assumed to influence the personality traits that people acquire through conditioning processes.

Endomorphic
Sociable, relaxed, affectionate, even-tempered

Mesomorphic
Energetic, competitive, aggressive, bold

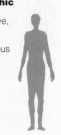

Ectomorphic
Inhibited, apprehensive, intellectual, introverted, self-conscious

Figure 12.10 Sheldon's biological theory. Sheldon described three basic types of physique and hypothesized that certain personality traits (such as those listed above) would be associated with each. His theory has not been supported by subsequent research.

453

Figure 12.11 Eysenck's model of personality structure. Eysenck describes personality structure as a hierarchy of traits. In this scheme, a few higher-order traits, such as extraversion, determine a host of lower-order traits, which determine our habitual responses.

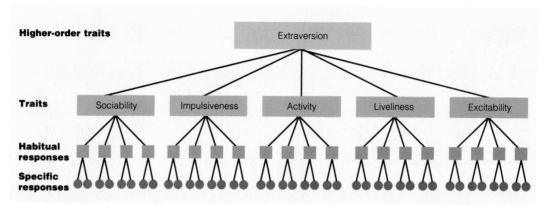

Eysenck's analysis of personality structure follows in the tradition established by Gordon Allport and Raymond Cattell, who both maintained that some traits are more important than others. Eysenck views personality as a hierarchy of traits, in which many superficial traits are derived from a smaller number of more basic traits, which are derived from a handful of fundamental higher-order traits, as shown in Figure 12.11. Like Cattell, Eysenck has used factor analysis to identify the fundamental dimensions of personality.

Eysenck has shown a special interest in explaining variations in *extraversion-introversion*, which is one of the fundamental personality traits in his model. He has proposed that introverts have an inherited tendency to condition more easily than extraverts. According to Eysenck, people who condition easily acquire more conditioned inhibitions than others. These inhibitions make them more bashful, tentative, and uneasy in social situations. This social discomfort leads them to turn inward. Hence, they become introverted.

Is there any empirical evidence to support Eysenck's theory? Yes. Eysenck and Levey (1972) found that introverts developed a classically conditioned eyeblink response more easily than extraverts, as predicted. There also is some evidence

that operant conditioning procedures (reinforcement) work more rapidly on introverts than extraverts (Eysenck, 1967).

Recent *twin studies* have also provided impressive support for Eysenck's hypothesis that personality is largely inherited. In one study, 573 pairs of twins responded to five personality scales that measured altruism, empathy, nurturance, aggressiveness, and assertiveness (Rushton et al., 1986). Figure 12.12 shows the mean correlations observed for identical and fraternal twins on several of the personality traits studied. Higher correlations are indicative of greater similarity on a trait. On all five traits, identical twins were found to be much more similar than fraternal twins.

Eysenck and his coworkers attribute the identical twins' greater personality resemblance to their greater genetic similarity. Figure 12.12 shows their estimates of the percentage of variation in each trait determined by genetic inheritance. These *heritability estimates* suggest that genetic factors account for about 56% to 72% of the variation in the traits studied.

As we noted in our discussion of the heritability of intelligence in Chapter 9, some skeptics wonder whether identical twins might exhibit more trait similarity than fraternal twins because they're treated more alike. In other words, they wonder whether environmental factors (rather than heredity) could be responsible for identical twins' greater similarity in many traits. This nagging question can only be answered by studying identical twins reared apart, which is why the twin study at the University of Minnesota is so important. The Minnesota researchers have been studying identical and fraternal twins *reared together* since 1970. They began to search for twins reared apart in 1979, offering to fly such twin pairs to Minneapolis for days of extensive interviews and psychological testing. Their project is the first study of personality resemblance among identical and fraternal twins reared apart, as well as together. Our Featured Study reports on some of the results from this project.

Figure 12.12 Heritability and personality. Selected results from the twin study of personality conducted by Rushton et al. (1986) are shown here. Identical twins showed stronger correlations in personality than fraternal twins, suggesting that personality is partly inherited. The correlational data yielded rather high heritability estimates for the personality traits examined in the study.

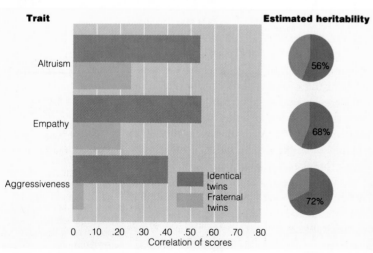

Is it all in the genes?

The investigators set out to assess the personality correspondence of identical and fraternal twins, some of whom were reared together and some of whom were reared apart. There have been a few other studies of personality in identical twins reared apart, but no previous study has managed to use the same personality test to compare all four possible groups (identical reared together, identical reared apart, fraternal reared together, and fraternal reared apart).

Method

Sample. The subjects included 217 pairs of identical twins reared together and 114 pairs of fraternal twins reared together, who were studied as part of an ongoing project between 1970 and 1984. They were compared to 44 pairs of identical twins reared apart and 27 pairs of fraternal twins reared apart, who were studied as part of an additional project between 1979 and 1986. Because twins are sometimes misclassified as identical or fraternal by appearance, the investigators double-checked their type of twinship with highly accurate blood tests and fingerprint comparisons.

The age of separation for the twins reared apart ranged from birth to 4½ years. Most were separated quite early in life, as the typical (median) age of separation was 2½ months. The twins reared apart remained separated for a median period of almost 34 years!

Measures. All subjects responded to the Multidimensional Personality Questionnaire developed by Tellegen—a 300-item self-report personality inventory that measures 11 personality traits and 3 more basic dimensions that underlie these traits. The three basic dimensions, which were identified through factor analysis, are (1) *positive emotionality* (extraverted, achievement-oriented, having a sense of well-being), (2) *negative emotionality* (anxious, angry, alienated), and (3) *constraint* (inhibited, cautious, deferential, conventional).

The investigators computed correlations to determine how similar the various types of twin sets were to each other with regard to each of the personality dimensions. The investigators also used sophisticated statistical modeling procedures to estimate the proportion of variability in each trait governed by (1) heredity, (2) shared family environment, and (3) unique aspects of experience.

Results

The correlations for all four types of twin sets with regard to the three basic dimensions of personality are shown in Figure 12.13. These correlations reveal that identical twins reared together are more similar on all three traits than fraternal twins reared together. More telling, though, are the results for the identical twins reared apart. On all three traits, identical twins reared apart are still more similar to each other than fraternal twins reared together.

Figure 12.13 also shows the proportion of variation in each trait allocated to heredity, family environment, and unique experience, as determined by the statistical modeling procedures. The genetic components, which are heritability estimates, range from 40% to 58%. A noticeable effect for family environment was found only for the positive emotionality trait, where the family component was estimated to be 22%. The remaining variance for the three traits, ranging from 38% to 43%, was attributed to the effect of unique

Investigators: Auke Tellegen, David T. Lykken, Thomas J. Bouchard, Jr., Kimberly J. Wilcox, Nancy L. Segal, and Stephen Rich (University of Minnesota)

Source: Personality similarity in twins reared apart and together. *Journal of Personality and Social Psychology* (1988), *54* (6), 1031–1039.

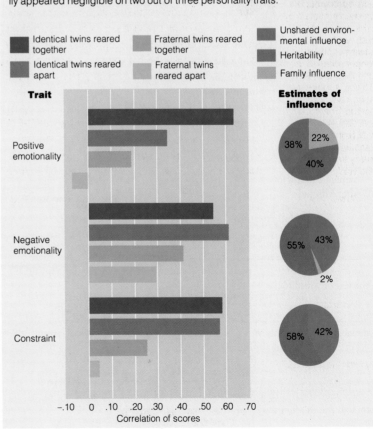

Figure 12.13 Personality resemblance in the Tellegen et al. (1988) study. On all three basic personality traits examined in this study, identical twins were more similar than fraternal twins—even if the identical twins were reared apart. These correlational data yielded relatively high estimates of heritability. Evidence of environmental influence on personality was also apparent in the data, but the investigators were surprised to find that the impact of one's family appeared negligible on two out of three personality traits.

experiences. Some of this "leftover" variance is also due to measurement error (the less-than-perfect reliability of any psychological test).

Discussion

The investigators maintain that their results support the hypothesis that our genetic blueprints shape the contours of our personalities. They estimate that the heritability of personality, as a whole, is at least 50% and that some traits may be influenced more by heredity than others. Stepping back to view the study's results as a whole, they conclude that "personality differences are more influenced by genetic diversity than they are by environmental diversity."

The researchers also draw attention to the surprisingly small impact of shared family environment. It's widely assumed that home environment is a potent force in shaping a child's personality. However, the findings in this study seriously undermine this common assumption. The results suggest that parents don't wield as much influence over their children's personalities as has been presumed.

Comment

As this research project progressed during the 1980s, the popular press reported on many highly publicized incidents of eerie resemblances between the separated identical twins in the study. These reports often suggested that personality is all in the genes. However, bizarre similarities observed in a few individuals have little value as scientific evidence. Uncanny parallels can occur between entirely unrelated people. Moreover, it's easy to focus on a few unusual parallels and forget about dozens of dissimilarities. So, psychologists around the world have eagerly awaited the actual findings of the study, which would measure the impact of heredity and environment with scientific precision.

The precise, quantitative data lived up to the expectations created by the anecdotal reports. This is a rigorous, carefully executed study that provides the best evidence to date that personality is molded to a significant degree by genetic inheritance. In the future, theories of personality will have to allocate a larger role to biological predispositions.

<table>
<tr><td>

CONCEPT CHECK 12.3
Understanding the Implications of Major Theories: Who Said This?

</td></tr>
<tr><td>

Check your understanding of the implications of the personality theories we've discussed by indicating which theorist is likely to have made the statements below. The answers are in Appendix A.

Choose from the following theorists.
Alfred Adler
Albert Bandura
Hans Eysenck
Sigmund Freud
Abraham Maslow
Walter Mischel

Quotes

_____ 1. "If you deliberately plan to be less than you are capable of being, then I warn you that you'll be deeply unhappy for the rest of your life."

_____ 2. "I feel that the major, most fundamental dimensions of personality are likely to be those on which [there is] strong genetic determination of individual differences."

_____ 3. "People are in general not candid over sexual matters . . . they wear a heavy overcoat woven of a tissue of lies, as though the weather were bad in the world of sexuality."

</td></tr>
</table>

Evaluating Biological Perspectives

Although early theories linking physique to personality were much too simple, subsequent researchers have compiled convincing evidence that biological factors help to shape personality. Nonetheless, we must take note of some weaknesses in biological approaches to personality:

1. As we discussed in Chapter 9, heritability estimates suffer from some conceptual problems. Critics of heritability studies, such as McGuire and Haviland (1985), have characterized heritability ratios as "notoriously biased and inaccurate" (p. 1435). Although their language may be a bit strong, heritability ratios should be regarded as ballpark estimates that will vary depending on sampling procedures and other considerations.
2. The results of efforts to carve behavior into genetic and environmental components are ultimately artificial. The effects of nature and nurture are twisted together in complicated interactions that can't be separated cleanly.
3. At present there's no comprehensive biological theory of personality. Eysenck's model doesn't provide a systematic overview of how biological factors govern personality development (and was never intended to). Additional theoretical work is needed to catch up with recent empirical findings on the biological basis for personality.

So far, our coverage has been devoted to grand, panoramic theories of personality. In this section we'll examine some contemporary empirical approaches that are narrower in scope. Modern personality research programs have tended to focus on specific traits. In these research programs investigators attempt to describe and measure an important personality trait, shed light on its development, and ascertain its relationship to other traits and behaviors.

In this research, psychologists have studied many widely discussed traits, such as independence, shyness, impulsiveness, optimism, introversion, and self-esteem. However, personality researchers take pride in their ability to discover subtle traits that are not readily apparent to everyone. Hence, they've focused much of their attention on personality traits that the average person probably doesn't think about. To get a sense of this kind of research, we'll take a look at three such traits in this section: (1) locus of control, (2) sensation seeking, and (3) self-monitoring. Research suggests that these are important aspects of personality.

Locus of Control: Life as a Pawn

Locus of control is a personality dimension that was first described by Julian Rotter (1966, 1975), a prominent social learning theorist. **Locus of control is a generalized expectancy about the degree to which we control our outcomes.** Individuals with an *external locus of control* believe that their successes and failures are governed by external factors such as fate, luck, and chance. "Externals" feel that their outcomes are largely beyond their control—that they're pawns of fate. In contrast, individuals with an *internal locus of control* believe that their successes and failures are determined by their actions and abilities (internal, or personal, factors). "Internals" consequently feel that they have more influence over their outcomes than people with an external locus of control.

Of course, locus of control is not an either-or proposition. Like any other dimension of personality, it should be thought of as a continuum. Some people are very external, some are very internal, and most people fall in between the extremes.

Which is healthier—an internal or an external locus of control? Using your intuition, you could probably make a case for either. In dealing with adversity and failure, an external locus of control might be beneficial. It would allow you to blame your setbacks on bad luck. When you're successful, though, an internal locus of control might look more attractive. It would help you to take credit for your success. Let's examine the evidence.

Studies indicate that people with an external locus of control develop psychological disorders more often than people characterized by an internal locus of control (Lefcourt, 1982). Externality correlates with feelings of both anxiety and depression. In one study, Boor (1976) found that suicide rates correlated positively (.68) with the average level of externality in a country. Why is externality associated with poor adjustment? We can only speculate that people tend to feel better about their life when they believe that they can exert some control over their outcomes.

Research also indicates that internality is related to higher academic achievement (Findley & Cooper, 1983). Youngsters with an internal locus of control get somewhat better grades than youngsters characterized by an external locus of control. Why? Probably because internals work harder than externals. If you're strongly external and you think that your grades are a matter of luck, you're not likely to work as hard as internals, who are more likely to think that their grades are determined by their efforts.

In a variety of contexts besides the academic arena, internals engage in more active efforts to control events than externals. Internals are more likely to actively confront a problem. For instance, Sims and Baumann (1972) found that internals react to tornado warnings by seeking information that can help them to protect themselves. In contrast, externals react with more fatalistic inactivity ("If it's going to hit us, it's going to hit us").

After a couple decades of research, it's becoming clear that a person's locus of control may not be quite as generalized as Rotter originally assumed. Some people display an internal locus of control regarding events in one domain of life while displaying an external locus of control regarding events in another domain. For instance, a person might feel very powerless (external) about influencing the political process, while feeling very responsible (internal) for more personal events. In light of this finding, some researchers are studying locus of control as it relates to specific domains of behavior.

The specific domain attracting the most attention centers around personal health. Health-related locus of control appears to affect how people deal with the threat of illness (Wallston & Wallston, 1981). Internals are more likely than externals to seek information about possible health problems. Internals also have a greater tendency to take preventive steps to maintain their health, such as giving up smoking, or embarking on an exercise program, or getting regular medical check-ups.

Sensation Seeking: Life in the Fast Lane

Perhaps you have some friends who prefer "life in the fast lane." If so, they're probably high in sensation seeking, a personality trait first described by Marvin Zuckerman (1971, 1979), a biologically oriented theorist influenced by Hans Eysenck's views. *Sensation seeking is a generalized preference for high or low levels of sensory stimulation.* People who are high in sensation seeking prefer a high level of stimulation, and they're always looking for new and exhilarating experiences. People who are low in sensation seeking prefer more modest levels of stimulation. They tend to choose tranquility over excitement.

Sensation seeking is distributed along a continuum, and many people fall in the middle.

Sensation-seeking tendencies are measured by Zuckerman's (1979) Sensation Seeking Scale (SSS). Figure 12.14 contains a simplified variation on the SSS that allows you to estimate your own sensation-seeking tendencies.

Boredom is the chief foe of high sensation seekers, who pursue adventure and challenge. They generally are more impulsive, uninhibited, extraverted, and nonconformist than low sensation seekers. Also, when compared to low sensation seekers, those high in sensation seeking display the following tendencies (Zuckerman, 1979; Zuckerman, Buchsbaum, & Murphy, 1980):

1. They're more willing to engage in activities that may involve a physical risk. Thus, they're more likely to go mountain climbing, skydiving, surfing, and scuba diving. They're more likely to ride motorcycles, and they drive their cars faster than others. They also are more likely to experiment with recreational drugs such as marijuana, LSD, and stimulants.

2. They're more willing to volunteer for unusual experiments or activities that they may know little about. Thus, they readily volunteer to participate in meditation, sensitivity groups, studies of hypnosis, and so forth.

Measuring Sensation Seeking

Answer "true" or "false" to each of the items listed below by circling "T" or "F." A "true" means that the item expresses your preference most of the time. A "false" means that you do not agree that the item is generally true for you. After completing the test, score your responses according to the instructions that follow the test items.

T F **1.** I would really enjoy skydiving.
T F **2.** I can imagine myself driving a sports car in a race and loving it.
T F **3.** My life is very secure and comfortable—the way I like it.
T F **4.** I usually like emotionally expressive or artistic people, even if they are sort of wild.
T F **5.** I like the idea of seeing many of the same warm, supportive faces in my everyday life.
T F **6.** I like doing adventurous things and would have enjoyed being a pioneer in the early days of this country.
T F **7.** A good photograph should express peacefulness creatively.
T F **8.** The most important thing in living is fully experiencing all emotions.
T F **9.** I like creature comforts when I go on a trip or vacation.
T F **10.** Doing the same things each day really gets to me.
T F **11.** I love snuggling in front of a fire on a wintry day.
T F **12.** I would like to try several types of drugs as long as they didn't harm me permanently.
T F **13.** Drinking and being rowdy really appeal to me on the weekend.
T F **14.** Rational people try to avoid dangerous situations.
T F **15.** I prefer Figure A to Figure B.

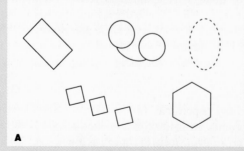

A

B

Give yourself 1 point for answering "true" to the following items: 1, 2, 4, 6, 8, 10, 12, and 13. Also give yourself 1 point for answering "false" to the following items: 3, 5, 7, 9, 11, 14, and 15. Add up your points, and compare your total to the following norms: 11–15, high sensation seeker; 6–10, moderate sensation seeker; 1–5, low sensation seeker. Bear in mind that this is a shortened version of the Sensation Seeking Scale and that it provides only a rough approximation of your status on this personality trait.

Figure 12.14 A brief scale to assess sensation seeking as a trait. Follow the instructions for this scale to obtain a rough estimate of your own sensation-seeking tendencies.

People high in sensation seeking engage in a variety of exciting activities that generate high levels of stimulation. Some of these activities, such as white-water rafting, skydiving, surfing, and mountain climbing, involve physical risks that most people find very unappealing.

3. They engage in a wider range of sexual activities with a greater variety of partners. They also report more sexual experimentation (varied practices) than others.

4. They show many other diverse preferences that promote high levels of stimulation. For instance, they relish extensive travel, gambling, spicy foods, provocative art, wild parties, and unusual friends.

Compatibility in sensation seeking may influence the progress of romantic relationships. Studies show that partners in intimate relationships tend to be fairly similar in terms of sensation seeking (Lesnik-Oberstein & Cohen, 1984). According to Zuckerman, this similarity occurs because incompatibility in sensation seeking places strain on intimate relationships. He theorizes that persons very high and very low in sensation seeking may have difficulty understanding and relating to each other, not to mention finding mutually enjoyable activities.

Self-Monitoring: Life as Theater

The trait of self-monitoring was originally unearthed by Mark Snyder and has been under investigation since the mid-1970s. **Self-monitoring refers to the degree to which people attend to and control the impression they make on others in social interactions.** According to Snyder (1979, 1986), people vary in how aware they are

of how they're being perceived by others. People who are high in self-monitoring are very sensitive to how their self presentation is going over. They seek information about how they're expected to behave in a situation. When necessary, they shrewdly adjust their behavior to create the right impression. For high self-monitors, "all the world's a stage."

People who are low in self-monitoring are much less concerned about the impression that they're making. They behave more spontaneously, are less skilled at figuring out what others want to see, and are less likely to alter their behavior in response to the social context.

Being tuned in to how others view you is one thing, but high self-monitors also show a gift for creating the right impression. They tend to be good actors. They control their emotions well and can feign emotions when necessary. They deliberately regulate nonverbal signals (for instance, facial expressions and gestures) that are fairly spontaneous in most people. As Snyder (1986, p. 4) puts it, "These people exhibit striking gaps and contradictions between the *public appearances* and the *private realities* of the self."

Ironically, people who are high in self-monitoring are good at spotting deceptive impression management *in other people*. For instance, they can tell when others are trying to "butter them up" (Jones & Baumeister, 1976). Their sensitivity to others' deception was demonstrated in a study in which subjects watched videotapes of the TV program *To Tell the Truth*. In this show, impostors try to deceive a panel of judges about their true identity. High self-monitors were better at picking out the impostors than low self-monitors (Ajzen, Timko, & White, 1982).

Self-monitoring appears to have some intriguing effects on interpersonal relationships. In dealing with friends, high self-monitoring persons decide who they want to spend time with based on situational demands (Snyder, Gangestad, & Simpson, 1983). If they're going to a football game, they want to go with someone who knows football. If they're going to a big party, they want to accompany an extraverted "party animal." In other words, their friendships are specialized, and their social world is compartmentalized. In con-

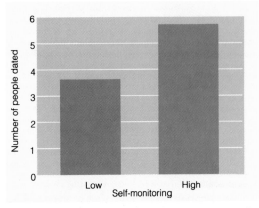

Figure 12.15 Self-monitoring and dating. Snyder and Simpson (1984) found that college students who were high in self-monitoring had dated more people in the preceding 12 months than students low in self-monitoring. Apparently, high self-monitors commit themselves to romantic relationships less readily than low self-monitors.

trast, people who are low in self-monitoring prefer to be with their best friends, regardless of the situation. They invite their favorite friends to participate in diverse activities, whether these friends are talented in these activities or not.

Self-monitoring also is related to patterns of dating. High self-monitors are relatively reluctant to make commitments in dating relationships (Snyder & Simpson, 1984). They date a greater variety of partners (see Figure 12.15), and they change partners more quickly when new opportunities arise. When they do stay in one relation-ship for a while, it's less likely to grow steadily in intimacy than when low self-monitors stay in a single relationship. Thus, it appears that people high in self-monitoring may make genuine emotional commitments less readily than those who are low in self-monitoring.

Similar patterns have been observed in regard to sexual behavior (Snyder, Simpson, & Gangestad, 1986). High self-monitors are more willing than low self-monitors to have sexual relations with someone they aren't especially close to. Thus, it's not surprising that high self-monitors usually have a history of involvement with more sexual partners than low self-monitors. In sum, those who are high in self-monitoring seem to be relatively calculating about their intimate relationships.

Contemporary researchers examining specific personality traits are making important contributions to our understanding of personality. It will be interesting to see whether their approach represents the wave of the future, or whether we'll once again see grand, sweeping theories in the tradition of Freud, Skinner, and Rogers.

PUTTING IT IN PERSPECTIVE

Our discussion of personality is ideally suited for embellishing on two of our unifying themes: psychology's theoretical diversity (theme 2) and the assertion that psychology evolves in a sociohistorical context (theme 3).

No other area of psychology is characterized by as much theoretical diversity as the study of personality, where there are literally dozens of insightful theories. Some of this diversity exists because different theories attempt to explain different facets of behavior. For example, there's only modest overlap between the theories of Jung, Bandura, and Eysenck, who are trying to account for different aspects of our behavior.

Of course, much of this theoretical diversity reflects genuine disagreement on basic questions about personality. Table 12.5 summarizes some areas of agreement and disagreement among the theories that we covered. The table compares the assumptions and emphases of the four major theoretical perspectives (psychodynamic, behavioral, humanistic, and biological) on the four key issues that we introduced at the beginning of the chapter.

This overview shows that the greatest consensus exists on the issues of *freedom versus determinism* and the importance of the *person versus the situation*. As you can see, only humanism does not embrace the assumption of determinism. Three out of four perspectives (behaviorism being the exception) also lean toward an emphasis on person variables, although they focus on quite different person variables, ranging from unconscious conflicts to self-concepts to genetically inherited traits. As a whole, this comparative overview reveals that there are more areas of disagreement than agreement among the major approaches to personality.

In previous chapters we've often seen movement toward reconciling contradictory theories. Has there been any movement toward such reconciliation in the the area of personality theory? Yes, but only a little. Eysenck has blended many behavioral concepts into his biological model. The humanistic perspective has left a mark on some of the more recent psychodynamic theories (for example, Kohut, 1971). Moreover, the emergence of social learning theory within the behavioral school of thought, with its focus on cognitive processes, has expanded the common ground shared by behaviorism and other theoretical approaches. Although these trends are encouraging, they represent only a few small steps toward reconciling and integrating modern theo-

Table 12.5 Comparison of the Basic Assumptions of Major Theoretical Perspectives on Personality

ASSUMPTION	PSYCHODYNAMIC PERSPECTIVE	BEHAVIORAL PERSPECTIVE	HUMANISTIC PERSPECTIVE	BIOLOGICAL PERSPECTIVE
Freedom versus determinism	*Determinism:* Are very mechanistic; past events in childhood determine present behavior.	*Determinism:* Classically, are very mechanistic; behavior is determined by environment. This position is softened by the social learning theory view of reciprocal determinism.	*Freedom:* Strongly emphasize freedom to chart our own courses of action and self-determination.	*Determinism:* See behavior as governed by evolution, heredity, and internal physiological functions.
Nature versus nurture	*Nature:* Moderately emphasize biology (instinctual drives, psychosexual stages).	*Nurture:* Strongly emphasize environmental factors, learning, and experience.	*Interaction:* Are interested in innate potentials and human nature; but humanists believe we can rise above our biological nature.	*Nature:* Strongly emphasize hereditary predispositions that shape our personalities.
Conscious versus unconscious	*Unconscious:* Assert that our behavior is dominated by unconscious, irrational wishes, needs, and conflicts.	*Varies:* Skinner ignores cognitive processes. Social learning theory allows for conscious, rational planning.	*Conscious:* Perceive behavior as guided by conscious, largely rational decision making.	*Unclear:* Haven't addressed this issue adequately.
Person versus situation	*Person:* Place strong emphasis on person variables (id, ego, superego, conflicts, defenses, and so forth).	*Situation:* Show the heaviest slant toward situational specificity of all the theories, although there is some allowance for person variables.	*Person:* Focus on self-concept, which is a stable person variable.	*Person:* Are interested in stable traits molded by heredity.

ries of personality. For the most part, the four major theoretical perspectives continue to provide four very different vantage points from which we can examine the mysteries of personality. These contrasts will also be apparent on the next two pages, where you'll find an illustrated, comparative overview of the ideas of Freud, Skinner, Rogers, and Eysenck, as representatives of the psychodynamic, behavioral, humanistic, and biological approaches to personality.

The study of personality also highlights the sociohistorical context in which psychology evolves. Personality theories have left many marks on our culture—we can mention only a handful as illustrations. The theories of Freud, Adler, and Skinner have had an enormous impact on child-rearing practices. The ideas of Freud and Jung have found their way into literature (influencing the portrayal of fictional characters in novels, for instance) and the visual arts (helping to inspire surrealism's interest in the world of dreams, for example). Social learning theory has become embroiled in the public policy debate about whether media violence should be controlled because of its effects on viewers' aggressive behavior. Maslow's hierarchy of needs and Skinner's affirmation of the value of positive reinforcement have given rise to new approaches to management in the world of business and industry.

The theories of Freud and Jung had considerable influence on the arts. For instance, their ideas about the unconscious guided the surrealists' explorations of the irrational world of dreams. Salvador Dali's 1936 painting *Soft Construction with Boiled Beans: Premonition of Civil War* is a bizarre image that symbolizes how a society can tear itself apart. Freud once commented, "I was tempted to consider the surrealists, who apparently have chosen me for their patron saint, as a bunch of complete nuts . . . [but] the young Spaniard [Dali], with the magnificent eyes of a fanatic and his undeniable technical mastery, has caused me to reconsider." (Quoted in Gerard, 1968) (Philadelphia Museum of Art: The Louise and Walter Arensberg Collection)

FOUR VIEWS OF PERSONALITY

Theorist and orientation	Source of data and observations	Key motivational forces

Sigmund Freud

A psychodynamic view

Case studies from clinical practice of psychoanalysis

Sex and aggression; need to reduce tension resulting from internal conflicts

B. F. Skinner

A behavioral view

Laboratory experiments, primarily with animals

Pursuit of primary (unlearned) and secondary (learned) reinforcers; priorities depend on personal history

Carl Rogers

A humanistic view

Case studies from clinical practice of client-centered therapy

Actualizing tendency (motive to develop capacities, experience personal growth) and self-actualizing tendency (motive to maintain self-concept and behave in ways that are consistent with self-concept)

Hans Eysenck

A biological view

Twin, family, and adoption studies of heritability; factor analysis studies of personality structure

No specific motivational forces singled out

Model of personality structure	View of personality development	Roots of disorders

Three interacting components (id, ego, superego) operating at three levels of consciousness

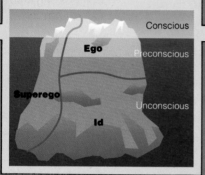

Emphasis on fixation or progress through psychosexual stages; experiences in early child-hood (such as toilet train-ing) can leave lasting mark on adult per-sonality

Unconscious fixa-tions and unresolved conflicts from child-hood, usually center-ing on sex and aggression

Collections of response tendencies tied to specific stimulus situations

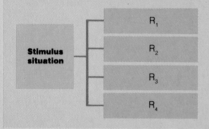

Personality evolves gradually over the lifespan (not in stages); responses (such as extraverted joking) followed by reinforcement (such as ap-preciative laughter) become more frequent

Maladaptive behav-ior due to faulty learning; the "symp-tom" *is* the problem, not a sign of underly-ing disease

Self-concept, which may or may not mesh well with actual experience

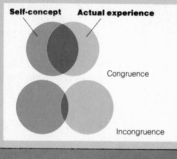

Children who receive unconditional love have less need to be defensive; they develop more accurate, congruent self-concept; conditional love fosters incongruence

Incongruence be-tween self and ac-tual experience (inaccurate self-concept); overde-pendence on others for approval and sense of worth

Hierarchy of traits, with specific traits derived from more fundamental, general traits

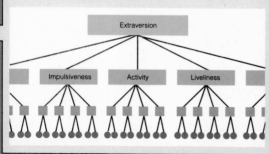

Emphasis on unfolding of genetic blueprint with maturation; inherited predisposi-tions inter-act with learning ex-periences

Genetic vulnerability activated in part by environmental factors

Sociohistorical forces also leave their imprint on psychology. This chapter provided many examples of how personal experiences, prevailing attitudes, and historical events contribute to the evolution of ideas in psychology. For example, Freud's pessimistic view of human nature and his emphasis on the dark forces of aggression were shaped to some extent by his exposure to the hostilities of World War I and prevailing anti-Semitic sentiments. Freud's emphasis on sexuality surely was influenced by the Victorian climate of sexual repression that existed in his youth. Adler's views also reflected the social context in which he grew up. His interest in inferiority feelings and compensation appear to have sprung from his own sickly childhood and the difficulties he had to overcome. His interest in birth order probably stemmed, in part, from the way in which he was overshadowed by his older brother. Likewise, it's reasonable to speculate that Jung's childhood loneliness and introversion may have sparked his interest in the introversion-extraversion dimension of personality. In a similar vein, we saw that both Rogers and Maslow had to resist parental pressures in order to pursue their career interests. Their emphasis on the need to achieve personal growth and fulfillment may have originated in these personal experiences.

Although sociohistorical forces influence the ideas of the theorists who push the frontiers of psychology forward, the effects of these forces depend on the unique personalities of the theorists. After all, behavior depends on both the situation and the person. For example, the devastating tragedies of World War I had very different effects on Freud and Adler. The war deepened Freud's pessimistic view of the fundamentally evil, animalistic quality of human nature. In contrast, Adler came away from the war impressed by humans' ability to bond together in cooperative efforts to achieve idealistic goals. Paradoxically, his experience of war contributed to his optimistic view of our innate social interest.

In a sense, optimism and pessimism about one's own personal nature lie at the core of our remaining topic in the chapter. In our Application, we'll explore the roots of self-esteem and discuss how people can work toward enhancing self-image.

UNDERSTANDING AND ENHANCING SELF-ESTEEM

Respond "yes" or "no" to the following statements.

☐ **1.** I have very little confidence in my abilities.

☐ **2.** I'm very sensitive to criticism.

☐ **3.** I tend to be highly critical of other people.

☐ **4.** I usually have a hard time accepting praise or flattery.

☐ **5.** I often dwell on my shortcomings.

If you answered "yes" to several of the questions above, you *may* be struggling with low self-esteem. This is a common and potentially very troublesome affliction. Self-esteem is an important element of your personality. Low self-esteem can contribute to many kinds of behavioral problems. An *overly positive* self-image can also be problematic, but conceited people don't suffer in the same way that highly self-critical people do. In this Application, we'll review research on the importance of self-esteem and discuss some advice on building higher self-esteem.

Self-esteem refers to a person's overall assessment of her or his personal adequacy or worth. It's the evaluative component of your self-concept. It's a global evaluation that blends many specific evaluations about your adequacy as a student, as an athlete, as a worker, as a spouse, as a parent, or as whatever is relevant for you. Figure 12.16 shows how specific elements of self-concept may contribute to self-esteem.

The Importance of Self-Esteem

Several lines of research suggest that it's important to develop a favorable

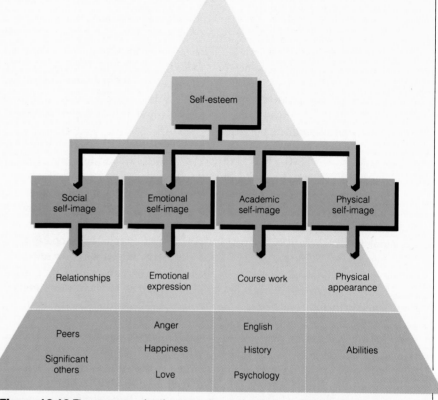

Figure 12.16 The structure of self-esteem. Our self-esteem, or global evaluation of ourselves, blends a number of dimensions of self-image, each of which is built up from many specific behaviors and experiences. Of course, the influence works both ways: our self-esteem influences our self-image and our behavior (see Figure 12.18). (Adapted from Shavelson et al., 1976)

self-concept. To appreciate the significance of self-esteem, let's look at some of the behavioral characteristics that tend to accompany *low* self-esteem:

1. People with low self-esteem develop more psychological problems than people with high self-esteem (Fitts, 1972; Rosenberg, 1965). Among other things, they're more likely to report that they're troubled by anxiety (see Figure 12.17), insomnia, unhappiness, and physical symptoms.
2. There's also a relationship between low self-esteem and relatively poor achievement. For instance, people with a negative self-image generally get lower grades in school than those with a favorable self-image (O'Malley & Bachman, 1979). It appears that

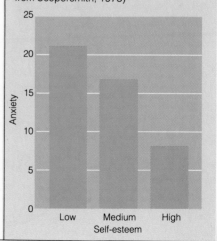

Figure 12.17 The inverse relation of anxiety and self-esteem. The amount of anxiety experienced by three groups of boys was measured by the frequency of their reported feelings of distress and the frequency of psychosomatic symptoms as reported by their mothers. (Data from Coopersmith, 1975)

this happens in part because people with low self-esteem set low goals for themselves.

3. In social interactions, people with low self-esteem are often awkward, self-conscious, and especially vulnerable to rejection (Rosenberg, 1965). They tend to be more sensitive to rejection than others. They may desperately want social acceptance, but they don't feel confident enough to pursue it vigorously.

4. Ironically, people who have a negative self-image tend to be more rejecting of others than people with a favorable self-concept (Baron, 1974). They look for flaws in others and try to "tear them down." Why would they engage in such self-defeating behavior? They're hypercritical of others because it allows them to feel better about themselves, for a brief time anyway. Unfortunately, these negative ways of relating to people compound their problems as they end up courting dislike from others (see Figure 12.18).

Admittedly, it's difficult to distinguish cause from effect in the relationships just discussed, as most of the data are correlational in nature. For instance, does low self-esteem cause low achievement, or does low achievement cause low self-esteem? Or are low achievement and low self-esteem both caused by a third variable, such as low ability? We lack definitive evidence on these possible causal relationships, but it's clear that low self-esteem is not a particularly desirable personality trait.

Determinants of Self-Esteem

The foundations for high or low self-esteem are laid down during childhood. The feedback we get from people around us, especially our parents, exerts considerable influence over our self-esteem. In comparison with parents of boys with low self-esteem, the parents of boys with high self-esteem tend to (1) be more affectionate and accepting toward their children, (2) show more interest in their children's activities, and (3) use consistent but democratic disciplinary procedures. These trends are illustrated in Figure 12.19, which summarizes some of the results from an influential study by Coopersmith (1967, 1975).

While parental feedback is important, it's clear that children and adults make their own judgments about themselves, as well. People who apply unrealistic standards in making these judgments often end up making very unfavorable appraisals of themselves. *Social comparison theory* sheds some light on the origins of these unrealistic standards (Goethals, 1986; Goethals & Darley, 1977).

Social comparison theory proposes that we compare ourselves with others to understand and evaluate our behavior. Of course, we don't choose just anyone as a basis for comparison. A *reference group* is a particular group of people used as a standard in social comparisons. Generally, we choose a reference group made up of people who are similar to us in certain key ways. The crucial dimensions of similarity depend on which aspects of our behavior we're trying to evaluate. If you want to evaluate your career progress, you'll probably compare yourself with people of roughly the same age who are in the same occupational area. However, some people choose unrealistic reference groups for their self-appraisals, comparing themselves to famous models, athletes, actors, investors, and so forth.

Our self-appraisals are influenced by our reference groups. Marsh and Parker (1984) compared the self-esteem of children of similar academic ability who attended high-quality or low-quality schools. The children in the low-quality schools, who compared themselves to a reference group of lesser ability, exhibited higher self-esteem than children of equal ability who came from high-quality schools. Thus, Marsh and Parker conclude that self-esteem may benefit if one is "a big fish in a small pond" rather than vice versa.

With these ideas about the determinants of self-esteem in mind, let's discuss what people with an unfavorable self-concept can do to raise their self-esteem.

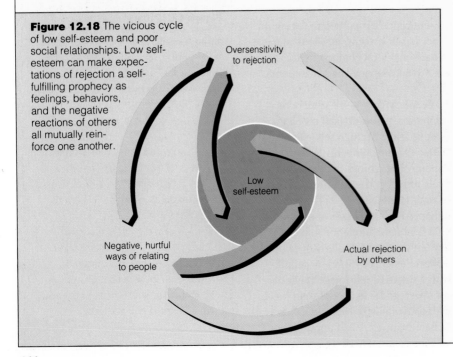

Figure 12.18 The vicious cycle of low self-esteem and poor social relationships. Low self-esteem can make expectations of rejection a self-fulfilling prophecy as feelings, behaviors, and the negative reactions of others all mutually reinforce one another.

Oversensitivity to rejection

Low self-esteem

Negative, hurtful ways of relating to people

Actual rejection by others

Improving Self-Esteem

Due to the importance of self-esteem, many prominent theorists in psychology have discussed advice on building higher self-esteem. The guidelines that follow are based on a distillation of the writings of a number of psychologists, including Rogers (1977), Ellis (1984), Jourard and Landsman (1980), Hamachek (1987), and Zimbardo (1977).

1. *Recognize that you control your self-image.* The first thing that you must do is recognize that *you* ultimately control how you see yourself. Thus, you *do* have the power to change your self-image. Sure, feedback from others can be very influential. But the final choice about whether to accept or reject such feedback rests with you. Your self-image resides in your mind. Although others may influence your self-esteem, you are the final authority.

2. *Don't let others set your standards.* People around us are constantly telling us that we ought to do this or we ought to do that. Thus, we hear that we should "study something practical," or "lose weight," or "move to a better neighborhood." Many of these suggestions may be well-intentioned. However, some of us too readily accept others' standards for our own. Consider a middle manager who sees himself in a negative light because he hasn't climbed as high in the corporate hierarchy as he thinks he should have by now. The crucial question is: Did he ever *really* want to make that climb? Perhaps he has gone through life thinking that he should pursue that kind of success only because everyone told him so. Maybe that isn't what he really wants out of life. Thus, you should think about the basis for your personal goals and standards. Do they really represent goals and ideals that you value? Or are they goals and ideals that you've passively accepted from others without thinking?

3. *Recognize unrealistic goals.* Even if

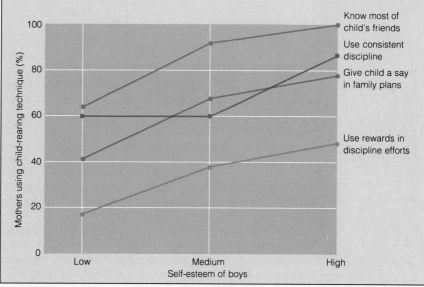

Figure 12.19 Self-esteem and parents' child-rearing techniques. Parents strongly influence their children's view of themselves, as suggested by this study of the relationship between the self-esteem of boys and their mothers' child-rearing practices. (Data from Coopersmith, 1975)

you sincerely want to achieve certain goals, another question remains. Are the goals realistic? Many people get into the habit of demanding too much from themselves. Some overly demanding people pervert the social comparison process by comparing themselves with the *best*, rather than similar others. They assess their looks by comparing themselves with famous models, and they judge their finances by comparing themselves with the wealthiest people they know. They select their reference groups in ways that are bound to end up undermining self-esteem.

4. *Modify negative thinking.* People who are low in self-esteem tend to engage in various types of negative thinking. On the one hand, when they succeed, they often attribute it to good luck. On the other hand, when they fail, they blame themselves. Thus, if they apply for a job and get it, they may say "Probably no one else applied." However, if they fail to get hired, they conclude, "I must be a terribly inept person." This negative thinking understandably has a negative impact on self-esteem. Thus, we should take credit for our successes and consider the possibility that our failures *may* not be our fault. More generally, it's important to recognize and combat irrational negative

thinking—a subject that we'll discuss in more detail in the next chapter.

5. *Work to improve yourself.* This sounds trite, but it brings up a point worth stressing. We've discussed that it's important to reassess your goals and discard those that are imposed by others or those that are unrealistic. However, this advice is *not* intended to provide a convenient rationalization for complacency. Many personal shortcomings *can* be conquered. It may be wise to accept those shortcomings you're powerless to change, but you should work on those that are potentially changeable. There are few things that can boost self-esteem as much as overcoming personal shortcomings.

6. *Approach others with a positive outlook.* People who are low in self-esteem often try to cut others down to their subjective size through constant criticism. As you can readily imagine, this faultfinding typically leads to bitter exchanges and rejection, and this rejection lowers self-esteem still further. Efforts to build self-esteem can be facilitated by breaking this vicious circle. If you approach people with a positive, supportive outlook, it will promote rewarding interactions and help you to earn their acceptance. There may be nothing that enhances self-esteem more than acceptance and genuine affection from others.

PERSONALITY: THEORY AND RESEARCH

KEY IDEAS

The Nature of Personality

• The concept of personality explains the consistency in our behavior over time and situations while also explaining individuals' distinctiveness. Personality traits are dispositions to behave in certain ways. Some traits are more basic than others. Allport differentiated between cardinal, central, and secondary traits. There is considerable debate about how many trait dimensions are necessary to fully describe personality. Personality theories are marked by great diversity because personality is such a broad concept and there is much to be explained.

Psychodynamic Perspectives

• Psychodynamic approaches include all the theories derived from Freud's insights. Freud's psychoanalytic theory emphasizes the importance of the unconscious. Freud described personality structure in terms of three components—the id, ego, and superego—that are routinely involved in an an ongoing series of internal conflicts.

• Freud theorized that conflicts centering around sex and aggression are especially likely to lead to significant anxiety. According to Freud, anxiety and other unpleasant emotions such as guilt are often warded off with defense mechanisms. Defenses such as repression, rationalization, projection, displacement, reaction formation, regression, and identification work primarily through self-deception.

• Freud believed that the first 5 years of life are extremely influential in shaping adult personality. He described a series of five psychosexual stages of development (oral, anal, phallic, latency, and genital). Certain experiences during these stages can have lasting effects on adult personality. Resolution of the Oedipal complex is thought to be particularly critical to healthy development.

• Jung's most innovative and controversial concept was that of the collective unconscious—a shared storehouse of archetypal memories inherited from our ancestral past. Jung's analytical psychology also provided the first description of introversion and extraversion. Adler's individual psychology emphasizes how we strive for superiority in order to compensate for our feelings of inferiority. His theory alerted researchers to the possible influence of birth order on personality.

Adler theorized that people have an innate social interest or sense of kinship with the human race.

• Overall, psychodynamic theories have produced many ground-breaking insights about the unconscious, the role of conflict, and the importance of early, formative childhood experiences. However, psychodynamic theories have been criticized for their poor testability, their inadequate base of empirical evidence, and their male-centered views of the human condition.

Behavioral Perspectives

• Behavioral theories explain how personality is shaped through learning. Skinner views personality as a collection of response tendencies that are tied to specific stimulus situations. He maintains that personality development is a lifelong process in which our response tendencies are shaped and reshaped by learning, especially operant conditioning.

• Social learning theory focuses on how cognitive factors such as expectancies and self-efficacy regulate learned behavior. Bandura's concept of observational learning accounts for the acquisition of responses from models. He has shown that observational learning can lead children to imitate the aggressive behavior modeled for them in violent media. Mischel has questioned the degree to which people display cross-situational consistency in behavior. Mischel's arguments have increased our awareness of the situational determinants of behavior.

• Behavioral approaches to personality are based on rigorous research. They have provided ample insights about how environmental factors and learning mold our personalities. The behaviorists have been criticized for their overdependence on animal research, their neglect of biological factors, and their fragmented analysis of personality.

Humanistic Perspectives

• Humanistic theories are phenomenological and take an optimistic view of our conscious, rational ability to chart our own courses of action. Rogers focuses on the self-concept as the critical aspect of personality. He maintains that anxiety can be attributed to incongruence between one's self-concept and reality. This incongruence is rooted in the belief that affection from others is conditional upon living up to their expectations.

- Maslow theorized that psychological health depends on fulfilling our need for self-actualization, which is our need to achieve our human potential. His work led to the description of self-actualizing persons as idealized examples of psychological health. Humanistic theories deserve credit for highlighting the importance of subjective views of oneself and for confronting the question of what makes for a healthy personality. Humanistic theories lack a firm base of research, are difficult to put to an empirical test, and may be overly optimistic about human nature.

Biological Perspectives

- Biological theories stress the genetic origins of personality. Eysenck attributes the genetic influence on personality to individual differences in physiological functioning that affect how easily one acquires conditioned responses. Our Featured Study on the personality resemblance of twins reared apart provides impressive evidence that genetic factors shape personality. The biological approach has been criticized because there are methodological problems with determining heritability ratios and because there is no systematic model of how our physiology governs our personality.

Contemporary Empirical Approaches to Personality

- Modern personality research programs have tended to focus on specific personality traits. Locus of control involves the degree to which people feel that they influence the outcome of events in their lives. An internal locus of control shows a modest correlation with better mental health, higher academic achievement, and active coping efforts.

- Sensation seeking involves the degree to which people seek high or low levels of sensory stimulation. High sensation seekers are impulsive, uninhibited, willing to take risks, sexually active, and open to new experiences. Self-monitoring involves the degree to which people attend to and control the impressions they make on others. High self-monitors are sensitive to how others see them and are skilled in self-presentation. Their social relations are marked by compartmentalization and deliberate calculation.

Putting It in Perspective

- The study of personality demonstrates that psychology is characterized by great theoretical diversity. There has been relatively little movement toward reconciling contradictory theories of personality. The study of personality also demonstrates that psychology leaves its mark on many aspects of everyday life and that ideas in psychology are shaped by sociohistorical forces.

Application: Understanding and Enhancing Self-Esteem

- Self-esteem refers to the evaluative component of our self-concept. Low self-esteem is associated with poor mental health, poor achievement, and self-defeating social interactions, although it's difficult to sort out cause and effect in these relations. Our self-esteem is shaped by feedback from others and by our own social comparisons.
- Advice on improving self-esteem emphasizes that you should (1) recognize that you control your self-image, (2) set your own standards, (3) watch out for unrealistic goals, (4) reduce pessimistic, negative thinking, (5) work toward self-improvement, and (6) approach others with a positive attitude.

KEY TERMS

Archetypes
Behaviorism
Cardinal trait
Central traits
Collective unconscious
Compensation
Conscious
Defense mechanisms
Displacement
Ego
Extraverts
Fixation
Humanism
Id
Identification
Incongruence
Inferiority complex
Introverts

Locus of control
Model
Need for self-
   actualization
Observational learning
Oedipal complex
Personal unconscious
Personality
Personality theories
Personality trait
Phenomenological
   approach
Pleasure principle
Preconscious
Projection
Psychodynamic theories
Psychosexual stages
Rationalization

Reaction formation
Reality principle
Reciprocal determinism
Reference group
Regression
Repression
Secondary traits
Self-actualizing persons
Self-concept
Self-efficacy
Self-esteem
Self-monitoring
Sensation seeking
Social comparison theory
Social interest
Striving for superiority
Superego
Unconscious

KEY PEOPLE

Alfred Adler
Gordon Allport
Albert Bandura
Hans Eysenck
Sigmund Freud
Carl Jung
Abraham Maslow
Walter Mischel
Carl Rogers
Julian Rotter
B. F. Skinner
Mark Snyder
Marvin Zuckerman

Stress, Coping, and Health

STRESS, COPING, AND HEALTH

You're in your car headed home from school with a classmate. Traffic is barely moving. A radio report indicates that the traffic jam is only going to get worse. You groan audibly as you fiddle impatiently with the radio dial. Another motorist nearly takes your fender off trying to cut into your lane. Your pulse quickens as you shout insults at the unknown driver, who can't even hear you. You think about the term paper that you have to work on tonight. Your stomach knots up as you recall all the crumpled drafts you tossed into the wastebasket last night. If you don't finish the paper soon, you won't be able to find any time to study for your math test, not to mention your biology quiz. Suddenly, you remember that you promised the person you're dating that the two of you would get together tonight. There's no way. Another fight looms on the horizon. Your classmate asks how you feel about the tuition increase that the college announced yesterday. You've been trying not to think about it. You're already in debt up to your ears. Your parents are bugging you about changing schools, but you don't want to leave your friends. Your heartbeat quickens as you contemplate the debate you're sure to have with your parents. You feel wired with tension as you realize that the stress in your life never seems to let up.

Like many other aspects of modern life, traffic jams add stress to our lives.

Many different circumstances can create stress in our lives. Stress comes in all sorts of packages: big and small, pretty and ugly, simple and complex. All too often, the package comes as a surprise. In this chapter we'll try to sort out these packages. We'll discuss the nature of stress, how people cope with stress, and the potential effects of stress. We'll examine questions like these:

• Why is the same event stressful for one person but not another?
• Is change in one's life inherently stressful?
• How do people typically cope with stress?
• How does stress affect our psychological and physical health?

Our examination of the relationship between stress and physical illness will lead us into a broader discussion of the psychology of health. The way people in health professions think about physical illness has undergone considerable change in the last 10 to 20 years. The traditional view of physical illness as a purely biological phenomenon has given way to a biopsychosocial model of illness. **The *biopsychosocial model* holds that physical illness is caused by a complex interaction of biological, psychological, and sociocultural factors.** This new model does not suggest that biological factors are unimportant. It simply asserts that these biological factors operate in a psychosocial context that is also influential.

What has led to this shift in thinking? In part, it's due to changing patterns of illness. Prior to the 20th century, the principal threats to health were *contagious diseases* caused by infectious agents—diseases like smallpox, typhoid fever, diphtheria, yellow fever, malaria, cholera, tuberculosis, and polio. Today, none of these diseases is among the leading killers in the United States (Shank, 1983). They were tamed by improvements in nutrition, public hygiene, sanitation, and medical treatment (Grob, 1983). Unfortunately, the void left by contagious diseases has been filled all too quickly by *chronic diseases* that develop gradually, like heart disease, cancer, and stroke (see Figure 13.1). Psychosocial factors, such as stress and lifestyle, play a much larger role in the development of chronic diseases than they do in contagious diseases.

The growing recognition that psychological factors influence our physical health has led to the emergence of a new specialty area within psychology. **Health psychology is concerned with how psychosocial factors relate to the promotion and maintenance of health and with the causation, prevention, and treatment of illness.** In the second half of this chapter, we'll explore this new domain of health psychology, tackling questions such as the following:

• How do patterns of behavior contribute to heart disease?
• How strong is the association between stress and physical illness?
• Why does stress lead to illness in some people, but not in others?
• Why do people continue to pursue health-impairing lifestyles, when they know that they're endangering their health?
• Why do people delay needed medical treatment, and why do they ignore the advice of their doctors?

In our chapter Application, we'll focus on strategies for improving stress management. However, you can't manage stress very effectively if you can't recognize it—so let's take an in-depth look at the nature of stress.

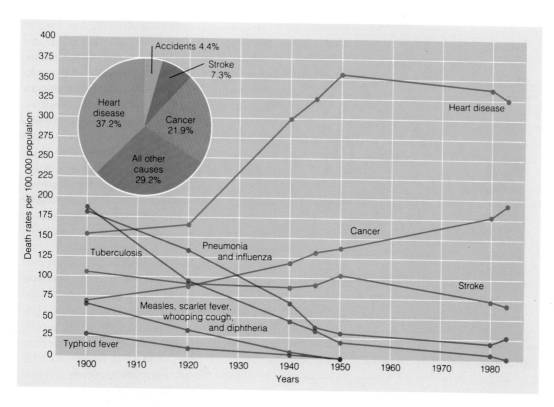

Figure 13.1 Changing patterns of illness. Trends in the death rates for various diseases during the 20th century reveal that contagious diseases (shown in green) have declined as a threat to our health. However, the death rates for stress-related chronic diseases (shown in red) have either remained stable (as in the case of stroke) or increased dramatically (as in the case of cancer and heart disease). The pie chart (inset) shows the results of these trends: three chronic diseases (heart disease, cancer, and stroke) account for 66% of all deaths.

THE NATURE OF STRESS

The term *stress* has been used in different ways by different theorists. Some, such as Thomas Holmes (1979), define stress as a *stimulus* event that presents difficult demands (for instance, a divorce). Others, such as Hans Selye (1976), define stress as the *response* of physiological arousal elicited by troublesome events. A point of view that lies between these extremes is gradually taking hold in psychology. It's the *transactional model of stress* advocated by Richard Lazarus and his colleagues, among others (Holroyd & Lazarus, 1982; Lazarus & Folkman, 1984).

Lazarus argues that stress is neither a stimulus nor a response, but a special stimulus-response transaction wherein one feels threatened. Lazarus points out that the same event may be stressful for one person but not another. For example, getting up to talk in front of a speech class is a "piece of cake" for some people. For others, however, it can be a paralyzing experience. If specific events are stressful only some of the time, then stress can't lie entirely in the stimulus events. In a similar vein, Lazarus argues against equating stress with the response of physiological arousal because we routinely experience such arousal in the absence of stress. For example, a beautiful sunset, lust, or a brisk walk can cause physiological arousal.

Thus, Lazarus concludes that "stress resides neither in the situation nor in the person; it depends on a transaction between the two. It arises

from how the person appraises an event and adapts to it" (Goleman, 1979, p. 52). In keeping with this theoretical perspective, we'll define **stress as any circumstances that threaten or are perceived to threaten our well-being and that thereby tax our coping abilities.** The threat may be to our immediate physical safety, our long range security, our self-esteem, our reputation, our peace of mind, or many other things that we value. This is a complex concept; so let's explore a little further.

Stress as an Everyday Event

The term *stress* tends to spark images of overwhelming, traumatic crises. People may think of hijackings, hurricanes, military combat, and nuclear accidents. Undeniably, these are extremely stressful events. However, these unusual events are only a small part of what stress is. Many everyday events such as waiting in line, having car trouble, shopping for Christmas presents, misplacing your checkbook, and staring at bills you can't pay are also stressful. In recent years, researchers have found that everyday problems and the minor nuisances of life are also important forms of stress (Burks & Martin, 1985).

You might guess that minor stresses would produce minor effects, but that isn't necessarily true. Research indicates that routine hassles may have

Table 13.1 The Ten Most Frequent Hassles

ITEM (HASSLE)	TIMES CHECKED (%)
1. Concerns about weight	52.4
2. Health of a family member	48.1
3. Rising prices of common goods	43.7
4. Home maintenance	42.8
5. Too many things to do	38.6
6. Misplacing or losing things	38.1
7. Yard work or outside home maintenance	38.1
8. Property, investment, or taxes	37.6
9. Crime	37.1
10. Physical appearance	35.9

Source: Kanner et al., 1981

"We developed the Hassle Scale because we think scales that measure major events miss the point. They don't tell us anything about what goes on day in and day out, hour after hour, in a person's life. The constant, minor irritants may be much more important than the large, landmark changes."

RICHARD LAZARUS

significant negative effects on our mental and physical health (Delongis, Folkman, & Lazarus, 1988; Kanner et al., 1981). Richard Lazarus and his colleagues have devised a scale to measure stress in the form of daily hassles. Their scale lists 117 everyday problems. Working with a sample of 100 middle-aged adults, Kanner et al. (1981) compared their hassles scale against another scale that assessed stress in the form of major life events. The ten hassles reported most frequently in this study are listed in Table 13.1. The investigators found that scores on their hassles scale were more strongly related to subjects' mental health than scores on the scale that measured major stressful events.

Why would minor hassles be more strongly related to mental health than major stressful events? The answer isn't entirely clear yet, but it may be because of the *cumulative* nature of stress. Stress adds up. Routine stresses at home, at school, and at work might be fairly benign individually, but collectively they could create great strain. Everyday hassles are common, frequent stressors that may pile up until "the last straw breaks the camel's back."

Appraisal: Stress Lies in the Eye of the Beholder

The experience of feeling threatened depends on what events we notice and how we choose to appraise or interpret them. Events that are stressful for one person may be "ho-hum" routine for another. For example, many people find flying in an airplane somewhat stressful, but frequent fliers may not be bothered at all. Some people enjoy the excitement of going out on a date with someone new; others find the uncertainty terrifying.

In discussing appraisals of stress, Lazarus and Folkman (1984) distinguish between primary and secondary appraisal. *Primary appraisal* is an initial evaluation of whether an event is (1) irrelevant to you, (2) relevant but not threatening, or (3) stressful. When you view an event as stressful, you're likely to make a *secondary appraisal*, which is an evaluation of your coping resources and options for dealing with the stress. Thus, your primary appraisal would determine whether you saw an upcoming job interview as stressful, and your secondary appraisal would determine how stressful this interview appeared, in light of your assessment of your ability to deal with the event.

Often, we're not very objective in our appraisals of potentially stressful events. A study of hospitalized patients awaiting surgery showed there was only a slight correlation between the objective seriousness of a person's upcoming surgery and the amount of fear experienced by the patient (Janis, 1958). Thus, stress lies in the eye (actually, the mind) of the beholder. Our appraisals of stressful events are highly subjective.

Marziali and Pilkonis (1986) found that carefully measuring these subjective appraisals can help us predict the effects of stress more accurately. They asked subjects to list major stressful events in their lives and to rate their subjective response to these events in terms of how helpless they felt, how angry they felt, how controllable they felt the events were, and so forth. The sum of these ratings of individuals' subjective reactions to stress was more strongly related to their mental health than was a more conventional, "objective" measure of stress based on the number of stressful events experienced. In light of the subjective nature of stress, we need to examine some of the factors that influence our appraisals of stress.

Key Factors in Our Appraisals of Stress

Quite a variety of factors influence our subjective appraisals of potentially stressful events. Three that stand out are (1) your familiarity with the challenge, (2) the controllability of the events, and (3) how predictable the events are.

FAMILIARITY
An important consideration in your appraisal of stress is your familiarity with the stressful demands. Generally, the less familiar you are with a potentially stressful event, the more threatened you're likely to feel (McGrath, 1977). Hence, a person's first major job interview or first appearance in a courtroom or first purchase of a home tends to be more stressful than subsequent similar

events. Familiarity with a challenge can make yesterday's crisis today's routine.

CONTROLLABILITY

Events are usually less stressful when we see them as being under our control. For example, when driving in icy, slippery weather, I prefer to be at the wheel rather than riding as a passenger. If I'm driving somewhere with my wife, there's no logic to this preference. I don't drive any slower than she would, and I have no illusions that I drive any better. However, I find it much less stressful if I feel that I'm in control. Consistent with this principle, Stern, McCants, and Pettine (1982) found that uncontrollable stressful events had more negative impact on subjects' health than controllable events.

Although most people experience less stress when troublesome events are more controllable, Folkman (1984) points out that this isn't universal. Apparently, some people would rather not have the increased responsibility—to take charge and cope—that comes with the potential for control.

PREDICTABILITY

If you experience a stressful event—for instance, being fired at work—is it more traumatic when the event comes out of nowhere (unpredictable stress) or when you can see the event coming for some time (predictable stress)? In general, it appears that we prefer predictable stress over surprise packages. Many animal studies show that unpredictable shock is more stressful than an equal amount of predictable shock (Weinberg & Levine, 1980). When the predictability of stress is studied with human subjects, the results are similar (Lazarus & Folkman, 1984). Major stressors, such as the death of a loved one or the loss of a job, seem to be less devastating when they can be anticipated over a period of time. We may prefer predictability because it allows us to engage in anticipatory coping to prepare for the stress.

Major Types of Stress

There's an enormous variety of events that can be stressful for one person or another. Although they're not entirely independent, the four principal types of stress are (1) frustration, (2) conflict, (3) change, and (4) pressure. As you read about each of these, you'll surely recognize four very familiar adversaries.

FRUSTRATION

I had a wonderful relationship with a married man for 3 months. One day when we planned to spend the entire day together, he called and said he wouldn't be meeting me. Someone had mentioned me to his wife, and he said that to keep his marriage together he would have to stop seeing me. I cried all morning. The grief was like losing someone through death. I still hurt, and I wonder if I'll ever get over him.

The scenario above illustrates frustration. As psychologists use the term, *frustration* **occurs in any situation in which the pursuit of some goal is thwarted**. In essence, you experience frustration when you want something and you can't have it. We all have to deal with frustration virtually every day. Traffic jams, for instance, are a routine source of frustration that can affect mood and blood pressure (Novaco et al., 1979). Fortunately, most of our frustrations are brief and insignificant. You may be quite upset when you go to a repair shop to pick up your ailing stereo and find that it hasn't been fixed as promised. However, a week later you'll probably have your stereo back, and the frustration will be forgotten.

Of course, some frustrations can be sources of significant stress. Failures and losses are two common kinds of frustration that are often very stressful. We all fail in at least some of our endeavors. Some of us make failure almost inevitable by setting unrealistically high goals for ourselves. People tend to forget that for every newly appointed vice president in the business world, there are dozens of middle-level executives who don't get promoted. Losses can be especially frustrating because we're deprived of something that we're accustomed to having. For example, there are few things more frustrating than losing a dearly loved boyfriend, girlfriend, or spouse.

CONFLICT

Should I or shouldn't I? I became engaged at Christmas. My fiancé surprised me with a ring. I knew if I refused the ring he would be terribly hurt and our relationship would suffer. However, I don't really know whether or not I want to marry him. On the other hand, I don't want to lose him either.

Like frustration, conflict is an unavoidable feature of everyday life. That perplexing question, "Should I or shouldn't I?" comes up in our lives again and again. **Conflict occurs when two or more incompatible motivations or behavioral impulses compete for expression.** Conflicts have been differentiated into three types, which were originally described by Kurt Lewin (1935) and investigated extensively by Neal Miller (1944; Dollard & Miller, 1950). The three basic types of conflict—approach-approach, avoidance-avoidance, and approach-avoidance—are diagrammed in Figure 13.2.

In an *approach-approach conflict* a choice

Figure 13.2 Types of conflict. Psychologists have identified three basic types of conflict. In approach-approach or avoidance-avoidance conflicts, a person is torn between two goals. In an approach-avoidance conflict, there is only one goal under consideration, but it has both positive and negative aspects.

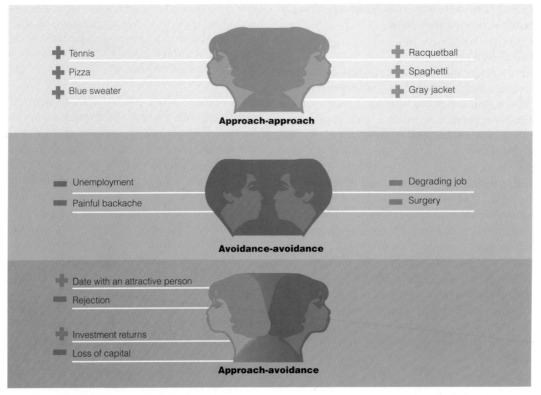

Tennis
Pizza
Blue sweater

Racquetball
Spaghetti
Gray jacket

Approach-approach

Unemployment
Painful backache

Degrading job
Surgery

Avoidance-avoidance

Date with an attractive person
Rejection

Investment returns
Loss of capital

Approach-avoidance

Many of the things we desire—including money, fame, and success—have their costs. This sign, which captures the essence of approach-avoidance conflict, was created by Jenny Holzer, an artist who uses language as a medium.

must be made between two attractive goals. The problem, of course, is that you can choose just one of the two goals. For example: You have a free afternoon; should you play tennis or racquetball? You're out for a meal; do you want to order the pizza or the spaghetti? You can't afford both; should you buy the blue sweater or the gray jacket?

Among the three kinds of conflict, the ap-proach-approach type tends to be the least stressful. People usually don't stagger out of restaurants exhausted by the stress of choosing which of several appealing entrees to eat. Approach-approach conflicts typically have a reasonably happy ending, whichever way you decide to go. Nonetheless, approach-approach conflicts centering on important issues may sometimes be troublesome. If you're torn between two appealing college majors or two attractive boyfriends, you may find the decision-making process quite stressful.

In an *avoidance-avoidance conflict* a choice **must be made between two unattractive goals**. Forced to choose between two repelling alternatives, you are, as they say, "caught between the devil and the deep blue sea." For example, should you continue to collect unemployment checks, or should you take that degrading job at the carwash? Or let's say you have very painful backaches; should you submit to surgery that you dread, or should you continue to live with the pain?

Obviously, avoidance-avoidance conflicts are most unpleasant and very stressful. Typically, people keep delaying their decision as long as possible, hoping that they'll somehow be able to escape the conflict situation. For example, you might delay the surgery to alleviate your backaches because you're hopeful that the backaches will disappear on their own.

In an *approach-avoidance conflict* a choice **must be made about whether to pursue a single goal that has both attractive and unattractive as-**

pects. For instance, imagine that you're offered a career promotion that will mean a large increase in pay, but you'll have to move to a city that you hate. Approach-avoidance conflicts are very common, and they can be very stressful. Any time you have to take a risk to pursue some desirable outcome, you're likely to find yourself in an approach-avoidance conflict. Should you risk rejection by asking out that attractive person in class? Should you risk your savings by investing in a new business that could fail?

Approach-avoidance conflicts often produce *vacillation*. That is, we go back and forth, beset by indecision. We decide to go ahead, then we decide not to, and then we decide to go ahead again. Humans are not unique in this respect. Many years ago, Neal Miller (1944) observed the same vacillation in his ground-breaking research with rats. Miller created approach-avoidance conflicts in hungry rats by alternately feeding and shocking them at one end of a runway apparatus. Eventually, these rats tended to hover near the center of the runway, alternately approaching and retreating from the goal box at the end of the alley.

In a series of studies of approach-avoidance conflict, Miller (1959) plotted how an organism's tendency to approach a goal (the approach gradient in Figure 13.3) and to retreat from a goal (the avoidance gradient in Figure 13.3) increase as the organism nears the goal. He found that avoidance motivation increases more rapidly than approach motivation (as reflected by the avoidance gradient's steeper slope in Figure 13.3). As a result of his analysis, Miller concluded that *in trying to resolve an approach-avoidance conflict, we should focus more on decreasing avoidance motivation than on increasing approach motivation.*

How would this insight apply to a complex human dilemma? Imagine that you're counseling a friend who is vacillating over whether to ask someone out on a date. Miller would say that you should downplay the negative aspects of possible rejection (thus lowering the avoidance gradient) rather than dwelling on how much fun the date could be (thus raising the approach gradient). In Figure 13.3, if the avoidance gradient is lowered far enough, the vacillation point will move very near the goal, indicating that the person should be able to reach the goal (make a decision and take action).

More recent research has revealed that avoidance tendencies don't *always* increase more rapidly than approach tendencies (Epstein, 1982). In light of this new finding, the best advice for resolving an approach-avoidance conflict may be to work on both aspects of the conflict. In other words, you may want to try to lower the avoidance tendency *and* raise the approach tendency.

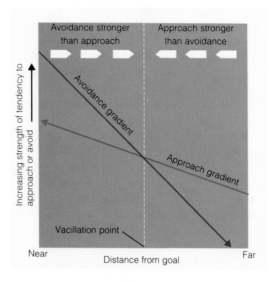

Figure 13.3 Vacillation in approach-avoidance conflict. According to Miller, as you near a goal that has positive and negative features, avoidance motivation tends to increase faster than approach motivation, sending you into retreat. However, if you retreat far enough, you'll eventually reach a point where approach motivation is stronger than avoidance motivation, and you may decide to go ahead once again. The ebb and flow of this process leads to vacillation.

CHANGE

After my divorce, I lived alone for 4 years. Six months ago I married a wonderful woman who has two children from her previous marriage. My biggest stress is suddenly having to adapt to living with three people instead of by myself. I was pretty set in my ways. I had certain routines. Now everything is chaos. I love my wife and I'm fond of the kids, and they're not really doing anything wrong, but my house and my life just aren't the same, and I'm having trouble dealing with it all.

There's evidence that life changes may represent a key type of stress. **Life changes are any noticeable alterations in one's living circumstances that require readjustment.** As we discussed in Chapter 2, Thomas Holmes, Richard Rahe, and their colleagues set out to explore the relations between stressful life events and physical

---

CONCEPT CHECK 13.1
Identifying Types of Conflict

Check your understanding of the three basic types of conflict by identifying the type experienced in each of the following examples. The answers are in Appendix A.

Examples

_____ 1. John can't decide whether to take a demeaning job in a car wash or to go on welfare.

_____ 2. Mary wants to apply to a highly selective law school, but she hates to risk the possibility of rejection.

_____ 3. Ellen has been shopping for a new car and is torn between a nifty little sports car and a classy sedan, both of which she really likes.

Types of conflict

a. approach-approach
b. avoidance-avoidance
c. approach-avoidance

illness (Holmes & Rahe, 1967; Rahe & Arthur, 1978). Theorizing that stress might make people more vulnerable to illness, they interviewed thousands of tuberculosis patients to find out what kinds of events had preceded the onset of their disease. Surprisingly, the frequently cited events were not uniformly negative. There were plenty of aversive events, as expected, but there were also many seemingly positive events, such as getting married, having a baby, or getting promoted.

Why would positive events, such as moving to a nicer home, produce stress? According to Holmes and Rahe, it's because they produce *change*. Their thesis is that disruptions of our daily routines are stressful. According to their theory, changes in personal relationships, changes at work, changes in finances, and so forth can be stressful even when the changes are welcomed.

Based on this analysis, Holmes and Rahe (1967) developed the Social Readjustment Rating Scale (SRRS) to measure life change as a form of stress. The scale assigns numerical values to 43 major life events. These values are supposed to reflect the magnitude of the readjustment required by each change (see Table 13.2). In using the scale, respondents are asked to indicate how often they experienced any of these 43 events during a certain time period (typically, the past year). The person then adds up the numbers associated with each event checked, and this sum is an index of the amount of change-related stress the person has recently experienced.

The SRRS has been used in more than 1000 studies by many different researchers all over the world (Holmes, 1979). Overall, these studies have shown that people with higher scores on the SRRS tend to be more vulnerable to many kinds of physical illness and many types of psychological problems as well (Barrett, Rose, & Klerman, 1979; Elliott & Eisdorfer, 1982). These results have attracted a great deal of attention, and the SRRS has been reprinted in many popular newspapers and magazines. The attendant publicity has led to the widespread conclusion that life change is inherently stressful.

More recently, however, experts have criticized this research, citing problems with the methods used (Schroeder & Costa, 1984) and problems in interpreting the findings (Perkins, 1982). At this point, it's a key interpretive issue that concerns us. Many critics have argued that the SRRS does not measure *change* exclusively. The main problem is that the list of life changes on the SRRS is dominated by events that are clearly negative or undesirable (death of a spouse, being fired from a job, and so on). These negative events probably generate great frustration. Although there are

Table 13.2 Social Readjustment Rating Scale

LIFE EVENT	MEAN VALUE
Death of spouse	100
Divorce	73
Marital separation	65
Jail term	63
Death of close family member	63
Personal injury or illness	53
Marriage	50
Being fired at work	47
Marital reconciliation	45
Retirement	45
Change in health of family member	44
Pregnancy	40
Sex difficulties	39
Gain of a new family member	39
Business readjustment	39
Change in financial state	38
Death of a close friend	37
Change to a different line of work	36
Change in number of arguments with spouse	35
Mortgage or loan for major purchase (home, etc.)	31
Foreclosure of mortgage or loan	30
Change in responsibilities at work	29
Son or daughter leaving home	29
Trouble with in-laws	29
Outstanding personal achievement	28
Spouse beginning or stopping work	26
Beginning or ending school	26
Change in living conditions	25
Revision of personal habits	24
Trouble with boss	23
Change in work hours or conditions	20
Change in residence	20
Change in school	20
Change in recreation	19
Change in church activities	19
Change in social activities	18
Mortgage or loan for lesser purchase (car, TV, and so on)	17
Change in sleeping habits	16
Change in number of family get-togethers	15
Change in eating habits	15
Vacation	13
Christmas	12
Minor violations of the law	11

Source: Holmes & Rahe, 1967

some positive events on the scale, it could be that frustration (generated by negative events), rather than change, creates most of the stress assessed by the scale.

To investigate this possibility, researchers began to take into account the desirability and undesirability of subjects' life changes. Subjects were

asked to indicate the desirability of the events that they checked off on the SRRS and similar scales. The findings in these studies clearly indicated that life change is *not* the crucial dimension measured by the SRRS. Undesirable or negative life events cause most of the stress tapped by the SRRS (Perkins, 1982; Zeiss, 1980).

In terms of the measurement and testing concepts that were discussed in Chapter 9, it boils down to this—the *construct validity* of the SRRS appears questionable. In other words, the scale doesn't measure exactly what it purports to measure. Given its ground-breaking nature, the SRRS represented a major step forward in the assessment of life stress. However, it was characterized inaccurately as a measure of life change. In reality, it assesses a wide range of different kinds of stressful experiences.

Should we discard the notion that change is stressful? Not entirely. There are other lines of research, independent of work with the SRRS, that support the hypothesis that change is an important form of stress. For instance, there's evidence linking geographic mobility to impaired mental and physical health (Brett, 1980). More research is needed, but it's quite plausible that change constitutes a major type of stress in our lives. However, at present, there's little reason to believe that change is *inherently or inevitably* stressful. Some life changes may be quite challenging, while others may be quite benign.

PRESSURE

My father questioned me at dinner about some things I didn't want to talk about. I know he doesn't want to hear my answers, at least not the truth. My father told me when I was little that I was his favorite because I was "pretty near perfect" and I've spent my life trying to keep up that image, even though it's obviously not true. Recently, he has begun to realize this, and it's made our relationship very strained and painful.

At one time or another, most of us have probably remarked that we're "under pressure." What does this mean? **Pressure involves expectations or demands that one behave in a certain way.** Pressure can be divided into two subtypes: the pressure to *perform* and the pressure to *conform*. You are under pressure to perform when you're expected to execute tasks and responsibilities quickly, efficiently, and successfully. For example, salespeople usually are under pressure to move merchandise, professors at research institutions are often under pressure to publish in prestigious journals, comedians are under pressure to be amusing, and secretaries are often under pressure to complete lots of clerical work in very little time. Pressures to conform to others' expectations are also common in our lives. Businessmen are expected to wear suits and ties, suburban home owners are expected to keep their lawns well manicured, teenagers are expected to adhere to their parents' values and rules, and workers are expected to laugh at their supervisors' jokes.

Pressure is found in virtually all walks of life, but some occupations involve more pressure than others. Trading on the commodities exchange involves intense pressure to perform quickly, efficiently, and successfully.

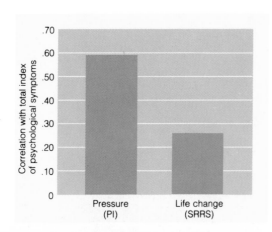

Figure 13.4 Pressure and psychological symptoms. A comparison of pressure and life change as sources of stress suggests that pressure may be more strongly related to mental health than change is. (Data from Weiten, 1988)

CONCEPT CHECK 13.2
Recognizing Sources of Stress

Check your understanding of the major sources of stress by indicating which type or types of stress are at work in each of the examples below. Bear in mind that the four basic types of stress are not mutually exclusive. There's some potential for overlap, so that a specific experience might include both change and pressure, for instance. The answers are in Appendix A.

Examples

_____ 1. Marie is late for an appointment, but is stuck in line at the bank.

_____ 2. Maureen decides that she won't be satisfied unless she gets straight A's this year.

_____ 3. Melvin has just graduated from business school and has taken an exciting new job.

_____ 4. Morris has just been fired from his job and needs to find another.

Types of stress

a. frustration
b. conflict
c. change
d. pressure

Although widely discussed by the general public, the concept of pressure has received scant attention from researchers. Specific aspects of pressure, such as work overload, have been examined in a few studies of work stress (Holt, 1982), but until recently there was no attempt to formally define pressure as a unique form of stress. However, in the 1980s, two research programs focused systematically on the concept of pressure.

In one of these programs, I devised a scale to measure pressure as a form of life stress (Weiten & Dixon, 1984; Weiten, 1988). The result is a 48-item self-report measure, called the Pressure Inventory, which assesses self-imposed pressure, pressure from work and school, and pressure from family relations, peer relations, and intimate relations. In the first two studies with this scale, a strong relationship has been found between pressure and a variety of psychological symptoms and problems. In fact, pressure has turned out to be more strongly related to measures of mental health than the SRRS and other established measures of stress (see Figure 13.4).

In the other research program, Roy Baumeister (1984; Baumeister & Steinhilber, 1984) has investigated how the pressure to perform affects performance of skilled tasks. Baumeister's research indicates that pressure often has a negative impact on task performance. To put it more bluntly, many of us "choke" under pressure. These two lines of research suggest that pressure may be an important form of stress that merits more attention from stress theorists. We'll look at some of Baumeister's research in detail later (see the Featured Study), after we discuss how people respond to stress.

RESPONDING TO STRESS

Our response to stress is complex and multidimensional. Stress affects us at several levels. Consider again the chapter's opening scenario, in which you're driving home in heavy traffic and thinking about overdue papers, tuition increases, and parental pressures. Let's look at some of the reactions we mentioned. When you groan audibly in reaction to the traffic report, you're experiencing an *emotional response* to stress, in this case annoyance and anger. When your pulse quickens and your stomach knots up, you're exhibiting *physiological responses* to stress. When you shout insults at another driver, your verbal aggression is a *behavioral response* to the stress at hand. Thus, we can analyze our reactions to stress at three levels: (1) our emotional responses, (2) our physiological responses, and (3) our behavioral responses. Figure 13.5 is a diagram of these three levels of response; it provides an overview of the stress process.

Emotional Responses

When we're under stress, we often react emotionally. More often than not, stress tends to elicit unpleasant emotions rather than pleasurable feelings.

The link between stress and emotion was apparent in a study of 96 women who filled out daily diaries about the stresses and moods that they experienced over a period of 28 days (Caspi, Bolger, & Eckenrode, 1987). The investigators found that daily fluctuations in stress correlated with daily fluctuations in mood. As stress increased, mood

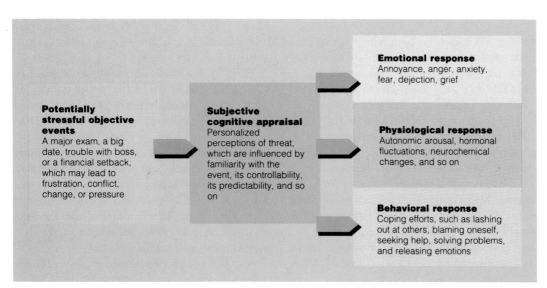

Figure 13.5 Overview of the stress process. A potentially stressful event, such as a major exam, elicits a subjective appraisal of how threatening the event is. If the event is viewed with alarm, the stress may trigger emotional, psychological, and behavioral reactions, as our response to stress is multidimensional.

tended to become more negative. As the researchers put it, "Some days everything seems to go wrong, and by day's end, minor difficulties find their outlet in rotten moods" (p. 184).

EMOTIONS COMMONLY ELICITED

There are no simple one-to-one connections between certain types of stress and particular emotions. Many different emotions can be evoked by stressful events, although some are certainly more likely than others. We'll use Plutchik's (1980) model of primary emotions to highlight the types of emotions that are especially common responses to stress. Figure 13.6 shows the eight primary emotions identified by Plutchik, including varying levels of intensity for some of the emotions (see Chapter 10 for more details). Although stress could elicit any of the primary emotions shown in Figure 13.6, Woolfolk and Richardson (1978) suggest that reactions along the following gradients are particularly likely: (1) annoyance, anger, and rage; (2) apprehension, fear, and terror; and (3) pensiveness, sadness, and grief.

ANNOYANCE, ANGER, AND RAGE Stress frequently produces feelings of anger ranging in intensity from mild annoyance to uncontrollable rage. Frustration is particularly likely to generate anger. Some people become visibly angry in response to nearly every trivial setback. The pressure to conform also seems likely to elicit anger and resentment.

APPREHENSION, FEAR, AND TERROR Stress probably evokes emotions on this gradient more frequently than on any other. *Anxiety* falls along this gradient, somewhere between apprehension and fear. Since Freud pinpointed the link between conflict and anxiety many years ago, psychologists have conducted thousands upon thousands of studies of anxiety. Although Freud emphasized that *conflict* causes anxiety, it's clear that apprehension, anxiety, and fear can be elicited by the pressure to perform, the threat of impending frustration, or the uncertainty associated with change. Thus, all of the major types of stress can evoke emotions in this category.

PENSIVENESS, SADNESS, AND GRIEF Sometimes stress simply "brings us down," evoking sadness and dejection. We all get depressed from time to time, especially in response to frustration. Sadness and depression are particularly likely when we feel powerless to do anything about the stress in our lives.

EFFECTS OF EMOTIONAL AROUSAL

Emotional responses are a natural and normal part of life. Even unpleasant emotions serve important purposes. Like physical pain, painful emotions

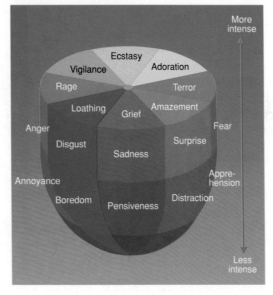

Figure 13.6 The dimensions of emotion. Plutchik's model of emotion provides a useful scheme for analyzing the emotional reactions evoked by stressful events. Reactions involving three of the eight primary emotions identified by Plutchik—anger, sadness, and fear—are commonly triggered by stress.

can serve as warnings that we need to take action. However, it's important to note that strong emotional arousal may sometimes interfere with efforts to cope with stress. For example, there's evidence that high emotional arousal may produce a narrowing of attention, poorer judgment, and less effective memory retrieval (Mandler, 1982).

The well-known problem of *test anxiety* illustrates how emotional arousal can hurt performance. Often students who score poorly on an exam will nonetheless insist that they know the material. Many of them are probably telling the truth. Many researchers have found a negative correlation between test-related anxiety and exam performance. Students who display high test anxiety tend to score low on exams (Wine, 1982). Test-anxiety can interfere with test taking in several ways, but the critical consideration appears to be the disruption of attention to the test (Sarason, 1984). Many test-anxious students waste too much time worrying about how they're doing and wondering whether others are having similar problems. In other words, their minds wander too much from the task of taking the test.

Although emotional arousal may hurt coping efforts, this isn't *necessarily* the case. Various theories of "optimal arousal" predict that task performance should improve with increased emotional arousal—up to a point, after which arousal becomes too high and is disruptive (Hebb, 1955; Malmo, 1975). The level of arousal at which performance peaks is characterized as the optimal level of arousal for a task.

This optimal level of arousal may depend in part on the complexity of the task at hand. The conventional wisdom is that *as a task becomes more complex, the optimal level of arousal (for peak performance) tends to decrease.* This relationship is depicted in Figure 13.7. As you can see, a fairly high level of arousal should be optimal on simple tasks (for example, driving 8 hours to help a friend in a crisis). However, performance should peak at a lower level of arousal on complex tasks (for example, making a major decision in which you have to weigh many factors).

Most of the research evidence on optimal levels of arousal comes from rather simple animal learning studies, so it may be risky to generalize these principles to human coping efforts. Nonetheless, optimal-arousal theories provide a plausible model of how emotional arousal could have either beneficial or disruptive effects on coping, depending on the nature of the stressful demands.

Physiological Responses

As we just discussed, stress frequently elicits strong emotional responses. Now we'll look at the important physiological changes that often accompany these emotional responses.

Figure 13.7 Arousal and performance. The effect of emotional arousal on task performance depends on the complexity of the task. On complex tasks, a relatively low level of arousal tends to be optimal. On simple tasks, however, performance may peak at a much higher level of arousal.

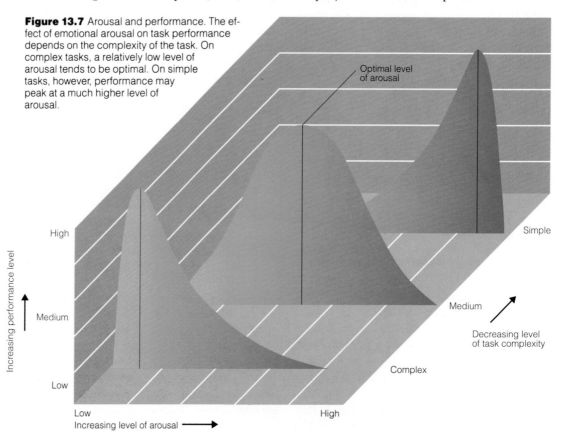

Optimal level of arousal

High

Increasing performance level

Medium

Low

Low
Increasing level of arousal ⟶

High

Simple

Medium

Decreasing level of task complexity

Complex

THE FIGHT-OR-FLIGHT RESPONSE

Walter Cannon (1932) was one of the first theorists to describe the fight-or-flight response. **The fight-or-flight response is a physiological reaction to threat in which the autonomic nervous system mobilizes the organism for attacking (fight) or fleeing (flight) an enemy.** As you may recall from Chapter 3, the autonomic nervous system (ANS) controls blood vessels, smooth muscles, and glands. The fight-or-flight response is mediated by the *sympathetic* division of the ANS. In one experiment, Cannon studied the fight-or-flight response in cats, by confronting them with dogs. Among other things, he noticed an immediate acceleration in breathing and heart rate and a reduction in digestive processes.

Elements of the fight-or-flight response are also seen in humans. In a sense, this automatic reaction is a "leftover" from our evolutionary past. It's clearly an adaptive response in the animal kingdom, where the threat of predators often requires a swift response of fighting or fleeing. But among humans, the fight-or-flight response appears less adaptive. Most of our stresses can't be handled simply through fight or flight. Work pressures, marital problems, and financial difficulties require far more complex responses. Moreover, our stresses often continue for lengthy periods of time, so that our fight-or-flight response leaves us in a state of enduring physiological arousal. Concern about the effects of prolonged physical arousal was first voiced by Hans Selye, a Canadian scientist who conducted extensive research on stress.

THE GENERAL ADAPTATION SYNDROME

The concept of stress was added to our language by Hans Selye (1936, 1956, 1982). Selye was born in Vienna, but spent his entire professional career at McGill University in Montreal. Beginning in the 1930s, Selye exposed laboratory animals to a diverse array of both physical and psychological stressors (heat, cold, pain, mild shock, restraint, and so on). The patterns of physiological arousal seen in the animals were largely the same, regardless of the type of stress. Thus, Selye concluded that stress reactions are *nonspecific*. In other words, he maintained that they did not vary according to the specific type of stress encountered.

Initially, Selye wasn't sure what to call this nonspecific response to a variety of noxious agents. In the 1940s he decided to call it *stress*, and the word has been part of our vocabulary ever since. As Selye traveled around the world giving lectures on his research, he was surprised at how quickly the word acquired popular use. He once remarked that "even if my scientific accomplishments should prove to be of little value, mine will be forever the glory of having enriched all these languages by at least one word" (Selye, 1976, p. 53).

In Selye's theory, stress refers to the body's *response* to threat. Ironically, late in his career, he admitted that he should have used the word *strain* to refer to the body's response to noxious stimuli and that he should have used the term *stress* to refer to the noxious stimulus events. But, as he explained, "my English was not yet good enough for me to distinguish between the words 'stress' and 'strain'" (Selye, 1976, p. 50). By the time his English had improved, the word was in widespread use, and it was too late to change.

As the years passed, other theorists began to use the term stress (in a more logical way) to refer to troublesome stimulus events, and this created some confusion. Because of the inconsistent use of the term *stress*, Selye was occasionally criticized (inaccurately) for theorizing that "stress causes stress." As we noted at the beginning of the chapter, most modern theorists sidestep this confusion by defining stress as neither a stimulus nor a response, but as a certain type of stimulus-response transaction.

Selye (1956, 1974) formulated an influential theory of stress reactions called the general adaptation syndrome. **The general adaptation syndrome is a model of the body's stress response, consisting of three stages: alarm, resistance, and exhaustion.** In the first stage of the general adaptation syndrome, an *alarm reaction* occurs when an organism first recognizes the existence of a threat. Physiological arousal occurs as the body musters its resources to combat the challenge. Selye's alarm reaction is essentially the fight-or-flight response originally described by Cannon.

However, Selye took his investigation of stress a few steps further by exposing laboratory animals to *prolonged* stress, similar to the chronic stress often endured by humans. As stress continues, the organism may progress to the second phase of the general adaptation syndrome, called the *stage of resistance*. During this phase, physiological changes stabilize as coping efforts get under way. Typically, physiological arousal continues to be higher than normal, although it may level off somewhat, as the organism becomes accustomed to the threat.

If the stress continues over a substantial period of time, the organism may enter the third stage, called the *stage of exhaustion*. According to Selye, the body's resources for fighting stress are limited. If the stress can't be overcome, the body's resources may be depleted, and physiological arousal will decrease. Eventually, there may be a collapse from exhaustion. During this phase, the organism's resistance declines, as shown in Figure 13.8.

"There are two main types of human beings: 'racehorses,' who thrive on stress and are only happy with a vigorous, fast-paced lifestyle; and 'turtles,' who in order to be happy require peace, quiet, and a generally tranquil environment."

HANS SELYE

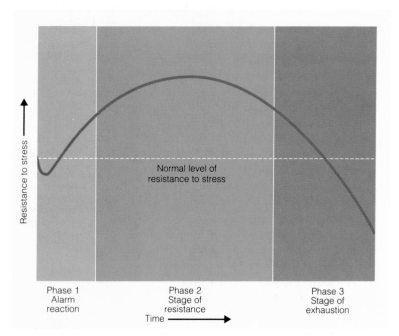

Resistance to stress →

Normal level of
resistance to stress

Phase 1
Alarm
reaction

Phase 2
Stage of
resistance

Phase 3
Stage of
exhaustion

Time →

Figure 13.8 The general adaptation syndrome. According to Selye, our psychological response to stress can be broken into three phases. During the first phase, the body mobilizes its resources for resistance after a brief initial shock. In the second phase, resistance levels off and eventually begins to decline. If the third phase of the general adaptation syndrome is reached, resistance is depleted, leading to health problems and exhaustion.

This reduced resistance may lead to what Selye called "diseases of adaptation."

Selye's theory and research forged a link between stress and physical illness. He demonstrated that physiological arousal that begins by being adaptive, if prolonged, can lead to diseases. Although his belief that stress reactions are nonspecific remains controversial (Mason, 1975), his model provided guidance for a generation of researchers who worked out the details of how stress reverberates throughout the body. Let's look at some of those details.

BRAIN-BODY PATHWAYS

Even in cases of moderate stress, you may notice that your heart has started beating faster, you've begun to breathe harder, and you're perspiring more than usual. How does all this (and much more) happen? It appears that there are two major pathways along which the brain sends signals to the endocrine system (Asterita, 1985). The *endocrine system* consists of glands located at various sites in the body that secrete chemicals called hormones (see Chapter 3). The hypothalamus is the part of the brain that appears to initiate action along these two pathways.

The first pathway (see Figure 13.9) is routed through the autonomic nervous system. Your hypothalamus activates the sympathetic division of the ANS. A key part of this activation involves stimulating the central part of the adrenal glands (the adrenal medulla) to release large amounts of *catecholamines* into the bloodstream. These hormones radiate throughout your body, producing many important physiological changes. The net result of catecholamine elevation is that your

body is mobilized for action. Heart rate and blood flow increase, and more blood is pumped to your brain and muscles. Respiration and oxygen consumption speed up, which facilitates alertness. Digestive processes are inhibited to conserve your energy. The pupils of your eyes dilate, increasing visual sensitivity.

The second pathway involves more direct communication between the brain and the endocrine system (see Figure 13.9). The hypothalamus sends signals to the so-called master gland of the endocrine system, your pituitary gland. The pituitary secretes a hormone (ACTH) that stimulates the outer part of the adrenal glands (the adrenal cortex) to release another important set of hormones—*corticosteroids*. These hormones stimulate the release of more fats and proteins into circulation, thus helping to increase your energy. They also mobilize chemicals that help to inhibit tissue inflammation in case of injury.

Stress can also produce other physiological changes that we're just beginning to understand. For instance, stress can trigger the release of endorphins in the brain or the suppression of immunal responding (Solomon, Amkraut, & Rubin, 1985; Veith-Flanigan & Sandman, 1985). The exact mechanisms underlying these physiological reactions remain a mystery for the moment. But it's becoming clear that our physiological responses to stress extend into all parts of our bodies. As you'll see, these physiological reactions can have an impact on both our mental and our physical health.

Behavioral Responses

Although we respond to stress at several levels, it's clear that our behavior is the crucial dimension of our reactions. Most behavioral responses to stress involve coping. **Coping refers to active efforts to master, reduce, or tolerate the demands created by stress.** Notice that this definition is neutral as to whether coping efforts are healthy or maladaptive. The popular use of the term often implies that coping is inherently healthy. When we say that someone "coped with her problems," we imply that she handled them effectively.

In reality, however, coping responses may be either healthy or unhealthy. For example, if you were flunking a history course at midterm, you might cope with this stress by (1) increasing your study efforts, (2) seeking special help from a tutor, (3) blaming your professor, or (4) giving up on the class without really trying. Clearly, the first two of these coping responses would be healthier than the last two. Thus, coping efforts may range from healthy to maladaptive.

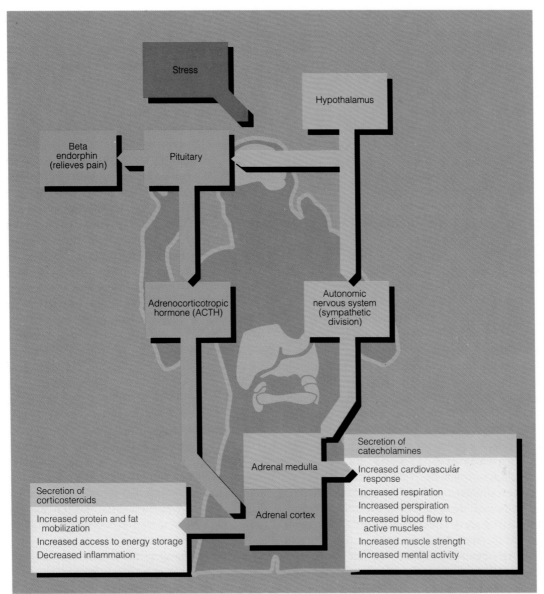

Figure 13.9 Brain-body pathways in stress. In times of stress, the brain sends signals along two pathways. The pathway through the autonomic nervous system controls the release of catecholamine hormones that help mobilize the body for action. The pathway through the pituitary gland and the endocrine system controls the release of corticosteroid hormones that increase energy and ward off tissue inflammation.

People cope with stress in a virtually endless variety of ways, and we can only highlight some of the more common patterns. In this section we'll focus most of our attention on styles of coping that tend to be less than ideal. We'll discuss a variety of healthier coping strategies in the chapter Application on stress management.

STRIKING OUT AT OTHERS

Often we respond to stressful events by striking out at others with aggressive behavior. **Aggression involves any behavior that is intended to hurt someone, either physically or verbally.** Many years ago, a team of psychologists (Dollard et al., 1939) proposed the *frustration-aggression hypothesis*, which held that aggression is always caused by frustration. Decades of research have verified their proposal that there's a causal link between frustration and aggression.

However, this research has also shown that there isn't an inevitable, one-to-one correspondence between frustration and aggression. In a discussion of qualifications to the frustration-aggression hypothesis, Leonard Berkowitz (1969) concluded (1) that frustration does not *necessarily* lead to aggression, (2) that many factors other than frustration (such as one's personality) influence the likelihood of aggression, and (3) that frustration may produce responses other than aggression (for example, apathy). Although these are important qualifications, it's clear that frustration often leads to aggression.

Frequently we lash out aggressively at others who had nothing to do with our frustration, apparently because we can't vent our anger at the real source of our frustration. For example, you'll probably suppress your anger rather than lash out verbally at your boss or at a police officer who's giving you a speeding ticket. Twenty minutes later, however, you might be verbally brutal to a colleague at work or to a gas station attendant. As we discussed in Chapter 12, this diversion of anger to a substitute target was noticed long ago by Sigmund Freud, who called it *displacement*.

GIVING UP

When confronted with stress, sometimes we simply give up and withdraw from the battle. This response of apathy and inaction tends to be associated with the emotional reactions of sadness and dejection. Martin Seligman (1974) has developed a model of this giving-up syndrome that appears to shed light on its causes.

In Seligman's research, animals are subjected to electric shocks that they can't escape. The animals are then given an opportunity to learn a response that will allow them to escape the shock. However, many of the animals have become so apathetic and listless that they don't even try to learn the escape response. When researchers made similar manipulations with *human* subjects using inescapable noise (rather than shock), they observed parallel results (Hiroto & Seligman, 1975). This syndrome is referred to as learned helplessness. **Learned helplessness involves passive behavior produced by exposure to unavoidable aversive events.**

Seligman originally viewed learned helplessness as a product of conditioning. However, research with human subjects has led Seligman and his colleagues to revise their theory. The current model proposes that our *cognitive interpretation* of aversive events determines whether we develop learned helplessness. Specifically, helplessness seems to occur when we come to believe that events are beyond our control. This belief is particularly likely to emerge when we attribute setbacks to personal inadequacies instead of situational factors (Abramson, Seligman, & Teasdale, 1978).

To summarize, stress sometimes leads to apathy, withdrawal, and surrender. Unfortunately, this tendency to give up may be transferred to situations in which we aren't really helpless. Hence, some people routinely respond to stress with fatalism and resignation. They passively accept setbacks that might instead be dealt with effectively.

INDULGING ONESELF

Stress sometimes leads to self-indulgence. When troubled by stress, many of us engage in excessive consummatory behavior—unwise patterns of eating, drinking, smoking, using drugs, spending money, and so forth. As I mentioned in Chapter 10, when I have an exceptionally stressful day, a frequent coping response on my part is to head for the refrigerator, the grocery store, or a restaurant in pursuit of something chocolate. I have a friend who copes similarly with stress by making a beeline for the nearest shopping mall to indulge in a spending spree.

It appears that my friend and I are not so unusual in our excessive consummatory behavior. In an influential classification of coping responses, Moos and Billings (1982) list *developing alternative rewards* as a common response to stress. It makes sense that when things are going poorly in one area of our lives, we may try to compensate by pursuing substitute forms of satisfaction. When this happens, consummatory responses probably rank high among the substitutes. They're relatively easy to execute, and they tend to be very pleasurable. Thus, it's not surprising that scientific evidence relates stress to increases in eating (Slochower, 1976), smoking (Tomkins, 1966), consumption of alcohol (Marlatt & Rose, 1980), and some types of drug use (Krueger, 1981).

DEFENSIVE COPING

Defensive coping is very common in response to stress. We noted in the previous chapter that Sigmund Freud originally developed the concept of the defense mechanism. Though rooted in the psychoanalytic tradition, this concept has gained widespread acceptance from psychologists of most persuasions. Building on Freud's initial insights, modern psychologists have broadened the scope of the concept and added to Freud's list of defense mechanisms.

Defense mechanisms are largely unconscious reactions that protect a person from unpleasant emotions such as anxiety and guilt. There are many specific mechanisms of defense. For example, Laughlin (1979) lists 49 different defenses. We described seven very common defense mechanisms in our discussion of Freud's theory in the previous chapter. Table 13.3 introduces another six defenses that people employ with some regularity.

Although widely discussed in the popular press, defense mechanisms are often misunderstood. To clear up misconceptions, we'll use a question-answer format to elaborate on the nature of defense mechanisms.

What exactly do defense mechanisms defend against? Above all else defense mechanisms shield us from the emotional discomfort that's so often elicited by stress. Their main purpose is to ward off unwelcome emotions or to reduce their intensity. Foremost among the emotions guarded against is *anxiety*. We're especially protective when the anxiety is due to some threat to our self-

Table 13.3 Six Common Defense Mechanisms, with Examples*

MECHANISM	EXAMPLE
Denial of reality. Protecting oneself from unpleasant reality by refusing to perceive or face it.	A smoker concludes that the evidence linking cigarette use to health problems is scientifically worthless.
Fantasy. Gratifying frustrated desires by imaginary achievements.	A socially inept and inhibited young man imagines himself chosen by a group of women to provide them with sexual satisfaction.
Intellectualization (isolation). Cutting off emotion from hurtful situations or separating incompatible attitudes by logic-tight compartments.	A prisoner on death row awaiting execution resists appeal on his behalf and coldly insists that the letter of the law be followed.
Undoing. Atoning for or trying to magically dispel unacceptable desires or acts.	A teenager who feels guilty about masturbation ritually touches door knobs a prescribed number of times following each occurrence of the act.
Overcompensation. Covering up felt weaknesses by emphasizing some desirable characteristic, or making up for frustration in one area by overgratification in another.	A dangerously overweight woman goes on eating binges when she feels neglected by her husband.
Acting out. Engaging in antisocial or excessive behavior without regard to negative consequences as a way of dealing with emotional stress.	An unhappy, frustrated sales representative has several indiscriminate affairs without regard to the negative effects of the behavior.

*See Table 12.3 for another list of defense mechanisms.
Source: Carson, Butcher, & Coleman (1988)

esteem. Defenses are also used to suppress dangerous feelings of anger so that they don't explode into acts of aggression. Guilt and dejection are two other emotions that we often try to evade through defensive maneuvers.

How do they work? Through *self-deception*. They accomplish their goals by distorting reality so that it doesn't appear so threatening. For example, let's say you're doing very poorly in school and you're in danger of flunking out. Initially you might use *denial* to block awareness of the possibility that you could flunk. This might temporarily fend off feelings of anxiety. If it becomes difficult to deny the obvious, you might resort to *fantasy*, daydreaming about how you'll salvage adequate grades by getting spectacular scores on the upcoming final exams, when the objective fact is that you're hopelessly behind in your studies. Thus, defense mechanisms work their magic by bending reality in self-serving ways.

Are they conscious or unconscious? Both. Freud originally assumed that our defenses operate entirely at an unconscious level. However, the concept of the defense mechanism has been broadened by other theorists to include maneuvers that we may be aware of. Thus, defense mechanisms may operate at varying levels of awareness, although they're largely unconscious.

Are they normal? Definitely. We all use defense mechanisms on a fairly regular basis. They're entirely normal patterns of coping. The notion that only neurotic people use defense mechanisms is inaccurate.

Are they healthy? This is a much more complicated question. More often than not, the answer is "no." Generally, defensive coping is less than optimal for a number of reasons. First, distorting reality rarely provides a genuine solution to our problems. Second, defensive tactics use up energy that could be spent more wisely in tackling the problem. In other words, defensive pseudo-solutions may prevent us from employing more constructive coping strategies. Third, defensive coping often leads us to delay facing up to a problem, and this delay may allow the problem to fester and grow.

Although defensive behavior *tends* to be relatively unhealthy, it can sometimes be adaptive. For example, *displacement* sometimes allows us to channel aggressive energy into socially acceptable outlets. If you worked in a frustrating job, you might start playing vicious racquetball games to release your smoldering anger in a harmless way. In a similar vein, *fantasy* might help you to endure a period of financial straits while you attend college. After studying denial and other defenses, Richard Lazarus acknowledges that sometimes "illusion and self-deception can have positive value in a person's psychological economy" (Goleman, 1979, p. 47).

Thus, it's hard to make sweeping generalizations about the adaptive value of defense mechanisms. Defensive coping tends to be less than ideal, but it can be either healthy or unhealthy, depending on the unique circumstances. Generally, the more your defenses prevent you from engaging in constructive coping, the more unhealthy they are. To fully appreciate this point, we need to consider what it is that makes coping "constructive."

CONSTRUCTIVE COPING

Our discussion thus far has focused on coping strategies that usually are less than ideal. Of course, we also exhibit many healthy strategies for dealing with stress. We'll use the term **constructive coping to refer to efforts that we make to deal with stressful events and that are judged to be relatively healthy**. No strategy of coping can *guarantee* a successful outcome. Even the healthiest coping responses may turn out to be ineffective in some circumstances. Thus, the concept of constructive coping is simply meant to connote a healthy, positive approach, without promising success.

What makes certain coping strategies constructive? Frankly, in labeling certain coping responses constructive or healthy, psychologists are making value judgments. It's a gray area in which opinions will vary to some extent. Nonetheless, among experts on stress and coping, there's some consensus about the nature of constructive coping. This consensus emerges from the sizable literature on stress management. Key themes in this literature include the following:

1. Constructive coping involves confronting problems directly. It's task relevant and action oriented. It involves a conscious effort to rationally evaluate your options so that you can try to solve your problems.
2. Constructive coping requires staying in tune with reality. It's based on a realistic appraisal of your stress and your coping resources, rather than on defensive self-deception.
3. Constructive coping involves learning to recognize, and in some cases inhibit, potentially disruptive emotional reactions to stress.
4. Constructive coping includes making efforts to ensure that your body is not especially vulnerable to the possibly damaging effects of stress.

The principles just described provide a rather general and abstract picture of constructive coping. We'll look at patterns of constructive coping in more detail in the chapter Application, which discusses various stress management strategies.

Thus far, we've probed the nature of stress and described how people typically respond to stress. We turn next to the possible outcomes of our struggles with stress. We'll look first at the effects of stress on our psychological functioning, and then we'll consider how stress affects our physical health.

THE EFFECTS OF STRESS ON PSYCHOLOGICAL FUNCTIONING

We struggle with many stresses every day. Most of them come and go without leaving any enduring imprint. However, when stress is severe or when many stressful demands pile up, stress may affect our psychological functioning.

Research on the effects of stress has focused mainly on negative outcomes, so you'll find our coverage slanted in that direction. However, it's important to emphasize that stress is not inherently bad for us. We'd probably "suffocate" from boredom if we lived a stress-free existence. Stress makes life challenging and interesting. Moreover, stress can have beneficial effects. Stress can force us to develop new skills, learn new insights, and acquire new personal strengths. Along the way, though, stress can be harrowing, sometimes leading to impairments in performance, burnout, and other problems.

Impaired Task Performance

Frequently, stress takes its toll on our ability to think and perform effectively on the task at hand.

Roy Baumeister's work on pressure shows how stress can interfere with performance. Baumeister's (1984) theory assumes that pressure to perform often makes us self-conscious and that this elevated self-consciousness disrupts our attention. He theorizes that attention may be distorted in two ways. First, elevated self-consciousness may divert attention from the demands of the task. In other words, the person is distracted. Second, on well-learned tasks that should be executed almost automatically, the self-conscious person may focus too much attention on the task. In other words, the person thinks *too much* about what he or she is doing.

Baumeister (1984) found support for his theory in a series of laboratory experiments in which he manipulated the pressure to perform well on a simple perceptual-motor task. However, in our Featured Study for this chapter, we'll take a detailed look at Baumeister's more entertaining investigation of the effects that the pressure to perform has on the actual performance of professional baseball and basketball teams.

CHOKING UNDER PRESSURE

This study was designed to test a surprising prediction derived from Baumeister's theory relating pressure to deterioration in skilled task performance. The prediction concerns performance in highly pressurized championship games in professional sports. According to Baumeister and Steinhilber, when a championship series such as the World Series in baseball goes to the final, decisive game, the home team is under greater pressure than the visiting team, and its performance will tend to decline. The greater pressure for the home team comes from the presence of a huge supportive audience of fans who have high expectations for their local heroes. Understandably, members of the home team desperately want to succeed in front of their fans, and they experience elevated self-consciousness.

The interesting aspect of Baumeister's prediction is that conventional wisdom suggests that home teams normally have the advantage in sports events because they're accustomed to the arena and have the emotional support of their cheering fans. Indeed, the presumed experts, sports writers and announcers, routinely refer to the home team *advantage* in championship games.

Nonetheless, Baumeister and Steinhilber hypothesized that analyses of past championship contests in professional baseball and basketball would show that playing at home is a disadvantage rather than an advantage when pressure mounts in the final game.

Method

The research method employed in this study is called *archival research*. Archival research involves the statistical examination of already existing records (the archives) to test hypotheses. The sports of professional baseball and basketball were selected for this study because they determine their championship with a *series* of games played at the home sites of the two teams. In both sports the series can go to a maximum of seven games; the first team to win four games is the victor.

This format permitted the investigators to compare the performance of the home team in the early games versus the final, decisive game. Baumeister and Steinhilber hypothesized that the normal home team advantage should be at work in the early games, but that it should be reversed by the intense pressure in the final game.

In baseball, World Series results from 1924 through 1982 were analyzed (the current scheduling format was adopted in 1924). In basketball, semifinal and championship series results were analyzed for the time period of 1967 through 1982. Both periods represent what could be char-

Investigators: Roy F. Baumeister and Andrew Steinhilber (Case Western Reserve University)

Source: Paradoxical effects of supportive audiences on performance under pressure: The home field disadvantage in sports championships, *Journal of Personality and Social Psychology, 47*(1) (1984), 85–93.

Are the baseball and basketball fans in these photos helping their hometown heroes by cheering for them? Perhaps not. According to Baumeister, the high expectations of sports fans put home teams under considerable pressure, and such pressure can disrupt performance.

Figure 13.10 The results of Baumeister and Steinhilber (1984). In early World Series and NBA championship contests that involve less pressure, the home team enjoys an advantage. But when it comes to the last game, the home team frequently chokes under pressure, as evidenced by the decreased winning percentages shown here.

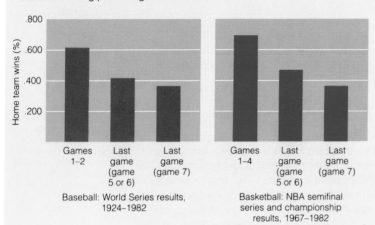

acterized as the "modern era" for each sport. Any series that resulted in a four-game sweep, wherein one team won the first four games, was excluded from the analyses. This was done because such sweeps were assumed to reflect mismatches in talent (if one team is far superior to the other, pressure effects are probably negligible).

The key dependent variable in the study was the home teams' winning percentage in championship games as compared to the teams' winning percentage in earlier home games. In baseball, games 1 and 2 were defined as the early games. In basketball, a different scheduling approach necessitated defining any home games in games 1 through 4 as the early games.

In both sports, the investigators also looked at certain performance variables besides winning percentage. The additional variables were examined because winning is determined by the *joint* performance of both teams. If team A loses, it's often hard to say whether this occurred because team A played poorly or because team B played well. To circumvent this problem, the researchers examined fielding error rates in baseball and free-throw shooting percentages in basketball as dependent variables. These are key performance measures that are not affected by the opponent team's play, making them relatively pure indicators of "choking" by the home team.

Results

As hypothesized, the winning percentage for home teams was significantly lower in final games than in early games in both sports. These results are summarized in Figure 13.10. Results are reported separately for those years in which a series went to a full seven games. Such years provide a particularly good test of the hypothesis because the 3–3 deadlock entering game 7 sug-

gests that the teams were evenly matched. In baseball, the home team's winning percentage drops from from .602 in early games to .385 in game 7. In basketball, the winning percentage for the home team drops from .701 in early games to .385 in game 7. Similar declines in performance were observed for the two supplementary dependent variables. In baseball, the home team made significantly more fielding errors in game 7 than in the early games. In basketball, the home team's free-throw shooting percentage went down significantly in the last game.

Discussion

The results clearly contradict the widespread assumption that playing at home provides an advantage in the final game of sports championships. Quite to the contrary, the home team seems to be at a substantial disadvantage. The most obvious explanation for this finding is that the home team frequently chokes under pressure, as predicted by Baumeister's theory. Of course, the home team's decline in winning percentage could conceivably be due to good performance by the visiting team rather than poor performance by the home team. However, this alternative explanation seems unlikely in light of the deterioration in fielding and free-throw shooting shown by the home teams. Thus, the home field disadvantage found in this study is probably due to the disruptive effects of stressful pressure.

Comment

This study is an impressive, creative example of the untapped potential of archival research. This method is probably underused in psychology. Analyzing sports records may strike you as trivial, but the theoretical issue relating stress to task performance is anything but trivial. Moreover, sports records are just one example of the diverse archival data kept by modern societies. There are mountains of census, economic, legal, educational, and medical records that can serve as a rich source of data to shed light on a variety of important empirical and theoretical questions.

One strength of archival research is that it examines records of behavior in the real world as opposed to behavior in the artificial world of the experimental laboratory. Thus, this study provides a very convincing demonstration that stress can impair performance. Of course, archival research has its weaknesses. In this case the available data provide little insight about whether Baumeister is correct in his analyses of *why* pressure tends to impair performance. We have no measures of the hypothesized explanatory variables, such as the athletes' self-consciousness or their attention. Understandably, there are limitations in what we can measure when we conduct our research after the fact.

A recent experimental study suggests that Baumeister is on the right track in looking to attention to explain how stress impairs task performance. In a study of stress and decision making, Keinan (1987) was able to measure three specific aspects of subjects' attention under stressful and nonstressful conditions. Keinan placed subjects under stress by telling them that they might receive painful but harmless electric shocks while working on a decision-making task at a computer keyboard. No one was actually shocked, and subjects were given the option of discontinuing their participation when they were told about the shock. Keinan found that stress disrupted two out of the three aspects of attention measured in the study. Stress increased subjects' tendency (1) to jump to a conclusion too quickly without considering all their options, and (2) to do an unsystematic, poorly organized review of their available options.

Keinan's research shows how stress can impair performance by affecting *cognitive functioning*. Unfortunately, stress is a versatile adversary. There are reasons to believe that stress can also impair performance by affecting *emotional functioning*, as seen in cases of burnout, which we'll discuss next.

Burnout

Burnout is an overused buzzword that means different things to different people. Nonetheless, Pines, Aronson, and Kafry (1981) have described burnout in a systematic way that has facilitated scientific study of the syndrome. According to their theory, **burnout involves physical, mental, and emotional exhaustion that is attributable to work-related stress.** The physical exhaustion includes chronic fatigue, weakness, and low energy. The mental exhaustion is manifested in highly negative attitudes toward oneself, one's work, and life in general. The emotional exhaustion includes feeling hopeless, helpless, and trapped.

What causes burnout? According to Pines and her colleagues, it "usually does not occur as the result of one or two traumatic events but sneaks up through a general erosion of the spirit" (p. 3). They view burnout as an emotional disturbance that's brought on gradually by heavy, chronic job-related stress.

Initially, theorists thought that burnout was unique to the helping professions, such as social work, clinical psychology, and counseling. The high burnout rate in the helping professions was blamed on the emotionally draining relations with clients. However, it has gradually become clear that burnout is a potential problem in all occu-

pational areas (Maslach, 1982). Indeed, work stress may not be the only cause of burnout. It's possible that chronic stress from other roles, such as parenting or being a student, may lead to burnout.

Posttraumatic Stress Disorders

The effects of stress are not necessarily apparent right away. There may be a time lag between the occurrence of stress and the appearance of its effects. **The *posttraumatic stress disorder* involves disturbed behavior that is attributed to a major stressful event but that emerges after the stress is over.** Posttraumatic stress disorders were seen often during the 1970s in veterans of the Vietnam war. Among Vietnam veterans, posttraumatic disorders typically began to surface anywhere from 9 to 60 months after a soldier's discharge from military service (Shatan, 1978). There were, of course, immediate stress reactions among the soldiers as well—but these were expected. The delayed reactions were something of a surprise.

Due to media attention, posttraumatic stress disorders are widely associated with the experiences of Vietnam veterans, but they have also been seen in response to other cases of severe stress. A recent study of mental health by Helzer, Robins, and McEvoy (1987) suggests that posttraumatic stress disorders have been experienced by roughly 5 out of 1000 men and 13 out of 1000 women in the general population.

Posttraumatic stress disorders were first recognized in Vietnam veterans. Research eventually showed that delayed stress reactions can be caused by a variety of highly stressful events other than combat. Two veterans are shown here at the New York City monument for their fallen comrades.

What types of stress besides combat are severe enough to produce posttraumatic disorders? Among females, the most common cause found by Helzer and his colleagues was a physical attack, such as a rape. Other causes among women included seeing someone die (or seriously hurt), close personal brushes with death, serious accidents, and discovering a spouse's affair. Among men, all the posttraumatic disorders were due to combat experiences or to seeing someone die.

In the study by Helzer and his colleagues (1987), a long time lag between the severe stress and the onset of the posttraumatic disorder was seen only in cases caused by war experiences. There may be something unique about how people cope with the stress of war. In all the other cases, the posttraumatic stress syndrome was seen soon after the occurrence of the extremely stressful event.

What are the symptoms of posttraumatic stress disorders? Common symptoms seen in combat veterans have included nightmares, paranoia, emotional numbing, guilt about surviving, alienation, and problems in social relations with others (Blank, 1982). In the more diverse collection of cases identified by the Helzer study team (1987), the most common symptoms were nightmares, difficulties in sleeping, and feelings of jumpiness.

Psychological Problems and Disorders

Posttraumatic stress disorders are caused by a single episode of extreme stress. Of greater relevance to most of us are the effects of chronic, prolonged everyday stress. On the basis of clinical impressions, psychologists have long suspected that chronic stress might contribute to many types of psychological problems and mental disorders. Since the late 1960s, advances in the measurement of stress have allowed researchers to verify these suspicions in empirical studies. In the domain of common psychological problems, studies indicate that stress may contribute to poor academic performance (Lloyd et al., 1980), insomnia (Hartmann, 1985), sexual difficulties (Malatesta & Adams, 1984), drug abuse (Krueger, 1981), and anxiety and dejection (Weiten, 1988).

Above and beyond these everyday problems, research reveals that stress often plays a role in the onset of full-fledged psychological disorders (Barrett, Rose, & Klerman, 1979; Neufeld & Mothersill, 1980). We'll discuss these relations between stress and mental disorders in detail in Chapter 14. Of course, stress is only one of many factors that may contribute to psychological disorders. Nonetheless, it's sobering to realize that stress can have a dramatic impact on our mental health.

It's every bit as sobering to realize that stress can have a dramatic impact on our physical health. We briefly mentioned the link between stress and physical illness before, but we now turn our attention to a systematic review of the evidence on the relationship between stress and physical health.

THE EFFECTS OF STRESS ON PHYSICAL HEALTH

The assertion that stress can contribute to physical diseases is not entirely new. Evidence that stress can cause physical illness began to accumulate back in the 1930s and 1940s. By the 1950s, the concept of psychosomatic disease was widely accepted. **Psychosomatic diseases are physical ailments with a genuine organic basis that are caused in part by psychological factors, especially emotional distress (they have also been called psychophysiological disorders).** The underlying assumption is that stress-induced autonomic arousal plays a key role in the development of most psychosomatic diseases. Please note, psychosomatic diseases are *genuine* physical ailments; the term is sometimes misused to refer to people whose ailments are "all in their head," an entirely different phenomenon, which we'll discuss in Chapter 14.

Common psychosomatic diseases include hypertension, ulcers, asthma, skin disorders such as eczema and hives, and migraine and tension headaches (Kaplan, 1985). These diseases do not *necessarily* have a strong psychological component in every affected individual. There's a genetic predisposition to most psychosomatic diseases, and in some people these diseases are largely physiological in origin (Weiner, 1977). More often than not, however, psychological factors contribute to psychosomatic diseases, and when they do, stress is the culprit at work.

Prior to the 1970s, it was thought that stress contributed to the development of only a few physical diseases (the psychosomatic diseases). However, in the 1970s, researchers began to uncover new links between stress and a great variety of diseases previously believed to be purely physiological in origin. Although there's room for debate on some specific diseases, there's reason to believe that stress *may* be related to the onset and course of heart disease, stroke, tuberculosis, arthritis, diabetes, leukemia, cancer, various types of infectious disease, and the common cold (Elliott & Eisdorfer, 1982). In this section we'll look at the evidence on the apparent link between stress and physical illness, beginning with heart disease, which is far and away the leading cause of death in North America.

Type A Behavior and Heart Disease

Heart disease accounts for nearly 40% of the deaths in the United States every year. *Coronary* heart disease involves a reduction in blood flow in the coronary arteries that supply the heart with blood. This type of heart disease accounts for about 90% of heart-related deaths.

Atherosclerosis is the principal cause of coronary disease. **Atherosclerosis involves a gradual narrowing of the coronary arteries.** A buildup of fatty deposits and other debris on the inner walls of the arteries is the usual cause of this narrowing. Atherosclerosis progresses slowly over periods of years. However, when a narrowed artery is blocked completely (by a blood clot, for instance) the abrupt interruption of blood flow can produce a heart attack.

In the 1960s and 1970s a pair of cardiologists, Meyer Friedman and Ray Rosenman (1974), were investigating the causes of coronary disease. Originally, Friedman and Rosenman were interested in the usual factors that were thought to produce a high risk of heart attack: smoking, obesity, physical inactivity, and so forth. Although they found that these factors were relevant, they eventually recognized that a piece of the puzzle was missing. Many people who smoked constantly, got little exercise, and were severely overweight avoided the ravages of heart disease. At the same time, other people who seemed to be in much better shape in regard to these risk factors experienced the misfortune of a heart attack.

Gradually, Friedman and Rosenman unraveled the riddle. What was their explanation for these perplexing findings? Stress! Specifically, they found a connection between coronary risk and a pattern of behavior that they called the *Type A pattern*, which involves self-imposed stress and intense reactions to stress.

ELEMENTS OF TYPE A BEHAVIOR

Friedman and Rosenman (1974) divided people into two basic types: Type A and Type B. **The type A pattern (also called the coronary-prone personality) is marked by competitive, aggressive, impatient, hostile behavior.** Type A's are ambitious, hard-driving perfectionists who are exceedingly time-conscious. They routinely try to do several things at once. Thus, a Type A person may watch TV, talk on the phone, work on a report, and eat dinner all at the same time. They're so impatient that they frequently finish others' sentences for them! Type A's fidget frantically over the briefest delays. They often are workaholics who drive themselves with many deadlines. They speak rapidly and emphatically. They're aggravated easily and get angry quickly. In contrast, **the type B pattern is marked by relatively relaxed, patient, easy-going, amicable behavior.** Type B's are less hurried, less competitive, and less easily angered than Type A's.

According to Glass (1978), the central feature of Type A behavior is the need to control situations. This need for control leads Type A's to

Measuring the Type A Personality

You can use the checklist below to *estimate* the likelihood that you might be a Type A personality. However, the checklist should be regarded as providing only a rough estimate, because Friedman and Rosenman (1974) emphasize that *how* you answer certain questions in their interview is often more significant than the answers themselves. Nonetheless, if you answer "yes" to a majority of the items below, you may want to consider reading their book *Type A Behavior and Your Heart*.

_____ **1.** Do you find it difficult to restrain yourself from hurrying others' speech (finishing their sentences for them)?

_____ **2.** Do you often try to do more than one thing at a time (such as eat and read simultaneously)?

_____ **3.** Do you often feel guilty if you use extra time to relax?

_____ **4.** Do you tend to get involved in a great number of projects at once?

_____ **5.** Do you find yourself racing through yellow lights when you drive?

_____ **6.** Do you need to win in order to derive enjoyment from games and sports?

_____ **7.** Do you generally move, walk, and eat rapidly?

_____ **8.** Do you agree to take on too many responsibilities?

_____ **9.** Do you detest waiting in lines?

_____ **10.** Do you have an intense desire to better your position in life and impress others?

Figure 13.11 The Type A personality. The ten questions shown here highlight some of the behavioral traits associated with the Type A personality.

expose themselves to an immense amount of avoidable stress, especially self-imposed pressure to perform. This heightened pressure to perform was apparent in a study that showed that Type A's set higher standards in evaluating their performance than Type B's (Grimm & Yarnold, 1984). Type A's also show a strong need for dominance in interpersonal relations (Palladino & Motiff, 1983). This pursuit of dominance, which would appear to reflect their need for control, has obvious potential for creating interpersonal hostilities and increased stress in their lives.

The strength of one's Type A tendencies can be measured with either structured interviews or questionnaires. There's quite a bit of debate about the best method for assessing Type A behavior (Matthews, 1982). The checklist in Figure 13.11 lists some representative questions like those used in measurements of Type A behavior. The Type A pattern is seen less frequently in women than men. When found among women, however, it appears to increase coronary risk about as much as in men (Haynes, Feinleib, & Eaker, 1983).

EVALUATING THE RISK

How strong is the link between Type A behavior and coronary risk? Based on preliminary data,

Friedman and his associates originally estimated that Type A's were *six* times as prone to heart attack as Type B's. At the other extreme, some studies have failed to find a clear association between Type A behavior and coronary risk (Shekelle et al., 1985), and one study even found that Type A's had a *lower* risk of a *second* heart attack than Type B's (Ragland & Brand, 1988).

What can we make of these inconsistent findings? Some of the inconsistency may be due to problems in accurately classifying people as Type A or Type B (Dimsdale, 1988), but the mixed findings suggest that the relationship between Type A behavior and coronary risk is more modest than originally believed. Taken as a whole, the data collected to date suggest that the increased coronary risk for Type A's is perhaps double that for Type B's (Weaver & Rodnick, 1986).

Actually, such ratios are misleading anyway. They're based on the assumption that you can divide the population neatly into just two categories. Behavior is rarely that simple. It's more accurate to think of the Type A and Type B patterns as endpoints of a continuum, with many people falling between the extremes. Thus, the elevation in coronary risk probably depends on the strength of one's Type A tendencies.

Which aspects of Type A behavior are most strongly related to increased coronary risk? Are need for control, time urgency, and hostility equally important? These are questions of current interest in research on the Type A syndrome. Thus far, the research suggests that the quick-tempered anger of Type A's may be more important than other elements of the Type A pattern (Dembroski et al., 1985). Hence, a "short fuse" may be a Type A's most deadly characteristic.

Stress and Other Diseases

The development of questionnaires to measure life stress has allowed researchers to look for correlations between stress and a variety of diseases. These researchers have uncovered many stress-illness connections. For example, in a sample of 22 female patients, Baker (1982) found an association between life stress and the onset of rheumatoid arthritis. Working with a sample of female students, Williams and Deffenbacher (1983) found that life stress was correlated with the number of vaginal (yeast) infections reported in the past year. In another study, investigators inoculated 52 volunteers with cold viruses and found that those under high stress experienced more colds (Totman et al., 1980). Yet another team of investigators observed a relationship between stress and the development of periodontal (gum)

disease in a sample of 50 male dental patients (Green et al., 1986).

These are just a handful of representative examples of studies relating stress to physical diseases. Table 13.4 lists some additional health problems that have been linked to stress. Many of these stress-illness connections are based on very tentative or inconsistent findings, but the sheer length and diversity of the list is remarkable.

The studies described thus far have looked at relations between stress and *specific* diseases. Many studies have also looked at the relationship between stress and illness of any kind. In other words, the outcome variable is not a particular disease, but any negative change in health. Typically, these studies have found significant correlations between high stress and a high incidence of physical illness in general (Holmes & Masuda, 1974). In one such study that used the SRRS to measure stress, only 37% of the subjects who endured mild stress became ill during the study, while 79% of those who experienced major stress became ill. Why should stress increase our risk for many different kinds of illness? A partial answer may lie in investigations of our immunal functioning.

Stress and Immunal Functioning

The apparent link between stress and illness raises the possibility that stress may undermine our immunal functioning. **The *immune response* involves the body's defensive reaction to invasion by bacteria, viral agents, or other foreign sub-**

Table 13.4 Some Health Problems That May Be Linked to Stress

HEALTH PROBLEM	REPRESENTATIVE EVIDENCE
Menstrual discomfort	Siegel, Johnson, & Sarason (1979)
Herpes	Robbins & Cotran (1979)
Chronic back pain	Holmes (1979)
Female reproductive problems	Fries, Nillius, & Petersson (1974)
Complications of pregnancy	Georgas et al. (1984)
Diabetes	Bradley (1979)
Hernias	Rahe & Holmes (1965)
Glaucoma	Cohen & Hajioff (1972)
Hyperthyroidism	Weiner (1978)
Hemophilia	Buxton et al. (1981)
Tuberculosis	Wolf & Goodell (1968)
Leukemia	Greene & Swisher (1969)
Stroke	Stevens et al. (1984)

Source: Weiten, 1986

stances. Our immune response works to protect us from many forms of disease. Immunal reactions are multifaceted, but they depend heavily on actions initiated by specialized white blood cells, called *lymphocytes.*

A wealth of studies indicate that experimentally induced stress can impair immunal functioning *in animals* (Ader & Cohen, 1984). Stressors such as crowding, shock, and restraint reduce various aspects of lymphocyte reactivity in laboratory animals.

Some studies have also related stress to suppressed immunal activity *in humans.* In one study, medical students provided researchers with blood samples so that their immune response could be assessed (Kiecolt-Glaser et al., 1984). They provided the baseline sample a month before final exams and contributed the high-stress sample on the first day of their finals. The subjects also responded to the SRRS to measure recent stress. Reduced levels of immune activity were found during the extremely stressful finals week. Reduced immunal activity was also correlated with higher scores on the SRRS. Thus, we're beginning to see some impressive evidence that stress may temporarily impair our immunal functioning. Immunosuppression may be the key to many of the links between stress and illness.

Sizing Up the Link Between Stress and Illness

A wealth of evidence shows that stress is related to our physical health, and converging lines of evidence suggest that stress contributes to the *causation* of illness, but we have to put this intriguing finding in perspective. Virtually all of the relevant research is correlational, so it can't demonstrate *conclusively* that stress causes illness (see Figure 13.12). Subjects' elevated levels of stress and illness could both be due to a third variable, perhaps some aspect of personality or some type of physiological predisposition (as you'll see, high autonomic reactivity would be a plausible candidate).

Moreover, critics of this research note that many of the studies employed methods that might have inflated the apparent link between stress and illness (Schroeder & Costa, 1984). For example, researchers often have subjects make after-the-fact reports of how much stress and illness they endured during the last year or two. If some subjects have a tendency to recall more stress than others *and* to recall more illness than others, the difference in subjects' memories would artificially increase the correlation between stress and illness.

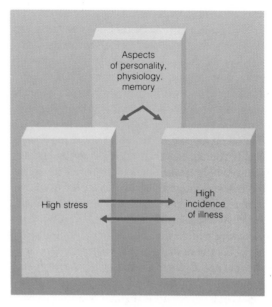

Figure 13.12 The stress-illness correlation. One or more aspects of personality, physiology, or memory could play the role of a postulated third variable in the relationship between high stress and high incidence of illness.

In spite of methodological problems favoring inflated correlations, the research in this area consistently indicates that the *strength* of the relationship between stress and health is modest (the correlations typically fall in the .20s and .30s). Clearly, stress is not an irresistible force that produces inevitable effects on our health. Actually, this should come as no surprise. Stress is only one factor operating in a complex network of biopsychosocial determinants of health, including one's genetic endowment, exposure to infectious agents and environmental toxins, nutrition, exercise, alcohol and drug use, smoking, use of medical care, cooperation with medical advice, and current health status. Furthermore, some people handle stress better than others, which is the matter we turn to next.

Factors Moderating the Impact of Stress

The effects of stress vary from one person to another. Some people seem to be able to withstand the ravages of stress better than others. Why? Because a number of *moderator variables* lessen the impact of stress on our physical and mental health. We'll look at three key moderator variables—social support, hardiness, and autonomic reactivity—to shed light on individual differences in how well people tolerate stress.

SOCIAL FACTORS: SOCIAL SUPPORT
Friends may be good for your health! This startling conclusion emerges from studies on social support as a moderator of stress. **Social support involves various types of aid and succor provided by members of one's social networks.** In one study of social support, Gore (1978) looked at the moderating role of support in 100 stably employed

495

married men who were facing a very powerful form of stress: the loss of their jobs after a plant shutdown. Social support from wives, friends, and relatives was assessed. Gore found that those with relatively strong social support showed (1) less emotional response to the frustration and (2) fewer symptoms of physical illness.

Many other studies have also found evidence that social support is favorably related to physical health (Broadhead et al., 1983). Social support seems to be good medicine for the mind as well as the body, as most studies find an association between social support and mental health (Leavy, 1983). It appears that social support serves as a protective buffer for us during times of high stress (reducing the negative impact of stressful events) and that social support has its own positive effects on health, which may be apparent even when we aren't under great stress (Cohen & Syme, 1985).

Researchers are now trying to figure out just *how* social support promotes health and eases the impact of stressful events. House (1981) has proposed that social support serves four important functions:

1. *Emotional support* involves expressions of affection, interest, and concern that tell us we're appreciated. It includes behaviors like listening sympathetically to our problems. It presumably bolsters our self-esteem.
2. *Appraisal support* involves helping people to evaluate and make sense of their troubles and problems. It includes efforts to clarify the nature of the problem and provide feedback about its significance.
3. *Informational support* involves providing advice about how to handle a problem. This kind of support includes discussing possible solutions and the relative merits of alternative coping strategies.
4. *Instrumental support* involves providing material aid and services. Instrumental support can include a wide range of activities, such as providing someone with a place to stay, lending money, going along to a social service agency, or helping to assume work or family responsibilities.

House's analysis raises the point that social *bonds* are not equivalent to social *support*. Some friends and family members may not provide the kinds of support described by House. Indeed, some people in our social circles may be a source of more *stress* than *support*. People close to us can put us under pressure, make us feel guilty, break promises, and so forth.

Pagel, Erdly, and Becker (1987) looked at both the good and the bad sides of social relations in measuring subjects' satisfaction with their social networks. They found that the helpfulness of friends and family wasn't as important as whether friends and family caused emotional distress. Adapting a line from an old Beatles song, the investigators concluded that "We get by with [*and in spite of*] a little help from our friends." To some extent, then, people who report good social support may really mean that their friends and family aren't driving them crazy.

PERSONALITY FACTORS: HARDINESS AND OPTIMISM

Another line of research indicates that certain personality traits may moderate the impact of stressful events. Suzanne Kobasa reasoned that if stress affects some people less than others, then some people must be *hardier* than others. She set out to determine whether personality factors might be the key to these differences in hardiness.

Kobasa (1979) used a modified version of the Holmes and Rahe (1967) stress scale (SRRS) to measure the amount of stress experienced by a group of executives. Like researchers in most other such studies, she found a modest correlation between stress and the incidence of physical illness. However, she carried her investigation one step further than previous studies. Specifically, she compared the high-stress executives who reported the expected high incidence of illness against the high-stress executives who reported *little* illness. She administered a battery of psychological tests, comparing the executives along 18 dimensions of personality. She found that the hardier executives "were more committed, felt more in control, and had bigger appetites for challenge" (Kobasa, 1984, p. 70). These personality traits, which have also shown up in other studies (Kobasa, Maddi, & Kahn, 1982; Kobasa & Pucetti, 1983), include the following:

1. *Commitment.* The hardy executives typically displayed a clear sense of values. They had well-defined goals and a commitment to the importance of those goals. In contrast, the less hardy executives were characterized as alienated (lacking direction and commitment to a value system).
2. *Challenge.* The stress-resistant executives tended to seek out and actively confront challenges. They viewed change, rather than stability, as the norm in life. They welcomed change instead of clinging to the past. In comparison, the less stress-resistant executives were more likely to view change as alarming.
3. *Control.* The hardy executives had a stronger belief in their ability to control their own destiny than the less stress-resistant executives, who were more likely to feel powerless. For instance, the

hardy executives tended to have an internal locus of control. As we noted in Chapter 12, people with an internal locus of control believe that the outcomes of life's events are governed by their own actions and behavior, as opposed to fate and luck.

Thus, **hardiness is a personality syndrome that is marked by commitment, challenge, and control and that is purportedly associated with strong stress resistance.** There is currently an active debate about the key elements of hardiness and about whether it buffers us against the impact of stress or has its own favorable effects on health (Funk & Houston, 1987; Hull, Treuren, & Virnelli, 1987). Nonetheless, Kobasa's work has stimulated research on how personality affects our health and our tolerance of stress. Of particular interest is recent work on optimism, a widely discussed trait that researchers have paid little attention to until recently.

Defining **optimism as a general tendency to expect good outcomes,** Michael Scheier and Charles Carver (1985) found a correlation between optimism and relatively good physical health in a sample of college students. In a pair of subsequent studies, they found that optimists cope with stress differently than pessimists (Scheier, Weintraub, & Carver, 1986). Specifically, optimists are more likely to (1) engage in action-oriented, problem-focused coping, (2) seek social support, and (3) emphasize the positive in their appraisals of stressful events. In comparison, pessimists are more likely to deal with stress by giving up or engaging in denial.

PHYSIOLOGICAL FACTORS: HOT REACTORS

In light of the physiological response that we often make to stress, it makes sense that our physical makeup might influence our stress tolerance. Ac-

cording to one line of thinking, those of us who have a relatively placid autonomic nervous system should be less affected by stress than those equipped with a highly reactive ANS. Thus far, most of the research on autonomic reactivity has focused on autonomically regulated cardiovascular (heart rate and blood pressure) reactivity in response to stress.

Subjects exposed to stressful tasks in laboratory settings show consistent personal differences in cardiovascular reactivity over a 1-year period (Manuck & Garland, 1980) and across different types of stressful tasks (Lawler, 1980). A recent twin study suggests that there's a genetic basis for these differences in cardiovascular reactivity (Smith et al., 1987).

These findings bolster the notion that some people are "hot reactors," as cardiologist Robert Eliot calls them (Eliot & Breo, 1984). According to Eliot, hot reactors display perfectly normal blood pressure most of the time, but their blood pressure skyrockets when they are confronted by stressful demands. From his clinical observations, he estimates that about one of every five persons is a hot reactor. This problem may overlap with the Type A behavior pattern that we discussed earlier. It appears that Type A's are somewhat more likely than Type B's to show high cardiovascular reactivity (Krantz & Manuck, 1984). Additional research is needed to relate these differences in cardiovascular reactivity to variations in health status.

Individual differences among people in social support, hardiness, and physiological makeup explain why stress doesn't have the same impact on everyone. Differences in lifestyle may play an even larger role in determining health. We'll examine some critical aspects of lifestyle in the next section.

HEALTH-IMPAIRING LIFESTYLES

Some people seem determined to dig an early grave for themselves. They do precisely those things that are bad for their health. For example, some people drink heavily even though they know that they're damaging their liver. Others eat all the wrong foods even though they know that they're increasing their risk of a second heart attack. Behavior that's downright *self-destructive* is surprisingly common. In this section we'll discuss how health is affected by smoking, nutrition, exercise, and drug use, and we'll look at lifestyle factors in AIDS. We'll also discuss *why* people develop health-impairing lifestyles.

Smoking

The smoking of tobacco is widespread in our culture. Current consumption in the United States is around 3300 cigarettes a year per adult. Smokers face a much greater risk of premature death than nonsmokers (Hammond & Horn, 1984). For example, a 30-year-old male who smokes two packs a day has an estimated life expectancy that is 8 *years shorter* than a 30-year-old male nonsmoker. The increased risk of smoking is positively correlated with the number of cigarettes smoked and with their tar and nicotine content. Why are

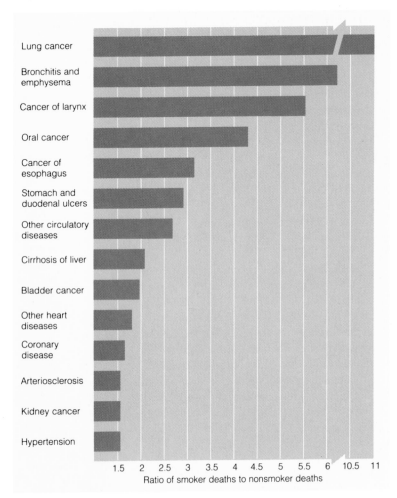

Lung cancer
Bronchitis and emphysema
Cancer of larynx
Oral cancer
Cancer of esophagus
Stomach and duodenal ulcers
Other circulatory diseases
Cirrhosis of liver
Bladder cancer
Other heart diseases
Coronary disease
Arteriosclerosis
Kidney cancer
Hypertension

1.5   2   2.5   3   3.5   4   4.5   5   5.5   6   10.5   11
Ratio of smoker deaths to nonsmoker deaths

Figure 13.13 Smoking and health. Smoking is associated with an increased risk for a diverse array of diseases. The magnitude of the elevated risk varies with the condition, ranging as high as 11 times normal in the case of lung cancer.

mortality rates higher for smokers? Because smoking increases one's risk for a surprisingly large range of chronic diseases, including heart disease, cancer, ulcers, bronchitis, emphysema, and stroke (see Figure 13.13).

Studies show that if people can give up smoking, their health risks decline reasonably quickly. Five years after people stop smoking, their health risk is already noticeably lower than that of people who have continued to smoke. The health risks of people who give up tobacco continue to decline until they reach a normal level after about 15 years (Rogot, 1974). Unfortunately, it's very difficult to give up cigarettes. Long-term success rates are in the vicinity of only 25%. In fact, as Figure 13.14 shows, relapse rates for quitting smoking often are as bad as those seen in efforts to give up heroin or alcohol (Hunt & Matarazzo, 1982).

Poor Nutritional Habits

Evidence is accumulating that patterns of nutrition influence susceptibility to a variety of diseases and health problems. Possible connections between eating patterns and diseases include the following:

1. Many factors influence the development of obesity, but chronic overeating usually plays a prominent role. Overweight people have an increased risk of heart disease, hypertension, stroke, respiratory ailments, arthritis, diabetes, and back problems (Jeffrey & Lemnitzer, 1981).

2. Heavy consumption of foods that elevate serum cholesterol level (eggs, cheeses, butter, shellfish, sausage, and the like) appears to increase the risk of heart disease (Hegsted, 1984).

3. High salt intake has long been thought to be a contributing factor to the development of hypertension (Friedewald, 1982), although there's still some debate about its role.

4. Diets high in fats and low in fiber have been implicated as possible contributors to some forms of cancer (Hegsted, 1984).

5. Certain patterns of sugar consumption (not sugar itself) may hasten the onset of diabetes (Mayer, 1980).

Of course, nutritional habits interact with other factors to determine whether one develops a particular disease. Nonetheless, the examples just described indicate that our eating habits are relevant to our physical health. Unfortunately, nutritional patterns are far from ideal in industrialized nations, especially the United States.

Lack of Exercise

The relationship between physical inactivity and increased risk of heart disease is well documented (Peters et al., 1983). The incidence of heart attacks among men (who are more prone to heart attacks than women) is noticeably higher among those who get little exercise. Lack of exercise also appears to contribute to other cardiovascular diseases such as hypertension and stroke.

Admittedly, exercise programs may carry their own hazards. For example, jogging can elevate one's risk of muscular and skeletal injuries (it's especially hard on the knees), and can elicit heat stroke and even a heart attack (Koplan et al., 1982). However, the potential hazards of exercise can be minimized easily by developing a workout regimen gradually and following it regularly. Most exercise-related problems occur when people work out sporadically and try to do too much in one session.

Alcohol and Drug Use

Recreational drug use is another very common health-impairing habit. The risks associated with the use of various drugs were discussed in detail in Chapter 5. Unlike smoking, poor eating habits,

498

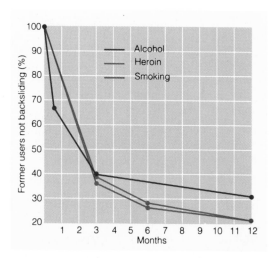

Figure 13.14 Relapse in efforts to quit smoking. As this figure shows, it is quite difficult to give up smoking. The relapse rates for returning to smoking are similar to those for returning to alcohol and heroin use (From Hunt & Matarazzo, 1982)

and inactivity, drugs can kill directly and immediately when they produce an overdose or cause an accident. In the long run, various recreational drugs may also elevate one's risk for infectious diseases; respiratory, pulmonary, and cardiovascular diseases; liver disease; gastrointestinal problems; cancer; neurological disorders; and pregnancy complications (see Chapter 5 to find out which drugs are associated with which risks). Ironically, the greatest physical damage in the population as a whole is caused by alcohol, the one recreational drug that's legal (Blum, 1984).

Lifestyle and AIDS

At present, the most problematic links between lifestyle and health may be those related to the Acquired Immunodeficiency Syndrome (AIDS). AIDS is caused by several related viruses that severely impair the body's immune response to infections. Unless there's a major research breakthrough, AIDS is likely to continue to be a fatal disease. AIDS is transmitted through the exchange of bodily fluids, primarily semen and blood. Cases of AIDS are increasing at an alarming rate, as shown in Figure 13.15.

The two principal modes of transmission have been sexual contact among homosexual and bisexual men and the sharing of needles by intravenous drug users. These two modes of transmission have accounted for about 90% of all AIDS cases (Castro, Hardy, & Curran, 1986; Castro et al., 1988). However, the virus *can* be transmitted through heterosexual contact with an affected individual. Thus, the disease is slowly diffusing into the population at large, and it's *not* just a "homosexual problem." Among urban Blacks, who have a somewhat higher rate of intravenous drug use than other groups, over half of AIDS cases are already occurring in heterosexuals (Bakeman et al., 1986).

Ironically, fear of AIDS is higher among low-risk groups that have relatively little knowledge about AIDS than among high-risk groups with more knowledge. Although San Francisco has the highest per capita incidence of AIDS in the United States, a sample of gay men and a heterosexual sample drawn from San Francisco both reported less fear of AIDS than heterosexual samples drawn from New York and London (Temoshok, Sweet, & Zich, 1987). As these investigators note, "Perhaps no medical phenomenon has been so feared or so misunderstood by the public." Although the myths persist, at present there's no evidence that AIDS can be transmitted through sneezing, shaking hands, sharing food, or other kinds of casual contact. Figure 13.16 contains a short quiz that you can take to test your knowledge of the facts about AIDS.

The lifestyle changes that will minimize one's risk for AIDS are fairly straightforward, although making the changes is often much easier said than done. In all groups, the more sexual partners a person has, the higher the risk that one will be exposed to AIDS. Thus, people can reduce their risk by having sexual contacts with fewer partners and by using condoms to control the exchange of semen. Among gay men it's also important to cur-

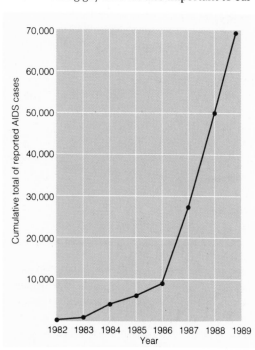

Figure 13.15 The prevalence of AIDS. Cases of AIDS are increasing at a rapid rate, with no plateau yet in sight.

A Quiz on AIDS

Answer the following "true" or "false."

T F **1.** AIDS is caused by a virus.

T F **2.** AIDS is caused by inheriting a bad gene or genes.

T F **3.** AIDS is caused by a kind of bacteria.

T F **4.** A person can "carry" and pass on whatever causes AIDS without necessarily having AIDS or looking sick.

T F **5.** Whatever causes AIDS can be passed on through semen.

T F **6.** Whatever causes AIDS can be passed on through blood or blood products.

T F **7.** You can catch AIDS like you catch a cold because whatever causes AIDS can be carried in the air.

T F **8.** You can catch AIDS by being in the same room as someone with AIDS.

T F **9.** You can catch AIDS by shaking hands with someone who has AIDS.

T F **10.** Having a monogamous relationship decreases the risk of AIDS.

T F **11.** Using condoms reduces the risk of getting AIDS.

T F **12.** A vaccine for AIDS will be available within a year.

Answers: 1. T 2. F 3. F 4. T 5. T 6. T 7. F 8. F 9. F 10. T 11. T 12. F

Figure 13.16 A quiz on knowledge of AIDS. Because misconceptions about AIDS abound, it may be wise to take this brief quiz to test your knowledge of AIDS. (Adapted from Temoshok et al., 1987)

tail certain sexual practices (in particular, anal sex) that increase the probability of mixing semen and blood. Intravenous drug users can greatly reduce their risk by abandoning their drug use, but this is unlikely, as most are physically dependent on the drugs. Alternatively, they need to improve the sterilization of their needles and quit sharing syringes with other users.

How Do Health-Impairing Lifestyles Develop?

It may seem puzzling that people behave in self-destructive ways. How does this happen? Several factors are involved. First, many health-impairing habits creep up on people slowly. For instance, drug use may grow imperceptibly over years, or exercise habits may decline ever so gradually. Second, many health-impairing habits involve activities that are quite pleasant at the time. Actions such as eating favorite foods, smoking cigarettes, or getting "high" are potent reinforcing events. Third, the risks associated with most health-impairing habits are chronic diseases such as cancer that usually lie 10, 20, or 30 years down the road. It's relatively easy to ignore risks that lie in the distant future.

REACTIONS TO ILLNESS

Some people respond to physical symptoms and illnesses by ignoring warning signs of developing diseases, while others engage in active coping efforts to conquer their diseases. Let's examine the decision to seek medical treatment, the sick role, and compliance with medical advice.

Finally, people have a curious tendency to underestimate the risks that accompany their own health-impairing behaviors, while viewing the risks associated with others' self-destructive behaviors much more accurately (Weinstein, 1984). In other words, many people are well aware of the dangers associated with certain habits, but when it's time to apply this information to themselves, they often discount it. They figure, for instance, that smoking will lead to cancer or a heart attack *in someone else.*

Changing Health-Impairing Habits

Health-impairing habits are often deeply entrenched. In general, it's not easy to alter health-impairing lifestyles. However, psychologists' training makes them well suited to confront this challenge. Thus, one of the major contributions of health psychology to medical treatment involves the design of programs to modify problematic behaviors.

These programs take many forms (Taylor, 1986). Some programs try to change bad habits by altering health beliefs. Thus, some psychologists with expertise in persuasion and attitude change are involved in efforts to improve the effectiveness of mass media campaigns for health promotion purposes (such as antismoking campaigns). Other programs involve helping individuals to directly alter their personal behavior. Health psychologists who deliver clinical services in medical settings often work with patients who need to conquer health-impairing habits. Although they use a wide range of techniques to assist these patients, behavioral techniqes based on the principles of learning have proven especially fruitful. The behavior modification procedures that we discussed in the Chapter 6 Application are well-suited to the task of changing health-impairing habits.

So far, we've seen that our physical health may be affected by stress and by aspects of our lifestyle. Next, we'll look at the importance of how we react to physical symptoms, health problems, and health care efforts.

The Decision to Seek Treatment

Have you ever experienced nausea, diarrhea, stiffness, headaches, cramps, chest pains, or sinus problems? Of course you have; we all experience some of these problems periodically. However, whether we view these sensations as *symptoms* is a matter of individual interpretation. The perception of pain is highly subjective, as we noted in Chapter 4. Pain perceptions are influenced by our expectations, our personality, and our level of anxiety or relaxation (Steger & Fordyce, 1982). When two persons experience the same unpleasant sensations, one may shrug them off as a nuisance while the other may rush to a physician. Thus, people differ greatly in their readiness to seek medical treatment.

In regard to treatment seeking, the biggest health problem is the tendency of many people to delay the pursuit of needed medical care. This is unfortunate because many health problems can be treated more effectively if they're diagnosed early. Males are more likely than females to put off needed medical consultation (Mechanic, 1972). Understandably, people who are fearful of doctors and hospitals often delay seeking treatment. People who believe strongly in self-care also tend to wait before obtaining professional care (Krantz, Baum, & Wideman, 1980).

The Sick Role

Although many people tend to delay medical consultations, some people are positively eager to seek care. These people have learned that there are potential benefits to adopting the "sick role" (Parsons, 1979). For instance, fewer demands are placed on sick people, who often can selectively decide which demands to ignore. Sick people may also find themselves to be the center of attention from friends and relatives. This increase in attention from others can be very rewarding, especially to those who have received little attention previously. Moreover, much of the attention a sick person receives is favorable, in that he or she is showered with affection, concern, and sympathy.

Thus, some people grow to *like* the sick role, although they may not be aware of this feeling. Such people readily seek professional care, but they also tend to behave in subtle ways that prolong their illness (Kinsman, Dirks, & Jones, 1982). For example, they may only pretend to go along with the medical advice that they're given, a common problem that we'll discuss next.

Compliance with Medical Advice

Many patients fail to follow the instructions they receive from physicians and other health care professionals. Noncompliance is not limited to people who have come to like the sick role, and it's a major problem in our medical care system. After their review of the evidence, DiMatteo and

Friedman (1982) estimated that noncompliance with medical advice may occur one-third to one-half of the time!

This point is not intended to suggest you should passively accept all professional advice from medical personnel. However, when you have doubts about a prescribed treatment, you should speak up and ask questions. Passive resistance can backfire. For instance, if a physician sees no improvement in a patient who falsely insists that he has been taking his medicine, the physician may abandon an accurate diagnosis in favor of an inaccurate one. The inaccurate diagnosis could lead to inappropriate treatments that might even be harmful to the patient.

Why don't people comply with the advice that they've sought out from highly regarded physicians? Three reasons are especially prominent (DiMatteo & Friedman, 1982):

1. Frequently, noncompliance is due to a failure by the patient to understand the instructions as given. Highly trained professionals often forget that what seems obvious and simple to them may be obscure and complicated for many of their patients.
2. Another key factor is how aversive or difficult the instructions are. If the prescribed regimen has unpleasant side effects, compliance will tend to decrease. And the more that following instructions interferes with routine behavior, the less probable it is that the patient will cooperate successfully.
3. If a patient has a negative attitude toward a physician, the probability of noncompliance will increase. When patients are unhappy with their interactions with the doctor, they're more likely to ignore the medical advice provided.

Many patients do not comply with the directions they receive from their physicians. Research suggests that improvements in doctor-patient communication can increase medical compliance.

In response to the noncompliance problem, some health psychologists are exploring how to increase patients' adherence to medical advice. They've found that the communication process between the practitioner and the patient is of crit-ical importance. Courtesy, warmth, patience, and a decreased reliance on medical jargon can im-prove compliance (DiNicola & DiMatteo, 1984). Thus, there's a new emphasis on enhancing health care professionals' communication skills.

PUTTING IT IN PERSPECTIVE

Which of our themes were prominent in this chapter? As you probably noticed, our discussion of stress and health illustrated multifactorial cau-sation (theme 4) and the subjectivity of experi-ence (theme 6).

The way in which multiple factors influence behavior was apparent in our discussion of the stress process. If you glance back at Figure 13.5, you'll see a complicated array of variables that are involved in our experience of stress.

Our discussion of the psychology of health pro-vided an even more complex illustration of mul-tifactorial causation. As we noted in Chapter 1, people are likely to think simplistically, in terms of single causes. In recent years, the highly publi-cized research linking stress to health has led many people to point automatically to stress as an explanation for illness. In reality, stress has only a modest impact on physical health. Stress *can* in-crease our risk for illness, but our health is gov-erned by a dense network of factors, including our inherited vulnerabilities; our physiological reac-tivity; our exposure to viruses, bacteria, and tox-ins; our healthful or health-impairing habits; our reactions to symptoms; our treatment-seeking be-havior; our compliance with medical advice; our hardiness; and our social support. In other words, stress is but one actor on a crowded stage. This should be apparent in Figure 13.17, which shows the multitude of biopsychosocial factors that jointly influence physical health. It illustrates multifactorial causation in all its complexity.

The subjectivity of experience was demon-strated by the frequently repeated point that stress lies in the eye of the beholder. The same promo-tion at work may be stressful for one person and invigorating for another. One person's pressure is another's challenge. When it comes to stress, ob-jective reality is not nearly as important as our subjective perceptions. More than anything else, the impact of stressful events seems to depend on how we view them. The critical importance of our stress appraisals will continue to be apparent in our Application on coping and stress manage-ment. Many stress-management strategies depend on altering our appraisals of events.

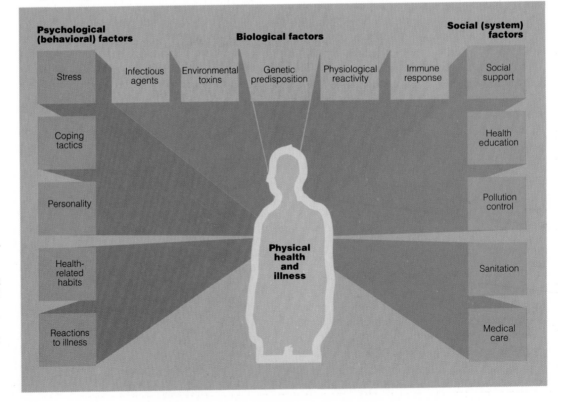

Figure 13.17 Biopsy-chosocial factors in health. Physical health can be influenced by a remarkably diverse set of variables, including biological, psychologi-cal, and social factors. The host of factors that affect health provide an excellent example of multifactorial cau-sation.

IMPROVING COPING AND STRESS MANAGEMENT

Answer the following "true" or "false."

[ ] **1.** The key to managing stress is to avoid or circumvent it.

[ ] **2.** It's best to suppress emotional reactions to stress.

[ ] **3.** Crying is a sign of maladaptive coping.

[ ] **4.** Laughing at one's problems is immature.

[ ] **5.** Leaning on others in times of stress is an ill-advised coping strategy.

Courses and books on stress management have multiplied at a furious pace in the last decade. They summarize experts' advice on how to cope with stress more effectively. How do these experts feel about the five statements above? Most would agree that all five are false. As you'll see, commonsense coping strategies such as crying, laughing, and leaning on others may be quite adaptive.

The key to managing stress does *not* lie in avoiding stress. Stress is an inevitable element in the fabric of modern life. As Hans Selye notes, "Contrary to public opinion, we must not—and indeed can't—avoid stress." Thus, most stress-management programs encourage people to confront stress rather than to sidestep it. This requires training people to engage in action-oriented, rational, reality-based *constructive coping*.

We cope with stress in many different ways. This variety was apparent in a study by Arthur Stone and John Neale (1984), who tabulated specific coping strategies employed by 120 married subjects who filled out questionnaires on their daily coping for 21 days. Stone and Neale focused on constructive coping, as they chose not to inquire about defensive coping or other tactics (such as aggression) that have little genuine value in handling stress. They found that their subjects' constructive coping strategies fell into eight categories, which are described in Table 13.5. We'll discuss most of these coping strategies and a few additional ones in this Application, beginning with Albert Ellis's ideas about

changing our appraisals of stressful events.

Reappraisal: Ellis's Rational Thinking

Albert Ellis (1977, 1985) is a prominent theorist who believes that we can short-circuit our emotional reactions to stress by altering our appraisals of stressful events. Stone and Neale call this strategy *situation redefinition* (see Table 13.5). Ellis's insights about stress appraisal are the foundation for a widely used system of therapy that he devised. **Rational-emotive therapy is an approach to therapy that focuses on altering clients' patterns of irrational thinking to reduce maladaptive emotions and behavior.**

Ellis maintains that *you feel the way you think.* He argues that problematic emotional reactions are caused by negative self-talk, which he calls catastrophic thinking. **Catastrophic thinking involves unrealistically pessimistic appraisals of stress that exaggerate the magnitude of one's problems.** Ellis uses a simple A-B-C sequence to explain his ideas (see Figure 13.18).

Table 13.5 Men's and Women's Coping Strategies

COPING STRATEGY	DESCRIPTION	INDIVIDUALS USING STRATEGY (%)	
		MALE	FEMALE
Distraction	Diverted attention away from the problem by thinking about other things or engaging in some activity.	23	30
Situation redefinition	Tried to see the problem in a different light that made it seem more bearable.	24	25
Direct action	Thought about solutions to the problem, gathered information about it, or actually did something to try to solve it.	48	43
Catharsis	Expressed emotions in response to the problem to reduce tension, anxiety, or frustration.	21	29
Acceptance	Accepted that the problem had occurred but that nothing could be done about it.	28	32
Seeking social support	Sought or found emotional support from loved ones, friends, or professionals.	11	18
Relaxation	Did something with the implicit intention of relaxing.	14	20
Religion	Sought or found spiritual comfort and support.	3	8

Source: Adapted from Stone & Neale, 1984

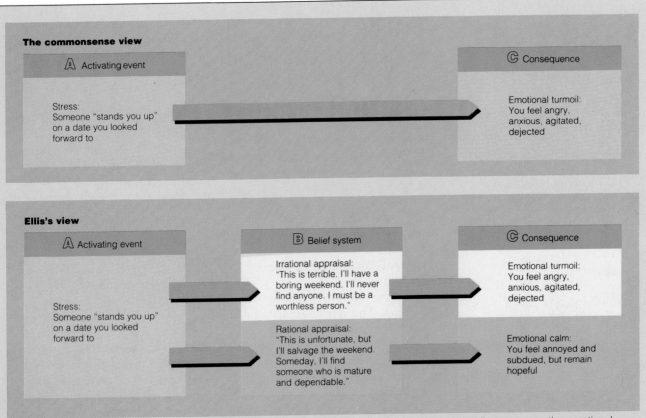

Figure 13.18 Albert Ellis's A-B-C model of emotional reactions. Although most of us are prone to attribute our negative emotional reactions directly to events, Ellis argues that we *feel* the way we *think*.

- A: *Activating event.* The A in Ellis's system stands for the activating event that produces the stress. The activating event may be any potentially stressful transaction. Examples might include an automobile accident, the cancellation of a date, a delay while waiting in line at the bank, or a failure to get a promotion you were expecting.
- B: *Belief system.* B stands for your belief about the event. This represents your appraisal of the stress. According to Ellis, we often view minor setbacks as disasters. Thus, we engage in catastrophic thinking: "How awful this is. I can't stand it! Things never turn out fair for me. I'll never get promoted."
- C: *Consequence.* C stands for the consequence of your negative thinking. When your appraisals of stressful events are terribly negative, the consequence tends to be emotional distress. Thus, we feel angry, or outraged, or anxious, or panic-stricken, or disgusted, or dejected.

Ellis asserts that most of us don't understand the importance of phase B in this three-stage sequence. We unwittingly believe that the activating event (A) causes the consequent emotional turmoil (C). However, Ellis maintains that A does *not* cause C. It only appears to do so. Instead, Ellis asserts, B causes C. Our emotional

"People largely disturb themselves by thinking in a self-defeating, illogical, and unrealistic manner."
ALBERT ELLIS

distress is actually caused by our catastrophic thinking in appraising stressful events.

According to Ellis, it's commonplace for people to turn inconvenience into disaster and to make "mountains out of molehills." For instance, imagine that someone "stands you up" on a date that you were looking forward to eagerly. You might think as follows: "Oh, this is terrible. I'm going to have

another rotten, boring weekend. People always mistreat me. I'll never find anyone to fall in love with. I must be a crummy, worthless person." Ellis would argue that such thoughts are terribly irrational. He would point out that it doesn't follow logically, just because you were stood up, that you (1) must have a lousy weekend, (2) will never fall in love, and (3) are a worthless person.

Ellis theorizes that unrealistic appraisals of stress are derived from irrational assumptions that we hold. He maintains that if you scrutinize your catastrophic thinking, you'll find that your reasoning is based on a logically indefensible premise, such as "I must have approval from everyone" or "I must perform well in all endeavors." These faulty assumptions, which we often hold unconsciously, generate our catastrophic thinking and our emotional turmoil. Ten such irrational assumptions that are especially common are described in Figure 13.19.

How can you reduce your unrealistic appraisals of stress? To accomplish this, Ellis asserts that you must learn

(1) how to detect catastrophic thinking and (2) how to dispute the irrational assumptions that cause it. Detection involves acquiring the ability to spot unrealistic pessimism and wild exaggeration in your thinking. Examine your self-talk closely. Ask yourself why you're getting upset. Force yourself to verbalize your concerns, silently or out loud. Look for key words that often show up in catastrophic thinking, such as *should, ought, never,* and *must.*

Disputing your irrational assumptions requires subjecting your entire reasoning process to scrutiny. Try to root out the assumptions from which you derive your conclusions. We're often unaware of these assumptions. Once they're unearthed, their irrationality may be quite obvious. If your assumptions seem reasonable, ask yourself whether your conclusions follow logically. Try to replace your catastrophic thinking with lower-key, more rational analyses. These strategies should help you to redefine stressful situations in ways that are less threatening. Strangely enough, another way to make stressful situations less threatening is to turn to humor.

Humor as a Stress Reducer

Not long ago, the Chicago area experienced its worst flooding in about a century. Thousands of people saw their homes wrecked when two rivers spilled over their banks. As the waters receded, the flood victims returning to their homes were subjected to the inevitable TV interviews. A remarkable number of victims, surrounded by the ruins of their homes, *joked* about their misfortune. When the going gets tough, it may pay to laugh about it. In a study of coping styles, McCrae (1984) found that 40% of his subjects used humor to deal with stress.

In analyzing the stress-reducing effects of humor, Dixon (1980) emphasized its impact on the appraisal of stress. Finding a humorous aspect in a stressful situation redefines the situation in a less threatening way. Dixon noted that laughter and mirth can also serve to discharge pent-up emotions.

These dual functions of humor may make joking about life's difficulties a particularly useful coping strategy.

While some psychologists have long suspected that humor might be a worthwhile coping response, empirical evidence to that effect has emerged only in recent years (Martin & Lefcourt, 1983; Nezu, Nezu, & Blissett, 1988). For instance, Martin and Lefcourt (1983) found that a good sense of humor functioned as a buffer to lessen the negative impact of stress on mood.

Releasing Pent-up Emotions

Try as we might to redefine situations as less stressful, we all go through times when we feel wired with stress-induced tension. When this happens, there's merit in the commonsense notion that you should try to release the emotions welling up inside, because the physiological arousal that accompanies emotions can become problematic. Often, it's inadvisable to let unconquered emotions seethe within. One study of high school students found that those who tended to hold their anger in tended to have relatively high blood pressure (Spielberger et al., 1985). Although there's no guarantee of it, you can sometimes reduce your physiological arousal by *expressing* your emotions. The key, of course, is to express your emotions in a mature and socially acceptable manner. This is particularly important when the emotion is anger.

Figure 13.19 Irrational assumptions that can cause and sustain emotional disturbance. Assumptions like these are often held unconsciously, and we may have to work at detecting them before we can change to a more positive way of thinking. (Adapted by Basil Najjar from Ellis, 1977)

Irrational assumption	Rational alternative
1. I must be loved or approved by everyone for everything I do.	It's best to concentrate on my own self-respect, on winning approval for practical purposes, and on loving rather than being loved.
2. I must be thoroughly competent, adequate, and achieving in order to be worthwhile.	I'm an imperfect creature who has limitations and fallibilities like anyone else—and that's okay.
3. It's horrible when things aren't the way I'd like them to be.	I can try to change or control the things that disturb me—or temporarily accept conditions I can't change.
4. There isn't much I can do about my sorrows and disturbances, because unhappiness comes from what happens to you.	I *feel* how I *think*. Unhappiness comes mostly from how I look at things.
5. If something is dangerous or fearsome, I'm right to be terribly upset about it and to dwell on the possibility of its occurring.	I can frankly face what I fear and either render it nondangerous or accept the inevitable.
6. It's easier to avoid facing difficulties and responsibilities than to face them.	The "easy way out" is invariably the much harder alternative in the long run.
7. I'm dependent on others and need someone stronger than I am to rely on.	It's better to take the risk of relying on myself and thinking and acting independently.
8. There's always a precise and perfect solution to human problems, and it's catastrophic not to find it.	The world is full of probability and chance, and I can enjoy life even though there isn't always an ideal solution to a problem.
9. The world—especially other people—should be fair, and justice (or mercy) must triumph.	I can work toward seeking fair behavior, realizing that there are few absolutes in life.
10. I must not question the beliefs held by society or respected authorities.	It's better to evaluate beliefs for myself—on their own merits, not on who happens to hold them.

If dejection and grief are the emotions that you're experiencing, it may be worthwhile to go ahead and "cry your heart out." We have a natural inclination to use this response. Unfortunately, many of us (especially men) are taught that crying is inappropriate behavior for an adult. However, there's nothing wrong with crying if the situation warrants it.

Verbalization can be especially valuable in releasing anxiety. Sometimes "talking it out" reduces tension. If you can find a good listener, you may be able to discharge some of your anxiety by letting your secret fears, misgivings, and suspicions spill out in a candid conversation. Sigmund Freud coined the term *catharsis* **to refer to the release of emotional tension.** He made use of this principle in his approach to psychotherapy, but you don't have to go to a therapist to experience catharsis. Of course, it does help to have some friends who are willing to listen, which brings us to the importance of using available social support.

Seeking Help

In your efforts to cope with problems, keep in mind that it's quite reasonable to ask for assistance from friends, family, colleagues, and so forth. Because of potential embarrassment, many people are reluctant to acknowledge their problems and seek help from others. This is unfortunate. The research on social support as a moderator of stress indicates that others can be a rich source of help during times of stress.

The strength of social support lies in its versatility. As we discussed earlier in the chapter, people can provide us with instrumental support, appraisal support, emotional support, and informational support (House, 1981). Seeking help from others is a strategy that has enormous potential because social support can facilitate coping in a variety of ways.

Learning to Relax

Relaxation is a very valuable stress-management technique that can soothe emotional turmoil and suppress problematic physiological arousal (Lehrer & Woolfolk, 1984). One study even suggests that relaxation training may improve the effectiveness of our immune response (Kiecolt-Glaser et al., 1985).

The value of relaxation became apparent to Herbert Benson (1975) as a result of his research on meditation. Benson, a Harvard Medical School cardiologist, believes that relaxation is the key to the beneficial effects of meditation. According to Benson, the elaborate religious rituals and beliefs associated with meditation are irrelevant to its effects. After "demystifying" meditation, Benson set out to devise a simple, nonreligious procedure that could provide similar benefits. He calls his procedure the *relaxation response.* Although there are several other worthwhile approaches to relaxation training, we'll examine Benson's procedure, as its simplicity makes it especially useful.

From his study of a variety of relaxation techniques, Benson concluded that four factors promote effective relaxation:

1. *A quiet environment.* It's easiest to induce the relaxation response in a distraction-free environment. After you become experienced with the relaxation response, you may be able to practice it in a crowded subway. Initially, however, you should practice it in a quiet, calm place.
2. *A mental device.* To shift attention inward and keep it there, you need to focus your attention on a constant stimulus, such as a sound or word that's recited repetitively.
3. *A passive attitude.* It's important not to get upset when your attention strays to distracting thoughts. You must realize that such distractions are inevitable. Whenever your mind wanders from your attentional focus, *calmly* redirect attention to your mental device.
4. *A comfortable position.* Reasonable body comfort is essential to avoid a major source of potential distraction. Simply sitting up straight generally works well. Lying down is too conducive to sleep.

Benson's simple relaxation procedure is described in Figure 13.20. For full benefit, it should be practiced daily.

Figure 13.20 Benson's relaxation procedure. (From Benson, 1975)

1. Sit quietly in a comfortable position.

2. Close your eyes.

3. Deeply relax all your muscles, beginning at your feet and progressing up to your face. Keep them relaxed.

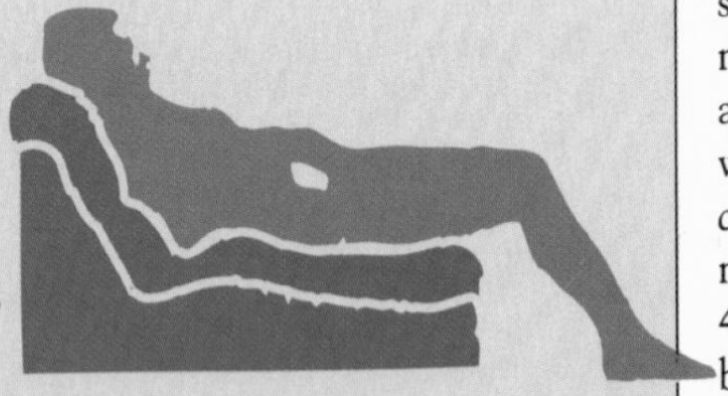

4. Breathe through your nose. Become aware of your breathing. As you breathe out, say the word "one" silently to yourself. For example, breathe in . . . out, "one"; in . . . out, "one"; and so forth. Breathe easily and naturally.

5. Continue for 10 to 20 minutes. You may open your eyes to check the time, but do not use an alarm. When you finish, sit quietly for several minutes, at first with your eyes closed and later with your eyes opened. Do not stand up for a few minutes.

6. Do not worry about whether you are successful in achieving a deep level of relaxation. Maintain a passive attitude and permit relaxation to occur at its own pace. When distracting thoughts occur, try to ignore them by not dwelling on them, and return to repeating "one." With practice, the response should come with little effort. Practice the technique once or twice daily but not within two hours after any meal, since the digestive processes seem to interfere with the elicitation of the relaxation response.

Figure 13.21 The effect of an aerobic-exercise program on depression. Exercise is one of the constructive-coping strategies that can improve how we feel emotionally as well a physically. In a study of mildly depressed women, McCann and Holmes (1984) found that an exercise regimen helped reduce depressive symptoms.

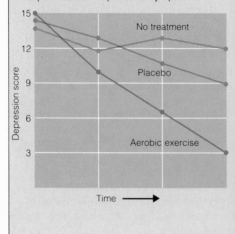

Minimizing Physiological Vulnerability

Our bodies are intimately involved in our response to stress, and the wear and tear of stress can be injurious to our health. To combat this potential problem, it helps to keep your body in relatively sound shape. It's a good idea to consume a nutritionally balanced diet, get adequate sleep, engage in at least a moderate amount of exercise, and learn how to control overeating and the use of tobacco, alcohol, and other drugs. Doing these things will not make you immune to the ravages of stress. However, failure to do them may increase your vulnerability to stress-related diseases. We discussed sleep and drugs elsewhere (see Chapter 5), so we'll limit our comments here to nutrition and exercise.

Nutrition

In modern, industrialized nations, our nutritional shortcomings are largely due to ignorance and poor motivation rather than to lack of food (although

an unfortunate minority of people suffer from hunger). Our schools tend to provide very little nutritional education, so that many of us are remarkably naive about the basic facts of nutrition. Our ignorance is often matched by our cavalier disregard for the importance of good nutritional habits. Typically, our eating is guided not by our nutritional needs, but by convenience, palatability, and clever advertising. For most people, then, the first steps toward improved nutrition involve changing attitudes and acquiring basic information.

Exercise

Like some of the other constructive coping tactics that we've discussed, exercise can provide diverse benefits. The most obvious benefits are increased physical endurance and improved cardiovascular fitness. The latter is especially important as it can reduce your susceptibility to deadly cardiovascular diseases.

Successful participation in an exer-

cise program can also have positive effects on mood and self-concept (Folkins & Sime, 1981). Figure 13.21 shows how an exercise regimen led to a decline in depression in a study of 43 female undergraduates who were mildly depressed when the study began (McCann & Holmes, 1984).

Embarking on an exercise program is difficult for many people. Exercise is time-consuming, and if you're out of shape, your initial attempts may be painful and discouraging. To avoid these problems, it's wise to do the following: (1) select an activity that you find enjoyable, (2) increase your participation gradually, (3) exercise regularly without overdoing it, and (4) reinforce yourself for your efforts (Greenberg, 1983). If you choose a competitive sport (such as basketball or tennis), try to avoid falling into the competition trap. If you become obsessed with winning, you'll put yourself under pressure and *add* to the stress in your life.

STRESS, COPING, AND HEALTH

The Nature of Stress

• Stress involves transactions with the environment that are perceived as threatening. Stress is a common, everyday event, and even seemingly minor stressors or hassles can be problematic. To a large degree, stress lies in the eye of the beholder. Whether we feel threatened by events depends on how we appraise them. Stressful events are usually viewed as less threatening when they are familiar, controllable, and predictable.

• Important types of stress include frustration, conflict, change, and pressure. Frustration occurs when an obstacle prevents us from attaining some goal. Failures and losses are common sources of frustration. There are three principal types of conflict: approach-approach, avoidance-avoidance, and approach-avoidance. The last is especially stressful. Vacillation is a common response to conflict. A large number of studies with the SRRS suggest that change is stressful. Although this may be true, it's now clear that the SRRS is a measure of general stress rather than just change-related stress. Two kinds of pressure (to perform and to conform) also appear to be stressful.

Responding to Stress

• Emotional reactions to stress typically involve anger, fear, or sadness. Emotional arousal may interfere with our coping. This interference appears to be the cause of poor test performance by test-anxious students. The optimal level of arousal on a task depends on the complexity of the task.

• Our physiological arousal in response to stress was originally called the fight-or-flight response by Cannon. This automatic response has limited adaptive value in our modern world. Selye's General Adaptation Syndrome describes three stages in our physiological reaction to stress: alarm, resistance, and exhaustion. Diseases of adaptation may appear during the stage of exhaustion. There are two major pathways along which the brain sends signals to the endocrine system in response to stress. Actions along these paths release two sets of hormones, catecholamines and corticosteroids, into the bloodstream.

• Our behavioral response to stress involves coping. Some coping responses are less than optimal. One of these is striking out at others with acts of aggression. Giving up and indulging oneself are two other coping patterns that tend to be of limited value. Defensive coping is particularly common. Defense mechanisms protect against emotional distress through self-deception. Ultimately, the adaptive value of any coping strategy depends on the exact situation in which it is applied. Relatively healthy coping tactics are called constructive coping.

The Effects of Stress on Psychological Functioning

• Research on the effects of stress has concentrated on negative outcomes, although positive effects may occur. Common negative effects in terms of psychological functioning include impaired task performance, burnout, posttraumatic stress disorders, and other psychological problems and disorders. Baumeister's study of choking under pressure illustrates how performance pressure can interfere with task performance, even by well-trained athletes. Burnout involves chronic exhaustion as a result of stress. Posttraumatic stress disorders are disturbances that surface in the aftermath of a major stressful event.

The Effects of Stress on Physical Health

• In regard to physical health, stress appears to play a role in many types of illness, not just psychosomatic diseases. Type A behavior has been implicated as a contributing cause of coronary heart disease. This competitive, impatient, hostile pattern of behavior may double one's coronary risk. However, the evidence is contradictory, and more research is needed.

• Researchers have found associations between stress and the onset of a great variety of specific diseases, although the evidence on many is highly tentative. Stress may play a role in a host of diseases because it can temporarily suppress the effectiveness of our immune system. While there is little doubt that stress can contribute to the development of physical illness, the link between stress and illness is modest in strength. Stress is only one factor in a complex network of biopsychosocial variables that shape health.

- There are individual differences in how much stress people can tolerate without experiencing ill effects. Social support is a key moderator of the relationship between stress and illness. Although social relationships are not equivalent to social support, people can be a valuable source of emotional, appraisal, informational, and instrumental support. The personality factors associated with hardiness—commitment, challenge, and a sense of being in control—may increase stress tolerance. In terms of personality, optimism may also lead to more effective coping with stress. Physiological factors, such as cardiovascular reactivity, may also influence stress tolerance.

Health-Impairing Lifestyles

- People frequently display health-impairing lifestyles. Smokers have much higher mortality rates than nonsmokers because they are more vulnerable to a host of diseases. Poor nutritional habits have been linked to obesity, heart disease, hypertension, cancer, and diabetes. Lack of exercise elevates one's risk for cardiovascular diseases. Alcohol and drug use carry the immediate risk of overdose and elevate the long-term risk of many diseases. Aspects of lifestyle also influence one's risk of AIDS.

- Health-impairing habits tend to develop gradually and often involve pleasant activities. The risks may be easy to ignore because the consequences lie in the distant future and because we underestimate risks as they apply to us personally. Health-impairing habits are difficult to change. Some programs try to alter health-related attitudes that underlie self-destructive behavior, while others use behavior modification techniques in direct efforts to alter behavior.

Reactions to Illness

- We all experience physical symptoms, but some of us tend to ignore them. This may result in a delay in obtaining needed medical treatment. At the other extreme, a minority of people learn to like the sick role because it earns them attention and allows them to avoid stress. Noncompliance with medical advice is a major problem. The likelihood of noncompliance is greater when instructions are difficult to understand, when recommendations are difficult to follow, and when patients are unhappy with their doctor.

Putting It in Perspective

- Two of our integrative themes were prominent in this chapter. First, we saw that behavior and health are influenced by multiple causes. Second, we saw that experience is highly subjective, as stress lies in the eye of the beholder.

Application: Improving Coping and Stress Management

- Action-oriented, realistic, constructive coping can be helpful in managing the stress of daily life. Ellis emphasizes the importance of reappraising stressful events to detect and dispute catastrophic thinking. According to Ellis, our emotional distress is often due to irrational assumptions that underlie our thinking. Recent evidence suggests that humor may be useful in efforts to redefine stressful situations.

- In some cases, it may pay to release pent-up emotions by expressing them. Crying and talking it out can help. It is also wise to remember the value of social support and to be willing to seek help and emotional sustenance from friends and family. Relaxation techniques, such as Benson's relaxation response, can reduce the wear and tear of stress. Physical vulnerability may also be reduced by getting enough sleep, consuming a nutritionally sound diet, engaging in regular exercise, and controlling overeating and drug use.

KEY TERMS

Aggression
Approach-approach conflict
Approach-avoidance conflict
Atherosclerosis
Avoidance-avoidance conflict
Biopsychosocial model
Burnout
Catastrophic thinking
Catharsis
Conflict
Constructive coping
Coping
Defense mechanisms
Fight-or-flight response
Frustration
General adaptation syndrome
Hardiness
Health psychology
Immune response
Learned helplessness
Life changes
Optimism
Posttraumatic stress disorder
Pressure
Primary appraisal
Psychosomatic diseases
Rational-emotive therapy
Secondary appraisal
Social support
Stress
Type A pattern
Type B pattern

KEY PEOPLE

Walter Cannon
Albert Ellis
Meyer Friedman & Ray Rosenman
Thomas Holmes & Richard Rahe
Suzanne Kobasa
Richard Lazarus
Neal Miller
Hans Selye

PSYCHOLOGICAL DISORDERS

PSYCHOLOGICAL DISORDERS

The government of the United States was overthrown more than a year ago! I'm the president of the United States of America, and Bob Dylan is vice president!" So said Ed, the author of a prominent book on journalism, who was speaking to a college journalism class as a guest lecturer. Ed also informed the class that he had killed both John and Robert Kennedy, as well as

Charles de Gaulle, the former premier of France. He went on to tell the class that all rock music songs were written about him, that he was the greatest karate expert in the universe, and that he had been fighting "space wars" for 2000 years. The students in the class were mystified by Ed's bizarre, disjointed "lecture," but they assumed that he was putting on a show that would eventually lead to a sensible conclusion. However, their perplexed but expectant calm was shattered when Ed pulled a hatchet from the props he had brought with him and hurled the hatchet at the class! Fortunately, he didn't hit anyone, as the hatchet sailed over the students' heads. At that point, the professor for the class realized that Ed's irrational behavior was not a pretense. The professor evacuated the class quickly while Ed continued to rant and rave about his presidential administration, space wars, vampires, his romances with female rock stars, and his personal harem of 38 "chicks." (Adapted from Pearce, 1974)

Clearly, Ed's behavior was abnormal. Even he recognized that later and agreed to be admitted to a mental hospital, signing himself in as the "President of the United States of America." What causes such abnormal behavior? Does Ed have a mental illness, or does he just behave strangely? What's the basis for judging behavior as normal versus abnormal? Are people who have psychological disorders dangerous? How common are such disorders? Can they be cured? These are just a few of the questions that we'll address in this chapter. We'll discuss many different types of psychological disorders and their complex causes. In the following chapter, we'll examine approaches to the treatment of psychological disorders.

Figure 14.1 Historical conceptions of mental illness. In the Middle Ages people who behaved strangely were sometimes thought to be in league with the devil. The drawing above depicts some of the cruel methods used to extract confessions from suspected witches and warlocks. Some psychological disorders were also thought to be caused by demonic possession. The illustration at the right is a detail from Di Benvenuto's *St. Catherine Exorcising Possessed Woman*. (Denver Art Museum Collection)

ABNORMAL BEHAVIOR: MYTHS, REALITIES, AND CONTROVERSIES

Misconceptions about abnormal behavior are common. Hence, we need to clear up some preliminary issues before we describe the various types of disorders. In this section, we'll discuss (1) the medical model of abnormal behavior, (2) the criteria of abnormal behavior, (3) stereotypes regarding psychological disorders, (4) the classification of psychological disorders, and (5) how common such disorders are.

The Medical Model Applied to Abnormal Behavior

In Ed's case, there's no question that his behavior was abnormal. But does it make sense to view his unusual and irrational behavior as a disease? This is a very controversial question. **The *medical model* proposes that it is useful to think of abnormal behavior as a disease.** This point of view is the basis for many of the terms that are used to refer to abnormal behavior, including mental *illness*, mental *disorder*, psychological *disorder*, and psycho*pathology* (pathology refers to manifestations of disease and to the study of diseases). The medical model gradually became the dominant way of thinking about abnormal behavior during the 18th and 19th centuries, and its influence remains pervasive today.

The advent of the medical model clearly represented progress over earlier models of abnormal behavior. Prior to the 18th century, most conceptions of abnormal behavior were based on superstition rather than science. People who behaved strangely were thought to be mortals possessed by demons, witches in league with the devil, or victims of God's punishment. Their disorders were "treated" with chants, rituals, exorcisms, and so forth. If their behavior was seen as threatening, they were candidates for chains, dungeons, torture, and death (see Figure 14.1).

The rise of the medical model brought great improvements in the treatment of people who exhibited abnormal behavior. Viewed as victims of an illness, they were treated with sympathy rather than hatred and fear. Although living conditions in early asylums were often deplorable, there was gradual progress toward more humane care of the mentally ill. It took time, but ineffectual approaches to treatment eventually gave way to scientific investigation of the causes and cures of psychological disorders.

PROBLEMS WITH THE MEDICAL MODEL
In recent decades, however, critics have suggested

that the medical model may have outlived its usefulness. A particularly vocal critic has been Thomas Szasz, author of *The Myth of Mental Illness* (1974). Szasz asserts that "Strictly speaking, disease or illness can affect only the body; hence there can be no mental illness. . . . Minds can be 'sick' only in the sense that jokes are 'sick' or economies are 'sick'" (p. 267). He further argues that abnormal behavior usually involves a deviation from social norms rather than an illness. He contends that such deviations are "problems in living," rather than medical problems. According to Szasz, the medical model's disease analogy converts moral and social questions about what is acceptable behavior into medical questions. Under the guise of "healing the sick," this conversion allegedly allows modern society to lock up deviant people and to enforce its norms of conformity.

The medical model has been criticized on additional grounds as well. Among the other bases for criticism, the following are especially prominent:

1. *Labeling.* Some critics are troubled because medical diagnoses of abnormal behavior pin potentially derogatory labels on people (Becker, 1973; Rothblum, Solomon, & Albee, 1986). Being labeled as psychotic, schizophrenic, or mentally ill carries a social stigma that can be difficult to shake. Even after a full recovery, someone who has been labeled mentally ill may have difficulty finding work or making friends. Deep-seated prejudice against people who have been labeled mentally ill is commonplace. This prejudice was apparent in a study in which a woman called landlords who had advertised rooms for rent (Page, 1977). When the woman mentioned that the prospective tenant (her brother) was about to be released from a mental hospital, the room suddenly became unavailable about three-quarters of the time. The stigma of mental illness is not impossible to shed (Gove, 1975), but it undoubtedly creates additional difficulties for many people who already have their share of problems.

Critics of the medical model also maintain that diagnostic labels such as alcoholic or neurotic can create unfortunate self-fulfilling prophecies (Scheff, 1975). Some people who are labeled alcoholic, for instance, seem to accept this designation as part of their identity and proceed to live out the "alcoholic role" created for them, instead of working to alter their behavior and conquer their problems.

"Minds can be 'sick' only in the sense that jokes are 'sick' or economies are 'sick.'"

THOMAS SZASZ

2. *Pseudoexplanations.* Other critics argue that the technical-sounding diagnoses that are part of the medical approach create an illusion that we understand more than we really do (Krasner & Ullmann, 1965). For instance, let's say that a fellow arrives at a psychiatric facility exhibiting a variety of symptoms that are characteristic of schizophrenic disorders; he says that he hears voices of nonexistent people, and he displays withdrawal, flat emotions, and disorganized, incoherent thinking. He is correctly diagnosed as having a schizophrenic disorder. Later, his bewildered family asks, "Doctor, why does he behave in these strange ways?" The doctor may often reply, "Because he is schizophrenic." That explanation may *sound* reasonable, but it's a pseudoexplanation involving circular reasoning. It's like saying that the reason a woman has red hair is that she's a redhead.

It's *not* accurate to say that a patient hears voices and is withdrawn, emotionally flat, and incoherent *because* he is schizophrenic. Quite the opposite is true. He is called "schizophrenic" because he hears voices and is withdrawn, emotionally flat, and incoherent. Schizophrenia and other diagnoses are only descriptive labels; they're not explanations of abnormal behavior.

3. *The patient role.* The medical model has also been criticized because it encourages people with behavioral problems to adopt the passive role of medical patient (Korchin, 1976). In this passive role mental patients are likely to wait for someone else to do the work to effect a cure. Such passiveness can be problematic even when an illness is purely physical. In psychological disorders, this passiveness can seriously undermine the likelihood of improvement in the person's condition. In general, people with psychological problems need to be actively involved in curative efforts.

PUTTING THE MEDICAL
MODEL IN PERSPECTIVE

So, what position should we take on the medical model? In this chapter, we'll assume an intermediate position, neither accepting nor discarding the model entirely. There certainly are significant problems with the medical model, and the questions raised by its critics deserve serious attention. However, in its defense, the medical model *has* stimulated scientific research on abnormal behavior. Moreover, some of the problems that are blamed on the disease analogy are not unique to this conception of abnormality. People who displayed strange, irrational behavior were labeled and stigmatized long before the medical model came along. Pseudoexplanations of psychological disorders were even more common and more primitive before the advent of the medical model.

In my estimation, applying the disease analogy to abnormal behavior can be useful, as long as we remember that it's *only* an analogy. Medical concepts such as *diagnosis*, *etiology*, and *prognosis* have proven useful in the treatment and study of abnormality. **Diagnosis involves distinguishing one illness from another. Etiology refers to the apparent causation and developmental history of an illness. A *prognosis* is a forecast about the probable course of an illness.** These concepts have widely shared meanings that permit clinicians, researchers, and the public to communicate more effectively in their discussions of abnormal behavior.

So, flawed though it may be, we 'll employ the disease analogy and use terms such as *abnormal behavior*, *mental illness*, and *psychological disorders* interchangeably. Do keep in mind, however, that the medical model is only an analogy. Most psychological disorders are not genuine diseases. Medical labels do not explain abnormal behavior, and we need to be wary of the negative stereotypes associated with these labels. Remember, too, that the passive role of medical patient is not well suited for the treatment of psychological problems. With these thoughts in mind, let's discuss the criteria that are employed in judgments of mental health and mental illness.

Criteria of Abnormal Behavior

If your next-door neighbor scrubs his front porch twice every day and spends virtually all of his time cleaning and recleaning his house, is he normal? If your sister-in-law goes to one physician after another to seek treatment for aches and pains that appear imaginary, is she psychologically healthy? If one of your coworkers became terribly depressed when his wife left him and his depression hasn't lifted after 18 months, does he have a disorder? How are we to judge what's normal and what's abnormal? More important, who's to do the judging?

These are complex questions. In a sense, we *all* make judgments about normality in that we all express opinions about others' (and perhaps our own) mental health. Of course, formal diagnoses of psychological disorders are made by mental health professionals, and official decisions about a person's sanity are made in our court system (with extensive input from psychiatrists and psychologists). In making these judgments, clinicians, legal authorities, and laypeople generally apply the same criteria, albeit with highly varied levels of knowledge and precision. Let's examine the three criteria that are most frequently used in judgments of abnormality. Although two or three criteria may apply in a particular case, people are often viewed as disordered when only one criterion is met.

DEVIANCE As Szasz has pointed out, people often are said to have a disorder because their behavior deviates from what their society considers acceptable. Standards for normality vary somewhat from one culture to another, but all cultures have such norms. When people ignore these standards and expectations, they may be labeled mentally ill. Consider transvestites, for instance. **Transvestism is a sexual disorder in which a man achieves sexual arousal by dressing in women's clothing.** This behavior is regarded as disordered because a man who wears a dress, brassiere, and nylons is deviating from our culture's norms. The example of transvestism illustrates the arbitrary nature of cultural standards regarding normality. In our society, it's normal for women to dress in men's clothing, but not vice versa—so exactly the same overt behavior (cross-sex dressing) is acceptable for women and deviant for men!

MALADAPTIVE BEHAVIOR In many cases, people are judged to have a psychological disorder because their everyday adaptive behavior is impaired. For example, this is the key criterion in the diagnosis of substance-use (drug) disorders. In and of itself, recreational drug use is not terribly unusual or deviant. However, when the use of cocaine, for instance, begins to interfere with a person's normal social or occupational functioning, a substance-use disorder exists. In such cases, it's the maladaptive quality of the behavior that makes it disordered.

PERSONAL DISTRESS Frequently, the diagnosis of a psychological disorder is based on an individual's report of great personal distress. This is usually the criterion met by people who are troubled by depression or various types of anxiety-related disorders. Depressed people, for instance, may or may not exhibit deviant or maladaptive behavior. Such people are usually labeled as having a disorder when they describe their subjective pain and suffering to friends, relatives, or mental health professionals.

NORMALITY AND ABNORMALITY AS A CONTINUUM

Antonyms such as normal versus abnormal, mental health versus mental illness, and psychological health versus psychopathology, imply that people can be divided neatly into two distinct groups:

those who are normal and those who are not. In reality, it's often difficult to draw a line that clearly separates normality from abnormality. On occasion, we all experience personal distress; we all act in deviant ways; and we all display maladaptive behavior. People are judged to have psychological disorders only when their behavior becomes *extremely* deviant, maladaptive, or distressing. However, it's difficult to spell out exactly how extreme one's depression has to be to qualify as a depressive disorder, or how impaired one has to be to have a drug disorder, or how anxious one has to be to have an anxiety disorder. Thus, normality and abnormality exist on a continuum, and it's a matter of degree rather than an either-or proposition (see Figure 14.2).

THE CULTURAL BOUNDS OF NORMALITY AND ABNORMALITY
To some extent, the criteria of psychological disorders are culture-bound. In other words,

Behavior that is deviant in one culture or context may be quite normal in another. Both of these men are wearing a dress, but only the man on the left is likely to be considered abnormal.

Figure 14.2 Normality and abnormality as a continuum. There isn't a sharp boundary between normal and abnormal behavior. Behavior is normal or abnormal in degree, depending on the extent to which one's behavior is deviant, personally distressing, or maladaptive.

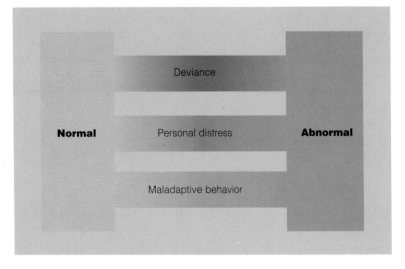

Vigorous campaigning by gay rights activists was one of several factors that led the American Psychiatric Association to delete homosexuality from its list of psychological disorders. Judgments regarding normality and abnormality reflect social trends and political forces, as well as scientific knowledge.

judgments of normality and abnormality are influenced by cultural norms and values. Behavior that's considered deviant or maladaptive in one society may be quite acceptable in another. For example, in modern Western society people who "hear voices" are assumed to be irrational and are routinely placed in mental hospitals. However, in some other cultures, hearing voices is commonplace and hardly merits a raised eyebrow.

Cultural norms regarding acceptable behavior may change over time. For example, consider how views of homosexuality have changed in our society. Homosexuality used to be listed as a sexual disorder in the American Psychiatric Association's diagnostic system. However, in 1973 a committee appointed by the association voted to delete homosexuality from the official list of psychological disorders. This action occurred because (1) attitudes toward homosexuality in our society became more accepting, (2) gay rights activists campaigned vigorously for the change, and (3) research findings showed that gays and heterosexuals did not differ overall on measures of psychological health (Rothblum, Solomon, & Albee, 1986). As you might guess, this change stimulated a great deal of debate.

Gays are not the only group that has tried to influence the diagnostic system for mental illness. For example, in recent years, womens' groups have lobbied successfully against adding a new diagnosis called *masochistic personality disorder*, because they thought it would be applied in sexist ways to women who were victims of wife battering.

The key point is this: Diagnoses of psychological disorders involve *value judgments* about what represents normal or abnormal behavior. The criteria of mental illness are not nearly as value free as the criteria of physical illness. In evaluating physical diseases, people usually can agree that a weak heart or a bad kidney is pathological, regardless of their personal values. However, judgments about mental illness reflect prevailing cultural values, social trends, and political forces, as well as scientific knowledge.

Stereotypes of Psychological Disorders

We've seen that mental illnesses are not diseases in a strict sense, that diagnoses are not explanations of abnormal behavior, and that judgments of mental health are not value free. However, there are still other myths about abnormal behav-

---

CONCEPT CHECK 14.1
Applying the Criteria of Abnormal Behavior

Check your understanding of the criteria of abnormal behavior by identifying the criteria met by each of the examples below and checking them off in the table provided. Remember, a specific behavior may meet more than one criterion. The answers are in Appendix A.

Behavioral examples

1. Alan's performance at work has suffered because he has been drinking alcohol to excess. Several co-workers have suggested that he should seek help for his problem, but he thinks that they're getting alarmed over nothing. "I just enjoy a good time once in a while," he says.
2. Monica has gone away to college and feels lonely, sad, and dejected. Her grades are fine, and she gets along okay with the other students in the dormitory, but inside she's choked with gloom, hopelessness, and despair.
3. Walter believes that he's Napoleon reborn. He believes that he is destined to lead the U.S. military forces into a great battle to recover California from aliens.
4. Phyllis panics with anxiety whenever she leaves her home. Her problem escalated gradually until she was absent from work so often that she was fired. She hasn't been out of her house in 9 months and is deeply troubled by her problem.

Criteria met by each example

	DEVIANCE	MALADAPTIVE BEHAVIOR	PERSONAL DISTRESS
1. Alan	_____	_____	_____
2. Monica	_____	_____	_____
3. Walter	_____	_____	_____
4. Phyllis	_____	_____	_____

ior that need to be exposed as such. Let's examine four stereotypes about psychological disorders that are largely inaccurate.

1. *Psychological disorders are a sign of personal weakness.* Psychological disorders are often seen as a manifestation of personal weakness and a source of shame. In reality, psychological disorders are a function of many factors—such as genetic predisposition, family background, and exposure to stress—over which we have little or no control. Mental illness can strike anyone. Mentally ill people are no more to blame for their troubles than people who develop leukemia or other physical illnesses.

2. *Psychological disorders are incurable.* Admittedly, there are mentally ill people for whom treatment is largely a failure. However, they're greatly outnumbered by people who *do* get better, either spontaneously or through formal treatment. The vast majority of people who are diagnosed as mentally ill eventually improve and lead normal, productive lives. Even the most severe psychological disorders can be treated successfully.

3. *People with psychological disorders are often violent and dangerous.* There appears to be little or no association between mental illness and violent tendencies (Cockerham, 1981). The stereotype that associates mental illness and violence exists because incidents of violence involving the mentally ill tend to command media attention. For example, our opening case history, which described Ed's breakdown and the incident with the hatchet, was chronicled in a national newsmagazine. People such as John Hinckley, whose mental illness led him to attempt an assassination of President Reagan, receive extensive publicity. However, these individuals are not very representative of the large number of people who have struggled with psychological disorders.

4. *People with psychological disorders behave in bizarre ways and are very different from normal people.* This is true only in a small minority of cases, usually involving relatively severe disorders. As noted earlier, the line between normal and abnormal behavior can be very difficult to draw. At first glance, people with psychological disorders usually are indistinguishable from those without disorders. This brings us to our Featured Study for the chapter, which showed that even mental health professionals may have difficulty distinguishing normality from abnormality.

QUESTIONING THE DISTINCTION BETWEEN NORMALITY AND ABNORMALITY

Voicing doubts about the validity of psychiatric diagnosis, David Rosenhan set out to demonstrate that "notions of normality and abnormality may not be quite as accurate as people believe they are" (p. 250). To test his thesis, he arranged for a number of normal people to seek admission to mental hospitals. He wanted to see how long it would take for the hospital staffs to recognize the normality of the "pseudopatients."

Method
Eight people with no history of psychiatric problems sought admission to a diverse collection of mental hospitals located in five states. The pseudopatients arrived at the hospitals complaining of one false symptom—hearing voices. Except for this single symptom, they acted as they normally would and gave accurate information when interviewed about their personal history and current mental status. The pseudopatients were instructed to stop simulating the symptom and behave in their usual manner if they were admitted to the hospital. Rosenhan wanted to find out what percentage of the pseudopatients would

be admitted and how long they would be kept hospitalized.

Results
The pseudopatients were admitted to the mental hospital every time. In all, Rosenhan's confederates were admitted to 12 different hospitals (some did it twice). The length of their hospitalization ranged from 7 to 52 days. The average stay was 19 days. In all but one case, the admitting diagnosis was schizophrenia, which is a very severe diagnosis. After the study was completed, the pseudopatients' hospital charts were obtained. The records indicated that they were discharged with a diagnosis of *schizophrenia—in remission.* The phrase "in remission" indicates that a disorder is currently abated or under control. In a sense, this means that the normality of the pseudopatients was unrecognized even when they were released after ample opportunity for observation by the staff.

Interestingly, the other patients recognized the normality of the pseudopatients more frequently than did the professional staff of psychiatrists,

Investigator: David L. Rosenhan (Stanford University)

Source: On being sane in insane places. *Science, 179* (1973), 250–258.

"How many people, one wonders, are sane but not recognized as such in our psychiatric institutions?"

DAVID ROSENHAN

psychologists, nurses, and attendants. Many patients came forward and said something like, "You're not crazy. You're a journalist or a professor checking up on the hospital." In part, this happened because the pseudopatients openly took notes on their experiences in the hospital. Their note-taking was not hidden from the hospital staff, but the examination of the patients' charts (after the study) revealed that the staff viewed the unusual note-taking as a *symptom* of the pseudopatients' mental disorder.

Discussion

The results support the assertion that it's not easy to distinguish normality from abnormality. The pseudopatients' notes about life on the psychiatric wards offer a clue as to why. They were impressed by the largely "normal" quality of the real patients' behavior. They concluded that people with genuine mental illness act normal most of the time, and act in a deviant manner only a small fraction of the time. The pseudopatients' notes also revealed that the hospital staff spent surprisingly little time interacting with patients. Most of the time they were segregated from the patients in a glassed-off enclosure known as "the cage." This lack of interaction presumably contributed to the staff's failure to detect that the pseudopatients were normal.

The study also showed that psychiatric diagnoses can be sticky labels that influence others' perceptions of one's behavior. The fact that pseudopatients were discharged with a diagnosis of schizophrenia in remission indicates that even perfectly normal people have difficulty shedding a psychiatric diagnosis. Furthermore, once the pseudopatients were labeled as schizophrenic, even innocuous behavior such as taking notes was viewed as a sign of pathology.

Comment

Rosenhan's study provoked a great deal of controversy. In defense of the hospitals' admission of the pseudopatients, Robert Spitzer (1975) argued that it would have been inhumane to turn away people who came to a psychiatric facility complaining of hearing voices. That's undeniably true. Spitzer also asserted that the symptom of hearing voices made schizophrenia the most probable diagnosis for the pseudopatients. That's also true. However, it overlooks the fact that the hospital staff did not have to make an immediate diagnosis. With most of the symptoms of schizophrenia absent, the hospital staff could have deferred their diagnosis pending further observation. If they had been more deliberate, some staff members might have detected the normality of the pseudopatients.

Rosenhan's study showed that our mental health system has a powerful bias toward seeing pathology in anyone who walks in the door. This slant toward seeing mental illness is not entirely unreasonable; after all, people don't go to mental hospitals because they're feeling terrific. However, this bias may need to be tempered. People often go to physicians with reports of physical symptoms and end up being assured that they're not really sick. In our mental health system, the slant toward seeing pathology should not be so powerful that it precludes a similar result.

Some critics of the medical model argued that Rosenhan's work demonstrated that the entire diagnostic system for mental disorders lacked validity. A more reasonable conclusion would be that Rosenhan showed that mental illness can be feigned easily. In any case, the diagnostic system for mental illness survived the controversy evoked by the Rosenhan study. Let's look at how this system has evolved into its current form.

Psychodiagnosis: The Classification of Disorders

Obviously, we can't lump all psychological disorders together without giving up all hope of understanding them better. Hence, a great deal of effort has been invested in devising an elaborate system for classifying psychological disorders.

A modern landmark in this classification effort was reached in 1952 when the American Psychiatric Association unveiled its *Diagnostic and Statistical Manual of Mental Disorders*, known as *DSM-I*, which described 60 disorders. Before the publication of *DSM-I*, a hodgepodge of conflicting classification systems were used in the United States. Major revisions, intended to enhance the utility of the *DSM* system, were completed in 1968 (*DSM-II*) and again in 1980 (*DSM-III*).

A useful diagnostic system, like a sound psychological test, should be characterized by *reliability*—that is, it should produce reasonably consistent results. In other words, different mental health professionals evaluating the same cases should arrive at the same diagnoses for most of the cases. *DSM-I* and *DSM-II*, which described classic "textbook cases" of each disorder, were characterized by mediocre reliability. Diagnostic reliability was improved considerably by *DSM-III* (Robins & Helzer, 1986). This improvement was achieved by listing all the common symptoms of a disorder along with explicit rules about which symptoms, and how many symptoms, are required to qualify for a specific diagnosis.

The current version of the *DSM* system, a modest revision of the third edition, known as *DSM-III-R*, was issued in 1987. Each revision of the *DSM* system has expanded the list of disorders

Diagnostic Criteria for Panic Disorder

A. At some time during the disturbance, one or more panic attacks (discrete periods of intense fear or discomfort) have occurred that (1) were unexpected (that is, they did not occur immediately before or on exposure to a situation that almost always causes anxiety) and (2) were not triggered by situations in which the person was the focus of others' attention.

B. Either four attacks, as defined in criterion A, have occurred within a 4-week period, or one or more attacks have been followed by a period of at least a month of persistent fear of having another attack.

C. At least four of the following symptoms developed during at least one of the attacks:
  1. Shortness of breath or smothering sensations
  2. Dizziness, unsteady feelings, or faintness
  3. Palpitations or accelerated heart rate
  4. Trembling or shaking
  5. Sweating
  6. Choking
  7. Nausea or abdominal distress
  8. Depersonalization (reduced sense of self)
  9. Numbness or tingling sensations
  10. Flushes (hot flashes) or chills
  11. Chest pain or discomfort
  12. Fear of dying
  13. Fear of going crazy or of doing something uncontrolled

D. During at least some of the attacks, at least four of the symptoms in C developed suddenly and increased in intensity within 10 minutes of the beginning of the first symptom in C noticed in the attack.

Figure 14.3 Example of the diagnostic criteria in *DSM-III-R*. This list of the conditions to be met for a diagnosis of panic disorder shows the degree of detail in the diagnostic criteria. (Adapted with permission from the *Diagnostic and Statistical Manual of Mental Disorders, Third Edition, Revised.* Copyright 1987 American Psychiatric Association.)

covered. *DSM-III-R* describes over 200 types of psychological disorders. As an example of the way the *DSM* system describes disorders, the diagnostic criteria for panic disorders are reprinted in Figure 14.3. As you can see, the diagnostic guidelines are explicit, concrete, and detailed, to facilitate reliability.

THE MULTIAXIAL SYSTEM

The publication of *DSM-III* in 1980 also introduced a new multiaxial system of classification. The multiaxial system asks for judgments about individuals on five separate dimensions, or "axes." Figure 14.4 provides an overview of the entire system and the five axes. The diagnoses of disorders are made on Axes I and II. Clinicians record any major disorders that are apparent on Axis I and use Axis II to list any personality or developmental disorders, which often coexist with Axis I syndromes. People may receive diagnoses on both axes. More than one diagnosis on a single axis is permitted, but rules built into the system discourage this practice.

The remaining axes are used to record information that supplements the diagnoses on Axes I and II. A patient's physical disorders are listed on Axis III. On Axis IV the clinician makes notations and ratings regarding the severity of stress experienced by the individual in the past year. On Axis V estimates are made of the individual's current level of adaptive functioning (social and occupational behavior, viewed as a whole) and of the individual's highest level of functioning in the past year. Figure 14.5 shows an example of a multiaxial evaluation.

Most theorists agree that the multiaxial system is a step in the right direction in that it recognizes the importance of information other than a traditional diagnostic label. However, in practice, it appears that clinicians make little use of Axis III (Maricle, Leung, & Bloom, 1987). Furthermore, Axes IV and V are poorly defined, and there is little evidence regarding their validity (Williams, 1985). Hopefully, research will lead to improvement of the supplementary axes in future editions of the DSM classification system.

CONTROVERSIES OVER NEW DIRECTIONS

Surely you've heard people described as neurotic. In the future, you'll probably hear such descriptions less frequently. In a controversial move, *DSM-III* did away with a long-standing distinction between *neuroses* and *psychoses*, making both terms somewhat dated. Essentially, the accumulated empirical evidence indicated that the disorders listed in each of these categories did not share enough in common to merit being grouped together. The disorders that were in each category still exist, but they've been subdivided into smaller groups that have more in common. For example, the neuroses listed in *DSM-II* were redistributed into groups called *anxiety disorders, somatoform disorders, dissociative disorders,* and *mood disorders*.

Although neurosis and psychosis are not official diagnostic categories any more, these concepts are still used informally as broad descriptions of different degrees of pathology. Hence, the term **neurotic refers to behavior marked by subjective**

Figure 14.4 Overview of the *DSM-III-R* system. Published by the American Psychiatric Association, *DSM-III-R* is the formal classification system used in the diagnosis of psychological disorders. It is a *multiaxial* system, which means that information is recorded on the five axes described here. (Adapted with permission from the *Diagnostic and Statistical Manual of Mental Disorders, Third Edition, Revised.* Copyright 1987 American Psychiatric Association.)

Axis I
Major Clinical Syndromes

1. *Disorders usually first evident in infancy, childhood, or adolescence*
   This category includes disorders that arise before adolescence, such as attention deficit disorders, bulimia, anorexia, enuresis, and stuttering.

2. *Organic mental disorders*
   These disorders are temporary or permanent dysfunctions of brain tissue caused by diseases or chemicals. Examples are delirium, dementia, and amnesia.

3. *Psychoactive substance use disorders*
   This category refers to the *maladaptive* use of drugs and alcohol. Mere consumption and recreational use of such substances are not disorders. This category requires an abnormal pattern of use, as with alcohol abuse and cocaine dependence.

4. *Schizophrenic disorders*
   The schizophrenias are characterized by psychotic symptoms (for example, grossly disorganized behavior, delusions, and hallucinations) and by over 6 months of behavioral deterioration.

5. *Delusional disorders*
   These disorders, of which paranoia is the most common, are characterized by persecutory delusions in the absence of other psychotic symptoms. In general, delusional patients are less impaired than schizophrenics.

6. *Mood disorders*
   The cardinal feature is emotional disturbance. Patients may, or may not, have psychotic symptoms. These disorders include major depression, bipolar disorder, dysthymic disorder, and cyclothymic disorder.

7. *Anxiety disorders*
   These disorders are characterized by physiological signs of anxiety (for example, palpitations) and subjective feelings of tension, apprehension, or fear. Anxiety may be acute and focused (panic disorder) or continual and diffuse (generalized anxiety disorder).

8. *Somatoform disorders*
   These disorders are dominated by somatic symptoms that resemble physical illnesses. The symptoms cannot be accounted for by organic damage. There *must* also be strong evidence that these symptoms are produced by psychological factors or conflicts. This category includes somatization and conversion disorders and hypochondriasis.

9. *Dissociative disorders*
   These disorders all feature a sudden, temporary alteration or dysfunction of memory, consciousness, identity, and behavior, as in depersonalization disorder, psychogenic amnesia, and multiple personality.

10. *Psychosexual disorders*
    Psychological factors play major etiological roles in all of these disorders. There are 3 basic types: gender identity disorders (discomfort with identity as male or female), paraphilias (preference for unusual acts to achieve sexual arousal), and sexual dysfunctions (impairments in sexual functioning).

Axis II
Personality and Developmental Disorders

Personality disorders
These disorders are patterns of personality traits that are long standing, maladaptive, and inflexible and involve impaired functioning or subjective distress. Examples include borderline, schizoid, and passive-aggressive personality disorders.

Specific developmental disorders
These are disorders of specific developmental areas that are not due to another disorder. Examples include mental retardation, autism, and reading, writing, and arithmetic disorders.

Axis III
Physical Disorders and Conditions

Physical disorders or conditions are recorded on this axis. Examples include diabetes, arthritis, and hemophilia.

Axis IV
Severity of Psychosocial Stressors

Code	Term	Adult example
1	None	No relevant events
2	Mild	Starting or graduating from school
3	Moderate	Loss of job
4	Severe	Divorce
5	Extreme	Death of loved one
6	Catastrophic	Devastating natural disaster

Axis V
Global Assessment of Functioning (GAF) Scale

Code	Symptoms
90	Absent or minimal symptoms, good functioning in all areas.
80	Symptoms are transient and expectable reactions to psychosocial stressors.
70	Some mild symptoms or some difficulty in social, occupational, or school functioning, but generally functioning pretty well.
60	Moderate symptoms or difficulty in social, occupational, or school functioning.
50	Serious symptoms or impairment in social, occupational, or school functioning.
40	Some impairment in reality testing or communication or major impairment in family relations, judgment, thinking, or mood.
30	Behavior is considerably influenced by delusions or hallucinations, serious impairment in communication or judgment, or inability to function in almost all areas.
20	Some danger of hurting self or others, occasional failure to maintain minimal personal hygiene, or gross impairment in communication.
10	Persistent danger of severely hurting self or others.

distress (usually chronic anxiety) and reliance on avoidance coping. People who are characterized as neurotic may be deeply troubled, but their reality contact is basically sound, and they don't show gross impairments in adaptive behavior. In contrast, the term **psychotic** refers to behavior **marked by impaired reality contact and profound deterioration of adaptive functioning.** Generally, psychotic behavior is more obvious than neurotic behavior, more problematic for society, and more debilitating for the individual.

DSM-III also sparked controversy by adding everyday problems to the diagnostic system. For example, *DSM-III-R* includes conditions such as an academic underachievement disorder (not performing up to ability in school), nicotine dependence (distress derived from quitting smoking), and caffeine intoxication (agitation and restlessness from drinking too much coffee) that are not traditionally thought of as mental illnesses. Critics argue that everyday problems such as these should not be listed in the diagnostic structure because this listing casts the shadow of pathology on normal behavior (McReynolds, 1979). However, critics of the *old* system (*DSM-II*) complained because it omitted many common problems that were being treated by psychologists and psychiatrists.

In part, everyday problems were added to the diagnostic system so that more people could bill their insurance companies for professional treatments of the conditions (Garfield, 1986). Many health insurance policies permit reimbursement only for the treatment of psychological conditions on the official (*DSM*) list of disorders. Although there's merit in making it easier for more people to seek needed professional help, the pros and cons of including everyday problems in *DSM* are complicated. The insurance industry's influence on this change illustrates once again that our conceptions of mental health and illness are shaped by cultural values, political realities, and economic necessities, as well as scientific findings (Schacht, 1985).

Shifting definitions of normality and abnormality inevitably affect estimates regarding the number of people who suffer from psychological disorders. The improved diagnostic reliability of *DSM-III* stimulated a flurry of research on the prevalence of specific mental disorders. Let's examine some of this research.

The Prevalence of Psychological Disorders

How common are psychological disorders? What percentage of the population is afflicted with men-

Example of a *DSM-III-R* Multiaxial Evaluation (Patient: 58-year-old male)

Axis I	Major depression
	Alcohol dependence
Axis II	Dependent personality disorder (provisional, rule out borderline personality disorder)
Axis III	Alcoholic cirrhosis of liver
Axis IV	Psychosocial stressors: anticipated retirement and change in residence, with loss of contact with friends
	Severity: 3—moderate
Axis V	Current global assessment of functioning (GAF): 44
	Highest GAF past year: 55

Figure 14.5 Example of a *DSM-III-R* evaluation. A multiaxial evaluation for a depressed man with a drinking problem might look like this. (Adapted with permission from the *Diagnostic and Statistical Manual of Mental Disorders, Third Edition, Revised.* Copyright 1987 American Psychiatric Association.)

tal illness? Is it 10%? Perhaps 25%? Could the figure range as high as 40% or 50%?

Such estimates fall in the domain of **epidemiology—the study of the distribution of mental or physical disorders in a population.** The epidemiology of mental illness is an interdisciplinary area of research, and epidemiological studies are conducted by psychologists, psychiatrists, sociologists, epidemiologists, and public health researchers. In epidemiology, **prevalence** refers to **the percentage of a population that exhibits a disorder during a specified time period.** In the case of mental disorders, the most interesting data are the estimates of *lifetime prevalence*, the percentage of people who endure a specific disorder at any time in their lives.

Obtaining sound estimates of the prevalence of psychological disorders is not a simple matter. The crucial problem is that many people with such disorders suffer in silence and don't seek treatment. Thus, we can't generalize accurately from statistics on the number of people who have been treated for a particular disorder. To get around this problem, researchers sometimes fan out into communities and interview people in their homes to assess their mental health. Although these studies have certain weaknesses, they provide our best estimates of the prevalence of psychological disorders in modern society (Dohrenwend, 1980).

Estimates from such surveys suggest that psychological disorders are more common than most people realize. Prior to the advent of *DSM-III*, studies suggested that about *one-fifth* of the population exhibited clear signs of mental illness (Neugebauer, Dohrenwend, & Dohrenwend, 1980). However, the older studies did not assess drug-related disorders very effectively, because

Figure 14.6 Prevalence of common psychological disorders in the United States. The estimated percentage of people who have, at any time in their life, suffered from one of four types of psychological disorders or from a disorder of any kind (*top bar*) is shown here. (Based on Robins et al., 1984)

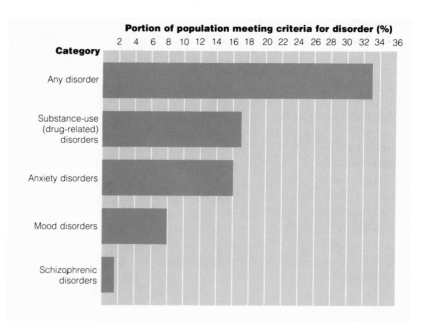

Portion of population meeting criteria for disorder (%)

DSM-I and DSM-II described these disorders only vaguely. More recent studies, employing the explicit criteria for substance-use disorders in DSM-III, have found psychological disorders in roughly *one-third* of the population! This increase in mental illness is more apparent than real, as it's due mostly to more effective tabulation of drug-related disorders.

The most ambitious research thus far on the prevalence of psychological disorders has emerged from the Epidemiological Catchment Area (ECA) studies (Kessler et al., 1987; Myers, Weissman, et al., 1984). The ECA studies have evaluated the mental health of more than 10,000 adults, who constitute a carefully selected sample from five major metropolitan areas in the United States. Figure 14.6 summarizes some of the results

from this series of studies. The data in Figure 14.6 indicate that the most common disorders are (1) substance-use disorders, (2) anxiety disorders, and (3) mood disorders (Robins et al., 1984).

The raw numbers are more dramatic than the prevalence rates in Figure 14.6. Estimates based on these prevalence rates suggest that the United States contains nearly 4 million people who will be troubled at some time by schizophrenic disorders, and roughly 20 million people with depressive disorders, 40 million with anxiety disorders, and 42 million with substance-use disorders. If you're thinking that these estimates add up to more than one-third of the population, you're right, but remember that some people have more than one disorder. In any case, it's clear that psychological disorders are widespread. When psychologists note that mental illness can strike anyone, they mean it quite literally.

We're now ready to start examining the specific types of psychological disorders. Obviously, we can't cover all 200 or so disorders listed in DSM-III. However, we'll introduce most of the major categories of disorders to give you an overview of the many forms abnormal behavior takes. Figure 14.7 categorizes the disorders that we'll discuss.

In discussing each set of disorders, we'll begin with brief descriptions of the specific syndromes or subtypes that exist within the category. Then we'll focus on the *etiology* of the disorders in that category. Although there are many paths that can lead to specific disorders, some paths are more common than others. We'll highlight some of the common ones to enhance your understanding of the roots of abnormal behavior.

Figure 14.7 An overview of the disorders covered in the chapter. This outline should help you keep the categories and subcategories organized.

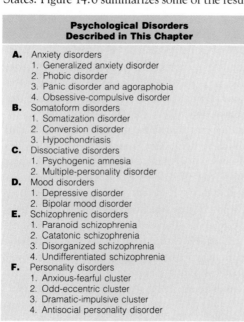

Psychological Disorders Described in This Chapter

A. Anxiety disorders
  1. Generalized anxiety disorder
  2. Phobic disorder
  3. Panic disorder and agoraphobia
  4. Obsessive-compulsive disorder
B. Somatoform disorders
  1. Somatization disorder
  2. Conversion disorder
  3. Hypochondriasis
C. Dissociative disorders
  1. Psychogenic amnesia
  2. Multiple-personality disorder
D. Mood disorders
  1. Depressive disorder
  2. Bipolar mood disorder
E. Schizophrenic disorders
  1. Paranoid schizophrenia
  2. Catatonic schizophrenia
  3. Disorganized schizophrenia
  4. Undifferentiated schizophrenia
F. Personality disorders
  1. Anxious-fearful cluster
  2. Odd-eccentric cluster
  3. Dramatic-impulsive cluster
  4. Antisocial personality disorder

ANXIETY DISORDERS

We all experience anxiety from time to time. Anxiety is a natural and common reaction to many of life's difficulties. For some people, however, anxiety becomes a chronic problem. These people experience high levels of anxiety with disturbing regularity. **Anxiety disorders are a class of disorders marked by feelings of excessive apprehension and anxiety.** Studies suggest that anxiety disorders are fairly common, occurring in roughly 10 to 15% of the population (Robins et al., 1984; Weissman, 1985). There are four principal types of anxiety disorders: the generalized anxiety disorder, phobic disorders, obsessive-compulsive disorders, and panic disorders.

Generalized Anxiety Disorder

The *generalized anxiety disorder* **is marked by a chronic, high level of anxiety that is not tied to any specific threat.** This anxiety is sometimes called "free-floating anxiety" because of its nonspecific nature. People with this disorder worry constantly about yesterday's mistakes and tomorrow's problems. They often dread decisions and brood over them endlessly. Their anxiety is frequently accompanied by physical symptoms, such as trembling, muscle tension, diarrhea, dizziness, faintness, sweating, and heart palpitations.

Phobic Disorder

In phobic disorders an individual's troublesome anxiety has a specific focus. **A *phobic disorder* is marked by a persistent and irrational fear of an object or situation that presents no realistic danger.** The following case provides an example of a phobic disorder.

Hilda is 32 years old and has a rather unusual fear. She's terrified of snow. She can't go outside in the snow. She can't even stand to see snow or to hear about it on the weather report. Her phobia severely restricts her day-to-day behavior. Probing in therapy revealed that her phobia was caused by a traumatic experience at age 11. Playing at a ski lodge, she was buried briefly by a small avalanche of snow. She had no recollection of this experience until it was recovered in therapy. (Adapted from Laughlin, 1967, p. 227)

As Hilda's unusual snow phobia illustrates, people can develop phobic responses to virtually anything. Nonetheless, certain types of phobias are relatively common, including most of those listed in Table 14.1. Particularly common are (1) claustrophobia (fear of small, enclosed places), (2) various animal phobias, and (3) social phobias (fears of humiliation in interpersonal situations). Claustrophobia tends to develop before age 35, animal phobias usually emerge during childhood, and social phobias usually appear during adolescence (Ost, 1987). Many people troubled by phobias realize that their fears are irrational, but they still are unable to calm themselves when confronted by a phobic object.

Panic Disorder and Agoraphobia

A *panic disorder* involves recurrent attacks of overwhelming anxiety that usually occur suddenly and unexpectedly. These paralyzing attacks are accompanied by various physical symptoms of anxiety, which are listed in the detailed description of the *DSM-III-R* criteria for panic disorders shown in Figure 14.3. After a number of anxiety attacks, victims often become very apprehensive, wondering when their next panic will occur. Their concern about exhibiting panic in public may escalate to the point where they're afraid to leave home, which creates a condition called agoraphobia, a common complication of panic disorders.

Agoraphobia is a fear of going out to public places (its literal meaning is "fear of the marketplace"). Because of this fear, some people become "prisoners" confined to their homes. As its name suggests, agoraphobia has traditionally been viewed as a phobic disorder, but recent studies

Table 14.1 Some Types of Phobias

PHOBIA	DEFINITION
Acrophobia	Fear of high places
Androphobia	Fear of men
Aviophobia	Fear of flying
Claustrophobia	Fear of closed or narrow spaces
Hydrophobia	Fear of water
Iatrophobia	Fear of doctors
Lalophobia	Fear of speaking (in public)
Mysophobia	Fear of dirt or contamination
Nyctophobia	Fear of darkness
Ombrophobia	Fear of rain
Pathophobia	Fear of disease
Phobophobia	Fear of fear
Sitophobia	Fear of food
Thanatophobia	Fear of death
Toxophobia	Fear of being poisoned
Xenophobia	Fear of strangers

have shown that agoraphobia shares more kinship with panic disorders than phobic disorders (Turner et al., 1986). Most agoraphobics are women, and the typical age of onset for the disorder is late adolescence or early adulthood (Barlow & Waddell, 1985).

Obsessive-Compulsive Disorder

Obsessions are *thoughts* that repeatedly intrude on one's consciousness in a distressing way. Compulsions are *actions* that one feels forced to carry out. Thus, an *obsessive-compulsive disorder* **is marked by persistent, uncontrollable intrusions of unwanted thoughts (obsessions) and urges to engage in senseless rituals (compulsions).** To illustrate, let's examine the bizarre behavior of a man once reputed to be the wealthiest person in the world.

The famous industrialist Howard Hughes was obsessed with the possibility of being contaminated by germs. This led him to devise extraordinary rituals to minimize the possibility of such contamination. He would spend hours methodically cleaning a single telephone. He once wrote a three-page memo instructing assistants on exactly how to open cans of fruit for him. The following is just a small portion of the instructions that Hughes provided for a driver who delivered films to his bungalow: "Get out of the car on the traffic side. Do not at

As a young man (shown in the photo), Howard Hughes was a handsome, dashing daredevil pilot and movie producer who *appeared* to be reasonably well adjusted. However, as the years went by, his behavior gradually became more and more maladaptive, as obsessions and compulsions came to dominate his life. In his later years (shown in the drawing), he spent most of his time in darkened rooms, naked, unkempt, and dirty, following bizzare rituals to alleviate his anxieties.

any time be on the side of the car between the car and the curb. . . . Carry only one can of film at a time. Step over the gutter opposite the place where the sidewalk dead-ends into the curb from a point as far out into the center of the road as possible. Do not ever walk on the grass at all, also do not step into the gutter at all. Walk to the bungalow keeping as near to the center of the sidewalk as possible. . . ." (Adapted from Barlett & Steele, 1979, pp. 227–237)

Obsessions often center on inflicting harm on others, personal failures, suicide, or sexual acts. People troubled by obsessions may feel that they've lost control of their mind. Compulsions usually involve stereotyped rituals that temporarily relieve anxiety. Common examples include constant handwashing, repetitive cleaning of things that are already clean, endless rechecking of locks, faucets, and such, or unusual rituals intended to bring good luck. Although many of us can be compulsive at times, full-fledged obsessive-compulsive disorders are relatively uncommon (Sturgis, 1984).

Etiology of Anxiety Disorders

Like most psychological disorders, anxiety disorders develop out of complicated interactions involving a variety of factors. Conditioning processes and aspects of child rearing appear especially important, but biological factors may also contribute to anxiety disorders.

BIOLOGICAL FACTORS
A handful of relatively recent studies suggest that there may be a slight genetic predisposition to anxiety disorders (Noyes et al., 1987; Torgersen, 1983). These findings are consistent with a long-discussed theory that inherited differences in autonomic reactivity might make some people more vulnerable than others to anxiety disorders (Martin, 1971). According to this theory, people with high autonomic reactivity are especially likely to develop anxiety-related problems because their bodies "overreact" to the normal, everyday stresses of life.

Thought-provoking connections have also been found between anxiety disorders and a common heart defect. The heart defect is *mitral valve prolapse*, an anatomical defect that makes people prone to heart palpitations, faintness, and chest pain. Pooling the results of the three relevant studies, Agras (1985) calculated that mitral valve prolapse showed up in 40% of anxiety-disorder patients, but only 9% of control group (nonanxious) subjects. This finding suggests that mitral valve prolapse may predispose some people to problems with anxiety.

Figure 14.8 Conditioning as an explanation for phobias. Many phobias appear to be acquired through classical conditioning, as a neutral stimulus becomes paired with an anxiety-arousing stimulus. Once acquired, a phobia may be maintained through operant conditioning: avoidance of the phobic stimulus reduces anxiety, resulting in negative reinforcement.

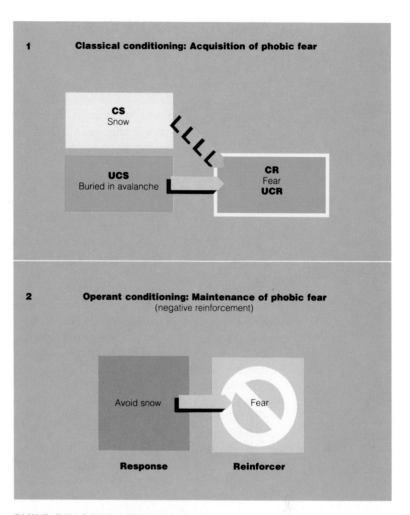

CONDITIONING

As we discussed in Chapter 6, many of our anxiety responses may be *acquired through classical conditioning and maintained through operant conditioning.* According to Mowrer (1947), an originally neutral stimulus (the snow in Hilda's case, for instance) may be paired with a frightening event (the avalanche) so that it becomes a conditioned stimulus eliciting anxiety (this is classical conditioning; see Figure 14.8). Once a conditioned fear is acquired, a person may start avoiding the anxiety-producing stimulus. This avoidance response is negatively reinforced because it's followed by a reduction in unpleasant anxiety (this is operant conditioning; see Figure 14.8). Thus, separate conditioning processes may create and then sustain specific anxiety responses (McAllister et al., 1986).

Our tendency to develop phobias of certain types of objects and situations can be explained by Martin Seligman's (1971) concept of *preparedness.* Like many theorists, Seligman believes that classical conditioning creates most phobic responses. *However, he theorizes that we are biologically prepared by our evolutionary history to acquire some fears much more easily than others.* His theory would explain why we develop phobias of ancient sources of threat (for example, snakes and spiders) much more readily than modern sources of threat (for example, electrical outlets or hot irons). Laboratory studies have provided some support for Seligman's theory of preparedness. Stimuli that humans should be "prepared" to fear produce relatively rapid acquisition of conditioned fear responses (Cook, Hodes, & Lang, 1986) and relatively slow extinction of these responses (Ohman, 1979).

The conditioning model of phobias is undermined by evidence that many people with phobias can't recall or identify a traumatic conditioning experience that led to their phobia (Marks, 1977). However, these failures to recall relevant conditioning experiences could reflect poor memory of childhood trauma, or unconscious repression, as in the case of Hilda's snow phobia. Although the details are still being worked out, there's ample evidence that conditioning often contributes to the development of anxiety disorders.

CHILD-REARING PATTERNS

How we are reared as children may affect our vulnerability to anxiety disorders. There are a variety of ways in which parents can unintentionally foster anxiety in their children. In some cases, children may acquire fears and anxieties through *observational learning* (Bandura & Rosenthal, 1966). For example, if a father hides in a closet every time there's a thunderstorm, his children may acquire their father's fear of storms. Laboratory studies have shown that conditioned fears can be created in animals through observational learning (Mineka & Cook, 1986).

Researchers have also found associations between overprotection by parents and elevated anxiety in their children (Poznanski, 1973). Overprotective parents may make their children feel like the world is a dangerous place. This sense of threat could predispose the children to anxiety reactions later in life. Howard Hughes, for instance, was raised by an extremely overprotective mother. She worried constantly about his health and tried to shelter him from the real world throughout his childhood (Fowler, 1986). She may have planted the seeds for her son's lifelong, chronic anxiety.

Chances are, you've met people who always seem to be complaining about aches, pains, and physical maladies of doubtful authenticity. You may have thought to yourself, "It's all in his head," and concluded that the person exhibited a "psychosomatic" condition. However, as we discussed in Chapter 13, the term psychosomatic is widely misused. **Psychosomatic diseases are physical ailments with a genuine organic basis that are caused in part by psychological factors.** These diseases, which include maladies such as ulcers, asthma, and high blood pressure, are recorded on the *DSM* axis for physical problems (Axis III). When physical illness appears *entirely* psychological in origin, we're dealing with somatoform disorders, which are recorded on Axis I. **Somatoform disorders are a class of disorders involving physical ailments with no authentic organic basis that are due to psychological factors.** Although their symptoms are more imaginary than real, victims of somatoform disorders are *not* simply faking illness. Deliberate feigning of illness for personal gain is another matter altogether, called *malingering*.

People with somatoform disorders typically seek treatment from physicians practicing neurology, internal medicine, and family medicine, instead of psychologists or psychiatrists. Making accurate diagnoses of somatoform disorders can be difficult because the causes of physical ailments are sometimes hard to identify. In some cases, an inaccurate diagnosis of somatoform disorder is made because a genuine organic cause for a person's physical symptoms goes undetected in spite of extensive medical examinations and tests. One

study found that 20 to 30% of patients given a somatoform diagnosis were later shown to have a genuine physical ailment that was related to their previously unexplained symptoms (Rubin, Zorumski, & Guze, 1986). Some physicians, when unable to identify an organic cause for a patient's complaints, may be overly likely to jump to the conclusion that the patient's problem is entirely psychological.

Diagnostic difficulties make it hard to obtain sound data on the prevalence of somatoform disorders, but they appear to be fairly common. We'll discuss three specific types of somatoform disorders: somatization disorders, conversion disorders, and hypochondriasis. Table 14.2 summarizes the similarities and differences among these disorders and psychosomatic diseases.

Somatization Disorder

Individuals with somatization disorders are often said to "cling to ill health." **A somatization disorder is marked by a history of diverse physical complaints that appear to be psychological in origin.** Somatization disorders occur mostly in women. Victims report an endless succession of minor physical ailments. They usually have a long and complicated history of medical treatment from many doctors. The distinguishing feature of this disorder is the diversity of victims' physical complaints. Over the years, they report a series of cardiovascular, gastrointestinal, pulmonary, neurological, and genitourinary symptoms, which eventually implicate nearly every organ system in the body. The unlikely nature of such a smorgas-

Table 14.2 Comparisons of Three Somatoform Disorders and Psychosomatic Diseases

CONDITION	PHYSICAL COMPLAINTS	ORGANIC BASIS	PSYCHOLOGICAL BASIS	TYPICAL SYMPTOM PATTERN	TYPICAL EXAMPLES
Psychosomatic diseases	Yes	Yes	Yes*	Varied stress-related diseases	Ulcers, high blood pressure
Somatization disorders	Yes	No	Yes	History of minor symptoms in many organ systems	Vague complaints of back pain, chest pain, dizziness
Conversion disorders	Yes	No	Yes	Major loss of function in a single organ system	Hysterical paralysis, glove anesthesia
Hypochondriasis	Yes	No	Yes	Preoccupation with health concerns	Unwarranted fear of infection

*The psychological component in diseases that are usually psychosomatic may be minimal in some cases.

Figure 14.9 Glove anesthesia. In conversion disorders, the physical complaints are sometimes inconsistent with the known facts of physiology. For instance, given the patterns of nerve distribution in the arm shown in (**a**), it is impossible that a loss of feeling in the hand exclusively (as shown in **b**) has a physical cause, indicating that the patient's problem is psychological in origin.

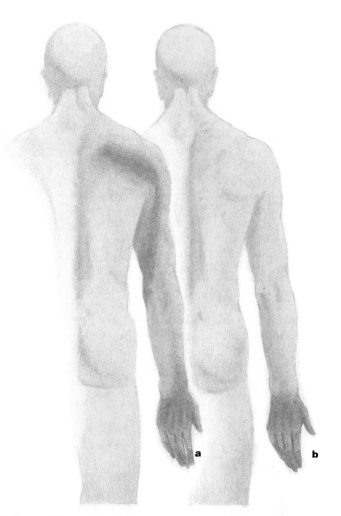

bord of symptoms is a key diagnostic clue that can alert a physician that the basis for the patient's problems may be psychological.

Conversion Disorder

Conversion disorder **involves a significant loss of physical function (with no apparent organic basis), usually in a single organ system.** Common symptoms include partial or complete loss of vision, partial or complete loss of hearing, partial paralysis, severe laryngitis or mutism, and loss of feeling or function in limbs, such as that seen in the following case.

Mildred was a rancher's daughter who lost the use of both of her legs during adolescence. Mildred was at home alone one afternoon when a male relative attempted to assault her. She screamed for help, and her legs gave way as she slipped to the floor. She was found on the floor a few minutes later when her mother returned home. She couldn't get up, so she was carried to her bed. Later, when she tried to walk on her own, her legs buckled. Due to her illness, she was waited on hand and foot by her family and friends. Neighbors brought her homemade things to eat or to wear. She became the center of attention in the household. (Adapted from Cameron, 1963, pp. 312–313)

People with conversion disorders are usually troubled by more severe ailments than people with somatization disorders. In some cases of conversion disorder, the telltale clue to the psychological origin of the illness is that the patient's symptoms are not consistent with medical knowledge about their apparent disease. For instance, the loss of feeling in one hand seen in "glove anesthesia" is inconsistent with the known facts of neurological organization (see Figure 14.9).

Hypochondriasis

Hypochondriacs constantly monitor their physical condition, looking for signs of illness. Any tiny alteration from their physical norm leads them to conclude that they've contracted a disease. *Hypochondriasis* **(more widely known as hypochondria) involves excessive preoccupation with health concerns and incessant worry about developing physical illnesses.** The following case illustrates the nature of hypochondria.

Jeff is a middle-aged man who works as a clerk in a drug store. He spends long hours describing his health problems to anyone who will listen. Jeff is an avid reader of popular magazine articles on medicine. He can tell you all about the latest medical discoveries. He takes all sorts of pills and vitamins to ward off possible illnesses. He's the first to try every new product on the market. Jeff is constantly afflicted with new symptoms of illness. His most recent problems were poor digestion and a heartbeat that he thought was irregular. He frequently goes to physicians, who can find nothing wrong with him physically. They tell him that he's healthy. He thinks they use "backward techniques," and he suspects that his illness is too rare to be diagnosed successfully. (Adapted from Suinn, 1984, p. 236)

When hypochondriacs are assured by their physicians that they don't have any real illness, they are often skeptical and disbelieving. As in Jeff's case, they frequently assume that the physician must be incompetent, and they go shopping for another doctor. Hypochondriacs don't subjectively suffer from physical distress as much as they *overinterpret* every conceivable sign of illness. Hypochondria often appears alongside other psychological disorders, especially anxiety disorders and depression (Turner, Jacob, & Morrison, 1984). For example, Howard Hughes's obsessive-

Check your understanding of the nature of anxiety and somatoform disorders by making very preliminary diagnoses for the cases described below. Read each case summary and write your tentative diagnosis in the space provided. The answers are in Appendix A.

1. Morris religiously follows an exact schedule every day. His showering and grooming ritual takes 2 hours. He follows the same path in walking to his classes every day, and he always sits in the same seat in each class. He can't study until his apartment is arranged perfectly. Although he tries not to, he thinks constantly about flunking out of school. Both his grades and his social life are suffering from his rigid routines.

Preliminary diagnosis: _____

2. Jane has been unemployed for the last 8 years because of poor health. She has suffered through a bizarre series of illnesses of mysterious origins. Troubles with devastating headaches were followed by months of chronic back pain. Then she developed respiratory problems, frequently gasping for breath. Her current problem is stomach pain. Physicians have been unable to find any physical basis for her maladies.

Preliminary diagnosis: _____

3. Nathan owns a small restaurant that's in deep financial trouble. He dreads facing the possibility that his restaurant will fail. One day, he suddenly loses all feeling in his right arm and the ability to control the arm. He's hospitalized for his condition, but physicians can't find any organic cause for his arm trouble.

Preliminary diagnosis: _____

compulsive disorder was coupled with profound hypochondria.

Etiology of Somatoform Disorders

The available evidence suggests that somatoform disorders are largely a function of personality and learning, although inherited aspects of physiological functioning may predispose people to these disorders (Jacob & Turner, 1984). Let's look at personality factors first.

PERSONALITY FACTORS
People with certain types of personality traits seem to be particularly likely to develop somatoform disorders. The prime candidates are people with *histrionic* personality characteristics (Nemiah, 1985). The histrionic personality tends to be self-centered, suggestible, excitable, highly emotional, and overly dramatic. Such people thrive on the attention that they get when they become ill.

REINFORCEMENT OF THE SICK ROLE
As we discussed in the previous chapter, some people grow fond of the role associated with being sick (Pilowsky, 1978). Their complaints of physical symptoms may be reinforced by indirect benefits derived from their illness. What are the benefits commonly associated with physical illness? One payoff is that becoming ill is a superb way to avoid having to confront life's challenges. Many people with somatoform disorders are avoiding facing up to marital problems, career frustrations, family responsibilities, and so on. After all, when you're sick, others can't place very great demands upon you.

Attention from others is another payoff that may reinforce complaints of physical illness. When people become ill, they command the attention of family, friends, coworkers, neighbors, and doctors. The sympathy that illness often brings may strengthen a person's tendency to feel ill. This clearly occurred in Mildred's case of conversion disorder. Her illness paid handsome dividends in terms of attention, consolation, and kindhearted assistance from others.

DISSOCIATIVE DISORDERS

Dissociative disorders are among the more unusual syndromes that we'll discuss. **Dissociative disorders are a class of disorders in which people lose contact with portions of their consciousness or memory, resulting in disruptions in their sense of identity.** These exotic and fascinating disorders are highly publicized, leading people to think that they are common, but in reality they are relatively rare. We'll describe two dissociative syndromes, psychogenic amnesia and multiple-personality disorder.

Psychogenic Amnesia

In our chapter on memory (Chapter 7), we discussed cases of amnesia caused by organic brain damage. However, pathological memory losses can also be caused by psychological factors, resulting in a syndrome called "psychogenic" amnesia. **Psychogenic amnesia is a sudden loss of memory for important personal information that is too extensive to be due to normal forgetting.** Memory losses in psychogenic amnesia may cover anything from a few hours to an entire lifetime, although the latter is rare.

Psychogenic amnesias differ from organic amnesias in that the memory losses center around one's identity or around a specific disturbing incident. When identity-related memory losses occur, people may forget their name, their family, where they live, and where they work. In spite of this wholesale forgetting, they remember matters unrelated to their identity, such as how to drive a car, the square root of 9, and the capital of the United States. When memory losses center around a traumatic incident (such as an automobile accident or a home fire), the person usually has a blank memory for the incident itself and events occurring in the next several hours to several days.

Multiple-Personality Disorder

Multiple-personality disorder involves the coexistence in one person of two or more largely complete, and usually very different, personalities. In multiple-personality disorders, the divergences in behavior go far beyond those that people normally display in adapting to different roles in life. People with multiple personality feel that they have more than one identity. Each personality has its own name, memories, traits, and physical mannerisms. Although rare, this "Dr. Jekyl and Mr. Hyde" syndrome is frequently portrayed in novels, movies, and television shows. In popular media portrayals, the syndrome is often referred to mistakenly as *schizophrenia*, but as you'll see later, schizophrenic disorders are entirely different.

In a multiple-personality disorder, the original personality often is not aware of the alternate personalities. In contrast, the alternate personalities usually are aware of the original one and have varying amounts of awareness of each other. The alternate personalities frequently display traits that are quite foreign to the original personality. For instance, a shy, inhibited person might develop a flamboyant, extraverted alternate personality. Transitions between personalities often occur suddenly, as in the following case.

Dazed and confused, Eric was found wandering about a Florida shopping mall. Admitted to a nearby psychiatric facility, the 29-year-old man soon began talking to doctors in two voices representing younger and older versions of Eric. One day his face twisted into a snarl and he started screaming out a series of obscenities. A new, insolent personality, demanding to be called Mark, had surfaced. In the ensuing months, he gradually unveiled 27 different personalities. They ranged in age from a fetus to an old man. They even included

three females. His personalities interact, but they don't necessarily get along very well. For instance, a pushy personality named Michael ripped the wires out of Eric's stereo so that he couldn't play any more classical music (Michael likes rock). One personality obsessed with athletics insisted on jogging 15 miles, much to the dismay of the other personalities, who had to use the same sore, worn-out body. (Adapted from Leo, 1982)

Starting in the 1980s, there was a dramatic increase in the diagnosis of multiple-personality disorders (Braun, 1986). Some theorists believe that multiple-personality disorders used to be underdiagnosed; that is, they frequently went undetected (Kluft, 1987). Other skeptics argue that a handful of clinicians began overdiagnosing the condition in the 1980s (Thigpen & Cleckley, 1984). The debate about the reason for the sudden upsurge in multiple-personality diagnoses is far from settled and probably won't be resolved without a great deal of additional research.

Etiology of Dissociative Disorders

Psychogenic amnesia is usually attributed to excessive stress, but relatively little is known about why this extreme reaction to stress occurs in certain people but not others. The causes of multiple-personality disorders are equally obscure. Some skeptical theorists believe that people with multiple personalities are engaging in intentional role playing to gain attention and to use mental illness as a face-saving excuse for their personal failings (Spanos, Weekes, & Bertrand, 1985). Indeed, there's evidence that multiple-personality disorders are faked with some regularity. However, various lines of evidence suggest to most theorists that at least some cases are authentic (Aalpoel & Lewis, 1984).

Multiple-personality disorders seem to be rooted in severe emotional trauma occurring during childhood. A substantial portion of people with this disorder have a history of disturbed home life, beatings and rejection from parents, sexual abuse, and forced repression of emotions (Aalpoel & Lewis, 1984). Such histories suggest that the emergence of multiple personalities might represent a person's desperate effort to deal with fundamental identity conflicts. The problem with this insight is that there are legions of people who struggle with identity conflicts and never develop multiple personalities.

The lack of research and information on multiple personality disorders stands in stark contrast to the wealth of information available on mood disorders, which are far more common. We examine the nature and causes of mood disorders in the next section.

MOOD DISORDERS

What did Abraham Lincoln, Marilyn Monroe, Ernest Hemingway, Winston Churchill, Janis Joplin, and Leo Tolstoy have in common? Yes, they all achieved great prominence, albeit in different ways at different times. But, more pertinent to our interest, they all suffered from severe mood disorders. Although mood disorders can be terribly debilitating, people with mood disorders can still achieve greatness, because such disorders tend to be *episodic*. In other words, emotional disorders often come and go, so that episodes of disturbance alternate with periods of normality.

Of course, we all have our ups and downs in terms of mood. Life would be dull indeed if our emotional tone was constant. All of us experience depression occasionally. Likewise, all of us have days that we sail through on an emotional high. Such emotional fluctuations are natural, but some people are prone to extreme distortions of mood. **Mood disorders are a class of disorders marked by emotional disturbances that may spill over to disrupt physical, perceptual, social, and thought processes.**

There are two basic types of mood disorders: unipolar and bipolar (see Figure 14.10). People with *unipolar disorders* experience emotional extremes at just one end of the mood continuum, as they are troubled only by *depression*. On the average, people troubled by recurrent depression go through three or four such episodes in their life-

time (Goodwin & Jamison, 1986). People with *bipolar disorders* experience emotional extremes at both ends of the mood continuum, going through periods of both *depression and mania* (excitement and elation). The mood swings in bipolar disorders can be patterned in many different ways, and people with bipolar mood disorders tend to go through more episodes of illness than those with unipolar disorders.

Recent studies suggest that periods of emotional disturbance may follow a seasonal pattern in some people. **In a *seasonal affective (mood) disorder* an individual's periods of depression or mania tend to repeatedly occur at about the same time of the year** (and are not associated with obvious seasonal variations in stress, such as seasonal unemployment). A seasonal pattern may be seen in either unipolar or bipolar disorders. The most common pattern appears to be recurrent depression in the fall and winter, alternating with normal or manic periods in the spring and summer (Rosenthal et al., 1986). Researchers suspect that seasonal patterns in mood disorders are tied to human biological rhythms that are presumably affected by exposure to daylight, which varies according to the time of year (Wehr et al., 1986). Evidence on these hypothesized relations between our biological rhythms and our vulnerability to emotional disturbance is still fragmentary and needs to be bolstered by additional studies.

Figure 14.10 Episodic patterns in mood disorders. Time-limited episodes of emotional disturbance come and go unpredictably in mood disorders. People with unipolar disorders suffer from bouts of depression only, while people with bipolar disorders experience both manic and depressed episodes. The time between episodes of disturbance varies greatly with the individual and the type of disorder.

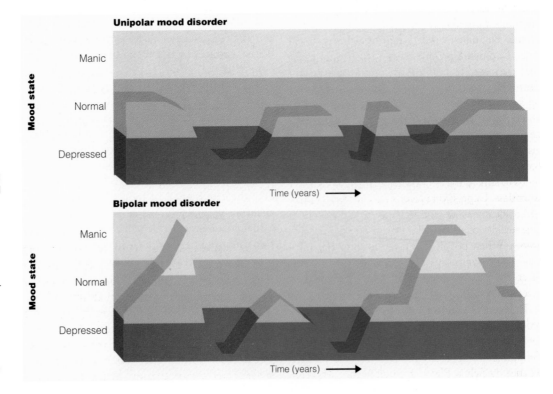

Table 14.3 Comparison of Common Symptoms in Manic and Depressive Episodes

CHARACTERISTICS	MANIC EPISODE	DEPRESSIVE EPISODE
Emotional	Elated, euphoric, very sociable, impatient at any hindrance	Gloomy, hopeless, socially withdrawn, irritable
Cognitive	Characterized by racing thoughts, flight of ideas, desire for action, and impulsive behavior; talkative, self-confident; experiencing delusions of grandeur	Characterized by slowness of thought processes, obsessive worrying, inability to make decisions, negative self-image, self-blame, and delusions of guilt and disease
Motor	Hyperactive, tireless, requiring less sleep than usual, showing increased sex drive and fluctuating appetite	Less active, tired, experiencing difficulty in sleeping, showing decreased sex drive and decreased appetite

Source: I. G. Sarason & B. R. Sarason, 1987

Depressive Disorder

It can be very difficult to draw the line between normal and abnormal depression. Ultimately, a subjective judgment is required. Crucial considerations in this judgment include the duration of the depression and its disruptive effects. When a depression significantly impairs everyday adaptive behavior for more than a few weeks, there's reason for concern.

In *depressive disorders* **people show persistent feelings of sadness and despair and a loss of interest in previous sources of pleasure.** Negative emotions form the heart of the depressive syndrome, but many other symptoms may also appear. Depressed people often give up activities that they used to find enjoyable. For example, a depressed person might quit going bowling or give up a favorite hobby like photography. Insomnia and reduced appetite are common. People with depression often lack energy—they move sluggishly and talk slowly. Anxiety, irritability, and brooding are frequently observed, and self-esteem tends to sink as the depressed person begins to feel worthless. Depression plunges people into feelings of hopelessness, dejection, and boundless guilt. The severity of abnormal depression varies considerably. When people display persistent but relatively mild symptoms of depression that do not meet the criteria for major depression, they're given a diagnosis of *dysthymic disorder*.

The most common symptoms of depressive disorders are summarized and compared to the symptoms of mania in Table 14.3. Many of these symptoms are apparent in the following passage written by Sylvia Plath, a gifted author who suffered from depression and eventually committed suicide:

I hadn't washed my hair for three weeks. I hadn't slept for seven nights. My mother told me I must have slept, it was impossible not to sleep in all that time, but if I slept, it was with my eyes wide open. . . . The reason I hadn't washed my clothes or my hair was because it seemed so silly. I saw the days of the year stretching ahead like a series of bright, white boxes, and separating one box from another was sleep, like a black shade. Only for me, the long perspective of shades that set off one box from the next had suddenly snapped up, and I could see day after day after day glaring ahead of me like a white, broad, infinitely desolate avenue. It seemed silly to wash one day when I would only have to wash again the next. It made me tired just to think of it. (Excerpted from Plath, 1971, pp. 142–143)

How common are depressive disorders? Very common. The ECA studies using *DSM-III* diagnostic criteria suggest that about 6 to 8% of the population endures a unipolar depressive disorder at some point in time (Robins, et al., 1984). The onset of unipolar disorder occurs throughout the life span and is *not* strongly related to age (Lewinsohn et al., 1986).

Bipolar Mood Disorder

Bipolar mood disorders **(formerly known as manic-depressive disorders) are marked by the experience of both depressed and manic periods.** The symptoms seen in manic periods generally are the opposite of those seen in depression (see Table 14.3 for a comparison). In a manic episode a person's mood becomes elevated to the point of euphoria. Self-esteem skyrockets as the person bubbles over with optimism, energy, and extravagant plans. People become hyperactive and may go for days without sleep. They talk rapidly and shift topics wildly, as their mind races at breakneck speed. Judgment is often impaired, and some people in manic periods gamble impulsively, spend money frantically, or become sexually reckless. Like depressive disorders, bipolar disorders vary considerably in severity. When people display persistent but relatively mild symptoms of a bipolar mood disturbance, they're given a diagnosis of *cyclothymic disorder*.

You may be thinking that the euphoria in manic episodes sounds appealing. If so, you're not entirely wrong. In their milder forms, manic states can seem attractive. The increases in energy, self-esteem, and optimism can be deceptively seductive. Because of the increase in energy, many bipolar patients report temporary surges of productivity and creativity (Jamison et al., 1980).

Although there may be some positive aspects to manic episodes, bipolar mood disorders ultimately prove to be very troublesome and terrifying for most victims. Manic periods often have a paradoxical negative undertow of uneasiness and irritability. Moreover, mild manic episodes usually escalate to higher levels that become scary and disturbing. Impaired judgment leads many victims to do things that they greatly regret later. You'll see an example of such a situation in the following case history of an individual with a bipolar disorder.

Robert, a dentist, awoke one morning with the idea that he was the most gifted dental surgeon in his tri-state area. He decided that he should try to provide services to as many people as possible, so that more people could benefit from his talents. Thus, he decided to remodel his two-chair dental office, installing 20 booths so that he could simultaneously attend to 20 patients. That same day he drew up plans for this arrangement, telephoned a number of remodelers, and invited bids for the work. Later that day, impatient to get rolling on his remodeling, he rolled up his sleeves, got himself a sledgehammer, and began to knock down the walls in his office. Annoyed when that didn't go so well, he smashed his dental tools, washbasins, and X-ray equipment. Later, Robert's wife became concerned about his behavior and summoned two of her adult daughters for assistance. The daughters responded quickly, arriving at the family home with their husbands. In the ensuing discussion, Robert—after bragging about his sexual prowess—made advances toward his daughters. He had to be subdued by their husbands. (Adapted from Kleinmuntz, 1980, p. 309)

Although not rare, bipolar disorders are much less common than unipolar depression. Bipolar disorders affect a little under 1% of the population (Boyd & Weissman, 1986). The onset of bipolar disorders is age related, with the peak of vulnerability occurring between the ages of 24 and 31 (Murphy, 1980).

Etiology of Mood Disorders

We know quite a bit about the etiology of mood disorders, although the puzzle hasn't been assembled completely. There appear to be a number of routes into these disorders, involving intricate interactions between psychological and biological factors.

GENETIC VULNERABILITY

The evidence strongly suggests that genetic factors influence one's likelihood of developing major depression or a bipolar mood disorder. In studies that assess the impact of heredity on psychological disorders, investigators look at *concordance rates* instead of the usual correlations. **A concordance rate indicates the percentage of twin pairs or other pairs of relatives that exhibit the same disorder.** If closely related relatives show higher concordance rates than more distant relatives, this finding suggests that genetic factors influence the disorder under scrutiny. Both twin and family studies of mood disorders support the genetic hypothesis (Nurnberger & Gershon, 1982). In twin studies, for example, concordance rates average around 65% for identical twins, but only 14% for fraternal twins, who share less genetic similarity (see Figure 14.11).

In a recent, widely heralded study, a research team headed by Janice Egeland has linked genetic material on a specific chromosome to bipolar mood disorder in a sample of Amish families (Egeland et al., 1987). The Amish group under study has kept exceptionally accurate genealogical records since the 1700s. Scrutiny of these records revealed that *all* 32 of the people in the current sample who exhibit a bipolar disorder have extensive family histories of this disorder going back many generations. One affected family of 81 relatives agreed to donate blood so that Egeland's team could examine the DNA structure of family members' chromosomes. The researchers found a specific gene segment on chromosome 11 that ap-

Figure 14.11 Twin studies of mood disorders. The concordance rate for mood disorders in identical twins is much higher than that for fraternal twins, who share less genetic overlap. These results suggest that there must be a genetic predisposition to at least some mood disorders. (Data from Nurnberger & Gershon, 1982)

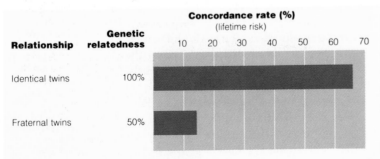

Relationship	Genetic relatedness	Concordance rate (%) (lifetime risk)
Identical twins	100%	
Fraternal twins	50%	

pears to transmit vulnerability to bipolar illness in this family.

Many experts feel that the Egeland et al. (1987) study is a major breakthrough. For instance, Darrel Regier, a director of the ECA studies on the epidemiology of mental disorders, asserts that this study "ushers in a new era of psychiatric research" (Hostetler, 1987, p. 16). Regier's enthusiasm is understandable, but these highly publicized findings should be interpreted cautiously.

Egeland's findings do *not* mean that a single gene leads to direct inheritance of bipolar disorders. Several sources of evidence, including the Egeland study, suggest that people inherit a *heightened vulnerability* to this disorder, not the disorder itself. In the Egeland study, only 63% of the family members who were "carriers" of the implicated gene segment exhibited bipolar illness. Thus, heredity creates a *predisposition* to mood disorders. Environmental factors probably determine whether this predisposition is converted into an actual disorder.

There also are reasons to be concerned about the generality of Egeland's results. The critical gene segment was identified in just one family, and that family is part of an unusually "closed" gene pool (few people marry into this Amish group). Two similar studies of other groups have failed to find a link between chromosome 11 and bipolar disorder (Hodgkinson et al., 1987; Detera-Wadleigh et al., 1987). Thus, vulnerability to mood disorders may be carried on entirely different chromosomes in different families. Many researchers in behavioral genetics predict that *many* genes will eventually be implicated as contributors to a predisposition for mood disorders. We have to conclude that we still have a long way to go before we fully understand the genetic basis for bipolar illness. However, addi-

Amish families, such as those studied by Egeland et al. (1987), offer two advantages in research on the inheritance of psychological disorders—they keep unusually thorough genealogical records, and they have a relatively "closed" gene pool because few outsiders marry into their group. The Egeland et al. study found a link between bipolar mood disorder and a specific chromosome in an Amish group, but additional research with other samples is needed to fully understand the genetic roots of mood disorders.

tional clues may come from studies relating brain chemistry to mood disorders, which we'll examine next.

NEUROCHEMICAL FACTORS

Heredity may influence susceptibility to mood disorders by creating a predisposition toward certain types of neuorochemical activity in the brain. As you learned in Chapter 3, secretions of chemical substances known as *neurotransmitters* permit neurons to communicate with each other. Correlations have been found between mood disorders and levels of three bioamine transmitters in the brain (norepinephrine, serotonin, and dopamine). *Norepinephrine* (NE) levels appear to be most critical, but investigators believe that mood disorders may be caused by intricate interactions between the bioamine neurotransmitters and perhaps other brain chemicals. Recent studies summarized by Schildkraut, Green, and Mooney (1985) suggest that altered neurotransmitter *release* may not be as important as changes in the sensitivity of the synaptic *receptors* that the neurotransmitters bind to (see Figure 14.12).

Although the details remain elusive, there's little doubt that there is a neurochemical basis for at

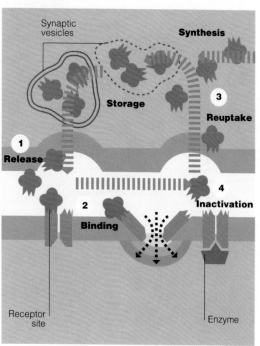

Figure 14.12 Hypotheses about the neurochemical bases for depression. Complex interactions involving several neurotransmitters have been implicated as factors in depression, but the most consistent finding is that depression appears to be associated with lowered levels of activation at norepinephrine (NE) synapses. Originally, it was assumed that the reduction in NE activity was due to decreased release of NE (**1**), but more recent studies suggest that alterations in the sensitivity of NE receptors (**2**) may also play a role. The hypothesis linking low NE levels to depression is also supported by evidence that both major classes of antidepressant drugs increase NE levels. Tricyclic antidepressants appear to inhibit reuptake (**3**), leaving more NE in the synapse, and MAO inhibitors seem to slow the inactivation of NE (**4**)

least some mood disorders. A variety of drug therapies are quite effective in the treatment of severe mood disorders. Most of these drugs are known to affect the availability (in the brain) of the neurotransmitters that have been implicated in mood disorders (Zis & Goodwin, 1982). This kind of drug action is unlikely to be a coincidence, and it bolsters the plausibility of the idea that neurochemical changes produce mood disturbances.

If alterations in neurotransmitter activity are the basis for many mood disorders, what causes the alterations in neurotransmitter activity? These neurochemical changes probably depend on our reactions to environmental events. Thus, a number of psychological factors have been implicated in the etiology of mood disorders. We'll examine evidence on patterns of thinking, interpersonal style, and stress.

COGNITIVE FACTORS: ATTRIBUTIONAL STYLE

A variety of theories emphasize how cognitive factors contribute to depressive disorders (Abramson, Metalsky, & Alloy, 1988; Beck, 1976; Ellis, 1962; Seligman, 1983). In recent years, theories that focus on our patterns of *attribution* have generated a great deal of research on the cognitive roots of depression. Perhaps you're wondering what an attribution is. **Attributions are inferences that people draw about the causes of events, others' behavior, and their own behavior.** We routinely make attributions because we want to *understand* our personal fates and the events that take place around us. For example, if your boss criticizes your work, you'll probably ask yourself why. Was your work really that sloppy? Was your boss just in a grouchy mood? Was the criticism a manipulative effort to motivate you to work harder? Each of these potential explanations is an attribution.

Attributions can be analyzed along a number of dimensions. Three important dimensions are illustrated in Figure 14.13. The most prominent dimension is the degree to which we attribute events to *internal, personal factors versus external, situational factors*. For instance, if you performed poorly on the Graduate Record Exam (GRE) Mathematics subtest (a critical admissions test for entrance into graduate school), you might attribute your poor showing to your lack of intelligence (an internal attribution) or to the horrible heat and humidity in the exam room (an external attribution).

Another key dimension is the degree to which we attribute events to factors that are *stable or unstable over time*. Thus, you might blame your

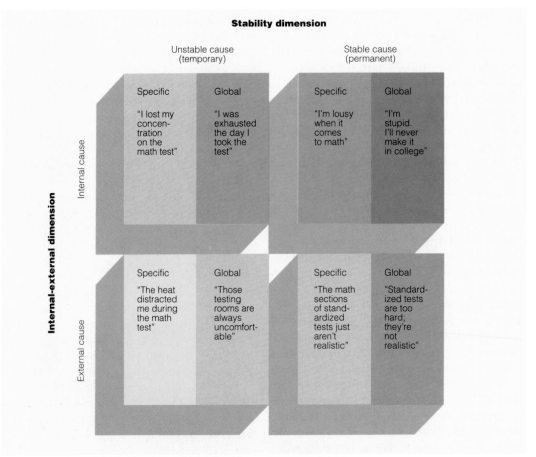

Figure 14.13 Attributional style and depression. Possible attributions for poor performance on a standardized math exam are shown here. Note how the explanations in each cell vary in terms of whether causes are seen as internal or external, stable or unstable, and specific or global. People who consistently explain their failures with internal, stable, and global attributions are particularly vulnerable to depression (hence, the deeper the color in the cell, the more depressing the attribution tends to be).

Stability dimension

Unstable cause (temporary) | Stable cause (permanent)

Internal-external dimension

Internal cause

Specific — "I lost my concentration on the math test"

Global — "I was exhausted the day I took the test"

Specific — "I'm lousy when it comes to math"

Global — "I'm stupid. I'll never make it in college"

External cause

Specific — "The heat distracted me during the math test"

Global — "Those testing rooms are always uncomfortable"

Specific — "The math sections of standardized tests just aren't realistic"

Global — "Standardized tests are too hard; they're not realistic"

poor test performance on exhaustion (an internal but unstable factor that could change next time) or on your low intelligence (an internal but stable factor). Some theorists are also interested in still another dimension—the degree to which our attributions have *global versus specific implications*. Thus, you might attribute your low test score to your lack of intelligence (which has very general, global implications) or your poor math ability (which has implications specific to math). Figure 14.13 provides additional examples of attributions that might be made for poor test performance.

Theories that link attribution to depression are interested in the *attributional style* that people display. In comparison to nondepressed individuals, depressed people *tend to make internal, stable, and global attributions for negative events and external, unstable, and specific attributions for positive events* (Robins, 1988; Sweeney, Anderson, & Bailey, 1986). In making internal, stable, and global attributions for negative events, people tend to blame their setbacks on personal inadequacies (internal) that they see as unchangeable (stable) and draw far-reaching conclusions (global) about their lack of worth as a human being. In other words, they draw depressing conclusions about themselves.

Thus, cognitive models of depression maintain that it's negative thinking that makes many people feel helpless, hopeless, and dejected. The principal problem with cognitive theories is their difficulty in separating cause from effect (see Figure 14.14). Does negative thinking cause depression? Or does depression cause negative thinking? Could both be caused by a third variable, such as neurochemical changes? Evidence can be mustered to support all three of these possibilities, suggesting that negative thinking, depression, and neurochemical alterations may feed off each other as a depression deepens.

Ironically, depressed individuals' negative thinking may be more *realistic* that nondepressed individuals' more positive thinking. This unexpected possibility first surfaced when Lauren Alloy and Lyn Abramson (1979) asked depressed and nondepressed subjects to work on a laboratory task in which the subjects estimated how much their responses (pressing or not pressing a button) influenced certain outcomes (turning on a light, winning money). As expected, the depressed subjects estimated that they had less control over the outcomes than the nondepressed subjects. However, this difference occurred because the nondepressed subjects overestimated their control, whereas the depressed subjects made fairly accurate estimates. Since then, numerous studies have shown that depressed subjects' self-evaluations,

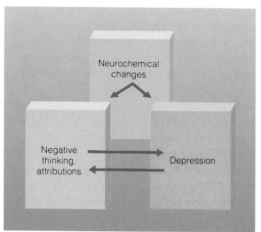

Figure 14.14 Interpreting the correlation between negative thinking and depression. Cognitive theories of depression assert that consistent patterns of negative thinking cause depression. Although these theories are highly plausible, depression could cause negative thoughts, or both could be caused by a third factor, such as neurochemical changes in the brain.

recall of feedback from others, and predictions of future outcomes tend to be more realistic than those made by nondepressed subjects (Alloy & Abramson, 1988). Thus, depressed individuals may not be overly pessimistic as much as nondepressed individuals are overly optimistic.

INTERPERSONAL ROOTS

Behavioral approaches to understanding depression emphasize that inadequate social skills put people on the road to depressive disorders (Lewinsohn, 1974). According to this notion, depression-prone people lack the social finesse needed to acquire many important kinds of interpersonal reinforcers, such as good friends, top jobs, and desirable spouses. This paucity of reinforcers could understandably lead to negative emotions and depression. Consistent with this theory, researchers have found correlations between poor social skills and depression (Blechman et al., 1986).

Another interpersonal factor that complicates depression is that depressed people tend to be depressing! Individuals suffering from depression often complain a lot, and they aren't very enjoyable companions. In a study by Coyne (1976), college women were asked to interact with both depressed and nondepressed females, whom they later evaluated. Depressed women were evaluated much more negatively by the subjects than were nondepressed women. Moreover, Coyne found that the subjects' own mood became more negative after talking to depressed individuals. Thus, depression, like other emotions, can be contagious. This "contagion" creates a tendency for people to reject and avoid depressed individuals, leaving depressed people with fewer sources of social support than nondepressed people (Billings, Cronkite, & Moos, 1983). In turn, this social rejection and lack of support may aggravate and deepen a person's depression (Klerman & Weissman, 1986).

PRECIPITATING STRESS

Mood disorders sometimes appear mysteriously "out of nowhere" in people who are leading benign, nonstressful lives. For this reason, experts used to believe that mood disorders were not influenced much by environmental stress. However, recent advances in the measurement of personal stress have altered this picture. The evidence available today suggests that there's a moderately strong link between stress and the onset of depression (Carson & Carson, 1984; Hammen et al., 1986). There is less evidence of a relationship between stress and bipolar illness, although one recent study of 50 manic patients found that 66% had experienced significant life stress in the month before the onset of their mania (Ambelas, 1987).

Stress seems to act as a precipitating factor that triggers depression in some people. Of course, many people endure great stress without getting depressed. The impact of stress varies, in part, because different people have different degrees of *vulnerability* to mood disorders. Variations in vulnerability appear to depend primarily on one's biological makeup. Similar interactions between stress and vulnerability probably influence the development of many kinds of disorders, including those that are next on our agenda—the schizophrenic disorders.

SCHIZOPHRENIC DISORDERS

Literally, *schizophrenia* means "split mind," but when Eugen Bleuler coined the term in 1911, he was referring to the fragmenting of thought processes seen in the disorder—not a "split-personality." Unfortunately, writers in the popular media often assume that the split-mind notion refers to the rare syndrome in which a person manifests two or more personalities. As you've already learned, the correct term for this syndrome is *multiple-personality disorder*. Schizophrenia is a much more common, and altogether different, type of disorder.

***Schizophrenic disorders* are a class of disorders marked by disturbances in thought that spill over to affect perceptual, social, and emotional processes.** People with schizophrenic disorders often display some of the same symptoms seen in people with severe psychotic mood disorders. However, disturbed *thought* lies at the the core of schizophrenic disorders, whereas disturbed *emotion* lies at the core of mood disorders.

How common is schizophrenia? Prevalence estimates suggest that about 0.5% to 1.5% of the population may suffer from schizophrenic disorders (Gottesman & Shields, 1982; Robins et al., 1984). That may not sound like much, but it means that in the United States alone, there may be 3 or 4 million people troubled by schizophrenic disturbances.

General Symptoms of Schizophrenia

There are a number of distinct schizophrenic syndromes, but they all share some general characteristics that we'll examine before looking at the subtypes. Many of these characteristics are apparent in the following case history.

Sylvia was first diagnosed as schizophrenic at age 15. She has been in and out of many different types of psychiatric facilities since then. She has never been able to hold a job for any length of time. During severe flare-ups of her disorder, her personal hygiene deteriorates. She rarely washes, she wears clothes that neither fit nor match, she smears makeup on heavily but randomly, and she slops food all over herself. Sylvia occasionally hears voices talking to her. Sylvia tends to be argumentative, aggressive, and emotionally volatile. Over the years, she has been involved in innumerable fights with fellow patients, psychiatric staff members, and strangers. Her thought can be highly irrational, as is apparent from the following quote:

"Mick Jagger wants to marry me. If I have Mick Jagger, I don't have to covet Geraldo Rivera. Mick Jagger is St. Nicholas and the Maharishi is Santa Claus. I want to form a gospel rock group called the Thorn Oil, but Geraldo wants me to be the music critic on *Eyewitness News*, so what can I do? Got to listen to my boyfriend. Teddy Kennedy cured me of my ugliness. I'm pregnant with the son of God. I'm going to marry David Berkowitz and get it over with. Creedmoor is the headquarters of the American Nazi Party. They're eating the patients here. Archie Bunker wants me to play his niece on his TV show. I work for Epic Records. I'm Joan of Arc. I'm Florence Nightingale. The door between the ward and the porch is the dividing line between New York and California. Divorce isn't a piece of paper, it's a feeling. Forget about Zip Codes. I need shock treatments. The body is run by electricity. My wiring is all faulty. A fly is a teen-age wasp. I'm marrying an accountant. I'm in the Pentecostal Church, but I'm considering switching my loyalty to the Charismatic Church." (Adapted from Sheehan, 1982; quotation from pp. 104–105)

Sylvia's case clearly shows that schizophrenic thinking can be bizarre and that schizophrenia can be a severe and debilitating disorder. Al-

The apathy, withdrawal, and severe deterioration in everyday adaptive behavior often seen in schizophrenic disorders leave many patients institutionalized for lengthy periods of time. Modern drug therapies have greatly reduced the amount of time that schizophrenic patients spend in mental hospitals, but these drug treatments can create their own problems (see Chapter 15).

though no single symptom is inevitably present, symptoms of irrational thought, deterioration of adaptive behavior, distorted perception, and disturbed emotion are commonly seen in schizophrenia.

IRRATIONAL THOUGHT

Disturbed, irrational thought processes are the central feature of schizophrenic disorders. Various kinds of delusions are common. **Delusions are false beliefs that are maintained even though they are clearly out of touch with reality.** For example, affected persons frequently believe that their private thoughts are being broadcast to other people. They may also believe that thoughts are being injected into their mind against their will. In delusions of grandeur, people maintain that they are extremely famous or important. Sylvia expressed an endless array of grandiose delusions, such as thinking that Mick Jagger wanted to marry her, that she dictated the hobbit stories to Tolkien, and that she was going to win the Nobel Prize for medicine.

In addition to delusions, the schizophrenic person's train of thought deteriorates. Thinking becomes chaotic rather than logical and linear. There is a "loosening of associations," as people shift topics in disjointed ways. The quotation from Sylvia illustrates this symptom dramatically. The entire quote involves a wild "flight of ideas," but at one point (beginning with the sentence "Creedmoor is the headquarters . . .") she rattles

off ten consecutive sentences, each of which has no apparent connection to the preceding sentence.

DETERIORATION OF ADAPTIVE BEHAVIOR

Schizophrenia usually involves a noticeable deterioration in the quality of one's routine functioning in areas such as work, social relations, and personal care. Friends will often make remarks such as "Hal just isn't himself anymore." This deterioration is readily apparent in Sylvia's inability to get along with others or function in the work world. It's also apparent in her neglect of personal hygiene.

DISTORTED PERCEPTION

A variety of perceptual distortions may occur in schizophrenia, with the most common being auditory hallucinations. **Hallucinations are sensory perceptions that occur in the absence of a real, external stimulus, or gross distortions of perceptual input.** Schizophrenics frequently report that they "hear voices" of nonexistent or absent people talking to them. Sylvia, for instance, heard messages from former Beatle Paul McCartney. These voices often provide an insulting, running commentary on the person's behavior ("you're an idiot for shaking his hand"). They may be argumentative ("you don't need a bath"), and they may issue commands ("prepare your home for visitors from outer space").

DISTURBED EMOTION

Normal emotional tone can be disrupted in schizophrenia in a variety of ways. Some victims show a flattening of emotions. In other words, they show little emotional responsiveness. Others show inappropriate emotional responses that don't jell with the situation or with what they're saying. For instance, a schizophrenic patient might cry about events in a Smurfs cartoon and then laugh about a news story describing how a child burned to death in a tragic home fire. People with schizophrenia may also become emotionally volatile. This pattern was displayed by Sylvia, who often overreacted emotionally in erratic, unpredictable ways.

OTHER FEATURES OF SCHIZOPHRENIA

People with schizophrenic disorders may display a variety of other, less central symptoms. Many exhibit *social withdrawal*, interacting with others only very reluctantly. Some experience a *disturbed sense of self* or individuality. Also common is *poverty of speech*, which involves hesitant, uncommunicative verbal interactions. Sometimes *abnormal motor behavior* is observed. A patient may rock back and forth constantly or become immobilized for great lengths of time.

Subtypes of Schizophrenia

Four subtypes of schizophrenic disorders are recognized, including a category for people who don't fit neatly into any of the first three categories.

PARANOID TYPE

As its name implies, *paranoid schizophrenia* **is dominated by delusions of persecution along with delusions of grandeur.** In this common form of schizophrenia, people come to believe that they have many enemies who want to harass and oppress them. They may become suspicious of friends and relatives or they may attribute the persecution to mysterious, unknown persons. They're convinced that they're being watched and manipulated in malicious ways. To make sense of this persecution, they often develop delusions of grandeur. They believe that they must be enormously important people, frequently seeing themselves as great inventors or as great religious or political leaders. For example, in the case described at the beginning of the chapter, Ed's belief that he was president of the United States was a delusion of grandeur.

CATATONIC TYPE

Catatonic schizophrenia **is marked by striking motor disturbances, ranging from muscular rigidity to random motor activity.** Some catatonics go into an extreme form of withdrawal known as a catatonic stupor. They may remain virtually motionless and seem oblivious to the environment around them for long periods of time. Others go into a state of catatonic excitement. They become hyperactive and incoherent. Some catatonics alternate between these dramatic extremes. The catatonic subtype of schizophrenia is not particularly common, and its prevalence seems to be declining.

DISORGANIZED TYPE

In *disorganized schizophrenia,* **a particularly severe deterioration of adaptive behavior is seen.**

"Schizophrenia disfigures the emotional and cognitive faculties of its victims, and sometimes nearly destroys them."

NANCY ANDREASEN

Prominent symptoms include emotional indifference, frequent incoherence, and virtually complete social withdrawal. Aimless babbling and giggling are common. Delusions often center on bodily functions ("my brain is melting out my ears").

UNDIFFERENTIATED TYPE

People who are clearly schizophrenic but who cannot be placed into any of the three previous categories are said to have **undifferentiated schizophrenia, which is marked by idiosyncratic mixtures of schizophrenic symptoms.** The undifferentiated subtype is fairly common.

New Directions in Classifying Subtypes

Some theorists are beginning to doubt the value of dividing schizophrenic disorders into the four subtypes just described (Pfohl & Andreasen, 1986). Critics note that the catatonic subtype is disappearing and that undifferentiated cases aren't a subtype as much as a hodgepodge of "leftovers." Critics also point out that there aren't meaningful differences between the classic schizophrenic subtypes in etiology, prognosis, or response to treatment. The absence of such differences casts doubt on the value of the current classification scheme.

Because of problems such as those just mentioned, Nancy Andreasen and others (Andreasen, 1982; Lewine, Fogg, & Meltzer, 1983) have proposed an alternative approach to subtyping that divides schizophrenic disorders into just two categories based on the predominance of negative versus positive symptoms. *Negative symptoms* involve behavioral deficits, such as flattened emotions, social withdrawal, apathy, impaired attention, and poverty of speech. *Positive symptoms* involve behavioral excesses or peculiarities, such as hallucinations, delusions, bizarre behavior, and wild flights of ideas.

The two categories in this classification scheme are simply called Type I (positive symptoms) and Type II (negative symptoms) schizophrenia. Andreasen believes that researchers will find consistent differences between these two subtypes in etiology, prognosis, and response to treatment. Table 14.4 outlines some of the hypothesized differences between Type I and Type II schizophrenia that researchers are currently investigating. It's hard to say whether the proposed subdivision based on positive versus negative symptoms will prove useful. The distinction is intriguing, but researchers are already having trouble just deciding which schizophrenic symptoms are positive and which are negative.

Course and Outcome of Schizophrenia

Schizophrenic disorders usually emerge during adolescence or early adulthood and only rarely after age 45 (Murphy & Helzer, 1986). The emergence of schizophrenia may be either very sudden or very gradual. A slow, gradual onset is seen in about one-half to three-quarters of the cases (Ciompi, 1980; Maxmen, 1986). In a gradual onset, a person usually exhibits increasingly frequent manifestations of odd, eccentric behavior, irrational ideas, difficulties in getting along with others, and deficiencies in everyday living skills. This gradual deterioration eventually culminates in a flare-up of psychotic disorientation, like that seen in Ed's case, described at the beginning of the chapter.

Once it clearly emerges, the course of schizophrenia is variable (Ciompi, 1980), but patients tend to fall into three broad groups. Some patients, presumably those with milder disorders, are treated successfully and enjoy a full recovery. In other patients treatment produces a partial recovery so that they can return to their normal life, but they experience frequent relapses and are in and out of treatment facilities for much of the remainder of their lives. Finally, a third group of patients endure chronic illness and continued deterioration that sometimes results in permanent hospitalization.

It's hard to generalize about the proportion of patients falling into each of the three groups just described because estimates of these proportions are changing due to advances in treatment, shifts in treatment strategies, and improved research on the issue. One recent study (Harding et al., 1987) suggests that substantial recoveries occur more frequently than previously believed, perhaps more than 50% of the time.

A number of factors are related to the likelihood of recovery from schizophrenic disorders (Lehmann & Cancro, 1985). A patient has a relatively *favorable prognosis* when (1) the onset of the disorder has been sudden rather than gradual, (2) the onset has occurred at a later age, (3) the patient's social and work adjustment were relatively good prior to the onset of the disorder, and (4) the patient has a relatively healthy, supportive family situation to return to. Three of these predictors of recovery relate to how the disorder develops, which is the matter we turn to next.

Etiology of Schizophrenia

Most of us can identify, at least to some extent, with people who suffer from mood disorders, somatoform disorders, or anxiety disorders. You probably can imagine events that could unfold

Table 14.4 Hypothesized Differences Between Type I and II Schizophrenia

	TYPE I	TYPE II
CHARACTERISTIC SYMPTOMS	Positive symptoms: delusions, hallucinations	Negative symptoms: flattening of affect, poverty of speech
TREATMENT	Good response to drugs	Poor response to drugs
PROGNOSIS	Potentially reversible	Irreversible?
ETIOLOGY	Increased number of D_2 dopamine receptors	Cell loss in temporal lobe structures

Source: Crow, 1985

that might leave you struggling with depression, or grappling with anxiety, or worrying about your physical health. But what could possibly have led Ed to believe that he had been fighting space wars and vampires? What could account for Sylvia's thinking that she was Joan of Arc? Or that Archie Bunker wanted her to appear on his show? As mystifying as these delusions may seem, you'll see that the etiology of schizophrenic disorders is not terribly different from the etiology of other disorders. We'll begin our discussion by examining the matter of genetic vulnerability.

GENETIC VULNERABILITY
Evidence is plentiful that hereditary factors play a role in the development of schizophrenic disorders. Family studies, twin studies, and adoption studies consistently indicate that there's a genetic basis for schizophrenia (Loehlin, Willerman, & Horn, 1988). For instance, in twin studies, concordance rates average around 46% for identical twins, compared to about 14% for fraternal twins (Gottesman & Shields, 1982). Family studies indicate that a child born to two schizophrenic parents has about a 46% probability of developing a schizophrenic disorder (compared to the general probability of about 1%). These and other findings that demonstrate the genetic roots of schizophrenia are summarized in Figure 14.15. Overall, the picture is similar to that seen for mood disorders. Several converging lines of evidence indicate that people inherit a genetically transmitted *vulnerability* to schizophrenia.

NEUROCHEMICAL FACTORS
Like mood disorders, schizophrenic disorders appear to be accompanied by neurochemical changes in the brain (Karson, Kleinman, & Wyatt, 1986). The onset of schizophrenia is thought to be related to excess activity at *dopamine* synapses. Dopamine has been implicated as the critical neurotransmitter because most of the

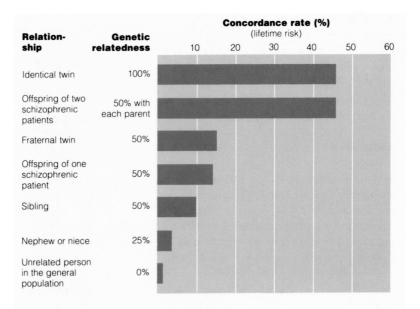

Figure 14.15 Genetic vulnerability to schizophrenic disorders. Relatives of schizophrenic patients have an elevated risk for schizophrenia. This risk is greater among closer relatives. Although environment also plays a role in the etiology of schizophrenia, the concordance rates shown here suggest that there must be a genetic vulnerability to the disorder. (Data from Nicol & Gottesman, 1983)

Relation-ship	Genetic relatedness	Concordance rate (%) (lifetime risk)
Identical twin	100%	
Offspring of two schizophrenic patients	50% with each parent	
Fraternal twin	50%	
Offspring of one schizophrenic patient	50%	
Sibling	50%	
Nephew or niece	25%	
Unrelated person in the general population	0%	

drugs that are useful in the treatment of schizophrenia are known to dampen dopamine activity in the brain. However, the evidence linking schizophrenia to neurotransmitter levels is riddled with interpretive problems and isn't nearly as strong as comparable evidence for mood disorders (Davidson, Losonczy, & Davis, 1986). Nonetheless, investigators continue to search for the neurochemical bases of schizophrenia.

STRUCTURAL ABNORMALITIES IN THE BRAIN

Various studies have suggested that schizophrenic individuals have difficulty in focusing their attention (Mirsky & Duncan, 1986). Some theorists believe that many bizarre aspects of schizophrenic behavior may be due mainly to an inability to filter out unimportant stimuli. This lack of selectivity supposedly leaves victims of the disorder flooded with overwhelming, confusing sensory input.

These problems with attention suggest that schizophrenic disorders may be caused by neurological defects (Lehmann, 1985). Until recently, this theory was based more on speculation than

actual research. However, new advances in brain-imaging technology are beginning to yield some intriguing data. Thus far, most of the data come from studies using the CAT scans or MRI scans introduced in Chapter 3. The findings suggest there's an association between enlarged brain ventricles (the hollow, fluid-filled cavities in the brain) and chronic schizophrenic disturbance (Andreasen, 1985; see Figure 14.16).

The significance of enlarged ventricles in the brain is hotly debated, however. Enlarged ventricles have been found in only about 20 to 25% of the schizophrenic persons tested (Weinberger, Wagner, & Wyatt, 1983). Moreover, enlarged ventricles are not unique to schizophrenia; they're a sign of many kinds of brain pathology. Furthermore, even if the association between enlarged ventricles and schizophrenia is replicated consistently, it will be difficult to sort out whether this brain abnormality is a cause or an effect of schizophrenia.

In sum, there's evidence linking schizophrenia to heredity, neurochemistry, and brain structure. However, evidence regarding the latter two factors is tentative, and it's clear that psychosocial factors also contribute to the development of schizophrenia. Let's look at the possible role of family dynamics.

FAMILY DYNAMICS: COMMUNICATION DEVIANCE

Over the years, hundreds of investigators have tried to relate patterns of family interaction to the development of schizophrenia. Popular theories have come and gone as empirical evidence has overturned once plausible hypotheses (Goldstein, 1988). Vigorous research and debate in this area continue today. The current emphasis is on fami-

Figure 14.16 Enlarged brain ventricles in a schizophrenic patient. These color-coded MRI brain scans were taken from a pair of identical twins, only one of whom suffers from schizophrenia. In comparison to the scan on the right, the one on the left, obtained from the schizophrenic twin, shows enlarged ventricles (note the large butterfly-shaped orange and yellow area).

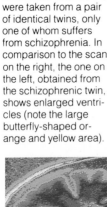
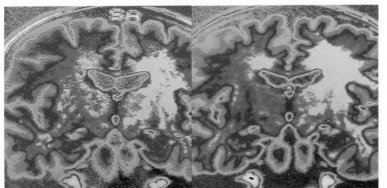

Figure 14.17 Communication deviance and schizophrenia. How does parental communication deviance contribute to the development of schizophrenia? One model suggests that confusing communication undermines a child's sense of reality, creates additional stress, and fosters peculiarities in thinking.

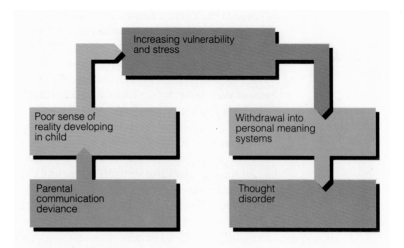

lies' communication patterns and their expression of emotions.

Various theorists assert that vulnerability to schizophrenia is increased by exposure to defective interpersonal communication during childhood. Studies have found a relationship between schizophrenia and diverse aspects of *communication deviance*, such as unintelligible speech, stories with no endings, heavy use of unusual words, extensive contradictions, and paying poor attention to children's communication efforts (Singer, Wynne, & Toohey, 1978). The evidence suggests that schizophrenia is more likely to develop when youngsters grow up in homes characterized by vague, muddled, fragmented communication. Researchers speculate that communication deviance gradually undermines children's sense of reality and encourages youngsters to withdraw into their own private world, setting the stage for schizophrenic thinking (see Figure 14.17).

A study by Michael Goldstein (1984) suggests that there's a causal connection between communication deviance and the eventual onset of schizophrenia. He followed up families first observed in the mid-1960s 15 years later. The 64 families originally came to a psychological clinic because they were having difficulties with a teenage child. Although many of the treated youngsters showed signs of disturbance, none were schizophrenic. During treatment, the extent of their parents' communication deviance was assessed. Fifteen years later, Goldstein was able to reestablish contact with 50 of the 64 families. He found that the number of schizophrenic disorders that had emerged in the interim was much higher in families characterized by high communication deviance.

FAMILY DYNAMICS:
EXPRESSED EMOTION

Studies of expressed emotion have primarily focused on how this element of family dynamics influences the *course* of schizophrenic illness after the onset of the disorder (Leff & Vaughn, 1985). *Expressed emotion* reflects the degree to which a relative of a schizophrenic patient displays highly critical or emotionally overinvolved attitudes toward the patient. Audiotaped interviews are used to assess relatives' expressed emotion. The interviews are carefully evaluated for the presence of critical comments, expressions of resentment toward the patient, and indications of excessive emotional involvement (overprotective, overconcerned attitudes).

CONCEPT CHECK 14.3
Distinguishing Schizophrenic and Mood Disorders

Check your understanding of the nature of schizophrenic and mood disorders by making very preliminary diagnoses for the cases described below. Read each case summary and write in your tentative diagnosis in the space provided. The answers are in Appendix A.

1. Max hasn't slept in 4 days. He's determined to write the "great American novel" before his class reunion, which is a few months away. He expounds eloquently on his novel to anyone who will listen, talking at such a rapid pace that no one can get a word in edgewise. He feels like he's wired with energy and is supremely confident about the novel, even though he's only written 10 to 20 pages. Last week, he charged $8000 worth of new computer software which is supposed to help him write his book.

Preliminary diagnosis: _____

2. Maurice maintains that he invented the atomic bomb, even though he was born after its invention. He says he invented it to punish homosexuals, Nazis, and short people. It's short people that he's really afraid of. He's sure that all the short people on TV are talking about him. He thinks that short people are conspiring to make him look like a Republican. Maurice gets in arguments with people frequently and is emotionally volatile. His grooming is poor, but he says it's okay because he's the Secretary of State.

Preliminary diagnosis: _____

3. Margaret has hardly gotten out of bed for weeks, although she's troubled by insomnia. She doesn't feel like eating and has absolutely no energy. She feels dejected, discouraged, spiritless, and apathetic. Friends stop by to try to cheer her up, but she tells them not to waste their time on "pond scum."

Preliminary diagnosis: _____

Studies show that a family's expressed emotion is a good predictor of the course of a schizophrenic patient's illness (Leff & Vaughn, 1981). After release from a hospital, schizophrenic patients who return to a family high in expressed emotion show relapse rates three or four times those of patients who return to a family low in expressed emotion. Part of the problem for patients returning to homes high in expressed emotion is that their families probably are sources of more stress than social support. And like virtually all mental disorders, schizophrenia is influenced to some extent by life stress (Schwartz & Myers, 1977).

PRECIPITATING STRESS
Most theories of schizophrenia assume that stress plays a key role in triggering schizophrenic dis-

orders (McGlashan, 1986; Zubin, 1986). According to this notion, various biological and psychological factors influence individuals' *vulnerability* to schizophrenia. High stress may then serve to precipitate a schizophrenic disorder in someone who is vulnerable. As we'll discuss later, the stress-vulnerability model can integrate the diverse array of factors known to be involved in the etiology of schizophrenia.

Schizophrenia is the last of the major, Axis I diagnostic categories that we'll consider. We'll complete our overview of different types of abnormal behavior with a brief look at the personality disorders, which are recorded on Axis II in the DSM classification system.

PERSONALITY DISORDERS

We've seen repeatedly that it's often difficult to draw that figurative line between healthy and disordered behavior. This is especially true in the case of personality disorders, which are relatively mild disturbances in comparison to most of the Axis I disorders. *Personality disorders* **are a class of disorders marked by extreme, inflexible personality traits that cause subjective distress or impaired social and occupational functioning.** Essentially, people with these disorders display certain personality traits to an excessive degree and in rigid ways that undermine their adjustment. Personality disorders usually emerge during late childhood or adolescence and often continue throughout adulthood. It's difficult to estimate the prevalence of these subtle disorders, but it's clear that they're common (Merikangas & Weissman, 1986).

In this section we'll describe three clusters of personality disorders, discuss some problems with the Axis II diagnostic categories, and take a close look at one personality disorder that has been the subject of considerable research—the antisocial personality disorder.

The Three Clusters of Personality Disorders

DSM-III-R lists 11 different personality disorders, which are grouped into three related clusters. All 11 disorders are described briefly in Figure 14.18. If you examine this figure, you'll find a diverse collection of maladaptive personality syndromes. You may also notice that some personality disorders are essentially mild versions of more severe

Axis I disorders. Let's examine the three broad clusters of personality disorders.

THE ANXIOUS-FEARFUL CLUSTER
All four of the disorders in the anxious-fearful cluster are marked by maladaptive efforts to control anxiety and fear about social rejection from others. People with an *avoidant personality disorder* tend to withdraw socially to reduce their anxiety about acceptance. People with a *dependent personality disorder* reduce their anxiety by always subordinating themselves to friends, coworkers, spouses, parents, and others. People with a *passive-aggressive personality disorder* deal with their anxiety by resisting conventional social expectations and demands by dawdling and forgetting. People with an *obsessive-compulsive personality* disorder cope with anxiety by imposing a rigid order on their lives and their interpersonal relationships.

The personality disorders in this cluster share some kinship with the anxiety disorders recorded on Axis I. For example, the diagnosis of obsessive-compulsive personality disorder may be given to people who have obsessive and compulsive traits, but don't meet the criteria for a full-fledged obsessive-compulsive disorder.

THE ODD-ECCENTRIC CLUSTER
People with the three personality disorders in this cluster are distrustful, socially aloof, and unable to "connect" with others emotionally. In a *schizoid personality disorder*, an individual shows a lack of interest in interpersonal intimacy, indifference to others' feelings, and a history of no close friendships. In a *schizotypal personality disorder*, similar

Figure 14.18 Per-
sonality disorders.
DSM-III-R describes
eleven different per-
sonality disorders that
fall into three clusters,
as shown here.

Personality Disorders

Cluster	Disorder	Description
Anxious/fearful	Avoidant personality disorder	Excessively sensitive to potential rejection, humiliation, or shame; socially withdrawn in spite of desire for acceptance from others
	Dependent personality disorder	Excessively lacking in self-reliance and self-esteem; passively allowing others to make all decisions; constantly subordinating own needs to others' needs
	Passive-aggressive personality disorder	Indirectly resistant to demands for adequate social and occupational performance; tending to procrastinate, dawdle, and "forget"
	Obsessive-compulsive personality disorder	Preoccupied with organization, rules, schedules, lists, trivial details; extremely conventional, serious, and formal; unable to express warm emotions
Odd/eccentric	Schizoid personality disorder	Defective in capacity for forming social relationships, showing absence of warm, tender feelings for others
	Schizotypal personality disorder	Showing social deficits and oddities of thinking, perception, and communication that resemble schizophrenia
	Paranoid personality disorder	Showing pervasive and unwarranted suspiciousness and mistrust of people; overly sensitive; prone to jealousy
Dramatic/impulsive	Histrionic personality disorder	Overly dramatic; tending to exaggerated expressions of emotion; egocentric, seeking attention
	Narcissistic personality disorder	Grandiosely self-important; preoccupied with success fantasies; expecting special treatment; lacking interpersonal empathy
	Borderline personality disorder	Unstable in self-image, mood, and interpersonal relationships; impulsive and unpredictable
	Antisocial personality disorder	Chronically violating the rights of others; failing to accept social norms, to form attachments to others, or to sustain consistent work behavior; exploitive and reckless

social deficits are seen along with eccentric qualities such as peculiar physical mannerisms, oddi-
ties in speech, and bizarre beliefs. In a *paranoid
personality disorder*, an individual is emotionally
cold, suspicious of virtually everyone, and constantly concerned about being slighted by others.
Obviously, there is some continuity between
the personality disorders in this cluster and the
schizophrenic disorders on Axis I.

THE DRAMATIC-IMPULSIVE CLUSTER

The four personality disorders in this cluster have
less in common with each other than those
grouped in the first two clusters. The histrionic
and narcissistic personalities share a flair for
overdramatizing everything. People with a *histrionic personality disorder* are egocentric, excitable,
erratic, exhibitionistic individuals who thrive on
attention. People with a *narcissistic personality disorder* manifest similar traits; they also are preoccupied with self-doubt, which they hide under
exaggerated feelings of self-importance.

Impulsiveness is the common ground shared by
the borderline and antisocial personality disorders. People with a *borderline personality disorder*

are characterized by impulsive, unpredictable behavior and instability in (1) emotions, (2) feelings
of self-worth, and (3) attitudes toward others.
People with an *antisocial personality disorder* are
impulsive, irresponsible, manipulative, exploitive, and frequently aggressive. The personality
syndromes in this cluster don't have close parallels
among the Axis I disorders.

Diagnostic Problems with Personality Disorders

Since the publication of *DSM-III* in 1980, many
critics have argued that the personality disorders
overlap too much with Axis I disorders and with
each other (Frances & Widiger, 1986). The extent of this problem was documented in a recent
study by Leslie Morey (1988). Morey reviewed the
cases of 291 patients who had received a specific
personality disorder diagnosis to see how many of
the patients could have met the criteria for any of
the other ten personality disorders. As Figure
14.19 shows, Morey found massive overlap among
the diagnoses. For example, among patients with
a diagnosis of histrionic personality disorder, 56%

	Patients qualifying for other *DSM-III-R* diagnosis (%)										
Actual diagnosis	Borderline	Narcis-sistic	Histrionic	Antisocial	Depen-dent	Avoidant	Obsessive-compulsive	Passive-aggressive	Paranoid	Schizoid	Schizo-typal
Borderline		30.9	36.1	8.2	34.0	36.1	2.1	13.4	32.0	6.2	9.3
Narcissistic	46.9		53.1	15.6	26.6	35.9	10.9	28.1	35.9	14.1	14.1
Histrionic	55.6	54.0		9.5	30.2	31.7	4.8	19.0	28.6	4.8	7.9
Antisocial	44.4	55.6	33.3		11.1	16.7	0.0	50.0	27.8	5.6	5.6
Dependent	50.8	26.2	29.2	3.1		49.2	9.2	16.9	29.2	9.2	12.3
Avoidant	44.3	29.1	25.3	3.8	40.5		16.5	15.2	39.2	21.5	20.3
Obsessive-compulsive	8.7	30.4	13.0	0.0	26.1	56.5		26.1	21.7	21.7	13.0
Passive-aggressive	36.1	50.0	33.3	25.0	30.6	33.3	16.7		30.6	16.7	11.1
Paranoid	48.4	35.9	28.1	7.8	29.7	48.4	7.8	17.2		23.4	25.0
Schizoid	18.8	28.1	9.4	3.1	18.8	53.1	15.6	18.8	46.9		37.5
Schizotypal	33.3	33.3	18.5	3.7	29.6	59.3	11.1	14.8	59.3	44.4	

Figure 14.19 Diagnostic overlap among personality disorders. Morey (1988) examined the symptom patterns of 291 patients who received the diagnoses listed in the vertical column on the left and determined the percentage of patients in each group who could also qualify for any of the other ten personality disorder diagnoses (listed across the top). Diagnoses with high (more than 40%) overlap are highlighted in orange, and diagnoses with moderate (20%–40%) overlap are highlighted in green. As you can see, the personality disorders described in *DSM-III-R* are plagued by an excessive amount of overlap.

also qualified for a borderline disorder, 54% for a narcissistic disorder, 32% for an avoidant disorder, 30% for a dependent disorder, and 29% for a paranoid disorder.

Clearly, there are fundamental problems with Axis II as a classification system, and revisions are sorely needed (Kiesler, 1986; Millon, 1986). The overlap among the personality disorders makes it virtually impossible to achieve adequate reliability for these diagnoses. Also, the poorly defined nature of personality disorders hinders research and is probably the main reason for our notable lack of information on the prevalence and etiology of most of these disorders. The only personality disorder that has a long history of extensive research is the antisocial personality disorder, which we'll examine next.

Antisocial Personality Disorder

The antisocial personality disorder has a misleading name. The antisocial designation does *not* mean that people with this disorder shun social interaction. Rather than shrinking from social interaction, many are sociable, friendly, and superficially charming. People with this disorder are *antisocial* in that they *reject widely accepted social norms* regarding moral principles and behavior.

DESCRIPTION

Antisocial personalities chronically violate the rights of others. They often use their social charm to cultivate others' liking or loyalty for purposes of exploitation. **The *antisocial personality disorder* is marked by impulsive, callous, manipulative, aggressive, and irresponsible behavior that reflects a failure to accept social norms.** Since they haven't accepted the social norms they vio-

late, antisocial personalities rarely feel guilty about their transgressions. Essentially, they lack an adequate conscience. The antisocial personality disorder occurs much more frequently among males than females. Studies suggest that it's a moderately common disorder, seen in roughly 2 to 3% of the population (Cadoret, 1986).

Many antisocial personalities get involved in illegal activities. Hare (1983) estimates that about 40% of convicted felons in prisons meet the criteria for an antisocial personality disorder. However, many antisocial personalities keep their exploitative, amoral behavior channeled within the boundaries of the law. Such people may even enjoy high status in our society (Sutker & Allain, 1983). In other words, the concept of the antisocial personality disorder applies to cutthroat business executives, scheming politicians, unprincipled lawyers, and money-hungry evangelists, as well as to con artists, drug dealers, thugs, burglars, and petty thieves.

Antisocial personalities rarely experience genuine affection for others. However, they may be skilled at faking affection so they can exploit people. Sexually, they're predatory and promiscuous. They also tend to be irresponsible and impulsive. They can tolerate very little frustration, and they pursue immediate gratification. These characteristics make them unreliable employees, unfaithful spouses, inattentive parents, and undependable friends. Many antisocial personalities have a checkered history of divorce, child abuse, and job instability.

ETIOLOGY

Many theorists believe that biological factors contribute to the development of antisocial personality disorders. Twin studies suggest that there's a genetic predisposition toward these disorders (Crowe, 1983). Eysenck (1982) has noted that antisocial personalities lack the inhibitions that most of us have about violating moral standards. Their lack of inhibitions prompted Eysenck to theorize that they might inherit relatively sluggish autonomic nervous systems, leading to slow acquisition of inhibitions through classical conditioning. Eysenck's ideas have been supported in empirical studies, but the findings are inconsistent (Brantley & Sutker, 1984), suggesting that biological factors may create a genuine but weak predisposition toward antisocial behavior.

Efforts to relate psychological factors to antisocial behavior have emphasized inadequate socialization and observational learning. It's easy to envision how antisocial traits could be fostered in homes where parents make haphazard or halfhearted efforts to socialize their children to be respectful, truthful, responsible, unselfish, and so forth. Consistent with this idea, Meyer (1980)

reports that antisocial personalities tend to come from homes where discipline is inconsistent, ineffective, or nonexistent. Antisocial personalities are also more likely to emerge from homes where one or both parents exhibit antisocial traits (Robins, 1966). These parents presumably model exploitive, amoral behavior, which their children acquire through observational learning.

Investigating the roots of antisocial personality disorders has proven difficult because people with these disorders generally don't voluntarily seek help from our mental health system. They feel little guilt and usually don't see anything wrong with themselves. Their antisocial traits may become apparent only when they run afoul of the law and are ordered into treatment by the courts. Such court-ordered treatment is only one example of the many interfaces between our mental health system and our legal system. We'll explore some of these interfaces in the next section, which focuses on abnormal behavior and the law.

PSYCHOLOGICAL DISORDERS AND THE LAW

Societies use the law to enforce their norms of conformity. Given this function, the law has something to say about many issues related to abnormal behavior. In this section we examine the concepts of insanity, competency, and involuntary commitment.

Insanity

Insanity is *not* a diagnosis; it's a legal concept. **Insanity is a legal status indicating that a person cannot be held responsible for his or her actions because of mental illness.** Why is this an issue in the courtroom? Because criminal acts must be intentional. The law reasons that people who are "out of their mind" may not be able to appreciate the significance of what they're doing. The insanity defense is used in criminal trials by defendants who admit that they committed the alleged crime but claim that they lacked intent.

There isn't any simple relationship between specific diagnoses of mental disorders and court findings of insanity. Most people with diagnosed psychological disorders would *not* qualify as insane. The people most likely to qualify are those troubled by severe, psychotic disturbances. The courts apply several different rules in making judgments about a defendant's sanity, depending on the jurisdiction. According to one widely used rule, called the M'naghten rule, *insanity exists when a mental disorder makes a person unable to distinguish right from wrong.* As you can imagine,

evaluating insanity as defined in the M'naghten rule can be difficult for judges and jurors, not to mention the psychologists and psychiatrists who are called into court as expert witnesses. Al-

After his attempt to assassinate President Reagan, John Hinckley was found not guilty by reason of insanity. The Hinckley verdict aroused controversy about the concept of insanity, which is a legal status and not a psychodiagnostic category.

though highly controversial, the insanity defense is actually used much less frequently than most people would estimate.

Competency

***Competency* (or fitness in some states) refers to a defendant's capacity to stand trial.** To be competent, defendants must be able to understand the nature and purpose of the legal proceedings and be able to assist their attorney. If they're not able, they're declared incompetent and can't be brought to trial unless they become competent once again.

What's the difference between insanity and incompetence? Insanity refers to a defendant's mental state *at the time of the alleged crime.* Competency refers to a defendant's mental state *at the time of the trial.* Given the potential for delay in our legal system, the crime and the trial may take place many months and even years apart. Insanity can't even become an issue unless a defendant is competent to stand trial. Far more people are found to be incompetent than insane.

What happens to defendants who are declared incompetent or insane? Essentially, they're turned over to the mental health system for treatment. However, this simple statement masks immense

variability in the handling of their cases. What happens to a defendant depends on the nature of the alleged offense, the nature of the mental disorder, the likelihood of recovery and a return to competence, and a host of other factors.

Involuntary Commitment

The issues of insanity and competency surface only in *criminal* proceedings. Far more people are affected by *civil* proceedings relating to involuntary commitment. **In *involuntary commitment* people are hospitalized in psychiatric facilities against their will.** What are the grounds for such a dramatic action? They vary some from state to state. Generally, people are subject to involuntary commitment when mental health professionals and legal authorities believe that a mental disorder makes them (1) dangerous to themselves (usually suicidal), (2) dangerous to others (potentially violent), or (3) in need of treatment (applied in cases of severe disorientation). In emergency situations psychologists, psychiatrists, and other physicians can authorize *temporary* commitment, usually for 24 to 72 hours. Orders for long-term involuntary commitment are usually set up for renewable 6-month periods and can be issued by a court only after a formal hearing. Mental

Figure 14.20 The stress-vulnerability model of schizophrenia. Multifactorial causation is readily apparent in current theories about the etiology of schizophrenic disorders. A variety of biological factors and personal history factors influence one's vulnerability to the disorder, which interacts with the amount of stress one experiences. Schizophrenic disorders appear to result from an intersection of high stress and high vulnerability.

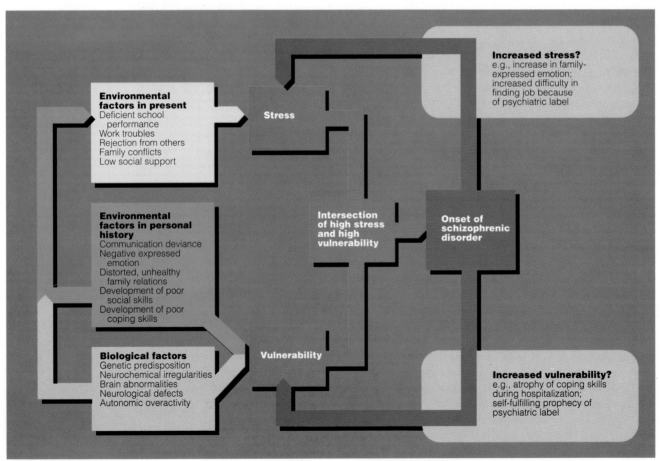

health professionals provide extensive input in these hearings, but the courts make the final decisions.

Most involuntary commitments occur because people appear to be *dangerous* to themselves or others. There's a problem, however, in that it's very difficult to predict dangerousness. Studies indicate that clinicians are not particularly accurate in predicting who will become violent (Cocker-

ham, 1981). This mediocrity in predicting dangerousness is unfortunate, because involuntary commitment involves the *detention* of people for what they *might* do in the future. Such detention goes against the grain of the American legal principle that one is *innocent until proven guilty.* The inherent difficulty in predicting dangerousness makes involuntary commitment a complex and controversial issue.

PUTTING IT IN PERSPECTIVE

Our examination of abnormal behavior and its roots has highlighted several of our organizing themes: multifactorial causation (theme 4), the interplay of heredity and environment (theme 5), and the sociohistorical roots of psychology (theme 3).

We can safely assert that every disorder described in this chapter has multiple causes. The development of mental disorders involves an interplay among a variety of psychological, biological, and social factors. Let's reconsider the etiology of schizophrenia to illustrate. The schematic diagram in Figure 14.20 provides an overview of how different factors are believed to contribute to the development of schizophrenia. As you can see, a host of variables (some of which we didn't discuss) have been implicated, including genetic predisposition, neurochemical changes, brain abnormalities, attention deficits, social deficits, coping skills, communication problems, family emotional atmosphere, styles of child rearing, life stress, social support, and society's response to the emergence of the disorder. The model depicted in the diagram shows not only that many variables are involved in the evolution of this disorder, but also that these variables interact in complex ways.

We also saw that most psychological disorders depend on an interaction of genetics and experience. This interaction shows up most clearly in the *stress-vulnerability models* for mood disorders and schizophrenic disorders. *Vulnerability* to these disorders seems to depend primarily on heredity, although experience contributes. *Stress* is largely a function of environment, although physiological factors may influence our stress reactions. According to stress-vulnerability theories, disorders emerge when high vulnerability intersects with

high stress, as shown in Figure 14.20. A high biological vulnerability may not be converted into a disorder if a person's stress is low, and high stress may not lead to a disorder if vulnerability is low. Thus, the impact of heredity depends on the environment, and the effect of environment depends on heredity.

Finally, this chapter clearly demonstrated that psychology evolves in a sociohistorical context. We saw that the formal definitions of normality and abnormality codified in the *DSM* system are not shaped exclusively by scientific research. For instance, because of changing social values and lobbying by a special-interest group, homosexuality is no longer classified as pathological. Some relatively minor problems in living are officially regarded as pathological to accommodate our insurance system. Currently, authorities are carefully reconsidering our definition of insanity because many people were outraged when John Hinckley was found not guilty by reason of insanity after attempting to shoot the president. These points are not raised to belittle the enormous contributions that science has made to our understanding of mental disorders. Our modern conceptions of normality and abnormality are largely shaped by empirical research, but social trends, cultural values, economic necessities, and political realities also play a role.

Indeed, a certain cultural orientation is implicit in our upcoming Application on suicide. Our culture views suicide as an abnormal act to be prevented whenever possible, while some cultures consider suicide to be an acceptable and even courageous act under certain circumstances. We'll take the traditional view in our culture and focus on suicide prevention.

UNDERSTANDING AND PREVENTING SUICIDE

Answer the following "true" or "false."

☐ **1.** People who talk about suicide don't actually commit suicide.

☐ **2.** Suicides usually take place with little or no warning.

☐ **3.** People who attempt suicide are fully intent on dying.

☐ **4.** People who are suicidal remain so forever.

The four statements above are all false. They're myths about suicide that we'll dispose of momentarily. First, however, let's discuss the magnitude of this tragic problem.

Prevalence of Suicide

There are about 200,000 suicide attempts in the United States each year. Roughly one in eight of these attempts is "successful." This makes suicide the eighth leading cause of death in the nation. Worse yet, official statistics may underestimate the scope of the problem. Many suicides are disguised as accidents, either by the suicidal person or by the survivors who try to cover up afterwards. Thus, experts estimate that there may be ten times more suicides than officially reported (Hirschfeld & Davidson, 1988).

Who Commits Suicide?

Anyone can commit suicide. No segment of society is immune. Nonetheless, some groups are at higher risk than others (Cross & Hirschfeld, 1986). For instance, the prevalence of suicide varies according to *marital status*. Married people commit suicide less frequently than divorced, bereaved, or single people. In regard to *occupational status*, suicide rates are

particularly high among people who are unemployed and among prestigious and pressured professionals, like doctors and lawyers.

Sex and *age* have complex relations to suicide rates. On the one hand, women *attempt* suicide more often than men. On the other hand, men are more likely to actually kill themselves in an attempt, so they *complete* more suicides than women. In regard to *age*, suicide attempts peak between ages 24 and 44, but completed suicides are most frequent after age 55. However, age trends are different for men and women, as you can see in Figure 14.21, which graphs suicide rates by sex and age group.

Unfortunately, suicide rates have doubled among adolescents and young adults in the last two decades (see Chapter 11). *College students* are at higher risk than their noncollege peers. Academic pressures and setbacks do *not* appear to be the principal cause of this elevated suicide rate among collegians. Interpersonal problems and loneliness seem to be more important.

Suicide is *not* committed only by people with severe mental illness, although elevated suicide rates are found for most categories of psychological disorders. As you might predict, suicide rates are highest for people with mood disorders, especially depression. Figure 14.22 shows how mood disorders and suicide attempts overlap.

Myths About Suicide

We opened this application with four false statements about suicide. Let's examine these myths discussed by Edwin Shneidman and his colleagues (1970):

Myth 1: People who talk about suicide don't actually commit suicide. Undoubtedly there are many people who threaten suicide without ever going through with it. Nonetheless, there's

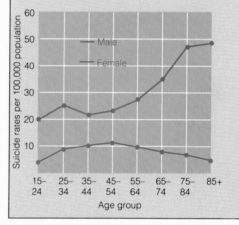

Figure 14.21 Suicide rates in the United States, by age and sex. At all ages, more men than women commit suicide. The age patterns for the two sexes are also noticeably different: whereas the rate of male suicides peaks in the retirement years, the rate of female suicides peaks in middle adulthood. (Data from Cross & Hirschfeld, 1986)

no group at higher risk for suicide than those who openly discuss the possibility. Many people who kill themselves have a history of earlier threats that they didn't carry out.

Myth 2: Suicide usually takes place with little or no warning. It's estimated that eight out of ten suicide attempts are preceded by some kind of warning. These warnings range from clear threats to vague statements. For example, at dinner with friends the night before he committed suicide, one prominent attorney cut up his American Express card, saying "I'm not going to need this anymore." The probability of an actual suicide attempt is greatest when a threat is clear, when it includes a detailed plan, and when the plan involves a relatively deadly method.

Myth 3: People who attempt suicide are fully intent on dying. It appears that only about 3 to 5% of those who attempt suicide definitely want to die. About 30% of the people who make an attempt seem ambivalent. They arrange things so that their fate is largely a matter of chance. The remaining two-thirds of suicide attempts are made by people who appear to have no interest in dying! They only want to send out a very dramatic distress signal. Thus, they arrange their suicide so that a rescue is quite likely. These variations in intent probably explain why only about one-eighth of suicide attempts end in death.

Myth 4: People who are suicidal remain so forever. Many people who become suicidal do so for a limited period of time. If they manage to ride through their crisis period, thoughts of suicide may disappear entirely. Apparently, time heals many wounds—if it's given the opportunity.

Preventing Suicide

There's no simple and dependable way to prevent someone from going ahead with a threatened suicide. One expert on suicide (Wekstein, 1979) makes the point that "perhaps nobody really knows *exactly* what to do when dealing with an imminent suicide" (p. 129). However, we'll review some general advice that may be useful if you ever have to help someone through a suicidal crisis (Farberow, 1974; Shneidman et al., 1970).

1. *Provide empathy and social support.* First and foremost, you must show the suicidal person that you care. People often contemplate suicide because they see the world around them as indifferent and uncaring. Hence, you must demonstrate to the suicidal person that you are genuinely concerned. Even if you're thrust into a situation where you barely know the suicidal person, you need to provide empathy. Suicide threats are often a last-ditch cry for help. It's therefore imperative that you offer to help.

2. *Identify and clarify the crucial problem.* The suicidal person is often terribly confused and feels lost in a sea of frustration and problems. It's a good idea to try to help sort through this confusion. Encourage the person to try to identify the crucial problem. Once it's isolated, the crucial problem may not seem quite so overwhelming. It also may help to point out that the person's confusion is clouding his or her ability to rationally judge the seriousness of the problem.

3. *Suggest alternative courses of action.* People thinking about suicide often see it as the "only solution" to their problems. This is obviously an irrational view. Try to chip away at this premise by offering other possible solutions for the problem that has been identified as crucial. Suicidal people often are too distraught and disoriented to do this on their own. Therefore, it may help if you assist them.

4. *Capitalize on any doubts.* For most people, life is not easy to give up. Most people in a suicidal crisis are racked by doubts about the wisdom of their decision. Many people will voice their unique reasons for doubting whether they should take the suicidal path. Zero in on these doubts; they may be your best arguments for life over death. For instance, if a person expresses concern about how her or his suicide will affect family members, capitalize on this source of doubt.

5. *Encourage professional consultation.* Most mental health professionals have at least some experience in dealing with suicidal crises. Many cities have suicide prevention centers with 24-hour hotlines. These centers are staffed with people who have been specially trained to deal with suicidal problems. It's important to try to get a suicidal person to seek professional assistance. The fact that you talk a person out of attempting a threatened suicide doesn't mean that the crisis is over. The contemplation of suicide indicates that a person is experiencing great distress, and so professional intervention is crucial.

There is no sure way to talk someone out of attempting suicide, but it's important to provide empathy and social support, clarify the person's problem, and capitalize on any doubts. If a person makes it through a suicidal crisis, thoughts of suicide may disappear, but it's always wise to encourage professional consultation.

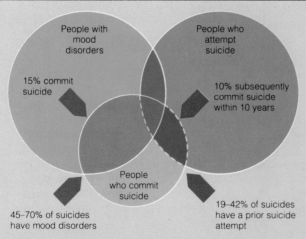

Figure 14.22 The relationship of suicide to mood disorders and prior suicide attempts. Two groups with elevated risk of suicide are people with mood disorders and people who have made prior suicide attempts. Between them, these groups account for a high percentage of suicides. (Adapted from Avery & Winokur, 1978)

People with mood disorders

15% commit suicide

45–70% of suicides have mood disorders

People who attempt suicide

10% subsequently commit suicide within 10 years

19–42% of suicides have a prior suicide attempt

People who commit suicide

PSYCHO-LOGICAL DISORDERS

Abnormal Behavior: Myths, Realities, and Controversies

• The medical model assumes that it is useful to view abnormal behavior as a disease. This view has been criticized on the grounds that it (1) turns ethical questions about deviance into medical questions, (2) stigmatizes those labeled mentally ill, (3) creates pseudoexplanations of psychological disorders, and (4) encourages the adoption of a passive patient role. Although there are serious problems with the medical model, the analogy is useful if one remembers that it is only an analogy.

• Three criteria are employed in deciding whether people suffer from psychological disorders: deviance, personal distress, and maladaptive behavior. Often, it is difficult to clearly draw a line between normality and abnormality. Contrary to popular stereotypes, people with psychological disorders are not particularly bizarre or dangerous. Psychological disorders are not a manifestation of personal weakness, and even the most severe disorders are potentially curable.

• Research by David Rosenhan, described in our Featured Study, showed that pseudopatients were routinely admitted to mental hospitals that were unable to detect the patients' normalcy. His study showed that the distinction between normality and abnormality is not clear cut.

• *DSM-III-R* is the official psychodiagnostic classification system in the United States. This system describes over 200 disorders and asks for information about patients on five axes, or dimensions. Controversies about *DSM* illustrate that judgments about psychological disorders are not value free and that they are influenced by social trends and political realities.

• It is difficult to obtain good data on the prevalence of psychological disorders. Nonetheless, it is clear that they are more common than widely believed, affecting roughly one-third of the population. According to the ECA studies, the most common syndromes are substance-use disorders, anxiety disorders, and mood disorders.

Anxiety Disorders

• The anxiety disorders include the generalized anxiety disorder, phobic disorder, panic disorder, and obsessive-compulsive disorder. These disorders may be more likely in people who have a highly reactive autonomic nervous system or in those with mitral valve prolapse. Parents who are overprotective or who model anxiety may promote these disorders. Many anxiety responses, especially phobias, can be caused by classical conditioning and maintained by operant conditioning.

Somatoform Disorders

• Somatoform disorders include somatization disorder, conversion disorder, and hypochondria. These disorders often emerge in people with highly suggestible, histrionic personalities. Somatoform disorders may be a learned avoidance strategy reinforced by attention and sympathy.

Dissociative Disorders

• Dissociative disorders include psychogenic amnesia and multiple personality. These disorders are uncommon, and their causes are not well understood. Multiple personality appears related to childhood trauma and identity conflict.

Mood Disorders

• The principal mood disorders are major (unipolar) depression and bipolar mood disorder. Mood disorders are episodic, and seasonal patterns have been observed in some patients. Unipolar depression is more common than bipolar disorders.

• Evidence indicates that people vary in their genetic vulnerability to the severe mood disorders. These disorders are accompanied by changes in neurochemical activity in the brain. Cognitive models posit that negative thinking contributes to depression. An attributional style emphasizing internal, stable, and global attributions has been implicated. Depression is often rooted in interpersonal inadequacies and setbacks and sometimes is stress related.

Schizophrenic Disorders

• Schizophrenic disorders are characterized by irrational thought, deterioration of adaptive behavior, distorted perception, and disturbed mood. Schizophrenic disorders are classified as paranoid, catatonic, disorganized, or undifferentiated. A new classification scheme based on the predominance of positive versus negative symptoms is under study. Schizophrenia is often a chronic illness, but substantial recoveries are not as infrequent as once believed.

• Research has linked schizophrenia to a genetic vulnerability, changes in neurotransmitter activity, and structural abnormalities in the brain. Precipitating stress and unhealthy family dynamics, including communication deviance and a negative emotional climate (high expressed emotion), may also contribute to the development of schizophrenia.

Personality Disorders

• There are 11 personality disorders that represent mild forms of disturbance allocated to Axis II in *DSM*. Personality disorders can be grouped into three clusters: anxious-fearful, odd-eccentric, and dramatic-impulsive. However, specific personality disorders are poorly defined, and there is excessive overlap among them, creating diagnostic problems and hindering research.

• The antisocial personality disorder involves manipulative, impulsive, exploitive, aggressive behavior. Research on the etiology of this disorder has implicated genetic vulnerability, autonomic reactivity, inadequate socialization, and observational learning.

Psychological Disorders and the Law

• Insanity is a legal concept applied to people who cannot be held responsible for their actions because of mental illness. Competency refers to a defendant's capacity to understand legal proceedings at the time of a trial. When people appear to be dangerous to themselves or others, courts may rule that they are subject to involuntary commitment in a hosptial.

Putting It in Perspective

• This chapter highlighted three of our unifying themes, showing that behavior is governed by multiple causes, that heredity and environment jointly influence mental disorders, and that psychology evolves in a sociohistorical context.

Application: Understanding and Preventing Suicide

• Suicide attempts result in death about one-eighth of the time, and suicide is the eighth leading cause of death in the United States. People with psychological disorders, especially those with mood disorders, show elevated suicide rates. Suicidal people usually provide warnings, often are not intent on dying, and may not remain suicidal if they survive their crisis. Efforts at suicide prevention emphasize empathy, clarification of the person's problems, and professional assistance.

KEY TERMS

Agoraphobia
Antisocial personality
  disorder
Anxiety disorders
Attributions
Bipolar mood disorder
Catatonic schizophrenia
Competency
Concordance rate
Conversion disorder
Delusions
Depressive disorder
Diagnosis
Disorganized
  schizophrenia
Dissociative disorders
Epidemiology

Etiology
Generalized anxiety
  disorder
Hallucinations
Hypochondriasis
Insanity
Involuntary commitment
Medical model
Mood disorders
Multiple-personality
  disorder
Neurotic
Obsessive-compulsive
  disorder
Panic disorder
Paranoid schizophrenia
Personality disorders

Phobic disorder
Prevalence
Prognosis
Psychogenic amnesia
Psychosomatic diseases
Psychotic
Schizophrenic disorders
Seasonal affective
  (mood) disorder
Somatization disorder
Somatoform disorders
Transvestism
Undifferentiated
  schizophrenia

KEY PEOPLE

Nancy Andreasen
Janice Egeland
David Rosenhan
Martin Seligman
Thomas Szasz

PSYCHOTHERAPY

What do you picture when you hear the term *psychotherapy*? If you're like most people, you probably picture a troubled patient lying on a couch in a therapist's office, with the therapist asking penetrating questions and providing sage advice about the patient's problems. Commonly, people believe that psychotherapy is only for "sick" people, that therapists have special knowledge and powers that allow them to "see through" people, that therapy requires years of deep probing into a client's innermost secrets, and that therapists routinely tell their clients how to lead their lives. Like most stereotypes, this picture is a mixture of fact and fiction, as you'll see in the upcoming pages.

In this chapter we'll take a down-to-earth look at the complex process of psychotherapy. We'll start by discussing some general questions about how therapy is provided. Who seeks therapy? What kinds of professionals provide therapy? How many different types of therapy are there? After we've considered these general issues, we'll examine a number of the more widely used approaches to psychotherapy, analyzing their goals, techniques, and effectiveness. Toward the end of the chapter, we'll discuss the changing role of institutions involved in the treatment of mental illness. The Application focuses on practical issues involved in seeking psychotherapy.

THE ELEMENTS OF PSYCHOTHERAPY: TREATMENT, CLIENTS, AND THERAPISTS

Sigmund Freud is widely credited with launching modern psychotherapy, although the landmark case that inspired Freud was actually treated by one of his colleagues, Josef Breuer. Around 1880, Breuer began to treat a young woman who came to be known in the annals of psychology as Anna O (a pseudonym). Anna exhibited a variety of physical maladies, including headaches, coughing, and a loss of feeling and movement in her right arm. Much to his surprise, Breuer discovered that Anna's physical symptoms cleared up when he encouraged her to talk about emotionally charged experiences from her past. Breuer and Freud discussed the case, and they speculated that talking things through enabled Anna to drain off bottled up emotions that had caused her symptoms. Breuer found the intense emotional exchange in this treatment not to his liking, so he didn't follow through on his discovery. However, Freud applied Breuer's insight to other patients, and his successes led him to develop a systematic treatment procedure, which he called *psychoanalysis*.

Freud's breakthrough ushered in a century of great progress for psychotherapy. Psychoanalysis spawned many offspring as Freud's followers developed their own systems of treatment. Since then, approaches to psychotherapy have steadily grown more numerous, more diverse, and more effective. Today, people can choose from a bewildering array of different therapies. But what do they have in common? What exactly is psychotherapy?

Anna O called her treatment "the talking cure," but psychotherapy isn't always curative, and many modern therapies place little or no emphasis on talking. Freud once characterized psychotherapy as a form of "re-education." Jerome Frank (1982) views psychotherapy as a "confiding interaction between a trained, socially sanctioned healer and a sufferer." In contrast, Albert Ellis (1987) emphasizes that psychotherapy should help people to "achieve a greater degree of happiness, pleasure, joy, and self-fulfillment than they would otherwise tend to achieve."

As you can see, there's little consensus among the experts about the essence of psychotherapy. Indeed, after organizing an unprecedented conference that brought together many of the world's leading authorities on psychotherapy, Jeffrey Zeig commented, "I do not believe there is any capsule definition of psychotherapy on which the 26 presenters could agree" (Zeig, 1987, p. xix). Thus, the immense diversity of psychotherapy defies definition.

In lieu of a definition, we can identify a few basic elements that the various approaches to therapy have in common. All psychotherapies involve a helping relationship (the treatment) between a professional with special training (the therapist) and a person in need of help (the client). As we look at each of these elements—the treatment, the therapist, and the client—you'll see the range and variability of modern psychotherapy.

Treatment: How Many Types Are There?

In their efforts to help people, psychotherapists employ many different methods of treatment, including discussion, emotional support, persuasion, conditioning procedures, relaxation training, role playing, drug prescription, biofeedback, group therapy, and a host of "unconventional" procedures like poetry therapy, primal therapy, and rebirthing. No one knows exactly how many approaches to treatment there are, but one handbook (Herink, 1980) lists over 250 distinct types of psychotherapy.

Fortunately, we can impose some order on this chaos. As varied as therapists' procedures are, approaches to treatment can be classified into three major categories:

1. *Insight therapies.* Insight therapy is "talk therapy" in the tradition of Freud's psychoanalysis. This is probably the approach to treatment that you envision when you think of psychotherapy. In insight therapies, clients engage in complex, often lengthy verbal interactions with their therapists. The goal in these discussions is to pursue increased insight regarding the nature of the client's difficulties and to sort through possible solutions. Insight therapy can be conducted with an individual client or with a group.

2. *Behavior therapies.* Behavior therapies are based on the principles of learning and conditioning. Instead of emphasizing personal insights, behavior therapists make direct efforts to alter problematic responses (phobias, for example) and maladaptive habits (drug use, for instance). Behavior therapists work on changing clients' overt behaviors. They employ different procedures for different kinds of problems, but most of their procedures involve either classical conditioning or operant conditioning.

3. *Biomedical therapies.* Biomedical approaches to therapy involve interventions into a person's biological functioning. The most widely used procedures are the prescription of drugs and electroconvulsive (shock) therapy. As the name biomedical therapies suggests, only physicians (usually psychiatrists) can provide these biological treatments.

We'll examine approaches to therapy that fall into each of the three categories just described. Although we'll find very different methods in each category, the three major classes of treatment are not entirely incompatible. For example, a client might be seen in insight therapy and be given medication at the same time.

Clients: Who Seeks Therapy?

In the therapeutic triad (therapists, treatments, clients), the greatest diversity of all is seen among clients, who bring to therapy the full range of human problems: anxiety, depression, unsatisfactory interpersonal relations, troublesome habits, poor self-control, irrational thinking, low self-esteem, marital conflicts, self-doubt, a sense of emptiness, feelings of boredom, and personal stagnation. Therapy is sought by people who feel troubled, but the nature and severity of that trouble varies greatly from one person to another. The two most common presenting problems are excessive anxiety and depression (Lichtenstein, 1980).

A client in treatment does *not* necessarily have an identifiable psychological disorder. Some people seek professional advice simply because they want help with everyday problems (career decisions, for instance) or vague feelings of discontent. Thus, therapy includes professional efforts to enhance personal awareness and foster personal growth, as well as professional interventions for mental disorders.

People vary considerably in their willingness to seek psychotherapy. Men are less likely than women to enter therapy, and people from the lower socioeconomic classes are more reluctant to seek therapy than those from the upper classes (Lichtenstein, 1980). *Unfortunately, it appears that many people who need therapy don't receive it.* As Figure 15.1 shows, research indicates that only a minority of people with disorders receive treatment (Shapiro et al., 1984). Many people who could benefit from therapy don't seek it because (1) they're unaware that it's available, (2) they believe that its cost is prohibitive, or (3) they equate being in therapy with admitting personal weakness.

A small portion of clients are essentially forced into psychotherapy. In most cases, this coercion involves pressure from a spouse, parent, friend, or

Figure 15.1 Patterns of seeking treatment. Not everyone who has a psychological disorder receives professional treatment. This graph shows the percentage of people with specific disorders who obtained mental health treatment during a 6-month period. As you can see, only a minority of people with disorders receive treatment. (Data based on Shapiro et al., 1984)

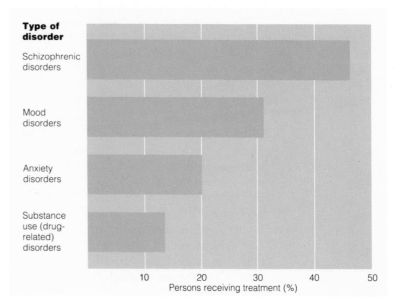

Type of disorder

Schizophrenic disorders

Mood disorders

Anxiety disorders

Substance use (drug-related) disorders

10   20   30   40   50
Persons receiving treatment (%)

Table 15.1 The Principal Mental Health Professions: Different Types of Therapists

TITLE	DEGREE*	YEARS BEYOND BACHELOR'S DEGREE	TYPICAL ROLES AND ACTIVITIES
Clinical or counseling psychologist	Ph.D. Psy.D. Ed.D.	5–7	Diagnosis, psychological testing, insight and behavior therapy
Psychiatrist	M.D.	8	Diagnosis; insight, behavior, and biomedical therapy
Social worker	M.S.W.	2	Insight and behavior therapy, family therapy, helping patients return to the community
Psychiatric nurse	B.S., B.A. M.A.	0–2	Inpatient care, insight and behavior therapy
Counselor	M.A.	2	Insight and behavior therapy, working primarily with everyday adjustment problems and marital and career issues

*Ph.D. = Doctor of Philosophy; Psy.D. = Doctor of Psychology; Ed.D. = Doctor of Education; M.D. = Medical Doctor; M.S.W. = Master of Social Work; B.S. = Bachelor of Science; B.A. = Bachelor of Arts; M.A. = Master of Arts.

employer. Sometimes, however, people are ordered into treatment by the courts, as in cases of involuntary commitment to a mental hospital.

Therapists: Who Provides Professional Treatment?

Friends and relatives may provide us with excellent advice about our personal problems, but their assistance doesn't qualify as therapy. Psychotherapy refers to *professional* treatment by someone with special training. However, a common source of confusion about psychotherapy is the variety of "helping professions" involved. Psychology and psychiatry are the principal professions involved in providing psychotherapy, but therapeutic services are also provided by psychiatric social workers, psychiatric nurses, and various types of counselors, as outlined in Table 15.1. Let's look at these mental health professions.

PSYCHOLOGISTS

Although widely associated wih psychotherapy, psychology is actually a latecomer to the mental health field. As we discussed in Chapter 1, psychology was predominantly an academic and research enterprise until World War II stimulated an unmet demand for therapeutic services and psychologists stepped into the breach. Today, two types of psychologists may provide therapy, although the distinction between them is more theoretical than real. **Clinical psychologists** and *counseling psychologists* specialize in the diagnosis and treatment of psychological disorders and everyday behavioral problems. In theory,

clinical psychologists' training emphasizes the treatment of full-fledged disorders, while counseling psychologists' training is slanted toward the treatment of everyday adjustment problems in normal people. In practice, however, clinical and counseling psychologists overlap so much in training, skills, and clientele that their roles are virtually interchangeable.

Both types of psychologists must earn a doctoral degree (Ph.D., Psy.D., or Ed.D.). A doctorate in psychology requires about 5 to 7 years of training beyond a bachelor's degree. The process of gaining admission to a Ph.D. program in clinical psychology is highly competitive (about as difficult as getting into medical school). Psychologists receive most of their training on university campuses, although they serve a 1-year or 2-year internship in a clinical setting such as a hospital.

In providing therapy, psychologists use either insight or behavioral approaches. In comparison to psychiatrists, they are more likely to use behavioral techniques and less likely to use psychoanalytic methods for insight therapy. Clinical and counseling psychologists do psychological testing as well as psychotherapy, and many also conduct research.

PSYCHIATRISTS

Psychiatrists are physicians who specialize in the treatment of psychological disorders. Many psychiatrists also treat everyday behavioral problems, although they tend to do so less often than psychologists. Figure 15.2, which compares the clientele seen by psychiatrists and psychologists,

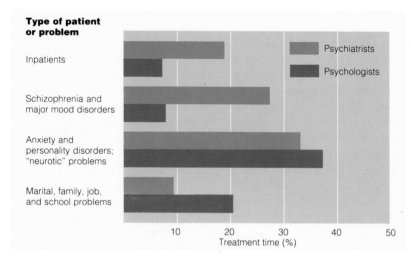

Type of patient or problem

Inpatients

Schizophrenia and major mood disorders

Anxiety and personality disorders; "neurotic" problems

Marital, family, job, and school problems

Psychiatrists
Psychologists

Treatment time (%)
10   20   30   40   50

Figure 15.2 Conditions treated by psychologists and psychiatrists. In comparison to psychologists, psychiatrists devote more of their time to the treatment of inpatients and more severe disorders, such as schizophrenia and major mood disorders. Although psychologists also treat these disorders, they devote more time than psychiatrists to the treatment of marital, family, work, and school problems. Note: The percentages for each profession do not add up to 100%, because there were other patient categories in the study and there was some overlap among categories. (Data from Knesper & Pagnucco, 1987)

shows that psychiatrists devote more of their time to inpatient care and relatively severe disorders (schizophrenia and mood disorders, for example) and less time to everyday marital, family, job, and school problems.

Psychiatrists have an M.D. degree. Their graduate training requires 4 years of course work in medical school followed by a 4-year "apprenticeship" in a residency at an approved hospital. Their psychotherapy training occurs during their residency, since the required course work in medical school is essentially the same for everyone, whether they're going into surgery, pediatrics, or psychiatry.

In providing therapy, psychiatrists tend to emphasize biomedical treatments that the other nonmedical helping professions can't provide (drug therapy, for instance). Psychiatrists employ a variety of insight therapies, but psychoanalysis and its descendants remain dominant in psychiatry. In comparison to psychologists, psychiatrists are less likely to use group therapies or behavior therapies.

OTHER MENTAL HEALTH PROFESSIONALS

Several other mental health professions provide psychotherapy services. In hospitals and other institutions, *psychiatric social workers* and *psychiatric nurses* often work as part of a treatment team with a psychologist or psychiatrist. Psychiatric nurses, who may have a bachelor's or master's degree in their field, play a large role in hospital inpatient treatment. Psychiatric social workers generally have a master's degree and typically work with patients and their families to ease the patient's integration back into the community.

Many kinds of *counselors* also provide therapeutic services. Counselors are usually found working in schools, colleges, and assorted human service agencies (youth centers, geriatric centers, family

planning centers, and so forth). Counselors typically have a master's degree. They often specialize in particular types of problems, such as vocational counseling, marital counseling, rehabilitation counseling, and drug counseling.

Although there are significant differences among the helping professions in education and training, their roles in the treatment process overlap considerably. In this chapter, we'll refer to psychologists or psychiatrists as needed, but otherwise we'll use the terms *clinician, therapist,* and *mental health professional* to refer to psychotherapists of all kinds, regardless of their professional degree.

Now that we've discussed the basic elements in psychotherapy, we can examine specific approaches to treatment in terms of their goals, procedures, and effectiveness. We'll begin with a few representative insight therapies.

A counselor comforting a patient in a day treatment program. Day treatment programs provide extensive therapeutic services on an outpatient basis, usually for people who have recently been hospitalized. Treatment teams in such programs may include therapists from any of the mental health professions, as well as paraprofessionals.

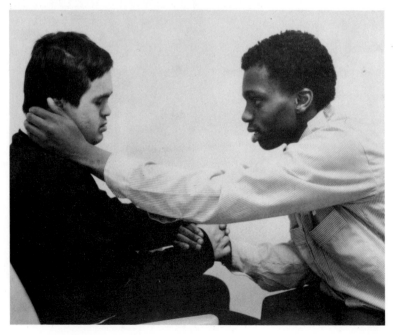

There are many schools of thought about how to do insight therapy. Therapists with different theoretical orientations use different methods to pursue different kinds of insights. However, what these varied approaches have in common is that *insight therapies* **involve verbal interactions intended to enhance clients' self-knowledge and thus promote healthful changes in personality and behavior.**

There probably are around 200 different insight therapies, but the leading eight or ten approaches appear to account for most of the treatment. In this section, we'll delve into psychoanalysis, related psychodynamic approaches, client-centered therapy, and cognitive therapy. We'll also discuss how insight therapy can be done with groups as well as individuals, and we'll evaluate evidence indicating how well insight therapy works.

Psychoanalysis

After the case of Anna O, Sigmund Freud worked as a psychotherapist for almost 50 years in Vienna. Through a painstaking process of trial and error, he developed innovative techniques for the treatment of psychological disorders and distress. His system of *psychoanalysis* came to dominate psychiatry, and it remains extremely influential today (Greenley, Kepecs, & Henry, 1981).

Psychoanalysis **is an insight therapy that emphasizes the recovery of unconscious conflicts, motives, and defenses through techniques such as free association and transference.** To appreciate the logic of psychoanalysis, we have to look at Freud's thinking about the roots of mental disorders. Freud mostly treated anxiety-dominated disturbances, such as phobic, panic, obsessive-compulsive, and conversion disorders, which were then called *neuroses*.

Freud believed that neurotic problems were caused by unconscious conflicts left over from early childhood. As explained in Chapter 12, he thought that these inner conflicts usually involved battles among the id, ego, and superego over sexual and aggressive impulses. According to Freud, people depend on defense mechanisms to avoid confronting these conflicts, which remain hidden in the depths of the unconscious. However, defensive maneuvers often lead to self-defeating behavior and are only partially successful in alleviating anxiety, guilt, and other distressing emotions. With this model in mind, let's take a look at the therapeutic procedures employed in psychoanalysis.

PROBING THE UNCONSCIOUS

Given Freud's assumptions, we can see that the logic of psychoanalysis is very simple. The analyst attempts to probe the murky depths of the unconscious to discover the unresolved conflicts causing the client's neurotic behavior. In a sense, the analyst functions as a "psychological detective." In

When most people think of psychotherapy, they envision a scene such as this—a therapist and one client engaged in intense discussion intended to foster personal insights. Although individual insight therapies are a common form of treatment, you'll see in this chapter that there are also many other approaches to treatment.

this effort to explore the unconscious, the therapist relies on two techniques: free association and dream analysis.

In *free association,* **clients spontaneously express their thoughts and feelings exactly as they occur, with as little censorship as possible.** Clients lie on a couch so that they'll be better able to let their mind drift and wander freely. Although Freud's legendary couch is widely associated with psychotherapy, psychoanalysts are about the only therapists who use the couch. In free associating, clients expound on anything that comes to mind, regardless of how trivial, silly, or embarrassing it might be. Gradually, most clients begin to let everything pour out without conscious censorship. The analyst studies these free associations for clues about what's going on in the unconscious.

In *dream analysis,* **the therapist interprets the symbolic meaning of the client's dreams.** For Freud, dreams were the "royal road to the unconscious," the most direct means of access to patients' innermost conflicts, wishes, and impulses. Clients are encouraged and trained to remember their dreams, which they then describe in therapy. The therapist analyzes the symbolism in these dreams to interpret their meaning.

To better illustrate these matters, let's look at an actual case treated through psychoanalysis (adapted from Greenson, 1967, pp. 40–41). Mr. N was troubled by an unsatisfactory marriage. He claimed to love his wife, but he preferred sexual relations with prostitutes. Mr. N reported that his parents had also endured lifelong marital difficulties, and his childhood conflicts about their relationship appeared to be related to his problems. Both dream analysis and free association can be seen in the following description of a session in Mr. N's treatment.

Mr. N reports a fragment of a dream. All that he can remember is that he is waiting for a red traffic light to change when he feels that someone has bumped into him from behind. . . . The associations led to Mr. N's love of cars, especially sports cars. He loved the sensation, in particular, of whizzing by those fat, old expensive cars. . . . His father always hinted that he had been a great athlete, but he never substantiated it. . . . Mr. N doubted whether his father could really perform. His father would flirt with a waitress in a cafe or make sexual remarks about women passing by, but he seemed to be showing off. If he were really sexual, he wouldn't resort to that.

As is characteristic of free association, Mr. N's train of thought meanders about with little apparent direction. Nonetheless, clues about his unconscious conflicts are apparent. What did Mr. N's therapist extract from this session? The therapist saw sexual overtones in the dream fragment, where Mr. N was bumped from behind, and detected a competitive orientation toward his father, based on the free association about whizzing by fat, old expensive cars. As you can see, analysts must *interpret* their clients' dreams and free associations. This is a critical process throughout psychoanalysis.

INTERPRETATION

Interpretation **involves the therapist's attempts to explain the inner significance of the client's thoughts, feelings, memories, and behaviors.** Contrary to popular belief, analysts do not interpret everything, and they generally don't try to dazzle clients with startling revelations. Instead, analysts move forward inch by inch, offering interpretations that should be just out of the client's own reach. Mr. N's therapist eventually offered the following interpretations to his client.

I said to Mr. N near the end of the hour that I felt he was struggling with his feelings about his father's sexual life. He seemed to be saying that his father was sexually not a very potent man. . . . He also recalls that he once found a packet of condoms under his father's pillow when he was an adolescent and he thought "My father must be going to prostitutes." I then intervened and pointed out that the condoms under his father's pillow seemed to indicate more obviously that his father used the condoms with his mother, who slept in the same bed. However, Mr. N *wanted* to believe his wish-fulfilling fantasy: mother doesn't want sex with father and father is not very potent. The patient was silent and the hour ended.

As you may already have guessed, the therapist has concluded that Mr. N's difficulties are caused by an unresolved Oedipal complex. He has sexual feelings toward his mother and hostile feelings about his father. These unconscious conflicts, which are rooted in Mr. N's childhood, are distorting his intimate relations as an adult.

RESISTANCE

How would you expect Mr. N to respond to his therapist's suggestion that he was in competition with his father for the sexual attention of his mother? Obviously, most clients would have great difficulty accepting such an interpretation. Freud fully expected clients to display some resistance to therapeutic efforts. *Resistance* **involves largely unconscious defensive maneuvers intended to hinder the progress of therapy.** Why do clients try to resist the helping process? Because they don't want to face up to the painful, disturbing conflicts that they've buried in their unconscious. Although they've sought help, they're reluctant to confront their real problems.

Resistance can take many forms. Patients may show up late for their sessions, merely pretend to engage in free association, or express hostility toward their therapist. For instance, Mr. N's therapist noted that after the session just described, "The next day he [Mr. N] began by telling me that he was furious with me. . . ." Analysts use a variety of strategies to deal with their clients' resistance to therapy. Often, a key consideration is the handling of transference, which we consider next.

TRANSFERENCE
Transference occurs when clients start relating to their therapist in ways that mimic critical relationships in their lives. Thus, a client might start relating to a therapist as if the therapist were an overprotective mother, a rejecting brother, or a passive spouse. In a sense, the client *transfers* conflicting feelings about important people onto the therapist. For instance, in his treatment, Mr. N transferred some of the competitive hostility he felt toward his father onto his analyst.

Psychoanalysts often encourage transference so that clients begin to reenact relations with crucial people in the context of therapy. These reenactments can help bring repressed feelings and conflicts to the surface, allowing the client to work through them. The therapist's handling of transference is complicated and difficult because transference may arouse confusing, highly charged emotions in the client.

Undergoing psychoanalysis is not easy. It can be a slow, painful process of self-examination that routinely requires 3 to 5 years of hard work. Ultimately, if resistance and transference can be handled effectively, the therapist's interpretations should lead the client to profound insights. For instance, Mr. N eventually admitted, "The old boy is probably right, it does tickle me to imagine that my mother preferred me and I could beat out my father. Later, I wondered whether this had something to do with my own screwed-up sex life with my wife." According to Freud, once clients recognize the unconscious sources of their conflicts, they can resolve these conflicts and discard their neurotic defenses.

Modern Psychodynamic Therapies

Though still available, classical psychoanalysis as done by Freud is not widely practiced anymore. Freud's psychoanalytic method was geared to a particular kind of clientele that he was seeing in Vienna many years ago. As his followers fanned out across Europe and America, many found that it was necessary to adapt psychoanalysis to differ-

"The news that reaches your consciousness is incomplete and often not to be relied on."
SIGMUND FREUD

ent cultures, changing times, and new kinds of patients. Thus, many variations on Freud's original approach to psychoanalysis have developed over the years. These descendants of psychoanalysis are collectively known as *psychodynamic approaches* to therapy.

Some of these adaptations, such as those by Carl Jung (1917) and Alfred Adler (1927), which we discussed in Chapter 12, were sweeping revisions based on fundamental differences in theory. Other variations, such as those devised by Melanie Klein (1948) and Heinz Kohut (1971), involved more subtle changes in theory. Still other revisions (Alexander, 1954; Stekel, 1950) simply involved efforts to modernize and streamline psychoanalytic techniques (rather than theory) as outlined in Table 15.2. Hence, today we have a rich diversity of psychodynamic approaches to therapy. Although examination of all of these many variations is beyond the scope of our review, we'll look at a few key trends seen in modern psychodynamic therapies, as highlighted by Kutash (1976) and Baker (1985).

First, many new approaches have tried to accelerate the pace of psychodynamic therapy. Modern approaches are less likely to assume that it will take 3 to 5 years of hard work to accomplish therapeutic gains.

Second, the goals of modern psychodynamic therapies usually go beyond the discovery of repressed conflicts and defenses. Analysts devote less attention to the workings of the unconscious. Instead, they focus on the conscious processes of the ego.

Third, client-therapist interactions have become more direct. Modern analysts depend less on the gradual, rambling process of free association. Many analysts have abandoned both the couch and free association in favor of face-to-face interaction that emphasizes candid communication.

Fourth, modern psychodynamic therapies no longer assume that neuroses grow out of conflicts centering around sex and aggression. Thus, analysts put less emphasis than formerly on probing into these areas, especially clients' sexuality.

Fifth, there also is less emphasis on delving into a client's distant past to reconstruct early childhood experiences. Instead, there's increased interest in understanding the client's present problems and current social relations.

Psychodynamic therapies have continued to evolve since Freud's era, but in recent decades most of the major innovations in insight therapy have emerged out of the humanistic tradition born in the 1950s. The most widely practiced humanistic therapy is Carl Rogers's *client-centered therapy*. Rogers's approach, which bears only slight resemblance to psychoanalysis, is next on our agenda.

Client-Centered Therapy

You may have heard of people going into therapy to "find themselves," or to "get in touch with their real feelings." These now popular phrases emerged out of the human potential movement, which was stimulated in part by Carl Rogers's work (Rogers, 1951, 1986). Employing a humanistic perspective, Rogers devised client-centered therapy (also known as person-centered therapy) in the 1940s and 1950s.

Client-centered therapy is an insight therapy that emphasizes providing a supportive emotional climate for clients, who play a major role in determining the pace and direction of their therapy. You may wonder why the troubled, untrained client is put in charge of the pace and direction of the therapy. Rogers (1961) provides a compelling justification:

It is the client who knows what hurts, what directions to go, what problems are crucial, what experiences have been deeply buried. It began to occur to me that unless I had a need to demonstrate my own cleverness and learning, I would do better to rely upon the client for the direction of movement in the process (pp. 11–12).

Rogers's theory about the principal causes of neurotic anxieties is quite different from the Freudian explanation. As discussed in Chapter 12, Rogers maintains that most personal distress is due to inconsistency, or "incongruence," between a person's self-concept and reality. According to his theory, incongruence makes people prone to feel threatened by realistic feedback about themselves from others. For example, if you inaccurately viewed yourself as a hardworking, dependable person and these perceptions were central to your self-concept, you would feel threatened by contradictory feedback from friends or coworkers. According to Rogers, anxiety about such feedback often leads to reliance on defense mechanisms, distortions of reality, and stifled personal growth. Excessive incongruence is thought to be rooted in clients' overdependence on others for approval and acceptance.

Given Rogers's theory, client-centered therapists stalk insights that are quite different from the repressed conflicts that psychoanalysts try to uncover. Client-centered therapists help clients to realize that they don't have to worry constantly about pleasing others and winning acceptance. They encourage clients to respect their own feelings and values. They help people to restructure

Table 15.2 Some Differences Between Classical and Modern Psychoanalysis

CLASSICAL PSYCHOANALYSIS	MODERN PSYCHOANALYSIS
Frequency of treatment is usually 4 to 5 times per week.	Frequency of treatment is typically 1 to 2 times per week.
Patient is treated "on the couch."	Patient is typically seen "face to face."
Treatment goals emphasize character reconstruction.	Treatment emphasizes problem resolution, enhanced adaptation, and support of ego functions with limited character change.
Treatment approach emphasizes the neutrality and nonintrusion of the analyst.	Therapist assumes an active and directive stance.
Technique emphasizes "free association," uncovering, interpretation, and analysis of transference and resistance.	A wide range of interventions are used, including interpretive, supportive, and educative techniques. Transference is typically kept less intense.

Source: Baker, 1985. (Baker divides contemporary psychodynamic therapies into three subgroups. "Modern psychoanalysis" refers to the group that has remained most loyal to Freud's ideas, while modifying clinical techniques.)

their self-concept to correspond better to reality. Ultimately, they try to foster self-acceptance and personal growth.

THERAPEUTIC CLIMATE

According to Rogers, the *process* of therapy is not as important as the emotional *climate* in which the therapy takes place. He believes that it's critical for the therapist to provide a warm, supportive, accepting climate. This creates a safe environment in which clients can confront their weaknesses and shortcomings without feeling threatened. The lack of threat should reduce clients' defensive tendencies and thus help them to open up. Rogers believes that to create this atmosphere of emotional support, client-centered therapists must provide three conditions:

1. *Genuineness.* The therapist must be genuine with the client, communicating in an honest and spontaneous manner. The therapist must not be phony or defensive.
2. *Unconditional positive regard.* The therapist must also show complete, nonjudgmental acceptance of the client as a person. The therapist should provide warmth and caring for the client with no strings attached. This doesn't mean that the therapist must approve of everything that the client says or does. A therapist can disapprove of a particular behavior while continuing to value the client as a human being.
3. *Empathy.* Finally, the therapist must provide accurate empathy for the client. This means that the therapist must understand the client's world from the client's point of view. Furthermore, the

therapist must be articulate enough to successfully communicate this understanding to the client.

THERAPEUTIC PROCESS

In client-centered therapy, the client and therapist work together as equals. The therapist provides relatively little guidance and keeps interpretation and advice to a minimum. So, just what does the client-centered therapist do, besides creating a supportive climate? Primarily, the therapist provides feedback to help clients sort out their feelings. The therapist's key task is *clarification*. Client-centered therapists try to function as a human mirror, reflecting statements back to their clients, but with enhanced clarity. They help clients to become more aware of their true feelings by highlighting themes that may be obscure in the clients' rambling discourse. The reflective nature of client-centered therapy can be seen in the following exchange between a client and therapist.

CLIENT: I really feel bad today . . . just terrible.

THERAPIST: You're feeling pretty bad.

CLIENT: Yeah, I'm angry and that's made me feel bad, especially when I can't do anything about it. I just have to live with it and shut up.

THERAPIST: You're very angry and feel like there's nothing you can safely do with your feelings.

CLIENT: Uh-huh. I mean . . . if I yell at my wife she gets hurt. If I don't say anything to her I feel tense.

THERAPIST: You're between a rock and a hard place—no matter what you do, you'll wind up feeling bad.

CLIENT: I mean she chews ice all day and all night. I feel stupid saying this. It's petty, I know. But when I sit there and try to concentrate I hear all these slurping and crunching noises. I can't stand it . . . and I yell.

"To my mind, empathy is in itself a healing agent."
CARL ROGERS

She feels hurt—I feel bad—like I shouldn't have said anything.

THERAPIST: So when you finally say something you feel bad afterward.

CLIENT: Yeah, I can't say anything to her without getting mad and saying more than I should. And then I cause more trouble than it's worth. (Duke & Nowicki, 1979, p. 565)

By working with clients to clarify their feelings, client-centered therapists hope to gradually build toward more far-reaching insights. In particular, they try to help clients to better understand their interpersonal relationships and to become more aware of and comfortable about their genuine selves. Obviously, these are very ambitious goals. Client-centered therapy resembles psychoanalysis in that both seek to help clients to "reconstruct" their personality. We'll see more limited and specific goals in cognitive therapy, which we consider next.

Cognitive Therapy

In the last two chapters, we saw that our cognitive interpretations of events make all the difference in the world in how well we handle stress and that cognitive factors play a key role in the development of depressive disorders. Citing the importance of findings such as these, Aaron Beck and his colleagues devised an approach to treatment that focuses directly on clients' cognitive processes (Beck 1987; Beck et al., 1979). **Cognitive therapy is an insight therapy that emphasizes recognizing and changing negative thoughts and maladaptive beliefs.** This approach resembles Albert Ellis's (1973; 1987) *rational-emotive ther-*

Table 15.3 Cognitive Errors and the Assumptions from Which They Are Derived According to Beck's Cognitive Theory

COGNITIVE ERROR	ASSUMPTION
Overgeneralizing	If it's true in one case, it applies to any case that's even slightly similar.
Selective abstraction	The only events that matter are failures, deprivation, and so forth. I should measure myself by errors, weaknesses, and so on.
Excessive responsibility (assuming personal causality)	I am responsible for all bad things, failures, and so forth.
Assuming temporal causality (predicting without sufficient evidence)	If it has been true in the past, then it's always going to be true.
Self-references	I am the center of everyone's attention, especially when my performance is bad.
Catastrophizing	Always think of the worst, because the worst is what's most likely to happen to you.
Dichotomous thinking	Everything is either one extreme or the other (black or white; good or bad).

apy. Since we covered Ellis's main ideas in our discussion of coping strategies (see the Chapter 13 Application), we'll focus exclusively on Beck's system here.

In recent years, cognitive therapy has been applied fruitfully to a wide range of disorders (Hollon & Najavits, 1988), but it was originally devised as a treatment for depression. According to Beck, depression is caused by "errors" in thinking (see Table 15.3). Among other things, he asserts that people make themselves depressed by (1) blaming their setbacks on personal inadequacies without considering circumstantial explanations, (2) focusing selectively on negative events while ignoring positive events, (3) making unduly pessimistic projections about the future, or (4) drawing negative conclusions, based on insignificant events, about their worth as a person. For instance, imagine that you earned a poor score on a minor quiz in a class. If you made the kinds of errors in thinking just described, you might blame the score on your woeful stupidity, dismiss comments from a classmate that it was an unfair test, hysterically predict that you'll surely flunk the course, and conclude that you're not genuine college material.

GOALS AND TECHNIQUES

The goal of cognitive therapy is to change the way the client thinks. At first, the therapist teaches clients to detect their automatic negative thoughts. These are self-defeating statements that people tend to make when analyzing problems. Examples might include "I'm just not smart enough," "No one really likes me," or "It's all my fault." Clients are then trained to subject these automatic thoughts to reality testing. The therapist helps them to see how unrealistically negative the thoughts are.

The therapist's goal is not to promote unwarranted optimism, but rather to help the client to employ more reasonable standards of evaluation. For example, a cognitive therapist might point out that a client's failure to get a desired promotion at work may be attributable to many factors and that this setback doesn't mean that the client is incompetent. Gradually, the therapist digs deeper, looking for the unrealistic assumptions that underlie clients' constant negative thinking. These, too, have to be changed.

Unlike client-centered therapists, cognitive therapists are actively involved in determining the pace and direction of treatment. They usually talk extensively in the therapy sessions. They may argue openly with clients as they try to persuade them to alter their patterns of thinking. The assertive nature of cognitive therapy is apparent in the following exchange between a patient and a therapist:

THERAPIST: What has your marriage been like?

PATIENT: It has been miserable from the very beginning . . . Raymond has always been unfaithful . . . I have hardly seen him in the past five years.

THERAPIST: You say that you can't be happy without Raymond . . . Have you found yourself happy when you are with Raymond?

PATIENT: No, we fight all the time and I feel worse.

THERAPIST: Then why do you feel that Raymond is essential for your living?

PATIENT: I guess it's because without Raymond I am nothing.

THERAPIST: Would you please repeat that?

PATIENT: Without Raymond I am nothing.

THERAPIST: What do you think of that idea?

PATIENT: . . . Well, now that I think about it, I guess it's not completely true.

THERAPIST: You said you are "nothing" without Raymond. Before you met Raymond, did you feel your were "nothing"?

PATIENT: No, I felt I was somebody.

THERAPIST: Are you saying then that it's possible to be something without Raymond?

PATIENT: I guess that's true. I can be something without Raymond.

THERAPIST: If you were somebody before you knew Raymond, why do you need him to be somebody now?

PATIENT: (*puzzled*) Hmmm . . . Well, I just don't think that I can find anybody else like him.

THERAPIST: Did you have male friends before you knew Raymond?

PATIENT: I was pretty popular then.

THERAPIST: If I understand you correctly then, you were able to fall in love before with other men and other men have fallen in love with you.

PATIENT: Uh huh.

THERAPIST: Why do you think you will be unpopular without Raymond now?

PATIENT: Because I will not be able to attract any other man.

THERAPIST: Have any men shown an interest in you since you have been married?

PATIENT: A lot of men have made passes at me but I ignore them.

THERAPIST: If you were free of the marriage, do you think that men might be interested in you—knowing that you were available?

PATIENT: I guess that maybe they would be. (Beck et al., 1979, pp. 217–219)

KINSHIP WITH BEHAVIOR THERAPY

Cognitive therapy borrows heavily from behavioral approaches to treatment, which we'll discuss shortly. Specifically, cognitive therapists often use

"Most people are barely aware of the automatic thoughts which precede unpleasant feelings or automatic inhibitions."
AARON BECK

"homework assignments" that focus on changing clients' overt behaviors. Clients may be instructed to engage in specified overt responses on their own, outside of the clinician's office. For example, one shy, insecure young man in cognitive therapy was told to go to a singles bar and engage three different women in conversations for up to 5 minutes each (Rush, 1984). He was instructed to record his thoughts before and after each of the conversations. This assignment elicited various maladaptive patterns of thought that gave the young man and his therapist plenty to talk about in subsequent sessions. As this example illustrates, cognitive therapy is a creative blend of "talk therapy" and behavior therapy, although it's primarily an insight therapy.

Cognitive therapy was originally designed as a treatment for individuals, but it has recently been adapted for use with groups (Covi & Primakoff, 1988). Many insight therapies can be conducted on either an individual or a group basis, so let's take a look at the dynamics of group therapy.

Group Therapy

Although it dates back to the early part of the 20th century, group therapy came of age during the 1950s and 1960s, when the expanding demand for therapeutic services forced clinicians to use group techniques. *Group therapy* **involves the simultaneous treatment of several clients in a group.** Most major insight therapies have been adapted for use with groups. In fact, the ideas underlying Rogers's client-centered therapy spawned the much publicized encounter-group movement. Although group therapy can be conducted in a variety of ways, we'll take a look at the process as it usually unfolds (see Fuchs, 1984; Grotjahn, Kline, & Friedmann, 1983).

PARTICIPANTS' ROLES

A therapy group typically consists of about five to ten participants. The therapist usually screens the group members. Most therapists exclude persons who seem likely to be disruptive. There's much debate about whether it's better to have a homogenous group (people who are similar in age, sex, and presenting problem) or a heterogenous group. Practical necessities usually dictate that groups are at least moderately heterogenous.

The therapist plays a subtle role in group therapy. Therapists often stay in the background and focus mainly on promoting group cohesiveness. They model supportive behaviors for the participants and try to promote a healthy climate. The therapist always retains a special status, but the therapist and clients are on much more equal footing in group therapy than in individual ther-

Insight therapy can be conducted with groups as well as individuals. Many approaches to group therapy rely on a variety of role-playing exercises to foster trust and open communication among participants. Group treatments have proven particularly useful in helping people with self-control problems. In peer self-help groups, such as Alcoholics Anonymous or Overeaters Anonymous, people with a common problem provide support and assistance for one another.

apy. The leader in group therapy expresses emotions, shares feelings, and copes with challenges from group members. In other words, group therapists participate in the group's exchanges and may "bare their own souls" to some extent.

In group therapy, participants essentially function as therapists for one another. Group members describe their problems, trade viewpoints, share experiences, and discuss coping strategies. Most importantly, they provide acceptance and emotional support for group members. In this supportive atmosphere, group members work at peeling away the social masks that cover their insecurities. Once their problems are exposed, members work at correcting them. As members come to value one another's opinions, they work hard to display healthy changes to win the group's approval of their behavior.

ADVANTAGES OF THE GROUP EXPERIENCE

Group therapies obviously save time and money, which can be critical in understaffed institutions. Therapists in private practice usually charge less for group than for individual therapy, making therapy affordable for more people. However, group therapy is not just a less costly substitute for individual therapy. Group therapy has unique strengths of its own. Irwin Yalom (1975), who has studied group therapy extensively, has described some of these advantages:

1. *In group therapy, participants often come to realize that their misery is not unique.* Clients often enter therapy feeling very sorry for themselves. They think that they alone have a terrible burden to bear. In the group situation, they quickly see that they're not unique. They're reassured to learn that many other people are coping with similar or even worse problems.

2. *Group therapy provides an opportunity for participants to work on their social skills in a safe environment.* Many personal problems essentially involve difficulties in relating effectively to people. Group therapy can provide a workshop for improving interpersonal skills that can't be matched by individual therapy.

3. *Certain kinds of problems are especially well suited to group treatment.* Specific types of problems and clients respond especially well to the social support that group therapy can provide. Peer self-help groups illustrate this advantage. In peer self-help groups, people who have a problem in common get together regularly to help one another. The original peer self-help group was Alcoholics Anonymous. Today, similar groups made up of former psychiatric patients, single parents,

or drug addicts, for example, work to help members deal with their unique types of problems.

Whether insight therapies are conducted on a group basis or an individual basis, clients usually invest considerable time, effort, and money. Are they worth the investment? In the next section, we examine the evidence on the effectiveness of insight therapy.

Evaluating Insight Therapies

In 1952, Hans Eysenck shocked mental health professionals by reporting that there was no sound evidence that insight therapy actually helped people. What was the basis for this startling claim? Eysenck (1952) reviewed numerous studies of therapeutic outcome for clients suffering from neurotic problems and found that about two-thirds of the clients recovered within two years. A two-thirds recovery rate wouldn't sound so bad, except that Eysenck found the same recovery rate among *untreated* neurotics. As we discussed in Chapter 14, psychological disorders sometimes clear up on their own. **In spontaneous remission a recovery from a disorder occurs without formal treatment.** Based on his estimate of the spontaneous remission rate for neurotic disorders, Eysenck concluded that "the therapeutic effects of [insight] psychotherapy are small or nonexistent."

In the ensuing years, critics pounced on Eysenck's (1952) article looking for flaws. They found a variety of shortcomings in his data. Eysenck made many arbitrary judgments about "recoveries" that were consistently unfavorable to the treated groups. Moreover, the untreated neurotics probably were not as severely disturbed as those who did pursue or require treatment. Ultimately, additional research indicated that Eysenck's estimate of the spontaneous remission rate was too high. More recent estimates suggest that the spontaneous remission rate for psychological disorders is in the vicinity of 30 to 40% (Bergin, 1971). Although Eysenck's conclusions were unduly pessimistic, he made an important contribution to the mental health field by sparking debate and research on the effectiveness of insight therapy.

Evaluating the effectiveness of any approach to psychotherapy is a complicated matter, but this is especially true for insight therapies. If you were to undergo insight therapy, how would you judge its effectiveness? By how you felt? By looking at your behavior? By asking your therapist? By consulting your friends and family? What would you be looking for? People enter therapy with different prob-

ically had some success in "curing" mental disorders with incantations, rituals, exorcisms, and so forth.

In spite of the difficulties inherent in evaluating the effects of therapy, hundreds of therapy outcome studies have been conducted since Eysenck's broadside prodded researchers into action. These studies consistently indicate that insight therapy *is* superior to no treatment. Two major reviews of the literature (Luborsky, Singer, & Luborsky, 1975; Meltzoff & Kornreich, 1970) conclude that therapy outshines an absence of treatment in about 80% of the studies. In an exceptionally comprehensive review, Smith, Glass, and Miller (1980) examined 475 studies and estimated that the average therapy client ends up better off than 80% of comparable, untreated controls.

Admittedly, this outcome research doesn't indicate that insight therapy leads to miraculous results. The superiority of therapy over no treatment is usually characterized as modest. In light of the price of therapy, there's room for debate about its cost-effectiveness. Overall, about 70 to 80% of clients appear to benefit from insight therapy while 20 to 30% fail to show any apparent improvement.

Some investigators have tried to figure out which clients are most likely to benefit from insight therapy. Schofield (1964) concluded that "YAVIS" clients are the best candidates for this type of therapy. What's a YAVIS? The letters are an abbreviation for young, attractive, verbal, intelligent, and successful. Schofield's findings make sense in that verbal therapy logically requires a client who is articulate, insightful, and motivated.

Clients' personal characteristics tend to be considerably less important when behavioral treatments are employed. As you'll see in the next section, behavior therapies can be useful with a wide range of clients, including some who are severely disturbed.

lems and needs. Different schools of thought seek to realize entirely different goals. Thus, measures of therapeutic outcome are inevitably subjective.

A key problem in assessing the effectiveness of insight therapy is that both therapists and clients are biased strongly in the direction of evaluating therapy favorably (Rachman & Wilson, 1980). Why? Therapists want to see improvement because it reflects on their professional competence. Obviously, they hope to see clients getting better as a result of their work. Clients tend to make a favorable evaluation because they want to justify their effort, their heartache, their expense, and their time.

Another problem that complicates the evaluation of psychotherapy is the occurrence of placebo effects. As explained in Chapter 2, if a client expects a treatment to help, it may help simply because of this expectation. This is presumably why witch doctors and medicine men have histor-

BEHAVIOR THERAPIES

Behavior therapy is different from insight therapy in that behavior therapists make no attempt to help clients achieve grand insights about themselves. Why not? Because behavior therapists believe that such insights are unnecessary to produce constructive change. For example, consider a client troubled by compulsive gambling. The behavior therapist doesn't care whether this behavior is rooted in unconscious conflicts or parental rejection. What the client needs is to get rid of the maladaptive behavior. Consequently, the

therapist simply designs a program to eliminate the compulsive gambling.

Actually, behavior therapists are not entirely uninterested in helping clients attain a better understanding of their behavior (Franks & Barbrack, 1983). They may work with clients to attain very limited insights about how environmental factors evoke troublesome behaviors such as excessive gambling, because information of this sort can sometimes be helpful in designing a behavioral therapy program.

The crux of the difference between insight therapy and behavior therapy is this: insight therapists treat pathological symptoms as signs of an underlying problem, whereas behavior therapists think that the symptoms *are* the problem. Thus, **behavior therapies involve the application of the principles of learning to direct efforts to change clients' maladaptive behaviors**.

Although behaviorism has been an influential school of thought in psychology since the 1920s, behaviorists devoted little attention to clinical issues until Joseph Wolpe launched behavior therapy in 1958 with his description of *systematic desensitization* (discussed a little later in this chapter). Since then, interest in behavioral approaches to psychotherapy has exploded. Today, more and more psychologists are using behavioral approaches, especially those who work with children (O'Leary, 1984).

General Principles

Behavior therapies are based on certain assumptions (Lazarus & Fay, 1984). *First, it's assumed that behavior is a product of learning.* No matter how self-defeating or pathological a client's behavior might be, the behaviorist believes that it's the result of past conditioning. *Second, it's assumed that what has been learned can be unlearned.* The same learning principles that explain how the maladaptive behavior was acquired can be used to get rid of it. Thus, behavior therapists attempt to change clients' behavior by applying the principles of classical conditioning, operant conditioning, and observational learning.

Behavior therapies are close cousins of the self-modification procedures described in the Chapter 6 Application. Both employ the same principles of learning to alter behavior directly. In discussing *self-modification*, we examined some relatively simple procedures that people can apply to themselves to improve everyday self-control. In our discussion of *behavior therapy*, we'll examine more complex procedures used by mental health professionals in the treatment of more severe problems.

Like self-modification, behavior therapy requires that clients' vague complaints ("My life is filled with frustration") be translated into concrete behavioral goals ("I need to acquire and increase my use of assertive responses in dealing with family and colleagues"). Once the troublesome behaviors have been targeted, the therapist designs a program to alter them. The nature of the therapeutic program depends on the types of problems identified. Behavior therapists employ different procedures for different problems. Some procedures depend on classical conditioning, while others depend on operant conditioning and observational learning.

Treatments Based on Classical Conditioning

A variety of behavioral procedures involve applications of the principles of classical conditioning, first described by Ivan Pavlov. We'll examine two examples: systematic desensitization and aversion therapy.

SYSTEMATIC DESENSITIZATION

Devised by Joseph Wolpe (1958, 1987), a treatment called systematic desensitization revolutionized the treatment of phobic disorders. **Systematic desensitization is a behavior therapy used to reduce clients' anxiety responses through counterconditioning.** The treatment assumes that most anxiety responses are acquired through classical conditioning (as we discussed in Chapters 6 and 14). According to this model, a harmless stimulus (for instance, a bridge) may be paired with a frightening event (lightning strikes it) so that the harmless stimulus becomes a conditioned stimulus eliciting anxiety. The goal of systematic desensitization is to weaken the association between the conditioned stimulus (the bridge) and the conditioned response of anxiety.

Systematic desensitization involves three steps. *First, the therapist helps the client to build an anxiety hierarchy* (see Figure 15.3). The hierarchy is a

"Neurotic anxiety is nothing but a conditioned response."
JOSEPH WOLPE

Figure 15.3 Example of an anxiety hierarchy. Systematic desensitization requires the construction of an anxiety hierarchy like the one shown here, which was developed for a woman who had a fear of heights and a penchant for hiking in the mountains.

Degree of fear	An Anxiety Hierarchy for Systematic Desensitization
5	I'm standing on the balcony on the top floor of an apartment tower.
10	I'm standing on a stepladder in the kitchen to change a light bulb.
15	I'm walking on a ridge. The edge is hidden by shrubs and treetops.
20	I'm sitting on the slope of a mountain, looking out over the horizon.
25	I'm crossing a bridge 6 feet above a creek. The bridge consists of an 18-inch-wide board with a handrail on one side.
30	I'm riding a ski lift 8 feet above the ground.
35	I'm crossing a shallow, wide creek on an 18-inch-wide board, 3 feet above water level.
40	I'm climbing a ladder outside the house to reach a second-story window.
45	I'm pulling myself up a 30-degree wet, slippery slope on a steel cable.
50	I'm scrambling up a rock, 8 feet high.
55	I'm walking 10 feet on a resilient, 18-inch-wide board, which spans an 8-foot-deep gulch.
60	I'm walking on a wide plateau, 2 feet from the edge of a cliff.
65	I'm skiing an intermediate hill. The snow is packed.
70	I'm walking over a railway trestle.
75	I'm walking on the side of an embankment. The path slopes to the outside.
80	I'm riding a chair lift 15 feet above the ground.
85	I'm walking up a long, steep slope.
90	I'm walking up (or down) a 15-degree slope on a 3-foot-wide trail. On one side of the trail the terrain drops down sharply; on the other side is a steep upward slope.
95	I am walking on a 3-foot-wide ridge. The slopes on both sides are long and more than 25 degrees steep.
100	I'm walking on a 3-foot-wide ridge. The trail slopes on one side. The drop on either side of the trail is more than 25 degrees.

list of anxiety-arousing stimuli centering around the specific source of anxiety—for example, flying, academic tests, snakes, or the other sex. The client ranks the stimuli from the least anxiety arousing to the most anxiety arousing. This ordered list of related, anxiety-provoking stimuli is the anxiety hierarchy. The example we've shown in Figure 15.3 is an anxiety hierarchy for one woman's fear of heights.

The second step involves training the client in deep muscle relaxation. This second phase may begin during early sessions while the therapist and client are still constructing the anxiety hierarchy. Different therapists use different relaxation training procedures. Whatever procedures are employed, the client must learn to engage in deep and thorough relaxation on command from the therapist.

In the third step, the client tries to work through the hierarchy, learning to remain relaxed while imagining each stimulus. Starting with the least anxiety-arousing stimulus, the client imagines the situation as vividly as possible while relaxing. If clients experience strong anxiety, they drop the imaginary scene and concentrate on relaxation. The clients keep repeating this process until they can imagine a scene with little or no anxiety. Once a particular scene is conquered, a client moves on to the next stimulus situation in the anxiety hierarchy. Gradually, over a number of therapy sessions, clients progress through the hierarchy, unlearning troublesome anxiety responses.

As clients conquer *imagined* phobic stimuli, they may be encouraged to confront the *real* stimuli. Although desensitization to imagined stimuli can be effective by itself, many behavior therapists advocate following it up with planned exposures to the real anxiety-arousing stimuli (Lazarus & Wilson, 1976). The desensitization to imagined stimuli should reduce anxiety enough so that clients will be able to confront situations they used to avoid at all costs. Usually, these real-life confrontations will prove harmless, and the per-

son's anxiety response should be diminished further. Without the desensitization, however, the client probably would have continued to avoid the feared stimulus situations.

The principle at work in systematic desensitization is simple. Anxiety and relaxation are incompatible responses. The trick is to recondition people so that the conditioned stimulus elicits relaxation instead of anxiety. This is counterconditioning—an attempt to reverse the process of classical conditioning by associating the crucial stimulus with a new conditioned response. Although it seems simple, systematic desensitization can be very effective in eliminating specific anxieties (Leitenberg, 1976).

AVERSION THERAPY

Aversion therapy is far and away the most controversial of the behavior therapies. It's not something that you would sign up for unless you were pretty desperate. Psychologists usually suggest it only as a treatment of last resort, after other interventions have failed. What's so terrible about aversion therapy? The client has to endure decidedly unpleasant stimuli, such as shock or drug-induced nausea.

Aversion therapy is a behavior therapy in which an aversive stimulus is paired with a stimulus that elicits an undesirable response. For example, alcoholic clients have had drug-induced nausea paired with their favorite drinks during therapy sessions (Cannon, Baker, & Wehl, 1981). By pairing an *emetic drug* (one that causes vomiting) with alcohol, the therapist hopes to create a conditioned aversion to alcohol (see Figure 15.4).

You may be thinking—"Wait a minute. The alcoholic clients know that when they go into their local tavern, they're not going to get a drink laced with an emetic. Why should the aversive conditioning treatment prevent them from drinking?" Aversive conditioning works because it can change reflexive, gut-level responses to stimuli. Perhaps you remember the anecdote in Chapter 6 about how Martin Seligman once experienced the onset of severe nausea from the flu in the midst of eating a sauce bearnaise. This single pairing of nausea with bearnaise sauce created a long-lasting distaste for bearnaise, even though Seligman "knew" that eating bearnaise wouldn't lead to nausea.

Aversion therapy takes advantage of the "automatic" nature of responses produced through classical conditioning. Sure, alcoholics treated with aversion therapy know that they won't be given an emetic outside of their therapy sessions. However, their reflex response to the stimulus of alcohol may be changed so that they respond to it

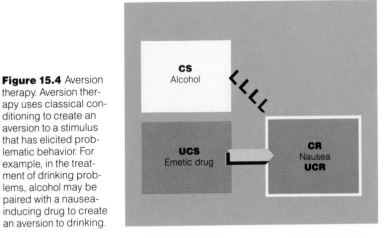

Figure 15.4 Aversion therapy. Aversion therapy uses classical conditioning to create an aversion to a stimulus that has elicited problematic behavior. For example, in the treatment of drinking problems, alcohol may be paired with a nausea-inducing drug to create an aversion to drinking.

Figure 15.5 An example of a token economy. Token economies are often used in institutional settings to promote desirable behavior. Patients are rewarded for appropriate behaviors with symbolic reinforcers that are subsequently exchanged for real reinforcers.

with nausea and distaste, making it much easier to go without drinking.

Aversion therapy can be helpful in reducing the frequency of clients' maladaptive responses. Troublesome behaviors treated successfully with aversion therapy include drug abuse, sexual deviance, self-mutilation, gambling, shoplifting, stuttering, cigarette smoking, and overeating (Lazarus & Wilson, 1976; Sandler, 1975). Typically, aversion therapy is only one element in a multifaceted treatment program. Of course, this procedure should be used only with willing clients and when other options have failed (Rimm & Cunningham, 1985).

Treatments Based on Operant Conditioning

The principles of operant conditioning described by B. F. Skinner and his followers are at work in many widely used behavior therapies, including some that also depend on observational learning. In this section we'll examine three treatments that depend primarily on operant principles: token economies, social skills training, and biofeedback.

TOKEN ECONOMIES

Token economies take advantage of the power of positive reinforcement. **A *token economy* is a behavior therapy designed to increase desirable responses by doling out symbolic reinforcers.** These symbolic reinforcers can later be converted into a variety of real reinforcers. Teodoro Ayllon and Nathan Azrin (1968) pioneered the use of token economies in mental hospitals to promote healthy, responsible behavior in patients, including severely disturbed psychotic patients who aren't likely respond to insight therapy.

A common problem with chronic psychotic patients is that they tend to be apathetic and their everyday adaptive behavior deteriorates. Although their apathy may not be the crux of their disorder, it often makes treatment difficult. A token economy can be used to penetrate patients' apathy while strengthening their normal adaptive behavior. In a token economy, hospital staff reward patients for voluntarily engaging in desirable responses such as taking care of personal hygiene,

cleaning their rooms, treating one another respectfully, taking scheduled medications, and cooperating with hospital personnel (see Figure 15.5). Staff members quickly reinforce appropriate behavior by awarding points or more concrete symbols of reinforcement, such as poker chips. Residents later trade these symbolic reinforcers for genuine reinforcers such as cigarettes, candy, magazines, recreational opportunities, and passes to leave the hospital. In some programs, patients have to give up tokens when they display disruptive behavior.

The token economy uses various principles of operant conditioning. The tokens are *secondary reinforcers* that acquire the capacity to strengthen desired responses by virtue of being paired with primary reinforcers. Staff members award token reinforcers immediately because operant research shows that *rapid reinforcement* works better than delayed reinforcement. The principle of *punishment* is at work when patients forfeit tokens because of troublesome behavior.

A well-run token economy can make a psychiatric ward a healthier environment by making it more like the "real world." Although token economies don't cure disorders, they can facilitate effective treatment. Studies indicate that token economies can lead to more rapid discharge of patients and lower readmission rates than traditional hospital environments (Curran, Monti, & Corriveau, 1982; Paul & Lentz, 1977). Token economies have proved useful in many kinds of institutionalized settings. They're commonly used in programs for retarded individuals, delinquent youngsters, and people with drug-abuse problems.

SOCIAL SKILLS TRAINING

Many psychological problems grow out of interpersonal difficulties. Behavior therapists point out

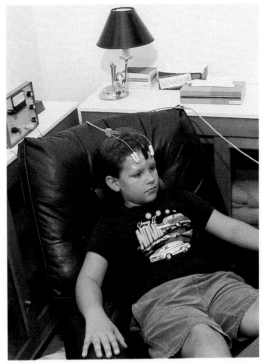

Biofeedback can be employed in a variety of ways with both adults and children. The EMG biofeedback device shown here monitors muscular tension recorded from the forehead and transforms this information into an auditory signal that increases and decreases in volume as one's level of muscular tension changes.

phasizes **shaping, modeling, and behavioral rehearsal.** This type of behavior therapy can be conducted with individual clients or in groups. Social skills training depends on the principles of operant conditioning and observational learning. *Modeling* is employed by encouraging clients to watch socially skilled friends and colleagues, so that responses (eye contact, active listening, and so on) can be acquired through observation.

In *behavioral rehearsal*, the client tries to practice social techniques in structured role-playing exercises. The therapist provides corrective feedback and uses approval to reinforce progress. Eventually, of course, clients try their newly acquired skills in real-world interactions. Usually, they're given specific homework assignments. *Shaping* is employed as clients are gradually asked to handle more complicated and delicate social situations. For example, a nonassertive client may begin by working on making requests of friends. Only much later will the client be asked to tackle standing up to his boss.

Comprehensive social skills training is a relatively recent innovation in behavior therapy, although it's similar to *assertiveness training*, which is an older, more specialized type of behavioral intervention. More research is needed, but available evidence suggests that social skills training can be very fruitful (Brady, 1984).

BIOFEEDBACK

Biofeedback is another promising therapy that has emerged from the behavioral tradition. **In *biofeedback* an aspect of a person's physiological functioning (such as heart rate) is monitored, and information about it is fed back to the person to facilitate improved control of the physiological process.** Armed with precise information about internal bodily functions, people are able to exert far more control over some of these functions than was previously thought possible. For example, many anxious people develop problematic high blood pressure. Obviously, it would be nice if these people could learn to control their blood pressure without depending on drugs that may have side effects. Evidence suggests that biofeedback *can* be used to train people to control their blood pressure (Shapiro, Schwartz, & Tursky, 1972).

To see how biofeedback works, let's look at *electromyograph* (EMG) feedback intended to enhance relaxation. An EMG is a device used to measure skeletal-muscular tension in the body. In a typical training session, a client is hooked up to an EMG, and its recordings are transformed into an auditory signal, such as a tone that increases and decreases in volume. The therapist explains

that we aren't born with social finesse; we acquire our social skills through learning. Unfortunately, some people don't learn how to be friendly, how to make conversation, how to express anger appropriately, how to turn away unreasonable requests, and so forth. Social ineptitude can contribute to anxiety, feelings of inferiority, and various kinds of disorders. In light of these findings, therapists are increasingly trying to devise treatments to improve patients' social abilities.

Social skills training is a behavior therapy designed to improve interpersonal skills; it em-

---

CONCEPT CHECK 15.2
Understanding Therapists' Goals

Check your understanding of therapists' goals by matching various therapies with the appropriate description of their therapeutic goals. The answers are in Appendix A.

Principal therapeutic goals

_____ 1. Elimination of maladaptive behaviors or symptoms

_____ 2. Acceptance of genuine self, personal growth

_____ 3. Recovery of unconscious conflicts, character reconstruction

_____ 4. Detection and reduction of negative thinking

Therapy

a. Psychoanalysis
b. Client-centered therapy
c. Cognitive therapy
d. Behavior therapy

to the client that changes in the tone will reflect changes in his or her level of muscular tension. The client is instructed to raise or lower the tone.

Although people often have difficulty describing how they do it, most can learn to exert better control over their level of muscular tension. Essentially, EMG feedback helps them to improve their ability to engage in deep muscle relaxation. Promising results have been obtained with EMG feedback in the treatment of anxiety (Raskin, Bali, & Peeke, 1981), tension headaches (Blanchard & Andrasik, 1982), and high blood pressure (Lustman & Sowa, 1983).

In some respects, biofeedback is a *biological* intervention and it could be classified as a biomedical therapy. However, it's usually grouped with the behavior therapies because it works directly on symptoms, its use is not limited to physicians, and the strategy emerged out of behavioral research. Studies have revealed that biofeedback can be used to help people exert some control over brainwave activity, skin temperature, blood pressure, heart rate, and muscle tension (Adler & Adler, 1984). Early proponents of biofeedback may have made overly extravagant claims about its benefits, but this unique intervention appears to have potential for treating many stress-related problems.

Evaluating Behavior Therapies

Ample evidence attests to the effectiveness of behavior therapy (Rachman & Wilson, 1980; Smith et al., 1980). Indeed, the evidence for the effectiveness of behavior therapy is stronger than the evidence for insight therapy. This is true for two reasons. First, being more research oriented, behavior therapists have historically placed greater emphasis than insight therapists have on the importance of measuring therapeutic outcomes. Second, behavior therapists can often measure progress more precisely than insight therapists because their therapeutic goals are more specific and concrete. Changes in overt behavior are much easier to assess than the profound insights pursued in verbal therapies.

A widely cited study by Gordon Paul (1966) illustrates how behavior therapists carefully evaluate their procedures. His study compared the effectiveness of systematic desensitization, insight therapy, and a placebo in the treatment of anxiety related to public speaking. The subjects were students who were fearful of speaking in front of groups. To assess their pretreatment speech phobias, they were asked to give a speech while various physiological, behavioral, and self-report measures of anxiety were made. The students were then assigned to one of four treatment con-

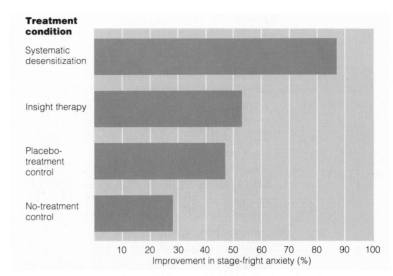

Treatment condition

Improvement in stage-fright anxiety (%)

ditions. After the completion of the treatments, subjects were asked to give another speech, and their anxiety was measured once again. Two years later, additional follow-up measures of speech anxiety were made. All the treatments, including the placebo, produced significant improvement. However, the results indicated that systematic desensitization was superior to the insight therapy and the placebo treatment in reducing stage fright (see Figure 15.6).

How does the effectiveness of behavior therapy compare to that of insight therapy? In direct comparisons of behavior therapy and insight therapy, the differences are usually small (Smith et al., 1980). However, these modest differences tend to favor behavioral approaches (Kazdin & Wilson, 1978). Of course, behavior therapies are not well-suited to the treatment of some types of problems (vague feelings of discontent, for instance). Furthermore, it's misleading to make global statements about the effectiveness of behavior therapies because they encompass a diverse array of very different procedures designed for different purposes. For example, the value of systematic desensitization for phobias is unrelated to the value of aversion therapy for sexual deviance.

For our purposes, it's sufficient to note that there is favorable evidence on the efficacy of most of the widely used behavioral interventions. Behavior therapies seem to be particularly effective in the treatment of anxiety problems, phobias, obsessive-compulsive disorders, sexual dysfunction, sexual deviance, drug-related problems, and obesity (Rachman & Wilson, 1980).

Only a few of these problems would be amenable to treatment with the biomedical therapies, which we'll consider next. To some extent, the three major approaches to treatment have different strengths. Let's see where the strengths of the biomedical therapies lie.

Figure 15.6 The effectiveness of systematic desensitization. When Paul (1966) compared systematic desensitization, insight therapy, and two control conditions in the treatment of public speaking phobias, he found that desensitization was the most effective intervention. Behavior therapies are often evaluated in formal studies such as this one.

BIOMEDICAL THERAPIES

In the 1950s, researchers synthesized an antihistamine drug called *chlorpromazine*. Antihistamines are generally used in the treatment of hay fever and other allergies, and are found in many over-the-counter cold remedies. However, a French surgeon looking for a drug that would reduce patients' autonomic response to surgical stress noticed that chlorpromazine produced a mild sedation. Based on this observation, Delay and Deniker (1952) decided to give chlorpromazine to hospitalized schizophrenic patients, to see if the drug might have calming effects on them.

Their experiment was a dramatic success; chlorpromazine became the first effective antipsychotic drug, and a revolution in psychiatry was begun. Hundreds of thousands of severely disturbed patients, who had appeared doomed to lead the rest of their lives in mental hospitals, were gradually sent home, thanks to the therapeutic effects of antipsychotic drugs. Today, biomedical therapies, such as drug treatment, lie at the core of psychiatric practice.

Biomedical therapies involve physiological interventions intended to reduce symptoms associated with psychological disorders. These therapies assume that psychological disorders are caused, at least in part, by biological malfunctions. As we discussed in Chapter 14, this assumption clearly has merit for many disorders, especially the more severe ones. We'll discuss two biomedical approaches to psychotherapy: drug therapy and electroconvulsive (shock) therapy.

Treatment with Drugs

Psychopharmacotherapy involves the treatment of mental disorders with medication, which we'll refer to more simply as *drug therapy*. Therapeutic drugs fall into three major groups with one notable "leftover" that doesn't fit neatly into any of the basic categories. The three major groupings are (1) antianxiety drugs, (2) antipsychotic drugs, and (3) antidepressant drugs, and the leftover is lithium, which is used in the treatment of bipolar mood disorders.

ANTIANXIETY DRUGS
Almost all of us know someone who pops pills to relieve anxiety. **Antianxiety drugs, which relieve tension, apprehension, and nervousness,** are the drugs involved in this common coping strategy. The most popular of these has been a drug known by the trade name Valium. Trade names are the names that pharmaceutical companies use in mar-

keting drugs. These names are often more widely known than the drugs' scientific or generic names. For example, the less well-known generic name for Valium is diazepam.

The drugs in the diazepam family are often called *tranquilizers*. They are routinely prescribed for people with anxiety disorders. They are also given to millions of people who simply suffer from chronic nervous tension. In the mid 1970s, U.S. pharmacists were filling nearly *100 million* prescriptions each year for Valium and similar antianxiety drugs, a level of use that many critics characterized as excessive (Lickey & Gordon, 1983).

Antianxiety drugs exert their effects almost immediately. They can be fairly effective in alleviating feelings of anxiety (Lader, 1984). However, their effects are measured in hours, so their impact is relatively short-lived. As noted in Chapter 3, their effects appear to be due to their impact on neurotransmitter activity at GABA synapses.

The principal side effects of antianxiety drugs are drowsiness and lethargy. There's some potential for abuse and dependency problems with these drugs. Some people get hooked on Valium and are unable to function without it (Lickey & Gordon, 1983). Problems with the abuse of tranquilizers led to a moderate decline in their use in the 1980s. Currently, researchers are studying the effects of a new antianxiety drug called Buspar (buspirone) that has less potential for abuse. Unlike Valium, Buspar is slow acting, exerting its effects in 7 to 10 days, but with fewer sedative effects (Newton et al., 1986).

ANTIPSYCHOTIC DRUGS
Antipsychotic drugs are used primarily in the treatment of schizophrenia, although they may also be given to people with severe mood disorders who become delusional. The trade names (and generic names) of some prominent drugs in this category are Thorazine (chlorpromazine hydrochloride), Mellaril (thioridazine), and Haldol (haloperidol). **Antipsychotic drugs are used to gradually reduce psychotic symptoms, including hyperactivity, mental confusion, hallucinations, and delusions.**

About two-thirds of psychotic patients respond favorably to antipsychotic medication (Baldessarini, 1984). When antipsychotic drugs are effective, they work their magic very gradually, as shown in Figure 15.7. Patients usually begin to respond within 2 days to a week. Further improvement may occur for several months. Many schizophrenic patients are placed on antipsychotics indefinitely because these drugs can reduce the likelihood of a relapse into an active schizophrenic episode. Antipsychotic drugs appear to work primarily by dampening activity at dopamine synapses in the brain (Davidson, Losonczy, & Davis, 1986).

Antipsychotic drugs undeniably make a major contribution to the treatment of severe mental disorders, but they're not without problems. They have many unpleasant side effects. Drowsiness, constipation, and cottonmouth (excess dryness) are common. Tremors, muscular rigidity, and impairment of coordination may also occur. After being released from a hospital, many schizophrenic patients who have been placed on antipsychotics discontinue their drug regimen because of the disagreeable side effects. Unfortunately, as Figure 15.8 shows, relapse into another schizophrenic episode often occurs within 3 to 18 months after a patient stops taking antipsychotic medication (Baldessarini, 1984; Davis, 1985).

In addition to minor side effects, antipsychotics may cause a severe and lasting problem called tardive dyskinesia. **Tardive dyskinesia is a neurological disorder marked by chronic tremors and involuntary spastic movements.** This debilitating syndrome resembles the well-known Parkinson's disease, and there is no cure. There has been a heated debate about how often this serious side effect occurs as a result of antipsychotic drug therapy (Brown & Funk, 1986). It may occur in as many as 25% of patients who take antipsychotics

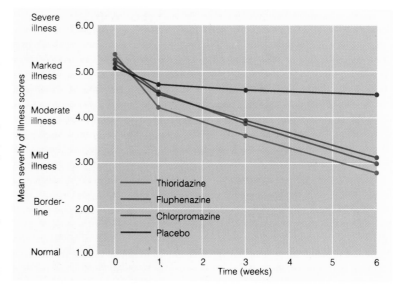

over a prolonged period (Jeste & Wyatt, 1982). As the prevalence of this problem has come to be recognized, experts have urged psychiatrists to become more conservative about prescribing antipsychotics on a long-term basis.

ANTIDEPRESSANT DRUGS

As their name suggests, **antidepressant drugs gradually elevate mood and help to bring people out of a depression.** There are two principal classes of antidepressants: *tricyclics* (such as Elavil) and *MAO inhibitors* (such as Nardil). These two sets of drugs appear to affect neurochemical activity in different ways and tend to work with different types of patients. The tricyclics are effective

Figure 15.7 The time course of antipsychotic drug effects. Antipsychotic drugs, such as thioridazine, fluphenazine, and chlorpromazine, reduce psychotic symptoms gradually over a span of weeks, as graphed here. In contrast, patients given placebo pills show noticeably less improvement. (Data from Cole, Goldberg, & Davis, 1966; Davis, 1985)

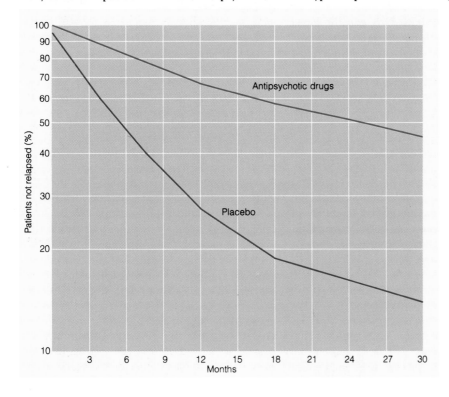

Figure 15.8 Schizophrenic relapse with and without drug treatment. Antipsychotic drugs can help to prevent relapse in schizophrenic patients. As this graph shows, over a period of 30 months the percentage of patients not relapsed is noticeably higher in the drug treatment group than in the placebo group. However, these results also reveal that antipsychotic drugs are far from completely successful in preventing relapse. (From Baldessarini, 1984)

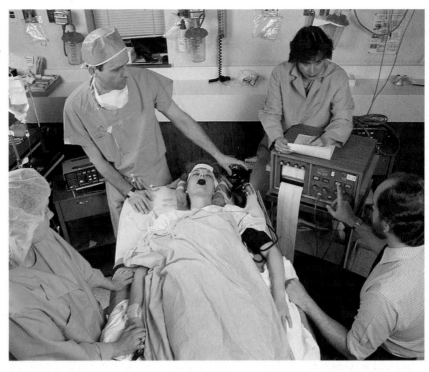

This patient is being prepared for electro-convulsive therapy (ECT). In ECT an electric shock is used to elicit a brief cortical seizure. The electric shock is delivered through electrodes attached to the patient's skull.

for a larger portion of depressed patients (perhaps as many as 85%) and have less problematic side effects than the MAO inhibitors (Glenn & Taska, 1984). Like antipsychotic drugs, antidepressants exert their effects gradually over a period of weeks, rather than immediately. Research is currently under way on several new classes of antidepressants that may yield more rapid therapeutic effects and fewer side effects (Feighner, 1986).

LITHIUM

Lithium is a chemical used to control mood swings in patients with bipolar mood disorders. Lithium has excellent value in preventing *future* episodes of both mania and depression in patients with bipolar illness. Lithium can also be used in efforts to gradually bring patients with bipolar illness out of *current* manic or depressed episodes, although antipsychotics and antidepressants are more frequently used for these purposes. On the negative side of the ledger, lithium does have some dangerous side effects if its use isn't managed carefully (Georgotas, 1985). Lithium levels in the patient's blood must be monitored carefully because high concentrations can be very toxic (and even fatal). Kidney damage and cardiac complications are the major problems associated with lithium therapy.

EVALUATING DRUG THERAPIES

Drug therapies can produce clear therapeutic gains for many kinds of patients. What's especially impressive is that they can be effective in severe disorders that otherwise defy therapeutic

endeavors. Nonetheless, drug therapies are controversial for two reasons.

First, some critics argue that drug therapies often produce superficial curative effects (Lickey & Gordon, 1983). For example, Valium doesn't really solve problems with anxiety. It merely provides temporary relief from an unpleasant symptom. Moreover, this temporary relief may lull patients into complacency about their problem, and prevent them from working toward a more lasting solution. Thus, drug therapies may be more of a "Band-Aid" than a cure for psychological disorders.

Second, critics charge that many drugs are overprescribed and many patients are overmedicated (Boutin, 1979; Leavitt, 1982). Drug interventions can be all too appealing to psychiatrists and other hospital personnel as apparent "solutions." Writing out a prescription is much less challenging than conducting insight therapy or designing a behavior therapy program. Thus, many psychiatrists habitually hand out prescriptions without giving adequate consideration to more complicated interventions. Also, drugs calm patients and make it easier for hospital staff to run their wards. Thus, critics argue that there's a tendency in some institutions to overmedicate patients to minimize disruptive behavior—a practice that represents unethical "crowd control" more than therapy.

Obviously, drug therapies have stirred up some debate. However, this controversy pales in comparison to the furious debates inspired by electroconvulsive (shock) therapy (ECT). The magnitude of the ECT controversy is indicated by the fact that the residents of Berkeley, California, voted to outlaw ECT in their city. (However, in subsequent lawsuits, the courts ruled that scientific questions can't be settled through a vote, and the law was overturned.) What makes ECT so controversial? You'll see in the next section.

Electroconvulsive Therapy (ECT)

In the 1930s, a Hungarian psychiatrist named Ladislas Meduna speculated that epilepsy and schizophrenia could not coexist in the same body. On the basis of this observation, which turned out to be inaccurate, Meduna theorized that it might be useful to induce epilepsylike seizures in schizophrenic patients. Initially, a drug was used to trigger these seizures. However, by 1938, two Italian psychiatrists (Cerletti & Bini, 1938) demonstrated that it was safer to elicit the seizures with electric shock. Thus, modern electroconvulsive therapy was born, creating a peculiar tribute to the old advertising slogan "better living through electricity."

***Electroconvulsive therapy (ECT)* is a biomedical treatment in which electric shock is used to produce a cortical seizure accompanied by convulsions.** In ECT, electrodes are attached to the skull over the temporal lobes of the brain. A light anesthesia is induced, and the patient is given a variety of drugs to minimize the likelihood of complications, such as spinal fractures. An electric current is then applied for about a second. The current should trigger a brief convulsive seizure (lasting 5 to 20 seconds), during which the patient usually loses consciousness. Patients normally awaken in an hour or two. People typically receive between 6 and 20 treatments as inpatients at a hospital.

The clinical use of ECT peaked in the 1940s and 1950s before effective drug therapies were widely available. ECT has long been controversial, and its use declined in the 1960s and 1970s. Nonetheless, there has been a recent resurgence in the use of ECT, and it's not a *rare* form of therapy (Sackeim, 1985). Estimates suggest that about 60,000 to 100,000 people receive ECT treatments yearly in the United States, mainly for depression.

Controversy about ECT is fueled by patients' reports that the treatment is painful, dehumanizing, and terrifying, and by reports that staff members at some hospitals use the threat of ECT to "keep patients in line" (Breggin, 1979). Using ECT for disciplinary purposes is unethical, but the essay in Figure 15.9 suggests that it has happened in some institutions. This essay on the experience

Figure 15.9 Effects of electroconvulsive therapy (ECT). Although some patients treated with ECT have much more favorable experiences, this moving memoir about ECT treatment paints a very unpleasant picture.

A Personal Experience with ECT

I'm not saying this is what all shock is about, or that it happens this way everywhere. I am saying that this is what happened to me in this particular institution.

Slang for shock in that institution was known as "gettin' Kentucky fried" and being taken to shock was known as "a visit to the Colonel." I was going for a visit.

Along the way, I always started making deals with God: "If you get me out of this one . . . " They never worked out. When the deals fell through, I started making every promise I knew I could keep, and just to be safe, a few I knew I couldn't. Looking back, it all seems kind of funny. At the time, I was sure they were trying to kill me.

The room where it was done was in the very center of the ward. This was not surprising. Almost all of our shock was done as a disciplinary measure, our very lives revolved around staff's ability to enforce discipline and order upon us. So to me, it was not too surprising that the Colonel set up shop where he did.

When the door opened, the intense whiteness of the fluorescent lights blinded me. Staff took advantage of this by leading me to the gurney where I was to lie down. By the time my eyes adjusted, I was on my back with several pairs of hands holding me down.

A mouthpiece was crammed rather indelicately into place, and the conductant was smeared on my temples. There was some technical talk and someone said "Now" (I wanted desperately to say wait a moment). And then there it was—one of the most excruciating pains I have ever felt. My back arched in an attempt to jump off the gurney, all the air squeezed out of my lungs, my legs flexed until they felt as if they would break, my head felt as if it would pop off. I was out of control; it was not me anymore.

I don't know how long it took but I finally passed out. When I opened my eyes again, I had the headache of headaches. I was confused, I couldn't connect two thoughts.

The next two or three days were a nightmare of confusion and awkward movements, always feeling like a thought was there, on the tip of your tongue, but not able to grab it. The more you grabbed at it, the more elusive it became, and the more frustrated you became.

Eventually, I returned to normal, but before that happened, I would go through a deep dark depression. I could fight the system, I could fight Staff, I could fight the drugs, the aides, and the other patients.

I could not fight this. I was beaten. My thoughts were exactly that, mine. Before shock they were untouched, now they had been reached and, worse still, disorganized externally. The depression then seemed to come from a sense of defeat, of being violated, and of being mentally raped.

How can I make you feel that?

of electroshock, written by one of my former students, provides a powerful description of how aversive ECT can be for some patients.

Unquestionably, many ECT patients don't find the treatment even remotely as unpleasant as my former student did, but this person's description is not terribly unusual either (Friedberg, 1976). Unfortunately, information regarding the therapeutic efficacy of ECT is marked by similar inconsistency.

THERAPEUTIC EFFECTIVENESS OF ECT

The effectiveness of ECT is hotly debated. There are ardent proponents who maintain that it's a remarkably effective treatment (Fink, 1988), and there are equally ardent opponents who argue that it's no more effective than a placebo (Friedberg, 1975). Reported improvement rates for ECT treatment range from negligible to very high (Friedberg, 1976; Small, Small, & Milstein, 1986). In part, these inconsistent findings are due to methodological weaknesses that are often found in ECT studies. Barton (1977) could only find *six* studies among hundreds on ECT that used appropriate control groups to assess therapeutic effects. Why are ECT studies so flawed? Probably because most investigators feel very strongly (pro or con) about ECT, and they let their biases affect their research, both intentionally and inadvertently.

In light of these problems, conclusions about the value of ECT must be tentative. Although ECT was once considered appropriate for a wide range of disorders, even most proponents now recommend it only for severe depression and bipolar mood disorders. Overall, there does seem to be enough favorable evidence to justify *conservative*

use of ECT in treating severe mood disorders (Weiner & Coffey, 1988).

Curiously, insofar as ECT may be effective, no one is sure why. The discarded theories about how ECT works could fill several books. Until recently, it was widely accepted that the occurrence of a cortical seizure was critical to the treatment, but this once "firm" conclusion is now being questioned by many theorists (Sackeim, 1988). Today, many ECT advocates theorize that the treatment must affect neurotransmitter activity in the brain. However, the evidence supporting this theory is fragmentary and inconclusive (Frankel, 1984). ECT opponents have a radically different, albeit equally unproven, explanation for why ECT might appear to be effective. They maintain that some patients find ECT utterly terrifying and that these patients muster all their willpower to climb out of their depression to avoid further ECT treatments.

The debate about whether ECT works, and how it works, does *not* make ECT unique among approaches to psychotherapy. Controversies exist regarding the effectiveness of many psychotherapies. However, this controversy is especially problematic because ECT may carry substantial risks.

PROBLEMS WITH ECT

Even ECT proponents acknowledge that memory losses, impaired attention, and other cognitive deficits are common short-term side effects of electroconvulsive therapy. However, proponents assert that these deficits are mild and usually last less than a month (Weeks, Freeman, & Kendell, 1981). In contrast, ECT critics maintain that these cognitive losses are significant and often permanent (Breggin, 1979). Complicating the issue considerably, recent studies using objective measures of patients' memory performance show that former ECT patients tend to subjectively overestimate their memory deficits (Sachs & Gelenberg, 1988).

So, what can we conclude about ECT and cognitive deficits? The truth probably lies somewhere in between the positions staked out by the proponents and opponents of ECT. In an unusually dispassionate review of the ECT controversy, Small et al. (1986) assert that "there is little doubt that ECT produces both short- and long-term intellectual impairment," but they conclude that this impairment isn't inevitable, and that in the vast majority of cases it isn't permanent.

Most of the other risks once associated with ECT have been minimized by modern improvements in the procedure. Fractures and dislocations used to be a problem, but medications administered prior to the treatment have virtually

Figure 15.10 The leading approaches to therapy among psychologists. The pooled data from a survey of 415 clinical and counseling psychologists (Smith, 1982) and another survey of 479 clinical psychologists (Norcross & Prochaska, 1982) indicate that the most widely employed approaches to therapy are (in order) eclectic, psychodynamic, behavioral, cognitive, and client-centered.

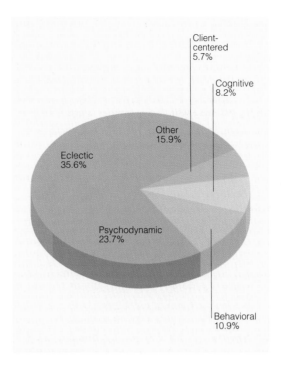

Client-centered 5.7%
Cognitive 8.2%
Other 15.9%
Eclectic 35.6%
Psychodynamic 23.7%
Behavioral 10.9%

eliminated these complications (Kramer, 1985). In competent hands, ECT is a reasonably safe procedure with a mortality rate well under 1 in 1000 (R. Weiner, 1985). The occasional deaths that occur are usually due to cardiac complications.

Because of the problems associated with ECT, there had been a trend toward more conservative use of the treatment (Weiner, 1984) until its recent resurgence in the mid 1980s. Let's hope more objective empirical research will be conducted in the future to resolve some of the controversies swirling around ECT.

BLENDING APPROACHES TO PSYCHOTHERAPY

There's no law that dictates that a client must be treated with just one approach to therapy. We've reviewed many different approaches separately, but they're by no means mutually exclusive. Often a clinician will use several different approaches in working with a client. For example, a depressed person might receive cognitive therapy (an insight therapy), social skills training (a behavior therapy), and antidepressant medication (a biomedical therapy). Multiple approaches are particularly likely when a treatment *team* provides therapy.

Studies suggest that there's merit in combining multiple approaches to treatment (Klerman, 1978; Luborsky et al, 1975). One representative study compared the value of insight therapy alone, drug therapy alone, and a combination of insight and drug therapy, for treating depression (Weissman et al., 1979). The subjects suffered from unipolar depression and were treated on an outpatient basis. The groups treated only with antidepressant medication or only with interpersonal therapy both responded well. However, the greatest improvement was found in the group treated with both. The two treatments complemented each other nicely. The drug therapy was particularly effective in relieving some symptoms (such as sleep and appetite disturbance), while the insight therapy was especially effective in relieving others (such as suicidal ideas and disinterest in work). Thus, there's much to be said for combining approaches to treatment.

The value of multiple approaches may explain a significant trend in the field of psychotherapy. There's a movement away from strong loyalty to individual schools of thought. Most clinicians used to depend exclusively on one system of therapy while rejecting the utility of all others. This era of fragmentation may be drawing to a close. In two surveys in the 1980s of psychologists' theoretical orientations (Norcross & Prochaska, 1982; Smith, 1982), researchers were surprised to find that the greatest proportion of respondents described themselves as *eclectic* in approach (see Figure 15.10).

***Theoretical eclecticism* involves selecting what appears to be best from a variety of theories or systems of therapy,** instead of committing to just one theoretical orientation. Eclectic therapists use ideas, insights, and techniques from a variety of sources. They adjust their strategy to the unique needs of each client. Eclecticism leads to a creative blending of different approaches to therapy. Some therapists, such as Arnold Lazarus (1987), have even developed systematic approaches to being eclectic.

Increasing eclecticism is only one of several recent trends in the field of psychotherapy. Many other changes have also occurred in the delivery of mental health services. We'll examine some of these changes in the next section, which discusses shifting patterns of institutional care for mental disorders.

INSTITUTIONAL TREATMENT IN TRANSITION

Traditionally, much of the treatment of mental illness has been carried out in institutional settings, primarily in mental hospitals. **A *mental hospital* is a medical institution specializing in providing inpatient care for psychological disorders.** In the United States, a national network of state-funded mental hospitals started to emerge in the 1840s through the efforts of Dorothea Dix and other reformers (see Figure 15.11). Prior to these reforms, the mentally ill who were poor were housed in jails and poorhouses, or left to wander the countryside. Dix was horrified by this lack of care and lobbied tirelessly to raise funds for public mental hospitals. Thanks to the movement that she began, nearly 300 state mental hospitals were established in the United States between 1845 and 1945. The people who built these hospitals believed that they would provide humane and effective treatment for those suffering from psychological disorders.

Today, mental hospitals continue to play an important role in the delivery of mental health services. However, since World War II, institutional care for mental illness has undergone a series of major transitions—and the dust hasn't settled yet. Let's look at how institutional care has evolved in recent decades.

Disenchantment with Mental Hospitals

By the 1950s, it had become apparent that public mental hospitals were not fulfilling their goals very well (Mechanic, 1980). Experts began to realize that hospitalization often *contributed* to the development of pathology instead of curing it.

What were the causes of these unexpected negative effects? Part of the problem was that the facilities were usually underfunded. In 1960, for instance, state mental hospitals made do with only one-sixth as much money per patient as general hospitals (Bloom, 1984). The lack of adequate funding meant that the facilities were overcrowded and understaffed. Hospital personnel were undertrained and overworked. They were hard-pressed to deliver minimal custodial care. Gallant efforts at treatment were made, but the demoralizing conditions made most public mental hospitals decidedly nontherapeutic. Although there certainly were *some* high-quality mental hospitals, most public facilities had degenerated

Figure 15.11 Dorothea Dix and the advent of mental hospitals in America. During the 19th century, Dorothea Dix campaigned tirelessly to obtain funds for building mental hospitals. Many of these hospitals, such as the New York State Lunatic Asylum shown here, were extremely large facilities. Although public mental hospitals improved the care of the mentally ill, they had a variety of shortcomings, which eventually prompted the deinstitutionalization movement.

THE STATE LUNATIC ASYLUM, UTICA, NEW YORK.

The deplorable deterioration of physical facilities seen here was one of several reasons why public mental hospitals failed to live up to expectations. State-funded psychiatric hospitals have generally been underfunded and overcrowded, making effective treatment difficult at best.

into nothing more than huge custodial warehouses.

As psychiatric hospitals were scrutinized closely, doubts were raised about the wisdom of hospitalization, even if adequate funding could be found (Korchin, 1976). Critics noted that hospitals placed people into a passive patient role, leading many to stop taking responsibility for their lives. Many patients adapted to this paternalistic care and became fearful of leaving the hospital. Their ability to manage their lives outside of an institutional setting declined rather than improved.

These problems were aggravated by the fact that state mental hospitals served large geographic regions, but were rarely placed near major population centers. Hence, most patients were uprooted from their community. Institutionalized 50, 100, or 300 miles from their homes, they lost contact with their families, friends, and employers. This deprived the patients of needed social support and made their potential return to the community more awkward and difficult. Thus, critics concluded that there were fundamental flaws in our system of mental hospitals.

The Community Mental Health Movement

Disenchantment with the state mental hospital system inspired the community mental health movement that emerged in the 1960s. The community mental health movement emphasizes (1) local, community-based care, (2) reduced dependence on hospitalization, and (3) the prevention of psychological disorders. The community mental health movement jumped into prominence in 1963 when John F. Kennedy became the first American president ever to address the nation on the subject of mental health. Kennedy enthusiastically endorsed the community mental health philosophy. He outlined a major plan to eventually build about 1500 community mental health centers that would operate according to this philosophy. Thus, in 1963, much of the responsibility for the treatment of psychological disorders was turned over to an entirely new kind of institution.

What do community mental health centers do? **Community mental health centers** provide com-

prehensive mental health care for their local communities. Their key services usually include the following:

1. *Short-term inpatient care.* Clearly, there are some people with severe disorders who require treatment on an inpatient basis. Community mental health centers are designed to provide this care locally.

2. *Outpatient therapy.* In keeping with their philosophy of reducing dependence on hospitalization, community mental health centers offer extensive outpatient therapy services. Whenever feasible, they provide treatment on an outpatient basis so that clients can keep their families intact, hang onto their jobs, and stay anchored in their community.

3. *Emergency services.* Crisis intervention services are based on a philosophical commitment to prevention. Because transient personal crises can grow into full-fledged psychological disorders, community mental health centers try to provide for early intervention. Thus, they set up telephone "hot lines" and offer counseling for personal problems (job loss, divorce, death of a loved one) to people who may have no signs of pathology.

4. *Education and consultation.* Taking prevention a step further, staff members often try to get out into the community to better educate people about mental health. This educational effort can range from talking about drug abuse at a high school to consulting with police departments to improve officers' handling of domestic disputes.

Community mental health centers provide diverse services for their local communities, including outpatient therapy (left) and emergency counseling (right) for rape, suicide, job loss, and other kinds of personal crises.

Community mental health centers supplement mental hospitals with decentralized and more accessible services. They were never intended to replace mental hospitals, although they did have an effect on patterns of hospitalization.

Deinstitutionalization

Although mental hospitals continue to care for many people troubled by chronic mental illness, their role in patient care has diminished. Since the 1960s, a policy of deinstitutionalization has been followed by the American mental health establishment. *Deinstitutionalization* **involves transferring the treatment of mental illness from inpatient institutions to community-based facilities that emphasize outpatient care.** This shift in responsibility was made possible by two developments: (1) the emergence of effective drug therapies for severe disorders and (2) the deployment of community mental health centers to coordinate local care (Wyatt, 1985).

The exodus of patients from mental hospitals has been dramatic (Kiesler, 1982). In 1955, about *one-half* of the hospital beds in the United States were occupied by psychiatric patients. Today that figure has declined to about one-quarter. The average inpatient population in state and county mental hospitals has dropped from a peak of nearly 550,000 to around 115,000 today (see Figure 15.12a). The average length of hospitalization has also declined. In Veterans Administration hospitals, for example, the average length of stay for psychotic patients peaked at 672 days in 1958. The average length of stay in these facilities fell to 92 days by 1980. Thus, as intended, deinstitutionalization has led to more outpatient and less inpatient care of psychological disorders (see Figure 15.12b).

These trends do *not* mean that hospitalization

for mental illness has become a thing of the past. A great many people are hospitalized, but there's been a shift toward placing them in local general hospitals instead of distant psychiatric hospitals (Kiesler & Sibulkin, 1984; see Figure 15.12c). Today, traditional mental hospitals (both public and private) account for only about 40% of psychiatric inpatient admissions (see Figure 15.12d). The patients admitted to general hospitals stay for relatively brief periods of time. The median stay is about 12 days. In keeping with the philosophy of deinstitutionalization, these facilities try to get patients stabilized and back into the community as swiftly as possible. Thus, hospitalization is still a frequent intervention, but long-term institutionalization is far less common today than it once was.

Evaluating Deinstitutionalization

How has deinstitutionalization worked out? It gets mixed reviews. On the positive side, many people have benefited by avoiding disruptive and unnecessary hospitalization. There's ample evidence that alternatives to hospitalization can be both more effective and less costly than inpatient care (Keisler, 1982). Moreover, many authorities maintain that treatment *inside* mental hospitals has improved because of deinstitutionalization (Schwartz & Swartzburg, 1976). This improvement would have been virtually impossible if the patient population hadn't been brought down to a more manageable size.

Unfortunately, there have been some unanticipated problems. Many patients suffering from chronic psychological disorders had nowhere to go when they were released. They had no families, friends, or homes to return to. Many had no work skills and were poorly prepared to live on their own. These people were supposed to be absorbed

a Declining inpatient population at state and county mental hospitals

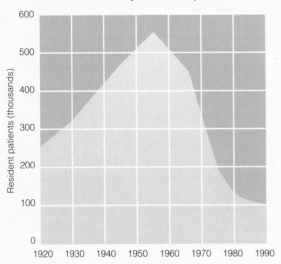

b Shift from inpatient to outpatient mental health care

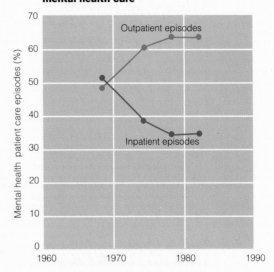

c Shift from mental hospitals to general hospitals for patient care

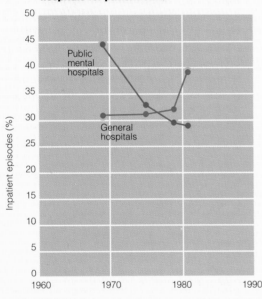

d Distribution of inpatient care episodes

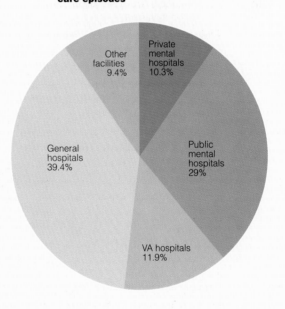

Figure 15.12 Trends in the institutional treatment of mental illness. (**a**) The inpatient population in public mental hospitals has declined dramatically since the late 1950s, as a result of deinstitutionalization and the use of drug therapy. (**b**) An increased emphasis on outpatient care is one of the main effects of deinstitutionalization. (**c**) Even when inpatient care is required, traditional mental hospitals provide less of it than in the past. (**d**) In recent years, general hospitals have handled as many psychiatric episodes as private and public mental hospitals combined. (**e**) The extent of the "revolving door problem" is apparent from these figures on the percentage of inpatient admissions that are readmissions at various types of facilities. (Data from the National Institute of Mental Health)

e Percentage of psychiatric inpatient admissions that are readmissions

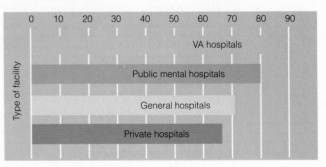

by "halfway houses," sheltered workshops, and other types of intermediate care facilities. Unfortunately, many communities were never able to fund and build the planned facilities. Meanwhile, the increased burden on community mental health centers left them strapped to provide needed services. This problem worsened in the 1980s, as federal funds for community mental health centers were reduced.

To some extent, patients were released into communities that weren't prepared to handle them. Thus, deinstitutionalization left two major problems in its wake: a "revolving door" population of people who flow in and out of psychiatric institutions, and a sizable population of homeless mentally ill people.

Mental Illness, the Revolving Door, and Homelessness

Although the proportion of hospital days due to mental illness has dwindled, admission rates for psychiatric hospitalization have actually climbed. What has happened? Deinstitutionalization and drug therapy have created a revolving door through which many mentally ill people pass again and again and again.

Most of the people caught in the mental health system's revolving door suffer from chronic, severe disorders (usually schizophrenia) that frequently require hospitalization. However, they respond well to drug therapies in the hospital. Once they're stabilized through drug therapy, they no longer qualify for expensive hospital treatment according to the new standards created by deinstitutionalization. Thus, they're sent back out the door, into communities that often aren't prepared to provide adequate outpatient care. Because they lack appropriate care and support, their condition deteriorates and they soon require readmission to a hospital, where the cycle begins once again. Studies reveal that 50% of the patients released from public mental hospitals are readmitted within 1 year (Keisling, 1983). Over two-thirds of all psychiatric inpatient admissions involve rehospitalizing a former patient (see Figure 15.12e).

Deinstitutionalization has also helped to create a large population of homeless mentally ill people. Although it's difficult to collect statistics on the homeless, many urban areas report sharp increases in the number of people living in the streets. The escalating number of homeless women or "bag ladies" has been particularly noticeable. A task force report from the American Psychiatric Association estimates that between one-quarter and one-half of the homeless people in the United States suffer from psychological disorders (Arce & Vergare, 1984). Many studies suggest that the prevalence of disorders among the homeless may even be higher. This brings us to our Featured Study, which investigated the connection between mental illness and homelessness.

CHAPTER FIFTEEN FEATURED STUDY	# FROM BACK WARDS TO BACK ALLEYS?

Investigators: Ellen L. Bassuk, Lenore Rubin, & Alison Lauriat (Harvard University)

Source: Is homelessness a mental health problem? *American Journal of Psychiatry, 141*(12) (1984), 1546–1550.

There's much debate about the extent of mental illness among the homeless. Before the 1970s, the urban homeless population was made up mostly of alcoholic males living in "skid row" areas. Since the advent of deinstitutionalization, this pattern seems to have changed. However, this assertion has largely been based on casual observation and anecdotal evidence. The present study attempted to collect systematic data on the question.

Method
A 1-day census of all the people using shelters for the homeless in the Boston area was conducted in February 1983. Local authorities collected demographic data on the "guests" using the 27 shelters serving the Boston area at the time. Based on these demographic data, the research team carefully selected a single shelter facility as the most representative of the lot. On one night

in April 1983, nine experienced mental health professionals interviewed all of the guests at this shelter to assess their mental health. The median age of the 78 subjects was 34. Most (83%) were male, and about two-thirds were at least high school graduates.

Results
The interviewers found psychological disorders in 91% of the subjects at the shelter that night. Major psychotic disorders (mostly schizophrenia) were found in 40% of the guests. Another 21% suffered from severe personality disorders, and 29% were chronic alcoholics. Most of the subjects with severe psychotic disorders were not receiving any form of treatment, even though many clearly belonged in some type of psychiatric facility. The investigators noted, "Many of the schizophrenic guests were so disorganized that they were unable to phrase even a few sentences coherently;

their stories were disjointed, rambling, unreal, at times grandiose, and almost always difficult to follow" (p. 1547).

The social isolation of the subjects was remarkable. Of those using the facility, 74% reported no existing family relationships, 73% indicated that they had no friends to lean on, and 40% said they had no ongoing social relations with anyone. The handful of healthy individuals in the shelter were either children accompanying their parents or adults who had just arrived in Boston looking for work.

Discussion
The authors understandably infer that there is a great deal of mental illness among the homeless. They acknowledge that their evidence did not clearly link this problem to deinstitutionalization. Only 28% of the shelter guests had ever been hospitalized for psychiatric reasons. Thus, most were not castaways from the mental health system. However, most of the subjects were young, and many had reached adulthood after deinstitutionalization changed patterns of hospitalization. Bassuk and her colleagues speculate that before the era of deinstitutionalization, many more of the guests would have been hospitalized. They conclude that "shelters have become 'open asylums' to replace the institutions of several decades ago" (p. 1549).

Casual observation suggests that homelessness among the mentally ill has increased in recent years. The study by Bassuk, Rubin, and Lauriat (1984) provides empirical documentation that homelessness and mental illness frequently go together.

Comment
Before Dorothea Dix's 19th-century crusade, the mentally ill were left to fend for themselves. The disheartening findings in this study suggest that we are moving backwards toward a similar state of affairs. Actually, the people living in the streets may be only the tip of the iceberg. Many other people with mental disorders live in decrepit flophouses. Thus, deinstitutionalization has apparently moved some disordered people from the back wards of our mental hospitals to the back alleys of our slums.

In light of the revolving door problem and homelessness among the mentally ill, what can we conclude about deinstitutionalization? It appears to be a worthwhile idea that has been poorly executed. Overall, the policy has probably been a benefit to countless people with milder disorders, and a cruel trick on countless others with severe, chronic disorders. Ultimately, it's clear that our society is not providing adequate care for a sizable segment of the mentally ill population. That's not a new development. Inadequate care for mental

illness has always been the norm. Societies always struggle with the problem of what to do with the mentally ill.

What's the solution? Few experts advocate returning to the era of custodial warehouses. Many *do* advocate increasing the quality and availability of intermediate care facilities (Bachrach, 1984; Talbott & Lamb, 1984). Only time will tell whether our society will be willing to make the financial commitment to follow through on this recommendation.

PUTTING IT IN PERSPECTIVE

In our discussion of psychotherapy, one of our unifying themes was particularly prominent: the benefits of theoretical diversity (theme 2). We have noted before that the tension between competing theoretical perspectives often stimulates advances in psychology, as well as in other fields. The value of theoretical diversity was readily apparent in this chapter.

Its value can be illustrated with a rhetorical question: Can you imagine what the state of modern psychotherapy would be if everyone in psychology and psychiatry had simply accepted

Freud's theories about the nature and treatment of psychological disorders? If not for theoretical diversity, psychotherapy might be in the "dark ages." Psychoanalysis can be a useful method of therapy, but it would be a tragic state of affairs if it were the *only* treatment available to people experiencing psychological distress. Multitudes of people have benefited from alternative approaches to treatment, such as client-centered therapy, cognitive therapy, behavior therapies, and biomedical therapies. These alternatives emerged out of tension between psychoanalytic

Table 15.4 Comparison of Major Approaches to Psychotherapy

TYPE OF PSYCHOTHERAPY	PRIMARY FOUNDERS	ORIGIN OF DISORDER	THERAPEUTIC GOALS	THERAPEUTIC TECHNIQUES
Psychoanalysis	Freud	Unconscious conflicts resulting from fixations in earlier development	Insights regarding unconscious conflicts and motives, personality reconstruction	Free association, dream analysis, interpretation, catharsis, transference
Client-centered therapy	Rogers	Incongruence between self-concept and actual experience, overdependence on acceptance from others	Congruence between self-concept and experience, acceptance of genuine self, self-determination, personal growth	Genuineness, empathy, unconditional positive regard, clarification, reflecting back to client
Cognitive therapy	Beck, Ellis	Irrational assumptions and negative, self-defeating thinking about events related to self	Detection of negative thinking, substitution of more realistic thinking	Thought stopping, recording automatic thoughts, refuting negative thinking, reattribution, homework assignments
Behavior therapies	Wolpe Bandura Azrin	Maladaptive patterns of behavior acquired through learning	Elimination of symptomatic, maladaptive behaviors; acquisition of more adaptive responses	Classical and operant conditioning, reinforcement, punishment, extinction, shaping, aversive conditioning, systematic desensitization, token economy, social skills training
Biomedical therapies		Physiological malfunction, primarily abnormal neurotransmitter activity	Elimination of symptoms, prevention of relapse	Antipsychotic, antianxiety, and antidepressant drugs, lithium, electroconvulsive therapy (ECT)

theory and the other four major theoretical perspectives identified in Chapter 1: the humanistic perspective (which generated client-centered therapy), the behavioral perspective (behavior therapies), the physiological perspective (biomedical therapies), and the cognitive perspective (cognitive therapy).

We've seen throughout this text that human existence is complex and highly varied. People have diverse problems, rooted in varied origins, that call for the pursuit of different therapeutic goals. Thus, it's fortunate that we can choose from a diverse array of approaches to psychother-

apy. Table 15.4 summarizes and compares the approaches that we've discussed in this chapter. The table shows that the major types of psychotherapy overlap relatively little. Each type has its own vision of the nature of human discontent and the ideal remedy.

Of course, diversity can be confusing. The range and variety of available treatments in modern psychotherapy leaves many people puzzled about their options. Thus, in our Application, we'll sort through practical issues involved in selecting a therapist.

LOOKING FOR A THERAPIST

Answer the following "true" or "false."

☐ **1.** Psychotherapy is an art as well as a science.

☐ **2.** The type of professional training a therapist has had is relatively unimportant.

☐ **3.** Psychotherapy can be harmful or damaging to a client.

☐ **4.** Psychotherapy doesn't have to be expensive.

☐ **5.** It's a good idea to shop around when choosing a therapist.

All of the above statements are true. Do any of them surprise you? If so, you're in good company. Many people know relatively little about the practicalities of selecting a therapist.

The task of finding an appropriate therapist is no less complex than shopping for any other major service. Should you see a psychologist or psychiatrist? Should you opt for individual therapy or group therapy? Should you see a client-centered therapist or a behavior therapist? Do you want to be treated by a man or a woman? The unfortunate part of this complexity is that people seeking psychotherapy often feel overwhelmed by personal problems. The last thing they need is to be confronted by yet another complex decision.

Nonetheless, the importance of finding a good therapist can't be overestimated. Therapy can sometimes have harmful rather than helpful effects. We've already discussed how drug therapies, electroconvulsive therapy, and hospitalization can sometimes be damaging, but problems are not limited to these interventions. Talking about your problems with a therapist may sound harmless, but studies indicate that insight therapies can also backfire (Bergin & Lambert, 1978; Strupp, Hadley, & Gomes-Schwartz, 1977).

Although a great many talented therapists are available, psychotherapy, like any other profession, has incompetent practitioners as well. Therefore, you should shop for a skilled therapist, just as you would for a good attorney or a good mechanic. In this application we'll go over some information that should be helpful if you ever have to look for a therapist for yourself, or for a friend or family member (based on Amada, 1985; Ehrenberg & Ehrenberg, 1977; Wiener, 1968).

When Should You Seek Professional Treatment?

There's no simple answer to this question. Obviously, people *consider* the possibility of professional treatment when they're psychologically distressed. However, there are other options besides psychotherapy. There's much to be said for seeking advice from family, friends, the clergy, and so forth. Insights about personal problems don't belong exclusively to people with professional degrees.

So, when should you turn to professionals for help? You should begin to think seriously about therapy (1) when you have no one to lean on, (2) when the people you lean on indicate that they're getting tired of it, (3) when you feel helpless and overwhelmed, or (4) when your life is seriously disrupted by your problems. Of course, you don't have to be falling apart to justify therapy. You may want to seek professional advice simply because you want to get more out of life.

Where Do You Find Therapeutic Services?

Psychotherapy can be found in a variety of settings. Contrary to general belief, most therapists are not in private practice. Many work in institutional settings such as community mental health centers, hospitals, human service agencies, schools, and workplaces. The principal sources of therapeutic services are described in Figure 15.13.

Figure 15.13 Principal sources of therapeutic services.

1. Private practitioners. Self-employed therapists are listed in the Yellow Pages under their professional category, such as psychologist or psychiatrist. Private practitioners tend to be relatively expensive, but they also tend to be highly experienced therapists.

2. Community mental health centers. Community mental health centers have salaried psychologists, psychiatrists, and social workers on staff. The centers provide a variety of services and often have staff available on weekends and at night to deal with emergencies.

3. Hospitals. Several kinds of hospitals provide therapeutic services. There are both public and private mental hospitals that specialize in the care of people with psychological disorders. Many general hospitals have a psychiatric ward, and those that do not will usually have psychiatrists and psychologists on staff and on call. Although hospitals tend to concentrate on inpatient treatment, many provide outpatient therapy as well.

4. Human service agencies. Various social service agencies employ therapists to provide short-term counseling. Depending on your community, you may find agencies that deal with family problems, juvenile problems, drug problems, and so forth.

5. Schools and workplaces. Most high schools and colleges have counseling centers where students can get help with personal problems. Similarly, some large businesses offer in-house counseling to their employees.

The exact configuration of therapeutic services available varies from one community to another. To find out what your community has to offer, you can consult friends and the local phone book. Community mental health centers, social service agencies, and school counseling centers are usually very helpful in explaining the range of services available in a particular area.

Is the Therapist's Profession Important?

As we noted earlier, psychotherapists may be trained in psychology, psychiatry, social work, psychiatric nursing, or counseling. Many talented therapists can be found in all of these professions. Thus, the kind of degree that a therapist holds doesn't need to be a crucial consideration in your selection process. It *is* true that only a psychiatrist can prescribe drugs for disorders that merit drug therapy. However, some critics (Wiener, 1968) argue that many psychiatrists are too quick to try drugs to solve everything. In any case, other types of therapists can refer you to a psychiatrist if they think that drug therapy would be helpful. If you have a health insurance policy that covers psychotherapy, you may want to check to see if it carries any restrictions about the therapist's profession. It's not a bad idea to inquire about a therapist's degrees to verify that she or he *does* have professional training. But the exact nature of that training isn't terribly important.

Is the Therapist's Sex Important?

If *you* feel that the therapist's sex is important, then for you it is. The therapeutic relationship must be characterized by trust and rapport. If you won't feel comfortable with a therapist of one sex or the other, this could inhibit the therapeutic process. Hence, you should feel free to look for a male or female therapist if you prefer to do so. This point is probably most relevant to female clients whose troubles may be related to the extensive sexism in our society. It's entirely reasonable for women to seek a therapist with a feminist perspective if that would make them feel more comfortable.

Speaking of sex, you should be aware that sexual exploitation is an occasional problem in the context of therapy. Studies indicate that a small minority of therapists take advantage of their clients sexually (Pope, Keith-Spiegel, & Tabachnick, 1986). Such incidents almost always involve a male therapist making advances to a female client, usually on the grounds that he's going to help her to experience or enjoy intimacy.

There are absolutely no situations in which therapist-client sexual relations are an ethical therapeutic practice. If a therapist makes sexual advances, a client should terminate treatment. Such a client should also consider writing a letter of complaint to the therapist's professional organization, or, in an institutional setting, to the therapist's supervisor.

Is Therapy Always Expensive?

Psychotherapy doesn't have to be prohibitively expensive. Private practitioners tend to be the most expensive, charging between $25 and $100 per (50-minute) hour. These fees may seem high, but they're in line with those of similar professionals, such as dentists and attorneys. As already discussed, however, private practitioners are not the only sources of therapeutic services.

Community mental health centers and social service agencies are usually supported by tax dollars and can charge lower fees than most therapists in private practice. Many of these organizations employ a sliding scale, so that clients are charged according to how much they can afford to pay. Thus, most communities have inexpensive opportunities for psychotherapy. Moreover, many health insurance plans provide at least partial reimbursement for the cost of psychotherapy.

Is the Therapist's Theoretical Approach Important?

The various approaches to therapy vary greatly in terms of goals, strate-

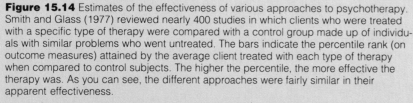

Figure 15.14 Estimates of the effectiveness of various approaches to psychotherapy. Smith and Glass (1977) reviewed nearly 400 studies in which clients who were treated with a specific type of therapy were compared with a control group made up of individuals with similar problems who went untreated. The bars indicate the percentile rank (on outcome measures) attained by the average client treated with each type of therapy when compared to control subjects. The higher the percentile, the more effective the therapy was. As you can see, the different approaches were fairly similar in their apparent effectiveness.

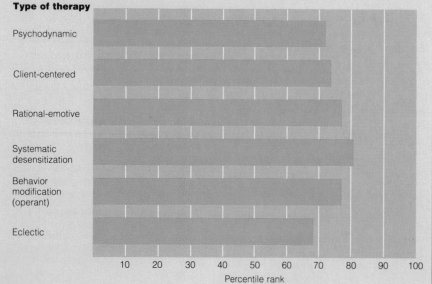

Type of therapy

Psychodynamic

Client-centered

Rational-emotive

Systematic desensitization

Behavior modification (operant)

Eclectic

10 20 30 40 50 60 70 80 90 100

Percentile rank

gies, and techniques. Logically, we might expect that the different approaches to therapy ought to vary in effectiveness. For the most part, this is *not* what researchers find, however. After reviewing the evidence, Luborsky et al. (1975) quote the dodo bird who has just judged a race in *Alice in Wonderland*. "Everyone has won and all must have prizes." Improvement rates for different theoretical orientations usually come out pretty close in most studies. In their massive review of outcome studies, Smith and Glass (1977) estimated the effectiveness of many major approaches to therapy. As you can see from the comparisons in Figure 15.14, the estimates cluster together closely.

These findings don't mean that all *therapists* do equally well. Some therapists unquestionably are more effective than others. However, these variations in effectiveness appear to depend on therapists' personal skills rather than differences in theoretical orientation. Good, bad, and mediocre therapists are found within each school of thought.

The key point is that effective therapy requires skill and creativity in execution. Arnold Lazarus, who devised multimodal therapy, emphasizes that therapists "straddle the fence between science and art" (Lazarus, 1987, p. 167). It's true that therapy is scientific in that interventions are based on extensive theory and empirical research (Forsyth & Strong, 1986). Ultimately, though, each client is a unique human being, and the therapist has to creatively fashion a treatment program that will help that individual. The stacks of scientific studies that serve as the basis for therapy techniques are relevant to this challenge, but they don't automatically provide answers. Therapy is more of a creative endeavor than many people realize.

What Should You Look for in a Prospective Therapist?

Some clients are timid about asking prospective therapists questions about their training, approach, fees, and so forth. However, these are reasonable questions, and the vast majority of therapists will be glad to answer them. You can usually ask your preliminary questions over the phone. If the result is positive, you can make an appointment for an interview (you'll probably have to pay for the interview). In this interview, the therapist will gather more information to determine the likelihood that he or she can help you, given the therapist's training and approach to treatment. At the same time, you should be making a similar judgment about whether *you* believe the therapist could help you with your problems.

What should you look for? First, you should look for personal warmth and sincere concern. Try to judge whether you'll be able to talk to this person in a candid, nondefensive way. Second, look for empathy and understanding. Is the person capable of appreciating your point of view? Third, look for self-confidence. Self-assured therapists will communicate a sense of competence without trying to intimidate you with jargon, or boasting needlessly about what they can do for you. When all is said and done, you should *like* your therapist. Otherwise, it will be difficult to establish the needed rapport.

What Is Therapy Like?

It's important to have realistic expectations about therapy, or you may be unnecessarily disappointed. Some people expect miracles. They expect to turn their life around quickly with little effort. Others expect their therapists to run their lives for them. These are unrealistic expectations. As Ehrenberg and Ehrenberg (1977) point out, "Psychotherapy takes time, effort, and courage" (p. 5).

Therapy is usually a slow process. Your problems are not likely to melt away quickly. Moreover, therapy is hard work, and your therapist is only a facilitator. Ultimately, *you* have to confront the challenge of changing your behavior, your feelings, or your

Figure 15.15 Signs of resistance in therapy. (Based on Ehrenberg & Ehrenberg, 1977)

If you're dissatisfied with your progress in therapy, resistance may be the problem when:

- You have nothing specific or concrete to complain about

- Your attitude about therapy changes suddenly just as you reach the truly sensitive issues

- You've had the same problem with other therapists in the past

- Your conflicts with the therapist resemble those that you have with other people

- You start hiding things from your therapist

personality. The process may not be pleasant; you may have to face up to some painful truths about yourself.

What If There Isn't Any Progress?

If you feel that your therapy isn't going anywhere, you should probably discuss these feelings with your therapist. Don't be surprised, however, if the therapist suggests that it may be your own fault. Freud's concept of resistance has some validity. Some clients *do* have difficulty facing up to their problems. Thus, if your therapy isn't progressing, you may need to *consider* whether your resistance may be slowing progress. This self-examination isn't easy, as you're not an unbiased observer. Some common signs of resistance identified by Ehrenberg and Ehrenberg (1977) are listed in Figure 15.15.

Given the very real possibility that poor progress may be due to resistance, you shouldn't be too quick to leave therapy when dissatisfied. However, it *is* possible that your therapist isn't sufficiently skilled or that the two of you are incompatible. Thus, after careful and deliberate consideration, you should feel free to terminate your therapy.

PSYCHO-THERAPY

The Elements of Psychotherapy: Treatment, Clients, and Therapists

• Although it is difficult to define the boundaries of psychotherapy, three elements are inevitably present: treatment, clients, and therapists. Approaches to treatment are diverse, but they can be grouped into three categories: insight therapies, behavior therapies, and biomedical therapies.

• Clients bring a wide variety of problems to therapy and do not necessarily have a disorder. Therapists come from a variety of professional backgrounds. Clinical and counseling psychologists, psychiatrists, social workers, psychiatric nurses, and counselors are the principal providers of therapeutic services. Each of these professions shows somewhat different preferences regarding treatment strategies.

Insight Therapies

• Insight therapies involve verbal interactions intended to enhance self-knowledge. Freudian approaches to therapy assume that neuroses originate from unresolved conflicts lurking in the unconscious. Therefore, in psychoanalysis, free association and dream analysis are used to explore the unconscious.

• When an analyst's probing hits sensitive areas, resistance can be expected. The transference relationship may be used to overcome this resistance so that the client can accept interpretations that lead to insight. Classical psychoanalysis is not widely practiced anymore, but Freud's legacy lives on in a rich diversity of modern psychodynamic therapies.

• Rogers's client-centered therapy assumes that neurotic anxieties are derived from incongruence between a person's self-concept and reality. Accordingly, the client-centered therapist tries to provide a supportive climate in which clients can restructure their self-concept. The process of client-centered therapy emphasizes clarification of the client's feelings and self-acceptance.

• Beck's cognitive therapy concentrates on changing the way clients think about events in their lives. Cognitive therapists reeducate clients to detect and challenge automatic negative thoughts that cause depression and anxiety. Cognitive therapists also use behavioral techniques in efforts to alter clients' overt behaviors.

• Most theoretical approaches to insight therapy have been adapted for use with groups. Group therapists usually play a subtle role, staying in the background and working to promote group cohesiveness. Participants essentially act as therapists for one another, exchanging insights and emotional support. Group therapy has unique advantages in comparison to individual therapy.

• Eysenck's work in the 1950s raised doubts about the effectiveness of insight therapy and stimulated research on its efficacy. Evaluating the effectiveness of any approach to therapy is complex and difficult. Nonetheless, the weight of the evidence suggests that insight therapies can be effective.

Behavior Therapies

• Behavior therapies use the principles of learning in direct efforts to change specific aspects of behavior. Wolpe's systematic desensitization, a treatment for phobias, involves the construction of an anxiety hierarchy, relaxation training, and step-by-step movement through the hierarchy, pairing relaxation with each phobic stimulus.

• In aversion therapy a stimulus associated with an unwanted response is paired with an unpleasant stimulus in an effort to eliminate the maladaptive response. Systematic desensitization and aversion therapy depend on classical conditioning, whereas token economies, social skills training, and biofeedback emphasize operant conditioning.

• The token economy, a system for doling out symbolic reinforcers, is useful in the management of institutionalized populations. Social skills training can improve clients' interpersonal skills through shaping, modeling, and behavioral rehearsal. Biofeedback involves providing information about bodily functions to a person so that he or she can attempt to exert some control over those physiological processes. There is ample evidence that behavior therapies are effective.

Biomedical Therapies

• Biomedical therapies involve physiological interventions for psychological problems. A great variety of disorders are treated with drugs. The principal types of therapeutic drugs are antianxiety drugs, antipsychotic drugs, antidepressant drugs, and lithium. Drug therapies can be very effective, but they have their pitfalls. Many drugs produce problematic side effects. Some critics maintain that drugs' curative effects are superficial and that some drugs are overprescribed.

- Electroconvulsive therapy is used to trigger a cortical seizure that is believed to have therapeutic value for mood disorders, especially depression. There is contradictory evidence and heated debate about the effectiveness of ECT and about possible risks associated with its use. Because of these controversies, psychiatrists use ECT less today than they once did.

Blending Approaches to Psychotherapy
- Combinations of insight, behavioral, and biomedical therapies are often used fruitfully in the treatment of psychological disorders. Many modern therapists are eclectic, using specific ideas, techniques, and strategies gleaned from a number of different theoretical approaches.

Institutional Treatment in Transition
- Institutional treatment of mental illness has changed a great deal in the last 40 years. Disenchantment with the negative effects of mental hospitals led to the establishment of more localized community mental health centers and a policy of deinstitutionalization.
- Long-term hospitalization for mental disorders is largely a thing of the past. Unfortunately, deinstitutionalization has left some unanticipated problems in its wake. Adequate outpatient facilities and care have not been provided for the mentally ill, and this lack has resulted in homelessness and the revolving-door problem. Our Featured Study suggested that mental disorders are commonplace among the homeless.

Putting It in Perspective
- Our discussion of psychotherapy highlighted the value of theoretical diversity. Conflicting theoretical orientations have generated varied approaches to treatment. Variety in treatment options allows clients to look for interventions suited to their unique needs.

Application: Looking for a Therapist
- Many practical considerations are relevant to the task of seeking professional treatment. Therapeutic services are available in many settings, and such services do not have to be expensive. Excellent therapists and mediocre therapists can be found in all of the mental health professions, using the full range of therapeutic approaches. Thus, therapists' personal skills are more important than their professional degree or their theoretical orientation.
- In selecting a therapist, warmth, empathy, confidence, and likability are desirable traits and it is reasonable to insist on a therapist of one sex rather than the other. If progress is slow, your own resistance may be the problem. Therapy requires time, hard work, and the courage to confront your problems.

KEY TERMS

Antianxiety drugs	Counseling	Psychiatrists
Antidepressant drugs	psychologists	Psychoanalysis
Antipsychotic drugs	Deinstitutionalization	Psychopharmacotherapy
Aversion therapy	Dream analysis	Resistance
Behavior therapies	Electroconvulsive	Social skills training
Biofeedback	therapy (ECT)	Spontaneous remission
Biomedical therapies	Free association	Systematic
Client-centered therapy	Group therapy	desensitization
Clinical psychologists	Insight therapies	Tardive dyskinesia
Cognitive therapy	Interpretation	Theoretical eclecticism
Community mental health	Lithium	Token economy
centers	Mental hospitals	Transference

KEY PEOPLE

Aaron Beck
Hans Eysenck
Sigmund Freud
Carl Rogers
Joseph Wolpe

Social Behavior

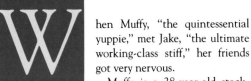

SOCIAL BEHAVIOR

hen Muffy, "the quintessential yuppie," met Jake, "the ultimate working-class stiff," her friends got very nervous.

Muffy is a 28-year-old stockbroker and a self-described "snob" with a group of about ten close women friends. Snobs all. They're graduates of fancy business schools. All consultants, investment bankers, and CPAs. All "cute, bright, fun to be with, and really intelligent," according to Muffy. They're all committed to their high-powered careers, but they all expect to marry someday, too.

Unfortunately, most of them don't date much. In fact, they spend a good deal of time "lamenting the dearth of 'good men.'" You know who the "good men" are. Those are the ones who are "committed to their work, open to the idea of marriage and family, and possessed of a good sense of humor."

Well, lucky Muffy actually met one of those "good men." Jake is a salesman. He comes from a working-class neighborhood. His clothes come from Sears.

He wasn't like the usual men Muffy dated. He treats Muffy the way she's always dreamed of being treated. He listens; he cares; he remembers. "He makes me feel safe and more cherished than any man I've ever known," she says.

So she decided to bring him to a little party of about 30 of her closest friends. . . .

Perhaps it was only Jake's nerves that caused him to commit some truly unforgivable *faux pas* that night. His sins were legion. Where do we start? First of all, he asked for a beer when everyone else was drinking white wine. He wore a worn turtleneck while everyone else had just removed the Polo tags from their clothing. He smoked. . . .

"The next day at least half of the people who had been at the party called to give me their impressions. They all said that they felt they just *had* to let me know that they thought Jake 'lacked polish' or 'seemed loud' or 'might not be a suitable match.'" Muffy says.

Now, you may think that Muffy's friends are simply very sensitive, demanding people. A group of princes and princesses who can detect a pea under the fluffiest stack of mattresses. But you'd be wrong. Actually, they've been quite accepting of some of the other men that Muffy has brought to their little parties. Or should we call them inquisitions? Winston, for example, was a great favorite.

"He got drunk, ignored me, and asked for other women's phone numbers right in front of me. But he was six-foot-four, the classic preppie, with blond hair, horn-rimmed glasses, and Ralph Lauren clothes."

And most important of all, he didn't ask for a Pabst Blue Ribbon.

So now Muffy is confused. "Jake is the first guy I've been out with in a long time that I've really liked. I was excited about him and my friends knew that. I was surprised by their reaction. I'll admit there's some validity to all their comments, but it's hard to express how violent it was. It made me think about what these women really want in a man. Whatever they say, what

they *really* want is someone they can take to a business dinner. They want someone who comes with a tux. Like a Ken doll."

Muffy may have come to a crossroads in her young life. It's clear that there's no way she can bring Jake among her friends for a while.

"I don't want their reaction to muddy my feelings until I get them sorted out," she says.

It just may be time for Muffy to choose between her man and her friends.

The preceding account is a real story, taken from a book about contemporary intimate relationships, entitled, *Tales From the Front* (Kavesh & Lavin, 1988, pp. 118–121). Muffy is on the horns of a difficult dilemma. Romantic relationships are very important to most people, but so are friendships, and Muffy may have to choose between the two. Muffy's story illustrates the significance of social relations in our lives and foreshadows each of the topics that we'll cover in this chapter, as we look at behavior in its social context.

Humans are social animals. We attend school and we work with others. We go to plays, concerts, and ball games with others. We try to impress others with our accomplishments and amuse them with our wit. We compete with others for parking spots, restaurant reservations, grades, and jobs. We share our streets and neighborhoods with others. As we saw in our chapter on motivation (Chapter 10), we have a fundamental need to affiliate with others and to maintain social bonds.

Social psychology is the branch of psychology concerned with the way individuals' thoughts, feelings, and behaviors are influenced by others. Of course, we haven't made our way through the first 15 chapters of this book without any mention of social behavior. As Table 16.1 shows, topics from the domain of social psychology—such as aggression, altruism, attribution, and affiliation—have surfaced in many of the preceding chapters. However, in this final chapter, we'll consider social behavior in earnest.

Our coverage of social psychology will focus on six broad topics, and an Application on prejudice will integrate ideas introduced in the main body of the chapter. Let's return to Muffy's story to get a glimpse of the various facets of social behavior that we'll examine in the coming pages.

• *Person perception.* The crux of Muffy's problem is that Jake didn't make a very good impression on her friends, primarily because her friends have preconceived views of "working-class stiffs." To what extent do our expectations color our impressions of others? Can a bad first impression be overcome?

Table 16.1 Social Psychology Topics from Previous Chapters

TOPIC	ISSUES DISCUSSED	CHAPTER
Affiliation	Effect of anxiety on desire to be with others	2
	Individual differences in need for affiliation and intimacy	10
	Situational determinants of affiliation	10
	Determinants of attachment in infancy	11
	Effect of social support from others on health	13
Aggression	Effect of physical punishment on aggressiveness in children	6
	Developmental patterns of aggressive behavior	11
	Effects of modeling on aggression	11
	Media violence and aggression	11
	Gender differences in aggressiveness	11
	Frustration-aggression hypothesis	13
Socialization	Socialization of high or low need for achievement	10
	Socialization of gender roles	11
Altruism	Developmental patterns of altruism	11
	Effects of modeling on altruism	11
Person perception	Biasing effect of expectations on impressions of others and events	1
	Gender stereotyping	11
	Relationship of self-monitoring to perceptions of others	12
Attribution	Two-factor theory of emotion, centering on attributions for physical arousal	10
	Social comparison, attributions for success and failure, and self-esteem	12
	Relation of attributional style to depression	14
Attraction	Factors in sexual attraction	10
	Relation of poor interpersonal skills to depression	14
	Therapeutic use of social skills training to improve interpersonal relations	15
Attitudes	Prejudicial attitudes and cultural differences in IQ	9
	Gender differences in influenceability	11
	Prejudice against victims of mental illness	14
Conformity	Pressure to conform as a form of stress	13
	Factors affecting compliance with medical advice	13
Groups	Processes and roles in group therapy	15

• *Attribution processes.* Muffy is struggling to understand her friends' rejection of Jake. When she implies that Jake's rejection is due to their snotty elitism, she's engaging in attribution, making an inference about the causes of her friends' behavior. How do we use attributions to explain social behavior? What kinds of bias are apparent in our attributional tendencies?

• *Interpersonal attraction.* Jake and Muffy are different in many important ways—is it true that opposites attract? Why does Jake's lack of similarity to Muffy's friends lead to such disdain?

• *Attitudes.* Muffy's girlfriends have negative attitudes about working-class men. How are our attitudes formed? What leads to attitude change? How do our attitudes affect our behavior?

• *Conformity and obedience.* Muffy's friends discourage her from dating Jake, putting her under pressure to conform to their values. What factors influence conformity? Can we be coaxed into doing things that contradict our values?

• *Behavior in groups.* Muffy belongs to a tight-knit group of friends who think along similar lines. Is our behavior in groups similar to our behavior when we're alone? Why do people in groups often think alike?

Social psychologists study how we're affected by the actual, imagined, or implied presence of others. Their interest is not limited to our *interactions* with others, as we can engage in social behavior even when we're alone. For instance, if you were driving by yourself on a deserted highway and tossed your trash out your car window, your littering would be a social action. It would defy social norms, reflect your socialization and attitudes, and have repercussions (albeit, small) for other people in your society. Thus, social psychologists often study *individual* behavior in a social context. This interest in understanding individual behavior should be readily apparent in our first section on person perception.

PERSON PERCEPTION: FORMING IMPRESSIONS OF OTHERS

Can you remember the first meeting of your introductory psychology class? What kind of impression did your professor make on you that day? Did your instructor appear to be confident? Easygoing? Pompous? Open-minded? Cynical? Friendly? Were your first impressions supported or undermined by subsequent interactions? When you interact with people, you're constantly engaged in **person perception, the process of forming impressions of others**. We show considerable ingenuity in piecing together clues about others' characteristics, but our impressions are often inaccurate because of the many biases and fallacies that occur in person perception. In this section we consider some of the factors that influence, and often distort, our perceptions of others.

In general, we have a bias toward viewing good-looking men and women as bright, competent, and talented. However, people sometimes downplay the talent of successful women who happen to be attractive, attributing their success to their good looks instead of to their competence.

Effects of Physical Appearance

"You shouldn't judge a book by its cover." "Beauty is only skin deep." We all know better than to let physical attractiveness determine our perceptions of others' personal qualities. Or do we? Studies have shown that our judgments of others' personality are often swayed by their appearance, especially their physical attractiveness. We tend to ascribe desirable personality characteristics to good-looking people, seeing them as more sensitive, kind, sociable, pleasant, likable, and interesting than those who are unattractive (Dion, 1986; Patzer, 1985).

We also tend to view good-looking people as more intelligent and competent. In a study of male employees in two large accounting firms, Ross and Ferris (1981) found that physical attractiveness was positively related to evaluations of the employees' performance and their salary increases. In another study, male subjects gave more favorable ratings to an essay when they thought it was written by an attractive woman than when they believed it was written by an unattractive woman (Landy & Sigall, 1974). However, physical attractiveness may occasionally backfire for

professional women, as some colleagues tend to downplay their talent while attributing their success to their good looks and their supposedly seductive behavior (Kaslow & Schwartz, 1978).

Some studies have examined the effects of specific aspects of appearance. For example, Pellegrini (1973) found a slight trend toward viewing bearded men as relatively confident, mature, and courageous. Greater height in men is associated with perceptions of leadership ability and competence (Patzer, 1985). A statistical analysis of starting salaries for male graduates at one university found that being over 6 feet 2 inches tall was more valuable than graduating with honors (Deck, 1968). While height is a plus, being overweight clearly isn't. For both sexes, obesity is associated with perceptions of laziness and lack of willpower (Cahnman, 1968).

Because physical appearance is readily apparent, it may have more impact on our first impressions of others than on our lasting perceptions of them. We focus on the significance of first impressions next.

First Impressions

When you want to impress someone, how damaging is it to "get off on the wrong foot"? Is a poor first impression something you can't overcome? Probably not. First impressions *do* tend to exert more influence on our judgments of people than subsequent information when experimenters hold other things, such as the amount of information, equal (Luchins, 1957; Friedman, 1983). However, outside of the research laboratory, first impressions are often pitted against a wealth of contradictory information from subsequent interactions. In such cases, most first impressions can probably be overcome.

Unfortunately, it tends to be harder to override unfavorable first impressions than favorable ones. Undesirable traits are quickly ascribed to people but are difficult to shed, while desirable trait descriptions are relatively difficult to earn but easily lost (Rothbart & Park, 1986). For example, you may want to see *consistent* hard work before you conclude that a new coworker is industrious, but *one* incident of loafing may lead you to characterize the person as lazy.

Cognitive Schemas

Although every individual is unique, we tend to label and categorize people. For instance, in our

Drinks fine wine | Hobby is travel | Drinks beer | Hobby is bowling
Patron of the arts | Health conscious | Sports fan | Smokes
Reads books often | | Watches TV often

Sophisticated professional   **Working-class stiff**

Figure 16.1 Examples of social schemas. We all have social schemas for different "types" of people, such as sophisticated professionals or working-class stiffs. Social schemas are clusters of beliefs that guide our information processing.

chapter-opening story, Muffy is characterized as "the quintessential yuppie." In another story in *Tales From the Front*, a man describes his date as a "BUP"—a "boring, uptight prude." These labels reflect our use of cognitive schemas in person perception.

As we discussed in our chapter on memory (Chapter 7), *schemas* are cognitive structures that guide our information processing. We have schemas for everything from inanimate objects (bicycles, apartments) to human activities (eating lunch, going to a gas station). We use schemas to organize the world around us—including our social world. **Social schemas are organized clusters of ideas about categories of social events and people.** We have social schemas for events like dates, picnics, committee meetings, and family reunions, as well as for certain categories of people, such as "dumb jocks," "social climbers," "frat rats," and "wimps" (see Figure 16.1).

When a schema is activated, it's likely to influence our perceptions of a person (Cantor & Mischel, 1979). For example, in our opening story, Muffy's friends apparently categorized Jake as a "working-class stiff." The activation of this schema probably increased their tendency to notice behaviors that fit their schema for working-class stiffs, such as beer drinking and smoking, while overlooking his kindness and other good points.

Stereotypes

Some of the schemas that we apply to people, such as "BUP," are unique products of our personal experiences, while other schemas, such as "yuppie," may be part of our shared cultural background. *Stereotypes* are special types of schemas that fall into the latter category (Anderson & Klatzky, 1987). **Stereotypes are widely held be-**

liefs that people have certain characteristics because of their membership in a particular group.

The most common stereotypes in our society are those based on sex and on membership in ethnic or occupational groups. Preconceived notions that Jews are mercenary, that Blacks have rhythm, that Germans are methodical, and that Italians are passionate are examples of common *ethnic stereotypes*. People who subscribe to traditional *gender stereotypes* tend to assume that women are emotional, submissive, illogical, and passive, while men are unemotional, dominant, logical, and aggressive. *Occupational stereotypes* suggest that lawyers are manipulative, accountants are conforming, artists are moody, and so forth.

Stereotypes are broad overgeneralizations that ignore the diversity within social groups and foster inaccurate perceptions of people (Hamilton, 1979). Obviously, all Jews, males, and lawyers do not behave alike. Most people who subscribe to stereotypes realize that all members of a group are not clones; they acknowledge that some Jews aren't mercenary, some men aren't competitive, and some lawyers aren't manipulative. However, they do tend to assume that Jews, males, and lawyers are *more likely* to have these characteristics. For instance, Figure 16.2 shows how gender stereotypes result in varied estimates of the probability that males and females will display certain personality traits.

Even if stereotypes mean only that people think in terms of slanted *probabilities*, their expectations may lead them to misperceive individuals with

Figure 16.2 Personality stereotypes of men and women. Gender stereotypes don't lead people to assume that all women (or men) are alike as much as they lead people to assume that there is a higher *probability* that one sex will exhibit certain traits. The probability judgments for four personality traits are graphed here. (From Deaux et al., 1985)

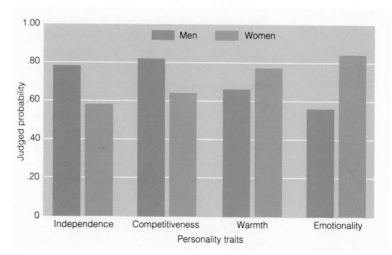

whom they interact. As we've noted in previous chapters, perception is subjective, and people often see what they expect to see.

Selectivity in Person Perception

Stereotypes and other schemas create numerous biases in person perception that frequently lead to confirmation of our expectations about others. If there's any ambiguity in someone's behavior, we're likely to interpret what we see in a way that's consistent with our expectations (Darley & Gross, 1983). Thus, after dealing with a pushy female customer, a salesman who believes in traditional gender stereotypes might characterize the woman as "emotional," while seeing a pushy male who exhibits exactly the same behavior as "aggressive."

We not only see what we expect to see, but we also tend to overestimate how often we see it (Hamilton & Gifford, 1976). **The illusory correlation effect occurs when we estimate that we have encountered more confirmations of an association between social traits than we have actually seen.** Statements like "I've never met an honest lawyer," illustrate this effect.

Memory processes make major contributions to our confirmatory biases in person perception. We may selectively recall facts that fit with the schemas that we apply to people. Evidence for such a tendency was found in a study by Cohen (1981). In this experiment, subjects watched a videotape of a woman, described as a waitress or a librarian,

who engaged in a variety of activities, including listening to classical music, drinking beer, and watching TV. When asked to recall what the woman did during the filmed sequence, subjects tended to remember activities consistent with their stereotypes of waitresses and librarians. For instance, subjects who thought the woman was a waitress tended to recall her beer drinking, while subjects who thought she was a librarian tended to recall her listening to classical music.

Not only do we recall information selectively, but we also tend to alter or *reconstruct* our memories of interactions to confirm our beliefs. Mc-Farland and Ross (1987) asked subjects to rate their dating partner on various personality traits, such as honesty, reliability and sociability. Two months later, the subjects were asked to rate their dating partners once again, and then were asked to recall their earlier ratings. Subjects who had become more negative about their partner during the 2-month period recalled making less favorable ratings than they had actually made. Subjects who had experienced a positive shift in their feelings about their partner recalled overly favorable ratings. Thus, subjects tended to reconstruct the past to make it more consistent with their present perceptions of their dating partners.

Our discussion of social schemas, stereotypes, and memory distortion in person perception shows that cognitive processes influence our impressions of others. This insight will be reinforced in the next section, where we discuss attribution processes.

ATTRIBUTION PROCESSES: EXPLAINING BEHAVIOR

It's Friday evening and you're sitting around at home feeling bored. You call a few friends to see whether they'd like to go out. They all say that they'd love to go, but they have other commitments and they can't. Their commitments sound vague, and you feel that their reasons for not going out with you are rather flimsy. How do you explain these rejections? Do your friends really have commitments? Are they worn out by school and work? Are they just lazy and apathetic about going out? When they said that they'd love to go, were they being sincere? Or do they find you boring? Could they be right? Are you boring? These questions illustrate a process that we engage in routinely: the explanation of behavior. *Attributions* play a key role in our explanatory efforts, and they have significant effects on our social relations.

Attributions: What? Why? When?

Although we discussed attributions briefly in Chapter 14, let's review what they are, elaborate on why we make them, and discuss when we're likely to engage in attributional thinking.

What are attributions? **Attributions are inferences that people draw about the causes of events, others' behavior, and their own behavior.** If you conclude that a friend turned down your invitation because she's overworked, you've made an attribution about the cause of her behavior (and, implicitly, rejected other possible explanations). If you conclude that you're stuck at home with nothing to do because you failed to plan ahead, you've made an attribution about the cause of an event (being stuck at home). If you conclude that you failed to plan ahead because you're a terrible procrastinator, you've made an attribution about the cause of your own behavior.

Why do we make attributions? We make attributions because we have a strong need to understand our experiences. We want to make sense out of our own behavior, others' actions, and the events in our lives. For instance, if you were explaining your friend's lack of interest in going out with you, it might be small consolation, but there would be some comfort in understanding why you were rejected. In addition to understanding for its own sake, attributions can serve other purposes. Explanations for our experiences may guide us in changing our behavior to improve our outcomes. Also, we sometimes make distorted attributions to maintain our self-image or to discount evidence that contradicts beliefs we cherish.

When do we make attributions? We don't attempt to explain everything that happens around us. You're not likely to mull over why a friend said "Hi" this morning or why a colleague took the elevator to get to the 20th floor of the building you work in. However, if your friend *did not* say "Hi," or if your colleague *walked* up 20 flights of stairs instead of taking the elevator, you might wonder why. A variety of factors influence whether we're stimulated to engage in attributional thinking (Fiske & Taylor, 1984; B. Weiner, 1985). Generally, we're more likely to make attributions (1) when unusual events grab our attention, (2) when events have personal consequences for us, such as success and failure, (3) when people behave in unexpected ways, and (4) when others ask us for our explanations of events.

Having looked at the what, why, and when of attribution, we'll devote the remainder of our discussion in this section to *how* we explain the causes of behavior. Specifically, we'll examine theoretical models that identify the key dimensions of our attributions and look at various sources of bias in our attributional thinking.

Internal Versus External Attributions

Fritz Heider (1958) was the first to describe how we make attributions. Heider asserted that we tend to locate the cause of behavior either *within a person*, attributing it to personal factors, or *outside of a person*, attributing it to environmental factors.

Elaborating on Heider's insight, various theorists have agreed that our explanations of behavior and events can be categorized as internal or external attributions (Jones & Davis, 1965; Kelley, 1967; Weiner, 1974). **Internal attributions ascribe the causes of behavior to personal dispositions, traits, abilities, and feelings. External**

An internal attribution would ascribe the cause of this young man's car accident to his personal traits (perhaps carelessness or incompetence). An external attribution would ascribe the accident to situational factors (perhaps slippery road conditions or poor highway markings). The attributions we make about events influence our social interactions.

attributions ascribe the causes of behavior to situational demands and environmental constraints. For example, if a friend's business fails, you might attribute it to your friend's lack of business acumen (an internal, personal factor) or to negative trends in the nation's economic climate (an external, situational explanation). Parents who find out that their teenage son has just banged up the car may blame it on his carelessness (a personal disposition) or on slippery road conditions (a situational factor).

Internal and external attributions can have a tremendous impact on our everyday interpersonal interactions. Blaming a friend's business failure on poor business acumen as opposed to a poor economy has a great impact on how you view your friend—not to mention whether you'll lend your friend money in the future. Likewise, if parents attribute their son's automobile accident to slippery road conditions, they're likely to deal with the event very differently than if they attribute it to his carelessness.

Given the importance of personal versus situational attributions, the next question should be obvious: What leads us to make an internal or external attribution? Let's examine a theory that attempts to address this question.

A "Rubik's Cube" for Attribution

Harold H. Kelley (1967, 1973) has devised a theory that identifies some of the important factors that we consider in making internal or external attributions. According to Kelley's model, when we attempt to infer the causes of an actor's behavior, we usually consider three types of informa-

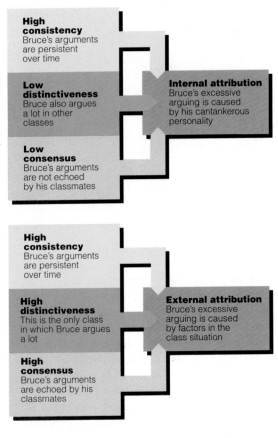

Figure 16.3 Examples of attributional thinking. In Kelley's model, high consistency, low distinctiveness, and low consensus should lead to an internal attribution, while high consistency, high distinctiveness, and high consensus should lead to an external attribution. These principles are applied here to the example in the text about Bruce's arguing in class.

High consistency
Bruce's arguments are persistent over time

Low distinctiveness
Bruce also argues a lot in other classes

Low consensus
Bruce's arguments are not echoed by his classmates

Internal attribution
Bruce's excessive arguing is caused by his cantankerous personality

High consistency
Bruce's arguments are persistent over time

High distinctiveness
This is the only class in which Bruce argues a lot

High consensus
Bruce's arguments are echoed by his classmates

External attribution
Bruce's excessive arguing is caused by factors in the class situation

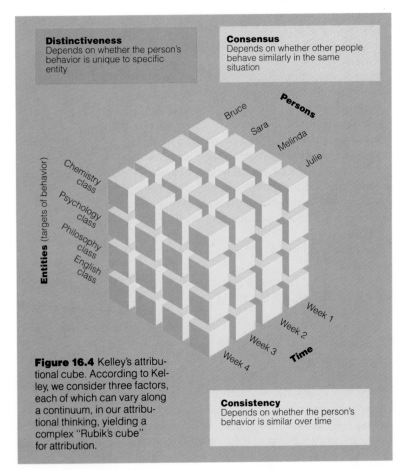

Distinctiveness
Depends on whether the person's behavior is unique to specific entity

Consensus
Depends on whether other people behave similarly in the same situation

Consistency
Depends on whether the person's behavior is similar over time

Figure 16.4 Kelley's attributional cube. According to Kelley, we consider three factors, each of which can vary along a continuum, in our attributional thinking, yielding a complex "Rubik's cube" for attribution.

tion: consistency, distinctiveness, and consensus. Let's look at how a professor might weigh each of these factors in figuring out why a hypothetical student (let's call him Bruce) is frequently argumentative in class.

Consistency refers to whether an actor's behavior in a situation is the same over time (across occasions). In our hypothetical case, the professor would ask, "Is Bruce always argumentative in my class meetings?"

Distinctiveness refers to whether a person's behavior is unique to the specific entity that is the target of the person's actions. Thus, the professor might ask, "Is Bruce argumentative only with me, or is he argumentative with all his professors?"

Consensus refers to whether other people in the same situation tend to respond like the actor. Thus, the professor might think, "Are Bruce's classmates also argumentative?"

According to Kelley, when distinctiveness and consensus are low, we tend to favor internal attributions and when they are high, we're more likely to make external attributions. Low consistency favors an external attribution, but high consistency is compatible with either an internal or external attribution. Thus, if Bruce's behavior is persistent over time (high consistency), not unique to the professor's class (low distinctiveness), and unlike the behavior of his classmates (low consensus), the professor probably will make an internal attribution and conclude that the excessive arguing is caused by Bruce's cantankerous personality (see Figure 16.3). In contrast, if Bruce's arguments are persistent (high consistency), but unique to the professor's class (high distinctiveness), and are echoed by Bruce's classmates (high consensus), the professor is more likely to make an external attribution and infer that something in the class situation stimulates Bruce's arguments (refer to Figure 16.3 again).

Kelley assumes that consistency, distinctiveness, and consensus each can vary along a continuum, and that we often juggle all three factors to arrive at our attributions. These assumptions mean that there are many possible combinations of consistency, distinctiveness, and consensus. These possibilities are usually depicted in a cube like that shown in Figure 16.4. In essence, then, Kelley's model suggests that we mentally manipulate a complex, imaginary "Rubik's cube" of attribution when we attempt to explain behavior.

Attributions for Success and Failure

Some psychologists have sought to discover additional dimensions of attributional thinking, besides the internal-external dimension. After studying the attributions that people make in explaining success and failure, Bernard Weiner and his colleagues concluded that we often focus on the *stability* of the causes underlying behavior (Weiner, 1974; Weiner et al., 1972). According to Weiner, the stable-unstable dimension in attribution cuts across the internal-external dimension, creating four types of attributions for success and failure, as shown in Figure 16.5.

Let's apply Weiner's model to a concrete event. Imagine that you're contemplating why you failed to get a job that you wanted. You might attribute your setback to internal factors that are stable (lack of ability) or unstable (inadequate effort to put together an eye-catching resumé). Or you might attribute your setback to external factors that are stable (too much outstanding competition) or unstable (bad luck). If you got the job, the explanations that you might offer for your success would fall into the same four categories: internal-stable (your excellent ability), internal-unstable (your hard work to assemble a superb resumé), external-stable (lack of top-flight competition), and external-unstable (good luck).

Weiner (1980) eventually added a third dimension—the *controllability* of events—to his model. Other theorists have built on Weiner's foundation in different ways. As we discussed in Chapter 14, attributional theories of depression focus on whether our attributions have *global* (far-reaching) or *specific* implications about our personal qualities. According to Abramson, Seligman, and Teasdale (1978), internal, stable, and global attributions for personal setbacks foster feelings of depression. According to their theory, people who exhibit this attributional style blame their setbacks on personal shortcomings (internal) that they see as permanent (stable) and then draw far-reaching conclusions (global) about their personal worth.

Clearly, attributions are complicated, and they have important implications for how we see ourselves and others. However, attributions are not entirely logical and objective. We turn next to the matter of biases in attribution processes.

Bias in Attribution

Attributions are only inferences. Your attributions may not be the correct explanations for events. Paradoxical as it may seem, we often arrive at inaccurate explanations even when we contemplate the causes of *our own* behavior. Attributions ultimately represent *guesswork* about the causes of events, and these guesses tend to be slanted in certain directions. Let's look the principal biases seen in attribution.

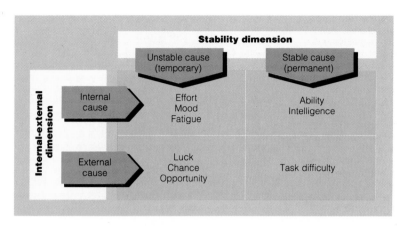

ACTOR-OBSERVER BIASES
Our view of our own behavior can be quite different from the view of someone else observing us. When an actor and an observer draw inferences about the causes of the actor's behavior, they often make different attributions. The *fundamental attribution error* **refers to the tendency of an observer to favor internal attributions in explaining the behavior of an actor** (Ross, 1977). Of course, in many instances, an internal attribution may not be an "error" (Harvey, Town, & Yarkin, 1981), but the point is that observers tend to assume that an actor's behavior reflects personal qualities rather than situational factors.

Figure 16.5 Attributions for success and failure. Weiner's model assumes that our explanations for success and failure emphasize internal versus external causes and stable versus unstable causes. Examples of causal factors that fit into each of the four cells in Weiner's model are shown in the diagram.

CONCEPT CHECK 16.1
Analyzing Attributions

Check your understanding of attribution processes by analyzing possible explanations for an athletic team's success. Imagine that the women's track team at your school has just won a regional championship that qualifies it for the national tournament. Around the campus, you hear different people attribute the team's success to a variety of different factors. Examine the attributions shown below and place each of them in one of the cells of Weiner's model of attribution (just record the letter inside the cell). The answers are in Appendix A.

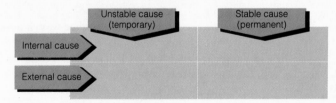

a. "They won only because the best two athletes on Central State's team were out with injuries—talk about good fortune!"

b. "They won because they have some of the best talent in the country."

c. "Anybody could win this region; the competition is far below average in comparison to the rest of the country."

d. "They won because they put in a great deal of last-minute effort and practice, and they were incredibly fired up for the regional tourney after last year's near miss."

As an example, imagine that you're visiting your bank and you fly into a rage over a mistake made on your bank account. Observers who witness your rage are likely to make an internal attribution and infer that you are surly, temperamental, and quarrelsome. They may be right, but if asked, you'd probably attribute your rage to the frustrating situation. Perhaps you're a calm, even-tempered, easygoing person, but you're late for an important appointment, you've been in line for 45 minutes, you just straightened out a similar error by the same bank last week, and you're being treated rudely by the teller. Observers often are unaware of situational considerations such as these, so they tend to make internal attributions for another's behavior.

In comparison to observers, actors are more aware of the situational factors that have influenced their behavior. Hence, they are more likely than observers to locate the cause of their behavior in the situation. In general, then, *actors favor external attributions for their behavior, while observers tend to explain the same behavior with internal attributions* (Jones & Nisbett, 1971).

DEFENSIVE ATTRIBUTION

In attempting to explain the calamities and setbacks that befall other people, an observer's tendency to make internal attributions becomes even stronger than normal. Let's say that a friend gets mugged and severely beaten. You may attribute the mugging to your friend's carelessness or stupidity ("He should have known better than to be in that neighborhood at that time") rather than to bad luck. Why? Because if you attribute your friend's misfortune to bad luck, you have to face the ugly reality that it could just as easily happen to you. To avoid disturbing thoughts such as these, we often attribute mishaps to victims' negligence (Thornton, 1984).

Defensive attribution **is a tendency to blame victims for their misfortune, so that we feel less likely to be victimized in a similar way.** Blaming victims for their calamities also helps us to maintain our belief that we live in a just world, where we're unlikely to experience similar troubles (Lerner & Miller, 1978). Unfortunately, when we blame victims for their setbacks, we view them in a very negative light. We unfairly attribute undesirable traits to them, such as incompetence, foolishness, laziness, greed, and so on. Thus, defensive attribution often leads us to derogate victims of misfortune.

SELF-SERVING BIAS

The self-serving bias in attribution comes into play when we attempt to explain success and fail-

ure. This bias may either strengthen or weaken our normal attributional tendencies, depending on whether we're trying to explain positive or negative outcomes (Bradley, 1978). **The *self-serving bias* is our tendency to attribute our positive outcomes to personal factors and our negative outcomes to situational factors.**

In explaining *failure*, the usual actor-observer biases are apparent. Actors tend to make external attributions, blaming their failures on unfavorable situational factors, while observers attribute the same failures to the actors' personal shortcomings. Thus, if you fail an exam, you may place the blame on the poorly constructed exam, lousy teaching, distractions in the hallway, or a bad week at work (all external attributions). However, an observer is more likely to attribute your failure to your lack of ability, or to your lack of study (both internal attributions).

In explaining *success*, the usual actor-observer differences are reversed to some degree. Thus, if you get a high exam score, you'll probably make an internal attribution, and point to your ability or your hard work (Forsyth & McMillan, 1981). In comparison, an observer may be more likely to infer that the test was easy or that you were lucky (external attributions). In other words, actors like to take credit for their success, while observers lean toward situational explanations for others' triumphs.

Attributional biases can have considerable impact on our interpersonal relations. For example, in recent years, researchers have learned that attributional bias may contribute to distress in intimate relationships. Let's find out how.

Attributional Bias and Intimate Relationships

Married people routinely make attributions to explain each other's behavior. For example, if a wife forgets her husband's birthday, he might conclude that she's self-centered and inconsiderate (an internal, stable attribution) or that she's drained by work overload at the office (an external, unstable attribution). Obviously, these attributions don't have the same implications for their relationship.

Research by Frank Fincham and his colleagues indicates that distressed spouses (usually defined as those seeking marital therapy) tend to explain their partners' negative behavior with internal, stable attributions that have global implications for their marriage ("she doesn't love me"). In contrast, they tend to explain their partners' positive behaviors with external, unstable attributions that have specific implications ("she was nice because she made a big sale today"). Patterns of

Check your understanding of bias in social cognition by identifying various types of errors that are common in person perception and attribution. Imagine that you're a nonvoting student member of a college committee at Southwest State University that is hiring a new political science professor. As you listen to the committee's discussion, you hear examples of: (a) the illusory correlation effect, (b) stereotyping, (c) the fundamental attribution error, and (d) defensive attribution. Indicate which of these is at work in the excerpts from committee members' deliberations below. The answers are in Appendix A.

_____ 1. "I absolutely won't consider the fellow who arrived 30 minutes late for his interview. Anybody who can't make a job interview on time is either irresponsible or hopelessly disorganized. I don't care what he says about the airline messing up his reservations."

_____ 2. "You know, I was very, very, impressed with the young female applicant, and I would love to hire her, but every time we add a young woman to the faculty in liberal arts, she gets pregnant within the first year." The committee chairperson, who has heard this line from this professor before replies, "You always say that, so I finally did a systematic check of what's happened in the past. Of the last 14 women hired in liberal arts, only one has become pregnant within a year."

_____ 3. "The first one I want to rule out is the guy who's been practicing law for the last 10 years. Although he has an excellent background in political science, I just don't trust lawyers. They're all ambitious, power hungry, manipulative cutthroats. He'll be a divisive force in the department."

_____ 4. "I say we forget about the two candidates who lost their faculty slots in the massive financial crisis at Western Polytechnic last year. I know it sounds cruel, but they brought it on themselves with their fiscal irresponsibility over at Western. Thank goodness we'll never let anything like that happen around here. As far as I'm concerned, if these guys couldn't see that crisis coming, they must be pretty dense."

attribution in happily married couples tend to be just the opposite (Bradbury & Fincham, 1988; Fincham, Beach, & Baucom, 1987). Thus, in comparison to happy couples, distressed spouses blame their problems on each other and view good behavior as a temporary aberration. Unhappy spouses' biases in attribution could be either a cause or an effect of marital distress, but their biases clearly aren't a promising foundation for marital bliss.

In a study of dating couples, the same attributional biases were found to be related to the couples' love, happiness, and commitment (Fletcher et al., 1987). Even more interesting, the investigators found that dating partners' attributional thinking about their relationship was most frequent during the early stages of their relationship, and at key choice points when they decided whether to break up, go steady, get engaged, and so forth.

These findings suggest that attributions play a key role in the growth, as well as the deterioration, of close relationships. In the next section, we'll look at the role of other factors in close relationships, as we discuss interpersonal attraction.

INTERPERSONAL ATTRACTION: LIKING AND LOVING

"I just don't know what she sees in him. She could do so much better for herself. I suppose he's a nice guy, but they're just not right for each other." Can't you imagine Muffy's friends making these comments in discussing her relationship with Jake? You've probably heard similar remarks on many occasions. These comments illustrate our interest in analyzing the dynamics of attraction. **Interpersonal attraction refers to positive feelings toward another.** Social psychologists use this term broadly to encompass a variety of experiences, including liking, friendship, admiration, lust, and love. In this section, we'll analyze key factors that influence attraction and examine several theoretical perspectives on the mystery of love.

Key Factors in Attraction

Many factors influence who is attracted to whom. We'll discuss factors that promote the development of liking, friendship, and love. Although these are different types of attraction, the interpersonal dynamics at work in each are surprisingly similar. Each is influenced by proximity, physical attractiveness, similarity, and reciprocity.

PROXIMITY EFFECTS

It would be difficult for you to develop a friendship with someone you never met. It happens occasionally (among pen pals, for instance), but attraction usually depends on people being in the same place at the same time, making proximity a major factor in attraction. **Proximity refers to geographic, residential, and other forms of spatial closeness** (seating charts, office arrangements, and so forth). Generally, we become acquainted with, and attracted to, people who live, work, shop, and play nearby.

The importance of spatial factors in living arrangements was apparent in a study of friendship patterns among married graduate students living in a university housing project (Festinger, Schachter, & Back, 1950). People whose doors were close together were most likely to become friends. Moreover, those whose homes faced the central court area had more than twice as many friends in the complex as those whose homes faced outward. Using the centralized court area apparently increased the likelihood that people would meet and befriend others.

Proximity effects may seem self-evident, but it's sobering to realize that our friendships and love interests are shaped by arbitrary desk arrangements in offices, dormitory floor assignments, and traffic patterns in apartment complexes. In spite of the increasing geographic mobility in modern society, people still tend to marry someone who grew up nearby (Ineichen, 1979).

PHYSICAL ATTRACTIVENESS

Although we often say that "beauty is only skin deep," the empirical evidence suggests that most of us don't care. The importance of physical attractiveness was demonstrated in a study of first-year college students whose dates for a dance were supposedly selected by a computer (Walster et al., 1966). Actually, the couples had been paired randomly, but the computer cover story provided a good rationale for asking students to rate their desire to go out with their dates again. These ratings were correlated with their dates' physical attractiveness (assessed by impartial judges) and a host of personality, interest, and background variables.

For both sexes, a partner's good looks was the *only* variable that predicted subjects' desire to go out with their date again. Subsequent studies have replicated the singular prominence of physical attractiveness in the initial stage of dating and have shown that it continues to influence the course of commitment as dating relationships evolve (Patzer, 1985).

The importance of good looks was also apparent in a recent study of the tactics people use in pursuing romantic relationships. David Buss (1988) asked 208 newlywed individuals to describe the things they did when they first met their spouse, and during the remainder of their courtship, to make themselves more appealing to their partner. Buss found that men were more likely than women to emphasize their material resources by doing things such as flashing lots of money, buying nice gifts, showing off expensive possessions, and bragging about their importance at work (see Figure 16.6). In contrast, women were more likely than men to work at enhancing their appearance by dieting, wearing stylish clothes, trying new hairstyles, and getting a tan. Although there were relative differences between the sexes in emphasis on physical appearance, the data in Figure 16.6 show that both sexes relied on tactics intended to enhance or maintain good looks.

Although we prefer physically attractive partners in romantic relationships, we may consider our own level of attractiveness in pursuing dates. **The *matching hypothesis* proposes that males and females of approximately equal physical attractiveness are likely to select each other as partners.** The matching hypothesis is supported by evidence that married couples tend to be very similar in level of physical attractiveness (Murstein, 1972). However, there's some debate about whether we match up by our own choice (Aron, 1988; Kalick & Hamilton, 1986). Some theorists believe that we mostly pursue high attractiveness in partners and that our matching is the result of social forces beyond our control, such as rejection by more attractive others.

Most of the studies of physical beauty and attraction have focused on dating relationships, and only a few have looked at friendship formation. However, the studies of friendship suggest that people prefer attractiveness in their friends as well as their dates (Lyman, Hatlelid, & Macurdy, 1981). Researchers have also found evidence for matching effects in same-sex friendships (Cash & Derlega, 1978).

SIMILARITY EFFECTS

Is it true that "birds of a feather flock together," or do "opposites attract"? Research provides far more support for the former than the latter.

According to the matching hypothesis, males and females who are similar in physical attractiveness are likely to be drawn together. This type of matching may also influence the formation of friendships.

TACTICS OF ATTRACTION	MEAN FREQUENCY (N = 102)	MEAN FREQUENCY (N = 106)
Tactics used significantly more by males	Men	Women
Display resources	0.67	0.44
Brag about resources	0.73	0.60
Display sophistication	1.18	0.88
Display strength	0.96	0.44
Display athleticism	1.18	0.94
Show off	0.70	0.47
Tactics used significantly more by females	Men	Women
Wear makeup	0.02	1.63
Keep clean and groomed	2.27	2.44
Alter appearance—general	0.39	1.27
Wear stylish clothes	1.22	2.00
Act coy	0.54	0.73
Wear jewelry	0.25	2.21
Wear sexy clothes	0.68	0.91
Tactics for which no significant sex differences were found	Men	Women
Act provocative	0.77	0.90
Flirt	2.13	2.09
Keep hair groomed	2.20	2.31
Increase social exposure	0.89	0.90
Act nice	1.77	1.86
Display humor	2.42	2.28
Act promiscuous	0.30	0.21
Act submissive	1.24	1.11
Dissemble (feign agreement)	1.26	1.09
Touch	2.26	2.16

Figure 16.6 Similarities and differences between the sexes in tactics of attraction. Buss (1988) asked newlywed subjects to rate how often they had used 23 tactics of attraction to make themselves more appealing to their partner. The tactics used by one sex significantly more often than the other are listed in the first two sections of the figure. Although there were significant differences between the sexes, there were also many similarities. The 11 tactics used most frequently by each sex (those above the median) are highlighted, showing that there is considerable overlap between males and females in the tactics they use most. (Note: Higher means in the data reflect higher frequency of use, but the numbers do not indicate frequency per day or week.)

Married and dating couples tend to be similar in age, race, religion, social class, education, intelligence, physical attractiveness, and attitudes (Brehm, 1985; Hendrick & Hendrick, 1983). Similarity is also seen among friends. For instance, adolescent best friends are similar in educational goals and performance, political and religious activities, and illicit drug use (Kandel, 1978).

The most obvious explanation for these correlations is that similarity causes attraction. Laboratory experiments on *attitude similarity*, conducted by Donn Byrne and his colleagues, suggest that similarity does cause liking (Byrne, 1971; Byrne, Clore, & Smeaton, 1986). In these studies, subjects who have previously provided information on their own attitudes are led to believe that they'll be meeting a stranger. They're given information about the stranger's views that has been manipulated to show various degrees of similarity to their own views. As attitude similarity increases, subjects' ratings of the likability of the stranger increase. This evidence supports the notion that similarity promotes attraction, but it's also consistent with a somewhat different explanation proposed by Rosenbaum (1986).

Rosenbaum has marshalled evidence which suggests that similarity effects occur in attraction, not because similarity fosters liking, but because *dissimilarity* leads us to *dislike* others. In one study of his "repulsion hypothesis," Rosenbaum found that Democrats did not rate other Democrats

(similar others) higher than controls as much as they rated Republicans (dissimilar others) lower than controls. Rosenbaum acknowledges that similarity sometimes causes liking, but he maintains that *dissimilarity causes disdain* more frequently. Additional research is needed to settle this interesting issue.

RECIPROCITY EFFECTS

In his book *How to Win Friends and Influence People*, Dale Carnegie (1936) suggested that people can gain others' liking by showering them with praise and flattery. However, we've all heard that "flattery will get you nowhere." Which advice is right? The evidence suggests that flattery will get you somewhere, with some people, some of the time.

In interpersonal attraction, **reciprocity involves liking those who show that they like us**. In general, it does appear that liking breeds liking and loving promotes loving (Byrne & Murnen, 1988). However, this principle must be qualified carefully.

People realize that others sometimes try to "butter them up." **Ingratiation is a conscious effort to cultivate others' liking by complimenting them, agreeing with them, and doing them favors.** If affection appears to be part of an ingratiation strategy rather than affection for its own sake, it's less likely to be reciprocated (Schlenker, 1980). Another qualification depends on the self-esteem of the person who receives praise. People low in self-esteem may soak up flattery eagerly, but those who have higher self-esteem may not be so easily swayed by positive treatment (Jacobs, Berscheid, & Walster, 1971).

Studies of proximity, physical attractiveness, similarity, and reciprocity shed some light on the formation and evolution of friendships and romantic relationships, but tell us very little about the mystery of love. We discuss some theoretical perspectives on love next.

Perspectives on the Mystery of Love

Wander through a bookstore and you'll see an endless array of titles, such as *How to Be Loved*,

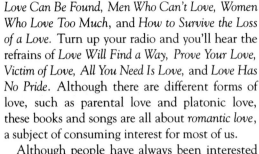

"The emotion of romantic love seems to be distressingly fragile. As a 16th-century sage poignantly observed, 'the history of a love affair is the drama of its fight against time.'"

ELLEN BERSCHEID

"Passionate love is like any other form of excitement. By its very nature, excitement involves a continuous interplay between elation and despair, thrills and terror."

ELAINE HATFIELD

Love Can Be Found, Men Who Can't Love, Women Who Love Too Much, and *How to Survive the Loss of a Love.* Turn up your radio and you'll hear the refrains of *Love Will Find a Way, Prove Your Love, Victim of Love, All You Need Is Love,* and *Love Has No Pride.* Although there are different forms of love, such as parental love and platonic love, these books and songs are all about *romantic love,* a subject of consuming interest for most of us.

Although people have always been interested in love and romance, the scientific study of love has a short history, which for all practical purposes, dates back only to the 1970s. Love has proven to be an elusive subject of study. It's difficult to define, difficult to measure, and frequently difficult to understand. Nonetheless, psychologists have begun to make some progress in their study of love. Let's look at their theories and research.

PASSIONATE AND COMPANIONATE LOVE
Perhaps no one has conducted more research on love than Elaine Hatfield (formerly Walster) and Ellen Berscheid (Berscheid, 1988; Berscheid & Walster, 1978; Hatfield, 1988; Walster & Berscheid, 1974). They propose that romantic relationships are characterized by two kinds of love: passionate love and companionate love. **Passionate love involves a complete absorption in another that includes tender sexual feelings and the agony and ecstasy of intense emotion. Companionate love is warm, trusting, tolerant affection for another whose life is deeply intertwined with our own.** Passionate and companionate love *may* coexist, but they don't necessarily go hand in hand.

Although they're rigorous researchers who have made major contributions to the scientific study of love, Berscheid and Hatfield have also been willing to offer down-to-earth, practical insights about the nature of love. For instance, they've identified some common myths about love that can foster disappointment in romantic relationships (Berscheid & Walster, 1978).

Myth 1: When you fall in love, you'll know it. People often spend a great deal of time agonizing over whether they're really in love or only experiencing infatuation. When people consult others about their doubts, they're frequently told, "If it were true love, you'd know it." This assertion, which amounts to replying, "You must not be in love," simply isn't true.

Berscheid and Hatfield use Schachter's two-factor theory of emotion to explain passionate love. Schachter's theory, described in Chapter 10, assumes that emotion consists of physiological arousal and the cognitive explanation we provide for it. This model assumes that we often aren't sure what our arousal should be attributed to. For instance, many people have difficulty distinguishing lust from love. As we saw earlier, dating couples engage in increased attributional guesswork at transition points in their relationships—in efforts to figure out their feelings. Hence, confusion about a romantic relationship is not the least bit unusual, and it does *not* mean that you aren't really in love.

Myth 2: Love is a purely positive experience. Our idealized views of love often suggest that it should be a purely enjoyable experience. In reality, pain, anger, and ambivalent feelings are common in love relationships, and it's unrealistic to expect love to be entirely pleasant. We often are more critical and less tolerant of lovers than we are of friends. The intense nature of passionate love means that love is capable of taking us to emotional peaks in *either* direction.

Myth 3: True love lasts forever. Love may last forever, but you certainly can't count on it. Some people perpetuate this myth in an interesting way. If their love relationship disintegrates, they conclude that it was never genuine love, but only infatuation or comfortable compatibility. Hatfield and Berscheid theorize that passionate love peaks early in a relationship and then declines rapidly, while companionate love is more likely to continue to grow. Robert Sternberg has built on this idea in some detail, so let's turn to his research.

A TRIANGULAR VIEW OF LOVE
The distinction between passionate and companionate love has been further refined by Robert Sternberg (1988), who suggests that love has three faces rather than just two. He subdivides companionate love into intimacy and commitment. **Intimacy refers to warmth, closeness, and sharing in a relationship. Commitment is an intent to maintain a relationship in spite of the difficulties and costs that may arise.** Thus, the three elements in Sternberg's triangular view of love are *passion, intimacy,* and *commitment.*

Figure 16.7 Sternberg's view of love over time. Sternberg's triangular theory breaks love into three components: passion, intimacy, and commitment. Sternberg theorizes that passion peaks early in a relationship, while intimacy and commitment build gradually.

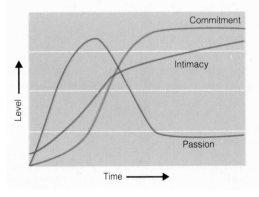

Sternberg has mapped out the probable relations between the passage of time and all three aspects of love, as shown in Figure 16.7. Like Hatfield and Berscheid, he suspects that passion reaches its zenith in the early phases of love and then erodes. Intimacy and commitment are thought to increase with time, although at different rates. Sternberg's relatively new model hasn't generated much research yet. However, one recent study of dating couples found that measures of their level of commitment and intimacy were among the best predictors of whether their relationships continued (Hendrick, Hendrick, & Adler, 1988).

STYLES OF LOVING

Instead of analyzing types of love, John Alan Lee (1974, 1988) has argued that people are characterized by different *styles* of loving. Lee suggests that love is like color mixing, with many varieties emerging out of mixtures of basic emotions, just as many hues emerge out of mixtures of the three primary colors. Figure 16.8 shows Lee's "color circle for love," and Table 16.2 describes the six basic styles of loving he has identified: eros, ludus, storge, mania, pragma, and agape. Lee (1974) theorizes that many romantic relationships fail because "too often people are speaking different languages when they speak of love" (p. 44). He asserts that satisfaction in intimate relationships depends on finding a partner who "shares the same approach to loving, the same definition of love" (p. 44).

Empirical studies of Lee's theory have only begun in earnest very recently, stimulated by the development of a practical scale to measure Lee's

six styles of loving (Hendrick & Hendrick, 1986). Thus far, a study of dating couples (Hendrick, Hendrick, & Adler, 1988) has indicated that eros is a positive predictor of relationship satisfaction and that ludus is a negative predictor of satisfaction (agape was also a weak positive predictor for women, as shown in Table 16.2). Future tests of Lee's hypotheses about the need for compatibility in styles of loving should prove interesting.

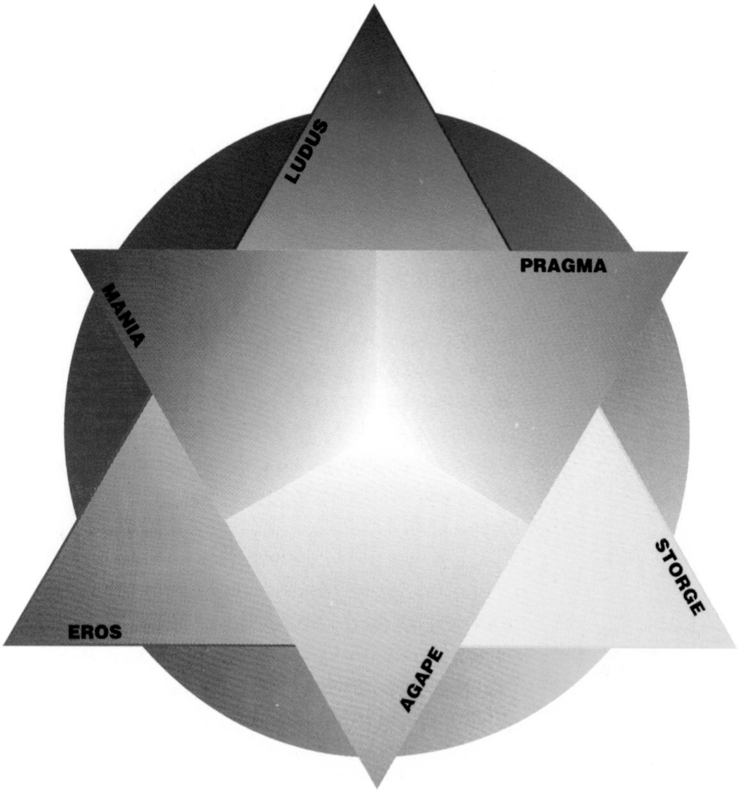

Figure 16.8 Lee's model of styles of loving. Lee draws an analogy between color mixing and styles of loving, asserting that many different styles can emerge out of mixtures of basic emotions. The six basic styles of loving that he has identified make up a "color circle for love," as shown here. Table 16.2 contains a brief description of each style and reports on correlations between subjects' styles of loving and their satisfaction with their intimate relationships.

Table 16.2 Description of Lee's Styles of Loving and Their Correlations with Relationship Satisfaction

NAME	STYLE OF LOVING	DESCRIPTION	CORRELATION WITH RELATIONSHIP SATISFACTION*	
			MEN	WOMEN
Eros	Romantic love	The search for the ideal mate, with emphasis on physical beauty	.49**	.51**
Ludus	Game-playing love	Playing the field; a search for many sexual conquests with little long-term involvement	−.60**	−.42**
Mania	Possessive love	Obsessive, jealous, emotionally extreme involvement with the lover	.10	−.16
Storge	Companionate love	Slow-developing affection and friendship culminating in a long-term relationship	.01	−.07
Agape	Altruistic love	Gentle, caring desire to give to another, without expectation of return	.18	.28**
Pragma	Pragmatic love	Practical, rational relationship based on mutual satisfaction	−.11	−.07

*As measured by the Relationship Assessment Scale in a study by Hendrick, Hendrick, & Adler (1988), using a sample of 57 men and 57 women.
**Statistically significant correlation ($p < .05$)

LOVE AS ATTACHMENT

The complexity of love is apparent from the variety of ways in which theorists have tried to analyze it. In another ground-breaking analysis of love, Cindy Hazan and Phillip Shaver (1987) have looked not at the components of love, nor at styles of loving, but at similarities between love and *attachment* relationships in infancy. We noted in Chapter 11 that infant-caretaker bonding, or attachment, emerges in the first year of life. Early attachments vary in quality, and infants tend to fall into 3 groups (Ainsworth et al., 1978). Most infants develop a *secure attachment*, but some are very anxious when separated from their caretaker, a syndrome called *anxious-ambivalent attachment*. A third group of infants, characterized by *avoidant attachment*, never connect very well with their caretaker.

According to Hazan and Shaver, romantic love is an attachment process, and our intimate relationships in adulthood follow the same form as our attachments in infancy. According to their theory, a person who had an anxious-ambivalent attachment in infancy will tend to have romantic relations marked by anxiety and ambivalence in adulthood. In other words, we relive our early bonding with our parents in our adult romances.

Hazan and Shaver's (1987) initial survey study provided some support for their theory. They found that adults' love relationships could be sorted into groups that paralleled the three patterns of attachment seen in infants. *Secure adults* found it relatively easy to get close to others and described their love relations as trusting. *Anxious-ambivalent adults* reported a preoccupation with love accompanied by expectations of rejection and described their love relations as volatile and marked by jealousy. *Avoidant adults* found it difficult to get close to others and described their love relations as lacking intimacy.

Hazan and Shaver (1987) found that the percentage of adults falling into each category was roughly the same as the percentage of infants in each comparable category. Also, subjects' recollections of their childhood relations with their parents were consistent with the idea that we relive our infant attachment experiences in adulthood.

The results of a single survey should always be regarded as tentative, and additional research is needed to further explore the link between attachment and romantic love. Nonetheless, Hazan and Shaver's ideas and results are thought provoking, to say the least.

As you can see, research on love is in its infancy. We have more theory than data and very little consensus on the directions in which future research should proceed. In contrast, we have mountains of data and a great deal of practical knowledge about another important element of social behavior—attitudes.

ATTITUDES: MAKING SOCIAL JUDGMENTS

In our chapter-opening story, Muffy's friends exhibited decidedly negative attitudes about working-class men. Their example reveals a basic feature of attitudes: they're evaluative. They involve making social judgments. Social psychology's interest in attitudes has a much longer history than its interest in attraction. Indeed, in its early days, social psychology was defined as the study of attitudes. In this section, we'll discuss the nature of attitudes, efforts to change attitudes through persuasion, and theories about the process of attitude change.

What are attitudes? William McGuire (1985) provides a succinct definition in *The Handbook of Social Psychology*: **Attitudes locate objects of thought on dimensions of judgment**. "Objects of thought" may include social issues (capital punishment or gun control, for example), groups (liberals, farmers), institutions (the Lutheran church, the Supreme Court), consumer products (yogurt, computers), and people (the President, your next-door neighbor). "Dimensions of judgment" refer to the various ways in which we might evaluate the objects of our thoughts. Although attitudes are social judgments, they're not exclusively cognitive in nature. Attitudes are complex mixtures of cognitive, emotional, and behavioral components.

Components of Attitudes

Has anyone ever suggested that you have a "bad attitude"? Years ago, one of my teachers told me that I had an "attitude problem." If we look at what he meant, we can see concrete examples of each of the three components of an attitude.

The *cognitive component* of an attitude is made up of the *beliefs* that we hold about the object of an attitude. I believed that my teacher was boring, incompetent, and uninterested in his students—you can imagine why he characterized my attitude as a "problem." The *affective component* of an attitude consists of the *emotional feelings* stimulated by an attitude object. At the time, my feelings for my teacher ranged from active dislike to contempt, with some occasional sympathy mixed in. The *behavioral component* of an attitude consists of *predispositions to act* in certain ways toward an attitude object. In the case of my attitude problem, my behavioral tendencies included ignoring lectures, talking in class, and not turning in assignments (see Figure 16.9 for another example of an attitude divided into its components).

Of course, people exhibit positive as well as negative attitudes. For instance, I had many teachers that I viewed as bright, dedicated individuals (cognitive component), who elicited feelings of liking and admiration (affective component), and who inspired rapt attention and hard work (behavioral component). Although attitudes include predispositions toward certain behaviors, the relations between attitudes and behavior can get complicated, as you'll see.

Attitudes and Behavior

In the early 1930s, when prejudice against Asians was common in the United States, Richard LaPiere journeyed across the country with a Chinese couple. He was more than a little surprised when they weren't turned away from any of the restaurants they visited in their travels—184 restaurants in all. About 6 months after his trip, the puzzled LaPiere surveyed the same restaurants and asked whether they would serve Chinese customers. Roughly half of the restaurants replied to the survey, and over 90% of them indicated that they would *not* seat Chinese patrons! Thus, LaPiere (1934) found that people who voice prejudicial attitudes may not behave in discriminatory ways. Since then, theorists have often asked: why don't attitudes predict behavior better?

Admittedly, LaPiere's study had a fundamental flaw that you may already have detected. The person who seated LaPiere and his Chinese friends may not have been the same person who responded to the mail survey sent later. Nonetheless, numerous followup studies, using more sophisticated methods, have shown that our attitudes are mediocre predictors of our behavior (McGuire, 1985). In other words, social psychologists have found that a favorable attitude toward a candidate may not translate into a vote for the candidate. Similarly, an unfavorable attitude about a product may not prevent its purchase, and a positive attitude about an organization may not mean that you'll contribute to it.

Why aren't attitude-behavior relations more consistent? One reason is that we often discuss

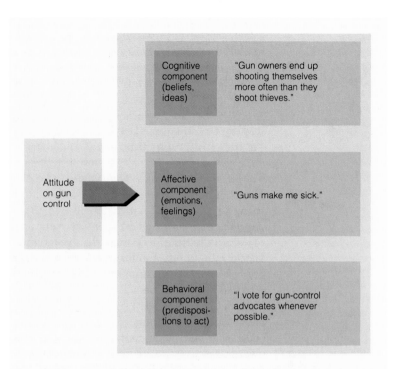

Figure 16.9 The components of attitudes. Attitudes can be broken into cognitive, affective, and behavioral components, as illustrated here for a hypothetical person's attitude about gun control.

the cognitive and affective components of our attitudes (beliefs and feelings) in a *general* way that isn't likely to predict *specific* behaviors (Weigel, Vernon, & Tognacci, 1974). Although you may express favorable beliefs and feelings about protecting civil liberties (a very general concept), when asked, you may not be willing to give $100 to the American Civil Liberties Union (a very specific action). Maybe you're a tightwad and your favorable feelings, although genuine, never translate into financial contributions to any organizations. If the ACLU asked you to donate time, though, you might give generously. In contrast, someone else who shares your beliefs and feelings about civil liberties may be willing to make financial contributions, but may never donate time. Thus, relations among the three components of attitudes are complex. Two people with very similar beliefs and feelings about a general issue may have different predispositions to specific actions, making for loose relations between attitudes and behavior.

Furthermore, the behavioral component in an attitude consists only of *predispositions* toward certain actions. Whether you follow through on these predispositions depends on situational constraints—especially your subjective perceptions of how people expect you to behave. Thus, Icek Ajzen and Martin Fishbein (1980) maintain that our attitudes interact with situational norms to shape our intentions, which then determine our behavior. Although you may be strongly opposed to marijuana use, you may not say anything when friends start passing a joint around at a party because you don't want to turn a party into an argument. However, in another situation governed by different norms, such as a class discussion, you may speak out forcefully against marijuana use. If so, you'll be trying to change others' attitudes, the process we'll discuss next.

Trying to Change Attitudes: Factors in Persuasion

The fact that our attitudes aren't always good predictors of our behavior doesn't stop others from trying to change those attitudes. Indeed, every day we're bombarded by efforts to alter our attitudes. To illustrate, let's trace the events of an imaginary morning. You may not even be out of bed before you start hearing radio advertisements intended to influence your attitudes about specific mouthwashes, computers, tennis shoes, and telephone companies. When you unfurl your newspaper, you find many quotes from government officials, which were carefully crafted to shape your opinions. On your way to school, you see billboards with attractive models draped all over automobiles and bottles of bourbon, in the hope that they'll affect your feelings about these products. When you arrive on campus, you find a group passing out leaflets that urge you to repent your sins and join them in worship. In class, your economics professor champions the wisdom of free markets in international trade. At lunch, the person you've been dating argues about the merits of an "open relationship." Your argument is interrupted by someone who wants both of you to sign a petition for nuclear disarmament. "Doesn't it ever let up?" you wonder. When it comes to persuasion, the answer is "no." In light of this reality, let's examine some of the factors that determine whether persuasion works.

Like other forms of communication, the process of persuasion includes four basic elements. **The *source* is the person who sends a communication, and the *receiver* is the person to whom the message is sent.** Thus, if you watched a presidential news conference on TV, the president would be the source, and you and millions of other listeners would be the receivers in this persuasive effort. **The *message* is the information transmitted by the source, and the *channel* is the medium through which the message is sent.** In examining communication channels, investigators have often compared face-to-face interaction with appeals sent via mass media (for example, television and radio). Although the research on communication channels is interesting, we'll confine our discussion to source, message, and receiver variables.

SOURCE FACTORS

Persuasion tends to be more successful when the source has high *credibility*. What gives a person credibility? Either expertise or trustworthiness. People try to convey their *expertise* by mentioning their degrees, their training, and their experience, or by showing an impressive grasp of the issue at hand (Hass, 1981).

Expertise is a plus, but *trustworthiness* is even more important (McGinnies & Ward, 1980). If you were told that your state needs to reduce corporate taxes to stimulate its economy, would you be more likely to believe it if the speaker was the president of a huge corporation in your state or an economics professor from out of state? Probably the latter. Trustworthiness is undermined when a source, such as the corporation president, appears to have something to gain. In contrast, trustworthiness is enhanced when people appear to argue against their own best interests (Eagly, Wood, & Chaiken, 1978). This effect explains why salespeople often make remarks like, "Frankly, my snowblower isn't the best, and they have a better brand down the street, if you're willing to spend a bit more . . ."

Likability also increases the effectiveness of a persuasive source, and some of the factors at work in attraction therefore have an impact on persuasion. Thus, the favorable effect of *physical attractiveness* on likability can make persuasion more effective. For instance, Chaiken (1979) asked students to obtain signatures for a petition and found that the more attractive students were more successful. We also respond better to sources who are *similar* to us in ways that are relevant to the issue at hand (Berscheid, 1966).

The importance of source variables can be seen in advertising. Many companies spend a fortune to obtain an ideal spokesperson, like Bill Cosby, who combines trustworthiness, expertise (a doctorate in education), likability, and a knack for connecting with the average person. Companies quickly abandon a spokesperson who acquires any hint of scandal. For example, when tennis star Billy Jean King's lesbian affair surfaced a number of years ago, her endorsements dropped immediately. Thus, source variables are extremely important factors in persuasion.

MESSAGE FACTORS

If you were going to give a speech to a local community group advocating a reduction in state taxes on corporations, you'd probably wrestle with a number of questions about how to structure your message. Should you look at both sides of the issue, or just present your side? Should you deliver a low-key, logical speech, or should you try to

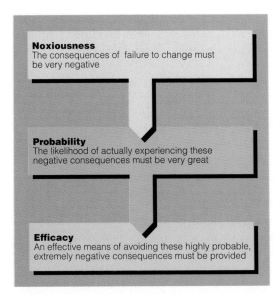

Noxiousness
The consequences of failure to change must be very negative

Probability
The likelihood of actually experiencing these negative consequences must be very great

Efficacy
An effective means of avoiding these highly probable, extremely negative consequences must be provided

Figure 16.10 When fear arousal works. As a method of persuasion, fear arousal tends to work most effectively when the conditions described here are met. (Based on Rogers & Newborn, 1976)

strike fear into the hearts of your listeners? Should you spell out your conclusions for your listeners, or use rhetorical questions to stimulate their thinking? Let's look at these message factors.

We'll assume that you're aware that there are two sides to the taxation issue. On the one hand, you're convinced that lower corporate taxes will bring new companies and factories to your state, stimulate economic growth, and increase jobs. On the other hand, you realize that reduced tax revenues may gradually hurt the quality of education and roads in your state (but you think the benefits will outweigh the costs). Should you present a *one-sided argument* that ignores the possible problems for education and road quality? Or should you present a *two-sided argument* that acknowledges concern about education and road quality, and then downplays the probable magnitude of these problems?

In general, two-sided arguments seem to be more effective. Just mentioning that there are two sides to an issue can increase your credibility with an audience (Jones & Brehm, 1970). One-sided messages work only when your audience is uneducated about the issue, or when they're already very favorably disposed to your point of view (Lumsdaine & Janis, 1953).

Persuasive messages frequently attempt to arouse fear. Opponents of nuclear power scare us with visions of meltdowns. Antismoking campaigns emphasize the threat of cancer, and deodorant ads highlight the risk of embarrassment. You could follow their lead and argue that if corporate taxes aren't reduced, your state will be headed toward economic ruin and massive unemployment. Does *fear arousal* work? Yes, studies involving a wide range of issues (nuclear policy, auto safety, dental hygiene, and so on) have shown that the arousal of fear often increases persuasion, but

there are limiting conditions (Leventhal, 1970; Rogers, 1975).

The conditions under which fear arousal is likely to work are outlined in Figure 16.10. Your listeners must view the dire consequences that you describe as exceedingly unpleasant, fairly probable if they don't take your advice, and avoidable if they do. In our hypothetical case, your listeners will surely agree that economic ruin is terrible, but you may have trouble convincing them that your state is headed toward this ruin, or that reduced taxes are the way to avoid it. If you aren't confident about the weight of evidence on these points, you shouldn't arouse fear in your audience, because it may make them defensive, so that they tune you out.

What about *drawing conclusions* versus *asking rhetorical questions*? Should you clearly spell out your conclusions for your listeners, making remarks like, "We must decrease corporate taxation to attract new business"? Or should you prod your listeners to draw their own conclusions (based on your arguments) by asking rhetorical questions like, "Will any companies consider building in our state if our taxes remain too high?" Research by Richard Petty and John Cacioppo (1986) suggests that rhetorical questions are helpful when you're addressing a neutral audience and you have strong arguments in your favor. In most cases, especially if your arguments are weak, you'd better try to draw your listeners' conclusions for them.

RECEIVER FACTORS

What about the receiver of the persuasive message? Are some people easier to persuade than others? Undoubtedly, but the personality traits that account for these differences interact with other considerations in complicated ways. Transient factors such as forewarning the receiver about a persuasive effort and a receiver's initial position on an issue seem to be more influential than a receiver's personality.

An old saying suggests that "to be forewarned is to be forearmed." The value of *forewarning* applies to targets of persuasive efforts (Freedman & Sears, 1965; McGuire, 1964). When you shop for a new TV, you *expect* salespeople to work at persuading you, and to some extent this forewarning reduces the impact of their arguments.

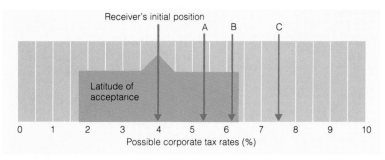

Receiver's initial position

Latitude of acceptance

Possible corporate tax rates (%)

Figure 16.11 Latitude of acceptance and attitude change. In relation to the receiver's initial stance on what the corporate tax rate should be, positions A and B both fall within the receiver's latitude of acceptance, but position B should produce a larger attitude shift. Position C is outside the receiver's latitude of acceptance and should fall on deaf ears.

The effect of a persuasive effort also depends on the discrepancy between a *receiver's initial position* on an issue and the position advocated by the source. Persuasion tends to work best when there's a moderate discrepancy between the two positions. Why? According to *social judgment theory*, people are usually willing to consider alternative views on an issue, if the views aren't too different from their own (Sherif & Hovland, 1961; Upshaw, 1969). **A *latitude of acceptance* is a range of potentially acceptable positions on an issue centered around one's initial attitude position.** Persuasive messages that fall outside a receiver's latitude of acceptance usually fall on deaf ears. When a message falls within a receiver's latitude of acceptance, successful persuasion is much more likely (Atkins, Deaux, & Bieri, 1967).

Moreover, within the latitude of acceptance, a larger discrepancy between the receiver's initial position and the position advocated should produce greater attitude change than a smaller discrepancy. The reason is that people often "meet part way" to resolve disagreement. Figure 16.11 shows how this theory about the relationship be-

Figure 16.12 Classical conditioning of attitudes in advertising. Advertisers routinely pair their products with likable celebrities, such as Bill Cosby, in the hope that their products will come to elicit pleasant emotional responses.

CS
Products
(e.g., autos)

UCS
Likable celebrity

CR
Pleasant emotional response
UCR

tween attitude change and discrepancy could apply to an audience member who heard your presentation advocating reduced corporate taxation.

Our review of source, message, and receiver variables has shown that attempting to change attitudes through persuasion involves a complex interplay of factors—and we haven't even looked beneath the surface yet. How do we acquire our attitudes in the first place? What dynamic processes within people produce attitude change? We turn to these theoretical issues next.

Theories of Attitude Formation and Change

Many theories have been proposed to explain the mechanisms at work in attitude change, whether it occurs in response to persuasion or not. We'll look at four theoretical perspectives: learning theory, balance theory, dissonance theory, and self-perception theory.

LEARNING THEORY

We've seen repeatedly that *learning theory* can help to explain a wide range of phenomena such as conditioned fears, the acquisition of sex roles, and the development of personality traits. Now we can add attitude formation and change to our list. The processes of classical conditioning, operant conditioning, and observational learning, which were described in Chapter 6, can all shed light on how our attitudes are formed and changed.

The affective, or emotional, component in an attitude can be created through *classical conditioning*, just like other emotional responses (Stalling, 1970). As we discussed in Chapter 6, advertisers routinely try to take advantage of classical conditioning by pairing their products with stimuli that elicit pleasant emotional responses, such as extremely attractive models, highly likable spokespersons, and cherished events (the Olympics, for instance). This conditioning process is diagrammed in Figure 16.12.

Operant conditioning may come into play when you openly express an attitude, such as "I believe that husbands should do more housework." Some people may endorse your view, while others may "jump down your throat." Agreement from other people generally functions as a reinforcer, strengthening your tendency to express a specific attitude (Insko, 1965). Disagreement often functions as a form of punishment, which may gradually weaken your commitment to your viewpoint.

Another person's attitudes may rub off on you through *observational learning* (Vidmar & Rokeach, 1974). If you hear your uncle say "Re-

Figure 16.13 Heider's balance theory. From Pam's point of view, the relations depicted on the left are imbalanced, creating an impetus for attitude change. If Pam's attitude toward Oliver changes as shown on the right, balance is restored.

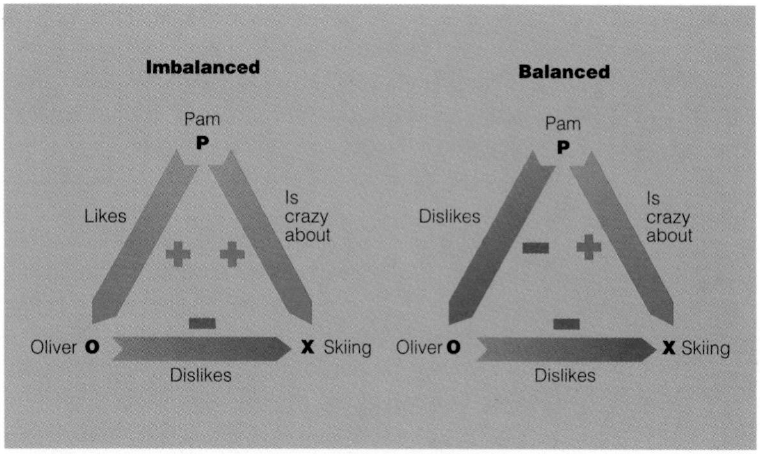

publicans are nothing but puppets of big business," and your mother heartily agrees, your exposure to your uncle's attitude and your mother's reinforcement of your uncle may influence your attitude toward the Republican party. Studies show that parents and their children tend to have similar political attitudes (Sears, 1975). Observational learning presumably accounts for much of this similarity. The opinions of teachers, coaches, coworkers, talk-show hosts, rock stars, and so forth are also likely to sway our attitudes through observational learning.

BALANCE THEORY

Fritz Heider's (1946, 1958) balance theory was the first of several *cognitive consistency theories* based on the assumption that we strive to maintain consistency among our attitudes. Characterizing them as either positive or negative, *balance theory* analyzes liking relationships between two people (labeled P and O) and an attitude object (labeled X) that could be an idea, a product, a group, an activity, or another person. Viewing balance from P's perspective, Heider proposed that the relations between P, O, and X may be either balanced or imbalanced. ***Balance* exists when liking relations fit together harmoniously.** Figure 16.13 shows examples of balanced and imbalanced relations. A simple rule of thumb is that a three-way relationship is imbalanced if the number of negative (−) signs is uneven.

The central ideas of balance theory are that we prefer balanced states, that imbalance creates tension, and that this tension motivates us to attempt to restore balance by changing one of our attitudes. Consider, for instance, the relations depicted in Figure 16.13. Pam (P) is attracted to Oliver (O), Pam lives to go skiing (X), and Oliver actively dislikes skiing. This state of affairs creates imbalance for Pam (note the uneven number of negative signs in the diagram) and an impetus for attitude change. According to balance theory, Pam will be motivated to change either her attitude toward Oliver or her attitude toward skiing. Because of his distaste for skiing, Pam may decide that Oliver isn't such an interesting guy, after all. The right side of Figure 16.13 shows the result of this attitude change. Balance is restored, and Pam's tension dissipates when her attitude about Oliver becomes negative.

The problem with balance theory is that it's too simple. It can only juggle three elements, doesn't allow for degrees of liking, and ignores the possibility that Pam could try to alter Oliver's attitude about skiing to restore balance. Dissonance theory, which is next on our agenda, is a more general and flexible model of cognitive consistency.

DISSONANCE THEORY

Like balance theory, Leon Festinger's dissonance theory assumes that inconsistency among our attitudes propels us in the direction of attitude change. Dissonance theory burst into prominence in 1959 when Festinger and J. Merrill Carlsmith published their famous study of counterattitudinal behavior. Let's look at their findings and at how dissonance theory explains them.

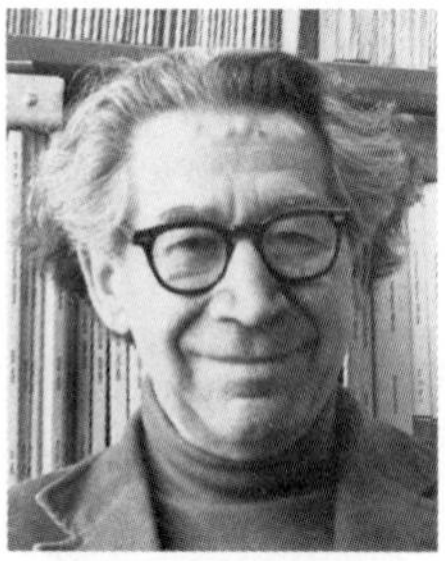

"Cognitive dissonance is a motivating state of affairs. Just as hunger impels a person to eat, so does dissonance impel a person to change his opinions or his behavior."
LEON FESTINGER

COUNTERATTITUDINAL BEHAVIOR Festinger and Carlsmith (1959) had male college students come to a laboratory, where they worked on excruciatingly dull tasks, like turning pegs repeatedly. When a subject's hour was over, the experimenter explained that he was studying how motivation affected performance, and he confided that some participants' motivation was being manipulated by telling them that the task was very interesting and enjoyable before they started it. Then, after a moment's hesitation, the experimenter asked if the subject could help him out of a jam. His usual helper was delayed and he needed someone to testify to the next "subject" (really an accomplice) that the experimental task was interesting. He offered to pay the subject if he would tell the person in the adjoining waiting room that the task was enjoyable and involving. Most subjects agreed to help.

This entire scenario was enacted to coax subjects into doing something that was inconsistent with their true feelings—that is, to engage in *counterattitudinal behavior.* Some subjects received a token payment of $1 for their effort, while others received a more substantial payment of $20 (an amount equivalent to about $60 today, in light of inflation). Later, a second experimenter inquired about the subjects' true feelings regarding the dull experimental task. Figure 16.14 summarizes the design of the Festinger and Carlsmith study.

Who do you think rated the task more favorably—the subjects who were paid $1 or those who were paid $20? Both common sense and learning theory would predict that the subjects who received the greater reward ($20) should come to like the task more. In reality, however, the subjects who were paid $1 exhibited a much more favorable attitude change than those paid $20—just as Festinger and Carlsmith had predicted. Why? Dissonance theory suggests an explanation.

According to Festinger (1957), *cognitive dissonance* **exists when related cognitions are inconsistent—that is, they contradict each other.** Festinger's model assumes that dissonance is possible only when cognitions are relevant to each other, as unrelated cognitions ("I am hardworking" and "Fire engines are red") can't contradict each other. However, when cognitions are related, they may be consonant ("I am hardworking" and "I'm staying overtime to get an important job done") or dissonant ("I am hardworking" and "I'm playing hooky from work"). Like imbalance, cognitive dissonance is supposed to create an unpleasant state of tension that motivates people to reduce their dissonance—usually by altering their cognitions.

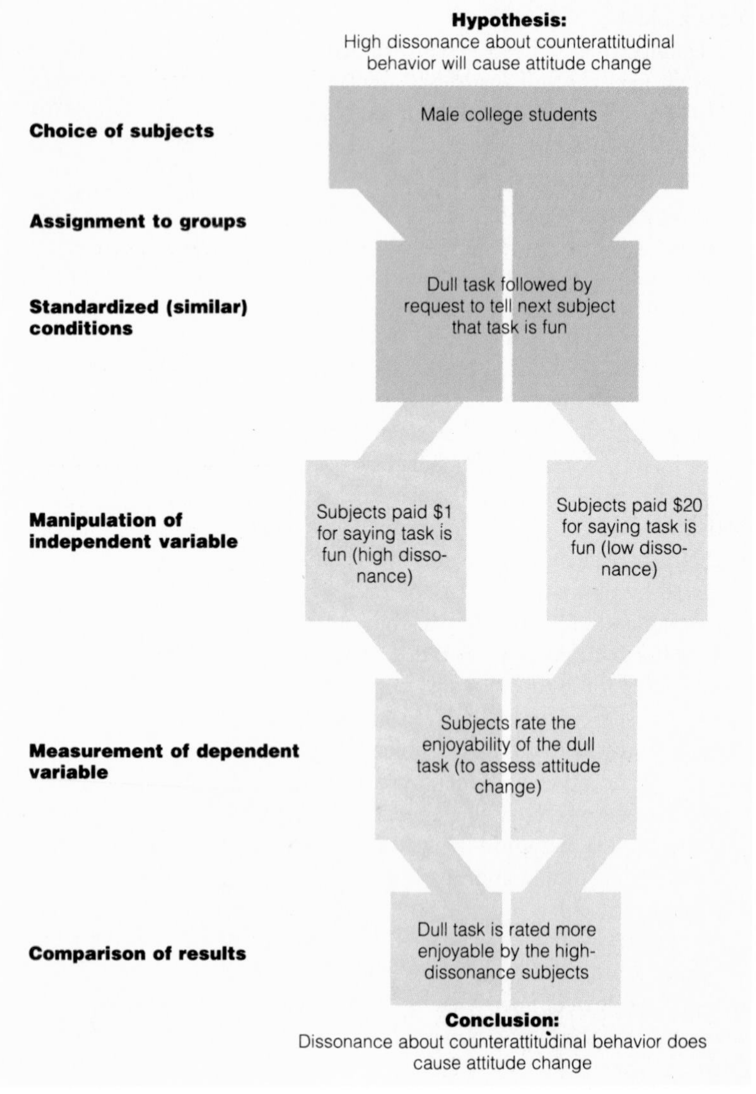

In the study by Festinger and Carlsmith (1959), the subjects' contradictory cognitions were "The task is boring" and "I told someone the task was enjoyable." However, the subjects who were paid $20 for lying felt less dissonance than those paid only $1. Being paid $20 for lying provided subjects with an obvious reason for behaving inconsistently with their true attitudes, so these subjects experienced little dissonance. In contrast, the subjects paid $1 had no readily apparent justification for their lie and experienced high dissonance. To get rid of their dissonance, they either had to convince themselves that they hadn't told someone that the task was enjoyable, or that the task wasn't really all that boring. Most chose the latter route and concluded that the task *was* more enjoyable than they had originally thought. In a sense, they came to believe their lie.

Similar results have been observed in many other studies. In one experiment (Nel, Helmreich, & Aronson, 1969), students who opposed the legalization of marijuana were induced to make a videotape describing the effects of the drug in a favorable way. The subjects who experienced the greatest dissonance (because they were given no readily apparent excuse for cooperating) showed dramatic attitude change. Indeed, many came to temporarily favor the legalization of marijuana! (Of course, they were debriefed afterwards.) Thus, dissonance sheds light on why people sometimes come to believe their own lies.

Counterattitudinal behavior that creates dissonance doesn't always involve lying. If you believe in the preservation of the environment but you leave litter all over your park campsite, your behavior is counterattitudinal. Similarly, if you're a political liberal, but vote for an appealing conservative candidate, your behavior runs counter to your attitudes.

POSTDECISIONAL DISSONANCE Cognitive dissonance also accounts for our curious tendency to work overtime justifying our decisions after the fact (Festinger, 1964). Decisions arouse dissonance. For instance, when people decide on an automobile purchase, they're immersed in con-

Figure 16.14 Design of the Festinger and Carlsmith (1959) study. The sequence of events in this landmark study of counterattitudinal behavior and attitude change is outlined here. The diagram omits a third condition (no dissonance), in which subjects were not induced to lie. The results in the no-dissonance condition were similar to those found in the low-dissonance condition.

Hypothesis:
High dissonance about counterattitudinal behavior will cause attitude change

Choice of subjects
Male college students

Assignment to groups

Standardized (similar) conditions
Dull task followed by request to tell next subject that task is fun

Manipulation of independent variable
Subjects paid $1 for saying task is fun (high dissonance)
Subjects paid $20 for saying task is fun (low dissonance)

Measurement of dependent variable
Subjects rate the enjoyability of the dull task (to assess attitude change)

Comparison of results
Dull task is rated more enjoyable by the high-dissonance subjects

Conclusion:
Dissonance about counterattitudinal behavior does cause attitude change

flicting cognitions, such as "The sports car would be great fun," "The sedan would be much more practical," "The sports car has better resale value," and so forth. Dissonance usually peaks right after we make a decision, leaving us in a state of *postdecisional dissonance*.

We reduce postdecisional dissonance by focusing on the good aspects of our chosen alternative and by focusing on the bad aspects of rejected alternatives. Thus, if you choose a sports car over a sedan, you'll tend to dwell on the sports car's beauty, handling, and speed, while dwelling on the sedan's poorly designed seat belts, inadequate engine size, and any other flaws you can find in it.

EFFORT JUSTIFICATION Cognitive dissonance is also at work when we turn attitudinal somersaults to justify efforts that haven't panned out, a syndrome called *effort justification*. Aronson and Mills (1959) studied effort justification by putting college women through a "severe initiation" before they could qualify to participate in what promised to be an interesting discussion of sexuality. In the screening test that represented the severe initiation, the women had to read obscene passages out loud to a male experimenter. After all that, the highly touted discussion of sexuality turned out to be a boring, taped lecture on reproduction in lower animals. Subjects in the severe initiation condition experienced highly dissonant cognitions ("I went through a lot to get here" and "This discussion is terrible"). How did they reduce their dissonance? Apparently by convincing themselves that the discussion was worthwhile, since they rated it more favorably than subjects in two control conditions.

Effort justification may be at work in many facets of everyday life. For example, people who wait in line for hours to get into an exclusive restaurant often praise the restaurant afterwards even if they are served a poorly prepared meal. Rock fans who pay $100 for scalped concert tickets will tend to rate the concert favorably, even if the artists show up in a stupor and play like a garage band. Unfortunately, similar patterns of dissonance reduction are probably seen when world leaders struggle to justify the effort that has gone into ill-chosen policies. It's easy to imagine a government official thinking, "We've lost thousands of lives. This war must be important."

REVISING DISSONANCE THEORY Dissonance theory has been tested in hundreds of studies with mixed, but largely favorable, results. The dynamics of dissonance appear to underlie many of our attitude changes (Aronson, 1980), and research has supported Festinger's claim that disso-

nance involves genuine physiological tension and arousal (Croyle & Cooper, 1983).

However, it's difficult to predict when dissonance will occur. If I learn that my favorite novelist is a child abuser, does this arouse dissonance? For me it does, because I expect a great novelist to be compassionate. For other people it might not, depending on their vision of a great novelist. To some extent, inconsistency between cognitions lies in the eye of the beholder. Thus, researchers continue to debate the factors that determine whether cognitive dissonance will occur (Aronson, 1980; Cooper & Fazio, 1984).

SELF-PERCEPTION THEORY
Research on cognitive dissonance led to an unexpected insight about the relationship between attitudes and behavior. After taking a close look at

---

CONCEPT CHECK 16.3
Understanding Attitudes and Persuasion

Check your understanding of the components of attitudes and the elements of persuasion by analyzing hypothetical political strategies. Imagine you're working on a political campaign and you're invited to join the candidate's inner circle in strategy sessions, as staff members prepare the candidate for upcoming campaign stops. During the meetings, you hear various strategies discussed. For each strategy below, indicate which component of voters' attitudes (cognitive, affective, or behavioral) is being targeted for change, and indicate which element in persuasion (source, message, or receiver factors) is being manipulated. The answers are in Appendix A.

1. "You need to convince this crowd that your program for regulating nursing homes is sound. Whatever you do, don't acknowledge the two weaknesses in the program that we've been playing down. I don't care if you're asked point blank. Just slide by the question and keep harping on the program's advantages."

_____

_____

2. "You haven't been smiling enough lately, especially when the TV cameras are rolling. Remember, you can have the best ideas in the world, but if you don't seem likable, you're not gonna get elected. By the way, I think I've lined up some photo opportunities that should help us create an image of sincerity and compassion."

_____

_____

3. "This crowd is already behind you. You don't have to alter their opinions on any issues. Get right to work convincing them to contribute to the campaign. I want them lining up to give money."

_____

_____

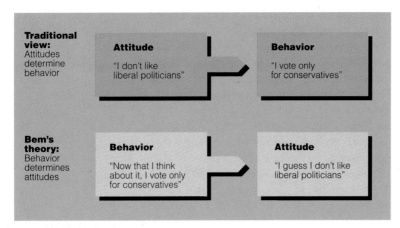

Figure 16.15 Bem's self-perception theory. The traditional view is that our attitudes determine our behavior. However, Bem proposed that behavior often determines (or causes us to draw inferences about) our attitudes.

studies of counterattitudinal behavior, Daryl Bem (1967) concluded that self-perception, rather than dissonance, explains why people sometimes come to believe their lies. According to Bem's *self-perception theory*, we often *infer* our attitudes from our own behavior. Thus, Bem argued that in the study by Festinger and Carlsmith (1959), the subjects paid $1 probably thought to themselves, "A dollar isn't enough money to get me to lie, so I must have found the task enjoyable."

This thinking isn't much different from what dissonance theory would predict. Both theories suggest that people often think, "If I said it, it must be true," but the two theories propose that similar patterns of thought may unfold for entirely different reasons. According to dissonance theory, subjects think along these lines because they're struggling to reduce tension caused by in-

consistency among their cognitions. According to self-perception theory, subjects are engaged in normal attributional efforts to better understand their own behavior. Bem originally believed that most findings explained by dissonance were really due to self-perception. However, studies eventually showed that self-perception is at work primarily when subjects do not have well-defined attitudes regarding the issue at hand (Chaiken & Baldwin, 1981).

Although self-perception theory did not replace dissonance theory, Bem's work shed new light on the relationship between attitudes and behavior. Conventional wisdom assumes that our attitudes determine our behavior. Thus, a person might say, "I don't like plays (attitude), and therefore I don't go to them" (behavior). However, Bem suggested that causation sometimes flows in the opposite direction: observing our own behavior leads to conclusions about what our attitudes must be (see Figure 16.15). For example, a person might say, "Gee, I don't go to any plays. I guess I don't like them." Research on attribution eventually showed that efforts to explain our own behavior *are* commonplace and that we often *do* infer our attitudes from our behavior.

Self-perception theory adds another complication to the complex relations between attitudes and behavior. We'll see more complications in the next section, which is concerned with related aspects of social influence—conformity and obedience.

CONFORMITY AND OBEDIENCE: YIELDING TO OTHERS

The mass suicide in Jonestown in 1978 was a shocking example of obedience to an authority figure.

I'll never forget the night of the Jonestown massacre in Guyana, when Jim Jones ordered his People's Temple followers to commit mass suicide by drinking cyanide-laced Kool-Aid. I was at a small

party watching *Saturday Night Live* when the show was interrupted to report the tragedy in Guyana. This dreadful example of obedience to authority seemed so implausible that people at the party assumed that it was one of the comedy show's fake news bulletins, just another cynical joke about religion from *Saturday Night Live*! It wasn't until sometime later, when a second news bulletin was broadcast, that we began to realize that we were dealing with reality.

As the Jonestown massacre demonstrates, the power of social influence can be astonishing. When the full story of Jonestown was assembled weeks later, it became apparent that a small minority of Jones's followers refused to cooperate (a few escaped, a few were shot), but most went along with their orders and took their own lives. How can we explain such extraordinary obedience? Was it due to the unique character of the people of Jonestown? Probably not. As you'll see, humans often are remarkably compliant. Both anecdotal and empirical evidence indicate that in the right circumstances most of us can be coaxed, pressured, or coerced into doing virtually anything. In this section, we'll analyze the dynamics of social influence at work in conformity and obedience.

Conformity

If you keep a well-manicured lawn and extoll the talents of the popular rock star Bruce Springsteen, are you exhibiting conformity? According to social psychologists, it depends on whether your behavior is the result of group pressure. **Conformity occurs when people yield to real or imagined social pressure.** For example, if you maintain a well-groomed lawn only to avoid complaints from your neighbors, you're yielding to social pressure. If you like Springsteen because you genuinely enjoy his records, that's *not* conformity. However, if you like Springsteen because it's "hip" and your friends would question your taste if you didn't, then you're conforming.

ASCH'S STUDIES

In the 1950s, Solomon Asch (1951, 1955, 1956) devised a clever procedure that minimized ambiguity about whether subjects were conforming, allowing him to investigate the variables that govern conformity. Let's re-create one of Asch's (1955) classic experiments. The subjects are male undergraduates recruited for a study of visual perception. A group of seven subjects are shown a large card with a vertical line on it, and then are asked to indicate which of three lines on a second card matches the original "standard line" in length (see Figure 16.16). All seven subjects are given a turn at the task, and they announce their choice to the group. The subject in the sixth chair doesn't know it, but everyone else in the group is an accomplice of the experimenter, and they're about to make him wonder whether he has taken leave of his senses.

The accomplices give accurate responses on the first two trials. On the third trial, line number 2 clearly is the correct response, but the first five "subjects" all say that line number 3 matches the standard line. The genuine subject is bewildered and can't believe his ears. Over the course of the experiment, the accomplices all give the same incorrect response on 12 out of 18 trials. Asch wants to see how the real subject responds in these situations. The line judgments are easy and unambiguous. Working alone, people achieve better than 95% accuracy in matching the lines, so if the subject consistently agrees with the accomplices, he isn't making honest mistakes—he's conform-

ing. Will the subject stick to his guns and defy the group? Or will he go along with the group?

Averaging across all 50 subjects, Asch (1955) found that the young men conformed on 37% of the trials. The subjects varied considerably in their tendency to conform, however. Of the 50 subjects, 13 never caved in to the group, while 14 conformed on more than half the trials.

In subsequent studies, *group size* and *group unanimity* turned out to be key determinants of conformity (Asch, 1956). To examine the impact of group size, Asch repeated his procedure with groups that included one to fifteen accomplices. Little conformity was seen when a subject was pitted against just one accomplice. Conformity increased rapidly as group size went from two to four, peaked at a group size of seven, and then leveled off (see Figure 16.17). Thus, Asch concluded that as groups grow larger, conformity increases—up to a point.

However, group size made little difference if just one accomplice "broke" with the others, wrecking their unanimous agreement. The presence of another dissenter lowered conformity to about one-quarter of its peak, even when the dissenter made *inaccurate* judgments that happened to conflict with the majority view. Apparently, the subjects just needed to hear someone else question the accuracy of the group's perplexing responses.

COMPLIANCE

At first, Asch wasn't sure whether conforming subjects were changing their beliefs in response to social pressure, or just pretending to change them. When subjects were interviewed later, many reported that they had begun to doubt their eyesight and that they thought "the majority must be right." These interviews suggested that the subjects had actually changed their beliefs, but critics asserted that the subjects may have been trying to rationalize their conformity after the fact. A study

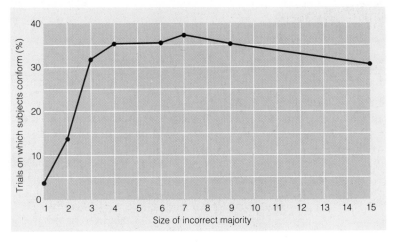

Figure 16.16 Stimuli used in Asch's conformity studies. Subjects were asked to match a standard line (*top*) with one of three other lines displayed on another card (*bottom*). The task was easy—until experimental accomplices started responding with obviously incorrect answers, creating a situation in which Asch evaluated subjects' conformity.

Figure 16.17 Conformity and group size. This graph shows the percentage of trials on which subjects conformed as a function of group size in Asch's research. Asch found that conformity became more frequent as group size increased up to about seven, and then conformity leveled off. (Data from Asch, 1955)

that included a condition in which subjects made their responses anonymously, instead of publicly, settled the question. Conformity declined dramatically when subjects recorded their responses privately, suggesting that subjects in the Asch studies were not really changing their beliefs (Deutsch & Gerard, 1955).

Based on this finding, theorists concluded that Asch's experiments evoked a particular type of conformity, called compliance. **Compliance occurs when people yield to social pressure in their public behavior, even though their private beliefs have not changed.** In the Asch studies, compliance resulted from subtle, implied pressure, but compliance usually occurs in response to explicit rules, requests, and commands. For example, if you agree to wear formal clothes to a fancy restaurant that requires formal attire, even though you despise such rules, you're displaying compliance. Similarly, if you reluctantly follow a supervisor's suggestions at work, even though you think they're lousy ideas, you're complying with a superior's wishes. This type of compliance with an authority figure's directions is commonplace, as we'll see in our next section.

Obedience

Obedience is a form of compliance that occurs when people follow direct commands, usually from someone in a position of authority. To a surprising extent, when an authority figure says "Jump!" many of us simply ask "How high?" Consider the following anecdote. Last year, the area I live in experienced a severe flood that required the mobilization of the National Guard and various emergency services. At the height of the crisis, a young man arrived at the scene of the flood, announced that he was from an obscure state agency

that no one had ever heard of, and proceeded to take control of the emergency. City work crews, the fire department, local police, municipal officials, and the National Guard followed his orders with dispatch for several days, evacuating entire neighborhoods—until an official thought to check, and found out that the man was just someone who had walked in off the street. The imposter, who had "small armies" at his beck and call for several days, had no history of training in flood control or emergency services, just a history of unemployment and psychological problems.

After news of the hoax spread, people criticized red-faced local officials for their compliance with the imposter's orders. However, many of the critics probably would have cooperated in much the same way, if they had been in the officials' shoes. For most people, willingness to obey someone in authority is the rule, not the exception.

MILGRAM'S STUDIES

Stanley Milgram wanted to study this tendency to obey authority figures. Like many other people after World War II, he was troubled by how readily the citizens of Germany had followed the orders of dictator Adolf Hitler, even when the orders required morally repugnant actions, such as the slaughter of millions of Jews. Milgram, who had worked with Solomon Asch, set out to design a standard laboratory procedure for the study of obedience, much like Asch's procedure for studying conformity. The clever experiment that Milgram devised became one of the most famous and controversial studies in the annals of psychology. It has been hailed as a "monumental contribution" to science, and condemned as "dangerous, dehumanizing, and unethical research" (Ross, 1988). Because of its importance, it's our Featured Study for this chapter.

"That we have found the tendency to conformity in our society so strong that reasonably intelligent and well-meaning young people are willing to call white black is a matter of concern."
SOLOMON ASCH

CHAPTER SIXTEEN FEATURED STUDY

"I WAS JUST FOLLOWING ORDERS"

Investigator: Stanley Milgram (Yale University)

Source: Behavioral study of obedience. *Journal of Abnormal and Social Psychology,* 67 (1963), 371–378.

"I was just following orders." That was the essence of Adolf Eichmann's defense when he was tried for his war crimes, which included masterminding the Nazis' attempted extermination of European Jews. Milgram wanted to determine the extent to which people are willing to follow authorities' orders. In particular, he wanted to identify the factors that lead people to follow commands that violate their ethics, such as commands to harm an innocent stranger.

Method

The subjects were a diverse collection of 40 men from the local community, recruited through advertisements to participate in a study at nearby Yale Univeristy. When a subject arrived at the lab, he met the experimenter and another subject, a likable, 47-year-old accountant, who was actually an accomplice of the experimenter. The "subjects" were told that the study would concern the effects of punishment on learning. They drew slips of paper from a hat to get their assignments, but the drawing was fixed so that the real subject always became the "teacher" and the accomplice the "learner."

The subject then watched as the learner was strapped into an electrified chair through which a shock could be delivered to the learner whenever he made a mistake on the task (left photo in Figure 16.18). The subject was told that the shocks were painful, but would not cause tissue damage, and was then taken to an adjoining room that housed the shock generator that he would control in his role as the teacher. This elaborate apparatus (right photo in Figure 16.18) had 30 switches designed to administer shocks varying from 15 to 450 volts, with labels ranging from "Slight shock" to "Danger: severe shock" and "XXX." Although the apparatus looked and sounded realistic, it was a fake, and the learner was never shocked.

As the "learning experiment" proceeded, the accomplice made many mistakes that necessitated shocks from the teacher, who was instructed to increase the shock level after each wrong answer. At 300 volts, the learner began to pound on the wall between the two rooms in protest and soon stopped responding to the teacher's questions. At this point, subjects ordinarily turned to the experimenter for guidance. The experimenter, a 31-year-old male in a gray lab coat, firmly indicated that no response was the same as a wrong answer, and the teacher should continue to give stronger and stronger shocks to the now silent learner. If the teacher expressed unwillingness to continue, the experimenter responded sternly with one of four prearranged prods, such

as, "It is absolutely essential that you continue."

When a subject refused to obey the experimenter, the session came to an end. The dependent variable was the maximum shock the subject was willing to administer before refusing to cooperate. After each session, the true purpose of the study was explained to the subject, who was reassured that the shock was fake and the learner was unharmed.

Results

No subjects refused to cooperate before the learner pounded on the wall, but 5 quit at that point. As the graph in Figure 16.18 shows, only 14 out of 40 subjects defied the experimenter before the series of shocks was completed. Thus, 26 of the 40 subjects (65%) administered all 30 levels of shock. Although they tended to obey the experimenter, many subjects voiced and displayed considerable distress about harming the learner. The horrified subjects groaned, bit their lips, stuttered, trembled, and broke into a sweat, but continued administering the shocks.

Discussion

Based on these results, Milgram concluded that obedience to authority was even more common than he or others anticipated. Before the study was conducted, Milgram described it to 40 psychiatrists and asked them to predict how much shock subjects would be willing to administer to their innocent victims. Most of the psychiatrists predicted that fewer than 1% of the subjects would continue to the end of the series of shocks! In interpreting his results, Milgram argued that

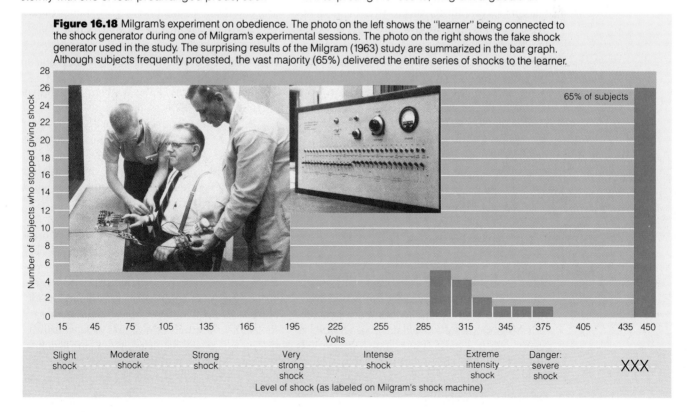

Figure 16.18 Milgram's experiment on obedience. The photo on the left shows the "learner" being connected to the shock generator during one of Milgram's experimental sessions. The photo on the right shows the fake shock generator used in the study. The surprising results of the Milgram (1963) study are summarized in the bar graph. Although subjects frequently protested, the vast majority (65%) delivered the entire series of shocks to the learner.

strong pressure from an authority figure can make decent people do terribly indecent things to others. Applying this insight to Nazi war crimes and other travesties, Milgram asserted that some sinister actions may not be due to actors' evil character so much as to situational pressures that can lead normal people to engage in acts of treachery and violence. Thus, he arrived at the disturbing conclusion that given the right circumstances, any of us might obey orders to inflict harm on innocent strangers.

Comment
In itself, obedience is not necessarily bad or wrong. Social groups of any size depend on a reasonable amount of obedience to function smoothly. Life would be chaotic if orders from police, parents, bosses, generals, and presidents were routinely ignored. However, Milgram's study suggested that many people are overly willing to submit to the orders of someone in command.

If you're like most people, you're probably confident that you wouldn't follow an experimenter's demands to inflict harm on a helpless victim. But the empirical findings indicate that you're probably wrong. After many replications, the results are deplorable, but clear: Most of us can be coerced into engaging in actions that violate our morals and values. This finding is disheartening, but it sharpens our understanding of moral atrocities, such as the Nazi persecutions of Jews and the mass suicide at Jonestown.

After his initial demonstration, Milgram (1974) tried about 20 variations on his experimental procedure, looking for factors that influenced subjects' obedience. In one variation, Milgram moved the study away from Yale's campus to see if the prestige of the university was contributing to the subjects' obedience. When the study was run in a seedy office building by the "Research Associates of Bridgeport," a small decrease in obedience was observed (only 48% of the subjects gave all the shocks).

In another version of the study, Milgram borrowed a trick from Asch's conformity experiments and set up teams of three teachers that included two more accomplices. When they drew lots, the real subject was always selected to run the shock apparatus in consultation with his fellow teachers. When both accomplices accepted the experimenter's orders to continue shocking the learner, the pressure increased obedience a bit. However, if the accomplices defied the experimenter and supported the subject's objections, obedience declined dramatically (only 10% of the subjects gave all the shocks), just as conformity had dropped rapidly when dissent surfaced in Asch's conformity studies. Dissent from another teacher turned out to be the only variation that reduced subjects' obedience appreciably. As a whole, Milgram was surprised at how stable subjects' obedience remained as he changed various aspects of his experiment.

THE ENSUING CONTROVERSY
Milgram's study evoked an enduring controversy that continues through today. Some critics argued that Milgram's results couldn't be generalized to apply to the real world (Baumrind, 1964; Orne & Holland, 1968). They maintained that subjects went along only because they knew it was an experiment and "everything must be okay." Or they argued that subjects who agree to participate in a scientific study *expect to obey* orders from an experimenter. Milgram (1964, 1968) replied by arguing that if subjects had thought "everything must be okay," they wouldn't have experienced the enormous distress that they clearly showed.

As for the idea that research subjects expect to follow an experimenter's commands, Milgram pointed out that so do soldiers and bureaucrats in the real world who are accused of villainous acts performed in obedience to authority. "I reject Baumrind's argument that the observed obedience doesn't count because it occurred where it is appropriate," said Milgram (1964). "That is precisely why it *does* count." Overall, the evidence supports the generalizability of Milgram's results, which were consistently replicated for many years, in diverse settings, with a variety of subjects and procedural variations (Miller, 1986).

Critics also questioned the ethics of Milgram's procedure (Baumrind, 1964). They noted that without prior consent, subjects were exposed to extensive deception that could undermine their trust in people and severe stress that could leave emotional scars. Moreover, most subjects also had to confront the disturbing fact that they caved in to the experimenter's commands to inflict harm on an innocent victim.

Milgram's defenders argued that the brief distress experienced by his subjects was a small price to pay for the insights that emerged from his obedience studies. Looking back, however, many psychologists seem to share the critics' concerns about the ethical implications of Milgram's work. His procedure is questionable by contemporary standards of research ethics, and at most universities it would be difficult to obtain permission to replicate Milgram's study today—a bizarre epitaph for what may be psychology's best-known experiment.

The studies on conformity and obedience foreshadow our last major topic in this chapter, behavior in groups. Social pressure, for instance, is often at work in group interactions, and being part of a group can have a dramatic impact on an individual's behavior (as it did in the Asch studies). Our review of behavior in groups will begin with a look at the nature of groups.

BEHAVIOR IN GROUPS: JOINING WITH OTHERS

Social psychologists study groups as well as individuals, but exactly what is a group? Are the divorced fathers living in Baltimore a group? Are three strangers moving skyward in an elevator a group? What if the elevator gets stuck? How about four students from your psychology class who study together regularly? A jury deciding a trial? The Boston Celtics? The U.S. Congress? Some of these collections of people are groups and others aren't. Let's examine the concept of a group and find out which of these collections qualify.

In social psychologists' eyes, a **group consists of two or more individuals who interact and are interdependent.** The divorced fathers in Baltimore aren't likely to qualify on either count. Strangers sharing an elevator might interact briefly, but they're not interdependent. However, if the elevator got stuck and they had to deal with an emergency together, they could suddenly become a group. Your psychology classmates who study together are a group, as they interact and depend on each other to achieve shared goals. So do the members of a jury, a sports team such as the Celtics, and a large organization such as the U.S. Congress.

Groups vary in many ways. Obviously, a study group, the Celtics, and the Congress are very different in terms of size, purpose, formality, how long they'll continue to exist, similarity of their members, and diversity of their activities. Can anything meaningful be said about groups if they're so diverse? Yes. In spite of their immense variability, groups share certain features that affect their functioning. Among other things, most groups have *roles* that allocate special responsibilities to some members, *norms* about suitable behavior, a *communication structure* that reflects who talks to whom, and a *power structure* that determines which members wield the most influence (Forsyth, 1983). For example, a study group and the Celtics may appear to have little in common, but both might have a "harmonizer" whose role is to smooth over conflicts among members, a norm that "everyone pulls his own weight," and an unequal distribution of power among members.

Thus, when we join together in groups, we create social organisms with unique characteristics and dynamics that can take on a life of their own.

The cornerstone idea of Gestalt psychology (discussed in Chapter 4), that "the whole is greater than the sum of its parts," definitely applies to groups. Indeed, "the parts" (people) that make up a group may function quite differently in a group context than they do on their own. One of social psychology's enduring insights is that in a given situation you may behave quite differently when you're in a group than when you're alone. To illustrate this point, let's look at some interesting research on helping behavior.

Behavior Alone and in Groups: The Case of the Bystander Effect

Imagine that you have a precarious medical condition and you have to go through life worrying about whether someone will leap forward to provide help if the need ever arises. Wouldn't you feel more secure when you were around larger groups? After all, there's "safety in numbers." Logically, as group size increases, the probability of having a "good samaritan" on the scene increases. Or does it?

We've seen before that human behavior isn't necessarily logical. When it comes to helping behavior, many studies have uncovered an apparent paradox called the **bystander effect: people are less likely to provide needed help when they are in groups than when they are alone.**

Evidence that your probability of getting help *declines* as group size increases was first described by John Darley and Bibb Latane (1968), who were conducting research on the determinants of altruism. As noted in Chapter 11, **altruism is selfless concern for the welfare of others that leads to helping behavior, without any expectation of personal gain.** In the Darley and Latane study, students in individual cubicles connected by intercom participated in discussion groups of three sizes. The separate cubicles allowed the researchers to examine each individual's behavior in a group context, a technique that minimizes confounded variables in individual-group comparisons. Early in the discussion, a student who was an experimental accomplice hesitantly mentioned that he was prone to seizures. Later in the discussion, the same accomplice feigned a severe seizure

619

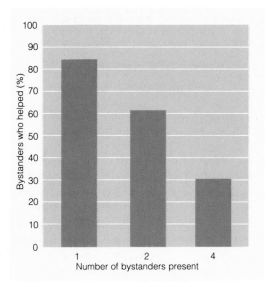

Figure 16.19 The bystander effect. As the number of apparent bystanders increased, the percentage of subjects who sought help for a victim of a (feigned) seizure declined. (Data from Darley & Latane, 1968)

Group Productivity and Social Loafing

Have you ever driven through a road construction project—at a snail's pace, of course—and become irritated because you see many workers, but they all seem to be standing around? Maybe the irony of the posted sign, "Your tax dollars at work," made you imagine that they were all dawdling. And then again, perhaps not. Individuals' productivity often *does* decline in larger groups (Latane, Williams, & Harkins, 1979).

Two factors appear to contribute to reduced individual productivity in larger groups. One factor is reduced *efficiency* due to the *loss of coordination* among workers' efforts. As you put more people on a yearbook staff, for instance, you'll probably create more and more duplication of effort and increase how often group members end up working at cross purposes.

Reduced coordination among workers can show up on the simplest of tasks, as demonstrated years ago by an agricultural engineer named Max Ringelmann. He measured the amount of pressure exerted by individuals and groups who pulled on a rope, as if they were playing tug-of-war. Ringelmann found that the amount of pressure produced by the group, per person, declined steadily as he increased group size (Kravitz & Martin, 1986). He pointed out that even on this simple task, some group members pulled when others paused, so that lack of coordination undermined their efficiency.

The second factor contributing to low productivity in groups involves *effort* rather than efficiency. **Social loafing is a reduction in effort by individuals when they work in groups as compared to when they work by themselves.** To investigate social loafing, Latane et al. (1979) measured the sound output produced by subjects who were asked to cheer or clap as loud as they could. So they couldn't see or hear other group members, subjects were told that the study concerned the importance of sensory feedback and were asked to don blindfolds and put on headphones through which loud noise was played. This manuever permitted a simple deception: subjects were *led to believe* that they were working alone or in a group of 2 or 6, when *individual* output was actually measured.

When subjects *thought* that they were working in larger groups, their individual output declined. Since lack of coordination could not affect individual output, the subjects' decreased sound production had to be due to reduced effort. Latane and his colleagues also had the same subjects clap and shout in genuine groups of 2 and 6 and found an additional decrease in production that was at-

and cried out for help. Although a majority of subjects sought assistance for the accomplice, Figure 16.19 shows that the tendency to seek help *declined* with increasing group size.

Similar trends have been seen in many other experiments, in which over 6000 subjects have had opportunities to respond to apparent emergencies including fires, asthma attacks, faintings, crashes, and flat tires, as well as less pressing needs, to answer a door or to pick up objects dropped by a stranger (Latane & Nida, 1981). Many of the experiments have been highly realistic studies conducted in subways, stores, and shopping malls, and many have compared individuals against groups in face-to-face interaction. Pooling the results of this research, Latane and Nida (1981) estimated that subjects who were alone provided help 75% of the time, while subjects in the presence of others provided help only 53% of the time. The only significant limiting condition on the bystander effect is that it's less likely to occur when the need for help is unambiguous.

What accounts for the bystander effect? A number of factors may be at work. Bystander effects are most likely in ambiguous situations because people look around to see if others think there's an emergency. If everyone hesitates, their inaction suggests that there's no real need for help. The *diffusion of responsibility* that occurs in a group is also important. If you're by yourself when you encounter someone in need of help, the responsibility to provide help rests squarely on your shoulders. However, if other people are present, the responsibility is divided among you, and everyone may say to themselves "someone else will help." A reduced sense of responsibility may contribute to other aspects of behavior in groups, as we'll see in the next section.

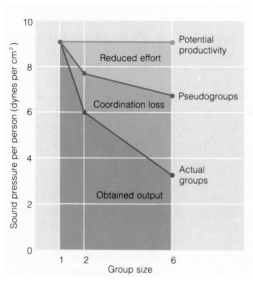

Figure 16.20 The effect of loss of coordination and social loafing on group productivity. The amount of sound produced per person declined noticeably when people worked in actual groups of two or six (*blue line*). This decrease in productivity reflects both loss of coordination and social loafing. Sound per person also declined when subjects merely *thought* they were working in groups of two or six (*red line*). This smaller decrease in productivity is due to social loafing. (Data from Latane, Williams, & Harkins, 1979)

tributed to loss of coordination. Figure 16.20 shows how social loafing and loss of coordination combined to reduce productivity as group size increased.

According to Latane (1981), the bystander effect and social loafing share a common cause: diffusion of responsibility in groups. As group size increases, the responsibility for getting a job done is divided among more people, and many group members ease up because their individual contribution is less recognizable. Thus, social loafing occurs in situations where individuals can "hide in the crowd." Social loafing can be minimized by allocating specific responsibilities to individuals in a group, so that their personal contributions remain recognizable (Weldon & Gargano, 1988).

In fairness to groups, although individual productivity usually declines, there may still be strength in numbers. The net productivity of 20 construction workers should dwarf that of 1 construction worker, barring inconceivable slacking off by the group. Obviously, there are many circumstances in which group performance is likely to exceed individual performance. The nature of the task is the principal determinant of whether groups or individuals tend to perform better (Steiner, 1976). Groups normally have an advantage on tasks in which individuals' efforts are added together (for example, sandbagging a flooded river).

Decision Making in Groups

Productivity is not the only issue that frequently concerns groups. When people join together in groups, they often have to make decisions about what the group will do and how it will use its resources. Whether it's your study group deciding

Many types of groups have to arrive at collective decisions. The social dynamics of group decisions are complicated, and a variety of factors can undermine effective decision making.

what type of pizza to order, a jury deciding on a verdict, or Congress deciding whether to pass a bill, groups make decisions.

Evaluating decision making is often more complicated than evaluating productivity. In many cases, the "right" decision may not be readily apparent. Who can say whether your study group ordered the right pizza or whether Congress passed the right bills? Nonetheless, social psychologists have discovered some interesting tendencies in group decision making. We'll take a brief look at *group polarization* and then discuss *groupthink* in more detail.

GROUP POLARIZATION

Who leans toward more cautious decisions: individuals or groups? Common sense suggests that groups will work out compromises that cancel out members' extreme views, so that the collective wisdom of the group should yield relatively conservative choices. Is common sense correct? Stoner (1961) investigated this question by asking individuals and groups to make decisions under conditions of uncertainty, like those seen in the following dilemma:

Mr. A., an electrical engineer who is married and has one child, has been working for a large electronics corporation since graduating from college 5 years ago. He is assured a lifetime job with a modest, though adequate, salary and liberal pension benefits upon retirement. On the other hand, it is very unlikely that his salary will increase much before he retires. While attending a convention, Mr. A. is offered a job with a small, newly founded company which has a highly uncertain future. The new job would pay more to start and would offer the possibility of a share in the ownership if the company survived the competition of the larger firms.

Imagine that you are advising Mr. A. Listed below are several probabilities, or odds, of the new company proving financially sound. *Please check the lowest probability that you would consider acceptable to make it worthwhile for Mr. A. to take the new job.*

_____ The chances are 1 in 10 that the company will prove financially sound.
_____ The chances are 3 in 10 that the company will prove financially sound.
_____ The chances are 5 in 10 that the company will prove financially sound.
_____ The chances are 7 in 10 that the company will prove financially sound.

Figure 16.21 A model of groupthink. The antecedent conditions and symptoms of groupthink are outlined here, along with the resultant effects on a group's decision making.

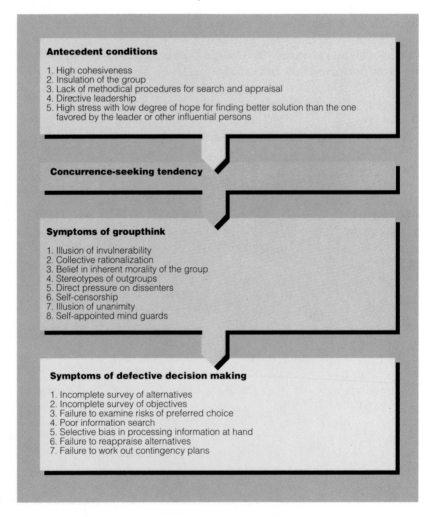

Antecedent conditions

1. High cohesiveness
2. Insulation of the group
3. Lack of methodical procedures for search and appraisal
4. Directive leadership
5. High stress with low degree of hope for finding better solution than the one favored by the leader or other influential persons

Concurrence-seeking tendency

Symptoms of groupthink

1. Illusion of invulnerability
2. Collective rationalization
3. Belief in inherent morality of the group
4. Stereotypes of outgroups
5. Direct pressure on dissenters
6. Self-censorship
7. Illusion of unanimity
8. Self-appointed mind guards

Symptoms of defective decision making

1. Incomplete survey of alternatives
2. Incomplete survey of objectives
3. Failure to examine risks of preferred choice
4. Poor information search
5. Selective bias in processing information at hand
6. Failure to reappraise alternatives
7. Failure to work out contingency plans

_____ The chances are 9 in 10 that the company will prove financially sound.

_____ Place a check here if you think Mr. A. should *not* take the new job no matter what the probabilities. (Kogan & Wallach, 1964)

Stoner had individual subjects give their recommendations and then asked the same subjects to engage in group discussion to arrive at a joint recommendation. When Stoner compared the average recommendation of a group's members against their group decision generated through discussion, he found that groups arrived at *riskier* decisions than individuals. Stoner's finding was replicated in other studies (Pruitt, 1971), and the phenomenon acquired the name *risky shift*.

However, investigators eventually determined that groups can shift either way, toward risk or caution, depending on which way the group is leaning to begin with (Myers & Lamm, 1976). It's a shift toward a more extreme position, an effect called *polarization*, that is the frequent result of group discussion. Thus, **group polarization occurs when group discussion strengthens a group's dominant point of view and produces a shift toward a more extreme decision in that direction.** Group polarization does *not* involve widening the gap between factions in a group, as its name might suggest. In fact, group polarization can contribute to consensus in a group, as we'll see in our discussion of groupthink.

GROUPTHINK

In contrast to group polarization, which is a normal process in group dynamics, groupthink is more like a "disease" that can infect decision making in groups. **Groupthink occurs when members of a cohesive group emphasize concurrence at the expense of critical thinking in arriving at a decision.** As you might imagine, groupthink doesn't produce very effective decision making. Indeed, groupthink often leads to major blunders that may look incomprehensible after the fact.

Irving Janis (1972) first described groupthink in his effort to explain how President Kennedy and his advisers could miscalculate so badly in deciding to invade Cuba at the Bay of Pigs in 1961. The attempted invasion failed miserably and, in retrospect, seemed remarkably ill-conceived. As Janis put it, "I was puzzled: How could bright men like John F. Kennedy and his advisers be taken in by such a stupid, patchwork plan as the one presented to them by the C.I.A. representatives?" (1973, p. 16).

Applying his many years of research and theory on group dynamics to the Bay of Pigs fiasco, Janis developed a model of groupthink, which is sum-

marized in Figure 16.21. When groups get caught up in groupthink, members suspend their critical judgment and the group starts censoring dissent as the pressure to conform increases. Soon, everyone begins to think alike. Moreover, "mind guards" try to shield the group from information that contradicts the group's view. For instance, at a critical meeting, President Kennedy did not give a key adviser who opposed the Cuban invasion an opportunity to speak.

If the group's view is challenged from outside, victims of groupthink tend to think in simplistic terms, dividing the world into the **ingroup—the group they belong to and identify with, and the outgroup—people who are not part of the ingroup.** When groups shift into this "us versus them" thinking, members begin to overestimate the ingroup's unanimity, and they begin to view the outgroup as the enemy. Groupthink also promotes incomplete gathering of information. The group's search for information is biased in favor of facts and opinions that support their decision.

What causes groupthink? The key precondition is high group cohesiveness. **Group cohesiveness refers to the strength of the liking relationships linking group members to each other and to the group itself.** Members of cohesive groups are close-knit, are committed, have "team spirit," and are very loyal to the group. Cohesiveness itself isn't bad; it can help groups to achieve great things. But Janis maintains that the danger of groupthink is greater when groups are highly cohesive. Groupthink is also more likely when a group works in relative isolation, when the group's power structure is dominated by a strong, directive leader, and when the group is under stress to make a major decision (see Figure 16.21). Under these conditions, group discussions can easily lead to group polarization, strengthening the group's dominant view.

After his description of groupthink, Janis and others reviewed other presidential blunders and found clear signs of groupthink underlying Franklin Delano Roosevelt's lack of preparation for Japan's attack on Pearl Harbor, President Lyndon Johnson's continued escalation of the Viet Nam war, and President Richard Nixon's cover-up of the Watergate break-in. Of course, groupthink is not limited to the highest levels of government. It may be even more prevalent in less public groups that make decisions every day in board rooms, committee rooms, courtrooms, and back rooms all over the world.

PUTTING IT IN PERSPECTIVE

Our discussion of social psychology provides a final embellishment on two of our six unifying themes. One of these themes (theme 1) is the value of psychology's commitment to empiricism—that is, its reliance on systematic observation through research to arrive at conclusions. The other theme that stands out (theme 6) is the extent to which our experience of the world is highly subjective. Let's consider the virtues of empiricism first.

It's easy to question the need to do scientific research on social behavior because studies in social psychology often seem to verify common sense. While most of us wouldn't presume to devise our own theory of color vision, question the significance of REM sleep, or quibble about the principal causes of schizophrenia, we all have our beliefs about first impressions, the nature of love, how to persuade others, the limits of obedience, and people's willingness to help in times of need. Thus, when studies demonstrate that credibility enhances persuasion, or that good looks facilitate attraction, it's tempting to conclude that social psychologists go to great lengths to document the obvious, and some critics say, "Why bother?"

You saw why in this chapter. Research in social psychology has repeatedly shown that the predictions of logic and common sense are often wrong. Consider just a few examples. Even psychiatric experts failed to predict the remarkable obedience to authority uncovered in Milgram's research. The bystander effect in helping behavior violates cold-blooded mathematical logic. Research on counterattitudinal behavior showed that (under the right conditions) the smaller the reward people are given for doing something, the more they like doing it. Dissonance research also showed that after a severe initiation, the bigger the letdown, the more favorable people's feelings are. These principles defy common sense.

Thus, research on social behavior provides dramatic illustrations of why psychologists put their faith in empiricism. The moral of social psychology's story is this: although scientific research often supports ideas based on common sense and logic, we can't count on this result. If we want to achieve sound understanding of the principles governing behavior, we have to put our ideas to an empirical test. Empiricism gives us a method for "separating the wheat from the chaff," a way to distinguish myth from reality.

Research in social psychology is also uniquely well suited for making the point that our view of the world is highly personal and subjective. In this chapter we saw how physical appearance can color our perception of a person's ability or personality, how social schemas can lead us to see what we expect to see in our interactions with others, how pressure to conform can make us begin to doubt our senses, and how groupthink can lead group members down a perilous path of shared illusions.

Subjectivity in social interaction is due in large part to processes that we've met before in earlier chapters, such as selective attention and the reconstructive nature of memory. However, our discussion of attribution processes introduced a new element that contributes to the subjectivity of our experience. Imagine that two people are exposed to the same event, an argument between their boss and one of their colleagues at work. Even if they *attend* to the event in the same way, *perceive* it in the same way, and *remember* it in the same way, when they make *attributions* about it, they may draw very different inferences about its causes and implications ("the boss is crabby," "everyone is on edge," "the heat is unbearable," and so forth). Thus, we encountered yet another factor that contributes to making our experience of the world highly subjective.

The subjectivity of attribution and social perception will surface once again in our chapter Application. It focuses on a practical problem that social psychologists have shown great interest in—prejudice.

UNDERSTANDING PREJUDICE

Answer the following "true" or "false."

☐ **1.** Prejudice and discrimination amount to the same thing.

☐ **2.** Stereotypes are always negative, or unflattering.

☐ **3.** Ethnic and racial groups are the only widespread targets of prejudice in modern society.

☐ **4.** We see members of our own ingroup as more alike than the members of outgroups.

Prejudice is a major social problem. It harms victims' self-concepts, suppresses human potential, creates tension and strife between groups, and even instigates wars. The first step toward reducing prejudice is to understand its roots. Hence, in this Application, we'll use concepts and principles from each of the chapter's six sections to achieve a better understanding of why prejudice is so common. Along the way, you'll learn the answers to the true-false questions above.

Prejudice and discrimination are closely related concepts, and the terms are nearly interchangeable in popular use. Social scientists, however, prefer to define their terms precisely, so let's clarify which is which. **Prejudice is a negative attitude held toward members of a group.** Like other attitudes, prejudice includes three components (see Figure 16.22): beliefs ("Indians are mostly alcoholic"), emotions ("I despise Jews"), and behavioral dispositions ("I wouldn't hire a Mexican"). Racial prejudice receives the lion's share of publicity, but prejudice is *not* limited to ethnic groups. Women, homosexuals, the aged, the handicapped, and the mentally ill are also targets of widespread prejudice. Thus, many of us hold prejudicial attitudes

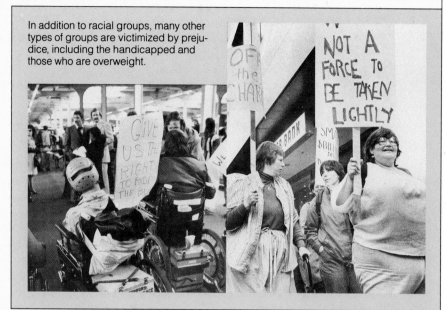

In addition to racial groups, many other types of groups are victimized by prejudice, including the handicapped and those who are overweight.

toward one group or another, and many of us have been victims of prejudice.

Prejudice may lead to *discrimination,* **which involves behaving differently, usually unfairly, toward the members of a group.** Prejudice and discrimination tend to go hand in hand, but as LaPiere's (1934) pioneering study of discrimination in restaurant seating showed, attitudes and behavior do not necessarily correspond (see Figure 16.23). In our discussion, we'll concentrate primarily on

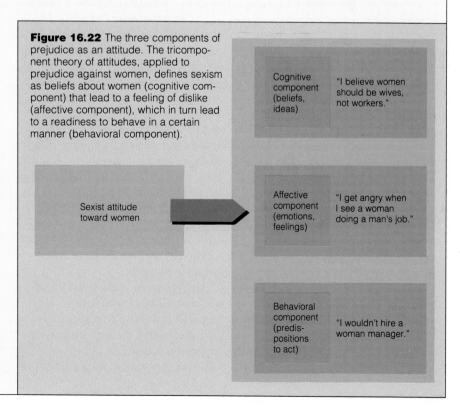

Figure 16.22 The three components of prejudice as an attitude. The tricomponent theory of attitudes, applied to prejudice against women, defines sexism as beliefs about women (cognitive component) that lead to a feeling of dislike (affective component), which in turn lead to a readiness to behave in a certain manner (behavioral component).

Sexist attitude toward women

Cognitive component (beliefs, ideas) — "I believe women should be wives, not workers."

Affective component (emotions, feelings) — "I get angry when I see a woman doing a man's job."

Behavioral component (predispositions to act) — "I wouldn't hire a woman manager."

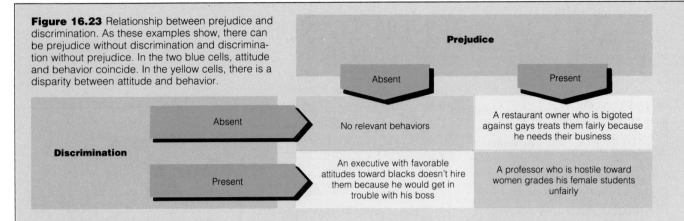

Figure 16.23 Relationship between prejudice and discrimination. As these examples show, there can be prejudice without discrimination and discrimination without prejudice. In the two blue cells, attitude and behavior coincide. In the yellow cells, there is a disparity between attitude and behavior.

Prejudice

Discrimination	Absent	Present
Absent	No relevant behaviors	A restaurant owner who is bigoted against gays treats them fairly because he needs their business
Present	An executive with favorable attitudes toward blacks doesn't hire them because he would get in trouble with his boss	A professor who is hostile toward women grades his female students unfairly

the attitude of prejudice. Let's begin by looking at processes in person perception that promote prejudice.

Stereotyping and Selectivity in Person Perception

Perhaps no factor plays a larger role in prejudice than *stereotypes*. However, stereotypes are not inevitably negative. As we saw earlier, good-looking people benefit from a favorable stereotype. Even ethnic stereotypes aren't all unflattering. Although it's a massive overgeneralization, it's hardly insulting to assert that Americans are ambitious or that the Japanese are industrious. Unfortunately, many people *do* subscribe to derogatory stereotypes of women and various ethnic groups. Studies suggest that racial stereotypes have declined over the last 50 years, but they're not a thing of the past (Dovidio & Gaertner, 1986; Karlins, Coffman, & Walters, 1969).

Unfortunately, the *selectivity* of person perception makes it likely that people will see what they expect to see when they actually come into contact with groups that they view with prejudice. For example, Duncan (1976) had white subjects watch and evaluate interaction on a TV monitor that was supposedly live (actually it was a videotape), and varied the race of a person who gets into an argument and gives another person a slight shove. The shove was coded as "violent behavior" by 73% of the white subjects when the actor was black, but by only 13% of the subjects when the actor was white. As we've noted before, our perceptions are highly subjective. Be-

cause of stereotypes, even "violence" may lie in the eye of the beholder.

Memory biases are also tilted in favor of confirming our prejudices. If a man believes that "women are not cut out for leadership roles," he may dwell with delight on his female supervisor's mistakes and quickly forget about her achievements. Obviously, actual interaction can do only so much to counteract stereotypes, since gender stereotypes remain commonplace, even though men and women interact profusely.

Biases in Attribution

Attribution processes can also help to perpetuate stereotypes and prejudice. Research taking its cue from Weiner's (1980) model of attribution has shown that we often make *biased attributions for success and failure*. For example, men and women don't get equal credit for their successes (Deaux, 1984). Observers often discount a woman's success by attributing it to good luck, sheer effort, or the ease of the task (except on traditional feminine tasks). In comparison, a man's success is more likely to be attributed to his outstanding ability. Figure 16.24 shows how sex bias tends to affect attributions for success and failure. These biased patterns of attribution help to sustain the stereotype that men are more competent than women.

Recall that the *fundamental attribution error* is a bias toward explaining events by pointing to the personal characteristics of the actors as causes (internal attributions). Pettigrew (1979) maintains that we're particu-

larly likely to make this error when evaluating targets of prejudice. Thus, when people take note of ethnic neighborhoods dominated by crime and poverty, the personal qualities of the residents are blamed for these problems, while other explanations emphasizing situational factors (job discrimination, poor police service, and so on) are downplayed or ignored. The old saying "they should be able to pull themselves up by their bootstraps" is a blanket dismissal of how situational factors may make it especially difficult for minorities to achieve upward mobility.

Defensive attribution, which involves unjustly blaming victims of misfortune for their adversity, can also contribute to prejudice. A prominent example in recent years has been the assertion by some people that homosexuals brought the AIDS crisis on themselves, and so deserve their fate. By blaming AIDS on gays' alleged character flaws, heterosexuals may be unknowingly seeking to reassure themselves that they're immune to a similar fate.

Proximity and Similarity Effects in Attraction

The dynamics of interpersonal attraction may foster prejudice and discrimination in at least two ways. First, *proximity effects* help to perpetuate ethnic prejudice wherever segregated patterns of housing limit opportunities for meaningful interracial contact. If people tend to become friends with those who live near them, they aren't likely to become friends with minorities who are excluded from their neighborhoods, schools, and country clubs.

Second, the contribution of *similarity effects* to prejudice may be considerable if Rosenbaum's (1986) "repulsion hypothesis" is correct. If dissimilarity causes disdain, this tendency would promote prejudice against many groups, including minorities, homosexuals, the handicapped, and the aged.

Forming and Preserving Prejudicial Attitudes

If prejudice is an attitude, where does it come from? Many of our prejudices appear to be handed down to us as a legacy from our parents (Ashmore & Del Boca, 1976). This transmission of prejudice across generations presumably depends to some extent on *observational learning*. For example, if a young boy hears his father ridicule homosexuals, his exposure to his father's attitude is likely to affect his attitude about gays. If the young boy then goes to school and makes disparaging remarks about gays that are reinforced by approval from peers, his prejudice will be strengthened through *operant conditioning*.

Once prejudicial attitudes are formed, *cognitive dissonance* may help to maintain them (Roberts, 1971). Most of us like to think of ourselves as fair-minded. However, if someone points out that you unfairly assume that blacks are lazy, this assertion and your belief in your fair-mindedness clash, creating dissonance. In theory, you could reduce your cognitive dissonance by concluding that you're less fair-minded than you thought. But

your belief about your fair-mindedness is likely to be a deeply entrenched feature of your self-concept, so you're more likely to conclude that blacks really are lazy. Thus, when our prejudices are challenged and dissonance is aroused, the resulting attitude changes may not be in the direction of less prejudice.

The Influence of Conformity

When stereotypic beliefs about groups are widely shared, people may run into *pressure to conform* to popular views. Thus, in some quarters of society, people may be pressured to express agreement with racist or sexist remarks. Even if people tell themselves they're just going along with others to avoid arguments, counterattitudinal behavior can lead to subtle shifts in attitudes. As we noted earlier, people sometimes think, "If I said it, it must be true."

Dividing the World into Ingroups and Outgroups

As noted in our discussion of groupthink, when we join together in groups, we sometimes divide the social world into "us versus them," or *ingroups versus outgroups*. These social dichotomies promote **ethnocentrism—a tendency to evaluate people in outgroups from the viewpoint of one's ingroup.**

As you might anticipate, we tend to evaluate outgroup members less favorably than ingroup members (Wilder,

1981). We also tend to think simplistically about outgroups; we see diversity among the members of our ingroup, but we overestimate the homogeneity of the outgroup (Judd & Park, 1988). At a simple, concrete level, the essence of this process is captured by the statement "they all look alike." Indeed, Brigham and Barkowitz (1978) found that blacks and whites do have more difficulty distinguishing the faces of outgroup members. The illusion of homogeneity in the outgroup makes it easier to sustain stereotypic beliefs about its members. This point disposes of our last unanswered question from the list that opened the Application. Just in case you missed one of the answers, they were: 1–false, 2–false, 3–false, 4–false.

Our discussion has shown that a plethora of processes conspire to create and maintain personal prejudices against a diverse array of outgroups. Most of the factors at work reflect normal, routine processes in social behavior, so most of us—whether privileged or underprivileged, minority members or majority members—probably harbor some prejudicial attitudes. Our analysis of the causes of prejudice may have permitted you to identify prejudices of your own or their sources. Perhaps it's wishful thinking on my part, but an enhanced awareness of your personal prejudices may help you to become a little more tolerant of the endless diversity seen in human behavior. If so, that alone would mean that my efforts in writing this book were amply rewarded.

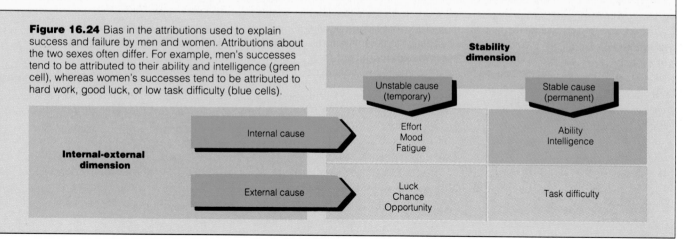

Figure 16.24 Bias in the attributions used to explain success and failure by men and women. Attributions about the two sexes often differ. For example, men's successes tend to be attributed to their ability and intelligence (green cell), whereas women's successes tend to be attributed to hard work, good luck, or low task difficulty (blue cells).

SOCIAL BEHAVIOR

Person Perception: Forming Impressions of Others

• Our perceptions of others can be distorted by a variety of factors, including a person's physical appearance. We tend to attribute desirable characteristics, such as intelligence, competence and kindness, to good-looking people. First impressions are especially likely to be influenced by physical appearance. It is harder to overcome negative first impressions than favorable ones.

• We use social schemas to categorize people into types. Stereotypes are widely held social schemas that lead us to expect that people will have certain characteristics because of their membership in a specific group. Gender, ethnic, and occupational stereotypes are common. In interacting with others, stereotypes may lead us to see what we expect to see and to overestimate how often we see it. The reconstructive nature of memory may also produce selective distortions in person perception.

Attribution Processes: Explaining Behavior

• Attributions are inferences about the causes of events and behavior. We make attributions to understand our social world, especially when behavior is unusual, unexpected, or has personal consequences for us. Internal attributions ascribe behavior to personal dispositions and traits, whereas external attributions locate the cause of behavior in the environment.

• Kelley's model of attribution suggests that internal attributions are more likely when one's behavior is consistent, not distinctive to an entity, and low in consensus value. Weiner's model proposes that attributions for success and failure should be analyzed in terms of the stability of causes, as well as the internal-external dimension.

• Observers favor internal attributions to explain another's behavior (the fundamental attribution error), while actors favor external attributions to explain their own behavior. In defensive attribution, we unfairly blame victims for their misfortune (with internal attributions) to reduce our own feelings of vulnerabilty. The self-serving bias is our tendency to attribute our good outcomes to personal factors and our bad outcomes to situational factors. Attributional patterns are related to marital distress, as unhappy spouses tend to attribute their problems to each other.

Interpersonal Attraction: Liking and Loving

• We tend to like and love people who live in close proximity to us, who are similar to us, who reciprocate our expressions of affection, and who are physically attractive. The matching hypothesis asserts that people who are similar in physical attractiveness are more likely to be drawn together than those who are not. Byrne's research suggests that attitude similarity causes attraction. Rosenbaum has argued that attitude dissimilarity also causes disdain.

• Berscheid and Hatfield have identified some popular myths about love, such as (1) when you fall in love, you'll know it, (2) love is a purely positive experience, and (3) true love lasts forever. Sternberg builds on their distinction between passionate and companionate love by dividing the latter into intimacy and commitment. Lee maintains that compatibility in basic styles of loving is critical to the success of romantic relationships. Hazan and Shaver's study suggests that love relationships in adulthood mimic our attachments in infancy.

Attitudes: Making Social Judgments

• Attitudes are made up of cognitive, affective, and behavioral components. Attitudes and behavior aren't as consistent as one might assume, in part because we expect very general attitudes to predict very specific behaviors, and in part because attitudes only create predispositions to behave in certain ways.

- A source of persuasion who is credible, expert, trustworthy, likable, physically attractive, and similar to the receiver tends to be relatively effective in stimulating attitude change. Although there are some situational limitations, two-sided arguments, fear arousal, and drawing conclusions are effective elements in persuasive messages. Persuasion is undermined when a receiver is forewarned, or when a receiver's initial position is very discrepant from the position advocated.
- Attitudes may be shaped through classical conditioning, operant conditioning, and observational learning. According to balance theory, attitude change is likely when attitudes do not fit together in harmony. Festinger's dissonance theory asserts that inconsistent attitudes cause tension and that people alter their attitudes to reduce cognitive dissonance. Dissonance theory has been used to explain attitude change following counterattitudinal behavior, major decisions, and efforts that haven't panned out. Some of these phenomena can be explained by self-perception theory, which posits that we may infer our attitudes from our behavior.

Conformity and Obedience: Yielding to Others

- Asch found that subjects often conform to the group, even when the group reports inaccurate judgments on a simple line-judging task. He found that conformity becomes more likely as group size increases, up to a group size of seven. If a small group isn't unanimous, conformity declines rapidly. To a large extent, Asch's experiments may have produced compliance in public, while subjects' private beliefs remained unchanged.
- In Milgram's landmark study of obedience to authority, adult men drawn from the community showed a remarkable tendency, in spite of their misgivings, to follow orders to shock an innocent stranger. Milgram concluded that situational pressures can make decent people do indecent things. Critics asserted that Milgram's results were not generalizable to the real world and that his methods were unethical. The generalizability of Milgram's findings have stood the test of time, but his work also helped to stimulate stricter ethical standards for research.

Behavior in Groups: Joining with Others

- The way you behave in a group may not correspond to the way you would behave if you were alone. For example, people who help someone in need when alone, are less likely to provide help when a group is present. This phenomenon, called the bystander effect, occurs primarily because a group creates diffusion of responsibility.
- Individuals' productivity often declines in larger groups because of loss of coordination and because of social loafing. Group polarization occurs when discussion leads a group to shift toward a more extreme decision in the direction the group was already leaning. In groupthink, a cohesive group suspends critical judgment in a misguided effort to promote agreement in decision making.

Putting It in Perspective

- Social psychology illustrates the value of empiricism because research in this area often proves that common sense is wrong. Additionally, several lines of research on social perception demonstrate that our experience of the world is highly subjective.

Application: Understanding Prejudice

- Prejudice is a negative attitude toward the members of a group. Prejudice is supported by stereotyping, the power of first impressions, and selectivity and memory biases in person perception. Attributional biases also contribute, including our tendency to assume that others' behavior reflects their dispositions, our tendency to attribute others' failures to personal factors, and our tendency to derogate victims.
- Proximity and similarity effects in attraction may also contribute to prejudice. Negative attitudes about groups are frequently acquired through observational learning. Pressure to conform, dissonance about not being fair-minded, and our tendency to see outgroups as homogeneous may all serve to strengthen prejudice.

KEY TERMS

Altruism	Group	Prejudice
Attitudes	Group cohesiveness	Proximity
Attributions	Group polarization	Receiver
Balance	Groupthink	Reciprocity
Bystander effect	Illusory correlation effect	Self-serving bias
Channel	Ingratiation	Social loafing
Cognitive dissonance	Ingroup	Social psychology
Commitment	Internal attributions	Social schemas
Companionate love	Interpersonal attraction	Source
Compliance	Intimacy	Stereotypes
Conformity	Latitude of acceptance	
Defensive attribution	Matching hypothesis	
Discrimination	Message	
Ethnocentrism	Obedience	
External attributions	Outgroup	
Fundamental attribution error	Passionate love	
	Person perception	

KEY PEOPLE

Solomon Asch	Fritz Heider
Ellen Berscheid	Harold Kelley
Leon Festinger	Irving Janis
Elaine Hatfield	Stanley Milgram

CHAPTER 1

Concept Check 1.1

1. c. John B. Watson (1930; p. 103) dismissing the importance of genetic inheritance while arguing that traits are shaped entirely by experience.

2. a. Wilhelm Wundt (1874/1904; p. v) campaigning for a new, independent science of psychology.

3. b. William James (1890) commenting negatively on the structuralists' efforts to break consciousness into its elements and putting forth his view of consciousness as a continuously flowing stream.

Concept Check 1.2

1. b. B. F. Skinner (1971; p. 17) explaining why he believes that freedom is an illusion.

2. a. Sigmund Freud (1905; pp. 77–78) arguing that it is possible to probe into the unconscious depths of the mind.

3. c. Carl Rogers (1961; p. 27) commenting on others' assertion that he has an overly optimistic (Pollyannaish) view of human potential and discussing humans' basic drive toward personal growth.

Concept Check 1.3

1. c **2.** a **3.** e **4.** b

CHAPTER 2

Concept Check 2.1

1. IV: Film violence (present vs. absent)
DV: There are two DVs—heart rate and blood pressure.

2. IV: Courtesy training (training vs. no training)
DV: Number of customer complaints

3. IV: There are 2 IVs—stimulus complexity (high vs. low) and stimulus contrast (high vs. low).
DV: Length of time spent staring at the stimuli

4. IV: Group size (large vs. small)
DV: Conformity

Concept Check 2.2

1. d. Surveys and psychological tests. You would probably measure many aspects of personality with a battery of personality tests and inquire about sleep habits with a questionnaire.

2. c. Case study. Using a case study approach, you could interview people with anxiety disorders and also interview their parents and examine their school records to look for similarities in childhood experiences. As a second choice, you might have people with anxiety disorders fill out a survey about their childhood experiences.

3. b. Naturalistic observation. To answer this question properly, you would want to observe baboons in their natural environment, without interference.

4. a. Experiment. To demonstrate a causal relationship, you would have to conduct an experiment. You would manipulate the presence or absence of food-related cues in controlled circumstances in which subjects had an opportunity to eat food, and monitor the amount eaten.

Concept Check 2.3

1. b and e. The other three conclusions all equate correlation with causation.

2. a. Negative. As age increases, more people tend to have visual problems, and acuity tends to decrease.

b. Positive. Studies show that highly educated people tend to earn higher incomes, and people with less education tend to earn lower incomes.

c. Negative. As shyness increases, the size of one's friendship network should decrease. However, research suggests that this inverse association may be weaker than widely believed.

Concept Check 2.4

Methodological flaw	Study 1	Study 2
Sampling bias	√	√
Placebo effects	√	___
Confounding of variables	√	___
Distortions in self-report data	___	√
Experimenter bias	√	___

Explanations for Study 1. Sensory deprivation is an unusual kind of experience that may intrigue certain potential subjects, who may be more adventurous or more willing to take risks than the population at large. Using the first 80 students who sign up for this study may not yield a sample that is representative of the population. Assigning the first 40 subjects who sign up to the experimental group may confound these extraneous variables with the treatment (students who sign up most quickly may be the most adventurous). In announcing that he will be examining the *detrimental* effects of sensory deprivation, the experimenter has created expectations in the subjects. These expectations could lead to placebo effects that have not been controlled for with a placebo group. The experimenter has also revealed that he has a bias about the outcome of the study. Since he supervises the treatments, he knows which subjects are in the experimental and control groups, thus aggravating potential problems with experimenter bias. For example, he might unintentionally give the control group subjects better instructions on how to do the pursuit-rotor task and thereby slant the study in favor of finding support for his hypothesis.

Explanations for Study 2. Sampling bias is a problem because the researcher has sampled only subjects from a low-income, inner-city neighborhood. A sample obtained in this way is not likely to be representative of the population at large. People are sensitive about the issue of racial prejudice, so distortions in self-report data are also likely. Many subjects may be swayed by social desirability bias and rate themselves as less prejudiced than they really are.

CHAPTER 3

Concept Check 3.1

1. E **2.** D **3.** A **4.** C **5.** B

Concept Check 3.2

1. Left hemisphere damage, probably to Wernicke's area.

2. Deficit in dopamine synthesis in an area of the midbrain.

3. Damage in the right hemisphere, which handles visual-spatial processing, or maybe damage in the midbrain area concerned with localizing where things are.

4. Disturbance in dopamine activity, possibly associated with enlarged ventricles in the brain (as discussed in "Brain-Imaging Procedures"), although this association requires much more investigation.

Please note that neuropsychological assessment is not as simple as this introductory exercise may suggest. There are many possible causes of most disorders, and we discussed only a handful of leading causes for each.

CHAPTER 4

Concept Check 4.1

___✓___ **1.** Interposition. The arches in front cut off part of corridor behind them.

___✓___ **2.** Height in plane. The back of the corridor is higher on the horizontal plane than the front of the corridor.

___✓___ **3.** Texture gradient. The more distant portions of the hallway are painted in less detail than closer portions.

___✓___ **4.** Relative size. The arches in the distance are smaller than those in the foreground.

___✓___ **5.** Light and shadow. Light shining in from the crossing corridor (it's coming from the left) contrasts with shadow elsewhere.

___✓___ **6.** Linear perspective. The lines of the corridor converge in the distance.

_____ **7.** Aerial haze.

___✓___ **8.** Object familiarity. The man and the doorways are assumed to be their usual size.

Concept Check 4.2

Dimension	Vision	Hearing
1. Stimulus	Light waves	Sound waves
2. Elements of stimulus and related perceptions	Wavelength/hue Amplitude/ brightness Purity/saturation	Frequency/pitch Amplitude/ loudness Purity/timbre
3. Receptors	Rods and cones	Hair cells
4. Location of receptors	Retina	Basilar membrane
5. Main location of processing in brain	Occipital lobe Visual cortex	Temporal lobe Auditory cortex
6. Spatial aspect of perception	Depth perception	Auditory localization
7. Typical Weber fraction	$1/60$ (brightness)	$1/10$ (loudness)

CHAPTER 5

Concept Check 5.1

Characteristic	REM sleep	NREM sleep
Type of EEG activity	"Wide awake" brain waves, mostly beta	Varied, lots of delta waves
Eye movements	Rapid, lateral	Slow or absent
Dreaming	Frequent, vivid	Less frequent
Depth (difficulty in awakening)	Difficult to awaken	Varied, generally easier to awaken
Percentage of total sleep (in adults)	About 20%	About 80%
Increases or decreases with age (as % of sleep)	% decreases	% increases
Timing in sleep cycle (dominates early or late)	Dominates later in cycle	Dominates early in cycle

Concept Check 5.2

1. Beta. Video games require alert information processing, which is associated with beta waves.

2. Alpha. Meditation involves relaxation, which is associated with alpha, and studies show increased alpha in meditators.

3. Theta. In stage 1 sleep, theta waves tend to be prevalent.

4. Delta. Sleepwalking usually occurs in deep NREM sleep, which is dominated by delta activity.

5. Beta. Nightmares are dreams, so you're probably in REM sleep, which paradoxically produces "wide awake" beta waves.

6. Beta. If you're a beginner, typing will be a "controlled process" requiring alert, focused attention, which should be associated with beta waves.

CHAPTER 6

Concept Check 6.1

1. CS: fire in fireplace
UCS: pain from burn   CR/UCR: fear

2. CS: brake lights in rain
UCS: car accident   CR/UCR: tensing up

3. CS: sight of cat
UCS: cat dander   CR/UCR: wheezing

Concept Check 6.2

1. Fixed ratio. Each sale is a response, and every third response earns reinforcement.

2. Variable interval. A varied amount of time elapses before the response of doing yard work can earn reinforcement.

3. Variable ratio. Reinforcement occurs after a varied number of unreinforced casts (time is irrelevant; the more casts Martha makes, the more reinforcers she will receive).

Concept Check 6.3

1. Punishment.

2. Positive reinforcement.

3. Punishment.

4. Negative reinforcement (for Audrey); the dog is positively reinforced for its whining.

5. Negative reinforcement.

Concept Check 6.4

1. Classical conditioning. Marcia's blue windbreaker is a CS eliciting excitement in her dog.

2. Operant conditioning. Playing new songs leads to negative consequences (punishment), which weaken the tendency of the band to play new songs. Old songs lead to positive reinforcers, which gradually strengthens the tendency to play old songs.

3. Classical conditioning. The song was paired with the passion of new love so that it became a CS eliciting emotional, romantic feelings.

4. Both. Ralph's workplace is paired with criticism so that his workplace becomes a CS eliciting anxiety. Calling in sick is operant behavior that is strengthened through negative reinforcement (because it reduces anxiety).

CHAPTER 7

Concept Check 7.1

Feature	Sensory memory	Short-term memory	Long-term memory
Maintenance of information	Not possible	Continued attention; rehearsal	Repetition; organization
Encoding format	Copy of input	Largely phonemic	Largely semantic
Storage capacity	Large	Small (7 ± 2 chunks)	No known limit
Storage duration	¼–2 seconds	Up to 30 seconds	Minutes to years

Concept Check 7.2

1. Ineffective encoding due to lack of attention.

2. Retrieval failure due to motivated forgetting.

3. Proactive interference (previous learning of Joe Cocker's name interferes with new learning).

4. Retroactive interference (new learning of sociology interferes with older learning of history).

CHAPTER 8

Concept Check 8.1

1. 2. One word is overextended to refer to a similar object.

2. 4. Words are combined into a sentence, but the rule for past tense is overgeneralized.

3. 3. The sentence is telegraphic.

4. 5. Words are combined into a sentence, and past tense is used correctly.

5. 1. One word is used to refer to an entity.

Concept Check 8.2

1. Functional fixedness.

2. Forming subgoals.

3. Insight.

4. Searching for analogies.

5. Arrangement.

Concept Check 8.3

1. Elimination by aspects.

2. Availability heuristic.

3. Shift to compensatory model.

4. Use of additive model.

CHAPTER 9

Concept Check 9.1

1. Test-retest reliability.

2. Criterion-related validity.

3. Content validity.

Concept Check 9.2

1. H. Given that the identical twins were reared apart, we conclude that their greater similarity in comparison to fraternals reared together can only be due to heredity. This comparison is probably the most important piece of evidence supporting the genetic determination of IQ.

2. E. We tend to associate identical twins with evidence supporting heredity; but in this comparison, genetic similarity is held constant since both sets of twins are identical. The only logical explanation for the greater similarity in identicals reared together is the effect of their being reared together (environment).

3. E. This comparison is similar to the previous one. Genetic similarity is held constant, and a shared environment produces greater similarity than being reared apart.

4. B. This is nothing more than a quantification of Galton's original observation that intelligence runs in families. Since families share both genes and environment, either factor or both could be responsible for the observed correlation.

5. B. The similarity of adopted children to their biological parents can be due only to shared genes, and the similarity of adopted children to their foster parents can be due only to shared environment, so these correlations show the influence of both heredity and environment.

Concept Check 9.3

1. Self-report inventory, specifically a single-trait inventory.

2. Reliability, specifically test-retest reliability.

3. Validity, specifically construct validity (obnoxiousness is the construct).

CHAPTER 10

Concept Check 10.1

Relevant theory	Level of needs
1. Drive theory (A deficit creates internal tension.)	Love and belongingness needs
2. Incentive theory (You're motivated by the triple bonus.)	Safety and security needs
3. Maslow's theory (Interests reflect higher, growth needs.)	Cognitive and aesthetic needs
4. Sociobiology (Self-sacrifice promotes welfare of close kin.)	Physiological needs

Concept Check 10.2

2. James-Lange theory.

3. Schachter's two-factor theory.

4. Evolutionary theories.

CHAPTER 11

Concept Check 11.1

1. b. Animism is characteristic of the preoperational period.

2. c. Mastery of hierarchical classification occurs during the concrete operations period.

3. a. Lack of object permanence is characteristic of the sensorimotor period.

Concept Check 11.2

1. c. Commitment to personal ethics is characteristic of postconventional reasoning.

2. b. Concern about approval of others is characteristic of conventional reasoning.

3. a. Emphasis on positive or negative consequences is characteristic of preconventional reasoning.

Concept Check 11.3

a. Moral reasoning changes as cognitive development progresses.

b. Youngsters who are in higher stages of moral development tend to display more altruistic social behavior.

c. Securely attached infants respond better to unfamiliar people and show more leadership. Emotionally deprived infants may have difficulty forming affectionate relationships (although this can be reversed).

CHAPTER 12

Concept Check 12.1

1. Regression.

2. Projection.

3. Reaction formation.

4. Repression.

5. Rationalization.

Concept Check 12.2

1. Bandura's observational learning. Sarah imitates a role model from television.

2. Maslow's need for self-actualization. Marilyn is striving to realize her fullest potentials.

3. Freud's Oedipal complex. Johnny shows preference for his opposite-sex parent and emotional distance from his same-sex parent.

Concept Check 12.3

1. Abraham Maslow (1971, p. 36) commenting on the need for self-actualization.

2. Hans Eysenck (1977, pp. 407–408) commenting on the biological roots of personality.

3. Sigmund Freud (in Malcolm, 1980) commenting on the repression of sexuality.

CHAPTER 13

Concept Check 13.1

1. b. A choice between two unattractive options.

2. c. Weighing the positive and negative aspects of a single goal.

3. a. A choice between two attractive options.

Concept Check 13.2

1. a. Frustration due to delay.

2. d. Pressure to perform.

3. c. Change associated with leaving school and taking a new job.

4. a. Frustration due to loss of job.
c. Change in life circumstances.
d. Pressure to perform (in quickly obtaining new job).

CHAPTER 14

Concept Check 14.1

	Deviance	Maladaptive behavior	Personal distress
1. Alan	_____	√	_____
2. Monica	_____	_____	√
3. Walter	√	_____	_____
4. Phyllis	√	√	√

Concept Check 14.2

1. Obsessive-compulsive disorder (key symptoms: frequent rituals, ruminations about school).

2. Somatization disorder (key symptoms: history of physical complaints involving many different organ systems).

3. Conversion disorder (key symptoms: loss of function in single organ system).

Concept Check 14.3

1. Bipolar mood disorder, manic episode (key symptoms: extravagant plans, hyperactivity, reckless spending).

2. Paranoid schizophrenia (key symptoms: delusions of persecution and grandeur, along with deterioration of adaptive behavior).

3. Major depression (key symptoms: feelings of despair, low self-esteem, lack of energy).

CHAPTER 15

Concept Check 15.1

1. c   **2.** a   **3.** b

Concept Check 15.2

1. d   **2.** b   **3.** a   **4.** c

Concept Check 15.3

1. c   **2.** a   **3.** b   **4.** d   **5.** b

CHAPTER 16

Concept Check 16.1

	Unstable	Stable
Internal	d	b
External	a	c

Concept Check 16.2

1. c. Fundamental attribution error (assuming that arriving late reflects personal qualities).

2. a. Illusory correlation effect (overestimating how often one has seen confirmations of the assertion that young, female professors get pregnant soon after being hired).

3. b. Stereotyping (assuming that all lawyers have certain traits).

4. d. Defensive attribution (derogating the victims of misfortune to minimize the apparent likelihood of undergoing a similar mishap).

Concept Check 16.3

1. Target: cognitive component of attitudes (beliefs about program for regulating nursing homes).

Persuasion: message factor (advice to use one-sided instead of two-sided arguments).

2. Target: affective component of attitudes (feelings about candidate).

Persuasion: source factor (advice on appearing likable, sincere, and compassionate).

3. Target: behavioral component of attitudes (making contributions).

Persuasion: receiver factor (considering audience's initial position regarding the candidate).

Concept Check 16.4

1. False. **4.** False. **7.** False.

2. False. **5.** False.

3. True. **6.** True.

Empiricism depends on observation, precise observation depends on measurement, and measurement requires numbers. Thus, scientists routinely analyze numerical data to arrive at their conclusions. Over 1000 empirical studies are cited in this text, and all but a few of the simplest studies required a statistical analysis. **Statistics involves the use of mathematics to organize, summarize, and interpret numerical data.** We discussed statistics briefly in Chapter 2, but in this Appendix we'll take a closer look.

To illustrate statistics in action, let's assume that we want to test a hypothesis that generated quite an argument in your psychology class. The hypothesis is that college students who watch a great deal of television aren't as bright as those who watch TV infrequently. For the fun of it, your class decides to conduct a correlational study of itself, collecting survey and psychological test data. Your classmates all agree to respond to a short survey on their TV viewing habits. Since everyone at your school had to take the Scholastic Aptitude Test (SAT), the class decides to use scores on the SAT Verbal subtest as an index of how bright students are. Everyone agrees to allow the records office at the college to furnish their SAT scores to the professor, who replaces each student's name with a subject number (to protect students' right to privacy). Let's see how we could use statistics to analyze the data collected in our pilot study (a small, preliminary investigation).

Graphing Data

After collecting our data, our next step is to organize the data to get a quick overview of our numerical results. Let's assume that there are 20 students in your class, and when they estimate how many hours they spend per day watching TV, the results are as follows:

3	2	0	3	1
3	4	0	5	1
2	3	4	5	2
4	5	3	4	6

One of the simpler things that we can do to organize data is to create a **frequency distribution— an orderly arrangement of scores indicating the frequency of each score or group of scores.** Figure 1a shows a frequency distribution for our data on TV viewing. The column on the left lists the possible scores (estimated hours of TV viewing) in order, and the column on the right lists the number of subjects with each score. Graphs can provide an even better overview of the data. One approach is to portray the data in a **histogram, which is a bar graph that presents data from a frequency distribution.** Such a histogram, summarizing our TV viewing data can be seen in Figure 1b.

Another widely used method of portraying data graphically is the **frequency polygon—a line figure used to present data from a frequency distribution.** Figures 1c and 1d show how our TV viewing data can be converted from a histogram

STATISTICAL METHODS

Figure 1 Graphing data. (**a**) Our raw data are tallied into a frequency distribution. (**b**) The same data are portrayed in a bar graph, called a histogram. (**c**) A frequency polygon is plotted over the histogram to show how they depict the same data. (**d**) The resultant frequency polygon is shown by itself.

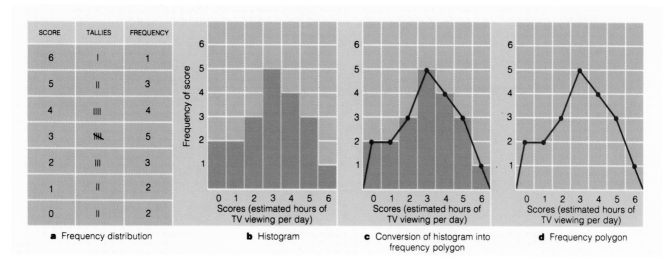

a Frequency distribution   **b** Histogram   **c** Conversion of histogram into frequency polygon   **d** Frequency polygon

Figure 2 Measures of central tendency. The mean, median, and mode usually converge, as in this case—unless a distribution is skewed, as shown in Figure 3.

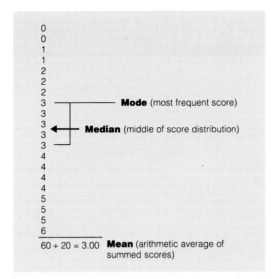

```
0
0
1
1
2
2
2
2
3 ─┐──── Mode (most frequent score)
3  │
3  │
3  ├──── Median (middle of score distribution)
3  │
3 ─┘
4
4
4
4
5
5
5
6
60 ÷ 20 = 3.00  Mean (arithmetic average of summed scores)
```

to a frequency polygon. In both the bar graph and the line figure, the horizontal axis lists the possible scores, and the vertical axis is used to indicate the frequency of each score. This use of the axes is nearly universal for frequency polygons, although sometimes it's reversed in histograms (the vertical axis lists possible scores, so the bars become horizontal).

Our graphs improve on the jumbled collection of scores that we started with, but **descriptive statistics, which are used to organize and summarize data,** provide some additional advantages. Let's see what the three measures of central tendency tell us about our data.

Measuring Central Tendency

In examining a set of data, it's routine to ask "What is a typical score in the distribution?" For instance, in this case we might compare the average amount of TV watching in our sample against national estimates, to determine whether our sub-

jects appear to be representative of the population. The three measures of central tendency—the median, the mean, and the mode—give us indications regarding the typical score in a data set. As explained in Chapter 2, the **median is the score that falls in the center of a distribution, the mean is the arithmetic average of the scores, and the mode is the score that occurs most frequently.**

All three measures of central tendency are calculated for our TV viewing data in Figure 2. As you can see, in this set of data the mean, median, and mode all turn out to be exactly the same score, which is 3. Although our example in Chapter 2 emphasized that the mean, median, and mode can yield different estimates of central tendency, the correspondence among them seen in our TV viewing data is quite common. Lack of agreement among them usually occurs when a few extreme scores pull the mean away from the center of the distribution, as shown in Figure 3. The curves plotted in Figure 3 are simply "smoothed out" frequency polygons based on data from many subjects. They show that when a distribution is symmetric, the measures of central tendency fall together, but this is not true in skewed or unbalanced distributions.

Figure 3b shows a **negatively skewed distribution,** in which most scores pile up at the high end of the scale (the negative skew refers to the direction in which the curve's "tail" points). A **positively skewed distribution,** in which scores pile up at the low end of the scale, is shown in Figure 3c. In both types of skewed distributions, a few extreme scores at one end pull the mean, and to a lesser degree the median, away from the mode. In these situations, the mean may be misleading, and the median usually provides the best index of central tendency.

Figure 3 Measures of central tendency in skewed distributions. In a symmetrical distribution (**a**), the three measures of central tendency converge. However, in a negatively skewed distribution (**b**) or in a positively skewed distribution (**c**), the mean, median, and mode are pulled apart as shown here. Typically, in these situations, the median provides the best index of central tendency.

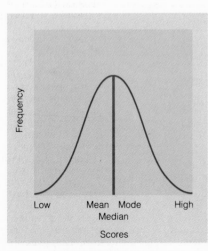

a Symmetrical distribution

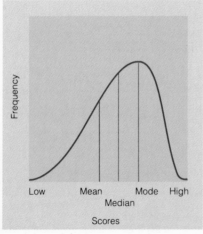

b Negatively skewed distribution

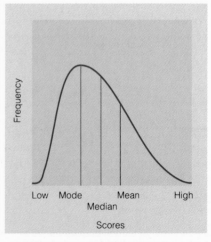

c Positively skewed distribution

In any case, the measures of central tendency for our TV viewing data are reassuring, since they all agree and they fall reasonably close to national estimates regarding how much young adults watch TV (Huston & Wright, 1982). Given the small size of our group, this agreement with national norms doesn't *prove* that our sample is representative of the population, but at least there's no obvious reason to believe that it is unrepresentative.

Measuring Variability

Of course, not everyone in our sample reported identical TV viewing habits. Virtually all data sets are characterized by some variability. **Variability refers to how much the scores tend to vary or depart from the mean score.** For example, the distribution of golf scores for a mediocre, erratic golfer would be characterized by high variability, while scores for an equally mediocre but consistent golfer would show less variability.

The **standard deviation is an index of the amount of variability in a set of data.** It reflects the dispersion of scores in a distribution. This principle is portrayed graphically in Figure 4, where the two distributions of golf scores have the same mean but the upper one has less variability because the scores are "bunched up" in the center (for the consistent golfer). The distribution in the bottom half of Figure 4 is characterized by more variability, as the erratic golfer's scores are more spread out. This distribution will yield a higher standard deviation than the distribution in the upper half of the figure.

The formula for calculating the standard deviation is shown in Figure 5, where d stands for each score's deviation from the mean and Σ stands for summation. A step-by-step application of this formula to our TV viewing data, also shown in Figure 5, reveals that the standard deviation for our TV viewing data is 1.64. The standard deviation has a variety of uses. One of these uses will surface in the next section as we discuss the normal distribution.

The Normal Distribution

The hypothesis in our study is that brighter students watch less TV than relatively dull students. To test this hypothesis, we're going to correlate TV viewing with SAT scores. But to make effective use of the SAT data, we need to understand what SAT scores mean, which brings us to the normal distribution.

The *normal distribution* is a symmetric, bell-shaped curve that represents the pattern in

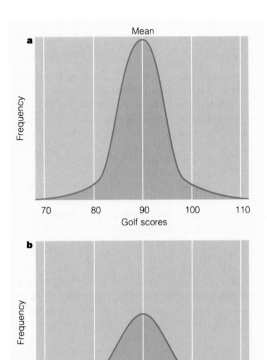

Figure 4 The standard deviation and dispersion of data. Although both these distributions of golf scores have the same mean, their standard deviations will be different. In (**a**) the scores are bunched together and there is less variability than in (**b**), yielding a lower standard deviation for the data in distribution (**a**).

TV VIEWING SCORES X	DEVIATION FROM MEAN d	DEVIATION SQUARED d^2
0	−3	9
0	−3	9
1	−2	4
1	−2	4
2	−1	1
2	−1	1
2	−1	1
3	0	0
3	0	0
3	0	0
3	0	0
3	0	0
4	+1	1
4	+1	1
4	+1	1
4	+1	1
5	+2	4
5	+2	4
5	+2	4
6	+3	9

$N = 20$

$$\Sigma X = 60 \qquad \Sigma d^2 = 54$$

$$\text{Mean} = \frac{\Sigma X}{N} = \frac{60}{20} = 3.0$$

$$\text{Standard deviation} = \sqrt{\frac{\Sigma d^2}{N}} = \sqrt{\frac{54}{20}}$$

$$= \sqrt{2.70} = 1.64$$

Figure 5 Steps in calculating the standard deviation. (1) Sum the scores (ΣX) and divide by the number of scores (N) to calculate the mean (which comes out to 3.0 in this case). (2) Calculate each score's deviation from the mean by subtracting the mean from each score (the results are shown in the second column). (3) Square these deviations from the mean and sum the results to obtain (Σd^2) as shown in the third column. (4) Insert the numbers for N and Σd^2 into the formula for the standard deviation and compute the results.

which many human characteristics are dispersed in the population. A great many physical qualities (for example, height, nose length, running speed) and psychological traits (for example, intelligence, spatial reasoning ability, introversion) are distributed in a manner that closely resembles this bell-shaped curve. When a trait is normally distributed, most scores fall near the center of the distribution (the mean), and the number of scores gradually declines as one moves away from the center in either direction. The normal distribution is *not* a law of nature. It's a mathematical function, or theoretical curve, that approximates the way nature seems to operate.

The normal distribution is the bedrock of the scoring system for most psychological tests, including the SAT. As we discussed in Chapter 9, psychological tests are *relative measures*; they assess how people score on a trait in comparison with other people. The normal distribution gives us a precise way to measure how people stack up in comparison to each other. The scores under the normal curve are dispersed in a fixed pattern, with the standard deviation serving as the unit of measurement, as shown in Figure 6. About 68% of the scores in the distribution fall within plus or minus 1 standard deviation of the mean, while 95% of the scores fall within plus or minus 2 standard deviations of the mean. Given this fixed pattern, if you know the mean and standard deviation of a normally distributed trait, you can tell where any score falls in the distribution for the trait.

Although you may not have realized it, you probably have taken many tests in which the scor-

ing system is based on the normal distribution. On the SAT, for instance, raw scores (the number of items correct on each subtest) are converted into standard scores that indicate where you fall in the normal distribution for the trait measured. In this conversion, the mean is set arbitrarily at 500 and the standard deviation at 100, as shown in Figure 7. Therefore, a score of 400 on the SAT Verbal subtest means that you scored one standard deviation below the mean, and a score of 600 indicates that you scored one standard deviation above the mean. Thus, SAT scores tell you how many standard deviations above or below the mean your score was. This system also provides the metric for IQ scales and many other types of psychological tests (see Chapter 9).

Test scores that place examinees in the normal distribution can always be converted to percentile scores, which are a little easier to interpret. A *percentile score* indicates the percentage of people who score below the score you obtained. For example, if you score at the 60th percentile, 60% of the people who take the test score below you, while the remaining 40% score above you. There are tables available that permit us to convert any standard deviation placement in a normal distribution into a precise percentile score. Figure 6 shows some percentile conversions for the normal curve.

Of course, not all distributions are normal. As we saw earlier in Figure 3, some distributions are skewed in one direction or the other. As an example, consider what would happen if a classroom exam were much too easy for the students, or much too hard. If the test were too easy, scores

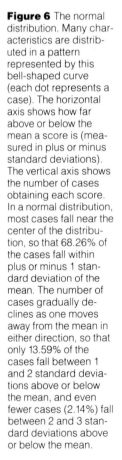

Figure 6 The normal distribution. Many characteristics are distributed in a pattern represented by this bell-shaped curve (each dot represents a case). The horizontal axis shows how far above or below the mean a score is (measured in plus or minus standard deviations). The vertical axis shows the number of cases obtaining each score. In a normal distribution, most cases fall near the center of the distribution, so that 68.26% of the cases fall within plus or minus 1 standard deviation of the mean. The number of cases gradually declines as one moves away from the mean in either direction, so that only 13.59% of the cases fall between 1 and 2 standard deviations above or below the mean, and even fewer cases (2.14%) fall between 2 and 3 standard deviations above or below the mean.

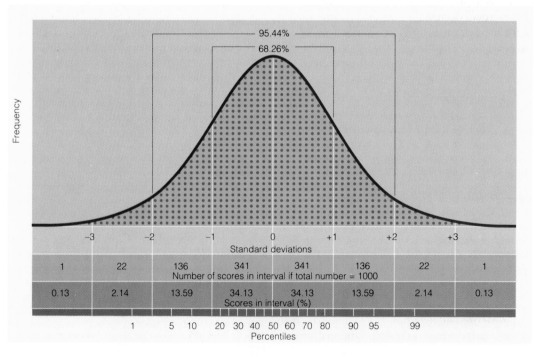

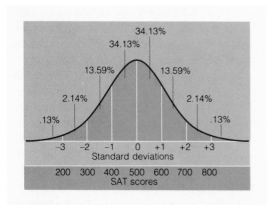

Figure 7 The normal distribution and SAT scores. As explained in Chapter 9, the normal distribution is the basis for the scoring system on many standardized tests. For example, on the Scholastic Aptitude Test (SAT), the mean is set at 500 and the standard deviation at 100. Hence, an SAT score tells you how many standard deviations above or below the mean you scored. For example, a score of 700 means you scored 2 standard deviations above the mean.

would be bunched up at the high end of the scale (see Figure 3b). If the test was too hard, scores would be bunched up at the low end (see Figure 3c).

Measuring Correlation

To determine whether TV viewing is related to SAT scores, we have to compute a **correlation coefficient**—a numerical index of the degree of relationship that exists between two variables. As discussed in Chapter 2, a *positive* correlation means that there's a *direct* relationship between two variables—say X and Y. This means that high scores on variable X are associated with high scores on variable Y, and that low scores on X are associated with low scores on Y. A *negative* correlation indicates that there is an *inverse* relationship between two variables. This means that people who score high on variable X tend to score low on variable Y, while those who score low on X tend to score high on Y. In our study, we hypothesized that as TV viewing increased, SAT scores would decrease, so we should expect a negative correlation between TV viewing and SAT scores.

The *magnitude* of a correlation coefficient indicates the *strength* of the association between two variables. This coefficient can vary between 0 and ± 1.00. The coefficient is usually represented by the letter r, (for example, $r = .45$). A coefficient near 0 tells us that there's no relationship between two variables. A coefficient of + 1.00 or − 1.00 indicates that there's a perfect, one-to-one correspondence between two variables. A perfect correlation is found only very rarely when we're working with real data. The closer the coefficient is to either − 1.00 or + 1.00, the stronger the relationship is.

The direction and strength of correlations can be illustrated graphically in scatter diagrams. **A scatter diagram is a graph in which paired X and Y scores for each subject are plotted as single points.** Figure 8 shows scatter diagrams for positive correlations in the upper half and for negative correlations in the lower half. A perfect positive correlation and a perfect negative correlation are shown on the far left. When a correlation is perfect, the data points in the scatter diagram fall exactly in a straight line. However, positive and negative correlations yield lines slanted in opposite directions because the lines map out opposite types of associations. Moving to the right in Figure 8, you can see what happens when the magnitude of a correlation decreases. The data points scatter farther and farther from the straight line that would represent a perfect relationship.

Figure 8 Scatter diagrams of positive and negative correlations. Scatter diagrams plot paired X and Y scores as single points. Score plots slanted in the opposite direction result from positive (*top row*) as opposed to negative (*bottom row*) correlations. Moving across both rows (to the right), you can see that progressively weaker correlations result in more and more scattered plots of data points.

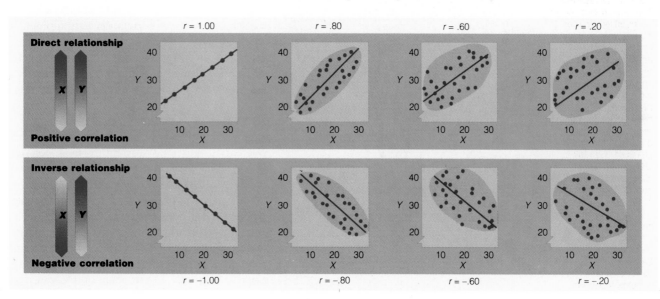

Figure 9 Scatter diagram of the correlation between TV viewing and SAT scores. Our hypothetical data relating TV viewing to SAT scores are plotted in this scatter diagram. Compare it to the scatter diagrams seen in Figure 8 and see if you can estimate the correlation between TV viewing and SAT scores in our data (see the text for the answer).

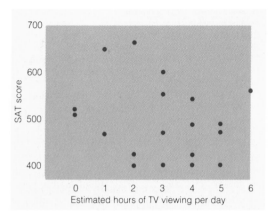

Figure 10 Computing a correlation coefficient. The calculations required to compute the Pearson product-moment coefficient of correlation are shown here. The formula looks intimidating, but it's just a matter of filling in the figures taken from the sums of the columns shown above the formula.

What about our data relating TV viewing to SAT scores? Figure 9 shows a scatter diagram of these data. Having just learned about scatter diagrams, perhaps you can estimate the magnitude of the correlation between TV viewing and SAT scores. The scatter diagram of our data looks a lot like the one seen in the bottom right corner of Figure 8, suggesting that the correlation will be in the vicinity of $-.20$.

The formula for computing the most widely used measure of correlation—the Pearson product-moment correlation—is shown in Figure 10,

SUBJECT NUMBER	TV VIEWING SCORE X	X^2	SAT SCORE Y	Y^2	XY
1	0	0	500	250,000	0
2	0	0	515	265,225	0
3	1	1	450	202,500	450
4	1	1	650	422,500	650
5	2	4	400	160,000	800
6	2	4	675	455,625	1350
7	2	4	425	180,625	850
8	3	9	400	160,000	1200
9	3	9	450	202,500	1350
10	3	9	500	250,000	1500
11	3	9	550	302,500	1650
12	3	9	600	360,000	1800
13	4	16	400	160,000	1600
14	4	16	425	180,625	1700
15	4	16	475	225,625	1900
16	4	16	525	275,625	2100
17	5	25	400	160,000	2000
18	5	25	450	202,500	2250
19	5	25	475	225,625	2375
20	6	36	550	302,500	3300

$N = 20$	$\Sigma X = 60$	$\Sigma X^2 = 234$	$\Sigma Y = 9815$	$\Sigma Y^2 = 4,943,975$	$\Sigma XY = 28,825$

Formula for Pearson product-moment correlation coefficient

$$r = \frac{(N)\Sigma XY - (\Sigma X)(\Sigma Y)}{\sqrt{[(N)\Sigma X^2 - (\Sigma X)^2][(N)\Sigma Y^2 - (\Sigma Y)^2]}}$$

$$= \frac{(20)(28,825) - (60)(9815)}{\sqrt{[(20)(234) - (60)^2][(20)(4,943,975) - (9815)^2]}}$$

$$= \frac{-12,400}{\sqrt{[1080][2,545,275]}}$$

$$= -.237$$

along with the calculations for our data on TV viewing and SAT scores. The data yield a correlation of $r = -.24$. This coefficient of correlation reveals that we have found a weak inverse association between TV viewing and performance on the SAT. Among our subjects, as TV viewing increases, SAT scores decrease, but the trend isn't very strong. We can get a better idea of how strong this correlation is by examining its predictive power.

Correlation and Prediction

As the magnitude of a correlation increases (gets closer to either -1.00 or $+1.00$), our ability to predict one variable based on knowledge of the other variable steadily increases. This relationship between the magnitude of a correlation and predictability can be quantified precisely. All we have to do is square the correlation coefficient (multiply it by itself) to get the **coefficient of determination, the percentage of variation in one variable that can be predicted from the other variable.** Thus, a correlation of .70 yields a coefficient of determination of .49 ($.70 \times .70 = .49$), indicating that variable X can account for 49% of the variation in variable Y. Figure 11 shows how the coefficient of determination goes up as the magnitude of a correlation increases.

Unfortunately, a correlation of .24 doesn't give us much predictive power. We can account for only a little over 6% of the variation in variable Y. So if we tried to predict individuals' SAT scores based on how much TV they watched, our predictions wouldn't be very accurate. Although a low correlation doesn't have much practical, predictive utility, it may still have theoretical value. Just knowing that there is a relationship between two variables can be theoretically interesting. However, we haven't yet addressed the question of whether our observed correlation is strong enough to support our hypothesis that there is a relationship between TV viewing and SAT scores. To make this judgment, we have to turn to inferential statistics and the process of hypothesis testing.

Hypothesis Testing

Inferential statistics go beyond the mere description of data. **Inferential statistics are employed to interpret data and draw conclusions.** They permit researchers to decide whether or not their data support their hypotheses.

In Chapter 2 we showed how inferential statistics can be used to evaluate the results of an experiment, but the same process can be applied to correlational data. In our study of TV viewing,

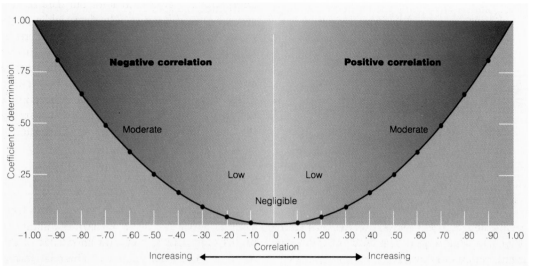

Figure 11 Correlation and the coefficient of determination. The coefficient of determination is an index of a correlation's predictive power. As you can see, whether positive or negative, stronger correlations yield greater predictive power.

we hypothesized that we would find an inverse relationship between amount of TV watched and SAT scores. Sure enough, that's what we found. However, we have to ask ourselves a critical question: Is this observed correlation large enough in magnitude to support our hypothesis, or might a correlation of this size have occurred by chance? We have to ask a similar question nearly every time we conduct a study.

Why do we have to ask this sort of question? Because we're working only with a sample. In research, we observe a limited *sample* (in this case, 20 subjects) to draw conclusions about a much larger *population* (college students in general). There's always a possibility that if we drew a different sample from the population, the results of our study might be different. Perhaps our results are unique to our sample, and not generalizable to the larger population. If we were able to collect data on the entire population, we wouldn't have to wrestle with this problem. But our dependence on a sample necessitates the use of inferential statistics to precisely evaluate the likelihood that our results are due to chance factors in sampling. Thus, inferential statistics are the key to making the inferential leap from the sample to the population (see Figure 12).

Although it may seem backwards, in hypothesis testing we formally test the *null* hypothesis. **The null hypothesis is that there is no true relationship between the variables observed.** In our study, the null hypothesis is that there is no genuine association between TV viewing and SAT scores. We want to determine whether our results will permit us to *reject* the null hypothesis, and thus conclude that our *research hypothesis* (that there *is* a relationship between the variables) has been supported. Why do we directly test the null hypothesis instead of the research hypothesis? Because our probability calculations depend on

assumptions tied to the null hypothesis. Specifically, we compute the probability of obtaining the results that we have observed if the null hypthesis is indeed true. The calculation of this probability hinges on a number of factors. A key factor is the amount of variability in the data, which is why the standard deviation is an important statistic.

Statistical Significance

When we reject the null hypothesis, we conclude that we have found *statistically significant* results. **Statistical significance is said to exist when the probability that the observed findings are due to chance is very low, usually fewer than 5 chances in 100.** This means that if the null hypothesis is correct and we conduct our study 100 times, drawing a new sample from the population each time, we will get results such as those observed only 5 times (at most) out of 100. If our calculations allow us to reject the null hypothesis, we conclude that our results support our research hypothesis.

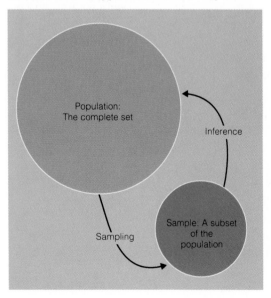

Figure 12 The relationship between the population and the sample. In research, we are usually interested in a broad population, but we can observe only a small subset of the population, so we obtain a sample from the population. After making observations of our sample, we draw inferences about the population, based on the sample. This inferential process works well as long as the sample is reasonably representative of the population.

Thus, statistically significant results are findings that usually support a research hypothesis.

The requirement that there be fewer than 5 chances in 100 that research results are due to chance is the *minimum* requirement for statistical significance. When this requirement is met, we say the results are significant at the .05 level. If researchers calculate that there is less than 1 chance in 100 that their results are due to chance factors in sampling, the results are significant at the .01 level. If there is less than a 1 in 1000 chance that findings are attributable to sampling error, the results are significant at the .001 level. Thus, there are several *levels* of significance that you may see cited in scientific articles.

Because we're dealing only in matters of probability, there is always the possibility that our decision to accept or reject the null hypothesis is wrong. The various significance levels indicate the probability of erroneously rejecting the null hypothesis (and inaccurately accepting the research hypothesis). At the .05 level of significance, there are 5 chances in 100 that we've made a mistake when we conclude that our results support our hypothesis, and at the .01 level of significance, the chance of an erroneous conclusion is 1 in 100. Although researchers keep the probability of this type of error quite low, the probability is never 0. This is one of the reasons why competently executed studies of the same question can yield contradictory findings. The contradictory findings may be due to chance variations in sampling that we can't prevent.

What do we find when we evaluate our data linking TV viewing to SAT scores? The calculations indicate that, given our sample size and the variability in our data, the probability of obtaining a correlation of $-.24$ by chance is greater than 20%. That's not a high probability, but it's *not* low enough to reject the null hypothesis. Thus, our findings are not strong enough to allow us to conclude that our results support our hypothesis.

Statistics and Empiricism

In summary, conclusions based on empirical research are a matter of probability, and there's always a possibility that the conclusions are wrong. However, two major strengths of the empirical approach are its precision and its intolerance of error. Scientists can give you precise estimates of the likelihood that their conclusions are wrong, and because they're intolerant of error, they hold this probability extremely low. It's their reliance on statistics that allows them to accomplish these goals.

GLOSSARY

A

Ablation Surgical removal of a piece of the brain.

Absolute refractory period The minimum length of time after an action potential during which another action potential cannot begin.

Absolute threshold The minimum amount of physical stimulation that an organism can detect for a specific type of sensory input.

Accommodation The process of changing existing mental structures to explain new experiences.

Achievement motive The need to master difficult challenges, to outperform others, and to meet high standards of excellence.

Achievement tests Standardized tests designed to gauge a person's mastery and knowledge of various subjects.

Acquisition The formation of a new conditioned response tendency.

Action potential A brief change in a neuron's electrical charge that travels along an axon.

Additive color mixing Formation of color by superimposing lights of different colors; such blending puts more light in the mixture than in any one light by itself.

Adoption studies Studies designed to assess hereditary influence by examining the resemblance between adopted children and both their biological and their adoptive parents.

Afferent fibers Axons that carry information inward to the central nervous system from the periphery of the body.

Affiliation motive The need to associate with others and to maintain social bonds.

Afterimage A visual image that persists after a stimulus is removed.

Aggression Any behavior that is intended to hurt someone, either physically or verbally.

Agonist A chemical that mimics the action of a neurotransmitter.

Agoraphobia Fear of going out to public places.

Alcohol A general term encompassing a variety of beverages that contain ethyl alcohol.

Altruism Selfless concern for the welfare of others that leads to helping behavior, without any expectation of personal gain.

Amnesia A significant memory loss that is too extensive to be due to normal forgetting.

Androgens The principal class of male sex hormones.

Animism The belief, characteristic of the preoperational stage of development, that all things are living.

Antagonist A chemical that opposes the action of a neurotransmitter.

Antecedents Events that typically precede a particular behavior.

Anterograde amnesia Loss of memory of events that occur after the injury that caused the memory loss.

Antianxiety drugs Drugs that relieve tension, apprehension, and nervousness.

Antidepressants Drugs that gradually elevate mood and help to relieve depression.

Antipsychotic drugs Drugs used to gradually reduce psychotic symptoms, including hyperactivity, mental confusion, hallucinations, and delusions.

Antisocial personality disorder A disorder marked by impulsive, callous, manipulative, aggressive, and irresponsible behavior that reflects a failure to accept social norms.

Anxiety disorders A class of psychological disorders marked by feelings of excessive apprehension and anxiety.

Aphasia A disorder marked by language and speech deficits attributable to brain damage.

Aphrodisiacs Substances thought to increase sexual desire.

Applied psychology That branch of psychology that applies the scientific findings of the field to everyday, practical problems.

Approach-approach conflict A conflict that requires that a choice be made between two attractive goals.

Approach-avoidance conflict A conflict that requires that a choice be made about whether to pursue a single goal that has both attractive and unattractive aspects.

Aptitude tests Tests designed to assess talent for specific kinds of learning.

Archetypes Emotionally charged images and thought forms that have universal meaning.

Ascending reticular activating system (ARAS) The afferent fibers running through the reticular formation; the ARAS influences physiological arousal.

Assimilation Interpretation of new experiences in terms of mental structures already available, without changing the mental structures.

Atherosclerosis A gradual narrowing of the coronary arteries as the result of fatty deposits.

Attachment A close, emotional bond of affection between an infant and its caregiver.

Attention The focusing of awareness on a narrowed range of stimuli or events.

Attitudes Social judgments that locate objects of thought on evaluative dimensions; these judgments include cognitive, affective, and behavioral components.

Attributions Inferences that people draw about the causes of events, others' behavior, and their own behavior.

Auditory system The organ system responsible for the sense of hearing.

Automatic processes Processes that occur with little awareness, require minimal attention, and do not interfere much with other activities.

Autonomic nervous system That part of the peripheral nervous system that is made up of nerves that connect to the heart, blood vessels, smooth muscles, and glands.

Aversion therapy A behavior therapy in which a noxious stimulus is paired with another stimulus to alter one's response to that stimulus; it is usually used to create a conditioned aversion to stimuli that previously elicited maladaptive behaviors, such as gambling, shoplifting, or sexual deviance.

Avoidance-avoidance conflict A conflict that requires that a choice be made between two unattractive goals.

Avoidance learning Learning that results in a response that prevents aversive stimulation from occurring.

Axon A long, thin fiber that transmits signals away from the soma of a neuron to other neurons, or to muscles or glands.

B

Balance The condition that exists when liking relations fit together harmoniously.

Basal metabolic rate The human body's rate of energy output at rest after a 12-hour fast.

Baseline period A span of time before a behavior modification program begins, during which a target behavior is systematically observed.

Basilar membrane A membrane that runs the length of the cochlea and holds the auditory receptors, called hair cells.

Behavior modification A systematic approach to changing behavior through the application of the principles of conditioning.

Behavior therapies The application of the principles of learning to direct efforts to change maladaptive behaviors.

Behavioral contract A written agreement outlining a promise to adhere to the contingencies of a behavior modification program.

Behaviorism A theoretical orientation based on the premise that scientific psychology should study only observable behavior.

Biaural listening An experimental technique in which a subject hears two separate auditory inputs that are sent simultaneously to both ears.

Binocular cues Clues about distance that are obtained by comparing the differing views of the two eyes.

Biofeedback A type of therapy in which an aspect of a person's physiological functioning (such as heart rate) is monitored, and information about it is fed back to the person to facilitate improved control of the physiological process.

Biological rhythms Periodic fluctuations in physiological functioning.

Biomedical therapies Treatment processes involving physiological interventions intended to reduce symptoms associated with psychological disorders.

Biopsychosocial model A theory that holds that physical illness is caused by a complex interaction of biological, psychological, and sociocultural factors.

Bipolar mood disorder A severe psychological disorder marked by the experience of both depressed and manic periods (formerly known as manic-depressive disorder).

Blocking Failure of a stimulus paired with a UCS to become a CS because it is redundant with an established CS.

Blood-brain barrier A semipermeable-membranelike mechanism that stops some chemicals from passing between the bloodstream and the brain.

Bottom-up processing In cognitive processing, a progression from elements to the whole.

Brainstorming A method of generating ideas that involves free expression of ideas while withholding criticism and evaluation.

Burnout Physical, mental, and emotional exhaustion that is attributable to work-related stress.

Bystander effect A paradoxical social phenomenon in which people are less likely to provide needed help when they are in groups than when they are alone.

C

Cannabis The hemp plant from which marijuana, hashish, and THC are derived.

Cardinal trait A dominant trait that characterizes nearly all of a person's behavior; cardinal traits are found in a minority of people.

Case study An in-depth investigation of an individual subject.

Catastrophic thinking Unrealistically pessimistic appraisal of stress that exaggerates the magnitude of one's problems.

Catatonic schizophrenia A type of schizophrenia marked by striking motor disturbances, ranging from muscular rigidity to random motor activity.

Catharsis In Freudian theory, the release of emotional tension.

Cell body See **Soma**

Central nervous system (CNS) The brain and the spinal cord.

Central traits Prominent, general dispositions that characterize one's personality.

Centration The tendency to focus on just one feature of a problem, thus neglecting other important aspects.

Cephalo-caudal trend The head-to-foot direction of motor development.

Cerebral cortex The convoluted outer layer of the cerebrum.

Cerebral hemispheres The right and left halves of the cerebrum.

Cerebrospinal fluid (CSF) A fluid that fills the hollow cavities (ventricles) of the brain and circulates around the brain and spinal cord.

Channel In the process of persuasion, the medium through which a message is sent.

Chromosomes Threadlike strands of DNA (deoxyribonucleic acid) molecules that carry genetic information.

Chunk A group of familiar stimuli stored as a single unit in memory.

Circadian rhythms The 24-hour biological cycles found in humans and many other species.

Classical conditioning A type of learning, first described by Ivan Pavlov, in which a neutral stimulus acquires the ability to evoke a response that was originally evoked by another stimulus; sometimes called *Pavlovian conditioning* in tribute to its discoverer.

Client-centered therapy A type of insight therapy developed by Carl Rogers that emphasizes providing a supportive emotional climate for clients, who play a major role in determining the pace and direction of their therapy.

Clinical psychologists Psychologists who specialize in the diagnosis and treatment of psychological disorders and everyday personal problems.

Clinical psychology The branch of psychology concerned with the diagnosis and treatment of psychological problems and disorders.

Clustering The tendency to remember similar or related items in groups.

Cochlea A fluid-filled, coiled tunnel within the bone of the skull; located in the inner ear, this structure plays a key role in hearing.

Coefficient of determination The percentage of variation in one variable that can be predicted from a correlated variable.

Cognition The mental processes involved in acquiring knowledge.

Cognitive development Age-related transitions in patterns of thinking, including reasoning, remembering, and problem solving.

Cognitive dissonance In dissonance theory, the condition that exists when related cognitions are inconsistent—that is, they contradict each other.

Cognitive therapy An insight therapy, developed by Aaron Beck, that emphasizes recognizing and changing negative thoughts and maladaptive beliefs.

Collective unconscious In Jung's personality theory, a storehouse of latent memory traces inherited from our ancestral past.

Commitment In interpersonal relations, an intent to maintain a relationship in spite of the difficulties and costs that may arise.

Community mental health centers Facilities that provide comprehensive mental health care for their local communities.

Companionate love Warm, trusting, tolerant affection for another whose life is deeply intertwined with one's own.

Compensation An effort to overcome imagined or real inferiorities by developing one's abilities.

Compensatory decision models In decision-making, strategies that allow attractive attributes to compensate for unattractive attributes.

Competency A defendant's capacity to stand trial; called *fitness* in some states.

Complementary colors Pairs of colors that can be additively mixed to produce gray.

Compliance Conforming one's public behavior to social pressure, even though one's private beliefs have not changed.

Conceptual hierarchy A multilevel classification system based on common properties among items.

Concordance rate The percentage of twin pairs or other pairs of relatives that exhibit the same disorder.

Conditioned reinforcer In operant conditioning, a previously neutral stimulus that has become a reinforcer; also called a *secondary reinforcer.*

Conditioned response (CR) A learned reaction to a conditioned stimulus that occurs because of previous conditioning.

Conditioned stimulus (CS) A previously neutral stimulus that has, through conditioning, acquired the capacity to evoke a conditioned response.

Conditioning The simplest form of learning; it involves learning associations between stimuli and responses.

Cones Specialized visual receptors, concentrated in the center of the retina, that play a key role in daylight vision and color vision.

Conflict A state in which two or more incompatible motivations or behavioral impulses compete for expression.

Conformity The tendency for people to yield to real or imagined social pressure.

Confounding of variables In research, a condition that exists when two or more variables vary together in a way that makes it difficult to sort out their independent effects.

Conscious The level of awareness that includes whatever internal or external events you are aware of at a particular point in time.

Consciousness Awareness of internal and external stimuli.

Conservation Piaget's term for the understanding that physical quantities remain constant when nothing is added or taken away, in spite of changes in their shape or appearance.

Construct validity The extent to which there is evidence that a test measures a particular hypothetical construct.

Constructive coping Efforts to deal with stressful events and that are judged to be relatively healthy.

Content validity The degree to which the content of a test is representative of the domain that the test is supposed to cover.

Continuous reinforcement A reinforcement schedule in which every instance of a designated response is reinforced.

Control group In an experiment, a group of subjects who do not receive the special treatment given to the experimental group.

Controlled processes Processes that require alert awareness, absorb our limited attention, and interfere with other ongoing activities.

Convergent thinking A thinking process in which one tries to narrow down a list of alternatives to converge on a single correct answer.

Conversion disorder A type of psychological disorder that involves a significant loss of physical function (with no apparent organic basis), usually in a single organ system.

Coping Active efforts to master, reduce, or tolerate the demands created by stress.

Corpus callosum The band of fibers that connects the two cerebral hemispheres of the brain.

Correlation An association or relationship between two variables.

Correlation coefficient A numerical index of the degree of relationship that exists between two variables.

Counseling psychologists Psychologists who specialize in the treatment of everyday behavioral problems, although they often diagnose and treat psychological disorders as well.

Creativity The generation of ideas that are original, novel, and useful.

Criterion-related validity The degree to which subjects' scores on a test correlate with their scores on an independent criterion (another measure) of the trait assessed by the test.

Critical period A brief time in development during which certain experiences must occur if development is to unfold normally.

Cross-sectional study In research on development, a study that compares groups of subjects of differing age who are observed at a single point in time.

Cumulative recorder An instrument that creates a graphic record of operant responding as a function of time.

D

Dark adaptation The process in which the eyes become more sensitive to light in low illumination.

Decay theory A theory of memory that proposes that forgetting occurs because memory traces fade with time.

Declarative memory Memory for factual information.

Defense mechanisms Largely unconscious reactions that protect a person from unpleasant emotions such as anxiety and guilt.

Defensive attribution A tendency to blame victims for their misfortune, so that we feel less likely to be victimized in a similar way.

Deinstitutionalization The transfer of treatment of mental illness from inpatient institutions to community-based facilities that emphasize outpatient care.

Delusions False beliefs that are maintained even though they are clearly out of touch with reality.

Dendrites Branchlike parts of a neuron that are specialized to receive neural signals.

Dependent variable In an experiment, the variable that is thought to be affected by the manipulation of the independent variable.

Depressive disorder A psychological disorder in which people show persistent feelings of sadness and despair and a loss of interest in previous sources of pleasure.

Depth perception Interpretation of visual cues to determine how near or far away objects are.

Descriptive statistics The use of mathematics to organize and summarize data.

Development The sequence of age-related changes that occur as a person progresses from conception to death.

Developmental norms The average ages at which people display various behaviors and abilities that change with age.

Deviation IQ scores IQ test scores that locate subjects precisely within the normal distribution, using the standard deviation as the unit of measurement.

Diagnosis The act of identifying a disease from its signs and symptoms; distinguishing one illness from another.

Dichotic listening An experimental technique in which a subject hears two separate auditory inputs that are sent simultaneously, with each sent to only one ear.

Discrimination Different, usually unfair, behavior toward the members of an identifiable group.

Discriminative stimuli Cues that influence operant behavior by indicating the probable consequences (reinforcement or nonreinforcement) of a response.

Disorganized schizophrenia A schizophrenic disorder in which a particularly severe deterioration of adaptive behavior is seen.

Displacement Diversion of emotional feelings (usually anger) from their original source to a substitute target.

Dissociation A splitting of mental processes into two separate, simultaneous streams of awareness.

Dissociative disorders A class of disorders in which people lose contact with portions of their consciousness or memory, resulting in disruptions in their sense of identity.

Distal stimuli Stimuli that lie in the distance (that is, in the world outside us).

Divergent thinking A type of thinking that expands the range of alternative answers to a question by generating many possible solutions.

Dominant gene The gene that is expressed when paired genes are heterozygous (different).

Double-blind procedure A research strategy in which neither subjects nor experimenters know which subjects are in the experimental or control groups.

Dream A mental experience during sleep that includes vivid visual images.

Dream analysis Interpretation of the symbolic meaning of dreams.

Drive An internal state of tension that motivates an organism to engage in activities that should reduce this tension.

Dual-coding theory A theory that holds that memory is enhanced by forming both semantic and visual codes, since either can lead to recall.

E

Efferent fibers Axons that carry information outward from the central nervous system to the periphery of the body.

Ego In Freudian theory, the decision-making component of personality that operates according to the reality principle.

Egocentrism A type of thinking characterized by a limited ability to share another person's viewpoint.

Elaboration A method of remembering by linking a stimulus to other information at the time of encoding.

Electrical stimulation of the brain (ESB) An experimental technique in which a weak electrical current is sent into a brain structure to stimulate (activate) it.

Electrocardiograph (EKG) An instrument that records the contractions of the heart.

Electroconvulsive therapy (ECT) A biomedical treatment in which electric shock is used to produce a cortical seizure accompanied by convulsions; used primarily in the treatment of depression.

Electroencephalograph (EEG) A device that monitors the electrical activity of the brain over time by means of recording electrodes attached to the surface of the scalp.

Electromyograph (EMG) An instrument that records muscular activity and tension.

Electro-oculograph (EOG) An instrument that records eye movements.

Elicit To draw out or bring forth; responses governed by classical conditioning are said to be elicited.

Embryonic stage The second stage of prenatal development, lasting from 2 weeks until the end of the second month.

Emit To send forth; responses governed by operant conditioning are said to be emitted.

Emotion A subjective conscious experience (the cognitive component) accompanied by bodily arousal (the physiological component) and by characteristic overt expressions (the behavioral component).

Emotional deprivation The condition that results when infants get little attention from adult caregivers and when circumstances prevent normal bonding.

Empiricism The premise that knowledge should be acquired through observation.

Encoding Formation of a memory code.

Encoding specificity principle The assumption that the value of a retrieval cue depends on how well it corresponds to the memory code originally used to store the information to be retrieved.

Endocrine system The system of glands that secrete chemicals into the bloodstream that help control bodily functioning.

Endorphins The family of internally produced chemicals that resemble opiates in structure and effects.

Epidemiology The study of the distribution of mental or physical disorders in a population.

Episodic memory The component of long-term memory that is made up of chronological, or temporally dated, recollections of personal experiences.

Erectile difficulties The persistent inability to achieve or maintain a penile erection adequate for intercourse.

Erotophiles People who have very favorable attitudes about sex.

Erotophobes People who have very negative attitudes about sex.

Escape learning Learning that takes place when an organism engages in a response that brings aversive stimulation to an end.

Estrogens The principal class of female sex hormones.

Ethnocentrism A tendency to evaluate people in outgroups from the viewpoint of one's ingroup.

Etiology The apparent causation and developmental history of an illness.

Eugenics Systematic efforts to control reproduction to gradually improve hereditary characteristics in a population.

Excitatory PSP An electric potential that increases the likelihood that a postsynaptic neuron will fire action potentials.

Experiment A reseach method in which the investigator manipulates one or more (independent) variables under carefully controlled conditions and observes whether there are changes in another (dependent) variable as a result.

Experimental group In an experiment, the subjects who receive some special treatment in regard to the independent variable.

External attributions Inferences that ascribe the causes of behavior to situational demands and environmental constraints.

Extinction The gradual weakening and eventual disappearance of a response tendency.

Extraneous variables In an experiment, any variables other than the independent variable that seem likely to influence the dependent variable in a specific study.

Extraverts Outer-directed people who tend to display an interest in the world of people and things.

F

Factor analysis Statistical analysis of correlations among many variables in order to identify groups of closely related variables.

Family studies Scientific studies in which researchers assess hereditary influence by examining blood relatives to see how much they resemble each other with regard to a specific trait.

Feature analysis A process in which we detect specific elements in visual input and assemble these elements into a more complex form.

Feature detectors Neurons that respond selectively to very specific features of more complex stimuli.

Fetal alcohol syndrome A collection of congenital (inborn) problems associated with excessive alcohol use during pregnancy.

Fetal stage The third stage of prenatal development, lasting from 2 months through birth.

Fetishism A form of sexual deviance in which a person is aroused by certain inanimate objects.

Fight-or-flight response A physiological reaction to threat in which the autonomic nervous system prepares the organism for attacking (fight) or fleeing (flight) an enemy.

Fixation A failure to move forward from one developmental stage to another as expected.

Fixed-interval (FI) schedule A schedule of reinforcement in which the reinforcer is given for the first appropriate response that occurs after a fixed time interval has elapsed.

Fixed-ratio (FR) schedule A schedule of reinforcement in which the reinforcer is given after a fixed number of (appropriate) nonreinforced responses.

Flashbulb memories Unusually vivid and detailed recollections of momentous events.

Forebrain The largest and most complicated region of the brain, encompassing a variety of structures including the thalamus, hypothalamus, limbic system, and cerebrum.

Forgetting curve A type of graph that tracks retention and forgetting over time.

Fovea A tiny spot in the center of the retina that contains only cones.

Free association A psychoanalytic procedure in which clients spontaneously express their thoughts and feelings exactly as they occur, with as little censorship as possible.

Frequency distribution An orderly arrangement of scores that indicates how often each score or group of scores occurs.

Frequency polygon A line figure used to present data from a frequency distribution.

Frequency theory A theory of hearing that holds that our perception of pitch corresponds to the rate, or frequency, at which the entire basilar membrane vibrates.

Frustration The blocking of motivated behavior; a situation in which the pursuit of a goal is thwarted.

Functional fixedness The tendency to perceive an object only in terms of its most common use.

Functionalism A school of thought based on the belief that psychology should investigate the function or purpose of consciousness, rather than its structure.

Fundamental attribution error The tendency of an observer to favor internal factors in explaining the behavior of an actor.

G

Galvanic skin response (GSR) An increase in the electrical conductivity of the skin that occurs when sweat glands increase their activity.

Gate-control theory A theory that holds that incoming pain sensations pass through a "gate" in the spinal cord that can be open (allowing perception of pain) or closed (blocking pain perception).

Gender differences Behavioral (rather than biological) disparities between females and males; also known as *sex differences*.

Gender roles Expectations about what is appropriate behavior for each sex; also known as *sex roles*.

General adaptation syndrome A model of the body's stress response, consisting of three stages: alarm, resistance, and exhaustion.

Generalized anxiety disorder A disorder marked by a chronic, high level of anxiety that is not tied to any specific threat.

Genes DNA segments that serve as the key functional units in hereditary transmission.

Genotype A person's genetic makeup.

Germinal stage The first phase of prenatal development, encompassing the first 2 weeks after conception.

Gestalt psychology A theoretical orientation, with a strong interest in perception, emphasizing that the whole may be greater than the sum of its parts.

Glia Cells found throughout the nervous system that provide structural support and insulation for neurons.

Glucose A simple sugar that is an important source of energy.

Glucostats Neurons sensitive to glucose in the surrounding fluid.

Group Two or more individuals who interact and are interdependent.

Group cohesiveness The strength of the liking relationships linking group members to each other and to the group itself.

Group polarization The strengthening, through group discussion, of a group's dominant point of view, with a resultant shift toward a more extreme decision in that direction.

Group therapy The simultaneous psychological treatment of several clients in a group.

Groupthink A process in which members of a cohesive group emphasize concurrence at the expense of critical thinking in arriving at a decision.

Gustatory system The organ system responsible for the sense of taste.

H

Hallucinations Sensory perceptions that occur in the absence of a real, external stimulus; gross distortions of perceptual input.

Hallucinogens A diverse group of drugs that have powerful effects on mental and emotional functioning, marked most prominently by distortions in sensory and perceptual experience.

Hardiness A personality syndrome that is marked by commitment, challenge, and control; hardiness is purportedly associated with strong stress resistance.

Health psychology A field of study concerned with how psychosocial factors relate to the promotion and maintenance of health, and with the causation, prevention, and treatment of illness.

Heritability ratio An estimate of the proportion of trait variability in a population that is determined by variations in genetic inheritance.

Heuristic A strategy or guiding principle used in solving problems.

Hierarchy of needs Maslow's systematic arrangement of needs according to priority, which assumes that basic needs must be met before less basic needs are aroused.

Higher-order conditioning A type of conditioning in which a conditioned stimulus (CS) functions as if it were an unconditioned stimulus (UCS).

Hindbrain A division of the brain that includes the cerebellum and two structures found in the lower part of the brain stem, the medulla and the pons.

Histogram A bar graph that presents data from a frequency distribution.

Holophrases Single-word utterances that represent the meaning of several words.

Homeostasis A state of physiological equilibrium or stability.

Hormones The chemical substances released by the endocrine glands.

Humanism A theoretical orientation that emphasizes the unique qualities of humans, especially their free will and their potential for personal growth.

Hypersomnia A condition marked by a consistent need for an excessive amount of sleep.

Hypnosis A systematic procedure used to produce a heightened state of suggestibility; also, the state of suggestibility produced by such techniques.

Hypochondriasis (hypochondria) Excessive preoccupation with health concerns and incessant worry about developing physical illnesses.

Hypothalamus A structure near the base of the forebrain that is involved in the regulation of basic biological needs such as hunger and thirst.

Hypothesis A tentative statement about the relationship between two (or more) variables.

I

Id In Freudian theory, the primitive, instinctive component of personality that operates according to the pleasure principle.

Identification The bolstering of one's self-esteem by forming an imaginary or real alliance with some other person or with a group.

Illusory correlation effect A misperception that occurs when we estimate that we have encountered more confirmations of an association between social traits than we have actually seen.

Immune response The body's defensive reaction to invasion by bacteria, viral agents, or other foreign substances.

Imprinting An "instinctive" form of learning that occurs when an animal forms a strong social attachment (usually to its mother) during a critical period shortly after birth.

Incentive An external goal that has the capacity to motivate behavior.

Incongruence In Carl Rogers's personality theory, the degree of disparity between one's self-concept and one's actual experience.

Independent variable A condition or event that an experimenter varies in order to see its impact on another (dependent) variable.

Inferential statistics The use of mathematics to interpret data and draw conclusions.

Inferiority complex Exaggerated feelings of weakness and inadequacy.

Information-processing theories Theories of memory that emphasize how information flows through a series of separate memory stores.

Ingratiation A conscious effort to cultivate others' liking by complimenting them, agreeing with them, or doing them favors.

Ingroup The group one belongs to and identifies with.

Inhibitory PSP An electric potential that decreases the likelihood that a postsynaptic neuron will fire action potentials.

Insanity A legal status indicating that a person cannot be held responsible for his or her actions because of mental illness.

Insight The sudden discovery of the correct solution to a problem following incorrect attempts based primarily on trial and error.

Insight therapies Approaches to psychotherapy in which verbal interactions between therapist and client are intended to enhance the client's self-knowledge and thus promote healthful changes in personality and behavior.

Insomnia A condition characterized by chronic problems in getting adequate sleep.

Instinctive drift The tendency for an animal's innate responses to interfere with conditioning processes.

Instincts Behavioral patterns that are (1) unlearned, (2) uniform in expression, and (3) universal in a species.

Instrumental learning *See* **Operant conditioning**

Insulin A hormone secreted by the pancreas, which is important in the body's ability to metabolize sugars.

Intelligence quotient (IQ) A child's mental age divided by chronological age, multiplied by 100.

Intelligence tests Tests devised to measure general mental ability.

Interference theory A theory of memory that proposes that people forget information because of competition from other material.

Intermittent reinforcement A reinforcement schedule in which a designated response is reinforced only some of the time; also called *partial reinforcement*.

Internal attribution Inferences that ascribe the causes of behavior to individuals' dispositions, traits, abilities, and feelings.

Interpersonal attraction Positive feelings toward another.

Interpretation In insight therapies, the therapist's attempts to explain the inner significance of the client's thoughts, feelings, memories, or behaviors.

Intimacy Warmth, closeness, and sharing in a relationship.

Intimacy motive The need to have warm, close exchanges with others marked by open communication.

Introspection Careful, systematic observation of one's own conscious experience.

Introverts Inner-directed people who tend to be preoccupied with the internal world of their own thoughts, feelings, and experiences.

Involuntary commitment Hospitalization in psychiatric facilities against the will of the individual who is hospitalized.

Irreversibility The inability to envision reversing an action.

J

Journal A periodical that publishes technical and scholarly material, usually in a narrowly defined area of inquiry.

Just noticeable difference (JND) The smallest difference in the amount of physical stimulation that a specific sense can detect.

K

Keyword method A method of memory encoding in which you associate a concrete word with an abstract word and generate an image to represent the concrete word.

Kinesthetic sense The sensory system that monitors the positions of the various parts of the body.

L

Language A collection of symbols and of rules for combining the symbols that can be used to create an infinite variety of messages.

Latent content The hidden or disguised meaning of the events in the plot of a dream.

Lateral antagonism Neural activity in a cell that opposes activity in surrounding cells.

Latitude of acceptance A range of potentially acceptable positions on an issue centered on one's initial attitude position.

Law of effect The assumption that if a response in the presence of a stimulus leads to satisfying effects, the association between the stimulus and the response will be strengthened.

Learned helplessness Passive behavior produced by exposure to unavoidable aversive events.

Learning A relatively durable change in behavior or knowledge that is due to experience.

Lens The transparent eye structure that focuses the light rays falling on the retina.

Lesioning Destruction of a piece of the brain.

Levels of processing theory The theory that proposes that deeper levels of processing result in longer-lasting memory codes.

Lexical decision task A task in which people are shown a string of letters and must decide as quickly as they can whether the string of letters forms a word.

Lie detector *see* **Polygraph**

Life changes Noticeable alterations in one's living circumstances that require readjustment.

Light adaptation The process whereby the eyes become less sensitive to light in high illumination.

Limbic system A loosely connected network of structures located beneath the cerebral cortex, involved in the control of emotion, motivation, and memory.

Link method Formation of a mental image of items to be remembered in a way that links them together.

Lithium A chemical used to control mood swings in patients with bipolar mood disorders.

Locus of control A generalized expectancy about the degree to which we control our outcomes.

Longitudinal study A study in which one group of subjects is observed repeatedly at different ages over a period of time.

Long-term memory (LTM) An unlimited capacity memory store that can hold information over lengthy periods of time.

M

Manifest content The plot of a dream at a surface level.

Matching hypothesis A hypothesis that proposes that males and females of approximately equal physical attractiveness are likely to select each other as partners.

Maturation Development that reflects the gradual unfolding of one's genetic blueprint.

Mean The arithmetic average of a set of scores.

Means/end analysis The process of identifying differences that exist between the current state and the goal state, and making changes that will reduce these differences.

Median The score that falls exactly in the center of a distribution of scores.

Medical model The view that it is useful to think of abnormal behavior as a disease.

Meditation A family of mental exercises in which a conscious attempt is made to focus attention in a nonanalytical way.

Mental age In intelligence testing, a score that indicates that a child displays the mental ability typical of a child of that chronological (actual) age.

Mental hospital A medical institution specializing in providing inpatient care for people with psychological disorders.

Mental retardation Subnormal general mental ability accompanied by deficiencies in everyday living skills originating prior to age 18.

Message In the process of persuasion, the information transmitted by the source.

Meta-analysis The process of combining the statistical results of many studies of the same question to yield an estimate of the size and consistency of a variable's effects.

Metalinguistic awareness The ability to reflect on the use of language.

Method of loci A method of recall that involves taking an imaginary walk along a familiar path where you have associated images of items you want to remember with certain locations.

Midbrain The segment of the brain stem that lies between the hindbrain and the forebrain.

Mnemonic devices Strategies and techniques for enhancing memory.

Mode The score that occurs most frequently in a set of scores.

Model A person whose behavior is observed and imitated by another.

Monocular cues Clues about distance that are obtained from the image in either eye alone.

Mood disorders A class of disorders marked by emotional disturbances that may spill over to disrupt physical, perceptual, social, and thought processes.

Morphemes The smallest units of meaning in a language.

Motivated forgetting Purposeful suppression of memories; also known as *repression*.

Motivation Goal-directed behavior.

Motor development The progression of muscular coordination required for physical activities.

Motor neurons Nerve cells that transmit messages to the muscles that actually move the body.

Multiple-personality disorder A psychological disorder in which two or more largely complete, and usually very different, personalities coexist within one person.

Myelin sheath Insulating material, derived from glial cells, that encases some axons.

N

Narcolepsy A disease marked by sudden and irresistible onsets of sleep during normal waking hours.

Narcotics Drugs derived from opium that are capable of relieving pain; also called *opiates*.

Naturalistic observation Careful, usually prolonged, observation of behavior by a researcher without direct intervention with subjects.

Need for self-actualization In Maslow's theory, the need to fulfill one's potential.

Negative reinforcement Reinforcement that occurs when a response is strengthened because it is followed by the removal of a (presumably) unpleasant stimulus.

Negatively skewed distribution A distribution in which most scores pile up at the high end of the scale.

Nerves Bundles of neuron fibers (axons) that travel together in the peripheral nervous system.

Neuromodulators Chemicals that increase or decrease (modulate) the activity of specific neurotransmitters.

Neurons Individual cells in the nervous system that receive, integrate, and transmit information.

Neurotic A term used to describe behavior marked by subjective distress (usually chronic anxiety) and reliance on avoidance coping.

Neurotransmitters Chemicals that transmit information from one neuron to another.

Night terrors Abrupt awakenings from NREM sleep accompanied by intense autonomic arousal and feelings of panic.

Nightmares Anxiety-arousing dreams that lead to awakening, usually from REM sleep.

Noncompensatory decision models Decision-making strategies that do not allow some attributes to compensate for others.

Noncontingent reinforcement Reinforcement that occurs when a response is strengthened even though delivery of the reinforcer was not a result of the response.

Non-REM (NREM) sleep Sleep stages 1 through 4, which are marked by an absence of rapid eye movements, relatively little dreaming, and variations in EEG activity.

Nonsense syllables In memory research, consonant-vowel-consonant letter arrangements that do not correspond to words.

Normal distribution A symmetric, bell-shaped curve that represents the pattern in which many characteristics are dispersed in a population.

Null hypothesis In inferential statistics, the postulate that there is no true difference between groups on the dependent variable, or no true relationship between the variables observed.

O

Obedience A form of compliance that occurs when people follow direct commands, usually from someone in a position of authority.

Object permanence A child's recognition that objects continue to exist even when they are no longer visible to the child.

Observational learning The type of learning that occurs when an organism's responding is influenced by the observation of others, who are called models.

Obsessive-compulsive disorder A psychological disorder marked by persistent, uncontrollable intrusions of unwanted thoughts (obsessions) and by urges to engage in senseless rituals (compulsions).

Occupational interest inventories Personality tests that examine interests as they relate to various vocations.

Oedipal complex In Freudian theory, a child's manifestation of erotically tinged desires for the opposite-sex parent, accompanied by feelings of hostility toward the same-sex parent.

Olfactory system The organ system responsible for the sense of smell.

Operant conditioning A form of learning in which voluntary responses come to be controlled by their consequences; also called *instrumental learning*.

Operational definition A definition that describes the actions or operations that will be made to measure or control a variable.

Operations In Piaget's theory, internal transformations, manipulations, and reorganizations of mental structures.

Opiates *See* **Narcotics**

Opponent process theory The theory of color vision that holds that color is perceived in three channels, where an either-or response is made to pairs of antagonistic colors.

Optic nerve A collection of axons from the retina that connect the eye with the brain.

Optimism A general tendency to expect good outcomes.

Orgasm The discharge of sexual tension in a series of muscular contractions that pulsate through the pelvic area.

Orgasmic difficulties A sexual dysfunction in which people experience sexual arousal but have persistent problems in achieving orgasm.

Outgroup People who are not part of an ingroup.

Overextension Incorrect use of a word to describe a wider set of objects or actions than its meaning encompasses.

Overlearning Continued rehearsal of material after first mastery of it.

P

Panic disorder A psychological disorder characterized by recurrent attacks of overwhelming anxiety that usually occur suddenly and unexpectedly.

Parallel play Side-by-side play among young children that goes on with little shared interaction.

Paranoid schizophrenia A type of schizophrenic disorder dominated by delusions of persecution along with delusions of grandeur.

Parasympathetic division The branch of the autonomic nervous system that generally conserves bodily resources.

Partial reinforcement *See* **Intermittent reinforcement**

Passionate love Complete absorption in another, including tender sexual feelings and the agony and ecstasy of intense emotion.

Pavlovian conditioning *See* **Classical conditioning**

Percentile score An indicator of the percentage of people taking a test who score below a particular score.

Perception The selection, organization, and interpretation of sensory input.

Perceptual constancy A tendency to experience a stable perception in the face of continually changing sensory input.

Perceptual hypothesis An inference about what distal stimuli could be responsible for the proximal stimuli sensed.

Perceptual set A readiness to perceive a stimulus in a particular way, due to one's expectations.

Peripheral nervous system All those nerves that lie outside the brain and spinal cord.

Person perception The process of forming impressions of others.

Personal unconscious According to Jung, the level of awareness that houses material that is not within one's conscious awareness because it has been repressed or forgotten.

Personality An individual's unique constellation of consistent behavioral traits.

Personality disorders A class of psychological disorders marked by extreme, inflexible personality traits that cause subjective distress or impaired social and occupational functioning.

Personality tests Tests designed to measure various aspects of personality, including motives, interests, values, and attitudes.

Personality theories Systems of related ideas used to explain the development, structure, and functioning of personality.

Personality trait A durable disposition to behave in a particular way in a variety of situations.

Phenomenological approach The assumption that we have to appreciate individuals' personal, subjective experiences to truly understand their behavior.

Phenotype The manifestation of a person's genotype in observable characteristics.

Pheromone A chemical secreted by one animal that affects the behavior of another.

Phi phenomenon The illusion of movement created by presenting visual stimuli in rapid succession.

Phobias Irrational fears of specific objects or situations.

Phobic disorder A psychological disorder marked by a persistent and irrational fear of an object or situation that presents no realistic danger.

Phonemes The smallest units of sound in a spoken language.

Phonemic code A memory code that emphasizes what a word sounds like.

Phrase-structure rules Rules of a language that specify how words can be combined into phrases and phrases into sentences.

Physical dependence A condition in which a person must continue to take a drug to avoid withdrawal illness.

Pituitary gland An endocrine gland, located near the hypothalamus, that releases a great variety of hormones that circulate throughout the body, stimulating actions in the other endocrine glands.

Place theory The theory of hearing that holds that our perception of pitch corresponds to the vibration of different portions, or places, along the basilar membrane.

Placebo effects Changes experienced by experimental subjects from an empty, fake, or ineffectual treatment and assumed to occur because of the subjects' expectations.

Placenta The structure that connects the circulation of the fetus and that of the mother.

Pleasure principle In Freudian theory, the id's demand for immediate gratification of its urges.

Polygenic traits Characteristics that are influenced by more than one pair of genes.

Polygraph A device that records autonomic fluctuations while a subject is questioned, to draw inferences about the truthfulness of the subject's responses; also called a *lie detector*.

Population In an empirical study, the collection of animals or people (that the researcher wants to generalize about from which a sample is drawn).

Positive reinforcement Reinforcement that occurs when a response is strengthened because it is followed by the arrival of a (presumably) pleasant stimulus.

Positively skewed distribution A distribution in which scores pile up at the low end of the scale.

Postsynaptic potential (PSP) A voltage change at the receptor site of a neuron; PSPs vary in magnitude and may be either excitatory or inhibitory.

Posttraumatic stress disorder Disturbed behavior that is attributed to a major stressful event but that emerges after the stress is over.

Preconscious The level of awareness that contains material just beneath the surface of conscious awareness that can easily be retrieved.

Prejudice An attitude, usually negative, held toward members of a specific group.

Premature ejaculation Impairment of sexual relations because a man consistently reaches orgasm too quickly.

Prenatal period The developmental period that extends from conception to birth, usually encompassing 9 months of pregnancy.

Preparedness A species-specific predisposition to be conditioned in certain ways and not in others.

Pressure Expectations or demands that one behave in a certain way.

Prevalence The percentage of a population that exhibits a disorder during a specified time period.

Primacy effect Better recall of items at the beginning of a list than of other items in the list.

Primary appraisal An initial evaluation of whether an event is (1) irrelevant to you, (2) relevant, but not threatening, or (3) stressful.

Primary reinforcers Stimulus events that are inherently reinforcing because they satisfy biological needs.

Proactive interference A memory effect in which previously learned information interferes with the retention of new information.

Procedural memory Memory for actions, skills, and operations.

Prognosis A forecast about the probable course of an illness.

Programmed learning An approach to self-instruction in which information and questions are arranged in a sequence of small steps to permit active responding by the learner.

Projection Attribution of one's own thoughts, feelings, or motives to another.

Projective tests A class of psychological tests that ask subjects to respond to vague, ambiguous stimuli in ways that may reveal the subjects' needs, feelings, and personality traits.

Proximal stimuli The stimulus energies that act directly on the sensory receptors.

Proximity Geographic, residential, or some other form of spatial closeness.

Proximo-distal trend The center-outward direction of motor development.

Psychiatrists Physicians who specialize in the diagnosis and treatment of psychological disorders.

Psychiatry A branch of medicine concerned with the diagnosis and treatment of psychological problems and disorders.

Psychoactive drugs Chemical substances that modify mental, emotional, or behavioral functioning.

Psychoanalysis A type of insight therapy, developed by Sigmund Freud, that emphasizes the recovery of unconscious conflicts, motives, and defenses through techniques such as free association and transference.

Psychoanalytic theory A theory developed by Sigmund Freud that attempts to explain personality, motivation, and psychological disorders by focusing on unconscious determinants of behavior.

Psychodynamic theories The diverse theories descended from the work of Sigmund Freud that focus on unconscious mental forces.

Psychogenic amnesia A sudden, abnormal loss of memory for important personal information that is not caused by organic damage.

Psycholinguistics The study of the psychological mechanisms underlying the acquisition and use of language.

Psychological dependence The need to continue to take a drug in order to satisfy intense emotional craving for the drug.

Psychological test A standardized measure of a sample of a person's behavior; used to measure individual differences in personality traits and mental abilities.

Psychology The science that studies behavior and the physiological and cognitive processes that underlie it, and the profession that applies the accumulated knowledge of this science to practical problems.

Psychopharmacotherapy The treatment of mental disorders with medication.

Psychophysics The study of how physical stimuli are translated into psychological (sensory) experience.

Psychosexual stages In Freudian theory, developmental periods with a characteristic sexual focus that leave their mark on adult personality.

Psychosomatic diseases Physical ailments with a genuine organic basis that are caused in part by psychological factors, especially emotional distress (also called *psychophysiological disorders*).

Psychotic A term used to describe behavior that is marked by impaired reality contact and profound deterioration of adaptive functioning.

Puberty The period of early adolescence marked by rapid physical growth and the development of sexual (reproductive) maturity.

Punishment The condition that occurs when an event that follows a response weakens or suppresses the tendency to make that response.

Pupil The opening in the center of the iris that helps regulate the amount of light passing into the rear chamber of the eye.

R

Random assignment of subjects Constitution of groups in a study so that all subjects have an equal chance of being assigned to any group or condition in the study.

Rational-emotive therapy An approach to therapy, developed by Albert Ellis, that focuses on altering clients' patterns of irrational thinking to reduce maladaptive emotions and behavior.

Rationalization Creating false but plausible excuses to justify unacceptable behavior.

Reaction formation Behaving in a way that is exactly the opposite of one's true feelings.

Reaction range Genetically determined limits on IQ or other traits.

Readability The ease with which different kinds of text can be read.

Reality principle In Freudian theory, the ego's attempt to delay gratification of the id's urges until appropriate outlets and situations can be found.

Recall measure A method of measuring memory retention that requires subjects to reproduce information on their own without any cues.

Receiver In the process of persuasion, the person to whom the message is sent.

Recency effect Better recall of items at the end of a list than of other items on the list.

Receptive field of a visual cell The retinal area that, when stimulated, affects the firing of a particular visual cell.

Recessive gene A gene that is masked when paired genes are heterozygous.

Reciprocal determinism In Bandura's social learning theory, the assumption that internal mental events, external environmental events, and overt behavior all influence each other.

Reciprocity Liking those who show that they like us.

Recognition measure A method of measuring memory retention that requires subjects to select previously learned information from an array of options.

Reference group A particular group of people used as a standard in social comparisons.

Refractory period A period of time following orgasm during which males are largely unresponsive to further stimulation.

Regression Reversion to immature patterns of behavior.

Rehearsal The process of repetitively verbalizing or thinking about information.

Reinforcement The condition that occurs when an event following a response strengthens the tendency to make that response.

Reinforcement contingencies Circumstances or rules that determine whether responses lead to the presentation of a reinforcer.

Relearning measure A method of measuring memory retention that requires a subject to memorize information a second time to determine how much time or effort is saved by having learned it before.

Reliability The measurement consistency of a test (or other kind of measurement technique).

REM rebound A sleep phenomenon in which a person spends extra time in REM periods for one or more nights after REM deprivation.

REM sleep A deep stage of sleep marked by rapid eye movements, high-frequency brain waves, and dreaming.

Replication The repetition of a study to see whether earlier results are duplicated.

Repression Keeping distressing thoughts and feelings buried in the unconscious.

Research method A strategy or procedure for collecting empirical data.

Resistance Largely unconscious defensive maneuvers intended to hinder the progress of therapy.

Resistance to extinction In operant conditioning, the effect demonstrated when an organism continues to make a response after delivery of the reinforcer for it has been terminated.

Respondent conditioning *See* **Classical conditioning**

Response set A systematic tendency to respond to questionnaire items in a particular way that is unrelated to the content of the questions.

Resting potential The stable, negative charge of a neuron when the cell in inactive.

Retention The proportion of material retained (remembered).

Retina The neural tissue lining the inside back surface of the eye.

Retrieval Recovery of information from memory stores.

Retroactive interference A memory effect in which new information impairs the retention of previously learned information.

Retrograde amnesia Loss of memory of events that occurred prior to the injury that caused the memory loss.

Reuptake A process in which neurotransmitters are taken up from the synaptic cleft by the presynaptic membrane.

Reversible figure A drawing that is compatible with two different interpretations that can shift back and forth.

Risky decision making Making decisions under conditions of uncertainty.

Rods Specialized visual receptors that play a key role in night vision and peripheral vision.

S

Sample The collection of subjects selected for observation in an empirical study.

Scatter diagram A graph in which paired X and Y scores for each subject are plotted as single points.

Schedule of reinforcement A specific pattern of presentation of reinforcers over time.

Schema An organized cluster of knowledge about a particular object or sequence of events.

Schizophrenic disorders A class of disorders marked by disturbances in thought that spill over to affect perceptual, social, and emotional processes.

Script A special type of schema that organizes what people know about common sequences of events.

Seasonal affective disorder A mood disorder in which periods of depression or mania tend to repeatedly occur at about the same time each year.

Secondary appraisal An evaluation of one's coping resources and options for dealing with a stressful event.

Secondary reinforcer *See* **Conditioned reinforcer**

Secondary sex characteristics Physical features that are associated with gender but that are not directly involved in reproduction.

Secondary traits Behavioral dispositions that surface in some situations but not others.

Sedatives Sleep-inducing drugs.

Self-actualizing persons In Maslow's theory, people with exceptionally healthy personalities, marked by continued personal growth.

Self-concept A collection of beliefs about one's own nature, unique qualities, and typical behavior.

Self-efficacy A person's belief about his or her own ability to perform behaviors that should lead to expected outcomes.

Self-esteem A person's overall assessment of her or his personal adequacy or worth.

Self-monitoring A personality trait that involves the degree to which people attend to and control the impression they make on others in social interactions.

Self-report inventories Personality tests that ask individuals to answer a series of questions about their characteristic behavior.

Self-serving bias The tendency to attribute one's positive outcomes to personal factors and one's negative outcomes to situational factors.

Semantic code A memory code that emphasizes the meaning of verbal input.

Semantic memory Memory of general knowledge that is not tied to the time when the information was learned.

Semantic network A model of memory organization in which concepts are joined together by links that show how the concepts are related.

Senility An abnormal deterioration in mental faculties seen in about 5% of people over 65.

Sensate focus An exercise in which partners take turns pleasuring each other sexually with guided verbal feedback, while certain kinds of stimulation are temporarily forbidden.

Sensation The stimulation of sense organs.

Sensation seeking A generalized preference for high or low levels of sensory stimulation.

Sensory adaptation A gradual decline in sensitivity to prolonged stimulation.

Sensory memory A memory store in which information is preserved in its original sensory form for a very brief time, usually only a fraction of a second.

Sensory neurons Neurons that receive information from outside the nervous system.

Separation anxiety Emotional distress seen in many infants when they are separated from people with whom they have formed an attachment.

Serial position effect Better recall for items at the beginning and end of a list than for items in the middle.

Set point A natural point of stability in body weight.

Sex differences *See* **Gender differences**

Sex roles *See* **Gender roles**

Sex therapy The professional treatment of sexual dysfunctions.

Sexual dysfunctions Impairments in sexual functioning that cause subjective distress.

Shaping In operant conditioning, the reinforcement of closer and closer approximations of the desired response.

Short-term memory (STM) A limited-capacity memory store that can maintain unrehearsed information for about 20 to 30 seconds.

Signal-detection theory The theory that sensory sensitivity depends on a variety of factors besides the physical intensity of a stimulus.

Skinner box A small enclosure in which an animal can make a specific response that is systematically recorded and in which the consequences of the response are controlled.

Sleep apnea Frequent, reflexive gasping for air that awakens a person and disrupts sleep.

Social comparison theory The theory that we compare ourselves with others to understand and evaluate our behavior.

Social desirability bias A tendency seen in some people to provide socially approved answers about oneself in responding to questionnaires.

Social interest In Alfred Adler's personality theory, an innate sense of kinship and belongingness with the human race.

Social loafing A reduction in effort by individuals when they work in groups as compared to when they work by themselves.

Social psychology The branch of psychology concerned with the way individuals' thoughts, feelings, and behaviors are influenced by others.

Social schemas Organized clusters of ideas about categories of social events and people.

Social skills training A behavior therapy designed to improve interpersonal skills.

Social support Aid and succor provided by members of one's social networks.

Socialization The acquisition of the norms, roles, and behaviors expected of people in a particular society (or smaller social group).

Sociobiology The study of the biological basis of social behavior in all organisms, including humans.

Soma The body of a cell, which contains the cell nucleus and much of the chemical machinery common to most cells; also called *cell body.*

Somatic nervous system That part of the nervous system that is made up of nerves that connect to voluntary skeletal muscles and sensory receptors.

Somatization disorder A psychological disorder marked by a history of diverse physical complaints that appear to be psychological in origin.

Somatoform disorders A class of mental disorders involving physical ailments with no authentic organic basis that are due to psychological factors.

Somnambulism The condition that occurs when a sleeping person arises and wanders about in deep NREM sleep (stages 3 and 4); also called *sleepwalking.*

Source In the process of persuasion, the person who sends a communication.

Split-brain surgery The cutting of the bundle of fibers that connects the cerebral hemispheres (the corpus callosum) to reduce the severity of epileptic seizures.

Spontaneous recovery In classical conditioning, the reappearance of an extinguished response after a period of nonexposure to the conditioned stimulus.

Spontaneous remission A recovery that occurs without formal treatment of the disorder.

SQ3R A study system designed to promote effective reading by means of five steps: survey, question, read, recite, and review.

Stage A developmental period during which characteristic patterns of behavior are exhibited and certain capacities become established.

Standard deviation An index of the amount of variability in a set of data.

Standardization The use of uniform procedures in the administration and scoring of a test.

State-dependent memory Improved recall that is attributed to being in the same emotional state during encoding and subsequent retrieval.

Statistical significance The condition in which the probability that observed findings are due to chance is very low, usually fewer than 5 chances in 100.

Statistics The use of mathematics to organize, summarize, and interpret numerical data.

Stereotaxic instrument A device used to implant electrodes in research animals at precise locations in their brains.

Stereotypes Widely held beliefs that people have certain characteristics because they belong to a particular group.

Stimulants Drugs that tend to increase central nervous system activation and behavioral activity.

Stimulus Any detectable input from the environment.

Stimulus contiguity The condition that occurs when there is a temporal (time) association between two stimulus events.

Stimulus discrimination The condition in which an organism does not respond to stimuli that are similar to the original stimulus used in conditioning.

Stimulus generalization The condition in which an organism responds to new stimuli that are similar to the original stimulus used in conditioning.

Storage Maintenance of encoded information in memory over time.

Stress Any circumstances that threaten or are perceived to threaten one's well-being and that thereby tax one's coping abilities.

Striving for superiority In Alfred Adler's theory of personality, a universal drive to adapt, improve oneself, and master life's challenges.

Structural code A memory code that emphasizes the physical structure of a stimulus.

Structuralism A school of thought that held that the task of psychology was to analyze consciousness into its basic elements and to investigate how these elements were related.

Subjects The persons or animals whose behavior is systematically observed in an empirical study.

Subtractive color mixing Formation of colors by removing some wavelengths of light, leaving less light than was originally there.

Superego In Freudian theory, the moral component of personality that incorporates social standards about what represents right and wrong.

Survey A structured questionnaire designed to solicit information about specific aspects of a subject's behavior.

Sympathetic division The branch of the autonomic nervous system that mobilizes the body's resources for emergencies.

Synapse A junction where information is transmitted from one neuron to the next.

Synaptic cleft A microscopic gap between the terminal button of the sending neuron and the cell membrane of the receiving neuron.

Syntax A system of rules that specify how words can be combined into phrases and sentences.

Systematic desensitization A behavior therapy used to reduce clients' anxiety responses through counterconditioning.

T

Tactile system The organ system responsible for the sense of touch.

Tardive dyskinesia A neurological disorder marked by chronic tremors and involuntary spastic movements that is a common side effect of treatment with antipsychotic drugs.

Telegraphic speech Speech that omits nonessential words, consisting mainly of content words.

Temperament A person's characteristic mood, energy level, and reactivity.

Terminal buttons Small knoblike projections at the end of an axon that secrete chemicals called neurotransmitters.

Test norms Standards that provide information about where a score on a psychological test ranks in relation to other scores on that test.

Test-retest reliability An estimate of a test's measurement consistency that is made by comparing subjects' scores on two administrations of the same test.

Testwiseness The ability to use the characteristics and formats of a cognitive test to maximize one's score.

Thalamus A structure in the forebrain through which all sensory information (except smell) must pass to get to the cerebral cortex.

Theoretical eclecticism Selection of what appears to be best from a variety of theories or systems of therapy.

Theory A system of interrelated ideas that is used to explain a certain set of observations.

Threshold A dividing point between energy levels that do and do not have a detectable effect.

Tip-of-the-tongue phenomenon A temporary inability to remember something accompanied by a feeling that the information is just out of reach.

Token economy A behavior therapy designed to increase desirable responses by doling out symbolic reinforcers for appropriate behaviors.

Tolerance A progressive decrease in a person's responsiveness to a drug.

Top-down processing In cognitive processing, a progression from the whole to its elements.

Transference In psychoanalysis, the process that occurs when clients start relating to their therapist in ways that mimic critical relationships in their lives.

Transformational rules Rules that specify how simple declarative sentences can be rearranged into questions, negatives, and other types of sentences.

Transvestism A sexual disorder in which a man achieves sexual arousal by dressing in women's clothing.

Trial In classical conditioning, any presentation of a stimulus or pair of stimuli.

Trichromatic theory A theory of color vision that proposes that the human eye has three types of receptors with differing sensitivities to different wavelengths of light.

Twin studies Empirical studies in which researchers assess hereditary influence by comparing the resemblance of identical twins and fraternal twins with respect to a trait.

Type A pattern A personality type marked by competitive, aggressive, impatient, hostile behavior; also called *coronary-prone personality.*

Type B pattern A personality type marked by relatively relaxed, patient, easy-going, amicable behavior.

U

Unconditioned response (UCR) An unlearned reaction to an unconditioned stimulus that occurs without previous conditioning.

Unconditioned stimulus (UCS) A stimulus that evokes an unconditioned response without previous conditioning.

Unconscious A level of awareness that contains thoughts, memories, and desires that are well below the surface of conscious awareness but that nonetheless exert great influence on behavior.

Undifferentiated schizophrenia A schizophrenic disorder marked by idiosyncratic mixtures of schizophrenic symptoms.

V

Validity The ability of a test to measure what it was designed to measure.

Variability A measure of how much the scores in a distribution tend to vary or depart from the mean score.

Variable-interval (VI) schedule A reinforcement schedule in which the reinforcer is given for the first appropriate response after a variable time interval has elapsed.

Variable-ratio (VR) schedule A reinforcement schedule in which the reinforcer is given after a variable number of (appropriate) nonreinforced responses.

Variables In an empirical study, any measurable conditions, events, characteristics, or behaviors that are controlled or observed.

Vasocongestion Engorgement of blood vessels.

Vestibular system The organ system that responds to gravity and keeps you informed of your body's location in space.

Visual cliff A glass platform that extends over a several-foot dropoff (the cliff); used to study the development of depth perception in infants.

Visual system The organ system responsible for the sense of sight.

Vocation An urge or commitment to work in a particular kind of occupation.

Volley principle The theory that groups of auditory nerve fibers fire neural impulses in rapid succession, creating volleys of impulses.

W

Weber's law The theory that states that the size of a just noticeable difference is a constant proportion of the size of the initial stimulus.

Z

Zygote A one-celled organism formed by the union of a sperm and an egg.

REFERENCES

A

Aalpoel, P. J., & Lewis, D. J. (1984). Dissociative disorders. In H. E. Adams & P. B. Sutker (Eds.), Comprehensive handbook of psychopathology. New York: Plenum Press.

Abeles, M., & Goldstein, M. H. (1970). Functional architecture in cat primary auditory cortex: Columnar organization and organization according to depth. Journal of Neurophysiology, 33, 172–187.

Abramson, L. Y., Metalsky, G. I., & Alloy, L. B. (1988). The hopelessness theory of depression: Does the research test the theory? In L. Y. Abramson (Ed.), Social cognition and clinical psychology: A synthesis. New York: Guilford Press.

Abramson, L. Y., Seligman, M. E. P., & Teasdale, J. (1978). Learned helplessness in humans: Critique and reformulation. Journal of Abnormal Psychology, 87, 32–48.

Acredolo, L. P., & Hake, J. L. (1982). Infant perception. In B. B. Wolman (Ed.), Handbook of developmental psychology. Englewood Cliffs, NJ: Prentice-Hall.

Adams, J. L. (1980). Conceptual blockbusting. San Francisco: W. H. Freeman.

Adcock, C. J. (1965). Thematic Apperception Test. In O. K. Buros (Ed.), Sixth mental measurements yearbook. Highland Park, NY: Gryphon Press.

Ader, R., & Cohen, N. (1981). Conditioned immunopharmacologic responses. In R. Ader (Ed.), Psychoneuroimmunology. New York: Academic Press.

Ader, R., & Cohen, N. (1984). Behavior and the immune system. In W. D. Gentry (Ed.), Handbook of behavioral medicine. New York: Guilford Press.

Adler, A. (1917). Study of organ inferiority and its psychical compensation. New York: Nervous and Mental Diseases Publishing.

Adler, A. (1927). Practice and theory of individual psychology. New York: Harcourt, Brace & World.

Adler, A. (1964). Superiority and social interest: A collection of later writings. Edited by H. L. Ansbacher & R. Ansbacher. New York: Viking Press.

Adler, C. S., & Adler, S. M. (1984). Biofeedback. In T. B. Karasu (Ed.), The psychiatric therapies. Washington, DC: American Psychiatric Association.

Agras, W. S. (1985). Stress, panic and the cardiovascular system. In A. H. Tuma & J. Maser (Eds.), Anxiety and the anxiety disorders. Hillsdale, NJ: Erlbaum.

Ainsworth, M. D. S. (1979). Attachment as related to mother–infant interaction. In J. S. Rosenblatt, R. A. Hinde, C. Beer, & M. Busnel (Eds.), Advances in the study of behavior (Vol. 9). New York: Academic Press.

Ainsworth, M. D. S., Blehar, M. C., Waters, E., & Wall, S. (1978). Patterns of attachment: A psychological study of the strange situation. Hillsdale, NJ: Erlbaum.

Ajzen, I., & Fishbein, M. (1980). Understanding attitudes and predicting behavior. Englewood Cliffs, NJ: Prentice-Hall.

Ajzen, I., Timko, C., & White, J. B. (1982). Self-monitoring and the attitude-behavior relation. Journal of Personality and Social Psychology, 42, 426–435.

Alexander, F. (1954). Psychoanalysis and psychotherapy. Journal of the American Psychoanalytic Association, 2, 722–733.

Alloy, L. B., & Abramson, L. Y. (1979). Judgment of contingency in depressed and nondepressed students: Sadder but wiser. Journal of Experimental Psychology: General, 108, 441–485.

Alloy, L. B., & Abramson, L. Y. (1988). Depressive realism: Four theoretical perspectives. In L. B. Alloy (Ed.), Cognitive processes in depression. New York: Guilford Press.

Allport, G. W. (1937). Personality: A psychological interpretation. New York: Holt.

Allport, G. W. (1961). Pattern and growth in personality. New York: Holt, Rinehart & Winston.

Amada, G. (1985). A guide to psychotherapy. Lanham, MD: Madison Books.

Ambelas, A. (1987). Life events and mania: A special relationship? British Journal of Psychiatry, 150, 235–240.

American Psychiatric Association. (1952). Diagnostic and statistical manual of mental disorders (1st ed.). Washington, DC: Author.

American Psychiatric Association. (1968). Diagnostic and statistical manual of mental disorders (2nd ed.). Washington, DC: Author.

American Psychiatric Association. (1980). Diagnostic and statistical manual of mental disorders (3rd ed.). Washington, DC: Author.

American Psychiatric Association. (1987). Diagnostic and statistical manual of mental disorders (3rd ed., rev.). Washington, DC: Author.

American Psychological Association. (1981). Ethical principles of psychologists. American Psychologist, 36, 633–638.

American Psychological Association. (1984). Behavioral research with animals. Washington, DC: Author.

Amoore, J. E. (1970). Molecular basis of odor. Springfield, IL: Charles C Thomas.

Anand, B. K., & Brobeck, J. R. (1951). Hypothalamic control of food intake in rats and cats. Yale Journal of Biology and Medicine, 24, 123–140.

Anderson, B. (1982). Test use today in elementary and secondary schools. In A. K. Wigdor & W. R. Garner (Eds.), Ability testing: Uses, consequences and controversies. Washington, DC: National Academy Press.

Anderson, B. F. (1980). The complete thinker. Englewood Cliffs, NJ: Prentice-Hall.

Anderson, J. R. (1980). Cognitive psychology and its implications. New York: W. H. Freeman.

Anderson, R. C., & Pichert, J. W. (1978). Recall of previously unrecallable information following a shift in perspective. Journal of Verbal Learning and Verbal Behavior, 17, 1–12.

Anderson, S. M., & Klatzky, R. L. (1987). Traits and social stereotypes: Levels of categorization in person perception. Journal of Personality and Social Psychology, 53(2), 235–246.

Andreasen, N. C. (1982). Negative versus positive schizophrenia: Definition and validation. Archives of General Psychiatry, 39, 789–794.

Andreasen, N. C. (1985). Structural brain abnormalities in schizophrenia. In M. N. Menuck & M. V. Seeman (Eds.), New perspectives in schizophrenia. New York: Macmillan.

Ansbacher, H. (1970). Alfred Adler, individual psychology. Psychology Today, 3(9), 42–44, 66.

Antrobus, J. S., Fein, G., Jordan, L., Ellman, S. J., & Arkin, A. M. (1978). Measurement and design in research on sleep reports. In A. M. Arkin, J. S. Antrobus, & S. J. Ellman (Eds.), The mind in sleep: Psychology and psychophysiology. Hillsdale, NJ: Erlbaum.

Arce, A. A., & Vergare, M. J. (1984). Identifying and characterizing the mentally ill among the homeless. In H. R. Lamb (Ed.), The homeless mentally ill.

Washington, DC: American Psychiatric Association.

Ardrey, R. (1966). The territorial imperative. New York: Atheneum.

Arentewicz, G., & Schmidt, G. (Eds.). (1983). The treatment of sexual disorders. New York: Basic Books.

Aron, A. (1988). The matching hypothesis reconsidered again: Comment on Kalick and Hamilton. Journal of Personality and Social Psychology, 54(3), 441–446.

Aronson, E. (1980). Large commitments for small rewards. In L. Festinger (Ed.), Retrospections on social psychology. New York: Oxford University Press.

Aronson, E., Brewer, M., & Carlsmith, J. M. (1985). Experimentation in social psychology. In G. Lindzey & E. Aronson (Eds.), Handbook of social psychology (3rd ed., Vol. 1). New York: Random House.

Aronson, E., & Mills, J. (1959). The effect of severity of initiation on liking for a group. Journal of Abnormal and Social Psychology, 59, 177–181.

Asch, S. E. (1951). Effects of group pressure on the modification and distortion of judgments. In H. Guetzkow (Ed.), Groups, leadership and men. Pittsburgh: Carnegie Press.

Asch, S. E. (1955). Opinions and social pressures. Scientific American, 193(5), 31–35.

Asch, S. E. (1956). Studies of independence and conformity: A minority of one against a unanimous majority. Psychological Monographs, 70(9, Whole No. 416).

Aschoff, J. (1981). Handbook of behavioral neurobiology: Vol. 4. Biological Rhythms. New York: Plenum Press.

Aschoff, J., & Wever, R. (1981). The circadian system of man. In J. Aschoff (Ed.), Handbook of behavioral neurobiology: Vol. 4. Biological rhythms. New York: Plenum Press.

Aserinsky, E., & Kleitman, N. (1953). Regularly occurring periods of eye mobility and concomitant phenomena during sleep. Science, 118, 273–274.

Ashmore, R. D., & Del Boca, F. K. (1976). Psychological approaches to understanding intergroup conflict. In P. A. Katz (Ed.), Towards the elimination of racism. Elmsford, NY: Pergamon Press.

Asterita, M. F. (1985). The physiology of stress. New York: Human Sciences Press.

Atkins, A., Deaux, K., & Bieri, J. (1967). Latitude of acceptance and attitude change: Empirical evidence for a reformulation. Journal of Personality and Social Psychology, 6, 47–54.

Atkinson, J. W. (1974). The mainsprings of achievement-oriented activity. In J. W. Atkinson & J. O. Raynor (Eds.), Motivation and achievement. New York: Wiley.

Atkinson, J. W. (1981). Studying personality in the context of an advanced motivational psychology. American Psychologist, 36, 117–128.

Atkinson, J. W., & Birch, D. (1978). Introduction to motivation. New York: Van Nostrand.

Atkinson, J. W., & Litwin, G. H. (1960). Achievement motive and test anxiety conceived as motive to approach success and to avoid failure. Journal of Abnormal and Social Psychology, 60, 52–63.

Atkinson, R. C., & Raugh, M. R. (1975). An application of the mnemonic keyword method to the acquisition of a Russian vocabulary. Journal of Experimental Psychology: Human Learning and Memory, 104, 126–133.

Atkinson, R. C., & Shiffrin, R. M. (1968). Human memory: A proposed system and its control processes. In K. W. Spence & J. T. Spence (Eds.), The psychology of learning and motivation (Vol. 2). New York: Academic Press.

Atkinson, R. C., & Shiffrin, R. M. (1971). The control of short-term memory. Scientific American, 225, 82–90.

Atwood, M. E., & Polson, P. G. (1976). A process model for water jar problems. Cognitive Psychology, 8, 191–216.

Ault, R. L. (1977). Children's cognitive development. New York: Oxford University Press.

Avery, D., & Winokur, G. (1978). Suicide, attempted suicide, and relapse rates in depression. Archives of General Psychiatry, 35, 749–753.

Axelrod, S., & Apsche, J. (1983). The effects of punishment on human behavior. New York: Academic Press.

Ayllon, T., & Azrin, N. H. (1968). Token economy. New York: Appleton-Century-Crofts.

B

Bachrach, L. L. (1984). The homeless mentally ill and mental health services: An analytical review of the literature. In H. R. Lamb (Ed.), The homeless mentally ill. Washington, DC: American Psychiatric Association.

Baddeley, A., & Hitch, G. (1974). Working memory. In G. H. Bower (Ed.), The psychology of learning and motivation (Vol. 8). New York: Academic Press.

Bakan, P. (1971). The eyes have it. Psychology Today, 4(3), 64–69.

Bakeman, R., Lumb, J. R., Jackson, R. E., & Smith, D. W. (1986). AIDS-risk group profiles in whites and members of minority groups. New England Journal of Medicine, 315, 191–192.

Baker, E. L. (1985). Psychoanalysis and psychoanalytic therapy. In S. J. Lynn & J. P. Garske (Eds.), Contemporary psychotherapies: Models and methods. Columbus, OH: Charles E. Merrill.

Baker, G. H. B. (1982). Life events before the onset of rheumatoid arthritis. Psychotherapy and Psychosomatics, 38, 173–177.

Baker, S. W. (1980). Psychosexual differentiation in the human. Biology of Reproduction, 22, 61–72.

Baldessarini, R. J. (1984). Antipsychotic drugs. In T. B. Karasu (Ed.), The psychiatric therapies. Washington, DC: American Psychiatric Association.

Bandura, A. (1973). Aggression: A social learning analysis. Englewood Cliffs, NJ: Prentice-Hall.

Bandura, A. (1977). Social learning theory. Englewood Cliffs, NJ: Prentice-Hall.

Bandura, A. (1982). The psychology of chance encounters and life paths. American Psychologist, 37, 747–755.

Bandura, A. (1986). Social foundations of thought and action: A social-cognitive theory. Englewood Cliffs, NJ: Prentice-Hall.

Bandura, A., & Rosenthal, T. L. (1966). Vicarious classical conditioning as a function of arousal level. Journal of Personality and Social Psychology, 3, 54–62.

Bandura, A., Ross, D., & Ross, S. (1963). Vicarious reinforcement and imitative learning. Journal of Abnormal and Social Psychology, 67(6), 601–607.

Barbach, L. G. (1975). For yourself: The fulfillment of female sexuality. Garden City, NY: Doubleday.

Barbach, L. G. (1982). For each other: Sharing sexual intimacy. New York: Doubleday.

Barber, T. X. (1969). Hypnosis: A scientific approach. New York: Van Nostrand.

Barber, T. X. (1979). Suggested ("hypnotic") behavior: The trance paradigm versus an alternative paradigm. In E. Fromm & R. E. Shor (Eds.), Hypnosis: Developments in research and new perspectives. New York: Aldine.

Bard, P. (1934). On emotional experience after decortication with some remarks on theoretical views. Psychological Review, 41, 309–329.

Barerra, M. E., & Maurer, D. (1981). Recognition of mother's photographed face by the three-month-old infant. Child Development, 52, 714–716.

Barlett, D. L., & Steele, J. B. (1979). Empire: The life, legend and madness of Howard Hughes. New York: Norton.

Barlow, D. H., & Waddell, M. T. (1985). Agoraphobia. In D. H. Barlow (Ed.), Clinical handbook of psychological disorders. New York: Guilford Press.

Baron, P. H. (1974). Self-esteem, ingratiation, and the evaluation of unknown others. Journal of Personality and Social Psychology, 30, 104–109.

Barrett, J. E., Rose, R. M., & Klerman, G. L. (Eds.). (1979). Stress and mental disorder. New York: Raven Press.

Barrett, M. D. (1982). The holophrastic hypothesis: Conceptual and empirical issues. Cognition, 11, 47–76.

Barron, F., & Harrington, D. M. (1981). Creativity, intelligence and personality. In M. R. Rosenzweig & L. W. Porter (Eds.), Annual Review of Psychology (Vol. 32). Palo Alto, CA: Annual Reviews.

Bartlett, F. C. (1932). Remembering: A study in experimental and social psychology. New York: Macmillan.

Barton, J. L. (1977). ECT in depression: The evidence of controlled studies. Biological Psychiatry, 12, 687–695.

Bartoshuk, L. M. (1968). Water taste in man. Perception and Psychophysics, 3, 69–72.

Bartoshuk, L. M. (1971). The chemical senses: I. Taste. In J. W. Kling & L. A. Riggs (Eds.), Experimental Psychology (3rd ed., Vol. 1). New York: Holt, Rinehart & Winston.

Bartus, R. T., Dean, R. L., Beer, B., & Lippa, A. S. (1982). The cholinergic hypothesis of geriatric memory dysfunction. Science, 217, 408–417.

Basbaum, A. I., & Fields, H. L. (1984). Endogenous pain control systems: Brainstem spinal pathways and endorphin circuitry. Annual Review of Neuroscience, 7, 309–338.

Bassuk, E. L., Rubin, L., & Lauriat, A. (1984). Is homelessness a mental health problem? American Journal of Psychiatry, 141(12), 1546–1550.

Baumeister, R. F. (1984). Choking under pressure: Self-consciousness and paradoxical effects of incentives on skillful performance. Journal of Personality and Social Psychology, 46(3), 610–620.

Baumeister, R. F., & Steinhilber, A. (1984). Paradoxical effects of supportive audiences on performance under pressure: The home field disadvantage in sports championships. Journal of Personality and Social Psychology, 47(1), 85–93.

Baumrind, D. (1964). Some thoughts on the ethics of reading Milgram's "Behavioral study of obedience." American Psychologist, 19, 421–423.

Baumrind, D. (1985). Research using intentional deception: Ethical issues revisited. American Psychologist, 40, 165–174.

Beahrs, J. O. (1983). Co-consciousness: A common denominator in hypnosis, multiple personality and normalcy. American Journal of Clinical Hypnosis, 26(2), 100–113.

Beck, A. T. (1976). Cognitive therapy and the emotional disorders. New York: International Universities Press.

Beck, A. T. (1987). Cognitive therapy. In J. K. Zeig (Ed.), The evolution of psychotherapy. New York: Brunner/Mazel.

Beck, A. T., Rush, A. J., Shaw, B. F., & Emery, G. (1979). Cognitive therapy of depression. New York: Guilford Press.

Becker, B. J. (1986). Influence again: An examination of reviews and studies of gender differences in social influence. In J. S. Hyde & M. C. Linn (Eds.), The psychology of gender: Advances through meta-analysis. Baltimore: Johns Hopkins University Press.

Becker, H. S. (1973). Outsiders: Studies in the sociology of deviance. New York: Free Press.

Beidler, L. M. (1963). Dynamics of taste cells. In Y. Zotterman (Ed.), Olfaction and taste. Oxford: Pergamon Press.

Bekesy, G. von. (1947). The variation of phase along the basilar membrane with sinusoidal vibrations. Journal of the Acoustical Society of America, 19, 452–460.

Bekesy, G. von. (1960). Experiments in hearing. New York: McGraw-Hill.

Bell, C. R., & Telman, N. (1980). Errors, accidents and injuries on rotating shift-work: A field study. International Review of Applied Psychology, 29, 271–291.

Bellisle, F. (1979). Human feeding behavior. Neuroscience and Biobehavioral Reviews, 3, 163–169.

Bem, D. J. (1967). Self-perception: An alternative interpretation of cognitive dissonance phenomena. Psychological Review, 74, 183–200.

Bem, D. J., & Allen, A. (1974). On predicting some of the people some of the time: The search for cross-situational consistencies in behavior. Psychological Review, 81, 506–520.

Bem, S. L. (1975). Sex-role adaptability: One consequence of psychological androgyny. Journal of Personality and Social Psychology, 31, 634–643.

Beneke, W. M., & Harris, M. B. (1972). Teaching self-control of study behavior. Behavior Research and Therapy, 10, 35–41.

Benjamin, L. T., Jr., Cavell, T. A., & Shallenberger, W. R., III. (1984). Staying with initial answers on objective tests: Is it a myth? Teaching of Psychology, 11(3), 133–141.

Benson, H. (1975). The relaxation response. New York: Morrow.

Berg, I. (1970). Education and jobs. New York: Praeger.

Berger, H. (1929). Über das elektrenkephalogramm des menschen. Archiv für Psychiatrie und Nervenkrankheiten, 99, 555–574.

Berger, P. A., & Dunn, M. J. (1986). The biology and treatment of drug abuse. In P. A. Berger & H. K. H. Brodie (Eds.), American handbook of psychiatry: Biological psychiatry (2nd ed., Vol. 8). New York: Basic Books.

Berger, T. W. (1984). Long-term potentiation of hippocampal synaptic transmission affects rate of behavioral learning. Science, 224, 627–630.

Bergin, A. E. (1971). The evaluation of therapeutic outcomes. In A. E. Bergin & S. L. Garfield (Eds.), Handbook of psychotherapy and behavior change: An empirical analysis. New York: Wiley.

Bergin, A. E., & Lambert, M. J. (1978). The evaluation of therapeutic outcomes. In S. L. Garfield & A. E. Bergin (Eds.), Handbook of psychotherapy and behavior change: An empirical analysis. New York: Wiley.

Berkowitz, L. (1969). The frustration-aggression hypothesis revisited. In L. Berkowitz (Ed.), Roots of aggression: A reexamination of the frustration-aggression hypothesis. New York: Atherton.

Bermant, G., & Davidson, J. M. (1974). Biological bases of sexual behavior. New York: Harper & Row.

Bernal, E. M. (1984). Bias in mental testing: Evidence for an alternative to the heredity-environment controversy. In C. R. Reynolds & R. T. Brown (Eds.), Perspectives on bias in mental testing. New York: Plenum Press.

Berscheid, E. (1966). Opinion change and communicator-communicatee similarity and dissimilarity. Journal of Personality and Social Psychology, 4, 670–680.

Berscheid, E. (1988). Some comments on love's anatomy: Or, whatever happened to old-fashioned lust. In R. J. Sternberg & M. L. Barnes (Eds.), The psychology of love. New Haven, CT: Yale University Press.

Berscheid, E., & Walster, E. (1978). Interpersonal attraction. Reading, MA: Addison-Wesley.

Bhatia, V. P., Katiyar, G. P., & Agarwal, K. N. (1979). Effect of intrauterine nutritional deprivation on neuromotor behavior of the newborn. Acta Paediatrica Scandinavica, 68, 561–566.

Billings, A. G., Cronkite, R. C., & Moos, R. H. (1983). Social-environment factors in unipolar depression. Journal of Abnormal Psychology, 92, 119–133.

Bindra, D. (1985). Motivation, the brain, and psychological theory. In S. Koch & D. E. Leary (Eds.), A century of psychology as science. New York: McGraw-Hill.

Binet, A. (1911). Nouvelle recherches sur la mesure du niveau intellectuel chez les enfants d'école. L'Année Psychologique, 17, 145–201.

Binet, A., & Simon, T. (1905). Méthodes nouvelles pour le diagnostic du niveau intellectuel des anormaux. L'Année Psychologique, 11, 191–244.

Binet, A., & Simon, T. (1908). Le développement de l'intelligence chez les enfants. L'Année Psychologique, 14, 1–94.

Binkley, S. (1979). A timekeeping enzyme in the pineal gland. *Scientific American, 204*, 66–71.

Birren, J. E., Woods, A. M., & Williams, M. V. (1980). Behavioral slowing with age: Causes, organization and consequences. In L. W. Poon (Ed.), *Aging in the 1980s: Psychological issues.* Washington, DC: American Psychological Association.

Blakeslee, T. R. (1980). *The right brain.* Garden City, NY: Doubleday/Anchor.

Blanchard, E. B., & Andrasik, F. (1982). Psychological assessment and treatment of the headache: Recent developments and emerging issues. *Journal of Consulting and Clinical Psychology, 50*, 859–879.

Blaney, P. H. (1986). Affect and memory: A review. *Psychological Bulletin, 99*, 229–246.

Blank, A. S., Jr. (1982). Stresses of war: The example of Viet Nam. In L. Goldberger & S. Breznitz (Eds.), *Handbook of stress: Theoretical and clinical aspects.* New York: Free Press.

Blasi, A. (1980). Bridging moral cognition and moral action: A critical review of the literature. *Psychological Bulletin, 88*, 1–45.

Blau, Z. S. (1981). *Black children/white children: Competence, socialization and social structure.* New York: Free Press.

Blechman, E. A., McEnroe, M. J., Carella, E. T., & Audette, D. P. (1986). Childhood competence and depression. *Journal of Abnormal Psychology, 95*(3), 223–227.

Bleuler, E. (1911). *Dementia praecox or the group F schizophrenias.* New York: International Universities Press.

Block, E. B. (1976). *Hypnosis: A new tool in crime detection.* New York: David McKay.

Block, J. (1981). Some enduring and consequential structures of personality. In A. I. Rabins, J. Aronoff, A. Barclay, & R. Zucker (Eds.), *Further explorations in personality.* New York: Wiley.

Block, N. J., & Dworkin, G. (1976). Heritability and inequality. In N. J. Block & G. Dworkin (Eds.), *The IQ controversy: Critical readings.* New York: Pantheon.

Bloom, B. L. (1984). *Community mental health: A general introduction.* Pacific Grove, CA: Brooks/Cole.

Bloom, B. S. (Ed.). (1985). *Developing talent in young people.* New York: Ballantine.

Bloomfield, H. H., & Kory, R. B. (1976). *Happiness: The TM program, psychiatry, and enlightenment.* New York: Simon & Schuster.

Blum, K. (1984). *Handbook of abusable drugs.* New York: Gardner Press.

Boehm, A. E. (1985). Educational applications of intelligence testing. In B. B. Wolman (Ed.), *Handbook of intelligence: Theories, measurements, and applications.* New York: Wiley.

Bogen, J. E. (1969). The other side of the brain II: An appositional mind. *Bulletin of the Los Angeles Neurological Society, 34*, 135–162.

Bolles, R. C. (1975). *Theory of motivation.* New York: Harper & Row.

Bolles, R. C., & Fanselow, M. S. (1980). A perceptual-defensive-recuperative model of fear and pain. *Behavioral and Brain Sciences, 3*, 291–323.

Bonnet, M. (1982). Performance during sleep. In W. B. Webb (Ed.), *Biological rhythms, sleep and performance.* New York: Wiley.

Boor, M. (1976). Relationship of internal-external control and national suicide rates. *Journal of Social Psychology, 100*, 143–144.

Booth, D. A. (1977). Satiety and appetite are conditioned reactions. *Psychosomatic Medicine, 39*, 76–81.

Borbely, A. (1986). *Secrets of sleep.* New York: Basic Books.

Boring, E. G. (1966). A note on the origin of the word psychology. *Journal of History of the Behavioral Sciences, 2*, 167.

Bouchard, T. J., Jr., & McGue, M. (1981). Familial studies of intelligence: A review. *Science, 212*, 1055–1059.

Bouchard, T. J., Jr., & Segal, N. L. (1985). Environment and IQ. In B. B. Wolman (Ed.), *Handbook of intelligence: Theories, measurements, and applications.* New York: Wiley.

Bousfield, W. A. (1953). The occurrence of clustering in the recall of randomly arranged associates. *Journal of General Psychology, 49*, 229–240.

Boutin, R. (1979). Psychoactive drugs: Effective use of low doses. *Psychosomatics, 20*, 403–405, 409.

Bower, G. H. (1970). Organizational factors in memory. *Cognitive Psychology, 1*, 18–46.

Bower, G. H. (1981). Mood and memory. *American Psychologist, 36*, 129–148.

Bower, G. H., Black, J. B., & Turner, T. J. (1979). Scripts in memory for text. *Cognitive Psychology, 11*, 177–220.

Bower, G. H., & Clark, M. C. (1969). Narrative stories as mediators of serial learning. *Psychonomic Science, 14*, 181–182.

Bower, G. H., & Springston, F. (1970). Pauses as recoding points in letter series. *Journal of Experimental Psychology, 83*, 421–430.

Bower, T. G. R. (1982). *Development in infancy.* San Francisco: W. H. Freeman.

Bowlby, J. (1969). *Attachment and loss: Vol. 1. Attachment.* New York: Basic Books.

Bowlby, J. (1973). *Attachment and loss: Vol. 2. Separation, anxiety and anger.* New York: Basic Books.

Bowlby, J. (1980). *Attachment and loss: Vol. 3. Sadness and depression.* New York: Basic Books.

Boyd, J. H., & Weissman, M. M. (1986). Epidemiology of major affective disorders. In J. H. Boyd & M. M. Weissman (Eds.), *Psychiatry: Vol. 5. Social, epidemiologic, and legal psychiatry.* New York: Basic Books.

Boynton, R. M., & Gordon, J. (1965). Bezold-Brucke hue shift measured by color naming technique. *Journal of the Optical Society of America, 55*, 78–86.

Bozarth, M. A., & Wise, R. A. (1985). Toxicity associated with long-term intravenous heroin and cocaine self-administration in the rat. *Journal of the American Medical Association, 254*(1), 81–83.

Bradburn, N. M. (1969). *The structure of psychological well-being.* Chicago: Aldine.

Bradbury, T. N., & Fincham, F. D. (1988). Individual difference variables in close relationships: A contextual model of marriage as an integrative framework. *Journal of Personality and Social Psychology, 54*(4), 713–721.

Bradley, C. (1979). Life events and the control of diabetes mellitus. *Journal of Psychosomatic Research, 23*, 159–162.

Bradley, G. W. (1978). Self-serving biases in the attribution process: A re-examination of the fact or fiction question. *Journal of Personality and Social Psychology, 35*, 56–71.

Bradley, R. H., & Caldwell, B. M. (1980). The relation of home environment, cognitive competence and IQ among males and females. *Child Development, 51*, 1140–1148.

Bradshaw, J. L. (1981). In two minds. *Behavioral and Brain Sciences, 4*, 101–102.

Bradshaw, J. L., & Nettleton, N. C. (1981). The nature of hemispheric specialization in man. *Behavioral and Brain Sciences, 4*, 51–91.

Brady, J. P. (1984). Social skills training for psychiatric patients: II. Clinical outcome studies. *American Journal of Psychiatry, 141*(4), 491–498.

Brady, J. P., & Levitt, E. E. (1966). Hypnotically induced visual hallucinations. *Psychosomatic Medicine, 28*, 351–368.

Braginsky, D. D. (1985). Psychology: Handmaiden to society. In S. Koch & D. E. Leary (Eds.), *A century of psychology as science.* New York: McGraw-Hill.

Bransford, J. D., & Johnson, M. K. (1973). Considerations of some problems of comprehension. In W. G. Chase (Ed.), *Visual information processing.* New York: Academic Press.

Bransford, J. D., & Stein, B. S. (1984). *The IDEAL problem solver.* New York: W. H. Freeman.

Brantley, P. J., & Sutker, P. B. (1984). Antisocial behavior disorders. In H. E. Adams & P. B. Sutker (Eds.), *Comprehensive handbook of psychopathology.* New York: Plenum Press.

Braun, B. G. (1986). Issues in the psychotherapy of multiple personality disorder. In B. G. Braun (Ed.), *Treatment of multiple personality disorder.* Washington, DC: American Psychiatric Press.

Bray, G. A., & York, D. A. (1979). Hypothalamic and genetic obesity in experimental animals: An autonomic and endocrine hypothesis. *Physiological Review, 59*, 719–809.

Breggin, P. R. (1979). *Electroshock: Its brain disabling effects.* New York: Springer.

Brehm, S. S. (1985). *Intimate relationships.* New York: Random House.

Breland, K., & Breland, M. (1961). The misbehavior of organisms. *American Psychologist, 16*, 681–684.

Breland, K., & Breland, M. (1966). *Animal behavior.* New York: Macmillan.

Bremer, T. A., & Wittig, M. A. (1980). Fear of success: A personality trait or a response to occupational deviance and role overload. *Sex Roles, 6*, 27–46.

Brett, J. M. (1980). The effect of job transfer on employees and their families. In C. L. Cooper & R. Payne (Eds.), *Current concerns in occupational stress.* New York: Wiley.

Brewer, W. F., & Nakamura, G. V. (1984). The nature and function of schemas. In R. S. Wyer & T. K. Sroll (Eds.), *Handbook of social cognition.* Hillsdale, NJ: Erlbaum.

Brigham, J. C. (1986). *Social psychology.* Boston: Little, Brown.

Brigham, J. C., & Barkowitz, P. B. (1978). Do "they all look alike"? The effect of race, sex, experience and attitudes on the ability to recognize faces. *Journal of Applied Social Psychology, 8*, 306–318.

Broadbent, D. E. (1954). The role of auditory localization in attention and memory span. *Journal of Experimental Psychology, 47*, 191–196.

Broadbent, D. E. (1958). *Perception and communication.* London: Pergamon Press.

Broadhead, W. E., Kaplan, B. H., James, S. A., Wagner, E. H., Schoenbach, V. J., Grimson, R., Heyden, S., Tibblin, G., & Gehlbach, S. H. (1983). The epidemiological evidence for a relationship between social support and health. *American Journal of Epidemiology, 117*(5), 521–537.

Brobeck, J. R., Tepperman, T., & Long, C. N. (1943). Experimental hypothalamic hyperphagia in the albino rat. *Yale Journal of Biology and Medicine, 15*, 831–853.

Brody, N. (1985). The validity of tests of intelligence. In B. B. Wolman (Ed.), *Handbook of intelligence: Theories, measurements, and applications.* New York: Wiley.

Bromage, B. K., & Mayer, R. E. (1986). Quantitative and qualitative effects of repetition on learning from technical text. *Journal of Educational Psychology, 78*(4), 271–278.

Bronson, F. H., & Whitten, W. (1968). Estrus accelerating pheromone of mice: Assay, androgen-dependency, and presence in bladder urine. *Journal of Reproduction and Fertility, 15*, 131–134.

Broverman, I. K., Vogel, S. R., Broverman, D. M., Clarkson, F. E., & Rosenkrantz, P. S. (1972). Sex roles stereotypes: A current appraisal. *Journal of Social Issues, 28*, 59–78.

Brown, P., & Funk, S. C. (1986). Tardive dyskinesia: Barriers to the professional recognition of an iatrogenic disease. *Journal of Health and Social Behavior, 27*, 116–132.

Brown, R. (1973). *A first language: The early stages.* Cambridge, MA: Harvard University Press.

Brown, R., & Hanlon, C. (1970). Derivational complexity and order of acquisition. In J. R. Hayes (Ed.), *Cognition and the development of language.* New York: Wiley.

Brown, R., & Kulik, J. (1977). Flashbulb memories. *Cognition, 5*, 73–99.

Brown, R., & McNeill, D. (1966). The "tip-of-the-tongue" phenomenon. *Journal of Verbal Learning and Verbal Behavior, 5*(4), 325–337.

Brownell, H. H., & Gardner, H. (1981). Hemisphere specialization: Definitions not incantations. *Behavioral and Brain Sciences, 4*, 64–65.

Bruce, B., Rubin, A., & Starr, K. (1981). *Why readability formulas fail.* Urbana, IL: Center for the Study of Reading.

Bruce, R. L. (1980). Biological psychology. In J. Radford & D. Rose (Eds.), *The teaching of psychology: Method, content and context.* New York: Wiley.

Bruner, J. S. (1968). *Processes of cognitive growth: Infancy*. Worcester, MA: Clark University Press with Barre Publishers.

Buchsbaum, M. S. (1986). Functional imaging of the brain in psychiatry: Positron emission tomography. In P. A. Berger & H. K. H. Brodie (Eds.), *American handbook of psychiatry: Biological psychiatry* (2nd ed., Vol. 8). New York: Basic Books.

Buhler, C., & Allen, M. (1972). *Introduction to humanistic psychology*. Pacific Grove, CA: Brooks/Cole.

Burks, N., & Martin, B. (1985). Everyday problems and life change events: Ongoing versus acute sources of stress. *Journal of Human Stress, 11*(1), 27–35.

Burt, C. (1955). The evidence for the concept of intelligence. *British Journal of Educational Psychology, 25,* 158–177.

Busch-Rossnagel, N. A., & Vance, A. K. (1982). The impact of the schools on social and emotional development. In B. B. Wolman (Ed.), *Handbook of developmental psychology*. Englewood Cliffs, NJ: Prentice-Hall.

Buss, D. M. (1988). The evolution of human intrasexual competition: Tactics of mate attraction. *Journal of Personality and Social Psychology, 54*(4), 616–628.

Bussey, K., & Bandura, A. (1984). Influence of gender constancy and social power on sex-linked modeling. *Journal of Personality and Social Psychology, 47,* 1292–1302.

Butcher, J. N. (1969). *MMPI: Research developments and clinical applications*. New York: McGraw-Hill.

Butcher, J. N. (1984). Current developments in MMPI use: An international perspective. In J. N. Butcher & C. D. Spielberger (Eds.), *Advances in personality assessment* (Vol. 4). Hillsdale, NJ: Erlbaum.

Butcher, J. N., & Keller, L. S. (1984). Objective personality assessment. In G. Goldstein & M. Hersen (Eds.), *Handbook of psychological assessment*. New York: Pergamon Press.

Buxton, M. N., Arkey, Y., Lagos, J., Deposito, F., Lowenthal, F., & Simring, S. (1981). Stress and platelet aggregation in hemophiliac children and their family members. *Research Communications in Psychology, Psychiatry and Behavior, 6*(1), 21–48.

Byrne, D. (1961). Anxiety and the experimental arousal of affiliation need. *Journal of Abnormal and Social Psychology, 63,* 660–662.

Byrne, D. (1971). *The attraction paradigm*. New York: Academic Press.

Byrne, D., Clore, G. L., & Smeaton, G. (1986). The attraction hypothesis: Do similar attitudes affect anything? *Journal of Personality and Social Psychology, 51*(6), 1167–1170.

Byrne, D., & Murnen, S. K. (1988). Maintaining loving relationships. In R. J. Sternberg & M. L. Barnes (Eds.), *The psychology of love*. New Haven, CT: Yale University Press.

C

Cadoret, R. J. (1986). Epidemiology of antisocial personality. In W. H. Reid, D. Dorr, J. I. Walker, & J. W. Bonner, III (Eds.), *Unmasking the psychopath: Antisocial personality and related syndromes*. New York: Norton.

Cahnman, W. J. (1968). The stigma of obesity. *Sociological Quarterly, 9,* 283–299.

Cain, W. S. (1979). To know with the nose: Keys to odor identification. *Science, 203,* 467–470.

Caligor, L., & May, R. (1968). *Dreams and symbols: Man's unconscious language*. New York: Basic Books.

Cameron, N. (1963). *Personality development and psychopathology*. Boston: Houghton Mifflin.

Campbell, D. P., & Hansen, J. C. (1981). *Manual for the SVIB-SCII Strong-Campbell Interest Inventory*. Stanford, CA: Stanford University Press.

Campbell, J. (1971). *Hero with a thousand faces*. New York: Harcourt Brace Jovanovich.

Campos, J. J., Langer, A., & Krowitz, A. (1970). Cardiac responses on the visual cliff in prelocomotor infants. *Science, 170,* 196–197.

Cannon, D. S., Baker, T. B., & Wehl, C. K. (1981). Emetic and electric shock alcohol aversion therapy:

Six- and twelve-month follow-up. *Journal of Consulting and Clinical Psychology, 49*(3), 360–368.

Cannon, W. B. (1927). The James-Lange theory of emotions: A critical examination and an alternate theory. *American Journal of Psychology, 39,* 106–124.

Cannon, W. B. (1929). *Bodily changes in pain, hunger, fear and rage*. New York: Appleton.

Cannon, W. B. (1932). *The wisdom of the body*. New York: Norton.

Cannon, W. B., & Washburn, A. L. (1912). An explanation of hunger. *American Journal of Physiology, 29,* 444–454.

Cantor, N., & Mischel, W. (1979). Prototypes in person perception. In L. Berkowitz (Ed.), *Advances in experimental social psychology* (Vol. 12). New York: Academic Press.

Carey, S. (1977). The child as a word learner. In M. Halle, J. Bresman, & G. A. Miller (Eds.), *Linguistic theory and psychological reality*. Cambridge, MA: MIT Press.

Carnegie, D. (1936). *How to win friends and influence people*. New York: Simon & Schuster.

Carroll, D. W. (1986). *Psychology of language*. Pacific Grove, CA: Brooks/Cole.

Carroll, J. B., & Horn, J. L. (1981). On the scientific basis of ability testing. *American Psychologist, 36*(10), 1012–1020.

Carroll, J. L., & Rest, J. R. (1982). Moral development. In B. B. Wolman (Ed.), *Handbook of developmental psychology*. Englewood Cliffs, NJ: Prentice-Hall.

Carson, R. C., Butcher, J. N., & Coleman, J. C. (1988). *Abnormal psychology and modern life*. Glenview, IL: Scott, Foresman.

Carson, T. P., & Carson, R. C. (1984). The affective disorders. In H. E. Adams & P. B. Sutker (Eds.), *Comprehensive handbook of psychopathology*. New York: Plenum Press.

Cartwright, R. D. (1974). The influence of a conscious wish on dreams: A methodological study of dream meaning and function. *Journal of Abnormal Psychology, 83,* 387–393.

Cartwright, R. D. (1977). *Night life: Explorations in dreaming*. Englewood Cliffs, NJ: Prentice-Hall.

Cartwright, R. D. (1978). Happy endings for our dreams. *Psychology Today, 12*(7), 66–76.

Cash, T. F., & Derlega, V. J. (1978). The matching hypothesis: Physical attractiveness among same-sexed friends. *Personality and Social Psychology Bulletin, 4,* 240–243.

Caspi, A., Bolger, N., & Eckenrode, J. (1987). Linking person and context in the daily stress process. *Journal of Personality and Social Psychology, 52*(1), 184–195.

Castro, K. G., Hardy, A. M., & Curran, J. W. (1986). The acquired immunodeficiency syndrome: Epidemiology and risk factors for transmission. In T. G. Cooney & T. T. Ward (Eds.), *Medical Clinics of North America* (Vol. 70). Philadelphia: Saunders.

Castro, K. G., Lifson, A. R., White, C. R., Bush, T. J., Chamberland, M. E., Lekatsas, A. M., & Jaffe, H. W. (1988). Investigation of AIDS patients with no previously identified risk factors. *Journal of the American Medical Association, 259*(9), 1338–1342.

Catania, A. C. (1979). *Learning*. Englewood Cliffs, NJ: Prentice-Hall.

Cattell, J. M. (1890). Mental tests and measurements. *Mind, 15,* 373–381.

Cattell, R. B. (1950). *Personality: A systematic, theoretical and factual study*. New York: McGraw-Hill.

Cattell, R. B. (1957). *Personality and motivation: Structure and measurement*. New York: Harcourt, Brace & World.

Cattell, R. B. (1965). *The scientific analysis of personality*. Baltimore: Penguin.

Cattell, R. B. (1966). *The scientific analysis of personality*. Chicago: Aldine.

Cattell, R. B., Eber, H. W., & Tatsuoka, M. M. (1970). *Handbook of the Sixteen Personality Factor questionnaire (16PF)*. Champaign, IL: Institute for Personality and Ability Testing.

Cattell, R. B., Kawash, S. F., & DeYoung, G. E. (1972). Validation of objective measures of ergic tension: Response of the sex erg to visual stimula-

tion. *Journal of Experimental Research in Personality, 6,* 76–83.

Cerletti, U., & Bini, L. (1938). Un nuevo metodo di shockterapie "L'elettro-shock." *Boll. Acad. Med. Roma, 64,* 136–138.

Chaiken, S. (1979). Communicator's physical attractiveness and persuasion. *Journal of Personality and Social Psychology, 37,* 1387–1397.

Chaiken, S., & Baldwin, M. W. (1981). Affective-cognitive consistency and the effect of salient behavioral information on the self-perception of attitudes. *Journal of Personality and Social Psychology, 41,* 1–12.

Charlesworth, W. R., & Kreutzer, M. A. (1973). Facial expression of infants and children. In P. Ekman (Ed.), *Darwin and facial expression*. New York: Academic Press.

Charrow, R. P., & Charrow, V. R. (1979). Making legal language understandable: A psycholinguistic study of jury instructions. *Columbia Law Review, 79,* 1306–1374.

Cherry, C. (1953). Some experiments on the recognition of speech with one and with two ears. *Journal of the Acoustical Society of America, 25,* 975–979.

Chi, M. T. H., Glaser, R., & Rees, E. (1982). Expertise in problem solving. In R. J. Sternberg (Ed.), *Advances in the psychology of human intelligence* (Vol. 1). Hillsdale, NJ: Erlbaum.

Chomsky, N. (1957). *Syntactic structures*. The Hague: Mouton.

Chomsky, N. (1959). A review of B. F. Skinner's "Verbal Behavior." *Language, 35,* 26–58.

Chomsky, N. (1965). *Aspects of theory of syntax*. Cambridge, MA: MIT Press.

Chomsky, N. (1968). *Language and mind*. New York: Harcourt Brace Jovanovich.

Chomsky, N. (1975). *Reflections on language*. New York: Pantheon.

Chorover, S. L. (1985). Psychology in cultural context: The division of labor and the fragmentation of experience. In S. Koch & D. E. Leary (Eds.), *A century of psychology as science*. New York: McGraw-Hill.

Chumlea, W. C. (1982). Physical growth in adolescence. In B. B. Wolman (Ed.), *Handbook of developmental psychology*. Englewood Cliffs, NJ: Prentice-Hall.

Ciompi, L. (1980). Catamnestic long-term study on the course of life and aging in schizophrenics. *Schizophrenia Bulletin, 6,* 607–618.

Clark, E. V. (1983). Meanings and concepts. In J. H. Flavell and E. M. Markman (Eds.), *Handbook of child psychology* (Vol. 3). New York: Wiley.

Clarke, A. M., & Clarke, A. D. B. (1976). Some continued experiments. In A. M. Clarke & A. D. B. Clarke (Eds.), *Early experience: Myth and evidence*. New York: Free Press.

Coates, T. J., & Thoresen, C. E. (1977). *How to sleep better*. Englewood Cliffs, NJ: Prentice-Hall.

Cockerham, W. C. (1981). *Sociology of mental disorder*. Englewood Cliffs, NJ: Prentice-Hall.

Cohen, C. E. (1981). Person categories and social perception: Testing some boundaries of the processing effects of prior knowledge. *Journal of Personality and Social Psychology, 40,* 441–452.

Cohen, D. (1983). *Piaget: Critique and reassessment*. New York: St. Martin's Press.

Cohen, S. (1980). *The substance abuse problem*. New York: Haworth Press.

Cohen, S., & Syme, S. L. (Eds.). (1985). *Social support and health*. New York: Academic Press.

Cohen, S. I., & Hajioff, J. (1972). Life events and the onset of acute closed-angle glaucoma. *Journal of Psychosomatic Research, 16,* 335–341.

Colby, A., Kohlberg, L., Gibbs, J., & Lieberman, M. (1983). A longitudinal study of moral development. *Monographs of the Society for Research in Child Development, 48*(1 & 2, Serial No. 200).

Cole, J. O., Goldberg, S. C., & Davis, J. M. (1966). Drugs in the treatment of psychosis. In P. Solomon (Ed.), *Psychiatric drugs*. New York: Grune & Stratton.

Cole, N. S. (1981). Bias in testing. *American Psychologist, 36*(10), 1067–1077.

Coleman, J., Herzberg, J., & Morris, M. (1977). Identity in adolescence: Present and future self-concepts. *Journal of Youth and Adolescence, 6*(1), 63–75.

Coles, R. (1970). *Erik H. Erikson: The growth of his work.* Boston: Little, Brown.

College Entrance Examination Board. (1979). *ATP guide for high schools and colleges: 1979–1981.* Princeton, NJ: Author.

Collins, A. M., & Loftus, E. F. (1975). A spreading activation theory of semantic processing. *Psychological Review, 82,* 407–428.

Colquhoun, W. P. (1984). Effects of personality on body temperature and mental efficiency following transmeridian flight. *Aviation, Space & Environmental Medicine, 55*(6), 493–496.

Colt, E. W., Wardlaw, S. L., & Frantz, A. G. (1981). The effect of running on plasma B-endorphin. *Life Sciences, 28,* 1637–1640.

Commons, M. L., Richards, F. A., & Kuhn, D. (1982). Systematic and metasystematic reasoning: A case for levels of reasoning beyond Piaget's stage of formal operations. *Child Development, 53,* 1058–1069.

Conrad, R. (1964). Acoustic confusions in immediate memory. *British Journal of Psychology, 55,* 75–84.

Cook, E. W., III, Hodes, R. L., & Lang, P. J. (1986). Preparedness and phobia: Effects of stimulus content on human visceral conditioning. *Journal of Abnormal Psychology, 95*(3), 195–207.

Cooper, J., & Fazio, R. H. (1984). A new look at dissonance theory. In L. Berkowitz (Ed.), *Advances in experimental social psychology* (Vol. 17). New York: Academic Press.

Cooper, J. R., Bloom, F. E., and Roth, R. H. (1986). *The biochemical basis of neuropharmacology* (5th ed.). New York: Oxford University Press.

Coopersmith, S. (1967). *The antecedents of self-esteem.* San Francisco: W. H. Freeman.

Coopersmith, S. (1975). Studies in self-esteem. In R. C. Atkinson (Ed.), *Psychology in progress: Readings from Scientific American.* San Francisco: W. H. Freeman.

Corballis, M. C. (1980). Laterality and myth. *American Psychologist, 35*(3), 284–295.

Corkin, S. (1984). Lasting consequences of bilateral medial temporal lobectomy: Clinical course and experimental findings in H. M. *Seminars in Neurology, 4,* 249–259.

Costa, P. T., Jr., & McCrae, R. R. (1980). Still stable after all these years: Personality as a key to some issues in aging. In P. B. Baltes & O. G. Brim (Eds.), *Life span development and behavior* (Vol. 3). New York: Academic Press.

Costello, C. C. (1982). Fears and phobias in women: A community study. *Journal of Abnormal Psychology, 91,* 280–286.

Cotton, J. L. (1981). A review of research on Schachter's theory of emotion and the misattribution of arousal. *European Journal of Social Psychology, 11,* 365–397.

Covi, L., & Primakoff, L. (1988). Cognitive group therapy. In A. J. Frances & R. E. Hales (Eds.), *Review of psychiatry: Volume 7.* Washington, DC: American Psychiatric Association.

Coyle, J. T., Price, D. L., and DeLong, M. R. (1983). Alzheimer's disease: A disorder of cortical cholinergic innervation. *Science, 219,* 1184–1190.

Coyne, J. C. (1976). Toward an interactional description of depression. *Psychiatry, 39,* 28–40.

Craik, F. I. M., & Lockhart, R. S. (1972). Levels of processing: A framework for memory research. *Journal of Verbal Learning and Verbal Behavior, 11,* 671–684.

Craik, F. I. M., & Tulving, E. (1975). Depth of processing and the retention of words in episodic memory. *Journal of Experimental Psychology: General, 104,* 268–294.

Craik, F. I. M., & Watkins, M. J. (1973). The role of rehearsal in short-term memory. *Journal of Verbal Learning and Verbal Behavior, 12,* 599–607.

Cregler, L. L., & Mark, H. (1986). Medical complications of cocaine abuse. *New England Journal of Medicine, 315*(23),1495–1500.

Crockett, H. (1962). The achievement motive and differential occupational mobility in the United States. *American Sociological Review, 27,* 191–204.

Cronbach, L. J. (1975). Five decades of public controversy over mental testing. *American Psychologist, 30,* 1–14.

Cross, C. K., & Hirschfeld, R. M. A. (1986). Epidemiology of disorders in adulthood: Suicide. In G. L. Klerman, M. M. Weissman, P. S. Appelbaum, & L. H. Roth (Eds.), *Psychiatry: Vol. 5. Social, epidemiologic, and legal psychiatry.* New York: Basic Books.

Crovitz, H. F. (1971). The capacity of memory loci in artificial memory. *Psychonomic Science, 24,* 187–188.

Crow, T. J. (1985). The two-syndrome concept: Origins and current status. *Schizophrenia Bulletin, 11,* 471–486.

Crowe, R. (1983). Antisocial personality disorder. In R. Tarter (Ed.), *The child at psychiatric risk.* New York: Oxford University Press.

Croyle, R. T., & Cooper, J. (1983). Dissonance arousal: Physiological evidence. *Journal of Personality and Social Psychology, 45,* 782–791.

Cunningham, S. (1985, June). Animals stolen, facility damaged in lab break-in. *APA Monitor,* pp. 1, 2.

Curran, D. K. (1987). *Adolescent suicidal behavior.* Washington, DC: Hemisphere.

Curran, J. P., Monti, P. M., & Corriveau, D. P. (1982). Treatment of schizophrenia. In A. S. Bellack, M. Hersen, & A. E. Kazdin (Eds.), *International handbook of behavior modification and behavior therapy.* New York: Plenum Press.

Czeisler, C. A., Moore-Ede, M. C., & Coleman, R. M. (1982). Rotating shift work schedules that disrupt sleep are improved by applying circadian principles. *Science, 217,* 460–463.

Czeisler, C. A., Weitzman, E. D., Moore-Ede, M. C., Zimmerman, J. C., & Knauer, R. S. (1980). Human sleep: Its duration and organization depend on its circadian phase. *Science, 210,* 1264–1267.

D

Daitzman, R., & Zuckerman, M. (1980). Disinhibitory sensation seeking, personality and gonadal hormones. *Personality and Individual Differences, 1,* 103–110.

Dansereau, D. F. (1985). Learning strategy research. In J. W. Segal, S. F. Chipman, & R. Glaser (Eds.), *Thinking and learning skills* (Vol. 1). Hillsdale, NJ: Erlbaum.

Darley, J. M., & Gross, P. H. (1983). A hypothesis-confirming bias in labeling effects. *Journal of Personality and Social Psychology, 44,* 20–33.

Darley, J. M., & Latane, B. (1968). Bystander intervention in emergencies: Diffusion of responsibility. *Journal of Personality and Social Psychology, 8,* 377–383.

Darwin, C. (1872). *The expression of emotions in man and animals.* New York: Philosophical Library.

Davidson, J. (1976). Physiology of meditation and mystical states of consciousness. *Perspectives in Biology and Medicine, 19,* 345–380.

Davidson, M., Losonczy, M. F., & Davis, K. L. (1986). Biological hypotheses of schizophrenia. In P. A. Berger & H. K. H. Brodie (Eds.), *American handbook of psychiatry: Biological psychiatry* (2nd ed., Vol. 8). New York: Basic Books.

Davis, H. P., & Squire, L. R. (1984). Protein synthesis and memory: A review. *Psychological Bulletin, 96,* 518–559.

Davis, J. M. (1985). Antipsychotic drugs. In H. I. Kaplan & B. J. Sadock (Eds.), *Comprehensive textbook of psychiatry/IV.* Baltimore: Williams & Wilkins.

Davitz, J. R. (1969). *The language of emotion.* New York: Academic Press.

Dawes, R. B. (1979). The robust beauty of improper linear models in decision making. *American Psychologist, 7,* 571–582.

Day, R. H. (1965). Inappropriate constancy explanation of spatial distortions. *Nature, 207,* 891–893.

Deaux, K. (1984). From individual differences to social categories: Analysis of a decade's research on gender. *American Psychologist, 39,* 105–116.

Deaux, K., Winton, W., Crowley, M., & Lewis, L. L. (1985). Level of categorization and content of gender stereotypes. *Social Cognition, 3,* 145–167.

DeCasper, A. J., & Fifer, W. P. (1980). Of human bonding: Newborns prefer their mother's voices. *Science, 208,* 1174–1176.

deCharms, R., & Moeller, G. H. (1962). Values expressed in American childrens' readers: 1800–1950. *Journal of Abnormal and Social Psychology, 64,* 136–142.

Deck, L. P. (1968). Buying brains by the inch. *Journal of College and University Personnel Association, 19,* 33–37.

de Groot, A. D. (1965). *Thought and choice in chess.* The Hague: Mouton.

de Groot, A. D. (1966). Perception and memory versus thought: Some old ideas and recent findings. In B. Kleinmuntz (Ed.), *Problem solving: Research, method and theory.* New York: Wiley.

Delay, J., & Deniker, P. (1952). *Trente-huit cas de psychoses traitees par la cure prolongee et continue de 4560 RP.* Paris: Masson et Cie.

Delgado, J. M. R. (1969). *Physical control of the mind.* New York: Harper & Row.

Dell, G. S. (1986). A spreading-activation theory of retrieval in sentence production. *Psychological Review, 93,* 283–321.

DeLongis, A., Folkman, S., & Lazarus, R. S. (1988). The impact of daily stress on health and mood: Psychological and social resources as mediators. *Journal of Personality and Social Psychology, 54*(3), 486–495.

Dembroski, T. M., MacDougall, J. M., Williams, B., & Haney, T. L. (1985). Components of Type-A, hostility, and anger-in: Relationship to angiographic findings. *Psychosomatic Medicine, 47,* 219–233.

Dement, W. C. (1978). *Some must watch while some must sleep.* New York: Norton.

Dement, W. C., & Kleitman, N. (1957). The relation of eye movements during sleep to dream activity: An objective method for the study of dreaming. *Journal of Experimental Psychology, 53,* 339–346.

Dement, W. C., & Wolpert, E. (1958). The relation of eye movements, bodily motility, and external stimuli to dream content. *Journal of Experimental Psychology, 53,* 543–553.

Dennis, W. (1960). Causes of retardation among institutional children: Iran. *Journal of Genetic Psychology, 21,* 1–8.

Dennis, W. (1966). Age and creative productivity. *Journal of Gerontology, 21*(1), 1–8.

De Silva, P., Rachman, S., & Seligman, M. E. P. (1977). Prepared phobias and obsessions: Therapeutic outcome. *Behavior Research and Therapy, 15*(1), 65–77.

Detera-Wadleigh, S. D., Berrettini, W. H., Goldin, L. R., Boorman, D., Anderson, S., & Gershon, E. S. (1987). Close linkage of c-Harvey-ras-1 and the insulin gene to affective disorder is ruled out in three North American pedigrees. *Nature, 325,* 806–808.

Deutsch, J. A., & Deutsch, D. (1963). Attention: Some theoretical considerations. *Psychological Review, 70,* 80–90.

Deutsch, M., & Gerard, H. B. (1955). A study of normative and informational social influences upon individual judgment. *Journal of Abnormal and Social Psychology, 51,* 629–636.

DeValois, R. L., Abramov, I., & Jacobs, G. H. (1966). Analysis of response patterns of LGN cells. *Journal of the Optical Society of America, 56,* 966–977.

De Villiers, P. (1977). Choice in concurrent schedules and a quantitative formulation of the law of effect. In W. K. Honig & J. E. R. Staddon (Eds.), *Handbook of operant behavior.* Englewood Cliffs, NJ: Prentice-Hall.

Deyoub, P. L. (1984). Hypnotic stimulation of antisocial behavior: A case report. *International Journal of Clinical and Experimental Hypnosis, 32*(3), 301–306.

Diamond, E. E. (1979). Sex equality and measurement practices. *New Directions for Testing and Measurement, 3,* 61–78.

Dillbeck, M. C., & Orme-Johnson, D. W. (1987, September). Physiological differences between transcendental meditation and rest. *American Psychologist,* pp. 879–881.

DiMatteo, M. R., & Friedman, H. S. (1982). *Social psychology and medicine*. Cambridge, MA: Oelgeschlager, Gunn & Hain.

Dimsdale, J. E. (1988). A perspective on Type-A behavior and coronary disease. *New England Journal of Medicine, 318*(2), 110–112.

DiNicola, D. D., & DiMatteo, M. R. (1984). Practitioners, patients, and compliance with medical regimens: A social psychological perspective. In A. Baum, S. E. Taylor, & J. E. Singer (Eds.), *Handbook of psychology and health: Vol. 4. Social psychological aspects of health*. Hillsdale, NJ: Erlbaum.

Dion, K. K. (1986). Stereotyping based on physical attractiveness: Issues and conceptual perspectives. In C. P. Herman, M. P. Zanna, & E. T. Higgins (Eds.), *Appearance, stigma and social behavior: The Ontario symposium on personality and social psychology* (Vol. 3). Hillsdale, NJ: Erlbaum.

Dixon, N. F. (1980). Humor: A cognitive alternative to stress? In I. G. Sarason & C. D. Spielberger (Eds.), *Stress and anxiety* (Vol. 7). Washington, DC: Hemisphere.

Dohrenwend, B. P. (1980). Introduction. In B. P. Dohrenwend, B. S. Dohrenwend, M. S. Gould, B. Link, R. Neugebauer, & R. Wunsch-Hitzig (Eds.), *Mental illness in the United States: Epidemiological estimates*. New York: Praeger.

Dollard, J., Doob, L. W., Miller, N. E., Mowrer, O. H., & Sears, R. R. (1939). *Frustration and aggression*. New Haven, CT: Yale University Press.

Dollard, J., & Miller, N. E. (1950). *Personality and psychotherapy: An analysis in terms of learning, thinking and culture*. New York: McGraw-Hill.

Domjan, M., & Burkhard, B. (1986). *The principles of learning and behavior*. Pacific Grove, CA: Brooks/Cole.

Dorfman, D. (1978). The Cyril Burt question: New findings. *Science, 201,* 1177–1186.

Dovidio, J. F., & Gaertner, S. L. (Eds.). (1986). *Prejudice, discrimination and racism*. New York: Academic Press.

Duclaux, R., & Kenshalo, D. R. (1980). Response characteristics of cutaneous warm receptors in the monkey. *Journal of Neurophysiology, 43,* 1–15.

Duke, M., & Nowicki, S., Jr. (1979). *Abnormal psychology: Perspectives on being different*. Pacific Grove, CA: Brooks/Cole.

Duncan, B. L. (1976). Differential social perception and attribution of intergroup violence: Testing the lower limits of stereotyping of blacks. *Journal of Personality and Social Psychology, 34,* 590–598.

Duncker, K. (1939). The influence of past experience upon perceptual properties. *American Journal of Psychology, 52,* 255–265.

Durlach, N. I., & Colburn, H. S. (1978). Binaural phenomenon. In E. C. Carterette & M. P. Friedman (Eds.), *Handbook of perception* (Vol. 4). New York: Academic Press.

Durrant, J., & Lovrinic, J. (1977). *Bases of hearing science*. Baltimore: Williams & Wilkins.

Dutton, D., & Aron, A. (1974). Some evidence for heightened sexual attraction under conditions of high anxiety. *Journal of Personality and Social Psychology, 30,* 510–517.

Dworkin, A. (1981). *Pornography: Men possessing women*. New York: Putnam.

E

Eagly, A. H., & Carli, L. L. (1981). Sex of researchers and sex-typed communications as determinants of sex differences in influenceability: A meta-analysis of social influence studies. *Psychological Bulletin, 90,* 1–20.

Eagly, A. H., Wood, W., & Chaiken, S. (1978). Causal inferences about communicators and their effect on opinion change. *Journal of Personality and Social Psychology, 36,* 424–435.

Ebbinghaus, H. (1885/1964). *Memory: A contribution to experimental psychology* (H. A. Ruger & E. R. Bussemius, Trans.). New York: Dover. (Original work published 1885)

Eccles, J. E. (1965). The synapse. *Scientific American, 212*(1), 56–66.

Edwards, B. (1979). *Drawing on the right side of the brain*. Los Angeles, CA: J. P. Tarcher.

Egan, D. E., & Schwartz, B. J. (1979). Chunking in recall of circuit diagrams. *Memory and Cognition, 7,* 149–158.

Egeland, J. A., Gerhard, D. S., Pauls, D. L., Sussex, J. N., Kidd, K. K., Allen, C. R., Hostetter, A. M., & Housman, D. E. (1987). Bipolar affective disorders linked to DNA markers on chromosome 11. *Nature, 325,* 783–787.

Ehrenberg, O., & Ehrenberg, M. (1977). *The psychotherapy maze: A consumer's guide to the ins and outs of therapy*. New York: Holt, Rinehart & Winston.

Eibl-Eibesfeldt, I. (1975). *Ethology: The biology of behavior*. New York: Holt, Rinehart & Winston.

Eibl-Eibesfeldt, I. (1979). *The biology of peace and war*. London: Thames and Hudson.

Eich, J. E., Weingartner, H., Stillman, R. C., & Gillin, J. C. (1975). State-dependent accessibility of retrieval cues in the retention of a categorized list. *Journal of Verbal Learning and Verbal Behavior, 14,* 408–417.

Einstein, G. O., Morris, J., & Smith, S. (1985). Note-taking, individual differences, and memory for lecture information. *Journal of Educational Psychology, 77*(5), 522–532.

Ekman, P. (1975). The universal smile: Face muscles talk every language. *Psychology Today, 9*(4), 35–39.

Ekman, P., & Friesen, W. V. (1975). *Unmasking the face*. Englewood Cliffs, NJ: Prentice-Hall.

Ekman, P., Levenson, R. W., & Friesen, W. V. (1983). Autonomic nervous system activity distinguishes among emotions. *Science, 221,* 1208–1210.

Eliot, R. S., & Breo, D. L. (1984). *Is it worth dying for?* New York: Bantam Books.

Elliott, G. R. (1986). Magnetic resonance and in vivo studies of the human brain. In P. A. Berger & H. K. H. Brodie (Eds.), *American handbook of psychiatry: Biological psychiatry* (2nd ed., Vol. 8). New York: Basic Books.

Elliott, G. R., & Barchas, J. D. (1986). Behavioral neurochemistry: The study of brain and behavior. In P. A. Berger & H. K. H. Brodie (Eds.), *American handbook of psychiatry: Biological psychiatry* (2nd ed., Vol. 8). New York: Basic Books.

Elliott, G. R., & Eisdorfer, C. (Eds.). (1982). *Stress and human health: Analysis and implications of research*. New York: Springer.

Ellis, A. (1962). *Reason and emotion in psychotherapy*. Seacaucus, NJ: Citadel Press.

Ellis, A. (1973). *Humanistic psychotherapy: The rational-emotive approach*. New York: Julian Press.

Ellis, A. (1977). *Reason and emotion in psychotherapy*. Seacaucus, NJ: Citadel Press.

Ellis, A. (1984). *Reason and emotion in psychotherapy*. Seacaucus, NJ: Citadel Press.

Ellis, A. (1985). *How to live with and without anger*. New York: Citadel Press.

Ellis, A. (1987). The evolution of rational-emotive therapy (RET) and cognitive behavior therapy (CBT). In J. K. Zeig (Ed.), *The evolution of psychotherapy*. New York: Brunner/Mazel.

Ellis, S., Rogoff, B., & Cromer, C. C. (1981). Age segregation in children's social interactions. *Developmental Psychology, 17,* 399–407.

Elstein, S. S., Shulman, L. S., & Sprafka, S. A. (1978). *Medical problem solving*. Cambridge, MA: Harvard University Press.

Engen, T. (1971). Psychophysics: 1. Discrimination and detection. In F. W. Kling & L. A. Riggs (Eds.), *Experimental Psychology* (3rd ed., Vol. 1). New York: Holt, Rinehart & Winston.

Enna, S. J., & Gallagher, J. P. (1983). Biochemical and electrophysiological characteristics of mammalian GABA receptors. *International Review of Neurobiology, 24,* 181–212.

Enroth-Cugell, C., & Robson, J. G. (1966). The contrast sensitivity of retinal ganglion cells of the cat. *Journal of Physiology, 187,* 517–552.

Epstein, S. (1980). The stability of confusion: A reply to Mischel and Peake. *Psychological Review, 90,* 179–184.

Epstein, S. P. (1982). Conflict and stress. In L. Goldberger & S. Breznitz (Eds.), *Handbook of stress: Theoretical and clinical aspects*. New York: Free Press.

Erikson, E. (1963). *Childhood and society*. New York: Norton. (First edition published in 1950)

Erikson, E. (1968). *Identity: Youth and crisis*. New York: Norton.

Eron, L. D. (1963). Relationship of TV viewing habits and aggressive behavior in children. *Journal of Abnormal and Social Psychology, 67,* 193–196.

Eron, L. D. (1982). Parent-child interaction, television violence, and aggression of children. *American Psychologist, 37,* 197–211.

Eron, L. D., Huesmann, L. R., Lefkowitz, M. M., & Walder, L. O. (1972). Does television violence cause aggression? *American Psychologist, 27,* 253–263.

Etaugh, C. F., & Harlow, H. (1975). Behaviors of male and female teachers as related to behaviors and attitudes of elementary school children. *Journal of Genetic Psychology, 127,* 163–170.

Evans, F. J. (1980). Phenomena of hypnosis: 2. Posthypnotic amnesia. In G. D. Burrows & L. Dennerstein (Eds.), *Handbook of hypnosis and psychosomatic medicine*. Amsterdam: Elsevier/North Holland Biomedical Press.

Exline, R. (1962). Need affiliation and initial communication behavior in problem-solving groups characterized by low visibility. *Psychological Reports, 10,* 79–89.

Eysenck, H. J. (1952). The effects of psychotherapy: An evaluation. *Journal of Consulting Psychology, 16,* 319–324.

Eysenck, H. J. (1967). *The biological basis of personality*. Springfield, IL: Charles C Thomas.

Eysenck, H. J. (1976). *Sex and personality*. London: Open Books.

Eysenck, H. J. (1981). Is intelligence inherited? In H. J. Eysenck versus L. Kamin, *The intelligence controversy*. New York: Wiley.

Eysenck, H. J. (1982). *Personality, genetics and behavior: Selected papers*. New York: Praeger.

Eysenck, H. J., & Levey, A. (1972). Conditioning, introversion-extraversion and the strength of the nervous system. In V. D. Nebylitsyn & J. A. Gray (Eds.), *Biological bases of individual behavior*. New York: Academic Press.

F

Fagley, N. S. (1987). Positional response bias in multiple-choice tests of learning: Its relation to testwiseness and guessing strategy. *Journal of Educational Psychology, 79*(1), 95–97.

Fagot, B. I. (1978). The influence of sex of child on parental reactions to toddler children. *Child Development, 49,* 459–465.

Fancher, R. E. (1979). *Pioneers of psychology*. New York: Norton.

Fancher, R. E. (1985). *The intelligence men: Makers of the IQ controversy*. New York: Norton.

Fanselow, M. S., & Baackes, M. P. (1982). Conditioned fear-induced opiate analgesia on the formalin test: Evidence for two aversive motivational systems. *Learning and Motivation, 13,* 220–221.

Fantino, E. (1973). Aversive control. In J. A. Nevin (Ed.), *The study of behavior: Learning, motivation, emotion and instinct*. Glenview, IL: Scott, Foresman.

Faraday, A. (1974). *The dream game*. New York: Harper & Row.

Farberow, N. L. (1974). *Suicide*. Morristown, NJ: General Learning Press.

Fasteau, M. F. (1974). *The male machine*. New York: McGraw-Hill.

Fechner, G. T. (1860). *Elemente der psychophysik* (Vol. 1). Leipzig: Breitkopf & Harterl.

Feder, H. H. (1984). Hormones and sexual behavior. In M. R. Rosenzweig & L. W. Porter (Eds.), *Annual review of psychology: 1984* (Vol. 35). Palo Alto, CA: Annual Reviews.

Feighner, J. P. (1986). The new generation of antidepressants. In A. J. Rush & K. Z. Altshuler (Eds.), *Depression: Basic mechanisms, diagnosis, and treatment*. New York: Guilford Press.

Ferster, C. S., & Skinner, B. F. (1957). *Schedules of reinforcement.* New York: Appleton-Century-Crofts.

Festinger, L. (1957). *A theory of cognitive dissonance.* Stanford, CA: Stanford University Press.

Festinger, L. (1964). *Conflict, decision and dissonance.* Stanford, CA: Stanford University Press.

Festinger, L., & Carlsmith, J. M. (1959). Cognitive consequences of forced compliance. *Journal of Abnormal and Social Psychology, 58,* 203–210.

Festinger, L., Schachter, S., & Back, K. (1950). *Social pressures in informal groups: A study of human factors in housing.* New York: Harper.

Field, D. (1981). Can preschool children really learn to conserve? *Child Development, 52,* 326–334.

Fields, H. L., & Levine, J. D. (1984). Placebo analgesia: A role for endorphins. *Trends in Neuroscience, 7,* 271–273.

Fincham, F. D., Beach, S. R., & Baucom, D. H. (1987). Attribution processes in distressed and non-distressed couples: 4. Self-partner attribution differences. *Journal of Personality and Social Psychology, 52(4),* 739–748.

Findley, M. J., & Cooper, H. M. (1983). Locus of control and academic achievement: A literature review. *Journal of Personality and Social Psychology, 44,* 419–427.

Finer, B. (1980). Hypnosis and anaesthesia. In G. D. Burrows & L. Dennerstein (Eds.), *Handbook of hypnosis and psychosomatic medicine.* Amsterdam: Elsevier/North Holland Biomedical Press.

Fink, M. (1988). Convulsive therapy: A manual of practice. In A. J. Frances & R. E. Hales (Eds.), *Review of psychiatry: Volume 7.* Washington, DC: American Psychiatric Press.

Fischler, I., Rundus, D., & Atkinson, R. C. (1970). Effects of overt rehearsal processes on free recall. *Psychonomic Science, 19,* 249–350.

Fisher, R. P., & Craik, F. I. M. (1977). Interaction between encoding and retrieval operations in cued recall. *Journal of Experimental Psychology: Human Learning and Memory, 3,* 701–711.

Fisher, W. A. (1984). Predicting contraceptive behavior among university men: The roles of emotions and behavioral intentions. *Journal of Applied Social Psychology, 14,* 104–123.

Fisher, W. A., & Byrne, D. (1978). Sex differences in response to erotica? Love versus lust. *Journal of Personality and Social Psychology, 36,* 119–125.

Fisher, W. A., Byrne, D., White, L. A., & Kelley, K. (1988). Erotophobia-erotophilia as a dimension of personality. *Journal of Sex Research, 25(1),* 123–151.

Fiske, S. T., & Taylor, S. E. (1984). *Social cognition.* Reading, MA: Addison-Wesley.

Fitts, W. (1972). *The self-concept and psychopathology.* Nashville, TN: Counselor Recording and Tests.

Flavell, J. H. (1982). On cognitive development. *Child Development, 53,* 1–10.

Flavell, J. H., Everett, B. H., Croft, K., & Flavell, E. R. (1981). Young children's knowledge about visual perception: Further evidence for the level 1–level 2 distinction. *Developmental Psychology, 17,* 99–103.

Fletcher, G. J. O., Fincham, F. D., Cramer, L., & Heron, N. (1987). The role of attributions in the development of dating relationships. *Journal of Personality and Social Psychology, 53(3),* 481–489.

Folkins, C. H., & Sime, W. (1981). Physical fitness training and mental health. *American Psychologist, 36,* 373–389.

Folkman, S. (1984). Personal control and stress and coping processes: A theoretical analysis. *Journal of Personality and Social Psychology, 46(4),* 839–852.

Forsyth, D. R. (1983). *An introduction to group dynamics.* Pacific Grove, CA: Brooks/Cole.

Forsyth, D. R., & McMillan, J. H. (1981). Attributions, affect, and expectations: A test of Weiner's three-dimensional model. *Journal of Educational Psychology, 73,* 393–403.

Forsyth, D. R., & Strong, S. R. (1986). The scientific study of counseling and psychotherapy: A unificationist view. *American Psychologist, 41(2),* 113–119.

Foulkes, D. (1985). *Dreaming: A cognitive-psychological analysis.* Hillsdale, NJ: Erlbaum.

Fowler, R. D. (1986). Howard Hughes: A psychological autopsy. *Psychology Today, 20(5),* 22–33.

Frances, A. J., & Widiger, T. (1986). The classification of personality disorders: An overview of problems and solutions. In A. J. Frances & R. E. Hales (Eds.), *Psychiatry Update: Annual Review* (Vol. 5). Washington, DC: American Psychiatric Press.

Frank, E., Anderson, C., & Rubinstein, D. (1978). Frequency of sexual dysfunction in "normal" couples. *New England Journal of Medicine, 299,* 111–115.

Frank, G. (1983). *The Wechsler enterprise: An assessment of the development, structure and use of the Wechsler tests of intelligence.* New York: Pergamon Press.

Frank, J. D. (1982). Therapeutic components shared by all psychotherapies. In J. H. Harvey & M. M. Parks (Eds.), *The master lecture series: Vol. 1. Psychotherapy research and behavior change.* Washington, DC: American Psychological Association.

Frank, L. K. (1939). Projective methods for the study of personality. *Journal of Psychology, 8,* 343–389.

Frankel, F. H. (1984). Electroconvulsive therapy. In T. B. Karasu (Ed.), *The psychiatric therapies.* Washington, DC: American Psychiatric Association.

Franks, C. M., & Barbrack, C. R. (1983). Behavior therapy with adults: An integrative perspective. In M. Hersen, A. E. Kazdin, & A. S. Bellack (Eds.), *The clinical psychology handbook.* New York: Pergamon Press.

Freedman, J. L., & Sears, D. O. (1965). Warning, distraction, and resistance to influence. *Journal of Personality and Social Psychology, 1,* 262–266.

French, E. G., & Thomas, F. H. (1958). The relation of achievement motivation to problem-solving effectiveness. *Journal of Abnormal and Social Psychology, 56,* 46–48.

Freud, S. (1900/1953). The interpretation of dreams. In J. Strachey (Ed.), *The standard edition of the complete psycholoical works of Sigmund Freud* (Vols. 4 and 5). London: Hogarth.

Freud, S. (1901/1960). *The psychopathology of everyday life.* In J. Strachey (Ed.), *The standard edition of the complete psychological works of Sigmund Freud* (Vol. 6). London: Hogarth.

Freud, S. (1905/1953). Fragment of an analysis of a case of hysteria. In J. Strachey (Ed.), *The standard edition of the complete psychological works of Sigmund Freud* (Vol. 7). London: Hogarth.

Freud, S. (1915/1959). Instincts and their vicissitudes. In E. Jones (Ed.), *The collected papers of Sigmund Freud* (Vol. 4). New York: Basic Books.

Freud, S. (1917/1955). *A difficulty in the path of psychoanalysis.* In J. Strachey (Ed.), *The standard edition of the complete psychological works of Sigmund Freud* (Vol. 17). London: Hogarth.

Freud, S. (1920). *A general introduction to psychoanalysis.* New York: Boni & Liveright.

Freud, S. (1923/1961). *The ego and the id.* In J. Strachey (Ed.), *The standard edition of the complete psychological works of Sigmund Freud* (Vol. 19). London: Hogarth.

Freud, S. (1924). *A general introduction to psychoanalysis.* New York: Boni & Liveright.

Freud, S. (1933/1964). *New introductory lectures on psychoanalysis.* In J. Strachey (Ed.), *The standard edition of the complete psychological works of Sigmund Freud* (Vol. 22). London: Hogarth.

Freud, S. (1940). An outline of psychoanalysis. *International Journal of Psychoanalysis, 21,* 27–84.

Fried, P. A. (1977). Behavioral and electroencephalographic correlates of the chronic use of marijuana—A review. *Behavioral Biology, 21,* 163–196.

Friedberg, J. (1975). Electroshock therapy—Let's stop blasting the brain. *Psychology Today, 9(3),* 18–23, 98–99.

Friedberg, J. (1976). *Shock treatment is not good for your brain.* San Francisco: Glide Publications.

Friedewald, W. T. (1982). Current nutrition issues in hypertension. *Journal of the American Dietetic Association, 80,* 17.

Friedman, H. S. (1983). Social perception and face-to-face interaction. In D. Perlman & P. C. Cozby (Eds.), *Social Psychology.* New York: Holt, Rinehart & Winston.

Friedman, M., & Rosenman, R. H. (1974). *Type-A behavior and your heart.* New York: Knopf.

Friedmann, J., Globus, G., Huntley, A., Mullaney, D., Naitoh, P., & Johnson, L. (1977). Performance and mood during and after gradual sleep reduction. *Psychophysiology, 14,* 245–250.

Fries, H., Nillius, J., & Petersson, F. (1974). Epidemiology of secondary amenorrhea. *American Journal of Obstetrics and Gynecology, 118,* 473–479.

Fritsch, G., & Hitzig, E. (1870). Über die elektrische erregbarkeit des grosshirns. *Archiv für Anatomie, Physiologie und Wissenschaftliche Medizin,* 300–332.

Fromm, E. (1979). The nature of hypnosis and other altered states of consciousness: An ego-psychological theory. In E. Fromm & R. E. Shor (Eds.), *Hypnosis: Developments in research and new perspectives.* New York: Aldine.

Fuchs, R. M. (1984). Group therapy. In T. B. Karasu (Ed.), *The psychiatric therapies.* Washington, DC: American Psychiatric Association.

Funch, P. G., and Faber, D. S. (1984). Measurement of myelin sheath resistances: Implications for axonal conduction and pathophysiology. *Science, 225,* 538–540.

Funk, S. C., & Houston, B. K. (1987). A critical analysis of the Hardiness Scale's validity and utility. *Journal of Personality and Social Psychology, 53(3),* 572–578.

Furst, C. (1979). *Origins of the mind.* Englewood Cliffs, NJ: Prentice-Hall.

Galin, D. (1974). Implications for psychiatry of left and right cerebral specialization: A neuropsychological context for unconscious processes. *Archives of General Psychiatry, 31,* 572–583.

Galin, D., and Ornstein, R. (1972). Lateral specialization of cognitive mode: An EEG study. *Psychophysiology, 9,* 412–418.

Galton, F. (1869). *Hereditary genius: An inquiry into its laws and consequences.* New York: Appleton.

Gantt, H. (1975). Unpublished lecture, Ohio State University, April 25, 1975. Cited in D. Hothersall (1984), *History of psychology.* New York: Random House.

Gantt, W. H. (1966). Conditional or conditioned, reflex or response? *Conditioned Reflex, 1,* 69–74.

Garcia, J., Clarke, J. C., & Hankins, W. G. (1973). Natural responses to scheduled rewards. In P. P. G. Bateson & P. Klopfer (Eds.), *Perspectives in ethology.* New York: Plenum Press.

Garcia, J., & Koelling, R. A. (1966). Learning with prolonged delay of reinforcement. *Psychonomic Science, 5,* 121–122.

Garcia, J., & Rusiniak, K. W. (1980). What the nose learns from the mouth. In D. Muller-Schwarze & R. M. Silverstein (Eds.), *Chemical signals.* New York: Plenum Press.

Gardner, H. (1975, August 9). Brain damage: Window on the mind. *Saturday Review,* pp. 26–29.

Gardner, H. (1983). *Frames of mind: The theory of multiple intelligences.* New York: Basic Books.

Gardner, M. (1969). *Perplexing puzzles and tantalizing teasers.* New York: Simon & Schuster.

Gardner, R. A., & Gardner, B. T. (1969). Teaching sign language to a chimpanzee. *Science, 165,* 664–672.

Garvey, C. R. (1929). List of American psychology laboratories. *Psychological Bulletin, 26,* 652–660.

Gawin, F. H. (1978). Pharmacological enhancement of the erotic: Implications of an expanded definition of aphrodisiacs. *Journal of Sex Research, 14,* 107–117.

Gazzaniga, M. S. (1970). *The bisected brain.* New York: Appleton-Century-Crofts.

Gazzaniga, M. S., Bogen, J. E., and Sperry, R. W. (1965). Observations on visual perception after disconnexion of the cerebral hemispheres in man. *Brain, 88(2),* 221–236.

Geiselman, R. E., Fisher, R. P., MacKinnon, D. P., & Holland, H. L. (1985). Eyewitness memory enhancement in the police interview: Cognitive retrieval mnemonics versus hypnosis. *Journal of Applied Psychology, 70,* 401–412.

Geldard, F. A. (1962). *Fundamentals of psychology.* New York: Wiley.

Geller, L. (1982). The failure of self-actualization theory: A critique of Carl Rogers and Abraham Maslow. *Journal of Humanistic Psychology, 22,* 56–73.

Georgas, J., Giakoumaki, E., Georgoulias, N., Koumandakis, E., & Kaskarelis, D. (1984). Psychosocial stress and its relation to obstetrical complications. *Psychotherapy and Psychosomatics, 41,* 200–206.

Georgotas, A. (1985). Affective disorders: Pharmacotherapy. In H. I. Kaplan & B. J. Sadock (Eds.), *Comprehensive textbook of psychiatry/IV.* Baltimore: Williams & Wilkins.

Gerard, M. (Ed.). (1968). *Dali.* Paris: Draeger.

Gerbner, G., Gross, L., Morgan, M., & Signorelli, N. (1980). The "mainstreaming" of America: Violence profile no. 11. *Journal of Communication, 30*(3), 10–29.

Gerner, R. H., & Bunney, W. E., Jr. (1986). Biological hypotheses of affective disorders. In P. A. Berger & H. K. H. Brodie (Eds.), *American handbook of psychiatry: Biological psychiatry* (2nd ed., Vol. 8). New York: Basic Books.

Geschwind, N. (1979). Specializations of the human brain. In *Scientific American* (Eds.), *The brain: Readings from Scientific American.* San Francisco: W. H. Freeman.

Gesteland, R. C. (1978). The neural code: Integrative neural mechanisms. In E. C. Carterette & M. P. Friedman (Eds.), *Handbook of perception* (Vol. 6). New York: Academic Press.

Ghiselli, E. (1966). *The validity of occupational aptitude tests.* New York: Wiley.

Gibson, E. J., & Walk, R. D. (1960). The "visual cliff." *Scientific American, 202,* 64–71.

Gibson, J. J. (1962). Observations on active touch. *Psychological Review, 69,* 477–491.

Gick, M. L., & Holyoak, K. (1980). Analogical problem solving. *Cognitive Psychology, 12,* 306–355.

Gilbert, C. D., & Wiesel, T. N. (1985). Intrinsic connectivity and receptive field properties in visual cortex. *Vision Research, 25,* 365–374.

Gilder, G. (1986). *Men and marriage.* New York: Pelican.

Gilgen, A. R. (1982). *American psychology since World War II: A profile of the discipline.* Westport, CT: Greenwood Press.

Gillberg, M. (1984). The effects of two alternative timings of a one-hour nap on early morning performance. *Biological Psychology, 19*(1), 45–54.

Gilligan, C. (1982). *In a different voice: Psychological theory and women's development.* Cambridge, MA: Harvard University Press.

Gilmer, B. V. H. (1975). *Applied psychology: Adjustments in living and work.* New York: McGraw-Hill.

Ginsburg, H. J., & Miller, S. M. (1982). Sex differences in children's risk-taking behavior. *Child Development, 53,* 426–428.

Ginzberg, E. (1972). Toward a theory of occupational choice: A restatement. *Vocational Guidance Quarterly, 20,* 169–176.

Glaser, R. (1984). Education and thinking: The role of knowledge. *American Psychologist, 39,* 93–104.

Glass, D. C. (1978). Pattern-A behavior and uncontrollable stress. In T. M. Dembroski, S. M. Weiss, J. L. Shields, S. G. Haynes, & M. Feinleib (Eds.), *Coronary prone behavior.* New York: Springer-Verlag.

Glenn, M., & Taska, R. J. (1984). Antidepressants and lithium. In T. B. Karasu (Ed.), *The psychiatric therapies.* Washington, DC: American Psychiatric Association.

Gmelch, G. (1978, August). Baseball magic. *Human Nature,* pp. 32–39.

Goddard, H. H. (1908). The Binet and Simon tests of intellectual capacity. *The Training School, 5,* 3–9.

Goddard, H. H. (1917). Mental tests and the immigrant. *Journal of Delinquency, 2,* 243–277.

Goethals, G. (1986). Social comparison theory: Psychology from the lost and found. *Personality and Social Psychology Bulletin, 12*(3), 261–278.

Goethals, G. R., & Darley, J. M. (1977). Social comparison theory: An attributional approach. In J. M. Suls & R. M. Miller (Eds.), *Social comparison processes: Theoretical and empirical perspectives.* Washington, DC: Hemisphere/Halsted.

Goldberg, H. (1983). *The new male-female relationship.* New York: Morrow.

Goldenberg, H. (1983). *Contemporary clinical psychology.* Pacific Grove, CA: Brooks/Cole.

Goldenthal, P. (1985). Posing and judging facial expressions of emotion: The effects of social skills. *Journal of Social and Clinical Psychology, 3*(3), 325–338.

Goldfarb, W. (1947). Variations in adolescent adjustment in institutionally reared children. *Journal of Orthopsychiatry, 17,* 449–457.

Goldstein, A. J., & Chambless, D. L. (1978). A reanalysis of agoraphobia. *Behavior Therapy, 9,* 47–59.

Goldstein, M. J. (1984). *Family factors that antedate the onset of schizophrenia and related disorders: The results of a fifteen-year prospective longitudinal study.* Paper presented at the Regional Symposium of the World Psychiatric Association Meeting, Helsinki, Finland.

Goldstein, M. J. (1988). The family and psychopathology. In M. R. Rosenzweig & L. W. Porter (Eds.), *Annual review of psychology: 1988* (Vol. 39). Palo Alto, CA: Annual Reviews.

Goleman, D. (1978). Special abilities of the sexes: Do they begin in the brain? *Psychology Today, 12*(6), 48–59, 120.

Goleman, D. (1979). [Interview with Richard S. Lazarus]. Positive denial: The case for not facing reality. *Psychology Today, 13*(6), 44–60.

Goleman, D. (1980). 1528 little geniuses and how they grew. *Psychology Today, 13*(9), 28–53.

Goleman, D. (1982). Staying up: The rebellion against sleep's gentle tyranny. *Psychology Today, 16*(3), 24–35.

Good, L., & Good, K. (1972). An objective measure of the motive to attain social power. *Psychological Reports, 30*(1), 247–251.

Goodall, K. (1972). Field report: Shapers at work. *Psychology Today, 6*(6), 53–63, 132–138.

Goodwin, F. K., & Jamison, K. R. (1986). *Manic-depressive illness.* New York: Oxford University Press.

Gore, S. (1978). The effect of social support in moderating the health consequences of unemployment. *Journal of Health and Social Behavior, 19,* 157–165.

Gottesman, I. I., & Shields, J. (1982). *Schizophrenia: The epigenetic puzzle.* Cambridge, MA: Cambridge University Press.

Gould, R. L. (1975). Adult life stages: Growth toward self-tolerance. *Psychology Today, 8*(9), 74–78.

Gould, R. L. (1978). *Transformations: Growth and change in adult life.* New York: Simon & Schuster.

Gould, S. J. (1981). *The mismeasure of man.* New York: Norton.

Gove, W. R. (1975). Labeling and mental illness: A critique. In W. R. Gove (Ed.), *The labeling of deviance: Evaluating a perspective.* New York: Halsted.

Green, L. W., Tryon, W. W., Marks, B., & Huryn, J. (1986). Periodontal disease as a function of life events stress. *Journal of Human Stress, 12*(1), 32–36.

Greenberg, J. S. (1983). *Comprehensive stress management.* Dubuque, IA: William C. Brown.

Greene, J. G., Fox, N. A., & Lewis, M. (1983). The relationship between neonatal characteristics and three-month mother–infant interaction in high-risk infants. *Child Development, 54,* 1286–1296.

Greene, W. A., & Swisher, S. N. (1969). Psychological and somatic variables associated with the development and course of monozygotic twins discordant for leukemia. *Annals of the New York Academy of Sciences, 164,* 394–408.

Greenfield, P. M. (1982). The role of perceived variability in transition to language. *Journal of Child Language, 9,* 1–12.

Greenfield, P. M., & Smith, J. H. (1976). *The structure of communication in early language development.* New York: Academic Press.

Greenley, J. R., Kepecs, J. G., & Henry, W. E. (1981). Trends in urban American psychiatry: Practice in Chicago in 1962 and 1973. *Social Psychiatry, 16,* 123–128.

Greeno, J. G. (1978). Natures of problem-solving abilities. In W. K. Estes (Ed.), *Handbook of learning and cognitive processes* (Vol. 5). Hillsdale, NJ: Erlbaum.

Greenson, R. R. (1967). *The technique and practice of psychoanalysis* (Vol. 1). New York: International Universities Press.

Gregory, R. L. (1973). *Eye and brain.* New York: McGraw-Hill.

Gregory, R. L. (1978). *Eye and brain.* New York: McGraw-Hill.

Griesinger, W. S., & Klene, R. R. (1984). Readability of introductory textbooks: Flesch versus student ratings. *Teaching of Psychology, 11*(2), 90–91.

Griffith, R. M., Miyago, O., & Tago, A. (1958). The universality of typical dreams: Japanese vs. Americans. *American Anthropologist, 60,* 1173–1179.

Grimm, L. G., & Yarnold, P. R. (1984). Performance standards and the Type-A behavior pattern. *Cognitive Therapy and Research, 8*(1), 59–66.

Grinker, J. A. (1982). Physiological and behavioral basis for human obesity. In D. W. Pfaff (Ed.), *The physiological mechanisms of motivation.* New York: Springer-Verlag.

Grob, G. N. (1983). Disease and environment in American history. In D. Mechanic (Ed.), *Handbook of health, health care, and the health professions.* New York: Free Press.

Grossman, S. P. (1979). The biology of motivation. In M. Rosenzweig & L. W. Porter (Eds.), *Annual review of psychology: 1979* (Vol. 30). Palo Alto, CA: Annual Reviews.

Grossman, S. P., Dacey, D., Halaris, A. E., Collier, T., & Routtenberg, A. (1978). Aphagia and adipsia after preferential destruction of nerve cell bodies in hypothalamus. *Science, 202,* 537–539.

Grotjahn, M., Kline, F. M., & Friedmann, C. T. H. (Eds.). (1983). *Handbook of group therapy.* New York: Van Nostrand Reinhold.

Guilford, J. P. (1939). *General psychology.* Princeton, NJ: Van Nostrand.

Guilford, J. P. (1959). Three faces of intellect. *American Psychologist, 14,* 469–479.

Guilford, J. P. (1985). The structure-of-intellect model. In B. B. Wolman (Ed.), *Handbook of intelligence: Theories, measurements, and applications.* New York: Wiley.

Gustavson, C. R., Kelly, D. J., Sweeney, M., & Garcia, J. (1976). Prey-lithium aversions I: Coyotes and wolves. *Behavioral Biology, 17,* 61–72.

Guyton, A. C. (1981). *Textbook of medical physiology.* Philadelphia: Saunders.

H

Hales, D. (1987). *How to sleep like a baby.* New York: Ballantine.

Hall, C. S. (1966). *The meaning of dreams.* New York: McGraw-Hill.

Hall, C. S. (1979). The meaning of dreams. In D. Goleman & R. J. Davidson (Eds.), *Consciousness: Brain, states of awareness, and mysticism.* New York: Harper & Row.

Hall, C. S., & Nordby, V. J. (1972). *The individual and his dreams.* New York: Mentor.

Hall, C. S., & Van de Castle, R. L. (1966). *Content analysis of dreams.* New York: Appleton-Century-Crofts.

Hall, E. (1987). *Growing and changing: What the experts say.* New York: Random House.

Hall, G. S. (1904). *Adolescence.* New York: Appleton.

Hall, J. A. (1978). Gender effects in decoding nonverbal cues. *Psychological Bulletin, 85,* 845–857.

Hall, J. A., & Halberstadt, A. G. (1986). Smiling and gazing. In J. S. Hyde & M. C. Linn (Eds.), *The psychology of gender: Advances through meta-analysis.* Baltimore: Johns Hopkins University Press.

Hamachek, D. E. (1987). *Encounters with the self.* New York: Holt, Rinehart & Winston.

Hamilton, D. L. (1979). A cognitive-attributional analysis of stereotyping. In L. Berkowitz (Ed.), *Advances in experimental social psychology* (Vol. 12). New York: Academic Press.

Hamilton, D. L., & Gifford, R. K. (1976). Illusory correlation in interpersonal perception: A cognitive basis of stereotypic judgments. *Journal of Experimental Social Psychology, 12,* 392–407.

Hammen, C., Mayol, A., deMayo, R., & Marks, T. (1986). Initial symptom levels and the life-event-depression relationship. *Journal of Abnormal Psychology, 95*(2), 114–122.

Hammond, E. C., & Horn, D. (1984). Smoking and death rates—Report on 44 months of follow-up of 187,783 men. *Journal of the American Medical Association, 251*(21), 2840–2853.

Hanson, R. A. (1975). Consistency and stability of home environmental measures related to IQ. *Child Development, 46*, 470–480.

Harding, C. M., Brooks, G. W., Ashikaga, T., Strauss, J. S., & Breier, A. (1987). The Vermont longitudinal study of persons with severe mental illness: II. Long-term outcome of subjects who retrospectively met DSM-III criteria for schizophrenia. *American Journal of Psychiatry, 144*(6), 727–735.

Hare, R. D. (1983). Diagnosis of antisocial personality disorder in criminals. *American Journal of Psychiatry, 140*, 887–890.

Harlow, H. F., & Harlow, M. (1962). Social deprivation in monkeys. *Scientific American, 207*(5), 136–146.

Harrell, T. W., & Harrell, M. S. (1945). Army General Classification Test scores for civilian occupations. *Educational and Psychological Measurement, 5*, 229–239.

Harris, L. J. (1980). Lateralized sex differences: Substrates and significance. *Behavioral and Brain Sciences, 3*, 236–237.

Harris, P. L. (1983). Infant cognition. In P. H. Mussen (Ed.), *Handbook of child psychology* (Vol. 2). New York: Wiley.

Harris, W. G. (1987). *Cary Grant: A touch of elegance.* New York: Doubleday.

Harrower, M. R. (1936). Some factors determining figure-ground articulation. *British Journal of Psychology, 26*(4), 407–424.

Hartline, H. K., & Ratliff, F. (1957). Inhibitory interaction of receptor units in the eye of limulus. *Journal of General Physiology, 40*, 357–376.

Hartman, W. E., & Fithian, M. A. (1974). *Treatment of sexual dysfunction: A bio-psycho-social approach.* New York: Aronson.

Hartmann, E. L. (1978). *The sleeping pill.* New Haven, CT: Yale University Press.

Hartmann, E. L. (1985). Sleep disorders. In H. I. Kaplan & B. J. Sadock (Eds.), *Comprehensive textbook of psychiatry* (4th ed.). Baltimore: Williams & Wilkins.

Hartup, W. W. (1974). Aggression in childhood: Developmental perspectives. *American Psychologist, 29*, 336–341.

Harvey, J. H., Town, J. P., & Yarkin, K. L. (1981). How fundamental is "the fundamental attribution error"? *Journal of Personality and Social Psychology, 40*(2), 346–349.

Haslam, D. R. (1981). The military performance of soldiers in continuous operations: Exercises "Early Call" I and II. In L. C. Johnson, D. I. Tepas, W. P. Colquhoun, & M. J. Colligan (Eds.), *Biological rhythms, sleep and shift work.* New York: Spectrum.

Hass, R. G. (1981). Effects of source characteristics on cognitive responses and persuasion. In R. E. Petty, T. M. Ostrom, & T. C. Brock (Eds.), *Cognitive responses in persuasion.* Hillsdale, NJ: Erlbaum.

Hastorf, A., & Cantril, H. (1954). They saw a game: A case study. *Journal of Abnormal and Social Psychology, 49*, 129–134.

Hatfield, E. (1988). Passionate and companionate love. In R. J. Sternberg & M. L. Barnes (Eds.), *The psychology of love.* New Haven, CT: Yale University Press.

Hathaway, S. R., & McKinley, J. C. (1943). *Manual for the Minnesota Multiphasic Personality Inventory.* New York: Psychological Corporation.

Haviland, S. E., & Clark, H. H. (1974). What's new? Acquiring new information as a process of comprehension. *Journal of Verbal Learning and Verbal Behavior, 13*, 512–521.

Hawton, K., Cole, D., O'Grady, J., & Osborn, M. (1982). Motivational aspects of deliberate self-poisoning in adolescents. *British Journal of Psychiatry, 141*, 286–290.

Hayes, K. J., & Hayes, C. (1951). The intellectual development of a home-raised chimpanzee. *Proceedings of the American Philosophical Society, 95*, 105–109.

Haynes, D. M. (1982). Course and conduct of normal pregnancy. In D. N. Danforth (Ed.), *Obstetrics and gynecology.* Philadelphia: Harper & Row.

Haynes, S. G., Feinleib, M., & Eaker, E. D. (1983). Type-A behavior and the ten-year incidence of coronary heart disease in the Framingham heart study. In R. H. Rosenman (Ed.), *Psychosomatic risk factors and coronary heart disease.* Bern: Huber.

Hazan, C., & Shaver, P. (1987). Romantic love conceptualized as an attachment process. *Journal of Personality and Social Psychology, 52*(3), 511–524.

Hearnshaw, L. S. (1979). *Cyril Burt: Psychologist.* Ithaca, NY: Cornell University Press.

Hearst, E. (1979). One hundred years: Themes and perspectives. In E. Hearst (Ed.), *The first century of experimental psychology.* Hillsdale, NJ: Erlbaum.

Heath, R. G. (Ed.). (1964). *The role of pleasure in behavior.* New York: Harper & Row.

Heath, R. G. (1976). Cannabis sativa derivatives: Effects on brain function of monkeys. In G. G. Nahas (Ed.), *Marijuana: Chemistry, biochemistry and cellular effects.* New York: Springer.

Hebb, D. D. (1955). Drives and the C.N.S. (conceptual nervous system). *Psychological Review, 62*, 243–254.

Hegsted, D. M. (1984). What is a healthful diet? In J. D. Matarazzo, S. M. Weiss, J. A. Herd, N. E. Miller, & S. M. Weiss (Eds.), *Behavioral health: A handbook of health enhancement and disease prevention.* New York: Wiley.

Heider, F. (1946). Attitudes and cognitive organization. *Journal of Psychology, 21*, 107–112.

Heider, F. (1958). *The psychology of interpersonal relations.* New York: Wiley.

Heiman, J. R. (1977). A psychophysiological exploration of sexual arousal patterns in females and males. *Psychophysiology, 14*, 266–274.

Helmholtz, H. von. (1852). On the theory of compound colors. *Philosophical Magazine, 4*, 519–534.

Helmholtz, H. von. (1863/1954). *On the sensations of tone as a physiological basis for the theory of music.* (A. J. Ellis, Trans.). New York: Dover.

Helson, R., & Moane, G. (1987). Personality change in women from college to midlife. *Journal of Personality and Social Psychology, 53*(1), 176–186.

Helzer, J. E., Robins, L. N., & McEvoy, L. (1987). Post-traumatic stress disorder in the general population: Findings of the epidemiologic catchment area survey. *The New England Journal of Medicine, 317*(26), 1630–1634.

Henderson, C. W. (1975). *Awakening: Ways to psychospiritual growth.* Englewood Cliffs, NJ: Prentice-Hall.

Henderson, N. D. (1982). Human behavior genetics. *Annual Review of Psychology, 33*, 403–440.

Hendrick, C., & Hendrick, S. S. (1983). *Liking, loving and relating.* Pacific Grove, CA: Brooks/Cole.

Hendrick, C., & Hendrick, S. S. (1986). A theory and method of love. *Journal of Personality and Social Psychology, 50*, 392–402.

Hendrick, S. S., Hendrick, C., & Adler, N. L. (1988). Romantic relationships: Love, satisfaction, and staying together. *Journal of Personality and Social Psychology, 54*(6), 980–988.

Henry, K. R. (1984). Cochlear damage resulting from exposure to four different octave bands of noise at three different ages. *Behavioral Neuroscience, 1*, 107–117.

Hering, E. (1878). *Zür lehre vom lichtsinne.* Vienna: Gerold.

Herink, R. (Ed.). (1980). *The psychotherapy handbook.* New York: New American Library.

Herrenkohl, R. C. (1972). Factor analytic and criterion study of achievement orientation. *Journal of Educational Psychology, 63*(4), 314–326.

Heth, C. D., & Rescorla, R. A. (1973). Simultaneous and backward fear conditioning in the rat. *Journal of Comparative and Physiological Psychology, 82*, 434–443.

Hilgard, E. R. (1965). *Hypnotic susceptibility.* New York: Harcourt, Brace & World.

Hilgard, E. R. (1986). *Divided consciousness: Multiple controls in human thought and action.* New York: Wiley.

Hilgard, E. R., & Bower, G. H. (1975). *Theories of learning.* Englewood Cliffs, NJ: Prentice-Hall.

Hilgard, J. R. (1970). *Personality and hypnosis: A study of imaginative involvement.* Chicago: University of Chicago Press.

Hilliard, A. G., III. (1984). IQ testing as the emperor's new clothes: A critique of Jensen's "Bias in Mental Testing." In C. R. Reynolds & R. T. Brown (Eds.), *Perspectives on bias in mental testing.* New York: Plenum Press.

Hineline, P. N. (1981). The several roles of stimuli in negative reinforcement. In P. Harzem and M. D. Zeiler (Eds.), *Predictability, correlation and continuity.* Chichester, England: Wiley.

Hiroto, D. S., & Seligman, M. E. P. (1975). Generality of learned helplessness in man. *Journal of Personality and Social Psychology, 31*, 311–327.

Hirschfeld, R. M. A., & Davidson, L. (1988). Risk factors for suicide. In A. J. Frances & R. E. Hales (Eds.), *Review of psychiatry* (Vol. 7). Washington, DC: American Psychiatric Press.

Hite, S. (1976). *The Hite report.* New York: Macmillan.

Hite, S. (1987). *The Hite report: Women and love—A cultural revolution in progress.* New York: Knopf.

Hobson, J. A., & McCarley, R. W. (1977). The brain as a dream state generator: An activation-synthesis hypothesis of the dream process. *American Journal of Psychiatry, 134*, 1335–1348.

Hodgkin, A. L., & Huxley, A. F. (1952a). Currents carried by sodium and potassium ions through the membrane of the giant axon of Loligo. *Journal of Physiology, 116*, 449–472.

Hodgkin, A. L., & Huxley, A. F. (1952b). The components of membrane conductance in the giant axon of Loligo. *Journal of Physiology, 116*, 473–496.

Hodgkin, A. L., & Huxley, A. F. (1952c). A quantitative description of membrane current and its application to conduction and excitation in nerve. *Journal of Physiology, 117*, 500–544.

Hodgkinson, S., Sherrington, R., Gurling, H., Marchbanks, R., Reeders, S., Mallet, J., McInnis, M., Petursson, H., & Brynjolfsson, J. (1987). Molecular genetic evidence for heterogeneity in manic depression. *Nature, 325*, 805–806.

Hoffman, L. W. (1974). Fear of success in males and females: 1965 and 1972. *Journal of Consulting and Clinical Psychology, 42*, 353–358.

Holden, C. (1986). The rational optimist. *Psychology Today, 20*(10), 55–60.

Holland, J. L. (1985). *Making vocational choices: A theory of careers.* Englewood Cliffs, NJ: Prentice-Hall.

Holley, C. D., Dansereau, D. F., McDonald, B. A., Garland, J. C., & Collins, K. W. (1979). Evaluation of a hierarchical mapping technique as an aid to prose processing. *Contemporary Educational Psychology, 4*, 227–237.

Hollon, S. D., & Najavits, L. (1988). Review of empirical studies on cognitive therapy. In A. J. Frances & R. E. Hales (Eds.), *Review of psychiatry* (Vol. 7). Washington, DC: American Psychiatric Press.

Holmes, D. S. (1984). Meditation and somatic arousal reduction: A review of the experimental evidence. *American Psychologist, 39*(1), 1–10.

Holmes, T. H. (1979). Development and application of a quantitative measure of life change magnitude. In J. E. Barrett, R. M. Rose, & G. L. Klerman (Eds.), *Stress and mental disorder.* New York: Raven.

Holmes, T. H., & Masuda, M. (1974). Life change and illness susceptibility. In B. S. Dohrenwend & B. P. Dohrenwend (Eds.), *Stressful life events: Their nature and effects.* New York: Wiley.

Holmes, T. H., & Rahe, R. H. (1967). The Social Readjustment Rating Scale. *Journal of Psychosomatic Research, 11*, 213–218.

Holroyd, K. A., & Lazarus, R. S. (1982). Stress, coping and somatic adaptation. In L. Goldberger & S. Breznitz (Eds.), *Handbook of stress: Theoretical and clinical aspects.* New York: Free Press.

Holt, R. R. (1982). Occupational stress. In L. Goldberger & S. Breznitz (Eds.), *Handbook of stress: Theoretical and clinical aspects.* New York: Free Press.

Hooper, J., & Teresi, D. (1986). *The 3-pound universe—The brain.* New York: Laurel.

Hopson, J. S. (1979). *Scent signals: The silent language of sex.* New York: Morrow.

Horn, J. L. (1976). Human abilities: A review of research and theory in the early 1970s. In M. R. Rosenzweig & L. W. Porter (Eds.), *Annual review of psychology* (Vol. 27). Palo Alto, CA: Annual Reviews.

Horn, J. L. (1979). Trends in the measurement of intelligence. In R. J. Sternberg & D. K. Detterman (Eds.), *Human intelligence: Perspectives on its theory and measurement.* Norwood, NJ: Ablex Publishing.

Horner, M. S. (1968). *Sex differences in achievement motivation and performance in competitive and non-competitive situations.* Unpublished doctoral dissertation, University of Michigan.

Horner, M. S. (1972). Toward an understanding of achievement-related conflicts in women. *Journal of Social Issues, 28,* 157–175.

Hostetler, A. J. (1987, May). Scientists warn role of biology miscast in wake of Amish study. *The APA Monitor, 18,* pp. 16–17.

Hothersall, D. (1984). *History of psychology.* New York: Random House.

House, J. S. (1981). *Work stress and social support.* Reading, MA: Addison-Wesley.

Houston, J. P., Bee, H., & Rimm, D. C. (1983). *Invitation to psychology.* New York: Academic Press.

Howard, A., Pion, G. M., Gottfredson, G. D., Flattau, P. E., Oskamp, S., Pfafflin, S. M., Bray, D. W., & Burstein, A. G. (1986). The changing face of American psychology: A report from the committee on employment and human resources. *American Psychologist, 41*(12), 1311–1327.

Hoyenga, K. B., & Hoyenga, K. T. (1979). *The question of sex differences: Psychological, cultural and biological issues.* Boston: Little, Brown.

Hubel, D. H., & Wiesel, T. N. (1962). Receptive fields, binocular interaction and functional architecture in the cat's visual cortex. *Journal of Physiology, 160,* 106–154.

Hubel, D. H., & Wiesel, T. N. (1963). Receptive fields of cells in striate cortex of very young visually inexperienced kittens. *Journal of Neurophysiology, 26,* 994–1002.

Hubel, D. H., & Wiesel, T. N. (1979). Brain mechanisms of vision. In *Scientific American* (Eds.), *The brain.* San Francisco: W. H. Freeman.

Hughes, J., Smith, T. W., Kosterlitz, H. W., Fothergill, L. A., Morgan, B. A., & Morris, H. R. (1975). Identification of two related pentapeptides from the brain with the potent opiate agonist activity. *Nature, 258,* 577–579.

Hull, C. L. (1943). *Principles of behavior.* New York: Appleton.

Hull, F. M., & Hull, M. E. (1973). Children with oral communication disabilities. In L. M. Dunn (Ed.), *Exceptional children in the schools.* New York: Holt, Rinehart & Winston.

Hull, J. G., Van Treuren, R. R., & Virnelli, S. (1987). Hardiness and health: A critique and alternative approach. *Journal of Personality and Social Psychology, 53*(3), 518–530.

Hunt, M. (1974). *Sexual behavior in the 1970s.* Chicago: Playboy Press.

Hunt, W. A., & Matarazzo, J. D. (1982). Changing smoking behavior: A critique. In R. J. Gatchel, A. Baum, & J. E. Singer (Eds.), *Handbook of psychology and health: Vol. 1. Clinical psychology and behavioral medicine, overlapping disciplines.* Hillsdale, NJ: Erlbaum.

Huston, A. C. (1983). Sex-typing. In P. H. Mussen (Ed.), *Handbook of child psychology* (4th ed., Vol. 4). New York: Wiley.

Huston, A. C., & Wright, J. C. (1982). Effects of communications media on children. In C. B. Kopp & J. B. Krakow (Ed.), *The child: Development in a social context.* Reading, MA: Addison-Wesley.

Hyde, J. S. (1981). How large are cognitive gender differences? *American Psychologist, 36,* 892–901.

Hyde, J. S. (1984). How large are gender differences in aggression? A developmental meta-analysis. *Developmental Psychology, 20,* 722–736.

Hyde, J. S. (1986). *Understanding human sexuality.* New York: McGraw-Hill.

Hygge, S., & Ohman, A. (1978). Modeling processes in the acquisition of fear: Vicarious electrodermal conditioning to fear-relevant stimuli. *Journal of Personality and Social Psychology, 36*(3), 271–279.

Hyman, B. T., Van Hoesen, G. W., Damasio, A. R., & Barnes, C. L. (1984). Alzheimer's disease: Cell-specific pathology isolates the hippocampal formation. *Science, 225,* 1168–1170.

Hyvarinen, J., & Poranen, A. (1978). Movement-sensitive and direction and orientation-selective cutaneous receptive fields in the hand area of the postcentral gyrus in monkeys. *Journal of Physiology, 283,* 523–537.

I

Ineichen, B. (1979). The social geography of marriage. In M. Cook & G. Wilson (Eds.), *Love and attraction.* New York: Pergamon Press.

Insko, C. A. (1965). Verbal reinforcement of attitudes. *Journal of Personality and Social Psychology, 2,* 621–623.

Izard, C. E. (1984). Emotion-cognition relationships and human development. In C. E. Izard, J. Kagan, & R. B. Zajonc (Eds.), *Emotions, cognition and behavior.* Cambridge, England: Cambridge University Press.

J

Jacklet, J. W. (1978). The cellular mechanisms of circadian clocks. *Trends in Neurosciences, 1,* 117–119.

Jackson, D. N. (1973). Structured personality assessment. In B. B. Wolman (Ed.), *Handbook of general psychology.* Englewood Cliffs, NJ: Prentice-Hall.

Jacob, R. G., & Turner, S. M. (1984). Somatoform disorders. In S. M. Turner & M. Hersen (Eds.), *Adult psychopathology and diagnosis.* New York: Wiley.

Jacobs, B. L. (1987). How hallucinogenic drugs work. *American Scientist, 75*(4), 386–392.

Jacobs, J. (1971). *Adolescent suicide.* New York: Wiley Interscience.

Jacobs, L., Berscheid, E., & Walster, E. (1971). Self-esteem and attraction. *Journal of Personality and Social Psychology, 17,* 84–91.

Jacobson, E. (1938). *Progressive relaxation.* Chicago: University of Chicago Press.

James, W. (1884). What is emotion. *Mind, 19,* 188–205.

James, W. (1890). *The principles of psychology.* New York: Holt.

James, W. (1902). *The varieties of religious experience.* New York: Modern Library.

Jamison, K. R., Gerner, R. H., Hammen, C., & Padesky, C. (1980). Clouds and silver linings: Positive experiences associated with the primary affective disorders. *American Journal of Psychiatry, 137*(2), 198–202.

Janis, I. L. (1958). *Psychological stress.* New York: Wiley.

Janis, I. L. (1972). *Victims of groupthink.* Boston: Houghton Mifflin.

Janis, I. L. (1973, January). Groupthink. *Yale Alumni Magazine,* pp. 16–19.

Janis, I. L., & Mann, L. (1977). *Decision making: A psychological analysis of conflict, choice, and commitment.* New York: Free Press.

Jeffrey, D. B., & Lemnitzer, N. (1981). Diet, exercise, obesity and related health problems: A macroenvironmental analysis. In J. M. Ferguson & C. B. Taylor (Eds.), *The comprehensive handbook of behavioral medicine: Vol. 2. Syndromes and special areas.* Jamaica, NY: Spectrum.

Jencks, C., Smith, M., Acland, H., Bane, M. J., Cohen, D., Gintis, H., Heyns, B., & Michaelson, S. (1972). *Inequality: A reassessment of the effect of family and schooling in America.* New York: Harper & Row.

Jenkins, J. G., & Dallenbach, K. M. (1924). Oblivescence during sleep and waking. *American Journal of Psychology, 35,* 605–612.

Jensen, A. R. (1969). How much can we boost IQ and scholastic achievement? *Harvard Educational Review, 39,* 1–23.

Jensen, A. R. (1980). *Bias in mental testing.* New York: Free Press.

Jernigan, T. L. (1986). Anatomical and CT scan studies of psychiatric disorders. In P. A. Berger & H. K. H. Brodie (Eds.), *American handbook of psychiatry: Biological psychiatry* (2nd ed., Vol. 8). New York: Basic Books.

Jeste, D. V., & Wyatt, R. J. (1982). *Understanding and treating tardive dyskinesia.* New York: Guilford Press.

Joffe, L. S., & Vaughn, B. E. (1982). Infant–mother attachment: Theory, assessment and implications for development. In B. B. Wolman (Ed.), *Handbook of developmental psychology.* Englewood Cliffs, NJ: Prentice-Hall.

Johnson, L. C. (1982). Sleep deprivation and performance. In W. B. Webb (Ed.), *Biological rhythms, sleep and performance.* New York: Wiley.

Johnson, M. K., Springer, S. P., & Sternglanz, S. H. (1982). *How to succeed in college.* Los Altos, CA: William Kaufmann.

Johnston, J. C., & McClelland, J. L. (1974). Perception of letters in words: Seek not and ye shall find. *Science, 184,* 1192–1194.

Johnston, L. D., O'Malley, P. M., & Bachman, J. G. (1987). *National trends in drug use and related factors among American high school students and young adults, 1975–1986.* Washington, DC: National Institute on Drug Abuse.

Johnston, L. D., O'Malley, P. M., & Bachman, J. G. (1988). *Illicit drug use, smoking, and drinking by America's high-school students, college students, and young adults, 1975–1987.* Washington, DC: National Institute on Drug Abuse.

Johnston, W. A., & Dark, V. J. (1986). Selective attention. In M. R. Rosenzweig & L. W. Porter (Eds.), *Annual review of psychology.* Palo Alto, CA: Annual Reviews.

Johnston, W. A., & Heinz, S. P. (1978). Flexibility and capacity demands of attention. *Journal of Experimental Psychology: General, 107,* 420–435.

Jones, E. E., & Baumeister, R. F. (1976). The self-monitor looks at the ingratiator. *Journal of Personality, 12,* 180–193.

Jones, E. E., & Davis, K. E. (1965). From acts to dispositions: The attribution process in person perception. In L. Berkowitz (Ed.), *Advances in experimental social psychology* (Vol. 2). New York: Academic Press.

Jones, E. E., & Nisbett, R. E. (1971). The actor and the observer: Divergent perceptions of the causes of behavior. In E. E. Jones, D. E. Kanouse, H. H. Kelley, R. E. Nisbett, S. Valins, & B. Weiner (Eds.), *Attribution: Perceiving the causes of behavior.* Morristown, NJ: General Learning Press.

Jones, J. S., & Oswald, I. (1968). Two cases of healthy insomnia. *Electroencephalography and Clinical Neurophysiology, 24,* 378–380.

Jones, M. C. (1965). Psychological correlates of somatic development. *Child Development, 36,* 899–911.

Jones, R. A., & Brehm, J. W. (1970). Persuasiveness of one- and two-sided communications as a function of awareness there are two sides. *Journal of Experimental Social Psychology, 6,* 47–56.

Jourard, S. M., & Landsman, T. (1980). *Healthy personality: An approach from the viewpoint of humanistic psychology.* New York: Macmillan.

Judd, C. M., & Park, B. (1988). Out-group homogeneity: Judgments of variability at the individual and group levels. *Journal of Personality and Social Psychology, 54*(5), 778–788.

Julien, R. M. (1985). *A primer of drug action.* New York: W. H. Freeman.

Jung, C. G. (1917/1953). On the psychology of the unconscious. In H. Read, M. Fordham, & G. Adler (Eds.), *Collected works of C. G. Jung* (Vol. 7). Princeton, NJ: Princeton University Press.

Jung, C. G. (1921/1960). *Psychological types*. In H. Read, M. Fordham, & G. Adler (Eds.), *Collected works of C. G. Jung* (Vol. 6). Princeton, NJ: Princeton University Press.

Jung, C. G. (1933). *Modern man in search of a soul*. New York: Harcourt, Brace & World.

K

Kagan, J. (1969). Inadequate evidence and illogical conclusions. *Harvard Educational Review, 39*, 274–277.

Kahana, B. (1982). Social behavior and aging. In B. B. Wolman (Ed.), *Handbook of developmental psychology*. Englewood Cliffs, NJ: Prentice-Hall.

Kahneman, D., & Tversky, A. (1984). Choices, values, and frames. *American Psychologist, 39*, 341–350.

Kail, R., & Hagen, J. W. (1982). Memory in childhood. In B. B. Wolman (Ed.), *Handbook of developmental psychology*. Englewood Cliffs, NJ: Prentice-Hall.

Kalant, H., & Kalant, O. J. (1979). Death in amphetamine users: Causes and rates. In D. E. Smith (Ed.), *Amphetamine use, misuse and abuse*. Boston: G. K. Hall.

Kales, A., & Kales, J. D. (1984). *Evaluation and treatment of insomnia*. New York: Oxford University Press.

Kales, J. D., Kales, A., Bixler, E. O., Soldatos, C. R., Cadieux, R. J., Kashurba, G. J., & Vela-Bueno, A. (1984). Biopsychobehavioral correlates of insomnia: V. Clinical characteristics and behavioral correlates. *American Journal of Psychiatry, 141*(11), 1371–1376.

Kalick, S. M., & Hamilton, T. E., III. (1986). The matching hypothesis reexamined. *Journal of Personality and Social Psychology, 51*(4), 673–682.

Kamin, L. J. (1965). Temporal and intensity characteristics of the conditioned stimulus. In W. F. Prokasy (Ed.), *Classical conditioning*. New York: Appleton-Century-Crofts.

Kamin, L. J. (1968). "Attention-like" processes in classical conditioning. In M. R. Jones (Ed.), *Miami symposium on the prediction of behavior: Aversive stimulation*. Miami, FL: University of Miami Press.

Kamin, L. J. (1969). Predictability, surprise, attention and conditioning. In B. A. Campbell & R. M. Church (Eds.), *Punishment and aversive behavior*. New York: Appleton-Century-Crofts.

Kamin, L. J. (1974). *The science and politics of IQ*. Hillsdale, NJ: Erlbaum.

Kamin, L. J. (1981). Some historical facts about IQ testing. In H. J. Eysenck versus L. Kamin, *The intelligence controversy*. New York: Wiley.

Kamiya, J. (1969). Operant control of the EEG rhythm and some of its reported effects on consciousness. In C. T. Tart (Ed.), *Altered states of consciousness*. New York: Wiley.

Kandel, D. B. (1978). Similarity in real-life adolescent friendship pairs. *Journal of Personality and Social Psychology, 36*, 306–312.

Kandel, E. R., & Schwartz, J. H. (1982). Molecular biology of learning: Modification of transmitter release. *Science, 218*, 433–442.

Kanner, A. D., Coyne, J. C., Schaefer, C., & Lazarus, R. S. (1981). Comparison of two modes of stress measurement: Daily hassles and uplifts versus major life events. *Journal of Behavioral Medicine, 4*, 1–39.

Kaplan, E., & Kaplan, G. (1971). The prelinguistic child. In J. Elliott (Ed.), *Human development and cognitive processes*. New York: Holt.

Kaplan, H. I. (1985). History of psychosomatic medicine. In H. I. Kaplan & B. J. Sadock (Eds.), *Comprehensive textbook of psychiatry/IV*. Baltimore: Williams & Wilkins.

Kaplan, H. S. (1979). *Disorders of sexual desire and other new concepts and techniques in sex therapy*. New York: Simon & Schuster.

Kaplan, H. S. (1983). *The evaluation of sexual disorders: Psychological and medical aspects*. New York: Brunner/Mazel.

Kaplan, R. M. (1985). The controversy related to the use of psychological tests. In B. B. Wolman (Ed.), *Handbook of intelligence: Theories, measurements, and applications*. New York: Wiley.

Karabenick, S. A. (1977). Fear of success, achievement and affiliation dispositions and the performance of men and women under individual and competitive conditions. *Journal of Personality, 45*, 117–149.

Karlins, M., Coffman, T. L., & Walters, G. (1969). On the fading of social stereotypes: Studies in three generations of college students. *Journal of Personality and Social Psychology, 13*, 1–16.

Karson, C. N., Kleinman, J. E., & Wyatt, R. J. (1986). Biochemical concepts of schizophrenia. In T. Millon & G. L. Klerman (Eds.), *Contemporary directions in psychopathology*. New York: Guilford Press.

Karwoski, C. J., & Proenza, L. M. (1980). Neurons, potassium, and glia in proximal retina of Necturus. *Journal of General Physiology, 75*, 141–162.

Kaslow, F. W., & Schwartz, L. L. (1978). Self-perceptions of the attractive, successful female professional. *Intellect, 106*, 313–315.

Katz, B. (1966). *Nerve, muscle, and synapse*. New York: McGraw-Hill.

Katz, D. (1951). Social psychology and group process. In C. P. Stone (Ed.), *Annual review of psychology*. Palo Alto, CA: Annual Reviews.

Kaufman, L., & Rock, I. (1962). The moon illusion I. *Science, 136*, 953–961.

Kavesh, L., & Lavin, C. (1988). *Tales from the front*. New York: Doubleday.

Kazdin, A. E. (1982). History of behavior modification. In A. S. Bellack, M. Hersen, & A. E. Kazdin (Eds.), *International handbook of behavior modification and behavior therapy*. New York: Plenum Press.

Kazdin, A. E., & Wilson, G. T. (1978). *Evaluation of behavior therapy: Issues, evidence and research strategies*. Cambridge, MA: Ballinger.

Keesey, R. E., Corbett, S. W., Hirvonen, M. D., & Kaufman, L. N. (1984). Heat production and body weight changes following lateral hypothalamic lesions. *Physiology & Behavior, 32*, 309–317.

Keesey, R. E., & Powley, T. L. (1975). Hypothalamic regulation of body weight. *American Scientist, 63*, 558–565.

Keesey, R. E., & Powley, T. L. (1986). The regulation of body weight. In M. R. Rosenzweig & L. W. Porter (Eds.), *Annual review of psychology: 1986* (Vol. 37). Palo Alto, CA: Annual Reviews.

Keinan, G. (1987). Decision making under stress: Scanning of alternatives under controllable and uncontrollable threats. *Journal of Personality and Social Psychology, 52*(3), 639–644.

Keisling, R. (1983). Critique of Kiesler articles. *American Psychologist, 38*(10), 1127–1128.

Keller, F. S. (1968). Goodbye teacher. . . . *Journal of Applied Behavior Analysis, 1*, 79–89.

Kelley, H. H. (1950). The warm-cold variable in first impressions of persons. *Journal of Personality, 18*, 431–439.

Kelley, H. H. (1967). Attribution theory in social psychology. *Nebraska Symposium on Motivation, 15*, 192–241.

Kelley, H. H. (1973). The processes of causal attribution. *American Psychologist, 28*, 107–128.

Kelley, K., Byrne, D., Przybyla, D. P. J., Eberly, C., Eberly, B., Greendlinger, V., Wan, C. K., Gorsky, J. (1985). Chronic self-destructiveness: Conceptualization, measurement and initial validation of the construct. *Motivation and Emotion, 9*(2), 135–151.

Kelley, K., Cheung, F. M., Rodriguez-Carrillo, P., Singh, R., Wan, C. K., & Becker, M. A. (1986). Chronic self-destructiveness and locus of control in cross-cultural perspective. *Journal of Social Psychology, 126*(5), 573–577.

Kelman, H. C. (1982). Ethical issues in different social science methods. In T. L. Beauchamp, R. R. Faden, R. J. Wallace, Jr., & L. Walters (Eds.), *Ethical issues in social science research*. Baltimore: Johns Hopkins University Press.

Kenrick, D. T., & Funder, D. C. (1988). Profiting from controversy: Lessons from the person-situation debate. *American Psychologist, 43*(1), 23–34.

Kenrick, D. T., & Stringfield, D. O. (1980). Personality traits and the eye of the beholder: Crossing some traditional philosophical boundaries in the search for consistency in all of the people. *Psychological Review, 87*, 88–104.

Kenshalo, D. R. (1970). Psychophysical studies of temperature sensitivity. In W. D. Neff (Ed.), *Contributions to Sensory Physiology* (Vol. 4). New York: Academic Press.

Kenshalo, D. R. (1971). The cutaneous senses. In J. W. Kling & L. A. Riggs (Eds.), *Experimental psychology*. New York: Holt, Rinehart & Winston.

Keppel, G. A. (1967). A reconsideration of the extinction-recovery theory. *Journal of Verbal Learning and Verbal Behavior, 6*, 476–486.

Kessler, L. G., Burns, B. J., Shapiro, S., Tischler, G. L., George, L. K., Hough, R. L., Bodison, D., & Miller, R. H. (1987). Psychiatric diagnoses of medical services users: Evidence from the epidemiologic catchment area program. *American Journal of Public Health, 77*, 18–24.

Keys, A., Brozek, J., Henschel, A., Mickelson, O., & Taylor, H. L. (1950). *The biology of human starvation*. Minneapolis: University of Minnesota Press.

Kiecolt-Glaser, J. K., Garner, W., Speicher, C., Penn, G. M., Holliday, J., & Glaser, R. (1984). Psychosocial modifiers of immunocompetence in medical students. *Psychosomatic Medicine, 46*(1), 7–14.

Kiecolt-Glaser, J. K., Glaser, R., Williger, D., Stout, J., Messick, G., Sheppard, S., Ricker, D., Romisher, S. C., Briner, W., Bonnell, G., & Donnerberg, R. (1985). Psychosocial enhancement of immunocompetence in a geriatric population. *Health Psychology, 4*(1), 25–42.

Kieras, D. E. (1978). Good and bad structure in simple paragraphs: Effects on apparent theme, reading time, and recall. *Journal of Verbal Learning and Verbal Behavior, 17*, 13–28.

Kiesler, C. A. (1982). Public and professional myths about mental hospitalization. *American Psychologist, 37*(12), 1232–1339.

Kiesler, C. A., & Sibulkin, A. E. (1984). Episodic rate of mental hospitalization: Stable or increasing? *American Journal of Psychiatry, 141*, 44–48.

Kiesler, D. J. (1986). The 1982 interpersonal circle: An analysis of DSM-III personality disorders. In T. Millon & G. L. Klerman (Eds.), *Contemporary directions in psychopathology: Toward the DSM-IV*. New York: Guilford Press.

Killeen, P. R. (1981). Learning as causal inference. In M. L. Commons & J. A. Nevin (Eds.), *Quantitative analyses of behavior: Vol. 1. Discriminative properties of reinforcement schedules*. Cambridge, MA: Ballinger.

Kimura, D. (1973). The asymmetry of the human brain. *Scientific American, 228*, 70–78.

Kimura, K., & Beidler, L. M. (1961). Microelectrode study of taste receptors of cat and hamster. *Journal of Cellular and Comparative Physiology, 58*, 131–140.

Kinsbourne, M. (1980). If sex differences in brain lateralization exist, they have yet to be discovered. *Behavioral and Brain Sciences, 3*, 241–242.

Kinsbourne, M. (1982). Hemispheric specialization and the growth of human understanding. *American Psychologist, 37*(4), 411–420.

Kinsman, R. A., Dirks, J. F., & Jones, N. F. (1982). Psychomaintenance of chronic physical illness: Clinical assessment of personal styles affecting medical management. In T. Millon, C. Green, & R. Meagher (Eds.), *Handbook of clinical health psychology*. New York: Plenum Press.

Kintsch, W. (1979). On modeling comprehension. *Educational Psychologist, 14*, 3–14.

Kintsch, W., & Vipond, D. (1979). Reading comprehension and readability in educational practice and psychological theory. In L. G. Nilsson (Ed.), *Perspectives on memory research*. Hillsdale, NJ: Erlbaum.

Klahr, D., & Wallace, J. G. (1976). *Cognitive development: An information processing view*. Hillsdale, NJ: Erlbaum.

Klein, K. E., Herrmann, R., Kuklinski, P., & Wegmann, H. M. (1977). Circadian performance rhythms: Experimental studies in air operations. In R. R. Mackie (Ed.), *Vigilance: Theory, operational performance and physiological correlates*. New York: Plenum Press.

Klein, M. (1948). *Contributions to psychoanalysis.* London: Hogarth.

Kleinmuntz, B. (1975). *Personality measurement: An introduction.* Huntington, NY: Robert E. Krieger.

Kleinmuntz, B. (1980). *Essentials of abnormal psychology.* San Francisco: Harper & Row.

Kleinmuntz, B., & Szucko, J. J. (1984). Lie detection in ancient and modern times: A call for contemporary scientific study. *American Psychologist, 39,* 766–776.

Klerman, G. L. (1978). Long-term treatment of affective disorders. In M. A. Lipton, A. DiMascio, & K. F. Killam (Eds.), *Psychopharmacology: A generation of progress.* New York: Raven.

Klerman, G. L., & Weissman, M. M. (1986). The interpersonal approach to understanding depression. In T. Millon & G. L. Klerman (Eds.), *Contemporary directions in psychopathology: Toward the DSM-IV.* New York: Guilford Press.

Klima, E. S., & Bellugi, U. (1966). Syntactic regularities in the speech of children. In J. Lyons & R. J. Wales (Eds.), *Psycholinguistic papers.* Edinburgh: Edinburgh University Press.

Kline, D. W., & Schieber, F. (1985). Vision and aging. In J. E. Birren & K. W. Schaie (Eds.), *Handbook of the psychology of aging* (2nd ed.). New York: Van Nostrand Reinhold.

Klinger, E. (1987). The power of daydreams. *Psychology Today, 21*(10), 36–44.

Kluft, R. P. (1987). Making the diagnosis of multiple personality disorder. In F. Flach (Ed.), *Diagnostics and psychopathology.* New York: Norton.

Knesper, D. J., & Pagnucco, D. J. (1987). Estimated distribution of effort by providers of mental health services to U.S. adults in 1982 and 1983. *American Journal of Psychiatry, 144,* 883–888.

Knittle, J. L. (1975). Early influences on development of adipose tissue. In G. A. Bray (Ed.), *Obesity in perspective.* Washington, DC: U.S. Government Printing Office.

Knittle, J. L., & Hirsch, J. (1968). Effect of early nutrition on the development of rat epididymal fat pads: Cellularity and metabolism. *Journal of Clinical Investigation, 47,* 209.

Kobasa, S. C. (1979). Stressful life events, personality, and health: An inquiry into hardiness. *Journal of Personality and Social Psychology, 37,* 1–11.

Kobasa, S. C., Maddi, S. R., & Kahn, S. (1982). Hardiness and health: A prospective study. *Journal of Personality and Social Psychology, 42*(1), 168–177.

Kobasa, S. C., & Pucetti, M. C. (1983). Personality and social resources in stress resistance. *Journal of Personality and Social Psychology, 45*(4), 839–850.

Kobasa, S. O. (1984, September). How much stress can you survive? *American Health,* pp. 64–77.

Koffka, K. (1935). *Principles of Gestalt psychology.* New York: Harcourt, Brace & World.

Kogan, N., & Wallach, M. (1964). *Risk taking: A study in cognition and personality.* New York: Holt, Rinehart & Winston.

Kohlberg, L. (1963). The development of children's orientations toward a moral order: I. Sequence in the development of moral thought. *Vita Humana, 6,* 11–33.

Kohlberg, L. (1964). Development of moral character and moral ideology. In L. W. Hoffman & M. L. Hoffman (Eds.), *Review of child development research* (Vol. 1). New York: Russell Sage Foundation.

Kohlberg, L. (1966). A cognitive-developmental analysis of children's sex-role concepts and attitudes. In E. E. Maccoby (Ed.), *The development of sex differences.* Stanford, CA: Stanford University Press.

Kohlberg, L. (1969). Stage and sequence: The cognitive-developmental approach to socialization. In D. A. Goslin (Ed.), *Handbook of socialization theory and research.* Chicago: Rand McNally.

Kohlberg, L. (1975, June). The cognitive-developmental approach to moral education. *Phi Delta Kappan,* pp. 670–677.

Kohlberg, L. (1976). Moral stages and moralization: Cognitive-developmental approach. In T. Lickona (Ed.), *Moral development and behavior: Theory, research and social issues.* New York: Holt, Rinehart & Winston.

Kohlberg, L. (1981). *Essays on moral development* (Vol. 1). New York: Harper & Row.

Kohut, H. (1971). *The analysis of self.* New York: International Universities Press.

Kolb, B., & Whishaw, I. Q. (1985). *Fundamentals of human neuropsychology.* New York: W. H. Freeman.

Kolodny, R. C., Masters, W. H., & Johnson, V. E. (1979). *Textbook of sexual medicine.* Boston: Little, Brown.

Kolodny, R. C., Masters, W. H., Kolodner, R. M., & Toro, G. (1974). Depression of plasma testosterone levels after chronic intensive marijuana use. *New England Journal of Medicine, 291,* 872–874.

Koplan, J. P., Powell, K. E., Sikes, R. K., Shirley, R. W., & Campbell, C. C. (1982). An epidemiologic study of the benefits and risks of running. *Journal of the American Medical Association, 248*(23), 3118–3121.

Korchin, S. J. (1976). *Modern clinical psychology: Principles of intervention in the clinic and community.* New York: Basic Books.

Krakauer, D., & Dallenbach, K. M. (1937). Gustatory adaptation to sweet, sour, and bitter. *American Journal of Psychology, 49,* 469–475.

Kraly, F. S. (1981). A diurnal variation in the satiating potency of cholecystokinin in the rat. *Appetite: Journal of Intake Research, 2,* 177–191.

Kramer, B. A. (1985). Use of ECT in California, 1977–1983. *American Journal of Psychiatry, 142*(10), 1190–1192.

Krantz, D. S., Baum, A., & Wideman, M. V. (1980). Assessment of preferences for self-treatment and information in health care. *Journal of Personality and Social Psychology, 39,* 977–990.

Krantz, D. S., & Manuck, S. B. (1984). Acute psychophysiologic reactivity and risk of cardiovascular disease: A review and methodologic critique. *Psychological Bulletin, 96*(3), 435–464.

Krasner, L., & Ullmann, L. P. (Eds.). (1965). *Research in behavior modification.* New York: Holt, Rinehart & Winston.

Kravitz, D. A., & Martin, B. (1986). Ringelmann rediscovered: The original article. *Journal of Personality and Social Psychology, 50,* 936–941.

Kretschmer, E. (1921). *Physique and character.* New York: Harcourt.

Kripke, D. F., Simons, R. N., Garfinkel, L., & Hammond, C. (1979). Short and long sleep and sleeping pills: Is increased mortality associated? *Archives of General Psychiatry, 36,* 103–116.

Kroger, W. S. (1977). *Clinical and experimental hypnosis.* Philadelphia: Lippincott.

Krueger, D. W. (1981). Stressful life events and the return to heroin use. *Journal of Human Stress, 7*(2), 3–8.

Krueger, W. C. F. (1929). The effect of overlearning on retention. *Journal of Experimental Psychology, 12,* 71–78.

Kuehnle, J., Mendelson, J. H., Davis, K. R., & New, P. F. J. (1977). Computerized tomographic examination of heavy marijuana smokers. *Journal of the American Medical Association, 237,* 1231–1232.

Kuffler, S. W. (1953). Discharge patterns and functional organization of mammalian retina. *Journal of Neurophysiology, 16,* 37–68.

Kutash, S. B. (1976). Modified psychoanalytic therapies. In B. B. Wolman (Ed.), *The therapist's handbook: Treatment methods of mental disorders.* New York: Van Nostrand Reinhold.

Kutchinsky, B. (1973). The effect of easy availability of pornography on the incidence of sex crimes: The Danish experience. *Journal of Social Issues, 29*(3), 163–181.

Kutchinsky, B. (1985). Pornography and its effects in Denmark and the United States. *Comparative Social Research, 8,* 281–300.

L

Lachman, R., Lachman, J. L., & Butterfield, E. C. (1979). *Cognitive psychology and information processing: An introduction.* Hillsdale, NJ: Erlbaum.

Lader, M. H. (1984). Antianxiety drugs. In T. B. Karasu (Ed.), *The psychiatric therapies.* Washington, DC: American Psychiatric Association.

Lakein, A. (1973). *How to get control of your time and your life.* New York: Peter H. Wyden.

Lamb, M. E. (1982). Parent–infant interaction, attachment and socioemotional development in infancy. In R. N. Emde & R. J. Harmon (Eds.), *The development of attachment and affiliative systems.* New York: Plenum Press.

Lamb, M. E., Thompson, R. A., Gardner, W., & Charnov, E. L. (1985). *Infant–mother attachment: The origins and developmental significance of individual differences in strange-situation behavior.* Hillsdale, NJ: Erlbaum.

Lamberg, L. (1986). A rescue kit for insomniacs. *American Health, 5*(2), 58–66.

Landy, D., & Sigall, H. (1974). Beauty is talent: Task evaluation as a function of the performer's physical attractiveness. *Journal of Personality and Social Psychology, 29,* 299–304.

Lange, C. (1885). One leuds beveegelser. In K. Dunlap (Ed.), *The emotions.* Baltimore: Williams & Wilkins.

LaPiere, R. T. (1934). Attitude and actions. *Social Forces, 13,* 230–237.

Larkin, J. H., & Reif, F. (1979). Understanding and teaching problem solving in physics. *European Journal of Science Education, 1,* 191–203.

LaRue, A., & Jarvik, L. F. (1982). Old age and biobehavioral changes. In B. B. Wolman (Ed.), *Handbook of developmental psychology.* Englewood Cliffs, NJ: Prentice-Hall.

Latane, B. (1981). The psychology of social impact. *American Psychologist, 36,* 343–356.

Latane, B., & Bidwell, L. D. (1977). Sex and affiliation in college cafeterias. *Personality and Social Psychology Bulletin, 3,* 571–574.

Latane, B., & Nida, S. A. (1981). Ten years of research on group size and helping. *Psychological Bulletin, 89,* 308–324.

Latane, B., Williams, K., & Harkins, S. (1979). Many hands make light the work: The causes and consequences of social loafing. *Journal of Personality and Social Psychology, 37,* 822–832.

Laughlin, H. (1979). *The ego and its defenses.* New York: Aronson.

Laughlin, H. (1967). *The neuroses.* Washington, DC: Butterworth.

Lavie, P. (1982). Ultradian rhythms in sleep and wakefulness. In W. B. Webb (Ed.), *Biological rhythms, sleep and performance.* New York: Wiley.

Lawler, K. A. (1980). Cardiovascular and electrodermal response patterns in heart rate reactive individuals during psychological stress. *Psychophysiology, 17*(5), 464–470.

Lazarus, A. A. (1987). The need for technical eclecticism: Science, breadth, depth, and specificity. In J. K. Zeig (Ed.), *The evolution of psychotherapy.* New York: Brunner/Mazel.

Lazarus, A. A., & Fay, A. (1984). Behavior therapy. In T. B. Karasu (Ed.), *The psychiatric therapies.* Washington, DC: American Psychiatric Association.

Lazarus, A. A., & Wilson, G. T. (1976). Behavior modification: Clinical and experimental perspectives. In B. B. Wolman (Ed.), *The therapist's handbook: Treatment methods of mental disorders.* New York: Van Nostrand Reinhold.

Lazarus, R. S., & Folkman, S. (1984). *Stress, appraisal and coping.* New York: Springer.

Leavitt, F. (1982). *Drugs and behavior.* New York: Wiley.

Leavy, R. L. (1983). Social support and psychological disorder: A review. *Journal of Community Psychology, 11,* 3–21.

LeBoeuf, M. (1980). *Imagineering.* New York: McGraw-Hill.

Lee, J. A. (1974). The styles of loving. *Psychology Today, 8*(5), 43–51.

Lee, J. A. (1977). A typology of styles of loving. *Personality and Social Psychology Bulletin, 3,* 173–182.

Lee, J. A. (1988). Love-styles. In R. J. Sternberg & M. L. Barnes (Eds.), *The psychology of love.* New Haven, CT: Yale University Press.

Leeper, R. W. (1935). A study of a neglected portion of the field of learning: The development of sensory organization. *Journal of Genetic Psychology, 46,* 41–75.

Lefcourt, H. M. (1982). *Locus of control: Current trends in theory and research.* Hillsdale, NJ: Erlbaum.

Leff, J., & Vaughn, C. (1981). The role of maintenance therapy and relatives' expressed emotion in relapse of schizophrenia: A two-year follow-up. *British Journal of Psychiatry, 139,* 102–104.

Leff, J., & Vaughn, C. (1985). *Expressed emotion in families.* New York: Guilford Press.

Lefkowitz, M. M., Eron, L. D., Walder, L. O., & Huesmann, L. R. (1977). *Growing up to be violent.* New York: Pergamon Press.

Legge, D. (1980). Cognitive psychology. In J. Radford & D. Rose (Eds.), *The teaching of psychology: Method, content and context.* New York: Wiley.

Le Grand, T. (1957). *Light, colour, and vision* (R. Hunt, T. Walsh, & F. Hunt, Trans.). New York: Wiley.

Lehmann, H. E. (1985). Current perspectives on the biology of schizophrenia. In M. N. Menuck & M. V. Seeman (Eds.), *New perspectives in schizophrenia.* New York: Macmillan.

Lehmann, H. E., & Cancro, R. (1985). Schizophrenia: Clinical features. In H. I. Kaplan & B. J. Sadock (Eds.), *Comprehensive textbook of psychiatry/ IV* (4th ed.). Baltimore: Williams & Wilkins.

Lehrer, P. M., & Woolfolk, R. L. (1984). Are stress reduction techniques interchangeable, or do they have specific effects? A review of the comparative empirical literature. In R. L. Woolfolk & P. M. Lehrer (Eds.), *Principles and practice of stress management.* New York: Guilford Press.

Leitenberg, H. (1976). Behavioral approaches to the treatment of neuroses. In H. Leitenberg (Ed.), *Handbook of behavior modification and behavior therapy.* Englewood Cliffs, NJ: Prentice-Hall.

Leo, J. (1982, October 25). The 27 faces of "Charles." *Time,* p. 70.

Leo, J. (1987, January 12). Exploring the traits of twins. *Time,* p. 63.

Lerner, M. J., & Miller, D. T. (1978). Just world research and the attribution process: Looking back and ahead. *Psychological Bulletin, 85,* 1030–1051.

Lesgold, A. M., Roth, S. F., & Curtis, M. E. (1979). Foregrounding effects in discourse comprehension. *Journal of Verbal Learning and Verbal Behavior, 18,* 291–308.

Lesnik-Oberstein, M., & Cohen, L. (1984). Cognitive style, sensation seeking and assortative mating. *Journal of Personality and Social Psychology, 46*(1), 112–117.

Lett, B. T. (1975). Long-delay learning in the T-maze. *Learning and Motivation, 6,* 80–90.

Leventhal, H. (1970). Findings and theory in the study of fear communications. In L. Berkowitz (Ed.), *Advances in experimental social psychology* (Vol. 5). New York: Academic Press.

Leventhal, H., & Tomarken, A. J. (1986). Emotion: Today's problems. In M. Rosenzweig & L. W. Porter (Eds.), *Annual review of psychology: 1986* (Vol. 37). Palo Alto, CA: Annual Reviews.

Levine, M. W., & Shefner, J. M. (1981). *Fundamentals of sensation and perception.* New York: Random House.

Levinger, G. (1966). Systematic distortion in spouses' reports of preferred and actual sexual behavior. *Sociometry, 29,* 291–299.

Levinson, D. J., Darrow, C. N., Klein, E. B., Levinson, M. H., & McKee, B. (1978). *The seasons of a man's life.* New York: Knopf.

Levy, J. (1985). Right brain, left brain: Fact or fiction. *Psychology Today, 19*(5), 38–44.

Levy, J., Trevarthen, C., & Sperry, R. W. (1972). Perception of bilateral chimeric figures following hemispheric disconnection. *Brain, 95,* 61–78.

Lewin, K. (1935). *A dynamic theory of personality.* New York: McGraw-Hill.

Lewine, R. J., Fogg, L., & Meltzer, H. Y. (1983). Assessment of negative and positive symptoms in schizophrenia. *Schizophrenia Bulletin, 9,* 968–976.

Lewinsohn, P. M. (1974). A behavioral approach to depression. In R. J. Friedman & M. M. Katz (Eds.), *The psychology of depression: Contemporary theory and research.* New York: Halsted.

Lewinsohn, P. M., Duncan, E. M., Stanton, A. K., & Hautzinger, M. (1986). Age at first onset for nonbipolar depression. *Journal of Abnormal Psychology, 95*(4), 378–383.

Lewis, D. O., Pincus, J. H., Feldman, M., Jackson, L., & Bard, B. (1986). Psychiatric, neurological, and psychoeducational characteristics of fifteen death-row inmates in the United States. *American Journal of Psychiatry, 143*(7), 838–845.

Lewis, S. A. (1969). Subjective estimates of sleep: An EEG evaluation. *British Journal of Psychology, 60,* 203–208.

Lewontin, R. C. (1976). Race and intelligence. In N. J. Block & G. Dworkin (Eds.), *The IQ controversy: Critical readings.* New York: Pantheon.

Lewontin, R. C., Rose, S., & Kamin, L. (1984). *Not in our genes: Biology, ideology and human nature.* New York: Pantheon.

Lichtenstein, E. (1980). *Psychotherapy: Approaches and applications.* Pacific Grove, CA: Brooks/Cole.

Lickey, M. E., & Gordon, B. (1983). *Drugs for mental illness: A revolution in psychiatry.* San Francisco: W. H. Freeman.

Liebert, R. M., Sprafkin, J. N., & Davidson, E. S. (1982). *The early window: Effects of television on children and youth.* New York: Pergamon Press.

Lindgren, H. C. (1969). *The psychology of college success: A dynamic approach.* New York: Wiley.

Lindsay, P. H., & Norman, D. A. (1977). *Human information processing.* New York: Academic Press.

Lindsley, D. B. (1970). The role of nonspecific reticulo-thalamocortical systems in emotion. In P. Black (Ed.), *Physiological correlates of emotion.* New York: Academic Press.

Linn, M. C., & Petersen, A. C. (1986). A meta-analysis of gender differences in spatial ability: Implications for mathematics and science achievement. In J. S. Hyde & M. C. Linn (Eds.), *The psychology of gender: Advances through meta-analysis.* Baltimore: Johns Hopkins University Press.

Livson, F. B. (1976). Patterns of personality development in middle-aged women: A longitudinal study. *International Journal of Aging and Human Development, 7*(2), 107–115.

Lloyd, C., Alexander, A. A., Rice, D. G., & Greenfield, N. S. (1980). Life events as predictors of academic performance. *Journal of Human Stress, 6*(3), 15–26.

Loehlin, J. C., & Nichols, R. C. (1976). *Heredity, environment and personality.* Austin: University of Texas Press.

Loehlin, J. C., Willerman, L., & Horn, J. M. (1988). Human behavior genetics. In M. R. Rosenzweig & L. W. Porter (Eds.), *Annual Review of Psychology: 1988* (Vol. 39). Palto Alto, CA: Annual Reviews.

Loftus, E. F., & Loftus, G. R. (1980). On the permanence of stored information in the human brain. *American Psychologist, 35*(5), 409–420.

Loftus, E. F., & Palmer, J. C. (1974). Reconstruction of automobile destruction: An example of the interaction between language and memory. *Journal of Verbal Learning and Verbal Behavior, 13,* 585–589.

Logue, A. W. (1986). *The psychology of eating and drinking.* New York: W. H. Freeman.

Londerville, S., & Main, M. (1981). Security of attachment, compliance, and maternal training methods in the second year of life. *Developmental Psychology, 17,* 289–299.

Long, J. (1987). *The essential guide to prescription drugs.* New York: Harper & Row.

Lorenz, K. (1937). The companion in the bird's world. *Auk, 54,* 245–273.

Lorenz, K. (1981). *The foundations of ethology.* New York: Springer-Verlag.

Luborsky, L., Singer, B., & Luborsky, L. (1975). Comparative studies of psychotherapies: Is it true that everyone has won and all must have prizes? *Archives of General Psychiatry, 32,* 995–1008.

Luce, G. G. (1971). *Biological rhythms in human and animal physiology.* New York: Dover.

Luchins, A. S. (1957). Experimental attempts to minimize the impact of first impressions. In C. I. Hovland (Ed.), *The order of presentation in persuasion.* New Haven, CT: Yale University Press.

Lumsdaine, A., & Janis, I. (1953). Resistance to counterpropaganda presentation. *Public Opinion Quarterly, 17,* 311–318.

Lustman, P. J., & Sowa, C. J. (1983). Comparative efficacy of biofeedback and stress inoculation for stress reduction. *Journal of Clinical Psychology, 31,* 191–197.

Lykken, D. T. (1981). *A tremor in the blood: Uses and abuses of the lie detector.* New York: McGraw-Hill.

Lyman, B., Hatlelid, D., & Macurdy, C. (1981). Stimulus-person cues in first-impression attraction. *Perceptual and Motor Skills, 52,* 59–66.

M

Maccoby, E. E., & Jacklin, C. N. (1974). *The psychology of sex differences.* Stanford, CA: Stanford University Press.

Machover, K. (1949). *Personality projection in the drawing of the human figure.* Springfield, IL: Charles C Thomas.

Mackenzie, B. (1984). Explaining race differences in IQ: The logic, the methodology, and the evidence. *American Psychologist, 39*(11), 1214–1233.

Madsen, K. B. (1968). *Theories of motivation.* Copenhagen: Munksgaard.

Madsen, K. B. (1973). Theories of motivation. In B. B. Wolman (Ed.), *Handbook of general psychology.* Englewood Cliffs, NJ: Prentice-Hall.

Malamuth, N. M. (1984). Violence against women: Cultural and individual cases. In N. M. Malamuth & E. Donnerstein (Eds.), *Pornography and sexual aggression.* New York: Academic Press.

Malamuth, N. M., & Donnerstein, E. (1982). The effects of aggressive-pornographic mass media stimuli. In L. Berkowitz (Ed.), *Advances in Experimental Social Psychology* (Vol. 15). New York: Academic Press.

Malatesta, V. J., & Adams, H. E. (1984). The sexual dysfunctions. In H. E. Adams & P. B. Sutker (Eds.), *Comprehensive handbook of psychopathology.* New York: Plenum Press.

Malcolm, J. (1980: Pt. 1, Nov. 24; Pt. 2, Dec. 1). The impossible profession. *The New Yorker,* pp. 55–133, 54–152.

Malmo, R. B. (1975). *On emotions, needs and our archaic brain.* New York: Holt, Rinehart & Winston.

Mandler, G. (1982). Stress and thought processes. In L. Goldberger & S. Breznitz (Eds.), *Handbook of stress: Theoretical and clinical aspects.* New York: Free Press.

Mandler, G. (1984). *Mind and body.* New York: Norton.

Mantyh, P. W. (1983). Connections of midbrain periaqueductal gray in the monkey: I. Ascending efferent projections. *Journal of Neurophysiology, 49,* 567–581.

Manuck, S. B., & Garland, F. N. (1980). Stability of individual differences in cardiovascular reactivity. *Physiology and Behavior, 24*(3), 621–624.

Maratsos, M. (1983). Some current issues in the study of the acquisition of grammar. In J. H. Flavell & E. M. Markham (Eds.), *Handbook of child psychology* (Vol. 3). New York: Wiley.

Marcia, J. E. (1966). Development and validation of ego identity status. *Journal of Personality and Social Psychology, 3,* 551–558.

Marcia, J. E. (1980). Identity in adolescence. In J. Adelson (Ed.), *Handbook of adolescent psychology.* New York: Wiley.

Maricle, R., Leung, P., & Bloom, J. D. (1987). The use of DSM-III axis III in recording physical illness in psychiatric patients. *American Journal of Psychiatry, 144*(11), 1484–1486.

Marks, I. (1977). Phobias and obsessions: Clinical phenomena in search of laboratory models. In J. D. Maser & M. E. P. Seligman (Eds.), *Psychopathology: Experimental models.* San Francisco: W. H. Freeman.

Marks, W. B., Dobelle, W. H., & MacNichol, E. F. (1964). Visual pigments of single primate cones. *Science, 143,* 1181–1183.

Marlatt, G. A., & Rose, F. (1980). Addictive disorders. In A. E. Kazdin, A. S. Bellack, & M. Hersen (Eds.), *New perspectives in abnormal psychology.* New York: Oxford University Press.

Marsh, H. W., & Parker, J. W. (1984). Determinants of student self-concept: Is it better to be a relatively large fish in a small pond even if you don't learn to swim well? *Journal of Personality and Social Psychology, 47*(1), 213–231.

Marshall, G. D., & Zimbardo, P. G. (1979). Affective consequences of inadequately explained physiological arousal. *Journal of Personality and Social Psychology, 37*(6), 970–988.

Marshall, J. C. (1981). Hemispheric specialization: What, how and why. *Behavioral and Brain Sciences, 4,* 72–73.

Martin, B. (1971). *Anxiety and neurotic disorders.* New York: Wiley.

Martin, R. A., & Lefcourt, H. M. (1983). Sense of humor as a moderator of the relation between stressors and moods. *Journal of Personality and Social Psychology, 45*(6), 1313–1324.

Marziali, E. A., & Pilkonis, P. A. (1986). The measurement of subjective response to stressful life events. *Journal of Human Stress, 12*(1), 5–12.

Maslach, C. (1979). Negative emotional biasing of unexplained arousal. *Journal of Personality and Social Psychology, 37*(6), 953–969.

Maslach, C. (1982). Understanding burnout: Definitional issues in analyzing a complex phenomenon. In W. S. Paine (Ed.), *Job stress and burnout: Research, theory and intervention perspectives.* Beverly Hills, CA: Sage Publications.

Maslow, A. H. (1954). *Motivation and personality.* New York: Harper & Row.

Maslow, A. H. (1962). *Toward a psychology of being.* Princeton, NJ: Van Nostrand.

Maslow, A. H. (1968). *Toward a psychology of being.* New York: Van Nostrand.

Maslow, A. H. (1970). *Motivation and personality* (2nd ed.). New York: Harper & Row.

Mason, J. W. (1975). A historical view of the stress field, Part 2. *Journal of Human Stress, 1,* 22–36.

Masters, W. H., & Johnson, V. E. (1966). *Human sexual response.* Boston: Little, Brown.

Masters, W. H., & Johnson, V. E. (1970). *Human sexual inadequacy.* Boston: Little, Brown.

Masters, W. H., & Johnson, V. E. (1980). *Human sexual inadequacy* (2nd ed.). New York: Bantam Books.

Matarazzo, J. D., & Herman, D. O. (1985). Clinical uses of the WAIS-R: Base rates of differences between VIQ and PIQ in the WAIS-R standardization sample. In B. B. Wolman (Ed.), *Handbook of intelligence: Theories, measurements, and applications.* New York: Wiley.

Matthews, K. A. (1982). Psychological perspectives on the Type-A behavior pattern. *Psychological Bulletin, 91,* 293–323.

Maxmen, J. S. (1986). *Essential psychopathology.* New York: Norton.

Mayer, J. (1955). Regulation of energy intake and the body weight: The glucostatic theory and the lipostatic hypothesis. *Annals of the New York Academy of Science, 63,* 15–43.

Mayer, J. (1968). *Overweight: Causes and control.* Englewood Cliffs, NJ: Prentice-Hall.

Mayer, J. (1980). The bitter truth about sugar. In C. Borg (Ed.), *Annual editions: Readings in health.* Guilford, CT: Dushkin.

McAdams, D. P. (1980). A thematic coding system for the intimacy motive. *Journal of Research in Personality, 14,* 413–432.

McAdams, D. P. (1982). Intimacy motivation. In A. J. Stewart (Ed.), *Motivation and society.* San Francisco: Jossey-Bass.

McAdams, D. P., & Constantian, C. A. (1983). Intimacy and affiliation motives in daily living: An experience sampling analysis. *Journal of Personality and Social Psychology, 45*(4), 851–861.

McAdams, D. P., Healy, S., & Krause, S. (1984). Social motives and patterns of friendship. *Journal of Personality and Social Psychology, 47*(4), 828–838.

McAdams, D. P., Jackson, R. J., & Kirshnit, C. (1984). Looking, laughing, and smiling in dyads as a function of intimacy motivation and reciprocity. *Journal of Personality, 52*(3), 261–273.

McAllister, W. R., McAllister, D. E., Scoles, M. T., & Hampton, S. R. (1986). Persistence of fear-reducing behavior: Relevance for the conditioning theory of neurosis. *Journal of Abnormal Psychology, 95*(4), 365–372.

McCann, I. L., & Holmes, D. S. (1984). Influence of aerobic exercise on depression. *Journal of Personality and Social Psychology, 46*(5), 1142–1147.

McClelland, D. C. (1961). *The achieving society.* Princeton, NJ: Van Nostrand.

McClelland, D. C. (1965). Achievement and entrepreneurship: A longitudinal study. *Journal of Personality and Social Psychology, 1,* 389–392.

McClelland, D. C. (1975). *Power: The inner experience.* New York: Irvington.

McClelland, D. C. (1985). How motives, skills and values determine what people do. *American Psychologist, 40,* 812–825.

McClelland, D. C., Atkinson, J. W., Clark, R. A., & Lowell, E. L. (1953). *The achievement motive.* New York: Appleton-Century-Crofts.

McClelland, D. C., & Winter, D. G. (1969). *Motivating economic achievement.* New York: Free Press.

McClelland, J. L., & Rumelhart, D. E. (1981). An interactive activation model of the effect of context in perception: Part 1. An account of basic findings. *Psychological Review, 88,* 375–407.

McClintock, M. K. (1971). Menstrual synchrony and suppression. *Nature, 299,* 244–245.

McConnell, J. V. (1962). Memory transfer through cannibalism in planarians. *Journal of Neuropsychiatry, 3*(Suppl. 1), 542–548.

McCormick, D. A., & Thompson, R. F. (1984). Cerebellum: Essential involvement in the classically conditioned eyelid response. *Science, 223,* 296–299.

McCrae, R., & Costa, P. T., Jr. (1985). Updating Norman's "adequate taxonomy": Intelligence and personality dimensions in natural language and in questionnaires. *Journal of Personality and Social Psychology, 49,* 710–721.

McCrae, R., & Costa, P. T., Jr. (1987). Validation of the five-factor model of personality across instruments and observers. *Journal of Personality and Social Psychology, 52*(1), 81–90.

McCrae, R. R. (1984). Situational determinants of coping responses: Loss, threat and challenge. *Journal of Personality and Social Psychology, 46*(4), 919–928.

McDaniel, M. A., & Einstein, G. O. (1986). Bizarre imagery as an effective memory aid: The importance of distinctiveness. *Journal of Experimental Psychology: Learning, Memory, & Cognition, 12,* 54–65.

McDougall, W. (1908). *An introduction to social psychology.* London: Methuen.

McFarland, C., & Ross, M. (1987). The relation between current impressions and memories of self and dating partners. *Personality and Social Psychology Bulletin, 13*(2), 228–238.

McGaugh, J. L. (1983). Preserving the presence of the past: Hormonal influences on memory. *American Psychologist, 38,* 161–174.

McGeoch, J. A., & McDonald, W. T. (1931). Meaningful relation and retroactive inhibition. *American Journal of Psychology, 43,* 579–588.

McGinnies, E., & Ward, C. D. (1980). Better liked than right: Trustworthiness and expertise as factors in credibility. *Personality and Social Psychology Bulletin, 6,* 467–472.

McGlashan, T. H. (1986). Schizophrenia: Psychosocial treatments and the role of psychosocial factors in its etiology and pathogenesis. In A. J. Frances & R. E. Hales (Eds.), *Psychiatry update: Annual review* (Vol. 5). Washington, DC: American Psychiatric Press.

McGlone, J. (1980). Sex-differences in human brain asymmetry: A critical review. *Behavioral and Brain Sciences, 3,* 215–263.

McGrath, J. E. (1977). Settings, measures and themes: An integrative review of some research on social-psychological factors in stress. In A. Monat & R. S. Lazarus (Eds.), *Stress and coping: An anthology.* New York: Columbia University Press.

McGuffin, P., & Reich, T. (1984). Psychopathology and genetics. In H. E. Adams & P. B. Sutker (Eds.), *Comprehensive handbook of psychopathology.* New York: Plenum Press.

McGuire, T. R., & Haviland, J. M. (1985). Further considerations on behavior-genetic analysis of humans. *Journal of Personality and Social Psychology, 49*(5), 1434–1436.

McGuire, W. J. (1964). Inducing resistance to persuasion. In L. Berkowitz (Ed.), *Advances in experimental social psychology* (Vol. 1). New York: Academic Press.

McGuire, W. J. (1985). Attitudes and attitude change. In G. Lindzey & E. Aronson (Eds.), *Handbook of social psychology* (3rd ed., Vol. 2). New York: Random House.

McReynolds, W. T. (1979). DSM-III and the future of applied social science. *Professional Psychology, 10,* 123–132.

Mechanic, D. (1972). Social psychologic factors affecting the presentation of bodily complaints. *New England Journal of Medicine, 286,* 1132–1139.

Mechanic, D. (1980). *Mental health and social policy.* Englewood Cliffs, NJ: Prentice-Hall.

Meeker, W. R., & Barber, T. X. (1971). Toward an explanation of stage hypnosis. *Journal of Abnormal Psychology, 77,* 61–70.

Melman, A., & Leiter, E. (1983). The urologic evaluation of impotence (male excitement phase disorder). In H. S. Kaplan (Ed.), *The evaluation of sexual disorders: Psychological and medical aspects.* New York: Brunner/Mazel.

Meltzoff, J., & Kornreich, M. (1970). *Research in psychotherapy.* New York: Atherton.

Melzak, R. (1973). *The puzzle of pain.* New York: Basic Books.

Mentzer, R. L. (1982). Response biases in multiple-choice test item files. *Educational and Psychological Measurement, 42,* 437–448.

Mercer, J. R. (1975). Sociocultural factors in educational labeling. In M. J. Begab & S. A. Richardson (Eds.), *The mentally retarded and society: A social science perspective.* Baltimore: University Park Press.

Mercer, J. R. (1984). What is a racially and culturally nondiscriminatory test? A sociological and pluralistic perspective. In C. R. Reynolds & R. T. Brown (Eds.), *Perspectives on bias in mental testing.* New York: Plenum Press.

Merikangas, K. R., & Weissman, M. M. (1986). Epidemiology of DSM-III axis II personality disorders. In A. J. Frances & R. E. Hales (Eds.), *Psychiatry update: Annual Review* (Vol. 5). Washington, DC: American Psychiatric Press.

Metcalfe, J. (1986). Feeling of knowing in memory and problem solving. *Journal of Experimental Psychology: Learning, Memory, & Cognition, 12,* 288–294.

Meyer, D. E., & Schvaneveldt, R. W. (1976). Meaning, memory structure, and mental processes. *Science, 192,* 27–33.

Meyer, R. (1980). The antisocial personality. In R. Woody (Ed.), *The encyclopedia of mental assessment.* San Francisco: Jossey-Bass.

Milgram, S. (1963). Behavioral study of obedience. *Journal of Abnormal and Social Psychology, 67,* 371–378.

Milgram, S. (1964). Issues in the study of obedience. *American Psychologist, 19,* 848–852.

Milgram, S. (1968). Reply to the critics. *International Journal of Psychiatry, 6,* 294–295.

Milgram, S. (1974). *Obedience to authority.* New York: Harper & Row.

Miller, A. G. (1986). *The obedience experiments: A case study of controversy in social science.* New York: Praeger.

Miller, C. T., Byrne, D., & Fisher, J. D. (1980). Order effects on sexual and affective responses to erotic stimuli by males and females. *Journal of Sex Research, 16,* 131–147.

Miller, G. A. (1956). The magical number seven, plus or minus two: Some limits on our capacity for processing information. *Psychological Review, 63,* 81–97.

Miller, G. A., Galanter, E., & Pribram, K. (1960). *Plans and the structure of behavior.* New York: Holt, Rinehart & Winston.

Miller, N. E. (1944). Experimental studies of conflict. In J. M. Hunt (Ed.), *Personality and the behavior disorders* (Vol. 1). New York: Ronald.

Miller, N. E. (1959). Liberalization of basic S-R concepts: Extension to conflict behavior, motivation, and social learning. In S. Koch (Ed.), *Psychology: A study of a science* (Vol. 2). New York: McGraw-Hill.

Miller, N. E. (1985). The value of behavioral research on animals. *American Psychologist, 40,* 423–440.

Miller, P. H., & Weiss, M. G. (1981). Children's attention allocation, understanding of attention, and performance on the incidental learning task. *Child Development, 52,* 1183–1190.

Millman, J., Bishop, C. H., & Ebel, R. (1965). An analysis of test-wiseness. *Educational and Psychological Measurement, 25,* 707–726.

Millon, T. (1986). A theoretical derivation of pathological personalities. In T. Millon & G. L. Klerman (Eds.), *Contemporary directions in psychopathology: Toward the DSM-IV.* New York: Guilford Press.

Milner, B. (1974). Hemispheric specialization: Scope and limits. In F. O. Schmitt & F. G. Worden (Eds.), *The neurosciences: Third study program.* Cambridge, MA: MIT Press.

Mineka, S. (1979). The role of fear in theories of avoidance learning, flooding and extinction. *Psychological Bulletin, 86,* 985–1010.

Mineka, S., & Cook, M. (1986). Immunization against the observational conditioning of snake fear in rhesus monkeys. *Journal of Abnormal Psychology, 95*(4), 307–318.

Mirsky, A. F., & Duncan, C. C. (1986). Etiology and expression of schizophrenia: Neurobiological and psychosocial factors. In M. R. Rosenzweig & L. W. Porter (Eds.), *Annual review of psychology: 1986.* Palo Alto, CA: Annual Reviews.

Mischel, W. (1961). Delay of gratification, need for achievement, and acquiescence in another culture. *Journal of Abnormal and Social Psychology, 62,* 543–552.

Mischel, W. (1968). *Personality and assessment.* New York: Wiley.

Mischel, W. (1973). Toward a cognitive social learning conceptualization of personality. *Psychological Review, 80,* 252–283.

Mischel, W. (1984). Convergences and challenges in the search for consistency. *American Psychologist, 39,* 351–364.

Mischel, W., & Mischel, H. N. (1976). A cognitive social learning approach to morality and self-regulation. In T. Lickona (Ed.), *Moral development and behavior: Theory, research, and social issues.* New York: Holt, Rinehart & Winston.

Mishkin, M. (1982). A memory system in the monkey. *Philosophical Transactions of the Royal Society of London, 298,* 85–95.

Mitler, M. M., Guilleminault, C., Orem, J., Zarcone, V. P., & Dement, W. C. (1975, December). Sleeplessness, sleep attacks, and things that go wrong in the night. *Psychology Today, 9*(7), 45–50.

Moates, D. R., & Schumacher, G. M. (1980). *An introduction to cognitive psychology.* Belmont, CA: Wadsworth.

Money, J., & Erhardt, A. A. (1972). *Man and woman, boy and girl: Differentiation and dimorphism of gender identity.* Baltimore: Johns Hopkins University Press.

Moore-Ede, M. C., Sulzman, F. M., & Fuller, C. A. (1982). *The clocks that time us.* Cambridge, MA: Harvard University Press.

Moos, R. H., & Billings, A. G. (1982). Conceptualizing and measuring coping resources and processes. In L. Goldberger & S. Breznitz (Eds.), *Handbook of stress: Theoretical and clinical aspects.* New York: Free Press.

Morey, L. C. (1988). Personality disorders in DSM-III and DSM-III-R: Convergence, coverage, and internal consistency. *American Journal of Psychiatry, 145*(5), 573–577.

Morgan, C. D., & Murray, H. A. (1935). A method for investigating fantasies: The Thematic Apperception Test. *Archives of Neurology and Psychiatry, 34,* 289–306.

Morris, P. E., Jones, S., & Hampson, P. (1978). An imagery mnemonic for the learning of people's names. *British Journal of Psychology, 69,* 335–336.

Moruzzi, G., & Magoun, H. (1949). Brain stem reticular formation and activation of the EEG. *Electroencephalography and Clinical Neurophysiology, 1,* 455–473.

Mosher, D. L., & Cross, H. J. (1971). Sex guilt and premarital sexual experiences of college students. *Journal of Consulting and Clinical Psychology, 36,* 27–32.

Mowrer, O. H. (1947). On the dual nature of learning: A reinterpretation of "conditioning" and "problem-solving." *Harvard Educational Review, 17,* 102–150.

Mozell, M. M. (1971). The chemical senses: II. Olfaction. In J. W. Kling & L. A. Riggs (Eds.), *Experimental Psychology* (3rd ed., Vol. 1). New York: Holt, Rinehart & Winston.

Mozell, M. M., Smith, B. P., Smith, P. E., Sullivan, R. L., & Swender, P. (1969). Nasal chemoreception in flavor identification. *Archives of Otolaryngology, 90,* 367–373.

Murphy, J. M. (1980). Continuities in community-based psychiatric epidemiology. *Archives of General Psychiatry, 37,* 1215–1223.

Murphy, J. M., & Helzer, J. E. (1986). Epidemiology of schizophrenia in adulthood. In G. L. Klerman, M. M. Weissman, P. S. Appelbaum, & L. H. Roth (Eds.), *Psychiatry: Vol. 5. Social, epidemiologic, and legal psychiatry.* New York: Basic Books.

Murray, H. A. (1938). *Explorations in personality.* New York: Oxford University Press.

Murray, H. A. (1943). *Thematic Apperception Test.* Cambridge, MA: Harvard University Press.

Murstein, B. (1972). Physical attractiveness and marital choice. *Journal of Personality and Social Psychology, 22,* 8–12.

Myers, D. G., & Lamm, H. (1976). The group polarization phenomenon. *Psychological Bulletin, 83,* 602–627.

Myers, J. K., Weissman, M. M., Tischler, G. L., Holzer, C. E., III, Leaf, P. J., Orvaschel, H., Anthony, J. C., Boyd, J. H., Burke, J. D., Jr., Kramer, M., & Stoltzman, R. (1984). Six-month prevalence of psychiatric disorders in three communities. *Archives of General Psychiatry, 41,* 959–967.

Myers, J. L., O'Brien, E. J., Balota, D. A., & Toyofuku, M. L. (1984). Memory search without interference: The role of integration. *Cognitive Psychology, 16,* 217–243.

N

Nahas, G. G. (1976). *Marijuana: Chemistry, biochemistry and cellular effects.* New York: Springer.

Naitoh, P. (1981). Circadian cycles and restorative power of naps. In L. C. Johnson, D. I. Tepas, W. P. Colquhoun, & M. J. Colligan (Eds.), *Biological rhythms, sleep and shift work.* New York: Spectrum.

Nakazima, S. (1962). A comparative study of the speech developments of Japanese and American English in children. *Studies in Phonology, 2,* 27–39.

Nash, M. R., Lynn, S. J., & Givens, D. L. (1984). Adult hypnotic susceptibility, childhood punishment and child abuse: A brief communication. *International Journal of Clinical and Experimental Hypnosis, 32*(1), 6–11.

Nass, G. D., & Fisher, M. P. (1988). *Sexuality today.* Boston: Jones and Bartlett.

Nathan, P. E., & Hay, W. M. (1984). Alcoholism: Psychopathology, etiology and treatment. In H. E. Adams & P. B. Sutker (Eds.), *Comprehensive handbook of psychopathology.* New York: Plenum Press.

Nathans, J., Piantanida, T. P., Eddy, R. L., Shows, T. B., & Hogness, D. S. (1986). Molecular genetics of inherited variation in human color vision. *Science, 232,* 203–210.

Neimark, E. D. (1982). Adolescent thought: Transition to formal operations. In B. B. Wolman (Ed.), *Handbook of developmental psychology.* Englewood Cliffs, NJ: Prentice-Hall.

Neisser, U. (1967). *Cognitive psychology.* New York: Appleton-Century-Crofts.

Nel, E., Helmreich, R., & Aronson, E. (1969). Opinion change in the advocate as a function of the persuasibility of his audience: A clarification of the meaning of dissonance. *Journal of Personality and Social Psychology, 12,* 117–124.

Nelson, T. O. (1978). Detecting small amounts of information in memory: Savings for nonrecognized items. *Journal of Experimental Psychology: Human Learning and Memory, 4,* 453–468.

Nemiah, J. C. (1985). Somatoform disorders. In H. I. Kaplan & B. J. Sadock (Eds.), *Comprehensive textbook of psychiatry/IV.* Baltimore: Williams & Wilkins.

Nesbitt, R. E. L., Jr., & Abdul-Karim, R. W. (1982). Coincidental disorders complicating pregnancy. In D. N. Danforth (Ed.), *Obstetrics and gynecology.* Philadelphia: Harper & Row.

Nestoros, J. N. (1980). Ethanol specifically potentiates GABA-mediated neurotransmission in feline cerebral cortex. *Science, 209,* 708–710.

Neufeld, R. W. J., & Mothersill, K. J. (1980). Stress as an irritant of psychopathology. In I. G. Sarason & C. D. Spielberger (Eds.), *Stress and anxiety* (Vol. 7). New York: Hemisphere.

Neugebauer, R., Dohrenwend, B. P., & Dohrenwend, B. S. (1980). Formulation about hypotheses about the true prevalence of functional psychiatric disorders among adults in the United States. In B. P. Dohrenwend, B. S. Dohrenwend, M. S. Gould, B. Link, R. Neugebauer, & R. Wunsch-Hitzig (Eds.), *Mental illness in the United States: Epidemiological estimates.* New York: Praeger.

Newell, A., Shaw, J. C., & Simon, H. A. (1958). Elements of a theory of human problem solving. *Psychological Review, 65,* 151–166.

Newell, A., & Simon, H. A. (1972). *Human problem solving.* Englewood Cliffs, NJ: Prentice-Hall.

Newsom, C., Favell, J. E., & Rincover, A. (1983). Side effects of punishment. In S. Axelrod & J. Apsche (Eds.), *The effects of punishment on human behavior.* New York: Academic Press.

Newton, R. E., Marunycz, J. D., Alderdice, M. T., & Napoliello, M. J. (1986). Review of the side-effect profile of Buspirone. *American Journal of Medicine, 80*(Suppl. 3b), 17–21.

Nezu, A. M., Nezu, C. M., Blissett, S. E. (1988). Sense of humor as a moderator of the relation between stressful events and psychological distress: A prospective analysis. *Journal of Personality and Social Psychology, 54*(3), 520–525.

Nichols, R. (1978). Twin studies of ability, personality and interests. *Homo, 29,* 158–173.

Nickerson, R. S., & Adams, M. J. (1979). Long-term memory for a common object. *Cognitive Psychology, 11,* 287–307.

Nicol, S. E., & Gottesman, I. I. (1983). Clues to the genetics and neurobiology of schizophrenia. *American Scientist, 71,* 398–404.

Nicoll, R. A., & Madison, D. V. (1982). General anesthetics hyperpolarize neurons in the vertebrate central nervous system. *Science, 217,* 1055–1057.

Niijima, A. (1982). Glucose-sensitive afferent nerve fibers in the hepatic branch of the vagus nerve in the guinea pig. *Journal of Physiology, 332,* 315–323.

Nisbett, R. E. (1968). Determinants of food intake in obesity. *Science, 159,* 1254–1255.

Nisbett, R. E. (1972). Hunger, obesity, and the ventromedial hypothalamus. *Psychological Review, 79,* 433–453.

Niswander, K. R. (1982). Prenatal care. In R. C. Benson (Ed.), *Current obstetric and gynecologic diagnosis and treatment.* Los Altos, CA: Lange Medical Publications.

Norcross, J. C., & Prochaska, J. O. (1982). National survey of clinical psychologists: Affiliations and orientations. *Clinical Psychologist, 35*(3), 1, 4–6.

Nordin, C., Siwers, B., & Bertilsson, L. (1982). Site of lumbar puncture influences levels of monoamine metabolites. *Archives of General Psychiatry, 39,* 1445.

Norman, D. A. (1976). *Memory and attention: An introduction to human information processing.* New York: Wiley.

Novaco, R. W., Stokols, D., Campbell, J., & Stokols, J. (1979). Transportation, stress and community psychology. *American Journal of Community Psychology, 7*(4), 361–380.

Novin, D., Robinson, B. A., Culbreth, L. A., & Tordoff, M. G. (1983). Is there a role for the liver in the control of food intake? *American Journal of Clinical Nutrition, 9,* 233–246.

Nowlis, D. P., & Kamiya, J. (1970). The control of electroencephalographic alpha rhythms through auditory feedback and the associated mental activity. *Psychophysiology, 6,* 476–484.

Noyes, R., Jr., Clarkson, C., Crowe, R. R., Yates, W. R., & McChesney, C. M. (1987). A family study of generalized anxiety disorder. *American Journal of Psychiatry, 144*(8), 1019–1024.

Nunnally, J. C. (1982). The study of human change: Measurement, research strategies, and methods of analysis. In B. B. Wolman (Ed.), *Handbook of developmental psychology*. Englewood Cliffs, NJ: Prentice-Hall.

Nurnberger, J. I., & Gershon, E.S. (1982). Genetics. In E. S. Paykel (Ed.), *Handbook of affective disorders*. New York: Guilford Press.

Nurnberger, J. I., & Zimmerman, J. (1970). Applied analysis of human behavior: An alternative to conventional motivational inferences and unconscious determination in therapeutic programming. *Behavior Therapy, 1*, 59–69.

O

Oakland, T., & Parmelee, R. (1985). Mental measurement of minority-group children. In B. B. Wolman (Ed.), *Handbook of intelligence: Theories, measurements, and applications*. New York: Wiley.

Odom, R. D. (1978). A perceptual-salience account of decalage relations and developmental change. In L. S. Siegel & C. J. Brainerd (Eds.), *Alternatives to Piaget*. New York: Academic Press.

Offer, D., & Offer, J. (1975). *From teenage to young manhood*. New York: Basic Books.

Ohman, A. (1979). Fear relevance, autonomic conditioning, and phobias: A laboratory model. In P. O. Sjoden & S. Bates (Eds.), *Trends in behavior therapy*. New York: Academic Press.

Ohman, A., Erixon, G., & Lofberg, I. (1975). Phobias and preparedness: Phobic versus neutral pictures as conditioned stimuli for human autonomic responses. *Journal of Abnormal Psychology, 84*(1), 41–45.

Olds, J. (1956). Pleasure centers in the brain. *Scientific American, 193*, 105–116.

Olds, J., & Milner, P. (1954). Positive reinforcement produced by electrical stimulation of the septal area and other regions of the rat brain. *Journal of Comparative and Physiological Psychology, 47*, 419–427.

Olds, M. E., & Fobes, J. L. (1981). The central basis of motivation: Intracranial self-stimulation studies. In M. R. Rosenzweig & L. W. Porter (Eds.), *Annual review of psychology: 1981*. Palo Alto, CA: Annual Reviews.

O'Leary, K. D. (1984). The image of behavior therapy: It is time to take a stand. *Behavior Therapy, 15*, 219–233.

O'Leary, K. D., Kent, R. N., & Kanowitz, J. (1975). Shaping data collection congruent with experimental hypotheses. *Journal of Applied Behavior Analysis, 8*, 43–51.

O'Leary, V. E. (1977). *Toward understanding women*. Pacific Grove, CA: Brooks/Cole.

Olsen, R. W. (1982). Drug interactions at the GABA receptor-ionophore complex. *Annual Review of Pharmacology and Toxicology, 22*, 245–277.

O'Malley, P. M., & Bachman, J. G. (1979). Self-esteem and education: Sex and cohort comparisons among high school seniors. *Journal of Personality and Social Psychology, 37*, 1153–1159.

Oomura, Y. (1976). Significance of glucose insulin and free fatty acid on the hypothalamic feeding and satiety neurons. In D. Novin, W. Wyrwicka, & G. Bray (Eds.), *Hunger: Basic mechanisms and clinical applications*. New York: Raven.

Orne, M. T. (1951). The mechanisms of hypnotic age regression: An experimental study. *Journal of Abnormal and Social Psychology, 46*, 213–225.

Orne, M. T. (1959). The nature of hypnosis: Artifact and essence. *Journal of Abnormal and Social Psychology, 58*, 277–299.

Orne, M. T., & Holland, C. C. (1968). On the ecological validity of laboratory deceptions. *International Journal of Psychiatry, 6*, 282–293.

Ornstein, R. E. (1977). *The psychology of consciousness*. New York: Harcourt, Brace and Jovanovich.

Osborn, A. F. (1963). *Applied imagination: Principles and procedures for creative problem solving* (3rd ed.). New York: Scribner's.

Ost, L. (1987). Age of onset in different phobias. *Journal of Abnormal Psychology, 96*(3), 223–229.

Oswald, I., & Adam, K. (1980). The man who had not slept for ten years. *British Medical Journal, 281*, 1684–1685.

P

Page, S. (1977). Effects of the mental illness label in attempts to obtain accommodation. *Canadian Journal of Behavioral Science, 9*, 84–90.

Pagel, M. D., Erdly, W. W., & Becker, J. (1987). Social networks: We get by with (and in spite of) a little help from our friends. *Journal of Personality and Social Psychology, 53*(4), 793–804.

Paivio, A. (1969). Mental imagery in associative learning and memory. *Psychological Review, 76*, 241–263.

Paivio, A. (1986). *Mental representations: A dual coding approach*. New York: Oxford University Press.

Paivio, A., Smythe, P. E., & Yuille, J. C. (1968). Imagery versus meaningfulness of nouns in paired-associate learning. *Canadian Journal of Psychology, 22*, 427–441.

Palkovitz, R. J., & Lore, R. K. (1980). Note taking and note review: Why students fail questions based on lecture material. *Teaching of Psychology, 7*(3), 159–161.

Palladino, J. J., & Carducci, B. J. (1984). Students' knowledge of sleep and dreams. *Teaching of Psychology, 11*(3), 189–191.

Palladino, J. J., & Motiff, J. P. (1983). Discriminant analysis of Type-A/Type-B subjects on the California Psychological Inventory. *Journal of Social and Clinical Psychology, 1*(2), 155–161.

Palmer, J. D. (1982, October). Biorhythm bunkum. *Natural History, 91*, 90–97.

Palmore, E. (1975). *The honorable elders*. Durham, NC: Duke University Press.

Paris, S. G., & Lindauer, B. K. (1982). The development of cognitive skills during childhood. In B. B. Wolman (Ed.), *Handbook of developmental psychology*. Englewood Cliffs, NJ: Prentice-Hall.

Parke, R. D. (1977). Some effects of punishment on children's behavior—revisited. In E.M. Hetherington & R. D. Parke (Eds.), *Contemporary readings in child psychology*. New York: McGraw-Hill.

Parke, R. D., & Slaby, R. G. (1983). The development of aggression. In P. H. Mussen (Ed.), *Handbook of child psychology* (4th ed, Vol. 4). New York: Wiley.

Parker, D. E. (1980). The vestibular apparatus. *Scientific American, 243*(5), 118–135.

Parlee, M. B. (1973). The premenstrual syndrome. *Psychological Bulletin, 80*, 454–465.

Parlee, M. B. (1982). Changes in moods and activation levels during the menstrual cycle in experimentally naive subjects. *Psychology of Women Quarterly, 7*, 119–131.

Parmelee, A. H., & Stern, E. (1972). Development of states in infants. In C. D. Clemente, D. P. Purpure, & F. E. Mayer (Eds.), *Sleep and the maturing nervous system*. New York: Academic Press.

Parsons, T. (1979). Definitions of health and illness in light of the American values and social structure. In E. G. Jaco (Ed.), *Patients, physicians and illness: A sourcebook in behavioral science and health*. New York: Free Press.

Patzer, G. L. (1985). *The physical attractiveness phenomena*. New York: Plenum Press.

Pauk, W. (1984). *How to study in college*. Boston: Houghton Mifflin.

Paul, G. L. (1966). *Insight versus desensitization in psychotherapy*. Stanford, CA: Stanford University Press.

Paul, G. L., & Lentz, R. J. (1977). *Psychosocial treatment of chronic mental patients: Milieu versus social-learning programs*. Cambridge, MA: Harvard University Press.

Paul, S. M., Crawley, J. N., & Skolnick, P. (1986). The neurobiology of anxiety: The role of the GABA/benzodiazepine receptor complex. In P. A. Berger & H. K. H. Brodie (Eds.), *American handbook of psychiatry: Biological psychiatry* (2nd ed., Vol. 8). New York: Basic Books.

Pavlov, I. P. (1906). The scientific investigation of psychical faculties or processes in the higher animals. *Science, 24*, 613–619.

Payne, J. W. (1976). Task complexity and contingent processing in decision making: An information search and protocol analysis. *Organizational Behavior and Human Performance, 16*, 366–387.

Pearce, L. (1974). Duck! It's the new journalism. *New Times, 2*(10), 40–41.

Pearlman, C. A. (1982). Sleep structure variation and performance. In W. B. Webb (Ed.), *Biological rhythms, sleep and performance*. New York: Wiley.

Pellegrini, R. J. (1973). Impressions of the male personality as a function of beardedness. *Psychology, 10*, 29–33.

Penfield, W., & Perot, P. (1963). The brain's record of auditory and visual experience. *Brain, 86*, 595–696.

Perkins, D. V. (1982). The assessment of stress using life events scales. In L. Goldberger & S. Breznitz (Eds.), *Handbook of stress: Theoretical and clinical aspects*. New York: Free Press.

Pernoll, M. I. (1982). Maternal and perinatal statistics. In R. C. Benson (Ed.), *Current obstetric and gynecologic diagnosis and treatment*. Los Altos, CA: Lange Medical Publications.

Perry, D. G., & Bussey, K. (1979). The social learning theory of sex differences: Imitation is alive and well. *Journal of Personality and Social Psychology, 37*, 1699–1712.

Persky, H. (1983). Psychosexual effects of hormones. *Medical Aspects of Human Sexuality, 17*(9), 74–101.

Persky, H., Lief, H. I., Straus, D., Miller, W. R., & O'Brien, C. P. (1978). Plasma testosterone level and sexual behavior of couples. *Archives of Sexual Behavior, 7*, 157–173.

Persons, R. W. (1970). The Mosher Guilt Scale: Theoretical formulations, research review and normative data. *Journal of Projective Techniques and Personality, 34*(4), 266–269.

Pert, C. B., & Snyder, S. H. (1973). Opiate receptor: Demonstration in the nervous tissue. *Science, 179*, 1011–1014.

Peters, R. K., Cady, L. D., Jr., Bischoff, D. P., Bernstein, L., & Pile, M. C. (1983). Physical fitness and subsequent myocardial infarction in healthy workers. *Journal of the American Medical Association, 249*(22), 3052–3056.

Petersen, A. C. (1987). Those gangly years. *Psychology Today, 21*(9), 28–34.

Peterson, C., Villanova, P., & Raps, C. S. (1985). Depression and attributions: Factors responsible for inconsistent results in the published literature. *Journal of Abnormal Psychology, 94*(2), 165–168.

Peterson, L. R., & Peterson, M. J. (1959). Short-term retention of individual verbal items. *Journal of Experimental Psychology, 58*, 193–198.

Pettigrew, T. F. (1979). The ultimate attribution error: Extending Allport's analysis of prejudice. *Personality and Social Psychology Bulletin, 5*, 461–476.

Petty, R. E., & Cacioppo, J. T. (1986). The elaboration likelihood model of persuasion. In L. Berkowitz (Ed.), *Advances in experimental social psychology* (Vol. 19). New York: Academic Press.

Pfaffmann, C. (1951). Taste and smell. In S. S. Stevens (Ed.), *Handbook of experimental psychology*. New York: Wiley.

Pfeiffer, E., & Davis, G. L. (1972). Determinants of sexual behavior in middle and old age. *Journal of the American Geriatric Society, 20*, 82–87.

Pfohl, B., & Andreasen, N. C. (1986). Schizophrenia: Diagnosis and classification. In A. J. Frances & R. E. Hales (Eds.), *Psychiatry update: Annual review* (Vol. 5). Washington, DC: American Psychiatric Press.

Piaget, J. (1929). *The child's conception of the world*. New York: Harcourt, Brace.

Piaget, J. (1932). *The moral judgment of the child*. Glencoe, IL: Free Press.

Piaget, J. (1952). *The origins of intelligence in children*. New York: International Universities Press.

Piaget, J. (1954). *The construction of reality in the child*. New York: Basic Books.

Piaget, J. (1983). Piaget's theory. In P. H. Mussen (Ed.), *Handbook of child psychology* (Vol. 1). New York: Wiley.

Pilowsky, I. (1978). A general classification of abnormal illness behaviors. *British Journal of Psychology, 51*, 131–137.

Pines, A. M., Aronson, E., & Kafry, D. (1981). *Burnout: From tedium to personal growth.* New York: Free Press.

Piotrowski, C., Sherry, D., & Keller, J. W. (1985). Psychodiagnostic test usage: A survey of the Society for Personality Assessment. *Journal of Personality Assessment, 49*(2), 115–119.

Pivar, W. H. (1978). *The whole earth textbook: A survival manual for students.* Philadelphia: Saunders.

Plath, S. (1971). *The bell jar.* New York: Harper & Row.

Plomin, R., & DeFries, J. C. (1980). Genetics and intelligence: Recent data. *Intelligence, 4*, 15–24.

Plutchik, R. (1980). A language for the emotions. *Psychology Today, 13*(9), 68–78.

Plutchik, R. (1984). Emotions: A general psychoevolutionary theory. In K. R. Scherer & P. Ekman (Eds.), *Approaches to emotion.* Hillsdale, NJ: Erlbaum.

Pocs, O., & Godow, A. G. (1977). Can students view parents as sexual beings? *Family Coordinator, 26,* 31–36.

Polivy, J. (1981). On the induction of emotion in the laboratory: Discrete moods or multiple affective states? *Journal of Personality and Social Psychology, 41,* 803–817.

Pope, H. G., Jr., Ionescu-Pioggia, M., & Cole, J. O. (1981). Drug use and life-style among college undergraduates. *Archives of General Psychiatry, 38,* 588–591.

Pope, K. S., Keith-Spiegel, P., & Tabachnick, B. G. (1986). Sexual attraction to clients. *American Psychologist, 41*(2), 147–158.

Posner, M. I., & Snyder, C. R. R. (1975). Attention and cognitive control. In R. L. Solso (Ed.), *Information processing and cognition: The Loyola symposium.* Hillsdale, NJ: Erlbaum.

Postman, L. (1971). Transfer, interference and forgetting. In J. W. Kling & L. A. Riggs (Eds.), *Experimental psychology* (3rd ed.). New York: Holt, Rinehart & Winston.

Postman, L. (1985). Human learning and memory. In G. A. Kimble & K. Schlesinger (Eds.), *Topics in the history of psychology.* Hillsdale, NJ: Erlbaum.

Potkay, C. R., & Allen, B. P. (1986). *Personality: Theory, research and applications.* Pacific Grove, CA: Brooks/Cole.

Poznanski, E. O. (1973). Children with excessive fears. *American Journal of Orthopsychiatry, 43*(3), 428–438.

Premack, D. (1971). Language in the chimpanzee? *Science, 172,* 808–822.

Pressley, M. (1982). Elaboration and memory development. *Child Development, 53,* 296–309.

Pribram, K. H. (1981). Emotions. In S. B. Filskov & T. J. Boll (Eds.), *Handbook of clinical neuropsychology.* New York: Wiley.

Prince, G. (1978). Putting the other half to work. *Training: The Magazine of Human Resources Development, 15,* 57–61.

Provence, S., & Lipton, R. C. (1962). *Infants in institutions.* New York: International Universities Press.

Pruitt, D. G. (1971). Choice shifts in group discussion: An introductory review. *Journal of Personality and Social Psychology, 20,* 339–360.

Pucetti, R. (1981). The case for mental duality: Evidence from split-brain data and other considerations. *Behavioral and Brain Sciences, 4,* 93–123.

Purvis, K., Landgren, B. M., Cekan, Z., & Diczfalusy, E. (1976). Endocrine effects of masturbation in men. *Journal of Endocrinology, 70,* 439–444.

Q

Quadagno, D. M. (1987). Pheromones and human sexuality. *Medical Aspects of Human Sexuality, 21*(11), 149–154.

Quigley, M. E., Sheehan, K. L., Wilkes, M. M., & Yen, S. S. C. (1979). Effects of maternal smoking on circulating catecholamine levels and fetal heart rates. *American Journal of Obstetrics and Gynecology, 133,* 685–690.

R

Rachman, S. (1966). Sexual fetishism: An experimental analogue. *Psychological Record, 16,* 293–296.

Rachman, S. J., & Wilson, G. T. (1980). *The effects of psychological therapy.* New York: Pergamon Press.

Ragland, D. R., & Brand, R. J. (1988). Type-A behavior and mortality from coronary heart disease. *The New England Journal of Medicine, 318*(2), 65–69.

Rahe, R. H., & Arthur, R. H. (1978). Life change and illness studies. *Journal of Human Stress, 4*(1), 3–15.

Rahe, R. H., & Holmes, T. H. (1965). Social, psychologic, and psychophysiologic aspects of inguinal hernia. *Journal of Psychosomatic Research, 8,* 487–491.

Rapaport, D., Gill, M., & Schafer, R. (1968). *Diagnostic psychological testing.* New York: International Universities Press.

Rapaport, K., & Burkhart, B. R. (1984). Personality and attitudinal characteristics of sexually coercive college males. *Journal of Abnormal Psychology, 93*(2), 216–221.

Raskin, R., Bali, L. R., & Peeke, H. V. (1981). Muscle biofeedback and transcendental meditation: A controlled evaluation of efficacy in the treatment of chronic anxiety. In D. Shapiro, Jr., J. Stoyva, J. Kamiya, T. X. Barber, N. E. Miller, & G. E. Schwartz (Eds.), *Biofeedback and behavioral medicine 1979/80: Therapeutic applications and experimental foundations.* Chicago: Aldine.

Rasmussen, T., & Milner, B. (1977). The role of early left-brain injury in determining lateralization of cerebral speech functions. *Annals of the New York Academy of Sciences, 299,* 355–369.

Ratliff, F. (1976). On the psychophysiological bases of universal color terms. *Proceedings of the American Philosophical Society, 120,* 311–330.

Read, J. D., & Bruce, D. (1982). Longitudinal tracking of difficult memory retrievals. *Cognitive Psychology, 14,* 280–300.

Reed, J. G., & Baxter, P. M. (1983). *Library use: A handbook for psychology.* Washington, DC: American Psychological Association.

Reed, S. K., Ernst, G. W., & Banerji, R. (1974). The role of analogy in transfer between similar problem states. *Cognitive Psychology, 6,* 436–450.

Reisenzein, R. (1983). The Schachter theory of emotion: Two decades later. *Psychological Bulletin, 94*(2), 239–264.

Relman, A. (1982). Marijuana and health. *New England Journal of Medicine, 306*(10), 603–604.

Renwick, P. A., & Lawler, E. E. (1978). What you really want from your job. *Psychology Today, 11*(12), 53–65, 118.

Repetti, R. L. (1984). Determinants of children's sex-stereotyping: Parental sex-role traits and television viewing. *Personality and Social Psychology Bulletin, 10*(3), 457–468.

Reschly, D. (1981). Psychological testing in educational classification and placement. *American Psychologist, 36*(10), 1094–1102.

Rescorla, R. A. (1978). Some implications of a cognitive perspective on Pavlovian conditioning. In S. H. Hulse, H. Fowler, & W. K. Honig (Eds.), *Cognitive processes in animal behavior.* Hillsdale, NJ: Erlbaum.

Rescorla, R. A. (1980). *Pavlovian second-order conditioning.* Hillsdale, NJ: Erlbaum.

Rescorla, R. A. (1987). A Pavlovian analysis of goal-directed behavior. *American Psychologist, 42*(2), 119–129.

Rescorla, R. A. (1988). Pavlovian conditioning: It's not what you think it is. *American Psychologist, 43*(3), 151–160.

Rescorla, R. A., & Solomon, R. L. (1967). Two-process learning theory: Relationships between Pavlovian conditioning and instrumental learning. *Psychological Review, 74,* 151–182.

Rescorla, R. A., & Wagner, A. R. (1972). A theory of Pavlovian conditioning: Variations in the effectiveness of reinforcement and nonreinforcement. In A. H. Black & W. F. Prokasky (Eds.), *Classical conditioning II: Current research and theory.* New York: Appleton-Century-Crofts.

Rest, J. R. (1983). Morality. In P. H. Mussen (Ed.), *Handbook of child psychology* (4th ed., Vol. 3). New York: Wiley.

Rest, J. R., & Thoma, S. J. (1985). Relation of moral judgment development to formal education. *Developmental Psychology, 21*(4), 709–714.

Restak, R. M. (1984). *The brain.* New York: Bantam Books.

Reynolds, G. S. (1975). *A primer of operant psychology.* Glenview, IL: Scott, Foresman.

Rezek, M. (1976). The role of insulin in the glucostatic control of food intake. *Canadian Journal of Physiology and Pharmacology, 54,* 650–665.

Richardson, J. G., & Simpson, C. H. (1982). Children, gender, and social structure: An analysis of the contents of letters to Santa Claus. *Child Development, 53,* 429–436.

Rimland, B., & Munsinger, H. (1977). Burt's IQ data. *Science, 195,* 248.

Rimm, D. C., & Cunningham, H. M. (1985). Behavior therapies. In S. J. Lynn & J. P. Garske (Eds.), *Contemporary psychotherapies: Models and methods.* Columbus, OH: Charles E. Merrill.

Roazen, P. (1976). *Erik H. Erikson: The power and limits of a vision.* New York: Free Press.

Robbins, D. (1971). Partial reinforcement: A selective review of the alleyway literature since 1960. *Psychological Bulletin, 76,* 415–431.

Robbins, S. L., & Cotran, R. S. (1979). *Pathologic basis of disease.* Philadelphia: Saunders.

Roberts, C. J., & Lowe, C. R. (1975, March 1). Where have all the conceptions gone? *Lancet,* pp. 498–499.

Roberts, S. O. (1971). Some mental and emotional health needs of Negro children and youth. In R. Wilcox (Ed.), *The psychological consequences of being a black American.* New York: Wiley.

Robins, C. J. (1988). Attributions and depression: Why is the literature so inconsistent? *Journal of Personality and Social Psychology, 54*(5), 880–889.

Robins, L. N. (1966). *Deviant children grow up.* Baltimore: Williams & Wilkins.

Robins, L. N., & Helzer, J. E. (1986). Diagnosis and clinical assessment: The current state of psychiatric diagnosis. In M. R. Rosenzweig & L. W. Porter (Eds.), *Annual review of psychology: 1986.* Palo Alto, CA: Annual Reviews.

Robins, L. N., Helzer, J. E., Weissman, M. M., Orvaschel, H., Gruenberg, E., Burke, J. D., Jr., & Regier, D. A. (1984). Lifetime prevalence of specific psychiatric disorders in three sites. *Archives of General Psychiatry, 41,* 949–958.

Robinson, F. P. (1970). *Effective study* (4th ed.). New York: Harper & Row.

Rodin, J. (1978). Has the distinction between internal versus external control of feeding outlived its usefulness? In G. A. Bray (Ed.), *Recent advances in obesity research* (Vol. 2). London: Newman.

Rodin, J. (1981). Current status of the internal-external hypothesis for obesity: What went wrong? *American Psychologist, 36*(4), 361–372.

Roe, A. (1956). *The psychology of occupations.* New York: Wiley.

Roediger, H. L. (1980). Memory metaphors in cognitive psychology. *Memory & Cognition, 8,* 231–246.

Roffwarg, H. P., Muzio, J. N., & Dement, W. C. (1966). Ontogenetic development of the human sleep-dream cycle. *Science, 152,* 604–619.

Rogers, C. R. (1951). *Client-centered therapy: Its current practice, implications, and theory.* Boston: Houghton Mifflin.

Rogers, C. R. (1961). *On becoming a person: A therapist's view of psychotherapy.* Boston: Houghton Mifflin.

Rogers, C. R. (1977). *Carl Rogers on personal power.* New York: Delacorte.

Rogers, C. R. (1980). *A way of being.* Boston: Houghton Mifflin.

Rogers, C. R. (1986). Client-centered therapy. In I. L. Kutash & A. Wolf (Eds.), *Psychotherapist's casebook*. San Francisco: Jossey-Bass.

Rogers, R. W. (1975). A protection motivation theory of fear appeals and attitude change. *Journal of Psychology, 91*, 93–114.

Rogers, R. W., & Newborn, R. (1976). Fear appeals and attitude change: Effects of a threat's noxiousness, probability of occurrence, and the efficacy of coping responses. *Journal of Personality and Social Psychology, 34*, 54–61.

Rogers, T. B., Kuiper, N. A., & Kirker, W. S. (1977). Self-reference and the encoding of personal information. *Journal of Personality and Social Psychology, 35*, 677–688.

Rogot, E. (1974). Smoking and mortality among U.S. veterans. *Journal of Chronic Diseases, 27*, 189–203.

Rorschach, H. (1942). *Psychodiagnostics: A diagnostic test based on perception*. Bern: Huber.

Rosenbaum, M. E. (1986). The repulsion hypothesis: On the nondevelopment of relationships. *Journal of Personality and Social Psychology, 51*(6), 1156–1166.

Rosenberg, M. (1965). *Society and the adolescent self-image*. Princeton, NJ: Princeton University Press.

Rosenfeld, A. H. (1986). A farewell to jet lag? *Psychology Today, 20*(10), 10.

Rosenhan, D. L. (1973). On being sane in insane places. *Science, 179*, 250–258.

Rosenthal, N. E., Carpenter, C. J., James, S. P., Parry, B. L., Rogers, S. L. B., & Wehr, T. A. (1986). Seasonal affective disorder in children and adolescents. *American Journal of Psychiatry, 143*, 356–358.

Rosenthal, R., & Fode, K. L. (1963). Three experiments in experimenter bias. *Psychological Reports, 12*, 491–511.

Rosenzweig, S. (1985). Freud and experimental psychology: The emergence of idiodynamics. In S. Koch & D. E. Leary (Eds.), *A century of psychology as a science*. New York: McGraw-Hill.

Ross, J., & Ferris, K. R. (1981). Interpersonal attraction and organizational outcome: A field experiment. *Administrative Science Quarterly, 26*, 617–632.

Ross, L. (1977). The intuitive psychologist and his shortcomings: Distortions in the attribution process. In L. Berkowitz (Ed.), *Advances in experimental social psychology* (Vol. 10). New York: Academic Press.

Ross, L. D. (1988). The obedience experiments: A case study of controversy. *Contemporary Psychology, 33*(2), 101–104.

Rothbart, M., & Park, B. (1986). On the confirmability and disconfirmability of trait concepts. *Journal of Personality and Social Psychology, 50*, 131–142.

Rothbart, M. K., & Derryberry, D. (1981). Development of individual differences in temperament. In M. E. Lamb & A. L. Brown (Eds.), *Advances in developmental psychology* (Vol. 1). Hillsdale, NJ: Erlbaum.

Rothblum, E. D., Solomon, L. J., & Albee, G. W. (1986). A sociopolitical perspective of DSM-III. In T. Millon & G. L. Klerman (Eds.), *Contemporary directions in psychopathology: Toward the DSM-IV*. New York: Guilford Press.

Rotter, J. B. (1966). Generalized expectancies for internal versus external control of reinforcement. *Psychological Monographs* (Whole No. 609).

Rotter, J. B. (1975). Some problems and misconceptions related to the construct of internal versus external control of reinforcement. *Journal of Consulting and Clinical Psychology, 43*, 56–67.

Rotter, J. B. (1982). *The development and application of social learning theory*. New York: Praeger.

Rotter, J. B., & Rafferty, J. E. (1950). *Manual: The Rotter incomplete sentence blank*. New York: Psychological Corporation.

Rubin, E. H., Zorumski, C. F., & Guze, S. B. (1986). Somatoform disorders. In T. Millon & G. L. Klerman (Eds.), *Contemporary directions in psychopathology: Toward the DSM-IV*. New York: Guilford Press.

Rubin, Z. (1981). Does personality really change after 20? *Psychology Today, 15*(5), 18–27.

Ruch, J. C. (1984). *Psychology: The personal science*. Belmont, CA: Wadsworth.

Rumelhart, D. E. (1970). A multicomponent theory of perception of briefly exposed stimulus displays. *Journal of Mathematical Psychology, 7*, 191–218.

Rundus, D. (1971). Analysis of rehearsal processes in free recall. *Journal of Experimental Psychology, 89*, 63–77.

Rush, A. J. (1984). Cognitive therapy. In T. B. Karasu (Ed.), *The psychiatric therapies*. Washington, DC: American Psychiatric Association.

Rushton, J. P. (1980). *Altruism, socialization and society*. Englewood Cliffs, NJ: Prentice-Hall.

Rushton, J. P., Fulker, D. W., Neale, M. C., Nias, D. K. B., & Eysenck, H. J. (1986). Altruism and aggression: The heritability of individual differences. *Journal of Personality and Social Psychology, 50*(6), 1192–1198.

Russell, M. J. (1976). Human olfactory communication. *Nature, 260*, 520–522.

Russell, M. J., Switz, G. M., & Thompson, K. (1980). Olfactory influences on the human menstrual cycle. *Pharmacology, Biochemistry and Behavior, 13*, 737–738.

Rutherford, W. (1886). A new theory of hearing. *Journal of Anatomy and Physiology, 21*, 166–168.

Rymer, R. (1987, September). Eavesdroppers in the O.R. *The New Physician*, pp. 29–30.

S

Sacerdoti, E. D. (1974). Planning in a hierarchy of abstraction spaces. *Artificial Intelligence, 5*, 115–135.

Sachs, G. S., & Gelenberg, A. J. (1988). Adverse effects of electroconvulsive therapy. In A. J. Frances & R. E. Hales (Eds.), *Review of psychiatry* (Vol. 7). Washington, DC: American Psychiatric Press.

Sackeim, H. A. (1985). The case for ECT. *Psychology Today, 19*(6), 35–40.

Sackeim, H. A. (1988). Mechanisms of action of electroconvulsive therapy. In A. J. Frances & R. E. Hales (Eds.), *Annual review of psychiatry* (Vol. 7). Washington, DC: American Psychiatric Press.

Sacks, O. (1985). *The man who mistook his wife for a hat*. New York: Harper & Row.

Sadava, S. W. (1984). Other drug abuse and dependence disorders. In H. E. Adams & P. B. Sutker (Eds.), *Comprehensive handbook of psychopathology*. New York: Plenum Press.

Samples, R. E. (1975, February). Are you teaching only one side of the brain? *Learning: The Magazine for Creative Teaching*, pp. 25–28.

Sanders, D., & Bancroft, J. (1982). Hormones and the sexuality of women—the menstrual cycle. In J. Bancroft, *Clinics in endocrinology and metabolism: Diseases of sex and sexuality*. Philadelphia: Saunders.

Sanders, G. S., & Simmons, W. L. (1983). Use of hypnosis to enhance eyewitness accuracy: Does it work? *Journal of Applied Psychology, 68*(1), 70–77.

Sandler, J. (1975). Aversion methods. In F. H. Kanfer & A. P. Goldstein (Eds.), *Helping people change: A textbook of methods*. New York: Pergamon Press.

Sarason, I. G. (1984). Stress, anxiety and cognitive interference: Reactions to stress. *Journal of Personality and Social Psychology, 46*(4), 929–938.

Sarason, I. G., & Sarason, B. G. (1987). *Abnormal psychology: The problem of maladaptive behavior*. Englewood Cliffs, NJ: Prentice-Hall.

Sarnacki, R. E. (1979). An examination of test-wiseness in the cognitive domain. *Review of Educational Research, 49*, 252–279.

Sarnoff, I., & Zimbardo, P. G. (1961). Anxiety, fear and social affiliation. *Journal of Abnormal and Social Psychology, 62*, 356–363.

Savage-Rumbaugh, S., McDonald, K., Sevcik, R. A., Hopkins, W. D., & Rupert, E. (1986). Spontaneous symbol acquisition and communicative use by pygmy chimpanzees (*Pan paniscus*). *Journal of Experimental Psychology: General, 115*, 211–235.

Scarr, S., & Carter-Saltzman, L. (1979). Twin method: Defense of a critical assumption. *Behavior Genetics, 9*, 527–542.

Scarr, S., & Carter-Saltzman, L. (1982). Genetics and intelligence. In R. J. Sternberg (Ed.), *Handbook of human intelligence*. Cambridge, MA: Cambridge University Press.

Scarr, S., & Kidd, K. K. (1983). Developmental behavior genetics. In P. H. Mussen (Ed.), *Handbook of child psychology* (Vol. 2) (M. M. Haith & J. J. Campos, Vol. Eds.). New York: Wiley.

Scarr, S., & Weinberg, R. A. (1977). Intellectual similarities within families of both adopted and biological children. *Intelligence, 32*, 170–190.

Scarr, S., & Weinberg, R. A. (1983). The Minnesota adoption studies: Genetic differences and malleability. *Child Development, 54*, 260–267.

Schacht, T. E. (1985). DSM-III and the politics of truth. *American Psychologist, 40*(5), 513–521.

Schachter, S. (1959). *The psychology of affiliation*. Stanford, CA: Stanford University Press.

Schachter, S. (1964). The interaction of cognitive and physiological determinants of emotional state. In L. Berkowitz (Ed.), *Advances in experimental social psychology* (Vol. 1). New York: Academic Press.

Schachter, S. (1971). *Emotion, obesity and crime*. New York: Academic Press.

Schachter, S., & Gross, L. (1968). Manipulated time and eating behavior. *Journal of Personality and Social Psychology, 10*, 98–106.

Schachter, S., & Rodin, J. (1974). *Obese humans and rats*. Hillsdale, NJ: Erlbaum.

Schachter, S., & Singer, J. E. (1962). Cognitive, social and physiological determinants of emotional state. *Psychological Review, 69*, 379–399.

Schachter, S., & Singer, J. E. (1979). Comments on the Maslach and Marshall-Zimbardo experiments. *Journal of Personality and Social Psychology, 37*(6), 989–995.

Schaie, K. W., & Geiwitz, J. (1982). *Adult development and aging*. Boston: Little, Brown.

Schank, R., & Abelson, R. (1977). *Scripts, plans, goals, and understanding*. Hillsdale, NJ: Erlbaum.

Scheff, T. (1975). *Labeling madness*. Englewood Cliffs, NJ: Prentice-Hall.

Scheflen, A. E., & Scheflen, A. (1972). *Body language and social order: Communication as behavioral control*. Englewood Cliffs, NJ: Prentice-Hall.

Scheier, M. F., & Carver, C. S. (1985). Optimism, coping and health: Assessment and implications of generalized expectancies. *Health Psychology, 4*, 219–247.

Scheier, M. F., Weintraub, J. K., & Carver, C. S. (1986). Coping with stress: Divergent strategies of optimists and pessimists. *Journal of Personality and Social Psychology, 51*(6), 1257–1264.

Schiffman, S. S. (1974). Physicochemical correlates of olfactory quality. *Science, 185*, 112–117.

Schildkraut, J. J. (1965). The catecholamine hypothesis of affective disorders: A review of supporting evidence. *American Journal of Psychiatry, 122*, 509–522.

Schildkraut, J. J., Green, A. I., & Mooney, J. J. (1985). Affective disorders: Biochemical aspects. In H. I. Kaplan & B. J. Sadock (Eds.), *Comprehensive textbook of psychiatry/IV*. Baltimore: Williams & Wilkins.

Schlenker, B. R. (1980). *Impression management: The self-concept, social identity, and interpersonal relations*. Pacific Grove, CA: Brooks/Cole.

Schlesinger, K. (1985). Behavioral genetics and the nature-nurture question. In G. A. Kimble & K. Schlesinger (Eds.), *Topics in the history of psychology* (Vol. 2). Hillsdale, NJ: Erlbaum.

Schlosberg, H. (1954). Three dimensions of emotion. *Psychological Review, 61*, 81–88.

Schmidt, F. L., & Hunter, J. E. (1981). Employment testing: Old theories and new research findings. *American Psychologist, 36*(10), 1128–1137.

Schofield, W. (1964). *Psychotherapy: The purchase of friendship*. Englewood Cliffs, NJ: Prentice-Hall.

Schooler, C. (1972). Birth order effects: Not here, not now! *Psychological Bulletin, 78*, 161–175.

Schroeder, D. H., & Costa, P. T., Jr. (1984). Influence of life events stress on physical illness: Substantive effects or methodological flaws? *Journal of Personality and Social Psychology, 46*(4), 853–863.

Schuckit, M. A. (1986). The biology and treatment of alcoholism. In P. A. Berger & H. K. H. Brodie (Eds.), *American handbook of psychiatry: Biological psychiatry* (2nd ed., Vol. 8). New York: Basic Books.

Schultz, J. H., & Luthe, W. (1959). *Autogenic training.* New York: Grune & Stratton.

Schwartz, A. H., & Swartzburg, M. (1976). Hospital care. In B. B. Wolman (Ed.), *The therapist's handbook: Treatment methods of mental disorders.* New York: Van Nostrand Reinhold.

Schwartz, C. C., & Myers, J. K. (1977). Life events and schizophrenia: I. Comparison of schizophrenics with a community sample. *Archives of General Psychiatry, 34,* 1238–1241.

Schwartz, D. G., Weinstein, L. N., & Arkin, A. M. (1978). Qualitative aspects of sleep mentation. In A. M. Arkin, J. S. Antrobus, & S. J. Ellman (Eds.), *The mind in sleep: Psychology and psychophysiology.* Hillsdale, NJ: Erlbaum.

Schwartz, G. E. (1974). The facts on transcendental meditation, part II: TM relaxes some people and makes them feel better. *Psychology Today, 7*(11), 39–44.

Schwartz, G. E., Weinberger, D. A., & Singer, J. A. (1981). Cardiovascular differentiation of happiness, sadness, anger, and fear following imagery and exercise. *Psychosomatic Medicine, 43*(4), 343–364.

Scoville, W. B., & Milner, B. (1957). Loss of recent memory after bilateral hippocampal lesions. *Journal of Neurology, Neurosurgery & Psychiatry, 20,* 11–21.

Sears, D. O. (1975). Political socialization. In F. I. Greenstein & N. W. Polsby (Eds.), *Handbook of political science* (Vol. 2). Reading, MA: Addison-Wesley.

Sears, R. (1977). Sources of life satisfaction of the Terman gifted men. *American Psychologist, 32,* 119–128.

Sekuler, R., & Blake, R. (1985). *Perception.* New York: Knopf.

Selfridge, O. G. (1959). Pandemonium: A paradigm for learning. In D. V. Blake & A. M. Uttley (Eds.), *Symposium on the mechanization of thought processes.* London: H. M. Stationery Office.

Seligman, M. E. P. (1971). Phobias and preparedness. *Behavior Therapy, 2,* 307–321.

Seligman, M. E. P. (1974). Depression and learned helplessness. In R. J. Friedman & M. M. Katz (Eds.), *The psychology of depression: Contemporary theory and research.* New York: Wiley.

Seligman, M. E. P. (1983). Learned helplessness. In E. Levitt, B. Rubin, & J. Brooks (Eds.), *Depression: Concepts, controversies and some new facts.* Hillsdale, NJ: Erlbaum.

Seligman, M. E. P., & Hager, J. L. (1972). Biological boundaries of learning (The sauce bearnaise syndrome). *Psychology Today, 6*(3), 59–61, 84–87.

Seligman, M. E. P., & Johnston, J. C. (1973). A cognitive theory of avoidance learning. In F. J. McGuigan & D. B. Lumsden (Eds.), *Contemporary approaches to conditioning and learning.* Washington, DC: V. H. Winston.

Selye, H. (1936). A syndrome produced by diverse nocuous agents. *Nature, 138,* 32.

Selye, H. (1956). *The stress of life.* New York: McGraw-Hill.

Selye, H. (1974). *Stress without distress.* Philadelphia: Lippincott.

Selye, H. (1976). *The stress of life.* New York: McGraw-Hill.

Selye, H. (1982). History and present status of the stress concept. In L. Goldberger & S. Breznitz (Eds.), *Handbook of stress: Theoretical and clinical aspects.* New York: Free Press.

Shaffer, D. R. (1989). *Developmental psychology: Childhood and adolescence.* Pacific Grove, CA: Brooks/Cole.

Shank, J. C. (1983). Disease incidence and prevalence. In R. B. Taylor (Ed.), *Family medicine: Principles and practice.* New York: Springer-Verlag.

Shapiro, D. H., Jr. (1984). Overview: Clinical and physiological comparison of meditation with other self-control strategies. In D. H. Shapiro, Jr., & R. N. Walsh (Eds.), *Meditation: Classic and contemporary perspectives.* New York: Aldine.

Shapiro, D. H., Jr. (1981). Meditation and psychotherapeutic effects: Self-regulation strategy and altered state of consciousness. In D. H. Shapiro, Jr., J. Stoyva, J. Kamiya, T. X. Barber, N. E. Miller, & G. E. Schwartz (Eds.), *Biofeedback and behavioral medicine 1979/80: Therapeutic applications and experimental foundations.* New York: Aldine.

Shapiro, D. H., Jr., Schwartz, G. E., & Tursky, B. (1972). Control of diastolic blood pressure in man by feedback and reinforcement. *Psychophysiology, 9,* 296–304.

Shapiro, S., Skinner, E. A., Kessler, L. G., Von Korff, M., German, P. S., Tischler, G. L., Leaf, P. J., Benham, L., Cottler, L., & Regier, D. A. (1984). Utilization of health and mental health services. *Archives of General Psychiatry, 41,* 971–978.

Shatan, C. F. (1978). Stress disorders among Viet Nam veterans: The emotional content of combat continues. In C. R. Figley (Ed.), *Stress disorders among Viet Nam veterans: Theory, research and treatment.* New York: Brunner/Mazel.

Shaver, P., & Klinnert, M. (1982). Schachter's theories of affiliation and emotion: Implications of developmental research. In L. Wheeler (Ed.), *Review of personality and social psychology* (Vol. 3). Beverly Hills, CA: Sage Publications.

Sheehan, S. (1982). *Is there no place on earth for me?* Boston: Houghton Mifflin.

Shekelle, R. B., Hulley, S. B., Neaton, J. D., Billings, J. H., Borhani, N. O., Gerace, T. A., Jacobs, D. R., Lasser, N. L., Mittlemark, M. B., & Stamler, J. (1985). The MRFIT behavior pattern study: II. Type-A behavior and incidence of coronary heart disease. *American Journal of Epidemiology, 122,* 559–570.

Sheldon, W. H. (with S. S. Stevens & W. B. Tucker). (1940). *The varieties of human physique: An introduction to constitutional psychology.* New York: Harper.

Sheldon, W. H. (with the collaboration of S. S. Stevens). (1942). *The varieties of temperament: A psychology of constitutional differences.* New York: Harper.

Shepherd, G. M. (1983). *Neurobiology.* New York: Oxford University Press.

Sheras, P. L. (1983). Suicide in adolescence. In C. E. Walker & M. C. Roberts (Eds.), *Handbook of clinical child psychology.* New York: Wiley.

Sherif, M., & Hovland, C. I. (1961). *Social judgment: Assimilation and contrast effects in communication and attitude change.* New Haven, CT: Yale University Press.

Sherman, M., & Key, C. B. (1932). The intelligence of isolated mountain children. *Child Development, 3,* 279–290.

Shertzer, B. (1977). *Career planning: Freedom to choose.* Boston: Houghton Mifflin.

Shneidman, E. S., Farberow, N. L., & Litman, R. E. (Eds.). (1970). *The psychology of suicide.* New York: Aronson.

Siegel, J. M., Johnson, J. H., & Sarason, I. G. (1979). Life changes and menstrual discomfort. *Journal of Human Stress, 5,* 41–46.

Siegel, O. (1982). Personality development in adolescence. In B. B. Wolman (Ed.), *Handbook of developmental psychology.* Englewood Cliffs, NJ: Prentice-Hall.

Siegler, R. S. (1984). Mechanisms of cognitive growth: Variation and selection. In R. J. Sternberg (Ed.), *Mechanisms of cognitive development.* New York: W. H. Freeman.

Siegler, R. S. (1986). *Children's thinking.* Englewood Cliffs, NJ: Prentice-Hall.

Silver, E. A. (1981). Recall of mathematical problem information: Solving related problems. *Journal for Research in Mathematics Education, 12,* 54–64.

Simon, H. A. (1957). *Models of man.* New York: Wiley.

Simon, H. A. (1974). How big is a chunk? *Science, 183,* 482–488.

Simon, H. A., & Gilmartin, K. (1973). A simulation of memory for chess positions. *Cognitive Psychology, 5,* 29–46.

Simon, H. A., & Reed, S. K. (1976). Modeling strategy shifts in a problem-solving task. *Cognitive Psychology, 8,* 86–97.

Sims, J. H., & Baumann, D. D. (1972). The tornado threat: Coping styles of the north and south. *Science, 176,* 1386–1392.

Sinclair, D. C. (1955). Cutaneous sensation and the doctrine of specific energy. *Brain, 78* (Pt. 4), 584–614.

Singer, J. L. (1975). Navigating the stream of consciousness: Research on daydreaming and related inner experiences. *American Psychologist, 30,* 727–738.

Singer, J. L., & Kolligian J., Jr. (1987). Personality: Developments in the study of private experience. In M. R. Rosenzweig & L. W. Porter (Eds.), *Annual review of psychology* (Vol. 38). Palo Alto, CA: Annual Reviews.

Singer, M. T., Wynne, L. C., & Toohey, M. L. (1978). Communication disorders and the families of schizophrenics. In L. C. Wynne, R. L. Cromwell, & S. Matthysse (Eds.), *The nature of schizophrenia: New approaches to research and treatment.* New York: Wiley Medical.

Skinner, B. F. (1938). *The behavior of organisms.* New York: Appleton-Century-Crofts.

Skinner, B. F. (1948). Superstition in the pigeon. *Journal of Experimental Psychology, 38,* 168–172.

Skinner, B. F. (1953). *Science and human behavior.* New York: Macmillan.

Skinner, B. F. (1957). *Verbal behavior.* New York: Appleton-Century-Crofts.

Skinner, B. F. (1967). Autobiography. In E. G. Boring & G. Lindzey (Eds.), *A history of psychology in autobiography* (Vol. 5). New York: Appleton-Century-Crofts.

Skinner, B. F. (1971). *Beyond freedom and dignity.* New York: Knopf.

Skinner, B. F. (1974). *About behaviorism.* New York: Knopf.

Skodak, M., & Skeels, H. M. (1947). A follow-up study of one hundred adopted children in Iowa. *American Psychologist, 2,* 278.

Sloane, K. D., & Sosniak, L. A. (1985). The development of accomplished sculptors. In B. S. Bloom (Ed.), *Developing talent in young people.* New York: Ballantine.

Slochower, J. (1976). Emotional labeling of overeating in obese and normal weight individuals. *Psychosomatic Medicine, 38,* 131–139.

Slochower, J., Kaplan, S. P., & Mann, L. (1981). The effects of life stress and weight on mood and eating. *Appetite, 2,* 115–125.

Slovic, P., Fischhoff, B., & Lichenstein, S. (1976). Cognitive processes and societal risk taking. In J. S. Carroll & J. W. Payne (Eds.), *Cognition and social behavior.* Potomac, MD: Erlbaum.

Small, I. F., Small, J. G., & Milstein, V. (1986). Electroconvulsive therapy. In P. A. Berger & H. K. H. Brodie (Eds.), *American handbook of psychiatry: Biological psychiatry* (2nd ed., Vol. 8). New York: Basic Books.

Smart, R. (1965). Social-group membership, leadership and birth order. *Journal of Social Psychology, 67,* 221–225.

Smith, D. (1982). Trends in counseling and psychotherapy. *American Psychologist, 37*(3), 802–809.

Smith, J. (1975). Meditation and psychotherapy: A review of the literature. *Psychological Bulletin, 32,* 553–564.

Smith, M. E. (1983). Hypnotic memory enhancement of witnesses: Does it work? *Psychological Bulletin, 94,* 387–407.

Smith, M. L., & Glass, G. V. (1977). Meta-analysis of psychotherapy outcome studies. *American Psychologist, 32,* 752–760.

Smith, M. L., Glass, G. V., & Miller, R. L. (1980). *The benefits of psychotherapy.* Baltimore: Johns Hopkins University Press.

Smith, T. W., Turner, C. W., Ford, M. H., Hunt, S. C., Barlow, G. K., Stults, B. M., & Williams, R. R. (1987). Blood pressure reactivity in adult male twins. *Health Psychology, 6*(3), 209–220.

Smolensky, M. H., Reinberg, A., Bicakova-Rocher, A., & Stanford, J. (1981). Chronoepidemiological search for circannual changes in the sexual activity of human males. *Chronobiologia, 8*(3), 217–230.

Snyder, M. (1979). Self-monitoring processes. In L. Berkowitz (Ed.), *Advances in experimental social psychology* (Vol. 12). New York: Academic Press.

Snyder, M. (1986). *Public appearances/Private realities: The psychology of self-monitoring.* New York: W. H. Freeman.

Snyder, M., Gangestad, S., & Simpson, J. A. (1983). Choosing friends as activity partners: The role of self-monitoring. *Journal of Personality and Social Psychology, 45*, 1061–1072.

Snyder, M., & Simpson, J. A. (1984). Self-monitoring and dating relationships. *Journal of Personality and Social Psychology, 47*, 1281–1291.

Snyder, M., Simpson, J. A., & Gangestad, S. (1986). Personality and sexual relations. *Journal of Personality and Social Psychology, 51*, 181–190.

Snyder, S. H. (1980). Brain peptides as neurotransmitters. *Science, 209*, 976–983.

Snyder, S. H. (1984). Drug and neurotransmitter receptors in the brain. *Science, 224*, 22–31.

Solnick, R., & Corby, N. (1983). Human sexuality and aging. In D. S. Woodruff & J. E. Birren (Eds.), *Aging: Scientific perspectives and social issues.* Pacific Grove, CA: Brooks/Cole.

Solomon, G. F., Amkraut, A., & Rubin, R. T. (1985). Stress, hormones, neuroregulation and immunity. In S. R. Burchfield (Ed.), *Stress: Psychological and physiological interactions.* New York: Hemisphere.

Solomon, R. L. (1982). The opponent-process in acquired motivation. In D. W. Pfaff (Ed.), *The physiological mechanisms of motivation.* New York: Springer-Verlag.

Solomon, R. L., & Corbit, J. D. (1974). An opponent-process theory of motivation: I. Temporal dynamics of affect. *Psychological Review, 81*, 119–133.

Solso, R. L. (1988). *Cognitive psychology.* Boston: Allyn & Bacon.

Sontag, L. W., Baker, C. T., & Nelson, V. L. (1958). Mental growth and personality. *Monographs of the Society for Research in Child Development, 23*(2, Serial No. 68).

Sotiriou, P. E. (1989). *Integrating college study skills: Reasoning in reading, listening, and writing.* Belmont, CA: Wadsworth.

Spanos, N. P., Weekes, J. R., & Bertrand, L. D. (1985). Multiple personality: A social psychological perspective. *Journal of Abnormal Psychology, 94*(3), 362–376.

Spearman, C. (1904). "General intelligence" objectively determined and measured. *American Journal of Psychology, 15*, 201–293.

Spearman, C. (1923). *The nature of "intelligence" and the principles of cognition.* London: Macmillan.

Sperling, G. (1960). The information available in brief visual presentations. *Psychological Monographs, 74*(11, Whole No. 498).

Sperling, G. (1967). Successive approximations to a model for short-term memory. *Acta Psychologica, 27*, 285–292.

Sperry, R. W. (1982). Some effects of disconnecting the cerebral hemispheres. *Science, 217*, 1223–1226, 1250.

Spiegel, D., & Spiegel, H. (1985). Hypnosis. In H. I. Kaplan & B. J. Sadock (Eds.), *Comprehensive textbook of psychiatry/IV.* Baltimore: Williams & Wilkins.

Spielberger, C. D., Gorsuch, R. L., & Lushene, R. E. (1970). *Manual for the State-Trait Anxiety Inventory.* Palo Alto, CA: Consulting Psychologists Press.

Spielberger, C. D., Johnson, E. H., Russell, S. F., Crane, R. J., Jacobs, G. A., & Worden, T. J. (1985). The experience and expression of anger. In M. A. Chesney, S. E. Goldston, & R. H. Rosenman (Eds.), *Anger and hostility in behavioral medicine.* New York: McGraw-Hill.

Spitzer, R. L. (1975). On pseudoscience in science, logic in remission and psychiatric diagnosis: A critique of Rosenhan's "On being sane in insane places." *Journal of Abnormal Psychology, 84*, 442–452.

Springer, S. P., & Deutsch, G. (1984). *Left brain, right brain.* New York: W. H. Freeman.

Squire, L. R. (1987). *Memory and brain.* New York: Oxford University Press.

Staats, A. W., & Staats, C. K. (1963). *Complex human behavior.* New York: Holt, Rinehart & Winston.

Stalling, R. B. (1970). Personality similarity and evaluative meaning as conditioners of attraction. *Journal of Personality and Social Psychology, 14*, 77–82.

Stalling, R. B., Ahles, T. A., Rutter, C. T., & Green, C. (1985, August). *Mood and pain: Evidence on the direction of the relationship.* Paper presented at the meeting of the American Psychological Association, Los Angeles, CA.

Stapp, J., & Fulcher, R. (1983). The employment of APA members: 1982. *American Psychologist, 38*(12), 1298–1320.

Stechler, G., & Halton, A. (1982). Prenatal influences on human development. In B. B. Wolman (Ed.), *Handbook of developmental psychology.* Englewood Cliffs, NJ: Prentice-Hall.

Steger, J., & Fordyce, W. (1982). Behavioral health care in the management of chronic pain. In T. Millon, C. Green, & R. Meagher (Eds.), *Handbook of clinical health psychology.* New York: Plenum Press.

Steiner, I. D. (1976). Task-performing groups. In J. W. Thibaut, J. T. Spence, & R. C. Carson (Eds.), *Contemporary topics in social psychology.* Morristown, NJ: General Learning Press.

Stekel, W. (1950). *Techniques of analytical psychotherapy.* New York: Liveright.

Stern, G. S., McCants, T. R., & Pettine, P. W. (1982). Stress and illness: Controllable and uncontrollable events' relative contributions. *Personality and Social Psychology Bulletin, 8*(1), 140–145.

Stern, W. (1914). *The psychological method of testing intelligence.* Baltimore: Warwick & York.

Sternberg, R. J. (1977). Component processes in analogical reasoning. *Psychological Review, 84*, 353–378.

Sternberg, R. J. (1984). Toward a triarchic theory of intelligence. *Behavioral and Brain Sciences, 7*, 269–315.

Sternberg, R. J. (1985). *Beyond IQ: A triarchic theory of human intelligence.* New York: Cambridge University Press.

Sternberg, R. J. (1986). *Intelligence applied: Understanding and increasing your intellectual skills.* New York: Harcourt Brace Jovanovich.

Sternberg, R. J. (1988). Triangulating love. In R. J. Sternberg & M. L. Barnes (Eds.), *The psychology of love.* New Haven, CT: Yale University Press.

Sternberg, R. J., Conway, B. E., Ketron, J. L., & Bernstein, M. (1981). People's conceptions of intelligence. *Journal of Personality and Social Psychology, 41*(1), 37–55.

Sternberg, R. J., & Powell, J. S. (1983). The development of intelligence. In P. H. Mussen (Ed.), *Handbook of child psychology: Vol. 3. Cognitive development* (4th ed.). New York: Wiley.

Stevens, D. P., & Truss, C. V. (1985). Stability and change in adult personality over 12 and 20 years. *Developmental Psychology, 21*(3), 568–584.

Stevens, J. H., Turner, C. W., Rhodewalt, F., & Talbot, S. (1984). The Type-A behavior pattern and carotid artery atherosclerosis. *Psychosomatic Medicine, 46*(2), 105–113.

Stevens, S. S. (1955). The measurement of loudness. *Journal of the Acoustical Society of America, 27*, 815–819.

Stevens, S. S. (1956). The direct estimation of sensory magnitudes: Loudness. *American Journal of Psychology, 69*, 1–25.

Stevens, S. S. (1957). On the psychophysical law. *Psychological Review, 64*, 153–181.

Stoddard, G. (1943). *The meaning of intelligence.* New York: Macmillan.

Stone, A. A., & Neale, J. M. (1984). New measure of daily coping: Development and preliminary results. *Journal of Personality and Social Psychology, 46*(4), 892–906.

Stoner, J. A. F. (1961). *A comparison of individual and group decisions involving risk.* Unpublished master's thesis, Massachusetts Institute of Technology.

Strongman, K. T. (1978). *The psychology of emotion.* New York: Wiley.

Strupp, H. H., Hadley, S. W., & Gomes-Schwartz, B. (1977). *Psychotherapy for better or worse: The problem of negative effects.* New York: Aronson.

Stunkard, A. J., Sorensen, T., Hanis, C., Teasdale, T. W., Chakraborty, R., Schull, W. J., & Schulsinger, F. (1986). An adoption study of human obesity. *New England Journal of Medicine, 314*, 193–198.

Sturgis, E. T. (1984). Obsessional and compulsive disorders. In H. E. Adams & P. B. Sutker (Eds.), *Comprehensive handbook of psychopathology.* New York: Plenum Press.

Sue, D. (1979). Erotic fantasies of college students during coitus. *Journal of Sex Research, 15*, 299–305.

Suinn, R. M. (1984). *Fundamentals of abnormal psychology.* Chicago: Nelson-Hall.

Sulin, R. A., & Dooling, D. J. (1974). Intrusion of a thematic idea in retention of prose. *Journal of Experimental Psychology, 103*, 255–262.

Super, D. E. (1972). Vocational development theory: Persons, positions and process. In J. M. Whitely & A. Resnikoff (Eds.), *Perspectives on vocational development.* Washington, DC: American Personnel and Guidance Association.

Sutker, P. B., & Allain, A. N. (1983). Behavior and personality assessment in men labeled adaptive sociopaths. *Journal of Behavioral Assessment, 5*, 65–79.

Sutker, P. B., & Archer, R. P. (1984). Opiate abuse and dependence disorders. In H. E. Adams & P. B. Sutker (Eds.), *Comprehensive handbook of psychopathology.* New York: Plenum Press.

Sweeney, P. D., Anderson, K., & Bailey, S. (1986). Attributional style in depression: A meta-analytic review. *Journal of Personality and Social Psychology, 50*, 974–991.

Swets, J. A., Tanner, W. P., & Birdsall, T. G. (1961). Decision processes in perception. *Psychological Review, 68*, 301–340.

Symons, D. (1979). *The evolution of human sexuality.* New York: Oxford University Press.

Szasz, T. S. (1974). *The myth of mental illness.* New York: Harper & Row.

T

Talbott, J. A., & Lamb, H. R. (1984). Summary and recommendations. In H. R. Lamb (Ed.), *The homeless mentally ill.* Washington, DC: American Psychiatric Association.

Tart, C. T. (1979). From spontaneous event to lucidity: A review of attempts to consciously control nocturnal dreaming. In B. B. Wolman (Ed.), *Handbook of dreams: Research, theories and applications.* New York: Van Nostrand Reinhold.

Tavris, C., & Sadd, S. (1977). *The Redbook report on female sexuality.* New York: Delacorte.

Taylor, S. E. (1986). *Health psychology.* New York: Random House.

Tedesco, N. S. (1974). Patterns in prime time. *Journal of Communication, 24*, 119–124.

Teichman, Y. (1973). Emotional arousal and affiliation. *Journal of Experimental Social Psychology, 9*, 591–605.

Teitelbaum, P., & Epstein, A. (1962). The lateral hypothalamic syndrome: Recovery of feeding and drinking after lateral hypothalamic lesions. *Psychological Review, 69*, 74–90.

Tellegen, A., Lykken, D. T., Bouchard, T. J., Jr., Wilcox, K. J., Segal, N. L., & Rich, S. (1988). Personality similarity in twins reared apart and together. *Journal of Personality and Social Psychology, 54*(6), 1031–1039.

Temoshok, L., Sweet, D. M., & Zich, J. (1987). A three city comparison of the public's knowledge and attitudes about AIDS. *Psychology & Health, 1*(1), 43–60.

Tepas, D. I. (1982). Work/sleep time schedules and performance. In W. B. Webb (Ed.), *Biological rhythms, sleep and performance.* New York: Wiley.

Terman, L. M. (1916). *The measurement of intelligence.* Boston: Houghton Mifflin.

Terman, L. M. (1922). The great conspiracy. *New Republic, 33*, 116–120.

Terman, L. M., Baldwin, B. T., & Bronson, E. (1925). *Genetic studies of genius: Vol. 1. Mental and physical traits of a thousand gifted children.* Stanford, CA: Stanford University Press.

Terman, L. M., & Merrill, M. A. (1937). *Measuring intelligence.* Boston: Houghton Mifflin.

Terman, L. M., & Merrill, M. A. (1960). *Stanford-Binet intelligence scale.* Boston: Houghton Mifflin.

Terman, L. M., & Merrill, M. A. (1973). *Stanford-Binet intelligence scale: 1972 norms edition.* Boston: Houghton Mifflin.

Terman, L. M., & Oden, M. H. (1959). *Genetic studies of genius: Vol. 5. The gifted group at mid-life.* Stanford, CA: Stanford University Press.

Terrace, H. S. (1986). *Nim: A chimpanzee who learned sign language.* New York: Columbia University Press.

Terrace, H. S., Petitto, L. A., Sanders, R. J., & Bever, T. G. (1979). Can an ape create a sentence? *Science, 206,* 891–901.

Teuber, M. (1974). Sources of ambiguity in the prints of Maurits C. Escher. *Scientific American, 231,* 90–104.

Thigpen, C. H., & Cleckley, H. M. (1984). On the incidence of multiple personality disorder: A brief communication. *International Journal of Clinical and Experimental Hypnosis, 32,* 63–66.

Thomas, A., & Chess, S. (1977). *Temperament and development.* New York: Brunner/Mazel.

Thomas, A., Chess, S., & Birch, H. G. (1970, August). The origin of personality. *Scientific American, 223*(2), 102–109.

Thomas, J. C. (1974). An analysis of behavior in the hobbits-orcs problem. *Cognitive Psychology, 6,* 257–269.

Thomson, J. R., & Chapman, R. S. (1977). Who is "Daddy"? The status of two-year-olds' over-extended words in use and comprehension. *Journal of Child Language, 4,* 359–375.

Thorndike, E. L. (1913). *Educational psychology: The psychology of learning* (Vol. 2). New York: Teachers College Press.

Thorndike, R. L., & Hagen, E. (1959). *Ten thousand careers.* New York: Wiley.

Thorndyke, P. W., & Hayes-Roth, B. (1979). The use of schemata in the acquisition and transfer of knowledge. *Cognitive Psychology, 11,* 83–106.

Thornton, B. (1984). Defensive attribution of responsibility: Evidence for an arousal-based motivational bias. *Journal of Personality and Social Psychology, 46*(4), 721–734.

Thurstone, L. L. (1938). *Primary mental abilities* (Psychometric Monographs No. 1). Chicago: University of Chicago Press.

Thurstone, L. L. (1955). *The differential growth of mental abilities* (Psychometric Laboratory Rep. No. 14). Chapel Hill: University of North Carolina Press.

Tinbergen, N. (1951). *The study of instinct.* Oxford: Clarendon.

Tolman, E. C. (1922). A new formula for behaviorism. *Psychological Review, 29,* 44–53.

Tolman, E. C. (1932). *Purposive behavior in animals and men.* New York: Appleton-Century-Crofts.

Tomkins, S. S. (1966). Psychological model for smoking behavior. *American Journal of Public Health, 56,* 17–20.

Tomkins, S. S. (1980). Affect as amplification: Some modifications in theory. In R. Plutchik & H. Kellerman (Eds.), *Emotion: Theory, research and experience* (Vol. 1). New York: Academic Press.

Torgersen, S. (1983). Genetic factors in anxiety disorder. *Archives of General Psychiatry, 40,* 1085–1089.

Totman, R., Kiff, J., Reed, S. E., & Craig, J. W. (1980). Predicting experimental colds in volunteers from different measures of life stress. *Journal of Psychosomatic Research, 24,* 155–163.

Tresemer, D. (1976). The cumulative record of research on "fear of success." *Sex Roles, 2,* 217–236.

Trivers, R. L. (1971). The evolution of reciprocal altruism. *Quarterly Review of Biology, 46,* 35–57.

Tulving, E. (1986). What kind of a hypothesis is the distinction between episodic and semantic memory? *Journal of Experimental Psychology: Learning, Memory and Cognition, 12,* 307–311.

Tulving, E., & Psotka, J. (1971). Retroactive inhibition in free recall: Inaccessibility of information available in the memory store. *Journal of Experimental Psychology, 87,* 1–8.

Tulving, E., & Thomson, D. M. (1973). Encoding specificity and retrieval processes in episodic memory. *Psychological Review, 80,* 352–373.

Turnbull, W. W. (1979). Intelligence testing in the year 2000. In R. J. Sternberg & D. K. Detterman (Eds.), *Human intelligence: Perspectives on its theory and measurement.* Norwood, NJ: Ablex.

Turner, S. M., Jacob, R. G., & Morrison, R. (1984). Somatoform and factitious disorders. In H. E. Adams & P. B. Sutker (Eds.), *Comprehensive handbook of psychopathology.* New York: Plenum Press.

Turner, S. M., McCann, B. S., Beidel, D. C., & Mezzich, J. E. (1986). DSM-III classification of the anxiety disorders: A psychometric study. *Journal of Abnormal Psychology, 95*(2), 168–172.

Tversky, A. (1972). Elimination by aspects: A theory of choice. *Psychological Review, 79,* 281–299.

Tversky, A., & Kahneman, D. (1973). Availability: A heuristic for judging frequency and probability. *Cognitive Psychology, 5,* 207–232.

Tversky, A., & Kahneman, D. (1980). Causal schemas in judgments under uncertainty. In M. Fishbein (Ed.), *Progress in social psychology.* Hillsdale, NJ: Erlbaum.

U

Underwood, B., & Moore, B. (1982). Perspective-taking and altruism. *Psychological Bulletin, 91,* 143–173.

Underwood, B. J. (1961). Ten years of massed practice on distributed practice. *Psychological Review, 68,* 229–247.

Underwood, B. J. (1970). A breakdown of the total-time law in free-recall learning. *Journal of Verbal Learning and Verbal Behavior, 9,* 573–580.

Upshaw, H. S. (1969). The personal reference scale: An approach to social judgment. In L. Berkowitz (Ed.), *Advances in experimental social psychology* (Vol. 4). New York: Academic Press.

V

Vaillant, G. E. (1977). *Adaptation to life.* Boston: Little, Brown.

Valenstein, E. S. (1973). *Brain control.* New York: Wiley.

Vance, E. B., & Wagner, N. N. (1976). Written descriptions of orgasm: A study of sex differences. *Archives of Sexual Behavior, 5,* 87–98.

VandenBos, G. R., & Stapp, J. (1983). Service providers in psychology: Results of the 1982 APA human resources survey. *American Psychologist, 38*(12), 1330–1352.

Vandenberg, S. G., & Vogler, G. P. (1985). Genetic determinants of intelligence. In B. B. Wolman (Ed.), *Handbook of intelligence: Theories, measurements, and applications.* New York: Wiley.

van der Post, L. (1975). *Jung and the story of our time.* New York: Vintage Books.

Van Houten, R. (1983). Punishment: From the animal laboratory to the applied setting. In S. Axelrod & J. Apsche (Eds.), *The effects of punishment on human behavior.* New York: Academic Press.

Van Oot, P. H., Lane, T. W., & Borkovec, T. D. (1984). Sleep disturbances. In H. E. Adams & P. B. Sutker (Eds.), *Comprehensive handbook of psychopathology.* New York: Plenum Press.

Vaughn, V. C., McKay, R. C., & Behrman, R. E. (1979). *Nelson textbook of pediatrics.* Philadelphia: Saunders.

Veith-Flanigan, J., & Sandman, C. A. (1985). Neuroendocrine relationships with stress. In S. R. Burchfield (Ed.), *Stress: Psychological and physiological interactions.* New York: Hemisphere.

Vernon, P. E. (1979). *Intelligence, heredity and environment.* San Francisco: W. H. Freeman.

Veroff, J., Atkinson, J. W., Feld, S., & Gurin, G. (1960). The use of thematic apperception to assess motivation in a nationwide interview study. *Psychological Monographs, 74*(12, Whole No. 499).

Vertes, R. P. (1984). Brainstem control of the events of REM sleep. *Progress in Neurobiology, 22,* 241–288.

Vidmar, N., & Rokeach, M. (1974). Archie Bunker's bigotry: A study in selective perception and exposure. *Journal of Communication, 24,* 36–47.

W

Wald, G., & Brown, P. K. (1965). Human color vision and color blindness. *Cold Spring Harbor Symposium on Quantitative Biology, 30,* 345–359.

Wallace, R. K., & Benson, H. (1972). The physiology of meditation. *Scientific American, 226,* 84–90.

Wallach, M. A., & Kogan, N. (1965). *Modes of thinking in young children.* New York: Holt, Rinehart & Winston.

Wallston, K. A., & Wallston, B. S. (1981). Health locus of control scales. In H. M. Lefcourt (Ed.), *Research with the locus of control construct* (Vol. 1). New York: Academic Press.

Walsh, D. A. (1983). Age differences in learning and memory. In D. S. Woodruff & J. E. Birren (Eds.), *Aging: Scientific perspectives and social issues.* Pacific Grove, CA: Brooks/Cole.

Walster, E., Aronson, V., Abrahams, D., & Rottmann, L. (1966). Importance of physical attractiveness in dating behavior. *Journal of Personality and Social Psychology, 4,* 508–516.

Walster, E., & Berscheid, E. (1974). A little bit about love: A minor essay on a major topic. In T. L. Huston (Ed.), *Foundations of interpersonal attraction.* New York: Academic Press.

Walters, C. C., & Grusec, J. E. (1977). *Punishment.* San Francisco: W. H. Freeman.

Wangensteen, O. H., & Carlson, A. J. (1931). Hunger sensation after total gastrectomy. *Proceedings of the Society for Experimental Biology, 28,* 545–547.

Wansell, G. (1983). *Haunted idol: The story of the real Cary Grant.* New York: Ballantine.

Warwick, D. P. (1975). Social scientists ought to stop lying. *Psychology Today, 8*(9), 38, 40, 105–106.

Waters, H. F., & Malamud, P. (1975, March 10). Drop that gun, Captain Video. *Newsweek, 85,* pp. 81–82.

Watkins, L. R., & Mayer, D. J. (1982). Organization of the endogenous opiate and nonopiate pain control systems. *Science, 216,* 1185–1193.

Watson, D. L., & Tharp, R. G. (1989). *Self-directed behavior: Self-modification for personal adjustment.* Pacific Grove, CA: Brooks/Cole.

Watson, J. B. (1913). Psychology as the behaviorist views it. *Psychological Review, 20,* 158–177.

Watson, J. B. (1930). *Behaviorism.* New York: Norton.

Watson, J. B., & Rayner, R. (1920). Conditioned emotional reactions. *Journal of Experimental Psychology, 3,* 1–14.

Watson, R. I. (1971). *The great psychologists.* Philadelphia: Lippincott.

Weaver, R. C., & Rodnick, J. E. (1986). Type-A behavior: Clinical significance, evaluation, and management. *Journal of Family Practice, 23*(3), 255–261.

Webb, W. B. (1975). *Sleep: The gentle tyrant.* Englewood Cliffs, NJ: Prentice-Hall.

Webb, W. B. (1982). Sleep and biological rhythms. In W. B. Webb (Ed.), *Biological rhythms, sleep and performance.* New York: Wiley.

Webb, W. B., & Bonnet, M. H. (1979). Sleep and dreams. In M. E. Meyer (Ed.), *Foundations of contemporary psychology.* New York: Oxford University Press.

Webb, W. B., & Cartwright, R. D. (1978). Sleep and dreams. In M. R. Rosenzweig & L. W. Porter (Eds.), *Annual review of psychology* (Vol. 29). Palo Alto, CA: Annual Reviews.

Webb, W. B., & Kersey, J. (1967). Recall of dreams and the probability of stage 1—REM sleep. *Perceptual and Motor Skills, 24,* 627–630.

Wechsler, D. (1939). *The measurement of adult intelligence.* Baltimore: Williams & Wilkins.

Wechsler, D. (1949). *Wechsler intelligence scale for children.* New York: Psychological Corporation.

Wechsler, D. (1955). *Manual, Wechsler adult intelligence scale.* New York: Psychological Corporation.

Wechsler, D. (1967). *Manual for the Wechsler preschool and primary scale of intelligence.* New York: Psychological Corporation.

Weeks, D., Freeman, C. P. L., & Kendell, R. E. (1981). Does ECT produce enduring cognitive deficits? In R. L. Palmer (Ed.), *Electroconvulsive therapy: An appraisal.* Oxford: Oxford University Press.

Weg, R. B. (1978). The physiology of sexuality in aging. In R. Solnick (Ed.), *Sexuality and aging*. Los Angeles: University of Southern California Press.

Wehr, T. A., Sack, D. A., Parry, B. L., & Rosenthal, N. E. (1986). The role of biological rhythms in the biology and treatment of insomnia and depression. In P. A. Berger & H. K. H. Brodie (Eds.), *American handbook of psychiatry: Biological psychiatry* (2nd ed., Vol. 8). New York: Basic Books.

Weigel, R. H., Vernon, D. T. A., & Tognacci, L. N. (1974). Specificity of the attitude as a determinant of attitude-behavior congruence. *Journal of Personality and Social Psychology, 30,* 724–728.

Weinberg, J., & Levine, S. (1980). Psychobiology of coping in animals: The effects of predictability. In S. Levine & H. Ursin (Eds.), *Coping and health*. New York: Plenum Press.

Weinberger, D. R., Wagner, R. J., & Wyatt, R. L. (1983). Neuropathological studies of schizophrenia: A selective review. *Schizophrenia Bulletin, 9,* 198–212.

Weiner, B. (Ed.). (1974). *Achievement motivation and attribution theory*. Morristown, NJ: General Learning Press.

Weiner, B. (1978). Achievement strivings. In H. London & J. E. Exner (Eds.), *Dimensions of personality*. New York: Wiley.

Weiner, B. (1980). *Human motivation*. New York: Holt, Rinehart & Winston.

Weiner, B. (1985). "Spontaneous" causal thinking. *Psychological Bulletin, 97,* 74–84.

Weiner, B., Frieze, I., Kukla, A., Reed, L., Rest, S., & Rosenbaum, R. M. (1972). Perceiving the causes of success and failure. In E. E. Jones, D. E. Kanouse, H. H. Kelley, R. E. Nisbett, S. Valins, & B. Weiner (Eds.), *Perceiving the causes of behavior*. Morristown, NJ: General Learning Press.

Weiner, H. (1977). *Psychobiology and human disease*. New York: Elsevier.

Weiner, H. (1978). Emotional factors. In S. C. Werner & S. H. Ingbar (Eds.), *The thyroid*. New York: Harper & Row.

Weiner, R. D. (1984). Does electroconvulsive therapy cause brain damage? *Behavioral and Brain Sciences, 7,* 1–53.

Weiner, R. D. (1985). Convulsive therapies. In H. I. Kaplan & B. J. Sadock (Eds.), *Comprehensive textbook of psychiatry/IV*. Baltimore: Williams & Wilkins.

Weiner, R. D., & Coffey, C. E. (1988). Indications for use of electroconvulsive therapy. In A. J. Frances & R. E. Hales (Eds.), *Review of psychiatry* (Vol. 7). Washington, DC: American Psychiatric Press.

Weinstein, N. D. (1984). Why it won't happen to me: Perceptions of risk factors and susceptibility. *Health Psychology, 3*(5), 431–458.

Weiskrantz, L., Elliott, J., & Darlington, C. (1971). Preliminary observations on tickling oneself. *Nature, 230,* 598–599.

Weiss, T. F. (1964). *A model for firing patterns at auditory nerve fibers* (Research Laboratory in Electronics Tech. Rep. No. 418). Cambridge, Mass: MIT Press.

Weissman, M. M. (1985). The epidemiology of anxiety disorders: Rates, risks and familial patterns. In A. H. Tuma & J. Maser (Eds.), *Anxiety and the anxiety disorders*. Hillsdale, NJ: Erlbaum.

Weissman, M. M., Prusoff, B. A., DiMascio, A., Neu, C., Goklaney, M., & Klerman, G. L. (1979). The efficacy of drugs and psychotherapy in the treatment of acute depressive episodes. *American Journal of Psychiatry, 136,* 555–558.

Weiten, W. (1984). Violation of selected item-construction principles in educational measurement. *Journal of Experimental Education, 51,* 46–50.

Weiten, W. (1986). *Psychology applied to modern life: Adjustment in the 80s*. Pacific Grove, CA: Brooks/Cole.

Weiten, W. (1988). Pressure as a form of stress and its relationship to psychological symptomatology. *Journal of Social and Clinical Psychology, 6*(1), 127–139.

Weiten, W., & Diamond, S. S. (1979). A critical review of the jury-simulation paradigm: The case of defendant characteristics. *Law and Human Behavior, 3,* 71–93.

Weiten, W., & Dixon, J. (1984, August). *Measurement of pressure as a form of stress*. Paper presented at the meeting of the American Psychological Association, Toronto, Ontario.

Wekstein, L. (1979). *Handbook of suicidology*. New York: Brunner/Mazel.

Weldon, E., & Gargano, G. M. (1988). Cognitive loafing: The effects of accountability and shared responsibility on cognitive effort. *Personality and Social Psychology Bulletin, 14*(1), 159–171.

Wellman, H. M., Ritter, R., & Flavell, J. H. (1975). Deliberate memory behavior in the delayed reactions of very young children. *Developmental Psychology, 11,* 780–787.

Wertheimer, M. (1912). Experimentelle stuidien über das sehen von beuegung. *Zeitschrift fuer Psychologie, 61,* 161–265.

Wertheimer, M. (1961). Psychomotor coordination of auditory and visual space at birth. *Science, 134,* 1692.

Wertheimer, M. (1970). *A brief history of psychology*. New York: Holt, Rinehart & Winston.

Wever, E. G., & Bray, C. W. (1937). The perception of low tones and the resonance-volley theory. *Journal of Psychology, 3,* 101–114.

White, K. R. (1982). The relation between socioeconomic status and academic achievement. *Psychological Bulletin, 91,* 461–481.

White, M. J. (1969). Laterality differences in perception: A review. *Psychological Bulletin, 72,* 387–405.

Wiener, D. N. (1968). *A practical guide to psychotherapy*. New York: Harper & Row.

Wiest, W. (1977). Semantic differential profiles of orgasm and other experiences among men and women. *Sex Roles, 3,* 399–403.

Wigdor, A. K., & Garner, W. G. (Eds.). (1982). *Ability testing: Uses, consequences and controversies: Part 1. Report of the committee*. Washington, DC: National Academy Press.

Wiggins, J. S., Wiggins, N., & Conger, J. S. (1968). Correlates of heterosexual somatic preference. *Journal of Personality and Social Psychology, 10,* 82–90.

Wilcoxon, H. G., Dragoin, W. B., Kral, P. A. (1971). Illness-induced aversions in rat and quail: Relative salience of visual and gustatory cues. *Science, 171,* 826–828.

Wilder, D. A. (1981). Perceiving persons as a group: Categorization and intergroup relations. In D. L. Hamilton (Ed.), *Cognitive processing in stereotyping and intergroup behavior*. Hillsdale, NJ: Erlbaum.

Williams, C. D. (1959). The elimination of tantrum behavior by extinction procedures. *Journal of Abnormal and Social Psychology, 59,* 269.

Williams, J. B. W. (1985). The multiaxial system of DSM-III, where did it come from and where should it go? II: Empirical studies, innovations, and recommendations. *Archives of General Psychiatry, 42,* 181–186.

Williams, N. A., & Deffenbacher, J. L. (1983). Life stress and chronic yeast infections. *Journal of Human Stress, 9*(1), 26–31.

Williams, R., Karacan, I., & Hursch, C. (1974). *EEG and human sleep*. New York: Wiley.

Williams, R. L. (1974). Scientific racism and IQ: The silent mugging of the black community. *Psychology Today, 7,* 32–41.

Williams, R. L., Dotson, W., Dow, P., & Williams, W. S. (1980). The war against testing: A current status report. *Journal of Negro Education, 49,* 263–273.

Wilson, E. O. (1975, October 12). Human decency is animal. *New York Times Magazine*, pp. 38–50.

Wilson, E. O. (1980). *Sociobiology: Abridged edition*. Cambridge, MA: Harvard University Press.

Wilson, G. T. (1982). Alcohol and anxiety: Recent evidence on the tension reduction theory of alcohol use and abuse. In K. R. Blankstein & J. Polivy (Eds.), *Self-control and self-modification of emotional behavior*. New York: Plenum Press.

Wine, J. D. (1982). Evaluation anxiety: A cognitive-attentional construct. In H. W. Krohne & L. Laux (Eds.), *Achievement, stress and anxiety*. New York: Hemisphere.

Winograd, T. (1975). Frame representations and the declarative-procedural controversy. In D. Bobrow & A. Collins (Eds.), *Representation and understanding: Studies in cognitive science*. New York: Academic Press.

Wolf, R. M. (1965). The measurement of environments. In C. W. Harris (Ed.), *Proceedings of the 1964 invited conference on testing problems*. Princeton, NJ: Educational Testing Service.

Wolf, S., & Goodell, H. (1968). *Stress and disease*. Springfield, IL: Charles C Thomas.

Wolpe, J. (1958). *Psychotherapy by reciprocal inhibition*. Stanford, CA: Stanford University Press.

Wolpe, J. (1987). The promotion of scientific therapy: A long voyage. In J. K. Zeig (Ed.), *The evolution of psychotherapy*. New York: Brunner/Mazel.

Women on Words and Images. (1972). *Dick and Jane as victims: Sex stereotyping in children's readers*. Princeton, NJ: Author.

Wood, F., Ebert, V., & Kinsbourne, M. (1982). The episodic-semantic memory distinction in memory and amnesia: Clinical and experimental observations. In L. Cermak (Ed.), *Human memory and amnesia*. Hillsdale, NJ: Erlbaum.

Woolfolk, R. (1975). Psychophysiological correlates of meditation. *Archives of General Psychiatry, 32,* 1326–1333.

Woolfolk, R. L., & Richardson, F. C. (1978). *Stress, sanity and survival*. New York: Sovereign/Monarch.

Wundt, W. (1874/1904). *Principles of physiological psychology*. Leipzig: Engelmann.

Wyatt, R. J. (1985). Science and psychiatry. In H. I. Kaplan & B. J. Sadock (Eds.), *Comprehensive textbook of psychiatry/IV*. Baltimore: Williams & Wilkins.

Wyler, A. R., Masuda, M., & Holmes, T. H. (1968). The seriousness of illness rating scale. *Journal of Psychosomatic Research, 11,* 363–374.

Wyler, A. R., Masuda, M., & Holmes, T. H. (1971). Magnitude of life events and seriousness of illness. *Psychosomatic Medicine, 33*(2), 115–122.

Wyrwicka, W., & Dobrzecka, C. (1960). Relationship between feeding and satiation centers of the hypothalamus. *Science, 132,* 805–806.

Y

Yalom, I. D. (1975). *The theory and practice of group psychotherapy*. New York: Basic Books.

Yates, F. A. (1966). *The art of memory*. London: Routledge & Kegan Paul.

Young, T. (1802). On the theory of light and colours. *Philosophical Transactions of the Royal Society of London, 92,* 12–48.

Z

Zajonc, R. B. (1980). Feeling and thinking: Preferences need no inferences. *American Psychologist, 35*(2), 151–175.

Zechmeister, E. B., & Nyberg, S. E. (1982). *Human memory: An introduction to research and theory*. Pacific Grove, CA: Brooks/Cole.

Zeig, J. K. (1987). Introduction: The evolution of psychotherapy—Fundamental issues. In J. K. Zeig (Ed.), *The evolution of psychotherapy*. New York: Brunner/Mazel.

Zeiler, M. (1977). Schedules of reinforcement: The controlling variables. In W. K. Honig & J. E. R. Staddon (Eds.), *Handbook of operant behavior*. Englewood Cliffs, NJ: Prentice-Hall.

Zeiss, A. M. (1980). Aversiveness versus change in the assessment of life stress. *Journal of Psychosomatic Stress, 24,* 15–19.

Zenhausen, R. (1978). Imagery, cerebral dominance and style of thinking: A unified field model. *Bulletin of the Psychonomic Society, 12,* 381–384.

Zeskind, P. S., & Ramey, C. T. (1981). Preventing intellectual and interactional sequelae of fetal malnutrition: A longitudinal, transactional and synergistic approach to development. *Child Development, 52,* 213–218.

Zigler, E., & Seitz, V. (1982). Social policy and intelligence. In R. J. Sternberg (Ed.), *Handbook of human intelligence.* Cambridge, MA: Cambridge University Press.

Zilbergeld, B., & Evans, M. (1980). The inadequacy of Masters and Johnson. *Psychology Today, 14*(3), 28–34, 37–43.

Zillmann, D. (1983). Transfer of excitation in emotional behavior. In J. T. Cacioppo & R. Petty (Eds.), *Social psychophysiology: A sourcebook.* New York: Guilford Press.

Zillmann, D., & Bryant, J. (1984). Effects of massive exposure to pornography. In N. M. Malamuth & E. Donnerstein (Eds.), *Pornography and sexual aggression.* New York: Academic Press.

Zimbardo, P. G. (1977). *Shyness: What it is, what to do about it.* Reading, MA: Addison-Wesley.

Zimmerman, I. L., & Woo-Sam, J. M. (1984). Intellectual assessment of children. In G. Goldstein & M. Hersen (Eds.), *Handbook of psychological assessment.* New York: Pergamon Press.

Zis, A. P., & Goodwin, F. K. (1982). The amine hypothesis. In E. S. Paykel (Ed.), *Handbook of affective disorders.* New York: Guilford Press.

Zubin, J. (1986). Implications of the vulnerability model for DSM-IV with special reference to schizophrenia. In T. Millon & G. L. Klerman (Eds.), *Contemporary directions in psychopathology: Toward the DSM-IV.* New York: Guilford Press.

Zubin, J., & Spring, B. (1977). Vulnerability—A new view of schizophrenia. *Journal of Abnormal Psychology, 86,* 103–126.

Zuckerman, M. (1971). Dimensions of sensation seeking. *Journal of Consulting and Clinical Psychology, 36,* 45–52.

Zuckerman, M. (1979). *Sensation seeking: Beyond the optimal level of arousal.* Hillsdale, NJ: Erlbaum.

Zuckerman, M., Buchsbaum, M. S., & Murphy, D. L. (1980). Sensation seeking and its biological correlates. *Psychological Bulletin, 88*(1), 187–214.

Zuckerman, M., & Wheeler, L. (1975). To dispel fantasies about the fantasy-based measure of fear of success. *Psychological Bulletin, 82,* 932–946.

Zunker, V. G. (1982). *Using assessment results in career counseling.* Pacific Grove, CA: Brooks/Cole.

Zwislocki, J. J. (1981). Sound analysis in the ear: A history of discoveries. *American Scientist, 69,* 184–192.

Woolfolk, R. L., 173, 481, 506
Woo-Sam, J. M., 312, 318
Wright, J. C., 219, 406, 639
Wundt, W., 5, 6, 23, 107
Wyatt, R. J., 74, 539, 573, 580
Wyatt, R. L., 540
Wyler, A. R., 35–37, 47, 49
Wynne, L. C., 541
Wyrwicka, W., 356

Y

Yalom, I., 564
Yarkin, K. L., 599
Yates, F. A., 262
York, D. A., 359
Young, T., 118
Yuille, J. C., 236

Z

Zajonc, R., 370
Zechmeister, E. B., 25, 263
Zeig, J., 554
Zeiler, M., 206
Zeiss, A. M., 479

Zenhausen, R., 100
Zeskind, P., 388
Zich, J., 499
Zigler, E., 317
Zilbergeld, B., 381
Zillmann, D., 362, 373
Zimbardo, P., 365, 375, 376, 467
Zimmerman, I. L., 312, 318

Zimmerman, J., 225
Zis, A. P., 534
Zorumski, C. F., 526
Zubin, J., 97, 542
Zuckerman, M., 361, 367, 458–459
Zunker, V. G., 342
Zwislocki, J., 134

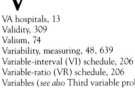

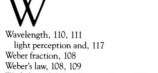

Y

Z

These pages constitute an extension of the copyright page.

PHOTO CREDITS

Contents

xvii: Archives of the History of American Psychology, University of Akron; **xviii:** Harvey Ginsberg, Ph.D. (see p. 44); **xx:** © 1988, The Salvador Dali Foundation, Inc. (see p. 146); **xxi:** Gene Sladek; **xxii:** © Harry Redl/Black Star; **xxiii:** Gary Bloomfield/The Picture Cube; **xxiv:** (left) © Herbert Terrace, Columbia University, (right) © Erika Stone 1987; **xxvi:** © Walter Hodges/Woodfin Camp & Associates; **xxvii:** © Enrico Ferorelli/DOT; **xxviii:** © Bill Ross/ TSW/Click/Chicago; **xxix:** © Michael Beasley/TSW/ Click/Chicago; **xxx:** Culver Pictures, Inc.; **xxxi:** © Michal Heron/Monkmeyer Press Photo Service; **xxxii:** © Arvind Gang/Photo Researchers, Inc.

Chapter One

xxxviii: © Robert Frerck/Odyssey Productions; **2:** (top left) © Richard Wood/The Picture Cube, (bottom left) © Hank Morgan/Rainbow, (right) Nicholas Shields, Jr; **3:** Musee Louvre/Giraudon/Art Resource; **5, 7, 8, 10, 12, 13** (portraits): Tom Voss; **6:** Archives of the History of American Psychology, University of Akron; **11:** Clark University Archives, all rights reserved, used with permission; **14:** telephone—Culver Pictures, Inc., Wundt lab—Archives of the History of American Psychology, University of Akron, Clark conference—Clark University Archives, all rights reserved, used with permission, Queen Victoria— Historical Picture Service, Wright Brothers— Historical Picture Service, Charlie Chaplin—Kobol Collection, silent movie—Culver Pictures, Inc., suffragetts—Culver Pictures, Inc., light bulb—Culver Pictures, Inc., Pavlov lab—Bettmann Archive, WWI—Culver Pictures, Inc.; **15:** protests—UPI/ Bettmann Newsphotos, Pearl Harbor—Culver Pictures, Inc., pigeon—B. F. Skinner/photo by W. Rapport, shuttle launch—NASA, apple seller— Culver Pictures, Inc., television—Culver Pictures, Inc., therapy—© Karen Preuss from *Life Time: A New Image of Aging*, published by Unity Press, Santa Cruz, California, 1978/Jeroboam, brain—© Dan McCoy/Rainbow, atomic bomb—Culver Pictures, Inc., Vietnam—Wide World Photos, Inc.; **22, 23:** H. Armstrong Roberts; **24:** © Richard Hutchings/ Photo Researchers, Inc.

Chapter Two

32: Carl Vanderschuit, (inset) © Tom McCarthey/The Stock Market; **34:** Craig McClain; **38**—Bodleian Library, Oxford, MS.Bodl. 211, fol. 5 r; **42:** From "Use of Hypnosis to Enhance Eye-Witness Accuracy: Does It Work?" G. S. Sanders & W. L. Simmons, State University of New York at Albany, 1983, courtesy, Glenn S. Sanders; **44:** Courtesy, Harvey Ginsburg, Ph.D. Southwest Texas State University; **52:** Courtesy, A. C. Nielson Media Research; **54:** Courtesy, Robert Rosenthal; **55:** © Ethan Hoffman/Archive Pictures, Inc.; **59:** Craig McClain.

Chapter Three

64: © Dan McCoy/Rainbow; **69:** © Charles Seaborn/ Odyssey Productions; **74:** © Duomo/Paul J. Sutton, 1986; **75:** Courtesy, Candace Pert; **78, 79:** © Dan McCoy/Rainbow; **81:** (top left and bottom) © Dan McCoy/Rainbow, (top right) © Hank Morgan/ Rainbow; **87:** © Dan McCoy/Rainbow; **89:** Courtesy, Roger Sperry; **97:** Virgil Apger/Kobal Collection.

Chapter Four

104: Cezanne, Paul, *Louis Guillaume*, circa 1882, National Gallery of Art, Washington, Chester Dale Collection; **106:** Craig McClain; **108:** Archives of the History of American Psychology, University of Akron; **109:** © Tom Tracy/After Image, Inc.; **116:** © Ira Wyman/Sygma; **117:** Craig McClain; **123:** (center right) Archives of the History of American Psychology, University of Akron, (top left) © Tony Freeman/ PhotoEdit; **127:** (top to bottom) © Michael Balderas 1985, © C. Colladay, © Mark Keller, © Michael H. Denny/all Photophile, San Diego; **128:** (top) van Gogh, Vincent, *Hospital Corridor at Saint Remy* (1889), gouche and watercolor, 24⅛ × 18⅝″ (61.3 × 47.3cm), Collection, The Museum of Modern Art, New York, Abby Aldrich Rockefeller Bequest, (center and bottom) Craig McClain; **130:** Photo by Ron Testa and Diane Alexander White, courtesy, Field Museum of Natural History (neg#GN-85079); **132:** © George Zimbel/Monkmeyer Press Photo Service; **142:** Maestro della Cattura di Cristo, Scala/Art Resource; **143:** (top) Gent. e Giov. Bellini in Egitto. Brera Predica di S. Marco Pinacoteca, Scala/Art Resource, (bottom) Monet, Claude, *Palazzo da Mula, Venice*, 1908, National Gallery of Art, Washington, Chester Dale Collection; **144:** Seurat, George, *Sunday Afternoon on the Island of La Grande Jatte* (without artist's border) and detail, 1884–1886, oil on canvas, 207.6 × 308.0 cm, Helen Birch Barlett Memorial Collection, 1926.224 © 1988 The Art Institute of Chicago, all rights reserved. **145:** (top) Picasso, Pablo, *Violin and Grapes* (1912) The Museum of Modern Art, New York, Copyright ARS N.Y./SPADEM, 1912. **145:** (bottom) Duchamp, *Nude Descending a Staircase, No. 2*, Copyright ARS N.Y./ADAGP 1912. **146:** (top) Dali, Salvador, *The Slave Market with Disappearing Bust of Voltaire* (1940), The Salvador Dali Museum, St. Petersburg, FL, © 1988 The Salvador Dali Foundation, Inc.; © DeMart Pro Arte/ARS N.Y. 1940; **146:** (bottom) and **147:** (top and bottom left) Courtesy, Haags Gemeentemuseum, © 1988 M. C. Escher % Cordon Art, Baarn; **147:** (right) *Les Promenades d'Eclid*, Copyright © Herscovici/ARS N.Y. 1955.

Chapter Five

150: Carl Vanderschuit, (clouds) © Tom Tracy/ Photophile, San Diego; **152:** Gene Sladek; **156:** © Dan McCoy/Rainbow; **157:** © Philip Jon Bailey/The Picture Cube; **159:** Michael O'Brien/© Archive Pictures, Inc.; **161:** Courtesy, Stanford News & Publications and William Dement; **165:** Craig McClain; **169:** Mary Evans Picture Library/Sigmund Freud Copyrights; **170:** Courtesy, Ernest Hilgard and News & Publications Service, Stanford University; **171:** (top) UPI/Bettmann Newsphotos, (bottom) Mario Cabera/Wide World Photos, Inc.; **172:** Courtesy, Theodore Barber; **178:** (left) © Ellis Herwig/ The Picture Cube, (right) Comstock, Inc./Tom Grill.

Chapter Six

188: Carl Vanderschuit; **193:** The Bettmann Archive; **194:** (left) Craig McClain, (right) M. Miller/H. Armstrong Roberts; **197:** Courtesy, Prof. Benjamin Harris; **202:** (top) TASS from Sovfoto, (bottom) Harry Redl/Black Star © 1988; **203:** Will Rapport/ courtesy B. F. Skinner; **205:** Courtesy, B. F. Skinner; **206:** (top left, bottom) Craig McClain, (top right) ©

Ken McVey/AfterImage, Inc.; **210:** © Robert Brenner/ PhotoEdit; **212:** Owen Franken/Stock, Boston; **213:** Courtesy, Prof. Stuart Ellins, California State University, San Bernardino; **215:** Courtesy, Robert Rescorla; **218:** (top) © R. Thompson/F.L./Bruce Coleman, Inc., (bottom) Robert V. Eckert, Jr. © 1982/The Picture Cube; **219:** Courtesy, Albert Bandura; **221:** (top left) Prof. Stuart Ellis, (top right) Prof. Benjamin Harris, (center left) TASS from Sovfoto, (center right) © Ken McVey/AfterImage, Inc., (bottom left) © R. Thompson/F.L./Bruce Coleman, Inc., (bottom right) Robert V. Eckert, Jr. © 1982/The Picture Cube.

Chapter Seven

228: Carl Vanderschuit; **231:** (bottom) Begis Bossu/ Sygma, (top) Craig McClain; **237:** Gary Bloomfield/ The Picture Cube; **238:** From *The Photo Issue 37*, p. 100, © Marshall Cavendish Ltd.; **241:** Courtesy, George Miller; **242:** (top) NASA, (bottom) Wide World Photos, Inc.; **244:** © Robert Frerck/Odyssey Productions; **245:** (top) © DRS Productions/The Stock Market, (bottom) By permission of the British Library; **250:** © Charles Steiner/Sygma; **251:** Courtesy, Gordon Bower; **253:** Courtesy, Elizabeth Loftus; **257:** Wellcome Institute Library, London.

Chapter Eight

268: Carl Vanderschuit; **270:** Courtesy, Herbert A. Simon; **271:** William Ritchie, courtesy of "MicroMom" (S. Rosenbaum, Plainfield, NY); **272:** (top) © Paul Fusco/Magnum Photos, Inc., (bottom) © Herbert Terrace, Columbia University; **274:** Courtesy, Language Research Center, Yerkes Regional Research Center; **278:** (top left) © Michal Heron 1982/Woodfin Camp & Associates, (bottom left) © Palmer/Kane 1985/The Stock Market, (right) © Erika Stone 1987; **281:** Courtesy, Noam Chomsky; **289, 290:** Craig McClain; **293:** (top) Michael L. Abramson/ Woodfin Camp & Associates, (center) © 1987 Martha Swope Photography, Inc., (bottom) From *One Woman's Power*, by Sondra Henry & Emily Taitz, © 1987 by Dillon Press, Minneapolis, photo by David Kaplan; **297:** Courtesy, Amos Tversky.

Chapter Nine

304: Copyright Kenneth Griffiths/G'Day Pictures Ltd., London; **307:** (left) © Erika Stone 1983, (right) Jet Propulsion Laboratory; **310:** Wellcome Institute Library, London; **311:** The Bettmann Archive; **312, 315:** Archives of the History of American Psychology, University of Akron; **318:** (right) © Lester Sloan/ Woodfin Camp & Associates, (center) Andrew Sacks/ Black Star © 1980, (left) © 1987 Rick Friedman/Black Star; **319:** Courtesy, Robert J. Sternberg; **320:** Courtesy, Arthur Jensen; **323:** UPI/Bettmann Newsphotos; **324:** Courtesy, Sandra W. Scarr/ University of Virginia Photographic Division; **334:** (top) © Ed Simpson 1977/AfterImage, Inc., (center) © 1988 Tony Freeman/PhotoEdit, (bottom) © Leverett Bradley 1979/AfterImage, Inc.; **336:** © Sepp Seiotz 1978/Woodfin Camp & Associates; **337:** Copyright © 1943 by The President and Fellows of Harvard College, © 1971 by Henry A. Murray; **343:** By permission of Consulting Psychologists Press, sample test results provided by Gene Hallongren, College of DuPage Testing Office.

Chapter Ten

346: © Comstock Inc./Michael Stuckey; 348: © Duomo/Daniel Forster 1978, all rights reserved; 349: Nina Leen, *Life* Magazine, © 1964 Time, Inc.; 350: Warren and Genny Garst/Tom Stack and Associates; 355: William Carter; 358: © Glasheen Graphics; 359: Courtesy, Judith Rodin, © Bill Hayward for *American Health*; 366: Courtesy, David McClelland; 369: (top) © Walter Hodges/Woodfin Camp & Associates, all rights reserved, (center) Courtesy, Radcliff College, Office of the President; 371: From *Unmasking the Face*, by P. Ekman and W. V. Friesen, © 1975 by Prentice-Hall, © 1984 by Consulting Psychologists Press, courtesy, Paul Ekman; 374: © Bill Apple, courtesy Stanley Schachter; 375: Courtesy, Donald D. Dutton, Department of Psychology, University of British Columbia.

Chapter Eleven

384: © John Blaustein 1979/Woodfin Camp & Associates; 386: Robert Coburn, RKO 1935, Kobal Collection; 388: © Lennart Nilsson, courtesy, Bonnier Fakta, Stockholm; 390: © Enrico Ferorelli/DOT; 394: (top) © Erika Stone 1987; 394 (bottom) and 395: Harlow Primate Laboratory, University of Wisconsin; 396: UPI/Bettmann Newsphotos, Inc.; 398: © 1980 Yves de Braine/Black Star; 399: © Doug Goodman/Monkmeyer Press Photo Service; 403: UPI/ Bettmann Newsphotos; 406: © Mary Kate Denny/ PhotoEdit; 407: © Marleen Ferguson/PhotoEdit; 412: UPI/Bettmann Newsphotos; 416: © George Will/ Monkmeyer Press Photo Service; 417: (left) © Christa Armstrong 1976/Rapho/Photo Researchers, Inc., (right) © 1984 Naoki Okamto/Black Star; 418: (left) © 1988 Lynn Johnson/Black Star, (right) © 1988 Bob Krist/Black Star; 419: (left) Paul Conklin/Monkmeyer Press Photo Service, (right) © 1987 Blair Seitz/Photo Researchers, Inc., all rights reserved; 425: (left) Capitol Cities/ABC, Inc., (center) Al Levine © NBC, photo courtesy of the National Broadcasting Company, Inc., all rights reserved, (right) courtesy, MacNeil/ Lehrer News Hour.

Chapter Twelve

428: Carl Vanderschuit; 431: © Santosh Basak/ Gamma/Liason Agency; 433: Historical Picture Service, Inc.; 439: Culver Pictures, Inc.; 440: (center) From *C. G. Jung: Word and Image*, edited by Aniela Jaffe, Bollingen Series xcvii.2, © 1979 by Princeton University Press, translated by Krishna Winston from *C. G. Jung: Bild und Wort*, © Walter-Verlag AG, Olten, Switzerland, 1977; 441: Culver Pictures, Inc.; 442: Manfred Kreiner/Black Star; 444: © Tony Freeman/PhotoEdit; 448: Courtesy, Walter Mischel; 451: William Carter; 452: Courtesy, Hans J. Eysenck, photo by Mark Gerson, FBIPP; 453: © Enrico Ferorelli/DOT; 459: © Bill Ross/TSW/Click/ Chicago, all rights reserved; 461: Dali, Salvador *Soft Construction with Boiled Beans*, Philadelphia Museum of Art: Louise and Walter Arensberg Collection; Copyright DeMart Pro Arte/ARS N.Y., 1936; 462: (top) Historical Picture Service, (top center) © Richard Wood/The Picture Cube, (bottom center) © Erich Hartman/Magnum Photos, Inc., (bottom) © 1980 Harvey Stein/Black Star; 463: © Erika Stone 1979, (top center) © Tony Freeman/Photo Edit, (bottom center) © 1979 Erika Stone.

Chapter Thirteen

470: Carl Vanderschuit; 472: © Glasheen Graphics; 474: Courtesy, Richard Lazarus; 476: Jenny Holzer, *Selections from TRUISMS*, 1986, "Protect me from what I want," reader board, Caesar's Palace, Las Vegas, Nevada, courtesy Barbara Gladstone Gallery, photo by Thomas Holder; 479: © Michael Beasley/TSW/Click/ Chicago; 483: © Karsh, Ottawa/Woodfin Camp & Associates; 489: (left) © Kirk Schlea/ALLSPORT USA, all rights reserved, (right) Rick Stewart/ ALLSPORT USA, all rights reserved; 491: © Joan Liftin/Archive Pictures, Inc.; 501: Mark Antman/The Image Works, all rights reserved; 504: Courtesy, Albert Ellis; 507: © Melanie Carr/ALLSPORT USA, all rights reserved.

Chapter Fourteen

510: Carl Vanderschuit; 512: (top) Culver Pictures, Inc., (bottom) di Benvenuto, Girolomo, *St. Catherine of Siena Exorcising a Possessed Woman*, Italian, Siena, 1500–1510, oil on wood panel, Denver Art Museum, Samuel H. Kress Foundation Collection; 513: photo by Joel Siegel, courtesy, Thomas Szasz; 515: (left) © Ferdinando Scianna/Magnum Photos, Inc., (right) © David Hurn/Magnum Photos, Inc.; 516: © Rose Skytta/Jeroboam, Inc.; 518: Courtesy, David Rosenhan, photo by Edward W. Souza/News & Publications Service, Stanford University; 524: Wide World Photos, Inc.; 533: David Strickler/The Picture Cube; 537: © Paul Fusco/Magnum Photos, Inc.; 538: Courtesy, Nancy Andreasen; 540: Courtesy, Dr. E. Fuller Towey and Dr. Manuel F. Casanova, CBDB-NIMH; 545: Wide World Photos, Inc.; 549: Hays/Monkmeyer Press Photo Service.

Chapter Fifteen

552: Carl Vanderschuit; 557: © Carrie Boretz/ Archive Pictures, Inc.; 558: © Erich Hartmann/ Magnum Photos, Inc.; 560: Mary Evans Picture Library/Sigmund Freud Copyrights; 562: Courtesy, Carl Rogers; 563: Courtesy, Aaron T. Beck; 564: (left) Craig McClain, (right) © Larry Mulvehill/Photo Researchers, Inc.; 567: Courtesy, Joseph Wolpe; 569: Courtesy, Robert Paul Liberman, M.D.; 570: Gene Sladek; 574: © James D. Wilson, all rights reserved/ Woodfin Camp & Associates; 578: Culver Pictures, Inc., (inset) detail of painting in Harrisburg State Hospital, photo by Ken Smith; 579: Culver Pictures, Inc.; 580: (left) © Michal Heron/Monkmeyer Photo Service, (right) © Billy E. Barnes/Jeroboam, Inc.; 583: © Joan Liftin/Archive Pictures, Inc.

Chapter Sixteen

590: © Richard Sullivan; 594: © Blair Seitz, all rights reserved/Photo Researchers, Inc.; 597: © 1988 Tony Freeman/PhotoEdit; 602: © 1987 Arvind Gang/Photo Researchers, Inc.; 604: (top) Courtesy, Ellen Berscheid, (bottom) Courtesy, Elaine Hatfield; 610: © E. Adams/Sygma; 611: © Karen Zebulon, courtesy, Leon Festinger; 614: Wide World Photos, Inc.; 616: Courtesy, Solomon Asch; 617: Copyright 1965 by Stanley Milgram, from the film *Obedience*, distributed by the New York University Film Division and the Pennsylvania State University, PCR; 621: © Tom Tracy/Photphile, San Diego; 625: © Rose Skytta/ Jeroboam, Inc.

FIGURE CREDITS

Chapter One

Figures 1.4 and 1.5: Adapted from data from the American Psychological Association by permission. Figure 1.8: Description from "The Warm-Cold Variable in First Impressions of Persons," by H. H. Kelley, 1950, *Journal of Personality*, 18, pp. 431–439. Reprinted by permission. Figure 1.10: Adapted from a figure in *How to Succeed in College*, by M. K. Johnson, S. P. Springer, and S. H. Sternglanz. Copyright © 1982 by William Kaufmann, Los Altos, CA. Adapted by permission. Figure 1.11: Adapted from *The Psychology of College Success: A Dynamic Approach*, by H. C. Lindgren, 1969. Copyright 1969. Adapted by permission of H. C. Lindgren. Figure 1.12: Adapted from "Note-Taking, Individual Differences and Memory for Lecture Information," by G. O. Einstein, J. Morris, and S. Smith, 1985, *Journal of Educational Psychology*, 77 (5), pp. 522–532. Copyright © 1985 by the American Psychological Association. Adapted by permission. Figures 1.13 and 1.14: Adapted from "Staying with Initial Answers on Objective Tests: Is It a Myth?" by L. T. Benjamin, Jr., T. A. Cavell, and W. R. Shallenberger III, 1984, *Teaching of Psychology*, 11 (3), pp. 133–141. Copyright © 1984 by Lawrence Erlbaum Associates, Inc. Adapted by permission of the author.

Chapter Two

Figure 2.7: Reprinted with permission of The Free Press, a division of Macmillan, Inc. from *The Psychotic Patient: Medication and Psychotherapy*, by David Greenfield, M.D., p. 94. Copyright © 1985 by The Free Press. Figure 2.16: Adapted from *Library Use: A Handbook for Psychology*, by J. G. Reed and P. M. Baxter, p. 57, 1983. Copyright © 1983 by the American Psychological Association. Adapted by permission. Figures 2.17 and 2.18: This material is reprinted with permission (fee paid) of the American Psychological Association, publisher of *Psychological Abstracts* and the PsycINFO Database (Copyright © 1967–1988 by the American Psychological Association), and may not be reproduced without its prior permission. Table 2.1: Adapted from "Personality and Attitudinal Characteristics of Sexually Coercive College Males," by D. Rapaport and B. R. Burkhart, 1984, *Journal of Abnormal Psychology*, 93 (2), pp. 216–221. Copyright © 1984 by the American Psychological Association. Adapted by permission.

Chapter Three

Figure 3.11: From "Current Concepts: The Sleep Disorders," by P. Hauri, 1982, The Upjohn Company, Kalamazoo, Michigan. Figure 3.29: Cartoon courtesy of Roy Doty. Figure 3.30: From *Drawing on the Right Side of the Brain*, by Betty Edwards, Jeremy P. Tarcher, Inc., Los Angeles. Copyright © 1979 by Betty Edwards. Reprinted by permission.

Chapter Four

Figure 4.4: From *Introduction to Psychology* by James W. Kalat, p. 94, 1986. Copyright © 1986 by Wadsworth, Inc. Reprinted by permission. Figure 4.16: Figure based on data from "Human Color Vision and Color Blindness," by G. Wald and P. K. Brown, 1965, *Symposium Cold Spring Harbor Laboratory of Quantitative Biology*, 30, 345–359 (p. 351). Copyright © 1965. Reprinted by permission. Figure 4.19: Adapted from "Perception of Letters in Words: Seek Not and Ye Shall Find," by J. C. Johnson & J. L. McClelland, 1974, *Science*, 184, 1192–1194. Copyright © 1974 by the American Association for the Advancement of Science. Adapted by permission of the AAAS. Figure 4.37: From Table 5-3, adapted from *Introduction to Psychology*, Ninth Edition, by Rita L. Atkinson, Richard C. Atkinson, Edward E. Smith, and Ernest R. Hilgard, copyright © 1987 by Harcourt Brace Jovanovich, Inc., reprinted by permission of the publisher. Table 4.2: From *Fundamentals of Psychology* by F. A. Geldard, 1962. Copyright © 1962 by John Wiley & Sons. Reprinted by permission of John Wiley & Sons, Inc. Table 4.3: From *Psychology: The Personal Science*, by John C. Ruch, p. 198, 1984. Copyright © 1984 by Wadsworth, Inc. Reprinted by permission.

Chapter Five

Figure 5.6: Adapted from "Rotating Shift Work Schedules That Disrupt Sleep Are Improved by Applying Circadian Principles," by C. A. Czeisler, M. C. Moore-Ede, and R. M. Coleman, 1982, *Science*, 217, 460–463. Copyright © 1982 by the American Association for the Advancement of Science. Adapted by permission of the author. Figure 5.7: From "Current Concepts: The Sleep Disorders," by P. Hauri, 1982, The Upjohn Company, Kalamazoo, Michigan. Figure 5.10: Figure adapted from a revision of "Ontogenetic Development of Human Sleep Dream Cycle," by H. P. Roffwarg, J. N. Muzio, and W. C. Dement, 1966. *Science*, 152, 604–609. Copyright © 1966 by the American Association for the Advancement of Science. Adapted and revised by permission of the author. Figure 5.12: Adapted from *Secrets of Sleep*, by Alexander Borbely. English Translation Copyright © 1986 by Basic Books, Inc. © 1984 Deutsche Verlags-Anstalt GmbH, Stuttgart. Reprinted by permission of Basic Books, Inc. Publishers. Figure 5.16: From Figure 4-6, adapted from *Hypnotic Susceptibility* by Ernest R. Hilgard, copyright © 1965 by Harcourt Brace Jovanovich, Inc., reprinted by permission of the publisher. Figure 5.19: Based on illustration on p. 86 by Lorelle A. Raboni from "The Psychology of Meditation," by R. K. Wallace and H. Bensen, February 1972, *Scientific American*, 226, 85–90.

693

Chapter Eleven

Figure 11.1: Adapted from Moore, K. L., *The Developing Human: Clinically Oriented Embryology*, 4th ed. Philadelphia, W. B. Saunders Co., 1988. Reprinted by permission. **Figure 11.5:** Adapted from Table 1 of "Sex Role Stereotypes: A Current Appraisal," by I. K. Broverman, S. R. Vogel, D. M. Broverman, F. E. Clarkson, and P. S. Rosenkrantz, 1972, *Journal of Social Issues*, 28, p. 63. Copyright © 1972 by the Society for the Psychological Study of Social Issues. Adapted by permission. **Figure 11.6:** Adapted from *The Developing Person Through the Lifespan*, by K. S. Berger, p. 176, 1983. Copyright © 1983 by Worth Publishers. Adapted by permission. **Figure 11.9:** After Kohlberg, "The Development of Children's Orientations Toward a Moral Order: I. Sequence in the Development of Moral Thought," by L. Kohlberg, 1963, *Vita Humana*, 6, 11–33. Copyright © 1963 by S. Karger AG, Basel. Reprinted by permission. **Figure 11.11c:** Adapted from "Motivational Aspects of Deliberate Self-Poisoning in Adolescents," by Howton, Cole, O'Grady, and Osborn, 1982, *British Journal of Psychiatry*, 141, 286–291. Copyright © 1982 by The Royal College of Psychiatrists. Adapted by permission. **Figure 11.12:** Adaptation of specified figure from page 57 from *The Seasons of a Man's Life*, by Daniel J. Levinson, et al. Copyright © 1978 by Daniel J. Levinson. Reprinted by permission of Alfred A. Knopf, Inc. **Figure 11.13:** Based on data from "Creative Productivity Between the Ages of 20 and 80 Years," by W. Dennis, 1966, *Journal of Gerontology*, 21 (1), 1–8. Copyright © 1966 by the Gerontological Society of America. Adapted by permission. **Figure 11.15:** Adapted from Figure 2.10 from *Psychology: A First Encounter*, by Dennis Krebs and Roger Blackman, p. 83, Copyright © 1988 by Harcourt Brace Jovanovich, Inc., adapted and reprinted by permission of the publisher. **Figure 11.16:** Adapted from "Children, Gender and Social Structure: An Analysis of the Contents of Letters to Santa Claus," by J. G. Richardson and C. H. Simpson, 1982, *Child Development*, 53, 429–436. Copyright © 1982 by The Society for Research in Child Development, Inc. Adapted by permission. **Table 11.1:** Adapted from *Developmental Psychology: Childhood and Adolescence*, by D. R. Schaffer, 1989. Copyright © 1989 by Wadsworth, Inc. Reprinted by permission of Brooks/Cole Publishing Company. **Table 11.2:** Adapted from *Childhood and Society*, by Erik H. Erikson, by permission of W. W. Norton & Company, Inc. Copyright © 1950, 1963 by W. W. Norton & Company, Inc. Copyright reviewed 1978 by Erik H. Erikson. **Table 11.6:** Adapted from John C. Brigham, *Social Psychology*, Table 10–4. Copyright © 1986 by John C. Brigham. By permission of Scott, Foresman and Company.

Chapter Twelve

Figure 12.9: Adapted from *Personality: Theory, Research and Application*, by C. R. Potkay and B. P. Allen, p. 246, 1986. Copyright © 1986 by Wadsworth, Inc. Adapted by permission of Brooks/Cole Publishing Company. **Figure 12.11:** From H. J. Eysenck, *The Biological Basis of Personality*, 1st ed., p. 36, 1967. Courtesy of Charles C Thomas, Publisher, Springfield, Illinois. **Figure 12.12:** Adapted from "Personality Similarity in Twins Reared Apart and Together," by A. Tellegen, D. T. Lykken, T. J. Bouchard, Jr., K. J. Wilcox, N. L. Segal, and S. Rich, 1988, *Journal of Personality and Social Psychology*, 54 (6), 1031–1039. Copyright © 1988 by the American Psychological Association. Adapted by permission. **Figure 12.14:** Reprinted by permission from *Adjustment and Competence: Concepts and Applications*, by A. F. Grasha and D. S. Kirschenbaum, p. 101, copyright © 1986 by West Publishing Company. All rights reserved. **Figure 12.16:** Based on R. J. Shavelson, et al. from "Self-Concept: Validation of Construct Interpretations," by R. J. Shavelson, et al., 1976, *Review of Educational Research*, 46, 407–411. Copyright © 1976 by the American Educational Research Association. Adapted

by permission. **Figures 12.17 and 12.19:** Adapted from "Studies in Self-Esteem," by S. Coopersmith, *Scientific American*, February 1968, from illustrations on p. 102, bottom left, top right, and p. 106, top and bottom. Copyright © 1968 by Scientific American, Inc. All rights reserved. Adapted by permission. **Table 12.1:** From "Validation of the Five-Factor Model of Personality Across Instruments and Observers," by R. R. McCrae and P. T. Costa, Jr., 1987, *Journal of Personality and Social Psychology*, 52 (1), 81–90. Reprinted by permission of the author. **Table 12.2:** From Table 2–4, from *Introduction to Personality: A New Look*, Fourth Edition, by Walter Mischel, copyright © 1986 by Holt, Rinehart and Winston, Inc., reprinted by permission of the publisher.

Chapter Thirteen

Figure 13.6: Based on art in "Language for Emotions," by R. Plutchik, 1980, *Psychology Today*, 13 (9), 68–78. Reprinted from Psychology Today Magazine. Copyright © 1980 American Psychological Association. **Figure 13.8:** Adapted from *The Stress of Life*, by Hans Selye, p. 121, 1956. Copyright © 1956 by McGraw-Hill, Inc. Adapted by permission. **Figure 13.10:** Based on "Paradoxical Effects of Supportive Audiences on Performance Under Pressure: The Home Field Disadvantages in Sports Championships," by R. F. Baumeister and A. Steinhilber, 1984, *Journal of Personality and Social Psychology*, 47 (1), 85–93. Copyright © 1984 by the American Psychological Association. Adapted by permission. **Figure 13.14:** Adapted from "Associative Learning, Habit and Health Behavior," by W. A. Hunt, J. D. Matarazzo, S. M. Weiss, and W. D. Gentry, 1979, *Journal of Behavioral Medicine*, 2 (2), 113. Copyright © 1979 by the Plenum Publishing Company. Adapted by permission. **Figure 13.16:** Adapted from "A Three City Comparison of the Public's Knowledge and Attitudes About AIDS," by L. Temoshok, D. M. Sweet, and J. Zich, 1987, *Psychology & Health*, 1 (1), 43–60. Copyright © 1987 by Harwood Academic Publishers GmbH. Adapted by permission. **Figure 13.20:** From Figure pp. 114–115 from *The Relaxation Response*, by Herbert Benson with Miriam Z. Klipper. Copyright © 1975 by William Morrow and Company, Inc. By permission of William Morrow and Company, Inc. **Table 13.1:** Adapted from "Comparison of Two Modes of Stress Measurement: Daily Hassles and Uplifts Versus Major Life Events," by A. D. Kanner, J. C. Coyne, C. Schaefer, and R. S. Lazarus, 1981, *Journal of Behavioral Medicine*, 4, 1–39. Copyright © 1981 by the Plenum Publishing Company. Adapted by permission. **Table 13.2:** From "The Social Readjustment Rating Scale," by T. H. Holmes and R. H. Rahe, 1967, *Journal of Psychosomatic Research*, 11, 213–218. Copyright © 1967 by Pergamon Press, Inc. Adapted by permission. **Table 13.3:** Adapted from *Abnormal Psychology and Modern Life* (8th ed.), by R. C. Carson, J. N. Butcher, and J. C. Coleman, pp. 64–65, 1988. Copyright © 1988 by Scott, Foresman and Company. Adapted by permission. **Table 13.5:** Adapted from "New Measure of Daily Coping: Development and Preliminary Results," by A. A. Stone and J. M. Neale, 1984, *Journal of Personality and Social Psychology*, 46 (4), 892–906. Copyright © 1984 by the American Psychological Association. Adapted by permission.

Chapter Fourteen

Excerpt p. 536: From *Is There No Place on Earth for Me?* by Susan Sheehan. This material originally appeared in slightly different form in *The New Yorker*, Spring 1981. Copyright © 1982 by Susan Sheehan. Reprinted by permission of Houghton Mifflin Company. Published by Houghton Mifflin Company and in paperback by Vintage. Reprinted by permission. **Figures 14.3, 14.4, and 14.5:** Adapted and reprinted with permission from the *Diagnostic and Statistical Manual of Mental Disorders*, Third Edition, Revised. Copyright © 1987 American Psychiatric Association. **Figure 14.15:** Adapted from "Clues to the Genetics and Neurobiology of Schizophrenia," by S. E. Nicol

and I. I. Gottesman, 1983, *American Scientist*, 71, 398–404. Copyright © 1983 by Sigma Xi. Adapted by permission of American Scientist. **Figure 14.17:** From Michael J. Goldstein, Bruce L. Baker, and Kay R. Jamison, *Abnormal Psychology: Experiences, Origins, and Interventions*, 2nd ed., p. 162, Fig. 6.7. Copyright © 1986 by Michael J. Goldstein, Bruce L. Baker, and Kay R. Jamison. Reprinted by permission of Scott, Foresman and Company. **Figure 14.19:** Adapted from "Personality Disorders in DSM III and DSM III-R: Convergence, Coverage and Internal Consistency," by L. C. Morey, 1988, *American Journal of Psychiatry*, 145 (5), 573–577. Copyright © 1988 by the American Psychiatric Association. Adapted by permission. **Figure 14.21:** Adapted from "Epidemiology of Disorders in Adulthood: Suicide," by C. K. Cross and R. M. A. Hirschfeld. In G. L. Klerman, M. M. Weissman, P. S. Appelbaum, and L. H. Roth (eds.), *Psychiatry (Vol. 5): Social, Epidemiologic, and Legal Psychiatry*, pp. 245–260, 1986. Copyright © 1986. Basic Books/J. B. Lippincott Company. **Figure 14.22:** Adapted from "Suicide, Attempted Suicide and Relapse Rates in Depression," by D. Avery and G. Winokur, 1978, *Archives of General Psychiatry*, June, 35, 749–753. Copyright © 1978 by the American Medical Association. Adapted by permission. **Table 14.3:** From Sarason/Sarason, *Abnormal Psychology: The Problem of Maladaptive Behavior*, 5/E, © 1987, p. 283. Reprinted by permission of Prentice-Hall, Inc., Englewood Cliffs, NJ.

Chapter Fifteen

Excerpt p. 562: From *Abnormal Psychology: Perspectives on Being Different*, by M. Duke and S. Nowicki, Jr., p. 565, 1979. Copyright © 1979 by Wadsworth, Inc. Reprinted by permission of Brooks/Cole Publishing. **Excerpt p. 563:** From *Cognitive Therapy of Depression*, by A. T. Beck, A. J. Rush, B. F. Shaw, and G. Emery, pp. 217–219, 1979, Guilford Press. Reprinted by permission. **Figure 15.3:** From *Methods of Self-Change: An ABC Primer*, by K. E. Rudestam, pp. 42–43, 1980. Copyright © 1980 by Wadsworth, Inc. Reprinted by permission of Brooks/Cole Publishing Company. **Figure 15.7:** From data in NIMH-PSC Collaborative Study I and reported in "Drugs in the Treatment of Psychosis," by J. O. Cole, S. C. Goldberg, and J. M. Davis, 1966. In P. Solomon (ed.) *Psychiatric Drugs*, Grune & Stratton. **Figure 15.8:** From "Antipsychotic Drugs," by R. J. Baldessarini. In T. B. Karasu (ed.) *The Psychiatric Therapies*, pp. 119–170, 1984. Copyright © 1984 by the American Psychiatric Association. Reprinted by permission. **Figure 15.14:** From "Meta Analysis of Psychotherapy Outcome Series," by M. L. Smith and G. V. Glass, 1977, *American Psychologist*, 32 (Sept.), 752–760. Copyright © 1977 by the American Psychological Association. Adapted by permission. **Table 15.2:** Adapted from "Psychoanalysis and Psychoanalytic Therapy," by E. L. Baker. In S. J. Lynn and J. P. Garske (eds.), *Contemporary Psychotherapies: Models and Methods*, p. 52. Copyright © 1985 Merrill Publishing Company, Columbus, Ohio.

Chapter Sixteen

Excerpt p. 592: From *Tales from the Front*, by Cheryl Lavin and Laura Kavesh. Copyright © 1988 by Cheryl Lavin and Laura Kavesh. Reprinted by permission of Doubleday, a division of Bantam, Doubleday, Dell Publishing Group, Inc. **Excerpt pp. 622–623:** From *Risk Taking: A Study in Cognition and Personality*, by Nathan Kogan and Michael Wallach, copyright © 1964 by Holt, Rinehart and Winston, Inc., reprinted by permission of the publisher. **Figure 16.2:** Adapted from "Level of Categorization and Content of Gender Stereotypes," by K. Deaux, W. Winton, M. Crowley, and L. L. Lewis, 1985, *Social Cognition*, 3, 145–167. Copyright © 1985 by Guilford Publications, Inc. Adapted by permission. **Figure 16.5:** "Perceiving the Causes of Success and Failure," by B. Weiner, I. Frieze, A. Kukla, L. Reed, and R. M. Rosenbaum. In E. E. Jones, D. E. Kanuouse, H. H. Kelley, R. E. Nisbett,

TO THE OWNER OF THIS BOOK:

I hope that I've been able to make this book likable. I'd like to learn your reactions to using this textbook. Only through your comments and advice and the comments and advice of others can I hope to improve the next edition of *Psychology: Themes and Variations.*

School: _____

Your instructor's name: _____

1. What did you like most about *Psychology: Themes and Variations*?

_____

_____

2. What did you like least about the book? _____

_____

3. Were all the chapters of the book assigned for you to read? _____

(If not, which ones weren't?) _____

4. How interesting and informative were the Application sections? _____

_____

_____

5. Did you use the Concept Checks? _____ Were they helpful? _____

_____

_____

_____

6. How helpful were the themes in fostering an understanding of basic insights about psychology? _____

_____

_____

_____

7. In the space below or in a separate letter, please let me know what other comments about the book you'd like to make. (For example, did you like the Featured Studies or Integrated Running Glossary?) I'd be delighted to hear from you!

_____

_____

_____

_____

Optional:

Your name: _____ Date: _____

May Brooks/Cole quote you, either in promotion for *Psychology: Themes and Variations* or in future publishing ventures?

Yes _____ No _____

Sincerely,

Wayne Weiten

FOLD HERE

BUSINESS REPLY MAIL

FIRST CLASS   PERMIT NO. 358   PACIFIC GROVE, CA

POSTAGE WILL BE PAID BY ADDRESSEE

ATT: Dr. Wayne Weiten _____

Brooks/Cole Publishing Company
511 Forest Lodge Road
Pacific Grove, California 93950-9968

FOLD HERE